WEST ACADEMIC PUBLISHING'S LAW SCHOOL ADVISORY BOARD

LLCs, Partnerships, and Corporations

■ ■ ■

Robert J. Rhee
John H. and Mary Lou Dasburg Professor of Law
University of Florida Levin College of Law

AMERICAN CASEBOOK SERIES®

WEST ACADEMIC PUBLISHING

444 Cedar Street, Suite 700
St. Paul, MN 55101
1-877-888-1330

Printed in the United States of America

ISBN: 978-1-68467-242-4

For Nicki, Piers, and Blake

PREFACE

Whenever an author decides to write a textbook, the first question is: Why? Most business associations courses tend to focus on corporation law and, implicitly, the public corporation chartered in Delaware. While the public corporation is the most important type of firm in the national and global economies, they number only a few thousand. The vast majority of firms are private and closely-held, a large segment being noncorporate entities. In modern business law practice, closely-held firms are ubiquitous, from small, simple storefront businesses to large, sophisticated multinational enterprises. They are the everyday clients of business lawyers. A business lawyer cannot practice law today without a sound understanding of noncorporate business entities. These firms and laws merit attention in the curriculum.

Despite the reality of modern practice, there is a dearth of casebooks that give proper attention to closely-held firms. The typical business organizations casebook focuses on corporations. Business forms such as partnerships and limited liability companies are taught as a brief introduction to business firms before a detailed study of the corporate form. One guesses that the coverage of closely-held firms is allocated perhaps 0.5 to 1 credit of a typical 3–4 credit business associations course. This is not enough. This book can support a 4-credit business organizations course, but with a stronger focus on noncorporate entities.

A teacher can use this book in two ways. First, the book can support an independent 2–3 credit course on noncorporate business entities. Suggested course titles are: "Noncorporate Business Entities," "Unincorporated Business Entities," "Closely-Held Firms," and "Partnerships and LLCs." Second, this book can support a traditional 4-credit business associations course, but one that places noncorporate entities on curricular par with corporations. Materials on corporation law and governance cover major topics such as the basic structural features of the corporate form, shareholder rights, duties of directors, and shareholder litigation. If a school's business law curriculum does not regularly offer a separate course on noncorporate entities, the use of this book in the introductory business associations course may be even more compelling.

Why might a professor teach the traditional business associations course in a way that balances corporations and noncorporate entities? Given market practice, a professor may believe that lawyers will spend as much time with noncorporate entities as they do with corporations and that, in light of the trend toward the freedom of contract, noncorporate forms can support complex business enterprises. Corporate law practice representing public companies is concentrated in big law firms in New York and several other major cities. In the rest of the country comprising the markets of the large majority of business lawyers, noncorporate entities, including subsidiaries and affiliates of public companies that are themselves sophisticated and complex entities, are just as prominent in practice, if not more.

This book provides the typical menu of cases and commentary on corporation law. The focus of the study of corporation law here is Delaware law because it is the quasi-national law. Many teachers agree on the most important principles and cases to present. The innovation here is that the materials is presented not only in its own right, but also in comparison to materials on noncorporate entities. Throughout the materials on noncorporate entities, rules and principles are compared to those of corporations. Each chapter begins with a short discussion of the rule under corporation law. A comparative analysis teaches the considerations involved in entity choice.

The presentation of noncorporate entities presents a challenge because there are fewer tested templates to model. The laws are broadly enabling, and statutes generally provide mostly default rules. Cases focus on unique contract terms, and many are an exercise in contract interpretation. How should materials be taught when a bespoke contract is often the core of the dispute? This book has two distinct pedagogical approaches.

First, the most important source laws of closely-held firms are the statutes. They provide the framework of substantive issues and rules to consider when drafting a partnership or operating agreement. This book excerpts statutory text liberally into the narrative of the book. This approach simplifies a teacher's syllabus and teaching plan. Students read statutes, case law, text commentary, and actual charter agreements together in a linear reading process. There are fewer seminal cases and old chestnuts in this subject area. Noncorporate business entities depend more heavily on the charter agreement as a form of contract. The law of limited liability companies is changing at a faster rate than corporation law. With these considerations in mind, selected cases are relatively new and many are state supreme court rulings, ensuring modern, up-to-date case law, rule durability, and authoritative commentary.

Second, this book is designed to teach an important practical skill: that is an understanding of entity choice, structure, and governance in a bespoke counseling process. The focus is on contracting and private ordering. In practice, sophisticated venturers and their lawyers will incorporate some rules in the statute and the case law, but will contract for other rules governing their internal affairs. A valuable skill is drafting and working with charter agreements. To this end, this book provides extensive examples of contract provisions, including an actual operating agreement used by FCA US LLC, formerly named Chrysler Group LLC, a subsidiary company owned by Fiat Chrysler Automobiles N.V., a public company traded on the New York Stock Exchange (ticker: FCAU). The Chrysler Group LLC's operating agreement is presented throughout this book. It provides examples of terms seen in business enterprises operating at the highest level of complexity and sophistication. To emphasize practical skills further, at the end of many chapters this book includes hypotheticals based on a common set of facts designed to be a single client representation and a continuing series of counseling sessions.

Note about case editing: Like most casebooks, presented cases have been edited. Readers are advised of the following editorial conventions. The most important editorial convention is that deletions of sections of opinions, sentences in paragraphs, sentence fragments, or individual words, and sections or fragments of statutes are not indicated by ellipses (. . .), and a change in capitalization in opinions and statutes are not indicated by brackets [ ]. Such deletions were made, obviously, to manage the page count of the book and the brevity of the reading, and to extract the precise lesson in the opinion. Most citations to authority, such as cases and statutes, are deleted unless the citation is materially relevant to the direct issue at hand or the cited case is presented elsewhere in the casebook. Citation conventions such as parentheticals to indicate "emphasis added" or "internal citations omitted" are deleted. Original quotation marks in opinions have been left to indicate that the court is quoting another source, but most internal quotation marks, brackets, and ellipses have been removed. Words supplied by the author for clarity are indicated by brackets. Other minor editorial changes were made to opinions: for example, identifying party names, citation consistency, and insertion of author's notes (which are specifically noted as "Author's note" in asterisk footnotes). Collectively, these editorial conventions streamline the reading process. They facilitate a better, more pleasant reading experience without changing the substance of the legal lessons in the opinions. Over the years, I have found exacting editorial conventions used in legal briefs to courts visually distracting and unnecessary for the purpose of reading specific lessons in law in a casebook. A casebook is not a brief or legal filing that must be subject to exacting editorial conventions. Students and readers can always reference the original opinion.

ROBERT J. RHEE
UNIVERSITY OF FLORIDA LEVIN COLLEGE OF LAW
YONSEI UNIVERSITY (FULBRIGHT U.S. SCHOLAR 2017–2018)

September 2020

used by FCA US LLC (formerly named Chrysler Group LLC), a subsidiary

ACKNOWLEDGMENTS

I began to write this book in connection with my teaching obligation as a Fulbright U.S. Scholar and Distinguished Lecturer at Yonsei University Law School in Seoul, Republic of Korea. My foreign students needed a book, and having fewer options in Korea I decided to write course materials for them. A draft of this book was used to teach American law to foreign students at Yonsei, and I thank students for their participation in the course, their patience with a draft book written in English, and their helpful feedback. I also thank the J. William Fulbright Foreign Scholarship Board, Yonsei University, Dean Laura Rosenbury, and the University of Florida College of Law for their support. This book would not have been possible without their collective support. I thank my colleagues Peter Molk and Daniel Sokol for their helpful comments.

I thank the following authors, publishers, and organizations for kindly granting permission to reproduce all or excerpts of the following materials:

Business Law Today, *Series LLCs: What Happens When One Series Fails?*, Michelle Harner, Jennifer Ivey-Crickenberger & Tae Kim, (February 2013)

FCA US LLC, formerly Chrysler Group LLC, *Operating Agreement of Chrysler Group LLC*, SEC Form 8-K (June 13, 2014)

Journal of Legal Studies, *State Law, Shareholder Protection, and the Theory of the Corporation*, Ralph K. Winter, volume 6, page 251 (1977)

Northwestern University Law Review, *Limited Liability and the Efficient Allocation of Resources*, Richard A. Booth, volume 40, page 140 (1994)

Northwestern University Law Review, *Director Primacy: The Means and Ends of Corporate Governance*, Stephen M. Bainbridge, volume 97, page 547 (2003)

William & Mary Law Review, *Bonding Limited Liability*, Robert J. Rhee, volume 51, page 1417 (2010)

Yale Law Journal, *Federalism and Corporate Law: Reflections Upon Delaware*, William L. Cary, volume 83, page 663 (1974)

Yale Law Journal, *The Essential Role of Organizational Law*, Henry Hansmann & Reinier Kraakman, volume 110, page 387 (2000)

SUMMARY OF CONTENTS

PREFACE V

ACKNOWLEDGMENTS IX

TABLE OF CASES XXV

Chapter 1. Overview of Business Entities 1
A. Relevance of Business Entities 1
B. Corporations and Noncorporate Business Entities 3
C. Differences Between Corporations and NBEs 10
D. Taxonomy of Corporations 15
E. Taxonomy of NBEs 17
F. Sources of Law and Internal Affairs 20
G. Two Choices at the Outset 32
H. Problem: Friends Consider a Startup 35

Chapter 2. Forming the Entity 37
A. Nature and Essential Attributes of Business Entities 37
B. Attorney Engagement 52
C. Forming General Partnerships 63
D. Forming Limited Liability Entities 81
E. Partnership and Operating Agreements 101
F. Contract Interpretation Principles 116
G. Issues to Consider for NBEs 119
H. Problem: Entrepreneurs Consider Forming a Firm 123

Chapter 3. Liability to Third Parties 125
A. Rule of Limited Liability in Corporations 125
B. Rule of Limited Liability in NBEs 137
C. Direct Liability for One's Own Conduct 155
D. Veil Piercing in NBEs 164
E. Successor Liability 181
F. Issues to Consider for NBEs 187
G. Problem: Entrepreneurs Think About Liability 189

Chapter 4. Finance 191
A. Introduction to Equity Financing 191
B. Shareholders 192
C. Members and Partners 198
D. Capital Accounts 209
E. Contributions 211
F. Profit and Loss, and Distribution 217
G. Improper Distribution and Liability 225
H. Admissions and Dissociations of Partners and Members 230

I. Interests as Securities 232
J. Issues to Consider for NBEs 240
K. Problem: Entrepreneurs Obtain Financing 244

Chapter 5. Agency 247
A. The Theory of Agency and Its Costs 247
B. Legal Definition of Agency and Agent 249
C. Authority, Estoppel, and Ratification 266
D. Principal's Liability for Agent's Contracts and Wrongful Acts 277
E. Agency and Limited Liability 288
F. Problem: Entrepreneurs Begin Managing 290

Chapter 6. Management Structure 293
A. Three Basic Forms of Management 293
B. Centralized Management and Corporations 295
C. Management Structures of NBEs 302
D. Voting Rights 316
E. Insurance and Indemnification 323
F. Information Rights 332
G. Issues to Consider for NBEs 337
H. Problem: Entrepreneurs Think Seriously About Governance 339

Chapter 7. Fiduciary Duty 341
A. Introduction to Fiduciary Duties 341
B. Traditional Approach in NBEs 344
C. Delaware Approach on Contracting for Fiduciary Duty 391
D. Obligation of Good Faith and Fair Dealing 403
E. Fiduciary Duty to Creditors 414
F. Actions by Partners and Members 420
G. Issues to Consider for NBEs 460
H. Problem: Entrepreneurs Find a Deal and a Problem 465

Chapter 8. Transfer of Interest and Dissociation 469
A. Transfers of Interest in Corporation 469
B. Transfers of Interest in NBEs 469
C. Dissociation 501
D. Buy-Sell Agreements 542
E. Issues to Consider for NBEs 546
F. Problem: Entrepreneurs Learn That Ownership Is Not Permanent 550

Chapter 9. Dissolution and Mergers 553
A. Dissolution 553
B. Mergers and Conversions 587
C. Issues to Consider for NBEs 599
D. Problem: Entrepreneurs Go Bigtime, Maybe 603

Chapter 10. Introduction to Corporations 605
A. Corporations in Society 605

B. Major Differences Between NBEs and Corporations 617
C. Why Corporations 622
D. Delaware Corporation Law 626

Chapter 11. Corporate Governance 633
A. Board of Directors 633
B. Officers 646
C. Shareholders 648
D. Corporate Governance 657

Chapter 12. Duty of Care 665
A. Care, Risk-Taking, and Business Judgment 665
B. Duty to Be Informed 672
C. Exculpation 685
D. Aiding and Abetting Breach of Duties 687

Chapter 13. Duty of Loyalty 695
A. Self-Dealing and Conflict of Interest Transactions 695
B. Bad Faith 716
C. Controlling Shareholders 747

Chapter 14. Shareholder Litigation 777
A. Information Rights 777
B. Direct and Derivative Suits 781
C. Plaintiff Standing in Derivative Actions 784
D. Demand and Demand Futility in Derivative Actions 793

Chapter 15. Issues in Mergers & Acquisitions 823
A. M&A Basics 823
B. Entrenchment and Defenses 837
C. Revlon and Its Progeny 844

Appendix A. Operating Agreement of Chrysler Group LLC 875

Appendix B. Revised Uniform Limited Liability Company Act (2006 & 2013 Harmonized) (Excerpted) 909

Appendix C. Revised Uniform Partnership Act (1997 & 2013 Harmonized) (Excerpted) 929

Appendix D. Uniform Limited Partnership Act (2001 & 2013 Harmonized) (Excerpted) 951

INDEX 977

TABLE OF CONTENTS

PREFACE V

ACKNOWLEDGMENTS IX

TABLE OF CASES XXV

Chapter 1. Overview of Business Entities 1
A. Relevance of Business Entities 1
B. Corporations and Noncorporate Business Entities 3
 1. Breakdown of Business Entities 5
 2. The Rise of LLCs 6
 Fraser v. Major League Soccer, L.L.C. 8
C. Differences Between Corporations and NBEs 10
 1. Taxation of Corporations and NBEs 11
 2. Management Structure 11
 3. Separation of Ownership and Control 12
 4. Fiduciary Duty 12
 5. Limited Liability 13
 6. Transferability of Interest 13
 7. Mandatory Rules and Elasticity of Private Ordering 14
D. Taxonomy of Corporations 15
 1. Private Corporations 15
 2. Public Corporations 16
E. Taxonomy of NBEs 17
 1. Partnership 18
 2. LP 18
 3. LLC 19
F. Sources of Law and Internal Affairs 20
 1. Corporation Law and Internal Affairs 20
 2. Sources of the Laws of NBEs 23
 3. Internal Affairs Doctrine in NBEs 24
 Azure Dolphin, LLC v. Barton 26
 Heaps v. Nuriche, LLC 30
G. Two Choices at the Outset 32
 1. Choice of Entity 32
 2. Choice of Law 33
H. Problem: Friends Consider a Startup 35
 Questions 36

Chapter 2. Forming the Entity 37
A. Nature and Essential Attributes of Business Entities 37
 1. Why Firms? 37
 The Essential Role of Organizational Law 39

2. Legal Personhood and Limited Liability 42
Corporation as Legal Entity 43
Reynolds v. Lyman 45
State v. Brelvis Consulting LLC 47
Notes 48
Gould v. City of Stamford 49
B. Attorney Engagement 52
In re Murrin Brothers 1885, Ltd. 59
C. Forming General Partnerships 63
Notes 66
Martin v. Peyton 66
Minuit Maid Corp. v. United Foods, Inc. 70
Energy Transfer Partners, L.P. v. Enterprise Products Partners, L.P. 76
D. Forming Limited Liability Entities 81
1. Filing Requirement for Corporations 82
2. Filing Requirement for NBEs 84
McDonough v. McDonough 86
Notes 90
3. Pre-Formation Legal Rights and Liabilities 90
In re Delaware Sports Complex, LLC 91
Notes 92
4. Filing for Foreign Limited Liability Entity 93
A Guy Named Moe, LLC v. Chipotle Mexican Grill of Colorado, LLC 95
Notes 99
E. Partnership and Operating Agreements 101
1. Definition of Charter Agreement 101
2. Function of Charter Agreement 103
In re Nantucket Island Assoc. Ltd. Partnership Unitholders Litig. 106
3. Elasticity of Private Ordering 111
4. Choice of Law Revisited 116
F. Contract Interpretation Principles 116
G. Issues to Consider for NBEs 119
1. Written Charter Agreement 119
2. Amendment of Charter Agreement 119
3. Assent to the Charter Agreement 120
4. Structure of the Charter Agreement 121
H. Problem: Entrepreneurs Consider Forming a Firm 123
Questions 124

Chapter 3. Liability to Third Parties 125
A. Rule of Limited Liability in Corporations 125
1. Shield Against Vicarious Liability 125
Bonding Limited Liability 126

2. Traditional Veil Piercing in Corporations 127
Walkovszky v. Carlton 127
Notes 129
ORT Associates v. IBC Services, Inc. 130
Freeman v. Complex Computing Co., Inc. 133
Notes 137
B. Rule of Limited Liability in NBEs 137
1. General Partnership 137
2. Limited Partnership 140
Gateway Potato Sales v. G.B. Investment Co 143
3. Limited Liability Company 145
4. "Series" LLC 147
Series LLCs: What Happens When One Series Fails? 151
Alphonse v. Arch Bay Holdings, L.L.C. 154
C. Direct Liability for One's Own Conduct 155
Fifth Third Mortgage Co. v. Kaufman 156
Cortez v. Nacco Material Handling Group, Inc. 158
D. Veil Piercing in NBEs 164
Dailey v. Ayers Land Development, LLC 165
GreenHunter Energy, Inc. v. Western Ecosystems Technology, Inc. 168
1. Reverse Veil Piercing 174
In re Phillips 175
2. Veil Piercing in LPs 180
E. Successor Liability 181
Alsco, Inc. v. Fatty's Bar, LLC 182
F. Issues to Consider for NBEs 187
1. Avoiding Veil Piercing 187
2. Personal Guarantees 188
3. Liability for One's Conduct and Indemnification 188
G. Problem: Entrepreneurs Think About Liability 189
Questions 190

Chapter 4. Finance 191
A. Introduction to Equity Financing 191
B. Shareholders 192
1. Characteristics of Stock 192
2. Issuing Stock 193
3. Classes and Series of Stock 194
C. Members and Partners 198
1. Becoming a Partner or Member 198
Kilpatrick v. White Hall on MS River, LLC 199
2. Addition of New Owners 204
In re Carlisle Etcetera LLC 205
D. Capital Accounts 209
E. Contributions 211
1. Default Statutory Rule 211

2. Liability for Contribution 212
Fox v. I-10 Ltd. 214
F. Profit and Loss, and Distribution 217
1. General Partnership 217
Kessler v. Antinora 218
Notes 220
2. Limited Partnership 221
3. Limited Liability Company 221
4. General Approaches to Profit and Loss Allocation 223
G. Improper Distribution and Liability 225
1. Rule Against Intentional Insolvency in Corporation Law 225
2. Improper Distribution NBEs 227
H. Admissions and Dissociations of Partners and Members 230
1. Admissions 230
2. Dissociations 231
I. Interests as Securities 232
SEC v. Merchant Capital, LLC 234
J. Issues to Consider for NBEs 240
1. Contributions 240
2. Profit and Loss, and Distributions 243
3. New Members and Partners 244
K. Problem: Entrepreneurs Obtain Financing 244
Questions 245

Chapter 5. Agency 247
A. The Theory of Agency and Its Costs 247
B. Legal Definition of Agency and Agent 249
Lang v. Lions Club of Cudahy Wisc., Inc. 251
Segal v. Genitrix, LLC 260
C. Authority, Estoppel, and Ratification 266
Gay Jenson Farms Co. v. Cargill, Inc. 272
D. Principal's Liability for Agent's Contracts and Wrongful Acts 277
Thomas D. Philipsborn Irrevocable Ins. Trust v. Avon Capital, LLC 280
Ira S. Bushey & Sons, Inc. v. U.S. 281
Burlington Industries, Inc. v. Ellerth 284
E. Agency and Limited Liability 288
Limited Liability and the Efficient Allocation of Resources 289
F. Problem: Entrepreneurs Begin Managing 290
Questions 292

Chapter 6. Management Structure 293
A. Three Basic Forms of Management 293
B. Centralized Management and Corporations 295
1. Reason for Centralized Management 295
Director Primacy: The Means and Ends of Corporate Governance 295

2. Management Structure of Corporations 298
3. Business Judgment Rule 299
C. Management Structures of NBEs 302
1. General Partnership 302
2. Limited Partnership 303
3. Limited Liability Company 305
Florida R & D Fund Investors, LLC v. Florida BOCA/Deerfield R & D Investors, LLC 310
D. Voting Rights 316
1. Purpose of Voting 316
2. Voting in Corporations 317
3. Voting in NBEs 318
4. Horizontal Voting in Owner-Managed Firms 319
5. Vertical Voting in Manager-Managed Firms 322
E. Insurance and Indemnification 323
Sandt v. Energy Maintenance Services Group I, LLC 324
Trascent Management Consulting, LLC v. Bouri 328
F. Information Rights 332
1. Corporations 332
2. NBEs 333
G. Issues to Consider for NBEs 337
1. Designing the Management Structure 337
2. Required Owner Approvals 338
3. Selecting and Removing Managers 338
H. Problem: Entrepreneurs Think Seriously About Governance 339
Questions 340

Chapter 7. Fiduciary Duty 341
A. Introduction to Fiduciary Duties 341
1. The Nature of Fiduciary Duties 341
2. Fiduciary Duties in Corporation Law 342
B. Traditional Approach in NBEs 344
1. General Partnership 344
Meinhard v. Salmon 344
2. Limited Partnership 349
In re USACafes, L.P. Litigation 354
Notes 357
Red River Wings, Inc. v. Hoot, Inc. 358
3. Limited Liability Company 362
In re Sky Harbor Hotel Properties, LLC 362
Notes 365
Acorn v. Moncecchi 368
4. Minority Oppression 374
Wilson v. Gandis 375
5. Contracting for Duties in NBEs 382
McConnell v. Hunt Sports Enterprises 384

C. Delaware Approach on Contracting for Fiduciary Duty ... 391
Bay Center Apartments Owner, LLC v. Emery Bay PKI, LLC ... 393
Norton v. K-Sea Transp. Partners L.P. ... 396
Notes ... 402
D. Obligation of Good Faith and Fair Dealing ... 403
Gerber v. Enterprise Products Holdings, LLC ... 406
Dieckman v. Regency General Partner LP ... 407
E. Fiduciary Duty to Creditors ... 414
CML V, LLC v. Bax ... 415
Notes ... 418
F. Actions by Partners and Members ... 420
1. General Partnership ... 420
2. Limited Partnership and Limited Liability Company ... 423
Fritchel v. White ... 428
Notes ... 432
Anglo American Security Funds, L.P. v. S.R. Global International Fund, L.P. ... 433
Notes ... 438
Saunders v. Briner ... 439
Notes ... 445
Marx v. Morris ... 446
Woodside Properties, LLC v. MKR Development, LLC ... 456
3. Arbitration ... 459
G. Issues to Consider for NBEs ... 460
1. General Drafting Consideration ... 460
2. Duty of Care ... 461
3. Duty of Loyalty ... 462
H. Problem: Entrepreneurs Find a Deal and a Problem ... 465
Questions ... 468

Chapter 8. Transfer of Interest and Dissociation ... 469
A. Transfers of Interest in Corporation ... 469
B. Transfers of Interest in NBEs ... 469
1. Transferable Interest ... 469
SP Investment Fund III, LLC v. Zell ... 472
Bauer v. Blomfield Co./Holden Joint Venture ... 476
Notes ... 478
Northeast Communications of Wisconsin, Inc. v. CenturyTel, Inc. ... 479
2. Charging Order ... 482
Weddell v. H2O, Inc. ... 484
Notes ... 487
Law v. Zemp ... 488
JPMorgan Chase Bank, N.A. v. McClure ... 494
3. Foreclosure of Charging Order ... 500

C. Dissociation 501
1. General Partnership 501
United States v. Sanofi-Aventis U.S. LLC 506
Gelman v. Buehler 514
Fredericks Peebles & Morgan LLP v. Assam 516
Congel v. Malfitano 522
Notes 531
2. Limited Partnership 532
3. Limited Liability Company 534
IE Test, LLC v. Carroll 535
D. Buy-Sell Agreements 542
E. Issues to Consider for NBEs 546
1. Transferable Interest 546
2. Dissociation 548
3. Exit Mechanisms 548
4. Price and Valuation 550
F. Problem: Entrepreneurs Learn That Ownership Is Not Permanent 550
Questions 552

Chapter 9. Dissolution and Mergers 553
A. Dissolution 553
1. Events of Dissolution 553
Dysart v. Dragpipe Saloon, LLC 555
Haley v. Talcott 559
Styslinger v. Brewster Park, LLC 566
Notes 569
In re Carlisle Etcetera LLC 569
2. Administrative Compliance 575
Beaudry v. Harding 575
Notes 576
3. Winding Up 577
Guenther v. Ryerson 581
B. Mergers and Conversions 587
1. Basics of Mergers and Conversions 587
Corwin v. KKR Financial Holdings LLC 590
2. Fiduciary Duties 592
Allison v. Eriksson 593
C. Issues to Consider for NBEs 599
1. Voluntary Dissolution 599
2. Judicial Dissolution 600
3. Specific Events Triggering Dissolution 602
D. Problem: Entrepreneurs Go Bigtime, Maybe 603
Questions 604

Chapter 10. Introduction to Corporations **605**
A. Corporations in Society 605
1. Separation of Ownership and Control 607
The Modern Corporation & Private Property 607
2. Constitutional Rights 611
Citizens United v. Federal Election Commission 611
Notes 616
B. Major Differences Between NBEs and Corporations 617
1. Representative Management 617
2. Mandatory Rules 619
3. Mandatory Fiduciary Duties 621
4. Taxes 622
C. Why Corporations 622
1. Standardized Mandatory Rules 622
2. Professional Management 623
3. Separation of Ownership and Control 623
4. Standardized Ownership Units and Free Transferability 624
D. Delaware Corporation Law 626
Federalism and Corporate Law: Reflections Upon Delaware 627
State Law, Shareholder Protection, and the Theory of the Corporation 630

Chapter 11. Corporate Governance **633**
A. Board of Directors 633
1. Basic Requirements and Function of Board 633
2. Business Judgment Rule 636
Cinerama, Inc. v. Technicolor, Inc 637
Notes 638
Joy v. North 639
Shlensky v. Wrigley 640
Kamin v. American Express Co. 643
B. Officers 646
C. Shareholders 648
1. Types of Shareholders 648
2. Voting Rights 651
3. Participation in Governance 656
D. Corporate Governance 657
1. The Problem of Agency 658
Bayer v. Beran 659
2. Mechanisms of Accountability 663

Chapter 12. Duty of Care **665**
A. Care, Risk-Taking, and Business Judgment 665
The Tort Foundation of Duty of Care and Business Judgment 666
In re Citigroup Inc. Shareholder Derivative Litigation 667
B. Duty to Be Informed 672
Smith v. Van Gorkom 673

Notes ... 683
C. Exculpation ... 685
D. Aiding and Abetting Breach of Duties ... 687
RBC Capital Markets, LLC v. Jervis ... 688

Chapter 13. Duty of Loyalty ... 695
A. Self-Dealing and Conflict of Interest Transactions ... 695
Benihana of Tokyo, Inc. v. Benihana, Inc. ... 697
Gantler v. Stephens ... 702
Notes ... 709
Broz v. Cellular Information Systems, Inc. ... 709
B. Bad Faith ... 716
1. Defining Bad Faith ... 717
In re Walt Disney Co. Derivative Litigation ... 719
2. Failure to Monitor Compliance ... 721
In re Caremark International Inc. Derivative Litigation ... 722
Stone v. Ritter ... 729
In re Citigroup Inc. Shareholder Derivative Litigation ... 731
Marchand v. Barnhill ... 735
Notes ... 742
3. Intentional Violation of Law ... 745
In re Massey Energy Co. Derivative Litigation ... 746
C. Controlling Shareholders ... 747
1. Determination of Control and Fiduciary Duty ... 748
Sinclair Oil Corp. v. Levien ... 749
2. Controlling Shareholder Cash-Out Transactions ... 752
Weinberger v. UOP Inc. ... 753
Notes ... 759
Solomon v. Pathe Communications Corp. ... 760
Kahn v. Lynch Communications System, Inc. ... 762
Notes ... 768
Kahn v. M & F Worldwide Corp. ... 769
Notes ... 775

Chapter 14. Shareholder Litigation ... 777
A. Information Rights ... 777
Seinfeld v. Verizon Communications, Inc. ... 778
Notes ... 780
B. Direct and Derivative Suits ... 781
Tooley v. Donaldson, Lufkin & Jenrette, Inc. ... 782
Notes ... 784
C. Plaintiff Standing in Derivative Actions ... 784
In re Fuqua Industries, Inc. Shareholder Litigation ... 785
Lambrecht v. O'Neal ... 787
D. Demand and Demand Futility in Derivative Actions ... 793
Aronson v. Lewis ... 796
Notes ... 801

1. Not Valid Exercise of Business Judgment 804
Cede & Co. v. Technicolor, Inc. 804
2. Disinterestedness and Independence of Directors 805
In re eBay, Inc. Shareholder Litigation 809
Beam ex rel. Martha Stewart Living Omnimedia v. Stewart 812
Kahn v. M & F Worldwide Corp. 820

Chapter 15. Issues in Mergers & Acquisitions 823
A. M&A Basics 823
1. Reasons for M&A Transaction 823
Bove v. Community Hotel Corp. of Newport, R.I. 825
2. Basic Transaction Structures 828
3. Voting in Dilutive Transactions 834
4. Role of Fiduciary Duties 835
B. Entrenchment and Defenses 837
Unocal Corp. v. Mesa Petroleum Co. 840
C. Revlon and Its Progeny 844
Revlon, Inc. v. MacAndrews & Forbes Holdings, Inc. 845
Notes 851
Paramount Communications, Inc. v. Time Inc. 852
Paramount Communications, Inc. v. QVC Network Inc. 858
Corporate Short-Termism and Intertemporal Choice 865
Air Products and Chemicals, Inc. v. Airgas, Inc 867
Notes 873

Appendix A. Operating Agreement of Chrysler Group LLC 875

Appendix B. Revised Uniform Limited Liability Company Act (2006 & 2013 Harmonized) (Excerpted) 909

Appendix C. Revised Uniform Partnership Act (1997 & 2013 Harmonized) (Excerpted) 929

Appendix D. Uniform Limited Partnership Act (2001 & 2013 Harmonized) (Excerpted) 951

INDEX 977

TABLE OF CASES

The principal cases are in bold type.

800 South Wells Commercial LLC v. Cadden, 344, 621
7222 Ambassador Road, LLC v. Nat. Ctr. On Institutions and Alternatives, Inc., 99
A Guy Named Moe, LLC v. Chipotle Mexican Grill of Colorado, LLC, 95
Acorn v. Moncecchi, 368, 419
Acree v. McMahan, 175
Adelphia Communications Corp., In re, 180
Air Products and Chemicals, Inc. v. Airgas, Inc., 865, **867**
Albright v. Jefferson County National Bank, 808
Allentown Ambassadors, Inc., In re, 7
Allison v. Eriksson, 593
Alphonse v. Arch Bay Holdings, L.L.C., 154
Alsco, Inc. v. Fatty's Bar, LLC, 182
ALT Hotel, LLC v. Diamondrock Allerton Owner, LLC, 174
Altobelli v. Hartmann, 155
Anastos v. Sable, 527
Anglo Am. Sec. Funds, L.P. v. S.R. Glob. Int'l Fund, L.P., 113, **433**, 619
Appraisal of Ford Holdings, Inc. Preferred Stock, Matter of, 112, 113
Arnold v. Soc'y for Sav. Bancorp, Inc., 851
Aronson v. Lewis, 299, 431, 637, 638, 665, 669, 678, 683, 725, 791, **796**, 804, 815, 822, 842, 848, 860
ASB Allegiance Real Estate Fund v. Scion Breckenridge Managing Member, LLC, 406
Atlas Energy Resources, LLC, In re, 465
Auld v. Estridge, 422
Auriga Capital Corp. v. Gatz Properties, LLC, 341, 365
Azure Dolphin, LLC v. Barton, 26
B&S MS Holdings, LLC v. Landrum, 459, 600
Backuswalcott v. Common Ground Community HDFC, Inc., 180
Bagdon v. Bridgestone/Firestone, Inc., 444
Baker v. Wood, Ris & Hames, Professional Corp., 53
Bandera Master Fund LP v. Boardwalk Pipeline Partners, LP, 351, 403
Bashford-Burmister Co. v. Hammons, 619
Bauer v. Blomfield Co./Holden Joint Venture, 476, 565
Bay Center Apartments Owner, LLC v. Emery Bay PKI, LLC, 392, **393**
Bayer v. Beran, 659, 808
Beam ex rel. Martha Stewart Living Omnimedia v. Stewart, 812, 820, 822
Beard v. Beard, 346
Beaudry v. Harding, 575
Belgard v. Manchac Techs., LLC, 212
Benihana of Tokyo, Inc. v. Benihana, Inc., 697
Benjamin v. Bierman, 569
Bentley-Wing Property W, LLC v. West Development Inc., 546
Board of Prof. Resp., Wyoming State Bar v. Casper, 53
Boeing Co. v. KB Yuzhnoye, 175
Bove v. Community Hotel Corp. of Newport, R.I., 825
Brehm v. Eisner, 300, 461, 666, 822
Brelvis Consulting LLC, State v., 47
Brobeck, Phleger & Harrison LLP, In re, 463
Brodie v. Jordan, 597
Broz v. Cellular Information Systems, Inc., 709
Burlington Industries, Inc. v. Ellerth, 284
Butler Law Firm, PLC v. Higgins, 306
Bynum v. Frisby, 470
C.F. Trust, Inc. v. First Flight L.P., 174, 178, 180
CA, Inc. v. AFSCME Employees Pension Plan, 112
Canter v. Lakewood of Voorhees, 180
Cantor Fitzgerald & Co. v. 8an Capital Partners Master Fund L.P., 180
Caremark Int'l Inc. Derivative Litig., In re, 300, 461, 665, **722**, 729, 731, 735, 739
Carlisle Etcetera LLC, In re, 14, **205**, 569

Cascade Energy & Metals Corp. v. Banks, 178
Cavalier Oil Corp. v. Harnett, 532
Cede & Co. v. Technicolor, Inc., 684, 706, 717, **804**, 822
CelestialRX Invs., LLC v. Krivulka, 393
Central Nat'l Bank & Trust Co. of Des Moines v. Wagener, 178
Channing Real Estate, LLC v. Gates, 45, 442, 443
Cinerama, Inc. v. Technicolor, Inc., **637**, 822
Citigroup Inc. Shareholder Derivative Litigation, In re, **667**, 731
Citizens United v. Federal Election Commission, 48, **611**
Clancy v. King, 341
Clancy v. State Bar of Cal., 53
Clovis Oncology, Inc. Derivative Litigation, In re, 742
CML V, LLC v. Bax, **415**, 419
CNL-AB LLC v. Eastern Property Fund I SPE (MS Ref) LLC, 464
Cohen v. Beneficial Indus. Loan Corp., 424, 794
Congel v. Malfitano, 522
Cortez v. Nacco Material Handling Group, Inc., 158
Corwin v. KKR Financial Holdings LLC, **590**, 709, 836
Crimson Exploration Inc. S'holder Litig., In re, 748
Crow Irvine #2 v. Winthrop California Investors L.P., 545
CSH Theatres, LLC v. Nederlander of San Francisco Associates, 392
Culverhouse v. Paulson & Co., Inc., 426
Dailey v. Ayers Land Development, LLC, 165
Del Monte Foods Co. Shareholders Litigation, In re, 687
Delaware Sports Complex, LLC, In re, 91
Dieckman v. Regency General Partner LP, 382, 402, **407**
Dohmen v. Goodman, 333
Dole Food Co. v. Patrickson, 43
Don King Prods., Inc. v. Douglas, 405
Donahue v. Rodd Electrotype Co. of New England, Inc., 4, 16, 404, 444, 597
Dougherty v. Snyder, 52
Dubroff v. Wren Hldgs., LLC, 749
Dunlap v. State Farm Fire & Cas. Co., 405
Duray Development, LLC v. Perrin, 92
Dysart v. Dragpipe Saloon, LLC, 555
eBay, Inc. Shareholder Litigation, In re, 809
Ederer v. Gursky, 474
Edgar v. MITE Corp., 21
Egle v. Egle, 174
Eight of Swords, LLC, In re, 212
El Paso Pipeline GP Co., L.L.C. v. Brinckerhoff, 426
Elf Atochem N. Am., Inc. v. Jaffari, 121, 326, 394, 459, 511
Ellingwood v. Wolf's Head Oil Refinery Co., 625
Emerald Partners v. Berlin, 686, 716
Empire Excavating Co. v. Maret Dev. Corp., 99
Energy Transfer Partners, L.P. v. Enterprise Products Partners, L.P., 76
Erie Insurance Exchange v. EPC MD 15, LLC, 146
Estudios, Proyectos e Inversiones de Centro America, S.A. v. Swiss Bank Corp., 178
F.B.I. Farms, Inc. v. Moore, 469
Feeley v. NHAOCG, LLC, 357, 392, 748
Fehl v. S.W.C. Corp., 833
Fenwick v. Unemployment Compensation Commission, 64
Fifth Third Mortgage Co. v. Kaufman, 156
First Nat. Bank of Boston v. Bellotti, 612
First Nat'l City Bank v. Banco Para El Comercio Exterior de Cuba, 155
Fisk Ventures, LLC v. Segal, 261, 264, 393
Flight Options International, Inc. v. Flight Options, LLC, 464
Flood v. Synutra International, Inc., 775
Flora Constr. Co. v. Fireman's Fund Ins. Co., 52
Florida R & D Fund Inv., LLC v. Fla. BOCA/Deerfield R & D Inv., LLC, 310
Floyd v. I.R.S. U.S., 175
Fontana v. TLD Builders, Inc., 137
Forsythe v. Clark USA, Inc., 174
Fox v. I-10 Ltd., 214
Fraser v. Major League Soccer, L.L.C., 8
Fredericks Peebles & Morgan LLP v. Assam, 516
Freeman v. Complex Computing Co., Inc., 133
Fritchel v. White, 428

Fuqua Industries, Inc. Shareholder Litigation, In re, 785
Gagliardi v. TriFoods Int'l, Inc., 300, 462, 665
Gantler v. Stephens, 342, 687, **702**, 835, 838
Gardener v. Henderson Water Park, LLC, 145
Gateway Potato Sales v. G.B. Investment Co., 143
Gatz Properties, LLC v. Auriga Capital Corp., 365
Gay Jenson Farms Co. v. Cargill, Inc., 272
Gelman v. Buehler, **514**, 525
Genesis Hospice Care, LLC v. Mississippi Division of Medicaid, 576
Gentile v. Rossette, 343
Gerber v. Enterprise Products Holdings, LLC, 406
Gilbert v. Perlman, 749
Glassman v. Unocal Exploration Corp., 776, 832
Glick, In re, 174, 175
Gorton v. Doty, 250
Gould v. City of Stamford, 49
Graham v. Allis-Chalmers Mfg. Co., 726
Grayson v. Imagination Station, Inc., 427, 784
Greb, In re Estate of, 92
GreenHunter Energy, Inc. v. Western Ecosystems Technology, Inc., **168**, 418
Grimes v. Donald, 816, 822
Guenther v. Ryerson, 581
Guilder v. Corinth Constr. Corp., 135
Guth v. Loft, Inc., 695, 706, 712, 750, 757, 804, 843, 848
Guttman v. Huang, 739
H & H Development, LLC v. Ramlow, 52
Hagerman, United States v., 52
Hale v. Henkel, 49
Haley v. Talcott, **559**, 573
Hamilton Partners, L.P. v. Englard, 342
Hampshire Gp., Ltd. v. Kuttner, 341
Harbison v. Strickland, 103
Harrison v. Wahatoyas, LLC, 52
Harwood, In re, 357
Hassiepen, In re Marriage of, 65
Hausman, In re, 92
Hawkins v. i-TV Digitális Távközlési zrt., 4
Haynes Family Trust, The v. Kinder Morgan G.P., Inc., 341
Heaps v. Nuriche, LLC, 30
Hermelin v. K-V Pharm. Co., 327
Horwitz v. Holabird & Root, 53
Howland, In re, 175
Hudson Farms, Inc. v. McGrellis, 98
IE Test, LLC v. Carroll, 535
Ingram v. Deere, 65, 79
Inter-Marketing Group USA, Inc. v. Armstrong, 402
IOENGINE LLC v. Imation Corp., 91
Ira S. Bushey & Sons, Inc. v. United States, 281
Island Recreational Dev. Corp. v. Republic of Tex. Sav. Ass'n, 81
Ivanhoe Partners v. Newmont Mining Corp., 297, 619, 748
James v. Jackson, LLC v. Willie Gary, LLC, 459, 600
Jesse v. Danforth, 54
Jones v. H. F. Ahmanson & Co., 343
Joy v. North, 639
JPMorgan Chase Bank, N.A. v. McClure, 494
Kahn v. Lynch Communications System, Inc., 748, **762**, 768, 771
Kahn v. M & F Worldwide Corp., **769, 820**
Kamen v. Kemper Fin. Servs., Inc., 431
Kamin v. American Express Co., 643
Kelly v. Blum, 392
Kendrick & Roberts v. Warren Bros. Co., 96
Kerbawy v. McDonnell, 342
Kessler v. Antinora, 218
Kilpatrick v. White Hall on MS River, LLC, 199
Kirksey v. Grohmann, 556
Klotz v. Warner Communications, Inc., 831
Koh v. Inno-Pacific Holdings, Ltd., 496
Kohannim v. Katoli, 547
Kovacik v. Reed, 219
Kurz v. AMCP-1, LLC, 148
Lambert v. Farmers Bank, Frankfort, Ind., 178
Lambrecht v. O'Neal, 787
Landreth Timber Co. v. Landreth, 469, 625
Lang v. Lions Club of Cudahy Wisc., Inc., 251
Lattanzio v. COMTA, 52
Law v. Zemp, 488
Leber Assocs., LLC v. Entm't Group Fund, Inc., 91, 92
Lehrman v. Cohen, 618
Leighton v. Poltorak, 301
Levine v. Smith, 798

Lewis v. Anderson, 784, 790
LFC Mktg. Group, Inc. v. Loomis, 178
Loft, Inc. v. Guth, 678
Lorillard Tobacco Co. v. Am. Legacy Found., 91
Lugosch v. Congel, 303
Lynn v. Lloyd A. Lynn, Inc., 50
Lyondell Chem. Co. v. Ryan, 851
Malone v. Brincat, 333, 717
Malpiede v. Townson, 687
Manion v. Nagin, 54
Mantle v. North Star Energy & Construction, 418
Marchand v. Barnhill, 735
Martin v. Peyton, 66, 226
Marx v. Morris, 441, **446**
Massey Energy Co. Derivative Litigation, In re, 746
Mattingly Law Firm, P.C. v. Henson, 137, 164, 175
McCall Stock Farms, Inc. v. United States, 178
McConnell v. Hunt Sports Enterprises, 384
McDermott Inc. v. Lewis, 22
McDonough v. McDonough, 86
McKay v. Longman, 174, 175
McMullin v. Beran, 716
Mease v. Warm Mineral Springs, Inc., 310
Meinhard v. Salmon, 341, **344**, 404, 695
Merrill Tenant Council v. Department of Housing and Urban Development, 280
Metro Communication Corp. BVI v. Advanced Mobilecomm Technologies Inc., 745
Metro Storage Int'l LLC v. Harron, 6
Metropolitan Life Insurance Co. v. RJR Nabisco, Inc., 226
Midwest Neurosciences Associates, LLC v. Great Lakes Neurosurgical Associates, LLC, 459, 600
Miller v. Am. Real Estate Partners, L.P., 112, 391, 392, 460
Mills Acquisition Co. v. Macmillan, Inc., 684, 685
Minich v. Gem State Developers, Inc., 178
Minneapolis & St. Louis Railway Co. v. Beckwith, 48
Minuit Maid Corp. v. United Foods, Inc., 70
MM Companies, Inc. v. Liquid Audio, Inc., 654
Moore, In re, 174
Moran v. Household International, Inc., 839
Morris v. Spectra Energy Partners (DE) GP, LP, 104
Murrin Brothers 1885, Ltd., In re, 59
Nantucket Island Assoc. Ltd. Partnership Unitholders Litig., In re, 106, 620
Nationwide Emerging Managers, LLC v. Northpointe Hldgs., LLC, 405
Nelson v. American-West African Line, 282
Nemec v. Shrader, 405
Nixon v. Blackwell, 300, 627, 685
Norris v. Besel, 65
North Am. Catholic Educ. Programming Found., Inc. v. Gheewalla, 415, 417
Northeast Communications of Wisconsin, Inc. v. CenturyTel, Inc., 479
Northeast Natural Energy LLC v. Pachira Energy LLC, 65
Norton v. K-Sea Transp. Partners L.P., 118, **396**, 511
Obeid v. Hogan, 114
Ohio State Bar Ass'n v. Cohen, 52
Ohio State Bar Ass'n v. Naumov, 52
Olson v. Halvorsen, 102, 119
Orman v. Cullman, 807
ORT Associates v. IBC Services, Inc., 130
Palmer v. Mellen, 600
Palmer v. Moffat, 314
Palsgraf v. Long Island R.R. Co., 284
Paramount Communications, Inc. v. QVC Network Inc., 592, **858**
Paramount Communications, Inc. v. Time Inc., 592, **852**, 858, 863, 865, 869, 870, 872
Payne v. Hall, 348
Pepper v. Litton, 343
Peterson Group, Inc. v. PLTQ Lotus Group, L.P., 181
Phillips, In re, 175
Pilling v. Travelers Insurance Co., 64
Pinebrook Props., Ltd. v. Brookhaven Lake Prop. Owners Ass'n, 180
Plank v. Cherneski, 438
Pogostin v. Rice, 807
Productivity Technologies Corp. v. Levine, 344, 621
Pucci v. Santi, 54
Puklich v. Puklich, 531
R & R Capital, LLC v. Buck & Doe Run Valley Farms, LLC, 101, 460, 601
Rales v. Blasband, 432, 791, 798, 801, 815, 822
Rawlings v. Apodaca, 364

RBC Capital Markets, LLC v. Jervis, 202, **688**
Red River Wings, Inc. v. Hoot, Inc., **358**
Remora Investments, LLC v. Orr, 445
Renberg v. Zarrow, 543
Revlon, Inc. v. MacAndrews & Forbes Holdings, Inc., 592, 693, **845**, 852, 855, 858
Reynolds v. Lyman, **45**
Rieder v. Woods, 44
Ritchie v. Rupe, 547
Ron Medlin Constr. v. Harris, 138
Rosman v. Shapiro, 54
Ross Holding and Management Company v. Advance Realty Group, LLC, 392
Rural Metro Corp. S'holders Litig., In re, 341
Sagarra Inversiones, S.L. v. Cementos Portland Valderrivas, S.A., 22
Sandt v. Energy Maintenance Services Group I, LLC, **324**
Sanofi-Aventis U.S. LLC, United States v., **506**
Santa Clara County v. South. Pac. R.R. Co., 48, 611
Sauer v. Xerox Corp., 405
Saunders v. Briner, **439**
Schnell v. Chris-Craft Industries, Inc., 112, 620, 627, 808, 843
Schoon v. Smith, 572, 784
Schwartz v. Broadcast Music, Inc., 54
Sciabacucchi v. Salzberg, 84
SEC v. Chenery Corp., 342
SEC v. Merchant Capital, LLC, **234**
SEC v. W.J. Howey Co., 233, 236
Segal v. Genitrix, LLC, **260**
Seidler v. Morgan, 180
Seinfeld v. Verizon Communications, Inc., 332, **778**
Seneca Invs. LLC v. Tierney, 596
Sertich v. Moorman, 422
Sheldon v. Pinto Tech. Ventures, L.P., 748
Shintom Co., Ltd. v. Audiovox Corp., 103
Shlensky v. Wrigley, **640**
Shuomali, In re, 165
SI Mgmt. L.P. v. Wininger, 118
Simmons v. Miller, 445
Simons v. Cogan, 414
Sinclair Oil Corp. v. Levien, 624, **749**, 804, 842, 862
Sky Cable, LLC v. Coley, 174
Sky Harbor Hotel Properties, LLC, In re, **362**
Skye Mineral Investors, LLC v. DXS Capital (U.S.) Ltd., 392, 393
Smith v. Rustic Home Builders, LLC, 52
Smith v. Van Gorkom, 461, 592, **673**, 804, 824, 835, 848, 852
Solomon v. Pathe Communications Corp., **760**
Southern Pacific Co. v. Bogert, 357
SP Investment Fund III, LLC v. Zell, **472**
Spring Real Estate, LLC v. Echo/RT Holdings, LLC, 833
Steinhausen v. HomeServices of Nebraska, Inc., 52
Stone v. Jetmar Properties, LLC, 92
Stone v. Ritter, 403, 404, 717, **729**, 732, 739
Styslinger v. Brewster Park, LLC, 439, 441, 445, 478, **566**
Sun-Times Media Grp. v. Black, 327
Sutherland v. Sutherland, 344, 621
SV Inv. Partners, LLC v. ThoughtWorks, Inc., 226
Swope v. Swope, 309, 619
Tavadia v. Mitchell, 146
Teamsters Local 443 Health Servs. & Ins. Plan v. Chou, 743
Thomas D. Philipsborn Irrevocable Ins. Trust v. Avon Capital, LLC, **280**
Thornton, In re, 129
Thrifty S'holder Litig., In re, 852
Tooley v. Donaldson, Lufkin & Jenrette, Inc., 426, 432, **782**
Tover v. 419 OCR, Inc., 121
Towe Antique Ford Found. v. IRS, 178
Trascent Management Consulting, LLC v. Bouri, **328**
True, Estate of v. Commissioner, 544
TW Services, Inc. v. SWT Acquisition Corp., 652, 654
Tzolis v. Wolff, 445
Unocal Corp. v. Mesa Petroleum Co., 112, 592, 804, **840**, 845, 848, 852, 858
USACafes, L.P. Litigation, In re, **354**
USG Corp. Stockholder Litig., In re, 836
Van Heusen v. Van Heusen Charles Co., 619
Veterans Parkway Developers, LLC v. RMW Development Fund II, LLC., 45
W.G. Platts, Inc. v. Platts, 178
Walkovszky v. Carlton, **127**
Wallop Canyon Ranch, LLC v. Goodwyn, 371, 429
Walt Disney Co. Derivative Litigation, In re, 717, **719**, 729

Washington v. Reliable Life Ins. Co., 81
Wasserman v. Kay, 365
Watson v. Button, 443, 445
Weddell v. H2O, Inc., 484
Weinberger v. UOP, Inc., 343, 673, 682, 684, 685, 694, **753**, 761, 765, 772, 805, 835, 861
Weinstein Enters., Inc. v. Orloff, 748, 760
Weinstein v. Colborne Foodbotics, LLC, 418
Wells Fargo Bank, N.A. v. Barber, 496
Westinghouse Elec. Corp. v. Kerr-McGee Corp., 54
Westland Police & Fire Retirement Sys., City of v. Axcelis Techns., Inc., 781
Westmas v. Creekside Tree Serv., Inc., 254
Wiggs v. Summit Midstream Partners, LLC, 464
Wilkes v. Springside Nursing Home, Inc., 374
Williams v. 5300 Columbia Pike Corp., 344
Williams v. Geier, 113
Williamson v. Tucker, 233, 236
Willie Gary LLC v. James & Jackson LLC, 459, 460, 600
Wilson v. Gandis, 375
Wood, United States ex rel. v. Allergan, Inc., 507
Woodside Properties, LLC v. MKR Development, LLC, 456
Zahra Spiritual Trust v. United States, 178
Zapata Corp. v. Maldonado, 803
Zisblatt v. Zisblatt, 178

LLCs, Partnerships, and Corporations

CHAPTER 1

OVERVIEW OF BUSINESS ENTITIES

■ ■ ■

A. RELEVANCE OF BUSINESS ENTITIES

Business entities such as corporations, partnerships, and limited liability companies are organizations formed through law that conduct business enterprise. "Organization" implies a set of rules or principles that organize participants in a common venture. Business entities are created by enabling laws. Partnership law enables the creation of partnerships: *i.e.*, without it, there can be no legal recognition of partnerships. The same is true for corporations and limited liability companies. These business entities exist because states permit them.

The laws of business organizations provide rules and principles that govern the internal affairs. To understand what "internal affairs" means, consider an association of 50 individuals who want to conduct a specific business in mind—perhaps the marketing and distribution of officially licensed English Premier League soccer merchandise in the U.S. These 50 persons are skilled and talented. The products are excellent and desirable. Soccer is the most popular sport in the world with increasing popularity in America. Good people, good products, and good market—the business venture is destined for success, right? Definitely not, at least not yet. Without an organization bound by some form of mutual understanding and system of governance rules, even a relatively simple business may fail. Important internal matters must be agreed upon among venturers. Consider some of these basic questions.

- **Economics.**—What is each person's economic claims?
    - On share of profits? Or losses?
    - On assets?
    - How are distributions of profits and assets made? A matter of right? Or a matter of discretion by others?
- **Liability.**—What liabilities may be imposed on each person by virtue of participation in this venture?
    - To each other?
    - To third parties?
    - On what grounds?

- **Management and agency.**—What is each person's management rights and powers?
  - Can a person conduct business on behalf of the firm, such as signing contracts?
  - How are ordinary and important business decisions made? By vote? By majority, supermajority, or unanimity? By selected individuals or group?
  - How are managers selected and removed? What are their powers?
  - What are the rights to information by all interested parties?
- **Duties.**—What are the duties that each person owes to the organization and others?
  - Can a person be sued for bad decisions or mismanagement?
  - Can a person use firm assets for personal reasons? Take business opportunities that belong or may be pursued by the firm? Engage in transactions with the firm that involve personal interests?
  - What are the potential liabilities of each person for these kinds of conducts?
- **Dissociation and transfer.**—How does a person leave the organization?
  - Can a person dissociate at will?
  - What is the person's rights? What economic interests do they receive upon exiting? What obligations remain?
  - Can a person be expelled? On what grounds?
  - Can a person sell her interest in the firm to a third party?
- **Dissolution.**—How does the firm dissolve?
  - What events trigger dissolution? Can a person seek to dissolve the firm? Can the government, such as the court, dissolve the firm?
  - How are the assets and liabilities of the firm dealt with upon dissolution?

The above issues are just some of the most basic questions that arise when venturers decide to form a firm, make an investment, and conduct business together. There is no single answer to the above questions. "Working things out" as venturers conduct business together is a recipe for legal and business disaster. Suppose they disagree on how to share profits and losses as the business soars or crashes. The rules of internal affairs should not be made up "on the fly" or based on a naïve faith in the goodwill or common thinking among economic actors seeking personal profit. One can imagine the discord, conflict, and opportunism—and perhaps tragicomedic episodes of confused misunderstandings and recriminations—if these questions are ignored at the outset only to spring up when one discovers that others do not view their stakes or roles in the enterprise as you do. Energy and cost are devoted to disputes rather than to the business.

The laws of business organizations provide the rules of internal affairs. Each entity form provides different answers to the above questions and many other rules. The law of each business form provides a comprehensive, if not entirely complete, set of rules unique to each entity form. We should understand each entity and its similarities to and differences with other entities. This broad understanding is important in the choice and maintenance of business forms.

B. CORPORATIONS AND NONCORPORATE BUSINESS ENTITIES

In the world of business enterprises, a clear dichotomy exists between public and private firms.[1] (A "firm" or a "company" herein simply means a business organization without reference to a specific legal form such as a corporation, partnership, or limited liability company.) Ownership interests can be publicly traded, typically on stock exchanges, and they are archetypically stock in public corporations. While public companies, such as Amazon and Google, are tremendously important in the national and global economies, they number less than 4,500 in the U.S.[2] The vast majority of firms are privately held. Interests in them such as shares of stock in a corporation or partners' interest in a partnership are not publicly traded under the auspice of federal securities law. Private firms can have many owners: *e.g.*, a law firm of many hundreds of partners. But the vast majority of private firms are closely-held firms whose equity is held by a

---

[1] Years ago, Henry Manne argued that there should be two theories of corporations, one for large public companies and the other for small private companies, in light of the fact that these two groups of firms were so different. Henry G. Manne, *Our Two Corporation Systems: Law and Economics*, 53 Va. L. Rev. 259, 259 & n.3 (1967). At that time, the major forms of firms were corporations (public and private companies) and partnerships (general partnerships and limited partnerships, virtually all of which were private ventures). Since then, the limited liability company form has grown to be a preferred entity form. Today, the dichotomy between public and private is not between private and public corporations or between corporations and partnerships, but is between public corporations and private firms of all entity forms.

[2] *See* Les Brorsen, *Looking Behind the Declining Number of Public Companies*, Harvard Law School Forum on Corporate Governance and Financial Regulation (May 18, 2017), available at https://corpgov.law.harvard.edu/2017/05/18/looking-behind-the-declining-number-of-public-companies/ ("Since the 2008 financial crisis, the total number of domestic US-listed companies has largely stabilized again, ranging between 4,100 and 4,400."); Craig Doidge, G. Andrew Karolyi, and René M. Stulz, *The U.S. Listing Gap*, NBER Working Paper No. 21181 (May 2015), available at http://www.nber.org/papers/w21181 (showing that from 1996 and 2012 the number of exchange-listed firms fell from 8,000 to 4,100).

relatively small number of owners: *e.g.*, a partnership between John and Jane to own a Sicilian pizza parlor, or a joint venture between Facebook and Google to develop biometric technology.

Corporations straddle both sides of the public-private divide. While virtually all publicly traded firms are corporations, the vast majority of all corporations are privately held. While few noncorporate business entities (NBEs) are publicly traded,[3] virtually all NBEs are private firms whose interests are closely held.

Corporations and NBEs constitute two spheres of the business world. In the well-known case of *Donahue v. Rodd Electrotype Co. of New England, Inc.*, 328 N.E.2d 505, 512 (Mass. 1975), the court characterized a close corporation, a corporation with a small group of shareholders, as an "incorporated partnership." This comment aptly described the limited menu of business entity choices in 1975. A general partnership at the time did not provide the benefit of limited liability. Only a corporation and a limited partnership provided this benefit, and the latter only as to limited partners. Given this limited choice, a close corporation permitted a partnership-style ownership and management structure with the benefit of limited liability to all shareholders. Much has changed since 1975, principally the addition of the limited liability company form as an entity choice. *See* Walter Frick, *A Brief Guide to U.S. Corporate Tax Reform*, Harv. Bus. Rev. (Sept. 7, 2017) ("In 1985, roughly half of companies were structured as C Corporations, meaning they were required to pay corporate taxes. Today, fewer than 20% of firms are C Corporations, meaning that the rest—representing half of business profits in the U.S.—are flow-through entities not eligible for corporate taxes."); Hawkins v. i-TV Digitális Távközlési zrt., 935 F.3d 211, 223 (4th Cir. 2019) ("Even for American entities, drawing a principled distinction between corporations and unincorporated associations is not always easy. The twentieth century saw the creation of new types of business entities that straddled the boundary separating traditional corporations from traditional partnerships: professional corporations, limited liability partnerships, limited liability companies, and so forth.").

Historically, NBEs were general partnerships and limited partnerships, and they were generally smaller, closely-held businesses. This is still accurate as a general statement. At the same time, NBEs are now regularly used to operate large and sophisticated businesses. For example, Chrysler and Major League Soccer are limited liability companies, and even large multinational corporations such as Amazon use limited liability companies to operate many of their ventures and subsidiaries. Large international law firms and other professional service

[3] Ownership interests in noncorporate entities can fall within the definition of "securities" under federal securities laws. Such securities can be publicly issued and traded. For example, The Blackstone Group L.P. (NYSE: BX) and The Carlyle Group L.P. (NYSE: CG) are publicly traded investment firms structured as limited partnerships.

firms, such as Skadden, Arps, Slate, Meagher & Flom, operate their businesses as limited liability partnerships. Major businesses, such as Bloomberg and many large investment funds, such as Blackstone and Carlyle, are operated as limited partnerships. In the modern world of business, NBEs are not simply the small partnerships of yore.

1. BREAKDOWN OF BUSINESS ENTITIES

Corporations come in all sizes and shapes. While many corporations are smaller firms or family-run enterprises, the archetypical corporation has always been the public corporations. Corporation law is important because public companies are vital to the national economy. Traditionally, NBEs have been the preferred entity forms for smaller, closely-held business enterprises. That is still the case. However, NBEs are becoming more prominent in larger and more sophisticated enterprises, principally due to the rise of limited liability companies as an entity form that can accommodate the needs of large or sophisticated business enterprises.

The chart below shows the changing percentages of the different types of entity from 1990 to 2012 according to IRS tax filings.

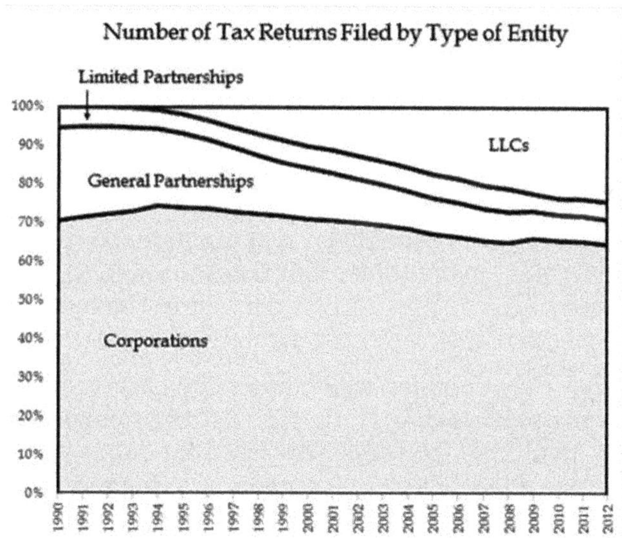

Jeffrey D. Bauman, Russell B. Stevenson, Jr. & Robert J. Rhee, Business Organizations Law and Policy: Materials and Problems 19 (West 2017).

As this chart indicates, there are three major types of NBEs: general partnership, limited partnership (LP), and limited liability company (LLC). They are the focus of this book. Each of these forms is distinct.

In 1990, general partnerships accounted for most of the NBEs with a small percentage of LPs. By 2012, however, LLCs accounted for most of the NBEs with smaller percentages of LPs and general partnerships. The trend is clear. General partnerships are declining and LLCs are more popular. We see a gradual decline in the percentage of corporate filings that is also correlated with the rapid increase in LLCs. Some businesspersons and their lawyers are choosing the LLC over the corporation.

Presently, corporations and LLCs are the two clearly preferred choice of entities in the United States, and the LLC is the fastest growing entity. No business law practitioner today can perform his or her job without at least a basic understanding of NBEs, including the LLC.

2. THE RISE OF LLCs

In 1977, Wyoming enacted the first LLC statute. The provision of limited liability for a noncorporate entity was the key innovation. Before this point, only limited partnerships provided limited liability for noncorporate entities. In 1991, Texas created the first limited liability partnership statute that provides limited liability to general partnerships, thus another noncorporate business entity with limited liability. However, partnerships require at least two owners. Unlike LPs and LLPs, LLCs are not partnerships and can be owned by a single owner.

With respect to LLCs, an important factor determining the utility of the LLC as a business entity form was its tax treatment. Under Subchapter C of the Internal Revenue Code (IRC), a "C" corporation is subject to a double taxation scheme: the corporation is taxed on its profit as a separate and distinct tax person, and a shareholder is a separate and distinct tax person and thus is taxed on any distributions, such as the receipt of dividends from the corporation. However, under Subchapter K of the IRC, partnerships are subject to a single level of taxation: the partnership is not taxed on its profit, and instead the profit flows through to the partners who are taxed on their income. When LLCs arrived in the business landscape, it was unclear whether they were tax corporations or tax partnerships.

In 1988, the IRS published a revenue ruling stating that a Wyoming LLC could be a tax partnership. With this confirmation, other states began enacting their own LLC statutes. By the mid-1990s, every state had enacted an LLC statute.[4] In 1997, in response to this rapid development in business organization law, the Treasury Department promulgated the "check-the-box" regulation. By checking a box, all noncorporate, multi-member business associations, such as a partnership or a multi-member LLC, could elect their federal tax treatment, either a tax partnership or a

[4] "The LLC was originally invented through the combined efforts of sophisticated corporate lawyers and savvy tax practitioners. Together, they convinced the State of Wyoming to adopt the first LLC statute in 1977 with the goal of delivering a combination of limited liability and partnership tax treatment. In 1988, the Internal Revenue Service ruled that this previously obscure entity could indeed deliver both features. After the IRS ruling and with the LLC gaining in popularity, a group of Delaware lawyers under the auspices of the Council of the Corporation Law Section of the Delaware State Bar Association began drafting the LLC Act. In 1992, the LLC Act became law." Metro Storage Int'l LLC v. Harron, 2019 WL 3282613, at *10 (Del. Ch. 2019).

tax corporation. Thus, multi-member LLCs can elect to be tax partnerships with the benefit of a single level of taxation. A single-member LLC is a disregarded entity (meaning that the IRS disregards the entity and thus the single member is treated as a sole proprietor for the purpose of taxes). Following the federal check-the-box regulations, LLCs grew rapidly. The IRS now provides the following information on its website:

> Depending on elections made by the LLC and the number of members, the IRS will treat an LLC as either a corporation, partnership, or as part of the LLC's owner's tax return (a "disregarded entity"). Specifically, a domestic LLC with at least two members is classified as a partnership for federal income tax purposes unless it files Form 8832 and affirmatively elects to be treated as a corporation. For income tax purposes, an LLC with only one member is treated as an entity disregarded as separate from its owner, unless it files Form 8832 and elects to be treated as a corporation. However, for purposes of employment tax and certain excise taxes, an LLC with only one member is still considered a separate entity.

Limited Liability Company (LLC), Internal Revenue Service, available at https://www.irs.gov/businesses/small-businesses-self-employed/limited-liability-company-llc (last visited July 19, 2020).

Importantly, tax treatment is not the only reason why LLCs became so popular. The tax issue is best understood as a precondition for the rapid rise of the LLC. If favorable tax treatment is the sole issue in entity choice, there would not have been a need for LLCs; general partnerships and LPs, which have long existed alongside corporations, provide a single level of taxation under Subchapter K. The rise of LLCs relative to other business forms is explained by their non-tax features. There was a need for an entity that combined the tax advantage of partnerships and the specific advantages of various existing business entities, including the corporation. Once the tax treatment of LLCs was clarified to provide a distinct advantage of LLCs over corporations, businesspersons and their lawyers could consider the other facets of the LLC form in comparison to corporations, general partnerships and LPs.

The LLC is a hybrid entity, a chameleon entity because its contractual flexibility permits great customization of the rules of internal affairs. It can acquire the features of a prototypical partnership with communitarian ownership and control, or a prototypical corporation with separation of ownership and control, or any other management and ownership structure in between these antipodes. The flexibility of the LLC form coupled with its favorable tax treatment presents a key advantage over other business entities. *See* In re Allentown Ambassadors, Inc., 361 B.R. 422, 442 (Bankr. E.D. Pa. 2007) ("An LLC is a conceptual hybrid, sharing some of the characteristics of partnerships and some of corporations. In particular, an

LLC combines the two most critical features of all of the other business organizations in a single business organization—a corporate-styled liability shield and the pass-through tax benefits of a partnership.").

The case below is an antitrust action involving Major League Soccer (MLS). It is presented not for the law, but for the facts. It provides an example of how a large, sophisticated business enterprise uses the LLC form. MLS was formed as an LLC in 1995, a time when the entity form was still relatively new. The court noted in 2002 that no team made a profit. In 2013, 19 MLS soccer teams had an aggregate value of $1.96 billion, earned $494 million in revenue and $34 million in operating profit. Chris Smith, *Major League Soccer's Most Valuable Teams*, Forbes (Nov. 20, 2013). In 2018, 23 MLS teams had an aggregate value of $5.53 billion, earned $763 in revenue and $63 million in operating loss. Chris Smith, *Major League Soccer's Most Valuable Teams 2018: Atlanta United Debuts on Top*, Forbes (Nov. 14, 2018). *Fútbol* is big business in America, and it will only get bigger. As of 2020, MLS had 26 teams including 3 Canadian teams, and fan interest is growing fast. American professional soccer, a multi-billion dollar sports industry, is organized as a single LLC structure.

In reading this case, think about these questions: (1) Major Leagues Soccer could have been organized in any number of ways—why was it organized in this way? (2) What role did the laws of business organizations, here LLCs, play in the organization of this soccer league?

FRASER V. MAJOR LEAGUE SOCCER, L.L.C.

284 F.3d 47 (1st Cir. 2002)

BOUDIN, CHIEF JUDGE.

Professional soccer players sued Major League Soccer, LLC ("MLS"), nine independent operator/investors in MLS, and the United States Soccer Federation, Inc. ("USSF"), alleging violations of Sherman Act sections 1 and 2, 15 U.S.C. §§ 1–2, and Clayton Act section 7, *id.* § 18, and seeking injunctive relief and monetary damages. The district court granted summary judgment for defendants on the section 1 and Clayton Act counts. After trial on the section 2 count, the jury returned a special verdict leading to judgment in favor of defendants. Players now appeal the disposition of all three counts. We begin with a statement of the background facts.

Despite professional soccer's popularity abroad, the sport has achieved only limited success in this country. Several minor leagues have operated here, but before the formation of MLS, only one other U.S. professional league—the North American Soccer League ("NASL")—had ever obtained Division I, or top-tier, status. Launched in 1968, the NASL achieved some success before folding in 1985; MLS attributes the NASL's demise in part to wide disparities in the financial resources of the league's independently owned teams and a lack of centralized control.

In 1988, the USSF, the national governing body of soccer was awarded the right to host the 1994 World Cup soccer tournament in the U.S. by the Federation Internationale de Football Association ("FIFA"), soccer's international governing body. In consideration for the coveted sponsorship rights, the USSF promised to establish a viable Division I professional soccer league in the U.S. as soon as possible.

In the wake of a successful World Cup USA, MLS was officially formed in February 1995 as a limited liability company ("LLC") under Delaware law. The league is owned by a number of independent investors (a mix of corporations, partnerships, and one individual) and is governed by a management committee known as the board of governors. Some of the investors are passive; others are also team operators as explained below.

MLS has, to say the least, a unique structure, even for a sports league. MLS retains significant centralized control over both league and individual team operations. MLS owns all of the teams that play in the league (a total of 12 prior to the start of 2002), as well as all intellectual property rights, tickets, supplied equipment, and broadcast rights. MLS sets the teams' schedules; negotiates all stadium leases and assumes all related liabilities; pays the salaries of referees and other league personnel; and supplies certain equipment.

At issue in this case is MLS's control over player employment. MLS has the "sole responsibility for negotiating and entering into agreements with, and for compensating, Players." In a nutshell, MLS recruits the players, negotiates their salaries, pays them from league funds, and, to a large extent, determines where each of them will play. For example, to balance talent among teams, it decides, with the non-binding input of team operators, where certain of the league's "marquee" players will play.

However, MLS has relinquished some control over team operations to certain investors. MLS contracts with these investors to operate nine of the league's teams (the league runs the other three). These investors are referred to as operator/investors. Each operator/investor has the "exclusive right and obligation to provide Management Services for a Team within its Home Territory" and is given some leeway in running the team and reaping the potential benefits therefrom.

The operator/investors hire, at their own expense and discretion, local staff (including the general managers and coaches of their respective teams), and are responsible for local office expenses, local promotional costs for home games, and one-half the stadium rent. They license local broadcast rights, sell home tickets, and conduct all local marketing on behalf of MLS; agreements regarding these matters do not require the prior approval of MLS. And they control a majority of the seats on MLS's board, the very same body which runs the league's operations. Among other things, the board is responsible for hiring the commissioner and approving national television contracts and marketing decisions, league rules and policies (including team player budgets), and sales of interests.

The operator/investors also play a limited role in selecting players for their respective teams. While the operating agreements provide that the operator/investors will not bid independently for players against MLS, they may trade players with other MLS teams and select players in the league's draft. Such transactions, however, must follow strict rules established by the league. Most importantly, no team may exceed the maximum player budget established by the management committee.

In return for the services of the operator/investors, MLS pays each a "management fee" that corresponds to the performance of their respective team. The management fee equals the sum of one-half of local ticket receipts and concessions; the first $1,125,000 of local broadcast revenues, increasing annually by a percentage rate, plus a 30% share (declining to 10% by 2006) of any amount above the base amount; all revenues from overseas tours; a share of one-half the net revenues from the MLS Championship Game and a share of revenues from other exhibition games.

The remaining revenues of the league are distributed in equal portions to all investors. While the investors qua investors share equally in the league's profits and losses, the individual team operators qua operators fare differently depending at least in part on the financial performance of their respective teams.

Although MLS retains legal title to the teams, the operator/investors may transfer their operating rights and retain much of the value created by their individual efforts and investments. Investors may transfer their ownership stakes and operating rights to other current investors without obtaining prior consent; transfers to outside investors require a two-thirds majority vote of the board. For its part, MLS may terminate any operating agreement on its own initiative if, by a two-thirds vote of the board, an operator/investor is determined to have failed to act in the best interests of the league. If so, it must still pay such operator/investor fair market value for its operating rights and ownership interest.

The league began official play in 1996. The following February of 1997, eight named players sued MLS, the USSF, and the operator/investors under various antitrust theories.

C. DIFFERENCES BETWEEN CORPORATIONS AND NBEs

There are many differences between corporations and NBEs. This book examines these differences. To provide an initial orientation, the following discussion outlines some of the most fundamental differences.

1. TAXATION OF CORPORATIONS AND NBEs

The tax rules apply differently to different business entities. Under Subchapter C of the IRC, a corporation is subject to a double taxation: tax on its profits and tax on shareholders. Under Subchapter K, an NBE is subject to a single level of tax: profits flow through to the owners who are then taxed. There are exceptions to these rules.

NBEs can be subject to the double taxation framework, under I.R.C. § 7704, if their securities are publicly traded. Conversely, corporations can elect flow through treatment and pass corporate income, losses, deductions, and credits through to their shareholders under Subchapter S. But the IRS limits the corporate attributes of an "S" corporation, including the following: (1) only domestic corporation are eligible; (2) shareholders may only be individuals, certain trusts, and estates; (3) there must be no more than 100 shareholders; (4) a corporation can only have one class of stock. Public corporations cannot meet these standards. Most S corporations are smaller, and by definition they are closely held firms. Many corporations today are S corporations. By electing to be an S corporation, the corporation chooses to limit its corporate attributes to the restrictions of tax law.

Tax is important. But it is just one important factor in the total set of considerations when choosing an entity. The distinctions between corporations and NBEs with respect to the rules of governance are important factors in entity choice.

2. MANAGEMENT STRUCTURE

The internal affairs of corporations are subject to corporation law, which does not reference or distinguish the tax status of corporations. The defining characteristic of a corporation is the requirement of a board of directors as the ultimate managerial authority. *See* Delaware General Corporation Law § 141(a) (DGCL) ("The business and affairs of every corporation shall be managed by or under the direction of a board of directors."); Model Business Corporation Act § 8.01(b) (MBCA) (functionally same).[5] A board structure constitutes a form of representative management: shareholders elect managers who, in public corporations at least, typically do not own a significant stake in the corporation.

With the exception of LPs, partnerships and LLCs do not have a required management structure. Instead, there are default statutory rules. "Default" means that the statute may provide a rule, but the parties may contractually change the default rule through the entity's partnership or operating agreement in the process of private ordering. An important

[5] Corporation law provides a way to limit the board's authority or to eliminate the board structure for close corporations. *See* DGCL § 102(b)(1), § 351; MBCA § 2.02(b)(2)(iii). However, there are limits to these means. *See* DGCL § 102(b)(1) (limited to nonstock corporation), § 342(a) (limited to a close corporation); MBCA § 7.32 (limited to shareholder agreement to limit the power of the board).

aspect of all laws of business organizations is a certain degree of contracting for internal rules of organization. Each law determines the degree of permissiveness. For example, LPs require a formal management structure that is similar in broad principle to a corporation, a general partner who manages the LP and a limited partner who is a passive investor. The assumption for both the corporation and the LP is that specialized management with centralized authority will manage the business on behalf of passive investors.

3. SEPARATION OF OWNERSHIP AND CONTROL

The requirement of a board reveals a fundamental premise of corporation law: the corporate form induces a separation of ownership and control. Modern scholars have recognized that a firm operated by professional managers on behalf of its owners provides a means to aggregate vast sums of capital and engage in large scale enterprise. *See* Adolf A. Berle & Gardiner C. Means, The Modern Corporation and Private Property (1932). Along with this benefit, scholars have also identified potential problems from such an arrangement—the nature of agency cost. Those in control, with little ownership stake, are not always incentivized to pursue the interest of the firm and its owners, but instead may sometimes pursue their own interests with their control.

NBEs start from a different fundamental premise: closely-held firms are operated by their owners. From this initial position, some NBE forms can assume hybrid qualities. Like corporations, LPs mandates a formal division between a manager (general partner) and a passive investor (limited partner), and LLCs can take the form of a manager-managed LLC wherein a manager, who may or may not be a member, operate the business like the board and officers of a corporation.

4. FIDUCIARY DUTY

Due to the separation of ownership and control and the special role and powers of directors and officers, corporate managers owe fiduciary duty to the corporation and shareholders. Shareholders are presumed to be passive investors and thus owe no fiduciary duty, unless they actually participate in the control of the company as controlling shareholders.

The rules for NBEs are more varied. Because partners in a general partnership manage the firm together, they owe fiduciary duty to the partnership and other partners. Because LPs have a formal separation of managers and investors, a general partner owes fiduciary duty, but a limited partner does not. An LLC is a hybrid entity and can be structured to look like a partnership or a corporation or anything in between. Accordingly, a member may or may not owe fiduciary duty depending on whether the member participates in the management of the LLC.

5. LIMITED LIABILITY

Corporations provide its shareholders with limited liability. The rule of limited liability means that shareholders are not vicariously liable for the debts and obligations of the corporation. The rule incentivizes risk taking. The separation of ownership and control is more palatable and practical if an investor, who is far removed from control and oversight authority, is limited in loss to the amount of investment, and no more.

Conversely, the rule of limited liability applies in some NBEs, but not others. General partnerships do not have limited liability, unless they file to become a limited liability partnership (LLP). LPs, which are different from LLPs, provide limited liability only to limited partners, subject to certain restrictions. LLCs provide broad protection against vicarious liability to members and managers. Thus, NBEs have different rules as to limited liability.

6. TRANSFERABILITY OF INTEREST

Each share of stock in a corporation constitutes the entire ownership interest, including all rights to governance and to economic claims. Shares, in their entirety, are presumed to be freely transferable. Historically, this rule permitted liquidity in shares such that ventures are fluidly financed with disparate groups of investors who readily enter and exit the investment. Corporation statutes permit certain restrictions on the transfer of shares. *E.g.,* Model Business Corporation Act § 6.27(c) (2016) (permitting restriction on transferability to maintain a corporation's particular status, preserve exemptions under securities laws, and "for any other reasonable purpose"). However, absent a specific limitation grounded in a valid statute or agreement, courts have disfavored restrictions on free transferability.

Conversely, the law of NBEs restrict free transferability as a default rule. Ownership interest in NBEs is deemed to have two components: the right to participate in the governance of the firm including voting and information rights, and the right to the economic interest. Only the latter is considered personal property and thus freely transferable. *E.g.*, Delaware Limited Liability Company Act § 18–701 ("A limited liability company interest is personal property."), § 18–702 ("The assignee of a member's limited liability company interest shall have no right to participate in the management of the business and affairs of a limited liability company."). The rationale behind this restriction is the policy that owners should select their business associates in closely-held ventures, which is the historical origin of NBEs.

7. MANDATORY RULES AND ELASTICITY OF PRIVATE ORDERING

The distinction between "must" and "may" is important in law. Laws are typically couched in the form of affirmative or negative obligations. For example, the obligations of criminal or environmental laws are not optional. But the laws of business organizations are, *in some respect*, enabling. They enable the creation of business firms and, *to varying degrees*, permit organizers, owners, and managers to create their own internal rules of governance. In this sense, they are more like contract law.

All corporation and NBE statutes provide a set mix of mandatory and default rules. Upon the creation of the entity, some statutory provisions are default rules that may be changed through the process of private ordering. But the laws of business organizations are not entirely in the nature of contract law. They also regulate because they mandate certain fixed rules for each entity. Mandatory rules are justified on the ground that the state provides certain important benefits and thus can dictate certain regulatory terms.

> To my mind, when a sovereign makes available an entity with attributes that contracting parties cannot grant themselves by agreement, the entity is not purely contractual. Because the entity has taken advantage of benefits that the sovereign has provided, the sovereign retains an interest in that entity. Put more directly, an LLC agreement is not an exclusively private contract among its members precisely because the LLC has powers that only the State of Delaware can confer.

In re Carlisle Etcetera LLC, 114 A.3d 592, 605–06 (Del. Ch. 2015). *See also* Robert J. Rhee, *Bonding Limited Liability*, 51 Wm. & Mary L. Rev. 1417, 1444 (2010) ("Private ordering cannot synthetically gin up the legal right of limited liability.").

Importantly, the set mix of mandatory and default rules in each law of business organization determines the elasticity of private ordering of the entity form. The greater the proportion of default rules relative to mandatory rules, the greater is the entity form's elasticity of private ordering. There is a sliding scale between the extreme end of purely regulatory (all mandatory rules provided by the government) and purely enabling (all default rules subject to contracting by private parties).

The above major differences provide a general orientation to the study of specific entity forms. Each entity form will have a specific set of rules that cover each of the major issues. A word of warning: because the laws of business organizations are state laws, even some fundamental rules for the same form may differ state to state.

Note on terminology: Some commentary in this book applies generally to partnerships and LLCs. Hereinafter, unless there is a specific discussion of a particular entity form, a general reference to "a partnership agreement and an operating agreement" will be referred to as the ***charter agreement***. Also, a general reference to "partners or members" in a partnership or an LLC will be referred to as ***owners*** or ***equityholders***.

D. TAXONOMY OF CORPORATIONS

A corporation is an entity created under state corporation law. Each state's law applies to all corporations chartered in the state. The size and shareholder ownership structure of corporations are legally and economically significant.

1. PRIVATE CORPORATIONS

Private corporations are distinguished from public corporations, and this distinction is significant under federal securities law. Federal securities law governs the issuance, purchase, and sale of securities, such as stock, in interstate commerce. The principal regulator of federal securities law is the Securities and Exchange Commission (SEC). If a corporation registers its securities with the SEC, they can be traded among the public. If they are traded on stock exchanges, such as the New York Stock Exchange or Nasdaq, anyone in the public can instantaneously transact in these securities. A private corporation, then, is a corporation whose securities are privately held among a limited number of shareholders, and federal securities law restricts the ability of companies and shareholders to issue, buy, or sell such securities to the broader public.

Private corporations have only a small number of shareholders.[6] Shareholders are typically a small group of affiliated persons, such as family members or entrepreneurs, employees, and financial investors. Private corporations are generally smaller than public corporations, but not always. Some are enormous in size and wealth, for example: Cargill Inc. (agriculture), Koch Industries Inc. (commodities), and Bechtel Corp. (engineering). As well, subsidiaries of a public corporation, which can be large enterprises, are generally private corporations since they are all or mostly owned by their parent public corporation.

Closely-held corporations are private corporations, and "closely-held" refers to the attribute that the ownership is held among a few shareholders. By virtue of a close group of shareholders, closely-held corporations can be

[6] Once the number of shareholders increase to large numbers, a corporation must register those securities under federal securities laws. Securities and Exchange Act of 1934 § 12(g)(1), codified in 15 U.S.C. § 78*l*(g)(1) (providing that "[e]very issuer [with] total assets exceeding $10,000,000 and a class of equity security (other than an exempted security) held of record by either (i) 2,000 persons, or (ii) 500 persons who are not accredited investors (as such term is defined by the [SEC]) [shall] register such security by filing with the Commission a registration statement.").

managed more informally than the archetypical public corporation defined by a separation of ownership and control, *i.e.*, a professional board of directors that is distinct from the shareholders for whom it manages the corporation. *See, e.g.*, Model Business Corporation Act § 7.32 (2016) (permitting a shareholder agreement to "eliminate the board of directors or restrict the discretion or powers of the board of directors"). By virtue of a closer connection between ownership and control, corporation law may impose certain duties on shareholders.

Close corporations are sometimes synonymously used to reference closely-held corporations. But some state corporation laws provide specific rules for a species identified as a "close corporation." For example, Subchapter XIV (§§ 341–356) of the Delaware General Corporation Law ("DGCL") is devoted to specific rules applicable to close corporations. DGCL § 342(a) defines a "close corporation" as, among other requirements, having no more than 30 shareholders. Under Delaware law, then, some closely-held corporations may not qualify as a close corporation. Massachusetts defines a "close corporation" as characterized by: "(1) a small number of stockholders; (2) no ready market for the corporate stock; and (3) substantial majority stockholder participation in the management, direction and operations of the corporation." Donahue v. Rodd Electrotype Co. of New England, Inc., 328 N.E.2d 505, 511 (Mass. 1975). This definition would encompass most, if not all, closely-held corporations. "The close corporation bears striking resemblance to a partnership and courts have noted that the close corporation is often little more than an 'incorporated' or 'chartered' partnership." *Id.* at 512. In cases where stock is closely held or a corporation meets a specific definition of a close corporation, special rules may apply. For example, because shareholders are active in management, Massachusetts law provides that "stockholders in the close corporation owe one another substantially the same fiduciary duty in the operation of the enterprise that partners owe to one another." *Id.* at 515. Also, the corporate charter in Delaware may provide that "the business of the [close] corporation shall be managed by the stockholders of the corporation rather than by a board of directors." DGCL § 351.

2. PUBLIC CORPORATIONS

Public corporations are corporations whose stock is traded in the public capital market. Federal securities law requires public companies to report periodically certain disclosures. These disclosures, among others, include Form 10-Q (quarterly disclosure of unaudited financial information), Form 10-K (annual disclosure of audited financial information), and Form 8-K (disclosures of matters related to current major events). Stock markets include well-known stock exchanges and trading systems such as the New York Stock Exchange and the Nasdaq. Public corporations are different in various aspects of economy and law.

Economically, public corporations are extremely important. They are the largest businesses and account for a great portion of the American economy. In 2017, the Fortune 500, a list of the 500 largest U.S. corporations, produced $12.8 trillion in revenue and $1.0 trillion in net profit, and held $42.1 trillion in assets. *Largest U.S. Corporations*, Fortune at F21 (June 2018). In the same year, the gross domestic product (GDP) of the U.S. economy was $19.5 trillion. With that said, the number of public companies is extremely small compared to the number of privately-held firms including the vast majority of NBEs. At yearend 2017, domestic companies listed on U.S. stock exchanges numbered 3,618. *Where Have All the Public Companies Gone?*, Bloomberg (Apr. 9, 2018). On the other hand, American privately-held operating business firms, regardless of their entity forms, number in the millions.[7] Public corporations are extremely important, but at the same time business lawyers will most likely work with privately-held firms on any given legal engagement.

Public corporations are subject to the same state corporation law applicable to a private corporation, but they are also subject to other laws. Federal securities law substantially applies to public corporations. The law requires disclosure of material information. Stock exchanges, subject to regulation by federal securities law, impose rules and requirements on listed companies. Collectively, these laws include rules on the structure and qualifications of corporate boards, shareholder voting on executive compensation, requirements of auditing and internal controls and certifications of them by auditors and senior executives. Also, state and federal laws related to takeovers apply to public companies or transactions or situations involving mostly public corporations. Public corporations are large and complex, and federal law addresses this fact by complementing or supplementing state corporation law.

E. TAXONOMY OF NBEs

The universe of NBEs can be categorized into three basic entities.

- **General partnership ("partnership")**
- **Limited partnership ("LP")**
- **Limited liability company ("LLC")**

Partnerships and LPs have long existed. The first iterations of the uniform statute for partnerships dates back to the Uniform Partnership Act of 1914, and for limited partnerships to the Uniform Limited Partnership Act of 1916. LLCs are the newest form of entity, with the first

[7] The website of Delaware Division of Corporations notes the following: "More than one million business entities take advantage of Delaware's complete package of incorporation services, including modern and flexible corporate laws, our highly-respected Judiciary and legal community, a business-friendly government, and the customer-service-oriented staff of the Division of Corporations." https://corp.delaware.gov/ (last visited February 13, 2019). Of course, Delaware is one of 50 states, and most local businesses are chartered in the state of their business operation.

iteration of the uniform law dating back to the Uniform Limited Liability Company Act of 1996.

NBEs are different in many ways. Some differences are fundamental. These differences, along with the differences in the corporate form, must be considered by businesspersons and their lawyers when they consider the suitability of any particular entity form.

Below is a brief outline of these entities and some of their most basic features. This initial orientation is sufficient to convey the idea that NBEs are quite varied. When reviewing these entity features, think about this question: What sort of business may benefit from each entity form?

1. PARTNERSHIP

A partnership is defined as "an association of two or more persons to carry on as co-owners a business for profit." Revised Uniform Partnership Act § 102(11). A partnership presumes, but does not mandate, a communitarian ownership and management of a business among equal partners. This presumption is reflected in key statutory default rules.

Management structure.—The default management structure is collective management among equal partners.

Management rights.—Each partner has equal rights in the management and conduct of the partnership business, irrespective of a partner's level of contribution. *Id.* § 401(h). Management responsibility requires that each partner is an agent of the partnership. *Id.* § 301.

Fiduciary duties.—Because partners manage the business, they owe fiduciary duties to the partnership and other partners. *Id.* § 409(a).

Finance.—Each partner is entitled to an equal share of partnership distributions and is chargeable with a share of losses in proportion to the partner's share of distributions. *Id.* § 401(a).

Liability.—Partners do not have the benefit of limited liability. All partners are liable jointly and severally for all obligations of the partnership. *Id.* § 306(a). In contrast to this rule, partnership law also permits the creation of a limited liability partnership (LLP). An LLP provides limited liability protection to all partners. *Id.* § 306(c).

2. LP

An LP is defined as a partnership, having at least one general partners and at least one limited partner, that is formed under the statute. Uniform Limited Partnership Act (2001) § 201(d). A basic presumption of the entity form is that an LP is an investment vehicle in which a general partner manages the business or investment on behalf of limited partners. This presumption is reflected in key statutory default rules.

Management structure.—Unlike a general partnership, an LP requires a two-class partner structure, which mandates a formal management structure between managers and passive investors. *Id.* § 201(d).

Management rights.—A limited partner does not have the right or the power as a limited partner to act for or bind the LP. *Id.* § 302. Instead, each general partner has equal rights in the management and conduct of the LP's activities. *Id.* § 406(a). Each general partner is an agent of the LP for the purposes of its activities. *Id.* § 402(a).

Fiduciary duties.—Because a limited partner does not exercise management authority, a limited partner does not owe fiduciary duty to the LP or to other partners. *Id.* § 305(b). Each general partner owes fiduciary duty to the LP and other partners. *Id.* § 409(a).

Finance.—Whenever the LP makes a distribution to partners, the distribution must be shared among the partners on the basis of the value of the stated contribution of each partner. *Id.* § 503(a).

Liability.—Limited partners have the benefit of limited liability against the debts and obligations of the LP. *Id.* § 303(a). Like partners in a general partnership, general partners in an LP are jointly and severally liable for the debts and obligations of the LP. *Id.* § 404(a). In contrast to this rule, some states also permit the creation of a limited liability limited partnership (LLLP), which provides limited liability protection to general partners in addition to limited partners. *Id.* § 404(c).

3. LLC

An LLC is defined simply as an entity formed under the statute. Revised Uniform Limited Liability Company Act § 102(8). The entity form is based on the concept of contractual flexibility. This flexibility is reflected in key statutory default rules.

Management structure.—LLCs can come in two basic structures. In a member-managed LLC, the members manage the LLC in a way that is similar to the default management structure of a general partnership. *Id.* § 407(b). In a manager-managed LLC, the managers, who can but need not be members, manage the LLC in a way that is similar to the LP and corporation structures. *Id.* § 407(c).

Management rights.—Management rights of members depend on whether the LLC is a member-managed or manager-managed LLC. If the former, members have management rights that are similar to a partner in a general partnership, except that a member is not an agent solely by virtue of being a member. *Id.* § 301(a), § 407(b). If the latter, members have no management rights. *Id.* § 407(c).

Fiduciary duties.—Fiduciary duties of members also depend on whether the LLC is a member-managed or manager-managed LLC. If the former, members owe fiduciary duties. *Id.* § 409(a). If the latter, managers owe fiduciary duties, but members do not. *Id.* § 409(i).

Finance.—Members share equally in any distributions. *Id.* § 404(a).

Liability.—All members and managers have limited liability. *Id.* § 304(a).

Ownership.—The concept of a partnership requires at least two partners. This requirement imposes a significant limitation because, obviously, a partnership cannot accommodate a single-person, wholly-owned enterprise. A person who wishes to operate a business venture and own it whole cannot use the partnership form. For example, a corporation that wishes to operate a business unit as a wholly-owned subsidiary can choose the corporation or an LLC as the entity form but not a partnership. An advantage of the LLC is that only a single owner is required. *See, e.g., id.* § 201(d) (requiring "at least one person has become a member"); New York Limited Liability Company Law § 203(c) ("at least one member"); New Hampshire Revised Limited Liability Company Act § 304–C:20 ("at least one member but may have any greater number of members").

F. SOURCES OF LAW AND INTERNAL AFFAIRS

1. CORPORATION LAW AND INTERNAL AFFAIRS

Corporation law is state statutory law as augmented by case law interpreting statutory provisions and providing supplementary common law. Both sources of law are important. Each state has its own corporation statute. When a corporation chooses to file its charter in a particular state, it becomes that state's corporation, *e.g.*, "a Delaware corporation."

Although there are 50 state corporation statutes, two statutes are highly influential. The Delaware General Corporation Law (**DGCL**) is important because Delaware is the preferred state of filing for public corporations. A majority of Fortune 500 companies are incorporated in Delaware.[8] The tiny state has an outsized influence because it provides the corporation law to some of the biggest, economically influential corporations in America. A notable aspect of Delaware corporation law is that, in addition to a complex and refined statute, the case law announced by the Delaware courts is an equally important part of Delaware corporation law. *See* Jill E. Fisch, *The Peculiar Role of the Delaware Courts*

[8] "Delaware has been the premier state of formation for business entities since the early 1900s. Today, more than one million business entities have made Delaware their legal home. Although the number of entities organized in Delaware is impressive, even more important is the fact that so many large and important corporations whose shares are listed on major stock exchanges are incorporated in Delaware. Indeed, more than 60 percent of the Fortune 500 companies are incorporated in Delaware." Delaware Division of Corporations, at https://corplaw.delaware.gov/why-businesses-choose-delaware/ (last visited Sept. 24, 2020).

in the Competition for Corporate Charters, 68 U. CINN. L. REV. 1061, 1074 (2000) ("The majority of Delaware's important legal rules are the result of judicial decisions. The scope of the business judgment rule, the analysis of transactions that implicate the duty of loyalty, the legal standards governing management's response to a hostile tender offer, all are based on legal principles articulated by the Delaware courts. Lawyers tend to think of corporate law as statutory, but there is a substantial common law component to Delaware corporate law.").

With respect to the other 49 states, the Model Business Corporation Act (2016) (**MBCA**), which is a model statute drafted by the American Bar Association, has been influential and adopted in some form by many states. A minority of Fortune 500 companies are likely subject to corporation law modeled under the MBCA. The DGCL and the MBCA are representative of American corporation laws. Furthermore, most state laws share a common understanding of important rules and principles, and they often borrow specific rules from Delaware or MBCA.

An important feature of the laws of business organizations is choice of law. There are 50 state laws of business organizations. Promoters seeking to create a limited liability entity are not required to file with a particular state, but instead can choose the state and thus the law applicable to the enterprise. This fact raises two issues: (1) Which state law governs the internal affairs of the entity? (2) Which state law should be chosen?

Under the American system of federalism, each state has its own laws of business organizations, including corporations, partnerships, and limited liability companies. There is the potential for conflicts of law among states with respect to the rules governing the internal affairs and governance of business entities. Suppose California imposes certain obligations on managers of an LLC but New York does not, and a firm operates in both states. Which law governs? The law deals with this potential conflict through the internal affairs doctrine. "The internal affairs doctrine is a conflict of laws principle which recognizes that only one State should have the authority to regulate a corporation's internal affairs—matters peculiar to the relationships among or between the corporation and its current officers, directors, and shareholders—because otherwise a corporation could be faced with conflicting demands." Edgar v. MITE Corp., 457 U.S. 624 (1982).

> In American corporation law, the internal affairs doctrine is a dominant and overarching choice of law principle. An important rationale for the doctrine is that, in order to prevent corporations from being subjected to inconsistent legal standards, the authority to regulate a corporation's internal affairs should not rest with multiple jurisdictions. The term "internal affairs" encompasses those matters that pertain to the relationships among or between the corporation and its officers, directors, and shareholders. The

> doctrine requires that the law of the state of incorporation must govern those relationships.

Sagarra Inversiones, S.L. v. Cementos Portland Valderrivas, S.A., 34 A.3d 1074, 1081–82 (Del. 2011).

MBCA § 15.01. Governing Law.

(a) The law of the jurisdiction of formation of a foreign corporation governs:

(1) the internal affairs of the foreign corporation; and

(2) the interest holder liability of its shareholders.

The practical import of the internal affairs doctrine is that "the law of the state of incorporation should determine issues relating to internal corporate affairs." McDermott Inc. v. Lewis, 531 A.2d 206, 215 (Del. 1987). For example, a Utah court must apply Delaware corporation law under these circumstances: (1) the corporation is Delaware chartered; (2) it has its principal office and major business activities in Utah; (3) a shareholder, who is a Utah resident, sues the board for a breach of the directors' fiduciary duty to the corporation and shareholders in Utah state court. The action involves the internal affairs of the corporation, and a local court (Utah) must apply the law of the foreign jurisdiction (Delaware). Clearly, the internal affairs doctrine is limited. Not all laws *affecting* the Delaware corporation are subject to Delaware law. If Utah determines that gaming (gambling) is against the policy of the state and prohibits it within state borders,[9] a Delaware corporation cannot operate a casino in Utah even if Delaware permits gaming within its borders. The same principle would apply to the innumerable areas of law and policy in which Utah, as a sovereign state, can pronounce laws that all persons within the state must obey: *e.g.*, criminal, employment, public safety, contracts, torts, environmental, etc. Foreign business entities must understand this distinction between internal affairs and external laws. *See* Revised Limited Liability Company Act § 801(c) ("A certificate of authority does not authorize a foreign limited liability company to engage in any business or exercise any power that a limited liability company may not engage in or exercise in this state.").

---

[9] *Compare* Utah Constitution, art. VI, § 27 ("The Legislature shall not authorize any game of chance, lottery or gift enterprise under any pretense or for any purpose."); Utah Code § 76-10-1102(1)(b) (providing that a "person is guilty of gambling if the person knowingly permits any gambling to be played, conducted, or dealt upon or in any real or personal property owned, rented, or under the control of the actor, whether in whole or in part"), *with* Nevada Revised Statutes § 463.0129 (stating that the "gaming industry is vitally important to the economy of the State and the general welfare of the inhabitants").

2. SOURCES OF THE LAWS OF NBEs

Like corporation law, the laws of NBEs are state law. All fifty states have their own statutes and case law of general partnerships, LPs, and LLCs. With respect to general partnerships and LPs, the uniform laws have been highly influential. The uniform laws are drafted by the National Conference of Commissioners on Uniform State Laws, a highly influential legal advisory body, and as its name suggests it seeks to promote uniform state laws. Virtually all states have adopted a version of the uniform laws for general partnerships and LPs, with the notable exception of Delaware whose business organization laws, including its corporation law, are *sui generis*. With respect to LLCs, however, the state laws are much more varied. The uniform laws have been adopted by a substantial number of states, but many other states have enacted their own statutes. The laws of LLCs are still evolving.

In light of the fact that the uniforms laws have been so influential, if students systematically learn the uniform laws, they will quickly understand the laws of NBEs of any state in which they practice. This book conducts a sustained study of three uniform statutes.[10]

- **RULLCA**: Revised Uniform Limited Liability Company Act of 2006. The RULLCA modernized an earlier uniform statute, the Uniform Limited Liability Company Act of 1996. As of September 2020, 20 states have adopted the RULLCA.
- **RUPA**: Revised Uniform Partnership Act of 1997 (amended 2013). The RUPA modernized an earlier uniform statute, the Uniform Partnership Act of 1914 ("UPA"). As of September 2020, 41 states have adopted the RUPA. Virtually all the other states have adopted the UPA.
- **ULPA (2001)**: Uniform Limited Partnership Act of 2001 (amended 2013). The ULPA (2001) modernized an earlier uniform statute, the Revised Uniform Limited Partnership Act of 1976 (with 1985 amendment) ("RULPA"). As of September 2020, 23 states have adopted the ULPA (2001). Virtually all the other states have adopted the RULPA.

The above statutes are the most modern versions. A mastery of these statutes will prepare lawyers to work with any state law in practice even though the law may differ from the above model statutes.

A note on the law of LPs is required. Many states have adopted a combination of two statutes for LPs: the RUPA, which governs general

[10] Each statute was amended in 2013 pursuant to the Harmonization of Business Entity Acts project, which seeks to harmonize the language in all uniform statutes. The harmonization process resulted in significant substantive amendments as well, and this book discusses some of these differences. Because each state adopts its statute individually, states may vary significantly even if they have adopted the uniform laws.

partnership, and the RULPA. The RULPA is *not* an independent, standalone statute. It provides special rules applicable to LPs, but otherwise "links" to the RUPA for the remaining rules on partnership. *See* RULPA § 1105 ("In any case not provided for in this [Act] the provisions of the Uniform Partnership Act govern."). The most recent version of the uniform law, the ULPA (2001), "delinks" LPs from the RUPA. It is a standalone statute that provides all the rules for LPs. Although many states still have the RUPA/RULPA scheme, this book focuses on the more modern statute. For thoroughness, this book highlights significant differences between the two statutes.

Since the uniform laws are model acts, they are not law until they are adopted by a state. States are not required to adopt any uniform law whole cloth. They may tweak the model acts however they like.

Note: This chapter introduces three basic NBEs and their most modern uniform statutes: general partnership with RUPA, LP with ULPA (2001), LLC with RULLCA. These acronyms constitute an alphabet soup. At first, the acronyms can be confusing, but they are convenient. Soon enough, they will become second nature.

3. INTERNAL AFFAIRS DOCTRINE IN NBEs

The internal affairs doctrine is not just limited to corporations. It also applies to the laws of NBEs. Like corporations, NBEs can operate in many states, each of which has its own laws of NBEs. The governing law depends on whether the firm is a limited liability entity or is a general partnership. Under RUPA, the applicable law of partnership is the state in which a partnership has its principal office. This rule changes, however, if the partnership elects to become an LLP, which provides limited liability protection to its partners. This election requires a filing with a state, and the law of the state of filing governs the internal affairs of the partnership and the partners' liability for the debts and obligations of the partnership.

RUPA § 104. Governing Law.

The internal affairs of a partnership and the liability of a partner as a partner for a debt, obligation, or other liability of the partnership are governed by:

(1) in the case of a limited liability partnership, the law of this state; and

(2) in the case of a partnership that is not a limited liability partnership, the law of the jurisdiction in which the partnership has its principal office.

The rule for limited liability entities follow the internal affairs doctrine for corporation law. The uniform laws on LPs and LLCs are the same.

ULPA (2001) § 104. Governing Law.

The law of this state governs:

(1) the internal affairs of a limited partnership; and

(2) the liability of a partner as partner for a debt, obligation, or other liability of a limited partnership.

RULLCA § 104. Governing Law.

The law of this state governs:

(1) the internal affairs of a limited liability company; and

(2) the liability of a member as member and a manager as manager for a debt, obligation, or other liability of a limited liability company.

Any foreign LP or LLC must registered to conduct business in the state. However, the statutes make clear that the internal affairs of a foreign LLP, LP, and LLC are governed by the laws of the foreign state. RUPA § 1001(a); ULPA (2001) § 1001(a); RULLCA § 901(a), § 902(a).

Although the law of the state of filing applies to the internal affairs, NBEs are still governed by external laws. The activities of any business entity may be regulated by state or federal laws. For instance, many states prohibit NBEs from engaging in banking, insurance, and other regulated activities. *See, e.g.*, Arizona Limited Liability Company Act § 29–609(a)–(b) (prohibiting banking and insurance); California Revised Limited Liability Company Act § 17701.04(b) (same); Delaware Limited Liability Company Act § 18–106(a) (prohibiting banking); New Hampshire Revised Limited Liability Company Act § 304–C:21 (prohibiting banking, railroad and insurance businesses).

In October 2014, Fiat and Chrysler automobile companies merged and formed one of the leading global automobile manufacturing companies, Fiat Chrysler Automobiles N.V., which is a public company traded on the New York Stock Exchange (ticker: FCAU). The public company principally operates its portfolio of Chrysler brands of cars and trucks, including Chrysler, Dodge, Jeep, and Ram, through a subsidiary LLC: FCA US LLC, formerly known as Chrysler Group LLC. The company is a Delaware LLC. The Italian-based subsidiary, FCA Italy, operates auto brands including Fiat and Alpha Romeo. As a sophisticated business enterprise advised by attorneys working at the highest level of business law practice, FCA US LLC (formerly Chrysler Group LLC) has a written operating agreement. The following is the LLC's choice of law provision.

CHRYSLER GROUP LLC OPERATING AGREEMENT

Section 12.4 Governing Law. This Agreement shall be governed by, and construed and enforced in accordance with, the Laws of the State of Delaware, without giving effect to any choice of law or conflict of law rules or provisions (whether of the State of Delaware or any other jurisdiction) that would cause the application of the Laws of any jurisdiction other than the State of Delaware.

The case below illustrates the application of the internal affairs doctrine. In reading this case, think about these questions: (1) Why were the entities involved here "foreign" firms from the perspective of North Carolina? (2) Why did the law of North Carolina not apply? (3) If the trial court erroneously applied North Carolina law, why did the court affirm the trial court's ruling anyway?

AZURE DOLPHIN, LLC V. BARTON

821 S.E.2d 711 (N.C. 2018)

ERVIN, JUSTICE.

The issues in this case are whether the trial court properly dismissed the claims that plaintiffs Azure Dolphin, LLC, and Jean-Pierre Boespflug asserted in their first amended complaint. After careful consideration of plaintiffs' challenges to the trial court's orders in light of the applicable law, we conclude that the challenged orders should be affirmed.

Boespflug and defendant Justin Barton began working together in the real estate investment business approximately thirty years ago. As part of their business strategy, Boespflug and Barton created "various entities to acquire and hold investment properties throughout the United States," including "large apartment complexes and commercial buildings." Among the investment entities that resulted from this process were defendants Hess Creek, LLC, an Oregon limited liability company; Royal Ascot, LLC, an Oregon limited liability company; and Barton Boespflug II and Vintage Oak II, both of which were California limited partnerships.

Barton served as manager or general partner for Hess Creek, Royal Ascot, Barton Boespflug, Vintage Oak, and the other investment entities, while Boespflug "contributed the majority of the capital" and served as either a member or limited partner of each of the investment entities. At some unspecified point in time, "Boespflug formed Azure Dolphin," a Nevada limited liability company, to which he transferred a portion of his economic interests in the investment entities that he and Barton had created and operated.

Boespflug moved to Paris. Barton e-mailed Boespflug for the purpose of requesting his assistance in securing a new loan and refinancing two existing loans. In his reply, Boespflug "explained to Barton that his financial position was no longer conducive to personally guaranteeing loans" relating to the investment entities. After a lender "demanded that both Azure [Dolphin] and Boespflug guaranty the new loans," Boespflug reiterated "that this was not an option."

Subsequently, Barton converted Boespflug's membership interests in the investment entities to notes payable with a face value that "was a fraction of the true value of Boespflug's membership interests." The promissory notes in question reflected the value of the interests that Boespflug and Azure Dolphin owned in the investment entities, which, according to appraisals that Barton had obtained, amounted to a total of $2,008,006. In plaintiffs' view, Barton "manipulated" the appraisals so as to undervalue Boespflug's interests in the investment entities.

After engaging in these transactions, Barton "unilaterally amended the operating agreements of the Investment Entities with terms considerably more favorable to him," "sold at least six of the properties" owned by the investment entities, and transferred properties held by the investment entities "into his own name and to different entities controlled by Barton and/or his immediate family members."

Boespflug, Azure Dolphin, and JPB Holdings, Inc., commenced this action by filing a complaint asserting fifteen claims, including individual and derivative claims for constructive fraud, breach of the duty of loyalty, breach of the duty of care, breach of the duty of good faith and fair dealing, civil conspiracy, fraudulent conveyance, and unfair and deceptive practices against twenty-one defendants, including Barton. [Among other things, the plaintiff sought to remove Barton as manager and general partner.]

Plaintiffs contend that the trial court erred by dismissing their claims for Barton's removal as manager or general partner of the investment entities based upon plaintiffs' purported failure to comply with "the North Carolina Limited Liability Company Act." Plaintiffs note that N.C.G.S. § 57D–8–06 provides that, "in any derivative proceeding in the right of a foreign [limited liability company], the matters covered by this Article will be governed by the law of the jurisdiction of the foreign [limited liability company's] organization," so that the [North Carolina] statutory pre-suit "demand requirement" is inapplicable to Barton, Boespflug, Hess Creek, Royal Ascot, and Vintage Oak, each of which was organized under either California or Oregon law. As a result, plaintiffs contend that Oregon law governs whether and to what extent plaintiffs must satisfy a statutory pre-suit demand requirement before commencing a derivative action on behalf of Hess Creek and Royal Ascot and note that Oregon law recognizes a futility exception to its statutory pre-suit demand requirement.

Plaintiffs assert that their "claims to remove Barton as general partner of Barton Boespflug II and Vintage Oak II are governed by California law" rather than North Carolina law. As a result of the fact that the relevant North Carolina statutory provisions apply to "a partnership formed by two or more persons *under the laws of this State*," N.C.G.S. § 59–102(8), plaintiffs assert that North Carolina's limited partnership pre-suit demand requirement does not extend to entities, such as Barton Boespflug and Vintage Oak, which were not organized under North Carolina law.

Plaintiffs contend that the common law-based "internal affairs doctrine would nevertheless vitiate the Business Court's holding" that plaintiffs' claims for the removal of Barton as manager or general partner of the investment entities were subject to the [North Carolina] pre-suit demand requirements. Plaintiffs argue that the internal affairs doctrine provides another basis for concluding that plaintiffs' removal claims are subject to Oregon and California, rather than North Carolina, law.

A limited liability company is defined as "an entity formed under [North Carolina law] that has not become another entity or form of entity by merger, conversion, or other means." N.C.G.S. § 57D–1–03(19) (2017). A "derivative action" is defined as "a proceeding brought in the superior court of this State in the right of [a limited liability company] or, to the extent provided in G.S. 57D–8–06, in the right of a foreign [limited liability company], to recover a judgment in favor of the [limited liability company] or, if applicable, the foreign [limited liability company]." *Id.* § 57D–8–01(b). A member of a limited liability company may initiate a derivative action when the member "[makes] written demand on the [limited liability company] to take suitable action," and either the demand is rejected or "90 days expire from the date the demand was made," or, alternatively, when "irreparable injury to the [limited liability company] would result by waiting for the expiration of the 90-day period." *Id.* § 57D–8–01(a)(2).

Similarly, a limited partnership is defined as "a partnership formed by two or more persons under the laws of this State and having one or more general partners and one or more limited partners, [including], for all purposes of the laws of the State of North Carolina, a limited liability limited partnership." *Id.* § 59–102(8). "A limited partner may bring an action in the right of a limited partnership to recover a judgment in its favor if general partners with authority to do so have refused to bring the action or if an effort to cause those general partners to bring the action is not likely to succeed." *Id.* § 59–1001. As a result, North Carolina law contains pre-suit demand requirements applicable to derivative claims asserted against both limited liability companies and limited partnerships.

As an initial matter, we are inclined to believe that plaintiffs' removal claims are, in fact, governed by foreign, rather than North Carolina, law. As far as limited liability companies are concerned, N.C.G.S. § 57D–8–06 provides that, "in any derivative proceeding in the right of a foreign [limited liability company], the matters covered by this Article will be governed by the law of the jurisdiction of the foreign [limited liability company's] organization." *Id.* § 57D–8–06. Similarly, with respect to limited partnerships, "the laws of the jurisdiction under which a foreign limited partnership is organized govern its organization and internal affairs." *Id.* § 59–901. The relevant North Carolina statutes indicate that plaintiffs' claims for Barton's removal as the manager of Hess Creek and Royal Ascot are governed by Oregon law and that plaintiffs' claims for Barton's removal as the general partner of Barton Boespflug and Vintage Oak are governed by California law. However, the fact that the trial court's decision rested upon North Carolina, rather than Oregon and California, law does not require reversal of the trial court's decision to dismiss plaintiffs' removal claims in this case.

According to the statutory provisions governing derivative actions brought against Oregon limited liability companies:

> a complaint in a proceeding brought in the right of a limited liability company must allege with particularity the demand made, if any, to obtain action by the managers or the members who would otherwise have the authority to cause the limited liability company to sue in its own right, and either that the demand was refused or ignored or the reason why a demand was not made.

Or. Rev. Stat. Ann. § 63.801(2). The California statute governing derivative claims in the limited partnership context provides that:

> A partner may bring a derivative action to enforce a right of a limited partnership if: (1) the partner first makes a demand on the general partners, requesting that they cause the limited partnership to bring an action to enforce the right, and the general partners do not bring the action within a reasonable time; or (2) a demand would be futile.

Cal. Corp. Code § 15910.02. The complaint filed in a derivative action involving a limited partnership must state "why demand is excused as futile." *Id.* § 15910.04. As a result, while plaintiffs are correct in noting that both Oregon Revised Statutes § 63.801(2) and California Corporations Code § 15910.02 contain what amounts to a "futility" exception to the otherwise-applicable pre-suit demand requirement, they overlook the fact that both Oregon and California law require that the plaintiff allege the basis for any claim of futility in any derivative complaint.

[The court determined that the plaintiffs' complaint did not plead demand futility as required under Oregon Revised Statutes § 63.801(2) and California Corporations Code § 15910.02.] Plaintiffs sought Barton's removal as the manager or general partner of the relevant investment entities . Plaintiffs' removal claims strike us as quintessentially derivative, rather than personal, in nature. As a result, we conclude that the trial court did not err by dismissing plaintiffs' removal claims.

The case below illustrates the divide between rules of internal affairs and external laws. In reading this case, think about this question: Why did Utah law govern on the liability of a Nevada LLC's managers?

HEAPS V. NURICHE, LLC

345 P.3d 655 (Utah 2015)

JUSTICE PARRISH, opinion of the Court:

This appeal requires us to decide whether the Utah Payment of Wages Act (UPWA) imposes personal liability on the managers of a limited liability company for unpaid wages. The UPWA imposes liability for unpaid wages on all employers. On summary judgment, the district court found that LLC managers qualify as employers under the UPWA, but nevertheless held that they are not liable for unpaid wages. We affirm the district court's ruling on the alternative ground that LLC managers do not qualify as employers under the UPWA.

In 2008, Ron Heaps and Phillip Sykes (collectively, Employees), along with others, founded Nuriche, LLC, a now-defunct limited liability company formed in Nevada and registered to do business in Utah. Employees allege that the other founding members promised them compensation and other benefits in connection with their employment by Nuriche, but that Nuriche and the remaining managers refused to provide the promised compensation upon Employees' termination in 2011.

The complaint alleged that Nuriche and those on its board of managers, David Heaps, Lavorn Sparks, Norm Clyde, Brad Holiday, and David Parker (collectively Managers), breached their agreement to pay Employees $150,000 in annual salaries and benefits. Employees also asserted a claim under the UPWA for failure to pay past-due wages following their termination.

[Managers] sought summary judgment. They argued first that Nevada limited-liability-company law controlled Employees' claim for unpaid wages and that, under Nevada law, LLC managers could not be held personally liable for unpaid wages. Alternatively, they argued that Utah wage law does not impose personal liability on managers for unpaid wages.

The district court granted Managers' motion for summary judgment. The court first undertook a conflict-of-laws analysis and concluded that Utah law applies because, under the most significant relationship test, "the majority of [the relevant] contacts were in Utah." Applying Utah law, the district court ruled that Managers were employers as defined by the

UPWA, but that the UPWA does not extend wage liability to individual managers. The district court explained that "there is simply no indication in the UPWA that it is intended to impose individual liability on officers or agents of a business."

Employees argue that the district court erred in granting Managers' motions for summary judgment because the UPWA imposes personal liability on LLC managers for unpaid wages. Managers respond that Nevada wage law should apply because Nuriche is a Nevada LLC and that, under Nevada law, LLC managers are not personally liable for unpaid wages. And if Utah law applies, Managers argue that the UPWA should not be read to impose personal liability on them because the statute does not evince an express legislative intent to override long-standing principles of corporate law. We address these arguments in turn.

In arguing that Nevada law applies, Managers rely on the governing law provision of the Utah Revised Uniform Limited Liability Company Act (URULLCA), which provides that "the law of the jurisdiction of formation of a foreign limited liability company governs the liability of a member as member and a manager as manager for a debt, obligation, or other liability *of the company*." Utah Code § 48–3a–901(1). Managers argue that unpaid wages are like any other debt, obligation, or liability of an LLC. Therefore, because Nuriche was formed in Nevada, the URULLCA requires that we apply Nevada law in determining whether Managers are personally liable for unpaid wages.

While it may be the case that Nevada law governs Managers' liability for the obligations of Nuriche, Employees are not seeking to hold Managers liable for an obligation of Nuriche. Instead, Employees argue that the UPWA imposes direct liability on Managers. Therefore, unlike claims that rely on derivative liability to render individual officers responsible for an obligation of a company, Employees' claims are premised on a theory of direct liability. Because the URULLCA's governing law provision limits its applicability to those cases implicating officer liability for the obligations of the company, it does not apply here.

"Registration of a foreign limited liability company to do business in this state does not authorize the foreign limited liability company to engage in any activities or affairs or exercise any power that a limited liability company may not engage in or exercise in this state." Utah Code § 48–3a–901(3). Because a foreign LLC employing individuals in Utah is required to follow Utah wage law, any claim of illegal wage practices filed by a Utah employee will be governed by Utah wage law. The question of Managers' liability for unpaid wages is governed by Utah law.

[The court then held that the individual managers of Nuriche cannot be held personally liable for the unpaid wages claimed by Employees under the Utah Payment of Wages Act.]

G. TWO CHOICES AT THE OUTSET

At the outset of the business venture, business organizers have two fundamental choices to make. They must choose the right entity form. Assuming that the entity form is a limited liability entity that requires a state filing, they must choose the state of filing and its laws.

1. CHOICE OF ENTITY

Why are there so many entities? NBE forms fundamentally differ from each other, and all NBEs fundamentally differ from the corporation. These legal packages of different features determine the choice of entity form. One may be better suited than the others given the circumstance and a set of needs. The table below provides a taxonomy of different firms using *just three* factors: tax, limited liability, and ownership base.

	Limited Liability	Tax	Equity Ownership
Corporations			
Nature of Shareholdings			
Close corporation	Yes	S or C	Limited number
Private corporation	Yes	S or C	Varies in number but limited
Public corporation	Yes	C	Large in number
Tax Status			
S Corporation	Yes	Flow-thru	Limited by IRS
C Corporation	Yes	Double	Large in number (public) Varies in number (private)
NBEs			
General partnerships	No	Flow-thru	At least 2, then varies
— LLP	Yes	Flow-thru	At least 2, then varies
Limited partnerships	Yes (limited partners) No (general partners)	Flow-thru	At least 2, then varies
— LLLP	Yes	Flow-thru	At least 2, then varies
Limited liability companies	Yes	Flow-thru or disregarded	At least 1, then varies

We see the panoply of different entity features with respect to *only three* factors, albeit important ones. A complete consideration of the spectrum of entities is needed for the critical decision of entity choice. What form of entity should businesspersons use to engage in enterprise? A corporation is just one option. For a public company, a corporation is the predominant default choice. However, if the entity is expected to be a closely-held enterprise among owners and it is an independent, standalone firm (*i.e.*, not a subsidiary or affiliate of a parent firm), the corporate form may not always be the best choice.

With respect to NBEs, the entity choice question has been fairly resolved by actual market practice. Over the years, general partnerships have seen substantial decline, and this phenomenon is inversely correlated to the rapid rise of LLCs. LPs have maintained a small, niche role. They are used in many real estate and financial investment businesses. There are good reasons for this phenomenon. A critical factor is that partners in a partnership do not have the benefit of limited liability whereas members and managers in an LLC have it. The LLC is contractually more flexible than general partnerships and LPs. This book discusses the different facets of these three entity forms in greater detail so that a business lawyer can conduct a sound analysis of entity choice and the continuing issues related to the management and maintenance of the entity.

If a partnership is now disfavored, why study it? Why not study just LLCs, and to a lesser extent LPs? The genealogical roots of business organizations are two: the corporation and the partnership. In this respect, the LP form was an early "hybrid" entity—hybrid in that it took facets of the corporation and the partnership and combined them. The LLC form is the newest hybrid form. We study partnership law because many default rules in LLC statutes come from the law of general partnership. It is not possible to fully understand NBEs without studying each entity form.

Given what we know about NBEs thus far, we can see the lawyer's role and job function in the business planning process. The business lawyer must advise clients on: (1) tax optimization, (2) entity choice, (3) jurisdictional choice, and (4) the entity's governance and economic design. To do this, the business lawyer must have a sound understanding of NBEs.

2. CHOICE OF LAW

The big implication of the internal affairs doctrine is that a business organizer for a limited liability entity can choose the state of filing, and thus the applicable law. This explains the many "Delaware corporations" even though Delaware is a small state and is not the physical situs of many industries or corporate headquarters. Most of these corporations are not physically located in Delaware (after all, it is the second smallest state by land area). The decision to be governed by Delaware corporation law or California LLC law is a choice of the business venturers.

A promoter can file to create a corporation, LLP, LP, and LLC in any jurisdiction. The choice of state is the choice of law. For corporation law, Delaware is a preferred choice for many large, sophisticated, or publicly traded corporations. The reasons are several: a highly developed body of corporation law including case law; a well-regarded judiciary that decides cases competently and expeditiously; a legislature that is focused on meeting the needs of the major constituents of corporation law. *See generally* Randy J. Holland, *Delaware's Business Courts: Litigation Leadership*, 34 J. Corp. L. 771 (2009).

Promoters may prefer Delaware laws of NBEs for all the reasons that make Delaware corporation law advantageous. The most distinct aspect of the Delaware NBE laws is the clearly expressed policy preference for maximum freedom of contract that includes the possibility of eliminating all fiduciary duties. *See* Delaware Limited Liability Company Act § 18–1101(b)–(c) (stating that the statutory policy is "to give the maximum effect to the principle of freedom of contract" and that "duties may be expanded or restricted or eliminated" in the limited liability company agreement); Delaware Revised Uniform Limited Partnership Act § 17–1101(c)–(d) (same). The practical effect of this policy is that the parties can custom design any aspect of the entity, including all aspects of fiduciary duty. Entities that would benefit from a Delaware choice of law are only a slice of the NBE world. Like their corporate counterparts, such entities are generally large, sophisticated, or publicly traded. Unlike the field of corporation law where Delaware is the dominant state, its influence is less pronounced in the sphere of NBEs.

Lawyers should generally recommend organizing under the laws of a state other than the situs of its business operations only when there is good reason to choose a particular law over another. For NBEs, the considerations in the choice of law are several.

First, there are administrative burdens of filing in a state where the NBE does not have substantial business operations, such as operations and customers. Every state requires that "foreign" limited liability entities (entities chartered in another jurisdiction) that are "doing business" in the state "qualify" to do business by registering with the state. Thus, a firm may be "local" in fact of presence and operation but foreign in law by virtue of chartering in another state. For example, a Delaware-chartered firm that does business only in Miami, Florida, would be considered a "foreign" firm in Florida, and thus it would have to register to conduct business in Florida. *See* Florida Revised Limited Liability Company Act § 605.0902(1) ("A foreign limited liability company may not transact business in this state until it obtains a certificate of authority from the department."). Due consideration must be given to the nature and scope of the entity's proposed business. If a firm is anticipated to conduct its business mostly intrastate or a localized region, organizing in the state of its situs will reduce filing, reporting, tax and fee burdens.

Second, the perceived advantage of Delaware law is less so in the realm of NBEs. The laws of general partnerships and LPs have long been established in all states, and the uniform laws have been by far the most influential body of law. Courts in all states are familiar with these entities and many states have well-developed bodies of case law on the different forms of partnerships. With respect to LLCs, the uniform laws have been somewhat less dominant, but is growing in influence. The LLC form is newest entity form, and some states are still experimenting with their laws. However, the LLC form is premised on contractual flexibility coupled with limited liability protection for members and managers. Virtually all state law provides these features in their state law and all state courts have routinely dealt with contracting and contract interpretation issues over the years. In other words, most state laws and courts are more than adequate to serve the needs of business enterprises requiring an NBE form.

The bottom line is when there are perceived advantages of a particular state law, and when this difference is consequential at the margin, filing in the advantageous state, if perceived, may be the proper choice. For large, sophisticated, or publicly traded entities, marginal differences in state law and judicial expertise may arguably be material, and the administrative and cost burden may be light in comparison to the marginal benefit from a perceived superior law or court. Delaware law comes to mind under this analysis. For most other businesses, the laws of NBEs in most states are sufficient for the needs of the business. Venturers and their lawyers should consider the adequacy of the law to structure the entity and the state courts to resolve legal conflicts, with the administrative burdens and costs of filing in a jurisdiction that has no relation to the firm's business operations.

H. PROBLEM: FRIENDS CONSIDER A STARTUP

"Damn," Piers cursed, pointing to the broken plastic eyeglass frame and scratched lenses. "My prescription glasses broke when I tripped on the stairs coming up here."

His longtime friend and roommate, Blake, looked over and shook his head slowly to commiserate. "That's $450 with lenses at least."

"I know . . . for basically molded plastic. I don't have that kind of money. I'm already maxed out on my student loans." Quizzically looking at his broken frame, he continued. "I don't understand why eyeglasses are so expensive. There's little high technology in the frames. I mean, look at this. Okay, the lenses have to be crafted to the prescription, but that can't cost *that* much. It's just plastic and steel."

"That's the market," Blake countered. "We just learned this in Managerial Economics. Competition, supply, and demand are factors that determine price. The market sets the price. Accept it and move on."

"Why should we accept that!" Piers was now animated. "Why can't I sell molded plastic for $150 and still make a profit? We are in business school. Why don't we think about disrupting this market? There has got to be a feasible, rational way to provide cheaper, quality frames and lenses. If we can figure out a way, we have a business model."

Curiosity piqued, Blake asked, "What are you suggesting?"

Piers pondered more, and then tentatively suggested, "Maybe like the Walmart of the eyeglass business." Both let this idea sink in.

"No!" Blake retorted excitedly. "Like the *Amazon* of the eyeglass market. An internet-based eyeglass shop. That's the business model!"

This was the *eureka!* moment for Piers and Blake, two second-year MBA students at the prestigious E.J. Song School of Business. Over the course of the next semester, they conducted market research. They learned that the market is dominated by a single company that has cornered much of the market. The following Wikipedia entry described this company:[11]

> Luxottica Group S.p.A. is an Italian eyewear company and the world's largest company in the eyewear industry. It is based in Milan, Italy.
>
> As a vertically integrated company, Luxottica designs, manufactures, distributes, and retails its eyewear brands, including LensCrafters, Sunglass Hut, Apex by Sunglass Hut, Pearle Vision, Sears Optical, Target Optical, Eyemed vision care plan, and Glasses.com. Its best known brands are Ray-Ban, Persol, and Oakley.
>
> Luxottica also makes sunglasses and prescription frames for designer brands such as Chanel, Prada, Giorgio Armani, Burberry, Versace, Dolce and Gabbana, Miu, DKNY, and Tory Burch.
>
> In January 2017, Luxottica announced a merger with Essilor. The combined entity would command more than one quarter of global value sales of eyewear. In March 2018, the European Commission unconditionally approved the merger of Essilor and Luxottica. On October 1, 2018, the new holding company EssilorLuxottica was born, resulting in combined market capitalization of approximately €57 billion.

At the end of semester exams, Piers and Blake returned to the idea of disrupting the market for eyeglasses and lenses, a market dominated by an industry giant. Rather than pursue careers in investment banking as they had planned, they committed to becoming entrepreneurs. They agreed to develop the business plan for their startup in the final spring semester before graduation. There was much to do.

QUESTIONS

1. What are some of the many business problems and issues that these entrepreneurs must work out?

2. At this point in time, what is the role of law? How can law specifically help these entrepreneurs initiate their startup?

---

11 https://en.wikipedia.org/wiki/Luxottica (last visited April, 3, 2019).

CHAPTER 2

FORMING THE ENTITY

■ ■ ■

A. NATURE AND ESSENTIAL ATTRIBUTES OF BUSINESS ENTITIES

1. WHY FIRMS?

When businesspersons decide to do business and hire a lawyer, they will invariably form a firm, *e.g.*, a corporation, partnership, or LLC. When layers of entities and other legal creations are peeled back, all enterprises ultimately involve the interests of natural persons. Presumably, these people can contract among themselves and do business together without forming a firm. We should consider the basic questions: Why form a firm? Why do firms exist? Why do business organization laws exist?

In a seminal article, Ronald Coase argued that firms exist because their hierarchical relationships can minimize the costs of establishing the economic relationships among factors of production.

> The main reason why it is profitable to establish a firm would seem to be that there is a cost of using the price mechanism. The most obvious cost of "organizing" production through the price mechanism is that of discovering what the relevant prices are. This cost may be reduced but it will not be eliminated by the emergence of specialists who will sell this information. The costs of negotiating and which takes place on a market must also be taken into account. Again, in certain markets, *e.g.*, produce exchanges, a technique is devised for minimising these contract costs; but they are not eliminated. It is true that contracts are not eliminated when there is a firm but they are greatly reduced. A factor of production (or the owner thereof) does not have to make a series of contracts with the factors with whom he is co-operating within the firm, as would be necessary, of course, if this co-operation were as a direct result of the working of the price mechanism. *For this series of contracts is substituted one.*

R. H. Coase, *The Nature of the Firm*, 4 Economica 386 (1937).

According to Coase, the firm (in whatever form venturers choose) provides a standard form contract.[1] The purpose of this contract is to

[1] This "contract" is not always the kind of binding, enforceable contract where there is mutual exchange of consideration, studied in Contracts in 1L. Rather, in economic terms, a

reduce the cost of organization associated with the unavoidable process of price discovery. This is econo-speak for the basic idea that venturers will want to know the terms and conditions of participating in the venture, and this knowledge will require effort and cost in the form of negotiating for terms and conditions, which is generally a process of price discovery. Thus, the purpose of the firm is to create a venture that is efficient because certain transaction costs of organizing the business affair are reduced. A venturer does not have to make a series of contracts with others in the venture: "For this series of contracts is substituted one."

Coase is credited with conceptualizing the firm as a series of contracts, which ultimately gave rise to the theory that a firm, such as a corporation, was in its essence a "nexus of contracts" among factors of production. Based on these economic ideas, a prominent law and economic theory of firms explains the laws of business organizations as providing a set of contract terms for participation in the firm.

> The dominant model of the corporation in legal scholarship is the so-called nexus of contracts theory. This model's origins fairly can be traced to Nobel Prize laureate Ronald Coase's justly famous article, The Nature of the Firm. Building on Coase's work, modern law and economics scholars view the corporation not as an entity but as an aggregate of various inputs acting together to produce goods or services. Employees provide labor. Creditors provide debt capital. Shareholders initially provide equity capital and subsequently bear the risk of losses and monitor the performance of management. Management monitors the performance of employees and coordinates the activities of all the firm's inputs. The firm is the nexus of explicit and implicit contracts establishing rights and obligations among the various inputs making up the firm.

Stephen M. Bainbridge, *The Board of Directors as Nexus of Contracts*, 88 Iowa L. Rev. 1, 9–10 (2002).

Efficient contracting does not wholly explain the need for a firm. There is no reason why, absent business organization laws provided by states, venturers cannot create "model contracts" that mimic the rules of internal affairs under the realm of contract law. If states eliminate business organization laws as we know them, the function of the law can presumably migrate to model contract terms existing in the commercial market in much the same way contract practice occurs today. But law and contract

"contract" simply notes the mutual assent among venturers to the terms and conditions of doing business together, some of which may be actual legal contracts and others simply implied understanding. *See* Frank H. Easterbrook & Daniel R. Fischel, The Economic Structure of Corporate Law 15 (1991) ("We treat corporate law as a standard-form contract, supplying terms most venturers would have chosen but yielding to explicit terms in all but a few instances. . . . The rhetoric of contract is a staple of political and philosophical debate. . . . Perhaps the corporate contract, like the social contract, is no more than a rhetorical device.").

are not coterminous. Contract law is limited when ventures must deal with parties outside of the venture. One of the most important reasons to form a firm is that the state can provide venturers the benefit of limited liability. The rule of limited liability is one of the major reasons—if not the most important reason—to form a limited liability entity such as corporations, LPs, and LLCs. Venturers cannot fully contract to bestow onto themselves the privilege of limited liability. The principle of limited liability is grounded in this question: Who bears the liabilities or losses incurred by the firm if the firm cannot pay them? While venturers can contract for the allocation of losses and liability as against *themselves*, they cannot fully limit the liability to themselves as against *third-parties*. In theory, limited liability can be achieved in contract transactions, such as the provision of credit, if a creditor agrees ex ante to provide credit without recourse to venturers personally. A creditor cannot achieve limited liability under tort law because most transactions in torts are involuntary.

> Tort law is a wrench in the smooth machinery of the contractarian explanation. Tort creditors do not assent to limited liability through voluntary transactions and are not factors of production in the corporate nexus of contracts. . . . Private ordering cannot synthetically gin up the legal right of limited liability. In the realm of torts and corporate law, the state can grant limited liability, abrogate it, or modify it.

Robert J. Rhee, *Bonding Limited Liability*, 51 Wm. & Mary L. Rev. 1417, 1426, 1444 (2010). The rule of limited liability is a fundamental rule of corporations, LLCs, and limited partnerships. These firms exist because only the state can provide the rule of limited liability through the filing to create a limited liability entity under state law.

One answer to the question—why firms?—is that firms are efficient ways to do business because they reduce the transaction cost of arranging participatory rights, obligations, and prices. Laws are also needed to grant venturers a set of default rules of internal affairs and the state-granted rule of limited liability. There is another abstract, but real, benefit provided by business organization laws.

THE ESSENTIAL ROLE OF ORGANIZATIONAL LAW

Henry Hansmann & Reinier Kraakman, 110 Yale L.J. 387 (2000)

In every developed market economy, the law provides for a set of standard-form legal entities. In the United States, these entities include, among others, the business corporation, the cooperative corporation, the nonprofit corporation, the municipal corporation, the limited liability company, the general partnership, the limited partnership, the private trust, the charitable trust, and marriage. To an important degree, these legal entities are simply standard-form contracts among the parties who participate in an enterprise—including, in particular, the organization's owners, managers, and creditors. It is therefore natural to ask what more, if anything, these entities offer. Do they—as the current literature increasingly implies—play essentially the same role performed by privately supplied standard-form contracts, just providing off-the-rack terms that simplify negotiation and drafting of routine agreements? Or do the various legal entities provided by organizational law permit the creation of relationships that could not practicably be formed by contract alone? In short, what, if any, essential role does organizational law play in modern society?

We offer an answer to that question here. In essence, we argue that the essential role of all forms of organizational law is to provide for the creation of a pattern of creditors' rights—a form of "asset partitioning"—that could not practicably be established otherwise. One aspect of this asset partitioning is the delimitation of the extent to which creditors of an entity can have recourse against the personal assets of the owners or other beneficiaries of the entity. But this function of organizational law—which includes the limited liability that is a familiar characteristic of most corporate entities—is, we argue, of distinctly secondary importance. The truly essential aspect of asset partitioning is, in effect, the reverse of limited liability—namely, the shielding of the assets of the entity from claims of the creditors of the entity's owners or managers. This means that organizational law is much more important as property law than as contract law. Surprisingly, this crucial function of organizational law has rarely been the explicit focus of commentary or analysis.

There are a variety of ways to coordinate the economic activity of two or more persons. One common approach is to have each of those persons enter into a contract with a third party who undertakes the coordination through design of the separate contracts and, most importantly, through exercise of the discretion given the third party by those contracts. A third party that serves this coordination function is what we commonly call a "firm." The firm therefore serves—not just metaphorically, but quite literally—as the requisite "nexus of contracts" for the persons whose activity is to be coordinated: It is the common party with whom each of those persons has an individual contract. . . .

To serve effectively as a nexus of contracts, a firm must generally have two attributes. The first is well-defined decisionmaking authority. More particularly, there must be one or more persons who have ultimate authority to commit the firm to contracts. We term those persons the "managers" of the firm. In a corporation, the managers (as we use the term here) are the members of the firm's board of directors; in a partnership, they are the firm's general partners. The firm's managers may or may not be distinct from the persons for whose benefit the managers are charged to act—namely, the firm's owners or, in the case of nonproprietary organizations, the firm's beneficial owners or beneficiaries.

The second attribute a firm must have, if it is to serve effectively as a locus of contracts, is the ability to bond its contracts credibly—that is, to provide assurance that the firm will perform its contractual obligations. Bonding generally requires that there exists a pool of assets that the firm's managers can offer as satisfaction for the firm'sx obligations.[7] We term this pool of assets the firm's "bonding assets." . . .

Legal entities, like individuals, are legal (or "juridical") persons in the sense that they also have the two attributes described above: (1) a well-defined ability to contract through designated managers, and (2) a designated pool of assets that are available to satisfy claims by the firm's creditors. Legal entities are distinct from natural persons, however, in that their bonding assets are, at least in part, distinct from assets owned by the firm's owners or managers, in the sense that the firm's creditors have a claim on those assets that is prior to that of the personal creditors of the firm's owners or managers.

In our view, this latter feature—the separation between the firm's bonding assets and the personal assets of the firm's owners and managers—is the core defining characteristic of a legal entity, and establishing this separation is the principal role that organizational law plays in the organization of enterprise. More particularly, our argument has four elements: (1) that a characteristic of all legal entities, and hence of organizational law in general, is the partitioning off of a separate set of assets in which creditors of the firm itself have a prior security interest; (2) that this partitioning offers important efficiency advantages in the creation of large firms; (3) that it would generally be infeasible to establish this form of asset partitioning without organizational law; and (4) that this attribute—essentially a property attribute—is the only essential contribution that organizational law makes to commercial activity, in the sense that it is the only basic attribute of a firm that could not feasibly be established by contractual means alone.

Asset partitioning has two components. The first is the designation of a separate pool of assets that are associated with the firm, and that are distinct from the personal assets of the firm's owners and managers. In essence, this is done by recognizing juridical persons (or, as we will usually say here, "legal entities") that are distinct from individual human beings and that can own assets in their own name. When a firm is organized as such an entity, the assets owned by that entity in its own name become the designated separate pool of firm assets.

The second component of asset partitioning is the assignment to creditors of priorities in the distinct pools of assets that result from the formation of a legal entity. This assignment of priorities takes two forms. The first assigns to the firm's creditors a claim on the assets associated with the firm's operations that is prior to the claims of the personal creditors of the firm's owners. We term this "affirmative" asset partitioning, to reflect the notion that it sets forth a distinct pool of firm assets as bonding assets for all the firm's contracts. The second form of asset partitioning is just the opposite, granting to the owners' personal creditors a claim on the owners' separate personal assets that is prior to the claims of the firm's creditors. We term this "defensive" asset partitioning, to reflect the common perception that it serves to shield the owners' assets from the creditors of the firm.

2. LEGAL PERSONHOOD AND LIMITED LIABILITY

The theory of asset partitioning has a practical implication. It supports the idea that firms are separate legal persons. Legal personhood separates and partitions assets among constituents in a business enterprise. The concepts of limited liability and legal personhood are linked.[2] The rule of limited liability states that equityholders are not liable for the debts and obligations of the firm solely by reason of their status as equityholders. They are not *vicariously* liable for the debts of the firm. For example, the debts of the Walt Disney Co. or the Coca-Cola Co. do not pass to their shareholders even if these companies cannot satisfy their obligations. A shareholder can safely invest $100 in these firms and know that her maximum loss is $100, and not $100,000. One justification for the rule of limited liability is that, as a separate legal person, the entity is "responsible" for or "bears" its own debts and obligations and these losses do not pass through to equityholders by virtue of the latter's status.

Limited liability segregates the liability of the firm and its owners. A related concept is that legal personhood segregates property rights among constituents. The owner's property is *not* the firm's property; conversely, the firm's property is *not* the owner's property. Once the firm acquires rights to property, the property belongs to the firm. Losses are charged against the firm's properties until such assets are exhausted. Then the rule of limited liability is triggered and creditors' pursuit of claims typically ends because the equityholders' properties, having been partitioned against claims by the firm, cannot be used to satisfy creditors' claims against the firm. Otherwise, consider these potential harms: (1) any single equityholder can claim the firm's property for personal use (an indicia that the firm is not separate and distinct from its equityholders); (2) the firm can reach into the personal assets of any single equityholder to satisfy its needs (an indicia that the rule of limited liability does not apply). Both situations are problematic. The firm's property and the equityholder's property are separate and distinct. The latter's property is her proportional

[2] Certain entities do not have limited liability. Partners in a general partnership and general partners in an LP do not have limited liability. RUPA § 306(a).

ownership in the firm, but this ownership is not the same as ownership of the firm's property or rights to govern the firm.

Legal personhood is an important *practical* concept. A business entity benefits from being considered a separate legal person because, among other things, it must be able to own property, sign contracts, and sue and be sued in its own name. To illustrate the importance of these functions, imagine a partnership of 50 partners, but partnership law prohibits the partnership from signing a contract in its own name. Who signs the contract? A single partner? All 50 partners? Who would want to sign? What are the potential personal liabilities? What if a partner leaves the partnership and seeks to be relieved of any obligation under the contract? What if a new partner joins? What are the considerations of the contract counterparty? Similar kinds of questions may apply to the ownership of property and the designation of parties in litigation. The concept of legal personhood has practical benefits that facilitate ordinary, day-to-day business transactions.

Corporations are legal persons. They are separate and distinct from its shareholders. A major function of this distinction is that it partitions assets among venturers. *See* Dole Food Co. v. Patrickson, 538 U.S. 468, 469 (2003) ("As a corporation and its shareholders are distinct entities, a corporate parent which owns a subsidiary's shares does not, for that reason alone, own or have legal title to the subsidiary's assets.").

CORPORATION AS LEGAL ENTITY

18 Corpus Juris Secundum § 6 (updated Sept. 2019)

The basic purpose of incorporation is to create a distinct legal entity, with legal rights, obligations, powers, and privileges different from those of the natural individuals who created it, who own it, or whom it employs.

A corporation is generally regarded as a legal entity, and a corporation and its shareholders are distinct entities. Thus, conceptually, a corporation is a separate entity having an existence distinct from its owners. Corporations and their shareholders are separate entities, even where one individual owns all of the corporation's stock. A corporate owner or employee, a natural person, is distinct from the corporation itself, which is a legally different entity with different rights and responsibilities due to its different legal status. The basic purpose of incorporation is to create a distinct legal entity, with legal rights, obligations, powers, and privileges different from those of the natural individuals who created it, who own it, or whom it employs. The natural persons who procure a corporation's creation and have a pecuniary interest in it are not the corporation.

An employee and the corporation for which the employee works are different persons, even where the employee is the corporation's sole owner. Also, a corporation is distinct from its shareholders even when it is professional service corporation. A corporation is further always a separate entity distinct from its investors. Additionally, corporations are separate legal entities even where one wholly owns the other and the two have mutual dealings. Courts will recognize the separate identities of corporations even when one corporation treats the other corporation as a mere department, instrumentality, or agency of the other. However, a corporation's use of a fictitious name does not create a separate legal entity.

The separate nature of the corporate existence must be respected. A corporation is a separate entity, distinct from the individuals who are its stockholders or who manage it as directors or officers, for the purposes of shielding a shareholder from liability, unless and until there is sufficient reason to the contrary. The notion of a corporation's legal entity, apart from the persons composing it, is introduced for convenience and to serve the ends of justice. A corporation is a legal fiction for the purpose of doing business, and this legal fiction may be disregarded when the purpose for which it was intended is abused.

Like corporations, all NBEs are entities that are separate and distinct from its owners.

RUPA § 201. Partnership as Entity.[3]

(a) A partnership is an entity distinct from its partners.

ULPA (2001) § 110. Nature, Purpose, and Duration of Entity.

(a) A limited partnership is an entity distinct from its partners.

RULLCA § 108. Nature, Purpose, and Duration of Limited Liability Company.

(a) A limited liability company is an entity distinct from its member or members.

NBEs and their owners and managers cannot be conflated. *See* Rieder v. Woods, 603 S.W.3d 86, 98 (Tex. 2020) (noting "the well-established legal principle that limited liability companies and their obligations are legally distinct from their members and managers"). Property belonging to the

[3] The older version of the general partnership statute, the Uniform Partnership Act of 1914 (UPA), did not have a similar provision. In some parts, the UPA envisioned a partnership as the aggregate of its partners. The dissociation of any partner caused a dissolution of the firm. UPA § 29. A dissolution does not automatically trigger wind up of the business, but it simply means a change in the legal relation among partners. *Id.* Only a small minority of jurisdictions continue to use the UPA.

firm is not property of the owner in his individual capacity. *See* Veterans Parkway Developers, LLC v. RMW Development Fund II, LLC., 793 S.E.2d 398, 401 (Ga. 2016) ("a member's stake in a LLC is not an interest in real property or an interest in any specific property of the LLC"). Members or managers do not have standing to sue on their individual capacities for an injury to the LLC. *See* Channing Real Estate, LLC v. Gates, 161 A.3d 1227, 1235–36 (Conn. 2017) ("A limited liability company is a distinct legal entity whose existence is separate from its members. A limited liability company has the power to sue or to be sued in its own name; or may be a party to an action brought in its name by a member or manager. A member or manager, however, may not sue in an individual capacity to recover for an injury based on a wrong to the limited liability company.").

The practical significance of personhood is that a firm can transact day-to-day without the complication of arranging and rearranging legal rights among potentially many constituents. As a single legal person, the firm can sue and be sued, execute contracts, and own property. ULPA (2001) § 111; RULLCA § 109. Because so many NBEs are closely held and many LLCs are single member firms, owners may not always appreciate the distinctness between entity and owner. Owners may assume that the firm's property is their personal property, but this would be wrong.

The cases below illustrate the concept of legal personhood in different contexts. In reading these cases, think about this question: What instrumental function is served by the rule of personhood?

REYNOLDS V. LYMAN

903 F.3d 693 (7th Cir. 2018)

WOOD, CHIEF JUDGE.

This appeal arises out of a malpractice suit that Brian Reynolds brought against the law firm Henderson & Lyman ("H&L"), alleging that H&L gave negligent advice to several LLCs that Reynolds co-owned and managed. According to Reynolds, H&L's bad advice led him to violate federal disclosure laws when he drafted the LLCs' financial statements. The district court granted summary judgment to H&L, explaining that Reynolds could not bring a malpractice suit on his own behalf because he did not have a personal attorney-client relationship with H&L.

Under Illinois law, a plaintiff must prove five elements to prevail on a claim for legal malpractice: "(1) an attorney-client relationship; (2) a duty arising out of that relationship; (3) a breach of that duty; (4) causation; and (5) actual damages."

The Illinois Supreme Court described the attorney-client relationship as "a voluntary, contractual relationship that requires the consent of both the attorney and client." Reynolds admits that he never asked H&L to represent him and that H&L never said anything that suggested it thought it was representing him. The parties never entered into any agreement that would have created an attorney-client relationship between them. H&L did have an attorney-client relationship with the LLCs that Reynolds co-owned and managed, but that is different. It was in his capacity as a managing member of these LLCs that Reynolds communicated with, and was advised by, H&L. Reynolds's primary argument on appeal is that H&L owed him something akin to a third-party duty of care arising out of its representation of the LLCs, because his personal interests were so closely bound with the interests of the LLCs as to be functionally indistinguishable. This theory might sound plausible on its face, but unfortunately for Reynolds it is foreclosed by decades of Illinois law.

Illinois courts consistently have held that neither shared interests nor shared liability gives rise to third-party liability. For third-party liability in Illinois, Reynolds must have been a direct and intended beneficiary, and "simply because the [officers of a business entity] were at risk of personal liability does not transform the incidental benefits of [the law firm's] representation of [the business entity] into direct and intended benefits for [the officers]." In fact, the only time an Illinois attorney owes a duty of care to a third party is when the attorney was hired for the primary purpose of benefitting that third party. Illinois courts have emphasized that the primary purpose of a retainer agreement between a business entity and a lawyer is to benefit the business entity, not to benefit that entity's owners or officers, however closely aligned their interests might be.

Illinois's courts are free to change the state's law or to carve out the exception that Reynolds seeks, but we are not. In fact, even if it were up to us, we would not do so, because the state's current rule makes good sense. A contrary rule would undermine the integrity of the attorney-client relationship by forcing attorneys to assume competing duties of care to non-clients. In addition, the rule that Reynolds asks us to adopt would chip away at the legal distinction between entities and individuals—a distinction that serves as the basis for the existence of many business structures, including that of the LLC. It would be bizarre indeed if a business's owners or officers could cloak themselves in the protections provided by the limited-liability corporate structure when they enter contracts or defend against a lawsuit, yet cast that structure aside when seeking to recover as plaintiffs for injuries sustained by the business. In law, as in life, double standards are frowned upon.

STATE V. BRELVIS CONSULTING LLC

430 P.3d 685 (Wash. App. 2018)

BJORGEN, J.

Brelvis Consulting LLC appeals from the superior court's order requiring it to comply with the civil investigative demand (CID) issued and served on Brelvis by the Attorney General's Office (AGO) pursuant to RCW 19.86.110. Brelvis argues that the superior court erred by compelling it to comply with the CID because it violates Brelvis' (1) right against self-incrimination, (2) right against intrusion into its private affairs, and (3) right against unreasonable search and seizure. Brelvis also argues that the CID is directed at the managing member of Brelvis, Bruce Mesnekoff, in his personal capacity.

We hold that the superior court properly required Brelvis to comply with the CID and consequently affirm its decision.

The AGO received a complaint regarding Student Loan Help Center LLC. The Student Loan Help Center does business under the name Brelvis Consulting LLC. Mesnekoff owns and operates Brelvis and is its registered agent. The AGO sent a CID to Brelvis pursuant to RCW 19.86.110 as part of its investigation into whether Brelvis had engaged in unfair or deceptive business practices in violation of RCW 19.86.020. The CID was addressed to Brelvis, in care of Mesnekoff. The AGO's investigation related to possible misrepresentations about student loan forgiveness and other possible violations of Washington's Debt Adjusting Act, chapter 18.28 RCW, and Consumer Protection Act, chapter 19.86 RCW. The CID included 12 interrogatories and 13 requests for production.

The CID noted that it was directed to "Brelvis Consulting LLC" and to Mesnekoff as its registered agent for service. The interrogatories and requests for production defined "You," "Your," and "Brelvis" as referring to Brelvis Consulting LLC, including any principals, owners, employees, officers, agents, and "any other persons or entities acting on behalf of or under the direction, authorization or control of Brelvis." Brelvis argues that because the definition of "You," "Your," and "Brelvis" encompasses Mesnekoff, "the CID applies to him personally." Brelvis asserts that

> the plain language of the CID equates Mesnekoff individually and personally with the word "Brelvis." Mesnekoff is therefore required by the terms of this CID to answer the interrogatories under oath.

Brelvis also argues that Mesnekoff is personally implicated because the CID was addressed to Brelvis in care of him.

A corporation is "artificial, invisible, intangible," and it exists only in law. Our case law recognizes that

> the invisible, intangible object of our legal contemplation cannot answer discovery or be effectively sanctioned if it does not. By necessity it acts through its officers, directors, employees, and other agents. As with a corporation's duties in every other sphere in which it operates, it is the corporate officers, directors, and other agents who must discharge its duties in a lawsuit.

A "corporation exists as an organization distinct from its shareholders." Accordingly, corporations acting through corporate officers and corporate officers acting in their personal capacity "maintain distinct legal obligations and interests." A corporation's separate legal identity is not lost because it is owned by one person or members of a single family.

Brelvis' claim that the CID targets Mesnekoff in his personal capacity is belied by case law. The United States Supreme Court has held that "without regard to whether the subpoena is addressed to the corporation, or as here, to the individual in his capacity as a custodian, a corporate custodian such as petitioner may not resist a subpoena for corporate records on Fifth Amendment grounds." Nevertheless, the "privilege against self-incrimination includes the right of a witness not to give incriminatory answers in any proceeding—civil or criminal, administrative or judicial, investigatory or adjudicatory."

Thus, Mesnekoff, in his capacity as Brelvis' custodian, may not resist a request for production of Brelvis' records on Fifth Amendment grounds. However, where the interrogatories propounded by the AGO might tend to incriminate Mesnekoff in future criminal proceedings, the Fifth Amendment privilege against self-incrimination permits Mesnekoff to refuse to answer official questions asked in the context of the CID.

NOTES

1. For corporations, the concept of legal personhood has a large political dimension. In addition to having the right to sign contracts, own property, and sue and be sued—the ordinary tasks of conducting business affairs—*corporations* have important constitutional rights such as equal protection, due process and free speech. *See* Santa Clara County v. Southern Pacific R.R. Co., 118 U.S. 394 (1886); Minneapolis & St. Louis Railway Co. v. Beckwith, 129 U.S. 26 (1888); Citizens United v. Fed. Elec. Comm'n, 558 U.S. 310 (2010). NBEs do not have equivalent rights under constitutional law. Corporate constitutional rights are not required to solve immediate practical problems related to day-to-day business problems. They embody a larger political judgment on the limits of governmental power over persons, most naturally considered in the context of the relationship between the government and natural persons, but also including the relationship between the government and corporations. But corporations do not have constitutional rights coextensive with natural persons. Some rights are considered personal. For example, the right against self-incrimination is a personal right.

> But it is further insisted that, while the immunity statute may protect individual witnesses, it would not protect the corporation of which appellant was the agent and representative. This is true, but the answer is that it was not designed to do so. The right of a person under the 5th Amendment to refuse to incriminate himself is purely a personal privilege of the witness. It was never intended to permit him to plead the fact that some third person might be incriminated by his testimony, even though he were the agent of such person. A privilege so extensive might be used to put a stop to the examination of every witness who was called upon to testify before the grand jury with regard to the doings or business of his principal, whether such principal were an individual or a corporation. The question whether a corporation is a "person" within the meaning of this amendment really does not arise, except, perhaps, where a corporation is called upon to answer a bill of discovery, since it can only be heard by oral evidence in the person of some one of its agents or employees. The amendment is limited to a person who shall be compelled in any criminal case to be a witness against *himself;* and if he cannot set up the privilege of a third person, he certainly cannot set up the privilege of a corporation.

Hale v. Henkel, 201 U.S. 43, 69–70 (1906).

GOULD V. CITY OF STAMFORD

203 A.3d 525 (Conn. 2019)

PALMER, J.

The issue that we must resolve in this appeal is whether the plaintiff, Peter Gould, the sole member of a single-member limited liability company, Intervale Group, LLC (Intervale), qualifies as Intervale's employee for purposes of the Workers' Compensation Act (act), General Statutes § 31–275 et seq., and is therefore eligible for concurrent compensation benefits from the defendant Second Injury Fund (fund) pursuant to General Statutes § 31–310.

The plaintiff formed Intervale, a limited liability company of which he is the sole member. Intervale provided various video production services to corporations. The plaintiff was solely responsible for completing the company's projects, which included field production work. He reported to no one other than Intervale's clients.

Intervale did not pay the plaintiff a fixed salary. Rather, when Intervale received a payment from a customer, the plaintiff would deposit the payment in Intervale's bank account and then withdraw funds as needed. In 2012 and 2013, the plaintiff reported his income from Intervale for federal tax purposes on schedule C of Internal Revenue Service Form 1040, which is the form used to report "Profit or Loss From Business (Sole Proprietorship)."

In 2012, a shopping mall in Massachusetts hired Intervale to shoot a video at the mall. As a condition of the engagement, the mall required Intervale to obtain workers' compensation insurance.

In 2013, in addition to his work in connection with Intervale, the plaintiff worked part-time for the city of Stamford as a park police officer. The plaintiff injured his back and legs during the course of his employment with the city. Thereafter, he filed a claim for compensation under the act based on both his earnings from the city and his earnings from Intervale. The fund denied the plaintiff's claim for concurrent employment benefits on the ground that there was no employer-employee relationship between the plaintiff and Intervale.

We consider the plaintiff's claim that the board incorrectly determined that the plaintiff was not Intervale's employee. We agree.

The fund claims that the commissioner correctly determined that the plaintiff is not Intervale's employee because the plaintiff, not Intervale, had "the right to control the means and methods used by the [plaintiff] in the performance of his" services. We recognize that the right to control test is the traditional test for determining the existence of an employer-employee relationship. The test generally has been used to distinguish between an independent contractor and an employee, which is not the issue presented in this case. Rather, the issue for us to decide is whether the sole member of a limited liability company who has the right to control the company and who also performs services for the company can be the company's employee. If the right to control test applied in this situation, then, contrary to the apparent legislative intent, the member of a single-member limited liability company could *never* be found to be the company's employee, because a single-member limited liability company can *only* exercise control over the member through the member.

The Missouri Court of Appeals addressed a similar problem in *Lynn* v. *Lloyd A. Lynn, Inc.*, 493 S.W.2d 363 (Mo. App. 1973). In that case, the widow of the sole owner and manager of a corporation who had been killed while performing services for the corporation claimed that the decedent was an employee of the corporation and, as a consequence, that she was eligible for death benefits under the workers' compensation laws of Missouri. The Industrial Commission and the state circuit court concluded that the decedent was not the corporation's employee because he did not satisfy the traditional controllable services test for employment under Missouri law. The Missouri Court of Appeals observed that "the policy behind the controllable services test, developed to distinguish between an employee and an independent contractor, was that an independent contractor is only temporarily and peripherally connected with the master's or employer's business." The court concluded that "the controllable services test was inappropriate as applied to executive officers. Such officers, by virtue of their managerial abilities, often accompanied by substantial stock ownership, are naturally apt to be under less control in the performance of their duties than the typical employee. But, unlike the independent contractor, the executive officer is intimately and permanently involved in the operation of the business. The criteria by which independent contractor status is determined [are] not adequate to meet the needs of the unique problems created by executive officers of corporations."

Lynn concluded that, under Missouri's workers' compensation law, which defined "employee" to include "every person in the service of any employer under any contract of hire, express or implied, oral or written, or under any appointment or election, including executive officers of corporations"; the word "employee" included "executive officers irrespective of whether these officers rendered controllable services or exercised control over the services of others.

Lynn further concluded that, "to hold that the decedent was not an employee at the time of his death because of the office he held and his stock ownership in the corporation is to disregard the separate and distinct legal identities of [the] decedent and [the corporation].

We agree that the right to control test is not an appropriate test for determining whether the member of a single-member limited liability company is an employee of the company. Rather, the test is whether the member performed services for the company and was subject to the hazards of the company's business.

Because there is no dispute in the present case that the plaintiff provided services to Intervale and was subject to the hazards of Intervale's business, the plaintiff was Intervale's employee for purposes of the act.

CHRYSLER GROUP LLC OPERATING AGREEMENT

Section 2.3 Purposes. The Company is formed for the object and purpose of, and the nature of the business to be conducted and promoted by the Company is, engaging in any lawful act or activity for which limited liability companies may be formed under the LLC Act, as such acts or activities may be determined by the Board of Directors (as herein defined) from time to time.

Section 2.4 Powers.

(a) The nature of the business or purposes to be conducted or promoted by the Company is to engage in any lawful act or activity for which limited liability companies may be organized under the LLC Act. The Company may engage in any and all activities necessary, desirable or incidental to the accomplishment of the foregoing. Notwithstanding anything herein to the contrary, nothing set forth herein shall be construed as authorizing the Company to possess any purpose or power, or to do any act or thing, forbidden by Law to a limited liability company organized under the Laws of the State of Delaware.

(b) Subject to the provisions of this Agreement and except as prohibited by Law, (i) the Company may enter into, deliver and perform any and all agreements, consents, deeds, contracts, proxies, covenants, bonds, checks, drafts, bills of exchange, notes, acceptances and endorsements, and all evidences of indebtedness and other documents, instruments or writings of any nature whatsoever, all without any further act, vote or approval of any Member, and (ii) the Company may authorize (including by general delegated authority) any Person to enter into, deliver and perform on behalf of the Company any and all agreements, consents, deeds, contracts, proxies, covenants, bonds, checks, drafts, bills of exchange, notes, acceptances and endorsements, and all evidences of indebtedness and other documents, instruments or writings of any nature whatsoever.

(c) Subject to the other provisions of this Agreement, the Company shall do all things necessary to maintain its existence separate and apart from each Member and any Affiliate of any Member and shall maintain its books and records separate from those of any Affiliate of the Company or any other Person.

Section 2.8 Duration. The period of the Company's duration commenced on April 28, 2009 and shall continue in full force and effect in perpetuity; provided that the Company may be dissolved and wound up in accordance with the provisions of this Agreement and the LLC Act.

B. ATTORNEY ENGAGEMENT

Business entities must or should retain attorneys to administer their legal matters. In matters before a court, business entities *must* be represented by an attorney. They cannot be represented *pro se* by a shareholder, partner, manager, or member,[4] even when the entity has a single owner, such as a single-member LLC or a sole shareholder.[5] Business entities are separate and distinct legal persons and they are not alter egos of their owners.

---

4 *See* Flora Constr. Co. v. Fireman's Fund Ins. Co., 307 F.2d 413, 414 (10th Cir. 1962) ("The rule is well established that a corporation can appear in a court of record only by an attorney at law."); Harrison v. Wahatoyas, LLC, 253 F.3d 552, 556 (10th Cir. 2001) ("As a general matter, a corporation or other business entity can only appear in court through an attorney and not through a non-attorney corporate officer appearing pro se."). *See also* Ohio State Bar Ass'n v. Naumov, 137 N.E.3d 84, 86–87 (Ohio 2019); Smith v. Rustic Home Builders, LLC, 826 N.W.2d 357, 359–60 (S.D. 2013); H & H Development, LLC v. Ramlow, 272 P.3d 657, 661 (Mont. 2012); Harrison v. Wahatoyas, LLC, 253 F.3d 552, 556 (10th Cir. 2001).

5 *See* Dougherty v. Snyder, 469 Fed.Appx. 71, 72 (3d Cir. 2012); United States v. Hagerman, 545 F.3d 579, 581–82 (7th Cir. 2008); Lattanzio v. COMTA, 481 F.3d 137, 139–40 (2d Cir. 2007); Steinhausen v. HomeServices of Nebraska, Inc., 857 N.W.2d 816, 825–26 (Neb. 2015); Ohio State Bar Association v. Cohen, 122 N.E.3d 172 (Ohio 2018).

In matters outside of litigation, such as entity formation and maintenance and other business dealings, there is no formal need for an attorney. For example, LLCs and partnerships, and even corporations, can be organized and formed without lawyers. But business entities *should* be represented by attorneys. Business dealings and transactions, including the formation and maintenance of a business entity, are complex tasks. The advice and service of a business lawyer are critically important to ensuring that important transactions, such as the formation and restructuring of an entity through the charter agreement, are done properly.

In both litigation and transactional contexts, lawyers are important. Before undertaking the work of forming and maintaining a business entity, the attorney and the participants must determine the most basic issue in attorney engagement: *Who is the client?*

An attorney is a client's fiduciary.[6] An attorney owes her client a number of duties, including the basic duties arising out of agency and professional ethics. These duties include the basic duty of care and duty of loyalty, embodied in professional rules of competence, diligence, and conflict of interest. *See* ABA Rules of Professional Conduct Rule 1.1 (Competence), Rule 1.3 (Diligence), Rule 1.7 (Conflict of Interest: Current Clients), Rule 1.8 (Conflict of Interest: Current Clients: Special Rules). An attorney owes the duty to maintain confidentiality of information. *See id.* Rule 1.6 (a) ("A lawyer shall not reveal information relating to the representation of a client unless the client gives informed consent, the disclosure is impliedly authorized in order to carry out the representation or the disclosure is permitted.").

Given this special relationship, the attorney and all parties should have a clear understanding of the attorney-client relationship. In the transactional setting of entity formation and maintenance, there are several possible clients: (1) the prospective and yet unformed new entity, (2) the group of organizers who would become owners in the new entity, (3) an individual prospective owner, or (4) any combination thereof.

With respect to the prospective and yet unformed new entity as the client, the attorney would work on the matter of entity formation before the client (a legal person) has come into existence. This complicates the matter, particularly when the lawyer is engaged by the organizers of the business. Rules of professional ethics may differ among state jurisdictions on whether the organizers are clients or whether the attorney-client relationship is formed when the entity comes into being.

---

[6] *See* Baker v. Wood, Ris & Hames, Professional Corp., 364 P.3d 872, 876 (Colo. 2016); Board of Prof. Resp., Wyoming State Bar v. Casper, 318 P.3d 790, 795 (Wyo. 2014); Horwitz v. Holabird & Root, 816 N.E.2d 272, 277 (Ill. 2004); Clancy v. State Bar of Cal., 454 P.2d 329, 333 (Cal. 1969).

State laws and the regulation of attorneys therein vary. Some states permit the entity rule, which states that an attorney does not actually represent organizers in their individual capacities where:

> (1) a person retains a lawyer for the purpose of organizing an entity and (2) the lawyer's involvement with that person is directly related to that incorporation and (3) such entity is eventually incorporated, the entity rule applies retroactively such that the lawyer's pre-incorporation involvement with the person is deemed to be representation of the entity, not the person.

Jesse v. Danforth, 485 N.W.2d 63, 67 (Wisc. 1992). *See* State Bar of Arizona, Opinion 02–06 (Sept. 2002) ("Can a lawyer represent an entity that does not yet exist? Yes, as long as the incorporators understand that they are retaining counsel on behalf of the yet-to-be-formed entity and will need to ratify this corporate action, nunc pro tunc, once the entity is formed."); Manion v. Nagin, 394 F.3d 1062, 1068–69 (8th Cir. 2005) (recognizing the entity rule, but holding that the attorney's representation may have went further to provide legal representation to the individual during the entity formation period).

Other states permit the aggregate theory of representation, which states that the attorney can represent the aggregate of the organizers and the entity. *See* Schwartz v. Broadcast Music, Inc., 16 F.R.D. 31, 32 (S.D.N.Y. 1954) ("ASCAP is an unincorporated association of which plaintiff Moore is a member. Each individual member of the association is a client of the association's lawyer."); Pucci v. Santi, 711 F.Supp. 916, 927 n.4 (N.D. Ill. 1989) ("The general view appears to be that where an entity is by law an aggregate of individuals, the lawyer has an attorney-client relationship with each of those individuals. Since a limited partnership is an aggregation of individual partners, this approach supports the plaintiffs' position that Litwin was the plaintiffs' lawyer.").

Another approach is the "reasonable expectations" test under which an attorney-client relationship is formed if an attorney leads a person to believe that the person is a client and the belief is reasonable under the circumstances, irrespective of whether the client enters into a formal engagement agreement. *E.g.,* Westinghouse Elec. Corp. v. Kerr-McGee Corp., 580 F.2d 1311, 1319 (7th Cir.1978) ("There are several fairly common situations where, although there is no express attorney-client relationship, there exists nevertheless a fiduciary obligation or an implied professional relation. The professional relationship hinges upon the client's belief that he is consulting a lawyer in that capacity and his manifested intention to seek professional legal advice."); Rosman v. Shapiro, 653 F.Supp. 1441, 1445 (S.D.N.Y. 1987) ("Rosman reasonably believed that Zisman was representing him. Although, in the ordinary corporate situation, corporate counsel does not necessarily become counsel for the corporation's shareholders and directors where, as here, the corporation is a close corporation consisting of only two shareholders with equal interests in the corporation, it is indeed reasonable for each shareholder to believe that the corporate counsel is in effect his own individual attorney.").

In determining whether an attorney can advise a prospective client, one must engage in a conflict of interest check. There should be no conflict of interest between the attorney and the prospective client: "The lawyer's own interests should not be permitted to have an adverse effect on representation of a client. For example, if the probity of a lawyer's own conduct in a transaction is in serious question, it may be difficult or impossible for the lawyer to give a client detached advice." ABA Rule of Professional Conduct Rule 1.7, cmt. 10 ("Personal Interest Conflicts").

A common problem is a potential conflict among prospective clients. This situation can arise when an attorney proposes to advise multiple clients in the same venture. For example, there may not be much conflict at the outset of a venture when contributions are exact and agreed upon, but the real world of business is not always so clear. Ownership of a business is measured by the allocation of economic and governance rights. Suppose Alex contributes $100,000 and agrees to provide valuable management service; Ben contributes $50,000 only; Claire contributes $200,000 and a valuable intellectual property. How are these contributions weighed in terms of the initial negotiation for economic and governance rights? Can an attorney advise these organizers in the aggregate during the formation of the entity?

ABA Model Rule of Professional Conduct Rule 1.7. Conflict of Interest: Current Clients.

(a) Except as provided in paragraph (b), a lawyer shall not represent a client if the representation involves a concurrent conflict of interest. A concurrent conflict of interest exists if:

(1) the representation of one client will be directly adverse to another client; or

(2) there is a significant risk that the representation of one or more clients will be materially limited by the lawyer's responsibilities to another client, a former client or a third person or by a personal interest of the lawyer.

(b) Notwithstanding the existence of a concurrent conflict of interest under paragraph (a), a lawyer may represent a client if:

(1) the lawyer reasonably believes that the lawyer will be able to provide competent and diligent representation to each affected client;

(2) the representation is not prohibited by law;

(3) the representation does not involve the assertion of a claim by one client against another client represented by the lawyer in the same litigation or other proceeding before a tribunal; and

(4) each affected client gives informed consent, confirmed in writing.

Comment on Rule 1.7

General Principles

[1] Loyalty and independent judgment are essential elements in the lawyer's relationship to a client. Concurrent conflicts of interest can arise from the lawyer's responsibilities to another client, a former client or a third person or from the lawyer's own interests. For specific Rules regarding certain concurrent conflicts of interest, see Rule 1.8. For former client conflicts of interest, see Rule 1.9. For conflicts of interest involving prospective clients, see Rule 1.18. For definitions of "informed consent" and "confirmed in writing," see Rule 1.0(e) and (b).

[2] Resolution of a conflict of interest problem under this Rule requires the lawyer to: 1) clearly identify the client or clients; 2) determine whether a conflict of interest exists; 3) decide whether the representation may be undertaken despite the existence of a conflict, *i.e.*, whether the conflict is consentable; and 4) if so, consult with the clients affected under paragraph (a) and obtain their informed consent, confirmed in writing. The clients affected under paragraph (a) include both of the clients referred to in paragraph (a)(1) and the one or more clients whose representation might be materially limited under paragraph (a)(2).

Identifying Conflicts of Interest: Directly Adverse

[7] Directly adverse conflicts can also arise in transactional matters. For example, if a lawyer is asked to represent the seller of a business in negotiations with a buyer represented by the lawyer, not in the same transaction but in another, unrelated matter, the lawyer could not undertake the representation without the informed consent of each client.

Identifying Conflicts of Interest: Material Limitation

[8] Even where there is no direct adverseness, a conflict of interest exists if there is a significant risk that a lawyer's ability to consider, recommend or carry out an appropriate course of action for the client will be materially limited as a result of the lawyer's other responsibilities or interests. For example, a lawyer asked to represent several individuals seeking to form a joint venture is likely to be materially limited in the lawyer's ability to recommend or advocate all possible positions that each might take because of the lawyer's duty of loyalty to the others. The conflict in effect forecloses alternatives that would otherwise be available to the client. The mere possibility of subsequent harm does not itself

require disclosure and consent. The critical questions are the likelihood that a difference in interests will eventuate and, if it does, whether it will materially interfere with the lawyer's independent professional judgment in considering alternatives or foreclose courses of action that reasonably should be pursued on behalf of the client.

Nonlitigation Conflicts

[26] Conflicts of interest under paragraphs (a)(1) and (a)(2) arise in contexts other than litigation. For a discussion of directly adverse conflicts in transactional matters, see Comment [7]. Relevant factors in determining whether there is significant potential for material limitation include the duration and intimacy of the lawyer's relationship with the client or clients involved, the functions being performed by the lawyer, the likelihood that disagreements will arise and the likely prejudice to the client from the conflict. The question is often one of proximity and degree. See Comment [8].

[28] Whether a conflict is consentable depends on the circumstances. For example, a lawyer may not represent multiple parties to a negotiation whose interests are fundamentally antagonistic to each other, but common representation is permissible where the clients are generally aligned in interest even though there is some difference in interest among them. Thus, a lawyer may seek to establish or adjust a relationship between clients on an amicable and mutually advantageous basis; for example, in helping to organize a business in which two or more clients are entrepreneurs, working out the financial reorganization of an enterprise in which two or more clients have an interest or arranging a property distribution in settlement of an estate. The lawyer seeks to resolve potentially adverse interests by developing the parties' mutual interests. Otherwise, each party might have to obtain separate representation, with the possibility of incurring additional cost, complication or even litigation. Given these and other relevant factors, the clients may prefer that the lawyer act for all of them.

A clear understanding of the attorney-client relationship is important as the attorney continues to work with the entity. When there are multiple owners or managers of an entity, they may believe that they are the clients when, in fact, the client may be the entity. When an entity retains an attorney, she represents the firm and not individuals therein even though they may have hired her. To avoid misunderstanding, clear communication between the lawyer and the owners or managers is required regarding the identity of the attorney's client.

ABA Model Rule of Professional Conduct Rule 1.13. Organization as Client.

(a) A lawyer employed or retained by an organization represents the organization acting through its duly authorized constituents.

(b) If a lawyer for an organization knows that an officer, employee or other person associated with the organization is engaged in action, intends to act or refuses to act in a matter related to the representation that is a violation of a legal obligation to the organization, or a violation of law that reasonably might be imputed to the organization, and that is likely to result in substantial injury to the organization, then the lawyer shall proceed as is reasonably necessary in the best interest of the organization. Unless the lawyer reasonably believes that it is not necessary in the best interest of the organization to do so, the lawyer shall refer the matter to higher authority in the organization, including, if warranted by the circumstances to the highest authority that can act on behalf of the organization as determined by applicable law.

(c) Except as provided in paragraph (d), if

(1) despite the lawyer's efforts in accordance with paragraph (b) the highest authority that can act on behalf of the organization insists upon or fails to address in a timely and appropriate manner an action, or a refusal to act, that is clearly a violation of law, and

(2) the lawyer reasonably believes that the violation is reasonably certain to result in substantial injury to the organization,

then the lawyer may reveal information relating to the representation whether or not Rule 1.6 permits such disclosure, but only if and to the extent the lawyer reasonably believes necessary to prevent substantial injury to the organization.

(d) Paragraph (c) shall not apply with respect to information relating to a lawyer's representation of an organization to investigate an alleged violation of law, or to defend the organization or an officer, employee or other constituent associated with the organization against a claim arising out of an alleged violation of law.

(e) A lawyer who reasonably believes that he or she has been discharged because of the lawyer's actions taken pursuant to paragraphs (b) or (c), or who withdraws under circumstances that require or permit the lawyer to take action under either of those paragraphs, shall proceed as the lawyer reasonably believes necessary to assure that the organization's highest authority is informed of the lawyer's discharge or withdrawal.

(f) In dealing with an organization's directors, officers, employees, members, shareholders or other constituents, a lawyer shall explain the identity of the client when the lawyer knows or reasonably should know that the organization's interests are adverse to those of the constituents with whom the lawyer is dealing.

(g) A lawyer representing an organization may also represent any of its directors, officers, employees, members, shareholders or other constituents, subject to the provisions of Rule 1.7. If the organization's consent to the dual representation is required by Rule 1.7, the consent shall be given by an appropriate official of the organization other than the individual who is to be represented, or by the shareholders.

The case below deals with the question of whether an attorney has a disqualifying conflict of interest when it represents one group of owners and purportedly the company in a derivative action brought by a dissenting group of owners. In reading this case, think about this question: In what way can an attorney represent both individual defendant owners and the company in an action brought by another group of individual owners who are also claiming that the action is on behalf of the company?

IN RE MURRIN BROTHERS 1885, LTD.

603 S.W.3d 53 (Tex. 2019)

JUSTICE BLACKLOCK delivered the opinion of the Court.

Billy Bob's is a historic entertainment venue located in the Fort Worth Stockyards. The three long-time owners of Billy Bob's—Steve Murrin, Don Jury, and Holt Hickman—decided to reorganize the company. They brought in additional owners and collectively formed Bill Bob's Texas Investments (BBT), a closely held LLC, to own and manage Billy Bob's. BBT's owners adopted a Company Agreement, which dictates BBT's structure and contains rules for the management of BBT. After adopting the Company Agreement, the owners received a Certificate of Formation for BBT from the Secretary of State. The Certificate of Formation lists six "Governing Persons" of BBT, all of whom are either owners of BBT or closely related to an owner or ownership entity.

Concho Minick, both an owner and a Governing Person, was unanimously elected President and Managing Member. Several years later, nine of BBT's twelve owners—and four of its six Governing Persons—became dissatisfied with Minick's performance. This opinion refers to the anti-Minick faction as the Hickman Group. The Hickman Group attempted to dismiss Minick by a majority vote of the Governing Persons.

Despite the Hickman Group's attempt to dismiss him, Minick claimed a right to remain as President and Managing Member. He claimed his dismissal was a "major decision" for which the Company Agreement required a unanimous vote of the owners. Three owners [including] Minick himself [and] two Governing Persons—Minick and Steve Murrin—opposed the dismissal as well. This opinion refers to the pro-Minick faction as the Murrin Group.

The Murrin Group responded to the Hickman Group's attempt to dismiss Minick by filing the underlying lawsuit against the Hickman Group [seeking injunctive and declaratory relief]. The suit contained claims asserted individually by the members of the Murrin Group and claims asserted derivatively on behalf of BBT.

The Hickman Group hired Kelly Hart & Hallman (KHH) to represent BBT in the litigation and to represent the defendants named in the Murrin Group's suit. The engagement letter with KHH was signed by BBT's CFO as well as nine of BBT's twelve owners and four of its six Governing Persons. KHH's legal fees have been paid from BBT's funds, both for its representation of BBT and at least to some extent for its representation of the individuals and entities comprising the Hickman Group.

The case was set for trial in April 2018. In January 2018, the Murrin Group filed a motion to disqualify KHH as counsel for BBT and as counsel for the Hickman Group. The motion alleged that because BBT is the "plaintiff" in the Murrin Group's derivative claims against the Hickman Group, KHH's representation of both BBT and the Hickman Group amounts to the impermissible representation of both sides in the same case. And because BBT is really a plaintiff, the Murrin Group alleged, KHH must also be disqualified from representing the individual Hickman Group defendants who are adverse to KHH's former client, BBT.

The trial court denied both motions.

The question is whether the trial court abused its discretion when it denied the motion to disqualify. We conclude that it did not.

Disqualification of counsel is a severe remedy that can result in significant expense to clients, disrupt the orderly progress of litigation, and deprive a party of the counsel of its choice. The Murrin Group alleges that KHH is violating several disciplinary rules, including Rule 1.06(a) and Rule 1.09, by representing parties on both sides of the same lawsuit. Although courts and litigants often "look to our disciplinary rules to decide disqualification issues," the rules "do not determine whether counsel is disqualified in litigation." Rather, the rules "provide helpful guidance" and "suggest the relevant considerations." Ultimately, a court "must consider all the facts and circumstances to determine whether the interests of justice require disqualification."

The foundation of the Murrin Group's disqualification argument is the notion that the Hickman Group and BBT are directly adverse to one another—that they are "opposing parties" for purposes of Rule 1.06(a). According to the Murrin Group, BBT is a plaintiff in the derivative action, and the members of the Hickman Group are the defendants. As the Murrin

Group sees it, if KHH represents both BBT and the Hickman Group, it is representing both the plaintiff and the defendant in the same case. Representing both sides in one case is the axiomatic conflict of interest, the Murrin Group contends, and it should never be tolerated. *See* Tex. Disciplinary Rules Prof'l Conduct R. 1.06(a) ("A lawyer shall not represent opposing parties to the same litigation.").

The battle lines are not so clear, however. Shareholder derivative actions provide a procedural pathway for a minority shareholder to sue on behalf of the company for wrongs committed against the company. Because the suit is to vindicate the company's rights, it is often said that the company is a "plaintiff" in a derivative action. Labeling the company a "plaintiff" does not tell the whole story, however. Most companies begin derivative litigation resistant to the minority shareholder's derivative claims. The resistance of the company's usual decisionmakers to the minority shareholder's claims is what causes derivative litigation in the first place. For this reason, in addition to sometimes being called plaintiffs, companies embroiled in derivative litigation are also commonly called "nominal defendants." Thus, companies in derivative litigation are simultaneously "plaintiffs" and "defendants," depending on how you look at it. Of course, if the company is literally both plaintiff and defendant, then no lawyer could ever represent it in derivative litigation because to do so would automatically place the lawyer on both sides of the case. Obviously, that is not the rule.

Rather than labor over which party label applies to a company in derivative litigation, the proper inquiry is to look to whether the substance of the challenged representation requires the lawyer to take conflicting positions or to take a position that risks harming one of his clients. Courts around the country are divided on whether such a risk is always present in derivative litigation. Some courts have concluded that representation by one law firm of both the company and the insider defendants is categorically impermissible. Other courts, including in Delaware, have taken a more practical approach, reasoning that the interests of the company and its controlling officers or directors are often aligned, and separate counsel is not necessary unless a divergence of those interests arises. Some courts have held that serious allegations of fraud or insider dealing against managers may trigger adversity between the company and its managers, requiring separate counsel.

We announce no categorical rule governing dual representation in derivative litigation. Whether a company and the individual defendants are "opposing parties" for purposes of Rule 1.06(a) in derivative litigation requires consideration of the true extent of their adversity under the circumstances. The definition of "directly adverse" representation provided in the comments to the disciplinary rules provides useful guidance in derivative litigation, as elsewhere:

> Within the meaning of Rule 1.06(b), the representation of one client is directly adverse to the representation of another client if the lawyer's independent judgment on behalf of a client or the lawyer's ability or willingness to consider, recommend or carry out a course of action will be or is reasonably likely to be adversely affected by the lawyer's representation of, or responsibilities to, the other client. The dual representation also is directly adverse if the lawyer reasonably appears to be called upon to espouse adverse positions in the same matter or a related matter.

Tex. Disciplinary Rules Prof'l Conduct R. 1.06 cmt. 6.

To use the comment's language, the Murrin Group contends that KHH's "independent judgment on behalf of" BBT will be "adversely affected" by KHH's simultaneous representation of the Hickman Group. It also contends, as it must, that the dual representation will prejudice the Murrin Group. Naturally, the Murrin Group claims to be aligned with BBT and acting on its behalf. Stripped of the conceptual and procedural baggage of its "derivative" claims, this case is about who controls the management of BBT—the Hickman Group by virtue of its majority interest, or the Murrin Group by virtue of the Company Agreement's unanimity provision. Either the Hickman Group is right, in which case its interests and BBT's are truly aligned, or the Murrin Group is right, in which case BBT is aligned with it instead.

Perhaps anticipating suits like this one—control-fights between LLC members couched as derivative actions—the legislature has provided that "if justice requires: a derivative proceeding brought by a member of a closely held limited liability company may be treated by a court as a direct action brought by the member for the member's own benefit." Tex. Bus. Orgs. C. § 101.463(c). For purposes of the disqualification motion, the trial court could have treated the derivative claims as claims "brought by the member for the member's own benefit," rather than disqualifying KHH based on the procedural complexities introduced by the derivative claims. Indeed, if the derivative claims are treated as direct claims, as the statute permits, the Murrin Group's case for disqualification essentially vanishes.

On top of that, none of the other "facts and circumstances" presented to the trial court supported disqualification. The case was nearly ready for trial. The Hickman Group and the Murrin Group were fully adverse. Both sought to control BBT. BBT's alignment as a party raised complex questions about the nature of derivative suits but was ultimately immaterial to the core merits question: Which ownership group has authority to control BBT? That question could be vigorously and fairly litigated by the parties and counsel currently before the court, and the resolution of it would resolve the nagging question of BBT's alignment. No showing was made that KHH possessed confidential information belonging to BBT that prejudiced the Murrin Group and could not have otherwise been obtained from the Hickman Group. The disqualification motion could have been brought much earlier in the litigation, as KHH's dual representation had long been known to all. All these facts and circumstances support the trial court's decision not to disrupt the existing alignment of parties and counsel on the eve of trial.

Gone are the days when a family feud over a dance hall and saloon in the Fort Worth Stockyards would be solved by six-shooters. These days, we use lawyers instead of lead. Thank goodness for that. As complicated, expensive, and frustrating as litigation can be, it sure beats a shootout at the stockyards. Today's denial of mandamus relief allows this dispute to proceed toward that peaceful alternative to shootouts known as trial, where both sides may be represented by their chosen lawyers.

C. FORMING GENERAL PARTNERSHIPS

A partnership is the association of two or more persons to carry on as co-owners of a business for profit. RUPA § 202(a). "Persons" include legal persons such as business entities. RUPA § 102(14). Thus, a partnership may be formed not only between natural persons, but also between businesses: for example, M-F Partners can be a partnership between Bill Gates and Mark Zuckerberg, or between Microsoft and Facebook.

Unlike a corporation or an LLC, which requires only one owner, a partnership requires at least two persons. This legal fact is important because the requirement places significant limitation on the venture. Suppose a person wants to own the entire business—clearly, she cannot do so through a partnership. The same applies to a parent corporation that seeks to run a business through a subsidiary. A one-person partnership is an oxymoron and a legal impossibility.

Co-owners means that partners have the attributes of ownership. There are two important attributes: owners have (1) control rights, and (2) are entitled to profits. Control rights do not mean that each partner can individually control the business or has veto rights on all decisions, but that partners collectively control, govern, and manage the partnership. If a person has such rights, that fact is a factor weighing in favor of concluding she is a partner.

Profit means that partners are entitled to the residual income after payment of all expenses, including the wages of employees. Profit means the difference between revenue (receipts from the sale of goods and service) and all expenses. For example, a firm sold 100 units of widgets priced at \$10 per unit, and incurred total expenses of \$8 per unit: profit is \$2 per unit multiplied by 100 units sold, which is \$200. If this difference is a negative number (*e.g.*, revenue of 100 and expenses of 120), then there is a loss. *See* Black's Law Dictionary (11th ed. 2019) (defining profit as the "excess of revenues over expenditures in a business transaction" whereas revenue is the total "income from any and all sources").

Partners do not need to have a specific intent to form a partnership. As long as partners satisfy the legal definition of a partnership, they have formed a partnership "whether or not the persons intend to form a partnership." RUPA § 202(a). If two persons do not satisfy this definition, they are not partners even if they profess or believe that they are partners. *E.g.*, Fenwick v. Unemployment Compensation Commission, 44 A.2d 172, 174–75 (N.J. App. 1945) (holding that persons had employer-employee relationship even though they called their arrangement a "partnership"). Persons can create a partnership *unwittingly*, and by doing so partnership law would apply to their relationship even if they never subjectively intended to invoke a set of legal rules to their business relationship.

"Accidental" partnerships occur more frequently among uninformed, unsophisticated, or unadvised businesspersons. For example, in *Pilling v. Travelers Insurance Co.*, 412 P.3d 252 (Ore. App. 2018), Pilling and his wife were engaged in a business together when he was injured on the job. He filed a claim as a "subject worker" under the state's works' compensation statute and sought benefits. The workers' compensation statute excludes from the definition of a "worker" persons who are partners in a partnership. The workers' compensation board denied benefits on the basis that Pilling was a partner in a partnership. Reviewing the board's decision, the court analyzed the issue under Oregon's partnership statute, modeled under RUPA § 202. The court noted that "accidental" partnerships were possible:

> The parties' intentions are not necessarily controlling in determining the existence of a partnership under ORS 67.055; "a partnership may be created unintentionally by the parties." The parties' "expression of an intent to be partners" is, instead, one of the factors to be considered by the finder of fact in determining whether persons have created a partnership.

Evidence from the case was mixed. Pilling and his wife may not have thought much about the nature of their business relationship, not uncommon among uninformed venturers. Ultimately, the court upheld the board's finding that Pilling was a partner in a partnership:

> There is also substantial evidence in support of the board's finding that claimant and Sandra were co-owners of the business and, therefore, partners. That includes undisputed evidence of the manner in which the business was operated, in particular, the parties' division and sharing of control and responsibilities, and their rights to share in the profits and losses.
>
> The board found that the sharing of profits gave rise to a presumption that claimant and Sandra were partners, implicitly rejecting claimant's contention that profits were "received in

> payment" of wages. That finding is supported by undisputed evidence that claimant never actually received "payment" of any kind; rather, the parties simply used funds remaining after payment of business expenses for household expenses. We conclude that substantial evidence supports the board's finding that claimant was in a partnership under Oregon law.

See also In re Marriage of Hassiepen, 646 N.E.2d 1348 (Ill. App. 1995) (holding that husband and wife were partners despite their lack of specific intent to form a general partnership, with the effect that only half of the husband's income was subject to his ex-wife's claim of child support); Norris v. Besel, 442 P.3d 60, 67 (Wyo. 2019) (holding that the wife of a contractor was not a partner because she did not co-own or control the husband contractor's business); Northeast Natural Energy LLC v. Pachira Energy LLC, 844 S.E.2d 133, 138 (W.Va. 2020) (ruling that "the conduct of the parties may have inadvertently created a partnership to co-own and operate the water system as a business for profit").

The word "partner" is a term used in common language. It can mean various things: partners in a marriage or a sports team, partners between supplier and customer, etc. But the use of the term "partners" to describe a relationship, without more, does not carry much legal significance. *See* Ingram v. Deere, 288 S.W.3d 886, 900 (Tex. 2009) ("Referring to a friend, employee, spouse, teammate, or fishing companion as a 'partner' in a colloquial sense is not legally sufficient evidence of expression of intent to form a business partnership.").

RUPA § 202. Formation of Partnership.

(a) The association of two or more persons to carry on as co-owners a business for profit forms a partnership, whether or not the persons intend to form a partnership.

(c) In determining whether a partnership is formed, the following rules apply:

(1) Joint tenancy, tenancy in common, tenancy by the entireties, joint property, common property, or part ownership does not by itself establish a partnership, even if the co-owners share profits made by the use of the property.

(2) The sharing of gross returns does not by itself establish a partnership, even if the persons sharing them have a joint or common right or interest in property from which the returns are derived.

(3) A person who receives a share of the profits of a business is presumed to be a partner in the business, unless the profits were received in payment:

(A) of a debt by installments or otherwise;

(B) for services as an independent contractor or of wages or other compensation to an employee;

(C) of rent;

(D) of an annuity or other retirement or health benefit to a deceased or retired partner or a beneficiary, representative, or designee of a deceased or retired partner;

(E) of interest or other charge on a loan, even if the amount of payment varies with the profits of the business, including a direct or indirect present or future ownership of the collateral, or rights to income, proceeds, or increase in value derived from the collateral; or

(F) for the sale of the goodwill of a business or other property by installments or otherwise.

NOTES

1. Consider RUPA § 202(c), subsections (1) and (2). Why does co-ownership of real property and sharing of gross returns "by itself" not establish a partnership?

2. With respect to subsection (3), what sort of persons are excluded from the definition of a partnership in enumerations (A) through (F)?

Most sophisticated businesses do not form partnerships unwittingly. One reason is that they are advised by business lawyers. Another reason is that in modern practice they typically choose to form limited liability entities, which always requires a conscious act of filing with the state.

The cases below concern whether a counterparty of a firm was really a partner in a partnership. Although "accidental" partnerships are typically formed by uninformed persons, even sophisticated businesses can be at risk of unwittingly forming a partnership. In reading these cases, think about these questions: (1) What practical difference does it make if one is a creditor, a counterparty, or a partner? (2) How is a partnership formed? (3) What business terms can lead to an unintended creation of a partnership?

MARTIN V. PEYTON

158 N.E. 77 (N.Y. 1927)

ANDREWS, J.

Partnership results from contract, express or implied. If denied it may be proved by the production of some written instrument; by testimony as to some conversation; by circumstantial evidence. If nothing else appears, the receipt of a share of the profits of the business is enough.

Assuming some written contract between the parties the question may arise whether it creates a partnership. If it be complete; if it expresses in good faith the full understanding and obligation of the parties, then it is for the court to say whether a partnership exists. It may, however, be a mere sham intended to hide the real relationship. Then other results follow. In passing upon it effect is to be given to each provision. Mere words will not blind us to realities. Statements that no partnership is intended are not conclusive. If as a whole a contract contemplates an association of two or more persons to carry on as co-owners a business for profit a partnership there is. If it be less than this no partnership exists. Passing on the contract as a whole, an arrangement for sharing profits is to be considered. It is to be given its due weight. But it is to be weighed in connection with all the rest. It is not decisive. It may be merely the method adopted to pay a debt or wages, as interest on a loan or for other reasons.

In the case before us the claim that the defendants became partners in the firm of Knauth, Nachod & Kuhne, doing business as bankers and brokers, depends upon the interpretation of certain instruments.

We are to remember that although the intention of the parties to avoid liability as partners is clear, although in language precise and definite they deny any design to then join the firm of K. N. & K.; although they say their interests in profits should be construed merely as a measure of compensation for loans, not an interest in profits as such; although they provide that they shall not be liable for any losses or treated as partners, the question still remains whether in fact they agree to so associate themselves with the firm as to "carry on as co-owners a business for profit."

In the spring of 1921 the firm of K. N. & K. found itself in financial difficulties. John Hall was one of the partners. He was a friend of William Peyton. From him he obtained the loan of almost $500,000 of Liberty bonds, which K. N. & K. might use as collateral to secure bank advances. This, however, was not sufficient. The firm and its members had engaged in unwise speculations, and it was deeply involved. Hall was also intimately acquainted with George Perkins and with Edward Freeman. All were anxious to help him. He, therefore, representing K. N. & K., entered into negotiations with them. While they were pending a proposition was made that Peyton, Perkins and Freeman* or some of them should become partners. It met a decided refusal. Finally an agreement was reached. It is expressed in three documents, executed on the same day, all a part of the one transaction. They were drawn with care and are unambiguous. We shall refer to them as "the agreement," "the indenture" and "the option."

---

* Author's note: The court's reference to Peyton, Perkins and Freeman as the "respondents" has been changed to "Peyton, Perkins and Freeman" for ease of reading.

We have no doubt as to their general purpose. Peyton, Perkins and Freeman were to loan K. N. & K. $2,500,000 worth of liquid securities, which were to be returned to them on or before April 15, 1923. The firm might hypothecate them to secure loans totalling $2,000,000, using the proceeds as its business necessities required. To insure Peyton, Perkins and Freeman against loss K. N. & K. were to turn over to them a large number of their own securities which may have been valuable, but which were of so speculative a nature that they could not be used as collateral for bank loans. In compensation for the loan Peyton, Perkins and Freeman were to receive 40 per cent of the profits of the firm until the return was made, not exceeding, however, $500,000 and not less than $100,000. Merely because the transaction involved the transfer of securities and not of cash does not prevent its being a loan within the meaning of section 11. Peyton, Perkins and Freeman also were given an option to join the firm if they or any of them expressed a desire to do so before June 4, 1923.

Many other detailed agreements are contained in the papers. Are they such as may be properly inserted to protect the lenders? Or do they go further? Whatever their purpose, did they in truth associate Peyton, Perkins and Freeman with the firm so that they and it together thereafter carried on as co-owners a business for profit? The answer depends upon an analysis of these various provisions.

As representing the lenders, Peyton and Freeman are called "trustees." The loaned securities when used as collateral are not to be mingled with other securities of K. N. & K., and the trustees at all times are to be kept informed of all transactions affecting them. To them shall be paid all dividends and income accruing therefrom. They may also substitute for any of the securities loaned securities of equal value. With their consent the firm may sell any of its securities held by Peyton, Perkins and Freeman, the proceeds to go, however, to the trustees. In other similar ways the trustees may deal with these same securities, but the securities loaned shall always be sufficient in value to permit of their hypothecation for $2,000,000. If they rise in price the excess may be withdrawn by the defendants. If they fall they shall make good the deficiency.

So far there is no hint that the transaction is not a loan of securities with a provision for compensation. Later a somewhat closer connection with the firm appears. Until the securities are returned the directing management of the firm is to be in the hands of John Hall, and his life is to be insured for $1,000,000, and the policies are to be assigned as further collateral security to the trustees. These requirements are not unnatural. Hall was the one known and trusted by the defendants. Their acquaintance with the other members of the firm was of the slightest. These others had brought an old and established business to the verge of bankruptcy. As Peyton, Perkins and Freeman knew, they also had engaged in unsafe speculation. Peyton, Perkins and Freeman were about to loan $2,500,000 of good securities. As collateral they were to receive others of problematical value. What they required seems but ordinary caution. Nor does it imply an association in the business.

The trustees are to be kept advised as to the conduct of the business and consulted as to important matters. They may inspect the firm books and are entitled to any information they think important. They may veto any business they think highly speculative or injurious. We hold this but a proper precaution to safeguard the loan. The trustees may not initiate any transaction as a partner may do. They may not bind the firm by any action of their own. Under the circumstances the safety of the loan depended upon the business success of K. N. & K. This success was likely to be compromised by the inclination of its members to engage in speculation. No longer, if Peyton, Perkins and Freeman were to be protected, should it be allowed. The trustees might prohibit it, and that their prohibition might be effective, information was to be furnished them. Not dissimilar agreements have been held proper to guard the interests of the lender.

As further security each member of K. N. & K. is to assign to the trustees their interest in the firm. No loan by the firm to any member is permitted and the amount each may draw is fixed. No other distribution of profits is to be made. So that realized profits may be calculated the existing capital is stated to be $700,000, and profits are to be realized as promptly as good business practice will permit. In case the trustees think this is not done, the question is left to them and to Hall, and if they differ then to an arbitrator. There is no obligation that the firm shall continue the business. It may dissolve at any time. Again we conclude there is nothing here not properly adapted to secure the interest of Peyton, Perkins and Freeman as lenders. If their compensation is dependent on a percentage of the profits still provision must be made to define what these profits shall be.

The "indenture" is substantially a mortgage of the collateral delivered by K. N. & K. to the trustees to secure the performance of the "agreement." It certainly does not strengthen the claim that Peyton, Perkins and Freeman were partners.

Finally we have the "option." It permits Peyton, Perkins and Freeman or any of them or their assignees or nominees to enter the firm at a later date if they desire to do so by buying 50 per cent or less of the interests therein of all or any of the members at a stated price. Or a corporation may, if Peyton, Perkins and Freeman and the members agree, be formed in place of the firm. Meanwhile, apparently with the design of protecting the firm business against improper or ill-judged action which might render the option valueless, each member of the firm is to place his resignation in the hands of Hall. If at any time he and the trustees agree that such resignation should be accepted, that member shall then retire, receiving the value of his interest calculated as of the date of such retirement.

This last provision is somewhat unusual, yet it is not enough in itself to show that a partnership was created. It is quite true that even if one or two or three like provisions contained in such a contract do not require this conclusion, yet it is also true that when taken together a point may come where stipulations immaterial separately cover so wide a field that we should hold a partnership exists. A question of degree is often the determining factor. Here that point has not been reached.

MINUIT MAID CORP. V. UNITED FOODS, INC.

291 F.2d 577 (5th Cir. 1961)

TUTTLE, CHIEF JUDGE.

This is an appeal from a judgment of the trial court, sitting without a jury, denying a recovery from Cold Storage Corp. by Minute Maid Corp. for the purchase price of commodities sold by it to United Foods, Inc.

Minute Maid's theory of recovery was that United Foods, Inc., a direct purchaser from it, was engaged in a partnership with the Cold Storage Corp., thus making Cold Storage liable for the unpaid purchase price.

United Foods was indebted to Minute Maid in the sum of $143,141 representing the purchase price of frozen food products sold to United Foods. The question whether Cold Storage is equally liable for this sum must be answered in the light of the following history of the relationship between the parties.

United Foods did not have the financial ability from its own resources plus normal credit sources to finance the carrying of a large inventory of frozen food products; that means that there were certain substantial price benefits that it could not get; Cold Storage did have and was willing to make funds available to assist United Foods in buying Minute Maid products in quantities that permitted the maximum discounts; the market conditions affecting frozen food products are such that the price of such goods tends to rise from the month of May to the end of the year, and such increases in price as to citrus food products are as high as 50% in years when weather conditions adversely affect citrus production; at all times pertinent to this action a direct buyer of frozen foods products, such as United Foods, was protected against price declines to the extent of inventories representing goods received during the last thirty day period; United Foods, without the knowledge of Minute Maid, operated so as to obtain an additional thirty days protection against price declines by taking goods owned by Minute Maid from warehouses approximately thirty days prior to notifying Minute Maid of the withdrawal. The effect of this relationship made it possible for a direct buyer, by buying large quantities, to profit as much as 50% on inventories by receiving notice from Minute Maid of proposed price increases a considerable time in advance of the price increase, whereas there was practically no risk of a loss on such inventories by reason of the sixty days protection against price declines. This made peculiarly attractive the speculation in inventories.

United Foods and Cold Storage entered into an agreement which spelled out their relationship with each other. Since we conclude that the essential question presented by this appeal must be resolved by reference to this written agreement we consider it essential to print the relevant portions of it in full as follows:

Memorandum of Agreement*

United Foods is a broker of frozen foods;

Cold Storage operates cold storage plants, and will extend finance services to United Foods on the following basis:

1. Staple commodities bought by United Foods, stored in Cold Storage plants, will be the collateral if acceptable to Cold Storage, together with acceptable (to Cold Storage) accounts receivable resulting from sales of the commodities, for loans to be made by Cold Storage. The aggregate amount of loans outstanding at both plants, taken together, shall not exceed $300,000.
2. The amount of loan to United Foods on any lot of product shall be United Foods's gross cost delivered to the warehouse of Cold Storage. The amount of the loan on any of United Foods accounts receivable shall be the amount of the invoices.
3. Notes to Cold Storage shall be given by United Foods for each loan and shall bear interest at 6% Until paid.
4. Notes for loans on commodities shall be paid when product is ordered from warehouse.
5. Notes for loans on accounts receivable shall be paid to Cold Storage by endorsement of check received from customer to Cold Storage provided that United Foods will itself pay Cold Storage for any invoices not otherwise paid in 45 days from date of invoice.
6. Warehouse charges on staple product on which loans are made on these terms shall be 15¢/100 lbs. handling and 12.5¢/100 lbs. per month storage, based on the gross weight of package and contents, and a lot delivery charge of 50¢ as current at each plant. Interest, interest service charges and insurance charges shall be at the rates current at each plant. Tariff rates will apply on all other products stored.

* Author's note: For better reading and consistency with the rest of opinion and the avoidance of confusion, the author changed the labeling of the parties in the contract from "United" to "United Foods" and from "U.S." to "Cold Storage."

7. All warehouse, interest and insurance charges shall be billed by Cold Storage monthly, and charged to the "Special Account" described below.

8. The "Special Account" on the books of Cold Storage is to be set up to accumulate charges as set forth in Paragraph 7 and to accumulate credits as follows:

    a. United Foods shall pay to Cold Storage the 6¢ per dozen packer allowance on retail merchandise or any other quantity allowance, advertising, freight, allowance, incentive and profit to the Special Account;

    b. United Foods shall pay to Cold Storage for the Special Account the incentive from any packer special proposals, as for instance, in forward buying, in anticipating of a price raise, or other inducements to move special product items, such as fish, shrimp, poultry and the like;

    c. United Foods is paid 20¢/100 lbs./month by Minute Maid on institutional merchandise and this allowance will be paid to Cold Storage for the Special Account to which also Cold Storage will debit the warehouse charges on this product;

    d. If United Foods shall charge any of its suppliers or customers for storage at a higher rate than Cold Storage is charging United Foods therefor, the excess shall be paid (upon collection) by United Foods to Cold Storage for credit to the Special Account.

    e. If the amount of any United Foods invoice pledged as an account receivable exceeds the amount of loan on the commodity so invoiced, United Foods shall pay the excess to Cold Storage for credit to the Special Account.

9. At the end of the calendar year, the Special Account shall be closed, and

    a. If there is a credit balance, 1/2 thereof shall be paid by Cold Storage to United Foods within 20 days and the remainder shall be retained by Cold Storage as its property.

    b. If there is a debit balance, Cold Storage shall so notify United Foods, who will pay Cold Storage 1/2 of the amount of such debit balance within 20 days of notification.

United Foods, as a food broker engaged in the business of selling Minute Maid products and handled in excess of $1,000,000 of these products. This business was carried on by United Foods at its own office, with its own employees, and at its own expense.

Minute Maid did not know of the relationship between United Foods and Cold Storage. It contends that the agreement between the parties and the course of dealing thereunder created a partnership relationship between United Foods and Cold Storage and that Cold Storage became liable with United Foods for all debts of the partnership. Minute Maid distinguishes between the regular sales business of United Foods in selling Minute Maid products to the trade from what it considers to be the subject of the partnership. It says that the partnership consisted of a joint endeavor by United Foods and Cold Storage under which United Foods would take advantage of its position as a direct purchaser of Minute Maid products and of the financing afforded it by Cold Storage to buy products in the quantities that would yield the greatest amount in allowances and discounts and if the market appeared right, to speculate on a possible price increase; that in return for Cold Storage's agreement to finance the transaction to the extent of advancing 100% of the purchase price of the products it would store the products in Cold Storage's warehouse at a profitable rate, it would pay interest of 6% on all advances and it and Cold Storage would share equally the profits that could thus be anticipated from the discounts and from profitable speculation, if indulged in.

Cold Storage, on the other hand, contends that the agreement created only a relationship at most of debtor and creditor between it and United Foods, or that the relationship was an ambiguous one which the trial court, on disputed evidence, found as a fact not to be a partnership.

A critical examination of the foregoing facts necessarily leads to the following conclusion:

(1) Cold Storage was to be repaid the principal amount of its advances to United Foods regardless of the success or failure of the enterprise.

(2) Cold Storage was to receive its warehouse charges, its interest at 6% and reimbursement for the cost of insurance out of the "special fund" set up under the contract. It seems plain that there could be no failure of the special fund to provide sufficient sums to meet these obligations and provide a profit, because the parties could in advance know exactly how much by way of special allowances and discounts would be paid into the special fund, and, of course, the charges would bear a direct relation to these same items. However, if there was a deficit in this special fund, it was to be shared by the parties equally.

(3) The advance of 100% of the invoice price of the merchandise was not a normal credit arrangement which would be available to United Foods by the payment of legal rates of interest.

(4) Both United Foods and Cold Storage would profit by increasing the purchases of United Foods made possible by the arrangement between

the two parties. United Foods' profit would come from its 50% participation in the profits in the special fund and Cold Storage's profit would come from the increasing of the inventory for which it received substantial warehouse fees, an increase in inventories for which it received its 6% interest and the anticipated profit arising by reason of the fact that it could be computed in advance that the special allowances and discounts paid into the fund would exceed the carrying charges. Cold Storage became the owner of one half of this excess.

(5) Cold Storage was undoubtedly in the relation of a creditor of United Foods; it was also in the relation of a bailee for hire.

(6) It is also clear, however, that the operation that here produced the sale of the volume of Minute Maid products to United Foods would not have occurred by reason of Cold Storage's willingness to engage in either or both of these two activities standing alone, and on normal terms—that is as a creditor receiving a legal rate of interest and a warehouseman receiving its stated warehouse charges.

(7) It is plain that Cold Storage was interested in assisting United Foods to create a larger indebtedness on which it would receive its interest and a larger volume of inventory on which it would receive its warehouseman's fees and that in order to assist in creating this larger volume of business for itself it participated with United Foods in making possible the larger purchases of Minute Maid products than United Foods could otherwise have accomplished.

Does this analysis cause us to conclude that the two parties, acting to their mutual interest to make possible an increased purchase of Minute Maid products, created a joint venture or partnership between them?

The parties do not disagree as to what constitutes a partnership under the law of Texas.

> Persons are partners who contribute either property or money to carry a joint business for their common benefit, and who own and share the profits thereof in certain proportions. If they do this, the incidents or consequences follow that the acts one in conducting the partnership business are the acts of all, that each is agent for the firm and for the other partners, that each receives part of the profits as profits, and takes part of the fund to which the creditors of the partnership have a right to look for the payment of their debts, that all are liable as partners upon contracts made by any of them with third persons within the scope of the partnership business, and that even an express stipulation between them that one shall not be so liable, though good between themselves, is ineffectual as against third persons. And participating in profits is presumptive, but not conclusive, evidence of partnership.

We take it to be the law of Texas that if the parties entered into a contract from which it is clear that the parties contemplated joining in a common business for their common benefit to be operated for their joint account and in which they as owners each of an interest would be entitled to share as principals in the profits as such, they would be partners.

Cold Storage is too preoccupied, we think, with its insistence that the relationship between United Foods and Cold Storage was that of debtor and creditor. This is undoubtedly correct, but it is equally undoubtedly indecisive. Cold Storage also relies strongly on the contention that there was no express obligation assumed under the written contract whereby Cold Storage was to share in the overall losses of the enterprise. This, of course, is the very question that this Court has to decide, for if the relationship between the parties constituted them partners, then the law imposes upon them the obligation to pay the losses.

It is the burden of Cold Storage's argument here that if there is nothing more than a lender relationship, coupled with an agreement that compensation for the loan is to be in the form of a sharing in profits, either in lieu of or in addition to normal interest, these facts are sufficient to rebut the presumption that arises by the profit sharing agreement. Cold Storage contends that additional indicia of an intent to create a partnership must be shown either in the nature of joint control by the person sought to be bound as a partner, or an express agreement to share in losses.

It is undeniably true that control over the particular enterprise in which these two parties were engaged was jointly held by United Foods and Cold Storage. We must bear in mind exactly what this enterprise was. It was not the commission food business carried on by United Foods. It was the arrangement whereby Cold Storage furnished the financing and warehouse facilities to make possible United Foods's use of its relationship as a direct buyer of Minute Maid products in such quantities and under such terms as would turn a profit for both of them. There can be no question but that the parties had joint control over this enterprise. This follows from the fact that United Foods initially determined how much to buy but such determination was subject to Cold Storage's right to determine whether the proposed collateral would be "acceptable." Also, it was provided that in case of pending price increases, which the court found would offer the opportunity to speculate on inventory, the parties would agree on the volume to be purchased. In point of fact the responsible officer for United Foods testified that, "they (Cold Storage) could have stepped in and written me (United Foods) off pretty damned fast."

We conclude that the relationship established by the written contract of the parties and by their conduct thereunder constituted a legal partnership or joint enterprise under the Texas law.

The case below concerns the dealings between two sophisticated businesses that specifically intended to form a business venture. In reading this case, think about these questions: (1) What is the relationship between the commercial contracts the parties executed and the formation of a partnership? (2) What were the transactional precursors to a partnership? (3) What is the implication of the rule that a partnership must be "a business for profit" under RUPA § 102(11), § 202(a)?

ENERGY TRANSFER PARTNERS, L.P. v. ENTERPRISE PRODUCTS PARTNERS, L.P.

593 S.W.3d 732 (Tex. 2020)

CHIEF JUSTICE HECHT delivered the opinion of the Court.

The issue in this case is whether Texas law permits parties to conclusively agree that, as between themselves, no partnership will exist unless certain conditions are satisfied. We hold that it does and that the parties here made such an agreement.

Cushing, Oklahoma is a major trading hub for crude oil. For decades, the United States imported most of its crude oil from abroad to its Gulf Coast refineries, where the oil was processed and shipped north through Cushing. In 2008, new technology enabled oil production in the Dakotas and Canada, resulting in oil being transported to Cushing from the north. But no pipeline existed to move oil stored at Cushing south. An excess supply accumulated, driving down the price of oil sold there. Sensing economic opportunity, major pipeline companies began exploring ways to move oil south from Cushing.

Among them were ETP and Enterprise, competitors that are among the ten largest energy companies in the United States. Enterprise co-owned with ConocoPhillips a pipeline called Seaway that sent oil north to Cushing from the Texas Gulf Coast. Enterprise lobbied ConocoPhillips for years to reverse the pipeline's direction, but ConocoPhillips refused. Enterprise also talked to Canadian pipeline company Enbridge about a joint project but to no result.

Enterprise approached ETP about converting a pipeline called Old Ocean into one that could move oil south from Cushing. Old Ocean transports natural gas from Sweeny, Texas, near the Coast, up to Maypearl, near Dallas. ETP owns the pipeline, but Enterprise holds a long-term lease on it. Converting the pipeline to one for transporting oil and extending it the rest of the way to Cushing would require a massive investment from the parties and committed customers willing to pay a sufficient tariff to justify the investment.

The parties agreed to explore the viability of the project, which they dubbed "Double E." In three written agreements, they reiterated their intent that neither party be bound to proceed until each company's board of directors had approved the execution of a formal contract. The Confidentiality Agreement recited that Enterprise and ETP had "entered into discussions with each other in connection with a possible transaction involving a joint venture to provide crude oil transportation [from Cushing to Houston] utilizing [the] Old Ocean Pipeline." The agreement laid out the parties' rights and responsibilities with respect to confidential information exchanged during the discussions and then stated:

> The Parties agree that unless and until a definitive agreement between the Parties with respect to the Potential Transaction has been executed and delivered, and then only to the extent of the specific terms of such definitive agreement, no Party hereto will be under any legal obligation of any kind whatsoever with respect to any transaction by virtue of this Agreement or any written or oral expression with respect to such a transaction by any Party or their respective Representatives, except, in the case of this Agreement, for the matters specifically agreed to herein.

The parties also signed a Letter Agreement with an attached "Non-Binding Term Sheet." The Letter Agreement again recited that the parties were "entering discussions regarding a proposed joint venture transaction involving the construction and operation of a pipeline to move crude oil" from Cushing to Houston, and that the "letter [was] intended only to set forth the general terms of the Transaction between the Parties, contained in the term sheet attached." The letter then stated:

> Neither this letter nor the JV Term Sheet create any binding or enforceable obligations between the Parties and, except for the Confidentiality Agreement, no binding or enforceable obligations shall exist between the Parties with respect to the Transaction unless and until the Parties have received their respective board approvals and definitive agreements memorializing the terms and conditions of the Transaction have been negotiated, executed and delivered by both of the Parties. Unless and until such definitive agreements are executed and delivered by both of the Parties, either [Enterprise] or ETP, for any reason, may depart from or terminate the negotiations with respect to the Transaction at any time without any liability or obligation to the other, whether arising in contract, tort, strict liability or otherwise.

The Non-Binding Term Sheet sketched out the basic features of the potential transaction and envisioned that a "mutually agreeable Limited Liability Company Agreement would be entered into" to govern the joint venture.

The parties also signed a Reimbursement Agreement that provided the terms under which ETP would reimburse Enterprise for half the cost of the project's engineering work. That agreement, like the other two, recognized that the parties were "in the process of negotiating mutually agreeable definitive agreements" for the project and stated that nothing in it would "be deemed to create or constitute a joint venture, a partnership, a corporation, or any entity taxable as a corporation, partnership or otherwise." ETP's pleadings acknowledge that "as of the date of [these agreements] the parties had not yet formed a partnership."

The parties had formed an integrated team to pursue Double E. The biggest piece of the puzzle was obtaining sufficient shipping commitments. To do so, the parties needed to convince shippers that their pipeline would be the first to market. They marketed Double E to potential customers as a "50/50 JV" and prepared engineering plans for the project. The parties also explored the possibility of building a new pipeline from scratch rather than retrofitting Old Ocean, but they continued to market the Old Ocean conversion to potential customers.

A Federal Energy Regulatory Commission rule governing new interstate pipelines requires an "open season" of 30 to 45 days in which shippers are asked to commit to daily barrel volumes and tariffs. For Double E to be viable, the parties needed shipping commitments of at least 250,000 barrels a day for ten years at a tariff of $3.00 per barrel. The initial open season was unsuccessful. The parties extended the open season twice more. On the last day of the second extended open season, Chesapeake Energy Corp. committed to ship 100,000 barrels daily. But days earlier, Enterprise had begun preparing its exit by resuming negotiations with Enbridge. Enterprise ended its relationship with ETP.

The next month, ConocoPhillips announced that it would sell its interest in the Seaway pipeline. Enbridge bought it, making Enbridge co-owner of the pipeline with Enterprise. Enterprise and Enbridge obtained an anchor shipper commitment from Chesapeake, which resulted in their securing many additional commitments during the open season. Enterprise and Enbridge invested billions to reverse the direction of the pipeline and make other modifications needed to move oil from Cushing to the Gulf. The new pipeline, called Wrangler, opened and it has been a financial success.

ETP sued. Its theory at trial was that despite the disclaimers in the parties' written agreements, they had formed a partnership to "market and pursue" a pipeline through their conduct, and Enterprise breached its statutory duty of loyalty by pursuing the Wrangler project with Enbridge. The jury answered "yes" to the question whether "ETP and Enterprise [had] created a partnership to market and pursue a pipeline project to transport crude oil from Cushing, Oklahoma to the Gulf Coast." It answered "no" to the question whether Enterprise had complied with its duty of loyalty. It found that $319,375,000 would compensate ETP for its damages and that the value to Enterprise of the benefit gained as a result of its misconduct was $595,257,433. The court reduced the disgorgement award to $150 million and otherwise rendered judgment on the verdict for ETP for a total of $535,794,777 plus postjudgment interest.

The court of appeals reversed and rendered judgment for Enterprise. The court concluded that the Texas Business Organizations Code (TBOC) allows parties to contract for conditions precedent to partnership formation; that the Letter Agreement in particular created two here that were not met—(1) execution of "definitive agreements memorializing the terms and conditions of the Transaction" that (2) have "received [each party's] respective board approvals"; and that ETP had the burden either to obtain a jury finding that the conditions were waived or to prove waiver conclusively, which it failed to do.

Section 152.051(b) of the TBOC states that "an association of two or more persons to carry on a business for profit as owners creates a partnership, regardless of whether: (1) the persons intend to create a partnership; or (2) the association is called a 'partnership,' 'joint venture,' or other name." Under § 152.052(a), "factors indicating that persons have created a partnership include the persons': (1) receipt or right to receive a share of profits of the business; (2) expression of an intent to be partners in the business; (3) participation or right to participate in control of the business; (4) agreement to share or sharing losses of the business or liability for claims by third parties against the business; and (5) agreement to contribute or contributing money or property to the business."

Section 152.003 provides that "the principles of law and equity and the other partnership provisions supplement this chapter unless otherwise provided by this chapter or the other partnership provisions."

In *Ingram v. Deere,* 288 S.W.3d 886 (Tex. 2009), we traced the evolution of Texas partnership law from the early common law, which required proof of five factors to establish a partnership, to TBOC Chapter 152, which sets out a nonexclusive list of factors to be considered in a totality-of-the-circumstances test. Under § 152.052(a)(2), "expression of an intent to be partners in the business" is just one factor of the totality-of-the-circumstances test. We acknowledged in *Ingram* that the statute "does not by its terms give the parties' intent or expression of intent any greater weight than the other factors." Moreover, under § 152.051(b), persons can create a partnership regardless of whether they intend to. This provision derives from Section 202(a) of the Revised Uniform Partnership Act. A comment to that section drafted by the Uniform Law Commission warns that parties "may inadvertently create a partnership despite their expressed subjective intention not to do so." But in *Ingram* we expressed skepticism that the Legislature "intended to spring surprise or accidental partnerships on independent businesspersons." Can persons override the default test for partnership formation in Chapter 152 by agreeing not to be partners until conditions precedent are satisfied? *Ingram* did not involve such an agreement, and our discussion there of the role of intent in the partnership-formation analysis did not contemplate one.

Section 152.003 imports other "principles of law and equity" into the partnership-formation analysis, and the use of the word "include" in § 152.052(a) makes the factors enumerated there nonexclusive. Against this backdrop of statutory law is a well-developed body of common law that "strongly favors parties' freedom of contract." Our decisions recognizing this policy are decades older than the TBOC or its predecessor statute.

> If there is one thing which more than another public policy requires it is that men of full age and competent understanding shall have the utmost liberty of contracting, and that their contracts when entered into freely and voluntarily shall be held sacred and shall be enforced by Courts of justice. Therefore, you have this paramount public policy to consider—that you are not lightly to interfere with this freedom of contract.

We reinforce this public policy virtually every Court Term. Texas courts regularly enforce conditions precedent to contract formation and reject legal claims that are artfully pleaded to skirt unambiguous contract language, especially when that language is the result of arm's-length negotiations between sophisticated business entities.

We have never squarely addressed whether parties' freedom to contract for conditions precedent to partnership formation can override the statutory default test, in which intent is a mere factor.

ETP argues that the TBOC's totality-of-the-circumstances test controls partnership formation to the exclusion of the common law and that the parties' intent with respect to the creation of a partnership is just one factor to be weighed with the others in § 152.052(a). The submission of the case to the jury reflects this theory. Question 1 instructed the jury on the rule of § 152.051(b) that parties can form a partnership even if they do not intend to and on the multi-factor test in § 152.052(a). Question 1 also told the jury that "no single fact may be stated as a complete and final test of partnership." It then asked the jury whether a partnership was created. Under ETP's view, submitted to the jury, parties cannot through contract language preclude the creation of a partnership until a specific condition has occurred or been performed. ETP argues that the key to avoiding an accidental partnership is to "avoid the conduct that establishes a partnership under the statute."

We maintain our view expressed in *Ingram* that the Legislature did not "intend to spring surprise or accidental partnerships" on parties. Section 152.003 expressly authorizes supplementation of the partnership-formation rules of Chapter 152 with "principles of law and equity," and perhaps no principle of law is as deeply engrained in Texas jurisprudence as freedom of contract. We hold that parties can contract for conditions precedent to preclude the unintentional formation of a partnership under Chapter 152 and that, as a matter of law, they did so here.

An agreement not to be partners unless certain conditions are met will ordinarily be conclusive on the issue of partnership formation. "Performance of a condition precedent, however, can be waived or modified by the party to whom the obligation was due by word or deed." Under Texas Rule of Civil Procedure 279, ETP was required either to obtain a jury finding on waiver or to prove it conclusively.[36] It has done neither.

Where waiver of a condition precedent to partnership formation is at issue, only evidence directly tied to the condition precedent is relevant. Evidence that would be probative of expression of intent under § 152.051(a)—such as "the parties' statements that they are partners, one party holding the other party out as a partner on the business's letterhead or name plate, or in a signed partnership agreement"—is not relevant. Nor is evidence of any of the other § 152.052(a) factors. Otherwise, a party in ETP's position could claim waiver in virtually every case.

ETP has not pointed to any evidence that Enterprise specifically disavowed the Letter Agreement's requirement of definitive, board-of-directors-approved agreements or that Enterprise intentionally acted inconsistently with that requirement.

We hold that parties can conclusively negate the formation of a partnership through contractual conditions precedent. ETP and Enterprise did so as a matter of law here, and there is no evidence that Enterprise waived the conditions. The judgment of the court of appeals is affirmed.

D. FORMING LIMITED LIABILITY ENTITIES

Unlike general partnerships, limited liability entities like LLPs, LPs, LLCs, and corporations cannot be unwittingly formed. They require a specific intent to form the entity because a promoter must file with the state. A general partnership does not require a filing by the partners because partners do not have limited liability.

A filing is required because only the state can grant the protection of limited liability. Private actors cannot bestow upon themselves the right to limited liability. *See* Robert J. Rhee, *Bonding Limited Liability*, 51 Wm. & Mary L. Rev. 1417, 1444 (2010) ("Private ordering cannot synthetically gin up the legal right of limited liability."). The filing requirement is not a special privilege in the sense that a successful application requires special grant from the state. The process of filing is ministerial. From the state's perspective, the most important aspects of filing are: (1) satisfaction of the

---

[36] *See* Tex. R. Civ. P. 279 ("Upon appeal all independent grounds of recovery or of defense not conclusively established under the evidence and no element of which is submitted or requested are waived."); *Island Recreational Dev. Corp. v. Republic of Tex. Sav. Ass'n*, 710 S.W.2d 551, 554 (Tex. 1986) ("We recognize that waiver is an independent ground of recovery or defense and must be pleaded and proved as such."); *Washington v. Reliable Life Ins. Co.*, 581 S.W.2d 153, 157 (Tex. 1979) ("Waiver was an affirmative defense upon which Washington had the burden of proof. No special issues were requested or submitted to the jury on this point. As stated above, a party generally waives an issue upon which he relies by failure to request its submission.").

minimal disclosure requirements; (2) the payment of fees to the state; (3) the notice to the world per the filing that the firm is a limited liability entity; and (4) the identification of a statutory agent for the purpose of receiving service of legal process.

1. FILING REQUIREMENT FOR CORPORATIONS

To form a corporation, an organizer must file with the state a certificate (or articles) of incorporation. Corporation law provides that the certificate *must* contain several mandatory items.

DGCL § 102(a). Contents of Certificate of Incorporation

(a) The certificate of incorporation shall set forth:

(1) The name of the corporation . . . ;

(2) . . . the corporation's registered office . . . and its registered agent . . . ;

(3) The nature of the business or purposes to be conducted or promoted. It shall be sufficient to state, either alone or with other businesses or purposes, that the purpose of the corporation is to engage in any lawful act or activity . . . , and by such statement all lawful acts and activities shall be within the purposes of the corporation, except for express limitations, if any;

(4) If the corporation is to be authorized to issue only 1 class of stock, the total number of shares of stock which the corporation shall have authority to issue and the par value of each of such shares, or a statement that all such shares are to be without par value. If the corporation is to be authorized to issue more than 1 class of stock, the certificate of incorporation shall set forth the total number of shares of all classes of stock which the corporation shall have authority to issue and the number of shares of each class and shall specify each class the shares of which are to be without par value and each class the shares of which are to have par value and the par value of the shares of each such class. . . . ;

(5) The name and mailing address of the incorporator . . . .

The most significant required disclosure pertains to stock. The certificate of incorporation requires a statement of the total number of shares a company is authorized to issue. This number constitutes the maximum number of shares a corporation can legally issue, unless the certificate is amended to permit a greater number. The certificate also requires a statement of the characteristics (designations, rights, powers, limitations, etc.) of different classes or series of stock. This provision in the certificate of incorporation is important, and there is no comparable requirement in the laws of NBEs.

In addition to the required information set forth in DGCL § 102(a), the certificate *may*, and typically do, contain other important provisions.

DGCL § 102(b). Contents of Certificate of Incorporation

(b) In addition to the matters required to be set forth in the certificate of incorporation by subsection (a) of this section, the certificate of incorporation may also contain any or all of the following matters:

(1) Any provision for the management of the business and for the conduct of the affairs of the corporation, and any provision creating, defining, limiting and regulating the powers of the corporation, the directors, and the stockholders, or any class of the stockholders, or the governing body, members, or any class or group of members of a nonstock corporation; if such provisions are not contrary to the laws of this State. . . .

(3) Such provisions as may be desired granting to the holders of the stock of the corporation, or the holders of any class or series of a class thereof, the preemptive right to subscribe to any or all additional issues of stock of the corporation of any or all classes or series thereof, or to any securities of the corporation convertible into such stock. . . .

(4) Provisions requiring for any corporate action, the vote of a larger portion of the stock or of any class or series thereof, or of any other securities having voting power, or a larger number of the directors, than is required by this chapter; . . .

(7) A provision eliminating or limiting the personal liability of a director to the corporation or its stockholders for monetary damages for breach of fiduciary duty as a director, provided that such provision shall not eliminate or limit the liability of a director: (i) For any breach of the director's duty of loyalty to the corporation or its stockholders; (ii) for acts or omissions not in good faith or which involve intentional misconduct or a knowing violation of law; (iii) under § 174 of this title; or (iv) for any transaction from which the director derived an improper personal benefit. No such provision shall eliminate or limit the liability of a director for any act or omission occurring prior to the date when such provision becomes effective. All references in this paragraph to a director shall also be deemed to refer to such other person or persons, if any, who, pursuant to a provision of the certificate of incorporation in accordance with § 141(a) of this title, exercise or perform any of the powers or duties otherwise conferred or imposed upon the board of directors by this title.

Section 102(b)(7) provides that the certificate may include a "provision eliminating or limiting the personal liability of a director to the corporation or its stockholders for monetary damages for breach of fiduciary duty as a director." Such exculpation clause is important to directors.[7] The certificate of many companies also include provisions related to indemnification and authority to issue securities. The filing of the certificate is important because it contains important substantive provisions.

A corporation is formed upon filing of a certificate of incorporation. *See* DGCL § 106 ("Upon the filing with the Secretary of State of the certificate of incorporation the incorporator or incorporators who signed the certificate shall, from the date of such filing, be and constitute a body corporate"); Sciabacucchi v. Salzberg, 2018 WL 6719718, at *18 (Del. Ch. 2018) ("For purposes of Delaware law, a corporation is a legal entity—a 'body corporate'—created through the sovereign power of the state.").

2. FILING REQUIREMENT FOR NBEs

Like corporations, noncorporate limited liability entities (LLPs, LPs, and LLCs) are formed upon filing with the state. However, unlike the certificate of incorporation for corporations, the certificate of formation for noncorporate limited liability entities is unimportant outside of the fact that its filing is required and is notice to the world. It does not require the disclosure of any important provisions that govern the internal affairs of the firm. The important charter document for noncorporate limited liability entities is the partnership and operation agreement.

RULLCA § 201. Formation of Limited Liability Company; Certificate of Organization.

(a) One or more persons may act as organizers to form a limited liability company by delivering to the [Secretary of State] for filing a certificate of organization.

(b) A certificate of organization must state:

(1) the name of the limited liability company, which must comply with Section 112;

(2) the street and mailing addresses of the company's principal office; and

---

[7] The certificate of incorporation for Alphabet Inc. (the parent company of Google), Article VII, Section 1, provides a typical formulation of the exculpation provision:

> To the fullest extent permitted by the General Corporation Law of Delaware as the same exists or as may hereafter be amended, a director of the Corporation shall not be personally liable to the Corporation or its stockholders for monetary damages for breach of fiduciary duty as a director. If the General Corporation Law of Delaware is amended to authorize corporate action further eliminating or limiting the personal liability of directors, then the liability of a director of the Corporation shall be eliminated to the fullest extent permitted by the General Corporation Law of Delaware, as so amended.

(3) the name and street and mailing addresses in this state of the company's registered agent.

(d) A limited liability company is formed when the certificate of organization becomes effective and at least one person has become a member.

ULPA (2001) § 201. Formation of Limited Partnership; Certificate of Limited Partnership.

(a) To form a limited partnership, a person must deliver a certificate of limited partnership to the [Secretary of State] for filing.

(b) A certificate of limited partnership must state:

(1) the name of the limited partnership, which must comply with Section 114;

(2) the street and mailing addresses of the partnership's principal office;

(3) the name and street and mailing addresses in this state of the partnership's registered agent;

(4) the name and street and mailing addresses of each general partner; and

(5) whether the limited partnership is a limited liability limited partnership.

(c) A certificate of limited partnership may contain statements as to matters other than those required by subsection (b), but may not vary or otherwise affect the provisions specified in Section 105(c) and (d) in a manner inconsistent with that section.

(d) A limited partnership is formed when:

(1) the certificate of limited partnership becomes effective;

(2) at least two persons have become partners;

(3) at least one person has become a general partner; and

(4) at least one person has become a limited partner.

RUPA § 901. Statement of Qualification.

(a) A partnership may become a limited liability partnership pursuant to this section.

(b) The terms and conditions on which a partnership becomes a limited liability partnership must be approved by the affirmative vote or consent necessary to amend the partnership agreement except, in the case of a partnership agreement that expressly addresses obligations to contribute to the partnership, the affirmative vote or consent necessary to amend those provisions.

(c) After the approval required by subsection (b), a partnership may become a limited liability partnership by delivering to the [Secretary of State] for filing a statement of qualification. The statement must contain:

(1) the name of the partnership which must comply with Section 902;

(2) the street and mailing addresses of the partnership's principal office and, if different, the street address of an office in this state, if any;

(3) the name and street and mailing addresses in this state of the partnership's registered agent; and

(4) a statement that the partnership elects to become a limited liability partnership.

The filing requirement to create a noncorporate limited liability entity is ministerial. It does not require a business lawyer. The essential functions of a filing are two. First, the filing notifies the world that the entity is a limited liability entity. The entity name is regulated for this reason and thus is a matter of administrative importance. *See* RULLCA § 112; RUPA § 902; ULPA (2001) § 114. Second, the filing designates a statutory agent for the purpose of service of process. For LPs, this function is further served by the identification of each general partner. ULPA (2001) § 201(b)(4)

The case below analyzes the effect of a dissolution date in the certificate of formation. In reading this case, think about these questions: (1) What function, if any, does the certificate of formation serve? (2) What function, if any, did the dissolution date in the certificate of formation serve? (3) Was there a conflict between the certificate of formation and the operating agreement with respect to dissociation?

MCDONOUGH V. MCDONOUGH

153 A.3d 187 (N.H. 2016)

DALIANIS, C.J.

The plaintiff, Mark McDonough, appeals an order of the Superior Court denying him summary judgment and granting summary judgment to the defendants, TASC Technical Services, LLC (TASC), Patrick McDonough, and Matthew McDonough. The trial court ruled that TASC was not required to dissolve. We affirm.

Brothers Mark, Matthew, and Patrick McDonough established TASC, a corporation that provides engineering services. In September 1995, the brothers converted TASC to a LLC. The New Hampshire Revised Limited Liability Company Act (the Act) governs TASC.

The brothers had a falling out. As a result, Mark sued the defendants seeking a declaration that TASC must dissolve by September 30, 2015, pursuant to its certificate of formation and operating agreement. TASC's certificate of formation states that "the latest date on which the limited liability company is to dissolve is September 30, 2015."* Section 5 of TASC's operating agreement states: "The Company shall have a term beginning on the date the Certificate of Formation is filed and shall continue in full force and effect for a term of twenty (20) years, unless sooner terminated or continued pursuant to the further terms of this Agreement."

Both parties moved for summary judgment. After a hearing, the trial court ruled that TASC was not required to dissolve because its operating agreement permits a majority of its members to continue the company. Consequently, it denied summary judgment to Mark and granted summary judgment to the defendants. This appeal followed.

TASC is governed by both its operating agreement and the Act. Therefore, to resolve the issues in this appeal, we need to construe both the Act and TASC's operating agreement.

Because the operating agreement is a form of contract, we will apply the general rules of contract interpretation. When interpreting a written agreement, we give the language used by the parties its reasonable meaning, considering the circumstances and the context in which the agreement was negotiated, and reading the document as a whole. We give an agreement the meaning intended by the parties when they wrote it. Absent ambiguity, however, the parties' intent will be determined from the plain meaning of the language used in the contract. The interpretation of a contract, including whether a contract term is ambiguous, is ultimately a question of law for this court to decide. Accordingly, we review a trial court's interpretation of a contract de novo.

Mark first argues that TASC's operating agreement and the Act required the company to dissolve by September 30, 2015. We disagree.

The Act requires an LLC's members to dissolve the company as provided for in the company's operating agreement. *See* RSA 304–C:129, I (2015) ("An [LLC] shall be dissolved as provided in the operating agreement."). Section 5 of TASC's operating agreement provides: "The

* Author's note: The members' insertion of the dissolution date in the certificate of formation is unusual. The statute does not require a dissolution date in the certificate of formation. But it provides that the "certificate of formation may set forth any other matters the members or managers decide to include." RSA § 304–C:31, II(e). In this case, the members inserted a dissolution date. The statute also provides: "The fact that a certificate of formation is on file with the secretary of state is notice that the entity formed in connection with the filing of the certificate of formation is a limited liability company legally formed under the laws of New Hampshire and is notice of all other facts set forth in the certificate which are *required to be set forth by RSA 304–C:31, II.*" *Id.* § 304–C:33. A dissolution date is not required information.

Company shall have a term beginning on the date the Certificate of Formation is filed and shall continue in full force and effect for a term of twenty (20) years, *unless sooner terminated or continued pursuant to the further terms of this Agreement.*"

Mark argues that, unless amended, the plain language of TASC's operating agreement required dissolution by September 30, 2015. This argument overlooks the language "unless sooner terminated or continued pursuant to the further terms of this Agreement." Although Mark is correct that the members could unanimously amend section 5 of TASC's operating agreement to remove or change the dissolution clause, that does not preclude other means of continuing TASC. If TASC's members had intended that the only means of continuing the company would be an amendment of section 5, they could have explicitly said so. Instead, they chose to more broadly state that TASC would exist for 20 years unless the company was "continued pursuant to the further terms of this Agreement."

TASC's operating agreement and the Act provide such a way for TASC's members to continue the company. Section 4 of TASC's operating agreement authorizes TASC to "have and exercise all powers now or hereafter conferred by [the Act]." This includes RSA 304–C:130, III, which provides: "After the members have dissolved the limited liability company under RSA 304–C:129, I,** they may revoke the dissolution at any time before completing the wind-up of the limited liability company." Thus, TASC's members have two means to avoid the effects of the September 30, 2015 dissolution. They can either revoke the dissolution pursuant to RSA 304–C:130, III, or unanimously amend section 5 of operating agreement.

Mark argues that a decision to revoke a dissolution pursuant to RSA 304–C:130, III also requires a unanimous vote. He asserts that because the legislature specifically included the word "majority" in RSA 304–C:130, I, the omission of that word in RSA 304–C:130, III demonstrates legislative intent that the phrase "the members" in paragraph III refers to all members of an LLC. Because accepting Mark's interpretation would require us to ignore the plain language of RSA 304–C:67, I, and add a unanimity requirement to RSA 304–C:130, III that is not present in the words of the statute, we conclude that a majority of members may revoke a dissolution pursuant to RSA 304–C:130, III.***

** Author's note: RSA 304–C:129, I, "Events of Dissolution—In General," provides: "A limited liability company shall be dissolved and its business and other activities and its internal affairs shall be wound up upon the first to occur of the events set forth in this section. A limited liability company shall be dissolved as provided in the operating agreement." Subsection II also provides: "Unless the operating agreement provides otherwise, a limited liability company shall be dissolved by majority vote of the members."

*** Author's note: RSA 304–C:67, "Voting Requirements," provides in full:

I. Unless paragraph II, RSA 304–C:68, RSA 304–C:69, RSA 304–C:87, V, or RSA 304–C:120, or the operating agreement provide otherwise, all matters that this act reserves for decision by the members shall be decided by majority vote of the members.

RSA 304–C:130, I, is one of a number of provisions in RSA chapter 304–C specifying that certain member decisions must be made by a majority vote. Other provisions in RSA chapter 304–C specify that the decisions to which they refer must be made by a unanimous vote. Still other provisions, like RSA 304–C:130, III, do not specify whether the member decision at issue must be made by majority or unanimous vote.

When a provision does not specify whether the member decision to which it refers must be made by majority or unanimous vote, RSA 304–C:67 applies. RSA 304–C:67, I, provides that, unless RSA 304–C:67, II or certain other enumerated provisions apply, or unless "the operating agreement provides otherwise, all matters that [the Act] reserves for decision by the members shall be decided by majority vote of the members."

To determine whether the decision to revoke a dissolution under RSA 304–C:130, III may be made by majority or unanimous vote, we first examine whether that decision is one of the decisions listed in RSA 304–C:67, II. RSA 304–C:67, II provides that, unless the operating agreement states otherwise, a unanimous vote of all of an LLC's members is required to: (1) amend a certificate of formation; (2) amend an operating agreement; (3) amend a promise to make a contribution; (4) grant additional membership rights to a member; or (5) admit a new member. Because RSA 304–C:130, III is not exempt, RSA 304–C:67, I, applies.

Section 5 of TASC's operating agreement does not specify whether TASC may be continued by majority or unanimous vote. Likewise, TASC's operating agreement is silent regarding how its members may decide to revoke a dissolution. Therefore, because TASC's operating agreement does not provide otherwise, RSA 304–C:67, I, controls, and TASC's members may by majority vote revoke a dissolution pursuant to RSA 304–C:130, III.

Mark argues that TASC's certificate of formation requires, without exception, that the company dissolve after 20 years. He argues that: (1) the plain language of the certificate of formation requires dissolution; and (2)

II. Unless the operating agreement provides otherwise, the affirmative vote of all members shall be required to:

(a) Amend a certificate of formation;

(b) Amend an operating agreement;

(c) Amend a promise to make a contribution;

(d) Grant additional membership rights to a member; or

(e) Admit a new member.

RSA 304–C:130, "Revocation of Dissolution by Majority of Members," provides in full:

I. Notwithstanding the dissolution of a limited liability company by majority vote of the members, and unless the operating agreement provides otherwise, a limited liability company shall not be dissolved and its internal affairs shall not be wound up if, before the filing of a certificate of cancellation of the limited liability company in the office of the secretary of state, the limited liability company is continued by majority vote of the members. . . .

III. After the members have dissolved the limited liability company under RSA 304–C:129, I, they may revoke the dissolution at any time before completing the wind-up of the limited liability company. . . .

allowing TASC's members to continue TASC without amending the certificate of formation renders the certificate of formation meaningless.

TASC's certificate of formation states that "the latest date on which the limited liability company is to dissolve is September 30, 2015." However, the Act does not require an LLC's members to dissolve the company when the duration listed in the certificate of formation expires. The Act requires an LLC's members to dissolve the company only as provided in its operating agreement. *See* RSA 304–C:129, I. Thus, there is no requirement that TASC's members dissolve the company after the twenty-year duration stated in its certificate of formation.

We disagree with Mark's argument that this interpretation renders the certificate of formation superfluous. Under the Act, an LLC's certificate of formation and its operating agreement are distinct documents that are separately defined and serve different purposes.

The primary purpose of an LLC's operating agreement is to govern how the parties will manage the internal affairs of the LLC and the LLC's business. By contrast, the primary purpose of the certificate of formation is to serve as notice to the secretary of state and the public that the company is operating as a New Hampshire LLC. *See* RSA 304–C:33. The certificate of formation is not rendered superfluous just because the Act looks to an LLC's operating agreement, not its certificate of formation, to determine when the LLC's members must dissolve the company.

We hold that TASC's operating agreement and the Act permit a majority of TASC's members to continue the company beyond September 30, 2015. Accordingly, we affirm the trial court's grant of summary judgment in favor of the defendants.

NOTES

1. The RULLCA anticipates that there might be a conflict between the articles of organization and the operating agreement. Section 107(d) provides: "if a record delivered by a limited liability company to the [Secretary of State] for filing becomes effective and conflicts with a provision of the operating agreement: (1) the agreement prevails as to members, persons dissociated as members, transferees, and managers; and (2) the record prevails as to other persons to the extent they reasonably rely on the record."

3. PRE-FORMATION LEGAL RIGHTS AND LIABILITIES

Ideally, business transactions will wait until the formal creation of the legal entity. But, intentionally or not, business transactions are executed in anticipation or assumed existence of the entity. The question arises: What is the firm's right or liability if a promoter signs a contract or transact on behalf of a firm that has not yet come into existence?

The case below discusses the allocation of liability for activities related to an entity that was not formed at the time of those activities. In reading this case, think about these questions: (1) What are the specific risks for the sponsor, the entity (yet to be formed), and the counterparty when a transaction is executed on behalf of a firm that does not yet exist? (2) How can a counterparty protect itself from the risk of a nonexistent entity?

IN RE DELAWARE SPORTS COMPLEX, LLC

573 B.R. 543 (Bankr. D. Del. 2017)

[The debtor in bankruptcy, Delaware Sports Complex, LLC, sought to develop 170 acres in Middletown, Delaware, as a sports complex. Debtor entered into the lease in question with the town in 2016. The Lease provided that Debtor represented and warranted that it "is a limited liability company duly formed and validly existing under the laws of Delaware." On February 1, 2017, the landlord issued a notice of default of the Lease. The LLC was not "formed and validly existing" until February 28, 2017. The LLC did not legally exist at the time of the signing of the Lease and even the notice of default.]

The Court asked the parties to address the question of whether the Lease was void *ab initio* because Debtor did not exist when it executed the Lease. What prompted the Court's question was a decision in *IOENGINE LLC v. Imation Corp.*, 2017 WL 39563 (D. Del. 2017). There, the District Court addressed a patent assignment to a non-existing limited liability company which was not formed until the day after the assignment. The District Court found that IOENGINE was a *de facto* limited liability company. The District Court held that a limited liability company is analogous to a corporation for which *de facto* status is recognized. The District Court found that there was a *bona fide* attempt to organize IOENGINE, and IOENGINE was formed long before the lawsuit in which it status was at issue. The District Court distinguished IOENGINE from the party in *Leber Assocs., LLC v. Entm't Group Fund, Inc.*, 2003 WL 21750211 (S.D.N.Y. 2003), where *de facto* status was denied because there was no evidence that anyone drafted or attempted to file a certificate of formation until after commencement of the lawsuit.

Here, the certificate of formation (the filing of which brought Debtor into existence per 6 *Del. C.* § 18–201(b)) was not filed until after the Town sent the notice of default. The Court is satisfied, however, that Debtor could enter into the Lease although it was not formed until later. When an agent contracts for a non-existent principal which is subsequently formed, the principal may assume the contract. The Debtor's original members were, in effect, promoters of the preformation entity. *See also Lorillard Tobacco Co. v. Am. Legacy Found.*, 903 A.2d 728, 744 (Del. 2006) (promoter allowed to enter into contracts that bind nascent corporation). The Town is now estopped[2] from denying the existence of Debtor, first, because it accepted Debtor as a limited liability company throughout; and second, because the Town conceded that Debtor's formation was sufficient to cure the default.

NOTES

1. The doctrine of de facto corporation states that "a de facto corporation exists when there has been a good faith attempt to organize the corporation, statutory requirements have been colorably complied with, and the corporation has exercised the functions or conducted the business that it was organized to perform." In re Estate of Greb, 848 N.W.2d 611, 620 (Neb. 2014). "The de facto corporation doctrine provides that a defectively formed corporation—that is, one that fails to meet the technical requirements for forming a de jure corporation—may attain the legal status of a de facto corporation if certain requirements are met." Duray Development, LLC v. Perrin, 792 N.W.2d 749, 755 (Mich. App. 2010). A legally defective corporation can still exist for the purpose of acquiring rights or incurring liabilities. Courts have recently recognize the application of the de facto corporation doctrine to LLCs. *See* In re Hausman, 921 N.E.2d 191, 193 (N.Y. 2009) ("The statutory schemes of the Business Corporation Law and the Limited Liability Company Law are very similar, and we see no principled reason why the de facto corporation doctrine should not apply to both corporations and limited liability companies."); Perrin, 792 N.W.2d at 759 ("The similarities between the Business Corporation Act and the Limited Liability Company Act support the conclusion that the de facto corporation doctrine applies to both."). Where, however, a state does not recognize the de facto corporation doctrine, the same would apply to LLCs unless the statute provides otherwise. *See* Stone v. Jetmar Properties, LLC, 733 N.W.2d 480, 486 (Minn. App. 2007) ("We reject Ortega's claim that even if the de facto-corporation doctrine was abolished for purposes of business corporations it has not been abolished for LLC purposes. The law relevant to corporations guides our interpretation and application of the law relevant to LLCs, the prohibition against de facto corporations must extend to LLCs.").

2. A related concept to the de facto corporation doctrine is corporation by estoppel. "Where a body assumes to be a corporation and acts under a particular name, a third party dealing with it under such assumed name is estopped to deny its corporate existence." Perrin, 792 N.W.2d at 755. This rule prevents a party who dealt with an association as though it were a corporation from denying its existence. By denying the argument that a corporation does not exist, the court prevents the party from reaching the constituents of the enterprise in their individual capacities.

---

[2] *See Leber Assocs., LLC v. Entm't Group Fund, Inc.*, 2003 WL 21750211, at *11 (S.D.N.Y. 2003), where, applying Delaware law, the court discussed estoppel and quoted the general proposition that "it is well settled that a person who contracts or otherwise deals with a body of people as a corporation thereby admits that they are a corporation and is estopped to deny their incorporation," citing 8 Fletcher Cyclopedia of the Law of Private Corporations § 3910 (2001).

4. FILING FOR FOREIGN LIMITED LIABILITY ENTITY

A foreign limited liability entity must file with the state to transact business in the state. "Foreign" does not mean a company based in a foreign country. It means an entity "formed under the law of a jurisdiction other than this state." RULLCA § 102(5); RUPA § 102(6); ULPA (2001) § 102(6). In Florida, a Delaware chartered entity is a foreign company even if the firm has its principal office and conducts all business in Miami. The filing requirement is ministerial, and the limited liability entity is subject to taxes and fees in the state where it does business.

If a foreign firm does not file with the state, the state may bring an action to enjoin it from doing business in the state. RULLCA § 912; RUPA § 1012; ULPA (2001) § 1012. Also, the firm may not maintain an action in the state. RULLCA § 902(b); RUPA § 1002(b); ULPA (2001) § 1002(b). Although these limitations are significant, a failure to file does not impair contracts or take away the benefit of limited liability. RULLCA § 902(c)–(d); RUPA § 1002(c)–(d); ULPA (2001) § 1002(c)–(d). Impairment of contract may harm innocent third parties. Although a contract is not impaired, the dilatory firm cannot maintain an action in the state to enforce it. With respect to limited liability, this protection is granted by the state of charter and thus another state cannot take it away.

The following are the RULLCA rules. The ULPA (2001) § 1001, § 1005, and RUPA § 1001, § 1005 provide functionally identical rules. The statute provides a safe harbor for activities that are not considered transacting business in the state, thus not requiring a filing and annual maintenance.

RULLCA § 901. Governing Law.

(a) The law of the jurisdiction of formation of a foreign limited liability company governs:

(1) the internal affairs of the company;

(2) the liability of a member as member and a manager as manager for a debt, obligation, or other liability of the company; and

(3) the liability of a series of the company.

(b) A foreign limited liability company is not precluded from registering to do business in this state because of any difference between the law of its jurisdiction of formation and the law of this state.

(c) Registration of a foreign limited liability company to do business in this state does not authorize the foreign company to engage in any activities and affairs or exercise any power that a limited liability company may not engage in or exercise in this state.

RULLCA § 905. Activities Not Constituting Doing Business.

(a) Activities of a foreign limited liability company which do not constitute doing business in this state under this [article] include:

(1) maintaining, defending, mediating, arbitrating, or settling an action or proceeding;

(2) carrying on any activity concerning its internal affairs, including holding meetings of its members or managers;

(3) maintaining accounts in financial institutions;

(4) maintaining offices or agencies for the transfer, exchange, and registration of securities of the company or maintaining trustees or depositories with respect to those securities;

(5) selling through independent contractors;

(6) soliciting or obtaining orders by any means if the orders require acceptance outside this state before they become contracts;

(7) creating or acquiring indebtedness, mortgages, or security interests in property;

(8) securing or collecting debts or enforcing mortgages or security interests in property securing the debts and holding, protecting, or maintaining property;

(9) conducting an isolated transaction that is not in the course of similar transactions;

(10) owning, without more, property; and

(11) doing business in interstate commerce.

(b) A person does not do business in this state solely by being a member or manager of a foreign limited liability company that does business in this state.

(c) This section does not apply in determining the contacts or activities that may subject a foreign limited liability company to service of process, taxation, or regulation under law of this state other than this [act].

The case below illustrates the relationship between filing to do business in the state and the LLC's power to engage in certain activities, in this case maintaining a legal action. In reading this case, consider this question: What may be the reason that a foreign LLC can file a suit but cannot "maintain" the action until it registers with the state?

A GUY NAMED MOE, LLC V. CHIPOTLE MEXICAN GRILL OF COLORADO, LLC

135 A.3d 492 (Md. 2016)

BATTAGIA, J.

We are asked to determine whether A Guy Named Moe, LLC, the Petitioner, a foreign limited liability company doing business in Maryland, having filed a civil action in the Circuit Court, although not registered to do business in Maryland, can continue to pursue its claims, once Chipotle Mexican Grill of Colorado, LLC, the Respondent, moved to dismiss the case because of Moe's failure to register.

The parties to this case are two foreign limited liability companies: A Guy Named Moe, LLC ("Moe") and Chipotle Mexican Grill of Colorado, LLC ("Chipotle"). Both companies operate a chain of restaurants, which are respectively known as "Moe's Southwest Grill" and "Chipotle Mexican Grill." The dispute between the parties began when Chipotle applied for a "special exception" to build a restaurant at 36 Market Space in Annapolis, Maryland, which is approximately 425 feet from Moe's Southwest Grill at 122 Dock Street. The Department of Planning and Zoning for the City of Annapolis recommended that the City's Board of Appeals approve Chipotle's application, but Moe opposed that recommendation. The Board, though, unanimously approved Chipotle's request.

Moe subsequently filed a petition for judicial review, asking that the Circuit Court review the Board's decision. Chipotle then filed a Motion to Dismiss in which it argued that Moe was unable to file a petition for judicial review because its right to do business had been forfeited, and, thus, could not "maintain" suit under Section 4A–1007(a) of the Corporations and Associations Article of the Maryland Code.

Moe, in response, filed an Amended Petition for Judicial Review and attached a "Certificate of Good Standing" issued by the State Department of Assessments and Taxation. Moe argued that, while it was not registered to do business in Maryland when it had filed its petition, it could still "maintain" the action under Section 4A–1007 because it had subsequently successfully registered and paid the associated penalty. Moe also argued that it did have standing, both as a taxpayer and as a person aggrieved.

It is undisputed that prior to filing suit, Moe's right to do business in Maryland was forfeited by the State Department of Assessments and Taxation pursuant to Section 4A–1013(a). Upon forfeiture of the right to do business a foreign limited liability company is treated as if it never registered. Section 4A–1013(d).

Under Section 4A–1009(a)(1), "doing business" does not include "maintaining suit":

> In addition to any other activities which may not constitute doing business in this State, for the purposes of this title, the following activities of a foreign limited liability company do not constitute doing business in this State: (1) Maintaining, defending, or settling an action, suit, claim, dispute, or administrative or arbitration proceeding.

"Unless the [foreign] limited liability company shows to the satisfaction of the court" that it has paid a penalty for noncompliance and complied with the registration requirements, it cannot "maintain" suit:

> If a foreign limited liability company is doing or has done any intrastate, interstate, or foreign business in this State without complying with the requirements of this subtitle, the foreign limited liability company and any person claiming under it may not maintain suit in any court of this State, unless the limited liability company shows to the satisfaction of the court that: (1) The foreign limited liability company or the person claiming under it has paid the penalty specified in subsection (d)(1) of this section; and (2)(i) The foreign limited liability company or a successor to it has complied with the requirements of this title; or (ii) The foreign limited liability company and any foreign limited liability company successor to it are no longer doing intrastate, interstate, or foreign business in this State.

Section 4A–1007(a).

The issue, thus, is queued up: If a foreign limited liability company had filed a judicial review action after it had forfeited its right to do business, could it then "maintain" the suit, after it cured the infirmity? The Circuit Court answered in the affirmative; the Court of Special Appeals determined that the suit was void *ab initio*.

Moe argues that the prohibition on *maintaining* suit does not prohibit it from *filing* suit and that its subsequent registration efforts would allow the suit to continue. Moe asserts that, not only is such an interpretation of "maintain" warranted by a plain meaning interpretation, but also that we concluded as much in *Kendrick & Roberts v. Warren Bros. Co.*, 72 A. 461, 463 (Md. 1909). Chipotle argues that the prohibition on "maintaining" suit includes a prohibition on commencing suit.

"Maintain," used in Section 4A–1007(a), means "to continue" something already in existence, Black's Law Dictionary 1097 (10th ed.2014), and coupled with "unless the limited liability company shows to the satisfaction of the court," indicates that the Legislature intended to permit a noncompliant foreign limited liability to "cure" its failure to comply with registration requirements, even though having failed to register before filing suit. The history of Section 4A–1007(a) after our decision in *Kendrick*, and the *Kendrick* case itself, as well as out of state cases interpreting the words "maintain" and "unless" or "until" in similar statutes support this analysis.

In *Kendrick* we analyzed an iteration of our foreign corporation statute, enacted in Section 109(d) of Chapter 270 of the Maryland Laws of 1898 and codified in Section 140 of Article 23 of the Code of Public General Laws of 1904, which stated that, "No such foreign corporation shall be permitted to maintain any action, either at law or equity, in the courts of this state, until the provisions of this Act shall have been complied with." In the case, Kendrick & Roberts Inc., a West Virginia corporation, had sued Warren Bros. Co., which in response stated that, "at the time of the institution of this suit in this Court the said foreign corporation had not filed in the office of the Secretary of the State of Maryland." Kendrick & Roberts Inc. alleged, thereafter "by way of replication," that two months after filing suit, "the plaintiff fully complied with all the requirements of the law of the state of Maryland relating to foreign corporations." The trial court allowed the action to proceed, and Kendrick & Roberts Inc. prevailed.

We affirmed and held that, "The statute does not forbid the institution or bringing of the action, but prevents the maintaining of such action until the provisions of the law shall have been complied with." We recognized that, "The meaning of the word 'maintain' has been defined in pleading, to support what has already been brought into existence." We concluded that, "omission on the part of the plaintiff does not operate to end a suit otherwise regularly instituted, or to destroy a right in other respects validly existing, and the greatest effect would be to suspend the prosecution of such suit until compliance was had with statute."

Both the foreign corporation statute and the statute governing foreign limited liability companies embody identical "may not maintain suit" language that we interpreted in *Kendrick*. Sections 4A–1007(a) and 7–301. Foreign limited liability companies and foreign corporations also suffer identical consequences upon failure "to file with the Department any report or failure to pay any late filing penalties required by law" such that the Department of Assessments and Taxation may forfeit the entities's right "to do business in this State." Sections 4A–1013(a) and 7–304(a). Upon forfeiture of the right to do business, a foreign limited liability company and a foreign corporation are "subject to the same rules, legal provisions, and sanctions as if [they] had never qualified or been licensed to do business in this State." Sections 4A–1013(d) and 7–304(d).

Our analysis that a foreign limited liability company may cure the infirmity of failure to register from the time of filing suit also finds support in our sister jurisdictions interpreting the words "maintain" and "unless" or "until" in statutes similar to ours.

A similar result was reached by the Delaware Supreme Court in interpreting its foreign corporation statute.[12] In *Hudson Farms, Inc. v. McGrellis,* 620 A.2d 215, 216 (Del. 1993), Hudson Farms Inc., a Pennsylvania corporation, filed a mechanic's lien against John McGrellis in Delaware at a time when Hudson Farms was not licensed to do business there. McGrellis filed a motion for summary judgment asserting that Hudson Farms was a foreign corporation not licensed to do business in Delaware, and was, therefore, barred from initiating the action. The trial court determined that Hudson Farms was not licensed at the time it filed the action and dismissed the action without prejudice, although, "the practical effect of the [trial court's] ruling was to defeat Hudson Farms' cause of action because the period for filing a mechanic's lien had expired."

The Supreme Court of Delaware reversed. The court interpreted *8 Del. C.* § 383:

> (a) A foreign corporation which is required to comply with §§ 371 and 372 of this title and which has done business in this State without authority *shall not maintain any action or special proceeding in this State unless and until such corporation has been authorized to do business in this State* and has paid to the State all fees, penalties and franchise taxes for the years or parts thereof during which it did business in this State without authority. This prohibition shall not apply to any successor in interest of such foreign corporation.

and stated that, "The great majority of courts which have construed such statutes have concluded that a court may stay a suit commenced by a non-qualified foreign corporation until the foreign corporation obtains the requisite authority." The court reasoned that, "It is not unreasonable to assume, as most courts do, that the word 'until,' as used in § 117, provides an inference that a proceeding may be stayed until compliance occurs."[14]

---

12 Delaware's foreign corporation statutes are similar to Maryland's provisions for foreign limited liability companies in its registration requirements and forfeiture provisions for failure to file annual reports. *8 Del. C.* §§ 371 and 375. It appears that the Delaware courts have not interpreted similar provisions applicable to foreign limited liability companies, *6 Del. C.* §§ 18–901 *et seq.* The limited liability company provisions are similar to the ones applicable to foreign corporations in the use of the "maintain" and "until" language: "A foreign limited liability company doing business in the State of Delaware may not maintain any action, suit or proceeding in the State of Delaware until it has registered in the State of Delaware, and has paid to the State of Delaware all fees and penalties for the years or parts thereof, during which it did business in the State of Delaware without having registered." *6 Del. C.* § 18–907(a).

14 The Delaware court also noted that the statute related to foreign corporations had a revenue enhancing purpose in the payment of "*all fees, penalties and franchise taxes* for the years or parts thereof during which it did business" in Delaware without authority. Our statute also has a revenue enhancing purpose. The statute requires that a penalty be paid in order to maintain suit and that the penalty be collected as a penalty under the Tax-Property Article: "(i) If a foreign limited liability company does any intrastate, interstate, or foreign business in this State without registering, the Department shall impose a penalty of $200 on the limited liability company. (ii) The penalty under this subsection shall be collected and may be reduced or abated under § 14–704 of the Tax-Property Article." Maryland Code (1975, 2007 repl. vol.), Section 4A–1007(d)(1) of the Corporations and Associations Article. Additionally, registration with the State Department of

In the case *sub judice,* we hold that a foreign limited liability company can "cure" its failure to comply with registration requirements and continue its suit even though not registered at the time of filing suit. What was true in *Kendrick* remains true today with respect to a foreign limited liability company: "omission on the part of the plaintiff does not operate to end a suit otherwise regularly instituted." Thus, once a foreign limited liability company comes into compliance with the statute, it may maintain its action even though not registered when initiating the suit.

[The court held that although Moe could file its petition for judicial review and then register in order to maintain its action, Moe was not a "person aggrieved" and thus did not have standing to pursue the action. Thus, it affirmed the dismissal of Moe's judicial review action.]

NOTES

1. In *7222 Ambassador Road, LLC v. Nat. Ctr. On Institutions and Alternatives, Inc.*, 233 A.3d 124 (Md. 2020), the court provided this description of the importance of properly maintaining an LLC by making necessary filing, which are ministerial in nature, and importantly payments to the state.

> To form an LLC in Maryland and reap the benefits of this form of business organization, its organizers must execute articles of organization and file them with the State Department of Assessment and Taxation ("SDAT"). CA § 4A–202. Among other general powers, an LLC may sue and be sued. CA § 4A–203(2). The members of an LLC may enter into an operating agreement that further elaborates the management, control, and operation of the LLC. CA § 4A–402.
>
> The LLC Act limits the right of an LLC to do business in the State if the LLC fails to make certain filings and payments required by law. CA § 4A–911. In particular, each year the Comptroller is to certify to SDAT a list of LLCs that have failed to pay by October 1 of that year a tax that is due; the Comptroller is to simultaneously notify each of those LLCs that its right to do business in Maryland is in jeopardy. CA § 4A–911(a). Similarly, each year the Secretary of Labor is to certify to SDAT a list of LLCs that have not made a required unemployment insurance contribution before October 1 of that year and simultaneously warn each of those LLCs that its right to do business in Maryland is in jeopardy. CA § 4A–911(b). SDAT itself is to certify a list of LLCs that have failed to file a required annual report with SDAT by October 1 each year. CA § 4A–911(c).

Assessments and Taxation helps facilitate the collection of taxes. Thus, dismissal of the action would undermine the incentive to pay the penalty and register. *See also Empire Excavating Co. v. Maret Dev. Corp.*, 370 F.Supp. 824, 827 (W.D. Pa. 1974) ("The generally stated purposes of corporate registration statutes are to facilitate the enforcement of tax laws and to subject foreign corporations to legal process. Obviously, the more effective the registration statute is in inducing compliance, the better those purposes will be accomplished.").

After the lists of delinquent LLCs are certified, SDAT issues a proclamation that each of those LLCs has forfeited the right to do business in Maryland and to use the LLC's name in Maryland. CA § 4A–911(d). Within 10 days of that proclamation, SDAT is to mail notice of the proclamation to each LLC that is the subject of the proclamation. CA § 4A–912. To regain the right to do business in Maryland, an LLC must make any required filings, pay delinquent taxes and unemployment insurance contributions, and file articles of reinstatement with SDAT. CA § 4A–915 through § 4A–917. If an LLC cures the deficiencies in its filings and payments within 60 days of forfeiture, its right to do business and to use its name in Maryland is retroactively restored as of the date of forfeiture. CA § 4A–912. The statute provides that it is a misdemeanor punishable by a fine for anyone to knowingly transact business on behalf of an LLC while the LLC's right to do business in Maryland is forfeited. CA § 4A–919.

Upon forfeiture of its right to do business, the LLC is not completely disabled. A savings provision in the LLC Act recognizes the validity of certain actions of the LLC and allows the LLC to defend itself in litigation. It provides: "The forfeiture of the right to do business in Maryland and the right to the use of the name of the limited liability company under [the Limited Liability Company Act] does not impair the validity of a contract or act of the limited liability company entered into or done either before or after the forfeiture, or prevent the limited liability company from defending any action, suit, or proceeding in a court of this State." CA § 4A–920.

In this case, the issue was whether an LLC that failed to file an annual report or to rectify the delinquency can pursue an appeal to the state appellate court upon losing at the lower court. The court held that the LLC could not pursue the appeal and that the savings clause of the statement did not apply.

Dismissal of this second-level appeal may seem like a harsh result. However, requiring a business entity to make a few timely filings and payments—or at least filings that are less than two months late after the entity is specially notified of its delinquency—is not an unfair price for its owners to have the shield against individual liability and the tax benefits, together with the organizational flexibility, that the LLC Act provides for a business organization. "The privileges associated with an LLC, such as tax benefits and liability protections, are afforded with the expectation that an LLC will fulfill its statutory obligations."

The failure of Ambassador Road LLC to fulfill its statutory obligations, compounded by its failure to rectify that delinquency during the statutory grace period, resulted in a period of nearly six months during which it lacked the authority to pursue an appeal it had initiated against NCIA. Unfortunately for Ambassador Road LLC, that period included the time during which it was permitted to file a petition for writ of certiorari to continue its appeal. The savings provision of the LLC Act did not preserve its right to do so.

E. PARTNERSHIP AND OPERATING AGREEMENTS

The Delaware Chancery Court colorfully characterized the importance of the partnership and operating agreements: "For Shakespeare, it may have been the play, but for a Delaware limited liability company, *the contract's the thing*. Ultimately, it is the contract that compels the Court's decision in this case because it is the contract that defines the scope, structure, and personality of limited liability companies." R & R Capital, LLC v. Buck & Doe Run Valley Farms, LLC, 2008 WL 3846318, at *1 (Del. Ch. 2008). The first rule of forming an NBE is unquestionably this: *The most important task in the formation of an entity is the drafting of the charter agreement among owners.* For any business that has some level of sophistication, complexity, or size, the charter agreement must be created through a bespoke process of attorney service. In the beginning, much of the lawyer's value-added service will focus on this function.

In practice, a business lawyer uses the applicable statute of the chosen entity as the template for intellectual analysis. In terms of mechanics, a lawyer will likely start with a template or model agreement that a firm may use or the lawyer used in prior engagements. Like a sculptor, the lawyer molds the statutory template and the model agreement into a shape that reflects the client's understanding of the entity structure and the relationship among its partners, members, or managers. This process requires eliminating and altering default statutory provisions and adding terms not found in the statute. The final product is the charter agreement.

The definition of a charter agreement in the statutes makes clear that the partnership or operating agreement does not have to be housed in a singularly contemplated or formalized document, though such systematic contemplation and recordation are obviously ideal and best practice.

1. DEFINITION OF CHARTER AGREEMENT

RUPA § 102(12) defines partnership agreement as an "agreement, whether or not referred to as a partnership agreement and whether oral, implied, in a record, or in any combination thereof, of all the partners of a partnership." ULPA (2001) § 102(14) and RULLCA § 102(13) provide functionally identical definitions of a partnership agreement and an operating agreement, except the RULLCA clarifies that an operating agreement can encompass "a sole member."

Whenever there is a dispute among partners, members, or managers, the first question must be whether the charter agreement governs the matter. The uniform laws broadly define a charter agreement to include "oral or implied" agreements. *See also* California Revised Limited Liability Company Act § 17701.02(s) (defining operating agreement as "whether oral, in a record, implied, or in any combination thereof"); Delaware Limited Liability Company Act § 18–101(7) ("any agreement, written, oral or implied, of the member or members as to the affairs of a limited liability company and the conduct of its business"). Clearly, the nature of unwritten agreements can be more ambiguous and contestable, and thus often requires fact-finding. One can easily imagine the different interpretations given to implied agreements based on professed course of conduct, implicit understanding, and oral communications, particularly when significant sums of money are involved. *See, e.g.,* Olson v. Halvorsen, 986 A.2d 1150, 1155–59 (Del. 2009) (holding that a departing member in a hedge fund was not entitled an oral earnout agreement over the course of several years and instead was only entitled under the written operating agreement to his capital account and current compensation, which was $100 million).

In a minority of states, the definition of a charter agreement is limited. For example, New York Limited Liability Company Law § 102 defines an operating agreement as "any *written* agreement of the members concerning the business of a limited liability company and the conduct of its affairs." Oral and implied agreements are not a part of the operating agreement, though "written agreement" could possibly encompass agreements in recorded form such as email and possibly audio and video forms.

In the ideal world of best practice, the charter agreement will be written in a single document and amendments thereto. The following is an example from the Chrysler Group LLC operating agreement.

CHRYSLER GROUP LLC OPERATING AGREEMENT

Section 12.3 Entire Agreement. This Agreement and the other documents referred to herein, constitute the entire agreement among the parties and contain all of the agreements among the parties with respect to the subject matter hereof as of the date of this Agreement and supersede all prior agreements, undertakings and negotiations (in each case, both oral and written) between the parties concerning the subject matter herein. Failure by any party hereto to enforce any covenant, duty, agreement, term or condition of this Agreement, or to exercise any right hereunder, shall not be construed as thereafter waiving such covenant, duty, term, condition or right; and in no event shall any course of dealing, custom or usage of trade modify, alter or supplement any term of this Agreement.

Section 12.5 Amendments. This Agreement may not be amended, modified, waived or supplemented except pursuant to a written instrument signed by the Company and the holders of a majority of the Membership Interests outstanding at such time.

2. FUNCTION OF CHARTER AGREEMENT

The charter agreement is a form of contract. *See* Harbison v. Strickland, 900 So.2d 385, 391 (Ala. 2004) ("Operating agreements of limited liability companies serve as contracts that set forth the rights, duties, and relationships of the parties to the agreement."). Ideally, it should contain all terms, conditions, rights, and duties—that is, the rules of internal affairs—of the parties. Partnership law makes clear that the parties to the partnership agreement are the partners. RUPA § 102(12); ULPA (2001) § 102(14). With respect to LLC, parties to the agreement are the members, who are deemed to assent to the operating agreement. *See* RULLCA § 106(b) ("A person that becomes a member is deemed to assent to the operating agreement."). Parties to the operating agreement include the entity and can include others such as non-owner managers. *See* RULLCA § 106(a) ("A limited liability company is bound by and may enforce the operating agreement, whether or not the company has itself manifested assent to the operating agreement.").

It is often said that corporation law is fundamentally enabling. *See* Shintom Co., Ltd. v. Audiovox Corp., 888 A.2d 225, 227 (Del. 2005) ("The Delaware General Corporation Law is an enabling statute."); William T. Allen, *Contracts and Communities in Corporation Law*, 50 Wash. & Lee L. Rev. 1395, 1400 (1993) ("United States corporate law is thus chiefly enabling in character, not regulatory."). However, corporation law fixes certain important aspects of the rules of internal affairs, such as a central manager in the form of a board of directors, fiduciary duties, governance procedures, and shareholder rights.

In contrast, the laws of NBEs are truly enabling in nature. They provide for greater latitude in contracting for the internal rules of the entity than under corporation law. Aside from certain limited number of mandatory provisions, the statute provides contractual gap filling provisions. The following passage, amusing and irreverent, highlights the importance of contracting in NBEs and a fundamental distinction between corporation law and the laws of NBEs.

> When a romantically-involved couple marries, they receive a basket of rights and responsibilities. Their legal duties, up to and including through a death or divorce, are defined by statute and case-law.[1] When couples forgo formal bonds, and pursue connubial pleasures au naturel, however, they are free to set their own bounds on the relationship. Behavioral flexibility is increased, of course, but so too is uncertainty, unless their agreements are explicit in a way unusual under the influence of

---

[1] As any long-married person can attest, these legal strictures leave ample room for disagreement, negotiation and compromise in the nature of the relationship.

> mutual attraction. Litigation in this Court over jointly-owned property is one unfortunate result.
>
> As with romantic parties, so with investing parties. Like a groom, an equity holder buying stock in a Delaware Corporation thereby receives strictures and rights, in that case provided by the Delaware General Corporation Law and a rather vast body of common law, and he can be reasonably confident of what to expect should his relationship with the company and its management and directors become a matter of tears and recriminations.
>
> A buyer of equity in an alternative entity, on the other hand, is free—to the extent the counterparty has agreed—to set the terms of the relationship as the parties find satisfactory. Again, flexibility is enhanced, but uncertainty may lurk unless the express terms of the relationship—the terms of the entity agreement—are both clear and understood by the investor. If the relationship grows less than affectionate, it is frequently the terms of that contract, and not corporate fiduciary duties, that control.

Morris v. Spectra Energy Partners (DE) GP, LP, 2017 WL 2774559, at *1 (Del. Ch. 2017).

RUPA § 105. Partnership Agreement; Scope, Function, and Limitations.

(a) Except as otherwise provided in subsections (c) and (d), the partnership agreement governs:

(1) relations among the partners as partners and between the partners and the partnership;

(2) the business of the partnership and the conduct of that business; and

(3) the means and conditions for amending the partnership agreement.

(b) To the extent the partnership agreement does not provide for a matter described in subsection (a), this [act] governs the matter.

ULPA (2001) § 105(a)–(b). Partnership Agreement; Scope, Function, and Limitations.

[Functionally the same]

RULLCA § 105(a)–(b). Operating Agreement; Scope, Function, and Limitations.

[Functionally the same]

The above provisions establish four principles: (1) the charter agreement provides the internal rules of governing the NBE; (2) each entity is subject to a high degree of private ordering by owners; (3) if owners do not have a charter agreement or do not have a provision on a specific issue, the statute provides the default rules; (4) the statute provides certain mandatory, nonwaivable rules that cannot be subject to contracting.

Other than mandatory provisions, the statute provides default and gap filling rules in the event that the owners did not contract for a particular issue. For example, partners who unwittingly form a partnership may not have a well-defined partnership agreement, and in that event the statute provides the rules of governance and internal affairs when the partnership agreement, including oral and implied agreements, does not provide.

The laws of NBEs enable a contracting process. While the uniform laws do not express the primacy of contract, some state laws explicitly state that the underlying policy is the freedom of contract. *See, e.g.*, Delaware Limited Liability Company Act § 18–1101(b) ("It is the policy of this chapter to give the maximum effect to the principle of freedom of contract and to the enforceability of limited liability company agreements."); Delaware Revised Uniform Limited Partnership Act § 17–1101(c) (same); Florida Revised Limited Liability Company Act § 605.0111(1) (same); Maryland Limited Liability Company Act § 4A–102(a) (same); Maine Limited Liability Company Act § 1507(1) (same).

Therefore, while the filing requirement is ministerial, the drafting of the charter document is critically important. This task should belong to the expertise of the business lawyer who should draft the agreements in consultation with clients and their needs.

CHRYSLER GROUP LLC OPERATING AGREEMENT

Section 2.2 Formation and Continuation.

(a) The Company was organized and hereby continues as a limited liability company under the LLC Act [Delaware Limited Liability Company Act], upon the terms and subject to the conditions set forth in this Agreement.

(b) The rights, duties and liabilities of the Members shall be as provided in the LLC Act, except as otherwise provided herein. To the extent that the rights, powers, duties, obligations and liabilities of any Members are different by reason of any provision of this Agreement than they would be in the absence of such provision, this Agreement shall, to the extent permitted by the LLC Act, control.

(c) This Agreement completely amends, restates and supersedes in all respects the 2012 Agreement and each of its predecessor agreements.

The case below discusses the importance of properly drafting the charter agreement and the provisions related to owner approval of certain actions by managers. In reading this case, consider these questions: (1) What was the basic scheme of managerial authority and owner approval with respect to financing through the issuance of new partnership interests? (2) What principles do courts apply in interpreting the charter agreement? (3) What was the role of the principle of *contra proferentem* in this case? (4) What was the general partner's scheme to take advantage of the limited partners? (5) With a properly drafted agreement (from the perspective of the general partner), could the general partner have legally executed that scheme?

IN RE NANTUCKET ISLAND ASSOC. LTD. PARTNERSHIP UNITHOLDERS LITIG.

810 A.2d 351 (Del. Ch. 2002)

STRINE, VICE CHANCELLOR.

Plaintiffs are limited partners in Nantucket Island Associates Limited Partnership (the "Partnership"). The Partnership was formed in 1987 to own and operate a portfolio of properties located on Nantucket Island, Massachusetts [the "Property"].

[The plaintiffs allege that the General Partner had decided to raise new capital. That transaction was a "Rights Offering," which gave the existing limited partners the opportunity to buy one "Preferred Unit" for each unit in the Partnership they held. The price of a Preferred Unit was $13,333 and the 785 Preferred Units equaled in number the then-outstanding limited partner units. Preferred Unitholders were to receive a cumulative preferred annual return of 8% on their purchase price and an aggregate cash distribution equal to 250% of their purchase price.]

The Rights Offering was guaranteed by an affiliate of the General Partner, defendant Zero Main Associates. Zero Main was a special purpose entity formed solely to purchase any Preferred Units not subscribed to by other limited partners of the Partnership. By this means, it was assured that the Partnership would sell all the Preferred Units. The Offering Prospectus informed the limited partners of this guarantee and of the fact that the guarantor was an affiliate of the General Partner. But the Offering Prospectus did not indicate whether officers and directors of the General Partner were investors, directly or indirectly, in the guarantor, Zero Main.

The Rights Offering was not conditioned on an affirmative vote of the limited partners. It proceeded solely by action of the General Partners. Once the Rights Offering was concluded, 83% of the new Preferred Units ended up in the hands of Zero Main, the General Partner's affiliate.

To implement the Rights Offering, the General Partner purported to adopt a "Second Amended and Restated Limited Partnership Agreement," which made several substantial changes to the Partnership Agreement.

The Amendment altered the distribution formula under the Partnership Agreement to subordinate the limited partners' right to receive distributions of net income or gains to the rights of the Preferred Unitholders to receive the 8% Annual Return and the 250% Return.

The Partnership used the new capital to make improvements to the Property. These included $4 million in expenditures to repair the bulkhead at the Boat Basin and to renovate the Hotel Properties.

[The real estate market in Cape Cod and the islands of Martha's Vineyard and Nantucket began to soar. Less than two years after the Rights Offering, the partnership sold several properties for $38,425,000, an amount that was $21.5 million more than the values noted in the Prospectus for the Rights Offering. The Sale proceeds were used to pay off the Preferred Unitholders, by providing them with their full 250% Return plus the 8% Annual Return. For each unit, they received the $13,333 initial investment, plus a $21,747 return. Because of its ownership of 83% of the Preferred Units, the General Partner's affiliate, Zero Main, received the overwhelming bulk of these proceeds.]

After the Sale was announced, this and other lawsuits were filed by limited partners who had not purchased Preferred Units.

The central basis for the plaintiffs' grievance is relatively simple. They contend that the General Partner exploited its superior knowledge and the weariness of a group of limited partners who had received no distributions for nine years to usurp the value of the Partnership largely for itself. Knowing that the limited partners would be reluctant to put more capital at risk without some prospect of a return, the General Partner downplayed the prospects of the Partnership in the Rights Offering, conscious that this would deter new investments by the limited partners and thereby allow its affiliate to buy most of the new Preferred Units. Not only that, the General Partner took it upon itself to amend the Partnership Agreement to advantage itself as a purchaser of Preferred Units, without seeking (what the plaintiffs argue was) the necessary approval of the limited partners.

The plaintiffs argue that the clear terms of the Partnership Agreement prevented the General Partner from adopting unilaterally the Amendment that accorded the Preferred Unitholders a preferential right to the 250% Return and the 8% Annual Return and that put in place the Removal Condition. The defendants argue that the General Partner had the clear authority to adopt the Amendment without a vote of the limited partners.

The interpretative principles relevant to resolving this dispute are familiar. Like other contracts, limited partnership agreements are to be construed in accordance with their literal terms.

Unlike negotiated bilateral agreements, most limited partnership agreements are drafted almost exclusively by their founding general partners—or perhaps more accurately, by the lawyers for their founding general partners. There is usually no drafting history that could shed light on the shared intentions of the contracting parties—the general partner and the limited partners. As a result, the court is required to resolve ambiguities against the drafting general partner and in favor of the reasonable expectations of the limited partners.

The application of these interpretative principles leads me to conclude that the Amendment was improperly adopted. The better reading of the literal terms of the Agreement is that the limited partners were required to approve the Amendment. Just as important, the Partnership Agreement is, at the very least, ambiguous on this question. Because the Agreement was drafted exclusively by the Partnership's original general partner, any ambiguity must be resolved in favor of the limited partners' reasonable expectations. Given the text of the Agreement, these expectations included the right to approve the Amendment.

The defendants argue that the General Partner's authority to effect the Amendment without approval of the limited partners is contained explicitly in § 4.3 of the Partnership Agreement, which states as follows:

> Section 4.3 *Additional Capital Contributions by Investor Limited Partners and Admission of Additional Investor Limited Partners.*
>
> A. In the event that the Managing General Partner determines that it is in the best interests of the Partnership to raise additional capital for the Partnership, the Managing General Partner may . . . without the Consent of the Limited Partners, sell additional limited partnership interests in the Partnership. Additional limited partnership interests may be sold on such terms and conditions, and additional Limited Partners shall have such rights and obligations, as the Managing General Partner shall determine.
>
> B. In the event that the Managing General Partner determines to issue and sell additional limited partnership interests as provided in Section 4.3.A, the Managing General Partner shall, prior to the offer or sale of such interests to Persons other than the Investor Limited Partners, offer such interests to the Investor Limited Partners pro rata in accordance with their Percentage Interests . . . .

According to the defendants, the portion of § 4.3 that permits the Managing General Partner to sell "additional limited partnership interests" on "such terms and conditions" and having "such rights and obligations, as the Managing General Partner shall determine" necessarily grants the General Partner the authority to amend the Partnership Agreement as necessary to secure the "rights" of the new partners.

The defendants believe that § 11.13.A. of the Agreement makes the existence of this power even clearer. That section states:

> A. *This agreement may be* modified or *amended* pursuant to Sections 5.5, 11.2, and 11.13.B, *or with the written consent of the General Partners and the Consent of the Limited Partners [determined by majority vote of Limited Partners],* provided that any modification or amendment which would . . .*
>
> (iv) *adversely affect (other than as permitted by Section 4.3) the rights of the Investor Limited Partners under Article IX,* or (v) amend this Section 11.13, *shall require the written consent of all of the Investor Limited Partners.*

They argue that the explicit reference to the General Partner's authority under § 4.3 acknowledges that the General Partner can amend the Agreement unilaterally when that is required to guarantee a right connected to a new issuance of partnership units. The defendants note that the original offering prospectus for the Partnership warned limited partners of the possibility of dilution and that the limited partners could only protect themselves from this risk by exercising their contractual right to participate on a *pro rata* basis in any future offering.

Whatever surface appeal the defendants' argument has largely vanishes when the issue is considered in view of the substance of the Preferred Units, the specific language of the Agreement, and the legal context in which the Partnership Agreement was drafted.

The Rights Offering did not involve an issuance of garden variety limited partnership units at, for example, a price that was more favorable than the initial sale of units in 1987. An offer on those terms would have been dilutive in the most common sense, [but] fully consistent with § 4.3, and would, it seems, have required no amendment to the Partnership Agreement at all.

In contrast to this traditional type of dilution, the Rights Offering involved the creation of what the Offering itself described as an entirely different class of "Preferred" partnership units, whose rights to certain returns had to be fully satisfied before the existing limited partner units could receive distributions. This is not dilution of the kind that reduces the existing limited partners from having a claim on 99% of the potential distributions to, for example, 47%. Rather, the effect of the Preferred Units on the limited partners is more aptly called "subordination" than "dilution."

* Author's note: The partnership agreement defined "Consent of the Limited Partners" as a majority vote of the limited partners. 810 A.2d at 367–68 & n.30.

It is conceivable that providing Preferred Unitholders with this type of superiority in distributions is a "right" of a "new limited partnership interest" within the intended meaning of § 4.3. But reading § 4.3 to empower the General Partner unilaterally to create a different class of limited partner units subordinating the rights of existing holders requires reading into that provision a more sweeping implicit meaning than obviously emerges from a reading of the provision's explicit terms.

It is important that one would expect the General Partner's right to create a new class of units to be articulated clearly, rather than as a component part of its authority to "Admit Additional Investor Limited Partners" and to "sell additional limited partnership interests." This expectation is grounded in the legal context in which the Partnership Agreement exists. For starters, the Delaware Revised Uniform Limited Partnership Act ("DRULPA") itself suggests the need for an explicit grant of authority if a general partner is to be empowered unilaterally to (i) create a new class of partnership units that has rights senior to those of the existing partners and (ii) amend the partnership agreement to include those rights. To wit, § 17–302(a) of DRULPA now states:

> A partnership agreement may provide for classes or groups of limited partners having such relative rights, powers and duties as the partnership agreement may provide, and may make provision for the future creation in the manner provided in the partnership agreement of additional classes or groups of limited partners having such relative rights, powers and duties as may from time to time be established, *including rights, powers and duties senior to existing classes and groups of limited partners.* A partnership agreement may provide for the taking of an action, *including the amendment of the partnership agreement,* without the vote or approval of any limited partner or class or group of limited partners, including an action to create under the provisions of the partnership agreement a class or group of partnership interests that was not previously outstanding.

At the time the Nantucket Island Partnership was created in 1987, § 17–302(a) did not include what now constitutes its last sentence. That last sentence says that a partnership agreement may provide for actions necessary to the creation of a new class or group of partnership interests, "including the amendment of the partnership agreement," to be taken without a vote of the existing limited partners. It was added to DRULPA, effective September 1, 1988, in the year after the Partnership Agreement was first executed.

As of that time period, the DRULPA contained no general provision addressing how partnership agreements could be amended. This factor contributed to uncertainty.

Then, in 1998, the General Assembly provided additional guidance about this issue, by adopting a new subsection (f) of § 17–302, which reads in pertinent part as follows:

> (f) If a partnership agreement provides for the manner in which it may be amended, it may be amended in that manner or with the approval of all the partners or as otherwise permitted by law. If a partnership agreement does not provide for the manner in which it may be amended, the partnership agreement may be amended with the approval of all the partners or as otherwise permitted by law.

This new subsection reinforced the need for a specific articulation of the manner in which partnership agreement amendments can be effected and clarified that the default rule requires approval of all the partners.

These various factors persuade me that the powers granted to the General Partner by § 4.3 are not nearly as sweeping as the defendants contend. The more obvious reading of § 4.3 is that it gives the General Partner authority to issue additional limited partner units at prices that reflect current market realities and some degree of discretion to grant rights to the new partners to the extent that those rights do not interfere with any right specifically secured to the limited partners by the other terms of the Agreement. When the issuance of new rights will impinge on contractual rights of the limited partners, however, the General Partner is required to amend the Agreement in accordance with the provision of the Agreement that generally governs amendments.

Although the General Partner retained important discretion to issue additional limited partner units that could dilute the interests of existing limited partners, it could not amend the Agreement unilaterally to subordinate the contractual rights of the limited partners to a new class of preferred unitholders. If a new issuance required an amendment to the Agreement affecting the substantive rights of the limited partners, the General Partner was required to obtain the necessary consent. Moreover, even if this is not the only reasonable reading of the Agreement, it is a reading that a reasonable investor could have discerned from the text.

The plaintiffs' motion for summary judgment on this issue is granted. Having failed to obtain the consent of the limited partners for the Amendment, the General Partner breached the Agreement and the Amendment was therefore invalidly adopted.

3. ELASTICITY OF PRIVATE ORDERING

All business organization laws permit contractual flexibility to varying degrees. Corporation law enables managers and shareholders to structure the company's capital structure and permits broad latitude in the details of how the company is managed with respect to internal procedures, liability of directors, and many other facets of managing a corporation. But this flexibility is also housed within a relatively fixed overall structure. Corporation law has certain mandatory rules, and business courts broadly regulate the underlying equities of managerial conduct through the framework of fiduciary duty. For example, corporation law mandates the following whereas the laws of NBEs generally do not:

- board of directors has ultimate managerial authority: *e.g.*, DGCL § 141(a)
- directors must be natural persons: *e.g.*, DGCL § 141(b); MBCA § 1.40, § 8.03(a)
- officers must be natural persons: *e.g.*, MBCA § 8.40(b)
- annual meeting of shareholders to elect directors must be held: *e.g.*, DGCL § 211(b); MBCA § 7.01(a)
- shareholders must approve any amendment to the certificate of incorporation: *e.g.*, DGCL § 242(b); MBCA § 10.03(b)
- shareholder power to adopt, repeal or amend the bylaws cannot be eliminated: *e.g.*, CA, Inc. v. AFSCME Employees Pension Plan, 953 A.2d 227 (Del. 2008)
- shareholders must vote on certain fundamental transactions such as merger, sale of all or substantially all assets, and dissolution: *e.g.*, DGCL § 251(c) (merger), § 271(a) (sale of substantially all assets), § 275(a) (dissolution)
- common shareholders have mandatory right to appraisal: *e.g.*, DGCL § 262(a); Matter of Appraisal of Ford Holdings, Inc. Preferred Stock, 698 A.2d 973, 976 (Del. Ch. 1997)
- fiduciary duties are not subject to private ordering: *e.g.*, DGCL § 102(b); MBCA § 2.02(b); Miller v. Am. Real Estate Partners, L.P., 2001 WL 1045643, at *8 (Del. Ch. 2001)
- takeover defenses are subject to judicial inquiry into reasonableness: *e.g.*, Unocal Corp. v. Mesa Petroleum Co., 493 A.2d 946 (Del. 1985)
- the equity of a particular situation is determined by the court, which regulates the conduct of managers and shareholder rights in virtually all facets of corporation law where the statute may not otherwise provide: *e.g.*, Schnell v. Chris-Craft Industries, Inc., 285 A.2d 437 (Del. 1971)

Limits on contracting is not the same as *prohibition* on contracting. Corporation law permits a good deal of contracting for the rules of internal affairs. For example, the following aspects of corporations, among many others, are subject to contracting: the size of the board, internal procedures for meetings and voting, capital structure such as classes of stock, structure of senior officers and management, insurance and indemnification, and exculpation of liability. In light of this, Delaware courts and judges have repeatedly said that corporation law is principally enabling.[8] Such comment carries the point only so far. In the relative apportionment of the mix of mandatory and default rules, corporation law imposes more mandatory rules than NBE laws. *See* Anglo Am. Sec. Fund, L.P. v. S.R. Global Int'l Fund, L.P., 829 A.2d 143, 150 (Del. Ch. 2003) ("Whereas corporations are largely creatures of statute with some limited contractual flexibility, limited partnerships offer greater contractual flexibility with only a few statutory constraints.").

The laws of NBEs provide fewer mandatory rules. Most statutory rules are default rules subject to change or elimination by the parties. The laws of NBEs thus enable a greater degree of private ordering. Whereas, generally speaking, the most important aspects of corporation law are found in the statute or case law, the most important rules of NBEs are found in the partnership and operating agreements.

> It is frequently observed that LLCs "are creatures of contract," which they primarily are. The Delaware Limited Liability Company Act (the "LLC Act") provides that "it is the policy of this chapter to give maximum effect to the principle of freedom of contract and to the enforceability of limited liability company agreements." 6 *Del. C.* § 18–110(b). Because of this freedom, "the parties have broad discretion to use an LLC agreement to define the character of the company and the rights and obligations of its members." One "attraction of the LLC form of entity is the statutory freedom granted to members to shape, by contract, their own approach to common business 'relationship' problems." "Virtually any management structure may be implemented through the company's governing instrument."
>
> Using the contractual freedom that the LLC Act bestows, the drafters of an LLC agreement can create an LLC with bespoke governance features or design an LLC that mimics the governance features of another familiar type of entity. The choices that the drafters make have consequences. If the drafters have embraced the statutory default rule of a member-managed governance arrangement, which has strong functional and historical ties to

[8] *E.g.*, Williams v. Geier, 671 A.2d 1368, 1381 (Del. 1996) ("At its core, the Delaware General Corporation Law is a broad enabling act which leaves latitude for substantial private ordering, provided the statutory parameters and judicially imposed principles of fiduciary duty are honored."); Matter of Appraisal of Ford Holdings, Inc. Preferred Stock, 698 A.2d 973, 976 (Del. Ch. 1997) ("Delaware's General Corporation Law, like most general laws of incorporation in the twentieth century U.S., is an *enabling statute*. That is, the philosophy that underlies it is that the public good is advanced by the provision of an inexpensive mechanism that allows all individuals to achieve the benefits that the corporate form provides (most importantly, centralized management and entity status, with its characteristics of indefinite duration and separately salable share interests) through establishing management and governance terms that appear advantageous to those designing the organization.").

> the general partnership (albeit with limited liability), then the parties should expect a court to draw on analogies to partnership law. If the drafters have opted for a single managing member with other generally passive, non-managing members, a structure closely resembling and often used as an alternative to a limited partnership, then the parties should expect a court to draw on analogies to limited partnership law. If the drafters have opted for a manager-managed entity, created a board of directors, and adopted other corporate features, then the parties to the agreement should expect a court to draw on analogies to corporate law. Depending on the terms of the agreement, analogies to other legal relationships may also be informative.

Obeid v. Hogan, 2016 WL 3356851, at *6 (Del. Ch. 2016).

American law generally tends to be enabling and permit a great deal of contracting, perhaps more so than the laws of other countries. There is a spectrum between purely enabling (private contracts) and purely regulatory (state mandates). Each entity form lies on a spectrum, and elasticity of contracting is relative. Corporation law lies on one end of that spectrum—it is more regulatory than the laws of other business entities. When the corporate form is used, all of corporation law come into play including its mandatory rules. Learning this mix of mandatory and default rules is important to understanding the entity form and its relationship to and differences with other entity forms. The following graph illustrates this elasticity of private ordering.

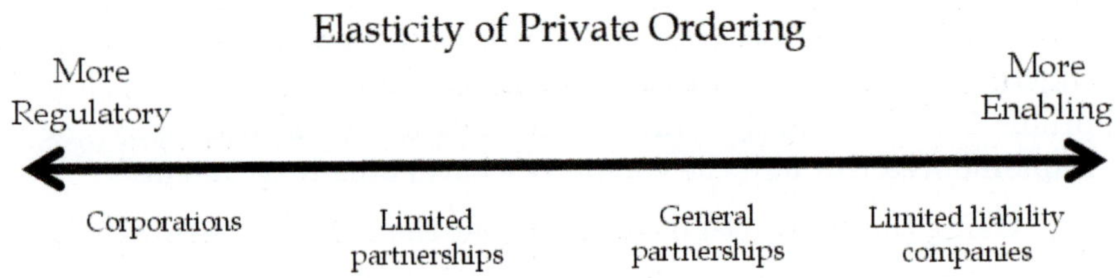

The following provision in the RULLCA states the mandatory terms of the statute, *i.e.*, provisions that are not subject to contracting in the operating agreement. The statutes for general partnerships and limited partnerships have similar provisions. RUPA § 105(c); ULPA (2001) 105(c).

RULLCA § 105. Operating Agreement; Scope, Function, and Limitations.

(c) An operating agreement may not:

(1) vary the law applicable under Section 104;

(2) vary a limited liability company's capacity under Section 109 to sue and be sued in its own name;

(3) vary any requirement, procedure, or other provision of this [act] pertaining to:

(A) registered agents; or

(B) the [Secretary of State], including provisions pertaining to records authorized or required to be delivered to the [Secretary of State] for filing under this [act];

(4) vary the provisions of Section 204;

(5) alter or eliminate the duty of loyalty or the duty of care, except as otherwise provided in subsection (d);

(6) eliminate the contractual obligation of good faith and fair dealing under Section 409(d), but the operating agreement may prescribe the standards, if not manifestly unreasonable, by which the performance of the obligation is to be measured;

(7) relieve or exonerate a person from liability for conduct involving bad faith, willful or intentional misconduct, or knowing violation of law;

(8) unreasonably restrict the duties and rights under Section 410, but the operating agreement may impose reasonable restrictions on the availability and use of information obtained under that section and may define appropriate remedies, including liquidated damages, for a breach of any reasonable restriction on use;

(9) vary the causes of dissolution specified in Section 701(a)(4);

(10) vary the requirement to wind up the company's activities and affairs as specified in Section 702(a), (b)(1), and (e);

(11) unreasonably restrict the right of a member to maintain an action under [Article] 8;

(12) vary the provisions of Section 805, but the operating agreement may provide that the company may not have a special litigation committee;

(13) vary the right of a member to approve a merger, interest exchange, conversion, or domestication under Section 1023(a)(2), 1033(a)(2), 1043(a)(2), or 1053(a)(2);

(14) vary the required contents of a plan of merger under Section 1022(a), plan of interest exchange under Section 1032(a), plan of conversion under Section 1042(a), or plan of domestication under Section 1052(a); or

(15) except as otherwise provided in Sections 106 and 107(b), restrict the rights under this [act] of a person other than a member or manager.

4. CHOICE OF LAW REVISITED

The choice of law is consequential because it provides default rules that become effective if parties (the entity, owners, managers, or lawyers) neglect to change the default rules in the charter agreement. For example, state laws providing default or mandatory rules vary on important issues:

Voting requirement to amend the charter agreement.—Compare Tex. Bus. Orgs. Code § 101.053 ("The company agreement of a limited liability company may be amended only if each member of the company consents to the amendment."), *with* Oklahoma Limited Liability Company Act § 2020(B)(3) ("A majority vote of the members shall be required to approve the following matters. An amendment to the articles of organization or operating agreement.").

Entitlement after dissociation.—Compare Delaware Limited Liability Company Act § 18–604 ("such [resigning] member is entitled to receive, within a reasonable time after resignation, the fair value of such member's limited liability company interest"), *with* California Revised Limited Liability Company Act § 17706.03 (a)(3) ("any transferable interest owned by the person immediately before dissociation in the person's capacity as a member is owned by the person solely as a transferee").

Elimination of fiduciary duty.—Compare Delaware Limited Liability Company Act § 18–1101(c) ("the member's or manager's or other person's duties may be expanded or restricted or eliminated by provisions in the limited liability company agreement"), *with* N.Y. Limited Liability Company Act § 417(a)(1) ("no such provision shall eliminate or limit the liability of any manager if a judgment or other final adjudication adverse to him or her establishes that his or her acts or omissions were in bad faith or involved intentional misconduct or a knowing violation of law or that he or she personally gained in fact a financial profit or other advantage to which he or she was not legally entitled").

Because most provisions in NBE laws are default rules, the operative effect of the statute becomes more important when parties neglect to contemplate matters that should have been subject to contracting.

F. CONTRACT INTERPRETATION PRINCIPLES

Because charter agreements in partnerships and LLCs are a type of contract, courts apply ordinary contract interpretation principles. The interpretation of a contract is a question of law for the court. Briefly, then, the following are some common contract interpretation principles that drafters and business lawyers should keep in mind. These concepts should have been introduced in the 1L contracts course. They are commonly described in judicial opinions before a court undertakes the process of interpreting and analyzing charter agreements.

Charter agreements are construed in accordance with their terms to give effect to the parties' intent, as ascertained by the language in the written agreement. To ascertain intent, a court construes the contract as a whole, looks to the entire instrument, and gives effect to every word in the agreement if reasonably possible. One particular meaning inferred from an isolated provision cannot control the contract if that inference conflicts with the contract's overall scheme and agreement as a whole.

When a contract is clear and unambiguous, a court must interpret it as a matter of law. Words are given their plain meaning unless the parties intended a special meaning and this intent is evident. Courts may rely on dictionary or common usage of terms unless a special meaning is evident. Plain terms control if a reasonable person would have no expectations that would be inconsistent with the common meaning. A contract is clear and unambiguous if it is subject to only one reasonable interpretation. In that case, the four corners of the contract govern, and extrinsic evidence such as the parties' course of dealings or oral communications is inadmissible. If the parties have fixed the language reflecting their understanding, a court will not consider parol evidence suggesting a different meaning. It will construe the contract as a matter of law.

A contract is ambiguous if it can be reasonably construed to have two or more meanings, where reasonable minds could differ as to the contract's meaning. A contract is not ambiguous just because a party disagrees with the plain meaning or its adverse application to the party. When a contract is ambiguous, a factual dispute results and the factfinder must consider extrinsic evidence to determine the intent of the parties.

In interpreting a contract, a court may rely on a number of principles of contract interpretation. A drafter should bear them in mind when drafting the charter agreement.

Expressio unius est exclusio alterius.—The expression of one thing is the exclusion of another. For example, a charter may provide that a partner can rightfully dissociate only upon: "(1) consent of a majority of partners, (2) the passage of two years upon execution of the partnership agreement, (3) death, incapacity, or submission into guardianship, or (4) bankruptcy, insolvency, or receivership." The application of the principle suggests that a partner does not have the right to dissociate at will. *Cf.* RUPA § 601(1) (providing a default rule of the right to dissociate upon "express will").

Contract read as a whole.—A court will not read specific terms out of context or in isolation. When possible, every part of the contract is read to have some meaning. An interpretation that results in superfluous terms is disfavored. As a corollary, words used throughout the contract are presumed to have a common meaning such that the contract is read as a whole and every part is integrated with common meanings.

Specific controls over general.—When a specific provision conflicts with a more general one, the specific controls because it is assumed to reflect the parties' intentions. For example, a charter agreement may provide these terms: (1) "unless otherwise provided in this agreement, the general partner shall have the sole discretion to make distributions from the annual profit"; (2) "cash distribution shall be made at the end of the year that shall be sufficient to provide for the payment of each partner's anticipated tax liability for the tax year." The second provision is more specific than the first, particularly in light of the qualifier "unless otherwise provided in this agreement," and thus it would control over the more general provision.

Contra proferentem.—Contracts are not always agreed upon after two parties, equally situated, negotiate for terms. Instead, one party may have bargaining power over the other, or the contract is presented as "take it or leave it." If the contract is ambiguous and thus susceptible to two reasonable interpretations, and if the party is deemed to not have negotiated for the agreement's terms, a court may apply the principle of *contra proferentem* and construe the ambiguous terms against the drafter. *See* Norton v. K-Sea Transp. Partners L.P., 67 A.3d 354, 360 (Del. 2013); SI Mgmt. L.P. v. Wininger, 707 A.2d 37, 43 (Del. 1998). It is incumbent upon the drafter to make terms clear.

The above contract principles apply to the interpretation of *written* agreements. Recall that the definition of a partnership agreement and an operating agreement may include oral and implied agreements as may be seen in the course of conduct. A written agreement may be supplemented by oral and implied agreements or terms because the existence of a written agreement does not necessarily mean that it constitutes the entire agreement among parties. In many contract disputes, extrinsic evidence may include oral statements and course of conduct, but in the context of NBE charter agreements they may be a part of the agreement itself, unless the written agreement explicitly provides that only the written agreement constitutes the entire charter agreement.

CHRYSLER GROUP LLC OPERATING AGREEMENT

Section 12.3 Entire Agreement. This Agreement and the other documents referred to herein, constitute the entire agreement among the parties and contain all of the agreements among the parties with respect to the subject matter hereof as of the date of this Agreement and supersede all prior agreements, undertakings and negotiations (in each case, both oral and written) between the parties concerning the subject matter herein. Failure by any party hereto to enforce any covenant, duty, agreement, term or condition of this Agreement, or to exercise any right hereunder, shall not be construed as thereafter waiving such covenant, duty, term, condition or right; and in no event shall any course of dealing, custom or usage of trade modify, alter or supplement any term of this Agreement.

G. ISSUES TO CONSIDER FOR NBEs

1. WRITTEN CHARTER AGREEMENT

Only a few states require a written operating agreement. *E.g.,* New York Limited Liability Company Act § 102(u). Most statutes provide that the charter agreement can be in oral form or implied from conduct. *See, e.g.,* RUPA § 102(12) (stating that "partnership agreement" may be in form of "oral, implied, in a record, or in any combination thereof"); RULLCA § 102(13) (same as to "operating agreement"). As a matter of best practice, the entity should have a *written* charter agreement, even if the charter largely mimics the statute. Without one, an entity must rely on ambiguous terms based on oral or implied understanding that might be easily contestable and, unless privately resolved, a contestable fact must be resolved through judicial fact-finding. A written agreement is no guarantee that it will be unambiguous, but in many cases when they were well drafted courts find them to be clear and unambiguous.

An executed written agreement would also comport with a state's statute of frauds.[9] The uniform statutes do not provide a rule on whether the charter agreement is exempt from the statute of frauds. Some state statutes specifically exempt partnership or operating agreements from the statute of frauds. *E.g.,* Delaware Limited Liability Company Act § 18–101(7) ("limited liability company agreement is not subject to any statute of frauds"); Florida Revised Limited Liability Company Act § 605.0106(b) (same); Colorado Limited Liability Company Act § 7–80–108(5) (same); New Hampshire Revised Limited Liability Company Act § 303–C:44 (same). However, other states may not provide a specific exemption from the statute of frauds or the law is not clear. *E.g.,* Olson v. Halvorsen, 986 A.2d 1150, 1159–62 (Del. 2009) (holding that "the statute of frauds applies to LLC agreements" in a decision prior to an amendment of the Delaware statute that exempts operating agreements from the statute of frauds). The best practice is: *Put it in writing.*

2. AMENDMENT OF CHARTER AGREEMENT

A charter agreement that suits needs now may not do so in the future. It may need to be amended to accommodate the dissociation or admission of an owner and changes in management structure, financial rights, fiduciary duties, etc. How can it be amended? *See* RUPA § 401(k) ("An

[9] The statute of frauds may apply in various context, including long duration service agreements and real estate transactions. *See* 6 Del.C. 2714(a) (requiring writing for "any contract or sale of lands, tenements, or any interest in or concerning them, or upon any agreement that is not to be performed within the space of 1 year from the making thereof").

amendment to the partnership agreement may be undertaken only with the affirmative vote or consent of all of the partners."); ULPA (2001) § 406(b)(1) (same); RULLCA § 407(b)(4)(B),(c)(3)(B) (same as to members). What should be the threshold vote on an amendment?

Unanimity works better when there are fewer voters. It becomes more unworkable with increasing number of voters. Once the number of voters reaches double digits, unanimity becomes practically unworkable. With many voters, the voting threshold should be supermajority or majority. Since the charter agreement is the fundamental contract that determines the rights and obligations of owners, one consideration is whether it should be easy to amend. Amendment may adversely change the rights of some owners, for example minority owners. If the owners deem this situation to be a potential problem, a supermajority voting requirement may provide the proper balance. Depending on the number of voters, the supermajority threshold can be anything, for example from 60% to 90%.

Should be a non-owner have a say in the amendment? *See* RULLCA § 107(a) ("The operating agreement may specify that its amendment requires the approval of a person that is not a party to the agreement or the satisfaction of a condition."). A creditor can try to negotiate veto rights when providing credit. It may seek a right to vote for an amendment of the charter agreement if such amendment would affect the credit contract. Such a right would have to be negotiated as a covenant of the original credit contract or an amendment thereof. In a more likely situation, a non-owner manager may have a significant interest in the charter agreement. She may wish to have a vote on an amendment, and the vote can be as a part of the collective whole with the owners or as a separate class vote of managers. Lastly, non-owners may have limited voting rights: for example, creditors can only vote on matters specifically related to their credit interest, or managers can only vote on certain specified matters such as financing, management structure, or fundamental transactions.

In light of the many cases in which there are purportedly different versions of charter agreement and amendments, the best practice is: *Have a clear amendment procedure and keep track of records.*

3. ASSENT TO THE CHARTER AGREEMENT

The charter agreement is a form of contract. Who is bound by it? Execution of a charter agreement would bind a party, but most statutes do not require a written charter agreement. Some statutes provide that the charter agreement is the agreement among owners. *See, e.g.,* RULLCA § 106(b) (providing that a "person that becomes a member is deemed to assent to the operating agreement"); New Hampshire Revised Limited Liability Company Act § 304–C:41 (same); Delaware Limited Liability Company Act § 18–101(7) ("member or manager or an assignee is bound by the limited liability company agreement whether or not the member or manager or assignee executes the limited liability company agreement"). If the statute does not address the issue, parties to the agreement should affirmatively execute the agreement.

The entity can also be bound by the charter agreement. Some statutes provide that the entity need not execute a charter agreement to be bound by it. *E.g.*, RULLCA § 106(a) (providing that a "limited liability company is bound by and may enforce the operating agreement, whether or not the company has itself manifested assent to the operating agreement"); Delaware Limited Liability Company Act § 18–101(7) (same); New Hampshire Revised Limited Liability Company Act § 304–C:42 (same). Absent a statutory provision, the question of whether the entity is bound and can enforce the charter agreement is subject to case law, which may diverge. *Compare* Tover v. 419 OCR, Inc., 921 N.E.2d 1249, 1254–55 (Ill. App. 2010) (holding that LLC is not a party to the operating agreement and thus is not bound by the arbitration clause therein unless it is a signatory), *with* Elf Atochem N. Am., Inc. v. Jaffari, 727 A.2d 286, 293 (Del. 1999) (holding that the LLC is bound by the arbitration clause in the operating agreement even though it was not a signatory). If the statute does not address the issue, the parties should affirmatively resolve the question of whether the entity should be a party to the charter agreement. If the entity is not a party to the agreement and a court determines so, among other effects, it cannot enforce the charter agreement. The easiest solution to the issue is to have the LLC execute the agreement as a party.

4. STRUCTURE OF THE CHARTER AGREEMENT

In terms of drafting the charter agreement, the broad organization can be gleaned from the statute. In practice, most lawyers will not draft a charter agreement from scratch. Like much of transactional practice, lawyers will start with a template form of some kind, such as a model agreement or a document used in prior transactions, and then tailor the agreement to the specific client needs. By providing default rules, the statutes identify most of the issues that lawyers and owners should consider. If so, the organizational framework of the charter agreement can and often do track, if only loosely, the subject matters covered in the applicable statute. Consider the organization in the table of contents of the Chrysler Group LLC's operating agreement.

ARTICLE I: DEFINITIONS

Section 1.1 Specific Definitions

Section 1.2 Other Definitions

ARTICLE II: ORGANIZATIONAL MATTERS; GENERAL PROVISIONS

Section 2.1 Name

Section 2.2 Formation and Continuation

Section 2.3 Purposes

Section 2.4 Powers

Section 2.5 Principal Business Office
Section 2.6 Registered Agent
Section 2.7 Limited Liability
Section 2.8 Duration
Section 2.9 Filings; Qualification in Other Jurisdictions

ARTICLE III: CAPITALIZATION; MEMBERSHIP INTERESTS

Section 3.1 Membership Interests; Capitalization; Capital Accounts
Section 3.2 Application of Article 8 of the Uniform Commercial Code
Section 3.3 Certification of Membership Interests

ARTICLE IV: CONTRIBUTION; ALLOCATIONS; DISTRIBUTIONS

Section 4.1 Additional Contributions
Section 4.2 Allocation of Profits and Losses
Section 4.3 Tax Matters
Section 4.4 Distributions

ARTICLE V: BOARD OF MANAGERS; OFFICERS

Section 5.1 Establishment of Board of Directors
Section 5.2 General Powers of the Board of Directors
Section 5.3 Election of Directors
Section 5.4 Meetings
Section 5.5 Notice of Meetings
Section 5.6 Quorum
Section 5.7 Voting
Section 5.8 Action Without a Meeting; Telephonic Meetings
Section 5.9 Compensation of Directors; Expense Reimbursement
Section 5.10 Committees of the Board of Directors
Section 5.11 Delegation of Authority
Section 5.12 Officers
Section 5.13 Standard of Care; Fiduciary Duties; Liability of Directors and Officers

ARTICLE VI: INDEMNIFICATION

Section 6.1 General Indemnity
Section 6.2 Rights Non-Exclusive
Section 6.3 Merger or Consolidation; Other Entities
Section 6.4 No Member Recourse

ARTICLE VII: ADMISSION OF ADDITIONAL MEMBERS

Section 7.1 Admission Requirements
Section 7.2 Acceptance of Prior Acts
Section 7.3 Transfers; Admission of Transferees

ARTICLE VIII: DISSOLUTION

Section 8.1 In General
Section 8.2 Reasonable Time for Winding Up

ARTICLE IX: RIGHTS AND DUTIES OF MEMBERS

Section 9.1 Members
Section 9.2 No Member Fiduciary Duties

ARTICLE X: MEETINGS OF MEMBERS

Section 10.1 Meetings of the Members

Section 10.2 Notice of Meetings
Section 10.3 Adjournments
Section 10.4 Quorum
Section 10.5 Organization
Section 10.6 Waiver of Notice of Meetings of Members
Section 10.7 Determination of Members of Record
ARTICLE XI: INFORMATION RIGHTS; BOOKS AND RECORDS
Section 11.1 Schedule of Members
Section 11.2 Books and Records; Other Documents
Section 11.3 Reports and Audits
Section 11.4 Financial Statements and Other Information
Section 11.5 Independent Auditor
ARTICLE XII: MISCELLANEOUS PROVISIONS
Section 12.1 Separability of Provision
Section 12.2 Notices
Section 12.3 Entire Agreement
Section 12.4 Governing Law
Section 12.5 Amendments
Section 12.6 Sole Benefit of Members
Section 12.7 Independent Contractors; Expenses
Section 12.8 Creditors
Section 12.9 Further Action
Section 12.10 Delivery by Facsimile or Email
Section 12.11 Interpretative Matters
DEFINITIONS ADDENDUM
SCHEDULE OF MEMBERS
ANNEX A—Form of Certificate
ANNEX B—Schedule of Authority

H. PROBLEM: ENTREPRENEURS CONSIDER FORMING A FIRM

After working hard on developing the business plan for their startup business in the spring semester, Piers and Blake graduated from business school with their MBAs. They built a rudimentary website, but still did not have an operating business. There was much to do in terms of figuring out the business problems of selling eyeglasses over the internet. Their finance professor, Professor Morgan Money, recommended that they need to think about the legal issues of starting up a business. Neither quite understood what this meant. Money suggested a visit to business attorney Lynn Law, who specializes in advising entrepreneurs and startups.

A week later, Piers and Blake met Law. They explained the basic business idea. They also characterized their business relationship: "We're partners. We have been friends since high school, and we originated this idea together. We're committed to this business, and we're in it together as partners in this startup."

During this conversation, Piers and Blake raised several issues related to how they want to set up their entrepreneurial venture.

Piers: "Both Blake and I were software engineers before business school. We can create the software architecture for this internet business."

Blake: "Prior to business school, I was also a part-time inventor. Inventing things was a hobby of mine. I was awarded several patents related to new ways to make hinges on fine delicate things like eyeglass frames, mechanical toys, and surgical devices. I think these patents can be used to make different kinds of glass frames that we can market under our brand. I'm willing to let our business use my patents."

Piers and Blake presented their business idea. Law listened intently.

Law: "I see. The idea sounds really exciting. Congratulations on the new venture. . . . So what can I do to help you?"

Piers and Blake traded uncertain glances.

Piers: "Well, we're not sure. Our finance professor recommended that we come see you. That's why we're here. We're businesspeople. We're not lawyers obviously. We think that we should form a company."

Law nodded: "Yes."

Blake: "So what do we need to do?"

QUESTIONS

1. Are there specific issues related to Law's potential representation of Piers and Blake?

2. What additional facts does Law need to continue the counseling process?

3. Counsel Piers and Blake on the information necessary to inform them of the legal issues relevant to the startup of their entrepreneurial venture.

4. What are the issues related to Blake's patents? Conceptualize the issues using the Hansmann-Kraakman concept of asset partitioning.

5. Explain the significance of the charter agreement to Piers and Blake.

CHAPTER 3

LIABILITY TO THIRD PARTIES

■ ■ ■

A. RULE OF LIMITED LIABILITY IN CORPORATIONS

1. SHIELD AGAINST VICARIOUS LIABILITY

The rule of limited liability precludes vicarious liability to owners of businesses. It states that a person cannot be held vicariously liable for the debts and obligations of a limited liability entity, such as a corporation or an LLC, solely by reason of one's status as a limited partner, member, manager, or shareholder. The rule of limited liability shields a person from vicarious liability based on one's status in the firm. It provides a floor on the potential downside risk of an investment in a firm.

The rule does not shield a person from *direct* liability for his or her own conduct. If a shareholder—or a limited partner or member or manager—commits a tort, she is not relieved of liability under the rule of limited liability (though she may be indemnified by the firm or covered by the firm's liability insurance).

The most fundamental rule of corporation law is that shareholders have limited liability. They are not held liable for the debts and obligations of the corporation solely on account of their status as shareholders. For example, when the Enron Corporation filed for bankruptcy, a shareholder is not liable for the company's debts and obligations and cannot be brought into an action by Enron creditors to satisfy their debts. When there is no limited liability, the owner would be held personally liable to the firm's creditors for the firm's debts and obligations. Shareholders are subject to a maximum loss of their investment, and no more.

DGCL § 102. Contents of Certificate of Incorporation

(b)(6) The stockholders of a corporation shall not be personally liable for the payment of the corporation's debts except as they may be liable by reason of their own conduct or acts;

MBCA § 6.22. Liability of Shareholders

(b) A shareholder of a corporation is not personally liable for any liabilities of the corporation (including liabilities arising from acts of the corporation) except that a shareholder may become personally liable by reason of the shareholder's own acts or conduct.

Historically, when the universe of business entities composed of the corporation and the partnership, limited liability was a foundational rule of corporation law. Partners in a general partnership did not and still do not have limited liability. They control their liability by actively managing the firm and monitoring its activities. Shareholders are passive investors in a company managed by the board of directors and officers. They cannot control the firm's liabilities through participation in management. Limited liability permits disparate, passive shareholders to invest in corporations without the fear that liability may be imposed on them for more money than the amount of the investment—a potentially risky proposition that may dissuade some investors altogether.

What specific characteristics of limited liability promote investment in firms? The following excerpt provides a summary of the benefits.

BONDING LIMITED LIABILITY

Robert J. Rhee, 51 William & Mary Law Review 1417 (2010)

Even the strongest proponents of limited liability recognize risk externalization is undesirable, but they argue that limited liability is justified because its many benefits outweigh the cost. These benefits are well known to most informed readers and only a short recital is necessary.

Limited liability decreases the cost of monitoring. A diversified shareholder need not closely monitor the managers of all companies in the investment portfolio. Limited liability also reduces the cost of monitoring other shareholders. In a world of unlimited liability, the expected return of each shareholder would be a function of the personal wealth of other shareholders. With limited liability, share prices reflect only information about the potential returns of corporate assets, rather than inaccessible, nonstandard information such as shareholder wealth. The rule creates a fungible, commoditized share, which promotes free transferability. Share liquidity creates a market for corporate control. Share prices correspond to quality of management, incentivizing agents to efficiently manage corporations. With personal liability, most investors would hold the least number of securities because any single bankruptcy could potentially wipe out their personal wealth. Limited liability incentivizes diversification, reducing an investor's exposure to firm specific risk. The ability to diversify also allows managers in turn to pursue any positive net present value project, thus increasing the overall return on any given portfolio.

These combined effects increase the value of the firm in several ways. They reduce agency cost, specifically the cost of monitoring by passive investors. Limited liability also reduces the cost of capital. The cost of equity is reduced when shares are freely alienable and there is a liquid market. The cost of debt is lowered because limited liability reduces the transaction cost of credit by providing a standard default contract term. These cost savings can then be directed toward economically productive activities of the firm. Lastly, we should not forget that the cost of equity is reduced as well because firms can externalize some of the cost of their activities to tort victims. While proponents of limited liability do not tout this reason, for it is obviously unappealing, tort victims clearly subsidize limited liability enterprises. Thus, proponents of limited liability argue that the rule is economically efficient and increases social wealth.

2. TRADITIONAL VEIL PIERCING IN CORPORATIONS

Courts occasionally set aside the rule of limited liability and permit creditors to seek claims directly against shareholders. Veil piercing is an equitable remedy. A creditor seeks it when the corporation does not have assets to satisfy its claim and it seeks to hold shareholders personally liable. Such a claim confronts the rule of limited liability. The rule exists for the purpose of shielding shareholders from the debts and obligations of the corporations and thus limiting their loss to the amount of the investment only. Veil piercing is an exception to the rule, and courts do not apply it casually. It permits creditors to pierce the corporate veil and thereby reach the personal assets of shareholders.

The cases below illustrate the doctrine of veil piercing. In reading these cases, consider these questions: (1) Is the fact that a corporation is ex post undercapitalized a basis to pierce the veil? (2) What are the factors that courts apply to determine whether to pierce the corporate veil?

WALKOVSZKY V. CARLTON

223 N.E.2d 6 (N.Y. 1966)

FULD, JUDGE.

This case involves what appears to be a rather common practice in the taxicab industry of vesting the ownership of a taxi fleet in many corporations, each owning only one or two cabs.

The complaint alleges that the plaintiff was severely injured four years ago in New York City when he was run down by a taxicab owned by the defendant Seon Cab Corporation and negligently operated. The individual defendant, Carlton, is claimed to be a stockholder of 10 corporations, including Seon, each of which has but two cabs registered in its name, and it is implied that only the minimum automobile liability insurance required by law (in the amount of $10,000) is carried on any one cab. Although seemingly independent of one another, these corporations are alleged to be "operated as a single entity, unit and enterprise" with regard to financing, supplies, repairs, employees and garaging, and all are named as defendants. The plaintiff asserts that he is also entitled to hold their stockholders personally liable for the damages sought because the multiple corporate structure constitutes an unlawful attempt "to defraud members of the general public" who might be injured by the cabs.

The defendant Carlton has moved to dismiss the complaint on the ground that as to him it "fails to state a cause of action." The court granted the motion but the Appellate Division reversed, holding that a valid cause of action was sufficiently stated. The defendant Carlton appeals to us.

The law permits the incorporation of a business for the very purpose of enabling its proprietors to escape personal liability but, manifestly, the privilege is not without its limits. Broadly speaking, the courts will disregard the corporate form, or, to use accepted terminology, "pierce the corporate veil," whenever necessary "to prevent fraud or to achieve equity." In determining whether liability should be extended to reach assets beyond those belonging to the corporation, we are guided, as Judge Cardozo noted, by "general rules of agency." In other words, whenever anyone uses control of the corporation to further his own rather than the corporation's business, he will be liable for the corporation's acts "upon the principle of Respondeat superior applicable even where the agent is a natural person." Such liability, moreover, extends not only to the corporation's commercial dealings but to its negligent acts as well.

The plaintiff has explicitly alleged that none of the corporations "had a separate existence of their own" and all are named as defendants. However, it is one thing to assert that a corporation is a fragment of a larger corporate combine which actually conducts the business. It is quite another to claim that the corporation is a "dummy" for its individual stockholders who are in reality carrying on the business in their personal capacities for purely personal rather than corporate ends. Either circumstance would justify treating the corporation as an agent and piercing the corporate veil to reach the principal but a different result would follow in each case. In the first, only a larger corporate entity would be held financially responsible while, in the other, the stockholder would be personally liable. Either the stockholder is conducting the business in his individual capacity or he is not. If he is, he will be liable; if he is not, then it does not matter—insofar as his personal liability is concerned—that the enterprise is actually being carried on by a larger "enterprise entity."

Reading the complaint in this case most favorably and liberally, we do not believe that there can be gathered from its averments the allegations required to spell out a valid cause of action against the defendant Carlton.

The individual defendant is charged with having "organized, managed, dominated and controlled" a fragmented corporate entity but there are no allegations that he was conducting business in his individual capacity. Had the taxicab fleet been owned by a single corporation, it would be readily apparent that the plaintiff would face formidable barriers in attempting to establish personal liability on the part of the corporation's stockholders. The fact that the fleet ownership has been deliberately split up among many corporations does not ease the plaintiff's burden. The corporate form may not be disregarded merely because the assets of the corporation, together with the mandatory insurance coverage, are insufficient to assure him the recovery sought. If Carlton were to be held individually liable on those facts alone, the decision would apply equally to the thousands of cabs which are owned by individual drivers who conduct their businesses through corporations and carry the minimum insurance required by the Vehicle and Traffic Law. These taxi owner-operators are entitled to form such corporations, and we agree that, if the insurance coverage required by statute "is inadequate for the protection of the public, the remedy lies not with the courts but with the Legislature."

The principle relied upon in the complaint to sustain the imposition of personal liability is not agency but fraud. If it is not fraudulent for the owner-operator of a single cab corporation to take out only the minimum required liability insurance, the enterprise does not become either illicit or fraudulent merely because it consists of many such corporations. The plaintiff's injuries are the same regardless of whether the cab which strikes him is owned by a single corporation or part of a fleet with ownership fragmented among many corporations. Whatever rights he may be able to assert against parties other than the registered owner of the vehicle come into being not because he has been defrauded but because, under the principle of respondeat superior, he is entitled to hold the whole enterprise responsible for the acts of its agents.

The complaint falls short of adequately stating a cause of action against Carlton in his individual capacity.

NOTES

1. Walkovszky involved a small business operating a bunch of taxi cabs. But can it be a microcosm for large corporate groups? What are the implications on corporate groups if the court held the other way and pierced the veil?

2. Should an intent to cabin in the risk of insolvency be a basis to pierce the veil? Suppose the veil is pierced in this case. How do we distinguish this case from the case where the owner of the company really only has two taxi cabs?

3. It is important to understand that ex post undercapitalization resulting in unsatisfied creditors is not a basis to pierce the veil. *See* In re Thornton, 2020 WL 1042027, at *5 (Bankr. C.D. Ill. 2020) ("Although insolvency is a factor to be considered, the failure of a business, in and of itself, is not determinative of whether the veil of a corporation or limited liability company should be pierced. If it were, then the veil of every failed entity could be pierced,

and the limited liability associated with corporations and limited liability companies would be rendered meaningless.").

ORT ASSOCIATES V. IBC SERVICES, INC.

801 A.2d 407 (N.J. App. 2002)

PRESSLER, P.J.A.D.

The single dispositive issue raised by this appeal is whether the trial court, based on its findings of fact following a bench trial, was justified, as a matter of law, in piercing the corporate veil and thus holding a parent corporation liable for the debt incurred by its wholly owned subsidiary. We are satisfied that the facts, both undisputed and as found, present a textbook illustration of circumstances mandating corporate-veil piercing.

Plaintiff OTR Associates, a limited partnership, owns a shopping mall in Edison, New Jersey, in which it leased space in 1985 for use by a Blimpie franchisee, Samyrna, Inc., a corporation owned by Sam Iskander and his wife. The franchise agreement, styled as a licensing agreement, had been entered into in 1984 between Samyrna and the parent company, then known as International Blimpie Corporation. The three names denote the same corporation at different stages of its existence, and we refer to it hereafter as Blimpie. Blimpie was the sole owner of a subsidiary named IBC Services, Inc. (IBC), created for the single purpose of holding the lease on premises occupied by a Blimpie franchisee. Accordingly, it was IBC that entered into the lease with OTR and, on the same day and apparently with OTR's consent, subleased the space to the franchisee. The history of the tenancy was marked by regular and increasingly substantial rent arrearages, and it was terminated by a dispossess judgment and warrant for removal. OTR commenced this action for unpaid rent, then in the amount of close to $150,000, against Blimpie under both its present name and its former name, International Blimpie Corporation. It also joined as defendants the leasing subsidiary, IBC, as well as Garden State Blimpie, Inc., another wholly-owned leaseholding subsidiary of Blimpie to whom IBC had assigned the lease without notice to the landlord in violation of the terms of the lease requiring such notice. The action was tried and judgment was entered in favor of OTR against Blimpie as well as the two judgment-proof subsidiaries in the full amount of the rent arrearages plus interest thereon, then some $208,000. Blimpie appeals, and we affirm.

We consider the well-settled principles respecting corporate-veil piercing. Nearly three-quarters of a century ago, the Court of Errors and Appeals made clear that while "ownership alone of capital stock in one corporation by another, does not create any relationship that by reason of which the stockholding company would be liable for torts of the other," nevertheless "where a corporation holds stock of another, not for the purpose of participating in the affairs of the other corporation, in the normal and usual manner, but for the purpose of control, so that the subsidiary company may be used as a mere agency or instrumentality for the stockholding company, such company will be liable for injuries due to the negligence of the subsidiary." The conceptual basis of the rule is simply that "it is where the corporate form is used as a shield behind which injustice is sought to be done by those who have control of it that equity penetrates the [corporate] veil." And, as the Supreme Court phrased it, "the purpose of the doctrine of piercing the corporate veil is to prevent an independent corporation from being used to defeat the ends of justice, to perpetrate fraud, to accomplish a crime, or otherwise to evade the law."

The basic finding that must be made to enable the court to pierce the corporate veil is "that the parent so dominated the subsidiary that it had no separate existence but was merely a conduit for the parent." But beyond domination, the court must also find that the "parent has abused the privilege of incorporation by using the subsidiary to perpetrate a fraud or injustice, or otherwise to circumvent the law." And the hallmarks of that abuse are typically the engagement of the subsidiary in no independent business of its own but exclusively the performance of a service for the parent and, even more importantly, the undercapitalization of the subsidiary rendering it judgment-proof.

Blimpie concedes that it formed IBC for the sole purpose of holding the lease on the premises of a Blimpie franchisee. It is also clear that IBC had virtually no assets other than the lease itself, which, in the circumstances, was not an asset at all but only a liability since IBC had no independent right to alienate its interest therein but was subject to Blimpie's exclusive control. It had no business premises of its own, sharing the New York address of Blimpie. It had no income other than the rent payments by the franchisee, which appear to have been made directly to OTR. It does not appear that it had its own employees or office staff. We further note that Blimpie not only retained the right to approve the premises to be occupied by the franchisee and leased by IBC, but itself, in its Georgia headquarters, managed all the leases held by its subsidiaries on franchisee premises. As explained by Charles Leaness, presently Executive Vice President of Blimpie and formerly corporate counsel as well as vice-president and secretary of IBC, in 1996, the year of IBC's eviction for non-payment of rent, he was Blimpie's Corporate Counsel Compliance Officer. Blimpie, he testified, is exclusively a franchising corporation with "hundreds and hundreds" of leases held by its wholly-owned leasehold companies, which are, however, overseen by Blimpie's administrative assistants, that is "people in our organization that do this [communicate with landlords] as their everyday job. Because we have—you know—there are various leases, various assignments." Leaness also made clear that the leasing companies, whose function he explained as assisting franchisees in negotiating leases, "don't make a profit. There's no profit made in a leasehold."

Domination and control by Blimpie of IBC is patent and was not, nor could have been, reasonably disputed. The question then is whether Blimpie abused the privilege of incorporation by using IBC to commit a fraud or injustice or other improper purpose. We agree with the trial judge that the evidence overwhelmingly requires an affirmative answer. The *leit motif* of the testimony of plaintiff's partners who were involved in the dealings with IBC was that they believed that they were dealing with Blimpie, the national and financially responsible franchising company, and never discovered the fact of separate corporate entities until after the eviction. While it is true that IBC never apparently expressly claimed to be Blimpie, it not only failed to explain its relationship to Blimpie as a purported independent company but it affirmatively, intentionally, and calculatedly led OTR to believe it was Blimpie. Illustratively, when OTR was pre-leasing space in the mall, the first approach to it was the appearance at its on-site office of two men in Blimpie uniforms who announced that they wanted to open a Blimpie sandwich shop. One of the men was the franchisee, Iskander. The other was never identified but presumably was someone with a connection to Blimpie. It is also true that the named tenant in the lease was IBC Services, Inc., but the tenant was actually identified in the first paragraph of the lease as "IBC Services, Inc. having an address at c/o International Blimpie Corporation, 1414 Avenue of the Americas, New York, New York." It hardly required a cryptographer to draw the entirely reasonable inference that IBC stood for International Blimpie Corporation, Blimpie's corporate name when the lease was executed. The suggestion, unmistakably, was that IBC was either the corporate name or a trading-as name and that International Blimpie Corporation was the other of these two possibilities.

The correspondence through the years between plaintiff and the entity it believed to be its tenant confirmed plaintiff's belief that Blimpie was its tenant. Blimpie's letters to OTR were on stationary headed only by the Blimpie logo. There is nothing in any of that correspondence that would have suggested the existence of an independent company standing between the franchisor and the franchisee, and the correspondence received by OTR from its lessee referred to the sub-tenant, Samyrna, as "our franchisee."

The inference is ineluctable and virtually conceded by Blimpie that IBC was created as a judgment-proof corporation for the sole purpose of insulating Blimpie from any liability on the lease in the event of the franchisee's default, a purpose found by the trial judge to have been deliberately concealed by Blimpie by its conduct in creating the impression from the outset of the tenancy relationship and throughout its duration that it and IBC were one and the same. We reject Blimpie's contention of the irrelevancy of its conduct after execution of the lease that tended to confirm to plaintiff that it was the actual tenant. The franchisee was habitually late and in arrears in its rent payments. We think it clear that if OTR had any suspicion that its tenant was a judgment-proof corporation, it would not have forborne over the years as the arrearages continued to accumulate but would have taken steps to regain possession long before the tenant's obligations reached $150,000.

Blimpie's asserts that it is entitled to the benefit of the separate corporate identities merely because IBC observed all the corporate proprieties—it had its own officers and directors albeit interlocking with Blimpie's, it filed annual reports, kept minutes, held meetings, and had a bank account. But that argument begs the question. The separate corporate shell created by Blimpie to avoid liability may have been mechanistically impeccable, but in every functional and operational sense, the subsidiary had no separate identity. It was moreover not intended to shield the parent from responsibility for its subsidiary's obligations but rather to shield the parent from its own obligations. And that is an evasion and an improper purpose, fraudulently conceived and executed. The corporate veil was properly pierced.

FREEMAN V. COMPLEX COMPUTING CO., INC.

119 F.3d 1044 (2d Cir. 1997)

MINER, CIRCUIT JUDGE:

Jason Glazier appeals from a judgment [on] claims made against him by Daniel Freeman. The claims were asserted under the provisions of a contract between Freeman and defendant Complex Computing Company, Inc. ("C3"). The court found that, although Glazier was neither an employee, officer, director, nor shareholder of C3, his control and dominion over C3 warranted the piercing of the corporate veil in order to impose personal liability upon him.

While pursuing graduate studies under a fellowship at Columbia University, Glazier co-developed computer software with potential commercial value and negotiated with Columbia to obtain a license for the software. Columbia apparently was unwilling to license software to a corporation of which Glazier was an officer, director, or shareholder. Columbia was willing to license the software to a corporation that retained Glazier as an independent contractor. The licensed corporation then could sublicense the product to others for profit.

C3 was incorporated, with an acquaintance of Glazier's as the sole shareholder and initial director, and Seth Akabas (a partner of Glazier's counsel in this action) as the president, treasurer and assistant secretary. Glazier, Inc., of which Glazier was the sole shareholder, entered into an agreement with C3 ("consulting agreement"). Under the consulting agreement, Glazier, Inc. was retained as an independent contractor (titled as C3's "Scientific Advisor") to develop and market Glazier's software, which was licensed from Columbia, and to provide support services to C3's clients. Glazier was designated the sole signatory on C3's bank account, and was given a written option to purchase all of C3's stock for $2,000.

C3 entered into an agreement with Freeman (the "C3-Freeman Agreement"), under which Freeman agreed to sell and license C3's computer software products for a five-year term. In exchange, C3 agreed to pay Freeman commissions on the revenue received by C3 over a ten-year period from the client-base developed by Freeman, including the revenue received from sales and licensing, maintenance and support services. The C3-Freeman Agreement included provisions relating to Freeman's compensation if C3 terminated the agreement prior to its expiration, or if C3 made a sale that did not result in revenues because of a future merger, consolidation, or stock acquisition.

Schedule 1 of the C3-Freeman Agreement listed the customers from whom Freeman would receive commissions. Although C3's president signed the C3-Freeman Agreement, Glazier personally signed the periodic amendments to Schedule 1.

C3 and Thomson Investment Software entered into a licensing agreement that granted Thomson exclusive worldwide sales and marketing rights of C3's products. Freeman contends that the licensing agreement resulted from efforts made by him over approximately nine months to bring the transaction to fruition.

C3 gave Freeman the notice of the termination of its agreement with him. The letter of termination, signed by Glazier, explained that C3's exercise of its option to terminate Freeman's employment was "an action to combat the overly generous termination clause we committed to, and to force a renegotiation of your sales contract."

Glazier was hired as Thomson Investment Software's Vice President and Director of Research and Development at a starting salary of $150,000 plus additional payments of "incentive compensation" based in part upon the revenues received by Thomson in connection with the sale or license of products developed by Glazier. On the same day, Thomson and C3 entered into an assets purchase agreement (the "Thomson Agreement" or "assets purchase agreement"). Thomson assumed C3's intellectual products, trademarks and tradenames. It also assumed most of the liabilities and obligations of existing agreements involving C3, including agreements with C3 customers such as Banker's Trust and Chemical Bank. The Thomson Agreement set forth a list of C3 agreements assumed by Thomson, but expressly excluded the C3-Freeman Agreement. Thomson paid a total of $750,000, from which Glazier was paid $450,000 as a "signing bonus" in connection with his new employment contract; and C3 was paid $300,000.

Freeman commenced the action giving rise to this appeal. Named as defendants were C3, Thomson, and Glazier. In his complaint Freeman alleged that C3 and Thomson terminated the licensing agreement and entered into the assets purchase agreement with the specific intent of depriving him of commissions due. Freeman asserted claims against C3 and, on successor liability theories, Thomson, for breach of contract. He sought relief from Glazier and Thomson for inducement of C3's alleged breach of contract and on a fraudulent conveyance theory.

Glazier contends that he should not be held personally liable under a veil-piercing theory because he is not a shareholder, officer, director, or employee of C3. We reject this argument.

New York courts have recognized for veil-piercing purposes the doctrine of equitable ownership, under which an individual who exercises sufficient control over the corporation may be deemed an "equitable owner," notwithstanding the fact that the individual is not a shareholder of the corporation. *See, e.g., Guilder v. Corinth Constr. Corp.*, 651 N.Y.S.2d 706, 707 (App. Div. 3d Dep't 1997) ("Even if the [principals] were not [the corporation's] legal owners, it is apparent that they dominated and controlled the corporation to such an extent that they may be considered its equitable owners."). A nonshareholder defendant may be, "in reality," the equitable owner of a corporation where the nonshareholder defendant "exercises considerable authority over [the corporation] to the point of completely disregarding the corporate form and acting as though [its] assets [are] his alone to manage and distribute."

Because Glazier "exercised considerable authority over [the corporation] to the point of completely disregarding the corporate form and acting as though [its] assets were his alone to manage and distribute," he is appropriately viewed as C3's equitable owner for veil-piercing purposes. If there were board meetings, no minutes were kept from August 1994 through May 1995. Glazier agreed to personally indemnify C3's sole shareholder and director against any liability arising from the performance of his duties as C3's director. The president of C3 never attended a meeting of the Board of Directors. No shareholder received dividends or other distributions, despite the corporate income of $563,257 in 1994 and $200,000 from the asset sale to Thomson.

Glazier used C3 to sell his intellectual product and powers, including the software that he had co-developed at Columbia and which Columbia licensed to C3. Through payments from C3 to Glazier, Inc., he received the vast majority of the resulting revenues. Both Glazier, Inc. and C3 were located at Glazier's apartment, and Glazier was the sole signatory on C3's bank account. Glazier, Inc.'s consulting agreement with C3 expressly provided that it was terminable if Glazier himself was unable to perform or supervise the performance of Glazier, Inc.'s obligations to C3, which were described as "marketing [C3's] software products, developing new software products, enhancing [C3's] existing software products, and providing support services to [C3's] clients." These obligations essentially described C3's entire business.

Glazier himself gave Thomson a resumé stating that Glazier was the principal, owner and manager of C3, and that Glazier, Inc. was the predecessor to C3. C3 paid over $8000 to the law firm that represented Glazier personally in his negotiations with Thomson. These negotiations resulted in Thomson employing Glazier and paying him a $450,000 signing bonus. C3 then paid Glazier, through Glazier, Inc., an additional $210,000 out of the proceeds of the assets and other funds that were in the C3 bank account following the assets purchase. After payment of taxes and other expenses, this left only $10,000 in C3's account. Freeman contends that this balance renders C3 unable to fulfill its alleged obligations to him. Additionally, Glazier had an option to purchase all the shares of C3 from its sole shareholder for $2000. Thus, at his discretion, he could have become the sole shareholder for a small payment.

The district court found that "to regard [Glazier] as anything but the sole stockholder and controlling person of C3 would be to exalt form over substance." Under the unique facts of the instant case, viewed in their totality, we agree that it is appropriate to treat Glazier as an "equitable owner" for veil-piercing purposes.

The presumption of corporate independence and limited shareholder liability serves to encourage business development. Nevertheless, that presumption will be set aside, and courts will pierce the corporate veil under certain limited circumstances. Specifically, such "liability may be predicated either upon a showing of fraud or upon complete control by the dominating [entity] that leads to a wrong against third parties." To pierce the corporate veil under New York law, a plaintiff must prove that "(1) [the owner] has exercised such control that the [corporation] has become a mere instrumentality of the [owner], which is the real actor; (2) such control has been used to commit a fraud or other wrong; and (3) the fraud or wrong results in an unjust loss or injury to plaintiff."

Veil-piercing will be allowed "in two broad situations: to prevent fraud or other wrong, or where a parent dominates and controls a subsidiary," the element of domination and control never was considered to be sufficient of itself to justify the piercing of a corporate veil. Unless the control is utilized to perpetrate a fraud or other wrong, limited liability will prevail. Even if a plaintiff showed that the dominator of a corporation had complete control over the corporation so that the corporation "had no separate mind, will, or existence of its own," New York law will not allow the corporate veil to be pierced in the absence of a showing that this control "was used to commit wrong, fraud, or the breach of a legal duty, or a dishonest and unjust act in contravention of plaintiff's legal rights, and that the control and breach of duty proximately caused the injury complained of."

In determining whether "complete control" exists, we have considered such factors as: (1) disregard of corporate formalities; (2) inadequate capitalization; (3) intermingling of funds; (4) overlap in ownership, officers, directors, and personnel; (5) common office space, address and telephone numbers of corporate entities; (6) the degree of discretion shown by the allegedly dominated corporation; (7) whether the dealings between the entities are at arms length; (8) whether the corporations are treated as independent profit centers; (9) payment or guarantee of the corporation's debts by the dominating entity, and (10) intermingling of property between the entities. No one factor is decisive. In this case, there is little question that Glazier exercised "complete control" over C3.

The record is replete with examples of Glazier's control over C3. The district court's finding of control was not erroneous. However, the district court erred in the decision to pierce C3's corporate veil solely on the basis of a finding of domination and control. "While complete domination of the corporation is the key to piercing the corporate veil, such domination, standing alone, is not enough; some showing of a wrongful or unjust act toward plaintiff is required." We remand to the district court the issue of whether Glazier used his control over C3 to commit a fraud or other wrong that resulted in unjust loss or injury to Freeman. Though there is substantial evidence of such wrongdoing, a finding on this issue must be made in the first instance by the district court before veil-piercing occurs. We therefore remand to the district court with instructions to determine whether Glazier used his control over C3 to commit a fraud or other wrong that resulted in an unjust loss or injury to Freeman.

NOTES

1. Other courts have applied the concept of equitable veil piercing. *See Fontana v. TLD Builders, Inc.*, 840 N.E.2nd 767, 778–81 (Ill.App. 2005) (holding that where a wife was the sole shareholder of the corporation, but where her non-owner husband exerted dominant control over the entity, the husband could be construed as the "equitable owner" of the company such that there was adequate "unity of interest and ownership" to allow piercing the corporate veil and hold the husband personally liable); Mattingly Law Firm, P.C. v. Henson, 466 P.3d 590, 597 (Oka.App. 2019) ("We find that the extension of the 'equitable ownership doctrine' to the piercing the veil analysis is consistent with principles of fairness and efficiency valued in Oklahoma corporate law. Applying the equitable ownership analysis here, we hold that Henson was an equitable owner of both Henson Farms LLC and Henson Insurance Group LLC.").

B. RULE OF LIMITED LIABILITY IN NBEs

1. GENERAL PARTNERSHIP

Unlike corporation law, partnership law does not provide partners with the benefit of limited liability. A partner is jointly and severally liable for the debts and obligations of the partnership. RUPA § 306(a). In the era before the LLC, when the choice of business form was basically between a partnership and a corporation, limited liability was a key consideration.

> Unlike a corporation that acts through its officers and directors, who may or may not be shareholders, partnerships act through their partners. Shareholders in a corporation are insulated from personal liability for acts of the corporation, but partners in a partnership are not insulated from liability. Stated differently, no corporate veil exists between a general partnership and its partners.

Ron Medlin Constr. v. Harris, 704 S.E.2d 486, 490 (N.C. 2010).

In the 1990s, states permitted the creation of a limited liability partnership (LLP). An LLP is simply a general partnership where the partners have limited liability, by virtue of filing with the state, to become a limited liability entity. *See* RUPA § 306(c).

RUPA § 306. Partner's Liability.

(a) Except as otherwise provided in subsections (b) and (c), all partners are liable jointly and severally for all debts, obligations, and other liabilities of the partnership unless otherwise agreed by the claimant or provided by law.

(b) A person that becomes a partner is not personally liable for a debt, obligation, or other liability of the partnership incurred before the person became a partner.

(c) A debt, obligation, or other liability of a partnership incurred while the partnership is a limited liability partnership is solely the debt, obligation, or other liability of the limited liability partnership. A partner is not personally liable, directly or indirectly, by way of contribution or otherwise, for a debt, obligation, or other liability of the limited liability partnership solely by reason of being or acting as a partner.

Arguably, the biggest drawback of forming a general partnership is the lack of limited liability. If a partnership is the chosen form, one must consider how to deal with the liability question. An answer might be that the partners themselves are limited liability entities. A partner can be any "person," who can be a legal person. RUPA § 102(10), (14). For example, Google and Facebook form the partnership G-F Partners. But this seems inefficient. Why expose their assets to the liabilities of G-F Partners? Why not simply form G-F LLC and thereby partition their assets from its liabilities? Even if Google and Facebook are enormous companies, they should still husband their assets.

Maybe G-F Partners is not concerned about liabilities. There might be several reasons for thinking this. It believes that its activities would not produce liabilities. But this is Pollyannaish since even the simple task of driving a car can potentially produce large liabilities and the potential liabilities of a technological venture like G-F Partners may be unknown. The firm can be well capitalized. But this presumes one's ability to divine the future and eliminate all risk. The firm can purchase cadillac insurance. Insurance is considered a form of capital (or more precisely insurance can substitute for capital because absent insurance, a firm may need to hold more capital). Or, due to the combination of these factors, the firm perhaps reasonably believes that the personal liabilities of partners can be managed. But even if this was the case, Google and Facebook must still contend with the question: Does a cost-benefit analysis justify the minimal administrative cost of filing to create a limited liability entity? In many (most) cases, the answer would be "yes."

If persons want to form a general partnership, there is the option of an LLP, which is created through a filing.[1] The LLP formed developed in the early 1990s in the wake of the bank and savings and loan failures in Texas, which has the spillover effect of potential liability against law and accounting firms, most of which were organized as partnerships. *See* Robert W. Hamilton, *Registered Limited Liability Partnerships: Present at Birth (Nearly)*, 66 U. Colo. L. Rev. 1065 (1995) (providing a history of the development of the LLP in all states in the wake of the failure of financial institutions in Texas in the 1980s and early 1990s). Partnership law permits the creation of an LLP.[2] Some states limit the type of businesses LLPs can conduct to professional services. *E.g.*, California Uniform Partnership Act § 16101(8)(A) (limited to "the practice of architecture, the practice of public accountancy, the practice of engineering, the practice of land surveying, or the practice of law"); New York Partnership Law § 121–1500(a)(1) (limited to "a partnership without limited partners each of whose partners is a professional authorized by law to render a professional service within this state"); Oregon Revised Partnership Act § 67.600(a)(1) (limited to a firm that "Renders professional service").

If the LLP is generally available to any business, is it functionally equal to an LLC for the purpose of entity choice? The answer is "no"—otherwise, the LLC would have had no commercial purpose. Instead, the

---

[1] *See* RUPA § 901(b)–(c) (requiring a vote of all partners and thereafter "a partnership may become a limited liability partnership by delivering to the [Secretary of State] for filing a statement of qualification").

[2] Certain regulated activities, external to laws of business organizations, may prohibit the use of particular forms of business entities. For example, some states prohibit banking or insurance activities through a partnership or an LLC. *E.g.*, Arizona Limited Liability Company Act § 29–609(a)–(b) (prohibiting banking and insurance); California Revised Limited Liability Company Act § 17701.04(b) (same); Delaware Limited Liability Company Act § 18–106(a) (prohibiting banking); New Hampshire Revised Limited Liability Company Act § 304–C:21 (prohibiting banking, railroad and insurance businesses). But some states permit these activities. *E.g.*, Nevada Limited Liability Company Act § 86.171(6) (permitting banking). If a business activity is regulated, the business lawyer who is not a specialist in the field must also consult with a specialist to ensure that the business structure is consistent with external regulation.

market for LLCs rapidly grew. When considering the entity form, *all aspects* of the entity must be considered. Partnerships, including LLPs, and LLCs differ in fundamental ways.

2. LIMITED PARTNERSHIP

An LP requires a dual class ownership structure. The general partner manages the firm, and the limited partner is a passive investor. This requirement explains the liability rules. A limited partner has limited liability, but a general partner does not. In some states, the rule has an exception: A limited partner who participates in the control of the LP can lose the limited liability protection because he is functionally a manager. In a minority of jurisdiction, a general partner can also acquire the benefit of limited liability alongside the limited partner.

ULPA (2001) § 303. No Liability as Limited Partner for Limited Partnership Obligations.

(a) A debt, obligation, or other liability of a limited partnership is not the debt, obligation, or other liability of a limited partner. A limited partner is not personally liable, directly or indirectly, by way of contribution or otherwise, for a debt, obligation, or other liability of the partnership solely by reason of being or acting as a limited partner, even if the limited partner participates in the management and control of the limited partnership. This subsection applies regardless of the dissolution of the partnership.

(b) The failure of a limited partnership to observe formalities relating to the exercise of its powers or management of its activities and affairs is not a ground for imposing liability on a limited partner for a debt, obligation, or other liability of the partnership.

ULPA (2001) § 404. General Partner's Liability.

(a) Except as otherwise provided in subsections (b) and (c), all general partners are liable jointly and severally for all debts, obligations, and other liabilities of the limited partnership unless otherwise agreed by the claimant or provided by law.

(b) A person that becomes a general partner is not personally liable for a debt, obligation, or other liability of the limited partnership incurred before the person became a general partner.

(c) A debt, obligation, or other liability of a limited partnership incurred while the partnership is a limited liability limited partnership is solely the debt, obligation, or other liability of the limited liability limited partnership. A general partner is not personally liable, directly or indirectly, by way of contribution or otherwise, for a debt, obligation, or other liability of the limited liability limited partnership solely by reason of being or acting as a general partner. This subsection applies:

(1) despite anything inconsistent in the partnership agreement that existed immediately before the vote or consent required to become a limited liability limited partnership under Section 406(b)(2); and

(2) regardless of the dissolution of the partnership.

(d) The failure of a limited liability limited partnership to observe formalities relating to the exercise of its powers or management of its activities and affairs is not a ground for imposing liability on a general partner for a debt, obligation, or other liability of the partnership.

Section 404(c) provides for the creation of a limited liability limited partnership (LLLP), which grants limited liability protection to general partners as well. However, unlike the LLP, which is permitted in all 50 states, only a minority of jurisdictions have adopted the ULPA (2001) and thus the LLLP form. It is unclear whether all states will adopt the LLLP as they did with the LLP. There may be good reasons why the LLLP is redundant and does not fill a market need. First, the LLC provides limited liability protection to members and managers, and the manager-managed LLC can mimic the management structure of an LP. Second, the general partner in an ordinary LP can also be a limited liability entity, thus providing limited liability protection to its owners.

The ULPA (2001) provides another innovation. Section 303(a) provides that a limited partner has limited liability "even if the limited partner participates in the management and control of the limited partnership." This rule rejects the "control" rule in the Revised Uniform Limited Partner Act (RULPA), an earlier statute but still prevalent in many states.

RULPA § 303. Liability to Third Parties.

(a) Except as provided in subsection (d), a limited partner is not liable for the obligations of a limited partnership unless he [or she] is also a general partner or, in addition to the exercise of his [or her] rights and powers as a limited partner, he [or she] participates in the control of the business. However, if the limited partner participates in the control of the business, he [or she] is liable only to persons who transact business with the limited partnership reasonably believing, based upon the limited partner's conduct, that the limited partner is a general partner.

(b) A limited partner does not participate in the control of the business within the meaning of subsection (a) solely by doing one or more of the following:

(1) being a contractor for or an agent or employee of the limited partnership or of a general partner or being an officer, director, or shareholder of a general partner that is a corporation;

(2) consulting with and advising a general partner with respect to the business of the limited partnership;

(3) acting as surety for the limited partnership or guaranteeing or assuming one or more specific obligations of the limited partnership;

(4) taking any action required or permitted by law to bring or pursue a derivative action in the right of the limited partnership;

(5) requesting or attending a meeting of partners;

(6) proposing, approving, or disapproving, by voting or otherwise, one or more of the following matters:

(i) the dissolution and winding up of the limited partnership;

(ii) the sale, exchange, lease, mortgage, pledge, or other transfer of all or substantially all of the assets of the limited partnership;

(iii) the incurrence of indebtedness by the limited partnership other than in the ordinary course of its business;

(iv) a change in the nature of the business;

(v) the admission or removal of a general partner;

(vi) the admission or removal of a limited partner;

(vii) a transaction involving an actual or potential conflict of interest between a general partner and the limited partnership or the limited partners;

(viii) an amendment to the partnership agreement or certificate of limited partnership; or

(ix) matters related to the business of the limited partnership not otherwise enumerated in this subsection (b), which the partnership agreement states in writing may be subject to the approval or disapproval of limited partners;

(7) winding up the limited partnership pursuant to Section 803; or

(8) exercising any right or power permitted to limited partners under this [Act] and not specifically enumerated in this subsection (b).

(c) The enumeration in subsection (b) does not mean that the possession or exercise of any other powers by a limited partner constitutes participation by him [or her] in the business of the limited partnership.

> (d) A limited partner who knowingly permits his [or her] name to be used in the name of the limited partnership, except under circumstances permitted by Section 102(2), is liable to creditors who extend credit to the limited partnership without actual knowledge that the limited partner is not a general partner.

RULPA § 303 states that a limited partner loses the limited liability shield if she "participates in the control of the business," but is liable "only to persons who transact business with the limited partnership reasonably believing, based upon the limited partner's conduct, that the limited partner is a general partner." The second condition was added in a 1985 amendment, and it requires a nexus between the limited partner's conduct and the creditor's reasonable belief that the limited partner is a general partner. In the original 1976 version, the RULPA stated: "if the limited partner's participation in the control of the business is not substantially the same as the exercise of the powers of a general partner, he is liable only to persons who transact business with the limited partnership with actual knowledge of his participation in control." Under this version, if the limited partner's participation in the control of the LP was "substantially the same" as a general partner, a creditor may impose liability even if the creditor may have been completely unaware of the limited partner's control. The 1985 amendment curtails potential liability to one of two situations: (1) a creditor can have direct dealings with limited partner; or (2) a creditor can observe the limited partner's conduct in the course of dealing with the LP. Either way, there must be a nexus between the limited partner's action and the creditor's belief.

Since RULPA § 303(a) exposes a limited partner to potential personal liability, it provides in section (b) a safe harbor listing activities not deemed to be, solely in themselves, participation in control.

The case below illustrates the "control" rule in an RULPA jurisdiction. In reading this case, consider this question: What conduct or actions constitute control?

GATEWAY POTATO SALES V. G.B. INVESTMENT CO.

822 P.2d 490 (Ariz. App. 1991)

TAYLOR, JUDGE.

[The limited partner, G.B. Investment, provided evidence that it had exerted no control over the daily management and operation of the LP. This evidence was contradicted, however, by the affidavit of the general partner, Ellsworth, who stated that the limited partner's employees, Darl Anderson and Thomas McHolm, controlled the LP's day-to-day affairs. Ellsworth's affidavit is provided below.]

[ELLSWORTH AFFIDAVIT]

a. During the early months of the Partnership, McHolm and/or Anderson were at the Partnership's offices on a daily basis directing the operation of the Partnership, and thereafter, they were at the Partnership's offices at least 2–3 times per week reviewing the operations of the business, directing changes in operations, and instructing me to make certain changes in operating the Partnership's affairs;

b. G.B. Investment Company was solely responsible for obtaining a $150,000.00 line-of-credit loan for the Partnership with Valley National Bank, and it signed documents guaranteeing the repayment of the loan;

c. As the President of the general partner, I was not permitted to make any significant independent business decisions concerning the operations of the Partnership, but was directed to have all business decisions approved with Anderson and/or McHolm, or was directed to carry out decisions made by Anderson and/or McHolm. For example, instead of using Partnership funds to pay certain creditors and suppliers, I was directed by Anderson and/or McHolm to use the Partnership funds to purchase additional machinery and equipment;

d. Prior to constructing improvements to the packaging facilities of the Partnership, McHolm and/or Anderson had to approve all construction bids, individually selected some of the suppliers and subcontractors, and individually selected the equipment to be installed;

e. McHolm and/or Anderson dictated the accounting procedures to be followed, reviewed the Partnership's books and accounts continually, dictated that the Partnership use the same accounting firm as that of G.B. Investment Company to do the Partnership accounting tasks, undertook the responsibility of having prepared all Partnership tax forms and returns, and I only signed tax returns after they had been prepared by G.B. Investment Company's accountants and reviewed by Anderson or some other employee/agent of G.B. Investment Company;

f. McHolm and/or Anderson oversaw the daily operations of the Partnership because I had to have all expenditures approved by McHolm and/or Anderson and Anderson had to approve and sign checks issued by the Partnership, including without limitation payroll checks and invoices for telephone charges, utilities, publications, interest payments, bank card charges, supplies, etc.;

g. After it was decided to add a hydrocooler to the processing and packaging facilities of the Partnership, McHolm selected the refrigeration equipment and chose the contractor to install the refrigeration equipment on the hydrocooler, and even saw to it that G.B. Investment Company (not the Partnership) directly paid the contractor for all of his services;

h. McHolm insisted that the Partnership use a particular supplier, to-wit: Allied Packaging, to supply packaging materials to the Partnership, he took an active role in reviewing and modifying the art work for use on the packaging items, and approved the bid submitted for the art work;

i. At least on two separate occasions, Anderson caused sums of monies to be withdrawn from the Partnership account with Valley National Bank without the prior knowledge or consent of myself. These monies were paid directly to G.B. Investment, and the withdrawals caused other checks of the Partnership to be dishonored due to insufficient funds and left the Partnership without sufficient funds to meet its payroll obligations;

j. Anderson and/or McHolm caused certain expenses of the Partnership to be paid directly by G.B. Investment Company, to-wit: refrigeration equipment; and

k. After the Partnership defaulted on its loan payments to Valley National Bank, a loan which had been guaranteed by G.B. Investment Company, Anderson, without my knowledge or consent, instructed the Valley National Bank to proceed with declaring the loan to be in default and to pursue its remedies under its Security Agreement with the Partnership, to-wit: to sell the equipment and machinery that it held as collateral at a foreclosure auction. At the foreclosure auction by Valley National Bank, Anderson, on behalf of G.B. Investment Company, bought the equipment and machinery previously owned by Sunworth Corp.

[COURT'S ANALYSIS]

Whether a limited partner has exercised the degree of control that will make him liable to a creditor has always been a factual question. Our statute lists activities that a limited partner may undertake without participating in controlling the business. It also states that other activities may be excluded from the definition of such control. Where activities do not fall within the "safe harbor" [of RULPA § 303(b)], it is necessary for a trier-of-fact to determine whether such activities amount to "control."

We conclude that the evidence [the creditor] presented should have allowed it to withstand summary judgment. The affidavit of Ellsworth raises the issue whether he was merely a puppet for the limited partner, G.B. Investment. While a few of the activities Ellsworth listed may have fallen within the protected areas listed in [RULPA § 303(b)], others did not. Ellsworth's detailed statement raises substantial issues of material facts.

3. LIMITED LIABILITY COMPANY

Members and managers have the benefit of limited liability. *See, e.g.,* Gardener v. Henderson Water Park, LLC, 399 P.3d 350, 351 (Nev. 2017) (holding that members are not liable for the torts of an LLC solely by virtue of being a member and personal liability attaches only when they were directly liable tort). Unlike the LP under the RULPA, there is no "control" rule even for members in a manager-managed LLC. Limited liability applies even when the LLC is a single-member LLC. *See* Erie Insurance Exchange v. EPC MD 15, LLC, 822 S.E.2d 351, 356–57 (Va. 2019) ("The LLC structure would have no meaning if single-member LLCs were one and the same with the single member."); Tavadia v. Mitchell, 564 S.W.3d 322, 328 (Ky. App. 2018) ("Such principle [of limited liability] is true even if the limited liability company has only a single member or manager.").

The only exception to the rule of limited liability is the veil piercing doctrine, which LLC law adopted from corporation law.

RULLCA § 304. Liability of Members and Managers.

(a) A debt, obligation, or other liability of a limited liability company is solely the debt, obligation, or other liability of the company. A member or manager is not personally liable, directly or indirectly, by way of contribution or otherwise, for a debt, obligation, or other liability of the company solely by reason of being or acting as a member or manager. This subsection applies regardless of the dissolution of the company.

(b) The failure of a limited liability company to observe formalities relating to the exercise of its powers or management of its activities and affairs is not a ground for imposing liability on a member or manager for a debt, obligation, or other liability of the company.

Because NBE laws, particularly LLC laws, vary by state, one can occasionally see unique features. For example, New York LLC law holds members personally liability for employee wages.

> The ten members with the largest percentage ownership interest of every limited liability company, shall jointly and severally be personally liable for all debts, wages or salaries due and owing to any of its laborers, servants or employees, for services performed by them for such limited liability company.

New York Limited Liability Company Law § 609(c).

CHRYSLER GROUP LLC OPERATING AGREEMENT

Section 2.7 Limited Liability. Except as otherwise provided by the LLC Act, the debts, obligations and liabilities of the Company, whether arising in contract, tort or otherwise, shall be solely the debts, obligations and liabilities of the Company, and no Member shall be obligated personally for any such debt, obligation or liability of the Company solely by reason of being a member of the Company.

4. "SERIES" LLC

A majority of states and the RULLCA do not permit the creation of a "series LLC." But some permit them.[3] A series LLC is an example of the continuing process of innovation in the laws of business organizations.

A series LLC is a single LLC entity. It can create "series" within the LLC that can hold their own assets, have their own members and managers, and most importantly internally contain their own liabilities without affecting the liabilities of the other series or the LLC in whole. An analogy is a corporate holding structure wherein a parent corporation is the sole shareholder of a group of subsidiary corporations. Each subsidiary is a separate entity with its own capital, management, and internally contained liability. But this analogy is not perfect. A corporate holding structure has several separate and distinct entities (the parent and all of its subsidiaries), but a series LLC is a single entity.

The purpose of a series LLC is to partition the assets and liabilities of a single LLC into legally segregated groups (called "series"). A series LLC provision permits a single LLC to create legal partitions around designated assets, existing liabilities, and potential future liabilities.

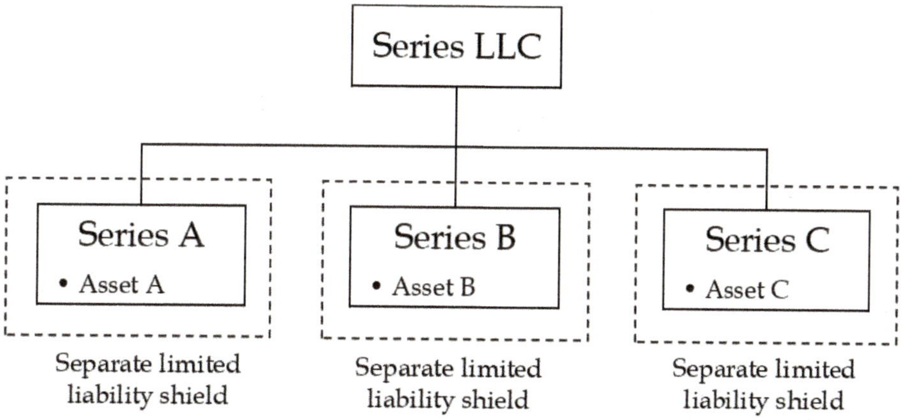

The ultimate rationale of a series LLC is not to enable a holding company structure. A traditional holding company structure is always possible. A single LLC can be the sole owner of many separate LLCs. What, then, is accomplished by a series LLC? One court provides this comment.

> Many of the benefits of a series LLC can be obtained by creating a family of traditional LLCs, with one master traditional LLC of which the members are, in turn, other traditional LLCs. The only

[3] *See, e.g.*, Delaware Limited Liability Company Act § 18–215; Illinois Limited Liability Company Act § 180/37–40; Texas Bus. Org. Code § 101.610 et seq. *See also* Bruce H. White, *Utah Series LLC—The Risk Continues to Be Uncertain*, Utah Bar J. (Sept./Oct. 2016) (counting 11 states as providing for series LLCs).

> differences that we perceive—at least in the abstract—are differences of nomenclature and the requirement for filing fees.

Kurz v. AMCP-1, LLC, 2016 WL 547146, at *7 (Md. App. 2016).

If a family of LLCs is composed of only several entities, then creating them separately may be the better choice in light of legal uncertainties associated with series LLCs (discussed below). But suppose one wanted to segregate a large number of assets and activities and partition liabilities therefrom. The efficiency of doing this through one LLC may be appealing. One can envision the use of series LLCs when assets are discrete and easily partitioned: *e.g.*, real estate, securities, financial contracts, etc. Businesses having these kinds of discrete assets are different from businesses that use a collection of assets in non-divisible ways. If there is a great number of discrete, divisible assets, the overall liability exposure can be lessened if the liability from one part of the business or asset can be "walled off" from other assets. In such cases, a traditional holding company structure may be feasible, but costly due to the great number of filings required.

The following is Delaware's series LLC provision. The statute section is heavily excerpted and not the complete provision. Like its corporation statute, the Delaware LLC statute in sui generis in terms of the "drafting style." It is dense, artful, and difficult to read. But the excerpted statute provides a sense of how a minority of states envision a series LLC.

Delaware Limited Liability Company Act § 18–215. Series of members, managers, limited liability company interests or assets.

(a) A limited liability company agreement may establish 1 or more designated series of members, managers, limited liability company interests or assets. Any such series may have separate rights, powers or duties with respect to specified property or obligations of the limited liability company or profits and losses associated with specified property or obligations, and any such series may have a separate business purpose or investment objective.

(b) In the event that a limited liability company agreement establishes 1 or more series, the debts, liabilities, obligations and expenses incurred, contracted for or otherwise existing with respect to a particular series shall be enforceable against the assets of such series only, and not against the assets of the limited liability company generally or any other series thereof, and, unless otherwise provided in the limited liability company agreement, none of the debts, liabilities, obligations and expenses incurred, contracted for or otherwise existing with respect to the limited liability company generally or any other series thereof shall be enforceable against the assets of such series.

(c) A series may carry on any lawful business, purpose or activity, whether or not for profit, with the exception of the business of banking shall have the power and capacity to, in its own name, contract, hold title to assets (including real, personal and intangible property), grant liens and security interests, and sue and be sued.

(e) A limited liability company agreement may provide for classes or groups of members or managers associated with a series having such relative rights, powers and duties as the limited liability company agreement may provide.

(g) The management of a series shall be vested in the members associated with such series in proportion to the then current percentage or other interest of members in the profits of the series owned by all of the members associated with such series, the decision of members owning more than 50 percent of the said percentage or other interest in the profits controlling; provided, however, that if a limited liability company agreement provides for the management of the series, in whole or in part, by a manager, the management of the series, to the extent so provided, shall be vested in the managers.

(i) A limited liability company may make a distribution with respect to a series. A limited liability company shall not make a distribution with respect to a series to a member to the extent that at the time of the distribution, after giving effect to the distribution, all liabilities of such series, other than liabilities to members on account of their limited liability company interests with respect to such series and liabilities for which the recourse of creditors is limited to specified property of such series, exceed the fair value of the assets associated with such series.

(j) A member shall cease to be associated with a series and to have the power to exercise any rights or powers of a member with respect to such series upon the assignment of all of the member's limited liability company interest with respect to such series. Any event under this chapter or a limited liability company agreement that causes a member to cease to be associated with a series shall not, in itself, cause such member to cease to be associated with any other series or terminate the continued membership of a member in the limited liability company or cause the termination of the series, regardless of whether such member was the last remaining member associated with such series.

(k) A series may be terminated and its affairs wound up without causing the dissolution of the limited liability company. The termination of a series shall not affect the limitation on liabilities of such series. A series is terminated and its affairs shall be wound up upon the dissolution of the limited liability company or otherwise upon the first to occur of the following:

(1) At the time specified in the limited liability company agreement;

(2) Upon the happening of events specified in the limited liability company agreement;

(3) Upon the vote or consent of members associated with such series who own more than ⅔ of the then-current percentage or other interest in the profits of the series of the limited liability company owned by all of the members associated with such series; or

(4) The termination of such series.

(*l*) A manager associated with a series or, if none, the members associated with the series or a person approved by the members associated with the series, in either case, by members who own more than 50 percent of the then current percentage or other interest in the profits of the series may wind up the affairs of the series; but the Court of Chancery, upon cause shown, may wind up the affairs of the series upon application of any member or manager associated with the series and in connection therewith, may appoint a liquidating trustee.

(m) On application by or for a member or manager associated with a series the Court of Chancery may decree termination of such series whenever it is not reasonably practicable to carry on the business of the series in conformity with a limited liability company agreement.

If a series LLC provides the benefit of a holding company structure at low cost, what's wrong with that? There are significant legal uncertainties associated with the use of a series LLC. Some questions are:

- What happens when a series fails?
- How will bankruptcy courts deal with a series?
- Can a series, as opposed to the LLC, file for bankruptcy?
- Is the bankruptcy estate the assets of the series or the entire LLC?
- How will creditors of other series and the LLC be treated relative to creditors of the failed series?
- How will creditors outside of bankruptcy deal with a series in the course of ordinary credit transactions?
- How will other jurisdictions that do have a series LLC provision in their statute treat a foreign series LLC?
- Are series subject to piercing in the same way that traditional entities structure are subject?
- What are the tax implications of a series?

Consider the following passage from Model Organization Checklist for a Limited Liability Company.

> Business clients want legal certainty. There is never certainty, but there are varying degrees of legal uncertainty. With series LLCs, there is currently a significant degree of the unknown. A report of the ABA's Limited Liability Company Subcommittee of the LLCs, Partnerships and Unincorporated Entities Committee provides the following observation.
>
> Still, there remain significant issues with respect to the utilization of the series, including with respect to (i) the treatment of the series under bankruptcy law; (ii) whether the "internal shields" will be respected in jurisdictions in which the series is not incorporated into the domestic LLC act; (iii) federal tax classification, including whether an individual series is an "eligible entity" able to independently elect its classification; (iv) issues of state tax classification; (v) issues of nexus for purposes of state tax treatment; (vi) issues of apportionment, for purposes of state taxation, between individual series and between a series and the parent LLC; (vii) issues with respect to the granting of a security interest in assets that are associated with but not titled in the names of a particular series; (viii) issues, in the states that do not expressly provide a rule, as to whether an individual series may contract in its own name, sue and be sued in its own name, or hold title to property in its own name.

69 Bus. Law. 1251, 1319 n.144 (2014). *See also* Bruce H. White, *Utah Series LLC—The Risk Continues to Be Uncertain*, Utah Bar J. (Sept./Oct. 2016) ("The reason the Utah Series LLC is not widely known or used is that the Utah Series LLC, and similar statutes across the country, have not yet been vetted by the legal system. A lack of case law, particularly under the Bankruptcy Code, should be reason enough for one to not take the risk of using the Series LLC form. Once case law has been developed, its use may very well become the norm.").

SERIES LLCS: WHAT HAPPENS WHEN ONE SERIES FAILS?

Michelle Harner, Jennifer Ivey-Crickenberger & Tae Kim, Business Law Today (American Bar Association, February 2013)

A handful of states permit companies to operate multiple businesses under a common organizational umbrella, referred to as a series LLC. These states are Delaware, Illinois, Iowa, Kansas, Nevada, Oklahoma, Tennessee, Texas, Utah, and Wisconsin. Both the District of Columbia and Puerto Rico have series LLC statutes as well. . . .

The nuances of the series LLC structure are beyond the scope of this article. Rather, this article focuses on a few of the key issues that arise when one series or the master LLC experiences financial distress and elects to file a petition for relief under the U.S. Bankruptcy Code. As discussed below, this scenario poses several challenging issues, many of which remain unresolved and open to interpretation.

The Bankruptcy Code provides two principal options for resolving the financial distress of business organizations—*i.e.*, liquidation under Chapter 7 and reorganization under Chapter 11. Sections 109(b) and (d) identify the category of "person" who may be a debtor in a Chapter 7 or Chapter 11 case. Those persons include "individuals, corporations and partnerships," and the term "corporation" includes, among others, "unincorporated organizations and associations." 11 U.S.C. §§ 101(9), (41). Courts have characterized LLCs as corporations under the Bankruptcy Code that generally are eligible to file a Chapter 7 or Chapter 11 case.

The primary challenge with a series LLC stems from the differing treatment of the structure under state law. For certain purposes, state law views the master LLC and the multiple series as one entity. Yet, for other purposes—primarily asset ownership and liability allocation—state law treats the master LLC and each series as separate and distinct entities. "For Secretary of State filing purposes, the series LLC is considered one entity that files a single annual report and pays a single fee. . . In other words, a series LLC is comparable to a structure with a parent LLC having multiple subsidiary LLCs except that the series LLC is considered one legal entity (at least for the Secretary of State filing purposes)." Whether courts will respect this united but separate characterization of the series LLC structure remains unclear.

The master LLC should qualify as a debtor under Sections 101 and 109 of the Bankruptcy Code. What then happens to the series if the master LLC seeks bankruptcy protection? Does each series remain a non-debtor entity, unaffected by the master LLC's bankruptcy case? Alternatively, is each series part of the master LLC's bankruptcy case but shielded from the debts of the master LLC and other series under applicable state law and the terms of their respective operating agreements? Or are the assets and liabilities of the master LLC and each series consolidated in one bankruptcy estate?

Similar questions exist with respect to the filing of a bankruptcy case by just one series. In addition, courts may raise the more basic question of whether a series is eligible to file independently from the master LLC. Relevant case law is limited, but some basic bankruptcy concepts may help guide the series LLC through these complex issues.

The law governing the rights and remedies of a financially-troubled series LLC is still developing. Parties using, or contemplating using, the series LLC structure should recognize the lingering uncertainty concerning the treatment of a master LLC and its series under federal bankruptcy law and proactively consider alternative structures and exit strategies in the planning stages. Although parties cannot necessarily avoid bankruptcy with advance planning, they can strengthen certain aspects of the series LLC structure with state law tools. For example, parties should clearly designate the allocation of asset ownership, liabilities, and the assets available to satisfy those liabilities; ensure that creditors' interests are properly perfected against the correct assets; and comply in all respects with the applicable series LLC statute.

In addition, parties should consider ways to use state LLC and commercial law to enhance the likelihood that the parties' intentions regarding the state law structure are respected in any subsequent bankruptcy case. For example, parties might endeavor to foster greater protection for the equity value of healthy series through contractual provisions—both in the operating agreement—concerning types and amount of debt that series may incur—and in creditor contracts—through acknowledgements of the assets available to pay obligations, waivers of deficiencies in the context of secured debt, and limiting the use of cross-collateralization and cross-acceleration provisions. These steps will not guarantee the protection of the series LLC structure in bankruptcy, but they will help all parties dealing with the series understand the construct and may foreclose certain arguments based on parties' expectations.

Similarly, sponsors and managers should evaluate their disclosure obligations to investors under applicable law and consider what information concerning insolvency risks might be required to satisfy such obligations. Although disclosing uncertainty in the series LLC structure might hold negative implications, those must be weighed against potential litigation involving sponsors and managers premised on inadequate disclosures. Moreover, lawyers should consider the effect of this uncertainty on the parameters and content of opinion letters.

Given the operational and financing advantages to the series LLC for some businesses, the uncertainty surrounding bankruptcy and series LLCs becomes part of the cost-benefit analysis. Parties should not necessarily avoid the structure because of this uncertainty, but they should consider its overall impact, including potential negative consequences on the rights and remedies of owners and certain creditors and on the cost of capital.

The case below illustrates the potential uncertainties revolving around the status of series LLCs in jurisdictions that do not provide for a series LLC. In reading this case, consider this question: What is the implication of a holding that the legal effect of a series LLC is a law that is "external" to a state's business organization statute?

ALPHONSE V. ARCH BAY HOLDINGS, L.L.C.

548 Fed.Appx. 979 (5th Cir. 2013) (per curiam)

Alphonse contends the district court erred when it held Arch Bay was the wrong party to sue because Arch Bay's wholly owned subsidiary, Series 2010B, is the separate entity that actually held the note. Alphonse argues that because he alleges in his complaint that Arch Bay and Series 2010B are not legally distinct entities, the district court erred by holding a Series LLC is a separate entity without evidence.

The district court held that, "taking all of plaintiff's factual claims as true, [Series 2010B] is a separate entity from [Arch Bay]" and dismissed Alphonse's LUTPA claims against Arch Bay Holdings LLC. The district court reasoned that Alphonse's allegation that "AB-Series 2010B is a financial instrument and not a separate juridical entity" is a "legal conclusion that is couched as a factual allegation." The district court cited the Delaware Corporate Code which provides in pertinent part:

> A limited liability company agreement may establish or provide for the establishment of 1 or more designated series of members, managers, limited liability company interests or assets. Any such series may have separate rights, powers or duties with respect to specified property or obligations of the limited liability company or profits and losses associated with specified property or obligations, and any such series may have a separate business purpose or investment objective.
>
> Unless otherwise provided in a limited liability company agreement, *a series* established in accordance with subsection (b) of this section *shall have the power and capacity to, in its own name,* contract, hold title to assets (including real, personal and intangible property), grant liens and security interests, and *sue and be sued.*

Del.Code Ann. tit. 6, § 18–215. The district court reasoned from these provisions that "AB-Series 2010B is a separate juridical entity from Arch Bay Holdings, LLC itself, [and is therefore] responsible for the trade practices at issue in the complaint."

Alphonse calls the district court's conclusion here the first of its kind and argues that Arch Bay did not produce sufficient evidence to show Series 2010B was a separate legal entity and thus failed to meet its burden on its motion to dismiss. Louisiana's applicable statute provides: "The laws of the state or other jurisdiction under which a foreign limited liability company is organized shall govern its organization, its internal affairs, and the liability of its managers and members that arise solely out of their positions as managers and members." La.Rev.Stat. Ann. § 12:1342.

The district court's conclusion that Delaware law applies does not necessarily follow because the district court has not yet considered the possibility that liability to a third party like Alphonse constitutes external rather than internal affairs. The district court concluded Delaware law applies by interpreting the Louisiana conflict-of-law statute that provides "the laws of the state under which a foreign limited liability company is organized shall govern its organization [and] its *internal affairs*." However, it is not clear that the liability of a limited liability company, or its "series," to third parties like Alphonse is *internal* rather than *external*. After all, "the law of the state of incorporation normally determines issues relating to the *internal* affairs of a corporation," but "different conflicts principles apply where the rights of third parties *external* to the corporation are at issue." *First Nat'l City Bank v. Banco Para El Comercio Exterior de Cuba*, 462 U.S. 611, 621 (1983).

The district court does not appear to have considered the issue of whether liability as between a third-party plaintiff with respect to a holding company LLC or its Series LLC constitutes internal or external affairs. *See also* Restatement (Second) of Conflict of Laws § 302 cmt. a, *cited with approval in First Nat'l City Bank*, 462 U.S. at 621 ("The 'internal affairs' of a corporation [involve] the relations inter se of the corporation, its shareholders, directors, officers or agents."). In light of the fact that the district court failed to consider the external—internal affairs conflict-of-law question under Louisiana law, dismissal without leave to amend was error. We remand for the district court to consider this question, perhaps with the benefit of factual development.

C. DIRECT LIABILITY FOR ONE'S OWN CONDUCT

Limited liability is a sovereign's grant of immunity, and the state determines the scope of any liability scheme within business organization law and outside of it. The rule of limited liability protects against only vicarious liability.[4] Through agency law, NBEs laws, or both, the firm is often held liable for the acts of its employees and agents. The line between vicarious and direct liability is sometimes unclear. The policies governing the rule of limited liability and the protection of others may compete.

The cases below analyze the limits of limited liability. In reading these cases, consider these questions: (1) Are the decisions consistent with the rule of limited liability? (2) Why did the rule of limited liability not protect

[4] *See* RULLCA § 304(a) ("A member or manager is not personally liable, directly or indirectly for a debt, obligation, or other liability of the company *solely by reason of* being or acting as a member or manager."); DGCL § 102(b)(6) ("stockholders shall not be personally liable for the corporation's debts *except by reason of their own conduct or acts*"); MBCA § 6.22(b) ("shareholder of a corporation is not personally liable *except by reason of the shareholder's own acts or conduct*"); Altobelli v. Hartmann, 884 N.W.2d 537, 545 n.9 (Mich. 2016) ("It is well established that corporate employees and officials are personally liable for all tortious and criminal acts in which they participate, regardless of whether they are acting on their own behalf or on behalf of a corporation.").

the defendants? (3) What is the interaction between external laws (*e.g.*, law of torts) and the rule of limited liability?

FIFTH THIRD MORTGAGE CO. V. KAUFMAN

934 F.3d 585 (7th Cir. 2019)

BAUER, CIRCUIT JUDGE.

Fifth Third Mortgage Company sued several individuals and businesses after it fell victim to a mortgage fraud scheme. At issue in this appeal is the personal liability of Ira Kaufman. Kaufman participated in numerous fraudulent closings as the attorney for the seller. Kaufman is also the owner of Traditional Title Company, LLC, which was the title company used for several closings that facilitated the fraud. For the reasons that follow, the judgment against Kaufman is affirmed.

The mortgage fraud scheme at issue began with Yaseen Ahmed, the president of High Point Developers, Inc. Ahmed also co-owned 4725 S. Michigan, LLC, which owned a condominium building located at 4725 S. Michigan Avenue. Ahmed obtained the proceeds of 35 mortgage loans through false statements and omissions made in loan applications and supporting documentation by purported buyers. Ahmed and five others pleaded guilty to criminal offenses related to the scheme.

Ahmed and another man, Eliot Higueros, recruited individuals to pose as buyers for units at 4725 S. Michigan Avenue. These straw buyers submitted fraudulent loan applications to various lenders, including Fifth Third. The participants in the scheme split the loan proceeds when disbursed; no payments were ever made on the loans.

Nine different borrowers purchased 26 properties at 4725 S. Michigan Avenue. 4725 S. Michigan, LLC was the seller and Kaufman was its attorney for each of the closings. The closings were conducted by Traditional Title, and took place at Kaufman's law office. The loan applications contained misrepresentations about the buyers' employment status, assets, and income. The applications also falsely indicated the units were going to be the primary residences of the buyers, despite each buyer purchasing multiple units in the building.

Traditional received closing instructions from Fifth Third that required it to notify the bank immediately of any misrepresentations that would influence the bank's decision to make the loan. The instructions also required Traditional Title to suspend the transaction and notify Fifth Third if "the loan is owner occupied and the closing agent has knowledge that the borrower does not intend to occupy the property." Kaufman failed to abide by either requirement by concealing the buyers' misrepresentations from Fifth Third and instructing closing agents to complete closings even when buyers were purchasing multiple properties.

Ahmed then extended the scheme to units in other buildings. Fifth Third was the lender for four of these properties. Kaufman participated in the transactions as the attorney for the seller; Traditional Title did not participate in these closings. These properties include: unit 5 at 6621 S. Ingleside Avenue; unit 2 at 7919 S. Phillips Avenue; unit 1 at 5416 S. Michigan Avenue; and unit G at 5416 S. Michigan.

Kaufman testified that he was not aware of the mortgage fraud scheme. He claimed that he reviewed the numbers for the sales but "didn't really look at the people." He also said that it was not his job as the seller's attorney to review the closing instructions or the buyer's loan application. Ahmed testified that Kaufman knew the buyers were part of the scheme. Two closing agents, Julio Martinez and Michael Lee, testified that they informed Kaufman about the misrepresentations in the loan applications. Kaufman testified that they never gave him that information.

Fifth Third filed claims of fraud against Kaufman, based on his knowledge that the individuals had been recruited as straw buyers, and that they made false representations in their loan applications. After a bench trial, the court entered judgment for Fifth Third against Kaufman.

Kaufman argues the district court erred in finding him personally liable for aiding and abetting the fraud in his capacity as owner of Traditional Title because Illinois law shields individuals for liability for torts committed in their capacity as members of an LLC. Section 10–10 of the Illinois LLC Act provides that "a member or manager is not personally liable for a debt, obligation, or liability of the company solely by reason of being or acting as a member or manager." 805 ILCS 180/10–10(a).

Kaufman concludes that his liability was derivative of his ownership of Traditional Title from several portions of the judgment. In describing Fifth Third's claim, the district court stated "Fifth Third claims that Kaufman—by virtue of his roles as owner of Traditional Title and attorney for the seller—knew that these individuals had been recruited to act as straw buyers and made material false representations to the bank in their loan applications." The court concluded that "based on all the evidence, that Kaufman was aware of the fraudulent scheme and his participation in it as both the owner of Traditional Title and the attorney for the sellers in the various transactions." The court stated that "through his ownership of Traditional Title, Kaufman substantially assisted the fraud regarding the two disputed purchases by Daugherty and Taylor."

Kaufman was sued in his individual capacity, and not as a member of Traditional Title and the judgment was entered against him in his individual capacity.

Kaufman participated individually in each of the closings as counsel for the seller. He also personally directed Traditional Title's employees to conceal the fraud from Fifth Third. In these dual roles he participated in the fraud for his own personal gain. The judgment against Kaufman was not derived solely from Traditional Title's liability, based on his membership in the LLC. Section 10–10 does not bar his liability here.

Kaufman argues that the district court erred in finding him personally liable for aiding and abetting the fraud as attorney for the seller, because under Illinois law there can be no conspiracy between an agent and his principal. Kaufman also argues that any actions he took as the closing attorney did not substantially assist the fraud scheme.

There is no authority supporting Kaufman's contention that a lawyer cannot aid and abet a client's fraud as a matter of law. On the contrary, Illinois courts have said

> we see no reason to impose a per se bar that prevents imposing liability upon attorneys who knowingly and substantially assist their clients in causing another party's injury. As we have recognized, one may not use his license to practice law as a shield to protect himself from the consequences of his participation in an unlawful or illegal conspiracy. The same policy should prevent an attorney from escaping liability for knowingly and substantially assisting a client in the commission of a tort.

The record supports the district court's conclusion that Kaufman was substantially involved in the scheme. Kaufman reviewed closing statements, hosted the fraudulent closings at his law firm, and attended the closings despite knowing the loans were obtained using straw buyers to defraud the lenders as a part of Ahmed's scheme. Without his participation, the scheme would have failed entirely.

Section 10–10 does not protect Kaufman from liability. Kaufman is also not shielded by being the attorney for the seller in these fraudulent transactions. The district court's judgment against him is affirmed.

CORTEZ V. NACCO MATERIAL HANDLING GROUP, INC.

337 P.3d 111 (Ore. 2014) (en banc)

KISTLER, J.

Plaintiff worked for a lumber mill, Sun Studs, LLC. One evening while he was walking from one area of the mill to another, a forklift hit and severely injured him. After receiving workers' compensation benefits, plaintiff brought this action against Swanson Group, Inc., which owns Sun Studs, as well as other defendants. Plaintiff alleged that Swanson was liable for negligently failing (or for negligently failing to require Sun Studs) to provide a safe workplace and for failing to provide competent safety personnel. Plaintiff also alleged that Swanson was liable under the Employers Liability Law (ELL), which requires employers to take certain safety measures. Swanson moved for summary judgment, and the trial court granted its motion on the ground that the workers' compensation statutes provided the exclusive remedy for plaintiff's injuries. The court entered a limited judgment in Swanson's favor.

Swanson Group, Inc., purchased a lumber mill, Sun Studs, Inc., and reorganized that business as a limited liability company. Swanson is the sole member of Sun Studs, LLC, and it elected to manage Sun Studs, making Sun Studs a member-managed LLC. Sun Studs is one of several timber-related LLCs that Swanson owns and manages. Swanson sets general policies and priorities for those LLCs. Sun Studs has its own employees, who are responsible for the day-to-day operation of the mill and also for implementing Swanson's general directives.

Regarding safety, Swanson provided the LLCs that it owned with a safety manual, which stated general policies and served as a "template" that each LLC could customize to its particular operations. Swanson delegated day-to-day responsibility for safety at Sun Studs to Sun Studs' mill manager and HR director. Specifically, Swanson delegated responsibility "to [Sun Studs' mill manager and HR director] to carry out the safety program and to follow as close as they can the template provided by [Swanson]." It was "up to [Sun Studs' mill manager and HR director] to identify and rectify any safety violations or unsafe workplace issues or safety hazard type issues" at the worksite.

Ash was Swanson's HR director and supervised his counterpart at Sun Studs. Swanson's executive vice president explained the relationship between Ash and Sun Studs' HR director:

> "So the practical way it works is that Ash would provide what I would say is oversight in the overall direct setting: [Ash would tell Sun Studs HR director,] you need to have these types of programs. Here's the steps you need to take to implement. Here's the things you need to do. Here's the programs you need to ensure you've implemented. I'm here at this point if you [Sun Studs' HR director] need any help. Or if you want any support on your safety committee meetings or in your training sessions, then I'll [Ash] help you with that."

Harris was Swanson's vice president of operations. In that capacity, Harris supervised Sun Studs' mill manager. Swanson's executive vice-president explained the relationship between Harris and Sun Studs' mill manager:

> "Harris was more of: You need to make sure you're doing what you have got to do safety-wise. You need to make sure that you're compliant. I'm going to be checking on you and making sure that I'm satisfied with your efforts in the safety program and the safety process."

Swanson's executive vice-president explained that the "primary responsibility for safety" rested with Sun Studs' HR director and mill manager.

Ash and Harris conducted periodic performance reviews of Sun Studs' managers. Ash and Harris also served as a resource to whom Sun Studs' HR director and mill manager could turn if they had a problem that required "corporate level upper-end" decision-making. On one occasion, Ash attended a safety committee meeting at Sun Studs to ensure that Sun Studs' supervisors did not need any help or further assistance. Otherwise, Swanson executives did not visit Sun Studs to monitor safety conditions or set safety policy. If Ash or Harris observed a safety violation when either of them was on Sun Studs' worksite, each person had authority to direct Sun Studs to correct the violation.

Plaintiff suffered severe injuries when another Sun Studs employee drove a forklift down a dark corridor and accidently hit him. Plaintiff filed a claim for and received workers' compensation benefits from Sun Studs. He then filed this action against Swanson. Plaintiff alleged that Swanson was negligent. Plaintiff also claimed that Swanson had violated the ELL.

Swanson does not dispute that a reasonable juror could infer from the evidence on summary judgment that Sun Studs was negligent. Swanson also does not dispute that a reasonable juror could infer from the evidence on summary judgment that it had the authority, as the member-manager of Sun Studs, to require Sun Studs to provide safer conditions. Swanson notes, however, that ORS 63.165(1) shields LLC members and managers from personal liability for "acting" as a member-manager.[12] Swanson reasons that, under ORS 63.165(1), "merely having the authority to require the LLC to prevent a workplace accident is not sufficient for personal liability to attach to a managing-member for every act of negligence that arises out of the operations of the LLC's business."

Swanson argues that it will be liable as Sun Studs' member-manager only when an officer or director of a corporation would be liable for a corporate employee's negligence—that is, only if Swanson "actively participated" in Sun Studs' negligence.

Plaintiff takes a different view of both ORS 63.165(1) and the evidence. He argues that the sole function of ORS 63.165(1) is to make clear that LLC members and managers are immune from vicarious liability for the LLC's debts, obligations, and liabilities. Plaintiff reasons that, to the extent a member or a manager is independently liable to an employee or a third

[12] An LLC member can be a passive owner of the LLC, much like a corporate shareholder. Alternatively, an LLC member can manage the LLC either in a member-managed LLC or in a manager-managed LLC, if the member is designated as the manager of the manager-managed LLC. We assume that the issues that arise from extending immunity to LLC members and managers for "acting" in those capacities primarily will involve persons (whether members or managers) who manage the LLC.

party, ORS 63.165(1) provides no protection from that liability. Plaintiff argues that a reasonable juror could infer that Swanson "retained control over job site safety" and, having retained control, failed to provide (or to require Sun Studs to provide) a safe workplace.

STATUTORY IMMUNITY UNDER ORS 63.165(1)

ORS 63.165(1) provides: "The debts, obligations and liabilities of a limited liability company, whether arising in contract, tort or otherwise, are solely the debts, obligations and liabilities of the limited liability company. A member or manager is not personally liable for a debt, obligation or liability of the limited liability company solely by reason of *being* or *acting* as a member or manager."

The two sentences in subsection (1) mirror each other. The first sentence provides that the "debts, obligations and liabilities" of an LLC are "solely" the debts, obligations, and liabilities of the LLC. The second sentence provides that a member or a manager of an LLC is not personally liable for the LLC's debts, obligations, and liabilities "solely by reason of being or acting as a member or manager" of the LLC. Each sentence makes clear that a member or a manager of an LLC is not vicariously liable for the LLC's debts, obligations, and liabilities, as a general partner will be vicariously liable for the partnership's obligations.

The use of the word "being" in the second sentence in ORS 63.165(1) is consistent with that interpretation. Merely "being" a member or manager does not make that person liable for the LLC's obligations. However, the use of the word "acting" interjects ambiguity into the text. On the one hand, "acting" could mean that a member or manager is not personally liable for any debts, obligations or liabilities of the LLC that arise solely by reason of the "actions" that a member or manager takes in that person's official capacity. Read broadly, the phrase "acting as a member or manager" would provide members and managers immunity not only from vicarious liability but also from personal liability for their actions in managing an LLC.

On the other hand, the word "acting" may play a more modest role. It may simply confirm that a member or manager of an LLC is not vicariously liable for the LLC's debts. The word "acting" could serve to make clear that, unlike a limited partner who will become vicariously liable if he or she participates in the control of the business, a member or manager of an LLC will not be vicariously liable for actively managing the LLC's business. *Cf.* ORS 70.135(1) (providing that, although a limited partner is ordinarily not vicariously liable for the limited partnership's liabilities, a limited partner will become vicariously liable for those liabilities if he or she participates in the control of the business). The word "acting" is capable of more than one interpretation, and we turn to the context.

In 1999, the legislature amended the part of ORS 63.165 (1993) at issue by adding the word "acting." The 1999 legislature relied on the recently published Uniform Limited Liability Company Act (ULLCA) (1996) and adopted verbatim subsections 303(a) and (b). The comment to those provisions sheds some light on the 1999 legislature's intent. The comment to Section 303 explains:

> "A member or manager is responsible for acts or omissions to the extent those acts or omissions would be actionable in contract or tort against the member or manager if that person were acting in an individual capacity. Where a member or manager delegates or assigns the authority or duty to exercise appropriate company functions, the member or manager is ordinarily not personally liable for the acts or omissions of the officer, employee, or agent [of the LLC] if the member or manager has complied with the duty of care set forth in Section 409(c)."

The first sentence in the comment makes clear that the use of the word "acting" in section 303 of the ULLCA, and by extension in ORS 63.165(1), was not intended to immunize members and managers from personal liability for their actions in managing an LLC. Rather, members and managers remain personally liable for the actions that they take on behalf of an LLC to the same extent that they would be liable "if [they] were acting in an individual capacity."

Having identified that, as a general rule, members or managers will remain personally liable for their own acts, the comment goes on to identify one instance in which members or managers ordinarily will not be personally liable. The second sentence quoted above recognizes that, when a member or manager of an LLC delegates authority to carry out company functions, as an officer or director of a corporation might, the member or manager ordinarily will not be personally liable for a subordinate's negligence. We do not read the second sentence as establishing statutory immunity in that situation. Rather, the second sentence recognizes that, as a matter of common law, a member or manager ordinarily will not be personally liable for a subordinate's negligence.

Unlike limited partners, members or managers who participate in or control the business of an LLC will not, as a result of those actions, be vicariously liable for the LLC's debts, obligations, or liabilities. However, a member or manager remains responsible for his or her acts or omissions to the extent those acts or omissions would be actionable against the member or manager if that person were acting in an individual capacity. Because ORS 63.165(1) does not shield Swanson from responsibility for its own negligent acts in managing Sun Studs, we turn to the question whether there was evidence from which a reasonable juror could find that Swanson was liable for the injuries that plaintiff suffered.

THE ELL

The ELL "imposes a heightened statutory standard of care on a person or entity who either is in charge of, or responsible for, any work involving risk or danger."[20] In this case, the "work involving risk or danger" was driving forklifts through the areas of the mill in which Sun Studs' employees customarily walked. The question on which plaintiff's ELL claim turns is whether Swanson was a person "having charge of, or responsibility for" that work. On that issue, this court has held that, in addition to a worker's direct employer, liability under the ELL "can be imposed on a person or entity who (1) is engaged with the plaintiff's direct employer in a common enterprise; (2) retains the right to control the manner or method in which the risk-producing activity was performed; or (3) actually controls the manner or method in which the risk producing activity is performed."

Swanson was not plaintiff's "direct employer." The Court of Appeals held that a reasonable juror could not infer that Swanson was engaged in a common enterprise with Sun Studs, that Swanson actually controlled the risk-producing activity, or that Swanson retained the right to control that activity. We agree with the Court of Appeals that Swanson was not liable under the ELL on a common-enterprise or actual-control theory of responsibility. We disagree, however, that a reasonable juror could not infer that Swanson retained the right to control the method or manner in which the risk-producing activity was performed.

To establish that Swanson "retained the right to control" a risk-producing activity, plaintiff must either "identify some source of legal authority for that perceived right" or evidence from which a retained right could be inferred. Swanson was the sole member-manager of Sun Studs. As such, the governing statutes gave Swanson the right to manage Sun Studs' business. Although Swanson chose to delegate responsibility for day-to-day decisions to Suns Studs' mill manager and HR director, Swanson retained the right, under ORS 63.130, to manage all aspects of Sun Studs' operation, including the way that forklifts operated in the mill and the safety conditions in their area of operation.

There was evidence from which a reasonable juror could infer that, even though Swanson had chosen to delegate primary authority to Sun Studs to operate the mill and regulate the way that forklifts were used, Swanson retained the right to do so itself. Swanson's executive vice president acknowledged that Swanson "could have made all of the [safety] changes" when it first acquired Sun Studs that Sun Studs later made in response to plaintiff's accident. The executive vice-president agreed "that

[20] The ELL provides: "Generally, all owners, contractors or subcontractors and other persons having charge of, or responsibility for, any work involving a risk or danger to the employees or the public shall use every device, care and precaution that is practicable to use for the protection and safety of life and limb, limited only by the necessity for preserving the efficiency of the structure, machine or other apparatus or device, and without regard to the additional cost of suitable material or safety appliance [*sic*] and devices." ORS 654.305.

if the Swanson group people wanted to change either the design or the equipment used in the yard at Sun Studs, they could do that." A reasonable juror could infer that, as the LLC statutes state, Swanson retained the right to manage the day-to-day operations of Sun Studs, including the operation of the forklifts and attendant safety procedures.

We recognize that some tension may exist between our resolution of plaintiff's negligence and ELL claims. Any tension results, however, from the differences between the common-law tort standards and the broader statutory standards that the legislature adopted in the ELL. Our negligence cases have held that, in the absence of knowledge or participation, corporate officers and directors are not liable for their employees' negligence. That is so even though corporate officers, having delegated responsibility to others to carry out tasks, retain the right to control how those tasks are carried out. Our ELL cases, however, have held that persons who retain the right to control how others carry out risk-producing activities are liable under the ELL. Our resolution of plaintiff's claims reflects those differing standards.

The judgment of the circuit court is affirmed in part [on the negligence claim] and reversed in part [on the ELL claim], and the case is remanded to the circuit court for further proceedings [on the ELL claim].

D. VEIL PIERCING IN NBEs

The doctrine of veil piercing is less applicable in partnerships for several reasons. General partners in either a general partnership or an LP do not have limited liability. Limited partners can be held liable for the debts and obligations of the LP under the control rule in an RULPA jurisdiction. Limited liability does not protect against outright fraud by a group of persons acting within a firm. Veil piercing is premised on the concept that the entity is an alter-ego of the owner or the owner has abused the entity form, and that as a result the situation perpetrates injustice or fraud. This situation naturally arises when there is a single or dominant owner. Because partners are co-owners, partnerships tend to have some natural checks and balances within the firm. Of course, as an equitable doctrine, veil piercing can potentially apply in any situation where the rule of limited liability is abused.

Veil piercing more naturally applies to LLCs. All courts that have considered the issue have ruled that veil piercing applies to LLCs.[5] No case has explicitly held that veil piercing does not apply to LLCs. Most courts

[5] *E.g.*, Mattingly Law Firm, P.C. v. Henson, 466 P.3d 590, 594–95 (Oka.App. 2019) ("The Oklahoma Supreme Court has never applied any form of veil piercing to LLCs. While the doctrine of traditional piercing the veil of corporations is well established in Oklahoma, Oklahoma has yet to apply this doctrine to the newer entity structure of LLCs. The Oklahoma LLC Act provides that the 'rules of law and equity' shall supplement the Act with regard to any case not addressed therein. Accordingly, we see no reason why the well recognized practice of piercing the corporate veil should not apply to LLCs.").

borrow from the state's corporation law to determine the precise standard. *E.g.*, North Dakota Limited Liability Company Act § 10–32.1–26(3) ("Except as relates to the failure of an LLC to observe any formalities relating exclusively to the management of its internal affairs, the case law that states the conditions and circumstances under which the corporate veil of a corporation may be pierced under North Dakota law also applies to limited liability companies."). There is one difference. In corporate veil piercing, courts have found the disregard of corporate formalities (such as not holding annual shareholder meetings) important in determining whether the corporate form has been disregarded or abused. A major benefit of LLCs is that the form does not require nearly as many mandatory rules and formalities as corporation law. Thus, RULLCA § 304(b) provides: "The failure of a limited liability company to observe any particular formalities relating to the exercise of its powers or management of its activities and affairs is not a ground for imposing liability on a member or manager for a debt, obligation, or other liability of the company."

> The application of veil-piercing principles is rather problematic when dealing with an individual's role with a limited liability company, particularly with a single-member LLC. Because many smaller LLC's are managed by few members, perhaps a single member, who are actively involved in all phases of the LLC's business, the disregard of corporate formalities—one of the key factors in veil-piercing determinations—is simply inapplicable. It makes no sense to imperil the shield simply because the members do not undergo meaningless formalities such as formal meetings.

In re Shuomali, 2016 WL 4991490, at *14 (Bankr. E.D. Tex. 2016).

The cases below provide examples of veil piercing in the context of LLCs. In reading these cases, consider these questions: (1) Since the failure "to observe any particular formalities" should not be a basis to pierce the veil, what are the critical factors in determining whether to pierce the veil or not? (2) What advice should a business lawyer give to clients seeking protection against the possibility of veil piercing? (3) For a single-member LLC in particular, how can the LLC be operated in a pragmatic manner that avoids the conflation of the member and the LLC?

DAILEY V. AYERS LAND DEVELOPMENT, LLC

825 S.E.2d 351 (W.Va. 2019)

HUTCHISON, JUSTICE:

The petitioners argue that the circuit court erred by finding that [for the purpose of summary judgment] they failed to produce sufficient evidence to pierce the veil of the respondent corporations and limited liability companies to hold Jerry Ayers, Roger Ayers, and Michael Frye personally liable [for the debts and obligations of their company RJM Holdings, LLC]. This Court has recognized that "a corporate shield may be pierced to subject a sole shareholder to liability for corporate acts or to make a corporation liable for behavior of another corporation within its total control." As we have explained:

> While a corporation constitutes an entity separate and apart from the persons who own it, such is a fiction of the law introduced for purpose of convenience and to subserve the ends of justice; and it is now well settled, as a general principle, that the fiction should be disregarded when it is urged with an intent not within its reason and purpose, and in such a way that its retention would produce injustices or inequitable consequences.

Whether the business is a corporation or a limited liability company, the same two-part test is applied to determine whether the veil may be pierced.

> To pierce the veil in order to impose personal liability on its member or manager, it must be established that (1) there exists such unity of interest and ownership that the separate personalities of the business and of the individual member or managers no longer exist and (2) fraud, injustice, or an inequitable result would occur if the veil is not pierced.

Application of the two-part test to determine whether to pierce the veil of a corporation or a limited liability company requires a fact-driven analysis that is specific to each case. Recognizing the multitude of considerations involved and the close scrutiny of the actions of the parties that is required, this Court has made clear that "decisions to look beyond, inside and through corporate facades must be made case-by-case, with particular attention to factual details." Likewise, "the analysis necessary to [pierce the veil of an LLC] is fact based and must be applied to LLCs on a case-by-case basis." To make the determination, we have outlined some of the relevant factors to be considered, which include:

> (1) commingling of funds and other assets of the corporation with those of the individual shareholders;
>
> (2) diversion of the corporation's funds or assets to noncorporate uses (to the personal uses of the corporation's shareholders);
>
> (3) failure to maintain the corporate formalities necessary for the issuance of or subscription to the corporation's stock, such as formal approval of the stock issue by the board of directors;
>
> (4) an individual shareholder representing to persons outside the corporation that he or she is personally liable for the debts or other obligations of the corporation;

(5) failure to maintain corporate minutes or adequate corporate records;

(6) identical equitable ownership in two entities;

(7) identity of the directors and officers of two entities who are responsible for supervision and management (a partnership or sole proprietorship and a corporation owned and managed by the same parties);

(8) failure to adequately capitalize a corporation for the reasonable risks of the corporate undertaking;

(9) absence of separately held corporate assets;

(10) use of a corporation as a mere shell or conduit to operate a single venture or some particular aspect of the business of an individual or another corporation;

(11) sole ownership of all the stock by one individual or members of a single family;

(12) use of the same office or business location by the corporation and its individual shareholder(s);

(13) employment of the same employees or attorney by the corporation and its shareholder(s);

(14) concealment or misrepresentation of the identity of the ownership, management or financial interests in the corporation, and concealment of personal business activities of the shareholders (sole shareholders do not reveal the association with a corporation, which makes loans to them without adequate security);

(15) disregard of legal formalities and failure to maintain proper arm's length relationships among related entities;

(16) use of a corporate entity as a conduit to procure labor, services or merchandise for another person or entity;

(17) diversion of corporate assets from the corporation by or to a stockholder or other person or entity to the detriment of creditors, or the manipulation of assets and liabilities between entities to concentrate the assets in one and the liabilities in another;

(18) contracting by the corporation with another person with the intent to avoid the risk of nonperformance by use of the corporate entity; or the use of a corporation as a subterfuge for illegal transactions;

(19) the formation and use of the corporation to assume the existing liabilities of another person or entity.

This Court has observed that "examination of the numerous relevant factors in a totality of the circumstances test provides a more enlightening analysis than merely applying metaphors, like 'simulacrum,' 'alter ego,' 'instrumentality,' etc., to describe the unity of the shareholder and the corporation justifying, where equitable, the piercing of the corporate veil." In addition, this Court has recognized that "this evidence must be analyzed in conjunction with evidence that a corporation attempted to use its corporate structure to perpetrate a fraud or do grave injustice on an innocent third party seeking to pierce the veil." Accordingly, "the propriety of piercing the corporate veil should rarely be determined upon a motion for summary judgment. Instead, the propriety of piercing the corporate veil usually involves numerous questions of fact for the trier of the facts to determine upon all of the evidence."

The petitioners have produced evidence that the respondents and RJM had no operating agreements with regard to the use of the same personnel, office space, equipment, phone lines, and marketing materials. The petitioners established that funds were transferred from the various respondents to RJM to pay its expenses. In fact, some of the funds contributed by one respondent were used to pay another respondent to do the infrastructure work for RJM. We recognize that "common ownership or common management without evidence of fraudulent conduct, total control, or a 'dummy' corporation [does not] justify piercing the corporate veil." Indeed, "the law presumes that two separately incorporated businesses are separate entities and that corporations are separate from their shareholders." Based on the record before us and given our express recognition of the fact-based nature of determining whether to "pierce the veil," we find this issue is a matter for the jury.

GREENHUNTER ENERGY, INC. V. WESTERN ECOSYSTEMS TECHNOLOGY, INC.

337 P.3d 454 (Wyo. 2014)

DAVIS, JUSTICE.

GreenHunter Energy, Inc. is the sole member of GreenHunter Wind Energy, LLC (LLC). It appeals from a district court decision piercing the LLC's veil to hold it liable for the LLC's contractual obligations to Western Echosystems Technology, Inc. (Western). We conclude that under the specific circumstances of this case, the evidence supports the use of this extraordinary equitable remedy. We therefore affirm.

Western and the LLC entered into a contract whereby Western undertook to provide the LLC consulting services related to the potential development of a wind turbine farm. While Western performed under the contract, the LLC paid nothing for Western's services. Western consequently brought a breach of contract action against the LLC and obtained a judgment in the amount of $43,646. The judgments cannot be satisfied because the LLC has no assets upon which Western can execute.

The district court found in favor of Western. It pierced the LLC's veil and awarded $45,807 against GreenHunter for the amount the LLC had not paid under its contract with Western.

The 2010 Wyoming Limited Liability Company Act recognized that the veil of limited liability companies may be pierced in certain circumstances:

> (a) The debts, obligations or other liabilities of a limited liability company, whether arising in contract, tort or otherwise:
>
> > (i) Are solely the debts, obligations or other liabilities of the company; and
> >
> > (ii) Do not become the debts, obligations or other liabilities of a member or manager solely by reason of the member acting as a member or manager acting as a manager.
>
> *(b) The failure of a limited liability company to observe any particular formalities relating to the exercise of its powers or management of its activities is not a ground for imposing liability on the members or managers for the debts, obligations or other liabilities of the company.*

Wyo. Stat. Ann. § 17–29–304.

The veil may be pierced under exceptional circumstances when: (1) the limited liability company is not only owned, influenced and governed by its members, but the required separateness has ceased to exist due to misuse of the limited liability company; and (2) an adherence to the fiction of its separate existence would, under the particular circumstances, lead to injustice, fundamental unfairness, or inequity.

This test is fact-driven and flexible, and it focuses on whether the limited liability company has been operated as a separate entity as contemplated by statute, or whether the member has instead misused the entity in an inequitable manner to injure the plaintiff.

In determining whether both prongs of this test have been met, courts can usually apply several factors. The first is whether there has been fraud. We have advised, however, that in certain cases, "although fraud in the classic sense requires an affirmative misrepresentation, this court has recognized that fraud may be perpetrated by silence as well as by affirmative representations; and when one has a duty to speak, the failure to speak may constitute fraud."

Constructive fraud may be an alternative to actual fraud. It "has been defined as consisting of all acts, omissions, and concealments involving breaches of a legal or equitable duty resulting in damage to another, and exists where such conduct, although not actually fraudulent, ought to be so treated when it has the same consequence and legal effects."

Second, inadequate capitalization, if there is evidence of it, may be considered. It is important to note, however, that undercapitalization alone will not suffice to pierce the veil. Basic business practice and societal policy call for a limited liability company to be financially responsible and require that it attempt to arrange for enough capital to reasonably cover its potential liabilities at various points of its existence.

Courts must compare the amount of capital to the amount of business to be conducted and the obligations which must be satisfied. If the LLC is undercapitalized, or if its members have never attempted to secure sufficient capital, these facts may be evidence that the company was used to screen members from legitimate debt because it is not in reality an autonomous company capable of carrying on its own business.

A third factor to consider is the degree to which the business and finances of the company and the member are intermingled. This factor may have numerous aspects which must be analyzed. Funds and assets should be separated and not commingled. Failure to maintain an arm's-length relationship between the member and company, as by not keeping separate bank accounts and bookkeeping records, may be weighed along with other factors. If the member treats limited liability company property as if it were that person's or company's personal property, a court should consider also this fact. Manipulation of assets and liabilities between the member and company so as to concentrate the assets in the former and the liabilities in the latter can be suggestive of improper use of the LLC as well.

Courts must be mindful of how limited liability companies are commonly operated in Wyoming, as they cannot ignore the realities of the marketplace. Because of the flexibility and decentralized management allowed by this innovative business entity, entrepreneurs find it attractive for small start-ups, and in many cases these legitimately do not require more than a single member with little capital. The limited liability company can be used for a variety of businesses with lawful purposes, from a member whose only assets are herded across the Wyoming prairie to one that is publicly traded and operates around the world. Accordingly, the test and factors considered must be attuned to the facts of a given case.

It bears repeating that limited liability is the rule, and piercing is the rare exception. This is one of those rare situations, although we must concede that it is a close call.

Undercapitalization

The district court did not rely solely on undercapitalization to determine that piercing the veil was warranted. Undercapitalization was one of several factors it considered in the totality of the circumstances of this case. The evidence supports the district court's findings that:

> In early 2009, LLC and [Western] entered into a Professional Services Contract, wherein [Western] contracted to provide consulting services to LLC relating to a wind energy project in Platte County, Wyoming. On June 8, 2009 [Western] submitted Invoice # 28355 to LLC in the amount of $5,022. As of June 9, 2009, LLC did not have any funds within its operating account. [Western] submitted subsequent invoices to LLC, which went unpaid. During the periods when these invoices were submitted to LLC, LLC often had $0.00 balances in its operating account and received periodic money transfers from [GreenHunter]. [It] at all times maintained the sole discretion to decide when funds would be transferred to LLC, to decide the amount of money that would be transferred to LLC, and to decide which bills of LLC would be paid with transferred monies. When [GreenHunter] stopped providing money transfers to LLC, LLC became insolvent and was unable to pay creditors, including [Western].

Based upon these facts, and other evidence introduced at trial, the district court correctly concluded that GreenHunter "failed to adequately capitalize LLC, that LLC was undercapitalized at all times relevant to this suit, and that LLC lacks corporate assets."

GreenHunter correctly points out that start-up companies, new business ventures, and early stage companies sometimes may not have initial capital or income sufficient to cover their expenses, and that they do in fact require periodic capital infusions from members to meet their financial obligations. However, the LLC had inadequate capital due to manipulation by its member, a publicly traded corporation, and GreenHunter used its position to control "the amount of money that would be transferred to LLC, and to decide which bills of LLC would be paid with transferred monies." Put another way, the LLC was continually undercapitalized by choice, not by external forces.

Intermingling of business and finances

GreenHunter and the LLC did maintain separate bank accounts and business records. If the analysis could end there, GreenHunter would have a convincing case. However, GreenHunter's argument ignores other facets of this factor which must be considered. In actions seeking to pierce the veil of a limited liability company, each case must be governed by its own facts. There is no rigid formula to which a court's analysis must conform; instead, each case requires a fact-intensive inquiry that must address the particular circumstances. Based upon the evidence presented at trial, the district court found the following with respect to intermingling:

- The overlap between the LLC's and GreenHunter's ownership and management was considerable and to an extent such that piercing was appropriate. GreenHunter and the LLC utilized GreenHunter's accounting department, and the same accountants managed the finances of both entities. They had the same business address and creditors of the LLC mailed their invoice to GreenHunter's address for processing. The LLC's tax returns were consolidated with the tax returns of GreenHunter.

- The LLC did not have any employees who were independent of GreenHunter; all of the LLC's functions were carried out by employees of GreenHunter. Employees of GreenHunter negotiated and entered into contracts on behalf of the LLC, and these same individuals decided which of the LLC's creditors to pay through contributions from GreenHunter.
- GreenHunter assigned its own employees to perform work of the LLC, and although GreenHunter "charged" the LLC for the labor performed by GreenHunter's personnel, GreenHunter directly paid its employees for that work.
- The LLC had no revenue separate from GreenHunter. Funds were commingled in the sense that the LLC's bills that GreenHunter wanted paid were settled with GreenHunter's funds which were "passed through" the LLC by periodic transfers. A particular bill was paid only if and when GreenHunter decided to transfer funds to pay it.
- The LLC entered into an agreement with Western to procure services for the purpose of supporting and benefitting GreenHunter's business. GreenHunter claimed a deduction in the amount of $884,092.00 attributable to the Platte County wind energy project and a loss on its corporate tax return in the amount of $61,047.00 attributable to the same project on its 2009 tax return.
- GreenHunter manipulated assets and liabilities in a manner such that GreenHunter improperly reaped all of the rewards and benefits of the LLC's activities, while simultaneously saddling the LLC with all of its losses and liabilities, including the unpaid bills for services rendered by Western. GreenHunter has enjoyed significant tax breaks attributable to the LLC's losses, without bearing any responsibility for the LLC's debt and obligations that contributed to such losses. Such a disparity in the risks and rewards resulting from this manipulation would lead to injustice.

Based upon this, and other evidence in the record, the LLC was not only owned, influenced and governed by GreenHunter, but the entities had ceased to be separate due to GreenHunter's misuse of the LLC. Adherence to the fiction of the LLC's separate existence would, under these particular circumstances, lead to an unjust and inequitable result.

GreenHunter raises a reasonable policy concern regarding the operational and management structure of a single-member limited liability company. A single-member company is owned and by default often managed by its sole member as expressly permitted by the 2010 Act. Because of the minimal requirements for creating and operating a single-member limited liability company, this form of business organization can be utilized by many different types of members, from an individual starting a business out of her home to a large corporation. The flexibility allowed in the operation of such an entity does not conflict with the use of a home address as the business's address in some cases. Nor is it inconceivable that the sole member may manage the company's finances as well as its own or be responsible for entering into agreements on the company's behalf. Indeed, that will likely be the case when the sole member manages the company. While the district court noted that the LLC's address was the same as GreenHunter's and that all finances and negotiations were handled by the latter, under the circumstances of this case, it did not assign inappropriate weight to this evidence in its overall analysis.

Fraud

A showing of fraud or an intent to defraud is not necessary to disregard the legal fiction of a separate entity. Our analysis could therefore stop here. However, the district court also found that GreenHunter's "course of conduct, which was executed in the name of the LLC, wherein it engaged and contracted with [Western] for valuable services knowing that it could not or would not pay [Western's] bill when received, constitutes a fraud that should not enjoy protection" behind the veil of limited liability.

While not a prerequisite for piercing [the]veil, fraud can be a powerful reason to do so. "It is in the public interest to disregard the legal fiction of a separate entity, whether that be a corporation or LLC, when those benefiting from that fiction commit fraudulent conduct."

There is no evidence that GreenHunter made false statements that Western relied upon in entering into the contract with the LLC or in continuing to perform services thereunder.

The district court found that GreenHunter misused the LLC in order to improperly manipulate the situation to avoid paying for services which benefitted it, that it failed to maintain adequate separation, and that to allow it to do so would be unjust and inequitable. Thus, even though there was no fraud in the classic and technical sense, the district court's decision to pierce the LLC's veil to hold GreenHunter responsible for a debt for services which benefitted it was legally correct and not clearly erroneous.

Based upon the totality of the circumstances, the evidence supports the determination that the LLC was not only owned, influenced and governed by GreenHunter, but that the LLC had ceased to be a separate entity due to GreenHunter's misuse of it in this transaction. Adherence to the fiction of the LLC's separate existence would, under these particular circumstances, lead to an unjust and inequitable result. Accordingly, we affirm the district court's judgment piercing the LLC's veil and imposing liability on GreenHunter for its debt to Western.

1. REVERSE VEIL PIERCING

Traditional veil piercing disregards the entity on equitable grounds to reach the owners. Disregard of the entity can also work in reverse. In "insider" reverse veil piercing, an insider of the entity seeks to disregard the veil to avail the insider of the rights or powers of the entity or to protect the entity's assets from third-party claims. In "outsider" reverse veil piercing (sometimes called "third-party reverse piercing"), a creditor of an owner seeks to satisfy the claim against the entity, which is the reverse of traditional veil piercing.

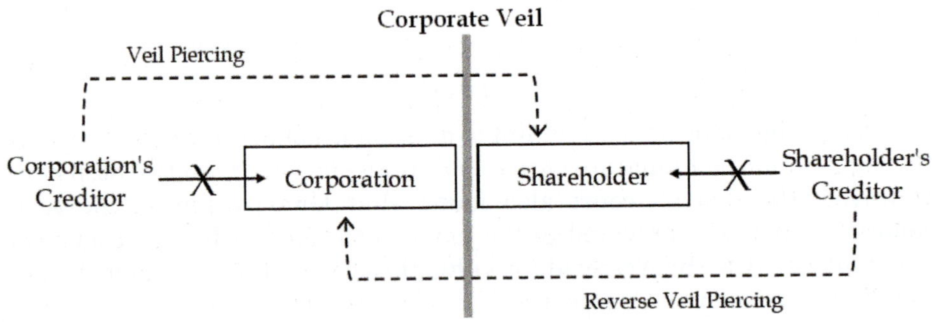

Reverse veil piercing in both forms is less settled than traditional veil piercing and is inconsistently adopted.[6] Where the business entity is simply an artifice of the owner, courts sometimes recognize reverse veil piercing.[7]

---

6 *E.g.,* In re Glick, 568 B.R. 634, 659 (Bankr. N.D. Ill. 2017) ("Outside reverse piercing occurs when a third party makes the alter ego argument, either to hold the corporation liable for the acts of its shareholder or subsidiary, or to pursue the shareholder or subsidiary in the name of the corporation. Inside reverse piercing occurs when a corporate insider, usually a shareholder, advances the alter ego theory to assert a corporate claim on behalf of himself against a third party. Of the two, inside reverse piercing is more common."); ALT Hotel, LLC v. Diamondrock Allerton Owner, LLC, 479 B.R. 781, 801–02 (Bankr. N.D. Ill. 2012). ("A significant minority of courts reject outside reverse piercing and courts are overwhelmingly hostile to insider reverse piercing."); In re Rehabilitation of Centaur Ins. Co., 1632 N.E.2d 1015, 1018 (Ill. 1994) (rejecting inside reverse veil piercing, a view the court reaffirmed in Forsythe v. Clark USA, Inc., 864 N.E.2d 227, 241–42 (Ill. 2007)).

7 *E.g.,* McKay v. Longman, 211 A.3d 20, 46 & n.27 (Conn. 2019) (holding that reverse veil piercing applied to actions filed before July 9, 2019, at which time such actions are precluded by Connecticut Pubic Act 19–181, § 3, which provides: "No domestic entity shall be responsible for a debt, obligation or other liability of an interest holder of such entity based upon a reverse veil piercing doctrine, claim or remedy."); In re Moore, 608 F.3d 253, 258–59 (5th Cir. 2010); Sky Cable, LLC v. Coley, 2016 WL 3926492, at *18 (W.D. Va. 2016); Egle v. Egle, 817 So. 2d 136, 140 (La. App. 2002). *See also* C.F. Trust, Inc. v. First Flight L.P., 580 S.E.2d 806, 811 (Va. 2003) (applying reverse veil piercing in the context of LPs and holding that "reverse veil piercing must prove the necessary standards by clear and convincing evidence"); In re Adelphia Communication Corp., 2006 WL 687153, at *20 (Bankr. S.D.N.Y. 2006) ("In the case of reverse veil piercing, a partner is attempting to use the limited partnership form to shield personal assets from the creditors of the

Reverse veil piercing is generally not as broadly accepted as traditional veil piercing.[8] A substantial consideration is the fact that outsider reverse veil piercing may have detrimental effects on innocent owners and creditors.[9]

The case below analyzes the policy rationale for reverse veil piercing. It arises out of corporation law. In reading this case, consider these questions: (1) What are the potential limitation of reverse veil piercing that would not apply in traditional veil piercing? (2) Are there good policy reasons why reverse veil piercing should not apply to LLCs?

IN RE PHILLIPS

139 P.3d 639 (Colo. 2006) (en banc)

JUSTICE MARTINEZ delivered the Opinion of the Court.

Appellant, Tom Connolly, is the Chapter 7 Bankruptcy trustee of Debtor Phillip Eugene Phillips's bankruptcy estate. In that capacity, Appellant seeks to avoid* certain transfers of real and personal property owned by Debtor and transfers of real and personal property owned by Philsax, Inc., a Colorado corporation. Prior to the property transfers, Debtor was the dominant and controlling shareholder of Philsax. To avoid the transfers made by Philsax and keep the property in the bankruptcy estate, Appellant seeks to show that Philsax is the alter ego of Debtor and,

individual partner, and not seeking to shield the limited partner from liability for the debts of the limited partnership, which is what Devon seeks to do in this matter.").

[8] *E.g.*, Connecticut Public Act 19–181, § 3 (statute providing that "reverse veil piercing doctrine" shall not apply); In re Glick, 568 B.R. 634, 659 (Bankr. N.D. Ill. 2017) ("Reverse piercing is controversial. Not all states endorse it."); In re Howland, 579 B.R. 411, 416 (Bankr. E.D. Ky. 2016) ("Reverse veil piercing is by no means a widely accepted legal principle."); Boeing Co. v. KB Yuzhnoye, 2016 WL 2851297, at *29 (C.D. Cal. 2016) ("Reverse veil piercing is a highly controversial and intensely debated corporate law doctrine."); Acree v. McMahan, 276 Ga. 880, 881, 585 S.E.2d 873 (Ga. 2003) ("we reject reverse piercing, at least to the extent that it would allow an 'outsider,' such as a third-party creditor, to pierce the veil in order to reach a corporation's assets to satisfy claims against an individual corporate insider").

[9] *See* McKay v. Longman, 211 A.3d 20, 52 (Conn. 2019) (permitting outsider reverse veil piercing while instructing courts to "consider the impact of reverse piercing on innocent shareholders and creditors"); Mattingly Law Firm, P.C. v. Henson, 466 P.3d 590, 594, 596 (Oka.App. 2019) ("We acknowledge the above-stated concerns associated with the practice of reverse piercing. We also acknowledge, however, that these concerns may be lessened or eliminated in the presence of particular facts, such as where a corporation is controlled by a single shareholder [and] there are no third-party shareholders to be unfairly prejudiced by disregarding the corporate form."); Floyd v. I.R.S. U.S., 151 F.3d 1295, 1299 (10th Cir. 1998) ("In addition, the reverse-pierce theory presents many problems. First, the theory bypasses normal judgment-collection procedures whereby judgment creditors attach the judgment debtor's shares in the corporation and not the corporation's assets. Second, third parties may be unfairly prejudiced if the corporation's assets can be attached directly. [One concern is] with non-culpable third-party shareholders of the corporation being unfairly prejudiced, [but] no greater culpability should attach to the third-party corporate creditors harmed by reverse-piercing in this case.").

* Author's note: "avoidance" in bankruptcy means the right of a bankruptcy trustee or the debtor in possession to avoid or nullify certain pre-bankruptcy transactions, thereby recovering certain transfers of property, including preferences, fraudulent transfers, and grant of liens.

therefore, actions taken by the corporation were, in effect, actions taken by the Debtor. The United States Bankruptcy Court for the District of Colorado dismissed Appellant's claim. The bankruptcy court held that absent clear Colorado precedent allowing reverse piercing, the court would not disregard Philsax's corporate status and invalidate the transfers.

Prior to May 2000, Debtor was the principal shareholder of Philsax, holding 51% of the outstanding shares. His wife, Margaret Phillips, owned the remaining 49% of the remaining shares. Debtor also owned 51% of Action Properties, Inc., prior to his November 2002 bankruptcy petition. Margaret Phillips owned the remaining Action Properties shares.

Although Margaret Phillips was the only other shareholder, officer, and director of Philsax and Action Properties, she could not testify as to her role in either corporation nor could she explain her duties or obligations as a director or officer in the entities.

While incorporated, Philsax had no bank account, no written bylaws, and maintained no written financial statements. Philsax failed to provide written notice of the board meetings and the Debtor removed and added directors at will.

Philsax's primary asset was the ownership of Parcel A and Parcel B, two parcels of real property. In early March 2000, Philsax entered into a written agreement to sell a 99.99% interest in Parcel A with the Veterans of Foreign Wars of the United States Post No. 32 ("VFW").

Although Philsax owned Parcel A, VFW executed a Promissory Note for $260,000 to Margaret Phillips at the closing. VFW also provided Margaret Phillips and Action Properties with a check for $90,000. Troy Brackeen, the Commander of the VFW, and Debtor, a member of the VFW, executed the check on behalf of the VFW. The VFW also made monthly payments to or for the benefit of Margaret Phillips.

At a March 8, 2000, special meeting of the board of directors of Philsax, Parcel B was transferred to Margaret Phillips and Action Properties. On March 13, 2000, the Philsax board of directors held a second special meeting. During the meeting, Debtor received approximately $90,000 for the transfer of 2000 shares to Troy Brackeen and 2000 to Troy Brackeen's wife, Ramona Brackeen. Ramona Brackeen is a niece by marriage of Debtor. Debtor also transferred 300 shares to Margaret Phillips, making her the majority shareholder of Philsax. Debtor used the money to pay personal expenses and transferred the remainder to Troy Brackeen.

A quit claim deed dated March 15, 2000, purportedly transferred VFW's 99.99% interest in Parcel A and Philsax's 0.01% interest in Parcel A to Margaret Phillips. Troy Brackeen and John Greenway signed the deed on behalf of the VFW. The deed was recorded on January 26, 2005.

Prior to these transfers, third parties sought and obtained a $135,000 civil judgment against Debtor. Action Properties and Philsax were both served with writs of garnishment. However, the transferring of Action Properties's and Philsax's assets rendered both corporations insolvent and the civil judgment creditors did not receive any payment.

Reverse Piercing

Colorado law permits trial courts to disregard the corporate form and pierce the corporate veil when a corporation and a shareholder are alter egos of each other. We are asked to expand this principle to disregard the corporate fiction and allow liability to be imposed on the corporation for acts of a dominant shareholder or other corporate insider.

Reverse piercing occurs when a claimant seeks to hold a corporation liable for the obligations of an individual shareholder. Two types of reverse piercing exist: inside and outside claims.

Inside claims involve a "controlling insider who attempts to have the corporate entity disregarded to avail the insider of corporate claims against third parties" or to protect corporate assets "from third party claims that are available only for assets owned by the insider." Inside reverse piercing claims allow a shareholder to disregard the corporate form.

Outside reverse piercing claims occur when a corporate outsider "pressing an action against a corporate insider seeks to disregard the corporate entity [and] to subject corporate assets to the claim" or when an outsider "with a claim against a corporate insider seeks to assert that claim against the corporation in an action between the claimant and the corporation." Outside reverse piercing actions involve a corporate outsider seeking to obligate a corporation for the debts of a dominant shareholder or other corporate insider.

We limit our review to outside claims due to the facts presented in this case. Appellant, an outsider to Philsax, seeks to hold the corporation liable for the obligations of Debtor.

Admittedly, the corporate interests at stake in traditional and outside reverse piercing differ, as does the entity pierced. In traditional veil piercing, the veil shields a shareholder who is abusing the corporate fiction to perpetuate a wrong. In outside reverse piercing, however, the corporate form protects the corporation which, through the acts of a dominant shareholder or other corporate insider, uses the legal fiction to perpetuate a fraud or defeat a rightful claim of an outsider. While traditional and outside reverse piercing affect diverse corporate interests, the purposes sought to be achieved are similar.

Both types of piercing strive to achieve an equitable result. In traditional piercing, equity requires the veil be pierced to impose liability on a shareholder who has abused the corporate form for his or her own advantage. Similarly, in outside reverse piercing, an equitable result is achieved by ignoring the corporate fiction to attach liability to the corporation. "Indeed, it is particularly appropriate to apply the alter ego doctrine in 'reverse' when the controlling party uses the controlled entity to hide assets or secretly to conduct business to avoid the preexisting liability of the controlling party." Thus, the purpose of obtaining a just result is furthered by permitting outside reverse piercing in Colorado.

Due to the similarities and parallel goals achieved in outside reverse piercing and traditional piercing, we hold that Colorado law permits outside reverse piercing when justice so requires.

We recognize that some jurisdictions refuse to allow outside reverse piercing of the corporate form because, when inartfully performed, outside reverse piercing has the potential to prejudice innocent shareholders and creditors, and to bypass normal judgment procedures. *See, e.g., Cascade Energy & Metals Corp. v. Banks*, 896 F.2d 1557, 1577 (10th Cir.1990). However, this concern is effectively alleviated by the requirement that piercing obtain an equitable result.

We note that a significant number of jurisdictions recognize outside reverse piercing. *See, e.g., McCall Stock Farms, Inc. v. United States,* 14 F.3d 1562, 1568 (Fed. Cir. 1993); *Towe Antique Ford Found. v. IRS,* 999 F.2d 1387, 1390–94 (9th Cir. 1993); *Zahra Spiritual Trust v. US,* 910 F.2d 240, 244 (5th Cir. 1990); *Estudios, Proyectos e Inversiones de Centro America, S.A. v. Swiss Bank Corp.*, 507 So.2d 1119, 1120–21 (Fla. App. 1987); *Minich v. Gem State Developers, Inc.*, 591 P.2d 1078, 1084 (Idaho 1979); *Lambert v. Farmers Bank, Frankfort, Ind.*, 519 N.E.2d 745 (Ind. App. 1988); *Central Nat'l Bank & Trust Co. of Des Moines v. Wagener,* 183 N.W.2d 678, 681–82 (Iowa 1971); *LFC Mktg. Group, Inc. v. Loomis,* 8 P.3d 841, 846 (Nev. 2000); *Zisblatt v. Zisblatt,* 693 S.W.2d 944, 955 (Tex. App. 1985); *C.F. Trust, Inc. v. First Flight L.P.*, 580 S.E.2d 806, 810 (Va. 2003); *W.G. Platts, Inc. v. Platts,* 298 P.2d 1107, 1110–11 (Wash. 1956).

Outside Reverse Piercing in Colorado

Having concluded that outside reverse piercing is appropriate, we proceed to discuss the limitations of the doctrine. A court may reverse pierce the corporate veil and obtain the assets of a corporation for the obligations of a controlling shareholder or other corporate insider only upon a clear showing that (1) the controlling insider and the corporation are alter egos of each other, (2) justice requires recognizing the substance of the relationship over the form because the corporate fiction is utilized to perpetuate a fraud or defeat a rightful claim, and (3) an equitable result is achieved by piercing. Only when a claimant makes a clear showing of each factor may the corporate form be disregarded.

In determining whether to outside reverse pierce the corporate veil, a court should review the same factors utilized in determining whether traditional veil piercing is appropriate.

The first factor to consider is whether Debtor and Philsax were alter egos of each other. In making this determination, our analysis suggests the Debtor's control over Philsax is relevant. Debtor removed and added directors without board approval and used the sale of corporate property to pay for his personal expenses. Margaret Phillips, the other shareholder, could not explain her role in the corporation. Also significant is Philsax's failure to operate as a distinct business entity, including the lack of a bank account and the intermingling with Action Properties and Debtor's personal affairs. Indeed, Action Properties and Margaret Phillips were paid for the sale of Philsax's property. Furthermore, Philsax's failure to observe many of the corporate formalities is germane; specifically the entity had no written bylaws, did not provide notice to directors or shareholders of board meetings, and did not maintain any written financial statements.

The second factor to review is whether justice requires recognizing the substance of the relationship between Debtor and Philsax over the form. Relevant to this inquiry is whether Philsax transferred its assets to defeat a third party judgment against Debtor.

The third determination is whether an equitable result would be achieved by piercing. As previously alluded to, some additional equitable considerations apply in the outside reverse piercing context.

When innocent shareholders or creditors would be prejudiced by outside reverse piercing, an equitable result is not achieved. Innocent shareholders possess legitimate expectations that corporate assets will be insulated from the claims of a controlling insider's creditors. Similarly, secured and unsecured creditors of the corporation have a cognizable legal interest in corporate assets, upon which they relied in lending money and selling goods and services to the corporation. Accordingly, equity requires that innocent shareholders and creditors be adequately protected before outside reverse piercing is appropriate under Colorado law.

Debtor identified the creditors of Philsax as identical to his personal creditors. The corporation has no other creditors. As the creditors of the entity are those of the Debtor, no creditors would be injured by outside reverse piercing. Our analysis does suggest, however, that if innocent shareholders would be prejudiced piercing would not be warranted.

As piercing the veil is an extraordinary remedy, the availability of alternative remedies must be considered by the trial court. These remedies may include, but are not limited to, conversion, fraudulent conveyance of assets, respondeat superior, and agency law. When a less invasive, adequate remedy is available, outside reverse piercing is discouraged.

We conclude that outside reverse piercing is appropriate when a claimant demonstrates that a controlling insider and a corporation are alter egos of each other and justice requires recognizing the substance of that relationship over the form to achieve an equitable result. An equitable result is not achieved when innocent shareholders or creditors are prejudiced by outside reverse piercing. A court should avoid outside reverse piercing when alternative, adequate remedies are available. In light of these limitations, this decision is unlikely to impact many business entities other than a limited number of closely held corporations with few shareholders or only a single shareholder.

2. VEIL PIERCING IN LPs

Courts are split on veil piercing for LPs. Some courts have applied it in situations where equity requires the prevention of fraud and abuse.[10] However, other courts have held that veil piercing does not apply due to the unique features of LPs.[11] The rationale revolves around the fact that the rule of limited liability in LPs is limited in scope.

> Appellants argue that the alter-ego ruling was in error because the alter-ego theory of veil-piercing simply does not apply to limited partnerships. Indeed, Texas courts have uniformly declined to apply the alter-ego theory to pierce a limited partnership's "veil" to impose the entity's liabilities on a limited partner. The need for any equitable veil-piercing doctrine is fundamentally dubious as applied to the liabilities of a limited partnership. Unlike a person doing business with a corporation, a person doing business with a limited partnership always has recourse against any general partner in the same manner as

---

[10] *See* C.F. Trust, Inc. v. First Flight L.P., 580 S.E.2d 806, 811 (Va. 2003) ("There is simply no language in the Act that prohibits a court from piercing the veil of a limited partnership."); Canter v. Lakewood of Voorhees, 22 A.3d 68, 70 (N.J. Super. 2011) ("Equitable principles, such as veil piercing, may apply to a New Jersey limited partnership but in limited circumstances, such as where a limited partner takes or attempts action not within the safe harbor of N.J.S.A. 42:2A–27b, or dominates and uses the limited partnership to perpetrate a fraud, injustice, or otherwise circumvent the law."); In re Adelphia Communications Corp., 376 B.R. 87, 108 (Bankr. S.D.N.Y. 2007) ("Although most veil-piercing cases have been decided in the context of corporations rather than partnerships, there is nothing about the nature of a limited partnership (where the limited partner is sometimes likened to a shareholder) that would preclude recourse to veil piercing as an equitable remedy in appropriate circumstances."); C.F. Trust, Inc. v. First Flight L.P., 580 S.E.2d 806, 811 (Va. 2003) ("A court considering reverse veil piercing must weigh the impact of such action upon innocent investors, in this instance, innocent limited partners or innocent general partners. A court considering reverse veil piercing must also consider the impact of such an act upon innocent secured and unsecured creditors.").

[11] *See* Cantor Fitzgerald & Co. v. 8an Capital Partners Master Fund L.P., 59 Mis.3d 1225(A) (N.Y. Sup. 2018) ("Veil piercing is not applicable to a limited partnership form as a matter of law given such a partnership has by its very nature no 'veil' to pierce."); Backuswalcott v. Common Ground Community HDFC, Inc., 104 F.Supp.2d 363, 369 n.3 (S.D.N.Y. 2000) ("the veil-piercing doctrine may not apply to limited partnerships"); Seidler v. Morgan, 277 S.W.3d 549, 558 n. 5 (Tex. App. 2009) ("Theory of piercing the corporate veil is inapplicable to limited partnerships."); Pinebrook Props., Ltd. v. Brookhaven Lake Prop. Owners Ass'n, 77 S.W.3d 487, 499 (Tex.App. 2002) ("The theory of piercing the corporate veil is inapplicable to partnerships.").

partners are liable for the liabilities of a partnership without limited partners. Tex. Bus. Orgs. Code § 153.152(b). The identities of the general partners of a limited partnership are readily ascertainable because they must be periodically reported to the secretary of state. *Id.* § 153.302(a)(1)(E).

In contrast to general partners, limited partners in a limited partnership are generally not responsible for the limited partnership's obligations unless they take some action to accept or subject themselves to such liability.[3] The statute expressly provides that a limited partner "is not liable for the obligations of a limited partnership unless" one of two circumstances applies: (1) the limited partner is also a general partner; or (2) in addition to the exercise of the limited partner's rights and powers as a limited partner, the limited partner participates in the control of the business. *Id.* § 153.102(a); *see also id.* § 153.003(c) ("A limited partner shall not have any obligation or duty of a general partner solely by reason of being a limited partner."). The plain implication of the statute is that a limited partner may become liable for the obligations of the limited partnership due to the limited partner's participation in the "control of the business," though that liability is limited by statute to "a person who transacts business with the limited partnership reasonably believing, based on the limited partner's conduct, that the limited partner is a general partner." *Id.* § 153.102(b). Unlike the few courts in foreign jurisdictions which have characterized the liability that can be imposed in such circumstances as an equitable exercise of limited-partnership veil-piercing, our view is that this liability is better characterized as an application of ordinary partnership principles, or, in other words, a limitation on the protection generally available to limited partners.

Significantly, the limited partnership statute also contains an extensive list of actions which do not constitute participation in "control of the business" for purposes of third-party liability pursuant to section 153.102. Such actions include acting as (A) a contractor for or an officer or other agent or employee of the limited partnership; (B) a contractor for or an agent or employee of a general partner; or (C) an officer, director, or stockholder of a corporate general partner. *Id.* § 153.103(1).

Peterson Group, Inc. v. PLTQ Lotus Group, L.P., 417 S.W.3d 46, 56–57 (Tex. App. 2013).

E. SUCCESSOR LIABILITY

When one company sells or otherwise transfers all its assets to another company, the general rule is that the acquiring company is not liable for the debts and liabilities of the transferring company, including liabilities under torts and contracts. However, the doctrine of successor liability is an exception to the general rule.

The case below deals with a situation in which an LLC continued a prior existing business. In reading this case, consider these questions: (1) What are the key facts that supported the application of successor liability? (2) In hindsight, how should the acquiring LLC have dealt with the trade counterparty to avoid the application of successor liability?

ALSCO, INC. V. FATTY'S BAR, LLC

461 P.3d 798 (Idaho 2019)

BEVAN, JUSTICE.

This appeal concerns the doctrine of successor liability and its applicability to a business known as "Fatty's Bar" ("Fatty's"). Tons of Fun, LLC opened Fatty's in October 2010 and a short time later its manager, Clay Roman, signed a textile services agreement (the "Agreement") with Alsco, Inc. ("Alsco"). The Agreement contained an automatic renewal clause, by which the Agreement would renew automatically for a period of 60 months if neither party terminated it in writing at least 90 days before its initial expiration. Fatty's fell on difficult financial times, and closed for a period in January 2013. Soon after, Steven and Jennifer Masonheimer created Fatty's Bar, LLC, and re-opened Fatty's in mid-February, 2013, continuing to receive textiles from Alsco. The Agreement automatically renewed in March 2016. In March 2017, Fatty's Bar, LLC terminated the Agreement, well before the 60-month term was set to expire.

Alsco sued Fatty's Bar, LLC and Clay Roman, seeking damages based on a liquidated damages provision in the Agreement. After trial, the district court held that both Fatty's Bar, LLC and Roman were jointly and severally liable to Alsco for damages under a liquidated damages clause that was also in the Agreement. Fatty's Bar, LLC appealed. We affirm.

Justin Zora filed a certificate of organization for a limited liability company called Tons of Fun, LLC. Zora listed himself as a member or manager on the filing. Later, Tons of Fun, LLC opened a bar called "Fatty's." Tons of Fun, LLC owned some equipment and Zora also leased a liquor license and some equipment from Colby Smith to operate Fatty's.

Roman executed the Agreement with Alsco. The customer name on the Agreement is "Fatty's," and under Roman's signature is the title "Partner Owner." The Agreement was an "exclusive" agreement, providing that Alsco "shall be the exclusive supplier to Customer of the services and goods listed." The Agreement also contained [a 60-month term].

Tons of Fun, LLC began experiencing financial difficulties and had to shut Fatty's down for a time due to a liquor license violation. Tons of Fun, LLC was also unable to secure a new lease for the space occupied by Fatty's. Zora began searching for a financial partner and asked Steven Masonheimer ("Steven") if he was interested in assisting. Steven and his wife Jennifer Masonheimer ("Jennifer") owned a limited liability company called The Drink, LLC, which owned another local bar in Boise called "The Drink." Zora and Roman both worked at The Drink. Notably, Alsco provided linen services to The Drink under a contract—also signed by Roman—identical to the Agreement at issue for Fatty's.

Steven declined Zora's offer to become a financial partner, but he and Zora did discuss opening what they called a new business at the same location of Fatty's, with Zora as the manager. The Masonheimers filed a certificate of organization for "Fatty's Bar, LLC."

Fatty's Bar, LLC negotiated a new five-year lease for the space occupied by Fatty's. Fatty's Bar, LLC also purchased the liquor license and some equipment that Tons of Fun, LLC had been leasing from Colby Smith. Fatty's Bar, LLC temporarily shut down Fatty's for about two months to remodel the space. Upon reopening, Fatty's Bar, LLC retained most of the employees but hired a new security team. Zora was hired back as the general manager. Fatty's Bar, LLC kept the name, "Fatty's," used the same signage, equipment, and vendors that Tons of Fun, LLC had used while operating Fatty's.

Once Fatty's Bar, LLC reopened Fatty's, Alsco continued to perform under the Agreement. At some point, Jennifer contacted Alsco to change the billing process under the Agreement from cash-on-delivery to monthly statements sent to Fatty's Bar, LLC's address. Jennifer was also listed as the customer representative for Fatty's in Alsco's system. Alsco sent billing statements for its services to Fatty's Bar, LLC's address and Fatty's Bar, LLC paid those statements for nearly four years.

Each statement Alsco sent to Fatty's Bar, LLC contained the total balance owing and the following language: "The services for which these charges are made are being furnished to you pursuant to a service agreement between our company as supplier and the above named customer." After taking ownership of Fatty's, Fatty's Bar, LLC amended the schedules under the written Agreement on at least one occasion to request new items or add inventory.

Fatty's Bar, LLC and Zora parted ways and Fatty's Bar, LLC executed an asset purchase agreement with Tons of Fun, LLC/Justin Zora. Fatty's Bar, LLC agreed to pay $10,000 for the following equipment owned by Tons of Fun, LLC, as set forth on the inventory list attached to the asset purchase agreement: "all televisions and brackets, beer pong tables, exterior and interior signage, lighting, sound equipment, decorations, electronic equipment, liquor/alcohol, fixtures (stationary or built in), glassware, and anything with the Fatty's logo on it." After Zora left, Roman returned to work as the manager for Fatty's Bar, LLC.

The Agreement automatically renewed for another 60 months after no party gave written notice terminating it. Fatty's Bar, LLC continued to accept and pay for services under the Agreement for another year, until Fatty's Bar, LLC found another vendor that could provide the same goods and services at a lower price. Fatty's Bar, LLC terminated the Agreement with Alsco at that time.

Alsco filed a verified complaint alleging breach of contract against Clay Roman, an individual d/b/a Fatty's, and Fatty's LLC. Alsco alleged "upon information and belief, FATTY'S BAR, LLC became the successor to Clay Roman d/b/a Fatty's in 2013."

The case proceeded to a bench trial. The court held that Fatty's Bar, LLC was liable to Alsco for breach of contract under the theory of successor liability because it impliedly assumed the Agreement. The district court held Fatty's Bar, LLC and Roman, jointly and severally liable to pay liquidated damages of $23,206. Fatty's Bar, LLC now appeals to this Court.

The doctrine of successor liability stems from equitable principles, and fairness is the prime consideration in application of the doctrine.

At the outset we recognize that the application of successor liability to a given set of facts is a fact-intensive exercise in a legal field nearly uncharted by this Court. That said, it is also an area of law fraught with potential pitfalls. As one commentator recognized:

> Successor liability law is mostly composed of state common law case-by-case decisions. These decisions fundamentally seek to balance two competing, and often conflicting, policy goals: to provide a necessary remedy to injured parties, often tort claimants, and to provide transactional clarity and certainty for business parties engaged in fundamental corporate transactions. As it has developed to date, however, successor liability law is so varied and unpredictable that it is not only a trap for the unwary, but a trap for the very wary, as well.

Such a trap may have caught the appellants here. Even so, we recognize and emphasize that this is an area of the law in which the trial court has broad discretion, and in which we are making a narrow decision based on (1) the record before us, and (2) the deferential standard of review that applies to such equitable results.

The district court's factual finding that Fatty's Bar, LLC was a successor in interest to Tons of Fun, LLC is supported by substantial evidence

Successor liability is generally considered an equitable doctrine. Cases involving claims of successor liability thus require a trial judge to weigh the competing equities of the case and make a reasoned and informed decision. As a result, appellate courts are deferential in reviewing a trial court's equitable decisions such as those made by the district court here.

The substantial evidence found by the district court is that in August 2013, Fatty's Bar, LLC executed an asset purchase agreement directly with Tons of Fun, LLC. Under the agreement, Fatty's Bar, LLC agreed to pay $10,000 for the equipment owned by Tons of Fun, LLC that was connected to its operation of Fatty's. The purchase included all the assets of the business, as itemized in the inventory list attached to the asset purchase agreement. Thus, despite Fatty's Bar, LLC's efforts to claim this agreement did not involve "all or substantially all" of the assets of Tons of Fun, LLC, it was reasonable for the district court to conclude that an agreement specifying "*all* televisions and brackets, *all* beer pong tables, *all* exterior and interior signage, *all* lighting, *all* sound equipment, *all* decorations, *all* electronic equipment, *all* liquor/alcohol, *all* fixtures (stationary or built in), *all* glass wear, and *anything* with the Fatty's logo on it" constituted substantially all of Tons of Fun, LLC's assets.

The question is whether Fatty's Bar, LLC, purchased all or substantially all of Tons of Fun, LLC's assets. There is no evidence in the record that any assets held by Tons of Fun, LLC were not transferred to Fatty's Bar, LLC. The district court was "responsible for determining factual issues that exist with respect to [successor liability] and for fashioning the equitable remedy." Based on the evidence, the district court did not abuse its discretion when it held that Fatty's Bar, LLC purchased or was the transferee of all or substantially all of Tons of Fun's assets. Thus, we affirm the district court's conclusion that Fatty's Bar, LLC was a successor in interest to Tons of Fun, LLC.

The district court did not abuse its discretion when it held that Fatty's Bar, LLC impliedly assumed the Agreement.

We must now assess the district court's legal conclusion in holding that Fatty's Bar, LLC is obligated under the written Agreement between Tons of Fun, LLC and Alsco.

The general rule, which is well settled in other jurisdictions, is that where one company sells or otherwise transfers all its assets to another company, the latter is *not* liable for the debts and liabilities of the transferor. We recognize this general principle and adopt it in a general sense in Idaho. However, the trap for the unwary in these cases is that successor liability also depends on the *particular facts and legal duties at stake in each case*; as a result, a buyer of assets "may be a successor for some purposes and not for others." Thus, a court acting in equity may make a discretionary decision that is within the outer limits of its discretion, but that goes against the general rule cited by Fatty's Bar, LLC.

There are four recognized exceptions which may require a successor entity to be liable as a successor: (1) the purchaser expressly or impliedly agrees to assume the liability; (2) the purchase is a de facto merger or consolidation; (3) the purchaser is a mere continuation of the seller; or (4) the asset transfer is for the fraudulent purpose of escaping liability. Here, the district court held that Fatty's Bar, LLC impliedly assumed liability for the Alsco Agreement, so the focus of our review is on that exception alone.

"Proof of an implied assumption of contractual liabilities is a heavily fact-intensive exercise." "An implied assumption requires consideration of all the circumstances, such as the subject matter of the contract, the assignee's acts and words, and whether he acquiesced in the terms of the contract, performed its obligations, or accepted its benefits." "In order for a promise to be implied, the conduct or representations relied upon must evidence an intention on the part of the purchasing company to assume the old corporation's liabilities in whole or in part."

Yet Fatty's Bar, LLC's continuous acceptance of and payment for Alsco's services for years after Tons of Fun, LLC ceased to exist can hardly be considered a "fortuitous debt payment." Here, as the district court found in its factual findings, Fatty's Bar, LLC continued to use and pay for all of Alsco's services under the Agreement for four years before it decided to terminate Alsco's services due to finding a cheaper option.

The district court [found] that Tons of Fun, LLC and Fatty's Bar, LLC had material connections before and after Fatty's Bar, LLC took over the operation, not the least of which were the ongoing operation of the bar in the identical leased space Fatty's used, using the same liquor license and equipment that Fatty's used, and using the identical name for the bar.

The district court [held] that Fatty's Bar, LLC impliedly assumed the entire Agreement, not just the term remaining until March 2016. We agree. To hold otherwise would undermine the basis of successor liability law. For successor liability, "liabilities" assumed include not only outstanding debts, but obligations arising under contracts assumed, including a contingent future liability on a contract.

We hold that the district court applied appropriate legal standards and acted within the boundaries of its discretion in concluding that Fatty's Bar, LLC impliedly assumed the liabilities under the Agreement. Once Fatty's Bar, LLC reopened Fatty's in March 2013, Alsco continued to perform under the Agreement, making weekly deliveries and pick-ups at Fatty's. Fatty's Bar, LLC accepted and paid for these services until March 2017. Fatty's Bar, LLC showed its ability to contact Alsco and modify the Agreement by: (1) notifying Alsco that Fatty's ownership had changed; (2) changing the billing process; and (3) amending the schedules under the Agreement to request new items or add inventory. The bottom line is that Fatty's Bar, LLC "acquiesced in the terms of the contract" by receiving benefits from Alsco and paying for those benefits for years. The district court did not abuse its discretion in holding that Fatty's Bar, LLC impliedly assumed the Agreement.

F. ISSUES TO CONSIDER FOR NBEs

1. AVOIDING VEIL PIERCING

Owners form limited liability entities to limit their liability exposure. The LLC is the form that provides blanket coverage to members and managers, unlike the LP where the general partner is vicariously liable for the debts and obligations of the firm. The rule of limited liability provides a shield, but courts have also held that the entity form cannot be abused, or else the rule of limited liability will be denied by equity. Advice on liability management is important.

Veil piercing is more commonly invoked in situations where there is one or a few dominant owners. Such situations are more conducive to abuse of the entity form. When there are many members, the possibility of inequitable conduct decreases because there is typically more monitoring. When there is a single owner, how can the risk of veil piercing be mitigated? An attorney and client should consider several principles.

First, a member should respect the entity form and conduct business affairs in a way that distinguishes the member and the firm. RULLCA § 304(b) provides that the "failure of a limited liability company to observe formalities relating to the exercise of its powers or management of its activities and affairs is not a ground" to pierce the veil. In corporations, certain formalities must be observed, such as the appointment of directors, holding board and shareholder meetings, and maintaining corporate records. The LLC form permits a more flexible and informal management practice. This does not mean that the LLC is simply an alter ego of the member. While formalities need not be observed, their observance would be evidence of a separate and distinct entity.

Second, one should avoid actions that indicate a prior scheme to defraud or engage in inequitable conduct. Such actions include ex ante undercapitalization. The rule of limited liability applies only when there is ex post undercapitalization. If it is apparent that the LLC was established with the intent to engage in transactions that benefit the member but load the LLC with unpayable debts and obligations, a court could see such conduct as a scheme to defraud and thus inequitable.

Third, the LLC should have a legitimate business enterprise. In a single-member LLC or an LLC with a dominant member, this business enterprise would also be the business of the member. However, the business should be operated as a business of the LLC. This means that the LLC exercises the powers of a legal person, such as executing contracts, owning property, using employees, and doing all other activities of a business. Although there may be a close or perfect alignment of the business interest of the LLC and the member, the activities between the two should not merge into an indistinguishable unity.

2. PERSONAL GUARANTEES

Although LLCs and LPs provide limited liability protection, there is no reason why the right to limited liability may not be waived. Such waivers are not seen ordinarily because a major reason for forming a limited liability entity is to get limited liability. However, creditors can and often do seek waivers of limited liability on transactional bases through the negotiation of personal guarantees of the entity's debt. Creditors often condition the provision of credit to the entity on the agreement by the owners of a personal guarantee.[12]

If a personal guarantee is given, it triggers some complications. What are the contribution requirements of other owners when a personal guarantee requires the guarantor owner's payment for the outstanding debt of the entity? Does the charter agreement's indemnification provision, if any, cover the payment of the guarantee? What are the obligations of a dissociating owner toward the personal guarantee of a remaining owner? What is the obligation of the firm or remaining owners if the dissociating member is the guarantor? Does the personal guarantee affect any buy-sell agreement in the charter agreement?

3. LIABILITY FOR ONE'S CONDUCT AND INDEMNIFICATION

Direct liabilities may arise under torts, contracts, regulations, or under any other laws that can impose liability on a person for his or her own actions. Given this possibility, the statute and the charter agreement may provide for indemnification. *See* RULLCA § 408(a) (providing for reimbursement "for any payment made by the member or manager in [compliance] with Sections 405, 407, and 409"); RUPA § 401(c) (providing indemnification for liabilities incurred by a partner); ULPA (2001) § 408(b) (same indemnification for a general partner).

---

12 *E.g.*, Russ Buettner, Susanne Craig & Mike McIntire, *The President's Taxes: Long-Concealed Records Show Trump's Chronic Losses and Years of Tax Avoidance*, N.Y. Times (Sept. 27, 2020) ("And within the next four years, more than $300 million in loans—obligations for which he is personally responsible—will come due. . . . What's more, the tax records show that Mr. Trump has once again done what he says he regrets, looking back on his early 1990s meltdown: personally guaranteed hundreds of millions of dollars in loans, a decision that led his lenders to threaten to force him into personal bankruptcy. This time around, he is personally responsible for loans and other debts totaling $421 million, with most of it coming due within four years.").

G. PROBLEM: ENTREPRENEURS THINK ABOUT LIABILITY

Piers and Blake continued to work on their business plan. They still have not decided on what form of business organization they will eventually form. That decision, they felt, could be held off for a while. The most pressing need was financing. Soon, they will graduate and will need funding to proceed with the business.

They approached Rittenhouse Bank to inquire about a bank loan for $500,000. They explained that they were entrepreneurs and needed financing. The banker, Bethaney Banks, was cautious, but continued the conversation, including eliciting personal financial information. The following conversation ensued.

Banks: "Have you formed a business yet?"

Piers: "Not yet. We're meeting with an attorney now. We have a few things to think about before forming an entity."

Banks: "Then, can I assume that the borrower will be both you in your personal capacities?"

Blake: "I don't know. Are you saying that I would be borrowing $500,000 in my personal capacity?"

Banks: "Well, without an entity, who would be the borrower?"

Piers: "Yes, we will be forming an entity. We don't know what that entity is just yet, but our lawyer said that limited liability is important."

Banks: "Even if you form a corporation or a limited liability entity, Rittenhouse Bank will require personal guarantees from both of you."

Blake: "What does that mean?"

Banks: "A personal guarantee means that both of you as individuals will provide a guarantee of your company's debt. At this point, it looks like your business is new. It has no other assets, or assets that can be liquidated to service the debt to Rittenhouse Bank. If the company goes insolvent like so many other new businesses, Rittenhouse Bank must have some assurance that the loan will be paid. We usually ask that the owners, such as yourselves, personally provide that guarantee."

Piers: "But the whole point of forming a limited liability entity is so that the owners would not be personally liable for the debts and obligations of the company solely because of our status as owners."

Banks: "That is true, but in cases of new startups and risky businesses our bank typically requires a personal guarantee by the owners. . . . Well, let me ask this. Will the company have an operating business right away? Will it be able to generate cash flows to service the interest on the loan and eventually the principal payment? What are its initial assets?"

Blake: "It's a new business. We don't know. But we're well aware of the potential problem of using debt in a new business."

Banks: "Yes. Your business will be risky, and that's why we'll require a personal guarantee. Rittenhouse Bank is willing to give you this loan, but we have our conditions."

Piers: "Thank you. Let us think about this."

QUESTIONS

1. Identify all the practical business issues that Piers and Blake should consider in deciding whether to accept the creditor's offer?

2. If Piers and Blake decide they need the bank loan, how might they go about negotiating the credit contract in a way that minimizes the personal exposure? What might be some of the negotiating points?

3. Even if no bank will provide a loan without personal guarantees, does the rule of limited liability provide a benefit to Piers and Blake who would be the owners of the firm?

CHAPTER 4

FINANCE

■ ■ ■

A. INTRODUCTION TO EQUITY FINANCING

Businesses must finance their ventures. Investors are either creditors or equityholders. Creditors provide debt financing. Debt is a legal contract providing financing to the firm for a promised interest payment and a return of principal at a maturity date. Equityholders provide equity financing. Equity represents a bundle of governance and economic rights. Equityholders are the "owners" of the firm in two ways.

First, equityholders have direct control or governance rights. Direct control rights mean that they participate in the management of the firm. *E.g.*, RUPA § 401(h) ("Each partner has equal rights in the management and conduct of the partnership's business."); RULLCA § 407(b)(2) ("In a member-managed limited liability company Each member has equal rights in the management and conduct of the company's activities and affairs."); ULPA (2001) § 406(a) ("Each general partner has equal rights in the management and conduct of the limited partnership's activities and affairs."). Governance rights mean that if the equityholders appoint a manager to manage the firm's day-to-day business and affairs (such as a board of directors in a corporation or a general partner in an LP), they still have certain voting rights that approve the appointment of managers or certain transactions. *E.g.*, DGCL § 211(b) (requiring annual election of directors by shareholders); RULLCA § 407(c)(4) ("In a manager-managed limited liability company. A manager may be chosen at any time by the affirmative vote or consent of a majority of the members."); ULPA (2001) § 801(a)(2) ("A limited partnership is dissolved, and its activities and affairs must be wound up, upon the affirmative vote or consent of all general partners and of limited partners owning a majority of the rights to receive distributions as limited partners").

Second, equity financing is characterized by an entitlement to the firm's profits and the net assets, which are assets of the firm net of liabilities owed to creditors. A fundamental attribute of a partner is that she is entitled to the profits of the partnership. *E.g.*, RUPA § 202(c)(3) ("A person who receives a share of the profits of a business is presumed to be a partner in the business."). Shareholders are entitled to distributions from the firm's surplus or profits. *E.g.*, DGCL § 170 (providing that dividends may be paid out of surplus or net profits). Upon dissolution and wind up, the equityholders are paid from assets after satisfying all liabilities to creditors, *i.e.*, assets net of liabilities (net assets). *E.g.*, *id.* § 281(a) ("Any remaining assets shall be distributed to the stockholders of the dissolved corporation."); ULPA (2001) § 810(a)–(b) (same as to partners); RULLCA § 707(a)–(b) (same as to members). Every firm requires a residual claimant. If the firm is successful and earns more than the interest and principal payments contractually obligated to creditors, *someone* must own the residual, which is the firm's profits and net assets.

B. SHAREHOLDERS

Shareholders provide equity financing by purchasing shares from the corporation. Once shares are purchased, they can, in compliance with securities law, subsequently sell their shares, which is personal property; the purchasers would then become new shareholders. If the corporation has a single class of stock, it is common stock. Common stockholders are entitled to all of the profits and surplus in the corporation. They are also entitled to full voting rights. *See* DGCL § 151(b) ("The corporation shall have outstanding 1 or more shares of 1 or more classes or series of stock, which share, or shares together, shall have full voting powers."); MBCA § 6.03(c) ("One or more shares that together have full voting rights and one or more shares that together are entitled to receive the net assets of the corporation upon dissolution must be outstanding."). If there are multiple classes of stock, some may have no, limited, or super voting rights. "Full voting rights" means that all shareholders, collectively, must have full voting powers. Among other things, shareholder voting is necessary to elect directors and approve fundamental governance matters and transactions such as amendment of certificate of incorporation, approval of mergers and sale of all or substantially all assets.

1. CHARACTERISTICS OF STOCK

Corporation law permits the rights to voting, profits, and net assets to be allocated among different classes and series of stocks. If there are two or more classes or series of stock, they may have different voting rights. Some shares may have super voting rights (*e.g.*, 10 votes per share while another class has 1 vote per share), or specific voting rights (*e.g.*, voting rights limited to approval of certain transactions such as mergers and acquisitions). Two or more classes or series of stock may have different rights to the corporation's economic production. Different series of a specific class of stock may have different dividend rates or other rights.

Stock is generally categorized into two broad classes: common stock and preferred stock. Preferred stock has certain preference rights and, usually, limitations as compared to common stock. Preferred stock is a contract-based instrument, and its rights, preferences, and limitations are set forth in the certificate of incorporation. The typical preference rights are priorities as to dividends and liquidation. Preferred stock has a fixed dividend that has a higher priority than dividends to common stock: *i.e.*, preferred stock dividends must be paid first before any dividends can be paid to the common stock. Preferred stock also has a liquidation preference wherein preferred stockholder are paid first in a liquidation from net assets before common stockholders are paid. Within these broad classes of stock, there may be different series having different rights. For example, preferred stock may have series "A" and "B" with different dividend amounts, liquidation values, and possibly other rights such as the right to convert into common stock at specific stated formulae.

Stock has two attributes that are different from the default rules of ownership interest in NBEs. First, absent a specific restriction on transferability, stock in its entirety is freely alienable. Stock is personal property. A shareholder can transfer the entire bundle of governance and economic rights embodied in the stock. For example, shareholder John sells his shares to Jane, and thereafter Jane is the new shareholder and can exercise all rights of a shareholder including the right to vote and participate in corporate governance. This trait of free alienability differs from the rules for NBEs. In NBEs, the default rule is that only the transferable interest, which is the right to received distributions, is personal property and thus transferable, and a transferee does not become a member owner.[1]

Second, each share of the same class or series of stock is fungible in terms of legal rights under corporation law. Each share is the same as other shares in the same class or series. A shareholder's stake in the corporation is simply the number of shares owned. The company founder may own shares identical to those owned by her employees, except she may own more shares than they do. Concessions, such as a board seat, may result from ownership of stock, but rights inherent in each unit of stock are common to all in the class or series. If a shareholder seeks a specific package of rights grafted into the ownership interest, the corporation must issue a class or series of stock that incorporates those specific demands into the security. If the certificate of incorporation does not provide such stock or the board is not authorized to issue such stock, then the corporation must amend the certificate of incorporation.

2. ISSUING STOCK

Corporation law requires that the certificate of incorporation state the maximum authorized shares that a corporation may issue. *See* DGCL

---

[1] *See* RULLCA § 102(24) (defining transferable interest as "the right to receive distributions"); *id.* § 501 (stating that a transferable interest "is personal property"); *id.* § 502(a) ("a transfer, in whole or in part, of a transferable interest is permissible" and "does not entitle the transferee to participate in the management or conduct of the company's activities and affairs"); *id.* § 502(g) ("if a member transfers a transferable interest, the transferor retains the rights of a member other than the transferable interest transferred and retains all the duties and obligations of a member").

§ 102(a)(4) (requiring disclosure of "the total number of shares of stock which the corporation shall be authority to issue"). When forming the corporation, an organizer should state a sufficient number of authorized shares that will not only satisfy the initial capitalization of the company but also future anticipated issuances of stock.[2] If the corporation issues all authorized shares and wishes to issue more shares, it must amend the certificate of incorporation to increase the number of authorized shares.

The board of directors may authorize stock to be issued for "consideration consisting of cash, any tangible or intangible property or any benefit to the corporation, or any combination thereof." DGCL § 152. In public companies, the most common consideration is obviously cash. However, consideration can be any form of property or benefit, *e.g.*, a building, a business unit, or service.

3. CLASSES AND SERIES OF STOCK

If there is one class of common stock, the shareholders have equal rights to distributions, dissolution and wind up, and voting. Each share is the same and the only distinction among shareholders is the number of shares they own. But a corporation may issue different classes and series of stock. Shareholders collectively have "full voting rights" under corporation law, but each class or series of stock may have different rights, powers, and preferences. Most public companies have only one class of common stock, thus equal rights, powers, and preferences inherent in each share. But some companies issue different classes of stock.

DGCL § 151(a). Classes and Series of Stock; Redemption; Rights.

Every corporation may issue 1 or more classes of stock or 1 or more series of stock within any class thereof, any or all of which classes may be of stock with par value or stock without par value and which classes or series may have such voting powers, full or limited, or no voting powers, and such designations, preferences and relative, participating, optional or other special rights, and qualifications, limitations or restrictions thereof, as shall be stated and expressed in the certificate of incorporation or of any amendment thereto, or in the resolution or resolutions providing for the issue of such stock adopted by the board of

---

[2] The number of authorized shares is a factor in the annual franchise tax a Delaware corporation must pay. *See* How to Calculate Franchise Taxes, Del. Division of Corporations, available at https://corp.delaware.gov/frtaxcalc/. Franchise taxes depends on whether the stock has no par value or a par value, and the number of authorized shares. The greater the number of authorized shares, the more annual franchise tax is owed. As of May 2020, the franchise tax is no less than $175 and no more than $200,000. For smaller companies, franchise taxes may affect the decision on setting the number of authorized shares. For larger public companies, the greater consideration would be the pragmatic need for the specific number of authorized shares irrespective of franchise taxes.

directors pursuant to authority expressly vested in it by the provisions of its certificate of incorporation.

Preferred stock is a commonly seen class of stock. It typically provides the holder preferred rights to dividends and in liquidation. It typically has a stated dividend (*e.g.*, 7% of face value). The right to dividends is typically cumulative, meaning that any dividend not paid accumulates as an obligation that must be paid first before dividends can be paid to common stockholders. Preferred stock can be issued in different series, each series having different terms with respect to dividends or other rights.

Another common form of stock is stock with supervoting rights. For example, one class of common stock may have 1 vote per share while another class has 10 votes per share. This structure is called *dual class stocks*. Dual class stocks are used to concentrate voting control in the hands of certain insiders. Some technology companies and other prominent companies use dual class stock: *e.g.*, Facebook, Google, and Ford Motor have dual class stock with one class having supervoting rights. Also, dual class is not limited to just differences in voting rights, but can be any differences in rights, powers, or preferences among common stocks: *e.g.*, Berkshire Hathaway has two classes to stock with different rights to the company's economic returns such that the Class B stock trades at much lower price than the Class A stock, thus affordable to smaller shareholders (as of Jan. 28, 2020, Class A stock closed on the NYSE at $336,000 per share, and Class B closed at $224.74 per share).

Preferred stock and dual class stocks are not the only kinds of securities. Corporation law permits a corporation to design any form of securities that fits its needs. *See* DGCL § 151(a) (permitting "voting powers, full or limited, or no voting powers, and such designations, preferences and relative, participating, optional or other special rights, and qualifications, limitations or restrictions").

Amended and Restated Certificate of Incorporation of Alphabet Inc. [Google]

ARTICLE IV

Section 1. Authorized Shares. This Corporation is authorized to issue nine billion (9,000,000,000) shares of Class A Common Stock, par value $0.001 per share (the "Class A Common Stock"), three billion (3,000,000,000) shares of Class B Common Stock, par value $0.001 per share (the "Class B Common Stock", and together with the Class A Common Stock, the "Common Stock"), three billion (3,000,000,000) shares of Class C Capital Stock, par value $0.001 per share (the "Class C Capital Stock"), and one hundred million (100,000,000) shares of Preferred Stock, par value $0.001 per share. The number of authorized shares of any class or classes of stock may be increased or decreased (but not below the number of shares thereof then outstanding) by the affirmative vote of the holders of at least a majority of the voting power of the issued and outstanding shares of Common Stock of the Corporation, voting together as a single class.

Section 2. Common Stock. A statement of the designations of each class of Common Stock and the powers, preferences and rights and qualifications, limitations or restrictions thereof is as follows:

(a) Voting Rights.

(i) Except as otherwise provided herein or by applicable law, the holders of shares of Class A Common Stock and Class B Common Stock shall at all times vote together as one class on all matters (including the election of directors) submitted to a vote or for the consent of the stockholders of the Corporation.

(ii) Each holder of shares of Class A Common Stock shall be entitled to one (1) vote for each share of Class A Common Stock held as of the applicable date on any matter that is submitted to a vote or for the consent of the stockholders of the Corporation.

(iii) Each holder of shares of Class B Common Stock shall be entitled to ten (10) votes for each share of Class B Common Stock held as of the applicable date on any matter that is submitted to a vote or for the consent of the stockholders of the Corporation.

(b) Dividends. Subject to the preferences applicable to any series of Preferred Stock, if any, outstanding at any time, the holders of Class A Common Stock and the holders of Class B Common Stock shall be entitled to share equally, on a per share basis, in such dividends and other distributions of cash, property or shares of stock of the Corporation as may be declared by the Board of Directors from time to time with respect to the Common Stock out of assets or funds of the Corporation legally available therefor; provided, however, that in the event that such dividend is paid in the form of shares of Common Stock or rights to acquire Common Stock, the holders of Class A Common Stock shall receive Class A Common Stock or rights to acquire Class A Common Stock, as the case may be, and the holders of Class B Common Stock shall receive Class B Common Stock or rights to acquire Class B Common Stock, as the case may be.

(c) Liquidation. Subject to the preferences applicable to any series of Preferred Stock, if any outstanding at any time, in the event of the voluntary or involuntary liquidation, dissolution, distribution of assets or winding up of the Corporation, the holders of Class A Common Stock and the holders of Class B Common Stock shall be entitled to share equally, on a per share basis, all assets of the Corporation of whatever kind available for distribution to the holders of Common Stock.

Section 4. Preferred Stock. The Board of Directors is authorized, subject to any limitations prescribed by law, to provide for the issuance of shares of Preferred Stock in series, and to establish from time to time the number of shares to be included in each such series, and to fix the designation, power, preferences, and rights of the shares of each such series and any qualifications, limitations or restrictions thereof. Except as otherwise required by law, holders of Common Stock shall not be entitled to vote on any amendment to this Certificate of Incorporation (including any certificate of designation filed with respect to any series of Preferred Stock) that relates solely to the terms of one or more outstanding series of Preferred Stock if the holders of such affected series are entitled, either separately or together as a class with the holders of one or more other such series, to vote thereon by law or pursuant to this Certificate of Incorporation (including any certificate of designation filed with respect to any series of Preferred Stock).

Section 5. Class C Capital Stock. A statement of the designation of the Class C Capital Stock and the powers, preferences and rights and qualifications, limitations or restrictions thereof is as follows:

(a) Voting. Except as otherwise required by applicable law, shares of Class C Capital Stock shall have no voting power and the holders thereof, as such, shall not be entitled to vote on any matter that is submitted to a vote or for the consent of the stockholders of the Corporation.

(b) Dividends. Subject to the preferences applicable to any series of Preferred Stock, if any, outstanding at any time, the holders of Class C Capital Stock shall be entitled to receive, on a per share basis, the same form and amount of dividends and other distributions of cash, property or shares of stock of the Corporation as may be declared by the Board of Directors from time to time with respect to shares of the Common Stock out of assets or funds of the Corporation legally available therefor; provided, however, that in the event that such dividend is paid in the form of shares of Common Stock or rights to acquire Common Stock, the holders of Class C Capital Stock shall receive Class C Capital Stock or rights to acquire Class C Capital Stock, as the case may be.

(c) Conversion upon Liquidation. Immediately prior to the earlier of (i) any distribution of assets of the Corporation to the holders of the Common Stock in connection with a voluntary or involuntary liquidation, dissolution, distribution of assets or winding up of the Corporation pursuant to Section 2(c) or (ii) any record date established to determine the holders of capital stock of the Corporation entitled to receive such distribution of assets, each outstanding share of the Class C Capital Stock shall automatically, without any further action, convert into and become one (1) fully paid and nonassessable share of Class A

Common Stock. The Corporation shall at all times reserve and keep available out of its authorized but unissued shares of Class A Common Stock, solely for the purpose of effecting the conversion of the shares of Class C Capital Stock pursuant to this Section 5(c), such number of its shares of Class A Common Stock as shall from time to time be sufficient to effect the conversion of all outstanding shares of Class C Capital Stock into shares of Class A Common Stock.

C. MEMBERS AND PARTNERS

1. BECOMING A PARTNER OR MEMBER

Upon entity formation, a person becomes a partner or a member by assent. For a general partnership, assent is the agreement to carry on as co-owners a business for profit. For an LP, at least one person must agree to be a general partner and another to be a limited partner. A member in an LLC becomes a member as agreed by that person. RULLCA § 401(a).

Like classes of stock, interests in an NBE can be apportioned into different classes with specific combinations of economic and governance rights. Some LLC statutes explicitly permit the creation of different classes of membership and interests.

Delaware Limited Liability Company Act § 18–302, Classes and Voting

(a) A limited liability company agreement may provide for classes or groups of members having such relative rights, powers and duties as the limited liability company agreement may provide, and may make provision for the future creation in the manner provided in the limited liability company agreement of additional classes or groups of members having such relative rights, powers and duties as may from time to time be established, including rights, powers and duties senior to existing classes and groups of members. A limited liability company agreement may provide for the taking of an action, including the amendment of the limited liability company agreement, without the vote or approval of any member or class or group of members, including an action to create under the provisions of the limited liability company agreement a class or group of limited liability company interests that was not previously outstanding. A limited liability company agreement may provide that any member or class or group of members shall have no voting rights.

(b) A limited liability company agreement may grant to all or certain identified members or a specified class or group of the members the right to vote separately or with all or any class or group of the members or managers, on any matter. Voting by members may be on a per capita, number, financial interest, class, group or any other basis.

At formation, the lawyers, owners and organizers should consider whether different classes of interests are needed. The utility of classes of interests is apparent. Owners may have heterogeneous preferences as to economic and governance rights. Even in a general partnership, partners may wish to organize themselves into managing partners who manage the internal affairs and business partners who produce goods and services. For an LP, the legally mandated two-tiered ownership structure (a general partner and a limited partner) may be further segregated into different subclasses. Limited partners may have different appetites for investment risk. Some may wish to have preferential rights to distributions and thus assume less risk, for which they may contract for lower returns relative to subordinated limited partners. An LLC has virtually unlimited contractual freedom to create different classes of members. *See* Delaware Limited Liability Company Act § 18–302(a)–(b) (above); New York Limited Liability Company Law § 418(a) ("The articles of organization may provide for classes or groups of members having such relative rights, powers, preferences and limitations as the operating agreement of such limited liability company may provide. The operating agreement may grant to or withhold from all or one or more classes of members the right to vote upon any matter on the basis of capital contributions, capital commitments or capital accounts or on a per capita, class or other basis.").

The case below discusses the question of whether a person became a member in the LLC. In reading this case, consider these questions: (1) Why did the plaintiff Kilpatrick demand a right to see the LLC's information? (2) In hindsight, how should the parties have handled the situation to avoid the lawsuit?

KILPATRICK V. WHITE HALL ON MS RIVER, LLC

207 So.3d 1241 (Miss. 2016)

COLEMAN, JUSTICE, for the Court:

Dennis Kilpatrick filed a complaint against White Hall on MS River, LLC, in the Chancery Court. The chancellor issued his final judgment, in favor of White Hall. The chancellor found that Kilpatrick was not a member of White Hall and that Kilpatrick was not entitled to the recovery of his capital contribution. Kilpatrick appeals. We find no error and affirm.

The parties do not dispute the initial facts of the case. The chancellor's judgment outlines the background of the case:

> The creation of White Hall began with an informal gentleman's deal in which there would be five initial contributors[1]

[1] The initial contributors were Dennis Kilpatrick, Murray Moran, Dominick Cvitanovich, Jackie Richards, and James McBeth.

> each putting up $500,000 with which to purchase land from International Paper. All of the parties were aware that the price per acre would increase substantially if the sale did not take place on or before December 31, 2007. Based on assurances from Kilpatrick as well as Moran, the sale did take place. Those assurances were that their remaining funds would be payable after the new year.
>
> However, due to the fact that there was only $2 million available at closing,[2] the interest rate at which the purchase could be made was substantially increased, and the entire acreage sought by White Hall would be encumbered by deeds of trust, thus making no collateral available, thus making the ability to use the timber on the land unavailable.

The land sale contract was executed by White Hall, LLC, with Dominick Cvitanovich as the "Managing Member," and by Sustainable Forests LLC, a subsidiary of International Paper. White Hall obtained the property for $2,050 an acre, achieving that below-market-value price by promising to close the deal by the end of 2007.

The sale closed on December 13, 2007. On December 17, Cvitanovich filed a certificate of formation with the Secretary of State to create White Hall on MS River, LLC. Cvitanovich drafted an Operating Agreement for White Hall in January 2008. All five men received a copy of the Operating Agreement ("the Agreement") by the first half of 2008, the time during which he was in the process of completing White Hall's tax returns for 2007 with his tax advisors.

In the end, only three of the men executed the agreement: Cvitanovich, Richards, and McBeth. The signature page provided signature lines only for them. Cvitanovich testified that he revised the signature page to reduce the number of signature lines from five to three between January and August of 2008, before the Agreement was executed. As only three of the five members of the limited liability company (LLC) executed the Agreement, its validity was a key issue disputed at trial.

The Agreement stated that "Establishment of a Membership has been defined as a cash contribution of $500,000 for a membership interest of two (2) shares." Exhibit A, attached to the operating agreement, showed the capital contributions by all five men. Cvitanovich, Richards, and McBeth each had contributed $500,000. The alleged ambiguity of White Hall's membership requirements arises because, while the Agreement stated that a $500,000 capital contribution must made to become a member of White Hall, it also stated that " 'Members' means the persons listed on attached

[2] Dennis Kilpatrick paid only $100,000 on December 19, 2007, at closing toward his $500,000 obligation. Murray Moran paid only $400,000 at the time of closing.

Exhibit A." Exhibit A included Kilpatrick, though it also showed that he possessed "0" ownership shares.

The Agreement provided no procedure for including a person who failed to make the initial $500,000 contribution. However, for existing members, it stated that, "except as provided in Article 6 [Transfer of Membership Interests], no Member shall be entitled to withdraw or resign from the company." The Agreement stated that "no Member shall have the right to receive any return of any Capital Contribution."

Kilpatrick, Cvitanovich, Richards, and McBeth testified that Kilpatrick alerted the other men about his inability to timely wire $500,000 only a few days before the date of closing. Cvitanovich stated that the group went ahead with the deal because of their belief that Kilpatrick's outstanding $400,000 would imminently arrive, and because several other members already had wired their nonrefundable contributions to International Paper. Kilpatrick testified he originally intended to draw the balance from his 401(k), but when the market crashed in 2008, his oil stocks depreciated in value and he did not want to cash them out. Though Kilpatrick never tendered his $400,000 balance, he did pay $84,500 toward the quarterly interest payments on the three-year balloon note. Kilpatrick made all four quarterly interest payments in 2008, but he ceased making those quarterly interest payments in 2009.

The White Hall tax records reported to the State of Mississippi and to the Internal Revenue Service indicate that Kilpatrick possessed an ownership interest in White Hall. The White Hall tax records stated that Kilpatrick was a 4.75% owner in the LLC at the start of 2008 and an 8.00% owner at the end of the year. The percentage decreased through 2009, and by the end of the year in 2010, Kilpatrick owned 0.00% of White Hall.

Kilpatrick admitted at trial that he had known that his initial $100,000 payment was a 20% down payment, and that his quarterly interest payments on the three-year balloon note were higher than the other men's payments because he still owed White Hall a balance of $400,000. Cvitanovich approached Kilpatrick first with queries about when the payment would be tendered, and then, as it became clear that the payment would not be forthcoming in full, with several payment plan proposals. Through 2009, Kilpatrick missed three quarterly interest payments. Thus, in November 2009, White Hall informed Kilpatrick that he could not continue to use the property without paying his contribution.

Kilpatrick removed his belongings from the hunting camp. During the course of 2010, Kilpatrick and his two sons formed an LLC and purchased a 460-acre hunting camp in Yazoo County for $650,000. White Hall offered Kilpatrick $43,225 to reimburse him for the amount of his quarterly payments that had gone toward the principal, which he refused. Unable to pay off in cash the deed of trust owed to International Paper, White Hall then sold 1,269 acres of the hunting camp to Soterra Corporation. White

Hall claims that its hand was forced to sell to Soterra because of Kilpatrick's failure to pay his full capital contribution.

Kilpatrick made a demand on White Hall to review the company records; White Hall refused. Kilpatrick filed his complaint, alleging that he was a member of White Hall and thus was entitled to inspect the company records. He sought a declaratory judgment validating his ownership interest in White Hall, a finding that White Hall had been unjustly enriched by retaining Kilpatrick's capital contribution of $186,500, and the establishment of an equitable lien or constructive trust to return that capital contribution to him.

After a trial, the chancellor found that Kilpatrick was not a member of White Hall, that he had come before a court of equity with unclean hands,* and that he had no right to the return of his capital contributions.

The Mississippi Limited Liability Company Act (MLLCA) provides the following for the admission of members:

> (1) A person becomes a member on the later of:
>
> > (a) The date the original certificate of formation is filed by the Secretary of State; or
> >
> > (b) The date stated in the records of the limited liability company as the date that person becomes a member.
>
> (2) After the filing by the Secretary of State, of a limited liability company's original certificate of formation, a person may be admitted as a member:
>
> > (a) In the case of a person acquiring a limited liability interest directly from the limited liability company, upon the compliance with the certificate of formation or the limited liability company agreement or, if the certificate of formation or the limited liability company agreement does not so provide, upon the written consent of all members.

Miss.Code Ann. § 79–29–301 (2009).

Kilpatrick begins his argument with the presumption that the Agreement is not and has never been valid, and thus statutory defaults must control. Under Kilpatrick's theory, because there is no valid operating agreement, the Court must look to default statutory provisions and the LLC's certificate of formation to determine how the LLC is managed, operated, and regulated. His argument begins with the proposition that he has always been a member of White Hall, so because he did not sign the Agreement, it is not enforceable under the MLLCA. His argument makes

* Author's note: "The doctrine of unclean hands is equity's maxim that a suitor who engaged in his own reprehensible conduct in the course of [a] transaction at issue must be denied equitable relief, a rule which in conventional formulation operated in limine to bar the suitor from invoking the aid of the equity court." RBC Capital Markets, LLC v. Jervis, 129 A.3d 816, 875-76 (Del. 2015).

sense only if the Court accepts Kilpatrick's assertion that he was indeed a member of White Hall. If Kilpatrick was never a vested member of the company, then whether or not he executed the Agreement is a moot point.

Section 79–29–301 does not require LLC agreements to be in force at the time of filing the certificate of formation, or that all potential members of the LLC be accounted for at [that] time. The Act provides two avenues by which membership may be established: by the date of the certificate of formation, or by the written agreement of all members.

White Hall's Agreement states that "establishment of Membership has been defined as a cash contribution of Five Hundred Thousand dollars ($500,000.00) for a membership interest of two (2) shares." The three members who executed the Agreement each had paid capital contributions of $500,000 by the date of execution—Cvitanovich, McBeth, and Richards. The signature page of the Agreement acknowledges capital contributions from nonmembers, stating that the three executing members

> wish to acknowledge that there are two (2) individuals that have made financial contributions in an effort to acquire membership in Whitehall on MS River, LLC. It is further acknowledged and understood according to this agreement that no one is named a member until the financial obligation of $500,000 is met, and that no rights and/or privileges to Whitehall property will be permitted to anyone other than a member.

The signature page lists Kilpatrick underneath, with an acknowledgment of his capital contribution of $100,000, which earned him zero membership shares. The signature page includes Moran as well, also possessing zero membership shares for his $400,000 capital contribution.

Kilpatrick points out that he *was* listed as a member of White Hall within the Agreement's attached exhibits and on White Hall's capital account ledger on the tax returns for the years 2007 through 2010. Exhibit B to the Agreement provides information about each man associated with White Hall, along with their addresses and their balances with White Hall. The "Members" column therein lists both Kilpatrick and Moran, though their contributions each are less than $500,000.

"An LLC operating agreement is a contract, subject to contract law." "Our law requires this Court to accept the plain meaning of a contract as the intent of the parties where no ambiguity exists." Kilpatrick's arguments about being named on the tax returns or on the Agreement's exhibits would hold weight if the Agreement were ambiguous; the Agreement's terms instead are *un*ambiguous. The clear language requires a $500,000 contribution to become a member. Kilpatrick had contributed less than $200,000 to White Hall, and so his membership interest is nonexistent under the plain language of the Agreement.

Cvitanovich testified that Kilpatrick had been listed as a member on the tax returns and as holding ownership units in the LLC only because Kilpatrick had continued to promise that the remaining $400,000 would soon arrive. Kilpatrick admitted at trial that he knew that he was responsible for a total of $500,000 to complete the purchase of land. Through the end of 2007 and into 2008, Cvitanovich had a good-faith belief that Kilpatrick would become a full member in White Hall based on the $100,000 already contributed, the promise that the rest of the money would arrive as soon as the oil stocks were sold, and the word of Richards that, Kilpatrick, his longtime friend, would uphold his end of the bargain.

To prove his membership interest, Kilpatrick points to the very evidence that exists only because of his own representations to White Hall. He is listed as a member on the exhibits attached to the Operating Agreement and on White Hall's tax returns because of his representations to the other members of the company that he would timely pay his outstanding balance. The chancellor stated that "he who comes into equity must come with clean hands. He who seeks equity must do equity." We agree. We note that equitable principles can be applied to contract law, and hold that, under the MLLCA and the White Hall Operating Agreement, the chancellor committed no reversible error in finding Dennis Kilpatrick was not a member of White Hall on the MS River, LLC.

[The court held that the members of White Hall relied to their detriment on Kilpatrick's never-fulfilled promise to contribute the remainder of his $500,000. It declined to establish a constructive trust or equitable lien to return to Kilpatrick any portion of his contribution.]

2. ADDITION OF NEW OWNERS

NBE laws provide that the only personal property a member or partner owns is a transferable interest, defined as the right to receive the economic benefits (distributions). *See* RUPA § 102(23), § 502; ULPA (2001) § 102(25), § 701; RULLCA § 102(24), § 501. An owner cannot transfer governance rights, which is not a part of personal property. He cannot freely transfer the entire interest in the LLC or partnership such that a transferee owns the entire interest. A person cannot become a new member or partner without the approval of other members or partners. *See* RUPA § 503(a)(3)(A); ULPA (2001) § 702(a)(3)(A); RULLCA § 502(a)(3)(A).

New owners are admitted to a firm because the firm anticipates that they will bring value to the firm and its existing owners. For example, they may bring a new book of business, new skills or services, additional financing, or contribution of important assets. The default rules of NBEs provide that a person can be admitted as a new owner per the charter agreement or unanimous consent. *See* RUPA § 402(b)(3) ("After formation of a partnership, a person becomes a partner as provided in the partnership agreement or with the affirmative vote or consent of all the partners");

ULPA (2001) § 301(b)(3) (same); RULLCA § 401(c)(3) (same). The policy principle is that the law should not thrust new owners onto closely held firms without their consent.

The case below provides an analysis of Delaware law on admission of a new member. In reading this case, consider these questions: (1) Is the holding consistent with the above rules? (2) Is there a possibility of a "de facto" member? (3) What is the role of equity in achieving the result here?

IN RE CARLISLE ETCETERA LLC

114 A.3d 592 (Del. Ch. 2015)

LASTER, VICE CHANCELLOR.

Petitioner Well Union Capital Limited ("WU Parent") and respondent Tom James Company ("James") formed Carlisle Etcetera LLC, a Delaware limited liability company ("Carlisle" or the "Company"). They executed a simple form of operating agreement (the "Initial LLC Agreement") in which they committed to work promptly on a more detailed operating agreement to replace the original one.

After the Company was formed, WU Parent transferred its member interest to a wholly owned subsidiary called Well Union U.S. Holdings, Inc. ("WU Sub"). James knew about the transfer, did not object, and treated WU Sub as a member from that point on. For purposes of the Delaware Limited Liability Company Act (the "LLC Act"), however, the transfer rendered WU Sub an assignee, rather than a member.

WU Parent and James never reached agreement on a replacement operating agreement. Other disputes arose, and the relationship deteriorated. Deadlock prevailed at the manager level, where the Initial LLC Agreement called for a board of directors (the "Board") to serve as the singular manager of the Company. The Board has four members, two appointed by WU Parent and two by James. They split 2–2 on key issues.

Both sides recognized that they could not manage the Company jointly and that one side needed to buy out the other. Despite some initially positive signs, they could not agree on a buyout procedure or a price.

WU Sub petitioned to dissolve the Company. James moved to dismiss on the grounds that WU Sub is an assignee, not a member, and that an assignee lacks standing to petition for dissolution under Section 18–802 of the LLC Act. 6 *Del. C.* § 18–802. WU Parent joined as a co-petitioner.

To petition for statutory dissolution under Section 18–802, WU Parent and WU Sub must be members or managers of the Company. Neither claims to be a manager. The Initial LLC Agreement makes clear that the

Board, acting collectively, is the manager of the Company. WU Parent and WU Sub do claim to be members.

Taking the allegations as true, WU Parent cannot be a member. WU Parent was a member of the Company, but it assigned its interest to WU Sub. Under Section 18–702(a) of the LLC Act, "a limited liability company interest is assignable in whole or in part except as provided in a limited liability company agreement." The Initial LLC Agreement was silent about assignability, so the interest was freely assignable.

WU Parent lost its status as a member of the Company when it assigned all of its interest in the Company to WU Sub. Under Section 702(b)(3) of the LLC Act, "unless otherwise provided in a limited liability company agreement: (3) a member ceases to be a member and to have the power to exercise any rights or powers of a member upon assignment of all of the member's limited liability company interest." By operation of law, once WU Parent assigned its interest in the Company to WU Sub, WU Parent "ceased to be a member" and could no longer exercise a member's right to seek statutory dissolution. Under the facts as pled, WU Parent cannot petition for statutory dissolution.

The analysis for WU Sub is more complex. As an initial matter, James is correct that WU Sub did not automatically become a member by receiving WU Parent's interest. Under Section 18–702(b)(1) of the LLC Act, "unless otherwise provided in a limited liability company agreement: (1) an assignment of a limited liability company interest does not entitle the assignee to become a member." The Initial LLC Agreement did not provide otherwise, so under the facts as pled, the transfer of WU Parent's interest made WU Sub an assignee, not a member.

By default under the LLC Act, only a member can petition for statutory dissolution, not an assignee. Section 18–702(b)(1) reinforces this reading by stating that "unless otherwise provided in a limited liability company agreement: (1) an assignment of a limited liability company interest does not entitle the assignee to exercise any rights or powers of a member." Section 18–702(a) similarly provides that

> the assignee of a member's limited liability company interest shall have no right to participate in the management of the business and affairs of a limited liability company except as provided in a limited liability company agreement or, unless otherwise provided in the limited liability company agreement, upon the affirmative vote or written consent of all of the members of the limited liability company.

The Initial LLC Agreement did not give assignees the right to seek statutory dissolution. Without more, therefore, WU Sub cannot claim to be a member or exercise the rights of a member, so WU Sub cannot seek statutory dissolution.

But there is more. The petition alleges that WU Sub became a *de facto* member by consent of the parties. Citing Section 18–301(b)(1) of the LLC Act, WU Sub argues that it became a member under the LLC Act once its status as a member was "reflected in the records of the limited liability company." WU Sub further argues that the tax forms and draft agreements that identified WU Sub as a member were "records of the [Company]." In my view, WU Sub jumps too hastily to this aspect of Section 18–301.

Several sections of the LLC Act bear on the admission of WU Sub as a member. Section 18–101(11) states that the term "'member' means a person who is admitted to a limited liability company as a member as provided in § 18–301 of this title." Section 18–301, entitled "Admission of members," addresses a variety of contexts in which persons may become members. Subsection 18–301(b) states:

> After the formation of a limited liability company, a person is admitted as a member of the limited liability company:
>
> (2) In the case of an assignee of a limited liability company interest, as provided in § 18–704(a) of this title and at the time provided in and upon compliance with the limited liability company agreement or, if the limited liability company agreement does not so provide, when any such person's permitted admission is reflected in the records of the limited liability company.

Through this language, Section 18–301(b) distinguishes between (i) the act of admitting an assignee as a member and (ii) the point when the admission becomes effective. First, the assignee must be admitted "as provided in § 18–704(a)." Once this has happened, the admission takes effect "at the time provided on and upon compliance with the limited liability company agreement." The subsection continues with an additional clause that addresses the point when the admission becomes effective if the operating agreement is silent, explaining that in that event, the admission becomes effective "when any such person's permitted admission is reflected in the records of the limited liability company." The phrase "permitted admission" relates back to the first step of the process—admission "as provided in § 18–704(a)"—which indicates that an assignee cannot establish membership simply by pointing to "records of the limited liability company." There must have been a "permitted admission."

The statutory path finishes with Section 18–704(a), which identifies two possibilities for a "permitted admission."

> An assignee of a limited liability company interest may become a member:
>
> (1) As provided in the limited liability company agreement; or

> (2) Unless otherwise provided in the limited liability company agreement, upon the affirmative vote or written consent of all of the members of the limited liability company.

The Initial LLC Agreement was silent on the admission of an assignee as a member. Under Section 18–704(a), WU Sub's only route to a "permitted admission" was "upon the affirmative vote or written consent of all of the members of the limited liability company." If that happened, then the "permitted admission" would become effective once WU Sub's admission was "reflected in the records of the limited liability company."

In my view, the reference in Section 18–704(a) to an "affirmative vote or written consent" means the type of formal action of members contemplated by Section 18–302 of the LLC Act, which addresses voting rights. Section 18–302(c) contemplates that action by members will take place at meetings and explains that

> a limited liability company agreement may set forth provisions relating to notice of the time, place or purpose of any meeting at which any matter is to be voted on by any members, waiver of any such notice, quorum requirements, voting in person or by proxy, or any other matter with respect to the exercise of any such right to vote.

Section 18–302(d) contemplates the alternative of members taking action by written consent without a meeting.

> Unless otherwise provided in a limited liability company agreement, on any matter that is to be voted on, consented to or approved by members, the members may take such action without a meeting, without prior notice and without a vote if consented to, in writing or by electronic transmission, by members having not less than the minimum number of votes that would be necessary to authorize or take such action at a meeting at which all members entitled to vote thereon were present and voted.

The correspondence between these two methods of action and the language of Section 18–704 leads me to conclude that the latter provision contemplates member action taking one of those forms. The phrase "affirmative vote or written consent" appears rarely in the LLC Act, and other appearances involve similar occasions for formal member action.

"A reason for the default rules in the [LLC] Act regarding the transferability of [member] interests may rest on the notion that one generally is entitled to select his own business associates in a closely held enterprise, like an LLC." "The policy that underlies § 18–702(b)(3) is that it is far more tolerable to have to suffer a new passive co-investor one did not choose than to endure a new co-manager without consent." It makes sense that the LLC Act would require formal member action to accept a new business partner, rather than contemplating *de facto* membership or the constructive admission of assignees.

In this case, the Company only had two members. Once WU Parent transferred its member interest and WU Sub became an assignee, James was the sole remaining member and controlled the vote on WU Sub's admission. The petition does not plead any formal action by which James voted or acted by written consent to admit WU Sub as a member. Assuming for purposes of analysis that the tax forms and draft agreements were "records" of the LLC for purposes of Section 301(b)(1), there was never a "permitted admission" that could be reflected on those records.

Based on the allegations of the petition, James is correct that WU Sub is not a member who can seek statutory dissolution. Neither petitioner can.

CHRYSLER GROUP LLC OPERATING AGREEMENT

Section 7.1 Admission Requirements. One or more additional Persons may be admitted to the Company as Members only upon furnishing to the Company: (i) a joinder agreement pursuant to which such Person agrees to be bound by all of the terms and conditions of this Agreement and (ii) such other documents or instruments as may be necessary or appropriate to effect such Person's admission as a Member (including entering into an investor representation agreement or such other documents as the Company may deem appropriate). Such admission shall become effective on the date on which the Company determines that the foregoing conditions have been satisfied and when any such admission is shown on the books and records of the Company. Upon the admission of an Additional Member, the Schedule of Members shall be amended to reflect the name, notice address, Membership Interests and other interests in the Company. Such Member's capital contributions and initial Capital Account shall be reflected in the Company's books and records.

Section 7.2 Acceptance of Prior Acts. Any Person who is admitted pursuant to Section 7.1 hereby accepts, ratifies and agrees to be bound by all actions duly taken pursuant to the terms and provisions of this Agreement by the Company prior to the date it was admitted to the Company and, without limiting the generality of the foregoing, specifically ratifies and approves all agreements and other instruments as may have been executed and delivered on behalf of the Company prior to such date and which are in force and effect on such date.

D. CAPITAL ACCOUNTS

Shareholders are given shares of stock that represent discrete units of ownership interest. Assuming the same class of stock, each share is fungible. Ownership interest and governance rights are measured by the number of shares owned as a percentage of the total shares outstanding. Only a record of shareholders and their holdings are needed.

Many NBEs follow the corporate model and issue "shares" or "units" representing a defined fixed interest in exchange for specific contributions by owners. However, the economic and governance arrangements may not always be represented in discrete, fungible units of ownership. Owners may have bespoke governance and economic rights. If economic interests are individually negotiated among owners, the entity must keep track of each person's economic interest. The laws of NBEs provide default rules for maintaining capital accounts.

RUPA § 401. Partner's Rights and Duties.

(a) Each partner is entitled to an equal share of the partnership distributions and, except in the case of a limited liability partnership, is chargeable with a share of the partnership losses in proportion to the partner's share of the distributions.

ULPA (2001) § 108. Required Information.

A limited partnership shall maintain at its principal office the following information:

(9) unless contained in a partnership agreement made in a record, a record stating:

> (A) a description and statement of the agreed value of contributions other than money made and agreed to be made by each partner;
>
> (B) the times at which, or events on the happening of which, any additional contributions agreed to be made by each partner are to be made;

The ULPA (2001) does not provide the specific method of keeping track of ownership interest. It simply requires that contributions and their values attributable to each partner must be recorded. This is required because LPs are most used as investment vehicles, and thus a record of investments made by each passive investor is a good idea. The RULLCA does not provide a provision at all. By its silence, it leaves the issue of accounting for interests to the LLC and its members.

Most NBEs keep capital accounts as a matter of good governance. Each partner has an account that keeps track of: (1) contributions ("+" value); (2) allocation of profit ("+" value); (3) allocation of loss ("–" value); (4) distributions ("–" value). A capital account is akin to each partner's or member's individual bank account. In theory at least, over the life of the firm, an owner's total distribution should be strongly, if not perfectly, correlated to her total contribution and total profit and loss allocation.

For example, Amy and Ben are partners. At the beginning of the partnership, each contribute 100 in capital. Consistent with the default rule of partnership, they agree to split profits and losses equally. During the first year of the partnership, the partnership made 300. At the end of the year, Amy takes 100 in a distribution, but Ben does not. Ben also makes another 50 in contribution to partnership capital. The firm's capital accounts would record these transactions as the following.

Partner	Beginning Capital	Profit Made		Capital Contribution	Draw and Distribution	Ending Capital
		%	Allocation			
Amy	100	50%	150	-	(100)	150
Ben	100	50%	150	50	-	300
Total	200	100%	300	50	(100)	450

CHRYSLER GROUP LLC OPERATING AGREEMENT

Section 3.1 Membership Interests; Capitalization; Capital Accounts.

(a) The Company shall have one authorized class of Membership Interests, consisting of 1,632,654 Membership Interests which may be issued in one or more series. A Membership Interest shall for all purposes be personal property. For purposes of this Agreement, Membership Interests held by the Company or any of its Subsidiaries shall be deemed not to be outstanding. The Company may issue fractional Membership Interests pursuant to the terms of this Agreement, and all fractional Membership Interests shall be rounded to the fourth decimal place.

(b) The Members of the Company consist of the Persons named as Members on the Schedule of Members. The Company shall update the Schedule of Members to reflect any changes in the Members, the Membership Interests and the Total Interest of the Members in accordance with the terms of this Agreement. The Company shall maintain a separate capital account (a "Capital Account") for each Member in accordance with [26 C.F.R.] Section 1.704–1(b)(2)(iv) of the Treasury Regulations.

E. CONTRIBUTIONS

1. DEFAULT STATUTORY RULE

Owners typically make contributions to the entity to capitalize the firm. However, a contribution is not a requirement to become an owner. *See*

RUPA § 402(c) ("A person may become a partner without: acquiring a transferable interest; or making or being obligated to make a contribution to the partnership."); RULLCA § 401(d) (same); ULPA (2001) § 301(c) (same), § 401(c) (same).

The statutes provide the default rules for the form of contribution. A contribution may be "property transferred to, services performed for, or another benefit provided to" to the entity. RUPA § 403; ULPA (2001) § 501; RULLCA § 402. The statutes broadly define contribution. *See, e.g.*, Belgard v. Manchac Techs., LLC, 92 So.3d 660, 664 (La. App. 2012) (stating that "the creation of an obligation to establish a $1.8 million line of credit was valid consideration for the transfer of 24% of the membership interest in Manchac"); In re Eight of Swords, LLC, 946 N.Y.S.2d 248, 249 (App. Div. 2d Dep't. 2012) (referring to "the petitioner's contributions to the LLC, which overwhelmingly consisted of services rendered to the LLC in the form of preparing and filing start-up documentation and performing activities associated with the renovation of the business's premises"). In firms where owners are anticipated to manage the firm, the manager's service often constitutes the contribution.

In practice, the form and amount of contribution and the obligation to make a contribution are subject to the agreement among owners. The charter agreement should answer these questions: (1) What is an acceptable form of contribution? (2) What interests are granted for the contribution (3) Is there a requirement to make additional contributions? Some of these questions may be answered by the degree of authority given to managers to accept contributions, determine their value, and make calls for additional contributions.

CHRYSLER GROUP LLC OPERATING AGREEMENT

Section 4.1 Additional Contributions. No Member shall be required to make any additional capital contribution to the Company in respect of the Membership Interests then held by such Member or to provide any financing to the Company; provided that a Member may, at the request or with the consent of the Company, make additional capital contributions or provide financing to the Company.

2. LIABILITY FOR CONTRIBUTION

With respect to additional capital contribution, there is a tension between the firm's managers and owners. Over the course of business, a firm may have additional capital needs. Managers may want to raise additional capital from the firm's owners, but the latter may want to limit their exposure to making additional investments. Also, additional capital calls may be unpredictable, coming at an inopportune time for an owner. The rules in the charter agreement must resolve this tension.

What is the consequence of failing to make a contribution? The answer depends in part on whether the contribution is required or not. If a capital call is voluntary, there should be a mechanism in the charter agreement to adjust the allocation of economic and, potentially, the governance right for all members. Consider that when a corporation sells stock to current shareholders, the interest in the corporation increases for those purchasing shareholders relative to nonparticipating shareholders.

If a capital call is required under the charter agreement, the statutes provide that an owner shall be liable for failure to make a contribution.

RUPA § 404. Liability for Contribution.

(a) A person's obligation to make a contribution to a partnership is not excused by the person's death, disability, termination, or other inability to perform personally.

(b) If a person does not fulfill an obligation to make a contribution other than money, the person is obligated at the option of the partnership to contribute money equal to the value of the part of the contribution which has not been made.

(c) The obligation of a person to make a contribution may be compromised only by the affirmative vote or consent of all the partners. If a creditor of a limited liability partnership extends credit or otherwise acts in reliance on an obligation described in subsection (a) without knowledge or notice of a compromise under this subsection, the creditor may enforce the obligation.

ULPA (2001) § 502. Liability for Contribution.

[Functionally the same]

RULLCA § 403. Liability for Contribution.

[Functionally the same]

The case below concerns a limited partner's liability for additional contribution. In the above Chrysler Group LLC operating agreement, Section 4.1 provides: "No Member shall be required to make any additional capital contribution." This declaration seems fixed in stone, but it is only definitive insofar as the agreement is fixed. Virtually all agreements can be amended and the ability to amend is necessary to address changed circumstance. The charter agreement is subject to amendment by whatever amendment mechanism is provided therein, or if not the statute. The partners in this case amended the partnership agreement to provide ever increasing capital contribution requirement. One partner did not like this change. In reading this case, consider this question: What is the relationship among the partnership agreement, the statute, and the certificate of limited partnership filed with the state?

FOX V. I-10 LTD.

957 P.2d 1018 (Colo. 1998) (en banc)

JUSTICE KOURLIS delivered the Opinion of the Court.

William Fox is a limited partner in I-10 Ltd. (the Partnership or I-10). Fox appeals a judgment of the court of appeals holding that the amendment provisions in the partnership agreement and applicable statutes allowed the limited partners to increase their capital contribution obligation by majority vote. We conclude that the majority vote provision plainly allows amendment of the limited partners' capital contributions; and this provision is not contrary to statutory provisions requiring capital contributions to be set forth in a certificate of limited partnership.

Fox purchased approximately 20% of the available limited partnership units in a Colorado limited partnership known as I-10 Ltd. Fox and several other limited partners (LPs) executed a limited partnership agreement with the general partner, MSP Investment Co. (the Agreement). The purpose of the Partnership was to acquire, develop and hold for resale 305 acres of land in Pima County, Arizona.

Article 4.09 of the Agreement provided:

> *Additional Assessments.* If at any time after the formation of the Partnership the General Partner determines that additional contributions to the capital of the Partnership are necessary or desirable for any purpose, the General Partner shall mail a notice to each Limited Partner specifying the aggregate amount of additional capital to be contributed to the Partnership, such Limited Partner's pro rata share of the additional capital required, the purpose for the assessment, the intended use of the proceeds thereof, and the penalty to be imposed for failure to meet the assessment. The total additional capital contribution required to be made by each Limited Partner hereunder shall not exceed an amount equal to four hundred percent (400%) of the initial capital contribution to the Partnership of each Limited Partner.

Article 7.00 dealing with amendments set forth two methods of amending the agreement depending upon the nature of the proposed change. Article 7.01 allowed the general partner, in its sole discretion, and as attorney in fact for the limited partners, to make certain "routine amendments" without the need for any partnership vote. These types of amendments related mainly to administrative matters such as preservation of proper status for federal income tax purposes.

Article 7.02 encompassed all other, non-routine amendments, and provided that, except for amendments affecting MSP's rights, all other amendments to the agreement would be made by majority vote:

> *Other Amendments.* All amendments, other than those set forth in paragraph 7.01 hereof, shall be proposed in writing by the General Partner or by Limited Partners owning not less than twenty-five percent (25%) of the Limited Partners' aggregate Interest in the Partnership for voting purposes. Any proposed amendment shall not become effective until it has been considered at a meeting of the Limited Partners duly held for that purpose and has received the affirmative vote of a majority of the Limited Partners' aggregate Interest in the Partnership and the approval of the General Partner. Notwithstanding the foregoing provisions of this paragraph to the contrary, no amendment shall be made to this Agreement which would deprive the General Partner of its Interest in the Partnership, or of any compensation or reimbursement of expenses due to the General Partner as provided herein.

The original certificate reflected that Fox had contributed a total of $85,000 and had agreed to potential future assessments not exceeding $340,000 (400% of $85,000). The certificate also stated that article 4.09 of the Agreement governed the times at which, or events upon the happening of which, the partners had agreed to make additional contributions.

[The Partnership found it necessary for various reasons to amend the Agreement several times. At the recommendation of MSP, all partners, including Fox, first voted to amend article 4.09 to increase potential assessments from 400% to 600% of the original investment. Any amendment is accomplished by majority vote as required in article 7.02 of the Agreement. Subsequently, MSP again proposed to amend article 4.09 by increasing the contribution cap to 800%, which would be $680,000 as to Fox and a total investment of $765,000. Fox objected, but all other partners voted to amend article 4.09 and increase the cap to 800%. After the vote, MSP sent Fox a notice of additional assessment for the additional 200%. Fox paid the assessment up to 600% of his initial contribution ($510,000), but refused to make the additional $170,000 contribution. Fox filed an action in the district court seeking a declaratory judgment that he had no obligation beyond the 600% cap.]

Our courts have recognized the sanctity of contracts and the court's role in enforcing them. Quoting the United States Supreme Court, we have held that: "the right of private contract is no small part of the liberty of the citizen, and the usual and most important function of courts of justice is rather to maintain and enforce contracts, than to enable parties thereto to escape from their obligation." Where a party enters into a contract absent fraud, duress or incapacity, the courts will not relieve that party of the consequences of the bargain simply because it may have been improvident.

The court's duty is to interpret and enforce contracts as written between the parties, not to rewrite or restructure them. The court will not interfere with the valid bargain of the parties:

> The impossibility of courts attempting to act as business clearing houses for the readjustment of legitimate profits and losses occurring in the marts of trade and commerce is obvious at a glance. To attempt it would be an unwarranted interference with the freedom of action of business men in their private affairs.

Parties to a contract, therefore, may agree on whatever terms they see fit so long as such terms do not violate statutory prohibitions or public policy. Additionally, where a contract is clear and unambiguous, courts must give effect to the plain and ordinary meaning of its terms.

Hence, we look first to the terms of the Agreement itself to determine whether Fox can be required, by majority vote, to increase his capital contribution. Fox asserts that there is tension between article 4.09, placing a definitive cap on contributions, and article 7.02, allowing amendment of the Agreement by majority vote, thereby creating an ambiguity with respect to the parties' intent. We do not agree.

Article 7.02 plainly states that "*all* amendments, other than those [routine amendments] set forth in paragraph 7.01" may be accomplished by majority vote. Article 7.02 goes on to specify that certain items are excluded from amendment by the majority vote procedure set out therein. Increase in capital contributions is not among the exclusions of article 7.02. Furthermore, article 2.04 specifically requires unanimous consent of the limited partners prior to allowing the general partner to take certain actions. Hence the parties clearly excluded certain items from amendment by majority vote, but did not exclude a change in capital contributions from this method of amendment. Neither the language in article 4.09, nor any other language in the Agreement, creates doubt about whether article 7.02 provides the proper procedure for amending article 4.09.

Fox argues that the ceiling on a limited partner's capital contribution is such a fundamental aspect of a limited partnership that, as a matter of law, it may not be amended by majority vote regardless of what the Agreement might state. We agree that the limit on an LP's liability represents a defining characteristic of a limited partnership interest. An LP's liability is limited by operation of law with respect to creditors of the partnership. An LP's liability to the partnership is also limited, but this limitation is defined, not by operation of law, but by the partnership agreement as the amount of capital which an LP agrees to contribute. While LPs may not, for example, agree among themselves to treat each other internally as general partners and still preserve their limited liability status with respect to creditors, there is no fundamental tenet of limited partnership law that prevents LPs from voluntarily agreeing, by majority vote or otherwise, to increase their capital contribution to the partnership.

We thus conclude that the plain language of the Agreement allows a majority of the partners to vote to amend the capital contribution amount, and no "fundamental right" invalidates that contractual term. Rather, if any fundamental right is implicated, it is the fundamental right to enter into a contract and expect its terms to be enforced.

CULPA requires limited partnerships to file a certificate of limited partnership with the secretary of state. Fox contends that the provisions in CULPA requiring identification of the limited partners' capital contributions on the certificate prohibit I-10, as a matter of law, from imposing additional capital contributions without Fox's consent.

Certificates of limited partnership serve the goal of giving third parties, specifically potential creditors, notice concerning matters of importance to them in dealing with the partnership. The certificate is not designed to protect or govern the rights of the partners as among themselves, and it cannot trump a valid contractual term.

The Agreement, by its plain language, allows the parties to amend article 4.09 by majority vote. Neither a "fundamental right" of limited partnership nor CULPA precludes parties from agreeing to such an amendment procedure. I-10 did not violate the certificate requirements of [the statute], and in any event, the partners' rights and obligations *inter se* are governed by the partnership agreement, not by the certificate.

F. PROFIT AND LOSS, AND DISTRIBUTION

NBE statutes provide threadbare provisions on profit and loss allocations and right to distributions. These matters are typically subject to contracting and the contract provisions depend heavily on tax considerations. In most ventures, and certainly all large or sophisticated ventures, the threadbare statutory default provisions will be irrelevant, and the contract provisions will be inextricably intertwined with partnership tax laws. Default statutory provisions on profit and loss allocation and distributions exist for smaller enterprises that, unfortunately, may not have properly planned the entity.

1. GENERAL PARTNERSHIP

The default statutory rule for the allocation of profit and loss is: "Each partner is entitled to an equal share of the partnership distributions and, except in the case of a limited liability partnership, is chargeable with a share of the partnership losses in proportion to the partner's share of the distributions." RUPA § 401(a). The rule reflects the communitarian view of partnership in which all partners are seen as co-equal owners.

The statutory rule is inappropriate in many commercial situations where investors expect risk-adjusted returns. For example, suppose a partner contributes $1 million and another partner contributes $100,000, and the latter is no more important to the partnership in terms of other attributes. One guesses that the partner contributing the larger amount would seek a larger allocation of profit.

The case below illustrates the importance of allocating both profit *and* loss. In reading this case, consider these questions: (1) What was the logic of the partners' economic arrangement? (2) Are there different conceptions of the loss suffered by the partnership? (3) What is the best allocation of loss in light of the partnership agreement (did the court get it right)?

KESSLER V. ANTINORA

653 A.2d 579 (N.J. Super. 1995)

KING, P.J.A.D.

Plaintiff Robert Kessler and defendant Richard Antinora entered into a written agreement for the purpose of building and selling a single-family residence on a lot in Wayne in Passaic County. The concept of the agreement seemed simple: Kessler was to provide the money and Antinora was to act as general contractor. Profits would be divided—60% to Kessler, 40% to Antinora—after Kessler was repaid. No thought was given to losses. The venture lost money. Kessler sued Antinora to recover 40% of his financial losses or $65,742. The Law Division judge ruled in Kessler's favor on summary judgment. The judge denied Antinora's cross-motion for summary judgment of dismissal. We disagree, reverse the judgment in Kessler's favor, and order judgment in Antinora's favor.

Kessler and Antinora executed a seven-page written agreement titled "Joint Venture Partnership Agreement." The agreement contemplated a single venture: buying a lot in Wayne and building and selling a residence on it. Under the agreement Kessler agreed to "provide all necessary funds to purchase land and construct a one-family dwelling and disburse all funds to pay bills." Antinora agreed to "actually construct the dwelling and be the general contractor of the job."

The agreement provided for distribution of the proceeds of the venture:

> *Distribution.* Upon or about completion of the dwelling it shall be placed for sale. Upon sale of same, and after deducting all monies expended by Robert Kessler . . . Robert Kessler and Richard Antinora, shall divide the net profits as follows: Robert Kessler 60%; Richard Antinora 40%.

The agreement was silent about losses. There was no provision to compensate Antinora for any services other than the 40% profit clause.

Both parties complied with the agreement. Kessler provided the funds; Antinora supervised and delivered the finished house. This took over three years. Meanwhile, the real estate market soured. The house sold for $420,000. The cost incurred in building and selling the house was $498,917.

Kessler was repaid all but $78,917 of the money he advanced pursuant to the contract. He also claimed unreimbursed interest of $85,440 for his self-characterized "loan" to the partnership. This claim for interest is disputed as to amount. Kessler thus claimed a total loss of $164,357. He sought and obtained his summary judgment for 40% of this amount, or $65,742. No amount was presented on the value of Antinora's services over the three-year period as general contractor.

We conclude that New Jersey's allegedly applicable section of the Uniform Partnership Law, *N.J.S.A.* 42:1–18a, does not control here because of the specific terms of the agreement between the parties.

We find the agreement controlling over the statute. The agreement said that upon sale of the house "and after deducting all monies expended by Robert Kessler plus interest," fees, and other costs the "parties [Kessler and Antinora] shall divide net profits" 60% and 40%. We conclude that the agreement evinced a clear intent that Kessler would be repaid his investment from the sale of the house only, not by Antinora. There is no suggestion in the agreement that any of Kessler's risked and lost money would be repaid in part by Antinora. Nor is there any suggestion that Antinora's risked labor would be repaid in part by Kessler.

We find persuasive the reasoning of the California Supreme Court in *Kovacik v. Reed,* 315 P.2d 314 (Cal. 1957). The parties orally agreed to participate in a kitchen remodeling venture for Sears Roebuck & Company. Kovacik agreed to invest $10,000 in the venture and Reed agreed to become the job estimator and supervisor. They agreed to share the profits on a 50–50 basis. Possible losses were not discussed. Despite their efforts, the venture was unsuccessful and Kovacik sued Reed to recover one-half the money losses he endured. Kovacik prevailed in the trial court and recovered $4,340, or one-half the net monetary loss of $8,680.

The California Supreme Court acknowledged the general rule that in the absence of an agreement, "the law presumes that partners and joint adventurers intended to participate equally in the profits and losses of the common enterprise, irrespective of any inequality in the amounts each contributed to the capital employed in the venture, with the losses being shared by them in the same proportions as they share the profits."

The California court observed that this "general rule" did not obtain where one party contributed the money and the other the labor, stating:

> In the cases in which the general rule has been applied, each of the parties had contributed capital consisting of either money or land or other tangible property, or else was to receive compensation for services rendered to the common undertaking which was to be paid before computation of the profits or losses. Where, however, as in the present case, one partner or joint adventurer contributes the money capital as against the other's skill and labor, all the cases cited, and which our research has discovered, hold that neither party is liable to the other for contribution for any loss sustained. Thus, upon loss of the money the party who contributed it is not entitled to recover any part of it from the party who contributed only services.

The rationale which the California decision and the earlier cited cases adopted was where one party contributes money and the other services, in the event of a loss, each loses his own capital—one in the form of money, the other in labor. A corollary view was that the parties have implicitly agreed, by their conduct and contract, to share profits and that their contributions of money and sweat equity have been valued in an equal ratio. Thus, upon the loss of both some money and labor, the loss falls upon each proportionately without any legal recourse. Thus, Kovacik lost $8,680 of his $10,000 while Reed lost all of his labor.

Likewise, in the case before us, Kessler lost some of his money—$65,472, plus disputed interest, but Antinora lost all of the value of his labor on the three-year project.

We conclude that the "Joint Venture Partnership Agreement" here did contemplate repayment to Kessler of his investment but only from the proceeds of the sale of the house, not from his coventurer Antinora. This is what the parties said, the only truly reliable evidence of what they intended. Our interpretation of the agreement between the parties accords with the result reached under the common-law cases discussed, and with our overall sense of fairness. Each party shoulders a loss, one in determinative dollars; the other in labor, difficult, if not impossible, to quantify. The parties did not think about losses in casting their agreement and any attempt by the law now to reconstruct their then non-existent intent on the subject would be speculative.

NOTES

1. There are several ways to theorize profit and loss in this case. Kessler's total loss of money capital was $164,357. His theory of loss allocation is a 60/40 split of the loss of money capital. Thus, he claimed that Antinora owed $65,742 (= $164,357 × 40%). The court rejected this theory. It held that Kessler and Antinora separately bore the loss of their capital contributions. Antinora did not owe any money because: "Each party shoulders a loss, one in determinative dollars; the other in labor, difficult, if not impossible, to quantity."

2. There is a third possible theory of loss allocation. Is it true that Antinora's labor was "difficult, if not impossible, to quantity"? Suppose we can value Antinora's labor. The value of labor can be implied by the amount of money capital. Kessler contributed money capital of $498,917, for which he claimed 60% of profit. It can be implied that Antinora provided the other 40% of capital in the form of service. If Kessler's capital contribution is grossed up to 100%, it would be $831,528 (= $498,917 ÷ 60%). Antinora's labor capital can be implied as $332,611. Kessler lost $164,357, and Antinora lost all of his labor capital of $332,611. The partnership's total loss could be theorized as $496,968. Kessler's portion of this total loss was 60%, which would be $298,181. Yet he incurred a loss of only $164,357. The difference could be Antinora's claim against Kessler to recoup his unpaid loss of $133,824. Antinora's share of loss of sweat equity was $198,787, but instead he lost all of his labor valued at $332,611. Under this theory, Kessler would be responsible for $133,824 of Antinora's lost labor.

Of course, the problem with this theory is that the total capital expended on the project is implied to be $831,528 when the house ultimately sold for $420,000. This gross mismatch between capital and return could imply that this theory of loss is unpersuasive, or perhaps that the partners did not evaluate the economic opportunity very well with respect to the amount of capital expended for the anticipated risk-adjusted returns.

2. LIMITED PARTNERSHIP

The ULPA (2001) does not have a specific rule on profit and loss allocation. The earlier version, RULPA § 503, provides that profit and loss allocation "shall be allocated on the basis of the value."

ULPA (2001) § 503. Sharing of and Right to Distributions Before Dissolution.

(a) Any distribution made by a limited partnership before its dissolution and winding up must be shared among the partners on the basis of the value, as stated in the required information when the limited partnership decides to make the distribution, of the contributions the limited partnership has received from each partner, except to the extent necessary to comply with a transfer effective under Section 702 or charging order in effect under Section 703.

The difference between a general partnership and an LP is clear. Whereas a general partnership emphasizes co-equal partners, an LP is envisioned as an investment vehicle where investors may contribute different investment amounts with commensurate returns.

3. LIMITED LIABILITY COMPANY

Although the RULLCA does not have a specific rule on profit and loss allocation, it provides a default rule for distributions: "Any distributions made by a limited liability company before its dissolution and winding up must be in equal shares among members and persons dissociated as members." RULLCA § 404(a).

The following are provisions from the Chrysler Group LLC operating agreement that deal with contribution, profit and loss allocation, and distribution. Note that it is excerpted. Some provisions are highly technical with respect to tax treatment, and such materials are outside the scope of this book.[3] This highlights an important point about business practice: the firm's financing and ownership interests are inextricably intertwined with tax issues. The laws of NBEs gives barebones treatment of financing issues because they recognize that financing issues are best left to partners, members, and managers to sort out in the charter agreement and tax laws are intertwined with the economic issues.

CHRYSLER GROUP LLC OPERATING AGREEMENT

Section 4.2 Allocation of Profits and Losses.

(a) Subject to the other provisions in this Section 4.2 and other than in the case of a liquidation of the Company, for each Fiscal Year or other shorter period in which allocations of profits and losses are to be made among the Members (an "Allocation Period"), the Company's Book Profits and Book Losses shall be allocated for each Allocation Period to the Members in proportion to the Total Interest of each Member.

Section 4.4 Distributions.

(a) Subject to Section 8.1, distributions may be made to the Members, at the times and in the aggregate amounts determined by the Board of Directors.

(b) Any distributions shall be made pro rata to the Members in proportion to their Total Interests at the record date established therefor by the Board of Directors (or if no such record date is established then at the time of such distribution), such that no Member receives under this Section 4.4(b) an amount less than such Member's Tax Amount[4] (*i.e.*, for the avoidance of doubt, the resulting distribution shall satisfy two conditions: (i) the distribution must be pro rata in proportion to the Members' Total Interests and (ii) each Member must receive no less than its Tax Amount).

---

[3] You can read these provisions in Section 4.2(b)–(g), Section 4.3, and Section 4.4(b)–(e) in the operating agreement in the Appendix A.

[4] "Tax Amount" is defined in the Definition Addendum as: "the product of (x) the sum of the highest U.S. Federal rate of tax (expressed as a percentage) generally applicable to corporations plus five (5) percent in respect of state and local taxes (reduced by the net federal tax benefit deemed to arise from such state and local taxes at the relevant assumed rates) and (y) the net amount of income allocable to such Member (excluding any allocations of income in respect of PDARs) for the applicable period."

4. GENERAL APPROACHES TO PROFIT AND LOSS ALLOCATION

Profit and loss allocation in NBEs are a matter of contract. The law provides only default rules. Partners and members can contract for whatever provisions that suit their needs. As a matter of practice, NBEs generally use four common methods.

The first method of profit and loss allocation mimics a corporate scheme in which ownership, the bundle of economic and governance rights, is embodied in units called "shares." In the course of a firm's lifecycle, the price of shares may vary as the firm value changes. An owner may buy into the firm at a share price of $100 per unit, but later another owner buys in at $200 per unit. Like shares in a corporation, each unit will have the same rights, powers, and limitations as every other unit, and the firm can issue different classes of units, such as preferred units that have certain preference rights or management units that have priority management rights. If this method is selected, the NBE can keep track of the number of shares owned by each member or partner and allocate profit and loss based on the ownership of shares.

The second method of profit and loss allocation is allocation based on a stated ratio. For example, assume that Amy initially contributes 30,000 in capital and Zach 10,000 in capital. In light of these contributions, they may decide that a 75% and 25% stated ratio of profit and loss is the best rule. An advantage of this method is simplicity. A disadvantage of this method is the fixed nature of the profit and loss allocation even though the nature of the firm and the fairness of the situation may change over time. For example, over time one owner may take more distributions or may provide additional contributions than the other owner. These events should change the stated ratio in the capital account.

The third method of profit and loss allocation is allocation based on current capital balance. For example, although Amy and Zach initially contributed capital in the ratio of 3 to 1, their capital accounts may change over time. If so, allocation based on changing ratio of capital accounts may be fairer. The formula may add nuance. The owners may want to consider whether allocation is based on only contributions or the total amount in the capital account. A disadvantage of allocation based on capital is that certain contributions may be devalued or unaccounted. Contribution can be in many forms: *e.g.*, property, benefit, or service. A service partner may not have contributions that are recorded in the capital account, unless an agreed method adequately compensates for service capital.

The fourth method of profit and loss allocation is the services, capital, and stated ratio method. It is a mixed method. It provides for different tiers of partner compensation. For example, the partnership may agree on tiers of compensation: first tier, services are compensated at stated amounts; second tier, a fixed interest rate on capital; third tier, a stated ratio.

An example illustrates how the services, capital, and stated ratio method works. Amy initially contributed 30,000 in capital and Zach 10,000 in capital. The partnership agrees that the salary allowance for service should be 36,000 to Amy and 24,000 to Zach based on an understanding that Amy's service is quite valuable. The interest allowance is at 10% for the amount of capital provided by the partners. Thereafter, the stated ratio is equal split of profit.

Suppose the partnership made net income of 100,000. The first 60,000 are allocated as salary allowance: 36,000 Amy, and 24,000 Zach. The remaining amount of profit is 40,000. The interest allowances of 10% on capital are: 3,000 Amy, and 1,000 Zach. The remaining profit is 36,000, which is allocated equally: 18,000 Amy, and 18,000 Zach. The total profit allocations are: 57,000 Amy, and 43,000 Zach.

	Amy	Zach	Total
Net income			100,000
Tier 1: Salary allowance			
Amy	36,000		
Zach		24,000	
Remaining income			40,000
Tier2: Interest allowance			
Amy (10% x 30,000)	3,000		
Zach (10% at 10,000)		1,000	
Remaining income			36,000
Tier 3: Stated ratio			
Amy (at 50%)	18,000		
Zach (at 50%)		18,000	
Remaining income			-
Income to each partner	57,000	43,000	100,000

After this profit allocation, Amy takes a distribution (a draw) of 20,000 and Zach of 12,000. The following would be the new capital account.

	Amy	Zach	Total
Beginning capital	30,000	10,000	40,000
Profit / (loss) allocation	57,000	43,000	100,000
Capital contribution	-	-	-
Distributions	(20,000)	(12,000)	(32,000)
Ending capital	67,000	41,000	108,000

Because the capital accounts have changed, the 10% rate on capital would reflect the new capital amounts in the next accounting period.

In the above example, we had the happy circumstance in which there was income at each of the three tiers. Suppose the partnership faces the less happy circumstance of earning profit of 50,000. This amount is short of the 60,000 needed to satisfy fully the tier 1 salary allowance of 36,000 to Amy and 24,000 to Zach, which is a 6:4 ratio. The 50,000 could simply be split on a pro rata basis of 60% and 40%, which would be 30,000 and 20,000. However, the partnership could also allocate profit tier by tier on a pro rata allocation. The full salary allocations are made: 36,000 Amy, and 24,000 Zach. Of course, there is a deficit of 10,000 in profit. The interest allocations are also made: 3,000 Amy, and 1,000 Zach. This leaves a total deficit in profit of 14,000. This deficit is shared equally under the stated ratio. Under this calculation, Amy's profit allocation is 32,000, and Zach's is 18,000.

	Amy	Zach	Total
Net income			50,000
Tier 1: Salary allowance			
Amy	36,000		
Zach		24,000	
Remaining income			(10,000)
Tier2: Interest allowance			
Amy (10% x 30,000)	3,000		
Zach (10% at 10,000)		1,000	
Remaining income			(14,000)
Tier 3: Stated ratio			
Amy (at 50%)	(7,000)		
Zach (at 50%)		(7,000)	
Remaining income			-
Income to each partner	32,000	18,000	50,000

G. IMPROPER DISTRIBUTION AND LIABILITY

1. RULE AGAINST INTENTIONAL INSOLVENCY IN CORPORATION LAW

Corporation law governs the internal affairs of the corporation and the relation among its shareholders and managers. It does not generally protect creditors. Creditors can best protect themselves through the credit contract. *See* American Bar Foundation, Commentaries on Indentures, at 2 (1971) ("Short of bankruptcy, the debt security holder can do nothing to protect himself against actions of the borrower which jeopardize its ability to pay the debt unless he establishes his rights through contractual provisions set forth in the debt agreement or indenture.").

Creditors are subject to the risk that shareholders and managers will engage in actions that effectively transfer wealth from creditors to shareholders. This can be done not by fraud, in which case ample legal remedies exist including fraudulent transfer statutes, tort law, and criminal law, but by choosing risks and allocating assets.[5] A corporation

[5] For example, suppose a corporation has assets of 1,000, and liabilities of 1,000 to a bank. Thus, equity is nil. The interest rate on the bank loan is 10% (100 per year). The corporation has two projects to deploy the assets. Project A has a 100% chance of earning operating profit of 100

can increase its risk and thereby effectively transfer economic value from creditors to shareholders. *E.g.*, Metropolitan Life Insurance Co. v. RJR Nabisco, Inc., 716 F.Supp. 1504 (S.D.N.Y. 1989) (firm engaged in an LBO transaction that resulted in the buyout of shareholders at a premium and a steep decline in the value of bonds resulting from the higher risk of greater leverage on the balance sheet). Creditors are always subject to the risk of how shareholders and managers will manage the venture, legitimately and lawfully. They can minimize some of this risk through contracting, such as debt covenants, but ultimately creditors assume credit risk as a part of lending money. *E.g.*, Martin v. Peyton, 158 N.E. 77 (N.Y. 1927) ("[A creditor] may veto any business they think highly speculative or injurious. This [is] a proper precaution to safeguard the loan. Under the circumstances the safety of the loan depended upon the business success of [debtor]. This success was likely to be compromised by the inclination of its members to engage in speculation.").

Corporation law provides one substantive protection for creditors, which can also be seen as benefiting the corporation as well. A corporation cannot make a distribution to shareholders that effectively causes the firm's insolvency. This concept is found in the common law.

> Since at least 1914, this Court has recognized that "the undoubted weight of authority" teaches that a "corporation cannot purchase its own shares of stock when the purchase diminishes the ability of the company to pay its debts, or lessens the security of its creditors." [There is] the legal principle that "a corporation should not be able to become a purchaser of its own stock when it results in a fraud upon the rights of or injury to the creditors."

SV Inv. Partners, LLC v. ThoughtWorks, Inc., 7 A.3d 973, 987 (Del. Ch. 2010). Statutes codify this common law prohibition against insolvency-inducing distributions.

> No distribution may be made if, after giving it effect:
>
> (1) the corporation would not be able to pay its debts as they become due in the usual course of business; or
>
> (2) the corporation's total assets would be less than the sum of its total liabilities plus (unless the articles of incorporation permit otherwise) the amount that would be needed, if the corporation were to be dissolved at the time of the distribution, to satisfy the preferential rights upon

per year. After debt service, no profit remains for shareholders. Project B has a 50/50 chance of earning operating project of 200 per year, or a loss of 100 per year. Clearly, a creditor would prefer Project A because it will be assured of getting paid. Shareholders, however, may rationally prefer Project B because ex ante it is more profitable, though there is a substantial chance that the creditor may be harmed if the "bet" loses. A corporate manager may pursue Project B to advance the interest of shareholders despite the creditor's clear preference.

> dissolution of shareholders whose preferential rights are superior to those receiving the distribution.

Model Business Corporation Act § 6.40(c). The rule against intentional insolvency serves two purposes.

First, the rule protects creditors against the most egregious form of shareholder opportunism. For example, a firm has assets of 1,000 in cash, liability to creditors of 500, and shareholder equity of 500. The board distributes 900 in cash to shareholders. The shareholders have effectively expropriated the creditor's money. Not only is this impermissible under corporation law, but such actions could violate fraudulent transfer statutes. *See* Bankruptcy Code, 11 U.S.C. § 548(a)(1); Uniform Fraudulent Transfer Act § 4 and § 5. The corporation can properly distribute 500 of assets, but the remaining 500 belongs to creditors.

Second, the rule against deliberate insolvency protects the firm as a legal person in light of the fact that the entity cannot speak for itself and the agents who purportedly act on its behalf may have ulterior interests that may jeopardize its solvency and creditors' claims. An underlying policy is the protection of the enterprise against deliberate insolvency, a policy preference to continue a going concern. A firm may voluntarily dissolve and wind up or be forced into bankruptcy, and both require an orderly process of paying creditors' claims. But this is different from terminating an otherwise going concern by expropriating creditors' claims.

2. IMPROPER DISTRIBUTION NBEs

The ULPA (2001) and the RULLCA provide a similar rule against deliberate insolvency. Below are RULLCA § 405 and § 406. The ULPA (2001) § 504 and § 505 provide functionally similar rules. The RUPA does not have a similar provision for a general partnership because general partners are personally liable for the debts and obligations of partnership. However, if a partnership is an LLP, the same limitation on and liability for improper distribution apply. RUPA § 406, § 407.

RULLCA § 405. Limitations on Distribution.

(a) A limited liability company may not make a distribution, including a distribution under Section 707, if after the distribution:

> (1) the company would not be able to pay its debts as they become due in the ordinary course of the company's activities and affairs; or
>
> (2) the company's total assets would be less than the sum of its total liabilities plus the amount that would be needed, if the company were to be dissolved and wound up at the time of the distribution, to satisfy the preferential rights upon dissolution and winding up of

members and transferees whose preferential rights are superior to the rights of persons receiving the distribution.

(b) A limited liability company may base a determination that a distribution is not prohibited under subsection (a) on:

(1) financial statements prepared on the basis of accounting practices and principles that are reasonable in the circumstances; or

(2) a fair valuation or other method that is reasonable under the circumstances.

RULLCA § 406. Liability for Improper Distributions.

(a) Except as otherwise provided in subsection (b), if a member of a member-managed limited liability company or manager of a manager-managed limited liability company consents to a distribution made in violation of Section 405 and in consenting to the distribution fails to comply with Section 409, the member or manager is personally liable to the company for the amount of the distribution which exceeds the amount that could have been distributed without the violation of Section 405.

(b) To the extent the operating agreement of a member-managed limited liability company expressly relieves a member of the authority and responsibility to consent to distributions and imposes that authority and responsibility on one or more other members, the liability stated in subsection (a) applies to the other members and not the member that the operating agreement relieves of the authority and responsibility.

(c) A person that receives a distribution knowing that the distribution violated Section 405 is personally liable to the limited liability company but only to the extent that the distribution received by the person exceeded the amount that could have been properly paid under Section 405.

(d) A person against which an action is commenced because the person is liable under subsection (a) may:

(1) implead any other person that is liable under subsection (a) and seek to enforce a right of contribution from the person; and

(2) implead any person that received a distribution in violation of subsection (c) and seek to enforce a right of contribution from the person in the amount the person received in violation of subsection (c).

(e) An action under this section is barred unless commenced not later than two years after the distribution.

Section 405(a) is identical to the MBCA § 6.40(c) (provided above). The first test is income-based: whether the firm can continue to service the debt (*i.e.*, pay interest and principal as they come due). The second test is balance sheet-based: whether the distribution would make assets less than liabilities, which means that the creditors' claims against the firm are larger than the firm's assets.

RULLCA § 405(a)(2) treats preferential rights upon dissolution of classes or series of memberships for distribution purposes as equivalent to liabilities rather than as equity. Preferential dissolution rights should be found in the certificate of organization or operating agreement. The liability from preferential rights must include arrearages in preferential distributions if the certificate of organization or operating agreement require such payment upon dissolution. The treatment of preferential dissolution rights is applicable only to the balance sheet test and is not applicable to the income-based test.

The income-based test is easier to apply. If a firm cannot timely service the debt at any point, it is insolvent. The balance sheet test can be more nuanced. At first glance, it should be pretty clear: Are assets less than liabilities to creditors? The answer is clear only if there is one definitive measure of assets. However, assets can have different values depending on the method or concept of valuation. The value of assets found in the financial statements (called "book value") may provide one figure. Asset value may be based on market prices (called "market value"). Market value may differ from "fair value" (sometimes called "theoretical value" or "intrinsic value"), which may be calculated under various methods.

A deeper understanding of these concepts is beyond the scope of this book. An example may illustrate the point. Assume that a firm purchased real estate in Manhattan in 1950 at value 100 and it has 400 of cash, and liabilities of 500. Clearly, the firm cannot make any distribution since all assets (500) are claimed by creditors (500). In 2010, the market value of the real property has increased to 600, but assume that under generally accepted accounting rules the real property is still recorded in the financial statements at the historical purchase price (book value) of 100. Assume that the firm still has 400 of cash and liabilities of 500. The book value of total assets is still 500, but the market value of total assets is now 1,000. Under book value, the firm cannot distribute anything to the owners because liabilities are 500. Under market value (1,000), the firm can distribute as much as 500 because liabilities are only 500. What is a permissible distribution?

Since there could be a range of plausible value of assets, Section 405(b) provides a manager some discretion to determine whether a distribution is improper or not: "A limited liability company may base a determination that a distribution is not prohibited on: (1) financial statements prepared on the basis of accounting practices and principles that are reasonable in the circumstances; or (2) a fair valuation or other method that is reasonable under the circumstances."

H. ADMISSIONS AND DISSOCIATIONS OF PARTNERS AND MEMBERS

An NBE can admit new owners. The default rule is unanimous consent of all owners to admit a new owner. *See* RUPA § 402(b)(3); ULPA (2001) § 301(b)(3), § 401(b)(3); RULLCA § 401(c)(3). The charter agreement can provide for any method for admitting new owners. These methods include majority vote, approval by a manager, or sale of the interest from one owner to someone outside the firm. The firm can permit these methods either through the charter agreement or consent of all other owners. Whenever a new owner joins the firm, it must account for contributions and new profit and loss allocation among all owners.

1. ADMISSIONS

If a firm permits the sale of an interest to an outsider who would then become a new owner, the transaction is between the owner and the outsider. The firm simply acknowledges the transaction in its books. For example, suppose Amy and Zach were equal partners. Amy sells half of her interest, which is 25% of the entire partnership interest, to Beth. With respect to the partnership, this is a sale between Amy and Beth. The partnership does not receive any additional contribution. The partnership simply acknowledges Beth as a new partner. The partnership interest would now be: 25% Amy, 25% Beth, and 50% Zach.

A transaction for the admission of a new owner can occur between the firm and the new owner. In such case, the new owner would typically contribute capital. Suppose Amy and Zach initially provided 30,000 and 10,000 in capital, and after profit allocation and distributions Amy and Zach had ending capital of 52,000 and 26,000. Beth joins the partnership by making a contribution of 22,000. The total equity is now 100,000. The equity ownership stakes by the partners are: 52% Amy, 26% Zach, and 22% Beth. The profit and loss allocation would be based on a new agreement among partners, who can adopt a number of methods as discussed before.

The price at which a new owner joins the firm can be greater than the price implied by the total owners' capital. This occurs when the firm value exceeds the value of the owners' total capital. Perhaps there is goodwill in the business. The new owner joins the firm and must pay the market value of equity. In this situation, the accounting for the transaction provides that the difference between the market value and the owners' capital is a bonus to the current owners.

Let's continue with the previous example. Amy and Zach had ending capital of 52,000 and 26,000. Beth joins as a new partner and contributes 42,000 in capital. This is total capital of 120,000. Beth's 42,000 contribution would imply a 35% claim to the equity (= 42,000 ÷ 120,000). However, suppose Beth agrees to a claim of 25% of the total equity. This means that out of the 120,000 in total capital, Beth's claim is 30,000. The additional 12,000 she contributed is a bonus to the current partners Amy and Zach. Assume that they share the bonus equally. Their capital accounts are credited with 6,000 each in bonus. After the admission of Beth, the equity claims are: 58,000 Amy, 32,000 Zach, and 30,000 Beth.

The reverse situation can also occur. A new owner can join a firm with the new owner receiving a bonus from the current owners. This situation may arise in two typical circumstances: first, when the market value of the firm is less the value of the owners' total capital; and second, when the new owner brings special skills or other attributes beyond simply the value of the contribution in property form. In this situation, the accounting for the transaction provides that the difference between the market value and the owners' capital is a bonus to the new owner.

Let's continue with the previous example. Amy and Zach had ending capital of 52,000 and 26,000. Beth joins as a new partner and contributes 22,000 in capital. Total capital is 100,000. Beth's contribution would imply a 22% claim to the equity. However, suppose the partnership agrees that Beth's claim to equity is 30%. This means that out of the 100,000 in total capital, Beth's claim is 30,000. She has received a bonus of 8,000. Assume that the contribution of this bonus was provided equally by Amy and Zach. The new capital structure is: 48,000 Amy, 22,000 Zach, and 30,000 Beth.

2. DISSOCIATIONS

Owners can withdraw or dissociate from the firm in two ways. First, if the firm permits, the owner can sell his entire interest to another person, who would then take his place as a new owner. Nothing changes in the firm's books except that it acknowledges the sale. The transaction is between the dissociating owner and the buyer. Second, the withdrawing owner can sell his interest back to the partnership. If the partnership had foresight, the charter agreement would have a buy-sell provision that would provide a clear formula for the transaction. Otherwise, the firm and the departing owner would have to negotiate a purchase price.

The accounting for dissociation is similar to that of admissions. It can be done with no bonus, a bonus to the remaining owners, or a bonus to the dissociating owner. Let's continue with the prior examples. The newest partner, Beth, joined the partnership with no bonus. After Beth's contribution, the partnership's capital accounts were: 52,000 Amy, 26,000 Zach, and 22,000 Beth. Suppose the capital accounts do not change. Beth decides to leave the partnership and the buyout price is 22,000. There is no bonus to anyone. The partnership's cash declines by 22,000, and the remaining partners' capital accounts are: 52,000 Amy, and 26,000 Zach.

Suppose the buyout price is 18,000, which is 4,000 less than the 22,000 in her capital account. There is a bonus to the remaining partners. Beth's capital account of 22,000 is eliminated. The firm's cash declines by 18,000.

Amy's and Zach's capital accounts are credited with a bonus of 2,000 each. Their capital accounts are: 54,000 Amy, and 28,000 Zach.

Suppose the buyout price is 26,000, which is 4,000 more than the 22,000 in her capital account. There is a bonus to Beth. Beth's capital account of 22,000 is eliminated. The firm's cash declines by 26,000. Amy's and Zach's capital accounts are deducted by 2,000 each. Their capital accounts are: 50,000 Amy, and 24,000 Zach.

I. INTERESTS AS SECURITIES

Stock in corporations are clearly securities within the definition of a "security" under federal and state securities laws. However, under securities laws, the definition of a "security" encompasses far more than clear examples of securities such as stocks and bonds. Among other things, any "investment contract" can be a security under securities laws. *See* Section 2 of the Securities Act of 1933, codified in 15 U.S.C. § 77b(a) ("The term 'security' means any investment contract."); Colo. Rev. Stat. § 11–51–201(17) (" 'Security' means any investment contract.").

When a financial interest is deemed to be a "security," securities laws apply. The most immediate concern—but certainly not all by any stretch—is whether the issuance of the security has been registered under securities laws or whether it is exempt. For example, under Section 5 of the Securities Act of 1933, codified in 15 U.S.C. § 77e, the sale of securities in interstate commerce is prohibited unless a registration statement filed with the SEC is in effect. The registration process is very entailed and expensive; it is not something that is undertaken lightly. Certain securities and transactions are exempt from this registration requirement. *See, e.g.*, Section 3 of the Securities Act of 1933, codified in 15 U.S.C. § 77c (exempting certain classes of securities); Section 4 of the Securities Act of 1933, codified in 15 U.S.C. § 77d (exempting certain transaction). When securities laws are violated, potential remedies available to investors are, among others, damages and rescission. Clearly, unhappy investors in NBEs, who may be otherwise trapped in an illiquid investment, may seek to frame their complaint as a sale of securities that violated securities laws for the purpose of seeking damages or rescission.

When is a partnership or member interest a "security"? The firm, its managers and lawyers must understand that securities laws could govern the marketing and sale of such interests and subsequent course of conduct, such as disclosure requirements. A complete review of all implications is learned in a separate course on securities regulation. However, a starting point in the analysis is the definition of a "security." This inquiry determines whether securities laws apply at all. If a partnership or member interest is a security, securities laws apply including the registration requirement and exemptions thereto.

The seminal case is *SEC v. W.J. Howey Co.*, 328 U.S. 293 (1946). It involved the sale of interests in citrus groves (of all things), under common management and control, to various disparate investors. The Court defined "investment contract," a term that securities laws include in the statutory definition of a "security," as the following:

> an investment contract for purposes of the Securities Act means a contract, transaction or scheme whereby [1] a person invests his money [2] in a common enterprise and [3] is led to expect profits solely from the efforts of the promoter or a third party, it being immaterial whether the shares in the enterprise are evidenced by formal certificates or by nominal interests in the physical assets employed in the enterprise.

Id. at 298–99. Clearly, an interest in an NBE could meet this definition of an investment contract, and thus be deemed a security. The critical inquiry is the third-prong of the *Howey* standard, *i.e.*, whether profits are gotten "solely from the efforts of" others.

With respect to specific investments in partnerships and LLCs, an influential case is *Williamson v. Tucker*, 645 F.2d 404 (5th Cir. 1981), which in light of *Howey* set forth the standard to determine whether an interest in a partnership was a security as:

> A general partnership or joint venture interest can be designated a security if the investor can establish, for example, that (1) an agreement among the parties leaves so little power in the hands of the partner or venturer that the arrangement in fact distributes power as would a limited partnership; or (2) the partner or venturer is so inexperienced and unknowledgeable in business affairs that he is incapable of intelligently exercising his partnership or venture powers; or (3) the partner or venturer is so dependent on some unique entrepreneurial or managerial ability of the promoter or manager that he cannot replace the manager of the enterprise or otherwise exercise meaningful partnership or venture powers.

Id. at 424. The case involved a real estate joint venture, a form of a general partnership. The court commented that none of the above factors appeared to be present in the case and that "the plaintiffs have an extremely difficult factual burden" to prove their joint venture interests were securities.

The unique management structures of each NBE is examined later in this book. A basic understanding for the moment informs the question of a security. *Howey* identified "solely from the efforts of the promoter or a third party" as a key factor, and the *Williamson* standard further delves into this issue. A key inquiry is the level of control rights held by the interest holder: To what degree are the investors passive investors who depend on others to gain profits?

In this respect, the default rule in general partnership is that "each partner has equal rights in the management and conduct of the partnership business." RUPA § 401(h). This rule clearly gives each partner governance and control rights, which are inconsistent with the *Williamson* standard. On the other hand, the defining characteristic of an LP is a two-tier partnership structure in which a general partner manages the LP and a limited partner is a passive investor with no management authority. ULPA (2001) § 302(a), § 406(a). A passive investment tends to satisfy the definition of a security under *Howey* and *Williamson*. This has been the finding in scholarly research. *See* Theresa A. Gabaldon, *A Sense of a Security: An Empirical Study*, 25 J. Corp. L. 307, 335 (2000) ("It is of interest, though no special surprise, to observe the frequency with which plaintiffs lose regarding general partnership or limited liability company interests (prevailing in approximately 25% of the cases) and win regarding limited partnership interests (triumphing at a rate of 80%).").

LLCs may present more complex analysis because, due to contractual flexibility, the rules permit a broader range of management structures. In a member-managed LLC, the company mimics a general partnership where all members participate in the management and conduct of the LLC. RULLCA § 407(b)(2). In a manager-managed LLC, the company mimics an LP or a corporation where managers manage the business and affairs of the company and members are passive investors. *Id.* § 407(c)(2).

The case below sets the standard for determining whether an interest in an NBE is a security under federal securities law. In reading this case, consider these questions: (1) What are the critical factors that would make an interest *not* a security? (2) How can the charter agreement be drafted in a way to avoid coming within the purview of securities law? (3) Are the written provisions of the charter agreement dispositive?

SEC v. MERCHANT CAPITAL, LLC

483 F.2d 747 (11th Cir. 2007)

ANDERSON, CIRCUIT JUDGE:

The SEC brought this enforcement action against defendants Steven Wyer, Kurt Beasley, and Merchant Capital, LLC ("Merchant"), alleging violations of the registration and antifraud provisions of the federal securities laws. Wyer and Beasley, through Merchant, sold interests in twenty-eight registered limited liability partnerships ("RLLPs") to 485 persons. The SEC asserted that these interests were "investment contracts" within the meaning of the federal securities laws, and that the defendants had committed securities fraud in marketing the interests. The district court concluded that the interests were not investment contracts and, regardless, that the defendants had not committed securities fraud. We reverse in part, vacate in part, and remand for further proceedings.

Wyer and Beasley formed Merchant in order to participate in the business of buying, collecting, and reselling charged-off consumer debt from financial institutions such as banks and credit card companies.

Wyer and Beasley formed Merchant, with Wyer owning seventy-five percent, and Beasley twenty-five percent. Wyer and Beasley planned to raise funds through Merchant and then buy fractional shares in debt pools ultimately purchased by New Vision. New Vision would aggregate money from Merchant and other sources, purchase debt pools through auction and forward-flow contracts, and then outsource the collection of the debt to Enhanced Asset Management ("EAM"). To formalize this relationship, Merchant entered into a services contract with New Vision.

Merchant began raising money by soliciting members of the general public to become partners in Colorado RLLPs. Merchant employed a network of recruiters to sell the RLLP interests, and provided the recruiters with scripts. These recruiters informed potential partners that, while they would be expected to participate in the operation of their partnership, their actual duties would be limited to checking a box on ballots that would be periodically sent to them. Merchant's offering materials also represented that the RLLP interests were not securities and that the federal securities laws did not apply to the interests.

Each RLLP was to have no more than 20 partners. Merchant organized twenty-eight RLLPs, containing 485 partners, with a total capitalization of over $26 million. The RLLP partners were all members of the general public with no demonstrated expertise in the debt purchasing business, and included a nurse, a housewife, and a railroad retiree.

Under the partnership agreement provided by Merchant, each partnership was scheduled to participate in the debt purchasing, collection, and resale business for three years, at which point it would be dissolved. The managing general partner ("MGP") would be the operational head of the partnership, with sole authority to bind the partnership.

The partnership materials told the partners that they were expected to have an active role in managing the business of their partnership. The agreement reserved certain powers for the partners. They had the ability to select the MGP. They had the exclusive right to approve any act obligating the partnership in an amount exceeding $5,000. They could remove the MGP upon a unanimous vote, for cause. Finally, they could inspect books and records and participate in various committee meetings.

Merchant prepared all the partnership materials and was the sole business contact for all of the partners. It was the only candidate for MGP and was named on one-hundred percent of the ballots. Merchant thus became MGP for each of the twenty-eight RLLPs.

Merchant also failed to operate the business successfully. Merchant and its principals knew that the existing partnerships were performing poorly. Despite the poor performance, no partnership replaced Merchant during the period before the SEC began its investigation.

The key issue is whether the RLLP interests marketed by Merchant were "investment contracts" covered by the federal securities laws. Both the Securities Act and the Exchange Act define "securities" to include "investment contracts." 15 U.S.C. §§ 77b(a)(1), 78c(a)(10). An investment contract is "a contract, transaction, or scheme whereby a person invests his money in a common enterprise and is led to expect profits solely from the efforts of the promoter or a third party." *SEC v. W.J. Howey Co.*, 328 U.S. 293, 298–99 (1946). The issue is whether the RLLP partners were led to expect their profits solely from the efforts of Merchant.

Under this prong of *Howey*, "solely" is not interpreted restrictively. "The Supreme Court has repeatedly emphasized that economic reality is to govern over form and that the definitions of the various types of securities should not hinge on exact and literal tests." *Williamson v. Tucker*, 645 F.2d 404, 418 (5th Cir. 1981). An interest thus does not fall outside the definition of investment contract merely because the purchaser has some nominal involvement with the operation of the business. Rather, "the focus is on the dependency of the investor on the entrepreneurial or managerial skills of a promoter or other party."

A general partnership interest is presumed not to be an investment contract because a general partner typically takes an active part in managing the business and does not rely solely on the efforts of others. *Williamson*, 645 F.2d at 422. But consistent with the substance over form principle of *Howey*, "a scheme which sells investments to inexperienced and unknowledgeable members of the general public cannot escape the reach of the securities laws merely by labeling itself a general partnership or joint venture." *Williamson*, 645 F.2d at 423. A general partnership interest may qualify as an investment contract if the general partner in fact retains little ability to control the profitability of the investment. *Williamson* recognized three situations where this would be the case: (1) "an agreement among the parties leaves so little power in the hands of the partner or venturer that the arrangement in fact distributes power as would a limited partnership"; (2) "the partner or venturer is so inexperienced and unknowledgeable in business affairs that he is incapable of intelligently exercising his partnership or venture powers"; or (3) "the partner or venturer is so dependent on some unique entrepreneurial or managerial ability of the promoter or manager that he cannot replace the manager of the enterprise or otherwise exercise meaningful partnership or venture powers."

The first *Williamson* factor requires us to analyze whether "an agreement among the parties leaves so little power in the hands of the partner or venturer that the arrangement in fact distributes power as would a limited partnership." Merchant relies primarily on the allegedly substantial powers reserved to the partners through the partnership agreement. The partnership materials informed partners that they were expected to take an active role in the business, and the agreement gave partners certain rights and powers. Partners had the ability to call meetings and hold regular quarterly meetings; the ability to participate in committees; the ability to elect the MGP; the ability to remove the MGP for cause upon a certain vote; the ability to inspect books and records; the ability to approve additional funding; the ability to amend the agreement or to dissolve the partnership upon a two-thirds vote; and the exclusive authority to approve obligations exceeding $5000.

The power to name the MGP was not a significant one in this case. Partners were required to turn in their ballots with their capital contribution, before their partnerships had even been formed. The power therefore reveals nothing about the partners' ability to control the business after their initial investment. Moreover, Merchant was the only option for MGP. The investors had no independent experience in the debt purchasing industry and no way of knowing about alternative MGPs. And, as a result, Merchant was named on all ballots. This power was not significant.

The partners did not have the practical ability to remove Merchant once it was installed as MGP. The agreement provided for removal only for cause. This meant that Merchant could not be removed readily, and even in the case of gross incompetence, the partners would have had to litigate any unconsented removal. We have previously found that where removal is only for cause, and the investors have no other ability to impact management, the interest is an investment contract as a matter of law.

There were further barriers to removing Merchant. The partnership agreement required a unanimous vote of the partners. The district court found that Merchant could be removed somewhat more easily, with a two-thirds vote of the partners in an individual partnership. Even if a two-thirds vote were enough, we would likely conclude that removal was practically impossible, when combined with the other factors. But we find that the district court clearly erred. The written materials are somewhat ambiguous: the partnership agreement seems to say that a two-thirds vote is enough, while the partnership application says that a unanimous vote is required. Wyer admitted at trial, however, that he told partners a unanimous vote is required. We hold Wyer's representation against him and conclude that a unanimous vote was required. It is clear that such a vote, combined with removal only for cause and the factors discussed below, rendered Merchant effectively unremovable.

Compounding the legal difficulty in removing Merchant, the investors in an individual partnership were geographically dispersed, with no preexisting relationships. *Howey* found it significant that the interests in that case were offered "to persons who reside in distant localities." *Howey,*

328 U.S. at 299. Similarly, in this case, the lack of face-to-face contact among the partners exacerbated the other difficulties and rendered the supposed power to remove Merchant illusory.

The next power reserved to the partners was the ability to approve all obligations over $5,000. If this power was real, it was a substantial one. The primary business of each partnership was purchasing fractionalized interests in pools of debt that generally exceeded $5,000 in value. However, as shown by Merchant's tenure as MGP, the ballot right also did not give the partners meaningful control over their investment.

First, Merchant controlled how much information appeared in the ballots, and did not submit sufficient information for the partners to be able to make meaningful decisions to approve or disapprove debt purchases. Each ballot indicated only the face value of the debt pool, the price per dollar of debt, and the name of the issuer. This information at most gave the partner the price of the pool and the name of the issuer. But unrebutted testimony at trial established that much more data is necessary to make an informed decision about how much a debt pool is really worth. The SEC's expert testified that many factors go into the price that should be paid for a debt pool, in addition to the name of the issuer: the reputation of the issuer, how the accounts were selected from the issuer's pool, the geographic distribution, the terms of the cardholder agreements, how old the debt is, when the last payment was, and whether a payment was ever made, among many others.

Second, the partners had no way to force Merchant to heed the results of the process. The SEC's expert testified, based on a sample of balloting data for five partnerships, that Merchant repeatedly abused the balloting process. Merchant purchased more debt than the ballots authorized thirty times; purchased debt before ballots were sent six times; and purchased before the ten-day return period expired seventy-three times. In part because the partners had no ability to remove Merchant, they also lacked the power to force Merchant to abide by the results of the ballots.

Finally, the voting process was tilted in Merchant's favor from the very start. The partnership agreement provided that unreturned and unvoted ballots were voted in favor of management. Until October 2002, the ballots had only a signature line, and no "no" box. Even after that, the ballots always contained insufficient information for investors to make informed decisions. The levers of the voting process were thus in Merchant's hands from the very beginning. It had control over the information in the ballots, did not have any incentive to heed the results of ballots, and was assured of victory in any balloting anyway because of the default rules. Unsurprisingly, no ballot ever went against Merchant's decisions. We therefore conclude that the voting process was a sham and did not give partners meaningful control over their investment.

The operation of the balloting process revealed that the partners from the very beginning lacked power to control Merchant's actions. The balloting process was a sham because the partnership agreement contained no way to force Merchant to conduct a meaningful ballot. The agreement did not require a particular form of ballot, which meant that Merchant could control the information partners received. The partners had no other influence over Merchant because they lacked a practical removal power. They could not force Merchant to give them a meaningful amount of information or to respect the results of the ballots. The RLLP partners lacked the ability to remove or control the manager from the inception of the enterprise. Nor did the RLLP partners ever expect to take an active role in managing the business, as the recruiters represented that the partners' duties would be limited to checking a box on the ballots that were periodically sent to them.

The remaining powers—the ability to inspect books and records, participate in committees, and hold meetings—did not on their own give the partners the potential to control Merchant's management of the business, and thus do not contribute to the *Williamson* analysis. We have previously held that "the opportunity to inspect records" and an "obligation to give periodic accountings" of income and expenses did not bear on an investor's ability to control the profitability of the investment, and were therefore irrelevant from the perspective of investment contract analysis. The inspection and meeting rights might have helped the partners make more informed decisions, if the partners also had the ability to effectuate those decisions. But because the appointment, approval, and removal powers were illusory, these other powers had no independent salience.

[The court also found the second and third factors of *Williamson* standard were met. The second factor asks whether "the partner or venturer is so inexperienced and unknowledgeable in business affairs that he is incapable of intelligently exercising his partnership or venture powers." In this case, the individual partners had no experience in the debt purchasing business. They were members of the general public, and included a railroad retiree, a housewife, and a nurse. They relied solely on Merchant to operate the business. The third factor asks whether "the partner or venturer is so dependent on some unique entrepreneurial or managerial ability of the promoter or manager that he cannot replace the manager of the enterprise or otherwise exercise meaningful partnership or venture powers." The RLLP partners did not have any realistic alternative to management by Merchant because Merchant effectively had permanent control over each partnership's assets.]

Because the RLLP interests were investment contracts, and the defendants sold the interests without filing a registration statement, the defendants violated the registration provisions of the securities laws.

J. ISSUES TO CONSIDER FOR NBEs

Consider the case of the corporation. The corporation issues shares to shareholders, and the board determines the issue price. The board has discretion to make distributions. Profit and loss are allocated based on pro rata ownership of shares. Shareholders are not required to buy additional shares. The corporation through the board can issue new shares. These rules answer most questions concerning a corporation's financing needs.

When drafting the charter agreement of an NBE, a lawyer must consider the same issues involving financing transactions among owners. There are broad questions to consider: Who has the duty to manage the firm's finances? What authority does the manager have to carry out this financial responsibility? What are the financial rights of owners? What are the tax consequences of any financing decision?[6]

1. CONTRIBUTIONS

When an entity is created, the owners make initial contributions. Initial contributions must be sufficient to begin business operations. They must determine the form, amount, and value of contributions:

- What form and amount of contribution must each owner make?
- If the contribution is not in cash, what is the value for the purpose of determining relative contributions by all?

Presumably, the issue of relative contribution and valuation will determine the profit allocation and distribution rights. For example, even in a general partnership, if Amy and Zach contribute 100 and 50, respectively, Amy would most likely seek greater profit allocation and perhaps also greater governance power despite the default rules in RUPA § 401(a) ("Each partner is entitled to an equal share of the partnership distributions") and § 401(h) ("Each partner has equal rights in the management").

A business may need additional capital in the future. The charter agreement should provide for how this can be done. Some owners may want to limit their financial commitment to the firm, but the firm may confront a situation in which it becomes undercapitalized. The agreement should provide for the possibility of additional calls and contributions.

- Are additional calls permitted or not?
- What are the current and anticipated future financing needs?
- Who has the authority to make a capital call?
- What process is used to authorize the capital call?

6 Tax law is not within the scope of this book, but obviously tax consequence is a critically important issue in practice in any financing provision and decision.

- Are capital calls mandatory or voluntary?
- What is the consequence or effect of not contributing in either a voluntary or mandatory capital call?

With respect to consequence or effect of not contributing, there are a number of potential options to consider:

- Reduction in profit allocation based on pro rata dilution noncontributing owner's interest
- Liability for failure to contribute
- Right of other owners to make the additional contribution
- Right of other owners or the firm to buyout the noncontributing owner's interest in the firm
- Suspension of noncontributing owner's management rights
- Forfeiture of noncontributing owner's entire interest

Assuming that the firm and its owners desire the option for future capital calls, a firm can pursue a number of potential options. The capital call can be mandatory or voluntary, unlimited or limited in amount, at the manager's discretion, upon a vote of owners, or upon some trigger in the charter agreement. In the event of voluntary contributions by some but not others, contributing owners would probably seek additional profit allocation and possibly governance rights, in the same way that a corporate shareholder will be entitled to additional economic interest and voting rights through the purchase of more shares. Nonparticipating owners would suffer dilution of their interests. Lastly, the agreement should provide for the specific adjustments to the interests of those who make a contribution, whether voluntary or mandatory, and those who do not.

If an owner does not make a mandatory contribution, the charter agreement should provide for the consequences of not making the required contribution. A lack of an enforcement mechanism would de facto make the action voluntary. What penalties must noncontributing owners incur? The following commentary provides some perspective.

> Advisors frequently want as harsh a remedy as possible. They want to be able to castrate the defaulting venturer, coat him in honey, and bury him in an anthill in the hot summer sun. Courts may not enforce these provisions. A court may not enforce forfeiture or dilution provisions that are unreasonably harsh, depending on the state law involved.

Terence Floyd Cuff, *Drafting Partnership and LLC Agreements: Part I*, 3 BUS. ENTITIES 22 (May/June 2001).

The harshest penalty is a forfeiture of the owner's interest. To include this provision into the charter agreement, the lawyer and the owners should be confident that courts will enforce a forfeiture provision. Some jurisdictions emphasize the primacy of freedom of contract. *E.g.*, Delaware Limited Liability Company Act § 18–1101(b) ("It is the policy of this chapter to give the maximum effect to the principle of freedom of contract and to the enforceability of limited liability company agreements."). These states may enforce forfeiture. Consider Delaware's LLC statute.

> Such penalty or consequence may take the form of reducing or eliminating the defaulting member's proportionate interest in a limited liability company, subordinating the member's limited liability company interest to that of nondefaulting members, a forced sale of that limited liability company interest, forfeiture of the defaulting member's limited liability company interest, the lending by other members of the amount necessary to meet the defaulting member's commitment, a fixing of the value of the defaulting member's limited liability company interest by appraisal or by formula and redemption or sale of the limited liability company interest at such value, or other penalty or consequence.

Id. § 18–502(c). *See also* Georgia Limited Liability Company Act § 14–11–402(b) ("Unless otherwise provided in the articles of organization or a written operating agreement, the obligation of a person to make a contribution to the capital of a limited liability company may be reduced or eliminated only with the unanimous consent of the members.").

The next level of severity in penalty would be a forced buyout of the defaulting owner. The charter agreement should provide the specific formula or method to determine the buyout price. Options can include, for example, return of the balance in the capital account or return of contribution only. The price can also incorporate a deduction similar to a liquidated damage provision. The lawyer and the owners should bear in mind that a buyout would result in capital leaving the firm and thus the possibility that the buyout would adversely affect the firm's finances in a way that may not have been contemplated at the time of drafting.

The least severe penalty for defaulting on a mandatory capital contribution would be additional dilution of interest. One should bear in mind that dilution should occur even without penalty due to the fact that some owners will make the mandatory contributions while others default on the obligation. Dilution as a penalty would be in addition to such ordinary dilution. The formula for dilution of either economic or governance interests should be stated in the charter agreement. Dilution will have economic effect due to changing profit allocations or distribution rights, and it may have potential tax consequences on both owners who accrete additional owner interests and those whose interest are diluted.

Lastly, lawyers and owners should consider the human aspect of business transactions. Outside of forfeiture, a noncontributing owner is still a participant in the venture. One must consider to what extent the penalty or liability for failure to make a mandatory contribution would result in hard feelings and potential dysfunction. This issue may be less relevant to owners who are passive investors, such as limited partners whose contribution to the venture is their capital, but may be more significant to ventures where the defaulting owner participates in management or provides other beneficial services.

2. PROFIT AND LOSS, AND DISTRIBUTIONS

Economic interests are the most important matter in an investment. They are subject to contracting. In this respect, corporations and NBEs are different. Each share of a specific class of stock has the same rights, preferences, and limitations as every other share in the class. However, in NBEs, the interest of each owner may be subject to bespoke contracting. The charter agreement should sort out the following questions.

- How should profit and loss be allocated among owners?
- How should profit and loss allocation be adjusted based on new events such as contributions and distributions?
- How should distributions be made in form and process?
- Does the manager have the authority to make a distribution, or does the owner have the contractual right to a distribution?
- Should distribution be made in proportion to contribution or some other measure?
- Should there be preferential rights to distribution from either the firm's earnings or a return of capital?
- Do owners have a right to draw from their capital accounts?
- What are distribution rights after specific transactions such as sale of capital assets, sale of company, or merger?
- What are distribution rights upon liquidation?
- Are owners entitled to tax distributions?

With respect to distribution upon liquidation, there are a number of possibilities for the distribution of net assets after payment of all liabilities. The following are some examples: (1) pro rata distribution by capital accounts, economic units, or contributions; or (2) distribution prioritized by return of contribution and followed by net profit and loss allocation.

With respect to tax distribution, earned income of the partnership entity flows through to owners under partnership tax law, and thus owners may be liable for taxes regardless of whether the entity has distributed the profit. This situation may result in a cash shortfall for owners who are have earned income for tax reporting but who have not received a distribution.

A tax distribution is designed to mitigate this liquidity problem by making a distribution sufficient to pay an owner's current tax liability.

3. NEW MEMBERS AND PARTNERS

When a firm has a small number of owners, the unanimous consent rule makes much sense. Such firms have close, intimate working relations among owners. The admission of a new person significantly changes the firm, and thus unanimous consent may be a good rule. However, when a firm has many owners, unanimous consent means that any owner has a veto and thus one person has the power to override the needs of the firm and the preferences of the many therein. The admission of a new owner should be subject to the charter agreement and the agreement should provide a practical rule. Where there are many owners, the possible mechanisms are several, for example: consent of owners where the approval threshold can be a minority, majority, or supermajority; consent of managers; manager recommendation followed by owner consent.

K. PROBLEM: ENTREPRENEURS OBTAIN FINANCING

After their disheartening meeting with Rittenhouse Bank, Piers and Blake thought hard about financing the venture. They still have not settled on the form of entity. At this point, they were leaning toward forming a limited liability company. As they represented to Rittenhouse Bank, they calculated that the company will need $500,000 in startup cash capital. After the sale of a condo he co-owned with his parents, Piers got $100,000 that could apply toward financing the venture. Blake was not as wealthy and he had no money. But Blake insisted on having equal ownership stake as Piers so that he did not become a "junior partner in this venture." Piers agreed. However, they needed to work out the issue of how to handle the fact that Piers would be contributing $100,000 more money to the venture and this money would not be a gratuitous gift to the business.

Piers: "I wholly agree that we have to be equal partners in every respect. But that still leaves me chipping in $100,000. How are we going to handle these two facts?"

Blake: "What about my patents for hinges? I have several patents for new ways to make hinges on fine delicate things like eyeglass frames. These hinges allow for folding things in multiple angles, which are perfect for new designs on glasses. In fact, when I received my patent, an eyeglass company, Craft Lenses, offered to buy it. We can use my patents."

Piers: "That's a great idea. Let's give some thought on how to handle this."

With $100,000 of Piers' funds, Piers and Blake still needed $400,000 in cash. While Piers' cash amount constitutes only 20% of the initial cash needed, Piers and Blake agreed that they must maintain control irrespective of Piers' 20% cash capital.

Piers and Blake began to seek out potential venturers on an individual basis. They first approached their finance professor Morgan Money. Seeing the promise of this venture, Money agreed to contribute $200,000. But Money placed the following condition on the contribution:

> I realize that both of you are the entrepreneurs, and you will be managing this venture. But I don't want to be an entirely passive investor. I'm a professor of business, and I think I can contribute to the vision, strategy, and business plan of this venture. At the same time, I have a daytime time, which is teaching. I can't devote as much time as the two of you. I also understand that the two of you will really want to control the venture and I can respect that. But I need to have a say. How do we achieve our mutual goals?

In addition to Money, Piers and Blake found another potential investor for the last $200,000. Nicki Song is an "angel investor." Angel investors are wealthy individuals who invest in the equity of startup ventures for profit. In their meeting, Song placed the following condition on any potential contribution to the venture:

> I'm a passive investor. I have money and I have a keen eye for talent. But I know that my entrepreneurs know their businesses far better than I do. Since I am passive, I want certain protections. I am most concerned about a situation in which the venture fails, and it has to liquidate. I also want the right to pull out my money if I see that the venture is not as promising as I had thought. What rights can you offer to protect my interest as a passive investor?

Piers and Blake have the potential to pull together their $500,000 in cash necessary to start the business: $100,000 Piers, $0 Blake, $200,000 Morgan Money, and $200,000 Nicki Song.

QUESTIONS

1. Assuming that Piers and Blake form an LLC, what are the basic issues that they must consider as the business organizers?

2. How can Piers and Blake structure the entire deal among themselves, Money, and Song?

3. Provide bullet point, initial term sheets for both Money and Song. A term sheet provides succinct description of the essential terms and conditions of the investment. How much money will each put in? What rights does each have? How do these rights relate to the rights of other investors?

4. Suppose that after the venture is started with the financing, Piers and Blake ran into an old friend, Art Estic, who graduated from art school and specialized in sculpting and crafting with plastic. They realized that Art would

be the perfect design and manufacturing manager for the new line of eyeglass frames. Art was a typical artist in the sense that he had no funds to make a business investment. But he did not want to work as an employee. As he said, "Making eyeglass frames is not what I had in mind when I went to art school. I realize that I might have to give up some psychic utility by foregoing my artist dreams to go work for a startup serving the mass consumer market. So I need to be compensated properly. I want equity in the venture." Piers and Blake thought that they can accommodate this. What are the issues to consider?

CHAPTER 5

AGENCY

■ ■ ■

A. THE THEORY OF AGENCY AND ITS COSTS

If a firm has only one individual-owner who conducts all activities herself without employees or agents, the utility of conducting business through a firm is limited. The business is still in large part a sole proprietorship. For tax purpose, the entity is disregarded. Statutory rules on management structure, fiduciary duties, and dissociation, among others, serve no function. Limited liability provides modest protection. When the firm is solely owned by a single individual, contract creditors will often seek a personal guarantee, and tort creditors will often be able to show that the individual owner participated in any wrongful acts.

Aside from the humblest individual-owner business, a business firm—corporation, partnership, or LLC—conducts business through employees and agents. They work for the firm and represent it in business dealings with third parties. Such representation generally benefits the firm. The following passage explains the specific benefits of agency.

> Agency allows us to live better in three different ways. First, we may not have time to pursue our own interests as vigorously as we would like. Many possibilities go unexplored and many of those we do explore go unexploited. Hiring an agent simply allows us to do more. Like an able research assistant or law firm associate, an agent can take advantage of opportunities that we ourselves would never have time to identify, evaluate, or enjoy. Two or more people—the right people, anyway—can simply do more than one.
>
> Second, even if we have the time, we may not have the knowledge and skills we need to pursue our own interests effectively. We may know what we want to do but not how to do it. Many of us, for example, engage others to invest our money not because we are pressed for time, but because we fear that we would make poor investment decisions. The right professional, we hope, will improve and steady our returns. In this way, a well-chosen agent may carry out our aims more effectively than we ourselves could. Just think of the difference between representing yourself in court and having an attorney represent you. Your attorney can not only make better legal decisions but can also

> make them more quickly. Unlike you, your attorney has a background of professional skills, knowledge, and experience to draw on. Even attorneys, in fact, know to hire attorneys to represent them.
>
> Third, agents can allow us to pursue our activities more cheaply. If we compartmentalize our projects, we can engage others to work on them who do not need the broad range of skills necessary to complete the overall projects. Such division of labor permits specialization, which brings its own returns and frees actors from having to master a wider range of knowledge than is necessary. Actors can thus focus more directly on serving us than on acquiring skills. Additionally, if our agents save us money, we ourselves will have more resources to devote to more of our own pursuits.

Samuel Issacharoff & Daniel R. Ortiz, *Governing Through Intermediaries*, 85 Va. L. Rev. 1627, 1635–36 (1999).

Although agency creates benefits for firms, it imposes costs as well. Economic theory posits that the interests of a principal and an agent are never perfectly aligned. The following articulates the idea of agency cost.

> We define an agency relationship as a contract under which one or more persons (the principal(s)) engage another person (the agent) to perform some service on their behalf which involves delegating some decision making authority to the agent. If both parties to the relationship are utility maximizers there is good reason to believe that the agent will not always act in the best interests of the principal. The *principal* can limit divergences from his interest by establishing appropriate incentives for the agent and by incurring monitoring costs designed to limit the aberrant activities, of the agent. In addition in some situations it will pay the *agent* to expend resources (bonding costs) to guarantee that he will not take certain actions which would harm the principal or to ensure that the principal will be compensated if he does take such actions. However, it is generally impossible for the principal or the agent at zero cost to ensure that the agent will make optimal decisions from the principal's viewpoint. In most agency relationships the principal and the agent will incur positive monitoring and bonding costs (non-pecuniary as well as pecuniary), and in addition there will be some divergence between the agent's decisions and those decisions which would maximize the welfare of the principal. The dollar equivalent of the reduction in welfare experienced by the principal due to this divergence is also a cost of the agency relationship, and we refer to this latter cost as the "residual loss." We define *agency costs* as the sum of:

> (1) the monitoring expenditures by the principal, (2) the bonding expenditures by the agent, (3) the residual loss.

Michael C. Jensen & William H. Meckling, *Theory of the Firm: Managerial Behavior, Agency Costs and Ownership Structure*, 3 J. Fin. Econ. 305, 308 (1976).

The above passage is written in econo-speak, but its core idea is simple enough. It assumes that an agent can never serve the principal's interest as well as the principal can if the latter could do all the work herself. The simplest example is the tension between employer and employee. Employees do not always work as hard as owners, and as a result sometimes owners need to monitor them. Bad behavior can range from mild missteps to malignant malice: *e.g.*, from surfing the internet on company time to defrauding the company. Because even the best agent's interest may diverge from the principal's interest, the principal must take certain steps to best align the interests. Principals can monitor agents through direct supervision, regular reporting, and appropriate surveillance. They can use contracting devices such as compensation and termination conditions, and bonding devices such as non-compete agreements or forbearance of the employee's other opportunities.

All of these control devices—compensation, supervision, monitoring, reporting, forbearance—affect the agent's production and thus the firm's as well. They also impose significant costs on principals and agents. For example, a firm incurs costs to institute a system of supervision and reporting, and a poorly structured compensation scheme can result in bad incentives and poor performance. The agent incurs costs of bonding and forbearance. These are real costs to on the firm and the agent.

Another significant cost on the principal is the residual loss from an agent's conduct. Agents can take actions that impose significant costs on the firm. In the most extreme case, they can destroy a business, such as the case of Enron. Residual loss includes the principal's legal liability resulting from the agency. Here, the loss has a direct nexus to "the law." In everyday situations, agents can impose liability on the firm by committing torts and entering into contracts even when the principal would not have approved of such conduct had it known or had the chance to intercede. Among other things, the law of agency exists to provide orderly, predictable rules dealing with the legal consequences on a principal for the acts of an agent or some other person affecting third parties.

B. LEGAL DEFINITION OF AGENCY AND AGENT

From a financial standpoint, agency is important because a firm needs agents to act on its behalf, but they can bind the principal and thus create liability. Agents impose cost on firms. The law of agency, like the laws of torts or contracts, applies to all firms. The legal form of firms and the structure of management may determine: (1) whether a principal-agent relationship exists, and (2) whether the firm as the principal is bound by the act of someone purportedly acting on its behalf. For example, absent contravening facts, all partners in a general partnership are agents, and public shareholders in a corporation are not agents. The law of agency provides the rules, but their application produces outcomes that are specific to the unique facts surrounding each transaction or event.

An agency relationship is created when a principal and an agent asset to such relationship. "Agency is the fiduciary relationship that arises when one person (a 'principal') manifests assent to another person (an 'agent') that the agent shall act on the principal's behalf and subject to the principal's control, and the agent manifests assent or otherwise consents so to act." Restatement (Third) of Agency § 1.01. The mutual manifestation of assent can be established through writing, oral agreement, or conduct. An agency relationship does *not* require an enforceable contract. Many agents serve the role gratuitously. *E.g.,* Gorton v. Doty, 69 P.2d 136, 140 (Idaho 1937) ("It is not essential to the existence of authority that there be a contract between principal and agent or that the agent promise to act as such, nor is it essential to the relationship of principal and agent that they, or either, receive compensation.").

An essential element of agency is the principal's right to control the agent's actions, though she may or may not exercise this right in the course of managing the business.

> Control is a concept that embraces a wide spectrum of meanings, but within any relationship of agency the principal initially states what the agent shall and shall not do, in specific or general terms. Additionally, a principal has the right to give interim instructions or directions to the agent once their relationship is established. Within an organization the right to control its agents is essential to the organization's ability to function, regardless of its size, structure, or degree of hierarchy or complexity.

Restatement (Third) of Agency § 1.01, cmt. f(1).

The law of agency imposes fiduciary duty on the agent when an agency is created. *See id.* cmt. e ("If the relationship between two persons is one of agency, the agent owes a fiduciary obligation to the principal."); *id.* § 8.01 ("An agent has a fiduciary duty to act loyally for the principal's benefit in all matters connected with the agency relationship."); *id.* § 8.08 ("Subject to any agreement with the principal, an agent has a duty to the principal to act with the care, competence, and diligence normally exercised by agents in similar circumstances."). In business organizations, agents owe fiduciary duties: *e.g.*, officers of a corporation, partners, and members and managers owe the fiduciary duties of care and loyalty.

The case below discusses the principles of agency within the context of statutory immunity. The opinion resulted in a robust dissent. In reading this case, consider these questions: (1) What are key points of disagreement among the majority and the dissent? (2) To what extent did the legislative policy affect the definition of "agent" in this case?

LANG V. LIONS CLUB OF CUDAHY WISC., INC.

939 N.W.2d 582 (Wisc. 2020)

PATIENCE DRAKE ROGGENSACK, C.J.

We review a decision of the court of appeals reversing an order of the circuit court that granted summary judgment in favor of Fryed Audio, LLC on the ground that it was entitled to recreational immunity pursuant to Wis. Stat. § 895.52(2) (2017–18). Fryed Audio is a member of Rhythm Method, LLC, with whom the Lions Club of Cudahy Wisconsin, Inc. contracted to provide music for its 2012 festival at a Milwaukee County park. The sole member of Fryed Audio, Steven Fry, laid Rhythm Method's electric cords on the floor of the music tent for the Lions Club event. Antoinette Lang allegedly tripped on a cord, which led to this lawsuit.

Because the Lions Club is a statutory owner pursuant to Wis. Stat. § 895.52(1)(d)1, Fryed Audio moved for summary judgment citing § 895.52(2), which provides that agents of owners have immunity from claims by those who enter land of a statutory owner.

We conclude that there are no issues of material fact in regard to the Lions Club's right to control Fryed Audio in regard to laying the cords for Rhythm Method's amplified sound and that Fryed Audio was an agent of the Lions Club who lawfully acted through its subagent, Steven Fry. Because the Lions Club was a statutory owner, Fryed Audio, as its agent, is entitled immunity pursuant to Wis. Stat. § 895.52(2).

The Lions Club is a nonprofit entity. Annually, it has organized a fundraising event called the Sweet Applewood Festival. The Festival has been a Lions Club event for fourteen years.

The Lions Club has controlled the grounds and determined how the Festival has run. Among other things, it controls how and where tents are placed; the selection of vendors; and ensures necessary services such as security, first responders, and garbage disposal are provided.

The Lions Club decided where the band was located and it set up the stage. The Lions Club was responsible for general electrical work.

The Lions Club contracted with Rhythm Method for music. The contract stated that "sound and lights" would be provided by Rhythm Method. It also stated, "professional covered stage and power by purchaser." The contract provided that each member of Rhythm Method was individually obligated to adhere to its terms and conditions and that the leader of Rhythm Method was an agent of the Lions Club:

> The Performer(s) are engaged *severally* on the terms and conditions of this agreement. The leader represents that the Performer(s) already designated have agreed to be bound by said terms and conditions. Each performer, not yet chosen, shall also be bound by said terms and conditions upon acceptance.
>
> The leader shall, as the *agent* of the Purchaser, enforce disciplinary measures for just cause and carry out instructions as to selections and manner of performance.

Rhythm Method, LLC had five people as members plus Fryed Audio, another LLC. Steven Fry was the sole member of Fryed Audio.

Lang allegedly tripped on a cord run by Steven Fry. She sued several parties for negligence. The only defendant remaining is Fryed Audio.

During a deposition, Steven Fry explained that he had not received specific instructions from the Lions Club on how to lay electric and electronic cords. [Frank Miller, a Lions Club member] said he had not provided "any prohibitions, or specific instructions, or directives as to how [those who set up the bands' equipment] are supposed to run their wires from that sound board in the middle of the tent to the stage at that time which they're performing."

In years past, before a Festival began, a Lions Club official performed a walkthrough looking for, among other things, trip hazards. Miller testified he did not specifically recall performing a walkthrough; however, he testified that it had been his practice each year.

Notably, Rhythm Method had a prior relationship with the Lions Club. It had played at the festival in past years. In the past, when the Lions Club determined that cords needed to be covered, it provided the mats to do that. It also placed orange cones to alert frequenters to a potential hazard.

Wisconsin Stat. § 895.52(2) states:

> No owner and no officer, employee or agent of an owner owes to any person who enters the owner's property to engage in a recreational activity:
>
> 1. A duty to keep the property safe for recreational activities.
>
> 2. A duty to inspect the property, except as provided under s. 23.115(2).
>
> 3. A duty to give warning of an unsafe condition, use or activity on the property.

The Lions Club was an owner under the statutory definition, [and] the festival was a recreational activity in which Lang was participating when she fell. [The parties] dispute centers on whether Fryed Audio was an "agent of an owner," *i.e.*, an agent of the Lions Club.

Agency

People and businesses sometimes act through others. As a general principle, a person or business acting on behalf of another, and subject to control of another, is an agent and the person or business they are acting on behalf of, a principal. Agency law provides a series of rules that apply to such relationships. Among these rules are provisions that govern when a principal is liable for the actions of its agent. "The foundational principle of agency law is that the principal, who has chosen to conduct her business through an agent, must bear the foreseeable consequences created by that choice." This principle arises from the benefit that the principal derives from acting through the agent whom the principal controls.

Wisconsin Stat. § 895.52 does not define agent. We have had few occasions to address the concept of agency within the confines of recreational immunity. When we have, however, we have given the word "agent" its plain meaning as a legal concept.

We have cited the Restatement Second's definition of agency with approval: "Agency [is] the fiduciary relation which results from the manifestation of consent by one person to another that the other shall act on his behalf and subject to his control, and consent by the other so to act."

An agency relationship "results from the manifestation of consent by one person to another that the other shall act on his behalf and subject to his control, and consent by the other so to act." An agent may be either an employee or an independent contractor; however, when "an independent contractor has no fiduciary obligations to and is not subject to control by the principal, no agency relationship has formed." [In this case, the parties] focus on whether the Lions Club had the right to control Fryed Audio, a member of the independent contractor, Rhythm Method.

The principal's right to control the injury causing conduct is crucial to both the existence of an agency relationship and the scope of the agency. It does not matter whether the conduct is complex or simple. What matters in forming an agency relationship is that the principal has the right to control that conduct. A principal is liable for the conduct of an agent when the injury causing conduct is "of the same general nature as authorized, or incidental to the conduct authorized." Restatement (Second) of Agency § 229(1). Stated otherwise, the principal is liable only if the principal had the "right to control" the injury causing conduct. A principal does not have to exercise that right; however, without the right to control the injury causing conduct, an agency cannot exist relative to that conduct.

In *Westmas v. Creekside Tree Serv., Inc.*, 907 N.W.2d 68 (Wisc. 2018), we interpreted the word agent within the context of recreational immunity. There, a property owner contracted with a tree-trimming service. The contract provided "no means or methods" controlling how the trees were to be trimmed or whether safety precautions were to be employed. We emphasized that the owner had "no background or knowledge on how to perform tree-trimming." The property owner did not know that the tree-trimming service was working at the time its conduct caused an injury.

In concluding that an agency relationship did not exist, we noted the lack of "reasonably precise specifications" for tasks that required knowledge about trimming trees and in regard to safety precautions that were needed for tree trimming. The question of agency is "fact-specific" and "fact-bound." The property owner merely had the right to expect a result as opposed to the right to control the injury causing conduct, *i.e.*, the means by which tree-trimming was accomplished. Therefore, although there was a contract between the tree trimmer and the property owner, no agency relationship existed because the property owner did not have the right to control the tree trimmer's conduct that caused the injury.

The right to control the conduct that caused the injury is critical to evaluating whether an agency exists, and if so, the scope of the agency. However, whether the injury-causing task is simple or requires some degree of specific knowledge by the contracting party affects the weight we give to the absence or presence of "reasonably precise specifications."

Fryed Audio's placement of electronic and electric cords was a simple task that Fryed Audio had performed at the Lyons Club's festivals in year's past, including the 2011 Festival. However, both the written contract and the testimony of Miller showed that the Lions Club had a right to control how the cords were placed and whether mats were used to cover them.

The contract specified that Rhythm Methods and its members, which included Fryed Audio, were "bound by the terms and conditions" of the contract, thereby subjecting them to the Lions Club's control.

> The Performer(s) are engaged severally on the terms and conditions of this agreement. The leader represents that the Performer(s) already designated have agreed to be bound by said terms and conditions. Each performer, not yet chosen, shall also be bound by said terms and conditions upon acceptance.

The contract, which bore the signature, "Steven Fry," on behalf of Rhythm Method, also specified that the leader of Rhythm Methods was "the agent" of the Lions Club:

> The leader shall, as the agent of the Purchaser, enforce disciplinary measures for just cause and carry out instructions as to selections and manner of performance.

Here, Fryed Audio was the leader of Rhythm Method for purposes of setting up the sound system, and its sole member, Steven Fry, was the leader in regard to contracting on behalf of Rhythm Method. As an agent of the Lions Club, Fryed Audio was subject to the Lions Club's right to control the injury causing conduct.

The testimony of Miller demonstrated the control that the Lions Club had on placing of cords needed for the amplified sound of Rhythm Method. He said that the Lions Club "requires sound companies to either cover their wiring or run it over head from the soundboards to the stages."

By contract, Fryed Audio, was individually bound to the contract's terms. As the leader of Rhythm Method in placing the electronic and electric cords, Fryed Audio was the "agent" of the Lions Club, thereby giving the Lions Club the right to control the conduct that is alleged to have caused injury. Miller's testimony further explained the relationship between Rhythm Method and the Lions Club that gave the Lions Club the right to control the injury causing conduct, *i.e.*, the placing and covering cords that were used to provide amplified sound. Fryed Audio was the agent of the Lions Club, because the Lions Club had the right to control Fryed Audio in many respects, including the placing of electronic and electrical cords for the amplified sound of Rhythm Method.

Subagency

Sometimes, an agent hires people or businesses to perform tasks on behalf of its principal. The hired people or businesses are known as subagents. 3 Am. Jur. 2d Agency § 7 (2019) ("A subagent is a person employed by the agent to assist him or her in conducting the principal's affairs."). As the Restatement (Third) of Agency illustrates:

> P Corporation retains A Corporation to manage its investment portfolio. S, a senior vice-president of A Corporation, is placed in charge of the management of P Corporation's portfolio. S is P Corporation's subagent.

Restatement (Third) of Agency § 3.15 cmt. b, Ill. 2.

> (1) A subagent is a person appointed by an agent to perform functions that the agent has consented to perform on behalf of the agent's principal and for whose conduct the appointing agent is responsible to principal. The relationships between a subagent and the appointing agent and between the subagent and the appointing agent's principal are relationships of agency.
>
> (2) An agent may appoint a subagent only if the agent has actual or apparent authority to do so.

Id., § 3.15; 3 C.J.S. Agency § 265 (1973) ("When one employs an agent who has either express or implied authority to employ a subagent, the subagent will also be the agent of the principal.").

A subagent owes duties to both the principal and the appointing agent. "A subagent owes a duty of obedience to the principal as well as to the appointing agent." Restatement (Third) of Agency § 3.15 cmt. d. The principal's rights as to the subagent are superior to rights of the appointing agent, even in the event of conflict or disagreement between principal and appointing agent."

"When an agent is itself a corporation or other legal person, its officers, employees, partners, or members who are designated to work on the principal's account are subagents." *Id.* cmt. b. When a principal creates an agency relationship with a legal person, such as an LLC, the principal implicitly consents to someone other than the agent performing the work, *i.e.*, a person that exists only as a matter of law must act through others. An LLC may act through its members, at least if it is member managed. Wis. Stat. § 183.0301(1)(a) ("Each member is an agent of the limited liability company for the purpose of its business."). A contract that creates an agency with an LLC necessarily implies an agency relationship with at least some of its members, officers, employees, or other agents.

When a subagent is an agent of the principal, a principal is liable for the tortious actions of a subagent.

> As between a principal and third parties, it is immaterial that an action was taken by a subagent as opposed to an agent directly appointed by the principal. In this respect, subagency is governed by a principle of transparency that looks from the subagent to the principal and through the appointing agent. As to third parties, an action taken by a subagent carries the legal consequences for the principal that would follow were the action instead taken by the appointing agent.

Restatement (Third) of Agency § 3.15 cmt. d (2006). Stated otherwise, "once a third party is validly appointed a subagent, the principal is liable for the subagent's actions." 3 Am. Jur. 2d Agency § 7.

Steven Fry laid the cables on which Lang tripped. He is the sole member of Fryed Audio, and Fryed Audio is a member of Rhythm Method, the band that the Lions Club contracted with to perform. Fryed Audio, through the actions of Steven Fry, connected the sound system that Rhythm Method needed to fulfill its contract with the Lions Club.

An agency relationship is driven by "the manifestation of consent by one person to another that the other shall act on his behalf and subject to his control, and consent by the other so to act." Restatement (Second) of Agency § 1(1) (1958). There is no dispute that the Lions Club requested Rhythm Method to act on its behalf to provide music for its festival and that Rhythm Method consented so to act. Furthermore, the Lions Club had broad contractual control.

First, the language of the contract gave the Lions Club the right to control each member of Rhythm Method, as they are severally bound to its terms and conditions. Second, it gave the Lions Club the right to control Rhythm Method and its members for everything from showing-up on time, to selecting music and its manner of performance, to disciplining members of Rhythm Method when its leader was instructed by the Lions Club that discipline was requested.

Steven Fry laid cords on the floor of the music tent. Fryed Audio, while severally bound by the Lions Club contract, could not actually lay the cords upon which Lang focuses. Fryed Audio, an LLC, is a legal person that required an actual person to place the cords for Rhythm Method's sound system. We conclude that Steven Fry was Fryed Audio's agent for that task and therefore, the subagent of the Lions Club for that task as well. Restatement (Third) of Agency § 3.15 cmt. d.

REBECCA FRANK DALLET, J. (dissenting).

The contract does not say that the Lions Club had "the right to" control the sound setup. It says the exact opposite: "Sounds and lights by band." Miller's deposition further confirms this understanding: "The sound companies who were providing services to the bands weren't contracted by us, so we did not get involved in how they set up their equipment." This evidence demonstrates the contract left the "means and methods" for setting up the band's sound to the band.

Essentially, the majority of this court is telling members of the public that when they enter any community festival, they do so at their own risk. This result is far afield from the immunity necessitated to achieve the stated purpose of the recreational immunity statute—to encourage property owners to open their lands to the public to engage in recreational activities. Fryed Audio played no part in opening the land and its liability here would not deter the Lions Club from hosting its festival again, yet the majority of this court extends to it immunity. This conclusion is contrary to the plain language of Wis. Stat. § 895.52(2)(b).

BRIAN HAGEDORN, J. (dissenting).

An agency relationship is not the same as a contract for services. The outcome in this case takes us further from that principle. The key question in agency law is whether the principal has the right to control the agent's activities—that is, the means and manner of the agent's work. Underlying this case, however, is an injury arising from a particular type of activity: negligent physical conduct. Our law has long distinguished between the physical conduct of the two types of agents—independent contractors and servants. An independent contractor is one whose physical conduct is not subject to the control of another, while a servant's physical conduct is.

The question of whether Fryed Audio, LLC was acting as an agent of the Lions Club of Cudahy Wisconsin, Inc. when carrying out the injury-causing conduct is premised on whether the Lions Club and Fryed Audio were in a master-servant relationship. Under our law, no such relationship was present here. Fryed Audio was therefore not acting within the scope of any agency relationship when laying the cords and is not entitled to immunity under Wis. Stat. § 895.52(2). I respectfully dissent.

Our law has distinguished between two types of agents. Agents may be either servants or independent contractors.

All servants are agents, but agents of a particular kind. "A servant is one employed to perform service for another in his affairs and who, with respect to his physical conduct in the performance of the service, is subject to the other's control or right to control." The typical example is the employee-employer relationship. When employees are acting within the scope of their employment, they are acting as agents of the employer. Restatement (Second) of Agency § 219. Masters have the right to control, and are therefore liable for, the physical conduct of their servants.

Independent contractors, in contrast, may or may not be agents. Restatement (Second) of Agency § 2(3). Sometimes independent contractors are simply hired to perform a service. The contract may contain reasonably precise specifications or other performance and quality-oriented details. It also may not. But none of that is key to whether the independent contractor is acting as an agent with respect to the independent contractor's physical activities.

While an independent contractor may enter into a contractual relationship to do something for another, the independent contractor "is not controlled by the other nor subject to the other's right to control with respect to his physical conduct." Restatement (Second) of Agency § 2(3). In other words, one who engages an independent contractor, whether an agent or not, does not have the right to control the physical conduct of the independent contractor. Even a contract that requires certain outcomes or appears to retain control over certain areas does not, with respect to the physical conduct of the independent contractor, constitute the right to control necessary to establish a fiduciary agency relationship. Hence, even an independent contractor agent is, with respect to his physical conduct, not acting within the scope of the agency relationship.

The key question is whether Fryed Audio was a servant of the Lions Club. If Fryed Audio was an independent contractor of the Lions Club (or something less), then by definition its physical conduct was not within the scope of any agency relationship, regardless of any contractual control or specifications. On the other hand, if Fryed Audio was a servant of the Lions Club, it was acting as an agent with respect to its physical conduct—the conduct that caused the injury.

The Restatement (Second) of Agency § 220(2) provides this framework: "In determining whether one acting for another is a servant or an independent contractor, the following matters of fact are considered: (a) the extent of control which, by the agreement, the master may exercise over the details of the work; (b) whether or not the one employed is engaged in a distinct occupation or business; (c) the kind of occupation, with reference to whether, in the locality, the work is usually done under the direction of the employer or by a specialist without supervision; (d) the skill required in the particular occupation; (e) whether the employer or the workman supplies the instrumentalities, tools, and the place of work for the person doing the work; (f) the length of time for which the person is employed; (g) the method of payment, whether by the time or by the job; (h) whether or not the work is a part of the regular business of the employer; (i) whether or not the parties believe they are creating the relation of master and servant; and (j) whether the principal is or is not in business."

The relationship between Fryed Audio and the Lions Club looks nothing like a master-servant relationship. At the outset, there is no formal relationship between Fryed Audio and the Lions Club at all. There is no contractual relationship between these two entities establishing the Lions Club's authority to determine how Fryed Audio carried out the means and manner of its sound system set-up responsibilities. No contractual language of this kind exists here.

None of the other related indicia of a master-servant relationship are found here either. The Lions Club does not purport to have told Fryed Audio when to do its job. Setting up band sound systems was not a normal part of the Lions Club operations, nor did it furnish equipment or training or expertise for such a task. This was a one-time job orchestrated by a different entity—Rhythm Method, LLC. Moreover, the Lions Club didn't even have an obligation to pay Fryed Audio. The Lions Club had no contractual right to fire Fryed Audio. There was no agreement for fees, no sharing of offices or billing, no shared or mandated insurance, and no oversight by the Lions Club in determining who Fryed Audio could serve.

The key question in agency is the right to control. [This] means the right to control the means and manner of accomplishing the work performed or at issue. Only masters have the requisite right to control the physical conduct of their servants. Independent contractors are not, with respect to their physical conduct, acting within the scope of any agency relationship that might exist. Because Fryed Audio was not in a master-servant relationship with the Lions Club, its negligent physical conduct cannot be said to be within any agency relationship. Therefore, Fryed Audio is not entitled to immunity under the recreational immunity statute.

The case below discusses the extent to which investors and directors *qua* individual directors of a firm are agents. In reading this case, consider these questions: (1) How does a firm's management structure determine whether a person is an agent or the extent of authority? (2) How did concepts from corporation law and corporate management structure affect the determination of agency authority in an LLC? (3) What are the implications of the holding and rationale on closely-held firms in which investors may also participate to varying degree in management?

SEGAL V. GENITRIX, LLC

87 N.E.3d 560 (Mass. 2017)

KAFKER, J.

A jury found the defendants, Fisk Johnson and Stephen Rose, two former board members and investors in Genitrix, LLC (Genitrix or company), personally liable under G. L. c. 149, § 148 (Wage Act), for failing to pay wages owed to the former president of Genitrix, Andrew Segal. We conclude that the Wage Act does not impose personal liability on board members, acting only in their capacity as board members, or investors engaged in ordinary investment activity. Rather, to impose such liability, the statute requires that the defendants be "officers or agents having the management" of a company. The defendants were not designated as company officers and had limited agency authority. The only officer having the management of the company was the plaintiff, not the defendants.

Segal and Johnson agreed to form a biotechnology startup company with Segal serving as president and chief executive officer (CEO) and Johnson providing initial funding. Rose was a representative for Johnson. Genitrix was established as a Delaware limited liability company (LLC).

Segal transferred his intellectual property rights to the company in exchange for a substantial equity interest. Johnson received a substantial equity interest in return for his initial investment in the company. Segal and Johnson each had authority to appoint two board members to Genitrix's four-member board of representatives. Most board decisions required a seventy-five per cent majority to pass.

Johnson began funding Genitrix through Fisk Ventures, LLC (Fisk), an entity owned entirely by Johnson and Rose. Fisk became the largest shareholder of Genitrix, and gained the authority to appoint a fifth member to the board. Johnson and Fisk's combined equity in Genitrix exceeded fifty per cent. Fisk and Johnson's board representatives, taken together, constituted sixty per cent of the board. Although their representatives comprised a majority on Genitrix's board, they were still short of the seventy-five per cent threshold required to pass most board resolutions.

Genitrix never employed more than five employees. As the president and sole officer, Segal was responsible for all day-to-day operations.

Segal informed the board that the company was running out of funds to pay its employees. He told the board they would need to lay off at-will employees the company could not afford to pay, so as to avoid liability under the Wage Act. Rose told Segal that Fisk would not invest more money in Genitrix if Segal continued to control the management of the company. Fisk did subsequently invest additional money in Genitrix, but unlike prior investments, Rose earmarked that investment for specific purposes: payroll, expenses necessary to comply with covenants in the LLC agreement, and the repair or replacement of a centrifuge. All subsequent Fisk investments were also earmarked for specific purposes, such as patent fees and other employees' salaries. Segal voted in favor of each board resolution authorizing Genitrix to accept these investments.

Genitrix was still short on money and struggling to make payroll. Segal stopped taking his salary in January 2007. He testified that he did so to help the company. When pressed about who made that decision, Segal testified, "Given the box I was in, I did."

At this point the company was out of money and apparently deadlocked on even how to conduct board business. As a result of the deadlock and the financial condition of the company, Rose filed a petition for the judicial dissolution of Genitrix on behalf of Fisk. The petition was filed in Delaware, where Genitrix was incorporated.

Segal actively opposed the dissolution.*

As the dissolution proceedings continued, Segal did some other work as president, including paying patent annuity fees and protecting the work associated with those patents, securing directors' and officers' insurance, and making necessary tax filings.

Segal raised the issue of unpaid wages with the board. A few months after Segal stopped paying himself, he informed the board that he was no longer taking a salary.

Segal filed suit against Rose and Johnson in Massachusetts under the Wage Act for unpaid wages from 2007 to 2009.

At trial the jury were instructed that the "duty to pay wages extends to the president and treasurer of a corporation and any officers or agents having the management of such corporation, which includes an LLC, such as Genitrix." The jury were instructed that a "person qualifies as an agent having the management of such corporation if he controls, directs, and participates to a substantial degree in formulating and determining policy

* Author's note: The Delaware Chancery Court ultimately dissolved the company. Fisk Ventures, LLC v. Segal, 2009 WL 73957, at *1 (Del. Ch. 2009) ("When such a company has no office, no employees, no operating revenue, no prospects of equity or debt infusion, and when the company's Board has a long history of deadlock as a result of its governance structure, more than ample reason and sufficient evidence exists to order dissolution. Accordingly, I will grant petitioner's motion for judgment on the pleadings and order that dissolution of the limited liability company occur as contemplated in the company's charter.").

of the corporation or LLC." The jury went on to find both defendants individually liable under the Wage Act.

The statutory language and legislative history of the Wage Act.

The Wage Act requires employers to compensate their employees for earned wages. An employer who violates § 148 may be sued by the aggrieved employees. Section 148 defines "employer" as a "person having employees in his [or her] service." For corporations, such persons are the "president and treasurer of [the] corporation and any officers or agents having the management of such corporation," in addition to the corporation itself. The statute does not include board directors or investors in its definition of "employer." We consider the omission of directors and investors to be significant.

Both parties agree that neither defendant was ever president or treasurer of Genitrix. Indeed, the *plaintiff* in this case was president of Genitrix. The defendants were also not officers of Genitrix. Accordingly, they could only be found liable if they were "agents having the management" of Genitrix under the statute.

In determining the meaning of "agents having the management" of the company, we examine the statutory language and legislative history, as well as our case law. The plain language of the provision indicates two important requirements: the defendant must both be an agent and have the management of the company.

The novel questions presented here.

We begin with the recognition that this case is quite unusual and removed from the core concerns of the Wage Act. An employee may always sue the president and treasurer of a company for unpaid wages. The plaintiff here, however, is the president and sole officer of the corporation and thus the only person expressly identified by virtue of his title as responsible for Wage Act violations. He was specifically charged with the management of the finances and the payroll function in his employment agreement. He also made the decision not to pay himself. As we consider whether the defendants were agents having the management of the company for the purposes of imposing personal liability under the Wage Act, we must carefully separate Segal's officer and agency powers, and his actions, from those of the defendants.

We must also for the first time apply the definition of "agents having the management of the corporation" to board members or investors.

How the statutory definition of "agents having the management of such corporation" would apply to board members and investors is by no means obvious. A board generally acts collectively, not individually. Also a board ordinarily sets policy and oversees management but does not perform the management function itself. Investors may exercise significant financial control over a company through their power over their investments, but they are generally acting as outsiders, not managers or agents of the corporation. With these overarching considerations in mind, we turn to the application of the phrase "agents having the management" of the company to board members and investors in general and, more specifically, Johnson and Rose.

Requirement that the defendants be agents.

Section 148 does not define "agent," but we assume the Legislature intended to give the term its ordinary common and corporate law meaning. At common law, an agency relationship exists where "there is mutual consent, express or implied, that the agent is to act on behalf and for the benefit of the principal, and subject to the principal's control." In the context of corporate law, an executive officer is generally considered an agent of the company, because he or she acts on the corporation's behalf, subject to the corporation's control, as exercised through the board of directors. See Restatement (Second) of Agency § 14C comments a, b (1958). By contrast, "neither the board of directors nor an individual director is, as such, an agent of the corporation." *Id.* at § 14C. This is because the board of directors, acting as a whole, is generally not subject to another's control. *Id.* at § 14C comment a. "An individual director, as such, has still less resemblance to an agent than has the board as a body. He has no power of his own to act on the corporation's behalf, but only as one of the body of directors acting as a board. Even when he acts as a member of the board, he does not act as an agent, but as one of the group which supervises the activities of the corporation." *Id.* at § 14C comment b.

Likewise, investors in a company are ordinarily not considered agents of the company. Much like board members, investors invariably exercise some control over the businesses they invest in. However, exercising one's rights as an outside investor is separate and distinct from being an agent of the corporation. 1 W.M. Fletcher, Fletcher Cyclopedia of the Law of Corporations § 30, at 100 (rev. ed. 2015) ("The mere fact that one is a shareholder or a majority or principal shareholder gives the individual no authority to represent the corporation as its agent in dealing with third persons"). Investors are acting on their own behalf, not that of the company. Neither the common understanding of the word "agent," nor its use in the Wage Act, encompasses ordinary investors or investment activity. This court accordingly will not attribute to the Legislature an intent to "alter the normal rules of corporate law in the absence of plain or necessarily implied intent to change the pre-existing law." If the Legislature intended for the Wage Act to reach investors and investment activity, it would have done so explicitly.

This is not to say that an individual director or investor can never be personally liable as an agent of the company. Rather, individual directors or investors may still be considered agents of the corporation if they are empowered to act as such, but any agency relationship stems from their appointment as an agent, not from their position as a director or investor. Restatement (Second) of Agency at § 14C comment b. For example, an individual director or investor could be appointed as an agent if the board exercised "its express or implied power to confer authority upon [the individual] to act for the corporation," or if the individual was appointed as an executive officer. *Id.* This does not mean that an individual director is immune from any Wage Act liability unless the board has passed an official board resolution appointing that director as an agent of the company. An agency relationship can arise from either express or implied consent.

In the instant case, neither defendant was appointed as an executive officer. The LLC agreement provided that "unless delegated by the board, all management powers over the business and affairs of the company shall be exclusively vested in the board." Those management powers, particularly over the payment of wages, were in turn expressly delegated to Segal, not individual board members. The agreement also expressly stated that investors did not have agency authority. The agreement specified that "no member in his or her capacity as a member shall have any power to represent, act for, sign for or bind the company or make any expenditures on behalf of the company."[10]

The significant powers the defendants had as board members and investors were distinct from the agency powers provided in the agreement. The board's powers are neither agency powers nor powers entrusted to individual board members. Collective board oversight and control over management, finances, and policy is not oversight and control by individual board members. The individual board members are not acting as the board's agents in the exercise of this board function. The statute specifically imposes personal liability on those who have assumed individual responsibility as officers or agents. It does not impose individual liability on board members, acting as board members, or outside investors overseeing their investments. This distinction reflects the Legislature's intention to exclude the ordinary performance of board or investor responsibilities, including board or investor oversight of management and the policymaking and financial controls, from personal liability under the Wage Act. Personal liability, particularly for board members, in corporate law is the exception, not the rule. See G. L. c. 156D, § 8.30 (c) ("A director is not liable for any action taken as a director, or any failure to take any action, if [the director] performed the duties of his office in compliance with this section"). The individuals targeted by the Wage Act reflect this careful consideration by the Legislature, particularly given that violations of its provisions may give rise to criminal as well as civil liability.

[10] The limited liability company (LLC) agreement defined "members" as "Segal, investor [Johnson], the other investors and any person who becomes a substituted or additional member as herein provided and who is listed as a member of the company in the books and records of the company, in such [p]erson's capacity as a member of the company."

Finally, our corporate statutes impose management oversight responsibility on boards. See, e.g., G. L. c. 156D, § 8.01 (b): "All corporate power shall be exercised by or under the authority of, and the business and affairs of the corporation shall be managed under the direction of, its board of directors, subject to any limitation set forth in the articles of organization." If board members, acting as board members, were to be considered agents of the company and their normal oversight responsibility were deemed to be "the management of the company," then they would always be agents having the management of the company. If that were the case, the Legislature would not have omitted board members and directors from the definition of corporate employers, as they would essentially have per se liability for every Wage Act violation.

Segal pointed to the behavior of Rose and Johnson's other board representatives, as well as Rose's communications on behalf of Johnson's representatives, as evidence of the defendants acting as agents having the management of the company. He emphasized that Rose and the other Johnson board representatives refused to authorize Segal's cost-cutting proposal to terminate the last employee other than Segal and to sell the company's laboratory equipment. This decision, according to Segal, limited Genitrix's ability to pay Segal.

Corporate boards are regularly required to make difficult decisions that have an impact on the company's finances; indeed, that is an important part of their responsibility as a board. Such decisions, however, are not the acts of individual board members as agents and do not impose personal Wage Act liability. We discern nothing exceptional in these board activities that would render Rose or Johnson individually liable under the Wage Act as agents having the management of the corporation.

To prove that Rose acted as an agent having the management of Genitrix, Segal relied on the conditions Rose imposed on new infusions of capital by Fisk. In 2006, as Genitrix was running out of funds, Segal sought more money from Fisk. Rose informed Segal that Fisk would not invest more money in Genitrix if Segal remained in control. Rose restricted Fisk's new investments to fund specific expenses, as decided by Rose. By 2007, Genitrix was so financially strapped that it needed more outside investment to fund its existing operations, including payroll. It was during this time period that Segal worked without pay.

Investors invariably exercise some control over the businesses in which they invest, particularly when that business is failing and seeking new funds from these investors. But exercising one's rights and leverage as an investor over infusions of new money are separate and distinct from being an agent having the management of the corporation that is seeking the additional financing. Investment restrictions limited to the use of new monies are not management direction and control over existing resources.

Fisk was a separate company from Genitrix. Fisk was not responsible for Genitrix's payroll; Genitrix was. Fisk had no contractual or other obligations to make these payments. As Fisk's representative, Rose undoubtedly had significant power over new investments in Genitrix, and how that money was spent, but his exercise of that power was not as an agent having the management of Genitrix. In fact, the LLC Agreement expressly prohibited the defendants from exercising agency authority on behalf of the company in their role as investors. It was Segal, not Rose, acting as the agent of Genitrix in these negotiations for infusions of new money from Fisk. Segal, as a board member, also voted in favor of each board resolution to accept capital from Fisk, including the conditions imposed on those monies. Finally, Rose imposing terms and conditions on new outside investment is not the same as Rose managing the company.

In sum, neither board members nor investors are officers or agents having the management of the company for Wage Act purposes unless they are so empowered by the corporation. The person expressly designated as an officer or agent of Genitrix, particularly in regard to the payment of wages, was the plaintiff, Segal, not the defendants Rose or Johnson. We conclude that the evidence at trial was insufficient to establish the defendants as liable under the Wage Act.

C. AUTHORITY, ESTOPPEL, AND RATIFICATION

There are generally five ways in which a person can be bound by another's act: (1) an agent has actual authority, (2) an agent has apparent authority, (3) an agent has inherent agency power, (4) a person is estopped from denying the agency relationship asserted by a third-party, and (5) a person ratifies another's act.

Actual authority is created when there is a manifestation from the principal to the agent for the latter to act as an agent. The principal's manifestation to the agent can be in writing, oral communications, or conduct. Actual authority does not require an expressed instruction: *e.g.*, "Go sign that contract." It can be implied from words or conduct, indicating the principal's manifestation of assent to the agency. Because agency created from implied words or conduct can be less clear than express instructions, whether an agent has actual authority depends on the agent's reasonable belief as to the principal's manifestation of assent.

Restatement (Third) of Agency § 2.01. Actual Authority.

An agent acts with actual authority when, at the time of taking action that has legal consequences for the principal, the agent reasonably believes, in accordance with the principal's manifestations to the agent, that the principal wishes the agent so to act.

Illustration 5

P drafts and executes a power of attorney authorizing A to sell a piece of property. Following a change of mind, P drafts and executes a second power authorizing A only to lease the property. P inadvertently sends the first power to A and does not otherwise communicate with A regarding the nature of A's authority. A has actual authority to sell the property.

Illustration 6

Same facts as Illustration 5, except that after A receives the power of attorney from P, P sends A a letter asking for a status report on A's efforts to lease the property. The letter also states that P is glad the property will not be sold. After receiving P's letter, A lacks actual authority to sell the property because it is not reasonable for A to believe that P wishes A to sell it.

Restatement (Third) of Agency § 2.02. Scope of Actual Authority.

(1) An agent has actual authority to take action designated or implied in the principal's manifestations to the agent and acts necessary or incidental to achieving the principal's objectives, as the agent reasonably understands the principal's manifestations and objectives when the agent determines how to act.

(2) An agent's interpretation of the principal's manifestations is reasonable if it reflects any meaning known by the agent to be ascribed by the principal and, in the absence of any meaning known to the agent, as a reasonable person in the agent's position would interpret the manifestations in light of the context, including circumstances of which the agent has notice and the agent's fiduciary duty to the principal.

(3) An agent's understanding of the principal's objectives is reasonable if it accords with the principal's manifestations and the inferences that a reasonable person in the agent's position would draw from the circumstances creating the agency.

Apparent authority is created when a third party reasonably believes the agent has authority to act on behalf of the principal and that belief is traceable to the principal's manifestations. Unlike actual authority where the inquiry focuses on the interaction between the principal and the agent and the agent's reasonable belief therefrom, the inquiry here focuses on the nexus between the principal and the third party. The key factor is the third party's belief that is traceable to the principal's conduct and that creates a third party's reasonable belief in the agency. Apparent authority is a form of authority that binds the principal even though the agent did not have actual authority. It is irrelevant that the principal would not have wanted the agent to engage in the transaction with the third party. The principal may be completely surprised by the agent's action. Nevertheless, she is bound by the agent's conduct under apparent authority.

Restatement (Third) of Agency § 2.03. Apparent Authority.

Apparent authority is the power held by an agent or other actor to affect a principal's legal relations with third parties when a third party reasonably believes the actor has authority to act on behalf of the principal and that belief is traceable to the principal's manifestations.

Illustration 5

P Corporation, a manufacturer of specialty food items, retains A, a commodity food broker, to purchase a large quantity of an expensive commodity, Q, for P Corporation's manufacturing needs. A enters into a contract on P Corporation's behalf to purchase a large quantity of Q from T. P Corporation does not itself communicate directly or indirectly with T concerning A's authority. It is customary in the Q trade for a broker to obtain the principal's consent before fixing a binding contract for Q because its price fluctuates sharply. It is also customary for a third party to confirm with the principal or someone else other than the broker that a broker has the principal's consent. A assures T that it will not be necessary for T to contact P Corporation because A has already done so. A does not have apparent authority to bind P Corporation to the contract, nor is it reasonable for T to believe that A has authority to represent that T has consented to the transaction.

Illustration 6

Same facts as Illustration 5, except that the custom in the Q trade is that brokers have authority to fix binding contracts for principals whom the broker has previously represented so long as the contracts are consistent in amount and in payment and delivery terms with the principal's prior purchases of Q. P Corporation, which has previously purchased Q through A, tells A not to commit it to any contract without P Corporation's consent. This limitation is known only to personnel at P Corporation and A. Disregarding P Corporation's instruction, A enters into a contract on P Corporation's behalf with T for a quantity of Q that is known to T to be consistent with P Corporation's prior purchases. A has apparent authority to make the contract. Thus, P Corporation is bound to the contract but has a claim against A for any loss suffered due to A's actions beyond A's actual authority. See § 8.09, Comment b.

Illustration 7

Same facts as Illustration 6, except that T learns that it is widely said in the industry that P Corporation has "placed A on a short leash." A does not have apparent authority because it would not be reasonable for T to rely on industry custom in light of specific information concerning A's authority.

Inherent agency power is the agent's power—as distinguished from authority—that derives solely from the agency relation. This concept is found in Restatement (Second) of Agency, but the Restatement (Third) has abandoned it in favor of strengthening other rules to cover some situations involving inherent agency power. The concept of inherent agency power arose when courts and commentators recognized a group of miscellaneous cases in which courts found no authority or other concepts binding the principal, but held that the agent's action bound the principal. The policy is the protection of innocent third parties. A common situation is when an agent improperly enters into contracts but there is no actual or apparent authority. More generally, inherent agency power deals with the problem of the rogue agent who violates instructions or expectations. Someone must bear the consequence of such action—the principal or the third party—and courts sometimes impose the cost on the principal.

Restatement (Second) of Agency § 8A. Inherent Agency Power.

Inherent agency power is a term used in the restatement of this subject to indicate the power of an agent which is derived not from authority, apparent authority or estoppel, but solely from the agency relation and exists for the protection of persons harmed by or dealing with a servant or other agent.

Comment (a), Rationale

Partnerships and corporations, through which most of the work of the world is done today, depend for their existence upon agency principles. The rules designed to promote the interests of these enterprises are necessarily accompanied by rules to police them. It is inevitable that in doing their work, either through negligence or excess of zeal, agents will harm third persons or will deal with them in unauthorized ways. It would be unfair for an enterprise to have the benefit of the work of its agents without making it responsible to some extent for their excesses and failures to act carefully. The answer of the common law has been the creation of special agency powers or, to phrase it otherwise, the imposition of liability upon the principal because of unauthorized or negligent acts of his servants and other agents. These powers or liabilities are created by the courts primarily for the protection of third persons, either those who are harmed by the agent or those who deal with the agent. In the long run, however, they enure to the benefit of the business world and hence to the advantage of employers as a class, the members of which are plaintiffs as well as defendants in actions brought upon unauthorized transactions conducted by agents.

Estoppel can bind a person when, despite the nonexistence of an agency relationship between the person and the actor or the latter's authority, the person induces a third party to make a detrimental change in position through a transaction between the third party and the actor, and the third party's action is justifiable because the third party believes the transaction with the actor is on the person's account and fault for this justifiable reliance can be attributable to the person. In other words, the actor whose action caused the third party's harm was not an agent or had authority, but the person is liable for the actor's action anyway because the person's faulty conduct caused the third party's justifiable reliance on the belief that the actor was the person's agent.

Restatement (Third) of Agency § 2.05. Estoppel to Deny Existence of Agency Relationship.

A person who has not made a manifestation that an actor has authority as an agent and who is not otherwise liable as a party to a transaction purportedly done by the actor on that person's account is subject to liability to a third party who justifiably is induced to make a detrimental change in position because the transaction is believed to be on the person's account, if

(1) the person intentionally or carelessly caused such belief, or

(2) having notice of such belief and that it might induce others to change their positions, the person did not take reasonable steps to notify them of the facts.

Illustration 1

P has two coagents, A and B. P has notice that B, acting without actual or apparent authority, has represented to T that A has authority to enter into a transaction that is contrary to P's instructions. T does not know that P's instructions forbid A from engaging in the transaction. T cannot establish conduct by P on the basis of which T could reasonably believe that A has the requisite authority. T can, however, establish that P had notice of B's representation and that it would have been easy for P to inform T of the limits on A's authority. T detrimentally changes position in reliance on B's representation by making a substantial down payment. If it is found that T's action was justifiable, P is estopped to deny B's authority to make the representation.

Ratification binds a person to a prior act done by another, where the person would not otherwise be bound because there was no authority or estoppel, if the person ratifies after-the-fact the act by manifesting assent to being bound by the act.

Restatement (Third) of Agency § 4.01. Ratification Defined.

(1) Ratification is the affirmance of a prior act done by another, whereby the act is given effect as if done by an agent acting with actual authority.

(2) A person ratifies an act by

(a) manifesting assent that the act shall affect the person's legal relations, or

(b) conduct that justifies a reasonable assumption that the person so consents.

(3) Ratification does not occur unless

(a) the act is ratifiable as stated in § 4.03,

(b) the person ratifying has capacity as stated in § 4.04,

(c) the ratification is timely as stated in § 4.05, and

(d) the ratification encompasses the act in its entirety as stated in § 4.07.

Illustration 3

P owns an import business, which A runs. P authorizes A to negotiate the terms of a sale of the business to T but does not authorize A to execute the sales agreement. A negotiates and executes an agreement to sell the business to T. A tells T that although A's authority does not extend to executing the agreement, A is certain that T will approve if A does so. P reviews the agreement after A executes it but does not tell T that P repudiates it. P has ratified the agreement.

It is an unavoidable fact of business that most firms require agents. When an agent represents the firm, the law of agency determines whether the principal is bound by the agent's conduct. Agents benefit the principal, and they can also create unwanted liabilities for the principal. The existence of an agency relationship has costs and benefits that each firm must weigh in creating and maintaining a principal-agent relationship.

A principal or a person can be bound by the act of an agent or an actor in many ways: (1) actual authority, (2) apparent authority, (3) inherent agency power, (4) estoppel, and (5) ratification.

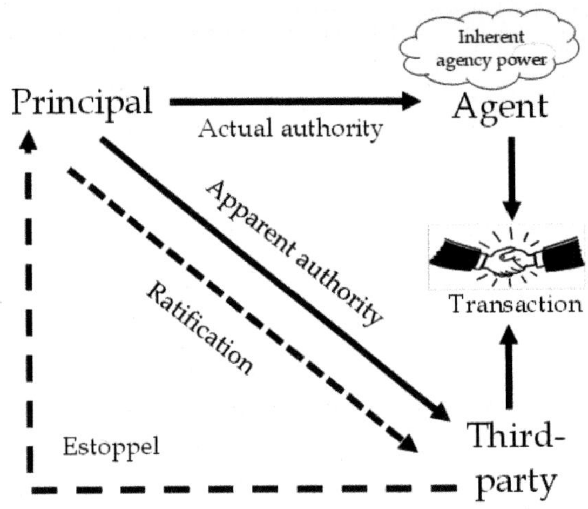

The case below illustrates the application of agency to impose liability on a principal. In reading this case, consider these questions: (1) Why was Cargill, a purchaser of Warren's products, dragged into a litigation for Warren's failure to pay its creditors when Warren was an independent company? (2) Why was Cargill, a putative purchaser of grain, considered a principal of the seller Warren? (3) In hindsight, how could Cargill have avoided liability, or stated differently, how could Cargill have reduced the overall ex ante cost of conducting business relations with Warren?

GAY JENSON FARMS CO. V. CARGILL, INC.

309 N.W.2d 285 (Minn. 1981)

PETERSON, JUSTICE.

Plaintiffs, 86 farmers, brought this action against defendant Cargill, Inc. and defendant Warren Grain & Seed Co. to recover losses sustained when Warren defaulted on the contracts made with plaintiffs for the sale of grain. After a trial by jury, judgment was entered in favor of plaintiffs, and Cargill brought this appeal. We affirm.

This case arose out of the financial collapse of defendant Warren, and its failure to satisfy its indebtedness to plaintiffs. Warren was operated by Lloyd Hill and his son, Gary Hill. Warren operated a grain elevator and was involved in the purchase of cash or market grain from local farmers. The cash grain would be resold through the Minneapolis Grain Exchange or to the terminal grain companies directly. Warren also stored grain for farmers and sold chemicals, fertilizer and steel storage bins. In addition, it operated a seed business which involved buying seed grain from farmers, processing it and reselling it for seed to farmers and local elevators.

Lloyd Hill decided in 1964 to apply for financing from Cargill. Cargill's officials from the Moorhead regional office investigated Warren's operations and recommended that Cargill finance Warren.

Warren and Cargill thereafter entered into a security agreement which provided that Cargill would loan money for working capital to Warren on "open account" financing up to a stated limit, which was originally set as $175,000. Under this contract, Warren would receive funds and pay its expenses by issuing drafts drawn on Cargill through Minneapolis banks. The drafts were imprinted with both Warren's and Cargill's names. Proceeds from Warren's sales would be deposited with Cargill and credited to its account. In return for this financing, Warren appointed Cargill as its grain agent for transaction with the Commodity Credit Corporation. Cargill was also given a right of first refusal to purchase market grain sold by Warren to the terminal market.

A new contract was negotiated in 1967, extending Warren's credit line to $300,000 and incorporating the provisions of the original contract. It was also stated in the contract that Warren would provide Cargill with annual financial statements and that either Cargill would keep the books for Warren or an audit would be conducted by an independent firm. Cargill was given the right of access to Warren's books for inspection.

In addition, the agreement provided that Warren was not to make capital improvements or repairs in excess of $5,000 without Cargill's prior consent. Further, it was not to become liable as guarantor on another's indebtedness, or encumber its assets except with Cargill's permission. Consent by Cargill was required before Warren would be allowed to declare a dividend or sell and purchase stock.

Officials from Cargill's regional office made a brief visit to Warren shortly after the agreement was executed. They examined the annual statement and the accounts receivable, expenses, inventory, seed, machinery and other financial matters. Warren was informed that it would be reminded periodically to make the improvements recommended by Cargill.[3] At approximately this time, a memo was given to the Cargill official in charge of the Warren account, Erhart Becker, which stated in part: "This organization (Warren) needs very strong paternal guidance."

In 1970, Cargill contracted with Warren and other elevators to act as its agent to seek growers for a new type of wheat called Bounty 208. Warren, as Cargill's agent for this project, entered into contracts for the growing of the wheat seed, with Cargill named as the contracting party. Farmers were paid directly by Cargill for the seed and all contracts were

[3] Cargill headquarters suggested that the regional office check Warren monthly. Also, it was requested that Warren be given an explanation for the relatively large withdrawals from undistributed earnings made by the Hills, since Cargill hoped that Warren's profits would be used to decrease its debt balance. Cargill asked for written requests for withdrawals from undistributed earnings in the future.

performed in full. In 1971, pursuant to an agency contract, Warren contracted on Cargill's behalf with various farmers for the growing of sunflower seeds for Cargill. The arrangements were similar to those made in the Bounty 208 contracts, and all those contracts were also completed. Both these agreements were unrelated to the open account financing contract. In addition, Warren, as Cargill's agent in the sunflower seed business, cleaned and packaged the seed in Cargill bags.

Cargill continued to review Warren's operations and expenses and recommend that certain actions should be taken.[4] Warren purchased from Cargill various business forms printed by Cargill and received sample forms from Cargill which Warren used to develop its own business forms.

Cargill wrote to its regional office in 1970 expressing its concern that the pattern of increased use of funds allowed to develop at Warren was similar to that involved in two other cases in which Cargill experienced severe losses. Cargill did not refuse to honor drafts or call the loan, however. A new security agreement which increased the credit line to $750,000 was executed in 1972, and a subsequent agreement which raised the limit to $1,250,000 was entered into in 1976.

Warren was at that time shipping Cargill 90% of its cash grain. When Cargill's facilities were full, Warren shipped its grain to other companies. Approximately 25% of Warren's total sales was seed grain which was sold directly by Warren to its customers.

As Warren's indebtedness continued to be in excess of its credit line, Cargill began to contact Warren daily regarding its financial affairs. Cargill headquarters informed its regional office in 1973 that, since Cargill money was being used, Warren should realize that Cargill had the right to make some critical decisions regarding the use of the funds. Cargill headquarters also told Warren that a regional manager would be working with Warren on a day-to-day basis as well as in monthly planning meetings. In 1975, Cargill's regional office began to keep a daily debit position on Warren. A bank account was opened in Warren's name on which Warren could draw checks in 1976. The account was to be funded by drafts drawn on Cargill by the local bank.

In early 1977, it became evident that Warren had serious financial problems. Several farmers, who had heard that Warren's checks were not being paid, inquired or had their agents inquire at Cargill regarding Warren's status and were initially told that there would be no problem with payment. In April 1977, an audit of Warren revealed that Warren was $4

[4] Between 1967 and 1973, Cargill suggested that Warren take a number of steps, including: (1) a reduction of seed grain and cash grain inventories; (2) improved collection of accounts receivable; (3) reduction or elimination of its wholesale seed business and its specialty grain operation; (4) marketing fertilizer and steel bins on consignment; (5) a reduction in withdrawals made by officers; (6) a suggestion that Warren's bookkeeper not issue her own salary checks; and (7) cooperation with Cargill in implementing the recommendations. These ideas were apparently never implemented, however.

million in debt. After Cargill was informed that Warren's financial statements had been deliberately falsified, Warren's request for additional financing was refused. In the final days of Warren's operation, Cargill sent an official to supervise the elevator, including disbursement of funds and income generated by the elevator.

After Warren ceased operations, it was found to be indebted to Cargill in the amount of $3.6 million. Warren was also determined to be indebted to plaintiffs in the amount of $2 million, and plaintiffs brought this action to seek recovery. Plaintiffs alleged that Cargill was jointly liable for Warren's indebtedness as it had acted as principal for the grain elevator.

The jury found that Cargill's conduct between 1973 and 1977 had made it Warren's principal. Warren was found to be the agent of Cargill with regard to contracts for: (1) the purchase and sale of grain for market; (2) the purchase and sale of seed grain; (3) the storage of grain. The court determined that Cargill was the disclosed principal of Warren. It was concluded that Cargill was jointly liable with Warren for plaintiffs' losses, and judgment was entered for plaintiffs.

The major issue in this case is whether Cargill, by its course of dealing with Warren, became liable as a principal on contracts made by Warren with plaintiffs. Cargill contends that no agency relationship was established with Warren, notwithstanding its financing of Warren's operation and its purchase of the majority of Warren's grain. We conclude that Cargill, by its control and influence over Warren, became a principal with liability for the transactions entered into by its agent Warren.

Agency is the fiduciary relationship that results from the manifestation of consent by one person to another that the other shall act on his behalf and subject to his control, and consent by the other so to act. In order to create an agency there must be an agreement, but not necessarily a contract between the parties. An agreement may result in the creation of an agency relationship although the parties did not call it an agency and did not intend the legal consequences of the relation to follow. The existence of the agency may be proved by circumstantial evidence which shows a course of dealing between the two parties. When an agency relationship is to be proven by circumstantial evidence, the principal must be shown to have consented to the agency since one cannot be the agent of another except by consent of the latter.

Cargill contends that the prerequisites of an agency relationship did not exist because Cargill never consented to the agency, Warren did not act on behalf of Cargill, and Cargill did not exercise control over Warren. We hold that all three elements of agency could be found in this case. By directing Warren to implement its recommendations, Cargill manifested its consent that Warren would be its agent. Warren acted on Cargill's behalf in procuring grain for Cargill as the part of its normal operations which were totally financed by Cargill. Further, an agency relationship was established by Cargill's interference with the internal affairs of Warren, which constituted de facto control of the elevator.

A creditor who assumes control of his debtor's business may become liable as principal for the acts of the debtor in connection with the business. Restatement (Second) of Agency § 14 O. It is noted in comment a to section 14 O that:

> A security holder who merely exercises a veto power over the business acts of his debtor by preventing purchases or sales above specified amounts does not thereby become a principal. However, if he takes over the management of the debtor's business either in person or through an agent, and directs what contracts may or may not be made, he becomes a principal, liable as a principal for the obligations incurred thereafter in the normal course of business by the debtor who has now become his general agent. The point at which the creditor becomes a principal is that at which he assumes de facto control over the conduct of his debtor, whatever the terms of the formal contract with his debtor may be.

A number of factors indicate Cargill's control over Warren, including the following:

(1) Cargill's constant recommendations to Warren by telephone;

(2) Cargill's right of first refusal on grain;

(3) Warren's inability to enter into mortgages, to purchase stock or to pay dividends without Cargill's approval;

(4) Cargill's right of entry onto Warren's premises to carry on periodic checks and audits;

(5) Cargill's correspondence and criticism regarding Warren's finances, officers salaries and inventory;

(6) Cargill's determination that Warren needed "strong paternal guidance";

(7) Provision of drafts and forms to Warren upon which Cargill's name was imprinted;

(8) Financing of all Warren's purchases of grain and operating expenses; and

(9) Cargill's power to discontinue the financing of Warren's operations.

We recognize that some of these elements are found in an ordinary debtor-creditor relationship. However, these factors cannot be considered in isolation, but, rather, they must be viewed in light of all the circumstances surrounding Cargill's aggressive financing of Warren.

On the whole, there was a unique fabric in the relationship between Cargill and Warren which varies from that found in normal debtor-creditor situations. There was sufficient evidence from which the jury could find that Cargill was the principal of Warren within the definitions of agency set forth in Restatement (Second) of Agency §§ 1 and 140.

D. PRINCIPAL'S LIABILITY FOR AGENT'S CONTRACTS AND WRONGFUL ACTS

A principal releases the agent to the world, and the agent can prove to be a force of destruction. An agent can create liabilities in torts, contracts, and other laws and thus bind the principal to liabilities to third parties, even if the principal was unaware of the agent's conduct or would have disapproved of the agent's conduct. The fundamental policy consideration in holding the *principal* liable is that an agency relationship is based on the right of the principal to control the agent for the benefit of the principal. The principal is often the least cost accident avoider, meaning that the principal is usually in the best position *ex ante* to prevent the problematic conduct. Since the principal is in a position to control, the principal can take measures to control the risk: *e.g.*, select good agents, train and instruct them, monitor them, and inform known or likely third parties of the limits of the agent's authority. When an agent acts in the course of the agency relationship, the risks and liabilities should fall on the principal.

CHAPTER 6: CONTRACTS AND OTHER TRANSACTIONS WITH THIRD PARTIES

Restatement (Third) of Agency § 6.01. Agent for Disclosed Principal.[1]

When an agent acting with actual or apparent authority makes a contract on behalf of a disclosed principal,

(1) the principal and the third party are parties to the contract; and

(2) the agent is not a party to the contract unless the agent and third party agree otherwise.

Comment c. When a disclosed principal is a corporation or other organization with separate legal personality, the corporation becomes a party to contracts made on its behalf by its agents. Corporate or other organizational agents, like agents for other disclosed principals, are not parties to a corporate contract unless the agent and the third party so agree.

[1] "A principal is disclosed if, when an agent and a third party interact, the third party has notice that the agent is acting for a principal and has notice of the principal's identity." Restatement (Third) of Agency § 1.04(2)(a).

Restatement (Third) of Agency § 6.02. Agent for Unidentified Principal.[2]

When an agent acting with actual or apparent authority makes a contract on behalf of an unidentified principal,

(1) the principal and the third party are parties to the contract; and

(2) the agent is a party to the contract unless the agent and third party agree otherwise.

Comment b. When a third party has notice that an agent deals on behalf of a principal but does not have notice of the principal's identity, it is not likely that the third party will rely solely on the principal's solvency or ability to perform obligations arising from the contract. Without notice of a principal's identity, a third party will be unable to assess the principal's reputation, assets, and other indicial of creditworthiness and ability to perform duties under the contract.

Restatement (Third) of Agency § 6.03. Agent for Undisclosed Principal.[3]

When an agent acting with actual authority makes a contract on behalf of an undisclosed principal,

(1) unless excluded by the contract, the principal is a party to the contract; and

(2) the agent and the third party are parties to the contract; and

(3) the principal, if a party to the contract, and the third party have the same rights, liabilities, and defenses against each other as if the principal made the contract personally, subject to §§ 6.05–6.09.

Comment b. When an agent acts on behalf of an undisclosed principal, the third party does not manifest assent to an exchange with the principal and the principal does not make a manifestation of assent to the third party. The third party's manifestation of assent is made to the agent to whom the third party expects to render performance and from whom the third party expects to receive performance. However, well-settled doctrine treats an undisclosed principal as a party to a contract that an agent makes on behalf of the principal, unless the contract excludes the principal as a party.

---

[2] "A principal is unidentified if, when an agent and a third party interact, the third party has notice that the agent is acting for a principal but does not have notice of the principal's identity." Restatement (Third) of Agency § 1.04(2)(c).

[3] A principal is undisclosed if the third party has no notice that the agent is acting for a principal. Restatement (Third) of Agency § 1.04(2)(b). Unlike section 6.01 and 6.02, section 6.03 states that the principal is bound only when the agent had actual authority. When the principal is undisclosed, there can be no apparent authority because the third party has no notice that there is a principal. The principal is bound under the contract only when the agent had actual authority. If the agent did not have actual authority, the principal cannot be bound. The parties to the contract are the agent acting with authority and the third party.

CHAPTER 7: TORTS—LIABILITY OF AGENT AND PRINCIPAL

Restatement (Third) of Agency § 7.01. Agent's Liability to Third Party.

An agent is subject to liability to a third party harmed by the agent's tortious conduct. Unless an applicable statute provides otherwise, an actor remains subject to liability although the actor acts as an agent or an employee, with actual or apparent authority, or within the scope of employment.

Restatement (Third) of Agency § 7.03. Principal's Liability—In General.

(1) A principal is subject to direct liability to a third party harmed by an agent's conduct when

(a) . . . the agent acts with actual authority or the principal ratifies the agent's conduct and

(i) the agent's conduct is tortious, or

(ii) the agent's conduct, if that of the principal, would subject the principal to tort liability; or

(b) . . . the principal is negligent in selecting, supervising, or otherwise controlling the agent; or

(c) . . . the principal delegates performance of a duty to use care to protect other persons or their property to an agent who fails to perform the duty.

(2) A principal is subject to vicarious liability to a third party harmed by an agent's conduct when

(a) . . . the agent is an employee who commits a tort while acting within the scope of employment; or

(b) . . . the agent commits a tort when acting with apparent authority in dealing with a third party on or purportedly on behalf of the principal.

The case below discusses the contractual liability of an agent. In reading this case, consider these questions: (1) What is the difference between tort and contract liability of an agent? (2) In what way are duties under tort and contract laws created to impose liability on agents?

THOMAS D. PHILIPSBORN IRREVOCABLE INS. TRUST V. AVON CAPITAL, LLC

699 Fed.Appx. 550 (7th Cir. 2017)

[The Thomas D. Philipsborn Irrevocable Insurance Trust purchased three policies on Philipsborn's life. The Trust's plan was to hold these policies for two years and then sell them into the life-settlement market. When the time arrived, Avon Capital offered about $4.5 million for the policies, which the Trust agreed to sell without a written contract. Things went awry, and the Trust sued Avon and its agent Donald Trudeau for breach of contract. The issue was whether Trudeau can be held liable for a breach of contract when Avon allegedly breached the contract.]

The Trust's theory is that Trudeau is responsible for Avon's breach of contract and therefore owes damages *as if* he were a principal. The district court instructed the jury that if Trudeau "took an active part in violating some duty Avon Capital owed to the Trust," then Trudeau is personally liable. The district court lifted this language from a 1953 treatise, 1 Ill. L. & Practice, Agency § 130 (1953), which declared: "It is considered a well settled principle of law in Illinois that an agent is not liable for the acts of a disclosed principal unless he takes an active part in violating some duty the principal owes to a third person." That sentence was quoted with approval in *Merrill Tenant Council v. Department of Housing and Urban Development*, 638 F.2d 1086, 1095 (7th Cir. 1981), and the district court deemed it the law of the circuit.

One problem is that *Merrill* did not hold what the second half of the quoted sentence says. It held that some of the defendants could be liable for violating their own statutory duties; that they were agents did not relieve them of those duties. That's different from holding that an agent can be liable for a violation of the principal's duties. A further problem is that the second half of the treatise's statement cannot be taken literally. A company's CEO who directs the business not to keep one of its promises, and instead to pay damages, does not become personally liable for those damages—at least we could not find any case in Illinois so holding. Corporations, partnerships, and limited liability companies can act *only* through agents, and if the second half of the sentence from the 1953 treatise were taken as gospel, then in *every* suit for breach of contract the right defendants would be the organization plus at least one agent, to be held personally liable. That would be a revolution in the law of agency.

And at least one intermediate appellate court has held that taking an "active part" in a breach of contract does not make an agent personally liable in Illinois. The *Restatement* suggests that an agent is liable for his own torts but not for a principal's breach of contract in which the agent played a role. (The current provisions on this subject are *Restatement (Third) of Agency* §§ 6.01 and 7.01 (2006).) The Trust does not contend that Trudeau committed a tort against it; its claim is contractual in nature. We do not see in Illinois law any general principle that declared agents for declared principals become personally liable if they take an "active part" in the principal's breach of contract.

The case below discusses the issue of whether an agent was acting within the scope of employment. In reading this case, consider these questions: (1) What factors led to the court's ruling that the sailor acted within the scope of employment? (2) As between the government and the dock, who was in the better position to avoid this accident at the least cost? (3) What is the ultimate policy rationale for the court's holding?

IRA S. BUSHEY & SONS, INC. v. U.S.

398 F.2d 167 (2d Cir. 1968)

FRIENDLY, CIRCUIT JUDGE:

While the United States Coast Guard vessel Tamaroa was being overhauled in a floating drydock located in Brooklyn's Gowanus Canal, a seaman returning from shore leave late at night, in the condition for which seamen are famed, turned some wheels on the drydock wall. He thus opened valves that controlled the flooding of the tanks on one side of the drydock. Soon the ship listed, slid off the blocks and fell against the wall. Parts of the drydock sank, and the ship partially did—fortunately without loss of life or personal injury. The drydock owner sought and was granted compensation by the District Court in an amount to be determined; the United States appeals. [We affirm.]

The Tamaroa had gone into drydock; her keel rested on blocks permitting her drive shaft to be removed and repairs to be made to her hull. The contract between the Government and Bushey provided in part:

> The work shall, whenever practical, be performed in such manner as not to interfere with the berthing and messing of personnel attached to the vessel undergoing repair, and provision shall be made so that personnel assigned shall have access to the vessel at all times, it being understood that such personnel will not interfere with the work or the contractor's workmen.

Access from shore to ship was provided by a route past the security guard at the gate, through the yard, up a ladder to the top of one drydock wall and along the wall to a gangway leading to the fantail deck, where men returning from leave reported at a quartermaster's shack.

Seaman Lane returned from shore leave. He had been drinking heavily. For reasons not apparent to us or very likely to Lane, he took it into his head, while progressing along the gangway wall, to turn each of three large wheels some twenty times; unhappily, these wheels controlled the water intake valves. After boarding ship at 12:11 A.M., Lane mumbled to an off-duty seaman that he had "turned some valves" and also muttered something about "valves" to another who was standing the engineering watch. Neither did anything; apparently Lane's condition was not such as to encourage proximity. At 12:20 A.M. a crew member discovered water coming into the drydock. By 12:30 A.M. the ship began to list, the alarm was sounded and the crew were ordered ashore. Ten minutes later the vessel and dock were listing over 20 degrees; in another ten minutes the ship slid off the blocks and fell against the drydock wall.

The Government attacks imposition of liability on the ground that Lane's acts were not within the scope of his employment. It relies heavily on § 228(1) of the Restatement of Agency 2d which says that "conduct of a servant is within the scope of employment if, but only if: it is actuated, at least in part by a purpose to serve the master." Courts have gone to considerable lengths to find such a purpose, as witness a well-known opinion in which Judge Learned Hand concluded that a drunken boatswain who routed the plaintiff out of his bunk with a blow, saying "Get up, you big son of a bitch, and turn to," and then continued to fight, might have thought he was acting in the interest of the ship. Nelson v. American-West African Line, 86 F.2d 730 (2d Cir. 1936). It would be going too far to find such a purpose here; while Lane's return to the Tamaroa was to serve his employer, no one has suggested how he could have thought turning the wheels to be, even if he was unaware of the consequences.

It is not at all clear, as the court below suggested, that expansion of liability in the manner here suggested will lead to a more efficient allocation of resources. As the most astute exponent of this theory has emphasized, a more efficient allocation can only be expected if there is some reason to believe that imposing a particular cost on the enterprise will lead it to consider whether steps should be taken to prevent a recurrence of the accident. And the suggestion that imposition of liability here will lead to more intensive screening of employees rests on highly questionable premises. The unsatisfactory quality of the allocation of resource rationale is especially striking on the facts of this case. It could well be that application of the traditional rule might induce drydock owners, prodded by their insurance companies, to install locks on their valves to avoid similar incidents in the future, while placing the burden on shipowners in much less likely to lead to accident prevention.[7] It is true, of course, that in many cases the plaintiff will not be in a position to insure, and so expansion of liability will, at the very least, serve respondeat superior's loss spreading function. But the fact that the defendant is better able to afford damages is not alone sufficient to justify legal responsibility, and this overarching

7 Although it is theoretically possible that shipowners would demand that drydock owners take appropriate action, see Coase, The Problem of Social Cost, 3 J.L. & Economics 1 (1960), this would seem unlikely to occur in real life.

principle must be taken into account in deciding whether to expand the reach of respondeat superior.

A policy analysis thus is not sufficient to justify this proposed expansion of vicarious liability. This is not surprising since respondeat superior, even within its traditional limits, rests not so much on policy grounds consistent with the governing principles of tort law as in a deeply rooted sentiment that a business enterprise cannot justly disclaim responsibility for accidents which may fairly be said to be characteristic of its activities. It is in this light that the inadequacy of the motive test becomes apparent. Whatever may have been the case in the past, a doctrine that would create such drastically different consequences for the actions of the drunken boatswain in Nelson and those of the/drunken seaman here reflects a wholly unrealistic attitude toward the risks characteristically attendant upon the operation of a ship.

Put another way, Lane's conduct was not so "unforeseeable" as to make it unfair to charge the Government with responsibility. We agree with a leading treatise that "what is reasonably foreseeable in this context (of respondeat superior) is quite a different thing from the foreseeably unreasonable risk of harm that spells negligence. The foresight that should impel the prudent man to take precautions is not the same measure as that by which he should perceive the harm likely to flow from his long-run activity in spite of all reasonable precautions on his own part. The proper test here bears far more resemblance to that which limits liability for workmen's compensation than to the test for negligence. The employer should be held to expect risks, to the public also, which arise out of and in the course of his employment of labor." Here it was foreseeable that crew members crossing the drydock might do damage, negligently or even intentionally, such as pushing a Bushey employee or kicking property into the water. Moreover, the proclivity of seamen to find solace for solitude by copious resort to the bottle while ashore has been noted in opinions too numerous to warrant citation. Once all this is granted, it is immaterial that Lane's precise action was not to be foreseen. Consequently, we can no longer accept our past decisions that have refused to move beyond the *Nelson* rule, since they do not accord with modern understanding as to when it is fair for an enterprise to disclaim the actions of its employees.

One can readily think of cases that fall on the other side of the line. If Lane had set fire to the bar where he had been imbibing or had caused an accident on the street while returning to the drydock, the Government would not be liable; the activities of the "enterprise" do not reach into areas where the servant does not create risks different from those attendant on the activities of the community in general. We agree with the district judge that if the seaman "upon returning to the drydock, recognized the Bushey security guard as his wife's lover and shot him," vicarious liability would not follow; the incident would have related to the seaman's domestic life, not to his seafaring activity, and it would have been the most unlikely happenstance that the confrontation with the paramour occurred on a drydock rather than at the traditional spot. Here Lane had come within the closed-off area where his ship lay to occupy a berth to which the Government insisted he have access, and while his act is not readily explicable, at least it was not shown to be due entirely to facets of his personal life. The risk that seamen going and coming from the Tamaroa might cause damage to the drydock is enough to make it fair that the enterprise bear the loss. It is not a fatal objection that the rule we lay down lacks sharp contours; in the end, as Judge Andrews said in a related context, "it is all a question (of expediency,) of fair judgment, always keeping in mind the fact that we endeavor to make a rule in each case that will be practical and in keeping with the general understanding of Mankind." Palsgraf v. Long Island R.R. Co., 162 N.E. 99, 104 (N.Y. 1928) (dissenting opinion).

The case below discusses the rules of agency in determining the liability of an employer when a supervising employee sexually harassed a subordinate employee. In reading this case, consider these questions: (1) Under what theory of agency can an employer be liable for a supervising employee's sexual harassment of a subordinate employee? (2) How could the analysis of the "aided in the agency relation" rule under Restatement (Second) of Agency § 219(2)(d) discussed in the case change under Restatement (Third) of Agency 7.03(2)(b)?

BURLINGTON INDUSTRIES, INC. V. ELLERTH

524 U.S. 742 (1998)

JUSTICE KENNEDY delivered the opinion of the Court.

We decide whether, under Title VII, 42 U.S.C. § 2000e *et seq.*, an employee who refuses the unwelcome and threatening sexual advances of a supervisor, yet suffers no adverse, tangible job consequences, can recover against the employer without showing the employer is negligent or otherwise at fault for the supervisor's actions.

[The district court granted summary judgment for the employer, but the Seventh Circuit reversed. The Supreme Court affirmed the Seventh Circuit's reversal of the district court's grant of summary judgment.]

The employer is Burlington Industries. The employee is Kimberly Ellerth. From March 1993 until May 1994, Ellerth worked as a salesperson. During her employment, she alleges, she was subjected to constant sexual harassment by her supervisor, one Ted Slowik.

Against a background of repeated boorish remarks and gestures which Slowik allegedly made, Ellerth places particular emphasis on three alleged incidents where Slowik's comments could be construed as threats to deny her tangible job benefits. While on a business trip, Slowik invited Ellerth to the hotel lounge, an invitation Ellerth felt compelled to accept because Slowik was her boss. When Ellerth gave no encouragement to remarks Slowik made about her breasts, he told her to "loosen up" and warned, "you know, Kim, I could make your life very hard or very easy at Burlington."

When Ellerth was being considered for a promotion, Slowik expressed reservations during the promotion interview because she was not "loose enough." The comment was followed by his reaching over and rubbing her knee. Ellerth did receive the promotion; but when Slowik called to announce it, he told Ellerth, "you're gonna be out there with men who work in factories, and they certainly like women with pretty butts/legs."

Ellerth called Slowik, asking permission to insert a customer's logo into a fabric sample. Slowik responded, "I don't have time for you right now, Kim—unless you want to tell me what you're wearing." Ellerth told Slowik she had to go and ended the call. A day or two later, Ellerth called Slowik to ask permission again. This time he denied her request, but added something along the lines of, "are you wearing shorter skirts yet, Kim, because it would make your job a whole heck of a lot easier."

A short time later, Ellerth's immediate supervisor cautioned her about returning telephone calls to customers in a prompt fashion. In response, Ellerth quit. She faxed a letter giving reasons unrelated to the alleged sexual harassment we have described. About three weeks later, however, she sent a letter explaining she quit because of Slowik's behavior.

We must decide whether an employer has vicarious liability when a supervisor creates a hostile work environment by making explicit threats to alter a subordinate's terms or conditions of employment, based on sex, but does not fulfill the threat. We turn to principles of agency law, for the term "employer" is defined under Title VII to include "agents." Congress has directed federal courts to interpret Title VII based on agency principles. We conclude a uniform and predictable standard must be established as a matter of federal law. We rely "on the general common law of agency, rather than on the law of any particular State, to give meaning to these terms."

The Restatement (Second) of Agency (1957) (hereinafter Restatement) is a useful beginning point for a discussion of general agency principles.

Section 219(1) of the Restatement sets out a central principle of agency law: "A master is subject to liability for the torts of his servants committed while acting in the scope of their employment."

An employer may be liable for both negligent and intentional torts committed by an employee within the scope of his or her employment. Sexual harassment under Title VII presupposes intentional conduct. While early decisions absolved employers of liability for the intentional torts of their employees, the law now imposes liability where the employee's "purpose, however misguided, is wholly or in part to further the master's business." W. Keeton, D. Dobbs, R. Keeton, & D. Owen, Prosser and Keeton on Law of Torts § 70, p. 505 (5th ed.1984). In applying scope of employment principles to intentional torts, however, it is accepted that "it is less likely that a willful tort will properly be held to be in the course of employment and that the liability of the master for such torts will naturally be more limited." The Restatement defines conduct, including an intentional tort, to be within the scope of employment when "actuated, at least in part, by a purpose to serve the [employer]," even if it is forbidden by the employer. Restatement §§ 228(1)(c), 230. For example, when a salesperson lies to a customer to make a sale, the tortious conduct is within the scope of employment because it benefits the employer by increasing sales, even though it may violate the employer's policies.

A supervisor acting out of gender-based animus or a desire to fulfill sexual urges may not be actuated by a purpose to serve the employer. The harassing supervisor often acts for personal motives, motives unrelated and even antithetical to the objectives of the employer. There are instances, of course, where a supervisor engages in unlawful discrimination with the purpose, mistaken or otherwise, to serve the employer.

The general rule is that sexual harassment by a supervisor is not conduct within the scope of employment.

Scope of employment does not define the only basis for employer liability under agency principles. In limited circumstances, agency principles impose liability on employers even where employees commit torts outside the scope of employment. The principles are set forth in the much-cited § 219(2) of the Restatement:

> A master is not subject to liability for the torts of his servants acting outside the scope of their employment, unless: (a) the master intended the conduct or the consequences, or (b) the master was negligent or reckless, or (c) the conduct violated a non-delegable duty of the master, or (d) the servant purported to act or to speak on behalf of the principal and there was reliance upon apparent authority, or he was aided in accomplishing the tort by the existence of the agency relation.

See also § 219, Comment *e* (Section 219(2) "enumerates the situations in which a master may be liable for torts of servants acting solely for their own purposes and hence not in the scope of employment").

Subsections (b) and (d) are possible grounds for imposing employer liability. Under subsection (b), an employer is liable when the tort is attributable to the employer's own negligence. Although a supervisor's sexual harassment is outside the scope of employment because the conduct was for personal motives, an employer can be liable where its own negligence is a cause of the harassment. An employer is negligent if it knew or should have known about the conduct and failed to stop it. Negligence sets a minimum standard for employer liability under Title VII; but Ellerth seeks to invoke the more stringent standard of vicarious liability.

Section 219(2)(d) concerns vicarious liability for intentional torts committed by an employee when the employee uses apparent authority, or when the employee "was aided in accomplishing the tort by the existence of the agency relation." In discussing vicarious liability for supervisor harassment, we begin with § 219(2)(d).

As a general rule, apparent authority is relevant where the agent purports to exercise a power which he or she does not have, as distinct from where the agent threatens to misuse actual power. In the usual case, a supervisor's harassment involves misuse of actual power, not the false impression of its existence. Apparent authority analysis therefore is inappropriate in this context. When a party seeks to impose vicarious liability based on an agent's misuse of delegated authority, the Restatement's aided in the agency relation rule, rather than the apparent authority rule, appears to be the appropriate form of analysis.

We turn to the aided in the agency relation standard. In a sense, most workplace tortfeasors are aided in accomplishing their tortious objective by the existence of the agency relation: Proximity and regular contact may afford a captive pool of potential victims. Were this to satisfy the aided in the agency relation standard, an employer would be subject to vicarious liability not only for all supervisor harassment, but also for all co-worker harassment. The aided in the agency relation standard, therefore, requires the existence of something more than the employment relation itself.

At the outset, we can identify a class of cases where, beyond question, more than the mere existence of the employment relation aids in commission of the harassment: when a supervisor takes a tangible employment action against the subordinate. Every Federal Court of Appeals to have considered the question has found vicarious liability when a discriminatory act results in a tangible employment action. We think it reflects a correct application of the aided in the agency relation standard.

In the context of this case, a tangible employment action would have taken the form of a denial of a raise or a promotion. A tangible employment action constitutes a significant change in employment status, such as hiring, firing, failing to promote, reassignment with significantly different responsibilities, or a decision causing a significant change in benefits.

When a supervisor makes a tangible employment decision, there is assurance the injury could not have been inflicted absent the agency relation. A tangible employment action in most cases inflicts direct economic harm. As a general proposition, only a supervisor, or other person acting with the authority of the company, can cause this sort of injury. A co-worker can break a co-worker's arm as easily as a supervisor, and anyone who has regular contact with an employee can inflict psychological injuries by his or her offensive conduct. Tangible employment actions fall within the special province of the supervisor. The supervisor has been empowered by the company as a distinct class of agent to make economic decisions affecting other employees under his or her control.

Tangible employment actions are the means by which the supervisor brings the official power of the enterprise to bear on subordinates. A tangible employment decision requires an official act of the enterprise, a company act. The decision in most cases is documented in official company records. The supervisor often must obtain the imprimatur of the enterprise and use its internal processes.

Whether the agency relation aids in commission of supervisor harassment which does not culminate in a tangible employment action is less obvious. Application of the standard is made difficult by its malleable terminology, which can be read to either expand or limit liability in the context of supervisor harassment. On the one hand, a supervisor's power and authority invests his or her harassing conduct with a particular threatening character, and in this sense, a supervisor always is aided by the agency relation. On the other hand, there are acts of harassment a supervisor might commit which might be the same acts a co-employee would commit, and there may be some circumstances where the supervisor's status makes little difference.

The aided in the agency relation standard is a developing feature of agency law, and we hesitate to render a definitive explanation of our understanding of the standard in an area where other important considerations must affect our judgment.

In order to accommodate the agency principles of vicarious liability for harm caused by misuse of supervisory authority, as well as Title VII's equally basic policies of encouraging forethought by employers and saving action by objecting employees, we adopt the following holding in this case. An employer is subject to vicarious liability to a victimized employee for an actionable hostile environment created by a supervisor with immediate (or successively higher) authority over the employee.

Ellerth should have an adequate opportunity to prove she has a claim for which Burlington is liable.

E. AGENCY AND LIMITED LIABILITY

The rule of limited liability is not an iron-clad protection against liabilities that arise from the operation of a firm. In a single-owner firm, the owner is exposed to liability in different ways. She might have done the act that results in liability: for example, she negligently drove the truck that hurt the pedestrian. *See* Restatement (Third) of Agency § 7.01 ("An agent is subject to liability to a third party by the agent's tortious conduct."); DGCL § 102(b)(6) (providing that shareholders are liable for "their own conduct or acts"). She might have signed the contract on behalf of the company without disclosing that the company was the principal. *See* Restatement (Third) of Agency § 6.03 ("When an agent acting with actual authority makes a contract on behalf of an undisclosed principal the agent and the third party are parties to the contract").

The article below discusses the limits of the rule of limited liability in a single-owner or small business enterprise. In reading the article, consider these questions: (1) Is there a relationship between the rule of limited liability and the law of agency where limited liability may protect the sole owner from liability that arises from agency? (2) If so, explain how.

LIMITED LIABILITY AND THE EFFICIENT ALLOCATION OF RESOURCES

Richard A. Booth, 89 Nw. U.L. Rev. 140 (1994)

Consider a one-person operation such as a small trucking company. Suppose that an entrepreneur—call him Ace—has the idea to buy a truck and to go into business for himself under the name of Ace Trucking Company. He will be the sole employee of the company. He will do the driving and the maintenance. He will load and unload the truck. He will keep the books, answer the phone, take the orders, and arrange for the advertising. Ace has heard that, by incorporating, he can get limited liability and protect himself against the possibility of bankruptcy.

How much of a benefit is limited liability in the context of a one-person start-up operation such as Ace Trucking Company? Not much. Voluntary creditors, parties who contract with the corporation, will likely insist on a personal guarantee from the principal. For example, if Ace tries to get a loan to buy a truck, the bank will probably insist that he sign the note in his personal capacity as well as for the corporation.

But what about involuntary creditors, those who are injured by the wrongful acts of the corporation? It is often supposed that involuntary creditors such as tort claimants are the real losers from limited liability, but that is not clearly so. In a one-person operation such as Ace Trucking Company in which the sole shareholder is an active participant in the business of the corporation, the shareholder is personally liable for damages inflicted on innocent bystanders, not because he is a shareholder but because he committed a tort.

The rule is the same as it is in the context of a simple employer and employee relationship. Of course, an employer is liable for damages caused by an employee acting within the scope of employment, and in most cases a plaintiff would choose to pursue the employer because the employer is more likely to be able to pay. But the employer's liability does not preclude the employee's liability. Indeed, employers are entitled to be indemnified by employees to the extent that the employer is required to pay damages owing to the acts of the employee even if they are within the scope of the business. Thus, limited liability affords little protection to the shareholder in a one-person corporation.

Limited liability may afford some protection in a corporation with non-shareholder employees. However, even here the protection afforded is not extensive. To the extent that the owner of the corporation exercises the authority to hire and fire, establishes rules of conduct, and supervises the activities of employees, he may be held liable for negligence in performing those functions. Thus, it is still unclear that limited liability constitutes a subsidy for somewhat larger private companies.

F. PROBLEM: ENTREPRENEURS BEGIN MANAGING

Things were moving fast. Piers and Blake secured the $500,000 initial funding. After much thought on entity form, they settled on the LLC form. They filed in the state of their residence, an RULLCA state, to create PB Optique Option LLC, affectionately known to them as "PBOO." The initial operating agreement contained the key terms negotiated among the entrepreneurs and their financiers. It provided these provisions.

Article I. Definitions

> "Board of Directors" shall manage the business and affairs of the Company and shall be composed of Members only. Directors shall be appointed by the majority of the Member Interests.
>
> "Manager" shall mean a person appointed by the Board to manage the business in the ordinary course of business, subject to the authority of the Board.

Article III. Management.

> The Board shall manage the business and affairs of the Company. The Board may appoint Managers, whose duties and responsibilities shall be determined by the Board. Managers have the authority to manage business in the ordinary course of business, subject to the authority of the Board. All matters outside the ordinary course of business shall be determined by the majority vote of each Member on the Board.

Piers, Blake, and Morgan Money appointed themselves to the board of directors with the title of "Director." The board appointed Piers and Blake as "Co-Presidents," which are the chief officers of the company. The board also appointed Art Estic as "Chief Design Officer."

Money's appointment as a Director was a point of some contention. Money wanted a board seat, but Piers and Blake were reluctant. They only acceded when Money threatened to not invest in the venture. However, Money assuaged Piers and Blake's concern about control of the company.

Money: "I understand and respect your concerns. You can trust me that I won't get in the way. My intent is to support your decisions and to bring my expertise in business as an asset to the venture in the boardroom and high-level strategic conversations. I'll always make sure to get your feedback on important matters in a collaborative process."

Piers: "It's important that Blake and I are running this company and making daily business decision."

Blake: "All matters outside the ordinary course of business will be determined by the majority of the Board, which includes you, Morgan."

Money: "I understand what the roles are. The two of you run the company and make the operational decisions."

Piers: "Great. We have an understanding."

PBOO began operations. Estic began to design eyeglass frames, using Blake's patented hinges. Piers began searching for a manufacturer that can handle production once PBOO secures a source of high-quality plastics. Blake began constructing the software architecture. Piers, Blake and Estic were busy with the process of design, manufacture, and distribution.

During the frenzy of activity, Money was feeling like the "third wheel." There was no specific assignment or task at hand. Wanting to be helpful, Money used business connections to set a meeting with Pacifico Plastic Recycling, Inc. Money met with the selling manager, Rey Repp. After initial pleasantries and exchanging company business cards, Money's indicating the title "Director" of PBOO. Repp gave Money a tour of the plastic recycling and manufacturing facility. Money examined the products and was immediately impressed. Afterwards, they had this conversation.

Repp: "What is it that you are seeking?"

Money: "PB Optique Option is seeking a source of high-quality plastic to manufacture into eyeglass frames."

Repp: "We make various grades of plastic. We are environmentally conscious. We source our plastic from Pacific Conservation, which is run by those surfer guys who collect plastics from the Pacific Ocean. Our raw materials are given to us free, but on the back-end we contribute 10% of our profits to conservation efforts. That is our agreement with Pacific Conservation. We do the recycling process. We have a proprietary process in which the plastic is strengthened during recycling. We are also the only manufacturer that has a zero-carbon footprint. Our manufacturing process relies entirely on solar and wind power that is plentiful there. Our customers can leverage our recycling process as a part of their marketing effort. As a result of our environmental commitment, our products are higher cost than most other sources. But we still have lots of customers."

Money: "This sounds great. I like the vision. Let's talk terms."

Repp: "What do you need?"

Thinking longterm, Money quickly calculated that the typical frame requires 1 ounce of plastic (there are 16 ounces per pound), including unavoidable waste in the molding process. He expects annual sales of 150,000 frames. With some cushion for surplus to handle demand in excess of expectation, Money calculated the plastic necessary for 160,000 frames.

Money: "We need 10,000 pounds per year."

Repp: "That's a small order. At that level, we can give you price of $20 per pound. It's a high price, to be sure. But we have to cover our costs with profit, 10% of which we contribute to conservation efforts. That's our corporate mission. Our customers partner with us on this mission. We have a policy of a 3-year contract. We require a contract for $200,000 of plastic order per year for at least 3 years. Thus, the total contract price is $600,000. The upside of the arrangement is that you secure a source of high quality raw materials for 3 year. We have been in business for the past 40 years, and we pride ourselves on dependability and sustainability."

Money: "I like the product. PBOO can leverage the environmental angle in our marketing strategy. That's a really good idea. The price is high, but the overall package is worth it. Let's sign that contract."

Repp drew up the supply agreement, and Money signed the agreement as "Morgan Money, Director, PB Optique Option LLC."

Upon returning, Money reported to Piers and Blake on his meeting with Pacifico Plastic Recycling. After presenting the signed contract and describing its terms, Piers and Blake sat silent, processing the whole thing.

QUESTIONS

1. Is PB Optique Option bound by Money's action? Under what theory?

2. Is Money personally liable for the contract to Pacifico Plastic Recycling?

3. If Money's action was not the model of good governance, in hindsight what could Piers and Blake have done to minimize the risk of this sort of situation?

4. In hindsight, was there a flaw in how the company was structured, keeping in mind that Piers and Blake still had to satisfy Money's original condition and concern related to the investment?

CHAPTER 6

MANAGEMENT STRUCTURE

■ ■ ■

A. THREE BASIC FORMS OF MANAGEMENT

Although many different kinds of management structures can be envisioned, there are three prototypical forms of management that are representative of corporations, LPs, and partnerships.

CORPORATION **Nonowner Centralized Management**	LIMITED PARTNERSHIP **Owner Centralized Management**	GENERAL PARTNERSHIP **Owner Collective Management**
a corporate form of centralized management with managerial power held by representative managers who may not always be owners	an LP form of centralized management with managerial power held by a designated class of owners who provide specialized service	a general partnership form of collective management with managerial power held by the entire group of owners

Corporation law places managerial authority in the board of directors. *See* DGCL § 141(a) ("The business and affairs of every corporation organized under this chapter shall be managed by or under the direction of a board of directors"). NBE statutes provide barebones default rules of management. A general partnership presumes a communitarian venture in which each partner has equal management rights. *See* RUPA § 401(h) ("Each partner has equal rights in the management and conduct of the partnership's business."). An LP requires at least one general partner who manages the business, and one limited partner who is presumed to be a passive investor. *See* ULPA (2001) § 406(a) ("Each general partner has equal rights in the management and conduct of the limited partnership's activities and affairs."); *id.* § 302(a) ("A limited partner is not an agent of a limited partnership solely by reason of being a limited partner."). An LLC can have either a member-managed LLC that resembles a general partnership or a manager-managed LLC that resembles an LP or a corporation. *See* RULLCA § 407(b)–(c).

All three NBE statutes permit significant degree of contractual freedom to shape the management structure. *See* RUPA § 105(a)(1) ("the partnership agreement governs relations among the partners as partners and between the partners and the partnership"); ULPA (2001) § 105(a)(1) (same); RULLCA § 105(a)(1) (functionally the same). A general partnership can be structured to resemble an LP; an LLC can be structured to resemble a corporate board structure; and so forth.

Business organizers must also consider other important matters such as: (1) the number of managers; (2) qualifications; (3) appointment and removal; (4) designation of authority and function. These matters should be in the charter agreement or other documents, such as employment agreements or bylaws.

New York Limited Liability Company Law § 419(a).

The articles of organization of a limited liability company may provide for classes or groups of managers having such relative rights, powers, preferences and limitations as the operating agreement may provide. The articles of organization may make provision for the future creation, in the manner provided in the operating agreement, of additional classes of managers having such relative rights, powers, preferences and limitations as may from time to time be established pursuant to the operating agreement, including rights, powers, preferences, limitations and duties senior to existing classes of managers. The operating agreement may provide for the classification of managers within classes of managers for the purpose of determining the terms of office of such managers and may grant to all or to one or more classes of managers the right to vote upon any matter on a per capita, class or other basis.

Delaware Limited Liability Company Act § 18–404(a).

A limited liability company agreement may provide for classes or groups of managers having such relative rights, powers and duties as the limited liability company agreement may provide, and may make provision for the future creation in the manner provided in the limited liability company agreement of additional classes or groups of managers having such relative rights, powers and duties as may from time to time be established, including rights, powers and duties senior to existing classes and groups of managers. A limited liability company agreement may provide for the taking of an action, including the amendment of the limited liability company agreement, without the vote or approval of any manager or class or group of managers, including an action to create under the provisions of the limited liability company agreement a class or group of limited liability company interests that was not previously outstanding.

Contractual flexibility means that the management structure is limited only by one's imagination. As a practical matter, most management structures tend to gravitate toward one of the three prototypical forms identified above. The LLC does not have a representative form because it is flexible and can mimic virtually any form of management.

When there are two or more owners, circumstances may dictate the form of management. Two equal co-owners would tend to be jointly managed. A small, intimate group of owners may fare better with a communitarian form of management rather than centralized management. The greater the number of owners, the greater is the tendency toward centralized management. A firm with 200 owners cannot realistically be managed as an Athenian democracy without some process that streamlines decisionmaking, suggesting some form of central authority with limits on such authority as the *demos* of owners deems fit. A firm with 2,000 owners cannot practically be managed without a centralized authority, whether that manager is an owner or a professional manager.

B. CENTRALIZED MANAGEMENT AND CORPORATIONS

1. REASON FOR CENTRALIZED MANAGEMENT

In large enterprises, centralized management authority is required as a pragmatic matter. The transaction cost of information conveyance, coordination, and deliberation among many owners to decide collectively day-to-day matters would be inefficient. Many owners provide capital, but otherwise prefer to be passive investors. Large enterprises generally tend to be complex as well, requiring specialized managers who are hired for their knowledge, skill, and expertise. Passive investors and specialized management result in the separation of ownership and control, which is a common phenomenon in corporations, particularly public corporations.

DIRECTOR PRIMACY: THE MEANS AND ENDS OF CORPORATE GOVERNANCE

Stephen M. Bainbridge, 97 Nw. U.L. Rev. 547, 555–59 (2003)

Despite their contractual nature, public corporations are not participatory democracies, but hierarchies in which decisions are made on a fairly authoritarian basis. Why? What survival advantages does a large corporation gain from bureaucratic hierarchy? An answer is suggested by Ronald Coase's fundamental insight into the difference between firms and markets. In a market, actors respond to changes in prices, but firms allocate resources via authoritative direction. Consequently, if a corporate employee moves from department Y to department X, he does so not because of a change in relative prices, but because he is ordered to do so. Accordingly, organizing economic activity within a firm is more efficient than doing so across markets when the costs of bargaining are higher than the costs associated with command-and-control.

There are several ways in which organizing economic activity via fiat can reduce transaction costs vis-à-vis organizing economic activity across markets. Where production requires some form of team effort, for example, bringing economic activity within the boundaries of a firm can reduce search and related bargaining costs. Bringing together employees, creditors, equity investors, and other necessary factors of production requires ongoing interactions too complex to be handled through a price mechanism. The firm solves that problem by creating a centralized contracting party, as some team member seeks out the necessary inputs and brings them together for productive labor.

Fiat can also lower costs associated with uncertainty, opportunism, and complexity. Given the limits on cognitive competence, as implied by "bounded rationality," incomplete contracts are the inevitable result of the uncertainty and complexity inherent in ongoing business relationships. In turn, incomplete contracts leave greater room for opportunistic behavior.

The Coasean central decisionmaker need not be an autocrat, however, as illustrated by the collegial decisionmaking processes of many small firms. Why, then, do large corporations tend to adopt hierarchical decisionmaking structures? The director primacy theory's answer to this question is based on Kenneth Arrow's seminal work on organizational decisionmaking. Arrow identifies two basic decisionmaking structures: "consensus" and "authority." In consensus-based structures, each member of the organization has identical information and interests, and will therefore select the course of action preferred by all the other team members. In contrast, in authority-based structures, team members have different interests and amounts of information. In response to that problem, authority-based decisionmaking structures provide a central agency to which all relevant information is transmitted and which is empowered to make decisions binding on the whole firm.

It is very hard (if not impossible) to imagine a modern public corporation that could be effectively run using consensus-based decisionmaking mechanisms. Consider the problems faced by shareholders who are conventionally assumed to be the corporate constituency with the best claim on control of the decisionmaking apparatus. At the most basic level, the mechanical difficulties of achieving consensus amongst thousands of decisionmakers impede shareholders from taking an active role. Even if those collective action problems could be overcome, however, active shareholder participation in corporate decisionmaking would still be precluded by the shareholders' widely divergent interests and differing levels of information. As to shareholder interests, although neoclassical economics assumes that shareholders invest in corporations with wealth maximization as their common goal, and most presumably do so, shareholder opinions are likely to differ once uncertainty is introduced as to which course will maximize share value for that company. As to shareholder incentives, most shareholders are rationally apathetic. A rational shareholder will expend the effort necessary to make informed decisions only if the expected benefits of doing so outweigh its costs. Given the length and complexity of corporate disclosure documents, the opportunity cost entailed in making informed decisions is both high and apparent. In contrast, the expected benefits of becoming informed are quite low, as most shareholders' holdings are too small to have significant effect on the outcome of shareholder votes.

It is hardly surprising then that the modern public corporation's decisionmaking structure precisely fits Arrow's model of an authority-based decisionmaking system that functions via fiat. This result is inevitable, because neither shareholders, employees, nor any other constituency have the information or the incentives necessary to make sound decisions on either operational or policy questions. Overcoming the collective action problems that prevent meaningful involvement by the corporation's various constituencies would be difficult and costly. Under these conditions, Arrow predicts, "it is cheaper and more efficient to transmit all the pieces of information once to a central place" and to have the central office "make the collective decision and transmit it rather than retransmit all the information on which the decision is based."

The fact that a firm has centralized management authority does not mean that the manager is an authoritarian who can run roughshod over non-managing owners. There must be some limits on authority. An important facet of all business organization laws is that each law provides a system of checks on authority.

All business organization laws impose fiduciary duties on those who control the firm including partners, members, managers, directors, officers, and controlling shareholders. Fiduciaries have a special duty, enforceable through legal action, to act in the best interest of the firm and its owners. Conversely, owners who are not in control do not owe fiduciary duties. *See* ULPA (2001) § 305(b) ("a limited partner does not have any duty to the limited partnership or to any other partner solely by reason of acting as a limited partner"); RULLCA § 409(i)(1) (stating that in a manager-managed LLC, fiduciary duties are owed by "managers and not the members"); Ivanhoe Partners v. Newmont Mining Corp., 535 A.2d 1334, 1344 (Del. 1987) ("A shareholder owes fiduciary duty only if it owns a majority interest in or exercises control over the business affairs of the corporation.").

The laws of business organizations may provide mechanisms to limit of a manager's authority such as the possibility of contracting for the firm's management structure. Although the firm may adopt a central management structure as a corporation, partnership, or LLC, it may impose certain limits on the manager's authority. *See* RULLCA § 105(a)(1) (stating that "the operating agreement governs relations among the members as members and between the members and the limited liability company"); ULPA (2001) § 105(a)(1) (functionally the same); DGLC

§ 141(a) (stating that the business and affairs of the corporation shall be managed by the board "except as may be otherwise provided in this chapter or in its certificate of incorporation").

The laws may provide that certain important or fundamental acts or transactions require the consent of owners. *E.g.*, RULLCA § 407(c)(3) ("The affirmative vote or consent of all members is required to: undertake an act outside the ordinary course of the company's activities and affairs; or amend the operating agreement."); ULPA (2001) § 801(a)(2) (providing that an LP is voluntarily dissolved upon "the affirmative vote or consent of all general partners and of limited partners owning a majority of the rights to receive distributions as limited partners"); DGCL § 251(c) (providing that a merger approved by the board of directors "shall be submitted to the stockholders for the purpose of acting on the agreement").

The laws may provide for rules to remove managers or periodic approval of their position through vote and consent. *See* RULLCA § 407(c)(4) ("A manager may be removed at any time by the affirmative vote or consent of a majority of the members without notice or cause."); ULPA (2001) § 603(4) (providing for the expulsion of a general partner "by the affirmative vote or consent of all the other partners" under certain circumstances); DGCL § 141(k) ("Any director or the entire board of directors may be removed, with or without cause, by the holders of a majority of the shares then entitled to vote at an election of directors").

The laws may provide that managers are required to provide accurate disclosures or information upon proper request. *See* RULLCA § 410 (providing members and managers the right to information); ULPA (2001) § 304, § 407 (same as to limited and general partners); DGCL § 220 (providing shareholders the right to inspect the corporation's books and records any proper purpose).

2. MANAGEMENT STRUCTURE OF CORPORATIONS

The prototypical firm with centralized management is the corporation. Managerial authority rests with the board of directors: "The business and affairs of every corporation shall be managed by or under the direction of a board of directors." DGCL § 141(a). A director can be a shareholder, but is not required to be. *Id.* § 142(b) ("Directors need not be stockholders unless so required by the certificate of incorporation or the bylaws."). In closely-held corporations, directors are often shareholders and employees as well. In large corporations, directors are generally not substantial owners. The board can and often do delegate managerial duties to corporate officers who generally operate the business on a day-to-day basis: "Every corporation shall have such officers with such titles and duties as shall be stated in the bylaws or in a resolution of the board of directors." *Id.* § 142(a). This basic structure of directors and officers facilitates management by professional managers, who may have little equity ownership.

An interesting feature of corporation law is that directors and officers must be natural persons. *Id.* § 141(b) ("The board of directors of a corporation shall consist of 1 or more members, each of whom shall be a natural person."); MBCA § 8.03(a) ("A board of directors shall consist of one or more individuals."), § 8.40(b) ("The board of directors may elect individuals to fill one or more offices of the corporation."), § 1.40 (defining "individual" as a natural person).

NBE laws differ. Partners, members, and managers can be legal entities. *See* RUPA § 102(10) (defining a "partner" as a "person"), § 102(14) (defining "person" as including "an individual, business corporation, nonprofit corporation, partnership, limited partnership, limited liability company"); ULPA (2001) § 102(7),(11),(15) (same as to "general partner" and "limited partner"); RULLCA § 102(9),(11),(15) (same as to "manager" and "member"). NBEs can be structured as layers of entities. For example, the two partners in M-F Partners, a joint venture, may be Microsoft and Facebook. On the other hand, M-F Inc. cannot have Microsoft and Facebook as its directors or officers. Directors and officers may be individuals affiliated with companies such as Bill Gates and Mark Zuckerberg, but not the companies themselves.

3. BUSINESS JUDGMENT RULE

When there is a centralized management authority, there is always a tension between authority and accountability. Authority is needed because collective management by a *demos* of many owners may be a road to internecine conflict or anarchy. But unaccountable authority means a dictator; in politics, social organizations, and business, an unconstrained authoritarian is most unfortunate, if not tragic. An unconstrained manager is a road to ruin, or at least regret. Yet complete accountability may mean the power to manage is illusory; shouldn't the ones holding the power to demand account simply run the firm themselves and bypass an enfeebled agent intermediary. There must be a balance between these notions.

The business judgment rule is corporation law's answer to striking this balance. It is a rule of substantial deference to managers, with caveats.

> *It is a presumption that in making a business decision the directors of a corporation acted on an informed basis, in good faith and in the honest belief that the action taken was in the best interests of the company.* Absent an abuse of discretion, that judgment will be respected by the courts. The burden is on the party challenging the decision to establish facts rebutting the presumption.

Aronson v. Lewis, 473 A.2d 805, 812 (Del. 1984).

The business judgment rule has a substantive and procedural component. Substantively, the rule provides that the exercise of business judgment is presumptively proper and thus not actionable. "Proper" does not mean that the business judgment was "correct" in some sense of the substance of a decision or good outcome. Properness is defined in terms of decisionmaking that was "on an informed basis, in good faith and in the honest belief that the action taken was in the best interests of the company." The question—did the director make the "right" or "correct" decision?—is irrelevant. Fiduciary duty is defined in terms of: Did the director acted on an informed basis? Did the director act in good faith? Did the director honestly believe that the action was in the best interest of the company? If the answers to these questions are "yes," there is no breach of duty, irrespective of poor substantive decision or outcome.[1] Motive and method of decisionmaking are important, but outcomes are not.

The business judgment rule imparts an initial presumption that a director acted in accordance with their fiduciary duties of care and loyalty. The action was proper, that is "in making a business decision the directors of a corporation acted on an informed basis, in good faith and in the honest belief that the action taken was in the best interests of the company."

An initial *presumption* suggests a procedural facet. Directors receive the initial benefit of the presumption. Their actions are entitled to the protection of the business judgment rule. The decision is given deference by courts, absent a plaintiff shareholder's *rebuttal* of that presumption by showing that the action was not informed, not in good faith, or not in the best interest of the corporation. The initial presumption of the business judgment rule is a powerful defense. Its application is said to be outcome determinative: "Because the effect of the proper invocation of the business judgment rule is so powerful and the standard of entire fairness so exacting, the determination of the appropriate standard of judicial review frequently is determinative of the outcome of derivative litigation." Nixon v. Blackwell, 626 A.2d 1366, 1376 (Del. 1993).

The business judgment rule has a gatekeeping function. It separates the wheat from the chaff at the outset of an action. The policy underlying the business judgment rule—deference to managerial decisions—would not work if all business decisions are subject to the ordinary rules of civil litigation, which permits liberal pleading rules and extensive (expensive) discovery process leading to pitched battles at summary judgment and

---

[1] *See* In re Caremark Int'l Inc. Deriv. Litig., 698 A.2d 959, 967 (Del. Ch. 1996) ("Whether a judge or jury considering the matter after the fact, believes a decision substantively wrong, or degrees of wrong extending through "stupid" to "egregious" or "irrational," provides no ground for director liability, so long as the court determines that the process employed was either rational or employed in a good faith effort to advance corporate interests."); Gagliardi v. TriFoods Int'l, Inc., 683 A.2d 1049, 1052 (Del. Ch. 1996) ("If, however, corporate directors were to be found liable for a corporate loss from a risky project on the ground that the investment was too risky (foolishly risky! stupidly risky! egregiously risky!—you supply the adverb), their liability would be joint and several for the whole loss."); Brehm v. Eisner, 746 A.2d 244, 264 (Del. 2000) ("As for the plaintiffs' contention that the directors failed to exercise substantive due care, we should note that such a concept is foreign to the business judgment rule. Courts do not measure, weigh or quantify directors' judgments. We do not even decide if they are reasonable in this context. Due care in the decisionmaking context is *process* due care only.").

trial. A derivative suit, the primary vehicle to enforce fiduciary duties, is not subject to the ordinary pleading rules in civil litigation. At the outset of pleadings, a shareholder's complaint must "*state with particularity* the reasons for not obtaining [a demand on the board] or not making the effort." Fed. R. Civ. P. 23.1.

Corporation law requires that a complaining shareholder first make a demand on the board. Once a demand is made, the fate of the litigation asset (*i.e.*, the substance of the complaint) rests in the board's hand. A board can take any action within its proper discretion, including not pursuing the matter on the ground that it would not be in the company's best interest. Obviously, a complaining shareholder will want to control the action and pursue the action himself in court. He can avoid a demand if he can show in the pleading "with particularity" that demand would be futile. Why might demand be futile? The plaintiff must show that the board is somehow materially compromised with respect to exercising its business judgment on the fate of the litigation asset. For example, the board is not independent and cannot exercise proper business judgment with respect to the complaint about a person to whom the board is beholden. Or the complaint states with particularity that the board breached its fiduciary duties and thus would not be inclined to sue itself. In other words, the plaintiff shareholder rebutted the initial presumption that the board's action was informed, in good faith, and in the best interest of the corporation. To avoid dismissal per a motion to dismiss for failure to make a demand under Rule 23.1, a plaintiff shareholder must show "with particularity" the merits of the complaint from the outset.

Although the business judgment rule originates from corporation law, it has been incorporated into the laws of business organizations that have centralized management authority. Specifically, the law of LLCs has embraced the concept. One version of the RULLCA (2006) incorporates the business judgment rule into the duty of care framework.

> Subject to the business judgment rule, the duty of care of a member of a member-managed limited liability company in the conduct and winding up of the company's activities is to act with the care that a person in a like position would reasonably exercise under similar circumstances and in a manner the member reasonably believes to be in the best interests of the company.

RULLCA § 409(c).[2] *See also* Leighton v. Poltorak, 2018 WL 2338789, at *8 (S.D.N.Y. 2018) (stating that those who manage an LLC, whether they be

---

[2] The harmonized version dated 2013, which is the version consistently cited in this book and appended in the appendix, does not incorporate the business judgment rule. The comments state that the 2013 amendments "replaced the 'ordinary care/business judgment rule' standard with the duty to 'refrain from engaging in grossly negligent or reckless conduct, willful or intentional misconduct, or knowing violation of law,' Section 409(c)."

members in a member-managed LLC or managers in a manager-managed LLC, are entitled to the protection of the business judgment rule).

C. MANAGEMENT STRUCTURES OF NBEs

1. GENERAL PARTNERSHIP

The default management structure of a partnership envisions partners as equal owner-managers. Each partner is an agent of the partnership with respect to carrying on in the ordinary course of partnership business.

RUPA § 401. Partner's Rights and Duties.

(h) Each partner has equal rights in the management and conduct of the partnership's business.

(k) A difference arising as to a matter in the ordinary course of business of a partnership may be decided by a majority of the partners. An act outside the ordinary course of business of a partnership and an amendment to the partnership agreement may be undertaken only with the affirmative vote or consent of all the partners.

RUPA § 301. Partner Agent of Partnership.

Subject to the effect of a statement of partnership authority under Section 303, the following rules apply:

(1) Each partner is an agent of the partnership for the purpose of its business. An act of a partner, including the signing of an instrument in the partnership name, for apparently carrying on in the ordinary course the partnership business or business of the kind carried on by the partnership binds the partnership, unless the partner did not have authority to act for the partnership in the particular matter and the person with which the partner was dealing knew or had notice that the partner lacked authority.

(2) An act of a partner which is not apparently for carrying on in the ordinary course the partnership's business or business of the kind carried on by the partnership binds the partnership only if the act was actually authorized by all the other partners.

The RUPA's default rule is premised on the assumption that a partnership is a closely held firm bound in a communitarian ethos. A partnership of five partners would probably do well with a rule of equal management. However, partnerships come in all sizes. Leading national and international law firms are operated as general partnerships (specifically LLPs), and they have hundreds of partners. Would a rule of "equal rights" in the management really work when the partnership is a sprawling business of national scale? Perhaps not.

Where the default rule does not work, the partnership agreement can provide rules of internal affairs that may be better suited for the circumstance. Centralized management becomes more efficient as the number of partners increase. Many large partnerships use an executive committee to manage the day-to-day business affairs, similar to the role of a board of directors and corporate officers. For example, the following is a provision from the partnership agreement in *Lugosch v. Congel*:

> The executive committee, with the authority granted to it under the agreement, shall have the exclusive right to manage the business of the Partnership and is hereby authorized to take any action of any kind and to do anything and everything in accordance with the provisions of this agreement. Except as expressly provided hereunder, the authority of any Partner to manage the business of the Partnership shall be exercised only by the Executive committee and, except as expressly so provided, no Partner other than the Executive Committee shall have any control over Partnership.

2006 WL 6651777, at *2 n.3 (N.D.N.Y. 2006).

The analogy to a corporation should not be taken too far. An executive committee or any other central management authority is purely a creature of the partnership agreement. The partnership statute does not require it. The authority of a manager would be defined in the partnership agreement, and not a mandatory rule in a statute. Generally, the RUPA imbues partners with significant governance role. *See* RUPA § 401(h) (providing for "equal rights in the management").

2. LIMITED PARTNERSHIP

The management structure of LPs requires two classes of partners. A general partner manages the business of the LP and has functionally the same default statutory powers as a partner in a general partnership. A limited partner is a passive investor. A partner can have dual capacity as a general partner and a limited partner. ULPA (2001) § 109. But an LP requires at least one of each.

ULPA (2001) § 406. Management Rights of General Partner.

(a) Each general partner has equal rights in the management and conduct of the limited partnership's activities and affairs. Except as otherwise provided in this [act], any matter relating to the activities and affairs of the partnership is decided exclusively by the general partner or, if there is more than one general partner, by a majority of the general partners.

(b) The affirmative vote or consent of all the partners is required to:

(1) amend the partnership agreement;

(2) amend the certificate of limited partnership to add or delete a statement that the limited partnership is a limited liability limited partnership; and

(3) sell, lease, exchange, or otherwise dispose of all, or substantially all, of the limited partnership's property, with or without the good will, other than in the usual and regular course of the limited partnership's activities and affairs.

ULPA (2001) § 402. General Partner Agent of Limited Partnership.

(a) Each general partner is an agent of the limited partnership for the purposes of its activities and affairs. An act of a general partner, including the signing of a record in the partnership's name, for apparently carrying on in the ordinary course the partnership's activities and affairs or activities and affairs of the kind carried on by the partnership binds the partnership, unless the general partner did not have authority to act for the partnership in the particular matter and the person with which the general partner was dealing knew or had notice that the general partner lacked authority.

(b) An act of a general partner which is not apparently for carrying on in the ordinary course the limited partnership's activities and affairs or activities and affairs of the kind carried on by the partnership binds the partnership only if the act was actually authorized by all the other partners.

ULPA (2001) § 302. No Agency Power of Limited Partner as Limited Partner.

(a) A limited partner is not an agent of a limited partnership solely by reason of being a limited partner.

(b) A person's status as a limited partner does not prevent or restrict law other than this [act] from imposing liability on a limited partnership because of the person's conduct.

Section 406(b) refers to the "consent of all the *partners*," and not just the general partner. It reserves management right to all partners, both general and limited, on certain fundamental matters. Thus, when drafting the partnership agreement, one should consider the kinds of matters that are not ordinarily within the exclusive authority of general partners—the checks and balance of authority and accountability when there is a centralized management authority. For example, the drafter may consider the following matters as requiring a vote of all partners.

- Dissolution and winding up

- Sale, exchange, lease, mortgage, pledge, or other transfer of all or substantially all of the assets
- Incurrence of indebtedness by the LP other than in the ordinary course of its business
- Change in the nature of the business
- Admission or removal of general and limited partners
- Transaction involving an actual or potential conflict of interest among partners or the LP
- Amendment to the partnership agreement or certificate of limited partnership
- Other matters subject to the approval or disapproval of limited partners

The functional split between management and passive investment explains the liability scheme. By virtue of their management power, general partners do not have limited liability. ULPA (2001) § 404(a) ("all general partners are liable jointly and severally for all debts, obligations, and liabilities of the limited partnership"). By virtual of their passive role, limited partners have limited liability. ULPA (2001) § 303(a) ("A debt, obligation, or liability of a limited partnership is not the debt, obligation, or liability of a limited partner."). In some states that still use the older RULPA, if a limited partner participates in the control of the LP, then limited partners lose their limited liability protection. *Compare* RULPA § 303(a) (providing for liability "if the limited partner participates in the control of the business"), *with* ULPA (2001) § 303(a) (providing limited liability "even if the limited partner participates in the management and control of the limited partnership").

3. LIMITED LIABILITY COMPANY

Most LLC statutes provide two basic forms of management structure: member-managed LLC and manager-managed LLC. *E.g.*, RULLCA § 407(b)–(c). Some states require that one of these structures must be declared and identified in the articles of organization filed with the state.[3] This requirement has three implications: (1) it requires a publicly declared choice of management structure; (2) by doing so, the choice may affect the application of the law of agency since the election can be deemed to provide notice to third parties of the LLC's management structure; (3) the election commits the firm to the management structure subject to an amendment

[3] *See, e.g.*, Texas Bus. Org. Code § 101.251 ("The governing authority of a limited liability company consists of: (1) the managers of the company, if the company's certificate of formation states that the company will have one or more managers; or (2) the members of the company, if the company's certificate of formation states that the company will not have managers."); Montana Limited Liability Company Act § 35–8–202(1) (same); Kentucky Limited Liability Company Act § 275.025(1) (same).

of the articles of organization. With respect to notice to third parties, some states provide that only the required information in the articles of organization constitutes notice to third parties.[4] However, many states do not have this binding election requirement, and the default rule is that an LLC is member-managed unless the company states otherwise.[5]

The model for a member-managed LLC is the general partnership. The model for a manager-managed LLC can be either the corporation or the LP.[6] Both have central management authority, but they are different and represent two variants of a centralized management structure.

In an LP, the manager is also a partner of the partnership. An LP must have at least one general partner. In this sense, the LP's management is structurally entrenched. A member can also be a manager. *See* RULLCA § 102(9) (defining a manager as "a person who under the operating agreement of a manager-managed limited liability company is responsible for performing the management functions"). In a manager-managed LLC, the operating agreement may, but is not required to, provide that only members can serve as managers. *Id.* § 407(c)(5) ("A person need not be a member to be a manager.").

In a corporation, directors and officers can be shareholders as well, but they generally serve in a representative capacity under a system in which shareholders assent and vote for directors. Directors in turn hire officers or delegate this task to other officers. A manager-managed LLC can mimic a corporate model of non-owner professional managers.

The LLC can be structured to adopt facets of three prototypical models of management structure. For example, a member-managed LLC can still incorporate aspects of central management authority while preserving significant aspects of control for the entire membership. A manager-managed LLC can have non-member managers, but the members can hold greater authority than the passive investors seen in LPs and corporations. The freedom of contract permits a great degree of entity design.

---

4 *See, e.g.*, Delaware Limited Liability Company Act § 18–207 (only required information in the certificate of formation constitutes notice, which are name, registered agent, and "series LLC" designation); Kentucky Limited Liability Company Act § 275.025(7) ("The fact that the articles of organization are on file with the Secretary of State is notice of all other facts set forth in the articles of organization which are required to be set forth.").

5 *See, e.g.*, Delaware Limited Liability Company Act § 18–402 ("Unless otherwise provided in a limited liability company agreement, the management of a limited liability company shall be vested in its members in proportion to the then current percentage or other interest of members in the profits of the limited liability company owned by all of the members.").

6 *See* Butler Law Firm, PLC v. Higgins, 410 P.3d 1223, 1229 (Ariz. 2018) ("An LLC's organizational flexibility is one of its central characteristics: an LLC may be managed directly by its members, making it more like a partnership, or it may be managed by a manager or group of managers, making it more like a corporation.").

RULLCA § 407. Management of Limited Liability Company.

(a) A limited liability company is a member-managed limited liability company unless the operating agreement:

(1) expressly provides that:

(A) the company is or will be "manager-managed";

(B) the company is or will be "managed by managers"; or

(C) management of the company is or will be "vested in managers"; or

(2) includes words of similar import.

(b) In a member-managed limited liability company, the following rules apply:

(1) Except as expressly provided in this [act], the management and conduct of the company are vested in the members.

(2) Each member has equal rights in the management and conduct of the company's activities and affairs.

(3) A difference arising among members as to a matter in the ordinary course of the activities and affairs of the company may be decided by a majority of the members.

(4) The affirmative vote or consent of all the members is required to:

(A) undertake an act outside the ordinary course of the activities and affairs of the company; or

(B) amend the operating agreement.

(c) In a manager-managed limited liability company, the following rules apply:

(1) Except as expressly provided in this [act], any matter relating to the activities and affairs of the company is decided exclusively by the manager, or, if there is more than one manager, by a majority of the managers.

(2) Each manager has equal rights in the management and conduct of the company's activities and affairs.

(3) The affirmative vote or consent of all members is required to:

(A) undertake an act outside the ordinary course of the company's activities and affairs; or

(B) amend the operating agreement.

(4) A manager may be chosen at any time by the affirmative vote or consent of a majority of the members and remains a manager

until a successor has been chosen, unless the manager at an earlier time resigns, is removed, or dies, or, in the case of a manager that is not an individual, terminates. A manager may be removed at any time by the affirmative vote or consent of a majority of the members without notice or cause.

(5) A person need not be a member to be a manager, but the dissociation of a member that is also a manager removes the person as a manager. If a person that is both a manager and a member ceases to be a manager, that cessation does not by itself dissociate the person as a member.

(6) A person's ceasing to be a manager does not discharge any debt, obligation, or other liability to the limited liability company or members which the person incurred while a manager.

RULLCA § 301. No Agency Power of Member as Member.

(a) A member is not an agent of a limited liability company solely by reason of being a member.

(b) A person's status as a member does not prevent or restrict law other than this [act] from imposing liability on a limited liability company because of the person's conduct.

The RULLCA provides flexible rules that permit LLCs to resemble general partnerships or LPs. Its provision on agency differs from the RUPA where partners are agents. Members are not agents by virtue of being a member, *viz.*, the statute does not automatically confer apparent agency authority. Instead, other laws, principally the law of agency, will determine the question of whether the LLC is bound by an act of a member.

This example illustrates the RULLCA approach of no statutory apparent authority. Ann and Bob are two members of A&B LLC. Ann orders office furniture from Chairs & Desks Inc. on behalf of the LLC, signing the purchase agreement as "Ann, member of A&B LLC." Under the RULLCA rubric, without additional facts, Ann does not have authority to bind the LLC solely by reason of being a member. The question of liability is resolved under the law of agency. In most similar cases, each owner would likely have actual authority over day-to-day decisions. Here, the issue is apparent authority. Chairs & Desks calls A&B LLC about payment, and in response Bob sends a check drawn from A&B LLC's bank account. A month later, Ann orders more furniture from Chairs & Desks. Based on the past dealing related to Ann's first order and payment by A&B LLC, Chairs & Desks reasonably believes that Ann has authority. Under the law of agency, absent other facts, Ann has apparent authority.

Why the divergence between partnership law and LLC law with respect to conferring agency authority under the statutes? One important reason is that LLCs are flexible entities that can mimic partnerships or an

LP or a corporation. These entities differ with respect to default agency authority. Partners in a partnership have agency authority. RUPA § 301 ("Each partner is an agent of the partnership for the purpose of its business."). General partners in an LP have agency authority, but limited partners do not. ULPA (2001) § 302(a) ("A limited partner is not an agent of a limited partnership solely by reason of being a limited partner."), § 402(a) ("Each general partner is an agent of the limited partnership for the purposes of its activities and affairs."). A shareholder of a corporation does not have agency authority. Levert v. Shirley Planting Co., 66 S. 301, 302 (La. 1914) ("Corporations can only act through their duly constituted agents. And stockholders are not such, and therefore cannot act for the corporation, except when it is necessary that somebody should do so, and the officers will not, though duly requested.").

With different default rules among corporations, partnerships, and LPs, what should be the default rule for an LLC, which can contractually mimic different entities? Should there be a default rule in light of the fact that a principal benefit of an LLC is its flexibility?

Further compounding the problem is that the RULLCA does not require a disclosure in the certificate of organization of the management structure. *See* RULLCA § 201(b). This approach is consistent with the majority of states that do not require such disclosure in the public filing,[7] though a significant number of states still require a statement in the filing of whether an LLC is member-managed or manager-managed.[8] In the many states where the LLC management structure is not required to be disclosed in the filing, a third-party has no way to discern the management structure other than to vet the LLC directly as to agency authority of members. The incentive placed on third parties by this reality aligns with a rule of no default agency. The rule places the onus of vetting agency on third parties that transact with the LLC.

There is another reason why the RULLCA declined to provide rules of agency. The statute incorporates many rules from corporation law, the most important of which is the concept of a manager-managed LLC that permits a corporate form of centralized management authority. The lack of default agency authority tracks the same rule applicable to shareholders, who *qua* shareholders, do not have agency authority.[9] In practice, the

---

[7] *See, e.g.,* Delaware Limited Liability Company Act § 201(a); Florida Revised Limited Liability Company Act § 605.0201(2); Illinois Limited Liability Company Act § 180/5–5(a); Maryland Limited Liability Company Act § 4A–204(a); Minnesota Revised Limited Liability Company Act § 322C.0201(2); New Jersey Revised Limited Liability Company Act § 42:2C–18(b); New York Limited Liability Company Act § 203(e); North Carolina Limited Liability Company Act § 57D–2–21(a); Pennsylvania Limited Liability Company Act § 8821(b); Virginia Limited Liability Company Act § 13.1–1011.

[8] *See, e.g.,* California Revised Limited Liability Company Act § 17702.01(b); Montana Limited Liability Company Act § 35–8–202(1)(e); New Hampshire Revised Limited Liability Company Act § 304–C:31 (II)(d); Texas Bus. Org. Code § 101.251.

[9] *See* Swope v. Swope, 739 P.2d 273, 280 (Idaho 1987) ("Stockholders are not agents of the corporation and do not make business decisions, but partners are agents of the partnership for the

manager-managed LLC is often selected by large or sophisticated ventures. Such firms do not manage their business like a general partnership. They desire a corporate style of management, but at the same time want the contractual flexibility of the LLC form along with other advantages of the LLC. Owners often elect a central management structure similar to a corporate board across all entity forms. Even in general partnerships, if a firm is large or has many partners, it often uses a central management authority in the form of an executive committee of partners. The lack of default rules of agency may better serve these preferences.

The case below discusses the nature of a manager's role in an LLC. In reading this case, consider these questions: (1) What is a "manager" in the statutory scheme? (2) What factors determine who is a manager?

FLORIDA R & D FUND INVESTORS, LLC V. FLORIDA BOCA/DEERFIELD R & D INVESTORS, LLC

2013 WL 4734834 (Del. Ch. 2013)

JOHN W. NOBLE, VICE CHANCELLOR.

Plaintiff Florida R & D Fund Investors, LLC ("R & D"), a member of Defendant Florida BOCA/Deerfield R & D Investors, LLC (the "Joint Venture") [holding about 87% of interest], brought a books and records action under 6 *Del. C.* § 18–305 and the Joint Venture's limited liability company agreement. R & D seeks two categories of books and records that are in the possession and control of Defendant HDG Mansur Investment Services, Inc. ("Investment Services"), which, until recently, managed the Joint Venture's assets. R & D offers two reasons to support its inspection requests: appointing a new asset manager and investigating and determining the extent of possible mismanagement at the Joint Venture.

[Investment Services moved to dismiss under Court of Chancery Rules 12(b)(2) for lack of person jurisdiction.] The primary question focuses on whether this Court has jurisdiction over Investment Services, an Indiana corporation, under either Delaware's Limited Liability Company Act (the "LLC Act"). Whether the LLC Act confers jurisdiction will depend upon whether Investment Services is a manager of the Joint Venture or whether its asset management activities constitute material participation in the management of the Joint Venture.

The Joint Venture is governed by the LLC Agreement, which allows for the books and records to be maintained by a third party selected by the Board of Directors. Section 5.3 of the LLC Agreement provides that:

purpose of its business."); Mease v. Warm Mineral Springs, Inc., 128 So.2d 174, 179 (Fla. App. 1961) ("Since stockholders of a corporation are not its agents, the admissions or declarations of individual stockholders are normally not binding upon the corporation.").

- The Board of Directors shall cause to be kept full and accurate records of the Group Companies' affairs.
- The Group Companies' books and records, this Agreement and the Certificate of Formation and all amendments thereto, the Master Lease Financing Documentation, and all other records required to be maintained by [the Joint Venture] and the other Group Companies pursuant to the LLC Act shall be maintained or caused to be maintained by the Board of Directors and shall be made available to the Members.
- The Members, their internal staff and accountants shall have the right at any time during normal business hours to inspect and audit all such books and records, to make copies thereof and to take extracts therefrom.
- The Board of Directors shall ensure that all deeds, Leases, contracts, title matters, surveys and other documentation, records and financial information relating to the ownership, maintenance, development and sale of Properties are maintained in safekeeping and accessible to the Members.
- The Board of Directors shall promptly deliver to the Members, upon request, and at the expense of [the Joint Venture], a copy of the information required to be maintained by the LLC Act and this Agreement.

The LLC Agreement anticipated that Investment Services would provide asset management services for the Group Companies. The Joint Venture and Investment Services executed the Asset Management Agreement, which was then incorporated into the LLC Agreement.

Investment Services was required under the Asset Management Agreement to "advise [the Joint Venture] and the other Group Companies on how best to preserve and enhance the asset value of the Properties and to provide asset management services to the Joint Venture and the other Group Companies." The Asset Management Agreement states that Investment Services "is an independent contractor and is not acting as agent, partner, joint venturer, lessee, coprincipal, or associate of any Group Company or any person claiming by, through or under any Group Company, in the conduct of any Group Company's businesses."

Although R & D characterizes Section 3 of the Asset Management Agreement as imposing an "obligation" on Investment Services to maintain the books and records of the Joint Venture, the Defendants instead contend that there is no such obligation, because Section 3: "(1) only addresses certain financial reporting requirements which are not at issue in this case; (2) does not mention maintenance of the Joint Venture's books and records; [and] (3) does not cite to or reference the LLC Agreement's Section 5.3 books and records clause."

Investment Services is an Indiana corporation with an Indiana address. The two categories of books and records sought by R & D were created, maintained, and held by Investment Services in either Indiana or Florida. R & D does not allege that the books and records were ever maintained or located in Delaware. Although Investment Services entered into the Asset Management Agreement with the Joint Venture, "a non-resident's entering into a contract with a domicile of the forum State has been held insufficient, in and of itself, to permit the exercise of personal jurisdiction over the [non-resident]." The Asset Management Agreement provides for the management of assets based in Florida, and the agreement is to be governed by New York law. R & D bears the burden of establishing a basis for the Court's exercise of jurisdiction over Investment Services. R & D argues that the Court may exercise jurisdiction over Investment Services under the service of process provisions of the LLC Act, 6 *Del. C.* § 18–109(a)(i) and (ii).

Section 18–109 of the LLC Act authorizes service of process on persons serving as managers of Delaware limited liability companies

> in all civil actions or proceedings brought in Delaware involving or relating to the business of the limited liability company, or a violation by the manager of a duty to the limited liability company or any member of the limited liability company, whether or not the manager is a manager at the time suit is commenced.

Service as a manager "constitutes such person's consent to the appointment of the registered agent of the limited liability company (or, if there is none, the Secretary of State) as such person's agent upon whom service of process may be made as provided in this section." 6 *Del. C.* § 18–109(a). Managers of Delaware limited liability companies are thus deemed to have consented to the jurisdiction of the Court in litigation arising out of their service as managers.

For purposes of service of process, "manager" refers:

> (i) to a person who is a manager as defined in § 18–101(10) of [the LLC Act] and
>
> (ii) to a person, whether or not a member of a limited liability company, who, although not a manager as defined in § 18–101(10) of [the LLC Act], participates materially in the management of the limited liability company.

R & D argues that the Court may exercise jurisdiction over Investment Services under either subsection.

Section 18–109(a)(i) identifies the managers of a Delaware limited liability company by reference to Section 18–101(10), which defines a manager as "a person who is named as manager of a limited liability company in, or designated as a manager of a limited liability company pursuant to, a limited liability company agreement or similar instrument under which the limited liability company is formed." The LLC Agreement provides in Section 6.1 that "the management of the business and affairs of the [Joint Venture] shall be vested in a board of directors of the [Joint Venture]" [and] that "for the purposes of the LLC Act, the management of the [Joint Venture] shall be vested in a Manager as defined in the LLC Act and not in the Members" and that "the Manager shall consist of the Board of Directors." Under Section 18–109(a)(i), the Joint Venture's manager is the Board of Directors. Because Investment Services is not listed in the LLC Agreement as a member of the Joint Venture's Board of Directors, it may not be considered a manager of the Joint Venture for the purposes of either Section 18–109(a)(i) or Section 18–101(10).

Section 18–109(a)(ii) of the LLC Act also provides that "a person, whether or not a member of a limited liability company, who, although not a manager as defined in § 18–101(10) of this title, participates materially in the management of the limited liability company" can nonetheless be served with process as a manager under Section 18–109(a). R & D argues that given Investment Services' broad authority to act on behalf of the Joint Venture under the Asset Management Agreement, and the fact that it thereby was to run the day-to-day operations of the Joint Venture, Investment Services can be said to have "participated materially" in the management of the Joint Venture.

The Asset Management Agreement provides that Investment Services "is an independent contractor and is not acting as agent, partner, joint venturer, lessee, coprincipal, or associate of any Group Company [including the Joint Venture] or any person claiming by, through or under any Group Company, in the conduct of any Group Company's businesses." As the HDG Defendants note, the fact that the Asset Management Agreement specifies Investment Services' role as an "independent contractor," and that it is "not acting as agent," detracts from R & D's contention that Investment Services had participated materially in the management of the Joint Venture.

Under the Asset Management Agreement, the role of Investment Services was confined to acting "as the asset manager and to provide the [listed] Services with respect to the Properties, Assets and Business in a manner consistent with the Business Plan." The management of the underlying assets of an LLC is analytically distinct from the management of the LLC itself for the purposes of Section 18–109(a)(ii). Under the Asset Management Agreement, the discretion and decision-making ability of Investment Services was contractually (and materially) constrained: for instance, Investment Services (i) had to "act in material compliance with the Business Plan and the applicable Annual Budget," and (ii) could not enter into any "sale, assignment, transfer, encumbrance, hypothecation, or pledge of any Property or other material asset of any Group Company."

The degree of involvement in a limited liability company that constitutes material participation in its management has not been defined with precision. Here, the Asset Management Agreement does give Investment Services relatively broad authority to engage in most of the operation and supervision of the Joint Venture. Yet, the Complaint does not allege—especially in a non-conclusory fashion—that Investment Services actually engaged in any of its contractually authorized conduct. Merely having the capacity to participate in management does not constitute material participation in management.[73] The Complaint offers very little, if anything, about Investment Services' actual role in the operation of the Joint Venture. There is an allegation that it maintains the books and records, but that alone does not constitute material participation in the management, especially in light of the designation of the board of directors as the Joint Venture's manager. There are other incidental steps taken by Investment Services that are alleged in the Complaint, but those allegations do not demonstrate the control or decision-making role necessary to satisfy the statutory standard for personal jurisdiction. In short, the Complaint does not allege that Investment Services materially participated in the management of the Joint Venture and, accordingly, jurisdiction may not be exercised over it by virtue of Section 18–109(a)(ii). R & D has not met its burden to make a *prima facie* showing of a statutory basis for personal jurisdiction over Investment Services under Section 18–109 of the LLC Act. Therefore, R & D's claim against Investment Services must be dismissed under Rule 12(b)(2) for lack of personal jurisdiction.

Below is the management provision of Chrysler Group LLC. It creates a board and officer structure. Obviously, this structure borrows directly from corporation law, but consider the following question: (1) What provisions differ from corporation law? (2) In what way do these differences reflect the reason why the parties used LLC form here?

[73] *See, e.g., Fisk Ventures, LLC v. Segal*, 2008 WL 19611156, at * 7–8 (Del. Ch. 2008) (declining to find that a party materially participated in management through the power to appoint members to the LLC's board, even where the party "offered comments via email to [the] appointed board representatives," because the agreement expressly provided that "all management powers over the business and affairs of the Company shall be exclusively vested in the board"); *see also Palmer v. Moffat*, 2001 WL 1221749, at * 2 (Del. Super. 2001) (finding that parties did not materially participate in management of the LLC, despite a broad contractual grant to them of the "full, exclusive and complete discretion, power and authority, subject in all cases to the provisions of this Agreement to manage, control, administer and operate the business and affairs of the company [and] to make all decisions affecting such business and affairs," because the agreement specifically provided that "the operations of the Company shall be conducted by the Management Committee [and] all Company decisions shall require the affirmative vote of the majority of the members of the Management Committee").

CHRYSLER GROUP LLC OPERATING AGREEMENT

Section 5.1 Establishment of Board of Directors. There is hereby established a committee of Member representatives (the "Board of Directors") comprised of natural Persons (the "Directors") having the authority and duties set forth in this Agreement. The Board of Directors shall number between five and thirteen persons as determined from time to time by the Members acting at a meeting or by written consent as contemplated in ARTICLE X. The Directors shall be elected pursuant to Section 5.3 for terms not to exceed one year; provided that Directors may serve an unlimited number of consecutive terms. Each Director elected shall hold office until a successor is duly elected and qualified or until his or her earlier death, resignation or removal as provided in this ARTICLE V.

Section 5.2 General Powers of the Board of Directors. The property, affairs and business of the Company shall be overseen by the Board of Directors, except as otherwise provided in this Agreement. Each Director shall be a "manager" (as such term is defined in the LLC Act) of the Company but, notwithstanding the foregoing, no Director shall have any rights or powers beyond the rights and powers granted to such Director in this Agreement or properly delegated to such Director by the Board of Directors. Except as such power is delegated pursuant to Section 5.11, no Director acting alone, or with any other Directors, shall have the power to act for or on behalf of, or to bind, the Company. For the avoidance of doubt, any act or thing that may be done under the authority or direction of the Board of Directors may also be done under the authority of a resolution duly adopted by Members holding a majority of the Membership Interests acting at a meeting or by written consent as contemplated in ARTICLE X.

Section 5.7 Voting.

(a) Each Director shall be entitled to cast one vote with respect to each matter brought before the Board of Directors (or any committee of the Board of Directors of which such Director is a member) for approval.

(b) Except as otherwise provided by this Agreement, the LLC Act, other Law or the Certificate of Formation, all matters to be determined by the Board of Directors shall be determined by a majority vote of the Directors present at a meeting at which a quorum is present. No Director shall be disqualified from voting on matters as to which such Director or any Member may have a conflict of interest, whether such matter is a direct conflict of interest in connection with which such Director or Member or any Affiliate of such Person will engage in a transaction with the Company or one or more of its Subsidiaries.

Section 5.12 Officers.

(a) The officers of the Company (the "Officers") shall consist of a Chief Executive Officer and such other Officers as the Chief Executive Officer may deem appropriate. Appointment of a Chief Executive Officer will require the prior written approval of Fiat Parent. Other Officers shall be approved and appointed by the Chief Executive Officer (which designation shall be in writing). One Person may hold, and perform the duties of, any two or more of such offices.

(b) Any Officer may be removed, with or without cause, at any time by the Board of Directors (in the case of the Chief Executive Officer) or by the Chief Executive Officer (in the case of other Officers), except that the Chief Executive Officer may be removed only with the prior written approval of Fiat Parent. For the avoidance of doubt, any of the Officers, including the Chief Executive Officer, may be employees of Fiat Parent or any of its Affiliates. Any seconded Officer may receive supplemental employment compensation from Fiat Parent or any of its Affiliates related to such secondment. The Board of Directors or the Chief Executive Officer may from time to time adopt a schedule of authority setting forth the specific powers and authorities delegated to each of the Officers and other authorized representatives (if any) of the Company. The initial schedule of authority is set forth in Annex B and shall be in force until amended, modified or terminated (in total or as applicable to any particular Officers(s) or other authorized representative(s)) by the Board of Directors, solely with respect to any power or authority delegated to the Chief Executive Officer, or the Chief Executive Officer (except as it applies to any power or authority delegated to the Chief Executive Officer).

D. VOTING RIGHTS

1. PURPOSE OF VOTING

An important aspect of managing the business and affairs of the firm is voting. Voting may be important even in a single-owner firm because the firm may employ several managers who may be required to resolve management decisions by vote. Voting serves several functions.

(1) Voting is an efficient mechanism to elicit information on preferences, especially among large groups. It is the best way to discern the aggregate preference for the purpose of deciding on a single action given a set of choices. Such preference may not be known until voting reveals it.

(2) Voting by owners legitimizes the recommendations or actions of managers. Managers may have significant powers. But without voting and the consent of owners on at least some particularly important matters, the separation of ownership and control may lose legitimacy and thus viability.

(3) Voting is a monitoring device. When matters are put before a vote, voters must be informed of the matter. This process facilitates review and monitoring of the matter at stake by owners and other stakeholders.

(4) Voting is an error correction device. Managers may decide on a course of action in the honest belief that it is in the firm's best interest, but upon being informed of the matter owners may disagree and conclude that the managers have erred. Voting provides a corrective mechanism.

(5) Voting is ultimately a power sharing arrangement. It reserves for owners some vestigial managerial or oversight power. Owners appoint managers and subject some managerial decisions to their consent, but may want to reserve power in certain important matters.

Collectively, these reasons explain why certain matters are more likely to be subject to the approval of owners. Owners may want to reserve certain powers, but at the same time they may not want to participate in, monitor, or check every managerial decision to the point of emasculating their authority altogether. The voting scheme in any firm must balance this tension between authority and accountability.

2. VOTING IN CORPORATIONS

Shareholders must have full voting power. *See* DGCL § 151(b) ("the corporation shall have outstanding 1 or more shares of 1 or more classes or series of stock, which share, or shares together, shall have full voting powers"); MBCA § 6.01(b)(1) (same).

The default rule is that each share of stock has equal right to one vote. *See* DGCL § 212(a) ("Unless otherwise provide in the certificate of incorporation each stockholder shall be entitled to 1 vote for each share of capital stock held by such stockholder"); MBCA§ 7.21(a) (same). The certificate of incorporation can provide for different classes or series of stock that have different rights, powers, limitations, and preferences.

> Every corporation may issue 1 or more classes of stock or 1 or more series of stock within any class thereof, any or all of which classes may be of stock with par value or stock without par value and which classes or series may have *such voting powers*, full or limited, or *no voting powers*, and such designations, preferences and relative, participating, optional or other special rights, and qualifications, limitations or restrictions thereof.

DGCL § 151(a). *See* MBCA§ 6.01(c) ("The articles of incorporation may authorize one or more classes or series of shares that have special, conditional, or limited voting rights, or no right to vote").

Shareholders must have full voting powers because corporation law grants shareholders the right to vote on and approve certain items. In the prototypical corporation, the board of directors and the officers manage the corporation; shareholders do not have a role in management. Due to the separation of ownership and control in the corporation, the typical shareholder does not have a real say in the company's management, affairs, or strategy.[10] Voting is an important component of monitoring corporate managers, keeping them accountable, and sharing power. Among other things, voting is required for the following matters: election of directors; amendment of the certificate of incorporation; approval of a merger; approval of a sale of all or substantially all assets; dissolution of the corporation. *See* DGCL §§ 211(b), § 242(b)(1), § 251(c), § 271(a), § 275(b).

With respect to the board, the default rule is that each director has one vote. Corporation law permits "the certificate of incorporation provides that 1 or more directors shall have more or less than 1 vote per director on any matter." *Id.* § 141(d). Different voting power among directors, albeit permitted, is not as common because a shareholder with significant voting power can achieve the same by negotiating greater board representation. The board may act when there is a quorum, which as a default rule is a majority of the board but can be set to a different threshold in the certificate of incorporation so long as a quorum is not less than one-third of the total directors. *Id.* § 141(b). When there is a quorum, a majority vote present at the meeting constitutes an action of the board. *Id.*

3. VOTING IN NBEs

In designing the management structure of an entity, thought must be given to the voting structure of the firm. The NBE statutes provide default rules for a partner's or member's voting power. The default rule originates from the general partnership. *See* RUPA § 401(h) ("Each partner has equal rights in the management and conduct of the partnership business."). The rules for LPs and LLCs provide equal voting power. *See* ULPA (2001) § 406(a) ("each general partner has equal rights in the management and conduct"); *id.* § 406(b) ("vote of all the partners is required" to amend the partnership agreement and approve sale of all or substantially all assets); RULLCA § 407(b)(2) ("each member has equal rights in the management [of a member-managed LLC]"); *id.* § 407(c)(2) ("each manager has equal rights in the management [of a manager-managed LLC]"); *id.* § 407(b)(4) ("vote of all the members is required" to amend the operating agreement and to undertake an act outside of the ordinary course).

The default rules of voting in NBEs reflect the partnership ethos of a communitarian enterprise. The per capita rule of one person, one vote is simpler. Unlike corporations that issue fungible, discrete units of stock, the economic ownership of owners may not be as simple as counting the number of shares. Contributions in all forms (*e.g.*, cash, property, service,

[10] Some corporations have controlling shareholders who can exert significant influence on the company's management. Also, in closely-held corporations, shareholders may have various roles including directors, officer, and employee. For a corporation with diffuse shareholders, an ordinary shareholder is passive except for certain voting rights under corporation law.

and other benefits) would have to be valued. For relatively unsophisticated entities, such exercises may be taxing. Per capita voting avoids these problems. However, if the enterprise is large or sophisticated, the expectation leans toward the corporate model. The partnership and operating agreements can provide different voting rights. *E.g.*, Delaware Limited Liability Company Act § 18–302(b) (permitting "a specified class or group of the members the right to vote separately or with all or any class or group of the members or managers, on any matter").

The voting scheme in partnerships and LLCs can adopt the corporate model of voting on the basis of per capital invested. *E.g.*, *id.* § 18–302(b) (permitting "voting by members may be on a per capita, number, financial interest, class, group or any other basis"); New York Limited Liability Company Law § 402(a) ("Each member shall vote in proportion to such member's share of the current profits of the limited liability company."). Per the charter agreement, voting rights can be based on profit allocation, contributions, capital account balance, or some other measure.[11] A firm must have a reliable method for continuous calculation of capital accounts and a "record date" to determine the date on which the capital account is calculated for the purpose of determining voting rights.

Like corporations, partnerships and LLCs can also create different classes of partners, members, and managers with different rights, including voting rights. Statutes implicitly permit this through the general provisions permitting contracting within the firm. *See, e.g.*, RULLCA § 105(a)(1) ("The operating agreement governs relations among the members as members and between members and the limited liability company."). Other statutes specifically permit for the possibility of different classes of owners. *E.g.*, Delaware Limited Liability Company Act § 18–302(a) (permitting "classes or groups of members having such relative rights, powers and duties as the limited liability company agreement may provide"); New York Limited Liability Company Law § 418(a) (same).

4. HORIZONTAL VOTING IN OWNER-MANAGED FIRMS

When a firm is managed by its owners in a communitarian fashion, there is horizontal voting among all owners, *i.e.*, voting across all owners either on a per capita or per capital invested bases. Owners must determine two large matters: (1) What level of vote is required to approve the item? (2) What items should be subject to such vote?

---

[11] Recall that the current balance in the capital account is calculated as: (1) credited with an amount equal to the money plus the value of any other property, net of the amount of any liabilities, the partner contributes to the partnership and the partner's share of the partnership profits; and (2) charged with an amount equal to the money plus the value of any other property, net of the amount of any liabilities, distributed by the partnership to the partner and the partner's share of the partnership losses.

On the threshold level, there are several obvious possibilities: majority vote (50% + 1), supermajority vote (*e.g.*, 67% or 75%), and unanimous vote (100%). There are several principles to consider. The more consequential the matter to the owners or some group thereof, the greater could be the threshold. The greater the number of voters, the lower should be the threshold. For example, an amendment of the charter document may be consequential, but unanimous consent on any matter in a firm with 100 owners would be impossible. Unanimity would grant each owner too much negative power, a veto. A supermajority threshold may be the best option.

The NBE statutes provide a default rule that matters in the ordinary course of business are decided by majority vote. *See* RUPA § 401(k) ("A difference arising as to a matter in the ordinary course of business of a partnership may be decided by a majority of the partners."); ULPA (2001) § 406(a) ("Any matter relating to the activities and affairs of the partnership is decided exclusively by a majority of the general partners."); RULLCA § 407(b)(3),(c)(1) (providing for majority vote of members and managers). In an LLC, managers are selected by a majority vote of members. RULLCA § 407(c)(4). The NBE statutes also provide various default rules that require unanimous consent to do the following:

- Admit a new owner: RUPA § 402(b)(3); ULPA (2001) § 301(b)(3); RULLCA § 401(c)(3)
- Amend the partnership or operating agreement: ULPA (2001) § 406(b)(1); RULLCA § 407(b)(4)(B), (c)(3)(B)
- Amend the certificate of organization filed with the state: ULPA (2001) § 406(b)(2)
- Take an action outside the ordinary course of business: RUPA § 401(k); RULLCA § 407(b)(4)(A),(c)(3)(A)
- Compromise an obligation to make a contribution: RUPA § 404(c); ULPA (2001) § 502(c); RULLCA § 403(c)
- Ratify a transaction that would otherwise violate the duty of loyalty: RUPA § 409(f); ULPA (2001) § 409(f); RULLCA § 409(f)
- Dissolve and wind up the firm: RUPA § 801(2)(B); ULPA (2001) § 801(a)(2); RULLCA § 701(a)(2)
- Sell all or substantially all assets: ULPA (2001) § 406(b)(3)
- Merge the partnership with another firm: RUPA § 1123(a)(1); ULPA (2001) § 1123(a)(1); RULLCA § 1023(a)(1)

On voting items, the above provisions provide broad guidance as to matters that could be subject to a vote. The charter agreement should indicate voting matters and voting thresholds. The following table provides a more detailed example of potential matters subject to vote and the voting threshold necessary for approval.

Action	Vote threshold			
	Majority	Super-majority	Unanimous	Other type
Financing decisions				
1. Require capital contributions (or in excess of $ ___)				
2. Incur indebtedness (or in excess of $ ___)				
3. Make distribution (or in excess of $ ___)				
4. Guarantee debt of another person or pledge property				
5. Lend money, including to partner, member, manager				
6. Invest funds (or in excess of $ ___)				
7. Open or close accounts				
8. Make tax election				
9. Choose auditor or accountant				
10. Waive obligation to make contribution				
Operational actions				
11. Acquire property (or in excess of $ ___)				
12. Enter into agreements (or in excess of $ ___)				
13. Commence litigation on behalf of the firm				
14. Approve compensation, distribution, or reimbursement to partners, members, or employees (or in excess of $ ___)				
15. Purchase or maintain insurance				
16. Hire employees (or specific levels of employees or salaries)				
17. Execute documents				
18. Expend funds (or in excess of $ ___)				

19. Construct capital improvements (or in excess of $ ___)				
Governance matters				
20. Admit new owner				
21. Expel owner for cause				
22. Modify economic or governance rights of current owners				
23. Amend charter agreement				
24. Exercise the firm's right of first refusal or right under buy-sell agreement				
25. Redeem an interest subject to a charging order with the firm's property				
26. Decide matters related to derivative suits, including approval of special litigation committee				
Extraordinary transactions				
27. Dissolve firm, including an action for judicial dissolution				
28. Merge, reorganize, or convert the firm				
29. Sell all or substantially all assets				
30. File for bankruptcy				
31. Do other acts or transactions outside of the ordinary course of business				

5. VERTICAL VOTING IN MANAGER-MANAGED FIRMS

Some firms are manager-managed businesses. When there are multiple managers, voting is both horizontal and vertical. Horizontal voting refers to the collective voting among the group of managers in matters and actions requiring their consent. There is also a vertical relationship between owners and managers. Vertical voting refers to decisions subject to consent of non-managing owners: (1) What managerial decisions and recommendations are subject to vertical voting? (2) What are the threshold voting levels for each consent? The following are some examples of vertical voting matters.

- Certain matters should clearly be subject to owner consent as a matter of logic or anticipated owner preference.
- Appointment of manager
- Amendment of charter agreement

- Modification of economic or governance rights of current owners
- Extraordinary transactions such as mergers, acquisitions, reorganizations, conversions, sale of all assets, or dissolution

Beyond these obvious matters, the allocation of authority between owners and managers is less clear. Recall that owner-voting may serve serval functions: eliciting owner preference, legitimization, monitoring, error correction, or power sharing. Based on these functions, what matters could be subject to vertical voting? Consider whether the following items should be subject to owner consent.

- Additional capital contribution
- Distributions
- Major expenditures and capital investments
- Admission of new owners

There is no right answer, only preferences. The answer will come through the client counseling process. An attorney should understand the circumstance of the firm and the aggregate preference of owners as to the amount of authority that should be granted to managers.

E. INSURANCE AND INDEMNIFICATION

Because employees, agents, and owners may incur liability while engaging in the firm's business, they may wish to have indemnification and insurance protection. *E.g.,* RULLCA § 408 (permitting indemnification and insurance). Firms commonly purchase liability insurance to protect owners, managers, employees, and agents. They also routinely provide for indemnification. Since the management structures of NBEs are different, the rules of indemnification and insurance are stated in a way that applies to those who manage. The following are the rules in RUPA. The provisions under the ULPA (2001) and RULLCA are substantially the same. ULPA (2001) § 408(b)–(d); RULLCA § 408(b)–(d).

RUPA § 401. Partner's Rights and Duties.

(c) A partnership shall indemnify and hold harmless a person with respect to any claim or demand against the person and any debt, obligation, or other liability incurred by the person by reason of the person's former or present capacity as a partner, if the claim, demand, debt, obligation, or other liability does not arise from the person's breach of this section or Section 407 or 409.

(d) In the ordinary course of its business, a partnership may advance reasonable expenses, including attorney's fees and costs, incurred by a person in connection with a claim or demand against the person by reason of the person's former or present capacity as a partner, if the person promises to repay the partnership if the person ultimately is determined not to be entitled to be indemnified under subsection (c).

(e) A partnership may purchase and maintain insurance on behalf of a partner against liability asserted against or incurred by the partner in that capacity or arising from that status even if, under Section 105(c)(7), the partnership agreement could not eliminate or limit the person's liability to the partnership for the conduct giving rise to the liability.

The case below discusses the policy difference between indemnification in corporations and Delaware LLCs. In reading this case, consider these questions: (1) What is the governing policy for indemnification in corporations? (2) What is it for Delaware LLCs?

SANDT V. ENERGY MAINTENANCE SERVICES GROUP I, LLC

534 S.W.3d 626 (Tex. App. 2017)

JANE BLAND, JUSTICE.

Jim Sandt was a former officer and shareholder of Energy Maintenance Services Group I, LLC, a closely held Delaware limited liability company. Timothy Nesler was the chief executive officer of Energy Maintenance. In 2005, Sandt sued Energy Maintenance and Nesler. The gravamen of Sandt's suit was that Energy Maintenance [and] Nesler wrongfully had diluted Sandt's ownership interest in Energy Maintenance, committing fraud and breach of fiduciary duty.

In 2007, while Sandt's suit was pending, Energy Maintenance's board of directors agreed to indemnify Nesler for any liability arising out of or relating to the *Sandt* litigation. The board memorialized that agreement in a company resolution:

> RESOLVED, that the Company shall indemnify Nesler in full against all damages, claims, judgments, fines and costs, including costs of defense, investigation and settlement and the cost of separate counsel, if any, together with all other expenses and damages of any kind, including punitive damages, if any, as and when incurred which arise out of or are related in any way to the Sandt litigation.

The resolution further recites that, as required by the limited liability company agreement as a precondition to indemnification, the board determined that Nesler had acted in good faith and in a manner that he reasonably believed was in, and not opposed to, Energy Maintenance's best interests:

> RESOLVED, that pursuant to Section 8.3 of the Company's LLC Agreement, and with respect to the events that are the subject of the Sandt litigation, the Board has determined that indemnification of Nesler is proper under the circumstances because he has met the standard of conduct set forth in Section 8.1 of the LLC agreement.

The *Sandt* lawsuit went to trial about two years after the board had agreed to indemnify Nesler. A jury found in favor of Sandt and against both Energy Maintenance and Nesler. The jury found that Nesler had breached his fiduciary duty to Sandt by diluting Sandt's interest in the company. It further found that Energy Maintenance and Nesler had committed statutory fraud against Sandt. The judgment awarded $780,000 in damages and attorney's fees to Sandt.

The defendants in the *Sandt* case appealed the judgment. While the appeal was pending, Energy Maintenance's primary creditor took control of the company and fired Nesler from his position as chief executive officer.

In 2011, a new board of directors voted by written consent to "revoke" the indemnification that the board had authorized in 2007 "effective as of the date indemnification was purportedly granted." In support of its revocation, the board passed a resolution stating that its "investigation to date indicates that Nesler misrepresented to the Board the facts, circumstances and status of the Sandt Matter."

[Subsequently, Energy Maintenance settled with Sandt, but Nesler did not. Nesler sought indemnity from Energy Maintenance. Energy Maintenance refused to provide it and sued Nesler, seeking a declaration that it did not owe him indemnity. Energy Maintenance contended that the jury's findings of fraud and breach of fiduciary duty against Nesler in the *Sandt* litigation alleviated the company's indemnification obligation, and it asserted that revocation of its agreement to indemnify Nesler was proper because Nesler had misled the board of directors about the *Sandt* litigation. Nesler counterclaimed for breach of contract, seeking indemnity and his attorney's fees. The trial court granted Nesler's summary judgment motion, ruling that Nesler was entitled to indemnity based on the board's 2007 indemnity resolution. Energy Maintenance appealed.]

Energy Maintenance is a limited liability company formed under Delaware law; thus, Delaware law controls the interpretation of the company's formation agreement. Under Delaware law, a limited liability company may indemnify any member, manager, or another "against any and all claims and demands whatsoever," subject to whatever standards or restrictions are included in its company agreement. 6 Del. Code § 18–108. For limited liability companies, Delaware law "defers completely to the contracting parties to create and delimit rights and obligations with respect to indemnification."

It is the express policy of Delaware's limited liability company statute "to give the maximum effect to the principle of freedom of contract and to the enforceability of limited liability company agreements." 6 Del. Code § 18–1101(b). A member's rights begin and end with the company agreement; once the agreement is executed, a member "can be virtually certain that the agreement will be enforced in accordance with its terms." This generally means "that only where the agreement is inconsistent with mandatory statutory provisions will the members' agreement be invalidated." *Elf Atochem N. Am. v. Jaffari*, 727 A.2d 286, 292 (Del. 1999).

With its passage of the resolution in 2007, the board obligated the company to indemnify Nesler for the *Sandt* litigation under the limited liability company agreement. Article VIII of the agreement contains provisions for the advancement of litigation expenses and indemnification of members. Section 8.6 obligates the company to advance a member's litigation expenses before the final disposition of a lawsuit. Section 8.1 obligates the company to indemnify a member in connection with threatened, pending, or completed civil suits if the member acted in good faith and in a manner reasonably believed to be in or unopposed to the company's best interests. Sections 8.1 and 8.3 vest the board of directors with the power to determine whether this good-faith standard is met.

Good faith is not defined by the company agreement, but Section 8.4 provides that a member or director shall be deemed to have acted in good faith if his actions were based on:

- the company's records or books;
- information supplied by the company's representatives;
- advice of the company's legal counsel; or
- information or records given or reports made to the company by an independent certified public accountant, appraiser, or other expert.

The board's discretion to find that the good-faith standard is satisfied is not confined to these instances; Section 8.4 provides that their enumeration does not limit the circumstances under which the board may decide that the standard is met.

Section 8.3 provides that if the member or director is successful on the merits or otherwise successfully defends against the suit, he is entitled to indemnity without the need for board authorization. Defeat, however, does not foreclose indemnification. Section 8.1 provides that the termination of the suit by judgment or settlement does not create a presumption that a member failed to act in good faith. Even a criminal conviction does not create an adverse presumption such that the board must find bad faith. Rather, Section 8.7 elaborates that it is Energy Maintenance's policy to indemnify its members and directors to the fullest extent permitted by law.

Once the board has granted indemnity for the expenses associated with any litigation and judgment, the agreement does not provide for the later revocation of that indemnity. Section 8.10 specifies that any advancement of expenses or indemnification granted by the board shall continue even after the person has ceased to be a member or director, unless the board provided otherwise when it initially authorized or ratified the advancement or indemnity.

Despite the company agreement that vests the board with the authority to determine whether the conditions for authorizing indemnification have been met, Energy Maintenance contends that the jury's unfavorable verdict and the judgment against Nesler for fraud disproved his good faith and thereby provided a basis for the board to revoke its earlier grant of indemnity. The company relies on Delaware decisions construing that state's corporate indemnification statute, 8 Del. Code § 145, for the proposition that a jury's finding of fraud negates good faith as a matter of public policy.*

But the statutes governing Delaware corporations and Delaware limited liability companies are different. Unlike Section 145, which applies to corporations, the statute governing limited liability companies allows indemnity "against any and all claims and demands whatsoever," subject only to the express terms of the company agreement. 6 Del. Code § 18–108 [providing in full: "Subject to such standards and restrictions, if any, as are set forth in its limited liability company agreement, a limited liability company may, and shall have the power to, indemnify and hold harmless any member or manager or other person from and against any and all claims and demands whatsoever."]. This statute does not purport to adopt or incorporate Delaware's public policy regarding indemnity in the corporate context, and instead defers to the contracting parties to place limits on indemnification.

Turning to Energy Maintenance's company agreement, its terms contemplate indemnification in the event that a jury finds that a member's or director's acts were not made in good faith. Though the company

* Author's note: DGCL § 145(a) provides: "A corporation shall have power to indemnify any person who was or is a party or is threatened to be made a party to any threatened, pending or completed action, suit or proceeding, whether civil, criminal, administrative or investigative (other than an action by or in the right of the corporation) by reason of the fact that the person is or was a director, officer, employee or agent of the corporation *if the person acted in good faith* and in a manner the person reasonably believed to be in or not opposed to the best interests of the corporation." Section 145 does not authorize "the use of contracts to grant advancement and indemnification rights that are contrary to the limitations or prohibitions set forth in the other section 145 subsections, other statutes, court decisions, or public policy [and that] as far as § 145 is concerned, Delaware corporations lack the power to indemnify a party who did not act in good faith or in the best interests of the corporation." Sun-Times Media Grp. v. Black, 954 A.2d 380, 404 n.93 (Del. Ch. 2008). *See* Hermelin v. K-V Pharm. Co., 54 A.3d 1093, 1112 (Del. Ch. 2012) ("If the prosecution or the plaintiff in the underlying proceeding established that the indemnitee acted in bad faith, particularly through a showing that the indemnitee knew that his actions were damaging to the company or that his conduct was unlawful, that would be conclusive evidence that the [indemnitee] is not entitled to indemnification.").

agreement obligates Energy Maintenance to indemnify members and directors who acted in good faith, it vests the board with the authority to decide if they did so. The agreement expressly specifies that an adverse judgment does not create a presumption of bad faith, and states a company policy of indemnifying corporate officers to the fullest extent legally possible. Energy Maintenance's company agreement does not, in express and affirmative terms, make members and directors ineligible for indemnification previously granted simply because a jury finds that they did not act in good faith, and we cannot rewrite its company agreement to say something it does not. The agreement provides the board with the option of advancing the costs of litigation and leaving the indemnification question for a later time. As Energy Maintenance's later board acknowledged, however, the 2007 resolution was one that obligated the company to indemnify its officers in the *Sandt* suit, not one that merely advanced the officers' litigation expenses.

Energy Maintenance has not identified any decision in which a Delaware court upheld a Delaware corporation's decision to rescind an agreement to indemnify one of its officers or directors after an adverse jury decision. Delaware law is to the contrary, providing that an indemnified person's continued service to the firm provides the consideration necessary to form a binding contractual agreement. This general principle of contract is equally applicable to limited liability companies, like Energy Maintenance. Accordingly, unless Energy Maintenance had a contractual right to reconsider its decision to indemnify Nesler, it could not do so. Neither its company agreement nor the board's 2007 indemnity resolution reserved a right to revisit Nesler's right to indemnity. Energy Maintenance therefore could not rescind its agreement to indemnify him.

The case below discusses the issue of whether an indemnification agreement can be invalidated because it was averred to have been induced by fraud. In reading this case, consider these questions: (1) How can an indemnification agreement be invalidated on the ground that it was induced by fraud? (2) Can such a theory be abused? (3) Are there procedural implications for advancing such a theory?

TRASCENT MANAGEMENT CONSULTING, LLC v. BOURI

152 A.3d 108 (Del. 2016)

STRINE, CHIEF JUSTICE:

[Trascent Management Consulting, LLC] hired a top executive—George Bouri—and installed him as a part owner, Managing Principal, and member of the Board of Managers of Trascent with responsibility for human resources, IT, and finance, positions Bouri occupied for about sixteen months. When Trascent terminated Bouri and sued him, for among other things, violating his employment agreement, Bouri sought advancement to defend himself in accordance with the plain language of both his employment agreement and Trascent's LLC agreement. Trascent argued that the same employment contract on which many of its claims against Bouri were premised was induced by fraud and that Bouri could not receive advancement because the employment agreement was thereby invalid (and presumably that he would not have become a member of Trascent's board, and thus be entitled to advancement, under the LLC agreement absent that contract). The Court of Chancery refused to countenance that defense to advancement, relying on the plain language of the agreements, which required that advancement be provided until a court made a final, nonappealable determination that indemnification was not required, and on the summary nature of the proceedings under 6 *Del. C.* § 18–108, the LLC analogue to 8 *Del. C.* § 145. Trascent has appealed, alleging that the Court of Chancery erred in making that ruling.

The sole argument of Trascent on appeal is that the Court of Chancery erred by enforcing the plain language of the employment agreement and LLC agreement, which contain almost identical language, giving Bouri a right to advancement:

> Unless a determination has been made by final, nonappealable order of a court of competent jurisdiction that indemnification is not required, [Trascent] shall, upon the request of Executive, advance or promptly reimburse Executive's reasonable costs of investigation, litigation or appeal, including reasonable attorneys' fees; provided, however, that Executive shall, as a condition of Executive's right to receive such advances or reimbursements, undertake in writing to repay promptly the Company for all such advancements and reimbursements if a court of competent jurisdiction determines that Executive is not entitled to indemnification.

The LLC Agreement's advancement provision varies only in its use of "Covered Person" instead of "Executive." Trascent argues that Bouri fraudulently induced the employment contract and LLC agreement by making misrepresentations to Trascent's founder during employment negotiations. Specifically, Trascent alleges that Bouri was not truthful about the circumstances surrounding his departure from his previous employer, and materially misstated his personal financial situation. Trascent argues that it relied on these misrepresentations and never would have entered into the employment agreement or made him a manager under the LLC agreement if it had known the truth. Yet, in the over sixteen months Bouri was associated with Trascent and its predecessor—much less the longer period where Rakesh Kishnan, Trascent's founder, had engaged with Bouri to encourage Bouri to join the firm—Trascent did not become aware of the alleged fraud.

The Court of Chancery reasoned that a plaintiff—Trascent—who had plainly promised its officer—Bouri—advancement could not escape that important obligation by suggesting that the employment contract was invalid, thereby delaying the officer's right to receive advancement until the plaintiff's plenary claim could be adjudicated. Rather, the Court of Chancery held that the right to advancement should be honored and enforced in accordance with the contract's plain terms to which Trascent and Bouri agreed at the beginning of Bouri's work, leaving Trascent with the right to proceed to prove that the contract was invalid and to recoup any improperly paid advancement in a plenary proceeding, such as a proceeding on indemnification or in the underlying suit for which advancement Bouri seeks to fund his defense. The Vice Chancellor tied this ruling to the plain language of the contract, stating "the contract language is clear: until a court determines that Trascent is not obligated to indemnify Bouri, Trascent must, upon Bouri's request and undertaking, cover both the legal fees and costs Bouri has incurred and those that he will incur as this litigation continues."

Trascent knew when it entered the contract that Bouri would be entitled to advancement "unless a determination has been made by final, nonappealable order of a court of competent jurisdiction that indemnification is not required." Thus, Trascent knew it agreed to provide a right, subject to expedited specific enforcement, and it could not reasonably believe that it could deny that right simply by alleging that the contract was invalid. Trascent may later show that Bouri is not entitled to indemnification by proving that the entire employment agreement or the advancement provision was invalid and fraudulently induced. But, Trascent cannot refuse to provide advancement by arguing that Bouri has the duty in an advancement proceeding to disprove Trascent's belated allegations. That is especially so in this case when Trascent sued Bouri to enforce its rights under the same contract in which Bouri's right to advancement is set forth, when it was Trascent's own decision to sue that triggered Bouri's right to advancement, and when there is a great deal of overlap with Trascent's substantive claims which seek to deprive Bouri of the benefits of his previous employment and lose any further rights under the employment agreement and LLC agreement, including advancement, on the grounds that he induced his hire by fraud.

Equity requires that any fraud in the inducement claim be brought with alacrity, because it hazards great prejudice to allow a party to reap the benefits of a contract for itself while reserving the right to claim the contract is invalid. Trascent not only employed Bouri as a Managing Principal for sixteen months without seeking to rescind the contract but then sued Bouri on the contract. Recognizing that allowing Trascent to avoid its contractual duty to make immediate advancement payments by making a belated fraudulent inducement claim would impair the public policies served by contractual advancement provisions made in reliance upon that provision of the DGCL as well as the Limited Liability Company Act, the Court of Chancery properly refused to delay enforcing the plain language of the contract. This determination was sound. "Advancement is an especially important corollary to indemnification as an inducement for attracting capable individuals into corporate service." Thus, we affirm the Court of Chancery's well-reasoned decision.

CHRYSLER GROUP LLC OPERATING AGREEMENT

Section 6.1 General Indemnity.

(a) To the fullest extent permitted by the LLC Act, the Company, to the extent of its assets legally available for that purpose, shall indemnify and hold harmless each Person who was or is made a party or is threatened to be made a party to or is involved in or participates as a witness with respect to any action, suit or proceeding, whether civil, criminal, administrative or investigative (each a "Proceeding"), by reason of the fact that he or she, or a Person of whom he or she is the legal representative, is or was a Director, an officer or employee, or is or was serving at the request of the Company as a manager, director, officer, employee, fiduciary or agent of another Entity (collectively, the "Indemnified Persons") from and against any and all loss, cost, damage, fine, expense (including reasonable fees and expenses of attorneys and other advisors and any court costs incurred by any Indemnified Person) or liability actually and reasonably incurred by such Person in connection with such Proceeding if such Person acted in good faith and in a manner such Person reasonably believed to be in or not opposed to the best interests of the Company and except that no indemnification shall be made in respect of any claim, issue or matter as to which such Person shall have been adjudged to be liable to the Company unless and only to the extent that the Court of Chancery of the State of Delaware or the court in which such action or suit was brought shall determine upon application that, despite the adjudication of liability but in view of all the circumstances of the case, such Person is fairly and reasonably entitled to indemnity for such expenses which the Court of Chancery or such other court shall deem proper. The termination of any Proceeding by judgment, order, settlement, conviction or upon a plea of nolo contendere or its equivalent, shall not, of itself, create a presumption that the Person did not act in good faith or in a manner such Person reasonably believed to be in or not opposed to the best interests of the Company.

(b) The Company shall pay in advance or reimburse reasonable expenses (including advancing reasonable costs of defense) incurred by an Indemnified Person who is or is threatened to be named or made a defendant or a respondent in a Proceeding; provided, however, that as a condition to any such advance or reimbursement, such Indemnified

Person shall agree that it shall repay the same to the Company if such Indemnified Person is finally judicially determined by a court of competent jurisdiction not to be entitled to indemnification under this ARTICLE VI.

(c) The Company shall not be required to indemnify a Person in connection with a Proceeding initiated by such Person against the Company or any of its Subsidiaries if the Proceeding was not authorized by the Board of Directors. The ultimate determination of entitlement to indemnification of any Indemnified Person shall be made by the Board of Directors in such manner as the Board of Directors may determine.

(d) Any and all indemnity obligations of the Company with respect to any Indemnified Person shall survive any termination of this Agreement. The indemnification and other rights provided for in this ARTICLE VI shall inure to the benefit of the heirs, executors and administrators of any Person entitled to such indemnification.

Section 6.2 Rights Non-Exclusive. The rights to indemnification and the payment of expenses incurred in defending any Proceeding in advance of its final disposition conferred in this ARTICLE VI shall not be exclusive of any other right which any Person may have or hereafter acquire under any Law, provision of this Agreement, any other agreement, any vote of Members or Directors or otherwise.

F. INFORMATION RIGHTS

Owners of firms have information rights. They should be informed of matters concerning the firm's business and governance. To vote on an informed basis, they require information pertaining to the matter on which they are asked to vote. They require information to monitor the firm and to exercise their governance rights.

1. CORPORATIONS

Shareholders have a right to demand an inspection of the corporation's books and records: "Any stockholder shall have the right to inspect for any proper purpose the corporation's stock ledger, a list of its stockholders, and its other books and records." DGCL § 220(b). This right is qualified by the requirement that the demand be for a "proper purpose." A shareholder's desire to investigate wrongdoing or mismanagement is a proper purpose. Courts may place procedural burdens to limit the potential for abuse or improper fishing expeditions. *See* Seinfeld v. Verizon Communications, Inc., 909 A.2d 117, 123 (Del. 2006) (requiring a "credible basis" for a proper claim based on "some evidence").

Directors have a continuing fiduciary duty to disclose information that is grounded in the board's fiduciary duties of care and loyalty.

> A director's duties of care and loyalty apply when directors communicate with stockholders. A director's specific disclosure obligations are defined by the context in which the director communicates. One context is a communication associated with a request for stockholder action. Stockholder action has included approving corporate transactions (mergers, sale of assets, or charter amendments) and making investment decisions (purchasing and tendering stock or making an appraisal election). When directors request discretionary stockholder action, they must disclose fully and fairly all material facts within their control bearing on the request. This application of the duties of care and loyalty is referred to as the "fiduciary duty of disclosure."

Dohmen v. Goodman, 234 A.3d 1161 (Del. 2020). The duty of disclosure requires "complete candor," which requires "no more than the duty to disclose all material facts when seeking stockholder action." Malone v. Brincat, 722 A.2d 5, 11 (Del. 1998).

Public companies are also subject to federal disclosure rules arising from federal securities law. Among other things, federal law requires continuing disclosures of financial results through the Form 10-Q (unaudited quarterly financial results) and Form 10-K (audited annual financial results), and major material events as they occur through the Form 8-K (current report). With respect to shareholder actions, companies must provide proxy statements containing disclosures on the matters upon which shareholder proxies are solicited. For public companies, federal securities law provides a vast, complex, and comprehensive requirement for the mandatory disclosure of information to public shareholders.

2. NBEs

NBE laws provide owners a right to information. RUPA § 408; ULPA (2001) § 304, § 407; RULLCA § 410. This right is nonwaivable and mandatory, and the charter agreement may not "unreasonably restrict" it. RUPA § 105(c)(4); ULPA (2001) § 105(c)(9); RULLCA § 105(c)(8).

The following are the RULLCA provisions on the right to information. The ULPA (2001) § 304, § 407 and RUPA § 408 provide functionally the same provisions as to partners as the RULLCA as to members and managers. The RULLCA provides elaborate procedures for making and meeting a demand for information. The procedures and the right to information are subject to contracting to the extent that they do not "unreasonably restrict" the core right to information.

RULLCA § 410. Rights to Information of Member, Manager, and Person Dissociated as Member.

(a) In a member-managed limited liability company:

(1) Any record regarding the company's activities, affairs, financial condition, and other circumstances, to the extent the information is material to the member's rights and duties under the operating agreement or this [act].

(2) The company shall furnish to each member:

(A) without demand, any information concerning the company's activities, affairs, financial condition, and other circumstances which the company knows and is material to the proper exercise of the member's rights and duties under the operating agreement or this [act]; and

(B) on demand, any other information concerning the company's activities, affairs, financial condition, and other circumstances, except to the extent the demand for the information demanded is unreasonable or otherwise improper under the circumstances.

(3) The duty to furnish information under paragraph (2) also applies to each member to the extent the member knows any of the information described in paragraph (2).

(b) In a manager-managed limited liability company:

(1) The informational rights stated in subsection (a) and the duty stated in subsection (a)(3) apply to the managers and not the members.

(2) A member may inspect and copy information regarding the activities, affairs, financial condition, and other circumstances of the company as is just and reasonable if:

(A) the member seeks the information for a purpose reasonably related to the member's interest as a member;

(B) the member makes a demand describing with reasonable particularity the information sought and the purpose for seeking the information; and

(C) the information sought is directly connected to the member's purpose.

(3) The company shall inform in a record the member that made the demand of:

(A) what information the company will provide in response to the demand and when and where the company will provide the information; and

(B) the company's reasons for declining, if the company declines to provide any demanded information.

(4) Whenever this [act] or an operating agreement provides for a member to vote on or give or withhold consent to a matter, before the vote is cast or consent is given or withheld, the company shall, without demand, provide the member with all information that is known to the company and is material to the member's decision.

(g) The rights under this section do not extend to a transferee.

(h) In addition to any restriction or condition stated in its operating agreement, a limited liability company, as a matter within the ordinary course of its activities and affairs, may impose reasonable restrictions and conditions on access to and use of information to be furnished under this section, including designating information confidential and imposing nondisclosure and safeguarding obligations on the recipient. In a dispute concerning the reasonableness of a restriction under this subsection, the company has the burden of proving reasonableness.

CHRYSLER GROUP LLC OPERATING AGREEMENT

Section 11.1 Schedule of Members. The Company shall maintain and keep at its principal office the Schedule of Members on which it shall set forth the name and notice address of each Member, and the aggregate number of Membership Interests of such Member at any time.

Section 11.2 Books and Records; Other Documents.

(a) The Company shall keep, or cause to be kept, (i) complete and accurate books and records of account of the Company, (ii) minutes of the proceedings of meetings of the Members, the Board of Directors and any committee thereof and (iii) a current list of the Directors and Officers and their notice addresses. Any of the foregoing books, minutes or records may be in written form or in any other form capable of being accurately and completely converted into written form within a reasonable time. The Company shall, and shall cause its Subsidiaries to, (A) make and keep financial records in reasonable detail that accurately and fairly reflect all financial transactions and dispositions of the assets of the Company and its Subsidiaries and (B) maintain a system of internal accounting controls sufficient to provide reasonable assurances that (1) transactions are executed in accordance with authorization by the Person in charge and are recorded so as to provide proper financial statements and maintain accountability for assets and (2) safeguards are established to prevent unauthorized persons from having access to the assets.

(b) At all times the Company shall maintain at its principal office a copy of the Certificate of Formation, including any amendments thereto, copies of this Agreement and all amendments hereto, and all other records required to be maintained pursuant to the LLC Act.

(c) The Company shall maintain books for the purpose of registering the Transfer of Membership Interests.

Section 11.3 Reports and Audits.

(a) Promptly upon request, the Company shall, at its cost and expense, furnish, or cause to be furnished, to each Member such information relating to the financial condition, operations of the Company or any other aspect of the Company or its business in possession of the Company as any such Member may from time to time reasonably request.

(b) Each Member shall have the right, at all reasonable times and upon reasonable notice during normal business hours, and at its own expense, so long as such access does not unreasonably interfere with the normal operation of the Company, to examine and make copies of or extracts from the books of account of the Company or any other Company record for any purpose reasonably related to such Member's interest as a Member of the Company, including to satisfy any public reporting obligations of such Member under applicable law and the rules of any securities exchange, and for federal, state, local or foreign income or franchise tax purposes. Such examination rights may be exercised through any designated agent or employee of such Members, as applicable, or their respective Affiliates. The parties agree that any such examination is not intended to duplicate in its entirety the audit conducted by the Independent Auditor.

Section 11.4 Financial Statements and Other Information.

(a) The Members shall be supplied with annual (audited) and condensed quarterly (unaudited but reviewed) consolidated financial statements of the Company in form and substance reasonably satisfactory to Fiat Parent, together with such other financial statements and supporting information as Fiat Parent may reasonably request to facilitate compliance with its financial reporting, record keeping and internal control requirements.

(b) The Members shall be supplied with all Company information reasonably necessary to enable each Member to prepare its federal, state, local and foreign income Tax Returns. Such information shall be prepared by the Company, and the Company shall use its reasonable best efforts to deliver such information to each Member promptly in light of the timing applicable to the purpose for which such information is to be used by such Member.

(c) If a Member or Affiliate of such Member is required by Law or any accounting principles (including GAAP) applied by such Member to consolidate or otherwise reflect the financial results of the Company into such Member's financial statements, then the Company shall provide to such Member, reasonably promptly upon request (and, so long as such Member has timely made such request, within a sufficient period of time so as to enable such Member to comply with any Law or accounting requirement applicable to it), any information reasonably requested for such purposes.

Section 11.5 Independent Auditor. The Company and its Subsidiaries shall engage a Person to audit its financial statements (the "Independent Auditor") that (a) is an independent public accounting firm within the meaning of the American Institute of Certified Public Accountants' Code of Professional Conduct (American Institute of Certified Public Accountants, Professional Standards, vol. 2, et seq. 101), (b) is a registered public accounting firm (as defined in Section 2(a)(12) of the Sarbanes Oxley Act of 2002 (the "Sarbanes-Oxley Act")), and (c) would not be in violation of the auditor independence requirements of the Sarbanes-Oxley Act by reason of its acting as the auditor of the Company and its Subsidiaries.

G. ISSUES TO CONSIDER FOR NBEs

1. DESIGNING THE MANAGEMENT STRUCTURE

The laws of NBEs permit a great degree of variation in management structures. Only the LP form requires a specific structure. The selection of the business form, however, is meaningful with respect to management structure. Some forms are better suited for particular businesses by virtue of the aggregate of default rules and case law.

By requiring a two-tier structure with the general partner serving as a manager, the LP is a vehicle for passive investment by limited partners. The LP form has been commonly used in investments that require significant capital provided by limited partners and specific managerial expertise provided by general partners. Such investments include real estate, investment management, and venture capital businesses.

A general partnership is better suited for a business in which all owners seek to retain some degree of agency authority, and managerial participation. Its default rules are conducive to collective management with authority held by all owners. A law firm is a quintessential example, and it is no surprise that many law firms are organized as LLPs, which is a general partnership with the benefit of limited liability. However, even in general partnerships, the number of partners may be so great that the partnership must institute some sort of centralized management structure to handle day-to-day business operations, which partnership law permits.

The LLC form is popular because the statute provides the greatest degree of contractual flexibility. A member-managed LLC can mimic a general partnership. A manager-managed LLC can mimic an LP or a corporation. This flexibility provides "room to grow" as the firm evolves in its lifecycle. Perhaps the firm starts small with just a few members, and then it grows and requires professional managers who may not be members. Such transitions may require entities to convert to other business forms, but the LLC form may accommodate such growth through rearrangements in the contract, *i.e.*, operating agreement.

In addition to the selection of the basic management form, an organizer should consider other details.

- Should owners or non-owner manage?
- Should there be a single layer of management or multiple layers as seen in a corporation with a board and officers?
- What are the limits of agency authority and scope of managerial decisions and functions?

2. REQUIRED OWNER APPROVALS

When owners are not managers, the organizer must consider the matters that require approval of owners. This is seen in corporation law where shareholders vote on their representative managers (the board of directors), and certain fundamental transactions such as mergers and sale of all or substantially all assets. The approval process provides a check on certain extraordinary transactions. In addition to all approval matters, the vote threshold is also another significant matter.

3. SELECTING AND REMOVING MANAGERS

Lawyers and owners must consider the selection and removal of managers. As to qualification and selection, they should consider:

- Must a manager also be an owner?
- Must a manager be a natural person?
- If a manager is an entity, what happens if there is a change of control in the entity?
- How is a manager selected?

With respect to the last question, the selection mechanism is some form of approval by owners. The selection process can involve a range of possibilities, for example: (1) for entities requiring a formal management structure, a periodic election with a formalized procedure for nomination and election; or (2) for less formal entities, an ad hoc process of selection upon need, such as a recommendation by other managers followed by a vote of owners or an owner-initiated hiring process. One should consider whether other managers should have a vote, whether voting should be class vote among identified groups or cumulative voting, and whether the voting threshold should be majority, supermajority, or unanimous.

As to removal of managers, these questions should be considered:

- What are the bases for removal of a manager?
- How is removal initiated?
- What are the voting structure and requirements for removal of a manager?

If removal of a manager is for cause only, the definition of cause should be set forth in the charter agreement. Possibilities include: all bases for dissociation of an owner (such as bankruptcy, material or willful violation of charter agreement, disability, or incapacity), violation of law, fraud, gross negligence or recklessness in performance of duties.

In smaller firms, the initiation of removal procedure may be informal. In larger firms, lawyers and owners should consider the removal process. The possibilities for the removal process are several, for example: majority vote of managers; manager recommendation voted upon by owners; owner-initiated vote upon recommendation of a threshold ownership stake. The vote threshold to approval the removal action should be considered.

H. PROBLEM: ENTREPRENEURS THINK SERIOUSLY ABOUT GOVERNANCE

After Morgan Money's foray into the plastic sourcing on behalf of PB Optique Option, Piers and Blake called a company retreat of all owners. While not ideal due to the premium cost, the contract with Pacifico Plastic Recycling, Inc., was "not a complete disaster." But it put pressure on the company to execute its business plan. The high cost also made it likely that they will have to seek more financing at some point in the future.

Based on initial financing, the members of the company were: Piers, Blake, Morgan Money, Art Estic, and Nicki Song. They unanimously agreed that "things have started off messily." The agenda for the company retreat was: "How should we govern PBOO?" They unanimously agreed that the company needed a "reset."

Since the company was still small, the members agreed that "all matter were on the table for negotiating a better agreement among the owners," and that an amended operating agreement may be needed. The amount of cash contributions provided by each owner were, of course, hard facts and a starting point of the company "reset": $100,000 Piers, $0 Blake, $200,000 Morgan Money, $200,000 Nicki Song, and $0 Art Estic. Another hard fact is that Piers and Blake must have management authority, each with equal authority, since they are the indispensable entrepreneurs in this venture. Piers and Blake are a unified interest group in the firm.

The retreat should focus on all issues: economics, governance, and management. Since the company has not started substantial operations and has had no economic returns as yet, which makes a "reset" a bit easier.

QUESTIONS

1. Is there a need to convert PB Optique Option LLC into another entity form due to differences in management structure of different entity forms?

2. What kind of a basic form of management structure would be best?

3. Should Money, Song, and Estic continue to have roles in management? What are some of the items that Money, Estic, and Song can negotiation in light of the unavoidable fact that Piers and Blake will have substantial management control? Indicate specific negotiation terms.

4. The Pacifico Plastic Recycling episode taught everyone the consequences of agency. How should the members deal with such possibilities?

CHAPTER 7

FIDUCIARY DUTY

■ ■ ■

A. INTRODUCTION TO FIDUCIARY DUTIES

1. THE NATURE OF FIDUCIARY DUTIES

The concept of fiduciary duty is one of the most important issues, if not *the* most important, in business organization laws. A fiduciary relationship exists when one person places special trust in and reliance on the judgment of another or where one person has a special duty to protect the interests of another. The law of agency provides an initial orientation: "An agent has a fiduciary duty to act loyally for the principal's benefit in all matters connected with the agency relationship." Restatement (Third) of Agency § 8.01. A fiduciary does not stand in a transactional relationship, but must consider the interest of those with whom she has a special relationship. Courts distinguish fiduciary relationships from arm's length commercial arrangements. A fiduciary is governed by, as Cardozo put it, "something stricter than the morals of the marketplace." Meinhard v. Salmon, 164 N.E. 545, 546 (N.Y. 1928) ("Not honesty alone, but the punctilio of an honor the most sensitive, is then the standard of behavior.").

Some courts have described fiduciary duties as an equitable "gap-filler." *See* The Haynes Family Trust v. Kinder Morgan G.P., Inc., 2016 WL 912184, at *1 n.2 (Del. 2016); Auriga Capital Corp. v. Gatz Properties, 40 A.3d 839, 853 (Del. Ch. 2012); Clancy v. King, 954 A.2d 1092, 1101 (Md. 2008). One conception of a firm is that it is a bundle of express and implied contracts among factors of production. Under this perspective, all contracts are said to be incomplete because parties cannot contract for all possible contingencies a business enterprise may encounter. Fiduciary duties address situations in which an incomplete contract leaves gaps in the agreement with respect to permissible and impermissible conduct among owners and managers based on an implied understanding of a relationship founded on trust. Courts fill in these gaps by applying principles of equity to *ex post* situations that the parties *ex ante* had not specifically addressed or considered in the contract.

Fiduciary duties have also been recognized to arise from principles of tort law. The Delaware courts have characterized a breach of fiduciary duty as an "equitable tort." In re Rural Metro Corp., 88 A.3d 54, 98 (Del. Ch. 2014). *See* Hampshire Gp., Ltd. v. Kuttner, 2010 WL 2739995, at *54 (Del. Ch. 2010) ("A breach of fiduciary duty is easy to conceive of as an equitable tort."); Hamilton Partners, L.P. v. Englard, 11 A.3d 1180, 1211 (Del. Ch. 2010) ("The underlying tort (albeit an equitable tort) is breach of fiduciary duty."); J. Travis Laster & Michelle D. Morris, *Breaches of Fiduciary Duty and the Delaware Uniform Contribution Act*, 11 Del. L. Rev. 71, 71 (2010) (noting that "a breach of a fiduciary duty is in fact a tort, although a unique species historically called an 'equitable tort' "); Robert J. Rhee, *The Tort Foundation of Duty of Care and Business Judgment*, 88 Notre Dame L. Rev. 1139, 1143 (2013) ("Tort theory provides not just the lexicon of liability, but the foundational principles of the duty and liability of corporate boards.").

When thinking about fiduciary duties in the context of business firms, Justice Felix Frankfurter's statement in *SEC v. Chenery Corp.*, 318 U.S. 80 (1943), is worth noting:

> But to say that a man is a fiduciary only begins the analysis; it gives direction to further inquiry. To whom is he a fiduciary? What obligations does he owe as fiduciary? In what respect has he failed to discharge these obligations? And what are the consequences of his deviation from duty? Determination of what is "fair and equitable" calls for the application of ethical standards to particular sets of facts. But these standards are not static.

Certain persons are placed in a position of trust and confidence by others such that law imposes fiduciary duties. Business organization laws provide specific rules on fiduciary duties: What are they? Who owes them? What constitutes a breach? Fiduciary duties are generally two: the duty of care and the duty of loyalty. As the Frankfurter quote implies, not all persons in a firm owe fiduciary duties. The law imposes duties on those persons who occupy a special position in the firm, a position that empowers the person to exercise the levers of control and management.

2. FIDUCIARY DUTIES IN CORPORATION LAW

Those who control the corporation are directors and officers, who together participate in its management. *See* DGCL § 141(a) ("The business and affairs of every corporation shall be managed by or under the direction of a board of directors"); *id.* § 142(a) ("Every corporation shall have such officers with such titles and duties as shall be stated in the bylaws or in a resolution of the board of directors"). Shareholders with small stakes—*e.g.*, most shareholders in public corporations—do not control the corporation. They do not owe fiduciary duties to the corporation or other shareholders. *See* Kerbawy v. McDonnell, 2015 WL 4929198, at *14 (Del. Ch. 2015) ("non-controlling stockholders generally do not owe fiduciary duties").

It is axiomatic that directors and officers owe the fiduciary duties of care and loyalty. *See* Gantler v. Stephens, 965 A.2d 695, 708–09 (Del. 2009) ("Officers of Delaware corporations, like directors, owe fiduciary duties of care and loyalty, and the fiduciary duties of officers are the same as those of directors."). Also, since a controlling shareholder exercises control, which may result in unfair benefit at the expense of minority shareholders, he owes fiduciary duties to the corporation and its minority shareholders. He has a duty to exercise control in a fair and equitable manner. He must exercise control to benefit all shareholders proportionately and may not benefit himself solely or harm minority shareholders.

> A director is a fiduciary. So is a dominant or controlling stockholder or group of stockholders. Their powers are powers in trust. Their dealings with the corporation are subjected to rigorous scrutiny and where any of their contracts or engagements with the corporation is challenged the burden is on the director or stockholder not only to prove the good faith of the transaction but also to show its inherent fairness from the viewpoint of the corporation and those interested therein. The essence of the test is whether or not under all the circumstances the transaction carries the earmarks of an arm's length bargain. If it does not, equity will set it aside. [A director] cannot manipulate the affairs of his corporation to their detriment and in disregard of the standards of common decency and honesty. He cannot by the intervention of a corporate entity violate the ancient precept against serving two masters. He cannot by the use of the corporate device avail himself of privileges normally permitted outsiders in a race of creditors. He cannot utilize his inside information and his strategic position for his own preferment. He cannot violate rules of fair play by doing indirectly through the corporation what he could not do directly. He cannot use his power for his personal advantage and to the detriment of the stockholders and creditors no matter how absolute in terms that power may be and no matter how meticulous he is to satisfy technical requirements. For that power is at all times subject to the equitable limitation that it may not be exercised for the aggrandizement, preference, or advantage of the fiduciary to the exclusion or detriment of the Cestuis. Where there is a violation of these principles, equity will undo the wrong or intervene to prevent its consummation.

Jones v. H. F. Ahmanson & Co., 460 P.2d 464, 471–72 (Cal. 1969) (en banc) (quoting Pepper v. Litton, 308 U.S. 295 (1939)). *See* Gentile v. Rossette, 906 A.2d 91, 103 (Del. 2006) ("The harm to the minority shareholder plaintiffs resulted from a breach of a fiduciary duty owed to them by the controlling shareholder, namely, not to cause the corporation to effect a transaction that would benefit the fiduciary at the expense of the minority stockholders."); Weinberger v. UOP, Inc., 457 A.2d 701, 710–11 (Del. 1983) (holding that a controlling shareholder, the parent company of a majority-owned subsidiary, did not fulfill its obligation to the minority shareholders of the subsidiary).

Corporation law does not permit private ordering of fiduciary duties. Directors and officers have no power to amend, alter, or eliminate these duties.[1] Fiduciary duties are mandatory and nonwaivable. *See* Sutherland v. Sutherland, 2009 WL 857468, at *4 (Del. Ch. 2009) ("While such a provision [eliminating fiduciary duty] is permissible under the Delaware Limited Liability Company Act and the Delaware Revised Uniform Limited Partnership Act, where freedom of contract is the guiding and overriding principle, it is expressly forbidden by the DGCL.").

B. TRADITIONAL APPROACH IN NBEs

1. GENERAL PARTNERSHIP

In a partnership, all partners are co-owners and co-managers. RUPA § 401(h) ("Each partner has equal rights in the management and conduct of the partnership's business."). They jointly control and manage the business. They owe fiduciary duty. *Id.* § 409(a) ("A partner owes to the partnership and the other partners the duties of loyalty and care"). Like the law of torts, the fact that duty exists is merely the start of the inquiry. The question is whether a fiduciary has breached that duty. The answer may depend on the scope of that duty.

The case below illustrates the application of common law fiduciary duty. In reading this case, consider these questions: (1) What was Salmon's conduct wrongful? (2) In hindsight, what should Salmon have done?

MEINHARD V. SALMON

164 N.E. 545 (N.Y. 1928)

CARDOZO, C. J.

Louisa Gerry leased to the defendant Walter J. Salmon the premises known as the Hotel Bristol at the northwest corner of Forty-Second street and Fifth Avenue in the city of New York. The lease was for a term of 20 years, commencing May 1, 1902, and ending April 30, 1922. The lessee

---

[1] *See* Delaware General Corporation Law § 102(b)(7) (prohibiting charter provision that eliminates the duty of loyalty, but permitting the elimination of money damages for a breach of the duty of care); 800 South Wells Commercial LLC v. Cadden, 103 N.E.3d 875, 885 (Ill. App. 2018) ("Plaintiff is not a regular corporation such that common-law propositions concerning officers and their duties dominate this conversation or are even relevant. When dealing with limited liability companies and the fiduciary duties owed to them, we must look—first, foremost, and primarily—to the Act."); Productivity Technologies Corp. v. Levine, 268 F.Supp.3d 940, 947 (E.D. Mich. 2017) ("The defendants have not cited any authority suggesting that Delaware's Limited Liability Company Act applies to corporations. And as the plaintiff notes, [DLLCA] section 18–1101(c), if applied to corporations, would conflict with a section of Delaware's General Corporation Law that does not allow directors to escape liability [which is] Del. Code tit. 8 § 102(7)."); Williams v. 5300 Columbia Pike Corp., 891 F.Supp. 1169, 1183 n.30 (E.D. Va. 1995) ("Yet, a by-law amendment surely cannot eliminate directors' fiduciary duty of loyalty and fairness to shareholders.").

undertook to change the hotel building for use as shops and offices at a cost of $200,000. Alterations and additions were to be accretions to the land.

Salmon, while in course of treaty with the lessor as to the execution of the lease, was in course of treaty with Meinhard, the plaintiff, for the necessary funds. The result was a joint venture with terms embodied in a writing. Meinhard was to pay to Salmon half of the moneys requisite to reconstruct, alter, manage, and operate the property. Salmon was to pay to Meinhard 40 percent of the net profits for the first five years of the lease and 50 percent for the years thereafter. If there were losses, each party was to bear them equally. Salmon, however, was to have sole power to "manage, lease, underlet and operate" the building. There were to be certain preemptive rights for each in the contingency of death.

The two were coadventurers, subject to fiduciary duties akin to those of partners. As to this we are all agreed. The heavier weight of duty rested, however, upon Salmon. He was a coadventurer with Meinhard, but he was manager as well. During the early years of the enterprise, the building, reconstructed, was operated at a loss. If the relation had then ended, Meinhard as well as Salmon would have carried a heavy burden. Later the profits became large with the result that for each of the investors there came a rich return. For each the venture had its phases of fair weather and of foul. The two were in it jointly, for better or for worse.

When the lease was near its end, Elbridge Gerry had become the owner of the reversion. He owned much other property in the neighborhood, one lot adjoining the Bristol building on Fifth Avenue and four lots on Forty-Second Street. He had a plan to lease the entire tract for a long term to someone who would destroy the buildings then existing and put up another in their place. In the latter part of 1921, he submitted such a project to several capitalists and dealers. He was unable to carry it through with any of them. Then, in January 1922, with less than four months of the lease to run, he approached the defendant Salmon. The result was a new lease to the Midpoint Realty Company, which is owned and controlled by Salmon, a lease covering the whole tract, and involving a huge outlay. The term is to be 20 years, but successive covenants for renewal will extend it to a maximum of 80 years at the will of either party. The existing buildings may remain unchanged for seven years. They are then to be torn down, and a new building to cost $3,000,000 is to be placed upon the site. The rental, which under the Bristol lease was only $55,000, is to be from $350,000 to $475,000 for the properties so combined. Salmon personally guaranteed the performance by the lessee of the covenants of the new lease until such time as the new building had been completed and fully paid for.

The lease between Gerry and the Midpoint Realty Company was signed and delivered on January 25, 1922. Salmon had not told Meinhard anything about it. Whatever his motive may have been, he had kept the negotiations to himself. Meinhard was not informed even of the bare existence of a project. The first that he knew of it was in February, when the lease was an accomplished fact. He then made demand on the defendants that the lease be held in trust as an asset of the venture, making offer upon the trial to share the personal obligations incidental to the guaranty. The demand was followed by refusal, and later by this suit.

Joint adventurers, like copartners, owe to one another, while the enterprise continues, the duty of the finest loyalty.* Many forms of conduct permissible in a workaday world for those acting at arm's length, are forbidden to those bound by fiduciary ties. A trustee is held to something stricter than the morals of the marketplace. Not honesty alone, but the punctilio of an honor the most sensitive, is then the standard of behavior. As to this there has developed a tradition that is unbending and inveterate. Uncompromising rigidity has been the attitude of courts of equity when petitioned to undermine the rule of undivided loyalty by the "disintegrating erosion" of particular exceptions. Only thus has the level of conduct for fiduciaries been kept at a level higher than that trodden by the crowd. It will not consciously be lowered by any judgment of this court.

The owner of the reversion, Gerry, had vainly striven to find a tenant who would favor his ambitious scheme of demolition and construction. Baffled in the search, he turned to the defendant Salmon in possession of the Bristol, the keystone of the project. He figured to himself beyond a doubt that the man in possession would prove a likely customer. To the eye of an observer, Salmon held the lease as owner in his own right, for himself and no one else. He held it as a fiduciary, for himself and another, sharers in a common venture. If this fact had been proclaimed, if the lease by its terms had run in favor of a partnership, Gerry, we may fairly assume, would have laid before the partners, and not merely before one of them, his plan of reconstruction. The pre-emptive privilege, or, better, the pre-emptive opportunity, that was thus an incident of the enterprise, Salmon appropriate to himself in secrecy and silence. He might have warned Meinhard that the plan had been submitted, and that either would be free to compete for the award. If he had done this, we do not need to say whether he would have been under a duty, if successful in the competition, to hold the lease so acquired for the benefit of a venture than about to end, and thus prolong by indirection its responsibilities and duties. The trouble about his conduct is that he excluded his coadventurer from any chance to compete, from any chance to enjoy the opportunity for benefit that had come to him alone by virtue of his agency. This chance, if nothing more, he was under a duty to concede. The price of its denial is an extension of the trust at the option and for the benefit of the one whom he excluded.

---

* Author's note: The court characterized the relationship between Meinhard and Salmon as joint adventurerers. A joint venture is a form of a partnership. *See* Beard v. Beard, 44 A.2d 469, 472 (Md. 1945) ("There is no real distinction between a joint adventure and what is termed a partnership for a single transaction.").

No answer is it to say that the chance would have been of little value even if seasonably offered. Such a calculus of probabilities is beyond the science of the chancery. Salmon, the real estate operator, might have been preferred to Meinhard, the woolen merchant. On the other hand, Meinhard might have offered better terms, or reinforced his offer by alliance with the wealth of others. Perhaps he might even have persuaded the lessor to renew the Bristol lease alone, postponing for a time, in return for higher rentals, the improvement of adjoining lots. All these opportunities were cut away from him through another's intervention. He knew that Salmon was the manager. As the time drew near for the expiration of the lease, he would naturally assume from silence, if from nothing else, that the lessor was willing to extend it for a term of years, or at least to let it stand as a lease from year to year. Not impossibly the lessor would have done so, whatever his protestations of unwillingness, if Salmon had not given assent to a project more attractive. At all events, notice of termination, even if not necessary, might seem, not unreasonably, to be something to be looked for, if the business was over [and] another tenant was to enter. In the absence of such notice, the matter of an extension was one that would naturally be attended to by the manager of the enterprise, and not neglected altogether. There was nothing in the situation to give warning to any one that while the lease was still in being, there had come to the manager an offer of extension which he had locked within his breast to be utilized by himself alone. The very fact that Salmon was in control with exclusive powers of direction charged him the more obviously with the duty of disclosure, since only through disclosure could opportunity be equalized. If he might cut off renewal by a purchase for his own benefit when four months were to pass before the lease would have an end, he might do so with equal right while there remained many years. He might steal a march on his comrade under cover of the darkness, and then hold the captured ground. Loyalty and comradeship are not so easily abjured.

We have no thought to hold that Salmon was guilty of a conscious purpose to defraud. Very likely he assumed in all good faith that with the approaching end of the venture he might ignore his coadventurer and take the extension for himself. He had given to the enterprise time and labor as well as money. He had made it a success. Meinhard, who had given money, but neither time nor labor, had already been richly paid. Salmon had put himself in a position in which thought of self was to be renounced, however hard the abnegation. He was much more than a coadventurer. He was a managing coadventurer. For him and for those like him the rule of undivided loyalty is relentless and supreme. A different question would be here if there were lacking any nexus of relation between the business conducted by the manager and the opportunity brought to him as an incident of management. For this problem, there are distinctions of degree. If Salmon had received from Gerry a proposition to lease a building at a location far removed, he might have held for himself the privilege. Here the subject-matter of the new lease was an extension and enlargement of the subject-matter of the old one. A managing coadventurer appropriating the benefit of such a lease without warning to his partner might fairly expect to be reproached with conduct that was underhand, or lacking, to say the least, in reasonable candor, if the partner were to surprise him in the act of signing the new instrument. Conduct subject to that reproach does not receive from equity a healing benediction.

A question remains as to the form and extent of the equitable interest to be allotted to the plaintiff. The trust has been held to attach to the lease which was in the name of the defendant corporation. We think it ought to attach at the option of the defendant Salmon to the shares of stock which were owned by him. An equal division of the shares might lead to other hardships. It might take away from Salmon the power of control and management which under the plan of the joint venture he was to have from first to last. The number of shares to be allotted to the plaintiff should, therefore, be reduced to such an extent as may be necessary to preserve to the defendant Salmon the expected measure of dominion.

The version of the RUPA below takes an "uncabined" approach to fiduciary duty, which means that the scope of the duties of care and loyalty "includes" the listed items. Some statutes take a "cabin in" approach, which seeks to limit duties to the listed items. *See* Payne v. Hall, 458 P.3d 1001 (Mont. 2020) (noting that the LLC statute limited statutory fiduciary duties when it provides "*the only* fiduciary duties are the duty of loyalty and the duty of care"). A "cabin in" approach seeks to contain duties within the statutory prescription. Each state construes its statute and has developed a body of law on the scope of fiduciary duty.

RUPA § 409. Standards of Conduct for Partners.

(a) A partner owes to the partnership and the other partners the duties of loyalty and care stated in subsections (b) and (c).

(b) The fiduciary duty of loyalty of a partner includes the duties:

(1) to account to the partnership and hold as trustee for it any property, profit, or benefit derived by the partner:

(A) in the conduct or winding up of the partnership's business;

(B) from a use by the partner of the partnership's property; or

(C) from the appropriation of a partnership opportunity;

(2) to refrain from dealing with the partnership in the conduct or winding up of the partnership business as or on behalf of a person having an interest adverse to the partnership; and

(3) to refrain from competing with the partnership in the conduct of the partnership's business before the dissolution of the partnership.

(c) The duty of care of a partner in the conduct or winding up of the partnership business is to refrain from engaging in grossly negligent or reckless conduct, willful or intentional misconduct, or a knowing violation of law.

(d) A partner shall discharge the duties and obligations under this [act] or under the partnership agreement and exercise any rights consistently with the contractual obligation of good faith and fair dealing.

(e) A partner does not violate a duty or obligation under this [act] or under the partnership agreement solely because the partner's conduct furthers the partner's own interest.

(f) All the partners may authorize or ratify, after full disclosure of all material facts, a specific act or transaction by a partner that otherwise would violate the duty of loyalty.

(g) It is a defense to a claim under subsection (b)(2) and any comparable claim in equity or at common law that the transaction was fair to the partnership.

(h) If, as permitted by subsection (f) or the partnership agreement, a partner enters into a transaction with the partnership which otherwise would be prohibited by subsection (b)(2), the partner's rights and obligations arising from the transaction are the same as those of a person that is not a partner.

2. LIMITED PARTNERSHIP

The rules of fiduciary duty in LPs are simply stated: (1) limited partners do not owe fiduciary duty solely by reason of being a limited partner; (2) general partners owe fiduciary duty as defined in the statute; (3) all partners bear the obligation of good faith and fair dealing. If limited partners participate in the control of the LP, this circumstance may give rise to limited partners owing fiduciary duty as courts determine under principles of equity and fairness.

ULPA (2001) § 305. Limited Duties of Limited Partners.

(a) A limited partner shall discharge any duties to the partnership and the other partners under the partnership agreement and exercise any rights under this [act] or the partnership agreement consistently with the contractual obligation of good faith and fair dealing.

(b) Except as otherwise provided in subsection (a), a limited partner does not have any duty to the limited partnership or to any other partner solely by reason of acting as a limited partner.

(c) If a limited partner enters into a transaction with a limited partnership, the limited partner's rights and obligations arising from the transaction are the same as those of a person that is not a partner.

ULPA (2001) § 409. Standards of Conduct for General Partners.

(a) A general partner owes to the limited partnership and, subject to Section 901, the other partners the duties of loyalty and care stated in subsections (b) and (c).

(b) The fiduciary duty of loyalty of a general partner includes the duties:

(1) to account to the limited partnership and hold as trustee for it any property, profit, or benefit derived by the general partner:

(A) in the conduct or winding up of the partnership's activities and affairs;

(B) from a use by the general partner of the partnership's property; or

(C) from the appropriation of a partnership opportunity;

(2) to refrain from dealing with the partnership in the conduct or winding up of the partnership's activities and affairs as or on behalf of a person having an interest adverse to the partnership; and

(3) to refrain from competing with the partnership in the conduct or winding up of the partnership's activities and affairs.

(c) The duty of care of a general partner in the conduct or winding up of the limited partnership's activities and affairs is to refrain from engaging in grossly negligent or reckless conduct, willful or intentional misconduct, or knowing violation of law.

(d) A general partner shall discharge the duties and obligations under this [act] or under the partnership agreement and exercise any rights consistently with the contractual obligation of good faith and fair dealing.

(e) A general partner does not violate a duty or obligation under this [act] or under the partnership agreement solely because the general partner's conduct furthers the general partner's own interest.

(f) All the partners of a limited partnership may authorize or ratify, after full disclosure of all material facts, a specific act or transaction by a general partner that otherwise would violate the duty of loyalty.

> (g) It is a defense to a claim under subsection (b)(2) and any comparable claim in equity or at common law that the transaction was fair to the limited partnership.
>
> (h) If, as permitted by subsection (f) or the partnership agreement, a general partner enters into a transaction with the limited partnership which otherwise would be prohibited by subsection (b)(2), the general partner's rights and obligations arising from the transaction are the same as those of a person that is not a general partner.

Partnership statutes do not require a fiduciary's selfless sacrifice. RUPA § 409(e) and ULPA (2001) § 409(e) state that a partner does not violate a duty or obligation "solely because the general partner's conduct furthers the general partner's own interest." *See* RULLCA § 409(e) (same as to "member"). These provisions protect partners who exercise their rights and powers held in their *individual capacities* as partners and members. For example, a partner may lend money as a creditor and as such exercise the rights of a creditor, despite the fact that such exercise may be against the interest of the other partners; or, a partner may exercise his right to vote, a right held in his individual capacity, despite the fact that such exercise of vote right works to the detriment of other partners. Some partnership agreement may make this distinction clear. In *Bandera Master Fund LP v. Boardwalk Pipeline Partners, LP*, 2019 WL 4927053, at *10 (Del. Ch. 2019), the partnership agreement provided this provision:

> Whenever the General Partner makes a determination or takes or declines to take any other action in its individual capacity as opposed to in its capacity as the general partner of the Partnership, then the General Partner [is] entitled to make such determination or to take or decline to take such other action free of any fiduciary duty or obligation whatsoever to the Partnership, any Limited Partner or Assignee, and the General Partner shall not be required to act in good faith or pursuant to any other standard imposed by this Agreement [or] any other agreement contemplated hereby or under the Delaware Act or any other law, rule or regulation or at equity.

The court ruled that this agreement reflected the statutory rule: "Under this provision, when acting in its individual capacity, the General Partner does not owe any duty to the Partnership or its limited partners, can act in its own interest, and does not have to believe in good faith that its actions are in the best interest of the Partnership." *Id.*

General partners manage assets, engage in transactions, and control private information. When someone holds these powers, the potential for self-dealing, conflict of interest, and opportunism generally is significant. To illustrate this risk, consider the following hypothetical. Venture capital firm Chelsea Venture, L.P. has made equity investments in three companies and also manages them as the general partner on behalf of different limited partners. Its ownership stakes in each vary. Assume that Chelsea engages in Transactions B and C in accordance with the managerial authority established in the partnership agreement.

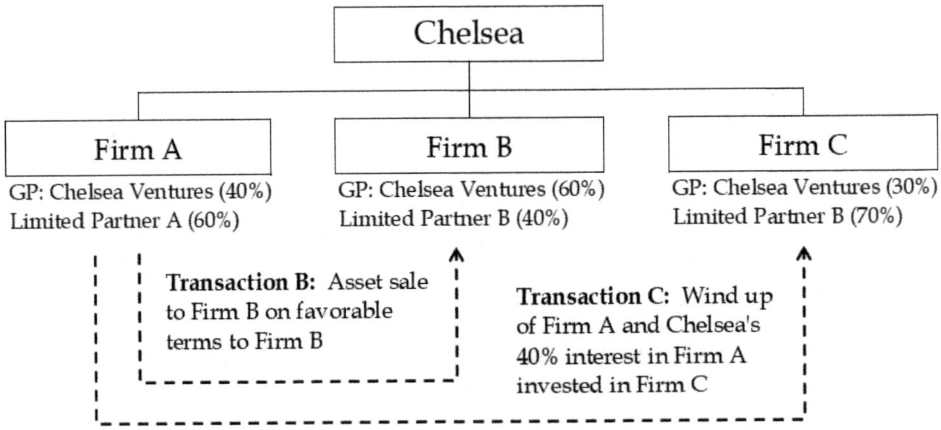

Consider Transaction B in which Firm A sells its assets to Firm B at favorable terms to Firm B. Chelsea benefits from a sweetheart deal because while it owns 40% of Firm A, it owns 60% of Firm B, thus net benefiting Chelsea by virtue of its greater ownership in Firm B.

Consider Transaction C in which Chelsea forces the dissolution and wind up of Firm A and uses the distribution to make an additional investment in Firm C, which would increase its ownership stake in Firm C. Why would it do so? Suppose Chelsea thought that Firm A was not as promising as it seemed at the time of the investment, but currently the outlook for Firm C looks highly promising. Clearly, there might be a conflict of interest between Chelsea and limited partner A.

The above hypothetical presents simple examples of the many possible ways in which control can result in opportunistic conduct. The Securities and Exchange Commission has warned about the potential conflict of interest in master limited partnerships.

> Generally, Master Limited Partnerships (MLPs) are exchange-traded investments that are focused on exploration, development, mining, processing, or transportation of minerals or natural resources. MLPs hold cash-generating assets such as oil and gas properties or pipelines. MLPs have certain characteristics that can make them attractive to some investors, including partnership tax consequences, limited liability to investors for the MLP's debts, and anticipated consistent distributions of cash. However, like all investments, MLPs have risks investors should consider before making an investment decision. *Those risks include governance features that can favor management over other*

investors, potential conflicts of interest, and concentrated exposure to a single industry or commodity.

Investor Bulletin: Master Limited Partnerships—An Introduction, U.S. Securities and Exchange Commission (May 18, 2016), *available at* https://www.sec.gov/oiea/investor-alerts-bulletins/ib_mlpintro.html.

In the course of time and experience, centralized management has proven to be a highly effective device for managing a venture in which there is diffuse ownership. Consider the success of the corporate form. There are many devices that can check potentially opportunistic conduct. The imposition of fiduciary duty and the means to enforce compliance through legal action are the most effective means. Contract devices can provide further checks. They could include the following:

- Removal of general partner by vote
- Voting requirement for certain fundamental transactions such as mergers and acquisitions, sale of substantially all assets, large capital raising
- Information disclosure requirement to further monitoring
- Approval of conflict of interest transactions
- Limitation on management powers of general partner
- Limitation on the purpose of the LP

Like corporate shareholders, partners and members are often legal entities. Corporation law requires that corporate managers must be natural persons. *See* DGCL § 141(b) (providing that a director shall be a "natural person"); Cal. Corp. Code § 164 (same); N.Y. Bus. Corp. L. § 701 (providing that a director "shall be at least eighteen years of age"); MBCA § 8.40(b) (providing that directors must be "individuals" which is defined as a natural person under § 1.40). Unlike corporate managers, managers and owners in NBEs can be, and often are, legal entities. *See* RULLCA § 102(9), (11), (15); RUPA § 102 (10), (14); ULPA (2001) § 102(13), (15). This means that bodiless, soulless legal fictions are said to owe fiduciary duties, which are founded on the notions of trust, honesty, fidelity, and confidence.

The case below deals with the issue of fiduciary duty in an LP when the general partner of the LP is a legal entity. In reading this case, consider these questions: (1) Who owes fiduciary duty? (2) What is the implication when fiduciary duty flows upstream to an ultimate natural person? (3) What is the underlying rationale for the court's ruling?

IN RE USACAFES, L.P. LITIGATION

600 A.2d 43 (Del. Ch. 1991)

ALLEN, CHANCELLOR.

These consolidated actions arise out of the purchase by Metsa Acquisition Corp. of substantially all of the assets of USACafes, L.P., a Delaware limited partnership at a cash price of $72.6 million or $10.25 per unit. Plaintiffs are holders of limited partnership units. They bring these cases as class actions on behalf of all limited partnership unitholders except defendants. The relief sought includes the imposition of constructive trusts on certain funds received by defendants in connection with the Metsa sale and an award of damages to the class resulting from the sale.

[The Partnership's general partner was USACafes General Partner, Inc., a Delaware corporation. Both the Partnership and the General Partner are named as defendants in this action. Additional defendants are individuals who sit on the board of directors of the General Partner, including the two shareholders who own all shares of the General Partner (the Wyly brothers). The plaintiffs allege that these persons received substantial cash payments, loan forgiveness, or other substantial personal benefits in connection with the Metsa purchase. The most central theory in the complaint involves an alleged breach of the duty of loyalty. It claims that the sale of the Partnership's assets was set at a low price, favorable to Metsa, because the directors of the General Partner all received substantial side payments, between $15 and $17 million, that induced them to authorize the sale of the Partnership assets for less than the price that a fair process would have yielded. Plaintiffs claim that some part at least of these "side payments" should have gone to the Partnership.]

The director defendants move under Rule 12(b)(6) to dismiss the breach of fiduciary duty claims asserting that, while the General Partner admittedly did owe fiduciary duties to the limited partners, they as directors of the General Partner owe no such duties to those persons.

The gist of this motion is the assertion that the directors of the General Partner owed the limited partners no duty of loyalty or care. In their view their only duty of loyalty was to the General Partner itself and to *its* shareholders (*i.e.*, the Wyly brothers). Thus, in alleging that the director defendants breached duties of loyalty and care running to them, the directors say the limited partners have asserted a legal nullity.

In my opinion the assertion by the directors that the independent existence of the corporate General Partner is inconsistent with their owing fiduciary duties directly to limited partners is incorrect.

While I find no corporation law precedents directly addressing the question whether directors of a corporate general partner owe fiduciary duties to the partnership and its limited partners, the answer to it seems to be clearly indicated by general principles and by analogy to trust law. I understand the principle of fiduciary duty, stated most generally, to be that one who controls property of another may not, without implied or express agreement, intentionally use that property in a way that benefits the holder of the control to the detriment of the property or its beneficial owner. There are, of course, other aspects—a fiduciary may not waste property even if no self interest is involved and must exercise care even when his heart is pure—but the central aspect of the relationship is, undoubtedly, fidelity in the control of property for the benefit of another.

The law of trusts represents the earliest and fullest expression of this principle in our law, but courts of equity have extended it to achieve substantial justice in a wide array of situations. Thus, corporate directors, even though not strictly trustees, were early on regarded as fiduciaries for corporate stockholders. When control over corporate property was recognized to be in the hands of shareholders who controlled the enterprise, the fiduciary obligation was found to extend to such persons as well.

While the parties cite no case treating the specific question whether directors of a corporate general partner are fiduciaries for the limited partnership, trust cases do stand for a principle that would extend a fiduciary duty to such persons in certain circumstances. The problem comes up in trust law because modernly corporations may serve as trustees of express trusts. Thus, the question has arisen whether directors of a corporate trustee may personally owe duties of loyalty to *cestui que trusts* of the corporation. A leading authority states the accepted answer:

> The directors and officers of [a corporate trustee] are certainly under a duty to the beneficiaries not to convert to their own use property of the trust administered by the corporation. Furthermore, the directors and officers are under a duty to the beneficiaries of trusts administered by the corporation not to cause the corporation to misappropriate the property. The breach of trust need not, however, be a misappropriation. Any officer [director cases are cited in support here] who knowingly causes the corporation to commit a breach of trust causing loss is personally liable to the beneficiary of the trust.
>
> Moreover, a director or officer of a trust institution who improperly acquires an interest in the property of a trust administered by the institution is subject to personal liability. He is accountable for any profit. Even where the trustee [itself] is not liable, however, because it had no knowledge that the director was making the purchase, the director is liable to the beneficiaries. The directors and officers are in a fiduciary relation not merely to the [corporation] but to the beneficiaries of the trust administered by the [corporation].

The theory underlying fiduciary duties is consistent with recognition that a director of a corporate general partner bears such a duty towards the limited partnership. That duty, of course, extends only to dealings with the partnership's property or affecting its business, but, so limited, its existence seems apparent in any number of circumstances. Consider, for example, a classic self-dealing transaction: assume that a majority of the board of the corporate general partner formed a new entity and then caused the general partner to sell partnership assets to the new entity at an unfairly small price, injuring the partnership and its limited partners. Can it be imagined that such persons have not breached a duty to the partnership itself? And does it not make perfect sense to say that the gist of the offense is a breach of the equitable duty of loyalty that is placed upon a fiduciary? It appears true that the same result might be rationalized as aider and abettor liability, but I am unsure what such indirection would add that is useful where a self-dealing transaction or other diversion of partnership property is alleged. Indeed in some instances, for example the use by a director of confidential information concerning the partnership's business not yet known by the board of the general partner, there may be no breach of loyalty or care by the general partner itself to abet, yet there may be director liability to the partnership by the director.

Two courts have held a sole shareholder/director of a corporate general partner personally liable for breach of fiduciary duty to limited partners.

While these authorities extend the fiduciary duty of the general partner to a controlling shareholder, they support as well, the recognition of such duty in directors of the General Partner who, more directly than a controlling shareholder, are in control of the partnership's property. It is not necessary here to attempt to delineate the full scope of that duty. It may well not be so broad as the duty of the director of a corporate trustee. But it surely entails the duty not to use control over the partnership's property to advantage the corporate director at the expense of the partnership. That is what is alleged here.

The amended complaint contains the following allegations:

> 16. The General Partner and its directors, the named individual defendants, are in a fiduciary relationship with the plaintiffs and the other Unitholders of USACafes.
>
> 17. Through their unit ownership and executive positions [the director defendants] have dominated and controlled the affairs of USACafes. Among other things, they have failed to adequately solicit or consider alternative proposals for USACafes, have failed to negotiate in good faith to enhance Unitholders' values and, instead, have agreed to sell all of its assets to Metsa, which will result in the minority limited partners receiving the grossly inadequate price of $10.25 per Unit. As inducement to the individual defendants to agree to the Metsa proposal, Metsa offered to pay and the individual defendants agreed to accept,

certain additional payments (approximately $17 million) that were not offered to the classes.

19. The individual defendants and the General Partner participated in the wrongdoing complained of in order to divert the valuable assets of USACafes for their own benefit by entering into highly favorable compensation arrangements with Metsa as part of the liquidation of USACafes.

The amended complaint does allege facts which if true establish that the director defendants have breached fiduciary obligations imposed upon them as directors of a Delaware corporation or have participated in a breach of such duties by the General Partner.

NOTES

1. Although the case specifically deals with an LP, the case holding can be extended to all NBEs in Delaware. *See* Feeley v. NHAOCG, LLC, 62 A.3d 649, 671 (Del. Ch. 2012) ("This Court's decisions also have extended the doctrine [of *USACafes*] to other alternative entities, such as LLCs.").

2. Other courts have also recognized the doctrine of fiduciary veil piercing seen in *USACafes. See, e.g.,* In re Harwood, 637 F.3d 615, 622 (5th Cir. 2011) ("We conclude that an officer of a corporate general partner who is entrusted with the management of the limited partnership and who exercises control over the limited partnership in a fashion analogous to Bennett and McBeth owes a fiduciary duty to the partnership that satisfies [Bankruptcy Code, 11 U.S.C. § 523(a)(4), exception to discharge for "for fraud or defalcation while acting in a fiduciary capacity, embezzlement, or larceny"]. We emphasize that it is not only the control that the officer actually exerts over the partnership, but also the confidence and trust placed in the hands of the controlling officer, that leads us to find that a fiduciary relationship exists sufficient for the purposes of Section 523(a)(4)."); Southern Pacific Co. v. Bogert, 250 U.S. 483, 491–92 (1919) (holding that the parent shareholder of the subsidiary, which is the controlling shareholder of the downstream corporation, owed fiduciary duty to the shareholders of the downstream corporation).

3. Several recent articles have discussed the issue. *See* Mohsen Manesh, *The Case Against Fiduciary Entity Veil Piercing*, 72 Bus. Law. 61 (2017); Colin P. Marks, *Piercing the Fiduciary Veil*, 19 Lewis & Clark L. Rev. 73 (2015).

The case below discusses the nature of fiduciary duty in LPs. The general partner owes duties, but limited partners generally do not. In reading this case, consider these questions: (1) Why did the limited partners owe duties? (2) What is the key inquiry that determines whether one owes duties or not? (3) In light of the fact that limited partners have limited liability, why was liability imposes on the limited partners?

RED RIVER WINGS, INC. V. HOOT, INC.

751 N.W.2d 206 (N.D. 2008)

KAPSNER, JUSTICE.

Thomas Lavelle is a Fargo restauranteur who owns and manages restaurants through LTM, Ltd. ("LTM"), a corporation whose only shareholder is Lavelle. Dyan Dockter and Shelly Dockter are employed by the company and they oversee LTM's management duties. Lavelle learned from Arthur Stern, who worked in the restaurant equipment supply business and had a long-standing business relationship with Lavelle, that Hooters of America was looking to expand into Canada. Hooters of America approved Lavelle as a franchisee, but as a condition for getting a first franchise in Edmonton, Lavelle had to purchase options for three additional franchises in Calgary, Winnipeg, and Banff. The franchise fee for the first restaurant was $75,000, plus a $10,000 nonrefundable fee for each of the additional option locations.

Lavelle decided to find investors and sought advice from a friend and retired securities broker, Louis Emerson. Emerson suggested a limited partnership as the best entity to finance and organize the venture and said he believed he could find a sufficient number of investors in the Fargo area. Emerson also recommended an attorney to draft the necessary legal documents. The attorney prepared a private placement memorandum for Canadian Wings Investment Limited Partnership ("Canadian Wings") and Lavelle formed Red River Wings, Inc. ("Red River Wings"), to serve as the general partner. The private placement memorandum informed potential investors that LTM would provide management services for the restaurants. Ownership units in Canadian Wings were offered for $80,000 per unit, and Emerson sold ten units to various investors. Many of the investors, including Richard Walstad, John Boulger, Hoadley Harris and the Harris Trust, David Butler, and ME Investments, LLP ("ME Investments"), a limited liability partnership formed by Curtis Kesselring and Dennis Leno, invested primarily because of Lavelle's reputation and involvement in the business. For their services, Stern and Emerson received fees and profits-only interests as special limited partners.

The Edmonton restaurant was profitable from the beginning and the limited partners received healthy returns on their investments.

Lavelle offered to all partners in Canadian Wings the opportunity to invest in Manitoba Wings Investment Limited Partnership ("Manitoba Wings"), a partnership formed to own a Hooters restaurant in Winnipeg. The investors received returns on their investment, but less than the returns from the Edmonton restaurant.

[Certain decisions by Lavelle antagonized Stern and Emerson, which led to discord between Lavelle and some limited partners.] ME Investments, Emerson, Stern, Jerry Baldwin, Jill Baldwin, Patricia

Corwin, and Clinton Emerson held a majority of the interests in the limited partnerships. Because the majority limited partners were dissatisfied with the performance of the Winnipeg restaurant, a meeting was held and their concerns were addressed by an accountant. The majority limited partners hired a certified public accountant to investigate the financial records of Canadian Wings and Manitoba Wings, but no evidence of wrongdoing was found. The majority limited partners were not satisfied with the report and decided to take over the management of the two partnerships.

The majority limited partners, through written action and without notice to minority limited partners, removed Red River Wings as the general partner of the two limited partnerships and appointed Hoot, Inc. ("Hoot"), as the replacement general partner. Hoot was a corporation formed by Kesselring and Leno for the sole purpose of serving as the replacement general partner for the limited partnerships. The majority partners also terminated the management contracts the partnerships had with LTM. The minority limited partners, which included Walstad, Boulger, Harris, and Butler, protested the takeover.

[After removing Red River Wings, the majority limited partners took physical control of Canadian Wings and Manitoba Wings restaurants. Under their control, the restaurants performed poorly.]

The minority limited partners sued the majority limited partners derivatively and individually for breach of the partnership agreements and breach of fiduciary duties, and sought dissolution and an accounting of the partnerships. The majority partners [filed] action against Red River Wings, LTM, Lavelle, and his associates in state court. Lavelle, through Red River Wings, also sued Hoot, the replacement general partner, for damages for wrongfully withholding distributions.

Following a trial, the district court awarded damages to the minority group and Lavelle from the majority group for breach of fiduciary duties.

[Analysis]

The majority partners argue they cannot be held liable under the circumstances of this case because of N.D.C.C. § 45–10.1–22(1), which provided in relevant part:

> A limited partner is not liable for the obligations of a limited partnership unless the limited partner is also a general partner or, in addition to the exercise of the limited partner's rights and powers as a limited partner, the limited partner participates in the control of the business. However, if the limited partner participates in the control of the business, the limited partner is liable only to persons who transact business with the limited partnership reasonably believing, based upon the limited partner's conduct, that the limited partner is a general partner.

We reject the majority partners' argument. This Court has said that "in a limited partnership, general partners, with unlimited liability, manage the business; limited partners contribute only investment capital without participating in the business and without liability beyond capital contributed." However, N.D.C.C. § 45–10.1–22(1) does not address fiduciary duties owed to a partnership and to limited partners, but addresses only the liability of a limited partner for the "obligations of a limited partnership." Section 45–10.1–27, N.D.C.C., retained fiduciary responsibilities by providing "a general partner of a limited partnership has the rights and powers and is subject to the restrictions and liabilities of a partner in a partnership without limited partners."

Courts have indicated that limited partners who participate in the business of the partnership or act in concert with the general partner are subject to the fiduciary duties of loyalty and care and the obligations of good faith and fair dealing applicable to partners in a general partnership.

The majority limited partners argue the district court erred in ruling they breached their fiduciary duties.

Whether a person has breached a fiduciary duty is a finding of fact subject to the clearly erroneous rule.

The district court found "limited partners Emerson, Stern, Kesselring and Leno were acting in concert with Hoot," "Emerson and Stern were deeply involved with the takeover and with the restaurant operation after the takeover," "Kesselring and Leno controlled Hoot and acted in concert by way of their controlling actions through the purported general partner," and "installing Hoot as general partner for both partnerships and running the partnerships under their own terms was a breach of the [majority] defendants' fiduciary duties to the minority partners." The court found the majority limited partners breached their fiduciary duties based on: (1) their "reckless action" of terminating the management contracts for both partnerships; (2) their knowledge that termination of the management contract with LTM would pose potential liability; (3) their "affirmative action to dominate and interfere with the partnerships" by taking them over and installing Hoot, a shell corporation controlled by Kesselring and Leno, as a general partner; (4) their authorizing reimbursement to the majority partners for attorney fees and expenses incurred in the federal litigation against Lavelle and his companies; (5) their causing the loss of the Hooters franchise and thereby significantly reducing the value of the two restaurants; (6) their refusals to cooperate with the court-appointed receiver; and (7) their taking these actions without calling meetings as required by the partnership agreements.

We cannot say the district court's findings of fact are clearly erroneous. The evidence reflects that the majority group planned a takeover of the limited partnerships and proceeded to do so in a reckless manner. They sought legal advice for the takeover from Kesselring and Leno's attorneys, but failed to secure unanimous consent for a new general partner after having been advised that unanimous consent was necessary. Emerson and Stern attempted to find reasons to remove Lavelle and his companies from the limited partnerships and traveled to the restaurants to accomplish the takeover. The majority disposed of Red River Wings without the required notice or consent of Hooters of America and later sued the franchiser. They hired two replacement management companies, Texas Wings and UD Management, without notice or a vote of all of the limited partners. After the takeover, Kesselring and Leno directly controlled Hoot, and Emerson and Stern were directly involved in controlling the partnerships. Hoot has no assets, no employees, and no separate office, and Stelzer, its sole officer, director, and shareholder, acted on behalf of and at the direction of his employers, Kesselring and Leno. Kesselring and Emerson's control of the partnerships was obvious to Lavelle and the minority limited partners, who dealt directly with Kesselring and Emerson after the takeover in an attempt to resolve the disputes. The majority limited partners authorized reimbursement from the limited partnerships for attorney fees and expenses in the federal lawsuit. Moreover, after the district court appointed a receiver for the limited partnerships, the majority limited partners continued to refuse to surrender control, forcing the receiver to seek a court order to gain control of the partnerships' Canadian bank accounts. The majority limited partners were ultimately held in contempt of court.

We conclude that the district court's findings that the majority limited partners took control and dominated the partnerships for their own interests and in doing so violated the fiduciary duties of good faith, fair dealing, loyalty, and care are not clearly erroneous.

The majority limited partners argue the district court erred in holding them personally liable because the court failed to perform an "entity piercing analysis." They contend the court was required to "pierce the limited partnership veil" before Stern, Emerson, and ME Investments could be held individually liable.

The majority partners are incorrect in their assertion that the "limited partnership veils" of Canadian Wings and Manitoba Wings needed to be "pierced" in order to hold Stern, Emerson, and ME Investments individually liable. In the context of a close corporation, minority shareholders are entitled to bring a direct action against majority shareholders for breach of fiduciary duties. The majority limited partners who controlled or acted in concert with the general partner can be held personally liable to the minority limited partners for damages for breach of fiduciary duties. Emerson, Stern, and ME Investments, through Kesselring and Leno, clearly participated in the takeover and installation of Hoot as the general partner, which the district court found "was an affirmative action to dominate and interfere with the partnerships."

We also are not persuaded by the majority partners' argument that Kesselring and Leno cannot be held personally liable because ME Investments was actually the limited partner in the partnerships. ME Investments, a limited liability partnership, was the vehicle used by Kesselring and Leno to invest in Canadian Wings and Manitoba Wings. It is obvious from the district court's decision that the court believed ME Investments to merely be the alter ego of Kesselring and Leno because the court refers to the limited liability partnership and the individuals as being one and the same. Principles for piercing a corporate veil apply to limited liability partnerships. *See* N.D.C.C. § 45–22–09(1). To apply the alter ego doctrine, "there must be such a unity of interest and ownership between the corporation and its equitable owner that the separate personalities of the corporation and the shareholder do not in reality exist," and "there must be an inequitable result if the acts in question are treated as those of the corporation alone." Given the evidence of Kesselring and Leno's participation in the takeover and their direct control and actions in concert with Hoot through their employee, Stelzer, we agree with the district court's implicit finding that it would be inequitable if Kesselring and Leno's acts were treated as those of the limited liability partnership alone. We conclude that the district court did not err in holding Kesselring and Leno individually responsible under these circumstances.

3. LIMITED LIABILITY COMPANY

Most LLC statutes provide statutory rules on fiduciary duties: What duties? Who owes them? To whom? A few state statutes do not provide statutory rules at all.

The case below discusses the applicability of common law fiduciary duties in the context of LLCs in the absence of statutory standards. Arizona subsequently revised its statute to provide statutory fiduciary duties. Statutory amendment notwithstanding, the case frames the relevant concepts. In reading this case, consider these questions: (1) What are the relative roles of the statute and common law in defining the contours of fiduciary duties? (2) In light of common law duties, what is the role of contracting for fiduciary duties in the operating agreement?

IN RE SKY HARBOR HOTEL PROPERTIES, LLC

443 P.3d 21 (Ariz. 2019)

CHIEF JUSTICE BALES, opinion of the Court:

These consolidated cases involve alleged breaches of fiduciary duties. To address these claims, the United States Bankruptcy Court for the District of Arizona certified the following questions to this Court:

1. Does a manager of an Arizona limited liability company ("LLC") owe common law fiduciary duties to the company?

2. Does a member of an Arizona LLC owe common law fiduciary duties to the company?

3. Can an Arizona LLC's operating agreement lawfully limit or eliminate those fiduciary duties?

We answer the first question in the affirmative. We answer the second question in the affirmative, provided that the member is an agent of the LLC. We answer the third question in the affirmative but note that the operating agreement may not eliminate the implied contractual duty of good faith and fair dealing.

Arizona enacted its first limited liability company act ("LLC Act") in 1992.

The LLC Act does not expressly impose any fiduciary duties on members or managers. By statute, however, "the law of agency" applies to the entire LLC Act. *See* A.R.S. § 29–854(B). We thus apply common law agency principles to answer the certified questions.

"Absent controlling authority to the contrary, we generally follow the Restatement when it sets forth sound legal policy." Under traditional agency rules, agency is the "fiduciary relation which results from the manifestation of consent by one person to another that the other shall act on his behalf and subject to his control, and consent by the other so to act." Restatement (Second) of Agency § 1 (Am. Law. Inst. 1958). The agent is the one who acts on behalf of another, the principal. *Id.* Agents are characterized by their "power to alter the legal relation between the principal and third persons and between the principal and" themselves. *Id.* § 12. Importantly, "an agent is a fiduciary with respect to matters within the scope of his agency." *Id.* § 13.

We have characterized a fiduciary duty as imposing "the obligation of loyalty," "the obligation of the utmost good faith in their dealings," and "requiring a high degree of care." Thus, the nature of the fiduciary relationship for agents includes a duty of loyalty, a duty of good faith, and a duty of care. Partnerships, joint ventures, and corporations are all owed fiduciary duties by those empowered to act on behalf of such businesses.

By default, the members of an LLC are agents of the LLC "for the purpose of carrying on its business in the usual way." A.R.S. § 29–654(A)(1). However, if an LLC's management is vested in one or more managers, members are not automatically agents "solely by reason of being a member except to the extent that authority has been delegated to the member by" the manager or the operating agreement. § 29–654(B)(1). If management is vested in one or more managers, by law they are deemed agents of the LLC "for the purpose of carrying on its business in the usual way." § 29–654(B)(2). Thus, if an LLC is managed by one or more managers, such managers are agents, and under § 29–854 and agency law, they would owe common law fiduciary duties to the LLC.

The answer to the second question depends on whether management has been vested in one or more managers. If not, then all members are deemed agents of the LLC and thus would owe common law fiduciary duties to the LLC. If, however, the LLC is managed by one or more managers, members are considered its agents to the extent they have been delegated authority by the managers or the operating agreement under § 29–654(B)(1). Thus, a member owes common law fiduciary duties to the LLC if the member acts as an agent of the LLC.

Although the common law recognizes that an LLC's managers or members, when acting as agents of the LLC, owe fiduciary duties to the company, these duties may be lawfully limited by a valid operating agreement.

The LLC Act provides for an operating agreement to govern relationships between members and managers and between managers, members, and the LLC itself. *See* A.R.S. § 29–682(B). The agreement "may contain any provision that is not contrary to law and that relates to the rights, duties or powers of its members, managers, officers, employees or agents." *Id.* However, an LLC is not required to adopt an operating agreement. § 29–682(A) (stating that an LLC "may" adopt an agreement). Neither the LLC Act nor any other applicable law broadly prohibits an operating agreement from altering or limiting fiduciary duties that otherwise would be owed to the LLC by its managers or members.

The defendants in both certified cases concede that, regardless of their arguments relating to common law fiduciary duties, the implied covenant of good faith and fair dealing cannot be eliminated by an operating agreement. Based on public policy and case law, this is a well-supported concession. *See Rawlings v. Apodaca*, 726 P.2d 565, 579 (Ariz. 1986) ("A covenant of good faith and fair dealing is implied in every contract. The covenant may be breached even though the express covenants of the contract are fully performed").

We answer the third question in the affirmative. An operating agreement may lawfully limit or eliminate common law fiduciary duties owed to the LLC by its members or managers, although it may not erase the covenant of good faith and fair dealing implied in every contract. We have no occasion here to address whether the provisions of any particular operating agreement are contrary to law in this respect or otherwise.

The LLC Act imposes common law fiduciary duties on managers and members serving as agents of the LLC. The LLC Act permits an LLC to limit or eliminate such common law duties through an operating agreement, except for the implied covenant of good faith and fair dealing.

NOTES

1. Arizona Limited Liability Company Act (ALLCA), codified in A.R.S. § 29–3101 *et seq.*, now provides statutory fiduciary duties in § 29–3409. Other courts, confronted with a silent statute, have imposed common law duties by referencing and importing the laws of partnership, corporation, or agency. *See* Wasserman v. Kay, 14 A.3d 1193, 1210 (Md. App. 2011) ("Unlike the corporate and general partnership context, there is no statute in Maryland expressly addressing LLC members' fiduciary duties. Nevertheless, managing members of LLCs owe common law fiduciary duties to the LLC and to the other members. Managing members are clearly agents for the LLC and each of the members, which is a fiduciary position under common law.").

2. Delaware faced a similar situation because its LLC statute was also silent on fiduciary duties. In *Auriga Capital Corp. v. Gatz Properties, LLC*, 40 A.3d 839, 851 (Del.Ch. 2012), the court stated in dictum: "because the LLC Act provides for principles of equity to apply, because LLC managers are clearly fiduciaries, and because fiduciaries owe the fiduciary duties of loyalty and care, the LLC Act starts with the default that managers of LLCs owe enforceable fiduciary duties." The gratuitous assertion (dictum) that default common law duties apply to Delaware LLCs drew a rebuke from the supreme court. *See* Gatz Properties, LLC v. Auriga Capital Corp., 59 A.3d 1206 (Del. 2012) ("We remind Delaware judges that the obligation to write judicial opinions on the issues presented Is not a license to use those opinions as a platform from which to propagate their individual world views on issues not presented."). *See also* Peter Lattman, *In Unusual Move, Delaware Supreme Court Rebukes a Judge*, N.Y. Times (Nov. 9, 2012). The Delaware legislature ultimately resolved the conflict by amending that statute to recognize default fiduciary duties. Delaware Limited Liability Company Act § 18–1104 ("the rules of law and equity, including *the rules of law and equity relating to fiduciary duties and* the law merchant, shall govern") (amendment in italics). Case like *Sky Harbor Hotel* and *Auriga Capital* illustrate the point that courts can develop fiduciary duties through the common law. The "uncabined" approach of NBE statutes recognizes that the statutory statement of duties is inclusive and not exclusive. *See* RUPA § 409; ULPA (2001) § 409; RULLCA § 409.

What is the role of the courts in defining the existence and scope of statutory fiduciary duties? Because the LLC can accommodate a range of management structures, the rules of fiduciary duty are complex. Consistent with the basic choice of a member-managed or manager-managed LLC, the rules track this split. In a member-managed LLC, the rules track the scheme of a general partnership in RUPA § 409 by imposing fiduciary duties on all members. RULLCA § 409(b)–(d). In a manager-managed LLC, the rules track the structure of duty between limited and general partners in an LP under ULPA (2001) § 305 and § 409 by imposing fiduciary duties on managers only. *Id.* § 409(i).

RULLCA § 409. Standards of Conduct for Members and Managers.

(a) A member of a member-managed limited liability company owes to the company and, subject to Section 801, the other members the duties of loyalty and care stated in subsections (b) and (c).

(b) The fiduciary duty of loyalty of a member in a member-managed limited liability company includes the duties:

(1) to account to the company and hold as trustee for it any property, profit, or benefit derived by the member:

(A) in the conduct or winding up of the company's activities and affairs;

(B) from a use by the member of the company's property; or

(C) from the appropriation of a company opportunity;

(2) to refrain from dealing with the company in the conduct or winding up of the company's activities and affairs as or on behalf of a person having an interest adverse to the company; and

(3) to refrain from competing with the company in the conduct of the company's activities and affairs before the dissolution of the company.

(c) The duty of care of a member of a member-managed limited liability company in the conduct or winding up of the company's activities and affairs is to refrain from engaging in grossly negligent or reckless conduct, willful or intentional misconduct, or knowing violation of law.

(d) A member shall discharge the duties and obligations under this [act] or under the operating agreement and exercise any rights consistently with the contractual obligation of good faith and fair dealing.

(e) A member does not violate a duty or obligation under this [act] or under the operating agreement solely because the member's conduct furthers the member's own interest.

(f) All the members of a member-managed limited liability company or a manager-managed limited liability company may authorize or ratify, after full disclosure of all material facts, a specific act or transaction that otherwise would violate the duty of loyalty.

(g) It is a defense to a claim under subsection (b)(2) and any comparable claim in equity or at common law that the transaction was fair to the limited liability company.

(h) If, as permitted by subsection (f) or (i)(6) or the operating agreement, a member enters into a transaction with the limited liability company which otherwise would be prohibited by subsection (b)(2), the member's rights and obligations arising from the transaction are the same as those of a person that is not a member.

(i) In a manager-managed limited liability company, the following rules apply:

(1) Subsections (a), (b), (c), and (g) apply to the manager or managers and not the members.

(2) The duty stated under subsection (b)(3) continues until winding up is completed.

(3) Subsection (d) applies to managers and members.

(4) Subsection (e) applies only to members.

(5) The power to ratify under subsection (f) applies only to the members.

(6) Subject to subsection (d), a member does not have any duty to the company or to any other member solely by reason of being a member.

CHRYSLER GROUP LLC OPERATING AGREEMENT

Section 9.2 No Member Fiduciary Duties.

(a) No Member shall, except as expressly required by the LLC Act and other applicable Law, owe any duties (including fiduciary duties) as a Member to (i) the other Members or (ii) the Company, except for duties arising under contracts between such Members and the Company, in each case notwithstanding anything to the contrary existing at Law, in equity or otherwise.

(b) Except as otherwise expressly provided in this Agreement, any Member may engage in or possess any interest in another business or venture of any nature and description, independently or with others, whether or not such business or venture is competitive with the Company or any of its Subsidiaries, and neither the Company nor any other Member shall have any rights in or to any such independent business or venture or the income or profits derived therefrom, and the doctrine of corporate opportunity or any analogous doctrine shall not apply to the Members and the members, shareholders, partners and Affiliates thereof. The pursuit of any such business or venture shall not be deemed wrongful, improper or a breach of any duty hereunder, at Law, in equity or otherwise. Any Member and the members, shareholders, partners and Affiliates thereof shall be able to transact business or enter into agreements with the Company to the fullest extent permissible under the LLC Act, subject to the terms and conditions of this Agreement.

(c) If a Member acquires knowledge of a potential transaction or matter that may be a business opportunity for both such Member and the Company or another Member, such Member shall have no duty to communicate or offer such business opportunity to the Company or any other Member and shall not be liable to the Company or the other Members for breach of any duty (including fiduciary duties) as a Member by reason of the fact that such Member pursues or acquires such business opportunity for itself, directs such opportunity to another Person, or does not communicate information regarding such opportunity to the Company.

(d) The provisions of this Agreement, to the extent that they restrict or eliminate the duties (including fiduciary duties) and liabilities of a Member otherwise existing or implied at law or in equity, are agreed by the Members to replace such duties and liabilities of such Member.

The case below analyzes a manager's duty of loyalty to the LLC. In reading this case, consider these questions: (1) In what way could Dino's interest conflict with the interest of the members of FHC? (2) Does the existence of a conflict always result in a finding of breach?

ACORN V. MONCECCHI

386 P.3d 739 (Wyo. 2016)

FOX, JUSTICE.

During the course of their marriage, M.W. "Bud" Federer and Margie Federer amassed a sizeable estate, predominantly comprised of apartment complexes throughout Wyoming. The Federers formed numerous entities to manage their holdings for their benefit during their lives, and for the benefit of their three daughters. As so often happens, the parents' attempt to impose harmony along with the assets they conveyed to the next generation was unsuccessful. The sisters disagreed about money, and those disagreements blossomed into accusations of misconduct and breaches of the duties. The sisters filed claims, counterclaims, and cross-claims.

Bud enjoyed a successful career as a businessman in Wyoming. He and his wife, Margie, had three daughters: Rebecca, Lori, and Tamra. Bud died in 2003. Margie was diagnosed with Alzheimer's disease and has not been able to manage her affairs since at least 2010. During Bud's life, and after he died, the family created a number of entities to hold and manage their business interests and to pass Bud and Margie's estate to their daughters and their families. [The fiduciary duty claim concerns the business dealings between two of those entities: Spartan Management, LLC (Spartan) and Federer Holding Company, LLC (FHC).]

The Federer family assets include nine low-income apartment complexes located throughout Wyoming. These apartments were or are managed in accordance with the United States Department of Housing and Urban Development (HUD). Each apartment complex operates as a separate limited liability partnership and is owned by various Federer trusts and other parties and entities.

Spartan was formed in 1972 to manage these apartment complexes. In 1993, Bud hired Dino Moncecchi to work for Spartan. Dino is married to Lori, the Federers' middle daughter. Spartan became an LLC in 1995, and Dino became its manager. Over time, Dino and Lori received Spartan ownership interests as compensation and purchased additional interests. At the time of the trial, the Moncecchis owned 65 percent of Spartan, and the Marital Trust owned the other 35 percent. The three Federer sisters are equal beneficiaries of the Marital Trust.

FHC was created in 2006 to serve as the general partner of the partnerships owning the apartment complexes and to "provide continuity of management and liability protection." FHC acquired a one percent interest in each of the apartment entities. The Moncecchis, Rebecca, and Tamra each own a one-third interest in FHC.

Prior to 2006, Spartan managed the apartment units pursuant to separate contracts with the various apartment entities. Because he had been managing the apartment complexes for the family as the manager of Spartan and in order to provide continuity to HUD, Dino was appointed the sole manager of FHC when it was formed and continued in that capacity until this litigation.

After the formation of FHC and under Dino's management, Spartan continued to manage the apartment complexes. The fees charged by Spartan were established by the original HUD contracts sometime between 1972 and 1995, and have not been changed, except as required by HUD in 2000 for five of the complexes that were in its Mark-to-Market program.

Spartan also owns laundry facilities in each of the apartment complexes, which were installed when the properties were constructed. Spartan owns and maintains the washers and dryers but pays the apartment owners about $15,000 per year to rent the laundry facilities. Dino testified that the laundry facilities generate a total of approximately $40,000 to $50,000 in annual income for Spartan.

[One claim in the litigation was that Dino breached his fiduciary duty to other members of FHC. At trial, the trial court rejected this claim.] The majority of the arguments raised by FHC concern its contentions that Dino should have solicited competitive bids for the management of the apartment complexes, and that Spartan should not have retained HUD incentive payments or operated the laundry facilities in the apartment complexes for its sole benefit.

The fiduciary duties owed to an LLC require the manager to act carefully and disinterestedly. Wyoming's Limited Liability Company Act, Wyo. Stat. Ann. §§ 17–29–101 through 17–29–1105, describes those duties:

> (b) The duty of loyalty of a [manager] in a [manager]-managed limited liability company includes the duties:
>
> (i) To account to the company and to hold as trustee for it any property, profit or benefit derived by the member:
>
> (A) In the conduct of the company's activities;
>
> (B) From a use by the [manager] of the company's property; or
>
> (C) From the appropriation of a limited liability company opportunity;
>
> (ii) To refrain from dealing with the company in the conduct of the company's activities as or on behalf of a person having an interest adverse to the company; and
>
> (iii) To refrain from competing with the company in the conduct of the company's activities before the dissolution of the company.

Wyo. Stat. Ann. § 17–29–409(b). The statute goes on to provide:

> (c) Subject to the business judgment rule, the duty of care of a [manager] of a [manager]-managed limited liability company in the conduct of the company's activities is to act with the care that a person in a like position would reasonably exercise under similar circumstances and in a manner the [manager] reasonably believes to be in the best interests or at least not opposed to the best interests of the company. In discharging this duty, a member may rely in good faith upon opinions, reports, statements or other information provided by another person that the member reasonably believes is a competent and reliable source for the information.
>
> (d) A [manager of] a [manager]-managed limited liability company shall discharge the duties under this chapter or under the operating agreement and exercise any rights consistently with the contractual obligation of good faith and fair dealing.

Wyo. Stat. Ann. § 17–29–409(c) and (d). Thus, a manager of a limited liability company has statutorily-imposed duties of loyalty, care, and good faith and fair dealing. Those duties require the manager to conduct business in a manner that the manager reasonably believes to be in the best interests or not opposed to the best interests of the company, to refrain from competing with the limited liability company, and to act in good faith.

Self-dealing in hiring Spartan as management company

The fact that the manager of an LLC enters into a contract with another entity owned, even partially, by the manager raises the question of whether that action was disinterested. *See* Wyo. Stat. Ann. § 17–29–409(b); Wallop Canyon Ranch, LLC v. Goodwyn, 351 P.3d 943, 958 (Wyo. 2015) (stating in partnership context that "self-dealing can form the basis for a finding of conflict of interest by a partner, even when the deals are with a separate entity, when that entity has substantial connections with the partner"). Thus, we turn to the question of whether Dino, as manager of FHC, engaged in prohibited self-dealing when he continued to engage Spartan, which is owned in part by Dino and Lori.

While our statutes governing limited liability companies do not specifically define conflicts of interest or self-dealing, they do prohibit a manager from dealing as a person "having an interest adverse to the company." Wyo. Stat. Ann. § 17–29–409(b)(ii). "It is a defense to a claim under [this provision] that the transaction was fair to or at least not opposed to the limited liability company." Wyo. Stat. Ann. § 17–29–409(e). Thus, once a party proves that a manager has an interest adverse to the limited liability company, the manager has the burden of establishing that the transaction was fair or not opposed to the company.

The district court recognized the existence of a "potential conflict" between Dino's position as the manager of FHC and his ownership interest in Spartan. This shifted the burden to Dino to prove that his continued use of Spartan to manage the apartment complexes was fair to FHC. The district court found that it was, and as a result, concluded that the fairness defense available under Wyo. Stat. Ann. § 17–29–409(e) applied and there was no violation of the statutory provision prohibiting dealing with persons who have an adverse interest.

The district court reasoned that Dino's continued use of Spartan was fair to FHC in part because there is common ownership between FHC and Spartan. Thus, if Spartan's management of the apartment complexes benefitted Dino, it also benefitted the other owners of FHC, namely Rebecca and Tamra, because of their interests in Spartan.[10] FHC takes issue with this rationale, arguing, without citation to authority, that such reasoning is contrary to law.

The fairness doctrine provides that "it is a defense to a claim under paragraph (b)(ii) of this section[11] and any comparable claim in equity or at

---

[10] Rebecca and Tamra are beneficiaries of the Marital Trust, which owns a 35 percent interest in Spartan.

[11] Wyo. Stat. Ann. § 17–29–409(b)(ii) provides that the duty of loyalty includes the duty to "refrain from dealing with the company in the conduct of the company's activities as or on behalf of a person having an interest adverse to the company."

common law that the transaction was fair to or at least not opposed to the limited liability company." Wyo. Stat. Ann. § 17–29–409(e). Thus, the Act does not prevent managers from transacting business with the LLC, but it does require that the terms of the transaction are fair *"to the limited liability company." Id.*

To the extent the district court determined that the use of Spartan was fair to FHC because it was fair to Rebecca and Tamra due to their status as beneficiaries of an owner of Spartan, that rationale was misplaced. The proper test is whether the transaction was fair to FHC. As summarized above, Dino testified regarding the services that Spartan performed, the origination of the fees charged to FHC, and the reasonableness of those fees. That evidence supports the district court's conclusion that the use of Spartan to manage the apartment complexes was fair.

Wyoming's Limited Liability Company Act provides that the operating agreement governs "the rights and duties under this chapter of a person in the capacity of manager," Wyo. Stat. Ann. § 17–29–110(a)(ii), and provides that "to the extent the operating agreement does not otherwise provide for a matter this chapter governs the matter." Wyo. Stat. Ann. § 17–29–110(b). Where the operating agreement contains specific provisions regarding a manager's rights and duties, it prevails. The Act also prohibits the operating agreement from eliminating the contractual obligation of good faith and fair dealing under Wyo. Stat. Ann. § 17–29–409(d).

The FHC Operating Agreement permits Dino, as the manager of FHC, to contract with entities owned by or affiliated with himself, such as Spartan. It states:

> "Agents, servants, employees, accountants, attorneys, investment advisors, independent contractors, *and management companies* hired under this Section may be Members of the Company or shareholders, members or employees of Company Members, or *entities owned by or directly or indirectly affiliated with Members or the Manager.*"

The operating agreement also contains the following provision:

> "No Exclusive Duty to Company. Manager and Officers are not required to manage the Company as their sole and exclusive function and they may have other business interests and may engage in other activities without violating their fiduciary duties under the Act and this Agreement." These terms of the operating agreement grant permission to Dino, as the manager of FHC, to use Spartan, which is owned in part by Dino, to manage the FHC apartment complexes. This is corroborated by the fact that the attorney who drafted the FHC limited liability documents anticipated that management of the properties after FHC was formed would not change when he stated that "Dino was

> appointed manager [of FHC] since he had been managing the HUD partnerships for the family and to provide continuity for HUD."

Because the operating agreement allows Dino to contract with entities he owns for the management of FHC, Dino's use of Spartan to manage the apartment complexes does not constitute improper self-dealing or a breach of his fiduciary duties. FHC failed to establish that use of Spartan violated Dino's duty of loyalty and good faith and fair dealing.

Self-dealing in business opportunities

FHC next argues that the district court erred when it concluded that Dino Moncecchi had not breached his fiduciary duty when he availed himself of business opportunities that allegedly should have been afforded to FHC. FHC claims that Dino appropriated business opportunities belonging to FHC in two respects: first, by having Spartan retain HUD incentive fees, and second, in Spartan's operation of laundry facilities in the apartment complexes.

The duty of loyalty includes a duty to "account to the company and to hold as trustee for it any property, profit or benefit derived by the [manager] from the appropriation of a limited liability company opportunity." Wyo. Stat. Ann. § 17–29–409(b)(i)(C). Other courts have held that this duty "includes the duty not to engage in enterprises directly in competition with and necessarily having an injurious or detrimental effect on the corporation's business." A party claiming breach of fiduciary duty through the appropriation of a business opportunity must

> establish that it had an actual or expected interest in an asset or property, and that it had the financial ability to acquire the asset or property. Even though a corporation might have had some rights with regard to the acquisition of property, in order for that opportunity to be usurped, *the acquisition must have been within the corporation's expectation.* Similarly, to establish an expectancy, it is not sufficient for plaintiff to show only that a proposed opportunity possesses value to it, but plaintiff must also show that there is a practical, not a mere theoretical, basis for the opportunity.

FHC relies solely on the following exchange to support its contention that Dino breached his duty of loyalty with respect to those fees:

> Q. [Attorney for FHC:] Now, the HUD agreements concerning the five HUD properties that [Spartan] is managing require that the property owners get to decide how the incentive performance fees are distributed, correct?
>
> A. [Dino:] Yes.
>
> Q. Who retained those incentive performance fees?

A. [Spartan] was paid the incentive performance fee according to the agreement.

Q. And is this the agreement that was entered into way back in 2004?

A. Well, yes, during the initial refinancing.

Q. And prior to the creation of [FHC]?

A. Yes.

Dino also testified that under his management of FHC, he continued operating under the terms of the prior management contracts. The evidence is uncontroverted that the payment of the HUD fees to Spartan was pursuant to Spartan's agreements with the owners of the apartments, and FHC had no expectation of receiving the fees. Because FHC had no expectation of receiving those fees, Dino did not "appropriate" the HUD incentive fees and thus did not contravene his fiduciary duty to FHC.

We now turn to the question of whether Spartan's management of the laundry facilities in the apartment complexes breached the duty of loyalty as an appropriation of FHC's opportunity. The laundry facilities also did not represent a corporate opportunity for FHC. The laundry facilities were installed when the properties were built, and they have been operated by Spartan pursuant to an agreement with the owners since that time, which was even prior to the time Dino began working for Spartan. There was no expectation that FHC would operate the laundry facilities in the apartment complexes. Therefore, Dino did not breach his duty of loyalty to FHC by continuing to have Spartan manage those facilities and receive the profits from doing so. The district court's finding that Dino did not violate his statutory and contractual fiduciary duties to FHC is supported by the record and is not clearly erroneous. We therefore affirm.

The district court's conclusion that Dino did not breach his duties to FHC was not clearly erroneous.

4. MINORITY OPPRESSION

In closely-held firms, a majority owner or a group of closely-aligned owners (such as family members) often controls the company. In this situation, a minority owner may be in a vulnerable position. Not only is an owner an investor, but she may also be an employee and the firm may constitute her entire livelihood. The majority owner can "freeze out" the minority owner. How? He can terminate the minority owner's employment, stop distributions to force a coercive sale of the minority stake, and freeze her out from decisionmaking processes. In the famous case of *Wilkes v. Springside Nursing Home, Inc.*, 353 N.E.2d 657 (Mass. 1976), the court observed in the context of a closely-held corporation:

> Several factors bear directly on the duty owed to Wilkes [the minority shareholder] by his associates. At a minimum, the duty of utmost good faith and loyalty would demand that the majority consider that their action was in disregard of a long-standing policy of the stockholders that each would be a director of the corporation and that employment with the corporation would go hand in hand with stock ownership; that Wilkes was one of the four originators of the nursing home venture; and that Wilkes, like the others, had invested his capital and time for more than fifteen years with the expectation that he would continue to participate in corporate decisions. Most important is the plain fact that the cutting off of Wilkes's salary, together with the fact that the corporation never declared a dividend, assured that Wilkes would receive no return at all from the corporation.

The case below discusses minority freeze out in the context of an LLC. In reading this case, consider these questions: (1) What actions constitute inequitable conduct as opposed to legitimate exercise of majority control? (2) What are the possible remedies for minority oppression?

WILSON V. GANDIS

844 S.E.2d 631 (S.C. 2020)

JUSTICE JAMES:

David Wilson, John Gandis, and Andrea Comeau-Shirley (Shirley) are members of Carolina Custom Converting, LLC (CCC). Wilson, a 45% member, brought an action against Gandis (also a 45% member), Shirley (a 10% member), and CCC alleging they engaged in oppressive conduct against him. Relief sought by Wilson included a forced buyout of his membership interest by Gandis, Shirley, and CCC.

During a five-day bench trial, the trial court found Gandis and Shirley engaged in oppressive conduct and ordered them to individually purchase Wilson's distributional interest in CCC for $347,863.

We find Wilson has proven that Gandis and Shirley engaged in oppressive conduct against him. Wilson is entitled to a buyout of his interest in CCC, and we agree with the trial court's valuation of Wilson's distributional interest. We modify the court's order to make CCC liable for the purchase of Wilson's interest in the first instance, with Gandis and Shirley being secondarily liable for the purchase, in proportion to their respective membership interests in CCC. We remand.

Wilson and Gandis formed CCC, a manager-managed limited liability company, with each man owning a 50% membership interest. Gandis served as president and manager, and Wilson served as vice-president. Wilson and Gandis never executed a formal operating agreement for CCC.

When CCC was formed, Wilson owned and operated Eastern Film Solutions (EFS), which bought and sold polyester, plastic, and metalized films. Gandis owned and operated DecoTex, which bought and sold decorative designs for vinyl film. Wilson and Gandis initially agreed that CCC would perforate and slit film. Wilson agreed to run some of EFS's slitting business through CCC.

Wilson and Gandis discussed expanding CCC's scope of operations and winding down their individual businesses. They discussed EFS buying film from CCC and selling it as an additional source of income to CCC. Wilson also agreed to make CCC the buyer and seller of film for one of EFS's major accounts, Minova, resulting in significant additional revenues for CCC. The Minova account prompted additional discussions between Gandis and Wilson about EFS winding down and running all new film business through CCC. However, Wilson advised Gandis he intended to keep three import accounts separate from CCC, namely Modular Metal, West Carrollton, and a portion of J.P. Lamborn. After CCC's expansion, Wilson led CCC's sales efforts, and Gandis managed its operations. Wilson completed the year-long process of winding down EFS.

In exchange for transferring EFS's accounts to CCC, Wilson received $12,000 per month. Gandis continued to own and operate DecoTex, and he agreed to fund CCC through credit lines from DecoTex and his other business, M-Tech. Gandis and Wilson both received distributions from CCC. CCC operated out of a building owned by M-Tech; since Gandis owned M-Tech, he received the benefit of rent payments.

Gandis engaged Shirley, a certified public accountant, to provide CCC with accounting and formation advice. Gandis and Wilson each transferred a 5% interest in CCC to Shirley in exchange for her services. Shirley did not have a formal voting interest; however, she took an active role in managing CCC. Shirley provided extensive personal counsel to Gandis about his operation of CCC. Gandis and Shirley largely excluded Wilson from their discussions about CCC's business operations. Gandis and Shirley exchanged a myriad of emails about the operation of CCC, and these emails provide evidence of their oppressive conduct against Wilson.

CCC's business grew, and CCC posted a profit of over $1 million in 2010. From the time CCC was formed in 2007 and through 2010, CCC reserved funds for the members to cover their individual tax liabilities. However, CCC had an operating loss in 2011. The high profits from 2010 combined with excess inventory created phantom income for the members, and the leaner revenue from 2011 resulted in a shortfall for the planned 2010 tax distributions.

Gandis had previously procured a line of credit for M-Tech, one of his other businesses. In private emails to Gandis, Shirley urged Gandis to use funds set aside by CCC for its members' 2010 tax liability to pay off CCC's obligation on the M-Tech line of credit. These reserved tax funds were typically kept on hand by CCC and distributed to members to cover their income tax liability. In one email to Gandis, Shirley stated, "What I want to do is to keep the cash balance [of CCC] relatively low so we don't get a request around tax time [from Wilson] to distribute any extra money instead it will already have been used to repay debt. Which is a better use!" She then advised Gandis to use the M-Tech line of credit to pay his own taxes, which Gandis did. Shirley told Wilson by email that no distributions would be made to CCC members to cover tax liability.

Trial testimony and emails between Shirley and Gandis from early 2011 reveal their plan to use CCC's employees to perform tasks for Gandis' other businesses, M-Tech and DecoTex. Also, Shirley and Gandis began secretly monitoring Wilson's emails.

On September 2011, Gandis retrieved [an] email sent to Wilson by Wilson's wife [which referenced Wilson hanging up on her during a telephone conversation and also expressed her frustration about Shirley's and Gandis' operation of CCC]. We agree with the trial court's conclusion that, "from this point forward, the emails between Gandis and Shirley evidence an effort to exclude Wilson from the benefits of ownership and to cease paying [Wilson] his monthly income as part of an effort to 'squeeze' [Wilson] to relinquish his ownership interest."

Shirley responded to Gandis that the email demonstrated marital discord, and she advised Gandis of a way to take advantage of the situation:

> This is probably your opportunity to make a RESTRUCTURING offer to him under which you restructure your relationship with him so that he gives up his equity ownership and converts to a structure where he is only taxed on what he receives! Now is the time to see if he wants to be in a different structure we can restructure so that he is not an owner as of [Jan. 1, 2012] and you can put him into a different deal that compensates him for his time and energy—maybe more like a regional sales manager is paid—so he gets paid on his sales and on the sales of the team.

The next morning, Shirley sent Gandis an even more detailed email expanding on her previous advice to restructure Wilson's position with CCC. She presented a framework that reflected the ultimate goal of Wilson becoming a salaried employee on terms that would allow CCC to terminate him for the smallest of reasons and with a noncompete agreement standing in his way to other employment. Even though Wilson held a 45% interest in CCC, Shirley admonished Gandis that Wilson "cannot continue to have access to the financial records" of CCC.

Wilson sent Gandis an email asking for a meeting with Gandis and Shirley. Wilson expressed his interest in knowing what "the game plan is for cash flow and taxes." Gandis forwarded the email to Shirley with the comment, "Now maybe the panic is setting in." Shirley responded to Gandis with her recommendation that Gandis continue to push Wilson toward relinquishing his membership interest and becoming an employee.

Wilson three options: (1) Wilson remains a member but foregoes the agreed-upon monthly compensation; (2) Wilson retires his membership interest, becoming a salaried at-will employee of CCC with a five-year noncompete agreement; or (3) CCC buys out Wilson's interest; however, the buyout would not eliminate Wilson's tax liability for 2010 or 2011. Unbeknownst to Wilson, Shirley revoked Wilson's authority to make wire transfers. Also, Wilson was removed as a signatory on CCC's bank account, and Gandis remained the only signatory on the account.

Shirley prepared a "Pro-Forma Balance Sheet" to accompany an offer to Wilson to buy his interest. The balance sheet contained questionable accruals and removed assets that had been listed on previous balance sheets. The balance sheet also devalued Wilson's interest in CCC. Gandis and Shirley indicated they would sell their membership interests at a price based upon this balance sheet; however, their actual offer to Wilson had materially different terms, including a requirement that Shirley be paid a $100,000 "preference on units" and the requirement that Wilson purchase M-Tech's building, which Shirley previously deemed a "burden."

The parties did not reach an agreement, and Wilson did not receive his $12,000 monthly compensation in January 2012.

January 17 emails between Gandis and Shirley reveal their decision to terminate Wilson and physically lock him out of his office but at the same time maintain the narrative that Wilson resigned.

On January 18, Gandis arrived at CCC's Greenville office with a law enforcement officer and a locksmith and advised Wilson his resignation was accepted. Wilson protested that he had not resigned. The officer did not force Wilson from the premises because Wilson was a co-owner of CCC; however, Wilson eventually left with two laptops, a Blackberry, files, his personal tax returns, and bank statements.

Immediately after locking Wilson out, Gandis and Shirley terminated Wilson's and his family's health insurance coverage and cell phone service. Gandis and Shirley increased CCC's monthly rent payments to M-Tech (wholly owned by Gandis) from $2,500 to $6,000. They also increased the interest rate on the M-Tech line of credit used by CCC, thereby increasing the return to Gandis.

Member Oppression

"A member or manager may maintain an action against a limited liability company or another member or manager for legal or equitable relief" to enforce his statutory rights under the Uniform Limited Liability Company Act of 1996 (the LLC Act), his rights under an operating agreement, and "the rights that otherwise protect the interests of the member." S.C. Code Ann. § 33–44–410(a). The comment to section 33–44–410 provides there is "broad judicial discretion to fashion appropriate legal remedies." If a member establishes that "the managers or members in control of the company have acted, are acting, or will act in a manner that is unlawful, oppressive, fraudulent, or unfairly prejudicial" to the member, a court may dissolve the limited liability company. S.C. Code Ann. § 33–44–801(4)(e). The comment to this section provides "the court has the discretion to order relief other than the dissolution of the company. Examples include the purchase of the distributional interest of the applicant." S.C. Code Ann. § 33–44–801 cmt.

"The terms 'oppressive' and 'unfairly prejudicial' are elastic terms whose meaning varies with the circumstances presented in a particular case." Determining if oppression exists requires "a fact-sensitive review and should therefore be determined through a case-by-case analysis, supplemented by various factors which may be indicative of oppressive behavior." The plaintiff is not required to prove illegal or fraudulent conduct by the majority shareholders. "The concern and focus in shareholder oppression cases is that the minority faces a trapped investment and an indefinite exclusion [from] participation in business returns." We hold these considerations also apply to a claim for oppression made by a minority member of a limited liability company.

The phrases "freeze out" or "squeeze out" are often used interchangeably and denote "the use by some of the owners or participants in a business enterprise of strategic position, inside information, or powers of control, or the utilization of some legal device or technique, to eliminate from the enterprise one or more of its owners or participants."

The trial court characterized Gandis' and Shirley's efforts as a "tightly controlled cabal to oust Wilson [that] could serve as a script for minority oppression." We agree. The record is replete with evidence of "freeze out" machinations. The emails between Gandis and Shirley reveal their explicit scheme to oust Wilson, and the emails unveil their step-by-step efforts to convert Wilson from a significant owner, with a promised $12,000 monthly compensation, to either a former owner or an employee bound by a noncompete agreement. The emails between Gandis and Shirley prove they calculated each move against Wilson. As the trial court observed, Shirley even posited to Gandis "we will freeze his capital account and provide that he will be paid out ONLY when the LLC has made distributions to you in excess of your guaranteed payment (and your tax liability)," and that "might mean that [Wilson] sits with a frozen capital account until the LLC liquidates (and he will still have a 2010 tax bill that he has to pay)."

Gandis and Shirley surreptitiously reviewed Wilson's email communications with his wife and used information gathered from this review to develop pressure tactics to squeeze out Wilson. They also deprived Wilson of the benefits of ownership when they withheld Wilson's distribution for his tax liability, while indirectly providing for Gandis to meet his tax liability, and when they withheld Wilson's promised monthly compensation beginning in January 2012. The accounts Wilson transferred from EFS to CCC were Wilson's investment in CCC. Wilson made clear to Gandis that he would transfer those accounts to CCC in exchange for monthly compensation because he was forfeiting income he would have received through EFS. By withholding Wilson's compensation, Gandis and Shirley trapped Wilson's investment in CCC.

Gandis and Shirley prevented Wilson from meaningfully participating in CCC operations by excluding him from many of their communications regarding CCC. Many times, Shirley advised Gandis to withhold important business information, such as financial and LLC formation information from Wilson, despite Wilson being a co-founder and a 45% owner of CCC. Gandis willingly followed along, as he did Shirley's other orchestrations. When they knew they had Wilson trapped, Gandis and Shirley presented Wilson with unfavorable alternatives for his future with CCC: (1) become an employee with an onerous noncompete, (2) remain an LLC member but forego the monthly compensation he relied upon, (3) accept a low buyout offer, or (4) buy Gandis and Shirley out on undesirable terms.

Also, Shirley and Gandis collaborated to physically lock Wilson out of CCC's premises and denied him access to CCC's financial information until they were compelled by the trial court to produce such information. After ousting Wilson, Gandis and Shirley routed CCC earnings to Gandis through higher rent and higher interest rates on the M-Tech line of credit. We also agree with the trial court's finding that Gandis and Shirley formed ZOi to compete with CCC in order to siphon profits from CCC.

We reject Gandis' and Shirley's argument that their actions are protected by the business judgment rule, as the rule only applies "absent a showing of a lack of good faith, fraud, self-dealing or unconscionable conduct." We completely agree with the trial court's conclusion that "the record—particularly the remarkable emails between Gandis and Shirley—abounds with evidence of calculated oppression." We find Wilson has proven Gandis and Shirley engaged in oppressive conduct against him.

Buyout of Wilson's Interest

"The LLC Act grants broad judicial discretion in fashioning remedies in actions by a member of an LLC against the LLC and/or other members." Importantly, subsection 33–44–410(a) specifically provides that an LLC member may maintain an action against the LLC or another member for legal or equitable relief "to enforce: (1) the member's rights under the operating agreement; (2) the member's rights under [the LLC Act]; and (3) the rights that otherwise protect the interests of the member." Courts have the authority under the LLC Act to order either the LLC or the oppressing member(s) to purchase the oppressed member's interest in the LLC.

We modify the trial court's order requiring Gandis and Shirley to individually purchase Wilson's interest. We first order CCC to purchase Wilson's interest in CCC, and Gandis and Shirley shall be obligated to purchase Wilson's interest only if CCC does not comply with our order that it do so. On remand, the trial court shall conduct a potentially two-step process for the buyout to take place. In the first (and perhaps only) step, CCC will first be responsible for purchasing Wilson's interest.

If CCC's purchase of Wilson's interest does not take place within a reasonable time after the remittitur is issued, the trial court shall take the second step and require Gandis and Shirley to complete the buyout in proportion to their respective membership interests in CCC. Even though Shirley owns a 10% interest in CCC and Gandis owns a 45% interest in CCC, the trial court concluded Gandis and Shirley were jointly and severally liable for the entire purchase price. Shirley argues, and Gandis agrees, that her responsibility to purchase any portion of Wilson's interest should be limited to the proportion her interest in CCC bears to the entire obligation to purchase. We agree.

Valuation of Wilson's Distributional Interest in CCC

The parties presented expert testimony on CCC's value and the value of Wilson's distributional interest. Wilson's expert, Catherine Stoddard, valued CCC's total equity at $1,018,753 and Wilson's interest at $408,335 as of December 31, 2011. Del Bradshaw (the trial court's appointed expert), Stoddard, and Charles Alford (the defense's expert) testified of possible adjustments to the value of CCC due to equipment moving costs, excess inventory, and advances.

The trial court noted CCC, Gandis, and Shirley failed to present evidence of CCC's then-current financial condition. The court found Stoddard's December 31, 2011 valuation credible but applied Alford's three downward adjustments to calculate the value of Wilson's interest as of that date. First, the trial court reduced CCC's $1,018,753 total value by $50,625, which was half the value of CCC's excess inventory. Second, the trial court reduced the value of CCC's equipment by 25% of its fair market value to account for moving costs. These two downward adjustments reduced the company's total value to $884,140, with Wilson's 45% interest valued at $397,863. The trial court then applied Alford's third adjustment by reducing the value of Wilson's interest by $50,000 for advances he previously received from CCC. Therefore, the trial court determined the fair value of Wilson's distributional interest in CCC was $347,863. We agree with the trial court's valuation of Wilson's interest.

Under the facts of this case, we find the most equitable valuation date is December 31, 2011. Gandis and Shirley initiated an exit strategy and ousted Wilson in January 2012; therefore, valuing CCC and Wilson's interest in CCC as of December 31, 2011, provides an accurate value of CCC when Wilson was an active member of CCC with an opportunity to impact CCC's financial condition.

5. CONTRACTING FOR DUTIES IN NBEs

Unlike corporation law where fiduciary duties are mandatory and nonwaivable, most NBE statutes permit a certain degree of contracting. This feature is one of the most critical distinctions between corporations and NBEs. *See* Dieckman v. Regency GP LP, 2016 WL 1223348, *8 (Del. Ch. 2016) ("But in stark contrast to the corporate context, in which fiduciary duties cannot be waived, a limited partnership may eliminate all fiduciary duties, including the duty of disclosure.").

Unless parties want to be bound by the statute and the entire common law of fiduciary duty applicable to the entity (and they may prefer this), they and their lawyers can contract for fiduciary duty. The contracting provisions are usually found in the section dealing with charter agreements. The following provisions in the RULLCA provide how parties can contract for duties. The RUPA and ULPA (2001) have corresponding and functionally identical provisions applicable to general partners. *See* RUPA § 105(c)–(e); ULPA (2001) § 105(c)–(e).

RULLCA § 105. Operating Agreement; Scope, Function, and Limitations.

(c) An operating agreement may not:

(5) alter or eliminate the duty of loyalty or the duty of care, except as otherwise provided in subsection (d);

(6) eliminate the contractual obligation of good faith and fair dealing under Section 409(d), but the operating agreement may prescribe the standards, if not manifestly unreasonable, by which the performance of the obligation is to be measured;

(7) relieve or exonerate a person from liability for conduct involving bad faith, willful or intentional misconduct, or knowing violation of law;

(8) unreasonably restrict the duties and rights under Section 410, but the operating agreement may impose reasonable restrictions on the availability and use of information obtained under that section

and may define appropriate remedies, including liquidated damages, for a breach of any reasonable restriction on use;

(d) Subject to subsection (c)(7), without limiting other terms that may be included in an operating agreement, the following rules apply:

(3) If not manifestly unreasonable, the operating agreement may:

(A) alter or eliminate the aspects of the duty of loyalty stated in Section 409(b) and (i);

(B) identify specific types or categories of activities that do not violate the duty of loyalty;

(C) alter the duty of care, but may not authorize conduct involving bad faith, willful or intentional misconduct, or knowing violation of law; and

(D) alter or eliminate any other fiduciary duty.

(e) The court shall decide as a matter of law whether a term of an operating agreement is manifestly unreasonable under subsection (c)(6) or (d)(3). The court:

(1) shall make its determination as of the time the challenged term became part of the operating agreement and by considering only circumstances existing at that time; and

(2) may invalidate the term only if, in light of the purposes, activities, and affairs of the limited liability company, it is readily apparent that:

(A) the objective of the term is unreasonable; or

(B) the term is an unreasonable means to achieve the term's objective.

The case below illustrates the role of the charter agreement in setting forth the scope of fiduciary duty. In reading this case, consider these questions: (1) What might have been the intent of drafting Section 3.3 of the operating agreement? (2) In hindsight, did the parties correctly draft Section 3.3, or did Section 3.3 work as originally intended?

MCCONNELL V. HUNT SPORTS ENTERPRISES

725 N.E.2d 1193 (Ohio App. 1999)

Author's summary of facts:* John McConnell and Wolfe Enterprises, Inc. filed a complaint for declaratory judgment against Hunt Sports Enterprises, Hunt Sports Enterprises, L.L.C., Hunt Sports Group, L.L.C. ("Hunt Sports Group"), and Columbus Hockey Limited ("CHL"). CHL was a limited liability company under Ohio law.

The National Hockey League ("NHL") sought applications for new hockey franchises. A consortium of persons sought to pursue this opportunity: Ronald Pizzuti, John, McConnell, Lamar Hunt, principal of Hunt Sports Group, and Wolfe Enterprises, Inc. Hunt was already the operating member of the Columbus Crew, a professional soccer team. CHL was formed to pursue the NHL franchise. The members of CHL were McConnell, Wolfe Enterprises, Inc., Hunt Sports Group, Pizzuti Sports Limited, and Buckeye Hockey, L.L.C. Each member made an initial capital contribution of $25,000. Pursuant to Section 2.1 of the written operating agreement, the general character of the business of CHL was to invest in and operate a franchise in the NHL.

CHL filed an application with the NHL. The application included Columbus's plan for an arena to house the hockey games. There was no facility at the time. Dimon McPherson, the CEO of Nationwide Insurance Enterprise ("Nationwide"), became interested in developing the arena and he approached Hunt. Hunt was interested. The NHL gave Columbus a deadline to come up with a plan for an arena. When Nationwide's plan was presented, Hunt Sports Group did not accept the lease proposal but indicated that it was still interested in pursuing the lease under different terms. McPherson then called McConnell. He told McConnell about Hunt Sports Group's rejection of the lease proposal and discussed the NHL's proposal deadline. McConnell stated that if Hunt would not accept lease and, therefore, get the franchise, McConnell would.

Nationwide informed the NHL that it would be building an arena in Columbus and that, if necessary, McConnell would purchase the franchise on his own. By this time, the Hunt Sports Group had not yet accepted the lease proposal. McConnell, in a conversation with the NHL, orally agreed to apply for a hockey franchise. The next day, McPherson returned a call from Hunt, and Hunt informed McPherson that he was still interested in pursuing an agreement with Nationwide. The NHL sent Hunt a letter requesting whether he was going forward with his franchise application. Hunt responded that CHL intended to pursue the franchise application but it was contingent upon entering into an appropriate lease.

* Author's note: For ease of reading, the opinion below has been edited to identify the parties by their names rather than their litigation positions (*i.e.*, "appellant" and "appellee"). These changes are not marked by brackets.

Matters came to a head when CHL held a meeting of members to discuss the matter, attended by McConnell, Hunt, Pizzuti, Wolfe Enterprises, and Buckeye Hockey, and Ameritech. Nationwide presented the lease term sheet to those present at the meeting, left the meeting, and went to a different room. The members of CHL split into two camps. Hunt, Ameritech and Buckeye Hockey indicated the lease was unacceptable. After this rejection, McConnell accepted the term sheet and signed it in his individual capacity. The executed term sheet was given to the NHL identified the ownership group as McConnell, majority owner, Pizzuti Sports, John Wolfe, and "up to seven (7) other members" (collectively "McConnell ownership group"). The NHL awarded Columbus a franchise to McConnell's group, and not to CHL.

McConnell and Wolfe Enterprises sought a declaration that Section 3.3 of the CHL operating agreement permitted members of CHL to compete with CHL. The trial court granted summary judgment in favor of McConnell and Wolfe Enterprises. It ruled that Section 3.3 of the operating agreement was unambiguous and permitted members to compete against CHL and to obtain the NHL franchise. The trial court also granted McConnell and Wolfe Enterprises, Inc.'s motion for directed verdicts on the issue of breach of fiduciary duty. An appeal followed.

TYACK, JUDGE.

The construction of written contracts is a matter of law. The purpose of contract construction is to discover and effectuate the intent of the parties, and the intent of the parties is presumed to reside in the language they chose to use in the agreement. If a contract is clear and unambiguous, there is no issue of fact to be determined, and the court cannot create a new contract by finding an intent not expressed in the clear language employed by the parties. Only where the language of a contract is unclear or ambiguous or when the circumstances surrounding the agreement invest the language of the contract with a special meaning, will extrinsic evidence be considered in an effort to give effect to the parties' intentions.

The test for determining whether a term is ambiguous is that common words in a written contract will be given their ordinary meaning unless manifest absurdity results or unless some other meaning is clearly evidenced from the face or overall content of the contract. A writing will be read as a whole, and the intent of each part will be gathered from a consideration of the whole. For the reasons that follow, we conclude that Section 3.3 is plain and unambiguous and allowed members of CHL to compete against CHL for an NHL franchise.

Section 3.3 of the operating agreement states:

> *Members May Compete.* Members shall not in any way be prohibited from or restricted in engaging or owning an interest in

any other business venture of any nature, including any venture which might be competitive with the business of the Company.

Hunt Sports Group emphasizes the word "other" in the above language and states, in essence, that it means any business venture that is different from the business of the company. Hunt Sports Group points out that under Section 2.1 of the operating agreement, the general character of the business is "to invest in and operate a franchise in the National Hockey League." Hence, Hunt Sports Group contends that members may only engage in or own an interest in a venture that is not in the business of investing in and operating a franchise with the NHL.

Hunt Sports Group's interpretation of Section 3.3 goes beyond the plain language of the agreement and adds words or meanings not stated in the provision. Section 3.3, for example, does not state "members shall not be prohibited from or restricted in engaging or owning an interest in any other business venture that is different from the business of the company." Rather, Section 3.3 states: "any other business venture *of any nature*." It then adds to this statement: "including any venture which might be competitive with the business of the Company." The words "any nature" could not be broader, and the inclusion of the words "any venture which might be competitive with the business of the Company" makes it clear that members were not prohibited from engaging in a venture that was competitive with CHL's investing in and operating an NHL franchise. Contrary to Hunt Sports Group's contention, the word "other" simply means a business venture other than CHL. The word "other" does not limit the type of business venture in which members may engage.

Hence, Section 3.3 did not prohibit McConnell from engaging in activities that may have been competitive with CHL, including McConnell's participation in McConnell ownership group. Accordingly, summary judgment in favor of McConnell was appropriate, and McConnell was entitled to a declaration that Section 3.3 of the operating agreement permitted McConnell to request and obtain an NHL hockey franchise to the exclusion of CHL.

We have already determined that Section 3.3 permitted McConnell to request and obtain an NHL franchise. Hunt Sports Group points to Section 4.1(c)(v) of the operating agreement in further support of its argument that McConnell breached the operating agreement in forming McConnell ownership group. Section 4.1 states:

> *Approval by Members.* No Member shall take any action *on behalf of the Company* unless such actions are approved by a vote of the specified number of Members:
>
> (c) The following actions require the approval of Members owning all of the Units allocated to the Members: (v) do any other

the duties created pursuant to such undertaking did not include a duty not to compete. Therefore, there was no duty on the part of McConnell to refrain from subjecting Hunt Sports Group to the injury complained of.

"Operating agreement" is defined in R.C. 1705.01(J) as all of the valid written or oral agreements of the members as to the affairs of a limited liability company and the conduct of its business. R.C. 1705.03(C) sets forth various activities limited liability companies may engage in and indicates such are subject to the company's articles of organization or operating agreement. Indeed, many of the statutory provisions in R.C. Chapter 1705 governing limited liability companies indicate they are, in various ways, subject to and/or dependent upon related provisions in an operating agreement. Here, the operating agreement states in its opening paragraph that it evidences the mutual agreement of the members in consideration of their contributions and promises to each other. Such agreement specifically allowed its members to compete with the company.

We conclude as a matter of law that it was not a breach of fiduciary duty for McConnell to form McConnell ownership group and obtain an NHL franchise to the exclusion of CHL. We are not stating that *no* act related to such obtainment could be considered a breach of fiduciary duty. In general terms, members of limited liability companies owe one another the duty of utmost trust and loyalty. However, such general duty in this case must be considered in the context of members' ability, pursuant to operating agreement, to compete with the company.

Theoretically, the charter agreement can strengthen the default statutory duties. In practice, however, the default fiduciary duties present the ceiling of the standard. Most contracting involve two kinds of changes: (1) clarifying or more precisely specifying duties generally consistent with the tenor of the statute; or (2) altering duties into an alternative standard, usually by weakening them.

Why would those who are owed fiduciary duties agree to contractual standards that are more lenient than the statutory standards? One answer may be the lack of bargaining power. Passive investors may be presented with an agreement as drafted by managers and their advisors as a take-it-or-leave-it proposition. Investors may calculate that the opportunity is sufficiently attractive that the cost of weaker fiduciary duties is simply a cost of investment, which on the whole may be net positive.

Another answer is that the default fiduciary duties do not optimally serve their purpose with respect to the particular circumstance. Business situations are not always conflict free. Even a simple partnership like the one in *Meinhard v. Salmon* presented a conflict of interest situation. Consider the situation in *McConnell v. Hunt Sports Enterprises*. Some of members of the LLC had outside interests including other sports teams, act that would make it impossible to carry on the business of the Company.

As to any argument that McConnell breached Secti forming McConnell ownership group and competing agains no genuine issue of material fact, and McConnell is entitled a matter of law. The voting requirements in Section 4.1 actions taken "on behalf of the Company." In forming McCor group and in obtaining the NHL franchise, McConnell wa taking action on behalf of CHL. Therefore, McConnell Section 4.1(c)(v) in failing to obtain the vote of all CHL m taking such action.

In summary, there are no genuine issues of material [is] entitled to judgment as a matter of law and reasonal only conclude that Section 3.3 of the operating agre McConnell to request and obtain an NHL franchise to the ex McConnell did not breach the operating agreement by forr ownership group and competing against CHL.

The term "fiduciary relationship" has been defined as a which special confidence and trust is reposed in the integ of another, and there is a resulting position of superior acquired by virtue of this special trust. In the case at bar, a company is involved which, like a partnership, invol relationship. Normally, the presence of such a relationship direct competition between members of the company. Ho have an operating agreement that by its very terms allo compete with the business of the company. Hence, the presented with is whether an operating agreement of a company may, in essence, limit or define the scope of the imposed upon its members. We answer this question in th

A fiduciary has been defined as a person having a dut *or her undertaking,* to act primarily for the benefit of an *connected with such undertaking.* A claim of breach of f basically a claim for negligence that involves a higher sta order to recover, one must show the existence of a duty o alleged wrongdoer not to subject such person to the injury failure to observe such duty, and an injury proxin therefrom. These principles support our conclusion that define the scope of fiduciary duties between parties to the

The injury complained of by Hunt Sports Group McConnell competing with CHL and obtaining the NH operating agreement constitutes the undertaking of the p becoming members of CHL, Hunt Sports Group and McC abide by the terms of the operating agreement, and specifically allowed competition with the company by its m and this fact may explain why they drafted the provisions of the operating agreement in question. The potential situations are endless.

- To attract a top person , the firm must accommodate her other business interests, which has the potential of conflicting with the firm's business.
- A business deal is brought to be firm by an owner or manager in which he has an interest, but the deal would actually benefit the firm.
- A competent manager wants to accept the firm's offer of employment, but does not want to be subject to duty of care claims without a high level of protection.

In each of these situations, the firm may benefit from contracting for fiduciary duties that provides relief from the specific anticipated situation. Contracting can narrowly tailor exceptions and exclusions for the circumstance. The firm may calculate that the opportunity is worth more than the cost of the specific relaxation of default fiduciary duties.

CHRYSLER GROUP LLC OPERATING AGREEMENT

Section 5.13 Standard of Care; Fiduciary Duties; Liability of Directors and Officers.

(a) The Board of Directors shall adopt corporate ethics, anti-bribery, anti-corruption, safety, environmental and other policies at least equivalent to those applicable to Fiat Parent.

(b) Any Director or Officer, in the performance of such Director's or Officer's duties, shall be entitled to rely in good faith on the provisions of this Agreement and on opinions, reports or statements (including financial statements, books of account or any other financial information, opinions, reports or statements as to the value or amount of the assets, liabilities, profits or losses of the Company and its Subsidiaries) of the following other Persons or groups: (i) one or more Officers or employees of such Member or the Company or any of their respective Subsidiaries, (ii) any legal counsel, accountants or other Person employed or engaged by any Member, the Board of Directors or the Company or any of its Subsidiaries or (iii) any other Person who has been selected with reasonable care as to matters which such relying Person reasonably believes to be within such other Person's professional or expert competence. The preceding sentence shall in no way limit any Person's right to rely on information to the extent provided in Section 18–406 of the LLC Act.

(c) On any matter involving a conflict of interest not provided for in this Agreement, each Director and Officer shall be guided by his or her good faith judgment as to the best interests of the Company and shall take such actions, if any, as are determined by such Person to be necessary or appropriate to ameliorate such conflict of interest.

(d) Subject to, and as limited by the provisions of this Agreement, the Directors and the Officers, in the performance of their duties as such, shall owe to the Company and its Members duties of loyalty and due care of the type owed under Law by directors and officers of a business corporation incorporated under the Delaware General Corporation Law; provided that the doctrine of corporate opportunity or any analogous doctrine shall not apply to the Directors and provided, further, that, no Director and no Person that elected such Director shall have any duty to disclose to the Company or the Board of Directors confidential information in such Director's or Person's possession even if it is material and relevant information to the Company and/or the Board of Directors and neither such Director nor such Person shall be liable to the Company or the Members for breach of any duty (including the duty of loyalty and any other fiduciary duties) as a Director or Person that has the right to nominate or elect such Director by reason of such lack of disclosure of such confidential information. The provisions of this Agreement, to the extent that they restrict or eliminate the duties (including the duty of loyalty and other fiduciary duties) and liabilities of a Director or Officer otherwise existing at Law or in equity or by operation of the preceding sentence, are agreed by the Members to replace such duties and liabilities of such Director or Officer. Notwithstanding the foregoing provisions and Section 5.13(f), except as otherwise expressly provided in this Agreement or any other written agreement entered into by the Company or any of its Subsidiaries and any Director, if a Director acquires knowledge of a potential transaction or matter that may be a business opportunity for the Company, such Director shall have no duty to communicate or offer such business opportunity to the Company and shall not be liable to the Company for breach of any duty (including the duty of loyalty and any other fiduciary duties) as a Director by reason of the fact that such Director directs such opportunity to any other Person, or does not communicate information regarding such opportunity to the Company, and any such direction of an opportunity by such Director, and any action with respect to such an opportunity by such Person, shall not be wrongful or improper or constitute a breach of any duty hereunder, at law, in equity or otherwise.

(e) Except as required by the LLC Act, no individual who is a Director or an Officer, or any combination of the foregoing, shall be personally liable under any judgment of a court, or in any other manner, for any debt, obligation or liability of the Company, whether that liability or obligation arises in contract, tort or otherwise by reason of being a Director or an Officer or any combination of the foregoing.

(f) No Director or Officer shall be liable to the Company or the Members (whether for monetary damages or otherwise) for any act or omission (including any breach of duty (fiduciary or otherwise)), including any mistake of fact or error in judgment taken, suffered or made by such Person if such Person acted in good faith and in a manner such Person reasonably believed to be in or not opposed to the best interests of the Company.

C. DELAWARE APPROACH ON CONTRACTING FOR FIDUCIARY DUTY

Under the uniform laws, fiduciary duties are subject to substantial contracting, but cannot be eliminated. Under Delaware laws of LPs and LLCs, the fiduciary duties of care and loyalty can be eliminated. Under both the uniform laws and Delaware law, the obligation of good faith and fair dealing may not be eliminated. However, the obligation is not a fiduciary duty (thus, the statutes distinguish "duty" and "obligation"), but is instead a contract principle. Only a small minority of states permits complete elimination of fiduciary duties. *E.g.*, Nevada Limited Liability Company Act § 86.286(7) ("An operating agreement may provide for the limitation or elimination of any and all liabilities for breach of contract and breach of duties, if any, of a member, manager or other person to a limited-liability company, to any of the members or managers, or to another person that is a party to or is otherwise bound by the operating agreement. An operating agreement may not limit or eliminate liability for any conduct that constitutes a bad faith violation of the implied contractual covenant of good faith and fair dealing."); Miller v. Am. Real Estate Partners, L.P., 2001 WL 1045643, at *8 (Del. Ch. 2001) ("The [Delaware limited partnership statute] puts investors on notice that fiduciary duties may be altered by partnership agreements, and therefore that investors should be careful to read partnership agreements before buying units. In large measure, [it] reflects the doctrine of *caveat emptor,* as is fitting given that investors in limited partnerships have countless other investment opportunities available to them that involve less risk and/or more legal protection. For example, any investor who wishes to retain the protection of traditional fiduciary duties can always invest in corporate stock.").

Delaware Limited Liability Company Act § 18–1101. Construction and application of chapter and limited liability company agreement.

(b) It is the policy of this chapter to give the maximum effect to the principle of freedom of contract and to the enforceability of limited liability company agreements.

(c) To the extent that, at law or in equity, a member or manager or other person has duties (including fiduciary duties) to a limited liability company or to another member or manager or to another person that is a party to or is otherwise bound by a limited liability company agreement, the member's or manager's or other person's *duties may be expanded or restricted or eliminated by provisions in the limited liability company agreement*; provided, that the limited liability company agreement may not eliminate the implied contractual covenant of good faith and fair dealing.

(e) A limited liability company agreement may provide for *the limitation or elimination of any and all liabilities for breach of contract and breach of duties (including fiduciary duties)* of a member, manager or other person to a limited liability company or to another member or manager or to another person that is a party to or is otherwise bound by a limited liability company agreement; provided, that a limited liability company agreement may not limit or eliminate liability for any act or omission that constitutes a bad faith violation of the implied contractual covenant of good faith and fair dealing.

Delaware Revised Uniform Limited Partnership Act § 17–1101. Construction and application of chapter and partnership agreement.

[Functionally the same as DLLCA § 18–1101(b), (c), (e).]

States like Delaware and Nevada follow the logical end of the policy to give maximum effect to the principle of freedom of contract in LPs and LLCs. "Delaware law recognizes the primacy of contract when addressing governance issues in the alternative entity space." Skye Mineral Investors, LLC v. DXS Capital (U.S.) Ltd., 2020 WL 881544, *25 (Del. Ch. 2020). Although the above Delaware statutes provide that fiduciary duties may be eliminated, elimination is a serious proposition. It means that passive investors and minority owners have no protection against a fiduciary's opportunism. Delaware courts have repeatedly stated that unless the elimination of duties is clearly expressed in the operating agreement, courts will not infer such elimination.[2]

[2] *See* CSH Theatres, LLC v. Nederlander of San Francisco Associates, 2015 WL 1839684, at *11 n.56 (Del. Ch. 2015) (stating that the elimination of fiduciary duties under the LLC statute "must be clear and unambiguous"); Ross Holding and Management Company v. Advance Realty Group, LLC, 2014 WL 4374261, at *13 n.138 (Del. Ch. 2014) (providing that the provision "clear and unambiguous"); Feeley v. NHAOCG, LLC, 62 A.3d 649, 664 (Del. Ch.2012) ("Drafters of an LLC agreement 'must make their intent to eliminate fiduciary duties plain and unambiguous.' ") (quoting Bay Ctr. Apartments Owner, LLC v. Emery Bay PKI, LLC, 2009 WL 1124451, at *9 (Del. Ch. 2009)); Kelly v. Blum, 2010 WL 629850, at *10 n.70 (Del. Ch. 2010) ("Having been granted great contractual freedom by the LLC Act, drafters of and parties to an LLC agreement should be expected to provide parties and anyone interpreting the agreement with clear and unambiguous provisions when they desire to expand, restrict, or eliminate the operation of traditional fiduciary duties."); Miller v. American Real Estate Partners, L.P., 2001 WL 1045643, at *1 (Del. Ch. 2001) (finding "that the drafters of the agreement did not make their intent to eliminate such duties

---

The case below illustrates an application of contract fiduciary duties in a conflict of interest situation. In reading this case, consider these questions: (1) What was the scope of contract fiduciary duty? (2) What conduct supported the court's conclusion that the general partner acted in bad faith? (3) In hindsight, how could the partnership agreement have been written to result in a conclusion of no breach of fiduciary duty? (4) Would such a provision have been commercially feasible?

BAY CENTER APARTMENTS OWNER, LLC v. EMERY BAY PKI, LLC

2009 WL 1124451 (Del. Ch. 2009)

STRINE, VICE CHANCELLOR.

This action arises out of a failed condominium development project based in Emeryville, California. The Project was a venture of two entities, plaintiff Bay Center LLC, and defendant Emery Bay PKI, LLC ("PKI"). PKI is owned and managed by defendant Alfred Nevis. Bay Center and PKI formed defendant Emery Bay Member, LLC ("Emery Bay") and designated PKI as the managing member.

The Emery Bay "LLC Agreement" gave PKI considerable power and authority to manage the affairs of Emery Bay. The LLC Agreement also contemplated that PKI would be responsible for managing the Project, but the parties defined those responsibilities through a separate agreement, the "Development Management Agreement." PKI was not required to sign the Development Management Agreement; instead, PKI designated one of its affiliates, defendant Emery Bay ETI, LLC ("ETI"), to be the entity bound by the terms of the Development Management Agreement. ETI's only counterparty in the Development Management Agreement was a wholly owned subsidiary of Emery Bay.

The Project encountered problems stemming from mismanagement and poor financial performance. Emery Bay defaulted on a loan it had obtained from a third-party bank and which Nevis had personally guaranteed. Bay Center alleges that the defendants secretly renegotiated this Loan on several occasions, resulting in the diversion of cash flow from the Project that was earmarked to repay an unsecured note from Emery

---

sufficiently clear to bar a fiduciary duty claim"); Fisk Ventures, LLC v. Segal, 2008 WL 1961156, at *11 (Del. Ch. 2008) ("The [limited liability company agreement] eliminates fiduciary duties to the maximum extent permitted by law by flatly stating that members have no duties other than those expressly articulated in the Agreement. Because the Agreement does not expressly articulate fiduciary obligations, they are eliminated."); CelestialRX Invs., LLC v. Krivulka, 2017 WL 416990, at *16 (Del. Ch. 2017) ("Thus, this Court has consistently found that removal of a manager's default fiduciary duties from an LLC agreement must be clear and unambiguous."); Skye Mineral Investors, LLC v. DXS Capital (U.S.) Ltd., 2020 WL 881544, at *21 (Del. Ch. 2020) ("Thus, this court has consistently found that removal of default fiduciary duties through an LLC agreement must be clear and unambiguous.").

Bay held by Bay Center. By renegotiating the Loan in this way, Nevis avoided triggering his Personal Guarantee, and PKI avoided capital calls.

The Project experienced a host of other problems, all supposedly resulting from mismanagement of the Project by PKI's affiliates, including budget overruns in excess of $10 million, vendor complaints, poor sales, and squatters and vandalism. The Project eventually failed under the weight of these troubles, and entered into receivership.

Bay Center seeks monetary damages from Nevis and the entities he controlled: PKI, ETI, and Emery Bay. Bay Center's most direct route to recovery is through a breach of contract claim under the LLC Agreement. But, this approach is limited because PKI is the only defendant who was a party to that Agreement. Bay Center therefore seeks to expand its remedial options by bringing claims for breach of fiduciary duty.

The defendants move to dismiss all of Bay Center's claims except those based on breach of contract. I deny the defendants' motion in its entirety. Bay Center has also sufficiently pled that PKI breached its fiduciary duties.

I address the disagreement between the parties as to what fiduciary duties existed under the LLC Agreement. The Delaware LLC Act gives members of an LLC wide latitude to order their relationships, including the flexibility to limit or eliminate fiduciary duties.[32] But, in the absence of a contrary provision in the LLC agreement, the manager owes the traditional fiduciary duties of loyalty and care to the members of the LLC.

The defendants claim that the parties took full advantage of this flexibility by eliminating all fiduciary duties in the LLC Agreement. Bay Center, in contrast, claims that the LLC Agreement specifically preserves the traditional fiduciary duties. To support these starkly opposite positions, the parties point to two separate and seemingly contradictory provisions of the LLC Agreement:

> Section 6.1 *Relationship of Members.* Each Member agrees that, to the fullest extent permitted by the Delaware Act and except as otherwise expressly provided in this Agreement or any other agreement to which the Member is a party: (b) *The Members shall have the same duties and obligations to each other that members of a limited liability company formed under the Delaware Act have to each other.*
>
> Section 6.2 *Liability of Members. Except for any duties imposed by this Agreement each Member shall owe no duty of any kind* towards the Company or the other Members in performing its duties and exercising its rights hereunder or otherwise.

[32] 6 *Del. C.* § 18–1101(e); *see also Elf Atochem N. Am., Inc. v. Jaffari,* 727 A.2d 286, 291 (Del.1999) ("The basic approach of the Delaware Act is to provide members with broad discretion in drafting the Agreement.").

The LLC Agreement states that the members of Emery Bay both owe each other the default fiduciary duties that exist between members of an LLC absent alteration in an LLC agreement, and at the same time owe each other no duty of any kind not imposed by the LLC Agreement itself.

On a motion to dismiss, the court cannot choose between reasonable interpretations of ambiguous contract provisions. Instead, defendants are only entitled to dismissal if "the interpretation of the contract on which their theory of the case rests is the *only* reasonable construction as a matter of law." The determinative question is therefore whether the defendants' position that the LLC Agreement eliminates their fiduciary duties is the only reasonable one. I find that it is not.

The defendants argue that under § 6.2, a duty must be expressly imposed by the LLC Agreement in order for PKI to be bound to it. According to the defendants, no fiduciary duty is expressly imposed on PKI in the LLC Agreement. But, it is reasonable to read § 6.1(b) as doing precisely that. Section 6.1(b) expressly imposes the default fiduciary duties on PKI, so the default fiduciary duties are carved out of § 6.2's elimination of duties by the "except for any duties imposed by this Agreement" language in that provision. The duties eliminated by § 6.2 are those that are not traditional duties or are otherwise not expressly contemplated in the LLC Agreement.

Because the existence of duties under § 6.1(b) can be reconciled with § 6.2's apparent elimination of them in this way, Bay Center's reading of the LLC Agreement is more reasonable than the defendants' reading. It is a maxim of contract interpretation that, "given ambiguity between potentially conflicting terms, a contract should be read so as not to render any term meaningless." The defendants have not offered a coherent argument for how the LLC Agreement can be read to eliminate fiduciary duties without rendering § 6.1(b) meaningless. The interpretive scales also tip in favor of preserving fiduciary duties under the rule that the drafters of chartering documents must make their intent to eliminate fiduciary duties plain and unambiguous. The defendants' interpretation of the LLC Agreement is not the most reasonable interpretation, let alone the only reasonable interpretation. Thus, I construe the LLC Agreement in favor of Bay Center and the LLC Agreement requires Emery Bay's members to act in accordance with traditional fiduciary duties.

The case below is another example of contract fiduciary duties in a conflict of interest situation. In reading this case, consider these questions: (1) What was the conflict of interest? (2) In what way could the partnership agreement's conflict of interest resolution mechanism have itself presented a conflict of interest? (3) If the contract mechanism was itself potentially tainted by an actual conflict, why was the transaction still valid?

NORTON V. K-SEA TRANSP. PARTNERS L.P.

67 A.3d 354 (Del. 2013)

STEELE, CHIEF JUSTICE.

The plaintiffs allege that the general partner obtained excessive consideration for its incentive distribution rights when an unaffiliated third party purchased the partnership. Importantly, the plaintiffs do not allege that the general partner breached the implied covenant of good faith and fair dealing. We conclude that the limited partnership agreement's conflict of interest provision created a contractual safe harbor, not an affirmative obligation. The general partner needed only to exercise its discretion in good faith, as the parties intended that term to be construed, to satisfy its duties under the agreement. The general partner obtained an appropriate fairness opinion, which, under the agreement, created a conclusive presumption that the general partner made its decision in good faith. We affirm the Court of Chancery's dismissal of the complaint.

This case arises out of the Merger of K-Sea Transportation Partners L.P. (K-Sea or the Partnership) and Kirby Corporation. K-Sea operates a barge and tugboat fleet that transports refined petroleum products between American ports. Before the Merger, K-Sea was a publicly traded Delaware limited partnership. The Fourth Amended and Restated Agreement of Limited Partnership (the LPA) created K-Sea's governance structure. Plaintiffs Edward Norton and Ken Poesl (Norton) represent a class consisting of K-Sea's unaffiliated former common unitholders.

K-Sea's general partner is K-Sea General Partner L.P. (K-Sea GP), which is also a Delaware limited partnership. K-Sea GP's general partner is K-Sea General Partner GP LLC (KSGP), a Delaware limited liability company that ultimately controls K-Sea. Anthony Abbate, Barry Alperin, James Baker, Timothy Casey, James Dowling, Brian Friedman, Kevin McCarthy, Gary Reaves, and Frank Salerno served on KSGP's board of directors (the K-Sea Board) during the Merger negotiations. Directors Abbate, Alperin, and Salerno comprised the K-Sea Board's Conflicts Committee. K-Sea, K-Sea GP, KSGP, and the K-Sea Board members are the Defendants in this action.

At the time of the Merger, K-Sea's equity was divided among K-Sea GP, the common unitholders, and a class of preferred units held by KA First Reserve, LLC (KAFR). The common unitholders held 49.8% of the total equity, KAFR held 49.9%, and K-Sea GP's general partner interest comprised the remaining 0.3%.

In addition to its general partner interest, K-Sea GP held incentive distribution rights (IDRs) through a wholly owned affiliate. These IDRs entitled K-Sea GP to increasing percentages of K-Sea's distributions once payments to the limited partners exceeded certain levels. K-Sea GP would not receive payments on the IDRs until *quarterly* distributions reached

$0.55 per unit. K-Sea's conservative estimates indicated that *annual* distributions would not reach $0.55 per unit until 2015. Norton extrapolates these projections to show that K-Sea would not reach the $0.55-per-unit quarterly threshold until the mid-2030s. Based on these projections, the IDRs were worth as little as $100,000.

Shortly after the phantom [IDR] unit grant, Kirby's CEO communicated with McCarthy to discuss a strategic transaction between Kirby and K-Sea. McCarthy informed Dowling, the K-Sea Board's Chairman, of those discussions. K-Sea and Kirby then extended a confidentiality agreement they had previously signed, and K-Sea provided Kirby with due diligence.

Kirby offered to pay $306 million for K-Sea's common and preferred units. McCarthy rejected it and informed Kirby that future offers should include consideration for K-Sea GP's general partner interest and its IDRs. Kirby responded the next day with a $316 million offer for all of K-Sea's equity interests, but McCarthy again rejected the offer as inadequate. Kirby offered $329 million for K-Sea, which included an $18 million payment for the IDRs (the IDR Payment).

When the K-Sea Board met to consider Kirby's new offer, it acknowledged that the IDR Payment created a "possible conflict of interest" and referred the proposed Merger to the Conflicts Committee for a recommendation. Under the LPA, the Conflict Committee's approval of a transaction would constitute "Special Approval," which purportedly would limit the unitholders' ability to challenge the transaction.

The Conflicts Committee hired Stifel, Nicolaus & Co. (Stifel) and DLA Piper LLP as its independent financial and legal advisors, respectively. After valuing the common units, Stifel opined that the consideration K-Sea's unaffiliated common unitholders received was fair from a financial viewpoint. The fairness opinion expressly did not consider "the fairness of the amount or nature of any compensation to any of the officers, directors or employees of K-Sea or its affiliates relative to the compensation of the public holders of K-Sea's equity securities."

After reviewing Stifel's fairness opinion, the Conflicts Committee unanimously recommended the Merger to the K-Sea Board, which also approved it. Like Stifel's fairness opinion, the Conflicts Committee's recommendation did not refer to the IDR Payment. K-Sea and Kirby then entered into a definitive merger agreement and [recommended] that the common unitholders vote in favor of the Merger. A majority of K-Sea's unitholders voted in favor of the transaction, and the Merger closed. As finally negotiated, K-Sea's common unitholders received $8.15 per unit and K-Sea GP received $18 million for the IDRs. The consideration represented a 26% premium over K-Sea's [pre-announcement] closing price.

Author's Note: diagram of entity relationships and economic stakes

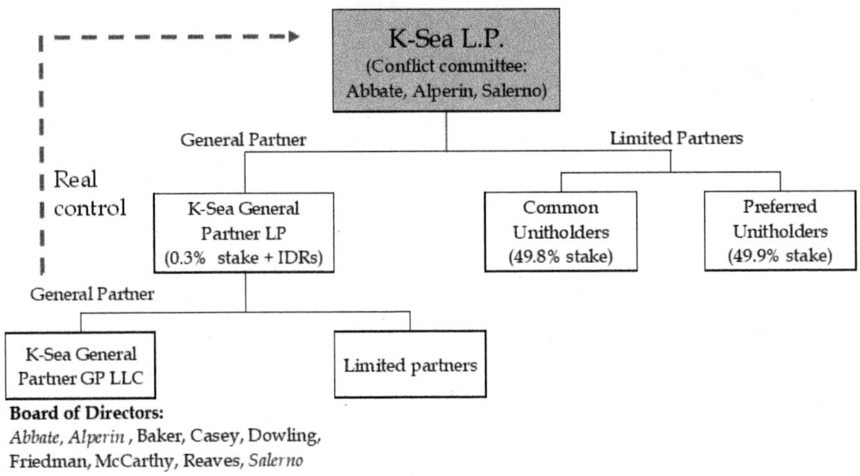

What Contractual Standards Apply to the Merger?

Limited partnership agreements are a type of contract. We, therefore, construe them in accordance with their terms to give effect to the parties' intent. We give words their plain meaning unless it appears that the parties intended a special meaning. When interpreting contracts, we construe them as a whole and give effect to every provision if it is reasonably possible. A meaning inferred from a particular provision cannot control the agreement if that inference conflicts with the agreement's overall scheme. We consider extrinsic evidence only if the contract is ambiguous. A contract is not ambiguous "simply because the parties do not agree upon its proper construction," but only if it is susceptible to two or more reasonable interpretations. If the contractual language at issue is ambiguous and if the limited partners did not negotiate for the agreement's terms, we apply the *contra proferentem* principle and construe the ambiguous terms against the drafter.

The Delaware Revised Uniform Limited Partnership Act (DRULPA) gives "maximum effect to the principle of freedom of contract and to the enforceability of partnership agreements." 6 Del. C. § 17–1101(c). Parties may expand, restrict, or eliminate any fiduciary duties that a partner or other person might otherwise owe, but they "may not eliminate the implied contractual covenant of good faith and fair dealing." 6 Del. C. § 17–1101(d).

The LPA's Provisions Governing Mergers and Creating Contractual Fiduciary Duties

Unfortunately, limited partnership agreements that attempt to modify, rather than eliminate, fiduciary duties often create a Gordian knot of interrelated standards in different sections of the agreement. This LPA requires us to parse several provisions to determine which standards apply to the Merger. The LPA creates procedures for mergers in Article XIV. Section 14.2 of Article XIV establishes that K-Sea GP must approve any proposed merger. K-Sea GP may consent to a merger "in the exercise of its discretion." Section 7.9(b), which attempts to clarify the nebulous "discretion" standard, provides:

> Whenever this Agreement provides that [K-Sea GP] is permitted or required to make a decision (i) in its "sole discretion" or "discretion," except as otherwise provided herein, [K-Sea GP] shall be entitled to consider only such interests and factors as it desires and shall have no duty or obligation to give any consideration to any interest of, or factors affecting, the Partnership [or] any Limited Partner [and] (ii) it may make such decision in its sole discretion (regardless of whether there is a reference to "sole discretion" or "discretion") unless another express standard is provided for.

When K-Sea GP decides whether to consent to a merger, it may "consider only such interests and factors as it desires and shall have no duty or obligation to give any consideration to any interest of, or factors affecting" K-Sea or its limited partners. The limited partners' ultimate right to reject a merger under Section 14.3 practically limits that discretion however.

The LPA limits Section 14.2's broad grant of discretion in Section 7.10(d), which provides:

> Any standard of care and duty imposed by [the LPA] or [DRULPA] shall be modified, waived or limited, to the extent permitted by law, as required to permit [K-Sea GP] to act under [the LPA] and to make any decision pursuant to the authority prescribed in [the LPA], *so long as such action is reasonably believed by [K-Sea GP] to be in, or not inconsistent with, the best interests of the Partnership.*

If K-Sea GP were subject to common law fiduciary duties, it could not consent to a merger in its sole discretion. Therefore, Section 7.10(d) eliminates any duties that otherwise exist and replaces them with a contractual fiduciary duty—namely, that K-Sea GP must reasonably believe that its action is in the best interest of, or not inconsistent with, the best interests of the Partnership.

The LPA broadly exculpates all Indemnitees so long as the Indemnitee acted in "good faith." Although the LPA regrettably does not define "good faith" in this context, we cannot discern a rational distinction between the parties' adoption of this "good faith" standard and Section 7.10(d)'s contractual fiduciary duty, *i.e.,* an Indemnitee acts in good faith if the Indemnitee reasonably believes that its action is in the best interest of, or at least not inconsistent with, the best interests of K-Sea. If we take seriously our obligation to construe the agreement's "overall scheme," we must conclude that the parties' insertion of a free-standing, enigmatic standard of "good faith" is consistent with Section 7.10(d)'s conceptualization of a reasonable belief that the action taken is in, or not inconsistent with, the best interests of the Partnership. In this LPA's overall scheme, "good faith" cannot be construed otherwise.

While the LPA does not require K-Sea GP to consider any particular interest or factor affecting the Partnership when exercising its discretion, K-Sea GP still must reasonably believe that its ultimate course of action is not inconsistent with K-Sea's best interests. Therefore, unless another provision supplants this standard, in order to state a claim that withstands Rule 12(b)(6), Norton must allege facts supporting an inference that K-Sea GP had reason to believe that it acted inconsistently with the Partnership's best interests when approving the Merger.

To state a claim that survives a motion to dismiss under Rule 12(b)(6), Norton must plead facts supporting a reasonable inference that K-Sea GP, the only defendant with a duty relating to the Merger's approval, acted inconsistently with the Partnership's best interests. If Norton's complaint cannot establish a breach of the contract's "good faith" standard, we need not reach whether the phantom unit grant disqualified the Conflicts Committee members and invalidated the Special Approval process.

Norton has alleged that the IDR Payment created a conflict of interest between K-Sea GP and the Partnership because K-Sea GP obtained consideration that did not flow to the common unitholders. At the motion to dismiss stage we must draw all inferences in Norton's favor. We therefore could conclude that K-Sea GP used its position to extract an excessive amount of consideration for its IDRs at the expense of the limited partners. That permits us to infer that K-Sea GP may not have acted in good faith when it approved the Merger and submitted it to the unitholders for approval. That raises the next issue, which is whether Norton has pled a cognizable claim that K-Sea GP did not act in good faith.

Did the Investment Banker's Fairness Opinion Create a Conclusive Presumption of Good Faith?

We must consider yet another LPA provision addressing K-Sea GP's obligation to act in "good faith." That provision creates a conclusive presumption that K-Sea GP has acted in good faith if K-Sea GP relies on a competent expert's opinion. Section 7.10(b) provides that

> [K-Sea GP] may consult with investment bankers and any act taken or omitted to be taken in reliance upon the opinion of such Persons as to matters that [K-Sea GP] reasonably believes to be within such Person's professional or expert competence *shall be conclusively presumed to have been done or omitted in good faith* and in accordance with such opinion.

The Conflicts Committee obtained Stifel's opinion that the consideration that Kirby paid to K-Sea's unaffiliated common unitholders was financially fair. No party alleges that Stifel lacked the requisite expertise to render that opinion. Norton nowhere claims that the opinion did not state that the Merger was fair, nor does he allege that the analyses underlying the fairness opinion were flawed. Rather, he alleges that K-Sea extracted a larger portion of the consideration than the IDRs' value justified. We note also that Norton does not claim on appeal that Defendants' actions breached the implied covenant of good faith and fair dealing.

Norton argues that K-Sea GP is not entitled to a conclusive presumption of good faith because Stifel did not specifically address the IDR Payment's fairness—the reason why K-Sea GP activated the Conflicts Committee. He concedes that the unaffiliated unitholders received a fair price, and he correctly notes that a limited partnership's value is not a single number, but a range of fair values. While we understand Norton's frustration, the LPA's provisions control.

The LPA does not require K-Sea GP to evaluate the IDR Payment's reasonableness separately from the remaining consideration. Section 7.9(a) explicitly states that nothing in the LPA shall be construed to require K-Sea GP to consider the interests of any person other than the Partnership. That Section authorizes (but does not require) K-Sea GP to consider the "relative interests of any party to such conflict." These provisions indicate that K-Sea GP was not required to consider whether the IDR Payment was fair, but only whether the Merger as a whole was in the best interests of the Partnership (which included the general partner and the limited partners). Because of those clear provisions, Norton had no reasonable contractual expectation that K-Sea GP or the Conflict Committee's retained investment banker would consider the IDR Payment's fairness.

Because Stifel's opinion satisfied the LPA's requirements, we next address whether that opinion entitles *K-Sea GP* to a conclusive presumption of good faith. Although the Conflicts Committee of the K-Sea Board actually obtained the fairness opinion, it is unreasonable to infer that the entire K-Sea Board did not rely on the opinion that a K-Sea Board subcommittee obtained. Similarly, because K-Sea GP is a "pass-through" entity controlled by KSGP, the only reasonable inference is that K-Sea GP relied on the fairness opinion. K-Sea GP is therefore conclusively presumed to have acted in good faith when it approved the Merger and submitted it to the unitholders for a vote. That process satisfied K-Sea GP's contractual duty to exercise its discretion in "good faith" (as this LPA defines the term).

Norton willingly invested in a limited partnership that provided fewer protections to limited partners than those provided under corporate fiduciary duty principles. He is bound by his investment decision. Here, the LPA did not require K-Sea GP to consider separately the IDR Payment's fairness, but granted K-Sea GP broad discretion to approve a merger, so long as it exercised that discretion in "good faith." Reliance on Stifel's opinion satisfied this standard. By opining that the consideration Kirby paid to the unaffiliated unitholders was fair, Stifel's opinion addressed the IDR Payment's fairness, albeit indirectly. Kirby presumably was willing to pay a fixed amount for the entire Partnership. If K-Sea GP diverted too much value to itself, at some point the consideration paid to the unaffiliated unitholders would no longer be "fair."

The LPA does not leave K-Sea's unitholders unprotected. K-Sea GP's approval merely triggered submission of the Merger to the unitholders for a majority vote. If the unitholders were dissatisfied with the Merger's terms, "their remedy [was] the ballot box, not the courthouse." Here K-Sea GP is conclusively presumed to have approved the Merger in good faith, and a majority of the unitholders voted to consummate it. The LPA required nothing more.

NOTES

1. In *Dieckman v. Regency GP LP*, 2019 WL 5576886, at *5 (Del. Ch. 2019), the court dealt with a limited partnership agreement that provided the same term seen in section 7.10(b) of *Norton v. K-Sea Transportation Partners L.P.*:

> The General Partner may consult with legal counsel, accountants, appraisers, management consultants, investment bankers and other consultants and advisers selected by it, and any act taken or omitted to be taken in reliance upon the opinion (including an Opinion of Counsel) of such Persons as to matters that the General Partner reasonably believes to be within such Person's professional or expert competence shall be conclusively presumed to have been done or omitted in good faith and in accordance with such opinion.

The court held that the defendants were not entitled to summary judgment based on the provision of an investment banker's fairness opinion because the plaintiff "has demonstrated that there is a genuine issue of fact about whether defendants *actually* relied on [the] fairness opinion." *Id.* at *7.

2. In *Inter-Marketing Group USA, Inc. v. Armstrong*, 2019 WL 417849, at *5–*6 (Del. Ch. 2019), the court found the below provision in the agreement functionally identical to language in *Norton v. K-Sea Transportation Partners L.P.* and held that it eliminated common law fiduciary duties.

> Any standard of care and duty imposed by this Agreement or under the Delaware Act or any applicable law, rule or regulation shall be modified, waived or limited, to the extent permitted by law, as required to permit the General Partner to act under this Agreement or any other agreement contemplated by this Agreement and to make any decision pursuant to the Authority prescribed in this Agreement, so long as such action is reasonably believed by the General Partner to be in, or not inconsistent with, the best interests of the Partnership.

Another example of a provision that eliminated all common law duties and replaced them with contractual duties is seen in *Bandera Master Fund LP v. Boardwalk Pipeline Partners, LP*, 2019 WL 4927053, at *8 (Del. Ch. 2019).

> Except as expressly set forth in this Agreement, neither the General Partner nor any other Indemnitee shall have any duties or liabilities, including fiduciary duties, to the Partnership or any Limited Partner or Assignee and the provisions of this Agreement, to the extent that they restrict, eliminate or otherwise modify the duties and liabilities, including fiduciary duties, of the General Partner or any other Indemnitee otherwise existing at law or in equity, are agreed by the Partners to replace such other duties and liabilities of the General Partner or such other Indemnitee.

D. OBLIGATION OF GOOD FAITH AND FAIR DEALING

In the laws of NBEs, the obligation of good faith and fair dealing is different from fiduciary duties. Notice that the uniform laws and Delaware laws provide that the obligation may not be eliminated, even though Delaware permits the elimination of fiduciary duties. *See* RUPA § 105(c)(6); ULPA (2001) § 105(c)(7); RULLCA § 105(c)(6); Delaware Limited Liability Company Act § 18–1101(c); Delaware Revised Uniform Limited Partnership Act § 17–1101(d). While the duty of care and duty of loyalty are identified as a "duty," the statutes identify good faith and fair dealing as an "obligation." Statutes further characterize the obligation as "contractual." *See* RUPA § 409(d) ("contractual obligation of good faith and fair dealing"); ULPA (2001) § 409(d) (same); RULLCA § 409(d) (same); Delaware Limited Liability Company Act § 18–1101(c) ("implied contractual covenant of good faith and fair dealing"); Delaware Revised Uniform Limited Partnership Act § 17–1101(d) (same).

These differences reveal an important conceptual distinction. In corporation law, the concept of "good faith" has for years been confusing. What does good faith mean? Is it a fiduciary duty? Is it an independent duty distinct from the duties of care and loyalty? Delaware resolved the confusion, at least conceptually and taxonomically. In *Stone v. Ritter*, the Delaware Supreme Court defined a breach of "good faith" as:

> A failure to act in good faith may be shown [1] where the fiduciary intentionally acts with a purpose other than that of advancing the best interests of the corporation, [2] where the fiduciary acts with the intent to violate applicable positive law, or [3] where the fiduciary intentionally fails to act in the face of a known duty to act, demonstrating a conscious disregard for his duties.

911 A.2d 362, 369 (Del. 2006). The court also held that directors "breach their *duty of loyalty* by failing to discharge that fiduciary obligation in good faith." *Id.* at 370. In Delaware corporation law, the concept of good faith is

a subset of the fiduciary duty of loyalty, and bad faith conduct including the above three variants constitutes a breach of the duty of loyalty.

In the realm of NBEs, the concept of good faith is entirely different. Although NBE statutes use the same term, the "contractual obligation of 'good faith' has nothing to do with the corporate concept of good faith." RUPA § 409, cmt. subsection (d). The concept is not grounded in fiduciary duty, but instead in contract. Contract law provides: "Every contract imposes upon each party a duty of good faith and fair dealing in its performance and its enforcement." Restatement (Second) Contracts § 205 (1981). Every contract, no matter how diligently drafted, is said to be incomplete. For example, even a simple contract to paint a house may not have specific provisions dealing with the terms upon which the painter may entry the house to perform the contract, but any dispute on entry may come down to whether the homeowner's denial of entry was consistent with the obligation of good faith and fair dealing in light to the bargained for fruit. The obligation of good faith fills in gaps that neither party anticipated at the time of contracting of the specific bargain.

> NBE laws conceptualize good faith as a contract principle.
>
> The contractual obligation of "good faith" has nothing to do with the corporate concept of good faith that for years bedeviled courts and attorneys trying to understand: (i) Delaware's famous corporate law exoneration provision; and (ii) that provision's exception "for acts or omissions not in good faith." [DGCL] § 102(b)(7). In that context, good faith is an aspect of the duty of loyalty. *See Stone v. Ritter*, 911 A.2d 362, 369–70 (Del. 2006).

Pennsylvania Uniform Limited Liability Company Act of 2016 § 8849.1, cmt. Moreover, the contractual obligation of good faith and fair dealing is not the same concept as fiduciary duties owed by partners and shareholders of closely-held businesses described as "utmost good faith," despite the common use of the term "good faith." *E.g.*, Meinhard v. Salmon, 164 N.E. 545, 551 (N.Y. 1928) ("Where parties engage in a joint enterprise each owes to the other the duty of the *utmost good faith* in all that relates to their common venture. Within its scope they stand in a fiduciary relationship."); Donahue v. Rodd Electrotype Co. of New England, Inc., 328 N.E.2d 505, 515 (Mass. 1975) ("Stockholders in the close corporation owe one another substantially the same fiduciary duty in the operation of the enterprise that partners owe to one another. In our previous decisions, we have defined the standard of duty owed by partners to one another as the *utmost good faith* and loyalty.").

Contractual obligation of good faith and fair dealing provides a gap filling provision. It applies as a counterfactual exercise. It provides implied contract terms consistent with the manner in which the parties would have decided had they considered the issue ex ante.

> The implied covenant of good faith and fair dealing involves a "cautious enterprise," inferring contractual terms to handle developments or contractual gaps that the asserting party pleads neither party anticipated. "One generally cannot base a claim for breach of the implied covenant on conduct authorized by the agreement." We will only imply contract terms when the party asserting the implied covenant proves that the other party has acted arbitrarily or unreasonably, thereby frustrating the fruits of the bargain that the asserting party reasonably expected. When conducting this analysis, we must assess the parties' reasonable expectations at the time of contracting and not rewrite the contract to appease a party who later wishes to rewrite a contract he now believes to have been a bad deal. Parties have a right to enter into good and bad contracts, the law enforces both.

Nemec v. Shrader, 991 A.2d 1120, 1125–26 (Del. 2010). *See* Don King Prods., Inc. v. Douglas, 742 F. Supp. 741, 767 (S.D.N.Y. 1990) ("It simply ensures that parties to a contract perform the substantive, bargained-for terms of their agreement and that parties are not unfairly denied express, explicitly bargained-for benefits.").

A contract claim for a breach of the implied covenant "may be brought, if at all, only where one party's conduct, though not breaching the terms of the contract in a technical sense, nonetheless deprived the other party of the benefit of its bargain." Sauer v. Xerox Corp., 95 F. Supp. 2d 125, 132 (W.D.N.Y. 2000). Since good faith is a gap filler, it does not apply when the contract expressly addresses the conduct or situation at issue. *See* Nationwide Emerging Managers, LLC v. Northpointe Holdings, LLC, 112 A.3d 878, 896 (Del. 2015) ("[The implied covenant of good faith and fair dealing] does not apply when the contract addresses the conduct at issue."); Dunlap v. State Farm Fire & Cas. Co., 878 A.2d 434, 441 (Del. 2005) ("Existing contract terms control, however, such that implied good faith cannot be used to circumvent the parties' bargain, or to create a free-floating duty unattached to the underlying legal document.").

The cases below illustrate the principle of implied covenant of good faith and fair dealing. In reading these cases, consider these questions: (1) What is the difference between fiduciary duties and the obligation of good faith and fair dealing? (2) In what situations do the concept apply? (3) What are the limits of its application? (4) Why is it that the obligation cannot be contractually eliminated even in Delaware?

GERBER V. ENTERPRISE PRODUCTS HOLDINGS, LLC

67 A.3d 400 (Del. 2013)

JACOBS, JUSTICE:

[Limited partners brought class action against managers. They challenged the sale of a portion of the partnership and subsequent merger of the LP. They argued that the transaction and the manager's action breached the partnership agreement and the implied covenant of good faith and fair dealing. The court quoted from *ASB Allegiance Real Estate Fund v. Scion Breckenridge Managing Member, LLC*, 50 A.3d 434, 440–42 (Del. Ch. 2012), and endorsed the excerpted quotation below on the distinction between fiduciary duty and the obligation of good faith and fair dealing as the correct statement of law in Delaware.]

The implied covenant seeks to enforce the parties' contractual bargain by implying only those terms that the parties would have agreed to during their original negotiations if they had thought to address them. Under Delaware law, a court confronting an implied covenant claim asks whether it is clear from what was expressly agreed upon that the parties who negotiated the express terms of the contract would have agreed to proscribe the act later complained of as a breach of the implied covenant of good faith—had they thought to negotiate with respect to that matter. While this test requires resort to a counterfactual world—what if—it is nevertheless appropriately restrictive and commonsensical.

The temporal focus is critical. Under a fiduciary duty or tort analysis, a court examines the parties as situated at the time of the wrong. The court determines whether the defendant owed the plaintiff a duty, considers the defendant's obligations (if any) in light of that duty, and then evaluates whether the duty was breached. Temporally, each inquiry turns on the parties' relationship as it existed at the time of the wrong. The nature of the parties' relationship may turn on historical events, and past dealings necessarily will inform the court's analysis, but liability depends on the parties' relationship when the alleged breach occurred, not on the relationship as it existed in the past.

An implied covenant claim, by contrast, looks to the past. It is not a free-floating duty unattached to the underlying legal documents. It does not ask what duty the law should impose on the parties given their relationship at the time of the wrong, but rather what the parties would have agreed to themselves had they considered the issue in their original bargaining positions at the time of contracting. "Fair dealing" is not akin to the fair process component of entire fairness, *i.e.*, whether the fiduciary acted fairly when engaging in the challenged transaction as measured by duties of loyalty and care whose contours are mapped out by Delaware precedents. It is rather a commitment to deal "fairly" in the sense of consistently with the terms of the parties' agreement and its purpose.

"Good faith" does not envision loyalty to the contractual counterparty, but rather faithfulness to the scope, purpose, and terms of the parties' contract. Both necessarily turn on the contract itself and what the parties would have agreed upon had the issue arisen when they were bargaining originally.

The retrospective focus applies equally to a party's discretionary rights. The implied covenant requires that a party refrain from arbitrary or unreasonable conduct which has the effect of preventing the other party to the contract from receiving the fruits of its bargain. *When exercising a discretionary right, a party to the contract must exercise its discretion reasonably.* The contract may identify factors that the decision-maker can consider, and it may provide a contractual standard for evaluating the decision. Express contractual provisions always supersede the implied covenant, but even the most carefully drafted agreement will harbor residual nooks and crannies for the implied covenant to fill. In those situations, what is "arbitrary" or "unreasonable"—or conversely "reasonable"—depends on the parties' original contractual expectations, not a "free-floating" duty applied at the time of the wrong.

DIECKMAN V. REGENCY GENERAL PARTNER LP

155 A.3d 358 (Del. 2017)

SEITZ, JUSTICE.

The plaintiff is a limited partner/unitholder in the publicly-traded master limited partnership ("MLP"). The general partner proposed that the partnership be acquired through merger with another limited partnership in the MLP family. The seller and buyer were indirectly owned by the same entity, creating a conflict of interest. Because conflicts of interest often arise in MLP transactions, those who create and market MLPs have devised special ways to try to address them. The general partner in this case sought refuge in two of the safe harbor conflict resolution provisions of the partnership agreement—"Special Approval" of the transaction by an independent Conflicts Committee, and "Unaffiliated Unitholder Approval."

In the MLP context, Special Approval typically means that a Conflicts Committee composed of members independent of the sponsor and its affiliates reviewed the transaction and made a recommendation to the partnership board whether to approve the transaction. Unaffiliated Unitholder Approval is typically just that—a majority of unitholders unaffiliated with the general partner and its affiliates approve the transaction. Under the partnership agreement, if either safe harbor is satisfied, the transaction is deemed not to be a breach of the agreement.

The partnership agreement required that the Conflicts Committee be independent, meaning that its members could not be serving on affiliate boards and were independent under the audit committee independence rules of the New York Stock Exchange. The plaintiff alleged in the complaint that the general partner failed to satisfy the Special Approval safe harbor because the Conflicts Committee was itself conflicted. According to the plaintiff, one of the Committee's two members began evaluating the transaction while still a member of an affiliate's board, and then resigned from the affiliate's board four days after he began his review to then become a member of the Conflicts Committee. On the same day the transaction closed, the committee member was reappointed to the seat left vacant for him on the affiliate's board.

The plaintiff also alleged that the general partner failed to satisfy the Unaffiliated Unitholder Approval safe harbor because the general partner made false and misleading statements in the proxy statement to secure that approval. In the 165-page proxy statement sent to the unitholders, the general partner failed to disclose the conflicts within the Conflicts Committee. Instead, the proxy statement stated that Special Approval had been obtained by an independent Conflicts Committee.

The general partner moved to dismiss and claimed that, in the absence of express contractual obligations not to mislead investors or to unfairly manipulate the Conflicts Committee process, the general partner need only satisfy what the partnership agreement expressly required—to obtain the safe harbor approvals and follow the minimal disclosure requirements. In other words, whatever the general partner said in the proxy statement, and whomever the general partner appointed to the Conflicts Committee, was irrelevant because only the express requirements of the partnership agreement controlled and displaced any implied obligations not to undermine the protections afforded unitholders by the safe harbors.

The Court of Chancery side-stepped the Conflicts Committee safe harbor, but accepted the general partner's argument that the Unaffiliated Unitholder Approval safe harbor required dismissal of the case.

We view the central issue in the dispute through a different lens than the Court of Chancery. The Court of Chancery was correct that the implied covenant of good faith and fair dealing cannot be used to supplant the express disclosure requirements of the partnership agreement. But the court focused too narrowly on the partnership agreement's disclosure requirements. Instead, the center of attention should have been on the conflict resolution provision of the partnership agreement.

We find that the plaintiff has pled sufficient facts, which we must accept as true at this stage of the proceedings, that neither safe harbor was available to the general partner because it allegedly made false and misleading statements to secure Unaffiliated Unitholder Approval, and allegedly used a conflicted Conflicts Committee to obtain Special Approval. Thus, we reverse the Court of Chancery's order dismissing the complaint.

[The case involves a complex web of cross-relationships among many entities. Adrian Dieckman is a unitholder of Regency Energy Partners LP

("Regency"), a publicly-traded Delaware LP. Regency General Partner LP ("General Partner LP") is the general partner of Regency. Regency is governed by a partnership agreement ("LP Agreement"). Energy Transfer Partners L.P. ("ETP") is the general partner of Sunoco LP and a 43% owner of limited partnership interests in Sunoco. Energy Transfer Equity, L.P. ("ETE") indirectly own Regency's general partner and ETP's general partner, which means that ETE indirectly controls both LPs. A simplified version of the complex cross-relationships is the following.

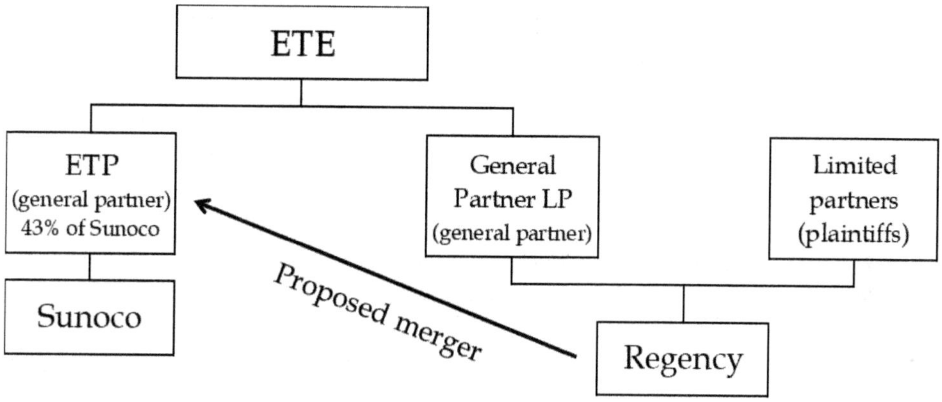

The other defendants are the six members of General Partner LP's board of directors including James Bryant and Richard Brannon, who served on the Conflicts Committee of the General Partner's board.]

The ETP and ETE boards met to discuss a merger between ETP and Regency. ETP eventually made a merger proposal to Regency, where Regency would be merged into ETP for a combination of cash and stock using an exchange ratio of 0.4044 ETP common units for one Regency common unit, and a $137 million cash payment. Because of the undisputed conflicts of interest in the proposed merger transaction, the General Partner looked to the conflict resolution provisions of the LP Agreement.

Under § 7.9(a) of the LP Agreement, entitled "Resolution of Conflicts of Interest; Standards of Conduct and Modification of Duties," the General Partner can resort to several safe harbors to immunize conflicted transactions from judicial review:

> Any resolution or course of action by the General Partner or its Affiliates in respect of such conflict of interest shall be permitted and deemed approved by all Partners, and shall not constitute a breach of this Agreement or of any duty stated or implied by law or equity, if the resolution or course of action in respect of such conflict of interest is (i) approved by Special Approval, (ii) approved by the vote of a majority of the Common Units (excluding Common Units owned by the General Partner and its Affiliates), (iii) on terms no less favorable to the Partnership than

those generally being provided to or available from unrelated third parties, or (iv) fair and reasonable to the Partnership, taking into account the totality of the relationships between the parties involved (including other transactions that may be particularly favorable or advantageous to the Partnership).

The General Partner sought the protections of the safe harbors by Special Approval under § 7.9(a)(i) and Unaffiliated Unitholder Vote under § 7.9(a)(ii). Special Approval is defined as "approval by a majority of the members of the Conflicts Committee." The Conflicts Committee must be:

> A committee of the Board of Directors of the general partner of the General Partner composed entirely of two or more directors who are not (a) security holders, officers or employees of the General Partner, (b) officers, directors or employees of any Affiliate of the General Partner, or (c) holders of any ownership interest in the Partnership Group other than Common Units and who also meet the independence standards required of directors who serve on an audit committee of a board of directors.

For purposes of subsection (b), "Affiliate" is defined as any person "that directly or indirectly through one or more intermediaries controls, is controlled by or is under control with, the Person in question." Sunoco and the General Partner are both controlled by ETE, and are "Affiliates," under the LP Agreement. Thus, Sunoco board members were not eligible to serve as members of the General Partner's Conflicts Committee.

The General Partner appointed Brannon and Bryant to the Conflicts Committee. The complaint alleges that before the proposed transaction, Brannon was a Sunoco director. On January 16, 2015, ETE appointed Brannon to the General Partner's board, while still a director of Sunoco. The plaintiff claims that, from January 16–20, while a member of both boards, Brannon consulted informally on the proposed transaction. Brannon then temporarily resigned from the Sunoco board on January 20, and on January 22, became an official member of the Conflicts Committee when formal resolutions were passed creating the Committee. Brannon and Bryant then negotiated on behalf of Regency with ETP and recommended the merger transaction to the General Partner. On April 30, 2015, the day that the merger closed, Brannon was reappointed to the Sunoco board, and Bryant was also appointed to Sunoco board.

The plaintiff claims that the negotiations between the Conflicts Committee and ETP were ceremonial and only lasted a few days. According to the complaint, between January 23 and January 25, the Conflicts Committee made a perfunctory and slightly increased counteroffer to ETP's offer, which would have achieved a 15% premium to the closing price of common units. ETP rejected the counteroffer, and the parties settled on ETP's opening bid of a 13.2% premium to the January 23 closing price. The Conflicts Committee recommended that the General Partner pursue the transaction on the original terms proposed by ETP, which the General Partner approved on January 25. The plaintiff alleges that the entire process from start to finish lasted nine days.

The LP Agreement only required minimal disclosure when a merger transaction was considered by the unitholders—a summary of, or a copy of, the merger agreement. But the General Partner went beyond the minimal requirements in the LP Agreement. To gain Unaffiliated Unitholder Approval and the benefit of the safe harbor, the General Partner filed a 165-page proxy statement and disseminated it and a copy of the merger agreement to the unitholders.

The proxy statement stated that the "Conflicts Committee consists of two independent directors: Richard D. Brannon (Chairman) and James W. Bryant." It also stated that the Conflicts Committee approved the transaction, and such approval "constituted 'Special Approval' as defined in the Regency partnership agreement." The proxy statement did not inform unitholders about the circumstances of Bryant's alleged overlapping and shifting allegiances, including reviewing the proposed transaction while still a member of the Sunoco board, his nearly contemporaneous resignation from the Sunoco board and appointment to the General Partner's board and then the Conflicts Committee, or Brannon's appointment and Bryant's reappointment to the Sunoco board the day the transaction closed. At a special meeting of Regency's unitholders on April 28, 2015, a majority of Regency's unitholders, including a majority of its unaffiliated unitholders, approved the merger.

[Analysis]

We start with the settled principles of law governing Delaware limited partnerships. The Delaware Revised Uniform Limited Partnership Act ("DRUPLA") gives "maximum effect to the principle of freedom of contract." DRUPLA § 17–1101(c). One freedom often exercised in the MLP context is eliminating any fiduciary duties a partner owes to others in the partnership structure. DRUPLA § 17–1101(d). The act allows drafters of Delaware limited partnerships to modify or eliminate fiduciary-based principles of governance, and displace them with contractual terms.

With the contractual freedom accorded partnership agreement drafters, and the typical lack of competitive negotiations over agreement terms, come corresponding responsibilities on the part of investors to read carefully and understand their investment. "With the benefits of investing in alternative entities often comes the limitation of looking to the contract as the exclusive source of protective rights." In other words, investors can no longer hold the general partner to fiduciary standards of conduct, but instead must rely on the express language of the partnership agreement to sort out the rights and obligations among the general partner, the partnership, and the limited partner investors.

Even though the express terms of the agreement govern the relationship when fiduciary duties are waived, investors are not without some protections. In the case of an ambiguous partnership agreement of a publicly traded limited partnership, ambiguities are resolved as with publicly traded corporations, to give effect to the reading that best fulfills the reasonable expectations an investor would have had from the face of the agreement. The reason for this is simple. When investors buy equity in a public entity, they necessarily rely on the text of the public documents and public disclosures about that entity, and not on parol evidence. Another protection exists. The DRUPLA provides for the implied covenant of good faith and fair dealing, which cannot be eliminated by contract.

The Court of Chancery decided that the implied covenant could not be used to remedy what the plaintiff alleged were faulty safe harbor approvals because the LP Agreement waived fiduciary-based standards of conduct and contained an express contractual term addressing what disclosures were required in merger transactions. According to the court, the implied covenant had "no work to do" because the express disclosure requirement displaced the implied covenant.

The Court of Chancery erred by focusing too narrowly on whether the express disclosure provision displaced the implied covenant. It should have focused on the language of the safe harbor approval process, and what its terms reasonably mean. Although the terms of the LP Agreement did not compel the General Partner to issue a proxy statement, it chose to undertake the transaction, which the LP Agreement drafters would have known required a pre-unitholder vote proxy statement. Thus, the General Partner voluntarily issued a proxy statement to induce unaffiliated unitholders to vote in favor of the merger. The favorable vote led not only to approval of the transaction, but allowed the General Partner to claim the protections of the safe harbor and immunize the merger from judicial review. Not surprisingly, the express terms of the LP Agreement did not address, one way or another, whether the General Partner could use false or misleading statements to enable it to reach the safe harbors.

We find that implied in the language of the LP Agreement's conflict resolution provision is a requirement that the General Partner not act to undermine the protections afforded unitholders in the safe harbor process. Partnership agreement drafters, whether drafting on their own, or sitting across the table in a competitive negotiation, do not include obvious and provocative conditions in an agreement like "the General Partner will not mislead unitholders when seeking Unaffiliated Unitholder Approval" or "the General Partner will not subvert the Special Approval process by appointing conflicted members to the Conflicts Committee." But the terms are easily implied because "the parties must have intended them and have only failed to express them because they are too obvious to need expression." Stated another way, "some aspects of the deal are so obvious to the participants that they never think, or see no need, to address them."

Our use of the implied covenant is based on the words of the contract and not the disclaimed fiduciary duties. Under the LP Agreement, the General Partner did not have the full range of disclosure obligations that a corporate fiduciary would have had. Yet once it went beyond the minimal disclosure requirements of the LP Agreement, and issued a 165-page proxy statement to induce the unaffiliated unitholders not only to approve the merger transaction, but also to secure the Unaffiliated Unitholder Approval safe harbor, implied in the language of the LP Agreement's conflict resolution provision was an obligation not to mislead unitholders.

The General Partner was required to form a Conflicts Committee comprised of members who:

> Are not (a) security holders, officers or employees of the General Partner, (b) officers, directors or employees of any Affiliate of the General Partner or (c) holders of any ownership interest in the Partnership Group other than Common Units and who also meet the independence standards required of directors who serve on an audit committee of a board of directors.

As with the contract language regarding Unaffiliated Unitholder Approval, this language is reasonably read by unitholders to imply a condition that a Committee has been established whose members genuinely qualified as unaffiliated with the General Partner and independent at all relevant times. Implicit in the express terms is that the Special Committee membership be genuinely comprised of qualified members and that deceptive conduct not be used to create the false appearance of an unaffiliated, independent Special Committee.

The LP Agreement's safe harbor provisions, if satisfied, would preclude judicial review of the transaction. But we find that the plaintiff has pled sufficient facts to support his claims that those safe harbors were unavailable to the General Partner. Instead of staffing the Conflicts Committee with independent members, the plaintiff alleges that the chair of the two-person Committee started reviewing the transaction while *still* a member of an Affiliate board. Just a few days before the General Partner created the Conflicts Committee, the same director resigned from the Affiliate board and became a member of the General Partner's board, and then a Conflicts Committee member.

After conducting the negotiations with ETE over the merger terms and recommending the merger transaction to the General Partner, the two members of the Conflicts Committee joined an Affiliate's board the day the transaction closed. The plaintiff also alleges that the Conflicts Committee members failed to satisfy the audit committee independence rules of the New York Stock Exchange, as required by the LP Agreement. In the proxy statement used to solicit Unaffiliated Unitholder Approval of the merger transaction, the plaintiff alleges that the General Partner materially misled the unitholders about the independence of the Conflicts Committee members. In deciding to approve the merger, a reasonable unitholder would have assumed based on the disclosures that the transaction was negotiated and approved by a Conflicts Committee composed of persons who were not "affiliates" of the general partner and who had the independent status dictated by the LP Agreement. This assurance was one a reasonable investor may have considered a material fact weighing in favor of the transaction's fairness.

The plaintiff has pled facts raising doubt about the General Partner's ability to use the safe harbors to shield the merger from judicial review.

E. FIDUCIARY DUTY TO CREDITORS

Corporate managers do not owe fiduciary duty to creditors. Debt is not equity. A creditor protects its interest principally through contracting. *See* Commentaries on Model Debenture Indenture Provisions, at 2 (Am. Bar Found. 1971) ("The second fundamental characteristic of long-term debt financing is that the rights of the holders of the debt securities are largely a matter of contract."). A debt instrument "does not represent an equitable interest in the issuing corporation necessary for the imposition of a trust relationship with concomitant fiduciary duties." Simons v. Cogan, 549 A.2d 300, 303 (Del. 1988).

However, Delaware courts have held that when a corporation is insolvent, creditors have standing to bring a derivative action on behalf of the corporation, but not a direct action.

> It is well settled that directors owe fiduciary duties to the corporation. When a corporation is *solvent,* those duties may be enforced by its shareholders, who have standing to bring *derivative* actions on behalf of the corporation because they are the ultimate beneficiaries of the corporation's growth and increased value. When a corporation is *insolvent,* however, its creditors take the place of the shareholders as the residual beneficiaries of any increase in value.
>
> The creditors of an *insolvent* corporation have standing to maintain derivative claims against directors on behalf of the corporation for breaches of fiduciary duties. The corporation's insolvency "makes the creditors the principal constituency injured by any fiduciary breaches that diminish the firm's value." Equitable considerations give creditors standing to pursue derivative claims against the directors of an insolvent corporation. Individual creditors of an insolvent corporation have the same

> incentive to pursue valid derivative claims on its behalf that shareholders have when the corporation is solvent.
>
> Recognizing that directors of an insolvent corporation owe direct fiduciary duties to creditors, would create uncertainty for directors who have a fiduciary duty to exercise their business judgment in the best interest of the insolvent corporation. To recognize a new right for creditors to bring direct fiduciary claims against those directors would create a conflict between those directors' duty to maximize the value of the insolvent corporation for the benefit of all those having an interest in it, and the newly recognized direct fiduciary duty to individual creditors. Directors of insolvent corporations must retain the freedom to engage in vigorous, good faith negotiations with individual creditors for the benefit of the corporation. We hold that individual *creditors* of an *insolvent* corporation have *no right to assert direct* claims for breach of fiduciary duty against corporate directors. Creditors may protect their interest by bringing derivative claims on behalf of the insolvent corporation or any *other* direct nonfiduciary claim that may be available for individual creditors.

N. Am. Catholic Educ. Programming Found., Inc. v. Gheewalla, 930 A.2d 92, 101–02 (Del. 2007).

The case below discusses the issue of whether creditors have standing to bring a derivative action against the managers of an LLC. In reading this case, consider this question: (1) Why can a creditor bring a derivative action on behalf of an insolvent corporation per *Gheewalla*, but cannot do so on behalf of an LLC? (2) Is there a plausible reason why different rules should apply as between corporations and LLCs?

CML V, LLC v. BAX

28 A.3d 1037 (Del. 2011)

STEELE, CHIEF JUSTICE:

CML V, LLC, a junior secured creditor of JetDirect Aviation Holdings, LLC, sued JetDirect's present and former officers directly and derivatively for breaching their fiduciary duties.

JetDirect, a Delaware limited liability company, was a private jet management and charter company. As part of a roll up strategy, JetDirect acquired a number of small to mid-sized competitor charter and service companies. This aggressive expansion left JetDirect with a highly leveraged balance sheet and volatile cash flows.

JetDirect's board of managers learned about serious deficiencies in its accounting system. JetDirect's auditor informed the officers of various weaknesses and deficiencies in internal controls. Later, JetDirect's new auditor—Ernst & Young LLP—declined to complete its audit because JetDirect's internal controls lacked sufficient integrity and the auditor could not rely on JetDirect's internal accounting books and records.

Despite lacking current information about JetDirect's true financial condition, the board approved four major acquisitions.

CML loaned JetDirect [$34,243,912] and became a junior secured lender. JetDirect defaulted on its loan to CML. JetDirect was insolvent.

JetDirect has not repaid any of its debt to CML, and after accounting for interest, the balance of CML's outstanding loan to JetDirect exceeds $40,000,000. CML filed a Complaint in the Court of Chancery asserting derivative claims against JetDirect's present and former managers.

The Vice Chancellor dismissed all claims on the basis that CML, as a creditor, lacks standing to pursue derivative claims on behalf of JetDirect.

The parties dispute the effect of the derivative standing provisions of the Limited Liability Company Act . The central provision at issue is 6 *Del. C.* § 18–1002, entitled "Proper plaintiff." That provision reads:

> In a derivative action, the plaintiff must be a member or an assignee of a limited liability company interest at the time of bringing the action and:
>
> (1) At the time of the transaction of which the plaintiff complains; or
>
> (2) The plaintiff's status as a member or an assignee of a limited liability company interest had devolved upon the plaintiff by operation of law or pursuant to the terms of a limited liability company agreement from a person who was a member or an assignee of a limited liability company interest at the time of the transaction.

This provision is unambiguous on its face. The provision dictates that a proper derivative action plaintiff "*must* be a member or an assignee of a limited liability company interest." The statutory language is clear, unequivocal, and exclusive, and operates to deny derivative standing to creditors who are not members or assignees of membership interests.

CML contends that section 18–1002 is limited to the context of section 18–1001, entitled "Right to bring action," which reads:

> A member or an assignee of a limited liability company interest may bring an action in the Court of Chancery in the right of a limited liability company to recover a judgment in its favor if the managers or members with authority to do so have refused to

bring the action or if an effort to cause those managers or members to bring the action is not likely to succeed.

In other words, one part of CML's contentions posits that section 18–1001 guarantees derivative standing to members or assignees, but does not limit standing to those groups. Reading the two sections together and consistently with each other, CML contends, demonstrates that the General Assembly intended merely to rephrase the language of section 327 of the [DGCL],[15] which does not bar creditors of insolvent corporations from derivative standing. *See N. Am. Catholic Educ. Programming Found., Inc. v. Gheewalla,* 930 A.2d 92, 101 (Del.2007) ("The creditors of an *insolvent* corporation have standing to maintain derivative claims against directors on behalf of the corporation for breaches of fiduciary duties."). According to CML, the combination of sections 18–1001 and 18–1002 shows that the General Assembly merely intended to take the corporate rule of derivative standing for creditors of insolvent corporations and apply it in the LLC context. We disagree. When statutory text is unambiguous, we must apply the plain language without any extraneous contemplation of, or intellectually stimulating musings about, the General Assembly's intent.

The text of section 18–1002 is unambiguous because it is not susceptible of two reasonable interpretations and because invoking its clear language does not yield an unreasonable or absurd result the General Assembly never contemplated. First, the General Assembly used the indefinite phrase "a derivative action" instead of the definite phrase "the derivative action" to describe those derivative actions to which section 18–1002 applies. We ascribe purpose to this choice. By making the choice, the General Assembly created an independent restriction on *all* derivative actions on behalf of LLCs—not merely those derivative actions that section 18–1001 seemingly authorizes. Moreover, in section 18–1002, the General Assembly used the mandatory and exclusive "must," rather than the permissive "may" that it used in section 18–1001. That is, in the LLC context, the "Proper Plaintiff" "*must* be a member or an assignee of a limited liability company interest." That is the only reasonable interpretation of the plain language of section 18–1002.

Finally, applying the plain language of section 18–1002 does not yield an unreasonable or absurd result. Sections 18–1001 and 18–1002 serve very different purposes. In section 18–1001, the General Assembly created the right to file a derivative action on behalf of an LLC and conferred derivative standing on LLC members and assignees. In section 18–1002, the General Assembly limited the scope of LLC derivative standing to members and assignees.

---

[15] 8 *Del. C.* § 327, Stockholder's Derivative Action: "In any derivative suit instituted by a stockholder of a corporation, it shall be averred in the complaint that the plaintiff was a stockholder of the corporation at the time of the transaction of which such stockholder complains or that such stockholder's stock thereafter devolved upon such stockholder by operation of law."

CML contends that this result is absurd because, given the policy underlying derivative standing, there should be no difference between LLCs and corporations. CML argues that unless the Court of Chancery can vest creditors of insolvent LLCs with derivative standing in equity, there will exist no stakeholders with incentive to enforce fiduciary duties through legal action. CML may be correct that in insolvency creditors become the ultimate risk bearers in LLCs. But the General Assembly is free to elect a statutory limitation on derivative standing for LLCs that is different than that for corporations, and thereby preclude creditors from attaining standing. The General Assembly is well suited to make that policy choice and we must honor that choice. In this respect, it is hardly absurd for the General Assembly to design a system promoting maximum business entity diversity. Ultimately, LLCs and corporations are different; investors can choose to invest in an LLC, which offers one bundle of rights, or in a corporation, which offers an entirely separate bundle of rights.

Only LLC members or assignees of LLC interests have derivative standing to sue on behalf of an LLC—creditors do not. Therefore, section 18–1002 precludes CML from suing derivatively, and the Vice Chancellor properly granted the motion to dismiss.

NOTES

1. Other courts have applied similar reasoning. In *Mantle v. North Star Energy & Construction, LLC*, 437 P.3d 758 (Wyo. 2019), the court provided the following analysis.

> The Colorado Supreme Court declined to extend fiduciary duties to creditors of insolvent LLCs, regardless of standing, in *Weinstein v. Colborne Foodbotics, LLC*, 302 P.3d 263 (Colo. 2013). The court observed that "an LLC is distinct from a corporation" and, unlike the provisions of Colorado's LLC Act, which "permits the operating agreement to override the LLC Act's provisions in all but a few instances, the provisions of the Colorado Business Corporation Act control over a corporation's articles of incorporation." The court noted that the only facet of corporation common law included in the LLC Act concerned veil-piercing. In contrast, the LLC Act contained no provision extending "the common law duty an insolvent corporation's directors owe to its creditors." Thus, the court held "absent statutory authority, the manager of an insolvent LLC does not owe the LLC's creditors the same fiduciary duty that an insolvent corporation's directors owe the corporation's creditors."
>
> Similar reasoning applies here. Wyoming created new types of business entities, such as the LLC, in part to avoid the "many formal requirements as to [a corporation's] structure and governance," and that "a limited liability company's operation is intended to be much more flexible than a corporation's." *GreenHunter Energy, Inc. v. Western Ecosystems Tech.*, 337 P.3d 454, 460–61 (Wyo. 2014). In

GreenHunter, we carried corporate common law over to LLCs with caution. Wyoming's LLC Act specifies that managers owe duties of loyalty and care "to the company," and is silent as to any extension of fiduciary duties to creditors. Our emphasis on the differences between corporations and LLCs, our apparent caution to extend corporate common law to LLCs, and the lack of statutory language extending fiduciary duties to creditors, all constrain us from imposing fiduciary duties on an LLC to its creditors.

Some courts have extended fiduciary duties to the creditors of insolvent LLCs. These cases are not persuasive. First, the sources cited above were all prior to the Delaware Chancery Court's decision in *CML V, LLC v. Bax*, 6 A.3d 238 (Del. Ch. 2010). Like *Gheewalla*, the decision will likely be persuasive to other courts considering the issue. Second, we have recognized the primacy of an LLC's operating agreement over the duties in Wyoming's LLC Act:

> Wyoming's Limited Liability Company Act provides that the operating agreement governs "the rights and duties under this chapter of a person in the capacity of manager," and provides that "to the extent the operating agreement does not otherwise provide for a matter this chapter governs the matter." *Thus, where the operating agreement contains specific provisions regarding a manager's rights and duties, it prevails.* However, the Act also prohibits the operating agreement from eliminating the contractual obligation of good faith and fair dealing under Wyo. Stat. Ann. § 17–29–409(d).

Acorn v. Moncecchi, 386 P.3d 739, 753–54 (Wyo. 2016). North Star's Operating Agreement explicitly states that its managers owe their duties to the company[:] "Each Manager shall perform the duties of Manager in good faith, in a manner he reasonably believes to be *in the best interests of the Company*"; "A Manager shall not have any liability by reason of being or having been a Manager of the Company, except as a result of a breach of the Manager's duties *to the Company*." Finally, refusing to recognize a fiduciary relationship between an LLC's managers and its creditors adheres to precedent concerning the creation of fiduciary relationships: "Fiduciary relationships are extraordinary and not easily created. We have been reluctant to impose additional duties and liability on lenders in a creditor/debtor relationship. The relationship between a lender and its customer is contractual in nature so we impose no duties higher than the morals of the marketplace."

F. ACTIONS BY PARTNERS AND MEMBERS

1. GENERAL PARTNERSHIP

A partner may sue the partnership or other partners for the breach of the partnership agreement or of any duties or obligations under the RUPA.

RUPA § 410. Action by Partnership and Partners.

(a) A partnership may maintain an action against a partner for a breach of the partnership agreement, or for the violation of a duty to the partnership, causing harm to the partnership.

(b) A partner may maintain an action against the partnership or another partner, with or without an accounting as to partnership business, to enforce the partner's rights and protect the partner's interests, including rights and interests under the partnership agreement or this [act] or arising independently of the partnership relationship.

(c) A right to an accounting on dissolution and winding up does not revive a claim barred by law.

Section 410(b) refers to an action for "without an accounting as to partnership business." An accounting is not an independent cause of action, but is instead a form of remedy. There must be an underlying cause of action, which can be "for a breach of the partnership agreement, or for the violation of a duty to the partnership, causing harm to the partnership." Upon the basis for a cause of action, an accounting provides a remedy. An accounting is a concept that traces back to the common law. It is not simply a review of the financial status of the partnership and the partners. It is a judicial review of *all disputed matters* pending among the partnership and partners. These matters may include claims for: allocation of profit and loss, indemnification, contributions, distributions, partnership property, status of debt, contract obligations, and breach of fiduciary duty.

At common law, an accounting was not available before dissolution. 59A Am.Jur.2d Partnership § 606 (Aug. 2017) ("Any partner is entitled to an accounting on dissolution or termination of the partnership, and in the absence of an agreement to the contrary, a partner's right to an accounting accrues at the date of dissolution or on an action for dissolution."). The older and now mostly superseded uniform statute, the Uniform Partnership Act of 1914 (UPA), modified this rule by specifying that under certain circumstances an accounting is available outside of dissolution. UPA § 22 provides: "Any partner shall have the right to a formal account as to partnership affairs: (a) if he is wrongfully excluded from the partnership business or possession of its property by his co-partners; (b) if the right exists under the terms of any agreement; (c) as provided by section 21;[3] (d) whenever other circumstances render it just and reasonable."

An accounting was traditionally subject to the "exclusivity rule." This rule established an accounting as a condition precedent to a partner's right to maintain an action at law concerning partnership matters. It arises from the earlier concept of a partnership as aggregation of partners, and not as a separate and distinct entity: accordingly, all proceedings to enforce partnership rights or obligations were cognizable only against the partners individually. This legal fact became problematic under the old distinction between law and equity and formal pleading requirements. The following passage explains the problem.

> No partner could sue another for moneys paid or liabilities incurred on behalf of the partnership for several reasons. Under the principles of common law pleading, a party could not be both plaintiff and defendant in the same suit. If partners sued copartners, they technically would be suing themselves. In addition, early courts were concerned that until all of the partnership concerns were ascertained and adjusted, it was impossible to determine whether a particular partner was a debtor or creditor of the firm. A settlement of the partnership concerns was unavailable at law, in part, because of the "serious inconvenience" of sorting out the potential cross claims. Also, an action at law to determine each partner's share of the final balance effectively changed the original contract from a joint contract between all partners to a several contract.
>
> Even in equity, an accounting ordinarily was not enforced except upon dissolution of the partnership. This practice reflected equity's reluctance to use its injunctive powers to enforce the positive covenants between partners. Thus, specific performance of the partnership contract was not an available remedy due to the potential for ongoing court involvement in the continuing partnership. If, however, the negative covenants were breached and the fiduciary relationship jeopardized, equity would consider the relationship severed and order a partnership accounting and dissolution.
>
> Despite the merger of law and equity in most jurisdictions, the early commentators noted that abolishing the distinctions between law and equity did not create a new cause of action at law. Over the years, this judicially created rule of convenience and

[3] UPA § 21(1), "Partner Accountable as Fiduciary," provides: "Every partner must account to the partnership for any benefit, and hold as trustee for it any profits derived by him without the consent of the other partners from any transaction connected with the formation, conduct, or liquidation of the partnership or from any use by him of its property."

> restriction on the forum available to enforce the remedies became a bar to a cause of action.
>
> Most courts applied the rule *pro forma* to hold that an accounting or settlement of partnership affairs was a prerequisite or condition precedent to a right of action at law among partners with regard to partnership affairs. Courts requiring an accounting gave various justifications, including: (1) the rule avoided premature and piecemeal judgments among partners; (2) a partner did not become a debtor or creditor of the copartner but of the firm in partnership transactions and, until a final settlement, no debt was due from one partner to another; (3) a party could not be both plaintiff and defendant; (4) one partner did not own or have a right to any specific portion of the partnership property; and (5) the complicated accounting required to establish the rights of partnership parties was not a proper subject for jury consideration and was better left to a court of equity.

Sertich v. Moorman, 783 P.2d 1199, 1201–02 (Ariz. 1989).

The merger of law and equity in modern courts of general jurisdiction eliminates the procedural problems associated with the accounting rule. In most states, courts have all powers formerly vested in separate courts and the judge sits as both chancellor in equity and judge at law. The merger of law and equity eliminated the formalism supporting the exclusivity rule.

Modern partnership law provides that, during the term of the partnership, partners may maintain a variety of legal or equitable actions, including an action for an accounting, as well as a final action for an accounting upon dissolution and winding up. Under RUPA § 410, a partner may bring a direct suit against the partnership or another partner for almost any cause of action arising out of the conduct of the partnership business. Section 410 reflects a policy choice that partners should have access to the courts during the term of the partnership to resolve claims against the partnership and the other partners, leaving broad judicial discretion to fashion appropriate remedies. An accounting is no longer a prerequisite to file suit and to seek other legal and equitable remedies. *See, e.g.*, Sertich v. Moorman, 783 P.2d 1199, 1205 (Ariz. 1989) ("This case illustrates that continued enforcement of the accounting rule is indeed illogical, impractical, and inequitable."); Auld v. Estridge, 382 N.Y.S.2d 897, 901 (N.Y. Sup. 1976) ("No purpose of justice is served by delaying the resolution here on empty procedural grounds").

Lastly, general partnership law does not provide partners with the right to bring a derivative suit. *See* RUPA § 410, cmt. 2. Partner have remedies in a direct action against the partnership and other partners in most disputes among partners.

2. LIMITED PARTNERSHIP AND LIMITED LIABILITY COMPANY

The ULPA (2001) and the RULLCA provide that an owner may bring either a direct action or a derivative action. A direct action is an action belonging to the plaintiff in her individual capacity. She has been injured and pursues a cause of action and remedy. A derivative suit is a concept from corporation law. It is one brought on behalf of the entity by one who has standing to bring such suit, typically an owner. Many state laws of LPs and LLCs permit derivative suits. *See, e.g.*, RULLCA § 802; RULPA § 1001; ULPA (2001) § 902; Delaware Limited Liability Company Act § 18–1001.The following passage describes the nature of a derivative suit.

> The background of stockholder litigation requires no more than general notice. As business enterprise increasingly sought the advantages of incorporation, management became vested with almost uncontrolled discretion in handling other people's money. The vast aggregate of funds committed to corporate control came to be drawn to a considerable extent from numerous and scattered holders of small interests. The director was not subject to an effective accountability. That created strong temptation for managers to profit personally at expense of their trust. The business code became all too tolerant of such practices. Corporate laws were lax and were not self-enforcing, and stockholders, in face of gravest abuses, were singularly impotent in obtaining redress of abuses of trust.
>
> Equity came to the relief of the stockholder, who had no standing to bring civil action at law against faithless directors and managers. Equity, however, allowed him to step into the corporation's shoes and to seek in its right the restitution he could not demand in his own. It required him first to demand that the corporation vindicate its own rights but when, as was usual, those who perpetrated the wrongs also were able to obstruct any remedy, equity would hear and adjudge the corporation's cause through its stockholder with the corporation as a defendant, albeit a rather nominal one. This remedy born of stockholder helplessness was long the chief regulator of corporate management and has afforded no small incentive to avoid at least grosser forms of betrayal of stockholders' interests. It is argued, and not without reason, that without it there would be little practical check on such abuses.
>
> Unfortunately, the remedy itself provided opportunity for abuse which was not neglected. Suits sometimes were brought not to redress real wrongs, but to realize upon their nuisance value. They were bought off by secret settlements in which any wrongs to the general body of share owners were compounded by the suing

stockholder, who was mollified by payments from corporate assets. These litigations were aptly characterized in professional slang as "strike suits." And it was said that these suits were more commonly brought by small and irresponsible than by large stockholders, because the former put less to risk and a small interest was more often within the capacity and readiness of management to compromise than a large one.

The very nature of the stockholder's derivative action makes it one in the regulation of which the legislature of a state has wide powers. Whatever theory one may hold as to the nature of the corporate entity, it remains a wholly artificial creation whose internal relations between management and stockholders are dependent upon state law and may be subject to most complete and penetrating regulation, either by public authority or by some form of stockholder action. Directors and managers, if not technically trustees, occupy positions of a fiduciary nature, and nothing in the Federal Constitution prohibits a state from imposing on them the strictest measure of responsibility, liability and accountability, either as a condition of assuming office or as a consequence of holding it.

Likewise, a stockholder who brings suit on a cause of action derived from the corporation assumes a position, not technically as a trustee perhaps, but one of a fiduciary character. He sues, not for himself alone, but as representative of a class comprising all who are similarly situated. The interests of all in the redress of the wrongs are taken into his hands, dependent upon his diligence, wisdom and integrity. And while the stockholders have chosen the corporate director or manager, they have no such election as to a plaintiff who steps forward to represent them. He is a self-chosen representative and a volunteer champion. The Federal Constitution does not oblige the State to place its litigating and adjudicating processes at the disposal of such a representative, at least without imposing standards of responsibility, liability and accountability which it considers will protect the interests he elects himself to represent. We conclude that the state has plenary power over this type of litigation.

Cohen v. Beneficial Indus. Loan Corp., 337 U.S. 541, 547–550 (1949).

The following are the provisions for LPs. The provisions for LLCs are functionally the same. RULLCA §§ 801–806.

ULPA (2001) § 901. Direct Action by Partner.

(a) Subject to subsection (b), a partner may maintain a direct action against another partner or the limited partnership, with or without an accounting as to the partnership's activities and affairs, to enforce the partner's rights and otherwise protect the partner's interests, including rights and interests under the partnership agreement or this [act] or arising independently of the partnership relationship.

(b) A partner maintaining a direct action under this section must plead and prove an actual or threatened injury that is not solely the result of an injury suffered or threatened to be suffered by the limited partnership.

(c) A right to an accounting on a dissolution and winding up does not revive a claim barred by law.

ULPA (2001) § 902. Derivative Action.

A partner may maintain a derivative action to enforce a right of a limited partnership if:

(1) the partner first makes a demand on the general partners, requesting that they cause the partnership to bring an action to enforce the right, and the general partners do not bring the action within a reasonable time; or

(2) a demand under paragraph (1) would be futile.

ULPA (2001) § 903. Proper Plaintiff.

A derivative action to enforce a right of a limited partnership may be maintained only by a person that is a partner at the time the action is commenced and:

(1) was a partner when the conduct giving rise to the action occurred; or

(2) whose status as a partner devolved on the person by operation of law or pursuant to the terms of the partnership agreement from a person that was a partner at the time of the conduct.

ULPA (2001) § 904. Pleading.

In a derivative action, the complaint must state with particularity:

(1) the date and content of plaintiff's demand and the response to the demand by the general partner; or

(2) why demand should be excused as futile.

ULPA (2001) § 906. Proceeds and Expenses.

(a) Except as otherwise provided in subsection (b):

(1) any proceeds or other benefits of a derivative action, whether by judgment, compromise, or settlement, belong to the limited partnership and not to the plaintiff; and

(2) if the plaintiff receives any proceeds, the plaintiff shall remit them immediately to the partnership.

(b) If a derivative action is successful in whole or in part, the court may award the plaintiff reasonable expenses, including reasonable attorney's fees and costs, from the recovery of the limited partnership.

(c) A derivative action on behalf of a limited partnership may not be voluntarily dismissed or settled without the court's approval.

The above provisions do not provide a clear definition of the distinction between direct and derivative actions. A direct action is one based on "rights and interests under the partnership agreement or this [act] or arising independently of the partnership relationship." ULPA (2001) § 901(a). Since the derivative suit is a borrowed concept, corporation law provides guidance on the matter. Delaware provides this test to determine whether a suit is direct or derivative.

> That issue must turn solely on the following questions: (1) who suffered the alleged harm (the corporation or the suing stockholders, individually); and (2) who would receive the benefit of any recovery or other remedy (the corporation or the stockholders, individually)?

Tooley v. Donaldson, Lufkin & Jenrette, Inc., 845 A.2d 1031, 1033 (Del. 2004). However, some courts, including Delaware courts, have stated that the *Tooley* test can be tweaked for application to NBEs.

> The *Tooley* direct/derivative test is substantially the same for claims involving limited partnerships. While the test may be substantially the same, cases involving limited partnerships often present unique facts relating to the provisions and structure of the limited partnership agreement and how it defines the rights and responsibilities of the limited partners.

El Paso Pipeline GP Co., L.L.C. v. Brinckerhoff, 152 A.3d 1248, 1255 (Del. 2016). *See* Culverhouse v. Paulson & Co., Inc., 133 A.3d 195, 198 n.9 (Del. 2016) (same).

The quintessential derivative suit alleges mismanagement, typically grounded in a claim for breach of the fiduciary duty of care or breach of the fiduciary duty of loyalty including claims for self-dealing. A direct claim arises when the "structural relationship" between the firm and owners is harmed by the actions of managers.

> The DGCL establishes a structural relationship between the corporation and its officers, directors, and shareholders. Although the DGCL empowers corporate directors and officers to act for the corporation, the DGCL also imposes certain restraints on the use of this authority. If a corporate officer acts in a manner that the

> DGCL prohibits, then the officer has violated this structural relationship by disregarding the specific restraints placed on him or her by the shareholders. It is consequently the rights of the shareholders, not those of the corporation, that are injured by the encroachment. Thus, any shareholder who was harmed by the violation of the structural relationship established between the corporation and the shareholder is harmed directly and has an individual cause of action.

Grayson v. Imagination Station, Inc., 2010 WL 3221951, at *5 (Del. Ch. 2010). Examples of direct claims include a failure to enforce a shareholder's voting agreement, interference with shareholder voting rights, unlawful withholding of dividends, discrimination against specific shareholders, denial of preferred shareholder's contract-based rights, challenges to a merger on the ground of price or process, and abdication of a board's duties.

Derivative actions have special procedures for determining control of the action. ULPA § 902(2) indicates that "a partner may maintain a derivative action if a demand would be *futile*." If not, the partner must make a demand on the general partner. To understand this procedure, start with the principle that decisions over a litigation asset is ordinarily a business decision. The law gives control of a claim belonging to the entity to the firm's managers—the board for a corporation, or partners, members, or managers who manage the firm for NBEs. A claimant must ordinarily make a demand on the manager who has the managerial authority to determine business matters, including the handling of a litigation asset. Once a claimant makes a demand, she loses control of the claim and the manager has the authority to decide the claim's fate—which may include a decision to pursue the action on behalf of the firm, to dismiss the action on the ground that it is meritless or not in the firm's best interest, or to settle the claim. A claimant and her attorney would prefer to control the claim. (Why else would she and her lawyer have brought it in the first place?).

How can she do so without encroaching on the principle that managers should manage the business and affairs of the firm including decisions regarding litigation assets? A claimant can aver that the managers are incapable of determining the fate of the litigation asset because they have a disqualifying disability. Suppose a claimant credibly asserts that the managers are incapable of evaluating the litigation asset because perhaps they are the alleged wrongdoers or cannot otherwise fairly evaluate the claims for some other reason such as when they are beholden to the wrongdoers. Suppose they are not disinterested in the action or independent of the alleged wrongdoers. The law recognizes the reality that managers would not investigate credible claims against themselves or sue themselves. When a claimant shows that demand would be futile, the law permits the claimant to avoid making a demand on the ground of futility and to control the derivative action.

However, even if the managers cannot control the litigation because a claimant can plead demand futility, they can still ensure that some other manager (but not them) controls the litigation as long as that manager is disinterested and independent. Conflicted managers can appoint a special litigation committee (SLC) composed of disinterested and independent managers. The SLC then makes a business decision with respect to the alleged injury to the firm. The uniform laws permit the use of an SLC. *See* ULPA (2001) § 905; RULLCA § 805.

The case below discusses the difference between a direct and a derivative action in the LP context. A derivative action is a corporation law concept. It is a suit brought on behalf of an entity by one who has standing to bring such a suit, typically the firm's equityholders. In reading this case, consider these questions: (1) What is the test for determining whether an action is direct or derivative? (2) What are the prototypical claims in a derivative action? (3) What is the key procedural implication if a suit is a derivative action? (4) What is demand futility?

FRITCHEL V. WHITE

452 P.3d 601 (Wyo. 2019)

BOOMGAARDEN, JUSTICE.

Appellants, a sub-group of limited partners in the John White Family Limited Partnership (the Limited Partnership), filed a direct action against the Appellees [the estate of the Decedent] to remedy losses incurred when John White (the Decedent) disposed of the Limited Partnership's real property. The Appellees moved to dismiss the complaint, arguing that the limited partners alleged derivative harms that had to be filed as a derivative action. The district court dismissed the complaint. Because the Decedent's property transaction injured the Limited Partnership, not the limited partners directly, Appellants must seek their remedy through a derivative action on behalf of the Limited Partnership. We affirm.

The dispositive issue is whether the Appellants' complaint asserts any facts which would entitle them to relief in the form of a direct action.

The Decedent created the Limited Partnership for estate planning purposes, gifting ownership interests to his four children, their spouses, and his grandchildren (the Limited Partners). He was the sole general partner. The Limited Partnership held in its name real property in Pueblo, Colorado (the Pueblo Property). The Decedent, acting alone as the sole general partner, sold the Pueblo Property to Robert Kennedy for $600,000 in a seller-financed transaction. The Limited Partnership retained a promissory note in its name for $545,000, with a deed of trust over the property as security. More than two years later, the Decedent, again acting alone as the sole general partner, consented to Kennedy's sale of the Pueblo Property directly to William Gradishar and Tiffany Moruzzi. Gradishar and Moruzzi assumed the promissory note with the Decedent's consent.

The critical event for this appeal occurred, when the Decedent, acting in his individual capacity, released Gradishar and Moruzzi from the "contract for deed purchase" and from "all real estate taxes, back payments, late payments charges, interest, etc." Instead of transferring the Pueblo Property to the Limited Partnership, however, Gradishar and Moruzzi deeded the Pueblo Property by quitclaim deed to Decedent in return for $30,000. At no point during this transaction did the Decedent reimburse or consult the Limited Partnership or its limited partners.

The Decedent died with the Pueblo Property in his estate. His estate plan—a combination of a pour-over will and a revocable trust—required distribution in equal shares to his four children. Per the terms of the Partnership Agreement, the Decedent's death constituted an event of withdrawal of the sole general partner—dissolving the Limited Partnership, and requiring it to wind up and terminate.

After discovering the transaction, all of the limited partners except the Decedent's children and two granddaughters filed a complaint. They allege four causes of action: Breach of Partnership Agreement; Breach of Fiduciary Duty; Constructive Fraud; and Conversion. Appellants also sought a Declaratory Judgment.

This case presents a new twist on an old conflict: whether the injury alleged gives rise to a direct or derivative action. We conclude that the injury is derivative, decline to adopt a discretionary rule, and determine that the demand rule can be met.

Appellants plead a derivative injury.

Although limited partnerships are distinct from corporations, we have looked to relevant corporate law to determine whether a claim is direct or derivative. *See Wallop Canyon Ranch, LLC v. Goodwyn*, 351 P.3d 943, 952 (Wyo. 2015). In corporate law, we look to the bearer of the injury to determine the nature of the claim: "When the director (or shareholder or member) seeks to remedy an injury to the corporation rather than himself, the action is derivative in nature."

The distinction between a direct and derivative action is important. A direct action is one to enforce a limited partner's rights against its limited partnership. A derivative action is one "by one or more stockholders to enforce a corporate cause of action."

In *Wallop Canyon Ranch, LLC*, we articulated the test to determine whether a claim is direct or derivative. We look to whether the plaintiff alleged a "special injury":

> A claim is derivative in nature where the plaintiff was not injured "directly or independently" of the partnership. Furthermore, in determining whether or not a claim is direct or derivative, the court must look ultimately to whether the plaintiff has alleged a special injury. Where a suit by a limited partner against a general partner clearly alleges wrongs to the partnership which have indirectly damaged the limited partner, the action asserts a derivative claim on behalf of the partnership, not one personal to the plaintiff.
>
> In ascertaining whether a cause of action arising in a limited partnership context is derivative, it is appropriate to look to corporate law for guidance. Under the latter law, the nature of the wrong alleged is what controls.

To determine the nature of the wrong alleged, "the prevailing criterion is whether the claimed injury is primarily to the partnership and only indirectly to the partners through their interest in the partnership—a partnership claim—or is direct and unique to the partner(s)—an individual claim." In the context of limited partnerships, a derivative suit is appropriate when the nature of the injury is to the limited partnership; and a direct suit is appropriate when the nature of the injury is to the limited partners. *See Wallop Canyon Ranch, LLC*, 351 P.3d at 951–52.

Viewing the facts of the complaint as true and in the light most favorable to the Appellants, the only injury alleged is the amount of money equal in value to the promissory note, plus interest, lost by the Limited Partnership: such an injury is derivative in nature.

Appellants argue they suffered a direct injury because the Decedent breached "the duty to account for any property the partner is holding in trust; the duty to refrain from competing with the partnership; the duty of loyalty; and the duty of good faith and fair dealing" when he purchased the Pueblo Property without reimbursing the Limited Partnership. This argument fails because that alleged injury stems from, and is not independent of, an injury first incurred by the Limited Partnership.

Subject to statute and partnership agreement, "a general partner of a limited partnership has the same duties as a partner in a general partnership." *Id.* at 956. Those duties are the duty of loyalty and the duty of care set forth in Wyoming Statute § 17–21–404. The general partner owes those duties "to the [limited] partnership and the [limited] partners." Wyo. Stat. Ann. § 17–21–404 (2019).

We have not considered whether a general partner's breach of a fiduciary duty owed to both the limited partnership and limited partners should be remedied by a direct or derivative action. The Appellants' alleged injury stems from the Decedent's alleged breach of fiduciary duties he owed to them, but they fail to identify how that injury is independent of the injury to the Limited Partnership. Consequently, the alleged breach of fiduciary duty in this case must be remedied through a derivative action.

Appellants also argue that a direct cause of action is appropriate because not all of the limited partners suffered the same injury. Appellants' precise argument tracks the distribution of the Pueblo Property: while the Decedent's children receive 25% of the Pueblo Property through his estate plan, the Appellants receive nothing through their devalued interests in the Limited Partnership. This argument fails because there is nothing special about this alleged injury.

A special injury occurs when the limited partner "suffered an injury that is special and distinct from not only any injury suffered by the entity but also any injury suffered by other" limited partners. While Appellants highlight potential inequities in "practical terms," the Decedent's dealing with the Pueblo Property devalues the children's interest in the Limited Partnership by the same amount as Appellants', notwithstanding the fact that the Decedent's children may recoup the loss through the Decedent's estate. Consequently, the Appellants do not allege a special injury that would entitle them to relief in the form of a direct action.

Appellants can satisfy demand by pleading "demand futility."

Appellants contend that they will be foreclosed from recovery if we require them to file a derivative action because they do not have a general partner on whom to make a demand and thus cannot satisfy the demand rule. We can imagine no more fitting a scenario for "demand futility."

Compliance with the demand rule is a statutory prerequisite to a derivative action. Limited partners can meet the demand rule if either: (1) "general partners with authority to do so have refused to bring the action" **or** (2) "an effort to cause those general partners to bring the action is not likely to succeed." Wyo. Stat. Ann. § 17–14–1101 (2019). Limited partners can meet the demand rule by making demand upon the general partner who has authority to bring an action, or by showing how demand is futile.

In the analogous corporate context, the United States Supreme Court has explained that "the purpose of the demand requirement is to afford the directors an opportunity to exercise their reasonable business judgment and waive a legal right vested in the corporation in the belief that its best interests will be promoted by not insisting on such right." *Kamen v. Kemper Fin. Servs., Inc.*, 500 U.S. 90, 96 (1991); *see also Aronson v. Lewis*, 473 A.2d 805, 812 (Del. 1984) ("The entire question of demand futility is inextricably bound to issues of business judgment and the standards of that doctrine's applicability."). "By permitting the shareholder to circumvent the board's business judgment on the desirability of corporate litigation, the 'futility' exception defines the circumstances in which the shareholder may exercise this particular incident of managerial authority." A shareholder may exercise this authority when a court determines that "the particularized factual allegations create a reasonable doubt that, as of the time the complaint is filed, the board of directors could have properly exercised its independent and disinterested business judgment in responding to a demand." *Rales v. Blasband*, 634 A.2d 927, 934 (Del. 1993). If the plaintiff satisfies this burden, then demand is futile.

Appellants can satisfy the demand rule by pleading futility. The Limited Partnership's Partnership Agreement states that "the withdrawal of the General Partner shall dissolve the Partnership unless another General Partner exists and consents to carry on the business of the Partnership [at] the time of the event of withdrawal." The Decedent's death constituted an event of withdrawal and he was the only general partner. *See* Wyo. Stat. Ann. § 17–14–502 (1997). Subsequent to the withdrawal of the sole general partner, the Partnership Agreement required the Limited Partnership to dissolve, wind up, and then terminate. After the Decedent's death, therefore, the Limited Partnership entered dissolution without a general partner—undoubtedly making Appellants' "effort to cause [the general partner] to bring the action" unlikely to succeed. Wyo. Stat. Ann. § 17–14–1101. Demand under these circumstances clearly would be futile.

Appellants' complaint fails to state any facts entitling them to relief in a direct action because they seek relief for an injury to the Limited Partnership, not an injury individual to them. Appellants can satisfy the demand rule by pleading demand futility. We affirm.

NOTES

1. In Wyoming, the determination of a direct or derivative action depends on whether the plaintiff suffered a "special injury." States may differ on the test. In *Tooley v. Donaldson, Lufkin & Jenrette, Inc.*, 845 A.2d 1031, 1035 (Del. 2004), the Delaware Supreme Court explicitly rejected the "special injury" test: "In our view, the concept of 'special injury' is not helpful to a proper analytical distinction between direct and derivative actions. We now disapprove the use of the concept of 'special injury' as a tool in that analysis."

The case below discusses the difference between a direct and derivative claim for a Delaware LP. Under Delaware corporation law, the test for this determination is: "Who suffered the alleged harm—the corporation or the suing stockholder individually—and who would receive the benefit of the recovery or other remedy?" Tooley v. Donaldson, Lufkin & Jenrette, Inc., 845 A.2d 1031, 1035 (Del. 2004). In reading this case, a lower court case decided before *Tooley*, consider these questions: (1) What is the court's test for determining whether a claim is direct or derivative? (2) How does the fact that the entity is an LP affect the determination of whether the claim is direct or derivative?

ANGLO AMERICAN SECURITY FUNDS, L.P. v. S.R. GLOBAL INTERNATIONAL FUND, L.P.

829 A.2d 143 (Del. Ch. 2003)

CHANDLER, CHANCELLOR.

Plaintiffs bring this action against defendants, S.R. Global International Fund, L.P. (the "Fund"), Sloane Robinson Investment (Cayman), Ltd., ("Sloane") the general partner of the Fund, and Ernst & Young LLP, ("E & Y") the Fund's independent auditors. Plaintiffs allege that Sloane breached its fiduciary duties to the limited partners of the Fund; that the Fund and Sloane breached the Fund's limited partnership agreement ("Agreement") and were negligent; that E & Y made negligent misrepresentations in the Fund's audited financial statements and aided and abetted Sloane's breach of fiduciary duty; and that all defendants engaged in fraud against the limited partners of the Fund. The defendants challenge the standing of the plaintiffs to bring these claims and have moved to dismiss the complaint for failure to state a claim.

The plaintiffs each became limited partners of the Fund, with initial capital investments ranging from over $0.4 million to approximately $11.9 million. The Fund is a Delaware limited partnership created "to serve as a fund through which the assets of its Partners may be utilized" in investing in various types of securities and other financial instruments or to act as what is commonly termed a hedge fund. The Fund establishes in its books a capital account for each partner consisting of the partner's original capital contribution, plus any additional capital contributions, minus any capital withdrawals, and adjusted at the end of each fiscal period for the partner's proportional share of net profits and losses. The Fund is obligated to provide the partners with unaudited quarterly reports and an audited annual financial statement as well as information necessary for federal income tax purposes. Limited partners of the Fund are not permitted to assign their interests without written consent of the general partner and must provide written notice to the Fund thirty business days prior to making any capital withdrawal. Sloane, the general partner of the Fund, is a company organized under the laws of the Cayman Islands. E & Y, the Fund's auditor, is a Delaware limited liability partnership.

As of December 31, 1999, Sloane's capital account in the Fund was credited with $22,350,704 or 15% of the net profits to the limited partners. On February 18, 2000, Sloane withdrew $22,350,704 from its capital account. The credit to Sloane's capital account was recorded in the Fund's audited 1999 financial statement ("1999 Statement"). The 1999 Statement was provided to the limited partners in March 2000. Although it did report other post-year-end capital contributions and withdrawals as "Subsequent Events," the 1999 Statement did not report Sloane's February 18 withdrawal. This withdrawal was reported in the Fund's quarterly statement for the first quarter of 2000, which statement was received by the limited partners on May 9, 2000.

The plaintiffs take issue with the withdrawal on the bases that (1) the withdrawal overdrew Sloane's capital account because substantial losses sustained by the Fund during January and February 2000 had reduced the available balance in Sloane's capital account below $22,350,704; (2) the Agreement permits the general partner to withdraw funds only on the last day of the month; and (3) the withdrawal should have been disclosed as a Subsequent Event in the 1999 Statement.

Standing of Plaintiffs

Defendants move to dismiss all claims on the basis that they are derivative in nature and the plaintiffs do not have standing to bring a derivative claim. Delaware partnership law requires in a derivative action that the plaintiff be a partner (or assignee of one) at the time of bringing the action and at the time of the challenged transaction. All plaintiffs had withdrawn from the fund by the time this action was filed.

The test for distinguishing direct from derivative claims in the context of a limited partnership is substantially the same as that used when the underlying entity is a corporation. The determination is made by careful application of a rather nuanced test. The test looks to the nature of the injury and to the nature of remedy that could result if the plaintiffs are successful. When a plaintiff alleges either an injury that is different from what is suffered by other shareholders (or partners) or one that involves a contractual right of shareholders (or partners) that is independent of the entity's rights, the claim is direct. If the injury is one that affects all partners proportionally to their *pro rata* interests in the corporation, the claim is derivative. In a derivative action the plaintiff sues for an injury done to the partnership and any recovery of damages is paid to the partnership. Conversely, in a direct action the plaintiff sues to redress an injury suffered by the plaintiff and damages recovered are paid directly to the plaintiff who was injured. In every case the court must determine from the complaint whether the claims are direct or derivative and may not rely on either party's characterization. Because harm to the entity will almost inevitably harm the stakeholders and because the entity itself is in some ways no more than an amalgamation of a certain subset of stakeholders' interests, differentiation of direct from derivative claims can be elusive.

To further complicate matters, whereas corporations are largely creatures of statute with some limited contractual flexibility, limited partnerships offer greater contractual flexibility with only a few statutory constraints. The structure and function of a limited partnership is sometimes analogous to the corporate model with the limited partners having similar rights and responsibilities as shareholders and the general partner acting in much the same capacity as a board of directors—but not necessarily so. Application of corporate law rules to disputes related to a limited partnership necessitates a bit of flexibility. This is true because the facts unique to a limited partnership dispute include the contents of the limited partnership agreement—how it specifies or modifies the entity's function and structure and the rights and responsibilities of the general and limited partners. "In the partnership context, the relationships among the parties may be so simple and the circumstances so clear-cut that the distinction between direct and derivative claims becomes irrelevant." In some instances, the relationships among the parties and the function and structure of the partnership itself may diverge from the corporate model so dramatically that some claims, which in a corporate context might be classified as derivative, *must* be brought as direct claims in order to enable the injured parties to recover while preventing a windfall to individuals or entities whose interests were not injured.

The essence of the plaintiffs' claims is that Sloane withdrew funds from its capital account in violation of the partnership agreement; that this withdrawal exceeded the balance in the account; and that timely disclosure of the withdrawal was not given to the limited partners. It is undisputed that on February 18, 2000, Sloane withdrew $22,350,704 from its capital account. The plaintiffs contend that this withdrawal breached the Agreement, which permits the general partner to make withdrawals only on the last day of the month. When the 1999 Statement was prepared and distributed to the limited partners, it disclosed (as "Subsequent Events") information about deposits and distributions related to the capital accounts of limited partners that occurred after December 31, 1999, but did not disclose that on February 18, 2000, the general partner withdrew over $22 million from its capital account. Plaintiffs claim that this withdrawal is material because it amounts to the general partner having "bailed out" of the Fund. Indeed, the plaintiffs contend that due to losses sustained by the Fund in January and February 2000, the balance of the capital account of the general partner, as of February 18, 2000, would have been less than the amount that was withdrawn, causing a negative balance in the account. Because the 1999 Statement contained other information of a similar nature (post-year-end withdrawals by limited partners) and because the withdrawal was material, the failure to disclose it in the 1999 Statement rendered the statement materially false and misleading.

The defendants point out that the various claims made by the plaintiffs allege only two distinct types of injury, either diminution in value of the fund or misdisclosure of the withdrawal, each of which constitute derivative rather than direct claims.

1. *Diminution of Value of the Fund*

Delaware corporate and limited partnership cases have agreed that a diminution of the value of a business entity is classically derivative in nature. I conclude that the operation and function of the Fund as specified in the Agreement diverge so radically from the traditional corporate model that the claims made in the complaint must be brought as direct claims.

"Superimposing derivative pleading requirements serves no useful or meaningful public policy purpose" in the context of certain narrow factual situations that may arise with respect to a non-corporate entity.

Due to the structure and operation of the Fund, whenever the value of the Fund is reduced, the injury accrues irrevocably and almost immediately to the current partners but will not harm those who later become partners. Although other types of injuries could harm the Fund as an entity in ways that appropriately could be challenged in a derivative action, injuries that result in a direct reduction of the Fund's assets will effect an almost immediate reduction in the capital accounts of each of the existing partners. Such losses confer only a fleeting injury to the Fund, one that is immediately and irrevocably passed through to the partners. When an injured partner withdraws from the partnership, the partner's capital account has already been diminished by any and all diminutions of value to the Fund from the time of entering the partnership until the time of withdrawal. There are no successors in interest to partners so injured because there are no "shares" sold to someone else, any withdrawing partner's interest in the entity is liquidated. Any recovery obtained by the Fund in a derivative action cannot provide a remedy to wronged former partners nor to their (non-existent) successors in interest. If additional partners are later admitted, they suffer no injury from previous reductions in the value of the fund because their capital accounts will reflect the full amount of their initial investments adjusted only for events occurring after their admission as partners. Such newly admitted limited partners would receive a windfall if the Fund were to recover damages for diminution of Fund value prior to their admission as limited partners. Characterizing the plaintiffs' claims as derivative would thus have the perverse effect of denying standing (and therefore recovery) to parties who were actually injured by the challenged transactions while granting ultimate recovery (and therefore a windfall) to parties who were not. This result is antithetical to the first purpose of derivative litigation identified in *Cencom,* does nothing to further the gatekeeping functions of derivative litigation requirements, and, in the words of Vice Chancellor Steele, "makes no sense." I hold that the plaintiffs' claims related to Sloane's February 18, 2000, withdrawal are direct claims.

2. *Misdisclosure in the 1999 Statement*

In support of their contention that claims related to non-disclosure of the withdrawal in the Fund's 1999 Statement are derivative, the defendants argue that if the plaintiffs' allegations were true, the plaintiffs have alleged only that they "experienced an injury suffered by all [investors] in proportion to their pro rata ownership interest." Here, plaintiffs allege that at least one effect of the two-month delay in disclosing to the limited partners that the general partner had bailed out of the Fund was to deprive the limited partners of the same opportunity to "cut their losses" promptly before the value of the Fund's investments declined further. The disclosure claim seems to implicate a contractual right of the limited partners that is not similarly a right of the Fund itself.

Under the terms of the Agreement, the limited partners have absolutely no control over the governance and management of the Fund; the limited partners are entitled to very limited routine disclosures regarding the activities and performance of the Fund; the limited partners' interests in the Fund are not freely transferable or tradable; the liquidity of the limited partners' investment is somewhat restricted and, perhaps, most importantly for purposes of this motion to dismiss, the Fund exists solely to utilize "the assets of its Partners" in various investment vehicles and maintains its books to account separately for the value of each partner's assets at all times. The Fund operates more like a bank with the individual partners each having accounts—albeit accounts that are not federally insured or afforded virtually any regulatory protections against loss of the assets invested. This is not a typical corporate business venture in which the value to the investors is based not only upon the physical assets of the entity but also upon the speculative value of the entity as a going concern. Other than a general partner's interest in management fees, there is no going-concern value. Yet, the limited partners have no capacity to replace a general partner that fails properly to represent the limited partners' interests. The only alternative available to a dissatisfied limited partner is to withdraw from the Fund.

Even withdrawing is impossible to implement instantaneously because the Agreement provides that limited partners may withdraw only on the last day of the month and only after giving thirty business days notice. This is six weeks at a minimum. The Fund is designed for the purpose of engaging in some highly speculative investments. This can be very rewarding as the partners found in fiscal year 1999 and highly risky as was discovered in 2000. Such investments tend to be highly volatile and a delay of six or more weeks in withdrawing one's funds from such a vehicle can lead to massive changes to the value of the account from the date the decision is made to withdraw until the funds may actually be withdrawn.

The plaintiff limited partners each appear to be sophisticated parties that understood and voluntarily accepted the terms of the Agreement and assumed the risks of investing in the Fund in order potentially to reap the rewards of undertaking such risks. As such, these sophisticated investors reasonably expected that the general partner would fulfill at least the obligations it voluntarily accepted under the Agreement and as a fiduciary. As the defendants correctly point out, the Agreement specifies the obligations of the general partner to report to the limited partners—unaudited quarterly reports of the fund performance, an audited financial report annually, and a year-end report to each partner indicating the necessary gain and loss information for Federal income tax purposes. Thus, the 1999 Statement was contractually required to be provided to the partners and any claims that it was incomplete, or materially false or misleading would state a direct claim.

NOTES

1. Since NBEs tend to owners who are closer to the management of the firm and more directly feel the impact of mismanagement and misconduct, courts may blur the line between direct and derivative actions. In *Plank v. Cherneski*, 231 A.3d 436 (Md. 2020), the court recognized an independent tort action for a breach of fiduciary duty in an LLC context.

> Does Maryland recognize an independent cause of action for breach of fiduciary duty?
>
> We answer the certified questions as follows. We hold that a breach of fiduciary duty may be actionable as an independent cause of action. To establish a breach of fiduciary duty, a plaintiff must demonstrate: (1) the existence of a fiduciary relationship; (2) breach of the duty owed by the fiduciary to the beneficiary; and (3) harm to the beneficiary. The remedy for the breach is dependent upon the type of fiduciary relationship, and the historical remedies provided by law for the specific type of fiduciary relationship and specific breach in question, and may arise under a statute, common law, or contract. The court should consider the nature of the fiduciary relationship and possible remedies afforded for a breach, on a case-by-case basis. If the plaintiff describes a fiduciary relationship, identifies a breach, and requests a remedy historically recognized by statute, contract, or common law applicable to the specific type of fiduciary relationship and the specific breach alleged, the court should permit the count to proceed. The cause of action may be pleaded without limitation as to whether there is another viable cause of action to address the same conduct. This does not mean that every breach will sound in tort, with an attendant right to a jury trial and monetary damages. The remedy will be dependent upon the specific law applicable to the specific fiduciary relationship at issue.

The court reasoned further: "Fiduciary relationship can be created by common law, by statute, or by contract, and can have different characteristics." They can exist between trustees and beneficiaries, guardians and wards, agents and principals, directors and corporations, and among partners.

The case below discusses whether the Connecticut LLC statute or its common law permits derivative suits. In a seven-member court, the case resulted in a dissent in which three justices dissented. In reading this case, consider these questions: (1) Should the law of LLCs be construed in the same way as corporation law with respect to derivative suits? (2) As a matter of policy, does it make sense to permit an exception to the requirement of filing a derivative suit for a single member LLC?

SAUNDERS V. BRINER

221 A.3d 1 (Conn. 2019)

KAHN, J.

[Roger Saunders, his son Sloan Saunders, and Clark Briner entered into the high yield commercial real estate lending business by setting up Revere Investments, LLC (Revere Investments), and related entities Revere High Yield Debt Fund, L.P. (Fund) and Revere High Yield, GP, LLC (Fund GP), to act as a servicer of the loans. The plaintiff, Roger Saunders, sued the defendants, Clark Briner and two entities solely owned by Briner, a Connecticut LLC (Revere Capital CT) and a Texas LLC (Revere Capital TX). Revere Investments profited by: (1) sourcing borrowers; (2) providing its own "inside" capital at high rates at the outset; (3) finding "outside" capital to participate in (sell portions of) at lower rates the loans funded by Revere Investments; (4) thus profiting by keeping the interest rate spread between the high and low rates and charging various "points" and service fees. Briner became dissatisfied with the fact that he was not making as much profit as the plaintiff and his son. He secretly found outside investors and disguised their capital as "inside" capital, thus profiting at the high rate for inside capital even though the source of the funding was from outside investors. This had the effect of reducing the profitability of Revere Investments and the plaintiff's interested in the company.]

We reverse the trial court's judgment in favor of the plaintiff [Roger Saunders] as to his derivative claims because we conclude that the plaintiff lacked standing to bring them under the CLLCA or the common law. We affirm the court's judgment in favor of the plaintiff as to his direct claims.

A. Derivative Standing

We begin by addressing whether, in the absence of authorization in the operating agreements of Revere Investments and Fund GP,[19] the plaintiff lacked standing to bring derivative claims under either General Statutes (Rev. to 2017) § 34–187 or, in the alternative, the common law.

On the basis of the plain language of the act, we conclude that the CLLCA does not permit members or managers to file derivative actions

[19] The parties could have authorized the filing of derivative actions in the operating agreements of Revere Investments and Fund GP. See *Styslinger* v. *Brewster Park, LLC*, 138 A.3d 257 (Conn. 2016) (noting that CLLCA provides default rules regarding operation of limited liability companies but permits "members to supplement these statutory provisions by adopting an operating agreement to govern the [company's] affairs"). Because the operating agreements of Revere Investments and Fund GP are silent as to the parties' abilities to bring a derivative action, no such contractual authorization exists in the present case, and the plaintiff's right to sue in a derivative capacity, if it exists, must emanate from the CLLCA or the common law.

but, rather, authorizes them to collectively commence an action in the name of the limited liability company upon a requisite vote of disinterested members or managers (member initiated action). [General Statutes (Rev. to 2017) § 34–187 provides:

> (a) Except as otherwise provided in an operating agreement, suit on behalf of the limited liability company may be brought in the name of the limited liability company by:
>
> > (1) Any member or members of a limited liability company, whether or not the articles of organization vest management of the limited liability company in one or more managers, who are authorized to sue by the vote of a majority in interest of the members, unless the vote of all members shall be required pursuant to subsection (b) of section 34–142; or
> >
> > (2) any manager or managers of a limited liability company, if the articles of organization vest management of the limited liability company in one or more managers, who are authorized to sue by the vote required pursuant to section 34–142.
>
> (b) In determining the vote required under section 34–142 for purposes of this section, the vote of any member or manager who has an interest in the outcome of the suit that is adverse to the interest of the limited liability company shall be excluded.]

Connecticut modeled the procedure set forth in § 34–187 on § 1102 of the Prototype Act. [Section 1102 of the Prototype Act provides that "a suit on behalf of the limited liability company may be brought only in the name of the limited liability company . . . [upon] the vote of more than one half by number of the members eligible to vote."] The drafters of the Prototype Act "emphasized that [§ 1102] does not permit derivative suits unless they are provided for in the operating agreement." Instead, the drafters intended to create a substitute for the derivative action, which they deemed more appropriate "in closely held firms like the typical [limited liability company in which] members can be expected to be actively interested in the firm, and can readily be coordinated for a vote on a suit by the firm." The "extra expense" and procedural hurdles required to bring a derivative action, the drafters reasoned, "may not be worth it" in the limited liability company context, which differs from that of "public corporations [where] the members are generally passive uninvolved in management and too numerous to coordinate effectively for action against errant managers."

We conclude that, in adopting a functionally identical provision to § 1102 of the Prototype Act, our legislature chose to omit the derivative action under the CLLCA for members and managers of limited liability companies. [The court held that the plaintiff did not meet the procedural requirement of a majority vote of members.]

The plaintiff asks this court, however, to look past the CLLCA and conclude that, despite our legislature's omission of a derivative remedy in the CLLCA, limited liability company members and managers may sue derivatively under the common law. We have recently explained, however, that "our common law does not recognize [LLCs], which were first created by [the enactment of the CLLCA]." *Styslinger* v. *Brewster Park, LLC*, 138 A.3d 257, 261 (Conn. 2016). The question we must resolve is "whether the recognition of [this] common-law remedy would conflict with or frustrate the purpose of the [CLLCA]." We conclude that it would. Consistent with our reasoning, we observe that other Prototype Act jurisdictions have held that members and managers of limited liability companies must follow the procedure for bringing a member initiated action and, as such, lack standing to bring derivative actions under the common law. See, e.g., *Marx* v. *Morris*, 925 N.W.2d 112 (Wisc. 2019) (declining to "judicially import corporate derivative standing provisions into the [limited liability company] context where the legislature has not done so"). We conclude that the trial court improperly exercised subject matter jurisdiction over the plaintiff's claims on behalf of Revere Investments and Fund GP.

B. Direct Standing

[The plaintiff loaned Revere Investment $398,000 of bridge financing through his single-member, solely owned company Saunders Capital. Revere Investment used this money to provide a loan to LR Global. The plaintiff later converted a portion of his bridge capital into a permanent investment in Revere Investment. After the parties began winding down the companies, the plaintiff learned that Briner failed to repay him the remainder of the amount on his LR Global bridge loan. The plaintiff claimed that Briner and Revere Capital TX breached their fiduciary duty and the implied covenant of good faith and fair dealing by failing to repay the remainder owed to the plaintiff on his LR Global bridge loan. The defendants claimed that the plaintiff [Saunders, in his individual capacity] lacked standing to seek damages with respect to the LR Global bridge loan because Saunders Capital provided the funding. The trial court ruled that Briner had failed to repay the plaintiff $55,000 of his bridge loan and, after including accrued interest, awarded him a total of $85,078.]

We next address whether the trial court incorrectly determined that the plaintiff had standing to bring direct claims alleging breach of fiduciary duty and breach of the implied covenant of good faith and fair dealing against Briner and Revere Capital TX for failure to repay one of his loans, the LR Global bridge loan. We conclude that, in the present case, the trial court correctly concluded that the plaintiff had standing to bring direct claims with respect to the LR Global bridge loan.

This court has not addressed the specific question of whether the member of a single-member limited liability company has standing to bring an action directly on behalf of the company. We derived the general rule outlined in *Channing Real Estate, LLC v. Gates*, 161 A.3d 1227 (Conn. 2017)—that members of limited liability companies cannot bring a direct action alleging harm to the company—from the direct injury requirements imposed on shareholders.[35] Consequently, the rationale behind the distinct and separate injury requirement as explained in the corporate law context provides an informative backdrop. We explained in *Channing Real Estate, LLC* that "a distinction must be made between the right of a shareholder to bring suit in an individual capacity as the sole party injured, and his right to sue on behalf of the corporation alleged to be injured." The distinction between a direct and derivative action turns on whether the alleged "injury sustained is peculiar to [that shareholder] alone" or whether, by virtue of harm suffered by the company, it affects all of the shareholders collectively. In the latter situation, the plaintiff must proceed "secondarily, deriving his rights from the corporation which is alleged to have been wronged."

We observe that the rule prohibiting shareholders from bringing a direct action to recover for a harm suffered by the corporation addresses the following policy rationales: (1) the protection of other shareholders and creditors; (2) the avoidance of multitudinous litigation; and (3) the equal distribution of recovery to injured parties. The American Law Institute explains that, if a shareholder sues directly for a harm that impacts multiple shareholders, the "injured shareholders other than the plaintiff will [not] share in the [plaintiff's] recovery [unless] the action is [brought as] a class action on behalf of all [of] these shareholders." 2 A.L.I., Principles of Corporate Governance: Analysis and Recommendations (1994) § 7.01, cmt. (d). A plaintiff's direct action can prevent creditors of the corporation from sharing in any recovery. Consequently, a direct action alleging harm to multiple shareholders can "unfairly expose the corporation or the defendants to a multiplicity of actions" by shareholders or creditors that later bring claims and affect the ability of those later plaintiffs to receive "a fair distribution of the recovery." *Id.*, § 7.01 (d).

An action brought by one shareholder on behalf of the company or derivative action alleviates the concerns posed by the direct action. It "distributes the recovery more broadly and evenly than a direct action [because it] goes to the corporation, [allowing] creditors and others having a stake in the corporation [to] benefit financially from [it]." *Id.*, § 7.01, comment (d). Because the corporation's recovery will be distributed to other shareholders, "[that derivative] action will have a preclusive effect that spares the corporation and the defendants from being exposed to a

[35] Our conclusion in *Channing Real Estate, LLC,* reflects the well-established corporate law principle that a shareholder must bring a derivative, rather than a direct, action to seek redress for injuries to the corporation.

multiplicity of suits." *Id.* Courts, therefore, can protect the interest of other shareholders and creditors of the corporation, avoid a multiplicity of actions, and distribute equal recovery to all the injured parties by requiring shareholders to bring an action on behalf of the corporation.

The law, however, has recognized some exceptions to this corporate rule. The Ninth Circuit recognized that, in some circumstances, the policy reasons for requiring shareholders to bring an action on behalf of the corporation may not be present even though the action alleges in substance a corporate injury. *Watson* v. *Button*, 235 F.2d 235, 237 (9th Cir. 1956) (concluding that Oregon law would permit individual recovery by shareholders, although injury belonged to corporation, where rights of creditors and other shareholders are not prejudiced and there exists no threat of multiplicity of actions). Partly in response to *Watson*, the American Law Institute promulgated a rule for actions brought by members of closely held corporations that permits trial courts to treat the shareholders' otherwise indirect claims as direct claims. See 2 A.L.I., § 7.01 (d). Before a trial court can "treat an action raising derivative claims as a direct action, exempt it from those restrictions and defenses applicable only to derivative actions, and order an individual recovery, it [must first find] that to do so will not (i) unfairly expose the corporation or defendants to a multiplicity of actions, (ii) materially prejudice the interests of creditors of the corporation, or (iii) interfere with a fair distribution of the recovery among all interested persons." *Id.*

These authorities persuade us that a narrowly tailored exception can provide a more flexible mechanism for addressing member standing. This is especially true under circumstances in which both the parties and the court system expended time and resources to litigate these matters and the "concept of a corporate injury that is distinct from any injury to [its sole member] approaches the fictional." We conclude that the trial court may permit the member of a single-member limited liability company to bring an action raising derivative claims as a direct action and may order an individual recovery if it finds that to do so will not (1) unfairly expose the company or defendants to a multiplicity of actions, (2) materially prejudice the interests of creditors of the company, or (3) negatively impact other owners or creditors of the company by interfering with a fair distribution of the recovery among all interested parties.

ROBINSON, C.J., with MCDONALD and MULLINS, JS., dissenting in part.

In *Channing Real Estate, LLC*, we observed that an LLC "is a distinct legal entity whose existence is separate from its members. We concluded that an individual defendant lacked standing to assert a counterclaim alleging a violation of the Connecticut Unfair Trade Practices Act (CUTPA) against the plaintiff because the facts established that the defendant had not demonstrated a specific, personal, and legal interest separate from that of an LLC of which he was a member. [The LLC] is therefore a distinct legal entity from the defendant, who is simply a member of that entity. Because a member of [an LLC] cannot recover for an injury allegedly suffered by the [LLC], we conclude that the defendant lacks standing to pursue a claim alleging a violation of CUTPA."

The majority, however, adopts an exception to this well settled general rule that is premised on American Law Institute's Principles of Corporate Governance § 7.01(d), which blurs the line between derivative and direct actions in certain cases involving closely held corporations.

In adopting this principle, the American Law Institute also found persuasive the Massachusetts Supreme Judicial Court's decision in *Donahue* v. *Rodd Electrotype Co. of New England, Inc.*, 328 N.E.2d 505 (Mass. 1975), which had observed that "the close corporation bears striking resemblance to a partnership," and that "the close corporation is often little more than an 'incorporated' or 'chartered' partnership"; in holding that stockholders in a close corporation owe each other a fiduciary duty akin to that of partners. *Id.*; see American Law Institute's Principles of Corporate Governance: Analysis and Recommendations § 7.01, comment (e). The American Law Institute considered that particular context and observed that, "in some circumstances, characterizing the action as direct will also be fairer to the defendants, as when the defendants wish to file a counterclaim against the plaintiff, because the general rule is to prohibit counterclaims in a derivative action. Also, in a direct action, each side must normally bear its own legal expenses, and the plaintiff, if successful, cannot ordinarily look to the corporation for attorney's fees. Such a rule seems more appropriate in cases that fundamentally involve disputes between a limited number of 'partners' in a closely held firm." Principles of Corporate Governance, supra, § 7.01, comment (e).

I respectfully disagree with the majority's decision to adopt the *Watson* v. *Button*/American Law Institute approach to close corporation standing to hold that the plaintiff had standing to raise the claims alleged in counts four, six, nine and ten of the second amended complaint. First, I do not believe that approach applies at all with respect to the factual predicate underlying those counts because it "is almost always employed in purely intracorporate disputes." The counts considered in the majority opinion do not present an intracorporate dispute, insofar as we consider whether the plaintiff sustained an injury separate and distinct from his own LLC, Saunders Capital, rather than one distinct from the other members of Revere Investments and Fund GP. Rather than presenting an occasion to make significant changes to corporate law in Connecticut, I believe that the present case is nothing more than a simple "wrong plaintiff" case.

Second, I find more persuasive the analysis of those courts that have rejected the *Watson*/American Law Institute approach to close corporation standing. The leading decision on this point is *Bagdon* v. *Bridgestone/Firestone, Inc.*, 916 F.2d 379 (7th Cir. 1990), in which the Seventh Circuit rejected, as a matter of Delaware law, the expansion of the "special injury" doctrine articulated in *Watson* "into a general exception for closely held corporations, treating them as if they were partnerships." The Seventh Circuit emphasized that the "premise of this extension may be questioned. Corporations are *not* partnerships. Whether to incorporate entails a choice of many formalities. Commercial rules should be predictable; this objective is best served by treating corporations as what they are, allowing the investors and other participants to vary the rules by contract if they think deviations are warranted. So it is understandable that not all states have joined the parade."

The Virginia Supreme Court "declined to adopt a closely held corporation exception to the rule requiring that suits for breach of fiduciary duty against officers and directors must be brought derivatively on behalf of the corporation and not as individual shareholder claims. Adherence to the general rule without this proposed exception prevents multiplicity of lawsuits by shareholders. A recovery by the corporation protects all shareholders as well as creditors. As expressed in *Bagdon*, consistent application of commercial rules promotes predictability. If shareholders and the corporation desire to vary commercial rules by contract, they are free to do so." *Simmons* v. *Miller*, 544 S.E.2d 666 (Va. 2001). Indeed, the Virginia Supreme Court has extended this analysis from *Simmons* to the LLC context. See *Remora Investments, LLC* v. *Orr*, 673 S.E.2d 845 (Va. 2009) (intracompany dispute between manager and member of LLC).

Particularly because LLCs are entirely creatures of statute, see, e.g., *Styslinger* v. *Brewster Park, LLC*, 138 A.3d 257 (Conn. 2016), I believe that action in this area that affects a party's rights and remedies is a uniquely legislative function. Because the legislature is active in this area, given its recent passage of the comprehensive Connecticut Uniform Limited Liability Company Act, and because there are natural constituencies that are well situated to advocate for legislative action in this area, I believe it best to stay our hand rather than make a public policy judgment expanding standing in civil cases involving LLCs.

NOTES

1. With respect to the question of whether the common law permits a derivative action when the LLC statute is silent on the issue, New York recognized standing under the common law. *See* Tzolis v. Wolff, 884 N.E.2d 1005, 1007–08 (N.Y. 2008) ("When fiduciaries are faithless to their trust, the victims must not be left wholly without a remedy. To determine that frauds of this kind are out of the reach of courts of law or equity would lead to an intolerable grievance. As shown above, courts have repeatedly recognized derivative suits in the absence of express statutory authorization. In light of this, it could hardly be argued that the mere absence of authorizing language in the Limited Liability Company Law bars the courts from entertaining derivative suits by LLC members.").

The case below discusses the issue of whether members of an LLC can pursue an action against another member based on an injury suffered primarily by the LLC. In a seven-member court, the case resulted in a dissent in which three justices dissented. In reading this case, consider these questions: (1) What policies determined the majority's and dissent's opinions? (2) Is there a difference between policies governing corporations and LLCs? (3) Although not mentioned in either the majority or dissenting opinions, is this a case of inside reverse veil piercing? (4) In what way does the principle of legal personhood apply or not apply?

MARX V. MORRIS

925 N.W.2d 112 (Wisc. 2019)

ROGGENSACK, C.J.

Two members of a limited liability company (LLC), Fracsand, LLC by Daniel Marx and Management Funds, LLC by Michael Murray, brought an action against another member, Richard Morris and his LLC, R.L. Co., LLC, after North Star Sand, LLC, sold valuable assets to a company owned by Morris. At the time of the sale, Morris was a manager of North Star.

Marx and Murray alleged that Morris willfully failed to deal fairly with them while having a material conflict of interest in the transaction, in violation of Wis. Stat. § 183.0402(1) [provision providing that a member or manager shall not engage in "willful failure to deal fairly . . . violation of criminal law . . . derive an improper personal profit . . . willful misconduct"]. They also alleged a number of common-law claims involving improper self-dealing. Marx and Murray brought all their claims in their individual LLC and personal capacities rather than in the name of North Star.

Morris moved for summary judgment. The circuit court denied Morris's motion, and the court of appeals certified [this] question:

> Does a member of [an] LLC have standing to assert a claim against another member of the same LLC based on an injury suffered primarily by the LLC, rather than the individual member asserting the claim?

We conclude the following: the members of an LLC have standing to assert individual claims against other members and managers of the LLC based on harm to the members or harm to the LLC. Corporate principles of derivative standing do not apply to the distinct business form of an LLC.

North Star is a limited liability company formed under Wisconsin law in November 2011. The company's goal was to own and mine land containing silica sand, a type of sand used in fracking operations.

North Star's membership consisted of six limited liability companies, which in turn were owned by six individuals. Fracsand, LLC was owned by Marx; R&R Management Funds, LLC owned by Murray; R.L. Co., LLC owned by Morris; [and three other LLCs owned by three other individuals]. Morris, an attorney, had previously represented both Murray and Johnson. Glorvigen had prepared Morris's personal taxes for at least 20 years.

Morris assisted in drafting North Star's Operating Agreement, and drafted two of the Amendments to the Operating Agreement. According to Marx and Murray, Morris was North Star's attorney. They allege that he was paid by North Star for his legal work on behalf of the company, and some of his equity in North Star was received in compensation for his legal work. Morris disputes this. However, it is undisputed that he was a manager of North Star in his capacity as a North Star director.

North Star's Operating Agreement reflected an understanding that the members would be free to pursue outside business opportunities. Transacting business with companies who had business relationships with North Star was permitted:

> Directors, as well as the Members and their respective officers, board of directors, directors, shareholders, partners, and affiliates, may engage independently or with others in other business ventures of every nature and description. Nothing in this Agreement shall be deemed to prohibit any Director, or the Members or their respective officers, board of directors, directors, shareholders, partners, and affiliates, from dealing or otherwise engaging in business with Persons transacting business with the Company. Neither the Company, any Director, or any Member shall have any right by virtue of this Agreement, or the relationship created by this Agreement, in or to such other ventures or activities, or to the income or proceeds derived from such other ventures or activities, and the pursuit of such ventures shall not be deemed wrongful or improper.

However, directors did not have the authority to: "Possess Company property, or assign rights in specific Company property, for other than a purpose of the Company."

North Star entered into a number of option agreements for the purchase of land in Jackson County, Wisconsin. The members decided to create a separate entity to control the purchase agreements for certain properties, called the Pine Creek Reserves, that contained substantial silica sand reserves. This entity became Westar Proppants, LLC, a wholly owned subsidiary of North Star. North Star assigned its Pine Creek purchase options to Westar on the same day Westar was formed.

Many of Westar's purchase options were set to expire. Concern was expressed that North Star and Westar had too much land under option contracts. The same day Westar's purchase options were set to expire, the members of North Star met by telephone to discuss Westar's future.

During this meeting, Morris informed the other members that he and two other people, Gerald Green and Scott Wesch, had formed an entity called DSJ Holdings, LLC. Morris also informed the group that he had an ownership interest in DSJ. He stated that DSJ was interested in purchasing Westar and was willing to pay $70,000. At this time, [one owner of a member LLC] made a motion for North Star to keep Westar. Marx seconded the motion, and it passed by vote of 4–2. Marx, Murray, [and two other owners of member LLCs] all voted in favor of the motion to keep Westar, while Morris and [another] voted against it.

Immediately after the vote, Morris indicated that he may withdraw from North Star. Marx and Murray allege that Morris became "very aggressive" and told Toy that "you're going to lose your million bucks." After a brief discussion, Morris made a motion for North Star to sell Westar to DSJ for $70,000. Murray immediately objected to Morris's motion, arguing that there had been insufficient notice, that a vote had already occurred, and that Morris was conflicted. Despite these objections, a second vote occurred, and Morris's motion passed 4–2. Morris [and three other owners of member LLCs] voted for North Star to sell Westar to DSJ, while Marx and Murray voted against the sale.

DSJ subsequently assigned Westar's membership units to R.L. Co., LLC (Morris's LLC) and to Wesch. Morris and Green then formed Hixton Trans-load Facility, LLC (Hixton Trans-load) for the purpose of securing purchase agreements for a new rail head site specifically for the Pine Creek Reserves property. Westar, along with Hixton Trans-load, was sold to Unimin Corporation for what has been alleged to be a substantial sum.

Marx and Murray alleged causes of action against Morris and his LLC [including] violation of Wis. Stat. § 183.0402, breach of fiduciary duty, and breach of implied covenant of good faith and fair dealing.

We consider whether Marx and Murray have standing to assert individual claims against Morris for injuries that are alleged to have occurred here. In order to have standing to sue, a party must have a personal stake in the outcome of the controversy. "Being damaged, however, without more, does not automatically confer standing." Instead, "plaintiffs must show that they suffered or were threatened with an injury to an interest that is legally protectable."

In the corporate context, we have long held that individual shareholders cannot directly sue a corporation's directors or officers when the "primary injury" resulting from the actor's wrong is to the corporation itself. Instead, a shareholder who wishes to seek redress for an injury "primarily" to the corporation must bring a derivative action.

Morris encourages us to read corporate principles of derivative standing into ch. 183 and hold that Marx and Murray's claims belong exclusively to North Star. We decline to do so. An LLC is a "creature of statute"; therefore, the absence of statutory procedures that limit actions against others for injuries to the LLC is significant. Additionally, North Star, LLC is a distinct business form that differs significantly from a corporation. Accordingly, we decline to import corporate principles of derivative standing into ch. 183 to preempt claims by individual North Star members. This conclusion is not driven by who "owns" the claim, but rather, by Wis. Stat. § 183.0402 and the partnership-like mode of operation North Star, LLC selected in its Operating Agreement.

In contrast to the statutes that limit standing to bring derivative actions in ch. 180, the only provision of ch. 183 relating to suits in the name of an LLC is Wis. Stat. § 183.1101. That section states in relevant part:

> Unless otherwise provided in an operating agreement, an action on behalf of a limited liability company may be brought in the name of the limited liability company by one or more members of the limited liability company, whether or not the management of the limited liability company is vested in one or more managers, if the members are authorized to sue by the affirmative vote as described in s. 183.0404(1)(a).

Wisconsin Stat. § 183.1101 does not require that claims against LLC members be brought in the name of the LLC, nor does it otherwise limit a member's ability to sue other members or managers in their individual capacities. It merely requires that *if* an action of any kind is to be brought *in the name of the LLC*, against anyone, it must be authorized by a majority vote of disinterested members. Section 183.1101, which is silent on a member's right to sue on his own behalf, does not abrogate the plain language of Wis. Stat. § 183.0402(1)(a), which prohibits the "willful failure to deal fairly with the limited liability company or its members."

An LLC is a business form created by statute. Other states have written standing rules that apply to corporations into their LLC statutes, including who may maintain an action for an injury to an LLC, demand requirements, and the role of the court. Wisconsin's legislature has not chosen to enact such statutes. We will not judicially import ch. 180's corporate derivative standing provisions into the LLC context where the legislature has not done so.

Morris's argument assumes that injuries to North Star, LLC and injuries to individual members are mutually exclusive. However, corporate principles of standing do not apply to LLCs. Injuries to North Star and to its members are not mutually exclusive because financial injury to North Star flows through to its members just as an injury would if North Star were a partnership rather than an LLC. The question is not whether the alleged injury is to the LLC or to its individual members. Rather, the question is simply whether the individual member bringing the action has suffered an injury to a legally protected interest.

In addition to the lack of statutory support for applying statutory corporate principles of derivative standing to an LLC, in a corporation, gains and losses do not flow through to the individual shareholders. Instead, the corporation's income is first taxed at the entity level. 26 U.S.C. § 11. Shareholders do not claim a corporation's gains and losses on their individual tax returns. They pay taxes only on the dividends, if any, they receive from the corporation, and are not taxed on capital gains and losses unless and until they choose to sell their corporate shares.

North Star has elected to be taxed as a partnership. This is the usual form of operation for an LLC. When treated as a partnership, the company's gains and losses flow through to individual members and are realized directly by each member on that member's individual tax return. North Star operates such that its gains and losses are directly credited to or deducted from each member's capital account, flowing through to each member's individual tax return. This is a concept used in partnership law that is not present in the corporate context. Each member's interest in North Star, LLC is that member's personal property, and includes the right to a share of the profits and losses of the LLC. Wis. Stat. §§ 183.0703, 183.0102(11). There is generally a much closer financial connection between harm to an LLC and harm to its members than between harm to a corporation and harm to its shareholders.

The members of an LLC have standing to assert individual claims against other members and managers of the LLC based on harm to the members or harm to the LLC. Corporate principles of derivative standing do not apply to the distinct business form of an LLC. There are genuine issues of material fact with regard to Marx and Murray's claim that Morris violated Wis. Stat. § 183.0402(1). We affirm the order of the circuit court and remand for further proceedings not inconsistent with this opinion.

KELLY, J. (concurring in part, dissenting in part [joined by ABRAHAMSON, J., and BRADLEY, J.]).

Our decision today is incompatible with the structure of limited liability companies and the laws that govern them.

Business Forms Matter

The distinction between LLCs and their members, of course, is why this case is here, so that's where I'll start. North Star is an LLC. It has six members, each one of which is itself an LLC. Each of the six LLC members has a single member, and in each case that member is a natural person. Two of the LLC members are plaintiffs in this case—Fracsand, LLC ("Fracsand"), and R & R Management Funds, LLC ("Management Funds"); one of the LLC members is a defendant—R.L. Co., LLC ("R.L."). Three individuals are parties to this case, none of whom are members of North

Star. Marx (Fracsand's sole member) and Murray (Management Funds' sole member) are plaintiffs. Morris (R.L.'s sole member) is a defendant.

The court's error started in the very first paragraph, in which it misapprehended the identity of the parties to this case:

> Two members of a limited liability company (LLC), Fracsand, LLC by Daniel Marx (Marx) and Management Funds, LLC by Michael Murray (Murray), brought an action against another member, Richard Morris (Morris) and his LLC, R.L. Co., LLC, after North Star Sand, LLC (North Star) sold valuable assets to a company owned by Morris.

No, Fracsand did not bring its claim "by Daniel Marx," nor did Management Funds bring its claim "by Michael Murray." Fracsand and Management Funds brought their claims under their own steam, because each one is a juridical entity with the ability to sue and be sued. Nothing in the amended complaint suggests that Marx and Murray are participating in this case simply as proxies for Fracsand and Management Funds. To the contrary, Marx and Murray asserted their own claims against the defendants. The complaint explicitly states there are four plaintiffs, not two: Marx, Fracsand, Murray, and Management Funds. Nonetheless, the court reduced them by half, referring to Marx and Fracsand as "Marx," and Murray and Management Funds as "Murray" throughout the opinion as though there is no legal difference between an LLC and its members. The court didn't fare much better with the defendants. It said the plaintiffs "brought an action against another member, Richard Morris (Morris) and his LLC, R.L. Co., LLC." That would certainly be news to the plaintiffs (all four of them), because they all understand that *R.L.* is the North Star member, not Morris. The apparent assumption behind the court's conflation of the LLCs involved in this case and their members is that our statutes make no distinction between them. But that's simply not true. In fact, the distinction between LLCs and their members is the very first thing for which we must account in deciding who may bring what types of claims against which defendants.

The first step in analyzing this case is determining who owns the causes of action asserted in the amended complaint. As a juridical entity, an LLC can buy, hold, and convey property in its own name. Wis. Stat. § 183.0701(3). Causes of action are a type of property recognized by Wisconsin law. Wis. Stat. § 990.01(27) (personal property "includes things in action"). Because LLCs have "the same powers as an individual to do all things necessary and convenient to carry out its business," and because they can own property as well as sue and be sued, it necessarily follows that they can own a cause of action just like an individual.

There's no need to judicially import derivative standing principles into Chapter 183, because the legislature has, in fact, already done so. The court's analysis is faulty because it didn't start at the beginning. The first statutory provision to consult on this subject is not Wis. Stat. § 183.1101 (which is where the court started), it is Wis. Stat. § 183.0305. Here we learn that one's status as a member of an LLC does not, by itself, provide the necessary authority to sue on behalf of the LLC:

> A member of a limited liability company is not a proper party to a proceeding by or against a limited liability company, solely by reason of being a member of the limited liability company, except if any of the following situations exists:
>
> (1) The object of the proceeding is to enforce a member's right against or liability to the limited liability company.
>
> (2) The action is brought by the member under s. 183.1101.

The first enumerated situation is not at issue here. The only other circumstance in which membership in an LLC confers authority to sue is through compliance with § 183.1101. That provision says:

> Unless otherwise provided in an operating agreement, an action on behalf of a limited liability company may be brought in the name of the limited liability company by one or more members of the limited liability company, whether or not the management of the limited liability company is vested in one or more managers, if the members are authorized to sue by the affirmative vote as described in s. 183.0404 (1) (a), except that the vote of any member who has an interest in the outcome of the action that is adverse to the interest of the limited liability company shall be excluded.

Consequently, § 183.0305 stands as a bar against members suing on behalf of their LLC unless they satisfy the terms of § 183.1101.

The primary reason the court's statutory analysis went where it did is because it never mentioned, much less analyzed, Wis. Stat. § 183.0305. Its narrow focus on the terms of Wis. Stat. § 183.1101, to the exclusion of all other statutory provisions, caused it to conclude that its provisions were optional, and that it "is silent on a member's right to sue on his own behalf." Yes, § 183.1101 is silent on that subject. The problem is, § 183.0305 is not. In fact, § 183.1101 simply operates as an exception to the rule in § 183.0305 that a member has no standing to sue on behalf of his LLC.

Ownership of the Claims

If our analysis had begun with the proper starting point, it would have looked something like the following.

Count I of the amended complaint claims that Morris and R.L. violated the obligations imposed on them by Wis. Stat. § 183.0402. That statute says, in relevant part:

> Unless otherwise provided in an operating agreement:

(1) No member or manager shall act or fail to act in a manner that constitutes any of the following:

(a) A willful failure to deal fairly with the limited liability company or its members in connection with a matter in which the member or manager has a material conflict of interest.

The plaintiffs say the violation occurred when R.L. and Morris influenced North Star to sell Westar Proppants, LLC ("Westar")—a wholly-owned subsidiary of North Star—to DSJ Holdings, LLC ("DSJ"), an entity owned by Morris. Specifically, they say Morris had a material conflict of interest in the sale of Westar to DSJ, and that the decision to sell was the consequence of a vote that was not preceded by the notice requirements of North Star's Operating Agreement.

By its explicit terms, Wis. Stat. § 183.0402 describes a potential injury to the LLC or its members. That automatically disqualifies Marx and Murray from bringing this claim, because they are not members of North Star. So the only potentially eligible plaintiffs are Fracsand and Management Funds. A proper analysis would next apply the primary injury rule to determine whether the claim belongs to North Star or, instead, the plaintiff LLCs.

The plaintiffs say that, because of the conflict of interest, Northstar sold Westar for inadequate consideration. If that is so, then Fracsand and Management Funds certainly suffered injury from that transaction, but not in a manner that affects their "rights in a manner distinct from the effect upon other" members' rights. Diminution of a company's value, and hence its value to the company's owner, describes a classic derivative injury: "That such primary and direct injury to a corporation may have a subsequent impact on the value of the stockholders' shares is clear, but that is not enough to create a right to bring a direct."

Further, our statutes treat any recovery upon such a claim in a way that unmistakably identifies this as a claim belonging to North Star. If Fracsand and Management Funds were to succeed in their claim, Wis. Stat. § 183.0402 requires the defendant to "hold as trustee" for the "limited liability company . . . any improper personal profit derived by that member or manager from any transaction connected with the organization." § 183.0402(2)(a). So the improper profits, if there are any, belong to North Star, not its members. Consequently, Fracsand and Management Funds must pursue North Star's claim in accordance with the procedures described in Wis. Stat. §§ 183.0305 and 183.1101, or not at all. Because they did not, they may not seek recovery for this alleged injury.

Breach of Fiduciary Duties

[Another] erroneous proposition is that fiduciary duties obtain between members of an LLC. They don't.

We conclude that Marx and Murray have no authority to pursue this claim. Neither one is a North Star member, and so it is not possible for intra-membership fiduciary duties (should there be any) to have anything to say about how non-members are treated. Similarly, we can eliminate Morris as a proper defendant with respect to this cause of action because he is not a member of North Star either. If this cause of action exists, it can obtain only between Fracsand, Management Funds, and R.L.

Nothing in Chapter 183 refers to fiduciary duties between members. So the only question before us was whether the nature of the relationship between LLC members necessarily implies the existence of fiduciary obligations.

Common law fiduciary duties arise out of the nature of the relationship between two or more parties. These duties mitigate the risk of self-dealing by the other members within the circle of fiduciary duties, and lower the monitoring costs of their conduct. We have recognized that "a fiduciary relationship arises from a formal commitment to act for the benefit of another or from special circumstances from which the law will assume an obligation to act for another's benefit." Typically, the law will assume such an obligation where there is an "entrustment of power or property in connection with the fiduciary's services." In "determining whether a fiduciary relationship has arisen, courts consider a variety of factors, including whether there is *dependence and inequality* or other conditions giving one side an advantage over the other."

These principles justify the imposition of fiduciary duties between, for example, members of a partnership. A partner can incur liabilities on behalf of other partners because (1) any partner can bind the partnership and (2) every partner is liable for all of the partnership's obligations. Wis. Stat. § 178.0306(1). Thus, in a partnership between "A" and "B," partner A depends on partner B to act in their combined best interest because if partner B chooses, he can incur liabilities for which partner A might ultimately be responsible. The relationship creates a "dependence" between the partners; the fiduciary duties between them ward against one partner taking advantage of the others.

If the members of an LLC stood in a position of "dependence and inequality" amongst themselves, that relationship would call into existence fiduciary duties between them. But LLC members do not relate to one another in the same way that partners do. Instead, the nature of the relationship between LLC members is much closer to that obtaining between shareholders of a corporation. An LLC member cannot bind another member of the LLC any more than a shareholder can bind fellow shareholders. Wis. Stat. § 183.0301(1)(a) ("Each member is an agent of the limited liability company, but not of the other members or any of them, for the purpose of its business."). A shareholder cannot bind a fellow shareholder because all corporate authority belongs to the corporation's board of directors. Wis. Stat. § 180.0801(2) ("All corporate powers shall be exercised by or under the authority of, and the business and affairs of the corporation managed under the direction of, its board of directors."). And because an LLC is a liability-limiting business entity, the obligations to which a member may bind an LLC do not reach the other members: "The debts, obligations and liabilities of a limited liability company, whether arising in contract, tort or otherwise, shall be *solely* the debts, obligations and liabilities of the *limited liability company*." Wis. Stat. § 183.0304(1). The same is true of corporations and their shareholders: "a shareholder of a corporation is not personally liable for the acts or debts of the corporation." § 180.0622(2). So while it is conceivable that an LLC member may owe a fiduciary duty to the LLC, there is nothing about membership in an LLC that can call fiduciary duties into existence between its members. Chapter 183 does not create those duties, and because there is a lack of "dependence and inequality" between LLC members, that relationship cannot make them fiduciaries.

Marx and Murray have no standing to pursue any of the claims in their complaint. With respect to fiduciary duties, we should have concluded that there is no fiduciary relationship amongst LLC members, and that an attorney owes fiduciary duties only to the LLC, not its members.

Because the court did not reach these conclusions, it affirmed the following six propositions, all of which are erroneous:

1. Marx and Murray, who are not North Star members, may nonetheless sue North Star's members for North Star's management decisions.

2. Marx and Murray (who are not North Star members) may sue Morris (who is also not a North Star member) based on North Star's management decisions.

3. Fracsand and Management Funds may sue Morris (who is not a North Star member), in his personal capacity, for North Star's management decisions.

4. The plaintiffs may sue North Star's members based on causes of action that belong to North Star, not the plaintiffs.

5. North Star's members owe each other fiduciary duties even though the membership relationship contains none of the particulars that call fiduciary obligations into existence in other contexts.

6. Morris (as North Star's attorney) owes fiduciary duties not only to North Star, but its members and its members' members.

The case below discusses the nature of the demand requirement and the rule of demand futility. In reading this case, consider these questions:

(1) What is the rationale for demand and demand futility? (2) Would demand have been futile in this case?

WOODSIDE PROPERTIES, LLC v. MKR DEVELOPMENT, LLC

814 S.E.2d 179 (Va. 2018)

STEPHEN R. MCCULLOUGH.

The circuit court dismissed without prejudice this derivative action on the ground that the plaintiff had failed to first make a demand for the limited liability company to take action. The plaintiff appeals from this ruling, arguing that the law does not require such a demand when doing so would be futile. The applicable statute, Code § 13.1–1042, and related provisions present us with a conundrum because competing canons of statutory construction point in opposite directions. We resolve this conundrum by concluding that the 2011 amendments to Code § 13.1–1042 did not abolish the futility exception to the demand requirement as established in case law preceding enactment of the statute. Consequently, we reverse and remand the case for further proceedings.

Melvin Davis Sr., the husband of Dorothy and the father of Kaye, Melvin Jr. and Rex, founded and owned Melvin L. Davis Oil Company. He sold the company stock to his three children. Melvin and Dorothy also owned real estate that the oil company leased. Melvin and Dorothy formed Woodside Properties as a limited liability company to take ownership of this real estate. Melvin and Dorothy intended to establish a vehicle through which they would receive income from Davis Oil's rental of these properties. The operating agreement for Woodside Properties appoints MKR Development, LLC as the manager of Woodside Properties. Under MKR's operating agreement, Rex, Melvin Jr., and Kaye are its managers.

Dorothy, who presently owns 72 percent of Woodside Properties, alleges that Woodside Properties should have received $1,374,147 in rent under the lease. Instead, she alleges, the bank account established for Woodside Properties had a balance of $35,000. She also asserts that funds that should have gone to Woodside Properties were used for improper purposes. When she asked Melvin Jr. and Rex for payment of funds due, they refused. They also refused to provide an accounting.

Dorothy filed a complaint against MKR Development, LLC and her two sons, Melvin Jr. and Rex, as well as Woodside Properties, LLC. She alleges that MKR and her sons, as managers, had breached their fiduciary duties towards Woodside Properties, were wasting corporate assets, and unjustly enriching themselves. She asked for MKR to be removed as manager of Woodside Properties, and for a decree imposing a constructive trust and requiring an accounting.

Significantly, the amended complaint states that:

> Davis did not make demand on MKR, Mel, and/or Rex to bring this action on behalf of Woodside Properties because such demand would have been a futile, wasteful, and useless act as they were the parties who authorized and ratified the alleged wrongful conduct complained of herein and were the direct beneficiaries thereof, and are incapable of making an independent and disinterested decision to institute and vigorously prosecute this action.

In response, the defendants filed a plea in bar and demurrer, alleging, among other things, that the complaint was barred because Dorothy had not made a "proper demand as required by" Code § 13.1–1042. The court agreed, granted the plea in bar, and dismissed the complaint on that basis. Dorothy appeals from this decision.

The derivative form of action permits an individual shareholder to bring "suit to enforce a *corporate* cause of action against officers, directors, and third parties." Devised as a suit in equity, the purpose of the derivative action is to place in the hands of the individual shareholder a means to protect the interests of the corporation from the misfeasance and malfeasance of "faithless directors and managers."

To prevent abuse of this remedy, however, equity courts required the shareholder to "allege and prove that a request or demand has been made upon the board of directors, or other body managing the corporation that they institute proceedings on the part of the corporation against the wrong-doers, and their refusal to do so after reasonable request, or demand." In the alternative, the stockholder could

> allege such a state of facts as will show that the defendants whom he charges with the wrong doing constitute a majority of the board of directors, or managing body at the time of the suit, or that they, or a majority of them, are under the control of the defendant wrong-doers, so that the court may infer that they would refuse to bring such suit; or he must allege such facts in his pleading as will show that it is reasonably certain that a suit by the corporation would be impossible, and that a demand to sue would be useless.

This became known as the "futility exception."

Effectively codifying this case law, Code § 13.1–1042 previously provided that a plaintiff could bring a derivative action "if members or managers with authority to do so have refused to bring the action or if an effort to cause those members or managers to bring the action is not likely to succeed." 1991 Va. Acts ch. 168 (enacting Virginia Limited Liability Company Act, Code § 13.1–1000 through –1069). In 2011, however, the General Assembly amended the statute, in pertinent part, as follows:

A. A member ~~may bring an action in the right of a limited liability company to recover a judgment in its favor to the same extent that a shareholder may bring an action for a derivative suit under the Stock Corporation Act, Chapter 9 (§ 13.1–601 et seq.) of this title. Such action may be brought if members or managers with authority to do so have refused to bring the action or if an effort to cause those members or managers to bring the action is not likely to succeed. The derivative action may not be maintained if it appears that the plaintiff does not~~ *shall not commence or maintain a derivative proceeding unless the member* fairly and adequately ~~represent~~ *represents* the interests of the ~~members and the~~ limited liability company in enforcing the right of the limited liability company *and is a proper plaintiff pursuant to § 13.1–1043.*

B. No member may commence a derivative proceeding until:

1. A written demand has been made on the limited liability company to take suitable action; and

2. Ninety days have expired from the date delivery of the demand was made unless (i) the member has been notified before the expiration of 90 days that the demand has been rejected by the limited liability company or (ii) irreparable injury to the limited liability company would result by waiting until the end of the 90-day period.

C. If the limited liability company commences a review and evaluation of the allegations made in the demand or complaint, the court may stay any derivative proceeding for such period as the court deems appropriate.

2011 Acts ch. 379 (newly enacted text in italics, deleted text stricken).

MKR argues that this amendment abolished the futility exception. As it presently reads, MKR notes, Code § 13.1–1042(B) requires a member to make a demand and wait 90 days prior to commencing a derivative suit. A longstanding canon of construction supports this view: "as a general rule, a presumption exists that a substantive change in law was intended by an amendment to an existing statute." There are two significant obstacles to [MKR's] interpretation of Code § 13.1–1042.

Code § 13.1–1044 sets forth pleading requirements for derivative suits. It states that "in derivative action, the complaint shall set forth with particularity the effort of the plaintiff to secure commencement of the action by a member or manager with the authority to do so *or the reasons for not making the effort.*" If Code § 13.1–1042 categorically requires a demand, this language in Code § 13.1–1044 would be superfluous. We resist a construction of a statute that would render part of a statute superfluous. "Every part of a statute is presumed to have some effect and no part will be considered meaningless unless absolutely necessary."

Code § 13.1–1001.1(A) provides that "the principles of law and equity supplement this chapter" except where they are "displaced by particular provisions of this chapter." The text of Code § 13.1–1042 as it presently exists does not expressly disclaim the futility exception. It is silent on the subject. Since derivative actions generally, and the futility exception specifically, developed on the equity side of the court, they constitute "principles of equity" under Code § 13.1–1001.1(A). Although derivative actions developed in connection with traditional corporations rather than limited liability companies, such a derivative action is closely analogous to a derivative action involving an LLC. By referring to "principles of law and equity [which] supplement this chapter," Code § 13.1–1001.1(A) embraces within its scope the futility exception, which has long been part of our law.

The General Assembly's 2011 enactment was not a futile gesture. The amendment reorganized and streamlined the statute. It created subsections A, B, and C, added a specific timeline in subsection B, and expressly provided the court with the power to stay an action in subsection C. With respect to the futility exception, the 2011 amendment had the effect of replacing an express textual provision in Code § 13.1–1042 with an incorporation by reference of a rule drawn from case law.

The combined force of the textual provisions of Code § 13.1–1001.1(A) and Code § 13.1–1044 lead us to conclude that the General Assembly did not abrogate the futility exception when it amended Code § 13.1–1042 in 2011. Therefore, the circuit court erred in dismissing Dorothy's complaint.

We remand with instructions to reinstate the plaintiff's complaint.

3. ARBITRATION

The charter agreement can provide for dispute resolution mechanisms. The most significant mechanism is arbitration. An arbitration is a binding alternative dispute resolution process in which the dispute is submitted to an arbitrator who has the power to make a binding decision. Most courts have upheld arbitration agreements in the charter agreement.[4] If the

[4] *See* Elf Atochem North America, Inc. v. Jaffari, 727 A.2d 286, 292 (Del. 1999) ("The arbitration provision of the Agreement in this case fosters the Delaware policy favoring alternate dispute resolution mechanisms, including arbitration."); James v. Jackson, LLC v. Willie Gary, LLC, 906 A.2d 76, 80–81 (Del. 2006) (recognizing that arbitration clauses in operating agreements are generally enforceable including "substantive arbitrability" issues, which are questions about the scope of an arbitration provision and its applicability, when there is a "clear and unmistakable intent"); Midwest Neurosciences Associates, LLC v. Great Lakes Neurosurgical Associates, LLC, 920 N.W.2d 767, 778–79 (Wisc. 2018) (noting that arbitration clauses in operating agreements are enforceable under general policies underlying the concept of arbitration). Even certain judicial powers, such as hearing claims for judicial dissolution, are subject to arbitration. *See* B&S MS Holdings, LLC v. Landrum, 302 So.3d 605 (Miss. 2020) (holding that when the operating agreement provided that all disputes "shall be finally and exclusively resolved by arbitration," a majority member must arbitrate a claim for judicial dissolution); Willie Gary LLC v. James & Jackson LLC, 2006 WL 75309, at *10 (Del. Ch. 2006) ("This court accepted that argument and

charter agreement provides that disputes must be arbitrated, it should also provide, among other matters: the process for arbitration including the selection of the arbitrator, the number of arbitrators, the forum to conduct arbitration, the costs of arbitration, and attorney fees and costs.

G. ISSUES TO CONSIDER FOR NBEs

1. GENERAL DRAFTING CONSIDERATION

In the realm of NBEs, the charter agreement is paramount. *See* R & R Capital, LLC v. Buck & Doe Run Valley Farms, LLC, 2008 WL 3846318, at *1 (Del. Ch. 2008) ("For Shakespeare, it may have been the play, but for a Delaware limited liability company, *the contract's the thing*. Ultimately, it is the contract that compels the Court's decision in this case because it is the contract that defines the scope, structure, and personality of limited liability companies."). When considering the alteration of fiduciary duties in the charter agreement, one should heed to advice of the Delaware Chancery Court.

> This court has made clear that it will not be tempted by the piteous pleas of limited partners who are seeking to escape the consequences of their own decisions to become investors in a partnership whose general partner has clearly exempted itself from traditional fiduciary duties. The [Delaware Revised Uniform Limited Partnership Act] puts investors on notice that fiduciary duties may be altered by partnership agreements, and therefore that investors should be careful to read partnership agreements before buying units. The [statute] reflects the doctrine of caveat emptor, as is fitting given that investors in limited partnerships have countless other investment opportunities available to them that involve less risk and/or more legal protection. For example, any investor who wishes to retain the protection of traditional fiduciary duties can always invest in corporate stock.

Miller v. Am. Real Estate Partners, L.P., 2001 WL 1045643, at *8 (Del. Ch. 2001) (Strine, V.C.).

The charter agreement constitutes the most important single source of rights and duties of a firm's owners and managers. Drafting and amending the charter agreement present opportunities to structure the firm.

---

found that a reference to a decree of judicial dissolution under the LLC Act did not mean that a dissolution claim was not subject to mandatory arbitration in the first instance, reasoning that such a judicial dissolution could be entered in accordance with, and following, dissolution proceedings before an arbitrator."). The rulings in *Landrum* and *Willie Gary*—that a claim for judicial dissolution can be arbitrated—are consistent with the RULLCA (harmonized 2013 version). *See* RULLCA § 105(c)(9) ("An operating agreement may not vary the *causes of dissolution* specified in Section 701(a)(4)"). However, another version of the RULLCA (without the harmonization amendments) would not permit arbitration of claims for judicial dissolution. *See* RULLCA § 110(c)(7) ("An operating agreement may not vary the *power of a court* to decree dissolution in the circumstances specified in Section 701(a)(4) and (5)").

Contracting requires care and consideration of all facets of relationships among owners, managers, and the firm.

2. DUTY OF CARE

In contracting for the duty of care, owners and managers must set forth the standard. There are a number of questions to address:

- What is the scope of the duty of care?
- Does the business judgment rule apply?
- What is the standard for determining liability for a breach of duty?

Does the duty subject managers to an ex post review of substantive business decisions? Does the duty subject managers to an ex post review of the process in which the business decision was made?

The LLC is a hybrid entity in several ways. It can resemble a general partnership, an LP, or a corporation, and whether duty attaches to a member or manager is a function of the management structure: Is the management organization structured like a partnership or a corporation? Some concepts from corporation law, such as the business judgment rule, may apply to the scrutiny of a fiduciary's conduct. However, other concepts of corporation law may not apply under the RULLCA. Specifically, even if the standard of care is "grossly negligent or reckless conduct," the RULLCA is ambiguous as to whether the "conduct" in question pertains to the substance of the business decision or the manner in which it was made.

Under Delaware corporation law, the duty of care is defined by a substantive-procedural dichotomy.

> As for the plaintiffs' contention that the directors failed to exercise "substantive due care," we should note that such a concept is foreign to the business judgment rule. Courts do not measure, weigh or quantify directors' judgments. We do not even decide if they are reasonable in this context. Due care in the decisionmaking context is process due care only.

Brehm v. Eisner, 746 A.2d 244 (Del. 2000). *See* Smith v. Van Gorkom, 488 A.2d 858, 873 (Del. 1985) ("We think the concept of gross negligence is also the proper standard for determining whether a business judgment reached by a board of directors was an informed one.").

Unlike the typical duty of care under tort law, which reviews the substance of conduct resulting in the accident, the scope of the duty of care under corporation law is limited to the process of informed decisionmaking, and not the substantive quality of the business decision. *See, e.g.,* In re Caremark Int'l Inc. Derivative Litig., 698 A.2d 959, 967 (Del. Ch. 1996) ("Whether a judge or jury considering the matter after the fact, believes a decision substantively wrong, or degrees of wrong extending through 'stupid' to 'egregious' or 'irrational,' provides no ground for director liability, so long as the court determines that the process employed was either rational or employed in a good faith effort to advance corporate interests."); Gagliardi v. TriFoods Int'l, Inc., 683 A.2d 1049, 1052 (Del. Ch. 1996) ("If, however, corporate directors were to be found liable for a corporate loss from a risky project on the ground that the investment was too risky (foolishly risky! stupidly risky! egregiously risky!—you supply the adverb), their liability would be joint and several for the whole loss.").

In light of the substantive-procedural dichotomy seen in corporation law, owners and managers and their lawyers must determine the scope of the duty of care, subject to the business judgment rule. Do they seek to permit a review of a manager's substantive business decisions? Is the duty of care limited to process of informed decisionmaking?

Also, corporation law permits the exculpation of money damages for breach of the duty of care.[5] The charters of a substantial majority of public corporations, and probably those of large or complex private corporations, have such exculpation provisions. Managers do not want to be held liable for honest mistakes, even if they were said to be negligent after-the-fact. The line between negligence and risk-taking is not always clear. In hindsight, good risk-taking can often look like negligence, and reckless action like brilliant strategy—it may all boil down to ex post outcome. On the one hand, owners may want to hold managers liable for bad decisions; on the other hand, managers may not want to work for firms where they are subject to potential liability for bad outcomes. In the public corporation market, this dynamic has resulted in most firms providing exculpation for money damages arising from a breach of the duty of care. For an NBE, owners and managers should consider whether imposing potential liability for a breach of the duty of care is desirable.

3. DUTY OF LOYALTY

Most NBE statutes permit contracting of the duty of loyalty. The statutes identify three categories of obligations under the duty of loyalty: (1) to account to the firm and hold as trustee for it any property, profit, or benefit derived by the owner in the conduct of the firm business, including

---

[5] *See* DGCL § 102(b)(7) ("[T]he certificate of incorporation may also contain a provision eliminating or limiting the personal liability of a director to the corporation or its stockholders for monetary damages for breach of fiduciary duty as a director, provided that such provision shall not eliminate or limit the liability of a director: (i) For any breach of the director's duty of loyalty to the corporation or its stockholders; (ii) for acts or omissions not in good faith or which involve intentional misconduct or a knowing violation of law; (iii) under § 174 of this title; or (iv) for any transaction from which the director derived an improper personal benefit."); MBCA § 2.02(b)(4) ("The articles of incorporation may set forth a provision eliminating or limiting the liability of a director to the corporation or its shareholders for money damages for any action taken, or any failure to take any action, as a director, except liability for (A) the amount of a financial benefit received by a director to which the director is not entitled; (B) an intentional infliction of harm on the corporation or the shareholders; (C) a violation of section 8.33; or (D) an intentional violation of criminal law.").

the appropriation of a firm opportunity; (2) to refrain from dealing with the firm in the conduct of the firm's business as or on behalf of a party having an interest adverse to the firm; and (3) to refrain from competing with the firm in the conduct of the firm's business. *See* RUPA § 409(b); ULPA (2001) § 409(b); RULLCA § 409(b). These duties can be subject to contracting so long as the alteration is not "if not manifestly unreasonable." RUPA § 105(d)(3); ULPA (2001) § 105(d)(2); RULLCA § 105(d)(3).

Owners and lawyer must consider whether the duty of loyalty includes a prohibition against competing with the firm. *See* RULLCA § 409(b)(3). The charter agreement may include a non-compete provision. But the enforceability of a non-compete agreement depends on state law. If drafted too broadly, a non-compete provision in a charter agreement runs the risk of unenforceability. Parties should tailor the non-compete provision to protect the firm while at the time be minimally intrusive to owners and managers who may at some point decide they want to leave the firm.

Statutes may provide that the charter agreement may eliminate certain aspects of the duty of loyalty, but again only if such a provision is "not manifestly unreasonable." *See* RULLCA § 105(d)(3) ("If not manifestly unreasonable, the operating agreement may: (A) alter or eliminate the aspects of the duty of loyalty stated in Section 409(b) and (i); (B) identify specific types or categories of activities that do not violate the duty of loyalty; (C) alter the duty of care, but may not authorize conduct involving bad faith, willful or intentional misconduct, or knowing violation of law; and (D) alter or eliminate any other fiduciary duty."); ULPA (2001) § 105(d)(2) (same); RUPA § 105(d)(3) (same). The statutes provide that courts should make the determination of "manifestly unreasonable" and provide further that a provision "may invalidate the term only if, in light of the purposes, activities, and affairs of the firm, it is readily apparent that: (A) the objective of the term is unreasonable; or (B) the term is an unreasonable means to achieve the term's objective." RULLCA § 105(e)(2); ULPA (2001) § 105(e)(2); RUPA § 105(e)(2). Section 105(e) provides a demanding standard because courts may invalidate a term only if it is *readily apparent* that the objective of the term is unreasonable. Case law has not dealt much with the scope of the concept of "manifestly unreasonable," and the few cases that have dealt with the issue have relied on commonsense to determine the meaning of manifestly unreasonable. *See, e.g.*, In re Brobeck, Phleger & Harrison LLP, 408 B.R. 318, 335 (Bankr. N.D. Cal. 2009) ("RUPA does not define what is 'manifestly unreasonable' and the parties have not cited, nor can the court locate, a decision that defines the term. Absent case law or even a dictionary definition, the court must rely on its common sense to recognize something as manifestly unreasonable.").

If a conflict of interest transaction is expected, one option is a provision to mimic an "arm's-length" deal. Such provision validates a conflict of interest transaction when the terms of the deal, including the price, "would have been the outcome of an arm's-length negotiation." Flight Options Int'l, Inc. v. Flight Options, LLC, 2005 WL 6799224, *7 n.32 (Del. Ch. 2005). The charter agreement should specify how to determine whether the terms of the transaction were consistent with an arm's-length transaction. For example, such mechanism can be an independent appraisal that determines price, an independent managerial body that negotiates with the conflicted manager, or ratification by owners after proper disclosure.

If a jurisdiction permits complete elimination of fiduciary duties (such as Delaware) and the parties desire it, a drafter must be careful to draft a provision that *really* eliminates duties. In Delaware, the following provisions of the operating agreement that purport to eliminate fiduciary duties have been upheld by its courts.

- "Summit shall have no duties (including fiduciary duties) or liabilities relating thereto to [Management] or to the other Members, except as may be specifically provided [in the Agreement] and required by any provisions of the [Delaware LLC] Act or other applicable law that cannot be waived. Accordingly, [Summit] shall be entitled to act solely on its own behalf, and in its own interests." *Wiggs v. Summit Midstream Partners, LLC*, 2013 WL 1286180, *10 (Del. Ch. 2013).
- "The execution, delivery or performance by the Managing Member of any agreement authorized or permitted under this Agreement shall be in the sole and absolute discretion of the Managing Member without consideration of any other obligation or duty, fiduciary or otherwise, of the Company or the Members and shall not constitute a breach by the Managing Member of any duty that the Managing Member may owe the Company or any Non-Managing Member or any other Persons under this Agreement or of any duty stated or implied by law or equity." *CNL-AB LLC v. Eastern Property Fund I SPE LLC*, 2011 WL 353529, *9 (Del. Ch. 2011).
- "Whenever a potential conflict of interest exists or arises between any Affiliate of the Company, on the one hand, and the Company or any Group Member, on the other, any resolution or course of action by the Board of Directors in respect of such conflict of interest shall be permitted and deemed approved by all Members, and shall not constitute a breach of this Agreement or of any duty existing at law, in equity or otherwise, including any fiduciary duty, if the resolution or course of action in respect of such conflict of interest is (i) approved by Special Approval, (ii) approved by the vote of holders of a majority of the Outstanding Common

Units (excluding Common Units held by interested parties), (iii) on terms no less favorable to the Company than those being generally available to or available from unrelated third parties or (iv) fair and reasonable to the Company, taking into account the totality of the relationships between the parties involved (including other transactions that may be particularly favorable to the Company)." *In re Atlas Energy Resources, LLC*, 2010 WL 4273122, *7 (Del. Ch. 2010).

While these provisions have been upheld, one should note that the entire operating agreement must always be read as a whole. If another provision in the operating agreement injects a duty, then it may nullify a provision such as the above to the extent of the duty prescribed elsewhere. For example, suppose the operating agreement purports to eliminate fiduciary duties altogether per a provision similar to the above. However, in a specific provision dealing with mergers and sale of the company, the operating agreement provides that the managers shall strive to ensure a "fair" price to members. A court could construe such a specific provision as inserting a duty to treat members "fairly" (and thus equitably) when managers engage in an M&A transaction.

H. PROBLEM: ENTREPRENEURS FIND A DEAL AND A PROBLEM

After the company retreat, PB Optique Option did a "reset." The company's operating agreement was amended to include this provision.

Article IV. Standard of Conduct.

(a) Managers owe fiduciary duties, which are the duty of care and the duty of loyalty.

(b) The fiduciary duty of loyalty of a Manager are limited:

(1) to account to the Company and hold as trustee for it any property, profit, or benefit derived by the Manager:

(A) in the conduct or winding up of the Company's activities and affairs;

(B) from a use by the Manager of the Company's property; or

(C) from the appropriation of a Company opportunity;

(2) to refrain from dealing with the Company in the conduct or winding up of the Company's activities and affairs as or on behalf of any person having an interest adverse to the Company; and

(3) to refrain from competing with the Company in the conduct of the Company's activities and affairs before the dissolution of the Company.

> (c) The fiduciary duty of care of a Manager in the conduct or winding up of the Company's activities and affairs is to refrain from engaging in grossly negligent or reckless conduct.
>
> (d) All Managers and Members shall discharge the duties and obligations under the operating agreement and exercise any rights consistently with the contractual obligation of good faith and fair dealing.

After the "reset," the company continued its business activities. Things were looking positive. There was a spurt of creativity from Art Estic, who produced an appealing line of frame designs. Arguing that Morgan Money did not have authority to sign the contract for PB Optique Option, Piers was able to renegotiate the contract with Pacifico Plastic Recycling, Inc., from 3-year, $200,000 per year to 2-year, $175,000 per year. He also found a manufacturer, Northwest Penn Industries, in Erie, Pennsylvania, that can handle "just-in-time" capability to step in to augment the source of plastics and ultimately to replace Pacifico Plastic Recycling once the two-year contract expires. Northwest Penn's prices were half that of Pacifico Plastic Recycling's prices. Blake constructed the PBOO's web page and software architecture. The company now had a product line, source of raw plastic, manufacturing capabilities, and online platform. It was near the launch of its business.

At this point, the business operated out of each owner's home, email address, and cellphone. At a teleconference meeting of owners, everyone agreed that a business office was needed. The new offices must be able to house financing, distribution and logistics, IT infrastructure, returned products warehousing, and administration. Piers and Blake were tasked with finding real estate for the new venture, either to purchase or to lease.

The need for a company office sparked an idea in Piers. He conveyed the following to Blake.

> Look, we've been friends since high school and roommates throughout business school, right? We've founded this company together. I'm going to share something private with you. I'm a bit reluctant to bring this up because it's complicated. My parents own a real estate company. Over the years, they have gifted me a minority stake in the company. I own 20% of Pro RE Solutions, LLC. My parents manage the business, and I'm rarely involved in the business even though I'm a designated manager. I know that Pro RE has a perfect building for us. It is an old warehouse, basically an empty shell, near the airport. It was originally a small manufacturing facility for the Camden Brass Company. I call it the "Brass House" because it has a huge brass sign that looks like a pipe fitting. It's perfect. It has 50,000 square feet. It is near the processing centers for FedEx and UPS. The structure of the building is great, old brick, iron, and huge industrial windows, all

in great condition. It doesn't have any amenities or a build out, which is actually a big plus for us. Because it hasn't been built out, Pro RE has had problems selling it. It's not listed for sale, but I know that my parents want to sell the building so that they can free up some cash for other investments. I could approach my parents about buying the building.

Blake: "Wow. I didn't know that you own other companies. . . . And how fortunately that you're bringing the opportunity to PBOO. The Brass House sounds like a fantastic opportunity. I'm entirely supportive."

Piers: "Well, I'm actually torn on this matter. I like the building so much that I was thinking about asking Pro RE Solutions, basically my parents, to buy out my interest in the company in exchange for the building. I see a lot of possibilities in the building. I'm still working through that possible transaction. If I do that deal with my parents, then I could either sell the Brass House to PBOO, or possibly lease it to PBOO for a period of time until I have a plan for developing it."

Blake: "The company can be flexible on any kind of a deal. We—you and I—are the company. I get the fact that a deal would only make sense if it's good for you."

Piers: "The problem is the financing."

Blake: "I agree. PBOO wouldn't have the money to buy the Brass House without additional financing."

Piers: "What do you think would be the deal parameters that would be satisfactory to you, Song, Estic, and Money?"

Blake: "What do you think is the value of the Brass House?"

Piers: "I don't know. I don't have an appraisal. My guess is $20 per square foot at 50,000 square feet, and so the value would be somewhere around $1 million. The $20 per square foot is the average price of bare industrial real estate, but of course, the Brass House would be perfect for PBOO, and so it wouldn't be unreasonable to expect a premium to value. After all, it's my property and I need to do what is in my best interest."

Blake: "I get it and I agree. . . . You're rich? All this time of being lifelong best friends and rooming together at business school and now founding PBOO together, and you never told me you were rich! You learn something every day."

Piers: "Well, I don't own the Brass House . . . not yet anyway. For the moment, I'm a minority owner of my parents' real estate company. Anyway, what do you think are some ideas about how to bring this deal to fruition? What would be the issues?"

QUESTIONS

1. With respect to any deal by PBOO for the Brass House, what are the different ways in which the deal can be structured?

2. What are the potential fiduciary duty issues raised by the possibility of doing a deal for Brass House?

3. If there are fiduciary duty issues, how might those issues be resolved?

4. If PBOO's "reset" resulted in Piers and Blake being the only designated "Managers" of the company, does that fact influence the analysis?

CHAPTER 8

TRANSFER OF INTEREST AND DISSOCIATION

■ ■ ■

A. TRANSFERS OF INTEREST IN CORPORATION

Corporation law is distinct from NBE laws with respect to the transfer of ownership interest. Stock embodies a shareholder's *entire interest*, which includes both the governance and economic rights. The whole share is considered a shareholder's personal property, and thus disposable at her will. *See* DGCL § 159 (providing that stock is "personal property and transferable"); F.B.I. Farms, Inc. v. Moore, 798 N.E.2d 440, 445 (Ind. 2003) ("Corporate shares are personal property."). A shareholder is entitled to distributions, increase in the value of shares, voting and other participatory rights. In the absence of a reasonable restriction on transfer, shares in their *entirety* are freely transferable.[1] The rule of free alienability is conducive to raising large amounts of capital and trading of shares among investors in an equity market.

B. TRANSFERS OF INTEREST IN NBEs

1. TRANSFERABLE INTEREST

Like stock in a corporation, an owner's interest in an NBE typically includes a bundle of governance and economic rights found in the charter agreement, the statute, and the common law including fiduciary duties owed to the holder. In an LP and a manager-managed LLC, the owners' governance rights may be limited, but their interests still include the rights to vote, inspect books and records, pursue judicial dissolution, file derivative action, and be owed fiduciary duty. A "transferable interest" is "the right, as initially owned by a person in the person's capacity as [an owner], to receive distributions." *See* RULLCA § 102(24); ULPA (2001)

---

[1] *See* MBCA § 6.27(c) (providing that restriction on transfer is authorized only for "reasonable purpose"); Landreth Timber Co. v. Landreth, 471 U.S. 681, 686 (1985) (identifying a common characteristic of stock as "negotiability"); Grynberg v. Burke, 378 A.2d 139, 143 (Del. Ch. 1977) (stating that, under the common law and DGCL § 202 "a restraint on the free transferability of corporate stock is permissible under our law provided it bears some reasonably necessary relation to the best interest of the corporation"); F.B.I. Farms, Inc. v. Moore, 798 N.E.2d 440, 445 (Ind. 2003) ("At common law, any restriction on the power to alienate personal property was impermissible. Despite this doctrine, Indiana, like virtually all jurisdictions, allows corporations and their shareholders to impose restrictions on transfers of shares. The basic theory of these statutes is to permit owners of a corporation to control its ownership and management and prevent outsiders from inserting themselves into the operations of the corporation.").

§ 102(25); RUPA § 102(23). Only the transferable interest is personal property. RULLCA § 501; RUPA § 502; ULPA (2001) § 701.

Under corporation law, stock is presumed to be freely transferable. The sale of stock transfers the entire bundle of economic and governance rights. Under NBE laws, the default rules do not permit the free transfer of an owner's entire interest such that the transferee becomes a new owner. Like personal relationships, business relationships in closely-held firms are based on actual assent. The idea of "one chooses one's partner" is fundamental. A partner cannot transfer her partnership interest to her spouse, thus thrusting the spouse onto the firm as a new partner much to the surprise of other partners. A person is admitted as a new owner by operation of the charter agreement or unanimous consent of all owners. RUPA § 402(b); RULLCA § 401(c); ULPA (2001) § 301(b), § 401(b).

NBE statutes permit only the transfer of an owner's "transferable interest." The transferee does not become a new owner, and his rights are limited to the ownership of the transferable interest. *See* Bynum v. Frisby, 311 P.2d 972, 975 (Nev. 1957) ("An assignment of a partnership interest from one partner to a stranger does not bring that stranger into fiduciary relationship with the remaining partners nor require them to resort to dissolution in order to prevent such a relationship from arising. The stranger remains a stranger entitled only to share in the partnership's worth and to demand an accounting upon dissolution.").

The RULLCA provides the typical provisions for NBEs. There are corresponding partnership rules. *See* RUPA § 102(23), § 502, § 503; ULPA (2001) § 102(25), § 701, § 702.

RULLCA § 102. Definitions.

"Transferable interest" means the right, as initially owned by a person in the person's capacity as a member, to receive distributions from a limited liability company, whether or not the person remains a member or continues to own any part of the right. The term applies to any fraction of the interest, by whomever owned.

RULLCA § 501. Nature of Transferable Interest.

A transferable interest is personal property.

RULLCA § 502. Transfer of Transferable Interest.

(a) Subject to Section 503(f), a transfer, in whole or in part, of a transferable interest:

(1) is permissible;

(2) does not by itself cause a person's dissociation as a member or a dissolution and winding up of the limited liability company's activities and affairs; and

> (3) subject to Section 504, does not entitle the transferee to:
>
> (A) participate in the management or conduct of the company's activities and affairs; or
>
> (B) except as otherwise provided in subsection (c), have access to records or other information concerning the company's activities and affairs.
>
> (b) A transferee has the right to receive, in accordance with the transfer, distributions to which the transferor would otherwise be entitled.
>
> (c) In a dissolution and winding up of a limited liability company, a transferee is entitled to an account of the company's transactions only from the date of dissolution.
>
> (d) A transferable interest may be evidenced by a certificate of the interest issued by a limited liability company in a record, and, subject to this section, the interest represented by the certificate may be transferred by a transfer of the certificate.
>
> (e) A limited liability company need not give effect to a transferee's rights under this section until the company knows or has notice of the transfer.
>
> (f) A transfer of a transferable interest in violation of a restriction on transfer contained in the operating agreement is ineffective if the intended transferee has knowledge or notice of the restriction at the time of transfer.
>
> (g) Except as otherwise provided in Section 602(5)(B), if a member transfers a transferable interest, the transferor retains the rights of a member other than the transferable interest transferred and retains all the duties and obligations of a member.
>
> (h) If a member transfers a transferable interest to a person that becomes a member with respect to the transferred interest, the transferee is liable for the member's obligations under Sections 403 and 406 known to the transferee when the transferee becomes a member.

An important distinction among the RUPA and the statutes for LPs and LLCs is that the RUPA permits a transferee "to seek a judicial determination that it is equitable to wind up the partnership business." RUPA § 503(b)(2). This is a significant right of a transferee. The ULPA (2001) and the RULLCA do not have a similar provision.

The case below discusses restrictions on the sale of a partnership interest. In reading this case, consider these questions: (1) Is the restriction on the sale of a partnership interest a default or mandatory rule? (2) What are the considerations when drafting a partnership agreement on the transfer of partnership interest or transferable interest?

SP INVESTMENT FUND III, LLC v. ZELL

2018 WL 6787328 (Cal. App. 2018)

EDMON, P.J.

William Zell, a New York resident, received an unsolicited offer from SP Investment Fund III, LLC to buy Zell's single-unit share of a New York limited partnership for $3,600. Zell accepted the offer and signed a one-page purchase agreement, which stated that he agreed to sell, and SP agreed to buy. A year and a half later, SP advised Zell that the partnership had not approved the transfer of Zell's unit, and thus Zell would remain its record owner. SP asserted, however, that the purchase agreement nonetheless remained in force, and Zell would be obligated to transfer to SP all income and distributions he received from the partnership and to vote his partnership interest as SP directed. SP resisted Zell's subsequent attempts to cancel the sale and return the purchase price with interest, instead suing Zell for specific performance, compensatory damages in excess of $290,000, and punitive damages.

The trial court concluded that the purchase agreement was unenforceable as a matter of law and granted summary judgment for Zell. We affirm.

Zell held one unit, or a 1.8333 percent interest, in Newport Highlands Associates, a New York limited partnership. Zell received [an] unsolicited letter from SP, dated April 12, 2011, offering to buy his interest in Newport Highlands for $3,600. Zell signed and returned the consent to transfer "all rights I own/represent related to Newport Highlands Associates (the Interest) to SP Investment Fund, LLC (SP) or its designee for $3,600."

On April 14, 2011, an attorney for Newport Highlands's operating general partner faxed a letter to SP's manager, Gil Seton. The letter said: "Please be advised that without the consent of the Operating General Partner the Limited Partners are not able to transfer [Zell's] interest to SP Investment Fund LLC."

By letter dated May 6, 2011, SP sent Zell a form purchase agreement and share assignment, which Zell was instructed to sign and return, and a check for $3,600. Zell signed and returned the purchase agreement and assignment to SP.

This apparently straightforward agreement was made considerably more complex by the attached two pages of "Terms and Conditions." Although the Purchase Agreement purported to transfer to SP "*all of* Seller's Rights and Claims" to Newport Highlands, the attached "Terms and Conditions" provided otherwise—namely, that if Newport Highlands did not approve the transfer to SP, Zell would remain the nominal owner of the partnership shares, but would be obligated to turn over all future distributions to SP, to provide SP with any information, documents, or correspondence he received from Newport Highlands, and to vote his Newport Highlands shares "only as [SP] directs."

On December 2012, a year and a half after Zell signed the purchase agreement, SP advised him that it had not been able to obtain "Necessary Approvals" from Newport Highlands. However, "this does not frustrate our transaction" because SP had elected to "waive the Conditions Precedent" and "continue to hold the Assignment in trust." As a result, Zell would remain "the owner of record of the Partnership Interest," but SP would be entitled to "all income, loss, distributions, proceeds, etc. received by you with respect to the Partnership Interest."

On June 2013, and again on June 2014, SP wrote to Zell, directing him to forward his K-1 and any distributions and/or ballots received from Newport Highlands.

In February 2015, Zell advised SP that he had become aware that Newport Highlands would not consent to the transfer of his shares to SP, and he thus was canceling the sale.

SP refused to cancel the purchase agreement or to accept return of the purchase price. Instead, it filed the present action against Zell. It asserted causes of action for breach of contract and conversion, and alleged that Zell had breached the purchase agreement by repudiating it and refusing to promptly deliver documents and turn over distributions to SP.

The issue is whether Newport Highlands's refusal to allow Zell to transfer his limited partnership interest rendered the purchase agreement between SP and Zell unenforceable as a matter of law.

New York's partnership law permits partnerships to restrict transfers of partnership rights in order to protect the right of partners to choose with whom they wish to associate. Enforcing the purchase agreement in present circumstances—that is, where Newport Highlands has explicitly *refused* to accept SP as a substitute limited partner—would fundamentally thwart the partnership's ability to choose with whom it does business. The purchase agreement therefore is unenforceable as a matter of law, and the trial court properly granted summary judgment for Zell.

SP contends that the transferability of limited partnership units is governed by New York substantive law, and we agree. It is undisputed that Newport Highlands is a limited partnership organized under the laws of New York. Under California Corporations Code section 15909.01, "the laws of the state under which a foreign limited partnership is organized govern relations among the partners of the foreign limited partnership and between the partners and the foreign limited partnership." New York law governs how and under what circumstances Zell, a limited partner, may transfer his partnership interest in Newport Highlands.

The New York Revised Limited Partnership Act (RLPA) provides that "except as provided in the partnership agreement," a limited partner may assign his or her "share of the profits and losses of [the] limited partnership [and] right to receive distributions." *Id.*, §§ 121–101(m), 121–702(a)(1). Such assignment does not "cause the partner to cease to be a partner or to have the power to exercise any rights or powers of a partner," nor does it "entitle the assignee to become or exercise any rights or powers of a partner." *Id.*, § 121–702(a)(2), (4). Instead, "the only effect of an assignment is to entitle the assignee to receive, to the extent assigned, the distributions and allocations of profits to which the assignor would be entitled." *Id.*, § 121–702(a)(3). An assignee may become a limited partner only if "(i) the assignor gives the assignee that right in accordance with authority granted in the partnership agreement, or (ii) all partners consent in writing, or (iii) to the extent that the partnership agreement so provides." *Id.*, §§ 121–702(a)(2), 121–704(a).

The RLPA thus distinguishes between the rights of limited partners to receive profits, losses, and distributions (which we will refer to as "distribution rights") and their rights to participate in the conduct of the partnership's activities, including by exercising voting rights, accessing information about partnership transactions, and inspecting partnership records (which we will refer to as "membership rights"). If the partnership agreement does not direct how distribution and membership rights may be transferred to third parties, such transfers are governed by the RLPA's default provisions. Those provisions state that a limited partner may freely transfer distribution rights, but must obtain partnership approval to transfer membership rights. If a partnership agreement *does* direct how distribution and membership rights may be transferred to third parties, the partnership agreement governs. See *Ederer v. Gursky*, 851 N.E.2d 204, 212 (N.Y. 2007) ("The Partnership Law's provisions are, for the most part, default requirements that come into play in the absence of an agreement").

The statutory proscription barring non-consensual assignments of membership in the partnership "is based upon the principle of *delectus personarum* (or *delectus personae*), the choice of person. At the heart of the partnership concept is the principle that partners may choose with whom they wish to be associated. A partnership is often an intimate business relationship likened to a marriage or a family. The assignment of economic rights does not violate the principle of *delectus personarum*, but it would be violated by the admission of a new speaking and voting member into the closely knit arrangement that typifies the general partnership."

The parties' obligations under the purchase agreement expressly were not conditioned on the partnership's consent to the transfer of Zell's limited partnership interest to SP. Instead, the purchase agreement provided that if the partnership did not consent to the transfer, Zell would assign his interest to SP "in trust," and would, in perpetuity:

(1) refrain from "disclosing the existence, pricing, and/or provisions of this Agreement" and from taking any action that would impair SP's rights;

(2) turn over to SP "all Economic Benefits" (distributions) received by Zell from the partnership;

(3) "consult with Buyer with respect to all opportunities to vote, elect or act with regard to the Partnership or the Partnership Interest and then to vote, elect, or act as, and only as, Buyer requests;" and

(4) deliver to SP "any information, documents, correspondence, conversations, etc. relating to the Partnership and/or Partnership Interest."

SP urges that the agreement is enforceable because none of these provisions violates New York's partnership law. SP is correct in part: The RLPA does not specifically prohibit a limited partner from remaining the nominal owner of a partnership interest, but agreeing to provide a third party with confidential partnership documents and to vote on partnership matters as the third party directs.

However, the RLPA permits partnerships to restrict transfers of partnership interests without consent. Newport Highlands has opted to exercise this statutory right: Its partnership agreement provides that a limited partner's transfer of distribution rights and withdrawal from the partnership, as well as a transferee's admission to the partnership, are "subject to the Consent of the Operating General Partner."

The general partner, on whose consent transfer is conditioned, has refused to consent to the transfer of Zell's limited partnership interest to SP. Newport Highlands's restrictions on transfer, and the general partner's ability to control with whom it does business, would be wholly frustrated if we were to enforce the purchase agreement in the present circumstances. That is, were we to enforce the purchase agreement according to its terms, SP, although not formally a member of the partnership, would have all the rights of a limited partner—to receive partnership profits and distributions, to review partnership documents, and to direct how Zell "votes, elects or acts with regard to the Partnership or Partnership Interest." As such, the partnership's ability to restrict with whom it does business—and specifically to choose *not* to do business with SP, which it repeatedly has expressed its desire to do—would be entirely thwarted.

The purchase agreement, although not in violation of "an express provision of law," plainly is contrary to "*the policy* of express law"—namely, that a partnership need not accept a member with whom it does not wish to associate. We will not enforce a contract under these circumstances, thus allowing SP to "to do indirectly that which it could not do directly." Because SP's causes of action for breach of contract and conversion both depend on an enforceable contract, our conclusion that the contract is *not* enforceable means that both causes of action necessarily fail as a matter of law.

The case below discusses the rights of a transferee and illustrates a transferee's potential vulnerability to opportunism by the entity and its owners. Of the five-member court, two judges dissented. In reading this case, consider these questions: (1) Should a transferee be owed fiduciary duties or an obligation of good faith? (2) How can a transferee protect himself against opportunism? (3) Which argument is better?

BAUER V. BLOMFIELD CO./HOLDEN JOINT VENTURE

849 P.2d 1365 (Alaska 1993)

BURKE, JUSTICE.

William Bauer, assignee of a partnership interest, sued the partnership and the individual partners, claiming that partnership profits were wrongfully withheld from him. The superior court granted summary judgment to the partnership and individual partners, and dismissed Bauer's complaint with prejudice. We affirm.

In 1986 William Bauer loaned $800,000 to Richard Holden and Judith Holden. To secure the loan, the Holdens assigned to Bauer "all of their right, title and interest" in a partnership known as the Blomfield Company/Holden Joint Venture. The other members of the partnership—Chuck Blomfield, Patricia Blomfield, Tony Blomfield and Richard Monsarrat—consented to the assignment. According to the consent document, their consent was given "pursuant to AS 32.05.220" [providing: "A conveyance of a partner's interest entitles the assignee to receive the profits to which the assigning partner would otherwise be entitled."].

When the Holdens defaulted on the loan, Bauer [notified the partners that] "he is exercising his rights to receive all distributions of income and principal from the Blomfield Company/Holden Joint Venture Partnership." Thereafter, for a time, the partnership income share payable to the Holdens was paid monthly to Bauer.

In January 1989, the partners stopped making income payments to Bauer. They agreed to use the income of the partnership to pay an $877,000 "commission" to partner Chuck Blomfield. Bauer was not a party to this agreement; he was notified of the agreement after the fact by means of a letter. Bauer was not asked to consent to the agreement, and he never agreed to forego payment of his assigned partnership income share or to pay part of the "commission" to Blomfield. The amount Bauer would have received, had the "commission" not been paid, was $207,567.

Blomfield's $877,000 commission represented 5% of the increased gross rental income earned by the partnership from lease extensions obtained from the state by Blomfield on partnership properties leased by the state. These and other lease extensions were obtained when a *private* claim made against the state by Chuck Blomfield and Patricia Blomfield for $1,900,000 was settled. Other lease extensions thus obtained were on properties not owned by the partnership; these properties were owned by the Blomfields and were leased by them to the state. One of the conditions upon which Chuck and Patricia Blomfield based their settlement was the agreement of the partners to pay Chuck Blomfield an $877,000 commission for the lease extensions that he obtained on the partnership's properties.

Bauer filed suit in superior court against the partnership and all of the partners except the Holdens. Bauer sought declaratory and injunctive relief, and damages. His claims were dismissed, with prejudice, when the court concluded that Bauer's assignment from the Holdens did not make him a member of the partnership. Therefore, he was not entitled to complain about a decision made with the consent of all the partners.

The assignment to Bauer of the Holdens' "right, title and interest" in the partnership, did not, in and of itself, make Bauer a partner in the Blomfield Company/Holden Joint Venture. We are unpersuaded by Bauer's argument that he should be considered a *de facto* partner.

As the Holdens' assignee, Bauer was not entitled "to interfere in the management or administration of the partnership business or affairs, or to require any information or account of partnership transactions or to inspect the partnership books." AS 32.05.220(a).[2]

The "interest" that was assigned to Bauer was the Holdens' "share of the [partnership's] profits and surplus." AS 32.05.210. The assignment only entitled Bauer to "*receive the profits to which the [Holdens] would otherwise be entitled.*" AS 32.05.220(a). Because all partners agreed that Chuck Blomfield was entitled to receive an $877,000 commission, to be paid out of partnership income, there *were no partnership profits* which the Holdens, and thus Bauer, were entitled to receive until the commission was paid.

MATTHEWS, JUSTICE, with RABINOWITZ, CHIEF JUSTICE, dissenting.

It is a well-settled principle of contract law that an assignee steps into the shoes of an assignor as to the rights assigned. Today, the court dismisses this principle in a footnote and leaves the assignee barefoot.

---

[2] We are unwilling to hold that partners owe a duty of good faith and fair dealing to assignees of a partner's interest. To do so would undermine the clear intent of AS 32.05.220(a). Partners should be able to manage their partnership without regard for the concerns of an assignee, who may have little interest in the partnership venture.

The court is correct in noting that Bauer has no management rights in the partnership. Bauer's attempt to enforce his right to profits under the assignment is not an interference with the management of the partnership. Requiring the partners to make decisions regarding distributions in good faith does not interfere with management, it merely requires that the partners fulfill their existing contractual duties to act in good faith.

The statute's intent is to assure that an assignee does not interfere in the management of the partnership while receiving "the profits to which the assigning partner would otherwise be entitled." AS 32.05.220(a). As interpreted by the court, the statute now allows partners to deprive an assignee of profits to which he is entitled by law for whatever outrageous motive or reason.

Upon formation of the Blomfield Company/Holden Joint Venture, a contractual relationship arose among the partners. This court has held that a covenant of good faith and fair dealing is implied in *all* contracts. We have noted that the basis for imposing this duty "is a hybrid of social policy and an effort to further the expectations of the contracting parties that the promises will be executed in good faith." The duty of good faith and fair dealing "requires that neither party do anything which will injure the right of the other to receive the benefits of the agreement."

One element of the contract between the Holdens and the partnership is the Holdens' right to receive their share of profits when a distribution is made. As an element of the partnership contract, this right is accompanied by the duty of the parties to deal fairly and in good faith. The partnership has a right to decide not to make a distribution, but in making this decision, the partnership must act in good faith.

The court's decision today effectively leaves an assignee with no remedy to enforce his right to receive partnership profits. I believe this result is contrary to basic contract and assignment law.

NOTES

1. In *Styslinger v. Brewster Park, LLC*, 138 A.3d 257 (Conn. 2016), excerpted later in this book, the Connecticut Supreme Court also discussed the issue of whether assignees have standing to force a dissolution and wind up of the LLC. What are the implications of permitting assignees to force a dissolution and wind up of an LLC? In light of cases like *Bauer v. Blomfield Co./Holden Joint Venture*, should assignees be able to force a dissolution and wind up?

CHRYSLER GROUP LLC OPERATING AGREEMENT

Section 7.3 Transfers; Admission of Transferees.

(a) No Member may Transfer its Membership Interests unless such Transfer complies with the provisions of this Agreement and any Certificate representing such Membership Interests. Notwithstanding the foregoing, any Member may Transfer its Membership Interests to any other Member.

(b) Upon admission as a Member pursuant to a Transfer conducted in accordance with this Agreement, a Transferee shall succeed to the rights, duties and obligations of the Transferor under this Agreement, the Certificate of Formation and the LLC Act and any references in this Agreement to the Transferor (unless such Transferor remains a Member) shall be deemed to refer to such Transferee for purposes of this Agreement.

(c) Until a Transferee is admitted as a Member pursuant to Section 7.1, the Transferor shall continue to be a Member and to be entitled to exercise any rights or powers of a Member with respect to the Membership Interest transferred.

Part I. Definitions.

"Membership Interest" means the limited liability company interests of a Member in the Company, as set forth opposite such Member's name on the Schedule of Members hereto, as amended from time to time, and also the right of such Member to any and all of the benefits to which such Member may be entitled as provided in this Agreement and the LLC Act, together with the obligations of such Member to comply with all the provisions of this Agreement and the LLC Act. The Company may issue whole or fractional Membership Interests pursuant to the terms of this Agreement.

The case below discusses the contractual aspect of drafting transfer and sale provisions in the charter agreement. In reading this case, consider these questions: (1) How did the court go about interpreting the charter agreements? (2) In hindsight, what was the drafting problem that led to the dispute, and how would one redraft the problematic sections?

NORTHEAST COMMUNICATIONS OF WISCONSIN, INC. V. CENTURYTEL, INC.

516 F.3d 608 (7th Cir. 2008)

EASTERBROOK, CHIEF JUDGE.

This litigation under the diversity jurisdiction, which is governed by Wisconsin law, presents the question whether a corporate merger involving the parent of one member of a limited partnership activated a right of first refusal. The district judge gave a negative answer and entered judgment for the member, which wants to retain its interest.

The partnership is Wisconsin RSA # 10 L.P. (Partnership), formed in 1989 as a joint venture among five firms that wanted to enter Wisconsin's cellular communications market. The five original members were Casco Telephone, Universal Cellular, Northeast Communications, Lakefield Communications, and Wayside Telecom. Three clauses of the agreement create rights of first refusal. Section 11.1 says that, before any member may sell its stake, any of the other members can step in to acquire that interest. Sections 11.3 and 11.5 qualify this rule by allowing subsets of the members to transfer interests among themselves: § 11.3 says that Northeast may sell to Wayside, or the reverse, without conferring a right of first refusal on the other three members, and § 11.5 deals with transactions among Casco, Universal, and Lakefield. Here is the text of § 11.5:

> Any provision of Section 11.1 to the contrary notwithstanding, it is understood and agreed that CASCO, UNIVERSAL and LAKEFIELD may transfer their respective partnership interest to one of their respective affiliates at any time without consent or restriction from any other partner. In the event of any sale, transfer, or other disposition of ownership or control by CASCO, UNIVERSAL or LAKEFIELD of their respective Partnership Interest, the non-selling entity, or affiliate of the non-selling entity, shall have, to the exclusion of all other partners, exclusive right to purchase the interest of the selling partner or a portion of said interest. Any interest not so purchased by CASCO, UNIVERSAL or LAKEFIELD shall be subject to purchase by any of the other partners. It is the intention of the parties that this paragraph shall apply only to sales by CASCO, UNIVERSAL or LAKEFIELD, or their affiliates to each other, or their affiliates, so as to give each of these entities the first right and option to purchase additional interests in the Partnership.

Universal Cellular has a parent, CenturyTel Wireless, Inc., and the acquisition of this parent by Alltel Corp. led to the current dispute. A reader of § 11.5 might be surprised to learn that the acquisition of a parent corporation could matter to rights of first refusal such as § 11.1, § 11.3, or § 11.5. But a state court has held that transfer of control at the level of a corporate parent can activate § 11.3, and the parties have assumed that this conclusion applies to § 11.5 as well—though they agree that it does *not* apply to § 11.1, a limitation that will become significant in a moment.

When Alltel acquired CenturyTel, Northeast tried to scoop up Universal's ownership interest in the Partnership. Universal protested that § 11.1 does not confer that option on Northeast, because it applies only when a member proposes to sell its interest, which Universal had not done. Northeast agreed with this reading of § 11.1. Still, Northeast insisted, the acquisition of Universal's parent activated § 11.5. Casco is no longer a member; its interest was divided among Universal and Lakefield some years back. As Northeast sees things, when Lakefield did not buy out Universal's interest, the penultimate sentence of § 11.5 came into play:

"Any interest not so purchased [by Lakefield] shall be subject to purchase by any of the other partners."

Universal thinks that making an interest "subject to purchase" just plops it back into the domain of § 11.1, which, everyone agrees, is irrelevant when a member is acquired by merger or tender offer. Universal maintains that using the "subject to purchase" language to give Northeast a right of first refusal would expand the limited scope of § 11.1 and disregard the difference, which Wisconsin's Court of Appeals perceived, between the scope of § 11.1 and the other two first-refusal clauses. Universal views § 11.5 as curtailing rather than expanding the scope of § 11.1. Northeast, for its part, contends that the "subject to purchase" language gives it an option on top of its rights under § 11.1.

The district judge relied principally on the last sentence of § 11.5: "It is the intention of the parties that this paragraph shall apply only to sales by UNIVERSAL or LAKEFIELD, or their affiliates *to each other*, or their affiliates, so as to give each of these entities the first right and option to purchase additional interests in the Partnership." Universal did not sell its membership to Lakefield, nor was CenturyTel acquired by Lakefield. Because none of the three members listed in § 11.5 transferred any asset to any other member specified in § 11.5, this paragraph drops out (the district judge held) and leaves only § 11.1—which, to repeat, everyone agrees does not afford Northeast a right of first refusal.

Northeast maintains that the district court's reading frustrates a major purpose of clauses such as § 11.5: to give the original partners a right to keep strangers out of their business ventures. Yet how does a change in its ownership structure make Universal Cellular a "stranger" to the Partnership? True, a new (indirect) owner may give Universal new marching orders, but so may a new CEO of a partner that has no corporate parent, and a change of CEO (or a new business plan adopted by an old CEO) does not give other partners a buyout right. Northeast's understanding of the reason why clauses such as § 11.5 are included in joint-venture agreements does more to call into question the state court's decision, which extends § 11.3 (and implicitly § 11.5) to transactions involving corporate parents, than to undermine the district court's decision in this case. But no matter. A contract's express language beats imputed purposes under Wisconsin's law. If Universal were to offer its interest to a stranger, then § 11.1 *would* grant Northeast a right of first refusal; that saves the district court's reading from any risk that it has sabotaged the main function of a first-refusal clause.

The reading that the district judge has given, which treats § 11.5 as a qualification rather than an extension of § 11.1, has much to commend it. For example, § 11.5 bears the caption: "Right of Limitation of Transfer and Right of First Refusal among Casco, Universal and Lakefield." This tells us that § 11.1 is about to be confined rather than expanded. What's more, the district judge's understanding of § 11.5 curtails the members' ability to engage in strategic behavior. Usually a right of first refusal comes into play only after the price of an asset has been negotiated in an arms'-length transaction. But when a corporate parent is acquired, no price is attached to a membership interest in Wisconsin RSA # 10 L.P. What price then would the interest fetch under a right of first refusal?

The absence of a market price would necessitate an appraisal under the cumbersome process outlined in § 11.5. Appraisals may miss the mark by a substantial margin. Section 11.5, as Northeast reads it, allows any member of the partnership to demand an appraisal as a speculative venture: if the appraisal comes in below the member's own estimate of the interest's value, then the interest will be snapped up; otherwise the original transaction will go through. Most businesses prefer to avoid situations in which their assets can be acquired for less than market value. Indeed, it is hard to understand CenturyTel's defense on any other ground. If it thought that the appraisal would give it full value, it would be indifferent between keeping the stake and selling to Northeast. The district judge's reading of § 11.5 reduces the opportunity for valuation errors. That plus the caption and the normal understanding of the phrase "to each other" suffice to support the judgment.

2. CHARGING ORDER

NBE statutes provide that a creditor may petition the court for a charging order against the debtor owner's transferable interest. *See* RUPA § 504; ULPA (2001) § 703; RULLCA § 503. A charging order is only a lien, but if the owner does not pay the debt a court may foreclose on the charging order resulting in a sale of the transferable interest.

RULLCA § 503. Charging Order.

(a) On application by a judgment creditor of a member or transferee, a court may enter a charging order against the transferable interest of the judgment debtor for the unsatisfied amount of the judgment. Except as otherwise provided in subsection (f), a charging order constitutes a lien on a judgment debtor's transferable interest and requires the limited liability company to pay over to the person to which the charging order was issued any distribution that otherwise would be paid to the judgment debtor.

(b) To the extent necessary to effectuate the collection of distributions pursuant to a charging order in effect under subsection (a), the court may:

(1) appoint a receiver of the distributions subject to the charging order, with the power to make all inquiries the judgment debtor might have made; and

(2) make all other orders necessary to give effect to the charging order.

(c) Upon a showing that distributions under a charging order will not pay the judgment debt within a reasonable time, the court may foreclose the lien and order the sale of the transferable interest. Except as otherwise provided in subsection (f), the purchaser at the foreclosure sale obtains only the transferable interest, does not thereby become a member, and is subject to Section 502.

(d) At any time before foreclosure under subsection (c), the member or transferee whose transferable interest is subject to a charging order under subsection (a) may extinguish the charging order by satisfying the judgment and filing a certified copy of the satisfaction with the court that issued the charging order.

(e) At any time before foreclosure under subsection (c), a limited liability company or one or more members whose transferable interests are not subject to the charging order may pay to the judgment creditor the full amount due under the judgment and thereby succeed to the rights of the judgment creditor, including the charging order.

(f) If a court orders foreclosure of a charging order lien against the sole member of a limited liability company:

(1) the court shall confirm the sale;

(2) the purchaser at the sale obtains the member's entire interest, not only the member's transferable interest;

(3) the purchaser thereby becomes a member; and

(4) the person whose interest was subject to the foreclosed charging order is dissociated as a member.

(g) This [act] does not deprive any member or transferee of the benefit of any exemption law applicable to the transferable interest of the member or transferee.

(h) This section provides the exclusive remedy by which a person seeking in the capacity of judgment creditor to enforce a judgment against a member or transferee may satisfy the judgment from the judgment debtor's transferable interest.

The case below discusses the nature of a charging order and its effects on the debtor member, the LLC, and its other members. In reading this case, consider this question: In what way can the operating agreement (or the partnership agreement) affect the debtor's status as a member (or partner) upon the issue of a charging order?

WEDDELL V. H2O, INC.

271 P.3d 743 (Nev. 2012)

CHERRY, J.:

Michael Stewart and Weddell entered into a business relationship concerning a number of different projects, ranging from garlic farming to geothermal energy. Several disputes arose among the two parties, leading to the collapse of their business relationship. Upon the relationship's demise, Weddell filed a complaint against Stewart. Stewart also asserted numerous counterclaims. After a bench trial, the district court found in Stewart's favor on all counts. Weddell filed this appeal.

Stewart and Weddell were both involved in some respect with Granite Investment Group and High Rock Holding, LLC. Weddell was elected manager of Granite. Stewart and Weddell signed an amended and restated operating agreement (Granite operating agreement).

Stewart received 1.5 votes and Weddell received 1 vote. Stewart used his majority voting power to allegedly remove Weddell as manager. Stewart ostensibly elected himself manager of Granite. However, pursuant to section 5.10 of the Granite operating agreement, a manager can only be removed by the unanimous affirmative vote of all of the members. Section 5.2 does not prohibit more than one manager at a time.

When Weddell was elected manager of the Granite Investment Group, he was also elected manager of High Rock Holding. To reflect the management changes at High Rock, Stewart and Weddell entered into an amended and restated operating agreement whereby Stewart had 1.5 votes and Weddell had 1 vote (High Rock operating agreement). Stewart used his superior voting power to remove Weddell as manager of High Rock. While the Granite operating agreement required a unanimous affirmative vote of the members, the similarly numbered section of the High Rock operating agreement only required an affirmative vote of the members.

The district court granted an application by a creditor to charge Weddell's membership interest in Granite and High Rock for over $6 million. Pursuant to NRS 86.401, the charging order entitled the creditor to any and all distributions, including interest, and all other rights of an assignee of the membership interest. Thereafter, Stewart purportedly purchased Weddell's remaining membership interest in Granite for $100 in accordance with section 10.2 of the Granite operating agreement.[3]

[3] Section 10.2 concerns voluntary transfers without the consent of the other members whereas section 10.4 concerns involuntary transfers, such as charging orders. Both sections would permit Stewart to buy out Weddell's membership interest. Under section 10.2, a transferring member is merely required to sell his or her membership interest for a purchase price of $100. On the other hand, section 10.4 includes an elaborate transferring scheme wherein the company must give written notice to the member and an appraisal must occur within thirty (30) days of the involuntary transfer.

The district court concluded that the charging order divested Weddell of *both* membership and managerial rights in Granite and High Rock upon the tender of purchase money made by Stewart.[4] The district court also concluded that Stewart is the sole manager of Granite and High Rock.

During the course of the litigation, Weddell filed a notice of lis pendens against Stewart and Empire Geothermal Power, among others, clouding the title to Empire Geothermal's real property. Weddell asserted that the action involved real property because he was entitled to 100 percent of the membership interest in Empire Geothermal, including a geothermal power plant and 20,000 acres of geothermal leases.

The district court focused on the language in Stewart and Weddell's option agreement: "Granite Investment Group, LLC, shall purchase from [Stewart] entities their membership interest in Empire Geothermal Power." The court ordered that the notice of pendency recorded by Weddell be canceled, finding that Weddell's alleged expectancy in the purchase of the membership interest in Empire Geothermal involved personal property interests, not real property interest. The court found that Weddell failed to establish that his action was for the foreclosure of a mortgage upon real property or that it affected the title or possession of real property as required by NRS 14.015(2)(a).

In Nevada, an LLC is formed by filing the articles of organization, together with the applicable filing fees, with the Secretary of State. An LLC may, but is not required to, adopt an operating agreement, which is defined as "any valid written agreement of the members as to the affairs of a limited-liability company and the conduct of its business." Unless the articles of organization or operating agreement provide otherwise, management of a limited-liability company is vested in its members in proportion to their contribution to capital. A member is "the owner of a member's interest or a noneconomic member." The term "member's interest" is defined as "a share of the economic interests in a limited-liability company, including profits, losses and distributions of assets."

The collection rights and remedies against a member's interest are governed by NRS 86.401. This provision recognizes the charging order as a remedy by which a judgment creditor of a member can seek satisfaction by petitioning a court to charge the member's interest with the amount of the judgment. A charging order directs the LLC to make distributions to the creditor that it would have made to the member. As a result, a charging order affects only the debtor's partnership interest and does not permit a creditor to reach partnership assets.

"Charging orders originated as a statutory solution to cumbersome common law collection procedures that were ill-suited for reaching

[4] The district court's language concerning the divestiture of both membership and managerial rights is troublesome. It appears that the district court has conflated the purpose of a charging order with the statutory provisions encompassed in the parties' operating agreements.

partnership interests." The charging order concept was first established in the 1914 Uniform Partnership Act and has since been replicated in some degree in nearly every United States jurisdiction.

Charging orders have been described as "nothing more than a legislative means of providing a creditor some means of getting at a debtor's ill-defined interest in a statutory bastard, surnamed 'partnership,' but corporately protecting participants by limiting their liability as corporate shareholders." In short, "a charging order gives the charging creditor only limited access to the partnership interest of the indebted partner." Consequently, the judgment creditor does not unequivocally step into the shoes of a limited-liability member. The limited access of a judgment creditor includes "*only* the rights of an assignee of the member's interest." NRS 86.401(1). A judgment creditor, or assignee, is only entitled to the judgment debtor's share of the profit and distributions, takes no interest in the LLC's assets, and is not entitled to participate in the management or administration of the business.[9] After the entry of a charging order, the debtor member no longer has the right to future LLC distributions to the extent of the charging order, but retains all other rights that it had before the execution of the charging order, including managerial interests.

The charging order levied by Weddell's creditor directed Granite to divert Weddell's rights to LLC profits and distributions to the creditor. The charging order divested Weddell of his economic opportunity to obtain profits and distributions from Granite—charging only his membership interest, not his managerial rights. Prohibiting the creditor from exercising Weddell's management rights reflects the principle that LLC members should be able to choose those members with whom they associate.

We further conclude that the charging order triggered the involuntary transfer provision of the Granite operating agreement, section 10.4. Section 10.4 explicitly included charging orders in its purview. Therefore, we remand this case to the district court to resolve whether Stewart properly complied with section 10.4 and whether, as a result, Weddell was divested of his membership interest in Granite.

Weddell argues that the district court improperly canceled his notice of lis pendens because the option agreement to purchase the membership interest and assets of the geothermal company "affected possession of real property." NRS 14.010(1).

The doctrine of lis pendens provides constructive notice to the world that a dispute involving real property is ongoing. "Lis pendens are not appropriate instruments for use in promoting recoveries in actions for personal or money judgments; rather, their office is to prevent the transfer

---

9 NRS 86.351(1) [provides]: "A transferee of a member's interest has no right to participate in the management of the business and affairs of the company [and] is only entitled to receive the share of profits or other compensation by way of income, and the return of contributions, to which the transferor would otherwise be entitled."

or loss of real property which is the subject of dispute in the action that provides the basis for the lis pendens." "It is fundamental to the filing and recordation of a *lis pendens* that the action involve some legal interest in the challenged real property." Therefore, under Nevada law the filing of a notice of pendency is limited to actions involving "the foreclosure of a mortgage upon real property, or affecting the title or possession of real property." NRS 14.010(1); NRS 14.015(2)(a).

The underlying complaint is not of the type envisioned under NRS 14.010(1) and NRS 14.015(2)(a) because it does not directly involve real property. Weddell seeks enforcement of an option to purchase the membership interest in the geothermal company, and even though the geothermal company apparently owned real property, membership interest is personal property. The district court did not abuse its discretion in canceling the notice of lis pendens.

NOTES

1. In *DuTac Community Credit Union v. Hefel*, 893 N.W.3d 282 (Iowa 2017), the Iowa Supreme Court held that an LLC had standing to challenge a charging order against its member. A member of an LLC (Star Properties) provided a guarantee to a creditor for a loan to the LLC. The LLC defaulted, and the member filed for bankruptcy. During the bankruptcy, the creditor learned that the member had a 50% interest in another LLC (Westgate), and the creditor applied for a charging order against the member's interest. Westgate filed a petition to intervene and resisted the charging order. The creditor argued that Westgate lacked standing. The Iowa Supreme Court held that Westgate had standing to intervene in the action. The member and Westgate also argued that the operating agreement prohibited a charging order because it prohibited a transfer of interest. The court held: "There is no language in Westgate's operating agreement that prevents the transfer of distributions. The operating agreement only prohibits the transfer of an ownership interest. Because the charging order does not transfer any ownership interest in Westgate, the operating agreement does not prevent the court from entering a charging order." *Id.* at 293.

2. In *Open Road Trucking, LLC v. Swanson*, 936 N.W.3d 72 (N.D. 2019), the court upheld a charging order against a debtor who owned interests in several LLCs. A bank executed against a guarantee provided by Swanson and Lund. The debtor agreed to a judgment in favor of the bank. Swanson fully paid the judgment, and then assigned his right to contribution from Lund to Lund's creditor, Open Road Trucking. Open Road Trucking sought a charging order, and the North Dakota Supreme Court upheld the charging order:

> A judgment debtor who has paid more than his or her proportionate share of the judgment should not have to bring a separate action against co-debtors to compel contribution from them. A co-debtor is already obligated to pay under the original judgment;

the interests of justice are not served by requiring the paying debtor to obtain another judgment for contribution against a co-debtor.

We hold that, in addition to a separate action for contribution under N.D.C.C. § 9–01–08, a judgment debtor, or an assignee of the judgment debtor, may take an assignment of the judgment for the purpose of enforcing contribution against co-debtors. The payment to the judgment creditor does not satisfy the judgment as between the debtor paying it and those jointly liable. The judgment may be used by the paying debtor to recover proportionate amounts from his or her co-debtors, and the paying debtor may enforce the judgment by execution or other lawful means.

We conclude the judgment was not satisfied as between Swanson and Lund, and Open Road was entitled to take an assignment of the judgment from Swanson to enforce Swanson's right of contribution from Lund for one-half of the judgment amount. The "unsatisfied amount of the judgment," as used in N.D.C.C. § 10–32.1–45(1), means Lund's proportionate share of the judgment amount.

The case below discusses the implementation of a charging order. In reading this case, consider this question: What are the competing policy considerations when a court issues ancillary provisions related to the execution of a charging order?

LAW V. ZEMP

408 P.3d 1045 (Ore. 2018)

WALTERS, J.

This review proceeding arises out of a post-judgment order charging a judgment debtor's interests in four limited partnerships and a limited liability company to satisfy the judgment creditor's judgment against him. The charging order was issued over the limited partnerships' and limited liability company's objections that ancillary provisions included in the charging order, which required them to refrain from certain kinds of transactions and provide extensive financial information to the judgment creditor, were not authorized under the controlling statutes. We hold that a trial court has either general or specific statutory authority to include, in a charging order, ancillary provisions that it finds necessary to allow a judgment creditor access to a debtor-partner's distributional interest in a company, as long as those provisions do not unduly interfere with the company's management. We further hold that the record does not establish that that standard was met and that the trial court erred in imposing the challenged ancillary provisions.

In 2012, plaintiff obtained a money judgment against defendant Ronald Zemp. After his initial attempts to collect the judgment were unsuccessful, plaintiff moved the trial court under ORS 70.295 and ORS 63.259 for an order directing Zemp to show cause why an order charging his interest in certain named companies to satisfy the judgment should not be entered. The named companies were four limited partnerships (LPs) and a limited liability company (LLC). In support of the motion, plaintiff submitted copies of public business registry records which identified Zemp as the general partner of each of the LPs and as the manager of the LLC. Plaintiff also submitted a proposed charging order which required the companies to pay all "distributions, credits, drawings or payments" they otherwise would have paid to Zemp to plaintiff until plaintiff's judgment against Zemp was satisfied in full. The proposed charging order also included the following ancillary provisions:

> "3. Until said judgments are satisfied in full, the companies shall make no loans to any partner or anyone else.
>
> "5. Until said judgments are satisfied in full, neither the companies nor its members shall undertake, enter into, or consummate any sale, encumbrance, hypothecation, or modification of any partnership interest without either Court approval or the approval of [plaintiff].
>
> "6. The companies shall supply to [plaintiff] full, complete, and accurate copies of the applicable membership or partnership agreements, including any and all amendments or modifications thereto; true, complete and accurate copies of any and all Federal and State income tax or informational income tax returns filed within the past two years; balance sheets and profit and loss statements for the past two years; and balance sheets and profit and loss statements for the most recent present periods for which same has been computed. Further, upon ten (10) days notice, all books and records shall be produced for inspection, copying examination in the office of [plaintiff].
>
> "7. Until said judgments are satisfied in full, all future statements reflecting cash position, balance sheet position, and profit and loss, the companies shall supply to [plaintiff] within thirty (30) days of the close of their respect accounting periods for which said data is or may be generated."

The companies filed objections and attended the hearing. The companies insisted that the [ancillary] provisions would invade the rights of the companies' other partners and members. The trial court adjusted certain due dates set in the proposed order, and instructed the parties to devise a protective order for the financial disclosure requirements. The court approved and issued the charging order as edited.

A. *A Court's Authority to Issue Ancillary Orders Directed to Limited Partnerships*

After setting out the charging order remedy, Oregon's partnership charging order statute, ORS 67.205(1), provides that a court issuing a charging order may also appoint a receiver and "make all other orders, directions, accounts and inquiries the judgment debtor might have made or that the circumstances of the case may require." The words by themselves can be read as authorizing a very broad range of orders, including ones that clothe the court (and, indirectly, the judgment creditor) with the rights of the debtor-partner and ones that otherwise touch on the partnership's management, if the "circumstances of the case [so] require."

But those words must be read in the broader context in which they appear—a provision that is directed first and foremost at furnishing judgment creditors with a mechanism for satisfying their judgments out of the partnership interests of their debtors. Notably, ORS 67.205(1) identifies the interest that may be charged to satisfy the judgment as "the *transferable interest* of the judgment debtor." The statute underscores the limited nature of the charging remedy: ORS 67.195 provides that "the *only* transferable interest of a partner in the partnership is the partner's share of the profits and losses of the partnership and the partner's right to receive distributions." ORS 67.200(1)(c), although not directly applicable in the context of charging orders, adds to the understanding that transferable rights are strictly limited. It provides that the actual transfer of a "transferable interest" to another person

> "does not, as against the other partners or the partnership, entitle the transferee, during the continuance of the partnership, to participate in the management or conduct of the partnership business, to require access to information concerning partnership transactions, or to inspect or copy the partnership books or records."

Taken together, ORS 67.195 and ORS 67.200(1)(c) point to a general legislative understanding that outsiders (creditors and assignees) should be excluded from participating in the conduct of partnership business and accessing partnership information even if, through a charging order or outright transfer of a partnership interest, they can obtain an interest in the partnership's profits and distributions. That notion of protecting the management of the partnership business from outside interference by creditors and assignees has long been understood as a bedrock principle underpinning the UPA and the RUPA.

ORS 67.205(1)'s grant of authority to "make all other orders, directions, accounts and inquiries the judgment debtor might have made or that the circumstances of the case may require" must be read in the context of the noted provisions and the broader principle that they convey. It seems highly unlikely that, while so clearly excluding management rights from the partnership interests that are subject to a charging order, the drafters of RUPA § 504 and the legislature that enacted it as ORS 67.205(1) would intend to authorize a court to issue ancillary orders that effectively override that exclusion.

Thus, it appears to us that the authority to issue orders "that the judgment debtor might have made" is qualified by the phrase "that the circumstances of the case may require." An "other order" may be required by the circumstances of the case when, without such an order or action, the underlying charging order would not be able to effectuate the statutory objective of allowing the judgment creditor to access a general partner's distributional interest in the company or of protecting the partnership's management from interference, or of drawing some balance between those purposes, if they cannot both be effectuated fully. "Other orders" are authorized under ORS 67.205 and ORS 70.295 only to the extent that they are "required" in that sense.[19]

B. *A Court's Authority to Issue Ancillary Orders Directed to Limited Liability Companies*

Charging orders directed to limited liability companies are governed by ORS 63.259. That statute contains no wording that expressly authorizes courts to issue ancillary orders in connection with charging orders, and, unlike charging orders directed at limited partnerships, it provides no basis for thinking that the legislature intended that its terms be supplemented by the terms in some other statute (such as ORS 67.205) that expressly provides such authority. The only question with respect to charging orders directed at limited liability companies under ORS 63.259 is whether courts have authority to issue ancillary orders in aid of a charging order under some other source of law.

ORS 63.259 directs a court, on application of a judgment creditor of a member of a limited liability company, to charge "the membership interest of the member" with payment of the judgment, and specifies that, "to the extent so charged, the judgment creditor has only the rights of an assignee of the membership interest." The referenced "rights of an assignee of a membership interest" are described in ORS 63.249(3). Under that provision, unless the assignee of the membership interest becomes a

[19] What that standard means, as a practical matter, is that, if a court has reason to believe that the charging order by itself cannot effectively convey to the judgment creditor the debtor-partner's right to distributions and profits—as might happen, for example, if the limited partnership exists only to shelter assets from creditors and has no business that will generate distributions or profits in the ordinary sense of the words, or has been structured in or operated in such a way as to allow money to be transferred to the debtor-partner or his or her agents through a mechanism other than formal distribution or profit sharing—the court may issue ancillary orders that will ensure that the charge on the judgment creditor's share is not evaded. And while the court would be expected to craft its orders, if possible, to avoid interference in the partnership's management, there may be circumstances in which it is not possible to effectuate the goal of charging the judgment creditor's share of distributions and profits without some degree of interference in the business. As long as the order effectuates a reasonable balance between the two objectives, it would be authorized.

member of the limited liability company (which generally requires the consent of the majority of the members):

> "the assignee shall have the assignor's right to receive and retain, to the extent assigned, the distributions, as and when made, and allocations of profits and losses to which the assignor would be entitled, *but shall not exercise any other rights of a member, including without limitation the right to vote or otherwise participate in the management and affairs of the limited liability company.*"

Considered in the context of ORS 63.249(3), ORS 63.259 directs courts to issue charging orders that accomplish two objectives—giving the judgment creditor of a member of a limited liability company access to the debtor-member's interest in the company's profits and distributions to satisfy his or her judgment, but, at the same time, excluding the judgment creditor from other rights of the member, including management rights. Those two objectives—and the further objective of striking a balance between them to the extent they are opposed—are at the heart of the charging order remedy, and are found in virtually every charging order statute, whether for general partnerships, limited partnerships or limited liability companies. The evident concern with preventing the transfer of management authority in all these statutes reflects the peculiar interests at play in the small, unincorporated business entities for which the charging order remedy was designed. In those entities—partnerships, limited partnerships, limited liability companies and a few others—a small number of owners invest in a business venture and agree to rely on each other, rather than on third parties (usually professionals), to manage the business's operations. For such entities, allowing a stranger to intrude into the business's operations and management is particularly problematic, undermining both the entity's foundational agreement and the principle that members of such organizations should be able to pick their own partners. The charging order mechanism, as provided in ORS 63.259 and in other similar statutes, seeks to balance that "pick your partner" principle against the judgment creditor's interest in reaching the debtor's assets by directing courts to charge the debtor-member's share of distributions and profits to satisfy the creditor's judgment while excluding the judgment creditor from participating in management.

As applied to ORS 63.259, the general authority of courts under ORS 1.160 to employ "all the means" necessary to carry their statutory jurisdiction into effect is circumscribed by the obligations imposed on the court by that statute to convey the debtor-member's right to the company's distributions and profits to the judgment creditor, to refrain from conveying the debtor-member's rights in the company's management, and, presumably, if those two obligations cannot both be perfectly served, to find some balance between them. An ancillary order is authorized by ORS

1.160, in this context, if it is needed to effectuate those objectives. Notably, that is the same standard that would apply under the "other orders" wording of ORS 67.205, as incorporated into ORS 70.295.

C. *The Standard's Application to the Ancillary Orders at Issue*

Our conclusions about the scope of a court's authority to make other orders in aid of a charging order issued under ORS 70.295 and ORS 63.259 have obvious implications for orders like those that are at issue, which preclude a limited partnership or limited liability company from engaging in certain kinds of transactions[22] or require a limited partnership or a limited liability company to provide details about their business and finances to the judgment creditor. But they do not provide a direct and immediate answer about the *particular* orders that are before us. On the one hand, we can imagine circumstances in which a carefully cabined order requiring a partnership or limited liability company to provide financial information or refrain from particular transactions would be truly necessary to make the charge against the debtor-partner's or debtor-member's distributional interest in the entity effective—so much so that any effect on the entity's management would be seen as incidental. On the other hand, in less compelling circumstances, an order of that sort—particularly if it is more broadly worded and appears to make the partnership accountable to the creditor, rather than the court—might be viewed as primarily working to transfer fundamental management rights of a debtor partner to the creditor, and properly disapproved on that ground. The trial court will have to carefully consider the judgment creditor's particular request and all of the circumstances to determine which side of the line the contemplated order falls on—and, thus, whether it is authorized either under the standard that we have announced.

With those conclusions in mind, we turn to the charging order in this case, which included ancillary provisions requiring both the LPs and the LLC to refrain from making any sort of loan to anyone, to refrain from selling, encumbering or otherwise modifying any partnership interest without permission from plaintiff or the court, to provide plaintiff with extensive information about the companies' structure and past finances, and to provide periodic updates regarding their internal finances until plaintiff's judgment should be satisfied in full. All of those provisions would seem to touch on matters of company management and therefore could only be properly included in the charging order if they were found to be necessary to the charging order's effectiveness under the standard that we

[22] The provisions in the charging order that precluded the LPs and LLC from engaging in certain transactions are particularly significant because they purport to control all transactions of a certain type *by the entire LP or LLC.* While plaintiff correctly observes that charging orders often include ancillary orders that "command that the debtor-member not take any loans, salary, fees, etc., or any other actions that would get money out of the LLC through the backdoor," those typical orders are different in that they are directed solely at the debtor-member or debtor-partner and transactions that might amount to distributions to the debtor-member or debtor-partner.

have discussed. Although we cannot say with certainty that the trial court did *not* consider the requested orders and the surrounding circumstances in the light of that standard, we *can* say that there was no evidence before the court that would have supported a determination that the orders were authorized under the standard. A broad range of evidence might have been relevant to that determination, including information about the structure of the companies and the interests of and relationships between Zemp partners and members, information about any past efforts to collect the judgment from Zemp, evidence supporting plaintiff's assertion that Zemp was using the companies as a device for protecting his assets from creditors and not for any recognizable business or commercial purpose, and information showing that Zemp had failed to respond fully and truthfully to a debtor's examination under ORS 18.265. The only actual evidence before the court when it made its decision was evidence that Zemp was a general partner of the four limited partnerships and the manager of the limited liability company. The court could not determine, on the basis of that evidence alone, that the ancillary orders were so crucial to the effectiveness of the remedy that the court sought to provide (*i.e.*, access to the debtor-partner's or debtor-member's distributional interest in the partnership or limited liability company) and their effect on the companies' management was so that incidental that, on balance, the orders were justified. It follows that none of the challenged ancillary orders were authorized. The trial court erred in refusing to strike them from the charging order, as the companies had requested.

The case below illustrates the issues related to the enforcement of a charging order when there are multiple charging orders in multiple states. In reading this case, consider this question: Why was Chase's Arizona charging order insufficient to compel a Colorado LLC to comply?

JPMORGAN CHASE BANK, N.A. V. MCCLURE

393 P.3d 955 (Colo. 2017) (en banc)

JUSTICE GABRIEL delivered the Opinion of the Court.

This case principally requires us to decide the relative priority of competing charging orders filed by multiple judgment creditors against a foreign judgment debtor's membership interests in several Colorado limited liability companies.

In July 2013, JPMorgan Chase Bank ("Chase") obtained an Arizona judgment of over $ 20 million against several defendants, including Reginald Fowler, an Arizona resident. Chase obtained Arizona orders charging Fowler's membership interests in three Colorado limited liability companies, Bridgeport Ethanol, LLC, Yuma Ethanol, LLC, and Sterling Ethanol, LLC ("the LLCs").

On December 3, 2013, Chase served its Arizona charging orders on the LLCs. Each of Chase's charging orders provided that the LLC (1) "shall make no further Distributions of any kind to Judgment Debtor with respect to his interests" in the LLC and (2) "shall make to [Chase] any and all Distributions to which Judgment Debtor is or would be entitled," with such distributions to be made within three business days following the date on which such distributions would or could have been made to Fowler or within three business days following the date on which Fowler would have been entitled to receive such distributions, whichever date is sooner.

In March 2014, Douglas McClure, Nancy McClure, and Mr. McClure's company, Spiral Broadcasting, LLC ("the McClures"), obtained a stipulated judgment for $1.5 million against Fowler, among others, in the Arizona Superior Court. In April 2014, the McClures domesticated their Arizona judgment in the District Court for Arapahoe County, Colorado, and between May and July 2014, they obtained and served Colorado orders charging Fowler's membership interests in the LLCs.

Now confronted with facially competing charging orders, the LLCs paid Fowler's then-due distributions into the Arapahoe County District Court registry. That same day, the McClures moved for release of the distribution funds to them, and several days later, Chase sought and obtained leave to intervene and opposed the McClures' motion.

The district court ultimately ordered the distribution funds released to the McClures. In so ruling, the court opined that Chase's domesticated Arizona judgment could only be enforced in Colorado by the means authorized by Colorado law, namely, by obtaining Colorado charging orders or by domesticating the Arizona charging orders.

On August 11, 2014, Chase domesticated its Arizona charging orders [in the District Court for the City of Denver pursuant to the Uniform Enforcement of Foreign Judgments Act, §§ 13–53–101 to –108, C.R.S. (2016)]. Chase then moved for reconsideration of the release order, arguing that its newly-domesticated charging orders should be deemed effective as of the date they were issued in Arizona and that therefore, those orders were entitled to priority over the McClures' competing charging orders.

The district court again ruled in the McClures' favor. Concluding that Chase's Arizona charging orders were unenforceable in Colorado until they were domesticated, the court ruled that the McClures' charging orders "were the first enforceable charging orders served on the [LLCs] and, hence, they have priority over [Chase's] Arizona charging orders."

Chase appealed. [The court of appeals] held that as a matter of first impression in Colorado, the priority of charging orders issued against an out-of-state debtor's membership interests in Colorado LLCs is based on first-in-time service of charging orders that are enforceable in Colorado. Because Chase did not domesticate its charging orders in Colorado before serving them, the [court] determined that the McClures' later-served but Colorado-issued charging orders had priority over Chase's charging orders.

A charging order is a statutorily created remedy that simultaneously (1) allows a judgment creditor to realize the value of a judgment debtor-LLC member's distributional interest in an LLC (*i.e.*, the debtor-member's right to profits and distributions from the LLC) and (2) protects the LLC's ability to continue to operate and the interests of its other members. Derived from the charging order remedy created for the personal creditors of partners in a partnership, a charging order allows a judgment creditor of an LLC member to obtain and enforce a lien on the "economic value that flows from membership in an LLC." The lien attaches to the judgment debtor's distributional interest and diverts to the judgment creditor, until the judgment is satisfied, the right to receive any distributions that would otherwise have been paid to the debtor-member. To the extent the debtor-member's interest is charged, the judgment creditor obtains only the rights of a transferee or assignee. Accordingly, the judgment creditor has no right to compel a distribution or otherwise participate in the LLC's management.

Under Colorado law, the lien created by a charging order generally attaches at the time the order is served on the LLC. That charging order is typically entitled to priority over later-served charging orders, regardless of the order in which the competing creditors' judgments were entered.

With these general principles in mind, we now consider the location of the LLC membership interests at issue and whether Chase's charging orders were effective to establish priority over the McClures' orders.

Location of Colorado LLC Membership Interests

A membership interest in an LLC constitutes the personal property of the member. Courts have divided, however, as to where this intangible property interest lies. [*Compare* Wells Fargo Bank, N.A. v. Barber, 85 F.Supp.3d 1308, 1314 (M.D. Fla. 2015) (membership interest in an LLC is intangible personal property that accompanies its owner); *with* Koh v. Inno-Pacific Holdings, Ltd., 54 P.3d 1270, 1271–72 (Wash. App. 2002) (relying on cases involving the situs of partnership interests, member's interest in an LLC is located where the LLC was formed).]

Resolving this long-standing debate has yielded no easy answer. As Justice Cardozo observed long ago:

> The situs of intangibles is in truth a legal fiction, but there are times when justice or convenience requires that a legal situs be ascribed to them. The locality selected is for some purposes, the domicile of the creditor; for others, the domicile or place of business of the debtor, the place, that is to say, where the obligation was created or was meant to be discharged; for others, any place where the debtor can be found. At the root of the

selection is generally a commonsense appraisal of the requirements of justice and convenience in particular conditions.

Here, for two reasons, we agree that for purposes of determining the enforceability of a charging order, a member's membership interest is located where the LLC was formed.

First, given that a charging order is a mechanism by which a judgment creditor may enforce its judgment by requiring an LLC to redirect the debtor-member's distributions to the creditor, as a practical matter, the charging order is directed to the LLC. Accordingly, we deem it more appropriate to place the membership interest in the state in which the LLC, and thus the membership interest, was created, as opposed to in whatever state the debtor-member happens to be domiciled at a given time.

Second, justice and convenience militate in favor of locating the membership interest in the state in which the LLC was formed. To conclude otherwise could result in substantial uncertainty and confusion. Consider, for example, a hypothetical scenario in which Fowler resided in New York, rather than Arizona, at the time the Arizona judgments were entered. If his membership interests were deemed to be located with him, then the case would involve an Arizona judgment that presumably would be domesticated in New York, followed by the issuance of New York charging orders that would be served on the Colorado LLCs. Such a scenario would understandably give the LLCs pause as to which, if any, of the foregoing orders were binding on them, particularly given the LLCs' or their members' or managers' potential liability were they to misdirect member distributions. And this scenario could become even more uncertain were Fowler to move to a different state while the judgment creditors were seeking to enforce their judgments against him.

In our view, such a scenario could place a substantial burden on the LLCs, contrary to the above-noted purpose of a charging order, which is to allow a judgment creditor to proceed against a debtor-member's membership interest without impairing the LLC's ability to continue to operate or the interests of its other members.

We believe that justice and convenience favor placing the membership interest in the LLC's state of formation, which is fixed, rather than placing it in the state of the debtor's domicile, which may not be. We conclude that the membership interests at issue are located in Colorado, where the LLCs were formed.

Priority of the Charging Orders at Issue

Chase sought and obtained its charging orders pursuant to section 29–655 of the Arizona Limited Liability Company Act, Ariz. Rev. Stat. §§ 29–601 to –858 (2016). That section provides, as pertinent here:

> On application to a court of competent jurisdiction by any judgment creditor of a member, the court may charge the member's interest in the limited liability company with payment of the unsatisfied amount of the judgment plus interest. To the extent so charged, the judgment creditor has only the rights of an assignee of the member's interest.

Chase principally contends that the [court] erred in determining that Chase's charging orders were unenforceable until domesticated in Colorado. Chase argues, instead, that a court with jurisdiction over the debtor-member (here, the Arizona court) may issue a valid and enforceable charging order against the debtor's economic interests in an LLC, regardless of where the LLC is organized. We are not persuaded.

Central to Chase's argument is the notion that the Arizona charging orders were simply liens on Fowler's right to receive distributions from the LLCs and thus were directed at Fowler, not the LLCs. Chase's argument, however, does not adequately consider the fact that the charging orders at issue not only served as liens on Fowler's right to receive distributions but also ordered the LLCs to pay to Chase any distributions to which Fowler was or would be entitled and to do so within specified time frames.

In our view, this distinction is material because it impacts the enforceability of the charging orders and, in turn, the relative priority of Chase's orders vis-à-vis the McClures' competing orders.

Determining the relative priorities of the competing charging orders requires us to ascertain when each order became effective or enforceable. Any assessment of the relative priorities of competing charging orders mandates comparing only effective and enforceable orders to one another (assuredly, an unenforceable or ineffective order could not take priority over an enforceable, effective one).

To be enforceable, a charging order that compels an LLC to act must bind the LLC such that ignoring the order would subject the LLC to remedial action. To hold otherwise would be to suggest that the charging order is effective even though it has no legal force against the LLC.

The question thus becomes what a judgment creditor must do to render a charging order effective as against an LLC from which the order compels action. The answer to this question turns on one's view as to the nature of the jurisdiction being exercised by the court issuing the charging order—namely, personal jurisdiction over the member, in rem jurisdiction over the membership interest, or personal jurisdiction over the LLC.

We note that the parties do not allege that the LLCs are registered to do business in Arizona, in fact do business in Arizona, or have any connection to Arizona other than that one of their members was sued in Arizona and had judgments entered against him there.

First, assuming without deciding that our analysis should be premised on the trial court's personal jurisdiction over Fowler, we do not see how such an exercise of jurisdiction by an Arizona court could force the Colorado LLCs to act, thereby rendering the charging orders at issue effective or enforceable against the LLCs.

Second, given that the membership interests to be charged are located in Colorado, the court's exercise of in rem jurisdiction also would not assist Chase here. The parties have cited no applicable authority suggesting that an Arizona state court may exercise in rem jurisdiction over a Colorado res, nor have we seen such authority. Accordingly, in an in rem jurisdiction scenario, a charging order would not be enforceable against a Colorado LLC unless it was issued by a Colorado court (*i.e.*, a court in the state in which the LLC (and, thus, the membership interest at issue) was formed).

Here, Chase did not obtain Colorado charging orders based on a domesticated foreign judgment. Chase domesticated its Arizona judgment and then domesticated its Arizona charging orders. Although it is unclear whether Chase's actions could properly be deemed the equivalent of obtaining Colorado charging orders based on a domesticated foreign judgment, even if they could, Chase would not have obtained enforceable Colorado charging orders until, at the earliest, August 11, 2014 (*i.e.*, when it domesticated its Arizona charging orders), which was after the McClures had obtained and served enforceable charging orders on the LLCs.

We note that if an LLC is not subject to personal jurisdiction in the state in which the judgment was entered and the creditor seeks a charging order, then the creditor must engage in a two-step process to obtain an effective charging order: "(1) Domesticate the money judgment in the LLC's state of formation [and] (2) Seek a charging order from a competent court in that state." After doing so, "the LLC would be clearly bound by the order, and ignoring it would invite a contempt penalty."

In this scenario, Chase would have needed to domesticate the Arizona judgment in Colorado and then to obtain and serve Colorado charging orders. Again assuming without deciding that domesticating the Arizona judgment and then domesticating the Arizona charging orders would suffice to satisfy these requirements, Chase did not acquire effective charging orders until, at the earliest, August 11, 2014, when it domesticated its Arizona charging orders in Colorado.

Whether we analyze this case as implicating either in rem jurisdiction over Fowler's membership interests or personal jurisdiction over the LLCs, Chase's charging orders did not become effective until, at the earliest, August 11, 2014, which was after the McClures had obtained and served effective charging orders on the LLCs.

3. FORECLOSURE OF CHARGING ORDER

RULLCA § 503(c) provides that the court may foreclose on a lien and order the sale of a transferable interest. It further provides that the "purchaser at the foreclosure sale obtains only the transferable interest, does not thereby become a member." The transferable interest is personal property, and a foreclosure results in the member's loss of this property.

An interesting situation arises when the LLC only has one member. The transferee owns the right to distribution, but the debtor is still the member and controls the LLC. Couple this fact with holding in *Bauer v. Bloomfield Co./Holden Joint Venture*. The sole member may have no incentive to make a distribution. Is there a solution to this problem?

Florida Revised Limited Liability Company Act § 605.0503. Charging Order.

(4) In the case of a limited liability company that has only one member, if a judgment creditor of a member or member's transferee establishes to the satisfaction of a court of competent jurisdiction that distributions under a charging order will not satisfy the judgment within a reasonable time, a charging order is not the sole and exclusive remedy by which the judgment creditor may satisfy the judgment against a judgment debtor who is the sole member of a limited liability company or the transferee of the sole member, and upon such showing, the court may order the sale of that interest in the limited liability company pursuant to a foreclosure sale. A judgment creditor may make a showing to the court that distributions under a charging order will not satisfy the judgment within a reasonable time at any time after the entry of the judgment and may do so at the same time that the judgment creditor applies for the entry of a charging order.

(5) If a limited liability company has only one member and the court orders a foreclosure sale of a judgment debtor's interest in the limited liability company or of a charging order lien against the sole member of the limited liability company pursuant to subsection (4):

(a) The purchaser at the court-ordered foreclosure sale obtains the member's entire limited liability company interest, not merely the rights of a transferee;

(b) The purchaser at the sale becomes the member of the limited liability company; and

(c) The person whose limited liability company interest is sold pursuant to the foreclosure sale or is the subject of the foreclosed charging order ceases to be a member of the limited liability company.

(6) In the case of a limited liability company that has more than one member, the remedy of foreclosure on a judgment debtor's interest in the limited liability company or against rights to distribution from the limited liability company is not available to a judgment creditor attempting to satisfy the judgment and may not be ordered by a court.

Pennsylvania Limited Liability Company Act of 2016 § 8853. Charging Order.

(c) Foreclosure. Upon a showing that distributions under a charging order will not pay the judgment debt within a reasonable time, the court may foreclose the lien and order the sale of the transferable interest. Except as provided in subsection (f), the purchaser at the foreclosure sale only obtains the transferable interest, does not thereby become a member, and is subject to section 8852 (relating to transfer of transferable interest).

(f) Foreclosure against sole member. If a court orders foreclosure of a charging order lien against the sole member of a limited liability company:

(1) the court shall confirm the sale;

(2) the purchaser at the sale obtains the member's entire interest, not only the member's transferable interest;

(3) the purchaser thereby becomes a member; and

(4) the person whose interest was subject to the foreclosed charging order is dissociated as a member.

The limitation on the charging order remedy is not intended to protect the debtor's assets. It is intended to protect the principle of "one chooses one's partner." A creditor cannot impose himself onto a debtor's fellow owners or firm. However, when the company is a single-member LLC, this problem does not exist. The foreclosure of such an interest can result in a foreclosure of the entire membership interest resulting in the transfer of ownership of the LLC from the debtor to the creditor.

C. DISSOCIATION

1. GENERAL PARTNERSHIP

Partners can leave the partnership, be fired, or be judicially expelled. Partners can leave the firm at will for any number of reasons in the same way that employees voluntarily quit their jobs. Partners can leave the firm involuntarily through various ways identified in the statute. The RUPA provides the basic rules on dissociation and its effects. The statutes for LPs and LLCs modify the RUPA framework to the extent that LPs and LLCs differ structurally and have different policy preferences.

NBE statutes provide default rules. The charter agreement should address dissociation and the effects on the dissociating owner and the firm. The default rules are highly specific because in the event the charter agreement does not provide contract terms, they must be specific enough to cover most situations involving partner dissociation and the legal consequences of dissociation. The statute only applies if the charter agreement is silent on the issue.

RUPA § 601. Events Causing Dissociation.

A person is dissociated as a partner when:

(1) the partnership knows or has notice of the person's express will to withdraw as a partner, but, if the person has specified a withdrawal date later than the date the partnership knew or had notice, on that later date;

(2) an event stated in the partnership agreement as causing the person's dissociation occurs;

(3) the person is expelled as a partner pursuant to the partnership agreement;

(4) the person is expelled as a partner by the affirmative vote or consent of all the other partners if:

(A) it is unlawful to carry on the partnership business with the person as a partner;

(B) there has been a transfer of all of the person's transferable interest in the partnership, other than:

(i) a transfer for security purposes; or

(ii) a charging order in effect under Section 504 which has not been foreclosed;

(C) the person is an entity and:

(i) the partnership notifies the person that it will be expelled as a partner because the person has filed a statement of dissolution or the equivalent, the person has been administratively dissolved, the person's charter or the equivalent has been revoked, or the person's right to conduct business has been suspended by the person's jurisdiction of formation; and

(ii) not later than 90 days after the notification, the statement of dissolution or the equivalent has not been withdrawn, rescinded, or revoked, or the person's charter or the equivalent or right to conduct business has not been reinstated; or

(D) the person is an unincorporated entity that has been dissolved and whose activities and affairs are being wound up;

(5) on application by the partnership or another partner, the person is expelled as a partner by judicial order because the person:

(A) has engaged or is engaging in wrongful conduct that has affected adversely and materially, or will affect adversely and materially, the partnership's business;

(B) has committed willfully or persistently, or is committing willfully or persistently, a material breach of the partnership agreement or a duty or obligation under Section 409; or

(C) has engaged or is engaging in conduct relating to the partnership's business which makes it not reasonably practicable to carry on the business with the person as a partner;

[Subsections (6) through (15) state that individuals or entities are dissociated as a partner if they become financially or otherwise incapacitated, including death, disability, dissolution, or merger.]

RUPA § 602. Power to Dissociate as Partner; Wrongful Dissociation.

(a) A person has the power to dissociate as a partner at any time, rightfully or wrongfully, by withdrawing as a partner by express will under Section 601(1).

(b) A person's dissociation as a partner is wrongful only if the dissociation:

(1) is in breach of an express provision of the partnership agreement; or

(2) in the case of a partnership for a definite term or particular undertaking, occurs before the expiration of the term or the completion of the undertaking and:

(A) the person withdraws as a partner by express will, unless the withdrawal follows not later than 90 days after another person's dissociation by death or otherwise under Section 601(6) through (10) or wrongful dissociation under this subsection;

(B) the person is expelled as a partner by judicial order under Section 601(5);

(C) the person is dissociated under Section 601(6); or

(D) in the case of a person that is not a trust other than a business trust, an estate, or an individual, the person is expelled or otherwise dissociated because it willfully dissolved or terminated.

(c) A person that wrongfully dissociates as a partner is liable to the partnership and to the other partners for damages caused by the dissociation. The liability is in addition to any debt, obligation, or other liability of the partner to the partnership or the other partners.

RUPA § 603. Effect of Partner's Dissociation.

(a) If a person's dissociation results in a dissolution and winding up of the partnership business, [Article] 8 applies; otherwise, [Article] 7 applies.

(b) If a person is dissociated as a partner:

(1) the person's right to participate in the management and conduct of the partnership's business terminates, except as otherwise provided in Section 802(c); and

(2) the person's duties and obligations under Section 409 end with regard to matters arising and events occurring after the person's dissociation, except to the extent the partner participates in winding up the partnership's business pursuant to Section 802.

(c) A person's dissociation does not of itself discharge the person from any debt, obligation, or other liability to the partnership or the other partners which the person incurred while a partner.

The RUPA provisions above answer three basic questions: What are the events that trigger dissociation? When is a dissociation wrongful for the purposing of imposing liability on the withdrawing partner? What are the legal effects when a partner dissociates? The events of dissociation can be categorized into several broad types.

First, a partner can voluntarily dissociate. This can be as a matter of right per the partnership agreement or consent of other partners, or as a matter of power since no one can be forced into unwanted association. A dissociation at will is not wrongful unless the partnership has a specific term or undertaking. Dissociation without a right is wrongful.

Second, a partner can be expelled per the partnership agreement or the unanimous vote of all partners. If the latter, the decision cannot be arbitrary. The statute identifies these reasons for partner-approved expulsion: it is unlawful to continue business with the partner; the partner has transferred all interest to another person; the partner is no longer a viable legal entity. Each of these reasons adversely affects the partnership and other partners.

Third, upon petition by the partnership or another partner, a partner can be judicially expelled for these reasons: the partner is engaging in wrongdoing that adversely affects the partnership, including the breach of fiduciary duties or the partnership agreement; or, it is not reasonably practicable to carry on the business in partnership with the partner.

Fourth, a partner is incapacitated in some form: death, incapacity, dissolution (death of a legal person), and financial distress. With respect to financial distress, a partner's financial condition is important. Partners are jointly and severally liable for the debts and obligations of the partnership. Each partner's financial situation affects the economic interests of other partners. The partnership may require future capital contributions and a financially distressed partner may not be able to perform this obligation. When a partner files for bankruptcy, the bankruptcy proceeding may also adversely affect the partnership.

If a dissociation is wrongful, Section 602(c) provides that a partner who "wrongfully dissociates as a partner is liable to the partnership and to the other partners for damages caused by the dissociation."

When a partner dissociates, the partnership has two paths forward: Article 7 and Article 8. RUPA § 603(a). Under Article 8, the partnership can dissolve and wind up. *Id.* § 801 to § 810. The partnership is wound up under certain conditions. *Id.* § 801. One such event is in a partnership at will "a person's express will to withdraw as a partner." *Id.* § 801(1). Under Article 7, the partnership can continue its business without the dissociating partner. *Id.* § 701 to § 705.[2] One such event is when a partnership causes "the person's interest to be purchased for buyout price," thus choosing to continue the partnership. *Id.* § 701(a).

The case below discusses the different conceptions of a partnership as seen in UPA (1914) and RUPA. In reading this case, consider these questions: (1) What is the practical consequence of conceptualizing the partnership as an aggregate or an entity in this case? (2) What is the role of contracting in the partnership agreement on the question of whether the partnership is an aggregate or an entity?

---

[2] Under the old UPA (1914), the partnership was seen as an aggregate of partners defined by a set of relations. The dissociation of a partner results in a dissolution of the partnership, which is defined simply as a "change in the relation of the partners caused by any partner ceasing to be associated in the carrying on as distinguished from the winding up of the business." UPA § 29. Upon dissolution, the partnership continues until wind up of the business. *Id.* § 30. The statutes do not mandate a wind up. It provides that "unless otherwise agreed the partners who have not wrongfully dissolved the partnership has the right to wind up the partnership affairs." *Id.* § 37. Although the statute does not require wind up, it exposes the partnership to a wind up. Partners have the right to wind up the partnership. To avoid this outcome, they must agree to continue the partnership as a new set of legal relations among the continuing partners.

UNITED STATES V. SANOFI-AVENTIS U.S. LLC

226 A.3d 1117 (Del. 2020)

VALIHURA, JUSTICE.

We are asked by the United States Court of Appeals for the Third Circuit to answer three questions of law certified to us:*

> 1. A limited liability partnership is formed to file and prosecute a specific lawsuit. Its formational documents say both that the partnership is not "a separate legal entity distinct from its Partners" under 6 Del. Code § 15–201(a) and that the "withdrawal of a Partner shall not cause a dissolution of the Partnership." If one of the partners leaves the partnership and a new partner joins, does it stay the same partnership? Or is it a new partnership?
>
> 2. If a "new" partnership was created upon the limited liability partnership's change in membership, was the "old" partnership terminated immediately such that it was actually the "new" partnership that filed the second amended complaint? Or did the "old" partnership continue to exist long enough in the winding-up process to file the second amended complaint?
>
> 3. If the "old" limited liability partnership did not survive the membership change, may the original partners continue to prosecute the lawsuit as part of the "winding up" process?

The Questions arise in connection with the prosecution of a *qui tam* action under the False Claims Act ("FCA"), *In re: Plavix Marketing, Sales Practices and Products Liability Litigation (No. II)*, brought against Sanofi-Aventis U.S. LLC, Sanofi-Aventis U.S. Services, Inc., Aventis, Inc., Aventis Pharmaceuticals, Inc., Bristol-Myers Squibb Company, and Bristol-Myers Squibb Pharmaceuticals Holding Partnership (together, the "Defendants"). The relator bringing the action, on behalf of the United States and several states, is JKJ Partnership 2011 LLP ["JKJ"], a Delaware limited liability partnership. The partnership consists of three individuals who allegedly are each an "original source" of knowledge upon which the allegations against Defendants are based.

The Questions arose when one of the partners was replaced by another partner, and an amended complaint was filed shortly thereafter. The

---

* Author's note: The Delaware Supreme Court has the jurisdiction to issue certain advisory opinions. Del. Const. § 11(8): "To hear and determine questions of law certified to it by other Delaware courts, the Supreme Court of the United States, a Court of Appeals of the United States, a United States District Court, a United States Bankruptcy Court, the United States Securities and Exchange Commission, the highest appellate court of any other state, the highest appellate court of any foreign country, or any foreign governmental agency regulating the public issuance or trading of securities, where it appears to the Supreme Court that there are important and urgent reasons for an immediate determination of such questions by it."

Defendants moved to dismiss, alleging that replacing the partner was impermissible the under the FCA's "first-to-file" bar.**

On October 26, 2011, two doctors and a Sanofi sales representative formed JKJ. According to JKJ's Partnership Agreement (the "Partnership Agreement"), JKJ was formed "to file and prosecute" a whistleblower action against the Defendants.

Section 1.03 of the Partnership Agreement states that "the Partnership shall not be a separate legal entity distinct from its Partners." The District Court explained the likely reason for this provision:

> Were JKJ a separate legal entity, the fact that it did not exist at the time the alleged fraud occurred would prevent it from being an "original source" with direct knowledge of the fraud under the pre-amendment FCA.

Nine days after it was formed, JKJ filed the original *qui tam* complaint (the "Complaint"), alleging that the Defendants failed to disclose, as required by law, certain information regarding Plavix,® an antiplatelet drug used to prevent heart attacks and strokes. The Complaint kept the partners' identities anonymous, identifying them as "Partner A," "Partner B," and "Partner C." The Partnership Agreement identified the partners as Jeffrey Stahl, Kelly Wood, and John Venditto.

On February 22, 2017, JKJ filed a second amended complaint (the "SAC"), further developing its claim of Plavix's® ineffectiveness for certain patients based on their genetic makeup.

After filing the Complaint, but before filing the SAC, Partner B (John Venditto) withdrew from JKJ, and was replaced by Dr. Paul Gurbel ("Partner G").

The District Court dismissed the SAC under Fed. R. Civ. P. 12(b)(1) for lack of jurisdiction. It held that because the JKJ that filed the SAC was a different partnership from the JKJ partnership that had filed the Complaint, there had been an "intervention" of a new private party in contravention of the first-to-file bar.

The Third Circuit submitted the following undisputed facts:

> a. JKJ Partnership 2011 LLP is the relator in this *qui tam* action. It is a limited liability partnership organized under Delaware's Revised Uniform Partnership Act.

** Author's note: "The FCA includes several other limiting provisions, in part a response to the possibility that the large profits available to *qui tam* relators created the danger of parasitic exploitation of the public coffers. To limit such abuses, Congress established several restrictions on FCA *qui tam* actions. One of these provisions, known as the 'first-to-file bar,' provides that 'when a person brings an action under [the FCA], no person other than the Government may intervene or *bring a related action* based on the facts underlying the pending action.' 31 U.S.C. § 3730(b)(5)." United States ex rel. Wood v. Allergan, Inc., 899 F.3d 163, 167 (2d Cir. 2018).

b. JKJ's partnership agreement says that its sole purpose "is to file and prosecute" this action.

c. One section of JKJ's partnership agreement says: "As authorized by Section 15–201(a) of the Act, the Partnership shall not be a separate legal entity distinct from its Partners. In the event of any conflict between the terms of this Section and the terms of any other Section of this Agreement, the terms of this Section shall control."

d. Another section of JKJ's partnership agreement says that the "withdrawal of a Partner shall not cause a dissolution of the Partnership."

e. After this action began, one of JKJ's founding partners withdrew. A new partner replaced him.

f. The new partner arrangement continued to prosecute this action by filing a second amended complaint.

A. If one of the partners leaves the partnership and a new partner joins, does it stay the same partnership? Or is it a new partnership?

We hold that the change in membership created a new partnership and caused a dissolution of the original JKJ.

For background purposes, we begin with the two models of partnership identified by the District Court: the aggregate and entity models. The Partnership Agreement at issue here contains elements of both.

Under the aggregate theory, "a partnership is an aggregate of individuals and does not constitute a separate legal entity." "The partnership has no legal existence apart from its members and cannot sue or be sued in the firm name." This is in contrast to the entity theory of partnership, where the partnership is a legal person, *i.e.*, an entity separate from its constituent partners.

The "aggregate concept of partnership was universally accepted" at common law. "Historically, a partnership, unlike a corporation, did not enjoy entity status, *i.e.*, it had not been considered a jural person but a collection of persons with aggregate rights." At common law, a partner dissociating from the partnership would cause dissolution of the partnership.

The Uniform Partnership Act ("UPA"), adopted in 1914, generally adopted the aggregate approach to partnerships. Although it adopted much of the aggregate approach, the UPA did not wholly embody it. The original drafting committee of the UPA initially was "split on philosophical grounds over whether the UPA should follow the separate entity theory or the aggregate theory." Within the regime are characteristics distinctly based in entity theory. For example, the UPA states that partners are agents of the partnership; partners must account to the partnership for profits arising from their individual use of partnership property; and the partners do not have individual rights to possess and use partnership property.

However, the UPA adopted the key aggregate principle of having partnerships be an aggregation of individuals. Section 6(1) of the UPA defined a partnership as "an association of two or more persons to carry on as co-owners a business for profit." Under the UPA, a partnership dissolved when a partner left the partnership. Section 29 of the UPA stated that "the dissolution of a partnership is the change in the relation of the partners caused by any partner ceasing to be associated in the carrying on as distinguished from the winding up of the business." Section 30 provided that, "on dissolution the partnership is not terminated, but continues until the winding up of partnership affairs is completed." Delaware enacted the DUPA, its version of the UPA, in 1947.

Delaware repealed the DUPA in 1999, and adopted the Delaware Revised Uniform Partnership Act, 6 *Del. C.* §§ 15–101 *et seq.* DRUPA is modeled after the model Revised Uniform Partnership Act ("RUPA"), but it also added features drawn from other states' versions of RUPA, from the Delaware Revised Uniform Limited Partnership Act, and the Delaware Limited Liability Company Act to increase flexibility and add clarity. It is clear that "RUPA embraces the entity theory of partnership." This was made explicit in Section 201(a) of RUPA, which states, "A partnership is an entity distinct from its partners." The Official Comments to RUPA explain the motivation behind the shift:

> Giving clear expression to the entity nature of a partnership is intended to allay previous concerns stemming from the aggregate theory, such as the necessity of a deed to convey title from the "old" partnership to the "new" partnership every time there is a change of cast among the partners. Under RUPA, there is no "new" partnership just because of membership changes.
>
> RUPA's move to the entity theory is driven in part by the need to prevent a technical dissolution or its consequences. Under RUPA, not every partner dissociation causes a dissolution of the partnership.

Under the RUPA's Section 801, a partnership generally will continue to exist notwithstanding the dissociation of a partner. The withdrawal of a partner is a "dissociation" that results in a dissolution of the partnership only in certain limited circumstances. Many dissociations result merely in a buyout of the withdrawing partner's interest, as opposed to a winding up of the partnership's business. The RUPA distinguishes departures that cause a winding up from those which only cause a buyout of the departing partners. Article 6 applies to all "dissociations;" Article 7 applies to all dissociations that result in a buyout of a partners; and Article 8 applies if there is a dissolution and winding up of the partnership business. Events causing a dissolution and winding up include a partnership at will having notice of a partner's express will to withdraw, the expiration of the term in a term partnership, events agreed to as resulting in the winding up of the partnership's business, and judicial dissolutions.

DRUPA modifies certain of RUPA's default rules, and also contains other provisions which have no counterpart in RUPA. Among the latter is Section 15–103(d), which provides that it is the policy of DRUPA to give maximum effect to the principal of freedom of contract and the enforceability of partnership agreements. Section 103 of RUPA provides that the partnership agreement controls in most circumstances. Section 15–103 of DRUPA similarly provides that except for certain mandatory provisions under DRUPA, "relations among the partners and between the partners and the partnership are governed by the partnership agreement," and that, "to the extent the partnership agreement does not otherwise provide, [DRUPA] governs relations among the partners and between the partners and the partnership." Thus, RUPA and DRUPA consist largely of default "gap-filler" provisions that govern when a partnership agreement is silent on an issue.

RUPA's Section 103 also enumerates what cannot be altered by the partnership agreement. Section 201(a) is not one of those mandatory provisions. Section 201 explicitly provides that a partnership is an entity distinct from its partners. Section 15–201(a) of DRUPA goes further and explicitly clarifies that it is a default provision that can be varied by the partnership agreement. It states:

> A partnership is a separate legal entity which is an entity distinct from its partners *unless otherwise provided in a statement of partnership existence or a statement of qualification and in a partnership agreement.*

In this case, the JKJ Partnership did vary the entity principle embodied in Section 15–201(a) of DRUPA.

Pursuant to Section 1.02 of the Partnership Agreement, JKJ was formed as a limited liability partnership pursuant to DRUPA. Thus, our analysis will proceed under DRUPA. Pursuant to Section 15–103 of DRUPA, we look to the Partnership Agreement and interpret its provisions relevant to the Questions. The principles we apply to our analysis are familiar. As noted above, Section 15–103(d) of DRUPA expressly states that, "it is the policy of [DRUPA] to give maximum effect to the principle of freedom of contract and to the enforceability of partnership agreements."[58]

---

[58] 6 *Del. C.* § 15–103(d). This Court has also stated in the context of the Delaware Limited Liability Company Act (noting that, "the following observations relating to limited partnerships applies as well to limited liability companies"):

> The Act's basic approach is to permit partners to have the broadest possible discretion in drafting their partnership agreements and to furnish answers only in situations where the partners have not expressly made provisions in their partnership agreement. Truly, the partnership agreement is the cornerstone of a Delaware limited partnership, and effectively constitutes the entire agreement among the partners with respect to the

With respect to our interpretation of the Partnership Agreement, partnership agreements are a type of contract.[59] "We, therefore, construe them in accordance with their terms to give effect to the parties' intent." "We give words their plain meaning unless it appears that the parties intended a special meaning." The "parties' intentions as reflected in the four corners of the agreement" are given priority. "When interpreting contracts, we construe them as a whole and give effect to every provision if it is reasonably possible."

Section 1.03 of the Partnership Agreement states in its entirety:

> No Separate Legal Entity. As authorized by Section 15–201(a) of the Act, the Partnership shall not be a separate legal entity distinct from its Partners. In the event of any conflict between the terms of this Section 1.03 and the terms of any other Section of this Agreement, the terms of Section 1.03 shall control.

Section 1.03 expresses an intent to adopt a key feature of the aggregate model, namely, that the Partnership not be distinct from its members. The plain meaning of "not a separate legal entity distinct from its Partners" means that JKJ consists of an association of Partners A, B, and C.

Despite its opt-out of entity status, Section 1.03 is premised on the notion that at least some provisions are, or could be viewed as being based on the entity model. This is evident as Section 1.03 attempts to address how to resolve conflicts between provisions that derive from the two competing models. In the event that provisions conflict, Section 1.03 gives primacy to the aggregate model by declaring that JKJ is not a separate legal entity distinct from its Partners, and it resolves any conflict by declaring that Section 1.03's preference for non-entity status trumps any other conflicting sections of the Partnership Agreement.

DRUPA gap-filler provisions provide, as the default, that a partnership, for a term or particular undertaking, generally can have partners withdraw without triggering dissolution of the partnership. Question 1 requires us to determine to what extent any "entity-based" provisions in the Partnership Agreement, and any applicable entity-based DRUPA default provisions, were overridden once the partners elected in Section 1.03 to provide that the partnership not be distinct from its partners. The replacement of Partner B with Partner G changed the composition of JKJ from an association of partners A, B, and C to an association of Partners A, C, and G. We conclude that if JKJ is "not distinct"

> admission of partners to, and the creation, operation and termination of, the limited partnership. Once partners exercise their contractual freedom in their partnership agreement, the partners have a great deal of certainty that their partnership agreement will be enforced in accordance with its terms.

Elf Atochem N. Am., Inc. v. Jaffari, 727 A.2d 286, 291 (Del. 1999).

[59] *Norton v. K-Sea Transp. P'rs L.P.*, 67 A.3d 354, 360 (Del. 2013).

from A, B, and C, then this new aggregation of partners A, C, and G resulted in a new partnership and dissolution of the old partnership.

B. *If a "new" partnership was created upon the limited liability partnership's change in membership, was the "old" partnership terminated immediately such that it was actually the "new" partnership that filed the second amended complaint? Or did the "old" partnership continue to exist long enough in the winding-up process to file the second amended complaint?*

Generally, under DRUPA, dissolution does not terminate the partnership, and the partnership continues after dissolution only for the purpose of winding up its business or affairs. Further, under DRUPA, the partnership is terminated when the winding up is complete. As we held in response to Question 1, the change in membership effected a dissolution of the old JKJ. However, we cannot determine from the undisputed facts whether the winding up was completed. Therefore, we leave that determination to the trial court.

We are asked whether the old JKJ continued to exist long enough in the winding up process to file the SAC. But we are told to accept, as an undisputed fact that, "the new partner arrangement continued to prosecute this action by filing a second amended complaint." Paragraph 26 of the SAC alleges that, "Plaintiff/Relator, a Delaware limited liability partnership, is named JKJ PARTNERSHIP 2011 LLP. There are three JKJ partners: Paul A. Gurbel, M.D., Jeffrey A. Stahl, M.D., and Kelly D. Evans." Based upon what we are told to accept as an undisputed fact, which is supported by the SAC itself, we conclude that the new partnership filed the SAC.

Perhaps the more critical question is, did the new partnership have ownership of the litigation asset so it could pursue the action and file the SAC? It appears that the action was partnership property at the outset of JKJ. Whether the action was retained by the original partnership or transferred to the new one is a fact-based question that we cannot determine based upon the undisputed facts.

C. *If the "old" limited liability partnership did not survive the membership change, may the original partners continue to prosecute the lawsuit as part of the "winding up" process?*

In our answer to Question 2, we concluded that the new partnership filed the SAC. Thus, it does not appear that the old partnership is prosecuting the action.

Notwithstanding our answer to Question 2, we are asked whether the old partnership can pursue the action. We hold that it cannot. Question 3 appears to assume that the winding up process has not been completed. We answer that question accepting that assumption.

Pursuant to Section 8.02(a) of the Partnership Agreement, and as consistent with DRUPA, dissolution triggers the winding up process. Section 8.02 of the Partnership Agreement addresses the "winding up" process and provides:

> Winding Up. Upon the dissolution of the Partnership, the Partnership's business shall be liquidated in an orderly manner. The Partners shall determine which Partnership property shall be distributed in-kind and which Partnership property shall be liquidated. The liquidation of Partnership property shall be carried out as promptly as is consistent with obtaining the fair value thereof.

The Partnership Agreement does not expressly address whether the Partnership can undertake the prosecution or defense of litigation in the winding up phase. Assuming *arguendo* that at least some litigation activity is generally permissible in the winding up phase, Section 8.02(a) requires the business of the Partnership to be *liquidated* promptly or distributed in-kind. The concept of "liquidating" Partnership property is inconsistent with continuing with carrying on the business for which the Partnership was established. The Partnership Agreement makes clear that for JKJ, pursuing the action is the singular purpose for which JKJ was formed. This purpose is explicitly stated in Section 1.06 of the Partnership Agreement entitled, "Purpose," which states that, "the purpose and business of the Partnership is to file and prosecute the Action." Although there is little Delaware case law precisely on point, the Official Comments to Section 801 of RUPA suggest that continuing with the main business of the partnership is not consistent with "winding up":

> Under RUPA, "dissolution" is merely the commencement of the winding up process. The partnership continues for the limited purpose of winding up the business. In effect, *that means the scope of the partnership business contracts to completing work in process and taking such other actions as may be necessary to wind up the business.* Winding up the partnership business entails selling its assets, paying its debts, and distributing the net balance, if any, to the partners in cash according to their interests. The partnership entity continues, and the partners are associated in the winding up of the business until winding up is completed. When the winding up is completed, the partnership entity terminates.

Generally, cases in both the partnership and the corporate context suggest that this allowance for litigation in the winding up phase is, more typically, ancillary to the main business of the entity, and, thus, normally would not extend to situations where the primary purpose of the partnership is to pursue that particular litigation. This would be especially true if the litigation were in its beginning stages.

The old JKJ may not continue to prosecute the action as a part of its winding up process, because to do so would be inconsistent with Section 8.02 of the Partnership Agreement, which directs that, "the liquidation of Partnership property shall be carried out as promptly as is consistent with obtaining the fair value thereof," and because the action is in its beginning phases and is the sole purpose for which JKJ was established.

Conclusion

The questions of law certified to the Court by the United States Court of Appeals for the Third Circuit are answered as follows:

ANSWER [to Question 1]: We hold that the change in membership created a new partnership and caused a dissolution of the original JKJ.

ANSWER [to Question 2]: The "old" partnership continues to exist until winding up is complete and it is terminated. We cannot determine from the undisputed facts whether it was terminated. We are told in the undisputed facts that the new partnership filed the SAC. We conclude that it was the "new" partnership that filed the SAC. Whether the new partnership possessed the litigation asset is another factual inquiry that we are unable to determine from the undisputed facts.

ANSWER [to Question 3]: We hold that the old JKJ may not continue to prosecute the action as a part of its winding up process, because to do so would be inconsistent with Section 8.02 of the Partnership Agreement, and because the action is in its beginning phases and is the sole purpose for which JKJ was established.

The case below discusses the issue of whether a partner can dissociate at will. In reading this case, consider this question: What is the practical consequence of a partner's exercise of the power and the right to dissociate?

GELMAN V. BUEHLER

986 N.E.2d 914 (N.Y. 2013)

GRAFFEO, J.

Partnership Law § 62(1)(b)[3] states that a partnership formed by oral agreement may be dissolved unilaterally if "no definite term or particular

[3] Dissolution is caused:

1. Without violation of the agreement between partners, (a) By the termination of the definite term or particular undertaking specified in the agreement, (b) By the express will of any partner when no definite term or particular undertaking is specified, (c) By the express will of all the partners who have not assigned their interests or suffered them to be charged for their separate debts, either before or after the termination of any specified term or particular undertaking, (d) By the expulsion of any partner from the business bona fide in accordance with such a power conferred by the agreement between the partners;

undertaking is specified" in the underlying agreement. Because the parties in this case did not sufficiently address either of these provisions in their oral contract, we conclude that there was no breach of contract when one party withdrew from the enterprise.

Plaintiff Geoffrey Gelman and defendant Antonio Buehler were recent business school graduates who decided to form a partnership in 2007. Buehler had proposed a plan to Gelman aimed at acquiring $600,000 from investors for the purpose of establishing a "search fund" to research and identify a business with growth potential. A second investor solicitation was contemplated to raise any additional funding needed to pay the purchase price of the targeted business. Buehler and Gelman were to manage the business with the goal of increasing its value until it could be sold at a profit—they referred to this future occurrence as the "liquidity event"—and the investors would share in the profits realized from the sale. Gelman accepted Buehler's proposal and the partnership was formed by oral agreement. Buehler and Gelman expected that the business plan would reach its objective in four to seven years.

The partners pursued prospective investors for several months. Buehler withdrew from the venture after Gelman refused his demand for majority ownership of the partnership. Gelman sued Buehler for breach of contract, claiming that Buehler could not unilaterally terminate his obligations under the agreement. Buehler moved to dismiss the complaint on the ground that dissolution was permissible under Partnership Law § 62(1)(b) because the oral agreement did not include a "definite term or particular undertaking." [The trial court] granted Buehler's motion to dismiss, concluding that the complaint failed to allege that the partnership agreement provided for a definite term or a defined objective.

Partnership Law § 62(1)(b) states that a partnership may be dissolved "by the express will of any partner when no definite term or particular undertaking is specified" in the partnership agreement. We are asked to decide whether the allegations in Gelman's complaint set forth a "definite term" or identify the particular objective sought to be achieved with the requisite specificity.

Since the enactment of the Partnership Law in New York, courts in other jurisdictions have held that the commonly-used statutory phrase—a "definite term"—is intended to be durational in nature and refers to an identifiable termination date. A "particular undertaking" has been defined

---

2. In contravention of the agreement between the partners, where the circumstances do not permit a dissolution under any other provision of this section, by the express will of any partner at any time;

3. By any event which makes it unlawful for the business of the partnership to be carried on or for the members to carry it on in partnership;

4. By the death of any partner;

5. By the bankruptcy of any partner or the partnership;

6. By decree of court under section sixty-three.

to require a specific objective or project that may be accomplished at some future time, although the precise date need not be known or ascertainable at the time the partnership is created.

Applying similar meanings to the terminology in Partnership Law § 62(1)(b), we believe that Gelman's complaint lacks a fixed, express period of time during which the enterprise was expected to operate. Instead, the complaint alleges a flexible temporal framework: the parties were to solicit investments for an indefinite length of time; conduct an open-ended (possibly two-year) search for an unidentified business in an unknown business sector or industry; secure additional capital investments over the course of an unspecified period of time; and then purchase and operate the enterprise for an indeterminate duration (perhaps four to seven years) until a liquidity event would hopefully occur. Since the complaint does not set forth a specific or even a reasonably certain termination date, it does not satisfy the "definite term" element of section 62(1)(b).

When the entire scheme is considered, the alleged sequence of anticipated partnership events detailed in the complaint are too amorphous to meet the statutory "particular undertaking" standard for precluding unilateral dissolution of a partnership. The stages of the plan were to: (1) raise money; (2) identify a business to buy; (3) raise more money to purchase the business; (4) "operate the business to increase its value"; (5) "achieve the liquidity event"; (6) "sell the business"; and (7) secure profit from the sale. But these objectives are fraught with uncertainty.

In the absence of a definite term of duration or a particular undertaking to be achieved, the partnership agreement at issue, however well-intended, was dissolvable at will by either partner under Partnership Law § 62(1)(b). Consequently, defendant Buehler is entitled to dismissal of the breach of contract cause of action.

The case below illustrates the manner in which a partner's interest is valued for the purpose of a buyout. In reading this case, consider these questions: (1) What factors go into the valuation of a firm? (2) What is the relevance of the writeoff of the accounts receivables? (3) Why were expert witnesses used? (4) Could the partnership agreement have been drafted in a way that might have reduced the possibility of a credible dispute?

FREDERICKS PEEBLES & MORGAN LLP V. ASSAM

915 N.W.2d 770 (Neb. 2018)

FUNKE, J.

This appeal concerns a determination of Fred Assam's ownership interest in the law firm of Fredericks Peebles & Morgan LLP (FPM). After Assam voluntarily withdrew from the firm, FPM filed suit seeking a declaration of the rights of FPM and Assam under the partnership agreement (Partnership Agreement). Following a bench trial, the district court for Douglas County declared the fair market value of Assam's interest in FPM to be $590,000. For the reasons stated herein, we affirm.

FPM is a limited liability partnership composed of legal professionals. FPM was organized under the laws of the District of Columbia, and its principal place of business is located in Omaha, Nebraska.

As of October 1, 2014, FPM had five equity partners: Thomas Fredericks, John Peebles, Lance Morgan, Conly Schulte, and Assam. Fredericks, Peebles, Schulte, and Assam each held a 23.25% interest in FPM, and Morgan held the remaining 7%. FPM traditionally implemented a team approach in servicing its clients' accounts, but nearly 90% of FPM's clients were brought in by Fredericks, Peebles, Morgan, and Schulte. Assam, a financial attorney, worked on accounts brought in by the other equity partners. Only three clients followed Assam when he left FPM, two of which maintained a relationship with FPM.

In early 2014, the partners began to discuss changes to their compensation structure in order to reward younger partners for bringing in new clients. Fredericks proposed that compensation should be based on client generation, while others proposed that compensation should be based upon equity ownership. The partners exchanged and refined proposals over a period of months, and FPM ultimately arrived at a hybrid of the two compensation structures.

As a result of his concerns, Assam hired the accounting firm Eide Bailly LLP to perform a valuation of his equity interest in FPM.

On the evening of October 2, 2014, Assam sent an email to his partners in which he voluntarily resigned from FPM.

FPM carried a significant amount of outstanding accounts receivable for an extended period of time. FPM decided to write off as uncollectable approximately $10 million in old accounts receivable.

After Assam's resignation, the partners made him an offer of payment intended to represent the fair market value of his equity interest as set out in the Partnership Agreement. However, the two sides could not agree as to the value of Assam's interest.

The parties agree that the provision [in the Partnership Agreement] which governs the determination of Assam's equitable interest in FPM is:

> In the event any Equity Partner gives a notice of voluntary withdrawal more than sixty months of July 1, 2003, such withdrawing Equity Partner will receive an amount equal to 100% of the fair market value of the Equity Partner's interest in the Partnership as of the date of such notice of voluntary withdrawal,

which amount will be paid out in six equal monthly installments without interest.

The court heard valuation testimony from several expert witnesses. FPM called William Brennan, a management consultant for the legal profession. Assam called Chad Flanagan and Jay Fullerton, of Eide Bailly.

(a) Brennan

Brennan's report demonstrated several different business valuation approaches for comparison. Brennan testified that although market-based, asset-based, and income-based approaches are each generally accepted, the income approach is best for valuing law firms. Brennan stated the market-based approach is not useful for valuing law firms, because such businesses are privately owned and therefore a firm's private transaction data is not publicly available to be used to compare value with other businesses in the market. As for an asset-based approach, Brennan testified firm assets must be adjusted down to their cash value in order to determine the asset's "net realizable value." Without this adjustment, assets such as encumbered assets and uncollectible accounts receivable would be overvalued.

Brennan testified that the income approach has several subsets, including the discounted cashflow approach and the "capitalization of economic income" approach. Brennan's methodology focused on future cashflows and relied on 5 years of historical income statements which were adjusted to normalize the income stream by removing nonrecurring expenses and adding liabilities not present on income tax forms. Brennan's analysis considered economic environment risks, government regulation risks, and risks specific to FPM such as sustainability, infrastructure, and technological and data security risks. Brennan employed the "Ibbotson Build-Up Method" to determine an appropriate discount rate which considered a risk-free rate, an equity premium, systemic environmental risk unique to the legal industry, and specific risks unique to FPM such as aging partners generating the majority of the client revenue and lower-than-average collection rates, coupled with an inability to pursue legal action against nonpaying clients. Brennan also emphasized that certain factors limit the control and marketability of a law firm, including that only attorneys can own law firms, that lawyers cannot ethically restrict their ability to serve clients through the use of noncompete agreements, and that most firms have partnership agreements which control compensation and/or admission into the firm. In considering all of these factors, Brennan applied a 60% discount to Assam's partnership interest. Brennan's ultimate opinion was a valuation of $590,000.

(b) Eide Bailly

Eide Bailly's opinion also employed a buildup rate which included industry risk and firm risk to reach a discount rate of 4 percent. The opinion also incorporated a 10% discount for lack of control as to nonoperating assets and a 5% discount for lack of marketability, because the Partnership Agreement provides a market for the sale of those shares.

[Flanagan and Fullerton performed Eide Bailly's valuation.] Flanagan admitted his valuation assumed that in a fair market value analysis, FPM should be understood as the specific hypothetical buyer of Assam's interest. Fullerton admitted this assumption was part of Eide Bailly's scope of engagement. In addition, Fullerton testified that Assam suggested to Eide Bailly that the reference to fair market value in the Partnership Agreement should equate to fair value. Fullerton further testified that fair value is essentially the same thing as fair market value without any discounts for lack of control or lack of marketability.

Flanagan and Fullerton used an income approach which utilized FPM's average normalized annual pretax revenue over a 4-year period. Eide Bailly also upwardly adjusted the value of the partnership due to its having a passthrough entity tax status. Flanagan testified that passthrough tax status is, in effect, a capitalization of taxes saved because FPM, as a limited liability partnership, is not subject to corporate taxation.

Eide Bailly's calculation engagement in 2014 concluded the value of Assam's interest in FPM to be $3,420,000. Eide Bailly's valuation engagement in 2016, using more recent revenue streams, concluded the value of Assam's interest to be $3,120,000. Eide Bailly's valuation accounted for FPM's nonoperating assets, such as an interest in real estate and dormant accounts receivable.

TRIAL COURT JUDGMENT

In its written order, the court found the proper remedy was declaratory judgment; it dismissed Assam's counterclaim and declined to award attorney fees. In doing so, the court found FPM's decision to write off approximately $10 million in old accounts receivable was not done in bad faith or with an intent to harm Assam, because the writeoff equally affected all equity partners and was set on the agenda for the partners' meeting prior to Assam's notice of resignation.

The court also determined, based on the language of the Partnership Agreement, that Assam's interest was the fair market value of his equity partnership interest in FPM as of the date of his notice of voluntary withdrawal, October 2, 2014.

The court declined to adopt Eide Bailly's opinion, because Flanagan and Fullerton had valued a law firm on only one other occasion; neither had ever worked at a law firm, been a chief financial officer for a law firm, or provided financial consulting services to a law firm; and neither had published any scholarly articles in the area of law firm valuation.

The court found that the testimony of Brennan was credible; Brennan's 60-percent lack-of-control and marketability discount was credible; Brennan's discounts were appropriate as part of a "fair market value" analysis, because they helped replicate a public marketplace for a private entity; Brennan's discount analysis was consistent with the fair market value standard of a hypothetical buyer's ability to convert the ownership interest to cash and control the investment; and Brennan was the only expert to weigh risk factors which were credible and relevant to determining the fair market value test of a fully informed hypothetical willing buyer's desire to maximize his economic interest.

The court found and declared that the fair market value of Assam's equity partner interest in FPM is $590,000; pursuant to the Partnership Agreement, FPM may pay Assam this amount.

DISTRICT COURT DID NOT ERR IN DETERMINING ASSAM'S EQUITY INTEREST

[Assam] claims the district court erred when it adopted the opinion of Brennan, because Brennan's opinion did not account for FPM's nonoperating assets. Assam claims the court erred by assigning no value to approximately $10 million in uncollectable accounts receivable and FPM's real estate investments.

"Fair market value" is the price that a willing buyer would pay a willing seller, both persons having reasonable knowledge of all relevant facts and neither person being under compulsion to buy or to sell. The willing buyer-willing seller rule presumes that a potential transaction is to be analyzed from the viewpoint of a hypothetical buyer whose only goal is to maximize his or her advantage. The willing buyer-willing seller rule is applied using the viewpoint of an objective hypothetical buyer, rather than a subjective buyer.

The evidence of fair market value included the opinions of Brennan, Flanagan, [and] Fullerton. Each expert posited a different fair market value, and each based his opinion on different factors. Just as the trial court did, we too find that there is evidence in conflict on material issues of fact concerning the appropriate considerations in valuing Assam's fair market value interest. Under our de novo review, we consider and give weight to the fact that the trial court observed the witnesses and accepted one version of the facts over another.

In regard to Eide Bailly's opinion as to fair market value, both Flanagan and Fullerton testified that it was premised upon FPM's being the hypothetical buyer. However, as mentioned above, fair market value is the price that a willing buyer would pay a willing seller. A willing buyer is presumed to be a hypothetical buyer whose only goal is to maximize his or her advantage. The willing buyer is considered from the viewpoint of an objective hypothetical buyer, rather than a subjective buyer. In using FPM as the willing buyer, Eide Bailly's opinion failed to fully consider discounts for lack of control and lack of marketability.

Eide Bailly employed 4 years of income instead of 5 years of income. In doing so, Eide Bailly disregarded 2010 income based on the determination that 2010 income was lower than the other years and was nonrepresentative of FPM's regular annual income. Both Brennan and Stadler testified that using the income figures over a 5-year period was preferred over using income figures over a 4-year period. Even Flanagan testified that, typically, they use 5 years of income. Additionally, Eide Bailly annualized 2014 income, because they did not have final figures for that year when preparing the report in May 2016. However, the record indicates that the 2014 income figures were finalized in March 2015.

Eide Bailly adjusted the value of FPM due to having a "pass-through entity tax status." However, Flanagan testified that this passthrough status had not been accepted by the U.S. Tax Court.

Though Flanagan and Fullerton are in the profession of preparing business valuation, neither had significant experience in valuating law firms. Flanagan had performed only one law firm valuation and Fullerton had performed no law firm valuations.

Each of these decisions by Eide Bailly upwardly impacted its valuation. As a result, we agree with the district court that the valuation determined by Eide Bailly of $3,120,000 does not accurately reflect the value of FPM as of October 2, 2014. Albeit for different reasons, Assam also testified that Eide Bailly's opinion should not be followed by the court.

In regard to Brennan's opinion, the trial court noted his vast experience in valuating law firms, including working for a law firm management consulting group dealing with over 500 law firms, working as an accountant and auditor, and serving as chief financial officer and executive director for two law firms. At the time of trial, Brennan had also performed approximately 25 law firm valuations and had testified in court seven times as an expert in law firm valuation. Ultimately, the trial court expressly based its findings on a credibility determination which accepted Brennan's version of the facts over Assam's and Eide Bailly's. The court found Brennan's testimony credible and controlling, because he implemented an approach which valued Assam's interest in the context of a market. The court therefore found the 60-percent discount for lack of control and marketability assigned by Brennan to be credible, because of the limitations presented by Assam's minority interest in a law firm with a specialized practice area and equity partnership makeup such as FPM. The court found that Assam and Eide Bailly sought to remove the need for a market from the fair market value analysis dictated by the Partnership Agreement and that, therefore, their small discounts for lack of control and marketability were not credible.

The record indicates that Brennan considered several different business valuation approaches for comparison, including market-based, asset-based, and income-based approaches. Brennan was able to articulate why the income approach was the most suitable valuation method. Brennan used income figures for 5 years as opposed to 4 years, and he did not apply the passthrough entity tax status calculation. Brennan employed the "Ibbotson Build-Up Method" to determine an appropriate discount rate, and his analysis considered economic environment risks, government regulation risks, and risks specific to FPM such as sustainability, infrastructure, and technological and data security risks. Though Brennan's capitalization and discount rates were significantly higher than those propounded by the other experts, Brennan was able to articulate why law firms should be valued differently from other professional services industries. We therefore agree with the district court that Brennan's opinion of value as to FPM is the most appropriate value.

We agree with the trial court that Brennan's testimony is persuasive and controlling. We find no merit to this assignment of error.

The case below discusses damages for wrongful dissolution. In reading this case, consider these questions: (1) What is the difference between the approaches taken by UPA and RUPA? (2) What are the policy considerations with respect to the application of a minority discount?

CONGEL V. MALFITANO

101 N.E.3d 341 (N.Y. 2018)

FAHEY, J.

A partnership is a voluntary, contractual association in which persons carry on a business for profit as co-owners. In the agreement establishing a partnership, the partners can chart their own course. New York's Partnership Law creates default provisions that fill gaps in partnership agreements, but where the agreement clearly states the means by which a partnership will dissolve, or other aspects of partnership dissolution, it is the agreement that governs the change in relations between partners and the future of the business.

Defendant, Marc Malfitano, and seven others entered into a written agreement (the agreement) to form a general partnership known as "Poughkeepsie Galleria Company" (the Partnership), for the ownership, operation, and management of a shopping mall. The mall continues to operate today. Defendant [had a 3.08%] ownership interest in the Partnership. The Partnership had a majority owner, Moselle Associates, which controlled a little over 56% of the Partnership.

The agreement provided that the Partnership "shall continue until it is terminated as hereinafter provided." In a subsequent provision, the agreement stated that the Partnership would dissolve upon "the election by the Partners to dissolve the Partnership" or "the happening of any event which makes it unlawful for the business of the Partnership to be carried on or for the Partners to carry it on in Partnership."

The agreement further stated that "all decisions to be made by the Partners shall be made by the casting of votes at a meeting of such Partners" and that "the affirmative vote of no less than fifty-one percent (51%)" of the partners "shall be required to approve any matter presented for decision." Day-to-day control of the Partnership was vested in a three-member Executive Committee, comprised of Robert Congel, Bruce Kenan, and James Tuozzolo, the plaintiffs in this case. The Executive Committee had "the exclusive right to manage the business of the Partnership," although a majority of partners had the authority to "overrule or modify" the Committee's decisions, "withdraw or modify" any power granted to the Committee, or remove its members.

Defendant decided to withdraw from the Partnership. Defendant asserts that certain conduct by plaintiffs related to the Partnership troubled him, and they did not address his concerns.

On November 24, 2006, defendant wrote to his partners: "In accordance with Section 62(1)(b) of the Partnership Law, and as a general partner of the Partnership I hereby elect to dissolve the Partnership and by this notice the Partnership is hereby dissolved."

Partnership Law § 62(1)(b) states that a partner may unilaterally dissolve a partnership, without violating the partnership agreement, if "no definite term or particular undertaking is specified" in the agreement and the partnership is therefore "at will." Defendant insisted that his partners were compelled to liquidate.

Plaintiffs, as the Partnership's Executive Committee and on behalf of the Partnership, commenced this action, seeking a declaratory ruling that defendant had wrongfully dissolved the Partnership, as well as damages.

Supreme Court granted summary judgment to plaintiffs, holding that the Partnership was not an "at-will" partnership, because it specified a "particular undertaking" within the meaning of Partnership Law § 62(1)(b), and that defendant's dissolution breached the agreement.

The Appellate Division affirmed, holding that defendant had dissolved the Partnership in contravention of the agreement. [It] remitted for further proceedings on the issue of damages for breach of contract.

Partnership Law § 69(2)(c)(II) states that when a partner dissolves a partnership in contravention of the partnership agreement, and the remaining partners continue the business, the dissolving partner has

> the right as against his copartners to have the value of his interest in the partnership, less any damages caused to his copartners by the dissolution, . . . and to be released from all existing liabilities of the partnership; but in ascertaining the value of the partner's

interest the value of the good-will of the business shall not be considered.

Consequently, Supreme Court conducted a bench trial to establish the value of defendant's interest in the Partnership, taking into account the value of goodwill, and the amount of damages, if any, that defendant owed to plaintiffs. The parties stipulated that the value of defendant's interest in the Partnership as of November 24, 2006 was $4,850,000.

Plaintiffs' valuation expert testified that the value of the Partnership contained goodwill of 44%, by which amount the value of defendant's interest should be proportionately reduced, and that his interest should be further reduced by, successively, a marketability discount of 35% and a minority discount of 66%. In testifying that a minority discount was applicable, based upon defendant's lack of control in the Partnership, the expert witness emphasized what he described as "draconian" restrictions on transferability under the agreement, and in particular a provision, which the expert testified he had never before seen in his 40-year career, that if a partner sold his or her interest, then for five years after the date of sale, the partner would be jointly and severally liable, with the buyer, for any capital costs. The expert testified that this restriction was relevant not only to the marketability of defendant's interest, but also to the minority status of the interest, in that a minority owner has no say in whether there would be a capital call.

Defendant's valuation expert testified that the Partnership—as a real estate holding company—did not have goodwill, but conceded that he did not regularly value assets of that type. He had been "advised, under the relevant statutes, that a minority discount was not applicable," adding that while a minority discount "would be applicable" if the court were determining "fair market value," it did not apply when determining "fair value." Because of this "advice," the expert witness did not argue, in the alternative, that the amount of the minority discount proposed by plaintiffs' expert, *i.e.*, 66%, was unreasonable or in error.

Conversely, defendant's expert did not contest that a marketability discount would apply, but valued it at 25%, rather than 35%. Notably, in post-trial papers, defendant failed to preserve any general objection to the marketability discount as legally inapplicable, focusing instead on the amount of that discount.

Supreme Court ruled that the stipulated value of $4,850,000 would be reduced by 15% or $727,500 to represent the value of the Partnership's goodwill. The court reasoned "that the partnership does indeed possess goodwill of its own," because the mall "and its tenants attract regular, loyal shoppers, which point towards the existence of some goodwill."

Next, Supreme Court applied a 35% or $1,442,875 marketability discount, to the stipulated value as reduced by goodwill, to account for the limited marketability of defendant's interest, generating a discounted value of $2,679,625. The trial court [took] into consideration all factors inhibiting transfer of defendant's partnership interest "resulting from a limited market." However, the court declined to apply a minority discount, citing cases that have barred the use of a minority discount in evaluation of a minority shareholder's stock in a closely held corporation.

Defendant contended that the holding that he had wrongfully dissolved the Partnership, in light of this Court's decision in *Gelman v. Buehler*, 986 N.E.2d 914 (N.Y. 2013), which provides a detailed analysis of the nature of an "at-will" partnership.[4] For their part, plaintiffs contended that a minority discount should have been applied to the valuation of defendant's interest in the Partnership.

The Appellate Division remitted to the trial court for a new calculation incorporating a 66% minority discount, applied to the discounted value of defendant's interest in the partnership, and for entry of a new judgment.

The Appellate Division adhered to its earlier determination that defendant had wrongfully dissolved the Partnership.

Upon remand, Supreme Court issued an amended judgment applying the minority discount and further reducing defendant's interest in the Partnership to $911,072.50 [= $2,679,625 × (1 − 66%)].

We granted defendant leave to appeal.

[WRONGFUL DISSOLUTION]

The governing law of partnerships in New York is the Partnership Law of 1919, which enacted into law the original Uniform Partnership Act (UPA). It is well established, however, that "the Partnership Law's provisions are, for the most part, default requirements that come into play in the absence of an agreement." The statutory scheme

> applies only when there is either no partnership agreement governing the partnership's affairs, the agreement is silent on a particular point, or the agreement contains provisions contrary to law. Where an agreement addresses a particular issue, the terms of the agreement control, and the rights and obligations of the parties are determined by reference to principles of contract law. Thus, an agreement specifying the circumstances under which a partnership may be dissolved is not at will.

The Partnership Law § 62(1)(a) provides that dissolution does not violate a partnership agreement if it occurs "by the termination of the

---

[4] Addressing the question of when a partnership agreement specifies a "definite term" or "particular undertaking" within the meaning of Partnership Law § 62, this Court adopted the rule that "a 'definite term' is intended to be durational in nature and refers to an identifiable termination date," while "a 'particular undertaking' requires a specific objective or project that may be accomplished at some future time, although the precise date need not be known or ascertainable at the time the partnership is created" (*Gelman*, 986 N.E.2d at 916).

definite term or particular undertaking specified in the agreement." Moreover, [§ 62(1)(b) provides that] if "no definite term or particular undertaking is specified" in the partnership agreement, then the partnership is said to be an "at-will" partnership, and a unilateral dissolution "by the express will of any partner" does not violate the partnership agreement. "When a partnership has no definite term or particular objective to be achieved, it may be dissolved at any time by the express will of one or more of the partners."

By contrast, the Partnership Law § 62(2) provides that a partnership is dissolved "in contravention of the agreement between the partners, where the circumstances do not permit a dissolution under any other provision of this section, by the express will of any partner at any time." In other words, "when the agreement specifies a durational term, or a defined project, an attempt unilaterally to dissolve the partnership would violate the partnership agreement."

Here, the agreement stated that the Partnership "shall continue until it is terminated as hereinafter provided," and, in a subsequent provision, stated that the Partnership would dissolve upon "the election by the Partners to dissolve the Partnership" or "the happening of any event which makes it unlawful for the business of the Partnership to be carried on or for the Partners to carry it on in Partnership." The partners clearly intended that the methods provided in the agreement for dissolution were the only methods whereby the partnership would dissolve *in accordance with the agreement*, and by implication that unilateral dissolution would breach the agreement. The agreement contemplated dissolution only in two instances, leaving no room for other means of dissolution that would be in accordance with its terms.

It follows that Partnership Law § 62(1)(b) has no application here, because the parties to the agreement clearly specified under what terms it could be properly dissolved, *i.e.*, what would constitute a dissolution under the agreement and what would constitute a dissolution in contravention of it. Accordingly, this was plainly not intended to be an "at-will" partnership.

Although the lower courts erred in applying Partnership Law § 62(1)(b), the conclusion they reached, *i.e.*, that defendant's dissolution was wrongful, is correct.

[GOODWILL]

With respect to the reduction for goodwill, Partnership Law § 69(2)(c)(II) gives a partner who dissolves a partnership in contravention of the partnership agreement the right "to have the value of his interest in the partnership, less any damages caused to his copartners by the dissolution, ascertained and paid to him in cash, but in ascertaining the value of the partner's interest the value of the good-will of the business shall not be considered." In other words, any goodwill component in the value of the partner's interest must be deducted. Defendant argues that he should not have been assessed a goodwill deduction.

Goodwill is an intangible asset of a business, corresponding in this context to what a buyer would pay for the business, over and above its value as a mere sum of tangible assets, because of the patronage and support of regular customers. Goodwill consists in "every positive advantage that has been acquired by a proprietor in carrying on [a] business, whether connected with the premises in which the business is conducted, or with the name under which it is managed, or with any other matter carrying with it the benefit of the business." It is, in Judge Cardozo's words, what people "will pay for any privilege that gives a reasonable expectancy of preference in the race of competition. Such expectancy may come from succession in place or name or otherwise to a business that has won the favor of its customers."

The goodwill question is a factual one. "In a case such as this, with affirmed findings of fact, our scope of review is narrow. This Court is without power to review findings of fact if such findings are supported by evidence in the record." The trial court found, based on the expert testimony and other evidence, that the shopping mall and the mall's tenants attract regular, loyal shoppers, and there is record support for the affirmed finding that the value of the Partnership included, in addition to its real property and cash, a goodwill component.

[MINORITY DISCOUNT]

The final question we must resolve is whether a minority discount may be applied in the calculation of the value of a wrongfully dissolving partner's interest in a partnership, pursuant to Partnership Law § 69(2)(c)(II), when the remaining partners continue the business under Partnership Law § 69(2)(b). A minority discount is a standard tool in valuation of a financial interest, designed to reflect the fact that the price an investor is willing to pay for a minority ownership interest in a business, whether a corporation or a partnership, is less because the owner of a minority interest lacks control of the business.

The Appellate Division relied on *Anastos v. Sable*, 819 N.E.2d 587 (Mass. 2004), in which the Massachusetts Supreme Judicial Court interpreted a UPA-based statute that is identical in all relevant respects to our Partnership Law § 69(2)(c)(II). There, the plaintiff dissolved a partnership in violation of the partnership agreement, and, as here, the other partners continued the partnership business, rather than liquidate. The trial court in *Anastos*, in determining the value of the plaintiff's interest, applied a minority discount to reflect that there was "no ready market for the purchase of an interest in a general partnership whose primary asset is real estate where the partnership agreement contains limitations and restrictions on the control that any minority owner can exercise." The Supreme Judicial Court upheld this decision, stating:

> In this case, the remaining partners chose to exercise their statutory right to continue the partnership business for the remainder of the partnership term, so the partnership business is not winding up and must therefore be treated as a going concern. Because the plaintiff cannot compel liquidation of the business at the point of dissolution, we read [Massachusetts G.L., ch. 108A, § 38(2)(c)(II)] as offering a nonliquidation based method of calculating the value of his partnership interest.

Similarly, Partnership Law § 69(2)(c)(II) contemplates a valuation of a wrongfully dissolving partner's interest based on treating the partnership as a going concern, rather than an asset to be liquidated. In other words, the statute does not contemplate a valuation of the entire business as if it were being sold on the open market, but rather a determination of the fair market value of the wrongfully dissolving partner's interest as if that interest were being sold piecemeal and the rest of the business continuing as a going concern.[12] Given that the focus is on one partner's interest in a persisting concern, we agree with the Massachusetts high court that a minority discount is applicable, because a minority interest is worth less to anyone buying that interest alone.

Notably, New York, like Massachusetts, has not adopted the 1997 Uniform Partnership Act commonly known as RUPA. The dissent's discussion of RUPA and of cases from states that have adopted RUPA does not illuminate the law in New York. In particular, while RUPA, "by focusing on a top-down valuation keyed to a sale of all of the assets of the partnership, directs the analysis away from a valuation of the interests of a particular partner," so that "a minority discount is inappropriate," we conclude that the same cannot be said of the UPA.

It is true, of course, that in the Partnership Law § 69(2)(c)(II) context the wrongfully dissolving partner's interest may simply be absorbed by the remaining partners. In our view, this does not render the value generated by application of a minority discount an inaccurate valuation of the intrinsic worth of that partner's interest. To repeat, the exiting partner's interest may appropriately be valued in light of the fair market value of that minority interest given that the partner is departing and the partnership continuing.

In sum, defendant provides no basis for concluding that a minority discount is inapplicable as a matter of law to the valuation of the interest of a wrongfully dissolving partner when the remaining partners continue the partnership. We note, finally, that the parties to a partnership agreement may contract out of application of a minority discount to the valuation of their interests, just as they may contract around statutory

12 "The fair market value is the price at which [an asset] would change hands between a willing buyer and a willing seller, neither being under any compulsion to buy or to sell and both having reasonable knowledge of relevant facts."

provisions. Defendant does not assert that the agreement precluded use of a minority discount in this manner.

For these reasons, Supreme Court properly determined the value of defendant's interest in the Partnership.

FEINMAN, J. (dissenting in part).

I do not join the majority's holding that the trial court was required to apply a minority discount to the value of a partner's interests.

The UPA left it unclear how a wrongful dissolver's buyout price should be calculated or whether any discounts should be applied. This ambiguity was explored during the process of drafting what would become the Uniform Partnership Act (1997) ("RUPA"), and attempts to arrive at an appropriate definition were made.

The RUPA resolved this ambiguity by explicitly defining the "buyout price" of a withdrawing partner as "the amount that would have been distributable to the dissociating partner if, on the date of dissociation, the assets of the partnership were sold at a price equal to the greater of the liquidation value or the value based on a sale of the entire business as a going concern" (RUPA § 701(b)). In other words, a dissociating partner would be entitled to its proportionate share in the value of the business as a going concern, set off against contractual damages, but without an individualized inquiry into the marketability of its particular slice of the partnership. Consistent with this definition, the Official Comment stated that "the notion of a minority discount in determining the buyout price is negated by valuing the business as a going concern."

"Partnership interests, unlike corporate stock, are not normally freely transferable. Giving each partner a right to sell his interest back to the firm, depending on how the buyout price is determined and the transaction costs of exercising the put, serves as a substitute for the efficient market for corporate stock in containing exploitation. In fact, a buyout price that represents the partner's pro rata share of the partnership is a better counter to exploitation than an efficient market price because the pro rata price prevents the controlling faction from taking advantage of its own exploitive conduct by purchasing the minority's interest at a discount."

Because this valuation would simply entitle the dissolving partner to its allocable share of the value of the partnership as a whole, it would be incompatible with a minority discount.

In the context of corporate appraisals and judicial dissolutions, minority discounts have been soundly rejected in New York and in the vast majority of jurisdictions across the country. In most states, including New York, minority stockholders must receive their "proportionate interest in the going concern value of the corporation as a whole, that is, what a willing purchaser, in an arm's length transaction, would offer for the *corporation* as an operating business." This valuation precludes a minority discount because "a minority discount would necessarily deprive minority shareholders of their proportionate interest in a going concern."

This wealth of corporate cases has produced a number of interlocking rationales for excluding minority discounts. Two primary rationales have emerged from the case law. First, many courts, including this one, have explained that the exclusion is partially motivated by a desire to deter unfair squeeze-outs and safeguard minority shareholders from oppression. The majority may be correct that these concerns are attenuated in the partnership context; a wrongful dissolution happens at the dissolving partner's initiative and is not necessarily triggered by a sale of the business or a determination that the partnership engaged in misconduct. Nevertheless, the dissenter-like status of a dissociating partner should not be completely ignored. By organizing their business as a general partnership, principals sacrifice limited liability and the free transferability of their equity interests in exchange for, among other things, a statutory right to cash out at any time, subject to their obligation to pay damages if the dissolution is wrongful. Imposing too great a punishment for exit "swings the pendulum toward permitting oppression of locked-in partners. Indeed, close corporations were long plagued by such problems." Again, although New York has not adopted the RUPA, it is noteworthy that "the strong support for the statutory buyout [in the RUPA] was influenced by trends in corporate law providing liquidity for a minority participant who wanted out of the business."

The second rationale transposes much more easily to the partnership context. There is an analytical flaw in applying a minority discount where the actual purchasers of the minority interest are the remaining shareholders, rather than a hypothetical "willing buyer." The purchasers are not entering into a noncontrolling position, but merely consolidating and increasing whatever degree of control they already have over the business. The Montana Supreme Court's analysis is commonly cited:

> Applying a discount is inappropriate when the shareholder is selling her shares to a majority shareholder or to the corporation. When selling to a third party, the value of the shares is either the same as or less than it was in the hands of the transferor because the third party gains no right to control or manage the corporation. However, a sale to a majority shareholder or to the corporation simply consolidates or increases the interests of those already in control. Therefore, requiring the application of a minority discount when selling to an 'insider' would result in a windfall to the transferee.

A number of authorities have criticized the feasibility of applying a minority discount. In the corporate context, "discounting individual share holdings injects into the appraisal process speculation on the various factors which may dictate the marketability of minority shareholdings."

Minority discounts would essentially randomize the partnership's liability in many wrongful dissolution cases, hindering the dissolving partner's ability to settle the dispute out of court based on a reliable and predictable computation of the "value of [its] interest."

In defining the value of [the partner's] interest, the question does not turn on whether a particular method of valuation is "accurate," but whether that valuation will lead to an allocation of wealth as between these partners that best advances the legislative scheme. "Value" can mean many different things, and the definition we embrace should be guided by the ends that the legislature sought to implement when it enacted the Partnership Law. Here, the court applied a minority discount of $1,768,552 to [defendant's] partnership interests, which were stipulated to be worth $4,850,000 without adjustments. The question is, in an action for wrongful dissolution, where the partnership is continued as a going concern, which party has the greater right to that $1,768,552 portion of interests—the controlling partners, or [defendant] himself? For the reasons discussed above, I believe this question should resolve in [defendant's] favor.

NOTES

1. In *Puklich v. Puklich*, 930 N.W.2d 593 (N. Dakota 2019), the court made the following analysis of minority discount in a general partnership.

> Elyse argues the district court erred in its valuation of PCI by accepting the valuation provided by Blayne as a penalty for Elyse's breach of a fiduciary duty and by rejecting the use of valuation discounts. The court concluded as follows:
>
> > Blayne's Count IV, that Elyse breached her duty of good faith and fair dealing in attempting to unfairly oppress Blayne as a minority shareholder in an effort to buy out his shares of PCI at below fair market value is proven. The Court awards no specific damages for the breach, but determines that the fair market value of Blayne's 19 percent ownership in PCI is $2,622,000. Elyse shall pay Blayne the sum of $2,622,000 for his 19 percent ownership interest in Puklich Chevrolet, Inc. The Court will not discount Blayne's interest as recommended by Sliwoski.
>
> After finding Elyse had breached her fiduciary duty with regard to PCI, the district court could dissolve the corporation or grant the equitable relief that it deemed to be just and reasonable under the circumstances of this particular case. The court selected a value for PCI within the range of evidence, but in a manner that favored Blayne, as an equitable remedy for Elyse's breach of fiduciary duty. The court's valuation was not induced by an erroneous view of the law, was within the range of evidence presented at trial, and we are

not left with a definite and firm conviction a mistake has been made. We conclude the valuation of PCI was not clearly erroneous.

Elyse also argues the district court erred in its valuation of PCI by rejecting the use of valuation discounts. This Court has previously noted the following regarding a district court's decision not to apply discounts for lack of control of a closely-held business when the business itself, or those with a controlling interest, have sought to purchase the minority interest:

> Almost all of the courts that have considered the question have refused to apply a discount in valuing stock to protect a minority shareholder. They realize the diminished value of a minority interest alone, but conclude that fact is irrelevant when the purchaser is the corporation or shareholders who control it. Those courts recognize the purpose of the corporate dissolution remedy intends no discount should be applied simply because the interest to be valued represents a minority interest in the corporation. The statutes suggest that a minority shareholder who brings an action for the involuntary dissolution of a corporation should not, by virtue of the controlling shareholder's invocation of the buy-out remedy, receive less than he would have received had the dissolution been allowed to proceed.

For shareholders dissenting from changes in a closely-held corporation, the courts fixing "fair value" have often refused to apply a minority discount. As the Delaware Supreme Court explained in *Cavalier Oil Corp. v. Harnett*, 564 A.2d 1137, 1145 (Del. 1989):

> Discounting individual share holdings injects into the appraisal process speculation on the various factors which may dictate the marketability of minority shareholdings. More important, to fail to accord to a minority shareholder the full proportionate value of his shares imposes a penalty for lack of control, and unfairly enriches the majority shareholders who may reap a windfall from the appraisal process by cashing out a dissenting shareholder, a clearly undesirable result.

We agree a trial court ascertaining "fair value" of minority shares under the Business Corporation Act should not automatically discount their value. The district court's rejection of discounts when valuing PCI was consistent with our case law.

2. LIMITED PARTNERSHIP

Because an LP has two classes of partners and the limited partner is a passive investor akin to a shareholder in a corporation, the rules of dissociation and effect of dissociation differ as between limited partners and general partners. Also, the ULPA (2001) and the RULPA have different rules as to whether a limited partner can dissociate at will.

ULPA (2001) § 601. Dissociation as Limited Partner.

(a) A person does not have a right to dissociate as a limited partner before the completion of the winding up of the limited partnership.

[Subsections (b) providing other grounds for dissociation that are similar to RUPA § 601.]

ULPA (2001) § 503. Sharing of and Right to Distributions Before Dissolution.

(b) A person has a right to a distribution before the dissolution and winding up of a limited partnership only if the partnership decides to make an interim distribution. A person's dissociation does not entitle the person to a distribution.

RULPA § 603. Withdrawal of Limited Partner.

A limited partner may withdraw from a limited partnership at the time or upon the happening of events specified in writing in the partnership agreement. If the agreement does not specify in writing the time or the events upon the happening of which a limited partner may withdraw or a definite time for the dissolution and winding up of the limited partnership, a limited partner may withdraw upon not less than six months' prior written notice to each general partner at his [or her] address on the books of the limited partnership at its office in this State.

RULPA § 604. Distribution Upon Withdrawal.

Except as provided in this Article, upon withdrawal any withdrawing partner is entitled to receive any distribution to which he [or she] is entitled under the partnership agreement and, if not otherwise provided in the agreement, he [or she] is entitled to receive, within a reasonable time after withdrawal, the fair value of his [or her] interest in the limited partnership as of the date of withdrawal based upon his [or her] right to share in distributions from the limited partnership.

There is a clear difference between the ULPA (2001), the RULPA and the RUPA. Under RUPA § 601(1), absent some specific limitation such as a partnership for a term or purpose, a partner can freely dissociate at will and the dissociation is not considered wrongful under the RUPA § 602(b). The RULPA follows the RUPA model. Under the RULPA § 603, a limited partner may withdraw with 6-month notice. Under the ULPA (2001) § 601(a), a limited partner does not have the right to dissociate "before the termination of the limited partnership." The implication is significant because, unless otherwise specified in the partnership agreement, an LP "has a perpetual duration" under ULPA (2001) § 110(c). Unless there is a contractual mechanism for an exit as a right, the limited partner has essentially committed to the venture indefinitely.

The ULPA (2001) and the RULPA express different policy preferences. The ULPA (2001) seeks to promote the business enterprise by locking in limited partners and their capital. Section 503(b) denies distribution upon dissociation. This rule locks in capital, but curtails partner freedom. The RULPA prefers freedom of limited partners to associate or not, and upon withdrawal a limited partner is entitled to "the fair value of his [or her] interest in the limited partnership as of the date of withdrawal." Capital may leave the firm at any time. This rule weakens the firm's capital structure, but promotes partner freedom.

Unlike the RUPA, the ULPA (2001) does not identify as a dissociation event a limited partner's bankruptcy and financial distress. The reason lies in the difference between a general partnership and an LP. Unlike the financial interrelations among general partners, a limited partner is not liable for the debts and obligations of the LP and also does not participate in the control of the business. The limited partner is a passive investor and provides only capital. Upon dissociation, the limited partner's interest is only in the personal property, which is the transferable interest. Accordingly, the financial situation of a limited partner is less connected to the LP and its partners. It is a concern to the extent that the LP may require additional capital from limited partners. In this regard, ULPA (2001) § 602(b) provides that the dissociation of "a limited partner does not of itself discharge the person from any debt, obligation, or other liability to the limited partnership or the other partners which the person incurred while a limited partner." If a limited partner is bankrupt, that may be bad luck for the LP to the extent of the limited partner's continuing commitment, but does not otherwise affect the partnership or its partners.

With respect to a general partner, the rules under ULPA (2001) § 603–605 track in basic respects the rules under the RUPA § 601–603.

3. LIMITED LIABILITY COMPANY

The rules of LLCs track in basic respects the rules under RUPA. *Compare* RULLCA §§ 601–603; *with* RUPA §§ 601–603.

In the Chrysler Group LLC operating agreement, there is no provision for the dissociation of a member. Why not? The omission was probably not inadvertent. A clue to the answer may be gleaned by reviewing the schedule of members. More pointedly, is there a risk that a member will unexpectedly dissociate from the LLC? Even if the omission was intentional, wouldn't the company want to draft the dissociation provision in the event that a non-affiliated member will join the company in the future? Without a provision in the operating agreement, the Delaware statute provides the default terms.

Delaware Limited Liability Company Act § 18–603. Resignation of Member.

A member may resign from a limited liability company only at the time or upon the happening of events specified in a limited liability company agreement and in accordance with the limited liability company agreement. Notwithstanding anything to the contrary under applicable law, unless a limited liability company agreement provides otherwise, a member may not resign from a limited liability company prior to the dissolution and winding up of the limited liability company. Notwithstanding anything to the contrary under applicable law, a limited liability company agreement may provide that a limited liability company interest may not be assigned prior to the dissolution and winding up of the limited liability company.

Delaware Limited Liability Company Act § 18–604. Distribution Upon Resignation.

Except as provided in this subchapter, upon resignation any resigning member is entitled to receive any distribution to which such member is entitled under a limited liability company agreement and, if not otherwise provided in a limited liability company agreement, such member is entitled to receive, within a reasonable time after resignation, the fair value of such member's limited liability company interest as of the date of resignation based upon such member's right to share in distributions from the limited liability company.

The case below discusses the legal standard for judicial expulsion of a member. In reading this case, consider these questions: (1) What is the standard for expelling a member because it "not reasonably practicable" to carry on the business? (2) Is the statutory provision for judicial expulsion a default rule or a mandatory rule under the RULLCA?

IE TEST, LLC v. CARROLL

140 A.3d 1268 (N.J. 2016)

JUSTICE PATTERSON delivered the opinion of the Court.

This appeal arises from a conflict among the three members of IE Test, LLC (IE Test). In the wake of a dispute about the terms of an operating agreement between defendant Kenneth Carroll (Carroll) and the LLC's other members, Patrick Cupo (Cupo) and Byron James (James), IE Test filed an action to expel Carroll as an LLC member, pursuant to the Limited

Liability Company Act (LLCA).* The trial court granted partial summary judgment and ordered that Carroll be disassociated from IE Test. It based its ruling on a provision of the LLCA that authorized the expulsion of a member by "judicial determination" if the court finds that the member has engaged in conduct relating to the LLC's business "which makes it not reasonably practicable to carry on the business" with the member remaining part of the LLC. *N.J.S.A.* 42:2B–24(b)(3)(c) (subsection 3(c)). The Appellate Division affirmed the trial court's judgment.

We construe the Legislature's intent when it enacted subsection 3(c) of the LLCA, and an analogous provision in the LLCA's successor statute, the Revised Uniform Limited Liability Company Act (RULLCA). We hold that a disagreement among members over the terms of an operating agreement does not necessarily compel the expulsion of a dissenting member. If members can manage the LLC without an operating agreement, invoking as necessary the default majority-rule provision of the LLCA, then a conflict among members may not warrant a member's expulsion under the LLCA. To assist trial courts in determining whether it is "not reasonably practicable" to operate an LLC in light of the member's conduct, we adopt a series of factors.

The dispute stemmed from the failure of a prior business in which IE Test's three LLC members were involved. In 2004, Carroll and Cupo formed Instrumentation Engineering, LLC pursuant to Delaware's LLC laws. Carroll owned a 51 percent interest, and Cupo owned the remaining 49 percent. James was employed as Vice President.

Following a series of financial setbacks, Instrumentation Engineering filed for Chapter 7 bankruptcy. Carroll claimed that Instrumentation Engineering owed him $2,543,318. The company did not repay the debt.

Shortly before Instrumentation Engineering filed for Chapter 7 bankruptcy, Cupo formed IE Test as a New Jersey LLC.

Carroll, Cupo, and James entered into a preliminary agreement. In that document, Carroll, Cupo, and James stated their intention to enter into an operating agreement for IE Test. They acknowledged that from the inception of IE Test, "the Members of the Company and their LLC Percentage Interests are: Carroll (33%), Cupo (34%) [and] James (33%)."

The LLC members were assigned divergent roles in the business of IE Test. Cupo managed the engineering, manufacturing, and financial components of the business. James was responsible for business development. Carroll's role was limited; he was not expected to become

* Author's note: The LLCA governed LLCs in New Jersey from its effective date, January 26, 1994, until March 18, 2013. The LLCA was repealed and replaced by the RULLCA, "a comprehensive, fully integrated second generation LLC statute that takes into account the best elements of first generation LLC statutes and two decades of legal developments in the field." *Sponsors' Statement to Assembly No. 1543* (2012). All LLCs in New Jersey are now subject to the RULLCA. However, the two statutes have the identical provisions at issue here.

involved in the day-to-day management of IE Test, and the record confirms that he did not do so. Carroll maintained no office at IE Test's facility and participated in only one sales call.

IE Test developed an increasingly successful business. After a modest beginning in 2009, during which it earned $396,597, IE Test reported revenue in the amount of $1,232,078 during the first half of 2010. Cupo and James drew salaries in the amount of $170,000 per year, and several $10,000 bonuses. IE Test paid Carroll no salary or bonus at any time.

Carroll's claim that Instrumentation Engineering owed substantial sums to him became a point of contention. Carroll acknowledged that IE Test had no legal obligation to repay him for losses sustained because of Instrumentation Engineering's bankruptcy. He pressed, however, for compensation that would allow him to recover some of his lost investment in Instrumentation Engineering.

An e-mail exchange between Cupo and James described the two options proposed by Carroll as alternative frameworks for an operating agreement: either an arrangement whereby Carroll would be paid an equal share of IE Test's profits with a premium, or the payment of a salary to Carroll plus an equal share of the profits. James and Cupo then agreed that they did not want to work with Carroll. James commented, however, that Carroll would not "walk away" from the business unless Cupo and James agreed to one of his alternative proposals for his compensation.

The three members met on January 7, 2010. According to Cupo and James, their plans for IE Test did not align with those of Carroll, and the company could not, then or in the foreseeable future, afford a third member. Carroll contends that Cupo and James declined to honor his ownership interest in IE Test and refused to enter into an operating agreement. At that point, the three members ceased communicating about the operation of their business.

IE Test filed this action. It sought the expulsion of Carroll as a member pursuant to *N.J.S.A.* 42:2B–24(b)(3)(a) (subsection 3(a)) or, in the alternative, under subsection 3(c).

No operating agreement for IE Test was ever executed.

IE Test filed a motion for partial summary judgment. It sought judgment in its favor on its claim for expulsion based upon two alternative theories. First, invoking subsection 3(a), IE Test contended that Carroll had engaged in "wrongful conduct that adversely and materially affected the limited liability company's business." *N.J.S.A.* 42:2B–24(b)(3)(a). Second, IE Test claimed that Carroll had engaged in conduct which made it "not reasonably practicable" to carry on IE Test's business, and that he should be expelled from the LLC pursuant to *N.J.S.A* 42:2B–24(b)(3)(c).

The trial court rejected IE Test's claim based on subsection 3(a). The court found that Carroll's insistence on specific compensation terms did not amount to "wrongful conduct" within the meaning of subsection 3(a). It concluded that although Carroll's demands may have been unreasonable, those demands were not unlawful, and inflicted no harm on IE Test.

The trial court found in IE Test's favor on its claim based on subsection 3(c). It reasoned that the "not reasonably practicable" language of subsection 3(c) imposed a less stringent standard than did subsection 3(a). The court concluded that Carroll's continued involvement would generate more controversy and further litigation. It therefore ruled that it was not "reasonably practicable" for the business to continue with Carroll involved.

The trial court conducted a bench trial to determine the value of IE Test, and valued the LLC at $683,173. The court entered final judgment for Carroll in the amount of $227,497, representing 33 percent of the total value of IE Test, plus prejudgment interest in the amount of $14,976.

Carroll appealed the trial court's judgment. An Appellate Division panel affirmed that judgment.

The LLCA provided for several alternative methods by which an LLC member may be disassociated from the LLC. One such procedure was expulsion of a member by "judicial determination" under *N.J.S.A.* 42:2B–24(b)(3). The statute provided that a member shall be disassociated from a limited liability company under the following circumstances:

> On application by the limited liability company or another member, the member's expulsion by judicial determination because:
>
> (a) the member engaged in wrongful conduct that adversely and materially affected the limited liability company's business;
>
> (b) the member willfully or persistently committed a material breach of the operating agreement; or
>
> (c) the member engaged in conduct relating to the limited liability company business which makes it not reasonably practicable to carry on the business with the member as a member of the limited liability company.

N.J.S.A. 42:2B–24(b)(3)(a)–(c).

In the wake of a judicial determination disassociating the member from the LLC, that member's interest is immediately limited to the "rights of an assignee of a member's limited liability interest," subject to the provisions of *N.J.S.A.* 42:2B–39, which addressed determination of the fair value of the LLC distribution. In that event, the member may no longer take part in decisions affecting the company, and may lose part or all of his or her investment in the business.

[Judicial Expulsion of Member]

We construe subsection 3(c), which authorized the expulsion of a member by judicial determination, based on the member's "conduct relating to the [LLC] which makes it not reasonably practicable to carry on the business with the member as a member of the [LLC.]"

The LLCA did not define the term "not reasonably practicable." Moreover, when the Legislature repealed the LLCA and replaced it with the RULLCA, retaining the "not reasonably practicable" language in the new statute, it did not define the term.

We are assisted in discerning the Legislature's intent by comparing subsection 3(c) with subsection 3(a), which provided an alternative ground for the expulsion of a member by "judicial determination." Subsection 3(a) required finding that "the member engaged in wrongful conduct that adversely and materially affected the limited liability company's business." Subsection 3(c) did not require that the member's conduct be "wrongful" in order to warrant expulsion of that member. In that regard, subsection 3(c) was more expansive than subsection 3(a).

The language of subsection 3(c) differed from the language of subsection 3(a) in a second respect. Subsection 3(a) involved any "wrongful conduct" by a member that has "adversely and materially affected [the LLC's] business." Under subsection 3(c), a court considers only conduct by the member "relating to the limited liability company business." Thus, the Legislature clearly did not intend that disagreements and disputes among LLC members that bear no nexus to the LLC's business will justify a member's expulsion under subsection 3(c).

Subsections 3(a) and 3(c) used different language to describe the impact that the member's "conduct" must have on the LLC in order to warrant expulsion. To disassociate a member under subsection 3(a), a court must find that the member's wrongful conduct has "adversely and materially affected" the company's business. That language suggests that to justify expulsion under subsection 3(a), the member's "wrongful conduct" must have damaged the LLC's business in the past. In contrast, subsection 3(c) did not mandate a finding that the member's conduct has materially affected the business. Under subsection 3(c), the court prospectively analyzes the impact of that conduct on the LLC's future.

The Legislature did not authorize a court to premise expulsion under subsection 3(c) on a finding that it would be more challenging or complicated for other members to run the business with the member than without him. Nor does the statute permit the members to expel a member to avoid sharing the LLC's profits with that member. Instead, the Legislature prescribed a stringent standard of prospective harm: the member's conduct must be so disruptive that it is "not reasonably practicable" to continue the business unless that member is expelled.

Interpreting the statutory text, "we ascribe to the statutory words their ordinary meaning and significance." Black's Law Dictionary defines "reasonable" to mean "fair, proper or moderate under the circumstances; sensible." *Black's Law Dictionary* 1456 (10th Ed. 2014). It defines "practicable" to denote "reasonably capable of being accomplished; feasible in a particular situation." Thus, the pivotal language suggests that it must be unfeasible, despite reasonable efforts, to keep the LLC operating while the disputed member remains affiliated with it.

A review of other components of the LLCA statutory scheme confirms that subsection 3(c) is not necessarily satisfied by the mere existence of a conflict among members. The LLCA's default provisions authorized majority rule in such matters as merger or consolidation, day-to-day management, and wind-up of affairs of an LLC, even if the members failed to reach consensus on the conduct of the business. Consequently, disputes among members on most issues relating to their business could be resolved by majority vote. Thus, it is possible that, despite an impasse among members regarding the company's management, an LLC could be effectively operated pursuant to the default provisions of the LLCA.

In short, members seeking to expel a fellow member under subsection 3(c), or its counterpart in the RULLCA, are required to clear a high bar. Neither provision authorizes a court to disassociate a member merely because there is a conflict. Instead, both provisions require the court to evaluate the member's conduct relating to the LLC, and assess whether the LLC can be managed notwithstanding that conduct, in accordance with the terms of an operating agreement or the default provisions of the statute.

In that inquiry, a trial court should consider the following factors, among others that may be relevant to a particular case:

(1) the nature of the member's conduct relating to the LLC's business;

(2) whether, with the member remaining a member, the entity may be managed so as to promote the purposes for which it was formed;

(3) whether the dispute among the members precludes them from working with one another to pursue the LLC's goals;

(4) whether there is a deadlock among the members;

(5) whether, despite that deadlock, members can make decisions on the management of the company, pursuant to the operating agreement or in accordance with applicable statutory provisions;

(6) whether, due to the LLC's financial position, there is still a business to operate; and

(7) whether continuing the LLC, with the member remaining a member, is financially feasible.

A trial court considering an application to expel a member under the LLCA, or the analogous "not reasonably practicable" standard of the RULLCA, should conduct a case-specific analysis using those factors, and other considerations raised by the record, with no requirement that all factors support expulsion, and no single factor determining the outcome.

We first review the nature of Carroll's conduct. By his own admission, Carroll had no legal right to recover his lost investment in Instrumentation Engineering through his interest in IE Test. Nonetheless, he sought a compensation arrangement that would accomplish that goal. He unsuccessfully attempted to persuade Cupo and James to sign an operating agreement to that effect, and thereby provoked a distracting dispute among the members that was never resolved. The record, however, is devoid of evidence that Carroll actively interfered with IE Test's business, or that he used the impasse over the compensation issue as an excuse to undermine that business by failing to cooperate when needed. He sought no role in the LLC's management, and participated in only one sales call on its behalf. There is no indication that he undermined IE Test to employees, vendors, or clients. In short, despite his insistence on generous compensation, Carroll permitted the LLC to operate unimpeded. The first factor does not weigh in favor of a finding that continuing IE Test's business with Carroll remaining a member was "not reasonably practicable."

Applying the second and third factors, the court considers whether the entity may be managed with the member remaining, so as to promote the purposes for which it was formed, and whether the dispute among the members precludes them from working with one another to pursue the LLC's goals. As to those issues, there are genuine issues of material fact.

It appears that the business operated with increasing revenue despite the deteriorating relationship between Carroll and the other members. Although IE Test maintains that because it has no operating agreement, it has been unable to secure a line of credit or bank financing, the proofs that it submitted to the trial court did not substantiate that claim. Moreover, Carroll contends that before the question was disputed in court, he was never informed by Cupo or James that IE Test had difficulty in obtaining a line of credit or financing. Carroll offers to assist in the LLC's financing, if necessary. In short, the parties dispute whether Carroll's insistence on being compensated for his prior losses precluded the members' common pursuit of IE Test's goals, or prevented the successful management of their business by obtaining necessary financing.

The fourth and fifth factors require a determination of whether there is a deadlock among the members and whether, notwithstanding such a deadlock, members can make decisions on the management of the company, pursuant to the operating agreement or in accordance with applicable statutory provisions. Those factors also weigh against the grant of partial summary judgment in this case. IE Test has not claimed, let alone established, that the three LLC members reached a deadlock regarding the company's management. Although IE Test contends that there is an impasse over the terms of an operating agreement, there is no evidence that Cupo and James proposed an alternative draft after rejecting Carroll's proposal. Moreover, even Carroll's failure to agree on a counterproposal would not, without more, justify his expulsion as a member; in accordance with the LLCA, IE Test has been effectively managed without an operating agreement. With all inferences drawn in favor of Carroll, the record does not demonstrate that any "deadlock" among the members threatened IE Test's business. Thus, the fourth and fifth factors do not support the trial court's grant of partial summary judgment.

Under the sixth and seventh factors, the court considers whether, due to the LLC's financial position, there is still a business to operate, and whether it is feasible for the company to continue in business with the member remaining a member. Those factors similarly weigh against the trial court's grant of summary judgment on the record of this case. There is no dispute that when the trial court ruled on IE Test's motion, the business remained in operation; indeed, its revenue evidently increased despite Carroll's continued involvement. Thus, the sixth and seventh factors do not favor the remedy imposed by the trial court.

In sum, when the record is viewed in accordance with the summary judgment standard, it does not support the trial court's finding that it was "not reasonably practicable" to carry on IE Test's business with Carroll remaining a member. IE Test was not entitled to a judicial determination expelling Carroll as a member. Accordingly, the trial court's grant of partial summary judgment constituted error.

D. BUY-SELL AGREEMENTS

Most multi-owner firms must anticipate the possibility of owners leaving. The charter agreement should address this possibility. Because NBEs are closely held entities, owners may be wary of admitting a new owner by the sale of a departing owner's interest to a stranger. This risk is reflected in the default statutory rules that permit the transfer of only the transferable interest and that require admission of new owners by unanimous consent. But owners also want viable exit options for investments that are generally illiquid. Many firms adopt a buy-sell agreement to deal with these competing tensions.

The discussion below provides examples of buy-sell agreements found in case law. These examples are not provided as exemplary model provisions. They are from prior litigation, some of which involved problems or issues concerning the wording of these provisions. Rather, they give a sense for the function and purpose of these agreements.

The following passage discusses the purpose of a buy-sell agreement in the context of a close corporation, but the comment on buy-sell agreements specifically applies to NBEs.

> Absolute restrictions forbidding the alienation of corporate stock are invalid, but reasonable restrictions are not.* The usual purpose of shareholders' agreements which restrict the sale of corporate stock is to prevent transfers to outsiders without first providing an opportunity for the shareholders to acquire the stock. The agreement evolved as a device to assure the succession in interest of persons most likely to act in harmony with the other stockholders. Stock creates a personal relationship analogous to a partnership, and shareholders in a close corporation should have the same right to choose one's associates in a corporation as in a firm. Restrictive agreements designed to prevent sale of stock to outsiders must be strictly construed and cannot be applied to transactions which are not expressly mentioned in the agreement; nor can they be enlarged by implication.
>
> A basic reason for buy-sell agreements is to provide methodology to determine the value of the stock. The difficulty of determining the price to be paid arises because shares of a close corporation are not traded on the open market and the value cannot be readily ascertained. To induce shareholders to purchase decedents' shares and to provide a market for the stock, the price must be attractive. A great deal of leeway is permitted because the shares represent more than a mere interest in property.
>
> The Sooner shareholders considered several factors other than income tax implications in the periodic revaluation of the option price. These included: the ability of the surviving shareholders to pay the purchase price; maintenance of the option price at a level which would be attractive enough to the survivors to exercise their options; and provision of a market for the shares.

Renberg v. Zarrow, 667 P.2d 465, 469–70 (Okla. 1983). The buy-sell agreement for the company's stock provided:

> The value of a share of stock of the Corporation for the purpose of computing the purchase price under paragraph II is hereby fixed by the Stockholders and agreed to be $270.00 per share. Hereafter, within ninety days after the close of each fiscal year of the Corporation, the value of each share of stock shall be fixed by resolution passed at a duly called meeting of the Stockholders by

* Author's note: This sentence reveals a major difference between corporations and NBEs. NBE laws provides that owners cannot freely transfer the entire ownership interest without the consent of all owners. An owner can only transfer his transferable interest.

a majority vote of the stock voted at such meeting. The resolution to be adopted shall be in the following form:

> "The value of each share of stock of the Corporation for the purpose of the Stock Purchase Agreement dated September 3rd, 1963, shall be $________, until and unless changed in accordance with the terms of the Stock Purchase Agreement."

It is agreed that the value of the stock is and shall be based upon consideration of all tangible and intangible assets, including good will, and all other factors relating to the value of the stock. It is further understood and agreed that the Trustee shall attach to its copy of this Stock Purchase Agreement, the resolutions setting forth the succeeding stock values.

> "If the Stockholders fail for any reason to pass a resolution as above provided fixing the value of the stock, the last valuation under the provisions of this Stock Purchase Agreement shall constitute the value of the stock until a subsequent resolution is passed in accordance with the terms of this stock purchase agreement."

Id. at 467 n.1.

Below is a buy-sell agreement in a partnership in *Estate of True v. Commissioner of Internal Revenue*, 2001 WL 761280, at *10 (Tax Ct. 2001):

> 5. No partner shall in any way attempt to dispose of, sell, encumber, or hypothecate his interest in the partnership except in accordance with the provisions of the Partnership Agreement relating to withdrawal or death of a partner, or, except in the normal course of business, any of the assets thereof.
>
> 6. If any partner shall resign, become legally disabled or bankrupt, assign his interest in the partnership for the benefit of his creditors, or institute any proceedings for temporary or permanent relief from his liabilities, or shall suffer an attachment or execution to be levied on his share or interest in the partnership, or a judgment shall be entered against him and stay of execution thereupon shall expire, or if he shall attempt to encumber or hypothecate his partnership interest, he shall be deemed to have filed a Notice of Intent to Withdraw, and his interest in the partnership shall be disposed of as provided in this Agreement.
>
> 7. In the event of the death of a partner or the filing with the partnership by a partner of Notice of Intent to Withdraw (the deceased partner or the partner filing such notice shall hereinafter be referred to as the "Selling Partner"), the Selling Partner shall be obligated to sell and the remaining partners shall

be obligated to purchase the Selling Partner's interest in the partnership for the purchase price described herein. The remaining partners shall purchase the Selling Partner's interest in proportion to their respective shares in the net profits of the partnership and the purchase price shall be payable within six months after death or the filing of the Notice of Intent to Withdraw. The purchase price of the Selling Partners's interest shall be the book value of the partnership multiplied by the Selling Partner's percentage interest in the net profits of the partnership, said book value to be determined as of the end of the month immediately preceding the date of the death or filing of Notice of Intent to Withdraw less any withdrawals made by the partners subsequent to end of the preceding month. The book value of the partnership shall be determined in accordance with the accounting methods and principles customarily followed by the partnership. Appropriate adjustments shall be made for over or under withdrawals by a partner.

8. The partnership shall continue in business and shall not be terminated unless the holders of 50% or more of the total interest in partnership capital and profits sell their interests as provided herein, or unless all of the partners agree to such termination.

9. In the event that a partner or partner's spouse ceases to devote all or a substantial part of his time to the business of the partnership, he shall be deemed to have filed with the partnership a Notice of Intent to Withdraw, unless the remaining partners unanimously agree to permit such partner to continue as a partner.

In *Crow Irvine #2 v. Winthrop California Investors L.P.*, 128 Cal.Rptr.2d 644, 646–47 (Cal. App. 2002), the court describes a buy-sell agreement that can best be described as "I cut, you choose" approach.

Section 6.6 also requires the terminating partner to "make a written offer to purchase the Interest of the other Partner [which] shall set forth a definite price for the other Partner's Interest." The price must "be based on a hypothetical sales price for the portion of the Excess Land and any Improvements thereon then owned by the Partnership and will equal the amount the Offeree Partner would receive if such portion of the Excess land and any Improvements thereon were sold at the hypothetical price for cash subject to existing debt and all allocations and distributions were made as prescribed by Article VIII."

Then, upon receipt of the offer, the offeree partner has the right to either accept the offer, or "purchase for cash the Interest of the Offeror Partner by paying an amount equal to the amount which the Offeror Partner would receive if such portion of the

> Excess Land and any Improvements thereon were sold at the hypothetical price upon which the Offered Amount was based."

Below is another iteration of the "I cut, you choose" approach found in *Bentley-Wing Property W, LLC v. West Development Inc.*, 2017 WL 1458970, at *4 (Cal. App. 2017):

> At any time after two (2) years from the date of this Agreement, any Member (the "Offering Member") may provide written notice to the other Member (the "Remaining Member") setting forth the fair market value of the Company. The value of the Interest of a Member to be sold or purchased pursuant to this Section 9.2 shall be based upon the remaining Distributions to be made pursuant to Section 4.1 (the "Distribution Value"). The Remaining Member shall within thirty (30) days from the written notice, either elect to purchase the Offering Member's Interest or sell its Interest to the Offering Member for an equivalent and proportionate price based upon the Distribution Value and shall give written notice of such election to the Offering Member, In the event the Remaining Member elects to sell its Interest to the Offering Member, the Offering Member shall purchase the Interest according to this Agreement. In the event the Remaining Member fails to timely make its election to buy or sell, then the Offering Member shall elect to sell the Offering Member's Interest or purchase the Remaining Member's Interest. A Member who is purchasing an offered Interest may assign that right to a third party on the terms and conditions as the purchasing Member so determines. The closing of the purchase and sale will be at the Company's offices on the ninetieth (90th) day following the written notice of election or deemed election by the Remaining Member and the purchase price shall be paid in cash at closing.

E. ISSUES TO CONSIDER FOR NBEs

1. TRANSFERABLE INTEREST

Lawyers and owners must consider the issue of transferable interest. In light of the statutory rules, the following are potential issues to consider:

- Should there be an absolute prohibition against transfer of any interest?
- Should the transferable interest be freely transferable?
- Should the entire interest be freely transferable?
- If the entire interest can be transferable, should there be an approval mechanism such as a threshold vote of owners or some limitation such as transfers only among family members or affiliated entities?

The firm's unique situation should answer these questions. For example, in a venture that is dominated by a family, the firm and its owners may wish to have free transferability of the entire interest to other family members. In a closely-knit professional organization, transferability of the entire interest may not be preferred absent consent of all owners. In a venture with passive investors, transferability may be desired on a case by case circumstance such that each proposed transfer should depend on a manager's approval or a vote of all owners.

The right to transfer an interest, whether the transferable interest or the entire interest, can be subject to certain conditions. For example, upon a proposed transfer to a third-party, the firm or its owners can have a right of first refusal. The exiting owner must first offer the interest to the firm or its remaining owners under the same terms and conditions given to the third-party. Only if the right is not exercised, a typical right of first refusal provision permit a transfer to a third-party. A right of first refusal is a compromise mechanism: it permits an owner to exit but also protects the firm and its remaining owners against unwanted new owners.

For a transferee (assignee), the issue is whether she is subject to potential opportunism by owners as may have been the case in *Bauer v. Blomfield Co./Holden Joint Venture*. The matter may come down to whether the charter agreement restrains the distributions rights of owners or managers and whether the transferee can pursue an action to force a distribution based on a breach of contract. For example, in *Kohannim v. Katoli*, 440 S.W. 3d 798, 813 (Tex. App. 2013), the defendant member paid himself $100,000 for management services that were not performed and failed to make any distributions to his former member or his assignee in a divorce decree even though more than $250,000 in undistributed profit had accumulated in the company's accounts. The operating agreement provided "for the distribution of 'available cash' to members quarterly provided that the available cash is not needed for a reasonable working capital reserve." *Id.* at 813. The court concluded that the member "oppressed"[4] the assignee's right to receive a distribution: "more than a scintilla of evidence supports the trial court's finding that [the member] failed to make profit distributions to [the assignee]." *Id.* It added further: "We agree with the trial court's conclusion that the established facts demonstrated [the member] engaged in wrongful conduct and exhibited a lack of fair dealing in the company's affairs to the prejudice of [the transferee]." *Id.*

---

[4] *Kohannim* was subsequently overruled with respect to the definition of "oppression." The court defined "oppression" as "burdensome, harsh, or wrongful conduct, a lack of probity and fair dealing in the company's affairs to the prejudice of some members, or a visible departure from the standards of fair dealing, and a violation of fair play on which every shareholder who entrusts his money to a company is entitled to rely." 440 S.W. 3d at 812. The Texas Supreme Court later ruled that "oppression" means "they abuse their authority over the corporation with the intent to harm the interests of one or more of the shareholders, in a manner that does not comport with the honest exercise of their business judgment, and by doing so create a serious risk of harm to the corporation." Ritchie v. Rupe, 443 S.W.3d 856, 871 & n.17 (Tex. 2014).

2. DISSOCIATION

The dissociation of an owner is an important consideration for drafting the charter agreement. When drafting an agreement, the lawyer should use the statutory framework: What events trigger a dissociation? When is a dissociation wrong? What is the effect of a dissociation?

The statutes provide a comprehensive set of default rules for an event of dissociation, and a drafter should start by examining the list and incorporating provisions therefrom. A critical question is whether an owner should be allowed to leave the firm at will as a matter of right. The RULPA and the ULPA (2001) provide the two choices. The answer will be easy if the owners agree on the point, or if the agreement is presented on a take-it-or-leave-it basis, such as passive investors. The options for withdrawal as a matter of right could be based on consent of owners or managers or both by some voting threshold, or at the will of the exiting owner.

If there is disagreement among owners, they must consider the consequences of the policy choice. A right to dissociate gives owners their economic freedom, but an obligation to stay promotes the business venture and financial stability. The two choices may not be as stark as "right" and "wrong." The process of contracting can soften the rough edges of each consequence. An owner may have the right to dissociate, but it can be conditioned to lessen the adverse consequence on the firm, for example:

- Sale of the interest to another owner or the firm in a "buy-sell" agreement
- Significant notice period to permit the firm to manage the transition
- Distribution rights that balances the interest of the withdrawing partner and the firm's financial needs

With respect to the last point, contracting permits the definition of different kinds of "right" or "wrong." For example, a partner may have a right to withdraw, but the distribution right depends on the nature of the withdrawal. If the withdrawal is based on the partner's will, then, for example, the distribution may be the amount in the partner's capital account. If the withdrawal is based on the firm's consent, the distribution may be some formula that provides a greater economic return.

3. EXIT MECHANISMS

Lawyers and owners must consider the possibility that owners will come and go. An absolute fixed ownership may be impossible. Dissociation by an owner at some is inevitable. People die or become disabled. Entities dissolve, become bankrupt, or are merged out of existence. In the most common circumstance, owners want to exit for various reasons.

If an exit is inevitable at some point, lawyers and owners need to think about the mechanism. There are various ways to think about an exit.

- Call option: the right, but not the obligation, of a firm to buy the dissociating owner's interest at some contractually defined price or mechanism to determine the price
- Put option: the right, but not the obligation, of a dissociating owner to sell his interest at some contractually defined price or mechanism to determine the price
- Buy-sell agreement: an agreement obligating the sale and purchase of the interest upon the dissociation of an owner

If an option, one should consider the fact that an option is a right, but not an obligation. What happens if the option is not exercised by the option holder? This is less of a problem for a put option held by the dissociating owner. If she does not want to sell at her option, then the fate of her interest in the firm is her problem. However, suppose the firm holds a call option and it does not exercise the option, what happens to the owner's interest?

In considering a buy-sell agreement, the firm and its owners should consider the basic questions.

- What is the right in the buy-sell agreement?
- What is the method to value the interest?
- What is the dispute resolution method?

Buy-sell agreements can be structured in a number of ways. In a deadlock situation between two owners, one common form of a buy-sell agreement is some sort of an "I cut, you choose" method. An owner may offer to buy out the other owner. This method elicits good faith and reveals truer information. The offeree can then sell the interest at the offered price or he can buy the interest at the price from the offering owner. In this way, the owner determining the sale price is kept honest by giving the offeree owner the choice of buying or selling the interest.

With the freedom of contract, the possibilities of exit mechanisms are endless. For example, consider these forms of collective selling rights or conditions: a "drag-along" right permits a selling owner to force other owners to sell their interests to the buyer on the same terms; or, "tag-along" right permits other owners to sell their interests to the buyer upon an agreement to buy a departing owner's interest. Such rights can work harsh or unintended results and the negotiation for them should involve a clear-eyed understanding of the potential outcomes. Do the owners want to give any single owner the option to force an exit by all owners? Do the owners want to condition a sale on the third-party's purchase of the interests of all owners, effectively requiring the purchase of the firm?

4. PRICE AND VALUATION

A sale to a third-party, if permitted, does not require a contractual provision on price because it does not involve the firm or its remaining owners. The sale is a matter of a private deal between the exiting owner and the third-party. However, many exit arrangements involve a transaction between the departing owner and the firm or its remaining owners. In such deals, the issue of price and valuation are paramount.

Price and valuation raise several issues. An owner can exit the firm under different situations: as rightfully, wrongfully, or per expulsion. Each of these situations could involve a different price under the agreement. Also, there can be different ways to value an exiting owner's interest. There are two basic approaches: the charter agreement can provide a fixed price, or it can provide a definition of a price and a methodology to calculate it.

A fixed price option includes a sum certain such as "$X per unit" or a method to specify a price such as the balance in an owner's capital account. The benefit of a fixed price is greater certainty. The potential risk is that the contractually fixed price may be substantially decoupled from the value of the interest. For example, suppose the price is set at $100 per unit in the charter agreement but the exiting owner's interest is really worth $50 or $200 per unit—either the owner or the firm may be unhappy with the outcome. A way to deal with this problem may be a provision where the fixed value is regularly updated such that the fixed price fairly represents actual value. The charter agreement can be regularly amended, or an independent appraiser can periodically conduct an appraisal.

The alternative is to define the price under a specific valuation method. For example, the charter agreement defines the price to be "fair value" and sets the procedure for determining that value. The procedure could be an agreement between the owner and the firm, an appraisal, or some dispute resolution mechanism. The charter agreement can specify a valuation method for parties to use, for example: book value, which is the value of the equity in the firm's financial statements; or, some formula such as a multiple of a firm's financial performance, for example 10x (ten times) the firm's last fiscal earning or 2x the firm's book value. The benefit of this approach is that price is coupled to some agreed methodology. The potential risk is that the determination of value and price may be subject to some uncertainty and potential disagreement, in which case the charter agreement should clearly specify the dispute resolution mechanism.

F. PROBLEM: ENTREPRENEURS LEARN THAT OWNERSHIP IS NOT PERMANENT

PBOO and Piers struck a deal for the Brass House, and soon PBOO began substantial business operations. As expected, sales were slow, though internet traffic through the company website was picking up. The company's strategy was to build up brand recognition as quickly as possible. In light of these positive developments, Piers and Blake were confident that they could meet the projected financial benchmarks by the end of the fiscal year: projected revenue of $1 million and net profit of $50,000, a 5% net income margin and a 10% return on the $500,000 of the initial cash contributions of the owners who provided cash. Much of the expenses were projected to be marketing costs.

While the company's operations were launching, an ordinary meeting of investors and managers became eventful. It became apparent that Morgan Money's deal with Pacifico Plastic Recycling, Inc. was going to put a dent in profitability, at least for the next two years of the contract term. It was an albatross around the company's neck, and everyone knew it, including Money. Nevertheless, Money continued to press for influence in management. Things came to a head at this meeting. Money sought to become involved in the company's marketing campaign. Piers and Blake resisted, thinking that marketing was absolutely crucial to the company's future and that they needed to control this function. Money had an expertise in finance, and not marketing. After a long, civil discussion on each owner's role in management, it became apparent that Money did not have support in the company for a more direct role in management.

The next day, Money wrote an email to Piers and Blake.

> Date: Tues 9/10/2xx0
>
> To: Piers; Blake
>
> Re: Moving on
>
> Hi Piers and Blake. It is apparent to me that my role in the company will be fairly diminished. This is inconsistent with the original understanding we had. I don't blame anyone for this misunderstanding, and my role in securing the contract with Pacifico Plastic may have diminished confidence in me, though I will say in my defense that the deal will eventually be very good for PBOO's brand and marketing. Our customer base cares about the environment and we can leverage the Pacifico brand. Being on the right side of the environment is always a good selling point! . . . In any event, in light to the reality that I have been pushed aside as a passive investor, which is contrary to our original understanding, I would like to leave PBOO and withdraw my capital. Consistent with our prior understanding, I am entitled to my percentage share of the company valued as a going concern.

Upon receiving this email, Piers and Blake hurriedly conferred. They both agreed that, while unfortunate, Money's departure was not a bad thing. He was a thorn in the side of the company. However, the departure of Money's capital at this crucial time would be a severe blow. Piers and Blake checked the written operating agreement to see the provisions dealing with dissociation. To their surprise and dismay, the PBOO's operating agreement did not contain any provisions related to dissociation. It dawned on Piers and Blake that they had no business writing the operating agreement themselves without a lawyer. In hindsight, they should have hired Lynn Law, the attorney who initially advised them on business entities in general, at the hourly fee of $700 per hour for approximately 15 hours of counseling and drafting, which would have been money well spent even for a cash-strapped entrepreneurial venture.

Piers: "What are we going to do?"

Blake: "What did Morgan Money mean with this comment, 'Consistent with our prior understanding, I am entitled to my percentage share of the company valued as a going concern' "?

Piers: "I don't know, but I suspect that it refers to a conversation we had during the initial negotiation for Money's investment on the subject."

Blake: "What did the two of you talk about?"

Piers: "I think I said that if Money ever became unhappy with the investment, pulling out was always a possibility."

Blake: "That's what you told Money?"

Piers: "Yeah, this was even before we formed the company. I intended that comment to be a general understanding. You can always leave an investment that you're not happy with. That's the Wall Street rule: Leave the investment that disappoints you. We learned that in business school, and I was just reminding Money that I was listening in his finance class."

Recall that PBOO is an LLC and it is chartered in an RULLCA state. Recall also that upon initial contributions of cash at the beginning of the year was the following: $100,000 Piers, $0 Blake, $200,000 Morgan Money, and $200,000 Nicki Song. Of course, these cash contributions were made before any operations and financial results described above here, and not including other forms of contributions by the members.

QUESTIONS

1. What are the business issues and problems?

2. What are the legal issues?

3. Propose a process for resolving the potential problems and for dealing with Money's exit.

CHAPTER 9

DISSOLUTION AND MERGERS

■ ■ ■

A. DISSOLUTION

1. EVENTS OF DISSOLUTION

NBE laws state that specific events result in dissolution. They provide four general ways in which a firm undergoes dissolution and wind up.

Voluntary dissolution.—The owners consent to a dissolution or the charter agreement provides for dissolution, such as when the entity ends its term or completes its particular undertaking. RUPA § 801(2); ULPA (2001) § 801(a)(1); RULLCA § 701(a)(1). Voluntary dissolution requires the consent of all members or partners. RUPA § 801(2)(B); ULPA (2001) § 801(a)(2); RULLCA § 701(a)(2).

No partner or member to continue.—The firm does not have owners to continue the business. RULLCA § 701(a)(3); RUPA § 801(6); ULPA (2001) § 801(a)(3)–(4). For example, in a two-partner partnership, one partner exercises his right to dissociate at will; in an LP, the sole general partner dies and cannot be replaced; in a single-member LLC, the member, a corporation, is dissolved and winds up its business. Unless a new owner is admitted, the entity cannot continue.

Administrative dissolution.—For limited liability entities, the state may dissolve an entity for failure to pay fees and taxes or comply with other requirements.[1] ULPA (2001) § 811; RULLCA § 708. There are provisions for administrative reinstatement upon remedying the deficiency of filing information or paying fees. ULPA (2001) § 812; RULLCA § 709.

Judicial dissolution.—Owners can petition the court for an order to dissolve the entity based on grounds set forth in the statute. RUPA § 801(4); ULPA (2001) § 801(a)(6); RULLCA § 701(a)(4). In the case of a general partnership, a transferee can also petition the court that "it is equitable to wind up the partnership business" in light of an existing

[1] General partnerships do not require a filing with the state, and there is no provision for administrative dissolution. But a partnership can choose to be a limited liability partnership (LLP) by filing with the state. RUPA § 901. If a partnership is an LLP, the state can revoke a partnership's qualification to be an LLP. *Id.* § 903(a). If an administrative revocation of qualification occurs, the partnership is not dissolved. *Id.* § 903(d). The partnership simply loses its limited liability status and reverts back to being an ordinary general partnership.

charging order. RUPA § 801(5). An equivalent provision is not found in the ULPA (2001) and the RULLCA.

RULLCA § 701. Events Causing Dissolution.

(a) A limited liability company is dissolved, and its activities and affairs must be wound up, upon the occurrence of any of the following:

(1) an event or circumstance that the operating agreement states causes dissolution;

(2) the affirmative vote or consent of all the members;

(3) the passage of 90 consecutive days during which the company has no members unless before the end of the period:

(A) consent to admit at least one specified person as a member is given by transferees owning the rights to receive a majority of distributions as transferees at the time the consent is to be effective; and

(B) at least one person becomes a member in accordance with the consent;

(4) on application by a member, the entry by [the appropriate court] of an order dissolving the company on the grounds that:

(A) the conduct of all or substantially all the company's activities and affairs is unlawful;

(B) it is not reasonably practicable to carry on the company's activities and affairs in conformity with the certificate of organization and the operating agreement; or

(C) the managers or those members in control of the company:

(i) have acted, are acting, or will act in a manner that is illegal or fraudulent; or

(ii) have acted or are acting in a manner that is oppressive and was, is, or will be directly harmful to the applicant; or

(5) the signing and filing of a statement of administrative dissolution by the [Secretary of State] under Section 708.

(b) In a proceeding brought under subsection (a)(4)(C), the court may order a remedy other than dissolution.

The case below provides an example of a petition for dissolution based on the ground that "it is not reasonably practicable" to continue the business. Such petitions are common, and the usual fact pattern involves dysfunction in the relationship among owners. In reading this case, consider these questions: (1) What is the legislative purpose of a statutory provision permitting judicial dissolution? (2) What are the policy boundaries of the rule permitting judicial dissolution?

DYSART V. DRAGPIPE SALOON, LLC

933 N.W.2d 483 (S.D. 2019)

SALTER, JUSTICE.

Two members of a limited liability company known as Dragpipe Saloon, LLC (Dragpipe) requested judicial dissolution ancillary to their efforts to sell their membership interests. Following a court trial, the circuit court ordered dissolution and the sale of Dragpipe's assets. The remaining members appeal, arguing the circuit court erred when it concluded that it was not reasonably practicable for Dragpipe to continue under the provisions of its operating agreement and that Dragpipe's economic purpose was unreasonably frustrated. We reverse.

Raymond Meyers, Penney Weast, Troy Dysart, and Richard Heinrich formed Dragpipe in 2003. Each member contributed $10,000 and received a 25% membership interest and voting rights. Dragpipe's operating agreement states that its purpose

> is to engage in all lawful activities, including, but not limited to, owning, purchasing, taking, leasing, or otherwise holding or acquiring real property and any interest or right in real property and any improvements thereon, and to hold, own, operate, control, maintain, manage and develop such property and interests in any manner that may be necessary, useful or advantageous [to the] company.

The operating agreement provides that Dragpipe may be dissolved and its affairs wound up with the unanimous vote of the members or by a decree of judicial dissolution pursuant to the Uniform Limited Liability Company Act. *See* SDCL ch. 47–34A. Individual members may also voluntarily resign their membership under the provisions of the operating agreement and obtain the "fair market value of [the member's] Ownership Interest, adjusted for profits and losses to the date of resignation." In the event of a resignation, the fair market value would be determined by a unanimous vote of the members or, failing that, by an independent appraiser.

The members purchased 74 acres of land off Highway 79 northeast of Sturgis for approximately $135,000 and built a bar that is open only during the Sturgis Motorcycle Rally (Rally), which runs for approximately ten days every year in August. Of the 74 acres purchased, 18 acres were used to operate the bar, and the remaining land was leased to a farmer. Dragpipe obtained a malt beverage license and opened for business during the 2004 Rally, selling beer, soft drinks, water, and t-shirts. The company also hosted food vendors and provided live entertainment.

Weast sold her membership interest to Patrick Kerwin. Dragpipe had its first profitable year in 2015 and posted modest profits in 2016 and 2017.

Each member has invested $80,000 in the company. The members also provide labor during the Rally without compensation. The members have not received income distributions. However, Dragpipe's net income from 2015 to 2017 did allow it to pay the mortgage expense previously contributed pro rata by the members. The profits also allowed Dragpipe to reimburse the members for their out-of-pocket expenses.

Following the 2015 Rally, Dysart and Heinrich (Appellees) advised Kerwin and Meyers (Appellants) that they wanted to sell their membership interests in Dragpipe. The Appellants expressed no objection. [The effort to sell the Appellees' membership interest eventually failed.]

Despite the apparent effort to end their membership, the Appellees did not invoke their right under the operating agreement to voluntarily resign their interests. Nor did the members vote to dissolve Dragpipe under the authority provided in the operating agreement.

Instead, the Appellees commenced this action, seeking judicial dissolution and an order authorizing the sale of Dragpipe's assets. The circuit court granted the request for dissolution. In its written findings of facts and conclusions of law, the circuit court found that "the profit made in [2015–2017] is insufficient to begin repaying the capital contributions made by the members." The court further found that the parties were "at a standstill" on whether to sell the property and determined that the only way for Dragpipe to make money was to sell its real estate. The court concluded that judicial dissolution was authorized under SDCL 47–34A–801(a)(4)(i) and (iii) because Dragpipe's economic purpose was unreasonably frustrated and because it was not reasonably practicable to carry on its business in conformity with the operating agreement.

The Appellants present one issue: Whether the circuit court erred in its interpretation of Dragpipe's operating agreement and its determination to order judicial dissolution pursuant to SDCL 47–34A–801.

Members of a limited liability company may choose to enter into an operating agreement "to regulate the affairs of the company and the conduct of its business, and to govern relations among the members, managers, and company." SDCL 47–34A–103. An LLC's operating agreement may specify the circumstances under which a limited liability company will be dissolved and its business wound up. Beyond this authority provided by agreement, the Legislature has given courts "limited power to order dissolution of an LLC if certain statutory standards are met." *Kirksey v. Grohmann*, 754 N.W.2d 825, 827 (S.D. 2008).

An LLC may be dissolved by judicial decree, as relevant here, "on application by a member or a dissociated member" if

> (i) The economic purpose of the company is likely to be unreasonably frustrated; [or]
>
> (iii) It is not otherwise reasonably practicable to carry on the company's business in conformity with the articles of organization and the operating agreement.

SDCL 47–34A–801(a)(4).

An involuntary judicial dissolution represents an exceptional level of intervention into the otherwise private agreement of an LLC's members. It should be unavailable merely to resolve disagreements among owners or relieve an owner of an investment decision later regarded as improvident. Rather, judicial dissolution is permitted only in those instances where it is expressly authorized under our statutes.

For example, in *Kirksey*, we held that judicial dissolution was authorized where the economic purposes of the LLC were likely to be unreasonably frustrated and because continuing the LLC's business was no longer practicable. The members in *Kirksey* were four sisters who had formed the LLC and contributed their equal interests in ranch land inherited from their mother. Two sisters were also tenants who leased the ranch land under terms that became increasingly favorable to them as the value of the land appreciated dramatically. They resisted efforts by the other two sisters to terminate the lease and sell the land, resulting in an "impenetrable deadlock" because there was no method of resolving the dispute under the articles of organization or the operating agreement. We recognized that "forced dissolution is a drastic remedy," but we concluded that the tenant-sister faction wielded disproportionate power over the other two sisters and that judicial dissolution was statutorily authorized.

We believe the circuit court incorrectly concluded that compulsory judicial dissolution was permitted under SDCL 47–34A–801(a)(4)(i) and (iii). As to the latter basis, we believe the court's findings fail to support the legal conclusion that it is no longer practicable for Dragpipe to continue to operate in accordance with its operating agreement. The agreement states Dragpipe's purpose as "owning, purchasing, taking, leasing, or otherwise holding or acquiring real property" and to "hold, own, operate, control, maintain, manage and develop such property and interests in any manner that may be necessary, useful or advantageous." Here, Dragpipe did "purchase real property" that it now "holds, owns, operates, maintains [and] manages." Continuing to do so is no less practicable now than it has been throughout Dragpipe's history of operation.

The fact that the Appellees believe it to be a prudent time to sell Dragpipe's real property and realize the gain from their investments does not mean Dragpipe is unable to continue to operate in accordance with its stated purposes. Nor do the historic losses or Dragpipe's failure to return income distributions to its members render its operation impracticable. In more recent years, Dragpipe's performance has improved and yielded profitable results, if not large cash returns, for its members. It may well be that the Appellees have grown weary of Dragpipe's lukewarm revenue outcomes over the years, but that does not, itself, mean that Dragpipe is not "carrying on the company's business in conformity with the operating agreement." *See* SDCL 47–34A–801(a)(4)(iii).

A similar analysis applies to the circuit court's determination that "the economic purpose of the LLC is likely to be unreasonably frustrated." *See* SDCL 47–34A–801(a)(4)(i). The court erred in its legal conclusion. In the absence of an order directing judicial dissolution, Dragpipe will continue to operate more or less as it has since its inception. Even if, as the circuit court found, the principal means of making money for Dragpipe's members will ultimately be through the sale of the real property, that does not mean that the members' failure to reach a consensus about a proposed sale is likely to frustrate Dragpipe's economic purpose.

Under the plain and unambiguous terms of the operating agreement, the Appellees can resign and receive the fair market value of their interests. In the event the members do not agree upon the fair market value, the operating agreement states that the value will be determined by an independent appraiser. Yet, the Appellees have not availed themselves of this option. Nor does it appear they have continued in their efforts to sell their interests outright. The other two members do not object to such a sale and, in fact, the prior sale of Weast's interest to Kerwin was successful without the need for judicial intervention or dissolution.

Beyond this, there is no "impenetrable deadlock" and no indication that a member or member-faction is benefitting from the disagreement regarding the proposed sale of Dragpipe's real estate to the prejudice of the other members. *See Kirksey*, 754 N.W.2d at 831. The circuit court's determination that the members were "at a standstill" is attached to the implicit legal conclusion that Dragpipe *must* sell its real estate now. However, we do not perceive the same degree of urgency when we interpret the text of Dragpipe's operating agreement and consider the legal standards for judicial dissolution.

We hold that the circuit court erred in its interpretation of the operating agreement and in its application of SDCL 47–34A–801(a)(4)(i) and (iii). The economic purpose is not likely to be unreasonably frustrated by Dragpipe's continued operation, and it is operating within the purposes stated in the operating agreement. The members are not effectively deadlocked and have multiple options for resolving their disagreement about the sale of Dragpipe's real estate. Under the circumstances, we conclude that the "drastic remedy" of judicial dissolution is not supported and that the circuit court's judgment of dissolution must be reversed.

The case below provides another example relational dysfunction as the basis of dissolution on the ground of "not reasonably practicable to carry on the business." In reading this case, consider these questions: (1) What is the standard for determining reasonable practicability? (2) How does the charter agreement affect the judicial determination of reasonable practicability? (3) If there was a contractual exit mechanism and the principle of "freedom of contract" governs, why did the court apply the statutory provision for judicial dissolution anyway?

HALEY V. TALCOTT

864 A.2d 86 (Del. Ch. 2004)

STRINE, VICE CHANCELLOR.

Plaintiff Matthew Haley moved for summary judgment of his claim seeking dissolution of Matt and Greg Real Estate, LLC ("the LLC"). Haley and defendant Gregory Talcott are the only members of the LLC, each owning a 50% interest in the LLC. Haley brings this action in reliance upon Delaware Limited Liability Company Act § 18–802 which permits this court to "decree dissolution whenever it is not reasonably practicable to carry on the business in conformity with a limited liability company agreement." The question is whether dissolution should be granted, as Haley requests, or whether, as Talcott contends, Haley is limited to the contractually-provided exit mechanism in the LLC Agreement.

Haley and Talcott have suffered, to put it mildly, a falling out. There is no rational doubt that they cannot continue to do business as 50% members of an LLC. But the path to separating their interests is complicated by a second company, Delaware Seafood, also known as the Redfin Seafood Grill ("Redfin Grill"), a restaurant that, at the risk of slightly oversimplifying, was owned by Talcott and, before the falling out, operated by Haley under an employment contract that gave him a 50% share in the profits. The LLC owns the land that the Redfin Grill occupies under an expired lease. The resolution of the current case and the ultimate fate of the LLC therefore critically affect the continued existence of a second business that one party owns and that the other bitterly contends, in other litigation pending before this court, wrongly terminated him.

Haley and Talcott have known each other since the 1980s. In 2001, Haley found the location for what would become the Redfin Grill. Talcott contributed substantial start-up money and Haley managed the Redfin Grill without drawing a salary for the first year.

The structure of the agreements between the parties forming the Redfin Grill is complex and the subject of additional litigation before this court. For reasons that are not relevant, Haley and Talcott chose to create and operate the Redfin Grill as an entity solely owned by Talcott, with Haley's rights and obligations being defined by a series of contracts. Those agreements, included an Employment Agreement, a Retention Bonus Agreement, and a Side Letter Agreement (together, the "Employment Contract"), as well as an Agreement regarding an option to purchase real estate (the "Real Estate Agreement").

The Employment Contract, although structured as an agreement between an employer and an employee, makes clear that the parties were operating the business as a joint venture. The Employment Contract specified that Haley reported to Talcott and that Talcott had the right to reevaluate and revise Haley's decisions, but indicated that "such action is not anticipated." It also provided that Haley's "bonus" would be one half of the net profits of the Redfin Grill, after the initial loan from Talcott was repaid. Moreover, Talcott would materially breach the Employment Contract, and Haley could end his employment for cause, if Talcott amended Haley's duties such that his position as "Operations Director" became one of "less dignity, responsibility, importance or scope." The Employment Contract further clarified Haley's importance to the enterprise by awarding him one half of any proceeds from any sale of the Redfin Grill. Finally, the Employment Contract limited Talcott's ability to remove Haley from his active role:

> Notwithstanding the language in the Employment Agreement relating to termination, individually, I [Talcott] will assure you that the Employment Agreement will not be terminable under any circumstances unless an event occurs that would entitle you payment of a Retention Bonus as set forth in the Retention Bonus Agreement that is part of this transaction. Such an event would be a "Business Sale."

The Employment Contract therefore establishes a relationship more similar to a partnership than a typical employer/employee relationship.

The equivalent nature of the parties' contributions is confirmed by the Real Estate Agreement. In that agreement, Talcott granted Haley the right to participate in an option to purchase the property where the Redfin Grill was situated which is located at 1111 Highway One in Bethany Beach, Delaware (the "Property"). Talcott had obtained the option personally when the Redfin Grill first leased the Property from the then-owner. Talcott provided this valuable right to participate for the nominal price of $10. The agreement provided that if the option were exercised, Haley would shoulder 50% of the burden of the purchase, and would be either a 50% owner of the land or a 50% owner of the entity formed to hold the land.

From late 2001 into 2003, under Haley's supervision, the Redfin Grill grew into a successful business. By the second year of its existence, the start-up money had been repaid to Talcott with interest, both parties were drawing salaries (Talcott's substantially smaller since he was not participating in day-to-day management), and the parties each received approximately $150,000 in profit sharing.

In 2003, the parties formed Matt & Greg Real Estate, LLC to take advantage of the option to purchase the Property that was the subject of the Real Estate Agreement. The option price was $720,000 and the new LLC took out a mortgage from County Bank in Rehoboth Beach, Delaware, for that amount, exercised the option, and obtained the deed to the Property. Importantly, both Haley and Talcott, individually, signed personal guaranties for the entire amount of the mortgage in order to secure the loan. The Redfin Grill continued to operate at the site, paying the LLC $6,000 per month in rent, a payment sufficient to cover the LLC's monthly obligation under the mortgage. By mid-2003, the parties appeared poised to reap the fruits of their labors; unfortunately, at that point their personal relationship began to deteriorate.

Haley, having managed the restaurant from the time it opened in May 2001, and having formalized his management position in the Employment Contract, apparently believed that the relationship would be reformulated to provide him a direct stock ownership interest in the Redfin Grill at some point. The reasons underlying that belief are not important here, but in late October they caused a rift to develop between the parties. On or about October 27, 2003, the conflict that had been brewing between the parties led to some kind of confrontation. As a result, Talcott sent a letter of understanding to Haley, purporting to accept his resignation and forbidding him to enter the premises of the Redfin Grill.

Haley responded with two separate letters from his counsel to Talcott. In the first, Haley asserts that he did not resign, and that he regarded Talcott's letter as terminating him without cause in breach of the Employment Contract. Haley goes on to express his intent to pursue legal remedies, an intent that he acted upon in the related case in this court.

In his second letter, Haley purported to take several positions expressly as a 50% member in the LLC including: (1) rejecting the new lease proposed by Talcott for the Redfin Grill; (2) voting to revoke any consent to possession by the Redfin Grill and terminating any lease by which the Redfin Grill asserts the right to possession; and (3) voting that the Property be put up for sale on the open market.

Of course, as a 50% member, Haley could not force the LLC to take action on these proposals because Talcott opposed them. The pre-existing status quo continued by virtue of the stalemate—a result that Talcott favored. The Redfin Grill's lease has expired and the Redfin Grill continues to pay $6,000 per month to the LLC in a month-to-month arrangement. The $6,000 rent exceeds the LLC's required mortgage payment by $800 per month, so the situation remains stable. With only a 50% ownership interest, Haley cannot force the termination of the Redfin Grill's lease and evict the Redfin Grill as a tenant; neither can he force the sale of the Property, land that was appraised as of June 14, 2004 at $1.8 million. In short, absent intervention by this court, Haley is stuck, unless he chooses to avail himself of the exit mechanism provided in the LLC Agreement.

That exit mechanism, like judicial dissolution, would provide Haley with his share of the fair market value of the LLC, including the Property. Section 18 of the LLC Agreement provides that upon written notice of election to "quit" the company, the remaining member may elect to purchase the departing member's interest for fair market value. If the remaining member elects to purchase the departing member's interest, the parties may agree on fair value, or have the fair value determined by three arbitrators, one chosen by each member and a third chosen by the first two arbitrators. Once a fair price is determined, it may be paid in cash, or over a term if secured by: (1) a note signed by the company and personally by the remaining member; (2) a security agreement; and (3) a recorded UCC lien. Only if the remaining member fails to elect to purchase the departing member's interest is the company to be liquidated.

The exit provision does not expressly provide a release from the personal guaranties that both Haley and Talcott signed to secure the mortgage on the Property. Nor does the exit provision state that any member dissatisfied with the status quo must break an impasse by exit rather than a suit for dissolution.

Rather than use the exit mechanism, Haley sought: (1) dissolution of the LLC; and (2) relief in an employment litigation filed against Talcott and Redfin Grill, a case also pending in this court. Haley does not view himself as being obligated by the LLC Agreement to be the one who exits; moreover, he would not release him from the guaranty.

Haley has expressed his desire to buy Talcott out of both the LLC and the Redfin Grill itself if given the opportunity. Talcott, by urging the exit remedy provided in the LLC Agreement, has expressed his desire to buy Haley out of the LLC and has no interest in selling the Redfin Grill. Haley continues to refuse to use the exit mechanism.

Pragmatically, the current impasse arises because we have two willing buyers and no willing sellers. Haley alleges that, given this practical dilemma, and his evident inability to effect his desired direction for the LLC, judicial dissolution is his only practicable remedy.

Haley alleges that pursuant to 6 Del. C. § 18–802 the court should exercise its discretion and dissolve the LLC because it is not reasonably practicable for it to continue the business of the company in conformity with the LLC Agreement. Section 18–802 provides in its entirety:

> On application by or for a member or manager the Court of Chancery may decree dissolution of a limited liability company whenever it is not reasonably practicable to carry on the business in conformity with a limited liability company agreement.

My decision turns on two legal issues: (1) if the doctrine of corporate deadlock is an appropriate analogy for the analysis of a § 18–802 claim on these facts; and (2) if so, and if action to break the stalemate is necessary to permit the LLC to function, whether, because of the contract-law foundations of the Delaware LLC Act, Haley should be relegated to the contractual exit mechanism provided in the LLC Agreement.

Case Law under § 273 of the Delaware General Corporate Law ("DGCL") Provides an Appropriate Framework for Analysis

Section 18–802 is a relatively recent addition to our law, and, as a result, there have been few decisions interpreting it. Nevertheless, § 18–802 has the obvious purpose of providing an avenue of relief when an LLC cannot continue to function in accordance with its chartering agreement. Thus § 18–802 plays a role for LLCs similar to the role that DGCL § 273 plays for joint venture corporations with only two stockholders. When a limited liability agreement provides for the company to be governed by its members, when there are only two members, and when those members are at permanent odds, § 273 provides relevant insight into what should happen. To wit, Section 273(a) provides, in relevant part, that:

> If the stockholders, having only 2 stockholders each of whom own 50% of the stock therein, shall be engaged in a joint venture and if such stockholders shall be unable to agree upon the desirability of discontinuing such joint venture and disposing of the assets used in such venture, either stock holder may file with the Court of Chancery a petition stating that it desires to discontinue such joint venture and to dispose of the assets used in such venture in accordance with a plan to be agreed on by both stockholders or that, if no such plan shall be agreed upon by both stockholders, the corporation be dissolved.

Section 273 sets forth three pre-requisites for a judicial order of dissolution: (1) the corporation must have two 50% stockholders, (2) those stockholders must be engaged in a joint venture, and (3) they must be unable to agree upon whether to discontinue the business or how to dispose of its assets. Here, each of the three provisions is indisputably met.

First, there is no dispute that the parties are 50% members of the LLC.

Second, there is no rational doubt that the parties intended to be and are engaged in a joint venture.

Haley never agreed to be a passive investor in the LLC who would be subject to Talcott's unilateral dominion. Instead, the LLC agreement provided that: "no member/managers may, *without the agreement of a majority vote of the managers' interest,* act on behalf of the company." Thus, Haley is entitled to a continuing say in the operation of the LLC.

Finally, the evidence clearly supports a finding of deadlock between the parties about the business strategy and future of the LLC.

There is no evidentiary support for Talcott's suggestion that the parties are not at an impasse. The parties have not interacted since their falling out in October 2003. Clearly, Talcott understands that the end of Haley's managerial role from the Redfin Grill profoundly altered their relationship as co-members of the LLC. After all, it has left Haley on the outside, looking in, with no power. Of course, Talcott insists that the LLC can and does continue to function for its intended purpose and in conformity with the agreement, receiving payments from the Redfin Grill and writing checks to meet its obligations under the mortgage on Talcott's authority. But that reality does not mean that the LLC is operating in accordance with the LLC Agreement. Although the LLC is technically functioning at this point, this operation is purely a residual, inertial status quo that just happens to exclusively benefit one of the 50% members, Talcott, as illustrated by the hands-tied continuation of the expired lease with the Redfin Grill. With strident disagreement between the parties regarding the appropriate deployment of the asset of the LLC, and open hostility as evidenced by the related suit in this matter, it is not credible that the LLC could, if necessary, take any important action that required a vote of the members. Abundant, uncontradicted documents in the record demonstrate the inability of the parties to function together.

For all these reasons, if the LLC were a corporation, there would be no question that Haley's request to dissolve the entity would be granted. But this case regards an LLC and more importantly, an LLC with a detailed exit provision. That distinguishing factor is considered next.

Even Given the Contractual Emphasis of the Delaware LLC Act, the Exit Remedy Provided in the LLC Agreement Is an Insufficient Alternative to Dissolution

The Delaware LLC Act is grounded on principles of freedom of contract. For that reason, the presence of a reasonable exit mechanism bears on the propriety of ordering dissolution under 6 Del. C. § 18–802. When the agreement provides a fair opportunity for the dissenting member who disfavors the inertial status quo to exit and receive the fair market value of her interest, it is at least arguable that the company may still proceed to operate practicably under its contractual charter because the charter itself provides an equitable way to break the impasse.

Here, that reasoning might be thought apt because Haley has already "voted" as an LLC member to sell the LLC's only asset, the Property, presumably because he knew he could not secure sole control of both the LLC and the Redfin Grill. Given that reality, so long as Haley can actually extract himself fairly, it arguably makes sense for this court to stay its hand in an LLC case and allow the contract itself to solve the problem.

Haley and Talcott created the LLC together and while the detailed exit provision provided in the formative LLC Agreement allows either party to leave voluntarily, it provides no insight on who should retain the LLC if both parties would prefer to buy the other out, and neither party desires to leave. In and of itself, however, this lack of priority might not be found sufficient to require dissolution, because of a case-specific fact; namely, that Haley has proposed—as a member of the LLC—that the LLC's sole asset be sold. But forcing Haley to exercise the contractual exit mechanism would not permit the LLC to proceed in a practicable way that accords with the LLC Agreement, but would instead permit Talcott to penalize Haley without express contractual authorization.

Why? Because the parties agree that exit mechanism in the LLC Agreement would not relieve Haley of his obligation under the personal guaranty that he signed to secure the mortgage from County Bank. If Haley is forced to use the exit mechanism, Talcott and he both believe that Haley would still be left holding the bag on the guaranty. It is therefore not equitable to force Haley to use the exit mechanism in this circumstance. While the exit mechanism may be workable in a friendly departure when both parties cooperate to reach an adequate alternative agreement with the bank, the bank cannot be compelled to accept the removal of Haley as a personal guarantor. The exit mechanism fails as an adequate remedy for Haley because it does not equitably effect the separation of the parties. It would leave Haley with no upside potential, and no protection over the considerable downside risk that he would have to make good on any future default by the LLC (over whose operations he would have no control) to its mortgage lender. Thus here, the parties do not, in fact, "have at their disposal a far less drastic means to resolve their personal disagreement."

I find that it is not reasonably practicable for the LLC to continue to carry on business in conformity with the LLC Agreement. The parties shall submit a plan for the dissolution of the LLC. The plan shall include a procedure to sell the Property owned by the LLC within a commercially reasonable time frame. Either party may, of course, bid on the Property.

The cases below discuss the issue of whether assignees or other non-members have standing to force a dissolution and wind up of the LLC. The uniform statutes for LLCs and LPs permit only members and partners to seek judicial dissolution.[2] ULPA (2001) § 801(a)(6) ("on application by a partner"); RULLCA § 701(a)(4) ("on application by a member"). In reading these cases, consider these questions: (1) What are the implications of permitting assignees to force a dissolution and wind up of an LLC? (2) In light of cases like *Bauer v. Blomfield Co./Holden Joint Venture*, 849 P.2d

---

[2] Unlike ULPA (2001) and RULLCA, RUPA permits a transferee to petition the court "on the ground that it is equitable to wind up the partnership business." RUPA § 801(5).

1365 (Alaska 1993), should assignees be able to force a dissolution and wind up? (3) In Delaware, what is the boundary between a statutory provision for judicial dissolution and a court's inherent power to provide equitable relief? (4) In Delaware, under what circumstances can a non-member petition for judicial dissolution?

STYSLINGER V. BREWSTER PARK, LLC

138 A.3d 257 (Conn. 2016)

VERTEFEUILLE, J.

We must determine whether the assignee of a membership interest in a Connecticut LLC has standing to seek a court order forcing the winding up of the affairs of an LLC in the absence of the LLC's dissolution. We conclude that the assignee does not have standing to do so.

The defendant, Brewster Park, LLC (Brewster Park), is an LLC that owns, maintains, and leases residential housing units in Bridgeport and Trumbull. It has two members: the defendant Michael Weinshel and Joyce Styslinger, a nonparty to this action who is the former spouse of the plaintiff, William Styslinger. As part of a marriage dissolution settlement agreement, Joyce Styslinger assigned her membership interest in Brewster Park to the plaintiff. The parties agree that, under General Statutes §§ 34–170 and 34–172,* the plaintiff, as assignee, has the right to receive distributions resulting from Joyce Styslinger's membership interest in Brewster Park, while Joyce Styslinger remains a member of Brewster Park unless and until the plaintiff is admitted to membership by Weinshel, the other member of Brewster Park. *See* General Statutes §§ 34–172 and 34–179. The plaintiff has requested membership status, but has not been granted it by Weinshel. Brewster Park also has not made any distributions to the plaintiff, despite the plaintiff's demand.

The plaintiff filed the present action against Brewster Park and Weinshel claiming that Weinshel has breached his fiduciary duties to Brewster Park and the plaintiff by refusing to make distributions to the plaintiff while taking distributions for himself, and by refusing to allow the plaintiff to inspect Brewster Park's books and records. The plaintiff sought the following forms of relief: (1) an order dissolving Brewster Park; (2) the appointment of a receiver to wind up its affairs and distribute its assets; and (3) "such other and further relief as in law or equity may appertain."

The trial court agreed with the defendants that the plaintiff did not have standing to seek a dissolution and wind up of Brewster Park's affairs. We affirm the trial court's judgment.

* Author's note: The statute has subsequently been repealed. The current statute is found in Connecticut Uniform Limited Liability Company Act, General Statutes, Chapter 613A, § 34–243 et seq. The new statutory provision, General Statutes § 34–267(a), does not change the analysis in this opinion.

The question of whether the plaintiff, as assignee of a membership interest in an LLC, has standing to bring his claims under the act, presents an issue of statutory construction.

An LLC is a distinct type of business entity that allows its owners to take advantage of the pass-through tax treatment afforded to partnerships while also providing them with limited liability protections common to corporations. The act establishes the right to form an LLC and all of the rights and duties of the LLC, as well as all of the rights and duties of members and assignees. It permits the members to supplement these statutory provisions by adopting an operating agreement to govern the LLC's affairs. It is undisputed in the present case, however, that Brewster Park does not have an operating agreement.

The provisions of the act relating to winding up an LLC's affairs inextricably link the winding up process to a dissolution, and therefore must be read together with the statutes governing the dissolution of an LLC. Reading the statutes together, the act creates a clear progression from dissolution to winding up the affairs, demonstrating that a winding up is not an independent event, but is an integral part of the dissolution process. Once an event of dissolution occurs, the LLC winds up its affairs, distributes its assets, and then terminates its business operations.

The act provides only a single mechanism for triggering a winding up of an LLC's affairs: an event of dissolution. Section 34–206 provides in relevant part that "a limited liability *company is dissolved and its affairs shall be wound up* upon the happening" of one of three events: (1) any event of dissolution specified in the LLC's articles of organization or operating agreement; (2) a vote to dissolve by the majority of the LLC's members; or (3) the entry of a decree of judicial dissolution under General Statutes § 34–207. Under § 34–207, only a member or someone on the member's behalf may apply for a decree of dissolution, and a decree may enter only if the court determines that "it is not reasonably practicable to carry on the business in conformity with the articles of organization or operating agreement."[3] General Statutes § 34–207. There are no other mechanisms in the act for triggering a winding up of the affairs.

The provisions of the act governing the winding up process presuppose that the LLC has already dissolved prior to winding up its affairs.

None of the events of dissolution specified in § 34–206 has occurred and the plaintiff therefore cannot trigger a winding up of Brewster Park's affairs. First, the plaintiff has not alleged that Brewster Park's articles of organization have triggered a dissolution and it has no operating

[3] By contrast, our Uniform Partnership Act, General Statutes § 34–300 et seq., expressly permits transferees of a partnership interest to ask a court to dissolve and wind up the affairs of a partnership. See, e.g., General Statutes §§ 34–348(b) and 34–372(6). We find this difference significant and strongly suggestive of the fact that the legislature did not intend to provide an assignee of a membership interest in an LLC with the right to wind up the affairs of the LLC.

agreement. Second, the plaintiff has not alleged that its members voted to dissolve. Third, because the plaintiff is not a member of Brewster Park, he cannot pursue a judicial dissolution under § 34–207. Unless the plaintiff is admitted to membership, Joyce Styslinger continues to hold the sole power to exercise the rights accompanying her membership interest; and she has not sought a judicial dissolution of Brewster Park in this action. Because no event of dissolution has occurred, and the plaintiff cannot force a judicial dissolution under § 34–207 as an assignee, the act does not grant the plaintiff standing to seek a winding up of Brewster Park's affairs.

The plaintiff argues that his right to force a winding up of Brewster Park's affairs is found in § 34–208(a). We disagree. That subsection pertains only to who may carry out the winding up process once it has been triggered by dissolution; it does not provide authority for an assignee to trigger a winding up in the first place. Section 34–208(a)(1) provides in relevant part that, by default, the winding up may be carried out "by the members or managers who have authority to manage the limited liability company prior to dissolution." Alternatively, "if one or more of the members or managers of the limited liability company have engaged in wrongful conduct, or upon other cause shown," the statute permits any member or an assignee to apply to the Superior Court to ask the court to carry out the winding up process in place of the members and managers. General Statutes § 34–208(a)(2). Under § 34–208(a), if an LLC has dissolved, but the members or managers had engaged in wrongful conduct or for other cause shown, an assignee can apply to have the court perform the winding up process instead of the members or managers. Nothing in § 34–208, however, permits an assignee to apply to force the commencement of a winding up process absent a dissolution under § 34–206.

The plaintiff's interpretation of § 34–208 allowing an assignee to force a winding up of affairs without a dissolution of the LLC would undermine the statutory scheme for LLCs, thus leading to absurd results. Under the act, an assignee is a passive recipient of the economic benefit of a membership interest and is barred by the act from participating in the management of the LLC's business or exercising any right of membership unless and until the assignee is admitted as a member. The act expressly provides that "an assignment of a limited liability company membership interest does not dissolve the limited liability company or entitle the assignee to participate in the management and affairs of the limited liability company or to become or exercise any rights of a member." Instead, the rights and duties of membership remain vested in the assignor until the assignee is admitted to membership. Recognizing that assignees have no role to play in managing the LLC's affairs, the act shields them from any liabilities that a member might have, including, for example, for capital contributions. Instead, the assignor member continues to hold the obligations of membership, including for capital contributions, and continues to owe a duty of good faith to the LLC.

We therefore conclude that the act does not provide an assignee such as the plaintiff with standing to seek the winding up of the affairs of an LLC in the absence of a dissolution of that LLC.[4] The trial court properly dismissed the plaintiff's complaint.

NOTES

1. In *Benjamin v. Bierman*, 943 N.W.2d 283 (Neb. 2020), the Nebraska statute, like the uniform statutes, provided:

> A limited liability company is dissolved, and its activities must be wound up, upon the occurrence of any of the following:
>
> (4) on application by a member, the entry by the district court of an order dissolving the company on the grounds that: it is not reasonably practicable to carry on the company's activities in conformity with the certificate of organization and the operating agreement; or
>
> (5) on application by a member, the entry by the district court of an order dissolving the company on the grounds that the managers or those members in control of the company: have acted or are acting in a manner that is oppressive and was, is, or will be directly harmful to the applicant.

Neb. Rev. Stat. § 21–147(a)(4)–(5). A personal representative of a deceased member brought a judicial action for dissolution. The Nebraska Supreme Court held that the representative lacked standing to seek dissolution.

IN RE CARLISLE ETCETERA LLC

114 A.3d 592 (Del. Ch. 2015)

LASTER, VICE CHANCELLOR.

In 2012, Well Union Capital Limited ("WU Parent") and Tom James Company ("James") formed Carlisle Etcetera LLC ("Carlisle" or the "Company"). They executed a simple form of operating agreement (the

---

[4] The plaintiff has also claimed that he is classically aggrieved under the common law or principles of equity, but we disagree. The act permits "principles of law and equity [to] supplement" the act only to the extent that they are not "displaced" by the act's provisions. General Statutes § 34–242(b). Thus, even if we assume, for the sake of argument, that the common law or equitable principles would otherwise grant an assignee standing to seek a winding up of an LLC's affairs, we nevertheless conclude that these principles are displaced by the provisions of the act discussed previously herein that expressly limit an assignee's role and prevent an assignee from forcing the dissolution or winding up of the LLC. In support of this claim, the plaintiff cites the Delaware Chancery Court decision in *In re Carlisle Etcetera LLC,* 114 A.3d 592 (Del. Ch. 2015), but we find that decision inapposite because Delaware law concerning assignments of membership interests in an LLC differs markedly from that in Connecticut. Under Delaware law, an assignment leaves both the member and the assignee without the power to assert the rights of membership at issue unless and until the assignee is admitted to membership. The court in *In re Carlisle Etcetera LLC* resolved this lacuna by granting equitable standing to the assignee. Connecticut law, by contrast, does not result in a similar void because the assignor continues to hold the exclusive power to exercise the rights of membership until the assignee becomes a member. General Statutes §§ 34–170(a)(4) and 34–172(d).

"Initial LLC Agreement") in which they committed to work promptly on a more detailed operating agreement to replace the original one.

After the Company was formed, WU Parent transferred its member interest to a wholly owned subsidiary called Well Union U.S. Holdings, Inc. ("WU Sub"). James knew about the transfer, did not object, and treated WU Sub as a member from that point on. For purposes of the Delaware Limited Liability Company Act (the "LLC Act"), however, the transfer rendered WU Sub an assignee, rather than a member.

WU Parent and James never reached agreement on a replacement operating agreement. Other disputes arose, and the relationship deteriorated. Deadlock prevailed at the manager level, where the Initial LLC Agreement called for a board of directors (the "Board") to serve as the singular manager of the Company. The Board has four members, two appointed by WU Parent and two by James. They split 2–2 on key issues.

Both sides eventually recognized that they could not manage the Company jointly and that one side needed to buy out the other. They could not agree on a buyout procedure or a price.

During the venture's halcyon days, the Board appointed a James executive as the Company's CEO. Through the CEO, James controls the Company's day-to-day operations. With the Board deadlocked, the CEO has been operating free of any oversight. Given its advantaged position, James does not see the deadlock as a problem and feels no urgency to alleviate it. During negotiations over the buyout, James sought to use its privileged position to extract concessions from WU Sub.

WU Sub turned to this court for assistance. It filed this action, in which it petitioned to dissolve the Company. James moved to dismiss on the grounds that WU Sub is an assignee, not a member, and that an assignee lacks standing to petition for statutory dissolution under Section 18–802 of the LLC Act. 6 *Del. C.* § 18–802. WU Parent joined as a co-petitioner.

James contends that WU Parent and WU Sub lack standing to seek dissolution because (i) Section 18–802 of the LLC Act only permits members and managers to seek dissolution, (ii) neither WU Parent nor WU Sub is a member or manager, and (iii) Section 18–802 is the exclusive extra-contractual method of dissolving an LLC. In my view, James is right on the first two points but wrong on the third.

Section 18–802 of the LLC Act addresses dissolution. It states that "on application by or for a member or manager the Court of Chancery may decree dissolution of a limited liability company whenever it is not reasonably practicable to carry on the business in conformity with a limited liability company agreement." By its terms, this language limits the right to seek statutory dissolution under Section 18–802 to members and managers of an LLC. As to this issue, James is correct.

To petition for statutory dissolution under Section 18–802, WU Parent and WU Sub must be members or managers of the Company. Neither claims to be a manager. The Initial LLC Agreement makes clear that the Board, acting collectively, is the manager of the Company. [After analysis of the LLC statute and the operating agreement, the court found that WU Parent and WU Sub are not now members*].

Equitable Standing To Seek Dissolution

James errs in contending that Section 18–802 is the exclusive extra-contractual means of obtaining dissolution of an LLC. Under the facts of this case, WU Sub has standing to seek dissolution in equity.

"This Court, as a court of equity, has the power to order the dissolution of a solvent company and appoint a receiver to administer the winding up of those assets." Justice Story described the "power to dissolve the partnership during the term for which it is stipulated" as one of the "strongest cases to illustrate the beneficial operation of the jurisdiction" of a court of equity. 2 Joseph Story, *Commentaries on Equity Jurisprudence* § 915 (14th ed. 1918). The implementation of a dissolution decree would require the appointment of a receiver, which is likewise an equitable remedy that forms part of this court's equitable powers. Courts of equity have long had the power to appoint receivers in cases "where the partners themselves are wholly unable to agree as to the management of the property and the settlement of the partnership affairs." Justice Story viewed the appointment of a receiver favorably in suits for dissolution when "one [partner] has wrongfully excluded the other from participation" in the management of the business.

For Section 18–802 to provide the exclusive method of dissolving an LLC, it would have to divest this court of a significant aspect of its traditional equitable jurisdiction. Section 18–802 does not state that it establishes an exclusive means to obtain dissolution, nor does it contain language overriding this court's equitable authority. To the contrary, the LLC Act elsewhere recognizes that equity backstops the LLC structure by

---

* Author's note: With respect to WU Parent, the court reasoned: "WU Parent lost its status as a member of the Company when it assigned all of its interest in the Company to WU Sub. Under Section 702(b)(3) of the LLC Act, 'unless otherwise provided in a limited liability company agreement: . . . member ceases to be a member and to have the power to exercise any rights or powers of a member upon assignment of all of the member's limited liability company interest.' " With respect to WU Sub, when WU Parent assigned all of its interest, WU Sub became an assignee under the statute. The court noted: "The Initial LLC Agreement was silent on the admission of an assignee as a member. Under Section 18–704(a), WU Sub's only route to a 'permitted admission' was 'upon the affirmative vote or written consent of all of the members of the limited liability company.' If that happened, then the 'permitted admission' would become effective once WU Sub's admission was 'reflected in the records of the limited liability company.' " WU Sub did not meet the statutory requirement for admission of an assignee as a member. Thus, the court concluded: "In this case, the Company only had two members. Once WU Parent transferred its member interest and WU Sub became an assignee, James was the sole remaining member and controlled the vote on WU Sub's admission."

providing generally that "the rules of law and equity" shall govern in "any case not provided for in this chapter."

If Section 18–802 did purport to establish an exclusive means to obtain dissolution and override a significant portion of this court's traditional equitable jurisdiction, then the validity of that aspect of the provision would raise serious constitutional questions. Article IV, Section 10 of the Delaware Constitution provides that this court "shall have all the jurisdiction and powers vested by the laws of this State in the Court of Chancery." The Delaware Supreme Court has held that this provision vested in the Court of Chancery "all the general equity jurisdiction of the High Court of Chancery of Great Britain as it existed prior to the separation of the colonies," except "where a sufficient remedy exists at law." In light of this provision, the high court held that the General Assembly cannot enact legislation that reduces this court's jurisdiction below the constitutionally established minimum, unless there is an adequate remedy at law. As the Delaware Supreme Court explained, Article IV, Section 10

> intended to establish for the benefit of the people of the state a tribunal to administer the remedies and principles of equity. They secured them for the relief of the people. This conclusion is in complete harmony with the underlying theory of written constitutions. Its result is to establish by the Judiciary Article of the Constitution the irreducible minimum of the judiciary. It secures for the protection of the people an adequate judicial system and removes it from the vagaries of legislative whim.

Although this court's equitable jurisdiction is measured by the "the general equity jurisdiction of the High Court of Chancery of Great Britain as it existed prior to the separation of the colonies," the Delaware Supreme Court has recognized that the scope of that jurisdiction is not limited by the extent of British scientific, technological, and legal knowledge at the time of the handover. "Historically, equity jurisdiction has taken its shape and its substance from the perceived inadequacies of the common law and the changing demands of a developing nation." *Schoon v. Smith*, 953 A.2d 196, 204 (Del. 2008). "It cannot be said too forcefully that the general powers of the Court of Chancery refer to that *complete system* of equity as administered by the High Court of Chancery of Great Britain." It is the "complete system" of equity that this court inherited and administers, not the temporally specific subject matter of eighteenth century cases.

The Delaware Supreme Court in *Schoon* quoted from a wide range of sources that demonstrate the continuing and evolving role of equity.

> The Chancellor always has had, and always must have, a certain power and freedom of action, not possessed by the courts of law, of adapting the doctrines which he administers. He can extend those doctrines to new relations, and shape his remedies to new circumstances, if the relations and circumstances come within the

> principles of equity, where a court of law in analogous cases would be powerless to give any relief.

The *Schoon* court similarly quoted from Justice Story, who explained that equity "has an expansive power, to meet new exigencies; and the sole question, applicable to the point of jurisdiction, must from time to time be whether such rights and wrongs do exist, and whether the remedies [therefore] in other courts, and especially in the courts of common law, are full, and adequate to redress." The high court [stated] that "the chancellors could adapt their system to meet changing needs without resorting to the fiction that they were merely interpreting and applying former rules, but the tendency to follow the path laid out by former chancellors was strong."

Given the weight of these authorities, I cannot accept the contention that because the nascent practice of entity law as it existed at the time of the colonies' separation had not yet envisioned LLCs, they fall outside the domain of equity. Decisions addressing the dissolution of LLCs have recognized the continuing role of equity. Most notably, in *Haley v. Talcott*, 864 A.2d 86 (Del. Ch. 2004), this court reviewed a contractual exit mechanism in a two-member operating agreement and determined that it did not provide the exiting member with "an adequate remedy." Chief Justice Strine, writing as a Vice Chancellor, explained that the existence of an exit mechanism was not sufficient; it had to be a "reasonable exit mechanism" that provided "a fair opportunity for the dissenting member who disfavors the inertial status quo to exit." On the facts of the case, the Chief Justice found that it was "not equitable to force [the locked-out member] to use the exit mechanism" and ordered dissolution.

Of particular relevance to dissolution, the purely contractarian view discounts core attributes of the LLC that only the sovereign can authorize, such as its separate legal existence, potentially perpetual life, and limited liability for its members. To my mind, when a sovereign makes available an entity with attributes that contracting parties cannot grant themselves by agreement, the entity is not purely contractual. Because the entity has taken advantage of benefits that the sovereign has provided, the sovereign retains an interest in that entity. That interest in turn calls for preserving the ability of the sovereign's courts to oversee and, if necessary, dissolve the entity. Put more directly, an LLC agreement is not an exclusively private contract among its members precisely because the LLC has powers that only the State of Delaware can confer. Those powers affect the rights of third parties, who at a minimum must take into account the LLC's separate legal existence and its members' limited liability shield. Just as LLCs are not purely private entities, dissolution is not a purely private affair. It involves third party claims, which have priority in the dissolution process. Because an LLC takes advantage of benefits the State of Delaware provides, and because dissolution is not an exclusively private matter, the

State of Delaware retains an interest in having the Court of Chancery available, when equity demands, to hear a petition to dissolve an LLC.

This case presents the type of situation where equity should intervene. If the opportunities for dissolution are limited to Section 18–802 and the specific terms of the Initial LLC Agreement, then dissolution is not an option. WU Parent and WU Sub lack standing to seek it, and James does not want it. The Company will continue, with [a party] locked-in as a silent and powerless passive investor.

That situation is contrary to the bargain the parties struck. WU Parent and James formed the Company as equal business partners. They contributed equal amounts of capital and brought comparable expertise, with one side acting as a major supplier and the other as a day-to-day manager. They agreed to start with a basic operating agreement in which they committed to negotiate a more detailed replacement agreement. As reflected by the Proposed LLC Agreement, the terms of that more detailed agreement contemplate that an affiliate transfer from WU Parent to WU Sub would result in the automatic admission of WU Sub as a substitute member. In other words, had the parties finalized the Proposed LLC Agreement, or acted in accordance with their agreement in principle, then WU Sub would be a member and have standing to seek dissolution under Section 18–802. Based on the allegations of the petition, WU Parent engaged in the affiliate transfer with James' knowledge and participation, and James subsequently treated WU Sub as a member.

"Equity always attempts to ascertain, uphold, and enforce rights and duties which spring from the *real* relations of parties." "Equity regards substance rather than form." Equity also "regards that as done which in good conscience ought to be done." The real relationship between the parties is a joint venture in which they are equal participants. Neither party intended to be a "passive investor subject to [the other party's] unilateral dominion." *Haley,* 864 A.2d at 95. In good conscience, WU Sub should be regarded as a member with the power to seek dissolution.

Likewise, the "*real* relations" of the parties point to a scenario warranting dissolution. For a time, both sides recognized the need to go their separate ways. James only changed its mind because of its fortuitous position as the entity's *de facto* manager. But that reality does not make the status quo a satisfactory alternative. "Although the LLC is technically functioning at this point, this operation is purely a residual, inertial status quo that just happens to exclusively benefit one of the 50% members." The Initial LLC Agreement made the Board the singular manager of the Company. Because its four members are deadlocked, the duly authorized manager of the Company cannot exercise its statutory and contractual authority or carry out its obligation to manage and direct the business and affairs of the entity. Brubaker may be managing the Company because of the power vacuum created by the deadlock, but Brubaker is not the Board.

Under the prevailing state of affairs, the Company is operating contrary to the governance structure set forth in its constitutive agreement.

I believe that WU Sub has standing in equity, as an assignee, to seek dissolution of the Company under the facts alleged in the petition.

WU Parent and WU Sub lack standing to seek statutory dissolution under Section 18–802. Nevertheless, because WU Sub has standing to seek dissolution in equity, the motion to dismiss is denied.

2. ADMINISTRATIVE COMPLIANCE

Although the administrative procedures for creating and maintaining a limited liability entity is ministerial as a matter of functional task, they are important nonetheless as a matter of consequence.

The case below provides an example of the consequence of the failure to maintain properly an LLC. In reading this case, consider this question: Why does an administratively dissolved LLC company still retain the right to defend an action?

BEAUDRY V. HARDING

104 A.3d 134 (Maine 2014)

SAUFLEY, C.J.

Paul Beaudry, individually and purportedly on behalf of Northern Maine Transport, LLC (NMT) appeals from a judgment of the Superior Court granting summary judgment to Alan Harding and Hardings Law Offices. The court concluded that Beaudry lacks the legal capacity to bring suit on behalf of an administratively dissolved LLC or derivatively and that Beaudry has no individual claim because he suffered no personal harm. Beaudry argues that Maine's Limited Liability Company Act specifically authorizes administratively dissolved LLCs to prosecute claims and that justice requires us to treat his derivative claim as a direct claim. Because we agree with the Superior Court that Maine law does not permit Beaudry to proceed on behalf of NMT under these circumstances, through a derivative action or individually, we affirm the judgment.

NMT [has] only two members, Paul Beaudry and Tyler Hallett. NMT was administratively dissolved on September 28, 2009.

Beaudry's complaint asserts claims against attorney Alan Harding for professional negligence and breach of fiduciary duty in 2010, when attorney Harding represented NMT and possibly Beaudry in facilitating a settlement between NMT and OneBeacon American Insurance to recover insurance proceeds after business property of NMT was destroyed by fire. Although OneBeacon and NMT eventually settled, Beaudry refused to honor the settlement agreement. In a separate matter, the United States District Court enforced the settlement agreement against Beaudry.

Beaudry filed this action, individually and purportedly on behalf of NMT, alleging that Beaudry would not have settled the OneBeacon litigation had attorney Harding not committed legal malpractice. Harding moved for summary judgment. The Superior Court granted Harding's motion for summary judgment on both counts. Beaudry timely appealed.

We focus on Beaudry's contention that Maine's Limited Liability Company Act specifically authorizes NMT, an administratively dissolved LLC, to prosecute claims to collect NMT's assets.

Administratively dissolved LLCs are those that the Secretary of State dissolves because the LLC fails to follow the procedures imposed by the Act, such as paying mandatory fees and penalties or filing annual reports. Section 1592 is entitled, "Procedure for and effect of administrative dissolution of limited liability company" and provides that "the administrative dissolution of a limited liability company under this section does not impair the right of the limited liability company to *defend* any action, suit, or proceeding in any court of this State." Unlike section 1592 addressing administratively dissolved LLCs, section 1596 [entitled "Effect of dissolution"] provides that the dissolution of an LLC does not "prevent the commencement of a proceeding by or against the limited liability company in its limited liability name."

Reading these sections in relation to the whole statutory scheme, the more specific statute governing the effect of administrative dissolution is controlling. Thus, NMT, as an administratively dissolved LLC, is not authorized to prosecute claims; it may only defend claims. To interpret the Act otherwise would be to render subsections of section 1592 superfluous. If the Legislature intended the effects of dissolution on administratively dissolved LLCs to be identical to the effects of judicially or voluntarily dissolved LLCs, there would be no reason for the Legislature to include the provision that specifically sets forth the effects of administrative dissolution in section 1592.

As a matter of law, Beaudry is barred from bringing suit on behalf of NMT—an administratively dissolved LLC—and the Superior Court did not err in granting summary judgment in Harding's favor.

NOTES

1. In *Genesis Hospice Care, LLC v. Mississippi Division of Medicaid*, 267 So.3d 779 (Miss. 2019), Genesis Hospice Care LLC, a Medicaid provider, appealed from a recoupment action brought by the state's Medicaid agency, for $1,941,285 of payments made to the provider for hospice care that was allegedly not medically necessary. The company was administratively dissolved three years before the company filed its notice of appeal to the

supreme court. The agency argued that the company had no authority to file the notice of appeal because it no longer legally existed.

> Medicaid cites Mississippi Code Section 79–29–831, the statute that spells out the effects of an administrative dissolution. Medicaid selectively hammers on one provision—"A limited liability company that has been administratively dissolved may not maintain any action, suit or proceeding in any court of this state until such limited liability company is reinstated." Medicaid argues this provision precluded Genesis from continuing to pursue its action against Medicaid without first being reinstated.
>
> Genesis has responded by citing another provision of Section 79–29–831—"The administrative dissolution of a limited liability company shall not prevent such limited liability company from *defending* any action, suit or proceeding with any court of this state." Genesis takes the position that, by appealing Medicaid's decision, it is not "maintaining an action" against Medicaid. Rather, Genesis continues to *defend* itself against Medicaid's administrative decision.
>
> We agree with Genesis. While Medicaid tries to characterize this matter as an original action, both the administrative regulation and the statute Medicaid cites clearly refer to Genesis' requests, first, for an administrative hearing and, next, for chancery court review as *appeals*. To follow Medicaid's logic, an administratively dissolved limited liability company loses its right to appeal—even in a proceeding in which the company began in a defensive posture. Since this position contradicts Section 79–29–831(2), which allows Genesis' appeal to proceed, Medicaid's motion to dismiss is denied.

3. WINDING UP

The wind up process is a termination of business and a settling up of all accounts. It requires payment first to the entity's creditors and a final distribution of remaining assets, if any, to the owners. Owners may petition for judicial supervision of the wind up process for "good cause." RULLCA § 702(e)(1); ULPA (2001) § 802(d)(2); RUPA § 802(e)(2).

The wind up process is a marshalling of assets, paying off liabilities, and distributing the remaining assets to owners. The rules for wind up differ depending on whether the firm has limited liability or not.

RUPA § 806. Disposition of Assets in Winding Up; When Contributions Required.

(a) In winding up its business, a partnership shall apply its assets, including the contributions required by this section, to discharge the partnership's obligations to creditors, including partners that are creditors.

(b) After a partnership complies with subsection (a), any surplus must be distributed in the following order, subject to any charging order in effect under Section 504:

(1) to each person owning a transferable interest that reflects contributions made and not previously returned, an amount equal to the value of the unreturned contributions; and

(2) among persons owning transferable interests in proportion to their respective rights to share in distributions immediately before the dissolution of the partnership.

(c) If a partnership's assets are insufficient to satisfy all its obligations under subsection (a), with respect to each unsatisfied obligation incurred when the partnership was not a limited liability partnership, the following rules apply:

(1) Each person that was a partner when the obligation was incurred and that has not been released from the obligation under Section 703(c) and (d) shall contribute to the partnership for the purpose of enabling the partnership to satisfy the obligation. The contribution due from each of those persons is in proportion to the right to receive distributions in the capacity of a partner in effect for each of those persons when the obligation was incurred.

(2) If a person does not contribute the full amount required under paragraph (1) with respect to an unsatisfied obligation of the partnership, the other persons required to contribute by paragraph (1) on account of the obligation shall contribute the additional amount necessary to discharge the obligation. The additional contribution due from each of those other persons is in proportion to the right to receive distributions in the capacity of a partner in effect for each of those other persons when the obligation was incurred.

(3) If a person does not make the additional contribution required by paragraph (2), further additional contributions are determined and due in the same manner as provided in that paragraph.

(d) A person that makes an additional contribution under subsection (c)(2) or (3) may recover from any person whose failure to contribute under subsection (c)(1) or (2) necessitated the additional contribution. A person may not recover under this subsection more than the amount additionally contributed. A person's liability under this subsection may not exceed the amount the person failed to contribute.

(e) If a partnership does not have sufficient surplus to comply with subsection (b)(1), any surplus must be distributed among the owners of transferable interests in proportion to the value of the respective unreturned contributions.

(f) All distributions made under subsections (b) and (c) must be paid in money.

ULPA (2001) § 810. Disposition of Assets in Winding Up; When Contributions Required.

(a) In winding up its activities and affairs, a limited partnership shall apply its assets, including the contributions required by this section, to discharge the partnership's obligations to creditors, including partners that are creditors.

(b) After a limited partnership complies with subsection (a), any surplus must be distributed in the following order, subject to any charging order in effect under Section 703:

(1) to each person owning a transferable interest that reflects contributions made and not previously returned, an amount equal to the value of the unreturned contributions; and

(2) among persons owning transferable interests in proportion to their respective rights to share in distributions immediately before the dissolution of the partnership.

(c) If a limited partnership's assets are insufficient to satisfy all of its obligations under subsection (a), with respect to each unsatisfied obligation incurred when the partnership was not a limited liability limited partnership, the following rules apply:

(1) Each person that was a general partner when the obligation was incurred and that has not been released from the obligation under Section 607 shall contribute to the partnership for the purpose of enabling the partnership to satisfy the obligation. The contribution due from each of those persons is in proportion to the right to receive distributions in the capacity of a general partner in effect for each of those persons when the obligation was incurred.

(2) If a person does not contribute the full amount required under paragraph (1) with respect to an unsatisfied obligation of the partnership, the other persons required to contribute by paragraph (1) on account of the obligation shall contribute the additional amount necessary to discharge the obligation. The additional contribution due from each of those other persons is in proportion to the right to receive distributions in the capacity of a general partner in effect for each of those other persons when the obligation was incurred.

(3) If a person does not make the additional contribution required by paragraph (2), further additional contributions are determined and due in the same manner as provided in that paragraph.

(d) A person that makes an additional contribution under subsection (c)(2) or (3) may recover from any person whose failure to contribute under subsection (c)(1) or (2) necessitated the additional contribution. A person may not recover under this subsection more than the amount additionally contributed. A person's liability under this subsection may not exceed the amount the person failed to contribute.

(e) All distributions made under subsections (b) and (c) must be paid in money.

RULLCA § 707. Disposition of Assets in Winding Up.

(a) In winding up its activities and affairs, a limited liability company shall apply its assets to discharge the company's obligations to creditors, including members that are creditors.

(b) After a limited liability company complies with subsection (a), any surplus must be distributed in the following order, subject to any charging order in effect under Section 503:

(1) to each person owning a transferable interest that reflects contributions made and not previously returned, an amount equal to the value of the unreturned contributions; and

(2) among persons owning transferable interests in proportion to their respective rights to share in distributions immediately before the dissolution of the company.

(c) If a limited liability company does not have sufficient surplus to comply with subsection (b)(1), any surplus must be distributed among the owners of transferable interests in proportion to the value of the respective unreturned contributions.

(d) All distributions made under subsections (b) and (c) must be paid in money.

The case below discusses the procedure for dissolution and wind up of a partnership. In reading this case, consider these questions: (1) What is the risk or potential inequity when a court orders that the partnership property can be purchased by a partner rather than a liquidation in a market sale? (2) What is the potential benefit of a sale to a partner? (3) Can a court fashion a remedy that maximizes the value for the partners and at the same time minimize the risk of inequity to a partner?

GUENTHER V. RYERSON

458 P.3d 184 (Idaho 2020)

BURDICK, CHIEF JUSTICE.

Joseph Guenther and Michelle Ryerson were in a relationship as an unmarried couple. Initially, they were not business partners; however, the couple purchased real property at 8571 N. Lost Sage Lane, and formed a partnership, West Foothills. There was no written partnership agreement. There was no clear agreement between the parties allocating contributions of labor or partnership expenses to either partner. Nor was there an agreement clearly delineating which partner was responsible for which partnership liability. Both parties agreed that the purpose of the partnership was to purchase the property and develop it into a vineyard for profit. Both parties agreed the property would be used to provide housing for [them]. The parties commingled their personal funds with partnership funds, paying for the partnership's liabilities using funds from individual checking accounts, personal credit cards, a joint checking account, and a credit card they held together.

Guenther and Ryerson obtained a $528,600 [mortgage] from Zions Bank. Both parties invested a considerable amount of personal funds and labor into development of the vineyard and construction of the house.

Guenther and Ryerson ended their relationship and decided they could not continue to operate the business as partners. Both parties agreed that the end of their business relationship on March 26, 2017, was a dissociative act requiring dissolution and winding up. [Guenther initiated a legal action, and Ryerson counterclaimed for judicial dissolution.]

The district court granted summary judgment determining the property to be worth $600,000 at the time of dissolution. The court also determined that the partnership had $144,789 of equity in the property.

[A trial took place on matters related to the wind up. The district court found Ryerson and Guenther contributed $101,514 and $330,163 to the partnership, respectively, for a total of $431,677. Thus, it found Ryerson's and Guenther's contributions to be 24 percent and 76 percent. It also found that any post-dissolution increase in equity in the property was 100 percent attributable to Guenther. The court granted Guenther's motion to purchase the property rather than have it be liquidated on the open market.]

The court reasoned that requiring the sale of the property on the open market would cause economic waste of the partnership's assets and unreasonably prolong the winding up process. The order provided that Guenther would be allowed to purchase the Lost Sage Lane property by July 31, 2018, if he refinanced through Zions Bank. If Guenther were unable or unwilling to purchase the property from the partnership, Ryerson would then have the opportunity to purchase the property "by August 31, 2018 for cash or by refinance."

If neither party purchased the property by August 31, 2018, then the order required it to be sold on the open market. In that case, the price would be set at an amount equal to "the real property value in the appraisal Guenther obtained in his efforts to refinance the property by July 31, 2018 plus six percent of that value."

After Zions Bank refused to go forward with financing Guenther's purchase of the property, Guenther sought alternative financing through Guild Mortgage. [Guenther could not meet the court's July 31 deadline, and the court rejected two motions by Guenther for an extension of time.]

Because Ryerson did not then purchase the property, it was set to be listed and sold on the open market with the price set at an amount equal to the value in the appraisal obtained by Guenther in his efforts to refinance the property ($725,000), plus six percent.

[The issues are:] Did the district court err in ordering the sale of the Lost Sage Lane property on the open market in winding up the partnership under the Idaho Uniform Partnership Act? Did the district court err in determining Guenther was entitled to 100 percent of any increase in equity in the Lost Sage Lane property that occurred after the date of dissolution?

A. In winding up the partnership, the district court erred in allowing each partner an opportunity to purchase the Lost Sage Lane property before requiring its sale on the open market.

In 1998, Idaho amended the Idaho Uniform Partnership Act ("the Act") to remodel it after the Revised Uniform Partnership Act (RUPA).

Under the Act, "a partnership is an entity distinct from its partners." Before Idaho adopted RUPA, a partner's withdrawal from a partnership automatically caused dissolution and winding up of the partnership. Now, "a partner who chooses to withdraw from the partnership is dissociated [under Idaho Code section 30–23–601(1)], but the dissociation of the partner does not require the dissolution of the partnership and the winding up of its affairs." That is, dissociation of a partner *can* cause dissolution and winding up of the partnership, but no longer automatically causes dissolution in all circumstances.

The Act provides two distinct statutory pathways to follow upon a partner's dissociation. *See* I.C. § 30–23–603(a) ("If a person's dissociation results in a dissolution and winding up of the partnership's business, part 8 of this chapter applies; otherwise, part 7 of this chapter applies."). If a partner's dissociation does not result in the dissolution and winding up of the partnership, the dissociation provisions in Part 7 of the Act govern the rights of the dissociating partner, the partnership, and its remaining partners. But when a partner's dissociation does result in the dissolution and winding up of the partnership, Part 8 of the Act applies.

Both parties sought judicial dissolution and further agreed that the Act governed the dissolution and winding up of their partnership.

Throughout the proceedings below, the district court relied on I.C. § 30–23–703(c) as providing it the authority to allow a partner to purchase partnership property during the winding up process.

However, I.C. § 30–23–703(c) does not apply to this case. Section 30–23–703(c) is a part of the dissociation pathway in the Act that applies when a partner dissociates from the partnership, but the partnership is not wound up and continues without the dissociating partner. Section 30–23–703(c) does not apply when a partnership is being dissolved and wound up pursuant to [Part 8]. The district court erred when it determined that it could enter an order allowing Guenther to buy the Lost Sage Lane property from the partnership under section 30–23–703(c).

The question remains as to whether a court may allow a partner to purchase partnership property during the judicial dissolution and winding up of a partnership under Part 8 of the Act.

[Part 8] govern the dissolution and winding up of a partnership in Idaho. *See* I.C. § 30–23–603(a). "Where partners mutually agree to a dissolution, any partner has the right to wind up partnership affairs in accordance with the [partnership] agreement." Upon the application of any partner who has not wrongfully dissociated, "the district court may order judicial supervision of the winding up of a dissolved partnership" for good cause shown. I.C. § 30–23–802(e).

"Winding up is the process of settling partnership affairs after dissolution, and generally involves an accounting and liquidation of the partnership's assets." The object of an accounting is to determine the value of each partner's interest in the partnership as of the date of dissolution and establish whether the partnership has any profits or losses. Ordinarily, the district court will order liquidation of partnership assets by sale and apply the proceeds according to the priorities set out in I.C. § 30–23–806.

I.C. § 30–23–802(b)(1) mandates that in winding up a partnership's affairs, the partnership "shall discharge the partnership's debts, obligations, and other liabilities, settle and close the partnership's business, and marshal and distribute the assets of the partnership." The Act provides the framework for distributing a partnership's assets during the winding up of a partnership:

> (a) In winding up its business, a partnership shall apply its assets, including the contributions required by this section, to discharge the partnership's obligations to creditors, including partners that are creditors.
>
> (b) After a partnership complies with subsection (a) of this section, any surplus must be distributed in the following order

> (1) To each person owning a transferable interest that reflects contributions made and not previously returned, an amount equal to the value of the unreturned contributions; and
>
> (2) Among partners in proportion to their respective rights to share in distributions immediately before the dissolution of the partnership, except to the extent necessary to comply with any transfer effective under section 30–23–503, Idaho Code.

Section 30–23–806(f) further requires that "*all* distributions made [to the partners] must be *paid in money.*"

The plain language of section 30–23–806(f) is unambiguous. If a distribution is made to a partner during the winding up of a partnership's business, the distribution must be paid in money. Such a requirement cannot reasonably be interpreted as allowing distributions to partners in any form other than money. To allow distributions in any other form would contradict the plain language of the statute.

While a rule requiring the forced sale of a partnership's assets upon its dissolution and winding up may seem harsh at first glance, its rigidity is lessened by the fact that the rules for winding up a partnership within section 30–23–806 are default provisions. *See* I.C. § 30–23–105 (with the exception of the specific provisions listed in sections 30–23–105(c) and (d), the partnership agreement governs "relations among the partners as partners and between the partners and the partnership" as well as "the business of the partnership and the conduct of that business"). A partnership agreement cannot change the requirements of section 30–23–802 that a dissolved partnership must be wound up, its liabilities discharged, and its assets marshalled and distributed. I.C. § 30–23–105(c)(13). But the partnership agreement can alter the default provisions for distribution of partnership assets to partners under section 30–23–806(b) and (c). *See* I.C. § 30–23–105(c)–(d) (where section 30–23–806 is not on the list of unmodifiable provisions). Therefore, partners who agree that liquidation of the partnership's surplus assets upon dissolution is undesirable may pursue an alternate path.

Guenther and Ryerson had no written partnership agreement and neither party alleged that their oral agreement provided for distributions of partnership assets in any form other than cash. Therefore, the default provisions of the Act control and the partnership's assets must be reduced to cash before being distributed to the partners. The district court erred in entering an order allowing Guenther and Ryerson each an opportunity to purchase the property at a given price before it was listed for sale.

We provide guidance for the district court in structuring the sale of the partnership property. Generally, the sale of partnership property is "held in such a manner and on such terms and conditions as the court deems proper." 59A Am.Jur.2d *Partnership* § 709. However, the district court's decision to fix the price at which the property may be listed is flawed. In winding up, the district court should seek to sell the partnership's assets at their fair market value. An asset's "fair market value" is "the amount that a willing buyer, who desires to buy but is under no obligation to buy, would pay a willing seller, who desires to sell but is under no obligation to sell." 59A Am.Jur.2d *Partnership* § 625. Thus, to obtain its fair market value, property should be sold at the highest price the market will bear.

B. The district court erred in assigning 100 percent of any post-dissolution increase in equity of the Lost Sage Lane property to Guenther.

"A partnership is an entity distinct from its partners." I.C. § 30–23–201. Therefore, partnership property "belongs to the partnership as an entity, rather than to the individual partners." *See* I.C. § 30–23–203 official cmt. A partnership does not terminate upon dissolution, but continues until its affairs have been completely wound up. I.C. § 30–23–802(a). Explained another way, before a partnership legally ends, three steps must be completed, (1) dissolution, (2) winding-up of the partnership's business or liquidation, and (3) termination of the partnership.

I.C. § 30–23–806 governs the distribution of assets during the winding up of a partnership. The partnership's assets should first be used to pay its obligations to any creditors. Once the partnership's creditors are satisfied, remaining partnership assets are used to repay any unreimbursed contributions made by partners. If the partnership does not have sufficient assets to repay all of the partners' unreimbursed contributions, the available assets should be distributed proportionally to the partners based on the amount of their respective contributions. Finally, if partnership assets remain, the surplus is distributed to the partners in proportion to their rights to share in partnership profits. Absent a partnership agreement to the contrary, every partner "is entitled to an equal share of the partnership profits." I.C. § 30–23–401(a). Therefore, the default rule is that partners share profits per capita, not in proportion to capital contributions. *See* I.C. § 30–23–401(a) official cmt.

In this case, the Lost Sage Lane property is partnership property, and any increase in value in the property, including from the date of dissolution until sale, belongs to the partnership. The partnership did not terminate upon dissolution, but continued for the sole purpose of winding up its business. Although Guenther has been the sole contributor to the development and upkeep of the property since the date of dissolution, that does not mean he is entitled to all increases in equity of the partnership property or that Ryerson has been divested of any interest in the partnership post-dissolution. That is not to say that Guenther should receive nothing for his post-dissolution contributions to the partnership.

Rather, his payment of partnership expenses, mortgage payments, development costs, and any other unreimbursed contributions made by him are to be taken into consideration if the partnership has surplus assets, distributable pursuant to I.C. § 30–23–806(b). Likewise, any benefit received by Guenther after the date of dissolution, such as the fair rental value of the property for the months he has continued to live there or any profits from the vineyard that have been distributed to him since dissolution, should be used to offset the amount of his total contributions to the partnership. Therefore, the district court erred in determining that Guenther was entitled to 100 percent of any gain in equity in the Lost Sage Lane property that accrued after the date of dissolution.

The district court determined that the partnership's surplus assets would be distributed on a pro rata basis, 76 percent to Guenther and 24 percent to Ryerson. This determination was based on the finding that the partnership's total surplus assets would not exceed the total amount of uncompensated capital contributions made by the partners. However, in conducting its analysis, the district court did not have the benefit of our holding that the property must be sold for its fair market value on the open market. Because the property has not been sold, any profits from its coming sale have not yet been realized by the partnership. The exact value of the partnership's assets after being converted to cash is still unknown. If there are surplus partnership assets after Zions Bank has been repaid, they must be distributed pursuant to I.C. § 30–23–806(b). Though the district court determined that Guenther had contributed 76 percent, and Ryerson 24 percent of the total partnership contributions, those percentages do not take into account either partner's contributions made after the date of dissolution. Therefore, only after all the partnership's assets have been reduced to cash and the costs of the sale have been paid from the proceeds of the sale can a final determination of each partner's capital contributions be made. Once each partner's right to distribution for uncompensated capital contributions has been satisfied, the remaining partnership assets must be distributed based on each partners right to share in the partnership's profits. Because there was no partnership agreement to the contrary, the default rule controls, Guenther and Ryerson have a right to share equally in the partnership's profits.

We hold that the Idaho Uniform Partnership Act requires the sale of partnership property upon dissolution unless otherwise agreed by the parties. We reverse the district court's order attributing 100 percent of post-dissolution increases in equity in the partnership's Lost Sage Lane property to Guenther. We remand for further proceedings.

B. MERGERS AND CONVERSIONS

1. BASICS OF MERGERS AND CONVERSIONS

Most laws of business organizations permit business entities to engage in mergers and conversions. In a merger, two existing entities combine to form one surviving entity. *E.g.*, Delaware Limited Liability Company Act § 18–209. For example, Alpha Inc. merges into Beta LLC where the latter becomes the surviving entity. In a conversion, an entity in one business form converts into another business form, and thus at any given time there is only one entity. *E.g.*, *id.* § 18–214. For example, Alpha Inc. converts into Alpha LLC. The reasons for a merger and a conversion are different.

Since a conversion involves one entity only, the transaction rationale is always a decision that the entity and its constituents are better served by operating the firm in another legal form. For example, partners in a general partnership may decide that they want the benefit of limited liability and thus convert the partnership into an LLC; or, a public corporation engages in a "going private" transaction in which managers and insiders buy out the public shareholders, and they decide to operate the business as an LLC in light of its greater contractual flexibility.

The reasons for a merger are more varied. The typical reason is to combine two businesses into one for the purpose of achieving some sort of synergy. For example, Firm A is prominent in the western half of the country and Firm B in the eastern half; together, they can become a national company. Or, Firm A sells a product that requires a key component manufactured by Firm B; together, Firm A can secure its supply chain and Firm B can diversify its product line. To execute a merger or conversion, there are three basic steps.

Plan of merger or conversion. This plan sets forth the terms and conditions of the transaction and the process used to achieve it. Unanimous consent of all owners is required to approve the plan. RUPA § 1123(a) (merger), § 1143(a) (conversion); ULPA (2001) § 1123(a) (merger), § 1143(a) (conversion); RULLCA § 1023(a) (merger), § 1043(a) (conversion). The voting threshold is a default rule. Unanimous voting requirement gives each person a veto, which means that each person has the significant hold up power. By contrast, corporate law provides for a majority approval of a merger as a default rule. DGCL § 251(c) ("a majority of the outstanding stock entitled to vote shall be voted for the adoption of the [merger agreement"). Terms and conditions in a plan of merger or conversion should answer two important questions: What does each owner get in terms of an interest in the merged or converted entity? What process is involved in the merger or conversion?

Filing. For limited liability entities, mergers and conversions require filing with the state. This filing requirement is ministerial and requires basic information, including name of the new entity, jurisdiction of the governing statute, and effective date of transaction. RUPA § 1125(a) (merger), § 1145(a) (conversion); ULPA (2001) § 1125(a) (merger), § 1145(a) (conversion); RULLCA § 1025(a) (merger), § 1045(a) (conversion).

Effectiveness. Once the merger or conversion becomes effective, a number of legal effects take place. The general principle is that while the merger or conversion may reorder the internal relationship among the owners and the new entity may be endowed with the rights and powers associated with the legal form of that entity, the surviving entity (in a merger) or the new legal form (in a conversion) does *not* affect prior relationship with respect to third parties and the world. Property rights, legal actions, contractual rights and obligations, and liabilities continue as if the transaction never happened. RUPA § 1126, § 1146; ULPA (2001) § 1126, § 1146; RULLCA § 1026, § 1046.

RULLCA § 1026. Effect of Merger.

(a) When a merger becomes effective:

(1) the surviving entity continues or comes into existence;

(2) each merging entity that is not the surviving entity ceases to exist;

(3) all property of each merging entity vests in the surviving entity without transfer, reversion, or impairment;

(4) all debts, obligations, and other liabilities of each merging entity are debts, obligations, and other liabilities of the surviving entity;

(5) except as otherwise provided by law or the plan of merger, all the rights, privileges, immunities, powers, and purposes of each merging entity vest in the surviving entity;

(6) if the surviving entity exists before the merger:

(A) all its property continues to be vested in it without transfer, reversion, or impairment;

(B) it remains subject to all its debts, obligations, and other liabilities; and

(C) all its rights, privileges, immunities, powers, and purposes continue to be vested in it;

(7) the name of the surviving entity may be substituted for the name of any merging entity that is a party to any pending action or proceeding;

(8) if the surviving entity exists before the merger:

(A) its public organic record, if any, is amended to the extent provided in the statement of merger; and

(B) its private organic rules that are to be in a record, if any, are amended to the extent provided in the plan of merger;

(9) if the surviving entity is created by the merger, its private organic rules are effective and:

(A) if it is a filing entity, its public organic record becomes effective; and

(B) if it is a limited liability partnership, its statement of qualification becomes effective; and

(10) the interests in each merging entity which are to be converted in the merger are converted, and the interest holders of those interests are entitled only to the rights provided to them under the plan of merger and to any appraisal rights they have under Section 1006 and the merging entity's organic law.

(b) Except as otherwise provided in the organic law or organic rules of a merging entity, the merger does not give rise to any rights that an interest holder, governor, or third party would have upon a dissolution, liquidation, or winding up of the merging entity.

(c) When a merger becomes effective, a person that did not have interest holder liability with respect to any of the merging entities and becomes subject to interest holder liability with respect to a domestic entity as a result of the merger has interest holder liability only to the extent provided by the organic law of that entity and only for those debts, obligations, and other liabilities that are incurred after the merger becomes effective.

(d) When a merger becomes effective, the interest holder liability of a person that ceases to hold an interest in a domestic merging limited liability company with respect to which the person had interest holder liability is subject to the following rules:

(1) The merger does not discharge any interest holder liability under this [act] to the extent the interest holder liability was incurred before the merger became effective.

(2) The person does not have interest holder liability under this [act] for any debt, obligation, or other liability that is incurred after the merger becomes effective.

(3) This [act] continues to apply to the release, collection, or discharge of any interest holder liability preserved under paragraph (1) as if the merger had not occurred.

(4) The person has whatever rights of contribution from any other person as are provided by this [act], law other than this [act], or the

operating agreement of the domestic merging limited liability company with respect to any interest holder liability preserved under paragraph (1) as if the merger had not occurred.

(e) When a merger becomes effective, a foreign entity that is the surviving entity may be served with process in this state for the collection and enforcement of any debts, obligations, or other liabilities of a domestic merging limited liability company as provided in Section 119.

(f) When a merger becomes effective, the registration to do business in this state of any foreign merging entity that is not the surviving entity is canceled.

The case below provides an example of how courts deal with challenges to a merger transaction between an LP and an LLC. The issue is whether courts should review a challenged merger under the business judgment rule or the entire fairness standard. The business judgment rule is the presumption that in making a business decision a manager was informed, acted in good faith and in the honest belief that the action was done in the best interest of the firm. It is a rule of judicial deference, providing that courts will not second-guess business decisions by presuming non-culpable conduct as a rebuttable prior. When a court applies the business judgment rule, the application is often outcome determinative because the case is subject to dismissal at the pleading stage absent an adequate rebuttal in the pleading. The presumption is rebutted when a plaintiff presents particularized facts showing that a court should not defer to managers because they breached their fiduciary duty of care or loyalty. In such case, the court applies a different standard of review—the entire fairness standard under which the court engages in a rigorous, independent, non-deferential analysis of the fairness of the process and price.

In reading this case, consider these questions: (1) When an owner challenges a transaction and seeks damages, what standard of review should courts apply to review the transaction? (2) Should the standard of review depend on how the transaction process is structured? (3) What is the implication of the court's ruling on how merger transactions should be structured to minimize the risk of post-agreement challenges?

CORWIN V. KKR FINANCIAL HOLDINGS LLC

125 A.3d 304 (Del. 2015)

STRINE, CHIEF JUSTICE:

The Court of Chancery held that the business judgment rule is invoked as the appropriate standard of review for a post-closing damages action when a merger that is not subject to the entire fairness standard of review has been approved by a fully informed, uncoerced majority of disinterested stockholders. The Chancellor was correct in finding that the voluntary judgment of the disinterested stockholders to approve the merger invoked the business judgment rule standard of review and that the plaintiffs' complaint should be dismissed. For sound policy reasons, Delaware corporate law has long been reluctant to second-guess the judgment of a disinterested stockholder majority that determines that a transaction with a party other than a controlling stockholder is in their best interests.

The plaintiffs filed a challenge in the Court of Chancery to a stock-for-stock merger between KKR & Co. L.P. ("KKR") and KKR Financial Holdings LLC ("Financial Holdings") in which KKR acquired each share of Financial Holdings's stock for 0.51 of a share of KKR stock, a 35% premium to the unaffected market price. The plaintiffs' primary argument was that the transaction was presumptively subject to the entire fairness standard of review because Financial Holdings's primary business was financing KKR's leveraged buyout activities, and instead of having employees manage the company's day-to-day operations, Financial Holdings was managed by KKR Financial Advisors, an affiliate of KKR, under a contractual management agreement that could only be terminated by Financial Holdings if it paid a termination fee. As a result, the plaintiffs alleged that KKR was a controlling stockholder of Financial Holdings, which was an LLC, not a corporation.

The Chancellor found that the defendants were correct that the plaintiffs' complaint did not plead facts supporting an inference that KKR was Financial Holdings's controlling stockholder. The Chancellor noted that KKR owned less than 1% of Financial Holdings's stock, had no right to appoint any directors, and had no contractual right to veto any board action. Financial Holdings had real assets its independent board controlled and had the option of pursuing any path its directors chose.

The Chancellor held: "There are no well-pled facts from which it is reasonable to infer that KKR could prevent the [Financial Holdings] board from freely exercising its independent judgment in considering the proposed merger or that KKR had the power to exact retribution by removing the [Financial Holdings] directors from their offices if they did not bend to KKR's will in their consideration of the proposed merger."

Because the Chancellor was correct in determining that the entire fairness standard did not apply to the merger, the effect of the uncoerced, informed stockholder vote is outcome-determinative.

The Court of Chancery noted that if the merger was not subject to the entire fairness standard, the business judgment standard of review was invoked because the merger was approved by a disinterested stockholder majority. The Chancellor adhered to precedent supporting the proposition that when a transaction not subject to the entire fairness standard is approved by a fully informed, uncoerced vote of the disinterested stockholders, the business judgment rule applies.

When a transaction is not subject to the entire fairness standard, the long-standing policy of our law has been to avoid the uncertainties and costs of judicial second-guessing when the disinterested stockholders have had the free and informed chance to decide on the economic merits of a transaction for themselves. There are sound reasons for this policy. When the real parties in interest—the disinterested equity owners—can easily protect themselves at the ballot box by simply voting no, the utility of a litigation-intrusive standard of review promises more costs to stockholders in the form of litigation rents and inhibitions on risk-taking than it promises in terms of benefits to them. The reason for that is tied to the core rationale of the business judgment rule, which is that judges are poorly positioned to evaluate the wisdom of business decisions and there is little utility to having them second-guess the determination of impartial decision-makers with more information (in the case of directors) or an actual economic stake in the outcome (in the case of informed, disinterested stockholders). In circumstances, therefore, where the stockholders have had the voluntary choice to accept or reject a transaction, the business judgment rule standard of review is the presumptively correct one and best facilitates wealth creation through the corporate form.

We affirm the Court of Chancery's judgment.

2. FIDUCIARY DUTIES

Fiduciary duties apply to all situations whenever a person acts in a fiduciary capacity. Those duties take on great significance in mergers or acquisitions because such transactions are fundamental. They change the firm and the owners' interest. Any breach may result in substantial harm. A fiduciary may breach the duty of care by acting uninformedly. He may breach the duty of loyalty by engaging in self-dealing. Many classic cases in corporation law dealing with fiduciary duties originate from mergers and acquisitions transactions. *E.g.*, Smith v. Van Gorkom, 488 A.2d 858 (Del. 1985); Unocal Corp. v. Mesa Petroleum Co., 493 A.2d 946 (Del. 1985); Revlon, Inc. v. MacAndrews & Forbes Holdings, Inc., 506 A.2d 173 (Del. 1986); Paramount Commc'ns Inc. v. Time Inc., 571 A.2d 1140 (Del. 1989); Paramount Commc'ns Inc. v. QVC Network Inc., 637 A.2d 34 (Del. 1994).

The case below illustrates the application of fiduciary duties in a merger. In reading this case, consider these questions: (1) What was the role of the operating agreement with respect to the scope of fiduciary duty? (2) In what way did the defendant breach his fiduciary duty?

ALLISON V. ERIKSSON

98 N.E.3d 143 (Mass. 2018)

KAFKER, J.

At issue is the remedy available for limited liability company (LLC) mergers undertaken in violation of fiduciary duties. The defendant, Elof Eriksson, contends that the exclusive remedy for dissenting members to such mergers is the distribution of their interest in the LLC, pursuant to G. L. c. 156C, § 60(b). The plaintiff, Robert Allison, contends that other equitable relief is available but that the judge erred in declining to rescind the merger. We conclude that § 60(b), provides the exclusive remedy for dissenting members so long as the merger is undertaken in accordance with §§ 59–63. Of relevance here is § 63(b), which provides that members of a limited liability company owe each other fiduciary duties, but that such duties may be enhanced or restricted according to the terms in the operating agreement. Where, as here, a member of an LLC conducts a merger in breach of his fiduciary and contractual duties, the merger has not been conducted in compliance with § 63, and the remedy provided by § 60(b), is not exclusive. Thus, the trial judge did not abuse his discretion in fashioning an equitable remedy.

Eriksson was looking to start a business based on technology he had developed at the hospital. He reached out to Allison, and the two eventually agreed to form Applied Tissue Technologies (ATT-MA), a Massachusetts LLC. Allison became the chief executive officer (CEO) of the company.

The membership interests in ATT-MA were as follows: Eriksson owned 55.5%; Eriksson's family trust owned 20%; Allison owned 14.66%; Allison's family trust owned 7.84%; and Baker [an employee] owned 2%.

Eriksson lent ATT-MA $200,000 to cover operating expenses. This sum was later repaid to him with 15% interest. Allison stepped down as CEO, and Karl Proppe, Eriksson's close friend, became the new CEO. Allison resigned as president and manager.

ATT-MA was almost out of cash. Eriksson was unwilling to lend the company any more money, but indicated he would be willing to invest money in exchange for additional equity. Allison was unwilling to have his interest diluted unless the investment came from an outside investor.

Eriksson eventually offered to invest $600,000 if Allison invested $200,000, but Allison rejected the proposal. Allison also refused to use personal assets to secure a bank loan for ATT-MA. Eriksson was frustrated by Allison's position and suggested that ATT-MA should be dissolved.

Eriksson's daughter arranged for him to meet with a senior attorney at her firm, Gary Schall, to discuss his concerns about the company. They ultimately decided that an appraisal of the company was necessary. Eriksson and Proppe retained Schall and his firm to represent ATT-MA.

The judge found that Eriksson, Proppe, and Schall all specifically decided not to let Allison know of Schall's engagement.

ATT-MA hired a firm to conduct the appraisal. Eriksson informed Allison of the appraisal, but not Schall's involvement or the purpose of the appraisal. The appraisal firm concluded that 100% of ATT-MA's equity had a value of $239,000, but only if $620,000 of additional funding was invested; without the additional $620,000, ATT-MA was worth $0.

Eriksson and Schall planned how they would deal with Allison. First, Eriksson would offer to purchase Allison's individual and trust membership interests based on the appraisal value. If Allison rejected the offer, Eriksson would form a new LLC under Delaware law (ATT-DE), and create a new operating agreement "that would accomplish Eriksson's goals." ATT-MA would then be merged into ATT-DE.

Eriksson offered to purchase Allison's collective membership interests, totaling 22.5%, for $53,775, *i.e.*, 22.5% of the $239,000 valuation. Allison rejected the offer.

Later the same month, ATT-DE was created. Proppe, now the manager and CEO of both ATT-MA and ATT-DE, executed the agreement and plan of merger. Eriksson and Proppe informed Allison of the merger. Up to this point, Allison had no prior notice of the merger or Schall's representation of ATT-MA.

The operating agreement for ATT-DE is significantly different from the operating agreement for ATT-MA. The ATT-DE operating agreement creates a class of preferred shares with liquidation preference over common shares. [Under § 6.01] the operating agreement establishes a board of directors to manage the company. Members have no rights other than to select the directors of the board. Directors are elected by a majority of the company's outstanding shares. As the holder of the majority of shares, Erickson could select the directors. As a minority member, Allison would not have the ability to successfully elect directors by himself. [Under § 6.04] members owe no fiduciary duty to ATT-DE or one another, and attempts to limit all other duties to the extent permitted by Delaware law.[7] [Under § 7.01] members do not have the right to access ATT-DE's books or records,

---

[7] Specifically, § 6.04(a) of the operating agreement states: "The Members' respective obligations to each other are limited to the express obligations set forth in this Agreement, subject only to the implied contractual covenant of good faith and fair dealing. *No Member shall have any duties or liabilities, including fiduciary duties, to [ATT-DE] or to any other Member*, or to the Board or any Director, and the provisions of this Agreement, to the extent that they restrict or otherwise modify, or eliminate, the duties and liabilities, including fiduciary duties, of the Members otherwise existing at law or in equity, are agreed by the Members to replace such other duties and liabilities of the Members. Any standard of care or duty imposed by or under the Act or any other law, rule or regulation (or any judicial decision based on or interpreting the same) shall be modified, waived or limited, to the extent permitted by law, as required to permit each Member to act under this Agreement and to make any decision such Member is authorized to make hereunder in such manner as such Member may determine in his, her or its sole and absolute discretion, subject only to the implied contractual covenant of good faith and fair dealing."

or to receive any information about ATT-DE's business or affairs, without the board's authorization. No membership interest may be transferred without board approval, even to family members.

Eriksson quickly purchased $250,000 of preferred shares in ATT-DE. Allison was given the opportunity to purchase enough preferred shares of ATT-DE to maintain his ownership interest, but declined to do so. Instead, Allison challenged the propriety of these transactions. Allison was denied further access to ATT-MA's offices, which now belonged to ATT-DE.

Eriksson purchased preferred shares in ATT-DE, totaling $923,536. As a result, Allison's combined interests in ATT-DE had been reduced to only 3.32%. His interests would also be subordinated to preferred shareholders' interests in the event of a liquidation.

Allison, Eriksson, Proppe, and Schall met to attempt to resolve Allison's claim that Eriksson had committed a breach of his fiduciary duties by authorizing the merger and purchasing preferred shares. Schall asked Allison if he would rather have 3.32% of an ongoing business or 22.5% of a defunct one. Allison responded that he would prefer a larger percentage of the failed business.

Eriksson was unwilling to reclassify his own investments as debt and restore Allison's prior ownership interests in the company. Allison would not agree to any compromise that did not include the restoration of his equity without the risk of dilution, except from a third-party investment.

Eriksson's son-in-law, Michael Broomhead, became CEO of ATT-DE. Broomhead actively looked for investors without success. Broomhead invested $10,000 in ATT-DE and Proppe invested $30,000.

After trial, Allison prevailed on his claim against Eriksson for breach of fiduciary duty, but lost on all other claims.

The judge granted equitable relief, ordering the following amendments to the operating agreement of ATT-DE: (1) the rescission of § 6.01, such that members shall have voting rights as provided under Delaware law; (2) the rescission of § 6.04 to the extent that it eliminated members' fiduciary duties to one another, and to directors, officers, and shareholders; (3) the rescission of the first two sentences of § 7.01, such that members may access the company's books and records; (4) the addition of a provision requiring the directors to "report to Allison either orally or in writing on the business and affairs of" ATT-DE, to timely advise him of anticipated extraordinary business events, and to provide him with a copy of ATT-DE's annual financial statements, if any. The judge also ordered that the combined membership interest of Allison and the Allison Trust be "grossed up" to 5% and not be subject to dilution without a bona fide outside investment. Any such dilution must be on the same terms as holders of common or preferred shares of ATT-DE. If ATT-DE should be liquidated before receiving any outside investment, Allison's interest must be "treated pari passus with the preferred shareholders."

a. **Relevant provisions of G. L. c. 156C.** We determine whether distribution is the exclusive remedy for a minority shareholder of an LLC who has objected to a merger that breaches fiduciary duties. The governing provision is § 60(b). Where a minority member objects to the merger, but the majority of members vote to merge anyway, § 60(b) provides:

> "The exclusive remedy of a member, who objects, shall be the right to resign as a member and to receive any distribution with respect to his limited liability company interest, as provided in [§§ 31–37], inclusive. Such members and the resulting or surviving entity shall have the rights and duties, and shall follow the procedure set forth in said sections."

The statute expressly provides for distribution of the dissenting member's interest in the LLC as an exclusive remedy where an LLC has voted to merge "under the provisions" of §§ 59–63. We must therefore consider the requirements of the cross-referenced sections, particularly § 63, to understand the scope of the exclusive remedy provision.

[Sections] 59–62, address the mechanics and consequences of merging or consolidating an LLC. By contrast, § 63 defines the scope of a member's or manager's duties and liabilities. Specifically, § 63(b) states:

> "To the extent that, at law or in equity, a member or manager has duties, including fiduciary duties, and liabilities relating thereto to a limited liability company or to another member or manager, (1) any such member or manager acting under the operating agreement shall not be liable to the limited liability company or to any such other member or manager for the member's or manager's good faith reliance on the provisions of the operating agreement, and (2) the member's or manager's duties and liabilities may be expanded or restricted by provisions in the operating agreement."

This provision establishes the rules governing fiduciary and contractual duties in LLCs, including the fiduciary duties applicable to mergers. The subsection's opening statement about "to the extent that" such duties exist "at law or in equity," is best read as an acknowledgement that the courts define and determine the nature of such duties, and that the courts provide for their enforcement as default rules. The LLC statute further allows, however, for the modification of these duties. According to § 63(b), such duties and liabilities "may be expanded or restricted by provisions in the operating agreement." This recognizes that "an LLC is primarily a creature of contract, and the parties have wide contractual freedom to structure the company as they see fit." Seneca Invs. LLC v. Tierney, 970 A.2d 259, 261 (Del. Ch. 2008). Additionally, § 63(b) provides that a member's or manager's good faith reliance on the operating agreement provides a defense to liability.

The merger here was done in contravention of the duties recognized in § 63(b) and does not fall under the good faith defense provision. As the trial judge correctly found, Eriksson clearly committed a breach of his fiduciary duties. Indeed, this is undisputed on appeal.

Although § 63(b) provided Allison and Eriksson the ability to restrict members' and managers' duties, they chose instead to expand them. ATT-MA's operating agreement expressly prohibited many of the consequences of this merger, such as the ability to dilute a member's interest without that member's consent, the ability to amend the operating agreement without the original members' consent, and the ability to cut members out of the management of the company. Thus, Eriksson was not acting in good faith reliance on the operating agreement when he conducted the merger in secret, so as to subvert each of these explicit protections.

The many minority protections provided in ATT-MA's operating agreement also indicate that the company was set up to establish protections akin to those provided at law to a close corporation.[13] Because close corporations often involve a small number of owners, who are "quite dependent on one another for the success of the enterprise, the relationship among the stockholders must be one of trust, confidence and absolute loyalty if the enterprise is to succeed." Donahue v. Rodd Electrotype Co. of New England, Inc., 328 N.E.2d 505, 512 (Mass. 1975). The nature of these close corporations imposes a duty of "utmost good faith and loyalty." *Id.* at 515. The minority protections in ATT-MA's operating agreement established an analogous relationship and duty among its members, and thus, the close corporation doctrine, and the strict fiduciary duty it imposes, applies here.[14]

The trial judge correctly found that "Eriksson certainly did not act with utmost good faith toward Allison." Eriksson does not challenge this finding, nor could he. Eriksson initiated the merger in secret, acting covertly in order to dilute Allison's interest in the company and remove Allison's minority rights, which were both expressly protected by ATT-MA's operating agreement.

"The danger of abuse of fiduciary duty is especially great in a freeze-out merger." In close companies and close corporations, such freeze-outs

---

[13] A closely held corporation is defined as having (1) a small number of shareholders; (2) no ready market for the corporation's shares; and (3) substantial majority shareholder participation in the management, direction, and operations of the corporation. *See Brodie v. Jordan*, 57 N.E.2d 1076 (Mass. 2006), quoting *Donahue v. Rodd Electrotype Co. of New England, Inc.*, 328 N.E.2d 505 (Mass. 1975).

[14] Not all LLCs are close companies. The test for whether a corporation is closely held, see note 13, *supra*, is not dispositive for determining whether an LLC is closely held. As LLCs are creatures of contract, determining whether an LLC is closely held is a more fact-specific determination that will depend on the way in which a particular LLC is structured.

defeat "the reasonable expectations" of minority shareholders. Here we have such a freeze-out merger.

We are presented with a merger that clearly contravenes the fiduciary and contractual duties recognized in § 63(b). The question that remains is whether such a merger may still be characterized as a merger "under the provisions of [§§ 59–63]," and therefore be covered by the exclusive remedy provision of § 60(b). We conclude that it cannot for the following reasons.

The exclusive remedy provision is expressly limited to mergers conducted "under the provisions of [§§ 59–63]." It would be anomalous to treat a merger conducted in contravention of the fiduciary and contractual duties identified in § 63(b) as a merger "under" § 63. This is especially true given the great flexibility provided to LLCs by statute either to restrict or enhance duties. Here, instead of restricting fiduciary duties, the operating agreement structured the LLC as a closely held company designed to prevent the very freeze-out accomplished by the merger.

We also have held that "a freeze-out merger in technical compliance" with G. L. c. 156B or 156D does not divest the courts of their equitable jurisdiction, and shareholders who dissented to the merger "are not limited to the statutory remedy of judicial appraisal [and distribution]," where the majority has violated its fiduciary duties. We conclude that the same principles apply here given how Erickson and Allison structured the LLC, imposing contractual and fiduciary duties on each other, including those designed not to allow the freeze-out and cash-out of one by the other.

We hold that in this case, where the merger of an LLC constitutes a breach of fiduciary and contractual duties in contravention of § 63(b), § 60(b) does not prevent the courts from providing the dissenting members with an equitable remedy other than the statutory right of distribution. Thus, a majority member may not rely on § 60(b) to exclude all other equitable relief when he or she has initiated a merger in breach of his or her existing fiduciary and contractual duties.

b. Propriety of the remedy. The proper remedy for a freeze-out merger is one that "will put [the minority member] in the position he would have been in had the freeze-out not occurred, and compensates him for the denial of his reasonable expectations." The remedy must also take into account the passage of time and changed circumstances. The LLC merger egg may not always be unscrambled. Courts have broad equitable powers in specifying the appropriate remedy.

Here, the trial judge carefully crafted an equitable remedy, amending specific provisions in ATT-DE's operating agreement that had diminished Allison's rights. The judge's amendments recreate Allison's minority member protections to the largest extent possible under Delaware law, within the existing structure of ATT-DE. Despite this, Allison insists that the only appropriate remedy was to rescind the merger and restore Allison's interest in ATT-MA. We disagree.

A judge need not order rescission of a freeze-out merger if it would not be in the best interest of the company. This litigation has gone on for five years, and concerns a merger that occurred six years ago. Despite being a sophisticated corporate attorney, Allison waited seven months after settlement negotiations had ended to file suit. By that point, the merger had been in place for nearly one year and Eriksson had already invested over $500,000 in ATT-DE. Rescinding the merger and backing out Eriksson's additional equity six years later would be complicated and inequitable. Under these circumstances we discern no abuse of discretion in the judge's decision to amend ATT-DE's operating agreement to restore Allison's minority protections instead of rescinding the merger.

In addition to amending ATT-DE's operating agreement, the judge increased Allison's ownership interest to 5%. Any such equitable change to Allison's ownership interest in ATT-DE should, in combination with the amendments to ATT-DE's operating agreement, "attempt to reset the proper balance between the majority's 'conceded rights to what has been termed 'selfish ownership,' and the minority's reasonable expectations of benefit from its shares." However, the judge did not explain how he settled on the 5% figure. The only potential basis for this increase is Allison's transfer of 2% of his interest to Eriksson after their disagreement over Baker's termination. Yet the judge's findings do not explain whether this was the reason for increasing Allison's interest. A 2% increase would give Allison a 5.32% interest in the company, not 5% exactly. Accordingly, we deem it appropriate to remand this matter on the question.

The judgment below is affirmed, except with respect to the issue of Allison's ownership interest percentage in ATT-DE. We remand for further explanation on the propriety of increasing Allison's interest to 5%.

C. ISSUES TO CONSIDER FOR NBEs

1. VOLUNTARY DISSOLUTION

Statutes may differ as to the threshold vote necessary for voluntary dissolution. Some states require a majority vote of the ownership interest. *See* Connecticut Uniform Limited Liability Company Act § 34–267(a)(1) ("The consent of a majority in interest of the members"); Rhode Island Limited Liability Company Act § 7–16–39(3) ("a majority of the capital values of all membership interests"); California Revised Limited Liability Company Act § 17707.01(b) ("By the vote of 50 percent or more of the voting interests of the members of the limited liability company"); New York Limited Liability Company Law § 701(a)(3) ("the vote or written consent of at least a majority in interest of the members"). These provisions refer to a majority of interest, and not a majority of owners.

Delaware requires a supermajority vote. *See* Delaware Limited Liability Company Act § 18–801(3) ("upon the vote or consent of members who own more than 2/3 of the then-current percentage or other interest in the profits of the limited liability company owned by all of the members").

Some states require unanimous consent. *See* Alabama Limited Liability Company Act of 2014 § 10A–5A–7.01(b) ("Consent of all members to dissolve"); Maryland Limited Liability Company Act § 4A–902(a)(2) ("the unanimous consent of the members"); Texas Business Organization Code § 101.552(b) ("The consent of all of the members of the limited liability company").

In light of these statutory differences, the charter agreement should provide the specific mechanism for voluntary dissolution.

- How is the question of voluntary dissolution introduced as a referendum item for deliberation and vote?
- What is the voting threshold for voluntary dissolution by owners?
- If there are different classes of owners, should there be separate class votes?
- Should voluntary dissolution also be subject to the consent of managers?

2. JUDICIAL DISSOLUTION

Many state statutes provide that a court's power to order judicial dissolution is mandatory and not waivable.[3] The rationale is that owners and managers cannot contract away a court's statutory power granted by the legislature. The uniform statutes provide that the power to order dissolution, by a court or an arbitrator, is a mandatory, nonwaivable term of the statute.[4]

[3] *E.g.*, Alabama Limited Liability Company Act of 2014 § 10A–5A–1.08(c)(11) ("A limited liability company agreement may not . . . vary the power of a court to decree dissolution in the circumstances specified in Section 10A–5A–7.01(d) or in Section 10A–5A–11.09(e)"); California Revised Limited Liability Company Act § 17701.10(c)(7) ("an operating agreement shall not . . . Vary the power of a court to decree dissolution in the circumstances specified in Section 17707.03(a)"). See also Palmer v. Mellen, 74 N.E.3d 1034, 1040 (Ill. App. 2017) ("The statute lists several nonwaivable provisions that cannot be varied or altered by a partnership agreement, including the requirement to wind up the partnership business.").

[4] *See* RULLCA § 105(c)(9) ("An operating agreement may not vary the causes of dissolution specified in Section 701(a)(4)"); RUPA § 105(c)(11) (same); ULPA (2001) § 105(c)(12) (same). Arbitration agreements in charter agreements are generally enforced. *See* Midwest Neurosciences Associates, LLC v. Great Lakes Neurosurgical Associates, LLC, 920 N.W.2d 767, 778–79 (Wisc. 2018); James v. Jackson, LLC v. Willie Gary, LLC, 906 A.2d 76, 80–81 (Del. 2006). Courts have held that dissolution can be issued by an arbitrator if the charter agreement provides for arbitration. *See* B&S MS Holdings, LLC v. Landrum, 302 So.3d 605 (Miss. 2020) (holding that when the operating agreement provided that all disputes "shall be finally and exclusively resolved by arbitration," a majority member must arbitrate a claim for judicial dissolution); Willie Gary LLC v. James & Jackson LLC, 2006 WL 75309, at *10 (Del. Ch. 2006) ("This court accepted that argument and found that a reference to a decree of judicial dissolution under the LLC Act did not

Delaware takes a different approach. The power of a court to grant judicial dissolution may be eliminated in the operating agreement. *See* R&R Capital, LLC v. Buck & Doe Run Walley Farms, LLC, 2008 WL 3846318, at *6 (Del. Ch. 2008) ("Because the waiver of a member's right to petition for dissolution or the appointment of a receiver does not violate the LLC Act and does not interfere with the rights of third parties, the waiver is valid and enforceable under the statute.").[5] This approach is consistent with Delaware's policy "to give the maximum effect to the principle of freedom of contract and to the enforceability of limited liability company agreements." Delaware Limited Liability Company Act § 18–1101(b). As long as third parties are not affected by the waiver of the court's power, Delaware takes the view that the availability of the judicial remedy should be a matter of contracting. In the states that either permit elimination or alteration of the judicial power to order judicial dissolution, there are several considerations.

- Should the court's power be eliminated?
- Should the charter agreement specify the standard that would permit a court to order judicial dissolution?

If the statute or case law is not clear on whether the remedy of judicial dissolution is waivable or the statute is silent, the charter agreement could provide such a provision, but of course it could be challenged.

With respect to contracting for the standard of judicial dissolution, if permitted, the following are some possibilities.

- Oppression of the minority owner by the majority owner
- Deadlock between two owners with equal management power
- Not reasonably practical to continue the business

Oppression, deadlock, and impracticability are not entirely self-defining terms. It is best that the charter agreement states, to the extent

mean that a dissolution claim was not subject to mandatory arbitration in the first instance, reasoning that such a judicial dissolution could be entered in accordance with, and following, dissolution proceedings before an arbitrator."). The uniform statutes provide that "the causes of dissolution" cannot be varied, which preserves the cause of action but leaves open the possibility of resolution by arbitration. Another version of the RULLCA (without the harmonization amendments) would not permit arbitration of claims for judicial dissolution. *See* RULLCA § 110(c)(7) ("An operating agreement may not vary the *power of a court* to decree dissolution in the circumstances specified in Section 701(a)(4) and (5)").

[5] The operating agreement, which the Delaware chancery court upheld as enforceable, provided:

> *Waiver of Dissolution Rights.* The Members agree that irreparable damage would occur if any member should bring an action for judicial dissolution of the Company. Accordingly, each member accepts the provisions under this Agreement as such Member's sole entitlement on Dissolution of the Company and waives and renounces such Member's right to seek a court decree of dissolution or to seek the appointment by a court of a liquidator for the Company.

R&R Capital, LLC v. Buck & Doe Run Walley Farms, LLC, 2008 WL 3846318, at *3 (Del. Ch. 2008).

possible, the definitions and the standards for determining these issues. Consider the issue of oppression:

- Does oppression mean that the majority owner must cede some degree of control to the minority owner?
- How do the owners balance the majority's right to govern and the minority's expectation in the investment?
- Is oppression conflated with a majority owner's fiduciary duty to the minority owner?
- Are there specific acts or conducts that the parties can agree ex ante do not constitute oppression?

A deadlock typically occurs when there are two owners with equal ownership interest and governance rights. When there is a third owner and no single owner owns a 50 percent stake, there is no mathematical possibility of a deadlock. Even with a single 50 percent owner, the chances of a deadlock become smaller with each additional owner in light of the fact that a single minority owner can deliver a majority vote. With two owners, the charter agreement should define the condition constituting a deadlock.

- Does any disagreement constitute a deadlock?
- If not, what sort of disagreement constitutes a deadlock?

With respect to the issue of not reasonably practicable to conduct business ("impracticability"), the owners should consider the standard. Deadlock and impracticability may be different.

- Does an inability to conduct business together constitute impracticability?
- Is impracticability tied to some external event such as a financial infeasibility or illegality of conducting the business?

3. SPECIFIC EVENTS TRIGGERING DISSOLUTION

In addition to the consent of owners, the charter agreement should specify the events triggering dissolution. The default terms are provided in the statutes. *See* RUPA § 801; ULPA (2001) § 701; RULLCA § 701. In addition to consideration of the default terms, some additional possibilities of specific events are:

- Sale of all or substantially all assets of the firm
- Dissociation of a key owner or manager
- Specific financial triggers such as a specific amount of loss
- Specific termination date or event

D. PROBLEM: ENTREPRENEURS GO BIGTIME, MAYBE

PBOO continued its operations and the marketing campaign began to takeoff. With innovative, eclectic designs, PBOO was starting to become a household name among millennials and Generation X. A huge boost came when a YouTube clip of the company's advertisement, featuring a link to Pacific conservation efforts and responsible plastic use, went viral. PBOO was starting to attract attention and a growing customer base. Piers and Blake were also featured at a nationally televised morning show. With a full year of operation behind it, the company is projected to double revenue to $2 million and increase profit from $50,000 in the prior year to $300,000 in the upcoming year, increasing net profit margin from 5% to 15%. The margin is expected to increase because brand recognition builds on itself and PBOO is expected to spend less on direct marketing costs.

Piers and Blake received a call from Crombie & Cink Co., a large national retailer that cater to a core consumer base that spans Generation X and millennials. Its brand is distinctive for colorful, almost irreverent designs that have become a signature for youthful chic. Crombie & Cink is seeking to enter the eyeglass frame business targeting Gen Xers and millennials. It has a small subsidiary that has been working on developing an online business, C&C See Inc. To advance this business strategy, the company seeks to acquire PBOO.

During an initial meeting with Stella Style, the CEO of Crombie & Cink, it was apparent that Crombie & Cink had certain priorities in mind.

Piers: "So tell us what you're thinking."

Style: "We are most interested in developing some momentum in this business. Most importantly, we want you guys and your team, especially Art Estic. There is no acquisition or deal if you guys cannot commit to the new company as the new management. As you know, our own business, C&C See, is fledgling, and to be honest flailing somewhat. The three of you can really take over and take the business to the next level."

Blake: "You're interested in hiring us? That's it?"

Style: "Well, that's one way to look at it. But we're also very much interested in PBOO's website and online infrastructure for dealing with an online eyeglass frame business. It's amazing that you have developed such a sophisticated platform for conducting an online business so quickly after only one year. We want that platform. As far as the actual PBOO brand. It's still in its infancy. At this point, we are indifferent between keeping the PBOO brand or developing our own brand under C&C See."

Piers: "Okay. Let us think about these issues."

Style: "Let's schedule a meeting for next week. I can bring along our businesspeople and deal team. We can begin to get to know each other a little bit more. We can talk about how we can do business together and maybe even deal structures that might work."

After the meeting with Style, Piers and Blake debriefed. There was much to consider. When Morgan Money departed the company on friendly terms with a negotiated buyout of Money's interest, the capital accounts of the members, including allocation of the first year's profits, showed the following balances: $110,000 Piers, $110,000 Blake, Art $10,000, and $210,000 Nicki Song. These amounts were recorded at book value, and did not include any increases in the value of the assets or any adjustments for goodwill. They are simply a record of contributions of tangible assets, profit and loss allocation, and distributions (which were none as to Piers, Blake, Art, and Nicki). Additionally, the company has debt of $300,000 owed to Rittenhouse Bank, debt financing which was required to buyout Morgan Money and to fund continuing operations. In addition to a cash balance of $100,000 and inventory of $100,000, PBOO's principal assets were the technology infrastructure, valued at fair market value of $1 million.

QUESTIONS

1. What are all the considerations in deciding to do a transaction with Crombie & Cink?

2. If Piers and Blake (and Art and Nicki) decide to do a deal with Crombie & Cink, how can the deal be structured? What are the options? (Assume that tax issues are not a problem.)

3. Suppose that Nicki is not so keen on the idea of doing a deal with Crombie & Cink, what are the implications? What legal points must be known to determine whether Nicki's potential opposition is a dispositive problem or not?

4. Suppose Piers, Blake, Art, and Nicki decide to do a deal with Crombie & Cink. What are the next steps?

CHAPTER 10

INTRODUCTION TO CORPORATIONS

■ ■ ■

A. CORPORATIONS IN SOCIETY

Corporations are important social and economic institutions. The largest companies tend to be public corporations.[1] They are socially the most significant business entities. They represent concentrations of economic and political power, and accordingly they can influence all aspects of society. Just consider the following facts.

- "The *Fortune Global 500* companies employ 67 million people worldwide. The industry with the most employees is commercial and savings banks, which employ more than 6.8 million people, or roughly 10.3% of the Global 500. The automotive industry is the second largest, with 5.3 million workers worldwide. *Fortune Global 500* companies had revenues [about $28 trillion] that equaled 37.8% of World GDP [about $73 trillion]—down from 40.1% last year." Christopher Tkaczyk et al., *Everything You Need to Know About the Global 500 in 6 Charts*, Fortune (July 22, 2016).
- "In total, *Fortune* 500 [U.S.] companies represent two-thirds of the U.S. GDP with $12.8 trillion in revenues, $1.0 trillion in profits, $21.6 trillion in market value, and employ 28.2 million people worldwide." *Fortune 500 2018*, available at https://fortune.com/fortune500/2018/.
- If the U.S. Fortune 500 companies were a single country, their aggregate revenue would constitute the second largest country in the world as measured by the GDPs of each country as of 2011: (1) U.S. $15.1 trillion, (2) Fortune 500 $11.8 trillion, (3) China $7.3 trillion, (4) Japan $5.9 trillion, (5) Germany $3.6 trillion, (6) France $2.8 trillion, (7) Brazil $2.5 trillion, (8) U.K. $2.4 trillion, (9) Italy $2.2 trillion, (10)

---

[1] Some very large corporations are privately held, for example (revenue, industry category, employees): Cargill ($115 billion, food, 155,000), Koch Industries ($110 billion, oil and gas, 120,000), Deloitte ($43 billion, business services, 263,900), PricewaterhouseCoopers ($41 billion, business services, 236,000), Mars ($35 billion, food, 100,000), Ernst & Young ($35 billion, business services, 247,570), Publix Super Markets ($35 billion, supermarket, 193,000), Reyes Holdings ($28 billion, food, 31,000), C&S Wholesale Grocers ($27 billion, food, 16,200). *America's Largest Private Companies*, Fortune (2018).

Russia $1.9 trillion. *If the Fortune 500 Were a Country*, Fortune (2011).

The overwhelming majority of firms in the U.S. are private firms, and many NBEs. From the perspective of the business of the practicing lawyer, NBEs are extremely important because they are many everyday clients. Smaller firms, operating locally or regionally, comprise much of the national economy from the standpoint of employing workers. But public corporations are the most important firms from the standpoint of size and scale of operations, and the impact on the society, the nation, and the world. Think about the influence of companies like Amazon, Google, and Facebook on our daily lives, or the reach of companies as diverse as McDonald's, Walmart, Bank of America, or ExxonMobile.

Public companies impart this influence even though they number only several thousand in the U.S. The table below shows a historical look at the number of public companies, most of which are traded on stock exchanges.

Bret Swanson, *Are Capital Markets Healthy? Some Thoughts on Corporate Concentration and Dwindling Public Firms*, U.S. Chamber of Commerce Found. (Mar. 27, 2018) ("The number of publicly listed U.S. firms is just one half what it was in the mid-1990s. Depending on the type of listings counted, the number of U.S. public firms has fallen to a range of 3,500–4,000 today from a range of 7,500–8,000 in 1996."). *See* Jason M. Thomas, *Where Have All the Public Companies Gone?*, Wall St. J. (Nov. 16, 2017) ("In 1996 there were 7,322 domestic companies listed on U.S. stock exchanges. Today there are only 3,671.").

Like the laws of NBEs, corporation law is state law. There is no general federal chartering system. Each state provides a statute that enables the creation of a corporation. The Delaware General Corporation

Law (DGCL) applies in the same way to both Facebook Inc. and Professor Kingsfield's Legal Outlines Inc. Like NBEs, corporations can engage in a wide spectrum of business activities, from complex global enterprises to simple storefront businesses. Notwithstanding the innumerable number of incorporated small businesses, corporation law is important because the vast majority of public companies are corporations.

1. SEPARATION OF OWNERSHIP AND CONTROL

The corporate form is *the* primary means of aggregating large pools of capital for large ventures, prototypically public corporations. In privately held firms, owners control the firm or are closer to those who control than shareholders are in public companies. A public corporation is characterized by a separation of ownership and control.

The excerpt below provides an analysis of large corporations. It was published in 1932, but is still a classic work in the field. It identifies the issues and frames policy agenda. Its message continues to raise the most fundamental issues concerning large corporations. In reading the passage, consider these questions: (1) In what way did large corporations "work a revolution" in the economic system? (2) In what way can "the interests of owner and of ultimate manager may, and often do, diverge"?

THE MODERN CORPORATION & PRIVATE PROPERTY

Adolf A. Berle & Gardiner C. Means

In its new aspect the corporation is a means whereby the wealth of innumerable individuals has been concentrated into huge aggregates and whereby control over this wealth has been surrendered to a unified direction. The power attendant upon such concentration has brought forth princes of industry, whose position in the community is yet to be defined. The surrender of control over their wealth by investors has effectively broken the old property relationships and has raised the problem of defining these relationships anew. The direction of industry by persons other than those who have ventured their wealth has raised the question of the motive force back of such direction and the effective distribution of the returns from business enterprise.

. . . The typical business unit of the 19th century was owned by individuals or small groups; was managed by them or their appointees; and was, in the main, limited in size by the personal wealth of the individuals in control. These units have been supplemented in even greater measure by great aggregations in which tens and even hundreds of thousands of workers and property worth hundreds of millions of dollars, belonging to tens even hundreds of millions of dollars, are combined through the corporate mechanism into a single producing organization under unified control and management. . . .

Such an organization of economic activity rests upon two developments, each of which has made possible an extension of the area
developments, each of which has made possible an extension of the area
under unified control. The factory system, the basis of the industrial revolution, brought an increasingly large number of workers directly under a single management. Then, the modern corporation, equally revolutionary in its effect, placed the wealth of innumerable individuals under the same central control. By each of these changes the power of those in control was immensely enlarged and the status of hoe involved, worker or property owner, was radically changed. The independent worker who entered the factory became a wage laborer surrendering the direction of his labor to his industrial master. The property owner who invests in a modern corporation so far surrenders his wealth to those in control of the corporation that he has exchanged the position of independent owner for one in which he may become merely recipient of the wages of capital.

In and of itself, the corporate device does not necessarily bring about this change. It has long been possible for an individual to incorporate his business even though it still represents his own investment, his own activities, and his own business transactions; he has in fact merely created a legal alter ego by setting up a corporation as the nominal vehicle. If the corporate form had done nothing more than this, we should have only an interesting custom according to which business would be carried on by individuals adopting for the purpose certain legal clothing. It would involve no radical shift in property tenure or in the organization of economic activity; it would inaugurate no "system" comparable to the institutions of feudalism.

The corporate system appears only when this type of private "close" corporation has given way to an essentially different form, the quasi-public corporation: a corporation in which a large measure of separation of ownership and control has taken place through the multiplication of owners. . . .

Growing out of this separation are two characteristics, almost typical of the quasi-public corporation as the separation itself—mere size and the public market for its securities. It is precisely this separation of control from ownership which makes possible tremendous aggregations of property. The Fords and the Mellons, whose personal wealth is sufficient to finance great enterprises, are so few, that they only emphasize the dependence of the large enterprise on the wealth more than the individual or group of individuals who may be in control. The quasi-public corporation commands its supply of capital from a group of investors frequently described as the "investing public." It draws these savings to itself either directly, as individuals purchase stocks or bonds, or indirectly as insurance companies, banks, and investment trusts receive these savings and invest them in corporate securities. To secure these funds it must commonly avail itself of an open market in its securities—usually by listing shares on a stock exchange, or, less importantly, by maintaining a private "unlisted" market. So essential, in fact, is the open market to the quasi-public corporation that it may be considered almost as characteristic of that type of corporation as the separation of ownership from control and the great aggregation of wealth. . . .

Though the American law makes no distinction between the private corporation and the quasi-public, the economics of the two are essentially different. The separation of ownership from control produces a condition where the interests of owner and of ultimate manager may, and often do, diverge, and where many of the checks which formerly operated to limit the use of power disappear. Size alone tends to give these giant corporations a social significance not attached to the smaller units of private enterprise. By the use of the open market for securities, each of these corporations assumes obligations towards the investing public which transform it from a legal method clothing the rule of a few individuals into an institution at least nominally serving investors who have embarked their funds in its enterprise. New responsibilities towards the owners, the workers, the consumers, and the State thus rest upon the shoulders of those in control. In creating these new relationships, the quasi-public corporation may fairly be said to work a revolution. It has destroyed the unity that we commonly call property—has divided ownership into nominal ownership and the power formerly joined to it. Thereby the corporation has changed the nature of profit-seeking enterprise. This revolution forms the subject of the present study. . . .

Outwardly the change is simple enough. Men are less likely to own the physical instruments of production. They are more likely to own pieces of paper, loosely known as stocks, bonds, and other securities, which have become mobile through the machinery of the public markets. Beneath this, however, lies a more fundamental shift. Physical control over the instruments of production has been surrendered in ever growing degree to centralized groups who manage property in bulk, supposedly, but by no means necessarily, for the benefit of the security holders. Power over industrial property has been cut off from the beneficial ownership of this property—or, in less technical language, from the legal right to enjoy its fruits. Control of physical assets has passed from the individual owner to those who direct the quasi-public institutions, while the owner retains an interest in their product and increase. We see, in fact, the surrender and regrouping of the incidence of ownership, which formerly bracketed full power of manual disposition with complete right to enjoy the use, the fruits, and the proceeds of physical assets. There has resulted the dissolution of the old atom of ownership into its component parts, control and beneficial ownership.

This dissolution of the atom of property destroys the very foundation on which the economic order of the past three centuries has rested. Private enterprise, which has molded economic life since the close of the middle ages, has been rooted in the institution of private property. Under the feudal system, its predecessor, economic organization grew out of mutual obligations and privileges derived by various individuals from their relation to property which no one of them owned. Private enterprise, on the other hand, has assumed an owner of the instruments of production with complete property rights over those instruments. Whereas the organization of feudal economic life rested upon an elaborate system of binding customs, the organization under the system of private enterprise has rested upon the self-interest of the property owner—a self-interest held in check only by competition and the conditions of supply and demand. Such self-interest has long been regarded as the best guarantee of economic efficiency. It has been assumed that, if the individual is protected in the right both to use his own property as he sees fit and to receive the full fruits of its use, his desire for personal gain, for profits, can be relied upon as an effective incentive to his efficient use of any industrial property he may possess.

In the quasi-public corporation, such an assumption no longer holds. As we have seen, it is no longer the individual himself who uses his wealth. Those in control of that wealth, and therefore in a position to secure industrial efficiency and produce profits, are no longer, as owners, entitled to the bulk of such profits. Those who control the destinies of the typical modern corporation own so insignificant a fraction of the company's stock that the returns from running the corporation profitably accrue to them in only a very minor degree. The stockholders, on the other hand, to whom the profits of the corporation go, cannot be motivated by those profits to a more efficient use of the property, since they have surrendered all disposition of it to those in control of the enterprise. The explosion of the atom of property destroys the basis of the old assumption that the quest for profits will spur the owner of industrial property to its effective use. It consequently challenges the fundamental economic principle of individual initiative in industrial enterprise. It raises for reexamination the question of the motive force back of industry, and the ends for which the modern corporation can be or will be run. . . .

This system bids fair to be as all-embracing as well as the feudal system in its time. It demands that we examine both its conditions and its trends, for an understanding of the structure upon which will rest the economic order of the future.

The problem of the separation of ownership and control is *the* fundamental in corporation law. More concretely, how can the rules of corporation law be formulated so that managers who own little or no equity in the firm relative to all shareholders are incentivized to maximize firm value on behalf of shareholders and other corporate constituents? Unlike NBEs, which tend to have owners who are closer to the control of the firm, in the public corporation "the interests of owner and of ultimate manager may, and often do, diverge, and where many of the checks which formerly operated to limit the use of power disappear." This divergence of interest results in what scholars call "agency cost." (The generic term "manager" herein refers to corporate directors and officers.)

Consider the many potential manifestations of agency cost: (1) excessive executive pay because managers control the process of awarding pay; (2) conflict of interest transactions benefiting the private interests of insiders because managers control the deal process; (3) taking of corporate assets or benefits, such as information or opportunities belonging to the corporation, because managers control such assets and benefits; (4) entrenchment of position because managers control the nomination of directors and hiring of officers. Much of corporation law deals with these kinds of situations created by the separation of ownership and control.

2. CONSTITUTIONAL RIGHTS

In addition to economic power, corporations have been granted some, but not all, constitutional rights endowed in natural persons. These rights include the right to due process. *See* Santa Clara County v. South. Pac. R.R. Co., 118 U.S. 394 (1886). A recent right earned by corporations is the right to free speech. Clearly, this right implicates the role of the corporation in the political process of the nation.

The case below holds that, under the free speech clause of the first amendment, corporations can spend unlimited money in independent expenditures in political campaigns. In reading this case, consider these questions: (1) Should the legal personality of corporations be extended to include the first amendment right of free speech? (2) What is the implication of corporations having the right of free speech under the constitution?

CITIZENS UNITED V. FEDERAL ELECTION COMMISSION

558 U.S. 310 (2010)

Author's summary of facts: Citizens United, a nonprofit corporation, sought to release a documentary, *Hillary: The Movie.* The Bipartisan Campaign Reform Act of 2002, codified in 2 U.S.C. § 411b, prohibited corporations and unions from using general treasury funds to make independent expenditures that expressly advocate the election or defeat of a candidate through the media under certain conditions. Citizens United sought to release the movie in contravention of section 441b and sought declaratory and injunctive relief. One issue was whether corporations have first amendment right to free speech such that section 411b infringed on that constitutional right. The court ruled that corporations have first amendment free speech rights: "Section 411b's restrictions on corporate independent expenditures are invalid and cannot be applied to *Hillary.*" One of the many questions in the opinion was whether corporations have a broad constitutional right to free speech to participate in the political process.

JUSTICE KENNEDY delivered the opinion of the Court.

First Nat. Bank of Boston v. Bellotti, 435 U.S. 765 (1978) reaffirmed the First Amendment principle that the Government cannot restrict political speech based on the speaker's corporate identity. *Bellotti* could not have been clearer when it struck down a state-law prohibition on corporate independent expenditures related to referenda issues:

> "We thus find no support in the First Amendment for the proposition that speech that otherwise would be within the protection of the First Amendment loses that protection simply because its source is a corporation that cannot prove, to the satisfaction of a court, a material effect on its business or property. [That proposition] amounts to an impermissible legislative prohibition of speech based on the identity of the interests that spokesmen may represent in public debate over controversial issues and a requirement that the speaker have a sufficiently great interest in the subject to justify communication.
>
> "In the realm of protected speech, the legislature is constitutionally disqualified from dictating the subjects about which persons may speak and the speakers who may address a public issue."

Bellotti rested on the principle that the Government lacks the power to ban corporations from speaking.

Bellotti did not address the constitutionality of the State's ban on corporate independent expenditures to support candidates. In our view, however, that restriction would have been unconstitutional under *Bellotti*'s central principle: that the First Amendment does not allow political speech restrictions based on a speaker's corporate identity.

The purpose and effect of this law is to prevent corporations, including small and nonprofit corporations, from presenting both facts and opinions to the public. "The First Amendment protects the right of corporations to petition legislative and administrative bodies." *Bellotti,* 435 U.S., at 792 n. 31. Corporate executives and employees counsel Members of Congress and Presidential administrations on many issues, as a matter of routine and often in private. An *amici* brief filed on behalf of Montana and 25 other States notes that lobbying and corporate communications with elected officials occur on a regular basis. When that phenomenon is coupled with

§ 441b, the result is that smaller or nonprofit corporations cannot raise a voice to object when other corporations, including those with vast wealth, are cooperating with the Government. That cooperation may sometimes be voluntary, or it may be at the demand of a Government official who uses his or her authority, influence, and power to threaten corporations to support the Government's policies. Those kinds of interactions are often unknown and unseen. The speech that § 441b forbids is public, and all can judge its content and purpose. References to massive corporate treasuries should not mask the real operation of this law.

Even if § 441b's expenditure ban were constitutional, wealthy corporations could still lobby elected officials, although smaller corporations may not have the resources to do so. And wealthy individuals and unincorporated associations can spend unlimited amounts on independent expenditures. Yet certain disfavored associations of citizens—those that have taken on the corporate form—are penalized for engaging in the same political speech.

When Government seeks to use its full power, including the criminal law, to command where a person may get his or her information or what distrusted source he or she may not hear, it uses censorship to control thought. This is unlawful. The First Amendment confirms the freedom to think for ourselves.

JUSTICE SCALIA, with whom JUSTICE ALITO joins, and with whom JUSTICE THOMAS joins in part, concurring.

Despite the corporation-hating quotations the dissent has dredged up, it is far from clear that by the end of the 18th century corporations were despised. If so, how came there to be so many of them? The dissent's statement that there were few business corporations during the 18th century—"only a few hundred during all of the 18th century"—is misleading. There were approximately 335 charters issued to business corporations in the United States by the end of the 18th century. This was a "considerable extension of corporate enterprise in the field of business," and represented "unprecedented growth." Moreover, what seems like a small number by today's standards surely does not indicate the relative importance of corporations when the Nation was considerably smaller. As I have previously noted, "by the end of the eighteenth century the corporation was a familiar figure in American economic life."

Even if we thought it proper to apply the dissent's approach of excluding from First Amendment coverage what the Founders disliked, and even if we agreed that the Founders disliked founding-era corporations, modern corporations might not qualify for exclusion. Most of the Founders' resentment toward corporations was directed at the state-granted monopoly privileges that individually chartered corporations enjoyed. Modern corporations do not have such privileges, and would probably have been favored by most of our enterprising Founders—

excluding, perhaps, Thomas Jefferson and others favoring perpetuation of an agrarian society. Moreover, if the Founders' specific intent with respect to corporations is what matters, why does the dissent ignore the Founders' views about other legal entities that have more in common with modern business corporations than the founding-era corporations? At the time of the founding, religious, educational, and literary corporations were incorporated under general incorporation statutes, much as business corporations are today. There were also small unincorporated business associations, which some have argued were the "true progenitors" of today's business corporations. Were all of these silently excluded from the protections of the First Amendment?

The lack of a textual exception for speech by corporations cannot be explained on the ground that such organizations did not exist or did not speak. To the contrary, colleges, towns and cities, religious institutions, and guilds had long been organized as corporations at common law and under the King's charter, and as I have discussed, the practice of incorporation only expanded in the United States. Both corporations and voluntary associations actively petitioned the Government and expressed their views in newspapers and pamphlets. For example: An antislavery Quaker corporation petitioned the First Congress, distributed pamphlets, and communicated through the press in 1790. The New York Sons of Liberty sent a circular to Colonies farther south in 1766. And the Society for the Relief and Instruction of Poor Germans circulated a biweekly paper from 1755 to 1757. The dissent offers no evidence—none whatever—that the First Amendment's unqualified text was originally understood to exclude such associational speech from its protection.

JUSTICE STEVENS, with whom JUSTICE GINSBURG, JUSTICE BREYER, and JUSTICE SOTOMAYOR join, concurring in part and dissenting in part.

The Framers conceived of speech more narrowly than we now think of it, but also they held very different views about the nature of the First Amendment right and the role of corporations in society. Those few corporations that existed at the founding were authorized by grant of a special legislative charter. Corporate sponsors would petition the legislature, and the legislature, if amenable, would issue a charter that specified the corporation's powers and purposes and "authoritatively fixed the scope and content of corporate organization," including "the internal structure of the corporation." Corporations were created, supervised, and conceptualized as quasi-public entities, "designed to serve a social function for the state." It was "assumed that [they] were legally privileged organizations that had to be closely scrutinized by the legislature because their purposes had to be made consistent with public welfare."

The individualized charter mode of incorporation reflected the "cloud of disfavor under which corporations labored" in the early years of this Nation. Thomas Jefferson famously fretted that corporations would subvert the Republic. General incorporation statutes, and widespread acceptance of business corporations as socially useful actors, did not emerge until the 1800's.

The Framers thus took it as a given that corporations could be comprehensively regulated in the service of the public welfare. Unlike our colleagues, they had little trouble distinguishing corporations from human beings, and when they constitutionalized the right to free speech in the First Amendment, it was the free speech of individual Americans that they had in mind. While individuals might join together to exercise their speech rights, business corporations, at least, were plainly not seen as facilitating such associational or expressive ends. Even "the notion that business corporations could invoke the First Amendment would probably have been quite a novelty," given that "at the time, the legitimacy of every corporate activity was thought to rest entirely in a concession of the sovereign." It seems to me implausible that the Framers believed "the freedom of speech" would extend equally to all corporate speakers, much less that it would preclude legislatures from taking limited measures to guard against corporate capture of elections.

As a matter of original expectations, it seems absurd to think that the First Amendment prohibits legislatures from taking into account the corporate identity of a sponsor of electoral advocacy. As a matter of original meaning, it likewise seems baseless—unless one evaluates the First Amendment's "principles," or its "purpose," at such a high level of generality that the historical understandings of the Amendment cease to be a meaningful constraint on the judicial task. This case sheds a revelatory light on the assumption of some that an impartial judge's application of an originalist methodology is likely to yield more determinate answers, or to play a more decisive role in the decisional process, than his or her views about sound policy.

Justice Scalia criticizes the foregoing discussion for failing to adduce statements from the founding era showing that corporations were understood to be excluded from the First Amendment's free speech guarantee. Justice Scalia adduces no statements to suggest the contrary proposition, or even to suggest that the contrary proposition better reflects the kind of right that the drafters and ratifiers of the Free Speech Clause thought they were enshrining. Although Justice Scalia makes a perfectly sensible argument that an individual's right to speak entails a right to speak with others for a common cause, he does not explain why those two rights must be precisely identical, or why that principle applies to electioneering by corporations that serve no "common cause." Nothing in his account dislodges my basic point that members of the founding generation held a cautious view of corporate power and a narrow view of corporate rights (not that they "despised" corporations), and that they conceptualized speech in individualistic terms. If no prominent Framer bothered to articulate that corporate speech would have lesser status than individual speech, that may well be because the contrary proposition—if not also the very notion of "corporate speech"—was inconceivable.

In fairness, our campaign finance jurisprudence has never attended very closely to the views of the Framers, whose political universe differed profoundly from that of today. We have long since held that corporations are covered by the First Amendment, and many legal scholars have long since rejected the concession theory of the corporation. But "historical context is usually relevant," and in light of the Court's effort to cast itself as guardian of ancient values, it pays to remember that nothing in our constitutional history dictates today's outcome. To the contrary, this history helps illuminate just how extraordinarily dissonant the decision is.

NOTES

1. To say that *Citizens United* has been broadly and fiercely criticized is an understatement. In many corners of society, *Citizens United* is a reviled Supreme Court opinion. Among other criticisms, the majority opinion is clearly undertheorized with respect to how constitutional rights relate to basic doctrines of corporation law, and whether the majority Supreme Court simply glossed over the implication of a corporate "speaker" so that the Court could reach a result it wanted for the purpose of constructing a desired design of a political society. The following critique is just one perspective by commentators of corporation law, one of whom (Strine) was the former chief justice of the Delaware Supreme Court.

> *Citizens United* ignored the entity theory of the corporation and adopted a view that the corporation is an aggregate of its shareholders. As Adam Winkler trenchantly observed, "not once" did Justice Kennedy in his opinion "mention corporate personhood."
>
>> He never said that corporations were people and nothing in his opinion turned on that notion. Corporate personhood—the idea that a corporation is an entity with rights and obligations separate and distinct from the rights and obligations of its members—is entirely missing from the court's opinion. The court afforded broad free speech rights to corporations, but not because they were people. Instead the *Citizens United* decision obscured the corporate entity and emphasized the rights of others, like shareholders and listeners. *Citizens United* repeatedly described the corporation as "an association that has taken on the corporate form."
>
> *Citizens United* treats the corporation as "a mere collection of men," attributing the rights and responsibilities of the corporation's shareholders to the corporation itself. This analysis confuses the traditional general partnership form of business organization, which is an association of partners whose individual rights and responsibilities are indistinguishable from those of the entity, with

> the corporate form of business organization, which is a separate juridical entity with distinct rights and responsibilities. The rights and responsibilities of corporations are limited by the states that create the legal framework that allows them to come into existence and that regulates their activities. The remainder of this Part introduces the two major ways in which the corporation has been viewed from a theoretical economic perspective: the "nexus of contracts" theory, and the "separation of ownership and control" theory. We observe that both of these economic views of the corporation reflect an understanding that the corporation is a separate entity distinct from its shareholders. As such, both these economic conceptualizations of the corporation should lead us to reject the reasoning of the *Citizens United* majority because their major thrust is to create entities distinct from their constituent shareholders.

Jonathan Macey & Leo E. Strine, Jr., *Citizens United as Bad Corporate Law*, 2019 Wisc. L. Rev. 451, 462–63 (2019).

B. MAJOR DIFFERENCES BETWEEN NBEs AND CORPORATIONS

1. REPRESENTATIVE MANAGEMENT

NBEs permit a wide range of management structures. It is common to see them adopt a management structure revolving around a "board of directors." These structures are contractual choices. A corporation mandates a board structure. Under DGCL § 141(a), the quintessential attribute of a corporation is that it is managed by a board of directors who are periodically elected by shareholders. It provides:

> The business and affairs of every corporation shall be managed by or under the direction of a board of directors, except as may be otherwise provided [1] in this chapter or [2] in its certificate of incorporation.

This provision provides two exceptions to the grant of full managerial authority to the board. These exceptions suggest that the management structure of corporations can be subject to significant contracting in the same way that a board structure may be chosen by partners and members in NBEs. The exceptions in section 141(a), however, are limited to closely-held corporations (which are firms that have close kinship with NBEs), but have no application to public corporations for all practical purposes.

First, the clause "otherwise provided in this chapter" principally refers to rules applicable if a corporation chooses to be a "close corporation" (*see* Subchapter XIV, "Close Corporations; Special Provisions," § 341 to § 356). Close corporations have closely held ownership. *See* DGCL § 342(a)(1) (requiring a close corporation to have no more than 30 shareholders). Rules applicable to close corporations permit management structures that resemble NBEs, including the elimination of a board structure altogether.[2] Of course, close corporations cannot be public corporations.

Second, the clause "otherwise provided in its certificate of incorporation" suggests that section 141(a)'s grant of managerial authority may be contractually limited by the certificate. *See* Lehrman v. Cohen, 222 A.2d 800, 805 (Del. 1966) (approving the concept that "the delegation of duty, if any, is made by stockholder action under § 141(a), via the certificate of incorporation").[3] This exception seems potentially broad because in theory any limitation could be incorporated into the certificate. In reality, it is seldom used, if ever, in public corporations. Virtually all corporations "going public" (in the process of an initial public offering (IPO)) will have a certificate that grants the board traditional management authority under section 141(a), even companies with strong controlling shareholders.[4] Pragmatically, professional managers and investors will expect broad grant of authority in the management structure, and an IPO is not the kind of a transaction to experiment with exotic or quirky management structures that can pose a risk to the transaction. Once the authority is in place in the certificate and the company is now a public company, a limitation on management authority would require an amendment of the certificate. An amendment requires a board resolution and a favorable

---

[2] *See, e.g.*, DGCL § 350 ("A written agreement among the stockholders of a close corporation holding a majority of the outstanding stock entitled to vote, whether solely among themselves or with a party not a stockholder, is not invalid, as between the parties to the agreement, on the ground that it so relates to the conduct of the business and affairs of the corporation as to restrict or interfere with the discretion or powers of the board of directors."); *id.* § 351 ("The certificate of incorporation of a close corporation may provide that the business of the corporation shall be managed by the stockholders of the corporation rather than by a board of directors.").

[3] In *Lehrman v. Cohen*, two equal factions of shareholders held AC stock and AL stock, entitling each faction to elect two directors. Because they anticipated a potential for a deadlock, they created a single share of a third class of stock (AD stock) entitling the holder to elect a tie-breaking fifth director. The stock was issued to the corporation's general counsel who elected himself as the arbiter director. One of the factions sued and argued that this tie-breaking mechanism constituted an improper delegation of statutory duty to the general counsel. The court rejected this argument: "The AD stock arrangement was created by the unanimous action of the stockholders of the Company by amendment to the certificate of incorporation. The stockholders thereby provided how the business of the corporation is to be managed, as is their privilege and right under § 141(a). It was this stockholder action which delegated to the AD director whatever powers and duties he possesses; they were not delegated to him by his fellow directors, either out of their own powers and duties, or otherwise." 222 A.2d at 805.

[4] Facebook, Inc. is a public company with a strong controlling shareholder (its founder Mark Zuckerberg). Presumably, Facebook's certificate could place limitations on the board of directors giving shareholders (presumably Zuckerberg) greater powers at the expense of diminution of board powers. But it does not do so. *See* Facebook, Inc. Restated Certificate of Incorporation, Art. VI, sec. 1 ("The business and affairs of the corporation shall be managed by or under the direction of the Board of Directors. In addition to the powers and authority expressly conferred upon them by statute or by this Restated Certificate of Incorporation or the Bylaws of the corporation, the directors are hereby empowered to exercise all such powers and do all such acts and things as may be exercised or done by the corporation."). There is no need to limit board authority, and doing so may have detrimental, unintended consequences. Of course, the concept of a controlling shareholder is not an oxymoron. Despite the grant of full managerial authority to the board, Zuckerberg *qua* shareholder can impart significant influence by virtue of the ownership of shares and thus voting control.

shareholder vote. *See* DGCL § 242(b); MBCA § 10.03(a)–(b). Absent strong external pressure from shareholders, a board will not be inclined to adopt a resolution limiting its authority. A shareholder that can impart such pressure will likely be a controlling shareholder who can exert control on the corporation via voting power of shares held. Aside from closely-held corporations, we would not expect to see corporate constituents limit the board's management authority via the certificate.

Public companies are managed by a board with full powers and authority under section 141(a). The prototypical form of management is representative management. The management structure is two-tiered: a board of directors provides oversight on a part-time basis of officers who manage the business on a day-to-day basis. Directors and officers generally have little ownership stake relative to all shareholders, thus the problem of the separation of ownership and control. The two-tier structure of managers in public companies is inherent in section 141(a)'s mandate that a corporation shall be managed by a board of directors.

The flip side of representative management is that shareholders do not participate in management and are not agents of the corporation.[5] This rule distinguishes corporation law from partnership law where partners are agents and can transact business on behalf of the partnership. *See* RUPA § 301 ("Each partner is an agent of the partnership for the purpose of its business."); *id.* § 401(h) ("Each partner has equal rights in the management and conduct of the partnership's business.").

2. MANDATORY RULES

Each business organization statute has a unique mix of default and mandatory rules. Corporation law imposes more mandatory rules. *See* Anglo Am. Sec. Fund, L.P. v. S.R. Global Int'l Fund, L.P., 829 A.2d 143, 150 (Del. Ch. 2003) ("Whereas corporations are largely creatures of statute with some limited contractual flexibility, limited partnerships offer greater contractual flexibility with only a few statutory constraints."). The table below provides examples of differences with respect to mandatory rules.

---

[5] *See* Bashford-Burmister Co. v. Hammons, 283 P. 926, 928 (Ariz. 1930) (noting that "the stockholders as such are not agents of the corporation and cannot sell or dispose of its property"); Swope v. Swope, 739 P.2d 273, 280 (Idaho 1987) ("Stockholders are not agents of the corporation and do not make business decisions"); Van Heusen v. Van Heusen Charles Co., 74 Misc. 292, 299 (N.Y. Sup. 1911) ("The legal title of the property is in the corporation, not in the stockholder, and a stockholder is not an agent of the corporation."). Because shareholders are ordinarily not an agent of the corporation, they do not owe fiduciary duties unless they exercise control of the company. *See* Ivanhoe Partners v. Newmont Mining Corp., 535 A.2d 1334, 1344 (Del. 1987) ("Under Delaware law a shareholder owes a fiduciary duty only if it owns a majority interest in or exercises control over the business affairs of the corporation.").

Matters	Corporation	NBE
Management	Representative managers in form of board of directors and officers: DGCL § 141(a), § 142(a)	Owner managers in member-managed LLC and partnership; representative managers possible, but not required in manager-managed LLC: RUPA § 401(h); ULPA (2001) § 406(a); RULLCA § 407(b)
Mandatory voting rights	One or more classes or series of stock that have full voting rights: DGCL § 151(b); MBCA § 6.01(b)	Voting rights subject to contracting through charter agreements: RUPA § 105; ULPA (2001) § 105; RULLCA § 105
Qualities of managers	Directors and officers must be natural persons: DGCL § 141(b); MBCA § 8.03(a), § 1.40, § 8.40(b)	Owners and managers are "persons" who can be legal persons: RUPA § 102(14); ULPA (2001) § 102(15); RULLCA § 102(15)
Procedural requirements	Annual shareholder meeting to elect directors must be held: DGCL § 211(b); MBCA § 7.01(a)	No statutory requirement to hold specific meetings
Transferring interest	"The shares of stock in every corporation shall be deemed personal property and transferable": DGCL § 159	Transferable interest is personal property, but the entire interest may not be transferred: RUPA § 502(a); ULPA (2001) § 702(a); RULLCA § 502(a)
Contracting for fiduciary duty	Duties not subject to private ordering: DGCL § 102(b); MBCA § 2.02(b)	Duties subject to much private ordering: RUPA § 105(d); ULPA (2001) § 105(d); RULLCA § 105(d)
Role of courts	The equity of a particular situation is determined by court, which regulates the conduct of managers and shareholder rights in all facets of corporation law where the statute may not provide and even when there is a legal right or a contract: *e.g.*, Schnell v.	Outside of a few mandatory rules, the principle of freedom of contract governs and often the court's role is to interpret the contract: *e.g.*, In re Nantucket Island Associates Ltd. Partnership Unitholders Litig., 810 A.2d 351 (Del. Ch. 2002); Delaware LLC Act § 18–

	Chris-Craft Industries, Inc., 285 A.2d 437 (Del. 1971)	1101(b); Delaware LP Act § 17–1101(c)

3. MANDATORY FIDUCIARY DUTIES

Directors and officers owe fiduciary duties to the corporation and shareholder. These duties are the duty of care and the duty of loyalty. One of the most important distinctions between corporations and NBEs is that fiduciary duties in corporation law are mandatory and not subject to private ordering.[6]

> Despite much academic debate, it is well settled that in Delaware at least, corporate law differs from unincorporated alternative entity law in one fundamental respect. Under Delaware corporate law, fiduciary duties are *mandatory*. These duties, owed by the managers of a corporation to the shareholders of the firm, in general cannot be waived or modified by contract. Under Delaware law governing limited liability companies (LLCs) and limited partnerships (LPs), however, fiduciary duties are merely *default* duties. Although managers of these alternative entity firms owe fiduciary duties, these duties may be modified or even wholly eliminated by the terms of the alternative entity governing agreement.

Mohsen Manesh, *What Is the Practical Importance of Default Rules Under Delaware LLC and LP Law?*, 2 Harv. Bus. L. Rev. Online 121, 121–22 (2012).

Mandatory fiduciary duties must be the logical rule. Imagine the havoc and mischief that would occur if managers of public companies, housing trillions of dollars of assets and wealth of numerous shareholders, can contract for their duties as they can in NBEs. The mandatory aspect of duties assures that *all* inequitable conduct by managers, as determined by courts, are subject to judicial review and remedy.

---

6 *See* Delaware General Corporation Law § 102(b)(7) (prohibiting charter provision that eliminates the duty of loyalty, but permitting the elimination of money damages for a breach of the duty of care). *See also* 800 South Wells Commercial LLC v. Cadden, 103 N.E.3d 875, 885 (Ill. App. 2018) ("Plaintiff is not a regular corporation such that common-law propositions concerning officers and their duties dominate this conversation or are even relevant. When dealing with limited liability companies and the fiduciary duties owed to them, we must look—first, foremost, and primarily—to the Act."); Productivity Technologies Corp. v. Levine, 268 F.Supp.3d 940, 947 (E.D. Mich. 2017) ("The defendants have not cited any authority suggesting that Delaware's Limited Liability Company Act applies to corporations. And as the plaintiff notes, [DLLCA] section 18–1101(c), if applied to corporations, would conflict with a section of Delaware's General Corporation Law that does not allow directors to escape liability '(i) for any breach of the director's duty of loyalty to the corporation or its stockholders; (ii) for acts or omissions not in good faith or which involve intentional misconduct or a knowing violation of law; (iii) under § 174 of this title; or (iv) for any transaction from which the director derived an improper personal benefit.' Del. Code tit. 8 § 102(7)."); Sutherland v. Sutherland, 2009 WL 857468, at *4 (Del. Ch. 2009) ("While such a provision [eliminating fiduciary duty] is permissible under the Delaware Limited Liability Company Act and the Delaware Revised Uniform Limited Partnership Act, where freedom of contract is the guiding and overriding principle, it is expressly forbidden by the DGCL.").

4. TAXES

Corporations can be subject to two-levels of taxation: tax at the corporate level on corporate profits, and tax at the shareholder level upon distribution or realization of profits on shares through capital gains on sale. *See* I.R.C. § 11(a) ("A tax is hereby imposed for each taxable year on the taxable income of every corporation."). However, NBEs can choose to be taxed as partnerships wherein profits flow-through to the partners.

C. WHY CORPORATIONS

The corporate form provides a distinctive set of rules. Why might the rules of corporations be better in some respects than the rules of NBEs as inferred when the corporate form is chosen? Before the rise of LLCs, the essential choice of entities boiled down to a choice between the corporation and the partnership. The two entities are very different, and the choice is stark. In yesteryear, limited liability was a major reason for the choice of the corporate form, but that is no longer the case. Limited liability is extremely important, but today there are multiple entity forms that provide limited liability. The LLC form provides limited liability, and the contractual flexibility to structure the entity in virtually any internal form the owners and managers desire. With this modern development, the question concerning entity choice changes somewhat: Why is the corporate form the dominant entity form for publicly-traded businesses?

Then and now, the corporate form has been the dominant form to amass large aggregations of assets from diffuse investors. By virtue of being owner-managed entities, partnerships and other closely-held entities generally are not mass aggregations of assets. Corporation law has rules that are conducive to public trading of ownership interests: (1) certain mandatory rules that protect passive owners consistently across all firms; (2) rules favoring professional, representative management; (3) rules begetting the separation of ownership and control; (4) standardized units of ownership conducive to free transfer of ownership interests.

1. STANDARDIZED MANDATORY RULES

Corporation law provides a number of mandatory rules that protect passive owners. A set of fixed rights protects shareholders, for example: mandatory voting rights with respect to director elections, fundamental transactions, and charter approval; power to amend the bylaws; mandatory right to appraisal in certain transactions; presumption of free transferability of shares. Fiduciary duties are mandatory and corporate managers cannot contract out of their duties.

Because virtually all publicly-traded businesses are corporations, corporation law provides a common set of rules applicable to all public companies.[7] Presumably, these rules have been tested over time by the market process and have been found (or are believed) to be effective at enhancing firm value. Firm values are enhanced when shareholders have a certain level of legal protection, if only because that protection induces investors to trust the market system and provide capital for all intent and purpose to strangers. Because a common set of legal rules applies to virtually all public firms, the factors of value are the economic and business attributes of firms such as management, strategy, profitability, and risk profile. In other words, because a common set of presumably good (market tested) laws applies across the board to virtually all firms, the market can ignore the law as a factor of value and instead focus on the qualities of the business when determining the market value of companies.

2. PROFESSIONAL MANAGEMENT

Under corporation law, the managerial authority rests in the board of directors: "The business and affairs of every corporation shall be managed by or under the direction of a board of directors." DGCL § 141(a). Directors can be any natural person, who can also be an officer and a shareholder. The board can and often do delegate managerial duties to corporate officers who generally operate the business on a day-to-day basis: "Every corporation shall have such officers with such titles and duties as shall be stated in the bylaws or in a resolution of the board of directors which is not inconsistent with the bylaws." *Id.* § 142(a). Like directors, officers can be any natural person, who can also be a director and a shareholder.

In large or sophisticated corporations, directors and officers are not substantial owners of the venture. They are professionals who work for the corporate enterprise. This basic structure of directors and officers facilitates the management of corporations by professional managers, who may have very little equity ownership.

3. SEPARATION OF OWNERSHIP AND CONTROL

According to Berle and Means, the separation of ownership and control begets the fundamental problem of agency and agency cost. At the same time, unless this separation has a substantial utility, it would not have survived for so long in the form of the public corporation. What positive benefits are begotten by separating ownership and control?

The separation in large ventures is inevitable because an owner will likely have only a small stake. Given this unavoidable fact, the choice of a manager should be a matter of meritocracy and specialized skill. In most cases, that choice would be a non-owner professional manager. Complex businesses may require highly specialized managerial skills that may not

---

7 A handful of publicly traded companies are organized as LPs or LLCs.

be found among shareholders. The requirement of a board embodies the idea that a specialized manager is needed.

Representative management has other benefits. Whereas owner management may be subject to the comings and goings of owners, professional management ensures a continuity of business subject only, in theory, to dismissal for poor performance. Professional management means that a multitude of shareholders are not competing to manage the company or to determine its strategy. Intra-firm competition for control and conflict are sometimes inevitable in owner-managed firms, but they may impose costs on the firm. Such competition and conflict are less prominent in corporations due to the hierarchy of the board system and officer ranks. The loser of any internal competition resigns or is fired.

4. STANDARDIZED OWNERSHIP UNITS AND FREE TRANSFERABILITY

Ownership interest is represented in shares of stock. If a corporation has only common stock, all shares have the same economic and governance rights. Each share is entitled to one vote. *Id.* § 212(a) ("each stockholder shall be entitled to 1 vote for each share of capital stock held by such stockholder"). Each share has the same right in the profits and in the distribution of assets upon liquidation. *See id.* § 170 ("The directors of every corporation, subject to any restrictions contained in its certificate of incorporation, may declare and pay dividends upon the shares of its capital stock."); Sinclair Oil Corp. v. Levien, 280 A.2d 717, 721–22 (Del. 19071) (holding that controlling shareholder was not self-dealing when it caused a large dividend that was equally paid to minority shareholders in the same proportion as the ownership stake).

Corporation law permits different classes of stock, each having different rights and preferences.

> Every corporation may issue 1 or more classes of stock or 1 or more series of stock within any class thereof, any or all of which classes may be of stock with par value or stock without par value and which classes or series may have such voting powers, full or limited, or no voting powers, and such designations, preferences and relative, participating, optional or other special rights, and qualifications, limitations or restrictions thereof, as shall be stated and expressed in the certificate of incorporation or of any amendment thereto, or in the resolution or resolutions providing for the issue of such stock adopted by the board of directors pursuant to authority expressly vested in it by the provisions of its certificate of incorporation.

DGCL § 151(a). If there are more than one class of stock, "the rights of stockholders are contract rights and it is necessary to look to the certificate of incorporation to ascertain what those rights are." Ellingwood v. Wolf's Head Oil Refinery Co., 38 A.2d 743, 747 (Del. 1944).

A share of stock represents the ownership interest in a corporation. Stock is fungible in that the rights, privileges, limitations, and powers are the same among the same class of stock. The standardization of ownership units differs from ownership in NBEs in two important ways.

First, in theory and in practice, the rights of partners and members in partnerships and LLCs can be and often are subject to individualized negotiation between the firm and its constituents. In corporations, the fungible bundles of rights are embedded in each share of stock. Corporate ownership is "contractual" in the abstract sense that the rights flow from corporation law and the certificate of incorporation; but the "contract" is not easily subject to a bespoke process of negotiation. The creation of a new class of stock requires an amendment of the certificate of incorporation, which requires a resolution of the board and a vote of shareholders. DGLC § 242(b). This requirement can be waived if the certificate of incorporation provides the board a "blank check" authority to designate the rights, preferences, limitations and powers of a newly issued class of stock. *Id.* § 151(a) (permitting a corporation to issue stock with terms "as shall be stated in the resolution or resolutions providing for the issue of such stock adopted by the board of directors pursuant to authority expressly vested in it by the provisions of its certificate of incorporation"); MBCA § 6.02(a) (permitting per the articles of incorporation the board to classify any unissued shares). The issuance of stock is a formal process. In practice and absent a significant investment by a shareholder, bespoken issuances at the shareholder level among multitude of shareholders are difficult to do.

Second, the laws of NBEs limit the transfer of ownership in the firm. Only the economic interest is transferable. *See* RULLCA § 501 ("A transferable interest is personal property."); RUPA § 502 (same); ULPA (2001) § 701 (same). Upon a transfer of the transferable interest, the transferee does not become an owner in the firm. *See* RULLCA § 502(a) ("a transfer, in whole or in part, of a transferable interest is permissible [but] does not entitle the transferee to participate in the management or conduct of the company's activities and affairs"); RUPA § 503(a) (same); ULPA (2001) § 702(a) (same). On the other hand, corporation law permits the transfer of the ownership in the company. *See* DGCL § 159 (providing that stock is "personal property and transferable"); MBCA § 6.27(c) (providing that restriction on transfer is authorized only for "reasonable purpose"); Landreth Timber Co. v. Landreth, 471 U.S. 681, 686 (1985) (identifying a common characteristic of stock as "negotiability"). Thus, corporation law is founded on the premise that ownership is presumptively fluid due to free negotiability, as would be the case in a public corporation, whereas the laws of NBEs are premised on the notion that firms are intimate associations in which consent is required to admit new owners. *See* RULLCA § 401(c)(3) ("a person becomes a member with the affirmative vote or consent of all the members"); RUPA § 402(b)(3) (same); ULPA (2001) § 301(b)(3) (same as to limited partners), § 401(b)(3) (same as to general partner).

D. DELAWARE CORPORATION LAW

Due to the internal affairs doctrine, incorporators can choose the jurisdiction to file the charter and thus the applicable law. Although Delaware is a small state by size and population, its corporation law is prominent because a substantial majority of public companies are filed in Delaware. *See* Jeffrey W. Bullock, *A Message from the Secretary of State, Annual Report Statistics*, Del. Div. Corps. (2018) ("Delaware remains the home of the vast majority of top U.S. companies, including more than two thirds of the Fortune 500 and 80 percent of all firms that go public."). Delaware corporation law is important, but does not represent a single national law in the way that federal law is. A significant minority, including very prominent companies, have chosen other states. For example, of the 2019 Fortune 50 companies, 19 companies were chartered in another jurisdiction.[8] Although there is not a true national corporation law, Delaware is the single most important state because it dominates incorporations and its law influences the development of laws of other states. *See* Mark J. Roe, *Delaware's Competition*, 117 Harv. L. Rev. 588, 590 (2003) (arguing that "Delaware has 'won' that race [among states, and that] Delaware's chief competitive pressure comes not from other states but from the federal government").

Although corporation law is statute based, the hallmark of Delaware law is the importance of its judiciary and judge-made law, particularly on the development of fiduciary duties as they apply in various contexts such as mergers and acquisitions. With the exception of a provision dealing with interested (conflicted) directors, DGCL § 144, the Delaware statute does not generally set standards of conduct for corporate fiduciaries.[9] Delaware courts thus play an important part in developing corporation law. Notably, the trial court, the Delaware Chancery Court, is a court of equity.[10] The

---

[8] ExxonMobile (#2, New Jersey), Apple (#3, California), Costco Wholesale (#14, Washington), Cardinal Health (#16, Ohio), Kroger (#20, Ohio), General Electric (#21, New York), Fannie Mae (#22, Federal), Microsoft (#26, Washington), Comcast (#32, Pennsylvania), Anthem (#33, Indiana), State Farm (#36, Illinois), Johnson & Johnson (#37, New Jersey), IBM (#38, New York), Target (#39, Minnesota), Freddie Mac (#40, Federal), Lowe's (#42, North Carolina), Procter & Gamble (#45, Ohio), PepsiCo (#48, North Carolina), Prudential Financial (#50, New Jersey).

[9] In contrast, many other corporation statutes take a different approach. *E.g.*, MBCA § 8.30 (Standards of Conduct for Directors), § 8.31 (Standards of Liability for Directors), § 8.42 (Standards of Conduct for Officers), Subchapter F (Director's Conflicting Interest Transactions, § 8.60 to § 8.63), Subchapter G (Business Opportunities, § 8.70).

[10] "The Court of Chancery has jurisdiction to hear and determine all matters and causes in equity. The general equity jurisdiction of the Court is measured in terms of the general equity jurisdiction of the High Court of Chancery of Great Britain as it existed prior to the separation of the American colonies. The General Assembly may confer upon the Court of Chancery additional statutory jurisdiction. In today's practice, the litigation in the Court of Chancery consists largely of corporate matters, trusts, estates, and other fiduciary matters, disputes involving the purchase

court applies equity to all situations. *E.g.,* Schnell v. Chris-Craft Industries, Inc., 285 A.2d 437, 439 (Del. 1971) (stating the principle that "inequitable action does not become permissible simply because it is legally possible"). A challenge of this approach of examining the equities in each unique context is that, sometimes, legal outcomes may be indeterminate.

> We are mindful of the elasticity inherent in equity jurisprudence and the traditional desirability in certain equity cases of measuring conduct by the "conscience of the court" and disapproving conduct which offends or shocks that conscience. Yet one must be wary of equity jurisprudence which takes on a random or ad hoc quality.
>
> > Equity is a rogish thing. For Law we have to measure, know what to trust to; Equity is according to the conscience of him that is Chancellor, and as that is larger or narrower, so it Equity. 'Tis all one as if they should make the standard for the measure we call a "foot" a Chancellor's foot; what an uncertain measure would this be! One Chancellor has a long foot, another a short foot, a third an indifferent foot. 'Tis the same thing in the Chancellor's conscience.

Nixon v. Blackwell, 626 A.2d 1366, 1378 n.17 (Del. 1993) (quoting John Selden, in *Equity*, Table-Talk (1689)).

There is a longstanding academic debate on whether Delaware law represents a "race to the bottom" or a "race to the top." William Cary famously argued that Delaware law leads a "race to the bottom." Ralph Winter responded by arguing that corporation law is a "race to the top."

FEDERALISM AND CORPORATE LAW: REFLECTIONS UPON DELAWARE

William L. Cary, 83 Yale L.J. 663 (1974)

Judicial decisions in Delaware illustrate that the courts have undertaken to carry out the "public policy" of the state and create a "favorable climate" for management. Consciously or unconsciously, fiduciary standards and the standards of fairness generally have been relaxed. In general, the judicial decisions can best be reconciled on the basis of a desire to foster incorporation in Delaware. It is not clear, however, that the revenue thermometer should replace the chancellor's foot. This trend should be reversed. This article examines Delaware laws and decisions, compares their underlying principles with those operating in federal cases,

---

and sale of land, questions of title to real estate, and commercial and contractual matters in general." https://courts.delaware.gov/chancery/jurisdiction.aspx. *See* Del. C., tit. 10, § 341 ("The Court of Chancery shall have jurisdiction to hear and determine all matters and causes in equity.").

and presents a proposal which would substantially alter the Delaware confluence.

Before proceeding to this inquiry certain underlying premises should be recognized. First, although there is not as much "free enterprise" as appears at first glance, ours is still a capitalist economy. At the same time, from the standpoint of legal rights and duties, we are tending toward a managerial, rather than a capitalist society—thanks in large part to the shift of authority to management.

Second, almost all of our business is transacted through corporations. For the year 1969 total business receipts amounted to $2.9 trillion, 84 percent of which was accounted for by active corporations. Moreover, a substantial and growing fraction of the major corporations is organized in Delaware. Of the approximately 1,250 concerns listed on the New York Stock Exchange in 1965, 433 or 35 percent were Delaware corporations. And the percentage is growing. As of January 5, 1973, there were 1,505 listed companies, of which 606 or 40 percent were organized in Delaware. For this reason alone Delaware decisions have a profound impact upon the development of corporation law. Furthermore, similar to its influence on statutory modernization, Delaware's case law is cited constantly and relied upon in other jurisdictions. Every corporation law casebook for students is filled with Delaware decisions because it is the state where great companies are organized and where there is the most corporate experience to draw upon.

Next, it is of obvious importance that business should be conducted fairly, honestly, and competently. Indeed, these ingredients are essential to raise capital and make the system work. In another context I have adverted to a discussion in Washington some years ago with the Ambassador from a South American country. He came to seek advice because he wanted to encourage the investment of outside capital into private firms in his country and wondered how that could be achieved. I asked first, "Are your stock exchange facilities inadequate?" And he replied, "No, that really isn't the question. We have to get back to fundamentals. My first concern is whether the public investor can trust anyone. The trouble with management in my country is that their only loyalty is to their relatives." This is not uncommon and it struck me forcefully; it emphasized the importance of confidence and a high standard of conduct by management as an essential ingredient before one can expect the private investor to entrust his funds to public companies. Such confidence can be sustained only by a combination of high standards coupled with disclosure and management accountability coupled with vulnerability to derivative or direct shareholder action.

Finally, we come back to a major focus of this article. It has been said that numerous members of the New York bar "felt Delaware was a more favorable forum than any other available." The necessary high standards of conduct cannot be maintained by courts shackled to public policy based upon the production of revenue, pride in being "number one," and the creation of a "favorable climate" for new incorporations. The view is widely held that Delaware corporate decisions lean toward the status quo and adhere to minimal standards of director responsibility both to the corporation and its shareholders. Although these generalizations are difficult to prove absolutely, a series of cases illustrates that this reputation is based upon an accurate analysis of the courts' decisions and that Gresham's law applies. One of the striking aspects of these opinions is that among the three supreme court justices there is rarely a dissent. . . .

However, in order to remedy the Delaware syndrome it does appear that federal standards of corporate responsibility are called for. This can best be achieved by prescribing minimum corporation law provisions which shall be applicable to companies doing business in interstate commerce and construed by federal judicial standards. Uniformity is of the essence. Efforts must be made to insure that provisions are not interpreted differently owing to varying state interpretations of public policy. There should also be wide-ranging service of process upon directors and officers of corporations. The participation of a government agency such as the Securities and Exchange Commission is not contemplated in this proposal.

Ideally, consideration should be given to a much broader inquiry perceptively suggested by Professor Eisenberg. In his opinion "Traditional corporate statutes fail to deal with many important structural decisions which are common in today's business world." We might go even farther and ask what representation the modern constituency of the corporation—employees, consumers, and the public, as well as shareholders—should have in the governance of the corporation. Consideration of this issue is not contemplated here. The first step is to escape from the present predicament in which a pygmy among the states prescribes, interprets, and indeed denigrates national corporate policy as an incentive to encourage incorporation within its borders, thereby increasing its revenue.

As an alternative, I propose a Federal Corporate Uniformity Act applying to all corporations having more than $1 million of assets and shareholders, thus paralleling the proposals made in the American Law Institute's proposed Federal Securities Code. To prevent disparity in the law, however, it might be preferable to make such an act apply to all public companies engaged in or affecting interstate commerce. . . .

The proposal is to continue allowing companies to incorporate in the jurisdiction of their choosing but to remove much of the incentive to organize in Delaware or its rival states. Such companies, nevertheless, must be subject to the jurisdiction of the federal courts under certain general standards. To illustrate, some of the major provisions of such a federal statute might include (1) federal fiduciary standards with respect to directors and officers and controlling shareholders; (2) an "interested directors" provision prescribing fairness as a prerequisite to any transaction; (3) a requirement of certain uniform provisions to be incorporated in the certificate of incorporation: for example, authority to amend by-laws, initiate corporate action, or draw up the agenda of shareholders' meetings shall not be vested exclusively in management; (4) a more frequent requirement of shareholder approval of corporate transactions, with limits placed upon the number of shares authorized at any one time; (5) abolition of nonvoting shares; (6) the scope of indemnification of directors specifically prescribed and made exclusive; (7) adoption of a long-arm provision comparable to § 27 of the Securities Exchange Act to apply to all transactions within the corporate structure involving shareholders, directors, and officers. . . .

In summary, as long as we operate within a capitalist society and as long as confidence in management is prerequisite to its continuance, there should be a federal interest in the proper conduct of the corporation itself as much as in the market for its securities. A civilizing jurisprudence should import lifting standards; certainly there is no justification for permitting them to deteriorate. The absurdity of this race for the bottom, with Delaware in the lead—tolerated and indeed fostered by corporate counsel—should arrest the conscience of the American bar when its current reputation is in low estate.

STATE LAW, SHAREHOLDER PROTECTION, AND THE THEORY OF THE CORPORATION

Ralph K. Winter, 6 J. Leg. Stud. 251 (1977)

It is not in the interest of Delaware corporate management or the Delaware treasury for corporations chartered there to be at a disadvantage in raising debt or equity capital relative to corporations chartered in other states. Management must induce investors freely to choose their firm's stock instead of, among other things, stock in companies incorporated in other states or other countries, bonds, bank accounts, certificates of deposit, partnerships (general or limited), individual proprietorships, joint ventures, present consumption, etc. As discussed in detail later, a corporation's ability to compete effectively in product markets is related to its ability to raise capital, and management's tenure in office is related to the price of stock. If management is to secure initial capital and have continuous access to ready capital in the future, it must attract investors away from the almost infinite variety of competing opportunities. Moreover, to retain its position management has a powerful incentive to keep the price of stock high enough to prevent takeovers, a result obtained by making the corporation an attractive investment.

The Cary analysis thus seems implausible at an *a priori* level, because, when analyzed, it appears as little more than a claim that Delaware can facilitate the monopolization of the capital market, just as it can grant exclusive franchises for taxicabs in Wilmington. But the market for capital is international in scope and involves an undifferentiated product with no transportation costs. Delaware cannot create barriers which prevent it from flowing to the most attractive investments; any attempt at monopolization will only drive capital from that state.

The fact that other states have found it necessary to change their law in response to Delaware, therefore, strongly suggests that investors do not share Professor Cary's view and in fact believe that they do better under Delaware law than under the laws of the other states.

The implausibility of the "race for the bottom" argument is obscured because the literature calling for stricter regulation stresses only expected benefits while ignoring costs and is in a real sense the victim of its own rhetoric. To say a legal system is marked by "laxity" implies a cost-benefit judgment about more stringent regulation but such rhetoric in the shareholder protection area is rarely accompanied by the analysis such judgments call for. In truth, a "lax" legal system is neither intuitively nor empirically inferior to a stringent one.

All regulation imposes costs in the way of consumed resources, such as the efforts of accountants or lawyers, which might be put to other uses. Where regulation is imposed on private transactions, such as the purchase of a car or investment in a corporation, those transactions are made more costly for all involved. For example, it has been argued that whatever reduction in securities fraud is caused by S.E.C. requirements is offset by the higher costs imposed on securities transactions.

Another way in which regulation imposes costs is in restricting the ability of private parties to arrange their affairs in the way they find most suitable. Often these costs result from well-meaning attempts to protect those parties. For example, assume that the quality of widgets can be determined only by extended use rather than consumer examination. Most consumers purchase widgets on the basis of a company brand name or on the advice of a local merchant, both of whom find it in their economic interest to maintain a good business reputation. Other consumers, however, purchase low quality widgets (at the high quality price) from manufacturers hoping to make a quick profit even at the cost of a bad reputation in the long run. Regulation designed to protect such consumers may operate by general rules applicable to all transactions, not just those the government seeks to prevent. For example, government testing of widgets would apply to all widgets, not just those of low quality, and would thus impose costs on (and thereby reduce in number) the beneficial transactions in high quality widgets. Regulation may deter blameless conduct as well as that which is conceded to have no social value, and those who call for regulation make an incomplete argument when they take account only of anticipated benefits.

Intervention in private transactions which impose no social cost can be justified only as a means of reducing the costs to the private parties. Thus, a prime function of state corporation codes is to supply standard terms which reduce the transaction costs, and thereby increase the benefits, of investing by eliminating costly bargaining which might otherwise accompany many routine corporate dealings. But substituting a mandatory legal rule for bargaining also may impose a cost in the form of the elimination of alternatives which the parties might prefer.

Much of the legal literature calling for further federal regulation either assumes that no costs will fall upon shareholders or merely undertakes a cursory "eyeballing" of the potential costs. To be sure, self-dealing and fraud exist in corporate affairs and their elimination is desirable. But at some point the exercise of control by general rules of law may impose costs on investors which damage them in both quantity and quality quite as much as self-dealing or fraud. A paradox thus results: maximizing the yield to investors generally may, indeed almost surely will, result in a number of cases of fraud or self-dealing; and eliminating all fraud or self-dealing may decrease the yield to shareholders generally.

CHAPTER 11

CORPORATE GOVERNANCE

■ ■ ■

A. BOARD OF DIRECTORS

1. BASIC REQUIREMENTS AND FUNCTION OF BOARD

The quintessential characteristic of a corporation is the board of directors. Corporation law provides basic directives. The business and affairs of the corporation is managed by or under the direction of the board. A director must be an individual, unlike a partner or member or manager in NBEs who can be a legal person. A board must consist of at least one director. The board may work through a committee of the board, which may have certain delegated powers of the board.

Delaware General Corporation Law: § 141. Board of directors; powers; number, qualifications, terms and quorum; committees; classes of directors; nonstock corporations; reliance upon books; action without meeting; removal.

(a) The business and affairs of every corporation organized under this chapter shall be managed by or under the direction of a board of directors, except as may be otherwise provided in this chapter or in its certificate of incorporation. . . .

(b) The board of directors of a corporation shall consist of 1 or more members, each of whom shall be a natural person. The number of directors shall be fixed by, or in the manner provided in, the bylaws, unless the certificate of incorporation fixes the number of directors, in which case a change in the number of directors shall be made only by amendment of the certificate. Directors need not be stockholders unless so required by the certificate of incorporation or the bylaws. The certificate of incorporation or bylaws may prescribe other qualifications for directors. Each director shall hold office until such director's successor is elected and qualified or until such director's earlier resignation or removal. . . . A majority of the total number of directors shall constitute a quorum for the transaction of business unless the certificate of incorporation or the bylaws require a greater number. Unless the certificate of incorporation provides otherwise, the bylaws may provide that a number less than a majority shall constitute a quorum which in no case shall be less than ⅓ of the total number of directors. The vote of the majority of the directors present at a meeting

> at which a quorum is present shall be the act of the board of directors unless the certificate of incorporation or the bylaws shall require a vote of a greater number.
>
> (c)(2) The board of directors may designate 1 or more committees, each committee to consist of 1 or more of the directors of the corporation. . . . Any such committee, to the extent provided in the resolution of the board of directors, or in the bylaws of the corporation, shall have and may exercise all the powers and authority of the board of directors in the management of the business and affairs of the corporation . . .; but no such committee shall have the power or authority in reference to the following matter: (i) approving or adopting, or recommending to the stockholders, any action or matter (other than the election or removal of directors) expressly required by this chapter to be submitted to stockholders for approval or (ii) adopting, amending or repealing any bylaw of the corporation.
>
> (e) A member of the board of directors, or a member of any committee designated by the board of directors, shall, in the performance of such member's duties, be fully protected in relying in good faith upon the records of the corporation and upon such information, opinions, reports or statements presented to the corporation by any of the corporation's officers or employees, or committees of the board of directors, or by any other person as to matters the member reasonably believes are within such other person's professional or expert competence and who has been selected with reasonable care by or on behalf of the corporation.

A public company must have more than one director. Pursuant to federal securities law, national stock exchanges require a board to have an audit committee and this committee must have at least three board members. Beyond this minimum number, boards of public companies will vary in the number of directors. The board size of many companies will be in the range of 7 to 15 members. For example, as of 2020, these randomly selected companies have the following number of directors:

- McDonald's: 12 directors
- Walt Disney: 9 directors
- General Motors: 11 directors
- Walmart: 12 directors
- Coca-Cola: 13 directors
- Boeing: 14 directors
- Nike: 13 directors
- Southwest Airlines: 11 directors
- Berkshire Hathaway: 7 directors
- JPMorgan Chase: 11 directors

While state corporation law mandates a board, the board structure of public companies is regulated by the national securities exchanges, which are themselves regulated by federal securities law and the Securities Exchange Commission (SEC). Both the New York Stock Exchange (NYSE) and the Nasdaq, the two major national exchanges, mandate specific aspects of board structure. Most large public companies are exchange listed and traded.[1] Stock exchanges have rules that companies must follow to be listed. For example, they have minimum threshold requirements of size, measured by various financial metrics. With respect to corporate governance, one such rule required by both the NYSE and the Nasdaq is that a majority of the board be comprised of independent directors. NYSE Listed Company Rule 303A.01 ("Listed companies must have a majority of independent directors."); Nasdaq Listing Rule 5605(b)(1) ("A majority of the board of directors must be comprised of Independent Directors").

Statutory corporation law tells us very little about how boards should function. It simply says that the board shall manage the business and affairs. The term "managed by" could imply that the board actively manages the business on a daily basis. In most public companies, a director is not a full-time employee, unless she is also an officer. A director works on a part-time basis, and the officers are the day-to-day managers.

> Directors spend considerable time preparing for and participating in board and committee meetings: the NACD estimates that on average a director spends approximately 223 hours per year on board and committee matters. The average number of board meetings per year has increased from seven in 1998 to almost nine in 2008. While nearly half of S&P 500 boards meet between six and eight times per year, more than 40 percent meet more frequently.

Report of the Task Force of the ABA Section on Business Law Corporate Governance Committee on Delineation of Governance Roles and Responsibilities, 65 Bus. Law. 107, 130–31 (2009).

> [T]he number of hours a director commits to preparing for and attending meetings of course varies, but for each board they serve we might reasonably expect a director to easily average somewhere around 300 to 350 hours of work per year for complex public companies, depending on committee service. . . . The change over the past years is marked, with the National Association of Corporate Directors (NACD) annual survey revealing the average director time commitment has grown by 46 percent, from 190 hours in 2005 to 278 hours in 2014.

Blake Stephenson, *Don't Go Overboard! Are Your Directors Serving on Too Many Boards?*, Nasdaq (Feb. 2, 2016).

---

[1] A publicly-traded company is not required to be listed on any stock exchange, no less listed on the two major national exchanges. The stock of public companies can be traded over-the-counter (OTC), which is trading of securities via a network of broker-dealers and not involving a listing on an exchange. Companies traded on the OTC are generally smaller and are not listed because they cannot meet the listing requirements of exchanges.

Given the part-time basis of a board's work, what is the function of a board in light of the law's directive to "manage the business and affairs"?

Model Business Corporation Law § 8.01, Requirement for and Functions of Board of Directors: Official Comment

The scope of the board's oversight responsibilities will vary depending on the nature of the corporation and its business. At least for public corporations, the board's responsibilities generally include oversight of the following:

- business performance, plans and strategy;
- management's assessment of major risks to which the corporation is or may be exposed;
- the performance and compensation of executive officers;
- policies and practices to foster the corporation's compliance with law and ethical conduct;
- management's preparation of the corporation's financial statements;
- management's design and assessment of effectiveness of the corporation's internal controls;
- plans for the succession of the chief executive officer and other executive officers;
- the composition of the board and of board committees; and
- whether the corporation has information and reporting systems in place to provide directors with appropriate information in a timely manner.

2. BUSINESS JUDGMENT RULE

Under DGCL § 141(a), the board manages the business and affairs of the corporation. A corollary to this concept is a rule that the board should have broad and ultimate authority to make decisions, subject to compliance with their fiduciary duties. Broad authority means that the board has wide-ranging powers. Ultimate authority means that, as long as that authority was properly exercised in conformity with their fiduciary duties, its exercise should not be challenged and thus should not result in liability. This concept is embodied in the business judgment rule. The business judgment rule is commonly stated as the following formulation:

> The business judgment rule is an acknowledgment of the managerial prerogatives of Delaware directors under Section 141(a). *It is a presumption that in making a business decision the directors of a corporation acted on an informed basis, in good faith*

> *and in the honest belief that the action taken was in the best interests of the company.* Absent an abuse of discretion, that judgment will be respected by the courts. The burden is on the party challenging the decision to establish facts rebutting the presumption.

Aronson v. Lewis, 473 A.2d 805, 812 (Del. 1984).

The case below discusses the dual procedural and substantive nature of the business judgment rule. In reading this case, consider this question: (1) In what way is the rule a substantive rule of law? (2) In what way does the rule serve an important procedural function when a corporate manager is sued? (3) What is the legal effect when a plaintiff shareholder rebuts the presumption of the business judgment rule?

CINERAMA, INC. V. TECHNICOLOR, INC.

663 A.2d 1156 (Del. 1995)

HOLLAND, JUSTICE:

The business judgment rule "operates as *both* a procedural guide for litigants and a substantive rule of law." As a *procedural* guide the business judgment presumption is a *rule of evidence* that places the initial burden of proof on the plaintiff. This Court described the rule's evidentiary, or procedural, operation as follows:

> If a shareholder fails to meet this evidentiary burden, the business judgment rule attaches to protect corporate officers and directors and the decisions they make, and our courts will not second-guess these business judgments. *See* 8 *Del.C.* § 141(a). If the rule is rebutted, the burden shifts to the directors, the proponents of the challenged transaction, to prove to the trier of fact the "entire fairness" of the transaction to the shareholder plaintiff.

Burden shifting does not create *per se* liability on the part of the directors. Rather, it "is a procedure by which Delaware courts of equity determine under what standard of review director liability is to be judged."

Where the presumption of the business judgment rule has been rebutted, the board of directors' action is examined under the entire fairness standard. This Court has described the dual aspects of entire fairness, as follows:

> The concept of fairness has two basic aspects: fair dealing and fair price. The former embraces questions of when the transaction was timed, how it was initiated, structured, negotiated, disclosed to the directors, and how the approvals of the directors and the stockholders were obtained. The latter aspect of fairness relates

> to the economic and financial considerations of the proposed merger, including all relevant factors: assets, market value, earnings, future prospects, and any other elements that affect the intrinsic or inherent value of a company's stock. However, the test for fairness is not a bifurcated one as between fair dealing and price. All aspects of the issue must be examined as a whole since the question is one of entire fairness.

The entire fairness standard requires the board of directors to establish "to the *court's* satisfaction that the transaction was the product of both fair dealing *and* fair price." The "fair price" aspect of an entire fairness analysis requires the board of directors to demonstrate "that the price offered was the highest value reasonably available under the circumstances."

Because the decision that the *procedural* presumption of the business judgment rule has been rebutted does not establish *substantive* liability under the entire fairness standard, such a ruling does not necessarily present an insurmountable obstacle for a board of directors to overcome. An initial judicial determination that a given breach of a board's fiduciary duties has rebutted the presumption of the business judgment rule does not preclude a subsequent judicial determination that the board action was entirely fair, and is, therefore, not outcome-determinative *per se*. To avoid substantive liability, *notwithstanding* the quantum of adverse evidence that has defeated the business judgment rule's protective procedural presumption, the board will have to demonstrate entire fairness by presenting evidence of the cumulative manner by which it otherwise discharged all of its fiduciary duties.

NOTES

1. The business judgment rule is the key obstacle that a complaining shareholder must overcome when pursuing a derivative action against a director or officer. Indeed, the most commonly cited quoted statement of the rule is found in *Aronson v. Lewis*, 473 A.2d 805 (Del. 1984), which is a case on the procedural requirement of pursing a derivative action.

The case below, written by the same author of *State Law, Shareholder Protection, and the Theory of the Corporation* excerpted in the previous chapter, discusses the reasons for the business judgment rule. In reading this case, consider this question: In what way does a cost-benefit, efficiency analysis support the business judgment rule?

JOY V. NORTH

692 F.2d 880 (2d Cir. 1982)

RALPH K. WINTER, CIRCUIT JUDGE:

While it is often stated that corporate directors and officers will be liable for negligence in carrying out their corporate duties, all seem agreed that such a statement is misleading. Whereas an automobile driver who makes a mistake in judgment as to speed or distance injuring a pedestrian will likely be called upon to respond in damages, a corporate officer who makes a mistake in judgment as to economic conditions, consumer tastes or production line efficiency will rarely, if ever, be found liable for damages suffered by the corporation. The fact is that liability is rarely imposed upon corporate directors or officers simply for bad judgment and this reluctance to impose liability for unsuccessful business decisions has been doctrinally labelled the business judgment rule. Although the rule has suffered under academic criticism, it is not without rational basis.

First, shareholders to a very real degree voluntarily undertake the risk of bad business judgment. Investors need not buy stock, for investment markets offer an array of opportunities less vulnerable to mistakes in judgment by corporate officers. Nor need investors buy stock in particular corporations. In the exercise of what is genuinely a free choice, the quality of a firm's management is often decisive. Since shareholders can and do select among investments partly on the basis of management, the business judgment rule merely recognizes a certain voluntariness in undertaking the risk of bad business decisions.

Second, courts recognize that after-the-fact litigation is a most imperfect device to evaluate corporate decisions. The circumstances surrounding a corporate decision are not easily reconstructed in a courtroom years later, since business imperatives often call for quick decisions, inevitably based on less than perfect information. The entrepreneur's function is to encounter risks and to confront uncertainty, and a reasoned decision at the time made may seem a wild hunch viewed years later against a background of perfect knowledge.

Third, because potential profit often corresponds to the potential risk, it is very much in the interest of shareholders that the law not create incentives for overly cautious corporate decisions. Some opportunities offer great profits at the risk of very substantial losses, while the alternatives offer less risk of loss but also less potential profit. Shareholders can reduce the volatility of risk by diversifying their holdings. In the case of the diversified shareholder, the seemingly more risky alternatives may well be the best choice since great losses in some stocks will over time be offset by even greater gains in others. Given mutual funds and similar forms of diversified investment, courts need not bend over backwards to give special protection to shareholders who refuse to reduce the volatility of risk by not diversifying. A rule which penalizes the choice of seemingly riskier alternatives thus may not be in the interest of shareholders generally.

Whatever its merit, however, the business judgment rule extends only as far as the reasons which justify its existence. It does not apply in cases, *e.g.*, in which the corporate decision lacks a business purpose, is tainted by a conflict of interest, is so egregious as to amount to a no-win decision, or results from an obvious and prolonged failure to exercise oversight or supervision. Other examples may occur.

The case below illustrates the boundaries of the business judgment rule and the substantive facet of the rule. In reading this case, consider these questions: (1) Who should have the ultimate authority to make business decisions—the board or shareholders? (2) Can there be ultimate authority if there can be legal challenges to the correctness of such decisions? (3) Are there circumstances in which a shareholder can successfully challenge a business decision?

SHLENSKY V. WRIGLEY

237 N.E.2d 776 (Ill. App. 1968)

SULLIVAN, JUSTICE.

This is an appeal from a dismissal of plaintiff's amended complaint on motion of the defendants. The action was a stockholders' derivative suit against the directors for negligence and mismanagement. The corporation was also made a defendant. Plaintiff sought damages and an order that defendants cause the installation of lights in Wrigley Field and the scheduling of night baseball games.

Plaintiff is a minority stockholder of defendant corporation, Chicago National League Ball Club, a Delaware corporation with its principal place of business in Chicago. Defendant corporation owns and operates the major league professional baseball team known as the Chicago Cubs. The corporation also engages in the operation of Wrigley Field, the Cubs' home park, the concessionaire sales during Cubs' home games, television and radio broadcasts of Cubs' home games, the leasing of the field for football games and other events and receives its share, as visiting team, of admission moneys from games played in other National League stadia. The individual defendants are directors of the Cubs and have served for varying periods of years. Defendant Philip Wrigley is also president of the corporation and owner of approximately 80% of the stock therein.

Plaintiff alleges that since night baseball was first played in 1935 nineteen of the twenty major league teams have scheduled night games. In 1966, out of a total of 1620 games in the major leagues, 932 were played at night. Plaintiff alleges that every member of the major leagues, other than the Cubs, scheduled substantially all of its home games at night. Allegedly this has been done for the specific purpose of maximizing attendance and thereby maximizing revenue and income.

The Cubs, in the years 1961–65, sustained operating losses from its direct baseball operations. Plaintiff attributes those losses to inadequate attendance at Cubs' home games. He concludes that if the directors continue to refuse to install lights at Wrigley Field and schedule night baseball games, the Cubs will continue to sustain comparable losses and its financial condition will continue to deteriorate.

Plaintiff alleges that, except for the year 1963, attendance at Cubs' home games has been substantially below that at their road games, many of which were played at night.

Plaintiff compares attendance at Cubs' games with that of the Chicago White Sox, an American League club, whose weekday games were generally played at night. The weekend attendance figures for the two teams was similar; however, the White Sox week-night games drew many more patrons than did the Cubs' weekday games.

Plaintiff alleges that the funds for the installation of lights can be readily obtained through financing and the cost of installation would be far more than offset and recaptured by increased revenues and incomes resulting from the increased attendance.

Plaintiff further alleges that defendant Wrigley has refused to install lights, not because of interest in the welfare of the corporation but because of his personal opinions "that baseball is a daytime sport and that the installation of lights and night baseball games will have a deteriorating effect upon the surrounding neighborhood." It is alleged that he has admitted that he is not interested in whether the Cubs would benefit financially from such action because of his concern for the neighborhood, and that he would be willing for the team to play night games if a new stadium were built in Chicago.

Plaintiff alleges that the other defendant directors have acquiesced in the policy laid down by Wrigley and have permitted him to dominate the board of directors, even though they knew he was not motivated by a good faith concern as to the best interests of defendant corporation, but solely by his personal views. It is charged that the directors are acting for a reason or reasons contrary and wholly unrelated to the business interests of the corporation; that such arbitrary and capricious acts constitute mismanagement and waste of corporate assets, and that the directors have been negligent in failing to exercise reasonable care and prudence in the management of the corporate affairs.

The question on appeal is whether plaintiff's amended complaint states a cause of action. It is plaintiff's position that fraud, illegality and conflict of interest are not the only bases for a stockholder's derivative action against the directors. Contrariwise, defendants argue that the courts will not step in and interfere with honest business judgment of the directors unless there is a showing of fraud, illegality or conflict of interest.

Plaintiff argues that the directors are acting for reasons unrelated to the financial interest and welfare of the Cubs. However, we are not satisfied that the motives assigned to Philip Wrigley, and through him to the other directors, are contrary to the best interests of the corporation and the stockholders. For example, it appears to us that the effect on the surrounding neighborhood might well be considered by a director who was considering the patrons who would or would not attend the games if the park were in a poor neighborhood. Furthermore, the long run interest of the corporation in its property value at Wrigley Field might demand all efforts to keep the neighborhood from deteriorating. By these thoughts we do not mean to say that we have decided that the decision of the directors was a correct one. That is beyond our jurisdiction and ability. We are merely saying that the decision is one properly before directors and the motives alleged in the amended complaint showed no fraud, illegality or conflict of interest in making that decision.

While all the courts do not insist that one or more of the three elements must be present for a stockholder's derivative action to lie, nevertheless we feel that unless the conduct of the defendants at least borders on one of the elements, the courts should not interfere. The trial court in the instant case acted properly in dismissing plaintiff's amended complaint.

We do not agree with plaintiff's contention that failure to follow the example of the other major league clubs in scheduling night games constituted negligence. Plaintiff made no allegation that these teams' night schedules were profitable or that the purpose for which night baseball had been undertaken was fulfilled. Furthermore, it cannot be said that directors, even those of corporations that are losing money, must follow the lead of the other corporations in the field. Directors are elected for their business capabilities and judgment and the courts cannot require them to forego their judgment because of the decisions of directors of other companies. Courts may not decide these questions in the absence of a clear showing of dereliction of duty on the part of the specific directors and mere failure to "follow the crowd" is not such a dereliction.

The order of dismissal entered by the trial court is affirmed.

The case below is another iconic case on the business judgment rule. The case involved American Express' disposal of a substantial stake in an investment bank, Donaldson Lufkin & Jenrette (DLJ). The following describes that divestiture.

> DLJ's stock, initially sold to the public at $15 a share, dropped to $1.75, and American Express, which owned 25 percent of the firm, was so disappointed that it spun off its holdings to its shareholders in the form of a stock dividend. "That was my lowest day," Jenrette later told a *New York Times* reporter. "American Express made us feel like the end of the world to me. But I had my pride on the line, and I didn't want it to be my epitaph that in the first year as chief executive, I broke the firm."

Donaldson, Lufkin & Jenrette, Inc. History, Funding Universe, available at http://www.fundinguniverse.com/company-histories/donaldson-lufkin-jenrette-inc-history/. The case is quite nuanced. The complexity is seen in this statement by the court: "What we have here as revealed both by the complaint and by the affidavits and exhibits, is that a disagreement exists between two minority stockholders and a unanimous board of directors as to the best way to handle *a loss already incurred on an investment.*"

In reading this case, consider these questions: (1) From an accounting perspective, what is the effect of a sale of the DLJ stake on the open market? (2) What would have been the effect of a decline in the market value of the DLJ stake on the stock price prior to the distribution to American Express shareholders? (3) From the perspective of generating more cash flow to American Express, which transaction (a market sale or distribution to shareholders) was better? (4) If the board made a demonstrably wrong decision, can it be subject to liability for making a clearly wrong business decision?

KAMIN V. AMERICAN EXPRESS CO.

86 Misc.2d 809 (N.Y. Sup. 1976)

EDWARD J. GREENFIELD, J.

The complaint is brought derivatively by minority stockholders of the American Express Company, asking for a declaration that a certain dividend in kind is a waste of corporate assets, directing the defendants not to proceed with the distribution, or, in the alternative, for monetary damages. The motion to dismiss requires the court to presuppose the truth of the allegations. It is the defendants' contention that, conceding everything in the complaint, no viable cause of action is made out.

The complaint alleges that in 1972 American Express acquired for investment 1,954,418 shares of common stock of Donaldson, Lufken and Jenrette, Inc. (hereafter DLJ), a publicly traded corporation, at a cost of $29,900,000. It is further alleged that the current market value of those shares is approximately $4,000,000. On July 28, 1975, it is alleged, the board of directors of American Express declared a special dividend to all stockholders of record pursuant to which the shares of DLJ would be distributed in kind. Plaintiffs contend further that if American Express were to sell the DLJ shares on the market, it would sustain a capital loss of $25,000,000 which could be offset against taxable capital gains on other investments. Such a sale, they allege, would result in tax savings to the company of approximately $8,000,000, which would not be available in the case of the distribution of DLJ shares to stockholders.

It is apparent that all the allegations of the complaint go to the question of the exercise by the board of directors of business judgment in deciding how to deal with the DLJ shares. The crucial allegation which must be scrutinized to determine the legal sufficiency of the complaint is paragraph 19, which alleges: "19. All of the defendant Directors engaged in or acquiesced in or negligently permitted the declaration and payment of the Dividend in violation of the fiduciary duty owed by them to Amex to care for and preserve Amex's assets in the same manner as a man of average prudence would care for his own property."

Examination of the complaint reveals that there is no claim of fraud or self-dealing, and no contention that there was any bad faith or oppressive conduct. The law is quite clear as to what is necessary to ground a claim for actionable wrongdoing. "In actions by stockholders, which assail the acts of their directors or trustees, courts will not interfere unless the powers have been illegally or unconscientiously executed, or unless it be made to appear that the acts were fraudulent or collusive and destructive of the rights of the stockholders. Mere errors of judgment are not sufficient as grounds for equity interference; for the powers of those entrusted with corporate management are largely discretionary."

The question of whether or not a dividend is to be declared or a distribution of some kind should be made is exclusively a matter of business judgment for the board of directors. "Courts will not interfere with such discretion unless it be first made to appear that the directors have acted or are about to act in bad faith and for a dishonest purpose. It is for the directors to say, acting in good faith of course, when and to what extent dividends shall be declared. The statute confers upon the directors this power, and the minority stockholders are not in a position to question this right, so long as the directors are acting in good faith."

A complaint must be dismissed if all that is presented is a decision to pay dividends rather than pursuing some other course of conduct. A complaint which alleges merely that some course of action other than that pursued by the board of directors would have been more advantageous gives rise to no cognizable cause of action. Courts have more than enough to do in adjudicating legal rights and devising remedies for wrongs. The directors' room rather than the courtroom is the appropriate forum for thrashing out purely business questions which will have an impact on profits, market prices, competitive situations, or tax advantages. The substitution of someone else's business judgment for that of the directors "is no business for any court to follow."

It is not enough to allege, as plaintiffs do here, that the directors made an imprudent decision, which did not capitalize on the possibility of using a potential capital loss to offset capital gains. More than imprudence or mistaken judgment must be shown. "Questions of policy of management, expediency of contracts or action, adequacy of consideration, lawful appropriation of corporate funds to advance corporate interests, are left solely to their honest and unselfish decision, for their powers therein are without limitation and free from restraint, and the exercise of them for the common and general interests of the corporation may not be questioned, although the results show that what they did was unwise or inexpedient."

Section 720 of the Business Corporation Law permits an action against directors for "the neglect of, or failure to perform, or other violation of his duties in the management and disposition of corporate assets committed to his charge." This does not mean that a director is chargeable with ordinary negligence for having made an improper decision, or having acted imprudently. The "neglect" referred to in the statute is neglect of duties (*i.e.*, malfeasance or nonfeasance) and not misjudgment. To allege that a director "negligently permitted the declaration and payment" of a dividend without alleging fraud, dishonesty or nonfeasance, is to state merely that a decision was taken with which one disagrees.

The objections raised by the plaintiffs to the proposed dividend action were carefully considered and rejected by the board. The minutes of the special meeting indicate that the defendants were fully aware that a sale rather than a distribution of the DLJ shares might result in the realization of a substantial income tax saving. Nevertheless, they concluded that there were countervailing considerations primarily with respect to the adverse effect such a sale, realizing a loss of $25,000,000, would have on the net income figures in the American Express financial statement. Such a reduction of net income would have a serious effect on the market value of the publicly traded American Express stock. This was not a situation in which the defendant directors totally overlooked facts called to their attention. They gave them consideration, and attempted to view the total picture in arriving at their decision. While plaintiffs contend that according to their accounting consultants the loss on the DLJ stock would still have to be charged against current earnings even if the stock were distributed, the defendants' accounting experts assert that the loss would be a charge against earnings only in the event of a sale, whereas in the event of distribution of the stock as a dividend, the proper accounting treatment would be to charge the loss only against surplus.

All directors have an obligation, using sound business judgment, to maximize income for the benefit of all persons having a stake in the welfare of the corporate entity. What we have here as revealed both by the complaint and by the affidavits and exhibits, is that a disagreement exists between two minority stockholders and a unanimous board of directors as to the best way to handle a loss already incurred on an investment. The directors are entitled to exercise their honest business judgment on the information before them, and to act within their corporate powers. That they may be mistaken, that other courses of action might have differing consequences, or that their action might benefit some shareholders more than others present no basis for the superimposition of judicial judgment, so long as it appears that the directors have been acting in good faith. The question of to what extent a dividend shall be declared and the manner in which it shall be paid is ordinarily subject only to the qualification that the dividend be paid out of surplus. The court will not interfere unless a clear case is made out of fraud, oppression, arbitrary action, or breach of trust.

In this case it clearly appears that the plaintiffs have failed as a matter of law to make out an actionable claim. The motion by the defendants for summary judgment and dismissal of the complaint is granted.

B. OFFICERS

Corporation statutes do not say much about officers. In the legal scheme, officers are mere senior employees, and the board is the ultimate authority. In practice, officers are the day-to-day corporate managers. An important board responsibility is to oversee "the performance and compensation of executive officers." MBCA § 8.01, cmt.

Delaware General Corporation Law: § 142 Officers; titles, duties, selection, term; failure to elect; vacancies.

(a) Every corporation organized under this chapter shall have such officers with such titles and duties as shall be stated in the bylaws or in a resolution of the board of directors which is not inconsistent with the bylaws and as may be necessary to enable it to sign instruments and stock certificates which comply with §§ 103(a)(2) and 158 of this title. One of the officers shall have the duty to record the proceedings of the meetings of the stockholders and directors in a book to be kept for that purpose. Any number of offices may be held by the same person unless the certificate of incorporation or bylaws otherwise provide.

(b) Officers shall be chosen in such manner and shall hold their offices for such terms as are prescribed by the bylaws or determined by the board of directors or other governing body. Each officer shall hold office until such officer's successor is elected and qualified or until such officer's earlier resignation or removal. Any officer may resign at any time upon written notice to the corporation.

By-Laws of McDonald's Corporation as Amended and Restated With Effect as of May 23, 2019

ARTICLE IV—OFFICERS

Section 1, Designation—The Corporation shall have a Chief Executive Officer. In addition, the Corporation shall have such other officers with such titles and duties as shall be stated in these By-Laws or in a resolution of the Board of Directors which is not inconsistent with these By-Laws and as may be necessary to enable him or her to sign instruments and stock certificates which comply with the DGCL. One of the officers of the Corporation shall have the duty to record the proceedings of the meetings of the stockholders and Directors in a book to be kept for that purpose. Officers shall be chosen in such manner and shall hold their offices for such terms as are prescribed in these By-Laws or determined by the Board of Directors. None of the officers, except the Chief Executive Officer, need be Directors. One person may hold more than one office at the same time provided the duties of such officer may be properly and consistently performed by one person.

Section 2, Chief Executive Officer—The Chief Executive Officer shall have responsibility for the general and active management of the business of the Corporation and shall do and perform such other duties as from time to time may be assigned to the Chief Executive Officer by the Board of Directors. In the event of the inability of the Chairman of the Board to act, the Chief Executive Officer shall preside at all meetings of the stockholders of the Corporation and of the Board of Directors of the Corporation.

In most companies, the most senior officers are the chief executive officer (CEO), the chief financial officer (CFO), and the general counsel (GC). All corporate officers report to the CEO. The CFO is responsible for all financial matters and is an important person with respect to financial reporting and auditing, an important matter for board oversight. The GC is the chief legal officer and the corporation's internal lawyer. Many companies may have other officers at this most senior level. They may hold various titles: *e.g.*, president, chief operating officer, chief technology officer, chief information officer, and chief marketing officer. Below this level are inferior senior officers, who may operate specific business units or functions. These officers may be a treasurer, chief accounting officer, chief investment officer, executive or senior vice president. Titles and functions vary considerably. The specific title, function and reporting line are determined by the board and the CEO.

C. SHAREHOLDERS

Shareholders own the equity securities—stock—in the corporation, and thus provide the equity capital to the firm. Corporation law enables the corporation to issue stock and provides rules protecting shareholders and their interests. Protections include mandatory structural checks such as the voting franchise and the imposition of mandatory fiduciary duties on corporate managers.

1. TYPES OF SHAREHOLDERS

Shareholders are broadly categorized into retail and institutional shareholders. Retail shareholders are the quintessential "moms, pops, uncles, aunts" who are said to be "Main Street" investors. Unfortunately, the majority of Americans do not own a significant investment in public companies. *See* Patricia Cohen, *We All Have a Stake in the Stock Market, Right? Guess Again*, N.Y. Times (Feb. 8, 2018) ("A whopping 84 percent of all stocks owned by Americans belong to the wealthiest 10 percent of households. And that includes everyone's stakes in pension plans, 401(k)'s and individual retirement accounts, as well as trust funds, mutual funds and college savings programs like 529 plans."). Most individuals with substantial wealth own some shares directly. However, most investments are in the form of indirect ownership through stakes in pension or mutual funds. Retail shareholders are the quintessential diffuse shareholder base that Berle and Means described. They are largely irrelevant to corporate governance precisely because they own minuscule stakes individually, are diffuse among many, and are not organized into a focused interest group. If they are dissatisfied with the company or its management, the easiest way to address this problem is to exercise the "Wall Street rule," *i.e.*, exit the investment by selling shares that disappoint.

By contrast, institutional shareholders are institutions that own shares. An institution holds a pool of money contributed by others (either institutions themselves or vast numbers of individuals), and it is charged with investing that money for its beneficiaries, who may be retail investors, retirees, sovereigns, universities, and shareholders in other corporations. The types of institutional shareholders are many. They can be conceptualized into several broad types and functions.

Mutual funds provide diversification benefits to mostly retail investors. Without delving into the technical details, diversification has the benefit of diversifying away certain risks that are unique to a specific investment.[2] Mutual funds provide diversification by pooling the funds of

---

[2] To understand intuitively the benefits of diversification, consider this example. You have the option of receiving $5,000 sum certain, or a 50/50 proposition where the correct guess on a coin flip will pay out $11,000 but a wrong guess will pay nothing. Most people will take the $5,000 sum certain because they do not want to be exposed to the specific risk of a single coin flip. On the other hand, if you were offered 100 coin flips, each flip for $110 or nothing, the specific risk is diversified away. You would probably be foolish to pass up the 100 coin flips in favor of the $5,000 sum certain

retail investors to hold various kinds of diversified portfolios, *e.g.*, portfolios holding baskets of stock that may mimic the broader market (such as S&P 500), international stocks (such as Asian or European companies), industry sectors (such as healthcare or technology), or companies by size (such as large or small capitalization companies). They are created and managed by asset management firms that cater to retail investors such Fidelity Investment and Vanguard.[3]

Pension funds are investment funds that are comprised of retirement savings of workers from specific organizations or entire sectors. They are funded by the retirement contributions of workers and perhaps their employers. For example, the California Public Employees' Retirement System (CalPERS) is an agency that manages the retirement of California's public employees, which is a massive fund, and Korea's National Pension Service and Norway's Government Pension Fund Global are public pension funds of each country's retirees and are among the largest single shareholders in the world.

Sovereign wealth funds, *endowments* and *foundations* are other kinds of funds holding the monies of specific investors, in these cases government entities, universities and charitable trusts. Sovereign wealth funds are investment funds of sovereigns, such as China Investment Corporation and Abu Dhabi Investment Authority. Endowments and foundations are funds that principally benefit educational and charitable organizations such as Harvard University and the Bill and Melinda Gates Foundation.

Corporations are also institutional shareholders. Insurance companies and other financial institutions receive large amounts of cash from policyholders and depositors, and they typically invest these monies to earn a return, some of which may be the stocks of other corporations. Investment banks and money center banks such as Goldman Sachs and JPMorgan Chase may have pools of money dedicated to investments in securities.

---

because you will mostly likely earn more than $5,000 and downside of earning less is not severe. For example, in 1999 an investor saving for retirement may have thought that investing in Enron Corp. was a good idea. *See* Bethany McLean & Peter Elkind, *The Guiltiest Guys in the Room*, Fortune (July 5, 2006) ("The most innovative company in corporate America. That's what *Fortune* called Enron for six years running, from 1995 through 2000."). But in hindsight this investment strategy would have been catastrophic as the investor would have lost his entire retirement savings. *See* Richard A. Oppel Jr. & Andrew Ross Sorkin, *Enron's Collapse: The Overview; Enron Corp. Files Largest U.S. Claim for Bankruptcy*, N.Y. Times (Dec. 3, 2001) ("Its stock, worth $90 at its peak last year, is now nearly worthless."); Richard A. Oppel Jr., *Employees' Retirement Plan Is a Victim as Enron Tumbles*, N.Y. Times (Nov. 22, 2001) ("The rapid decline of the Enron Corporation has devastated its employees' retirement plan, which was heavy with company stock, and has infuriated workers, who were prohibited from changing their investments as the stock plunged."). But suppose the investor invested in portfolio of 100 stocks, only 1 of which was Enron. The bankruptcy would have had adversely affected the portfolio, but not by much and the stellar performance of other stocks may offset the losses related to Enron.

[3] A concept that is related to a mutual fund investment is an exchange-traded fund (ETF). An ETF is a security that is based on a basket of stock, thus providing diversification. For example, the basket of stock may be a broad market-based portfolio such as the S&P 500, or various industries such as technology or pharmaceuticals. ETFs are listed on exchanges and can be bought and sold on them.

Nonfinancial corporations can also hold large sums of cash and they invest in stock, *e.g.*, in 2018, Alphabet Inc. (the parent company of Google) and Apple Inc. respectively held $92.4 billion and $40.4 billion of securities in other firms, some of which were stock in corporations.

Some institutional shareholders exist to serve specific functions and market niches. *Venture capital funds* are funds that specialize in providing early equity financing of new or growing companies. They specialize in seeding equity capital in promising startup companies. Much of the mature technology sector is an outgrowth of venture capital investments, including for example Google and Facebook. *Private equity funds* are funds that specialize in providing capital, whether equity or debt, to a broader range of companies. The investments are often in the form of private offerings (vis-à-vis publicly traded securities), and they are made at various stages of a firm's life cycle. Deals in venture capital and private equity are typically bespoke transactions with securities that are tailored to the investor's needs. *Hedge funds* are funds that seek riskier investments for the purpose of generating higher returns. There is no single investment strategy. Hedge funds may be merger arbitrageurs (speculators in mergers), commodities and currency traders, traders in exotic securities such as derivatives, activist shareholders that seek to implement corporate governance changes for the purpose of enhancing value, or any other investment strategy that can produce abnormal returns. The pool of capital held by venture capital, private equity, and hedge funds are typically provided by other institutions (such as endowments, pension funds, and corporations) and high net worth (very rich) individuals.

Venture capital, private equity, and activist hedge funds will typically have some role in corporate governance, either through voting rights or specific negotiations for board seats. The corporation may view venture capital and private equity investors as active partners in the business venture, as would be the case in venture capital and private equity investments since they are welcomed and solicited by the company's management. The nature of these investments typically requires active participation in corporate governance. On the other hand, an activist hedge fund may invest in the public companies regardless of invitation, and thus its relationship with the company may be quite nuanced.

Because institutional shareholders can hold large stakes in any given company, their participation in corporate governance can be meaningful. The vote of a 3% holder is significant, especially since many shareholders do not vote. Corporate managers must respect that voice. The degree of participation in governance by institutional shareholders depends on each firm's individual investment philosophy. Some investors, such as pension funds associated with unions or labor organizations, actively seek to participate in governance (particularly on matters related to the interest of their employee constituents), while other investors may be more passive and, like retail investors, rely on the Wall Street rule.

Lastly, *inside shareholders* are shareholders who are insiders of the corporation, typically the founder, key employees, officers, and directors, or their affiliates. In many private corporations, these individuals control the company. In some public companies, these individuals may be controlling shareholders, either individually or as a group. But even if they are not, they may hold a substantial stake. For example, if they hold 10% stake, that holding is meaningful.

2. VOTING RIGHTS

Corporation law provides: "Unless otherwise provided in the certificate of incorporation each stockholder shall be entitled to 1 vote for each share of capital stock held by such stockholder." DGCL § 212(a). *See* MBCA § 7.21(a) ("Except as provided in subsections (b) and (d) or unless the articles of incorporation provide otherwise, each outstanding share, regardless of class or series, is entitled to one vote on each matter voted on at a shareholders' meeting."). If there are two or more classes of stock, the certificate of incorporation may provide different voting rights, including stock with limited voting rights (*e.g.*, approval of certain transactions only), supervoting rights, and no voting rights at all.[4] A capital structure in which several classes of stock form the equity capital is called dual class stock structure. Frequently, dual class stock structure exists to grant variable voting rights to different groups of shareholders.

Shareholders have voting power, but other constituents such as creditors generally do not. Delaware permits a corporation to confer the right to vote to creditors, but the MBCA prohibits voting by persons other than shareholders. *Compare* DGCL § 221 ("Every corporation may confer upon the holders of any bonds, debentures the power to vote."); *with* MBCA § 7.21(a) ("Only shares are entitled to vote."). Regardless of the difference, granting creditors the right to vote would be unusual. It would indicate that creditors have unusual bargaining leverage as may be the case in a financially troubled company. In ordinary practice, only shareholders vote. Shareholders have voting rights because they are the "residual claimants" of the firm whereas creditors have superior priority in distributions and dissolution. Shareholders claim the remaining assets and income after all other claimants, such as employees and creditors, are paid. Employees must be paid wages lest they quit or stop working. The interest on debt must be paid lest creditors pursue legal rights under the credit contract or

[4] For example, the following are the voting provisions for the three classes of stock for Alphabet Inc. (Google) found in the Amended and Restated Certificate of Incorporation (§§ 2(a)(ii), 2(a)(iii), 5(a)): "each holder of shares of Class A Common Stock shall be entitled to one (1) vote for each share of Class A Common Stock"; "each holder of shares of Class B Common Stock shall be entitled to ten (10) votes for each share of Class B Common Stock"; "shares of Class C Capital Stock shall have no voting power."

bankruptcy law. Upon dissolution and wind up, creditors are paid first from the liquidation of assets, and shareholders are entitled to the residual assets. Because shareholders are proverbially "the last in line" in the financial queue, they are most incentivized to maximize firm value. Only when the firm has residual income and assets do they economically gain.

Economic theory says that creditors and shareholders have an inherent conflict of interests, and that firm value is maximized when the residual claim is maximized. If so, shareholders should have the voting rights. For example, assume that the corporation has a creditor who is owed $50 in interest per year on a debt of 1,000. The corporation must choose between two potential projects with probabilities and payouts.

Project A		Project B	
Outcome 1: 50%	50	Outcome 1: 50%	0
Outcome 2: 50%	150	Outcome 2: 50%	240
Expected value	100	Expected value	120

The creditor would prefer Project A because even in the worst case (Outcome 1), the company would generate $50, sufficient to pay the creditor's interest. Project B has a 50% probability that the creditor would not be paid (Outcome 1). A diversified shareholder should clearly prefer Project B because, based on ex ante expected value, Project B enhances firm value. Because the enhancement of firm value is seen as a normative end, the law vests shareholders with the control rights and the duties owed. The vote helps to align the motive force of a manager's actions with the interest of shareholders. Thus, corporation law grants them voting rights.

Shareholders, as a group, have full voting power. *See* DGCL § 151(b) ("The corporation shall have outstanding 1 or more shares of 1 or more classes or series of stock, which share, or shares together, shall have full voting powers."); MBCA § 6.03(c) ("One or more shares that together have full voting rights and one or more shares that together are entitled to receive the net assets of the corporation upon dissolution must be outstanding."). If a company issues only one class of stock (common stock), shareholders must be permitted to vote. With a dual class stock structure, voting power may vary and some shareholders may have little or no voting power. "Full voting power" means that shareholders, collectively, must be permitted to vote on matters that corporation law requires their assent.

Shareholders do not manage the corporation because that authority is vested in the board. *See* TW Servs., Inc. v. SWT Acquisition Corp., 1989 WL 20290, at *8 n.14 (Del. Ch. 1989) ("While corporate democracy is a pertinent concept, a corporation is not a New England town meeting; directors, not shareholders, have responsibilities to manage the business and affairs of the corporation, subject however to a fiduciary obligation.").

Voting power, therefore, is a check on the broad authority of corporate managers. Some of the items requiring assent are election of directors, amendments of the certificate of incorporation, and certain fundamental transactions such as mergers, sale of all assets, or dissolution. *See* DGCL § 211(b) ("an annual meeting of stockholders shall be held for the election of directors"); *id.* § 242(b)(1) (requiring a "meeting of the stockholders entitled to vote in respect thereof for the consideration of such amendment [of the certificate]"); *id.* § 251(c) (requiring a merger agreement to "be submitted to the stockholders"); *id.* § 271(a) (requiring approval of "the holders of a majority of the outstanding stock" for sale of all or substantially all assets); *id.* § 275(a) (requiring "stockholders to take action" upon proposal for dissolution).

When shareholders vote, there must be a quorum, which is a minimum percentage of shares, based on total shares held by shareholders, present in person or represented by proxy for an action to be valid and binding. A quorum is a "majority of the shares entitled to vote." DGCL § 216(1). With respect to voting matters other than voting for directors, "the affirmative vote of the majority of shares present in person or represented by proxy at the meeting and entitled to vote on the subject matter shall be the act of the stockholders." *Id.* § 216(2). Both the quorum and the voting thresholds are statutory default rules. The bylaws or the certificate of incorporation can provide different quorum and voting thresholds. However, there is a minimum quorum requirement. DGCL § 216 ("in no event shall a quorum consist of less than 1/3 of the shares entitled to vote at the meeting, except that, where a separate vote by a class or series or classes or series is required, a quorum shall consist of no less than 1/3 of the shares of such class or series or classes or series").

The election of directors is different from other voting items. "Directors shall be elected by a plurality of the votes of the shares present in person or represented by proxy at the meeting and entitled to vote on the election of directors." *Id.* § 216(3). This is a default rule, and the bylaws or the certificate of incorporation can provide for a different threshold, *e.g.*, the majority of the shares present and entitled to vote. Plurality voting means that the candidate for each position that receives the most votes wins the election. This is distinguished from a majority vote rule where the candidate must receive a majority of the shares present and entitled to vote. The practical significance of the plurality rule is apparent when one considers the fact that most elections are uncontested. At the annual meeting of shareholders, the incumbent management submits a slate of director nominees they seek to elect, one nominee for each open board seat. Each shareholder will vote on each board seat. For each position, whoever receives the plurality of the votes is elected. In an uncontested election, there is no competition and thus each nominee needs at least one affirmative vote to satisfy the plurality rule. The commonly cited policy rationale for the plurality rule is that it curtails the possibility of a "failed" election because a candidate cannot meet a specified threshold.[5]

In light of the plurality rule, is voting in corporate elections a Potemkin village? There is a temptation to think so if an "election" presents no choice to express an actual preference. By imperfect analogy, election in a one-party political system is undemocratic.[6] With that said, there is no good reason why *every* corporate election has to be vigorously contested. A contest implies a conflict of some sort—of vision, strategy, priorities, etc. A policy question is whether such conflict or competition is always a good thing. There is no legal impediment to creating a choice if a shareholder is willing to engage in a proxy contest, which is a contest for securing the proxies of shareholders. Any shareholder can attempt to present and elect an alternative slate of nominees. There is an economic impediment. The real issue is one of cost and (dis)incentives. The incumbent management holds an annual meeting of shareholders and controls the process for proxy solicitation for shareholder votes and communication with shareholders, at the corporation's cost. A shareholder engaging in a proxy contest bears its own cost to communicate with shareholders and solicit their proxies in favor of its nominees. These costs are substantial. A shareholder must have a strong motivation to challenge an incumbent management. A proxy contest for board seats is usually a tactic in a hostile takeover bid by an acquirer when the stake for the acquirer—the acquisition of the target—is substantial enough to bear the cost of the proxy contest.

Given this background, the policy question is: Should shareholders have more power to replace directors through a contested election? They would gain more power to have a greater say on who is elected to the board if the economic disincentive is removed through some form of cost-bearing by the corporation. Corporation law permits such a scheme.

---

5 *See* Robert S. Saunders, *Why Majority Voting in Director Elections Is a Bad Idea*, 1 Va. L. & Bus. Rev. 107, 123 (2006) ("Under plurality voting, stockholder groups cannot extract wealth transfers, or further other private agendas, by threatening the corporation with a failed election."); Report of Committee on Corporate Laws, ABA Section of Business Law, *Changes in Model Business Corporation Act—Proposed Amendments to Chapters 8 and 10 Relating to Voting by Shareholders for Election of Directors*, 61 Bus. Law. 399, 402 (2005) ("Any such change in the statutory plurality default rule would apply universally to all corporations governed by the Model Act's provisions where those corporations have not opted out of the plurality default rule in their articles of incorporation. For reasons specified in detail in this Report, the Committee has concluded that the "failed election" consequences for some corporations and other concerns make it unwise to propose a universally applicable change in the statutory plurality default rule.").

6 *Compare* MM Companies, Inc. v. Liquid Audio, Inc., 813 A.2d 1118, 1127 (Del. 2003) ("if the stockholders are not satisfied with the management or actions of their elected representatives on the board of directors, the power of corporate democracy is available to the stockholders to replace the incumbent directors when they stand for re-election"); *with* TW Services, Inc. v. SWT Acquisition Corp., 1989 WL 20290, at *8 n.14 (Del.Ch. 1989) ("'Shareholder democracy' is an appealing phrase, and the notion of shareholders as the ultimate voting constituency of the board has obvious pertinence, but that phrase would not constitute the only element in a well articulated model. While corporate democracy is a pertinent concept, a corporation is not a New England town meeting; directors, not shareholders, have responsibilities to manage the business and affairs of the corporation, subject however to a fiduciary obligation.").

DGCL § 112. Access to proxy solicitation materials.

The bylaws may provide that if the corporation solicits proxies with respect to an election of directors, it may be required, to the extent and subject to such procedures or conditions as may be provided in the bylaws, to include in its proxy solicitation materials (including any form of proxy it distributes), in addition to individuals nominated by the board of directors, 1 or more individuals nominated by a stockholder. Such procedures or conditions may include any of the following:

(1) A provision requiring a minimum record or beneficial ownership, or duration of ownership, of shares of the corporation's capital stock, by the nominating stockholder, and defining beneficial ownership to take into account options or other rights in respect of or related to such stock;

(2) A provision requiring the nominating stockholder to submit specified information concerning the stockholder and the stockholder's nominees, including information concerning ownership by such persons of shares of the corporation's capital stock, or options or other rights in respect of or related to such stock;

(3) A provision conditioning eligibility to require inclusion in the corporation's proxy solicitation materials upon the number or proportion of directors nominated by stockholders or whether the stockholder previously sought to require such inclusion;

(4) A provision precluding nominations by any person if such person, any nominee of such person, or any affiliate or associate of such person or nominee, has acquired or publicly proposed to acquire shares constituting a specified percentage of the voting power of the corporation's outstanding voting stock within a specified period before the election of directors;

(5) A provision requiring that the nominating stockholder undertake to indemnify the corporation in respect of any loss arising as a result of any false or misleading information or statement submitted by the nominating stockholder in connection with a nomination; and

(6) Any other lawful condition.

DGCL § 113. Proxy expense reimbursement.

(a) The bylaws may provide for the reimbursement by the corporation of expenses incurred by a stockholder in soliciting proxies in connection with an election of directors, subject to such procedures or conditions as the bylaws may prescribe, including:

(1) Conditioning eligibility for reimbursement upon the number or proportion of persons nominated by the stockholder seeking

reimbursement or whether such stockholder previously sought reimbursement for similar expenses;

(2) Limitations on the amount of reimbursement based upon the proportion of votes cast in favor of 1 or more of the persons nominated by the stockholder seeking reimbursement, or upon the amount spent by the corporation in soliciting proxies in connection with the election;

(3) Limitations concerning elections of directors by cumulative voting pursuant to § 214 of this title; or

(4) Any other lawful condition.

(b) No bylaw so adopted shall apply to elections for which any record date precedes its adoption.

3. PARTICIPATION IN GOVERNANCE

Along with directors and officers, shareholders participate in corporate governance because corporation law requires their vote and assent on certain matters. Unlike directors who are required to exercise their powers vested under corporation law and officers who are hired to manage day-to-day business, shareholders are voluntary participants. They can be passive investors whose "participation" is simply the choice of staying invested or not. This choice is not as inconsequential as one may think. If enough shareholders sell shares, their collective shared preference, presumably reflected in the stock price in an efficient market, would signal disapproval of management's handling of the corporation. Most managers are sensitive to the stock price, particularly over the longterm. Shareholders can also more actively participate in governance by regularly voting on matters. Or they can be activist shareholders who seek to participate directly in corporate governance by influencing the manner in which corporate managers operate the corporation.

Shareholders with an insignificant stake can participate in corporate governance, if they desire, through the voting franchise. But many are rationally passive. They do not vote or participate in governance. This does not mean that they are apathetic to their investments; they clearly care about economic returns. As between participation and apathy, the latter is more rational for many based on an individual cost-benefit analysis. Active participation is not costless; it requires time and effort. Suppose a shareholder owns a 0.1% stake. The firm's equity is valued at $100 million. The shareholder owns a substantial $100,000 stake. Suppose he incurs a modest cost of $100 in terms of time and effort related to voting and participation in governance. This effort results in a minute positive difference in the firm's value of 0.01%, a value increase to the firm of $10,000 (= 0.01% × $100 million). The shareholder's portion of this value increase is $10 (= 0.1% × $10,000). Clearly, expending $100 to gain a benefit of $10 is irrational. Thus, when retail shareholders get their voting materials in the mail, the proxies are tossed in the recycle bin.

The calculus changes as the stake increases. Suppose the stake is not 0.1%, but instead 1%. The shareholder's claim to the value increase would be $100. The cost-benefit analysis is now in equipoise. In most public companies, only institutional shareholders have the financial resources to hold stakes that are significant, such as 1%. This does not mean that most institutional shareholders are active participants in corporate governance beyond merely voting shares. They are subject to the same cost-benefit analysis as retail shareholders. The better choice for a disappointing investment is often the Wall Street rule, *i.e.*, sell. Another factor is that most institutional investors, including traditional investors such as mutual and pension funds, invest in any given company for a short period of time. *See* Mark Roe, *Are Stock Markets Really Becoming More Short Term?*, Project Syndicate (Feb. 21, 2013) (the average hold period for longterm investors like Fidelity and Vanguard was a year and a half in 2010). Given an expected turnover of shares in a portfolio, some investors may decide that the investment of time and cost to participate actively in governance may be unwarranted. For example, if an investor pushes for a new strategic direction that may require five years to develop, it may not immediately see the payout of that new strategy but may suffer the immediate consequences of any potential uncertainty related to the new strategy, which may manifest in short-term stock price decline. Thus, institutional shareholders often defer to management and vote for management proposals including director nominees, amendments to certificate of incorporation, approval of transactions, and executive pay packages.

In contrast to passive retail and institutional shareholders, activist shareholders seek to participate in corporate governance. With a significant stake, for example 3%, they seek to influence management through direct conversation and input. Recall that since not all shares vote, a voting shareholder's actual influence on voting outcomes is greater than their percentage stake. An activist shareholder may recommend business strategies, financial decisions, and specific transactions such as mergers and acquisitions. Management's reception to these interventions may vary, but it is fair to assume that management would be at least somewhat cautious or wary of uninvited participants in the boardroom.

D. CORPORATE GOVERNANCE

Corporate governance is a broad term used to capture the entire set of rules, norms, facts, devices, institutions, and mechanisms—anything and everything—that affect how corporations are governed. "Every device, institution, or mechanism that exercises power over decision-making within a corporation is a part of the system of corporate governance for that firm." Jonathan R. Macey, Corporate Governance: Promises Kept,

Promises Broken 2 (2008). Corporate governance is not restricted to corporation law. It is affected by, among other things: federal securities law that governs disclosures, proxies, and securities fraud; stock exchange rules that govern listing requirements including standards related to governance such as director independence and board structure; norms and interactions among institutional shareholders and corporate managers such as modes of communication between the company and investors; the influence of professional advisers and market actors such as lawyers, bankers, accountants, proxy advisory firms, and credit rating agencies; the workings of the capital markets such as the impact of managerial decisions and governance on the company's stock price; and executive compensation policies that may affect incentives by managers. A major goal of corporate governance is to produce management decisions and behaviors that enhance firm value. A key problem is the factual reality that large business organizations are run by agents who work on their behalf.

1. THE PROBLEM OF AGENCY

The separation of ownership and control is inevitable because it is the essential trait of public corporations. Large aggregations of assets and investments may require many investors, and such ventures may require professional management. As Berle and Means noted, the separation of ownership and control "produces a condition where the interests of owner and of ultimate manager may, and often do, diverge." What does this mean concretely? Consider the following examples.

Example 1: Interested transactions.—A director of Firm A has a significant ownership stake in Firm B. He owes fiduciary duty to Firm A, but his only economic interest is director fees. He causes Firm A to sell assets worth $200 to Firm B for $150. Is there a problem?

Example 2: Care in transactions.—The CEO of Firm A wants the company to do a deal with Firm B. The board must consider and approve the deal. Rather than independently vetting the transaction, the board approves the transaction because it believes in good faith that the CEO knows best and has confidence in her. Is there a problem?

Example 3: Executive compensation.—The CEO of a company typically has significant influence on the board by virtue of a close working relationship and her indirect influence on the nomination process and board composition. The board sets the compensation of senior executives. Is there a problem?

The separation of ownership and control results in a fundamental problem of agency: the divergence of the interests of the agent and the principal, the manager and the corporation.

The case below is an older case, but still teaches the basic framework for thinking about the problem of agency in corporations and its relationship to fundamental rules of corporation law. It is a challenge to a company's expenditure for a radio advertisement campaign that employed the company president's spouse. The case provides an example of the potential for a conflict between the company's insiders and most other shareholders. In reading this case, consider these questions: (1) What is the general rule when a shareholder seeks to challenge the board's business decision? (2) What is the potential cost of a conflict of interest transaction involving a manager? (3) What is the rule when a shareholder presents some credible evidence that a manager engaged in a potential conflict of interest transaction? (4) If a transaction on its face presents a potential conflict of interest, should it be void as a matter of law?

BAYER V. BERAN

49 N.Y.S.2d 2 (Sup. Ct. 1944)

SHIENTAG, JUSTICE.

Directors of a corporation are not trustees and are not held to strict accountability as such. Nevertheless, their obligations are analogous to those of trustees. Directors are agents; they are fiduciaries. The fiduciary has two paramount obligations: responsibility and loyalty. Those obligations apply with equal force to the humblest agent or broker and to the director of a great and powerful corporation. They lie at the very foundation of our system of free private enterprise.

The concept of loyalty, of constant, unqualified fidelity, has a definite and precise meaning. The fiduciary must subordinate his individual and private interests to his duty to the corporation whenever the two conflict. The fiduciary principle of undivided loyalty was, in effect, "the precept as old as Holy Writ, that a man cannot serve two masters. More than a century ago equity gave a hospitable reception to that principle and the common law was not slow to follow in giving it recognition. No thinking man can believe that an economy built upon a business foundation can long endure without loyalty to that principle." "The separation of ownership from management, the development of the corporate structure so as to vest in small groups control of resources of great numbers of small and uninformed investors, make imperative a fresh and active devotion to that principle if the modern world of business is to perform its proper function."

A director is not an insurer. On the one hand, he is not called upon to use an extraordinary degree of care and prudence; and on the other hand it is established by the cases that it is not enough for a director to be honest, that fraud is not the orbit of his liability. The director may not act as a dummy or a figurehead. He is called upon to use care, to exercise judgment, the decree of care, the kind of judgment that one would give in similar situations to the conduct of his own affairs.

The director is given a wide latitude of action. The law does not seek to deprive him of initiative and daring and vision. Business has its adventures, its bold adventures; and those who in good faith, and in the interests of the corporation they serve, embark upon them, are not to be penalized if failure, rather than success, results from their efforts. The law will not permit a course of conduct by directors, which would be applauded if it succeeded, to be condemned with a riot of adjectives simply because it failed. Directors may take chances, the same kind of chances that a man would take in his own business. Because they are given this wide latitude, the law will not hold directors liable for honest errors, for mistakes of judgment. The law will not interfere with the internal affairs of a corporation so long as it is managed by its directors pursuant to a free, honest exercise of judgment uninfluenced by personal, or by any considerations other than the welfare of the corporation.

To encourage freedom of action on the part of directors, or to put it another way, to discourage interference with the exercise of their free and independent judgment, there has grown up what is known as the business judgment rule. "Questions of policy of management, expediency of contracts or action, adequacy of consideration, lawful appropriation of corporate funds to advance corporate interests, are left solely to their honest and unselfish decision, for their powers therein are without limitation and free from restraint, and the exercise of them for the common and general interests of the corporation may not be questioned, although the results show that what they did was unwise or inexpedient." Indeed, although the concept of "responsibility" is firmly fixed in the law, it is only in a most unusual and extraordinary case that directors are held liable for negligence in the absence of fraud, or improper motive, or personal interest.

The business judgment rule, however, yields to the rule of undivided loyalty. This great rule of law is designed "to avoid the possibility of fraud and to avoid the temptation of self-interest." It is "designed to obliterate all divided loyalties which may creep into a fiduciary relation." "Included within its scope is every situation in which a trustee chooses to deal with another in such close relation with the trustee that possible advantage to such other person might influence, consciously or unconsciously, the judgment of the trustee." The dealings of a director with the corporation for which he is the fiduciary are therefore viewed "with jealousy by the courts." Such personal transactions of directors with their corporations, such transactions as may tend to produce a conflict between self-interest and fiduciary obligation, are, when challenged, examined with the most scrupulous care, and if there is any evidence of improvidence or oppression, any indication of unfairness or undue advantage, the transactions will be voided. "Their dealings with the corporation are subjected to rigorous scrutiny and where any of their contracts or engagements with the corporation are challenged the burden is on the director not only to prove the good faith of the transaction but also to show its inherent fairness from the viewpoint of the corporation and those interested therein."

While there is a high moral purpose implicit in this transcendent fiduciary principle of undivided loyalty, it has back of it a profound understanding of human nature and of its frailties. It accomplishes a practical, beneficent purpose. It tends to prevent a clouded conception of fidelity that blurs the vision. It preserves the free exercise of judgment uncontaminated by the dross of divided allegiance or self-interest. It prevents the operation of an influence that may be indirect but that is all the more potent for that reason. The law has set its face firmly against undermining "the rule of undivided loyalty by the disintegrating erosion of particular exceptions."

The first cause of action charges the directors with negligence, waste and improvidence in embarking upon a radio advertising program beginning in 1942 and costing about $1,000,000 a year. It is further charged that they were negligent in selecting the type of program and in renewing the radio contract for 1943. More serious than these allegations is the charge that the directors were motivated by a noncorporate purpose in causing the radio program to be undertaken and in expending large sums of money therefor. It is claimed that this radio advertising was for the benefit of Miss Jean Tennyson, one of the singers on the program, who in private life is Camille Dreyfus, the wife of the president of the company and one of its directors; that it was undertaken to "further, foster and subsidize her career"; to "furnish a vehicle" for her talents.

Eliminating for the moment the part played by Miss Tennyson in the radio advertising campaign, it is clear that the character of the advertising, the amount to be expended therefor, and the manner in which it should be used, are all matters of business judgment and rest peculiarly within the discretion of the board of directors. Under the authorities previously cited, it is not, generally speaking, the function of a court of equity to review these matters or even to consider them. Had the wife of the president of the company not been involved, the advertising cause of action could have been disposed of summarily. Her connection with the program, however, makes it necessary to go into the facts in some detail.

The directors decided to resort to the radio and to have the company go on the air with a dignified program of fine music, the kind of program which they felt would be in keeping with what they believed to be the beauty and superior quality of their products. The radio program was not adopted on the spur of the moment or at the whim of the directors. They acted after studies reported to them, made by the advertising department. A radio consultant was employed to advise as to time and station. An advertising agency of national repute was engaged to take charge of the formulation and production of the program. It was decided to expend about $1,000,000 a year, but the commitments were to be subject to cancellation every thirteen weeks, so that the maximum obligation of the company would be not more than $250,000.

So far, there is nothing on which to base any claim of breach of fiduciary duty. Some care, diligence and prudence were exercised by these directors before they committed the company to the radio program. It was for the directors to determine whether they would resort to radio advertising; it was for them to conclude how much to spend; it was for them to decide the kind of program they would use. It would be an unwarranted act of interference for any court to attempt to substitute its judgment on these points for that of the directors, honestly arrived at. The expenditure was not reckless or unconscionable. It bore a fair relationship to the total amount of sales and earnings of the company. That a program of classical and semiclassical music was selected, rather than a variety program, or a news commentator program, furnishes no ground for legal complaint.

Now we have to take up an unfortunate incident, one which cannot be viewed with the complacency displayed by some of the directors of the company. The Doctors Dreyfus and their families own about 135,000 shares of common stock, the other directors about 10,000 shares out of a total outstanding issue of 1,376,500 shares. Some of these other directors were originally employed by Dr. Camille Dreyfus, the president of the company. His wife, to whom he has been married for about twelve years, is known professionally as Miss Jean Tennyson and is a singer of wide experience.

Dr. Dreyfus, as was natural, consulted his wife about the proposed radio program; he also asked the advertising agency, that had been retained, to confer with her about it. She suggested the names of the artists, all stars of the Metropolitan Opera Company, and the name of the conductor, prominent in his field. She also offered her own services as a paid artist. All of her suggestions as to personnel were adopted by the advertising agency. While the record shows Miss Tennyson to be a competent singer, there is nothing to indicate that she was indispensable or essential to the success of the program. She received $500 an evening. It would be far-fetched to suggest that the directors caused the company to incur large expenditures for radio advertising to enable the president's wife to make $24,000 in 1942 and $20,500 in 1943.

It is not improper to appoint relatives of officers or directors to responsible positions in a company. But where a close relative of the chief executive officer, and one of its dominant directors, takes a position closely associated with a new and expensive field of activity, the motives of the directors are likely to be questioned. The board would be placed in a position where selfish, personal interests might be in conflict with the duty it owed to the corporation. That being so, the entire transaction, if challenged in the courts, must be subjected to the most rigorous scrutiny to determine whether the action of the directors was intended or calculated "to subserve some outside purpose, regardless of the consequences to the company, and in a manner inconsistent with its interests."

After such careful scrutiny I have concluded that, up to the present, there has been no breach of fiduciary duty on the part of the directors. The president undoubtedly knew that his wife might be one of the paid artists on the program. The other directors did not know this until they had approved the campaign of radio advertising and the general type of radio program. The evidence fails to show that the program was designed to foster or subsidize "the career of Miss Tennyson as an artist" or to "furnish a vehicle for her talents." That her participation in the program may have enhanced her prestige as a singer is no ground for subjecting the directors to liability, as long as the advertising served a legitimate and a useful corporate purpose and the company received the full benefit thereof.

The musical quality of Celanese Hour has not been challenged, nor does the record contain anything reflecting on Miss Tennyson's competence as an artist. There is nothing in the testimony to show that some other soprano would have enhanced the artistic quality of the program or its advertising appeal. There is no suggestion that the present program is inefficient or that its cost is disproportionate to what a program of that character reasonably entails. Miss Tennyson's contract with the advertising agency retained by the directors was on a standard form, negotiated through her professional agent. Her compensation, as well as that of the other artists, was in conformity with that paid for comparable work. She received less than any of the other artists on the program. Although she appeared with a greater regularity than any other singer, she received no undue prominence, no special build-up. Indeed, all of the artists were subordinated to the advertisement of the company and of its products. The company was featured. It appears also that the popularity of the program has increased since it was inaugurated.

It is clear that the directors have not been guilty of any breach of fiduciary duty, in embarking upon the program of radio advertising and in renewing it. It is unfortunate that they have allowed themselves to be placed in a position where their motives concerning future decisions on radio advertising may be impugned. The corporation has not been wronged by the radio advertising attacked in the complaints.

The directors acted in the free exercise of their honest judgment and their actions did not constitute negligence, waste or improvidence. The complaint is accordingly dismissed on the merits.

2. MECHANISMS OF ACCOUNTABILITY

If managers are susceptible to a potential divergence of interest, what can be done? Corporate governance requires accountability mechanisms. The central tension is between authority and accountability. In much of law, accountability is achieved through legal sanctions. Think about tort, criminal, securities, or environmental laws. In each field, legal enforcement are the principal means of achieving compliance. In corporate governance, the procurement of ideal decisions and behaviors by agents is not wholly achieved by litigation under corporation law alone. The mechanisms of accountability are multi-faceted. Shareholders, directors, and markets play roles in achieving the ideals of corporate governance.

Shareholder derivative actions: Directors and officers owe fiduciary duties to the corporation and shareholders. If they breach these duties, shareholders may bring a derivative suit on behalf of the corporation. Like tort or criminal law, the potential for legal liability deters conduct that is not in keeping with the fiduciary obligations of corporate managers.

Independent directors: If officers are the day-to-day managers and their undue influence on directors is seen as a potential problem, directors can be immunized through a requirement of independence. At least, they should not be beholden to or controlled by other directors or officers or to the corporation such that their independent judgment may be compromised by divided loyalty or their own economic or personal incentives.

Capital markets: The markets can be an accountability mechanism if corporate managers are sensitive to stock price performance. Corporate executives are now routinely fired for poor performance or bad behavior. There is a market for corporate control. If managers perform poorly, the capital markets can hold them accountable through the mechanism of stock price, which would decline with poor performance, and a takeover of the firm by an acquirer who can install new, presumably better managers. *See* Henry G. Manne, *Mergers and the Market for Corporate Control*, 73 J. Pol. Econ. 110 (1965). Thus, the markets incentivize managers to perform.

No single mechanism is a perfect solution to the problem of agency cost. Even in the realm of private wrongs such as torts, the law applies a multi-faceted approach to minimize wrongs and social cost: private tort law; public criminal law; compliance through regulation; even social norms. Derivative litigation, independent directors, and capital markets are each a partial solution to the problem of agency. Their scope and effectiveness have limitations. Derivative suits are limited by the contours of the duties and the unique restrictions placed on the derivative litigation process, which are dictated by countervailing policy considerations. Director independence is an ideal, but the law may be limited in testing for it just the way truthful testimony in court is not always achieved despite best efforts of judges, lawyers, and factfinders. Hostile takeovers are limited by the availability of defense mechanisms, which are legal based on countervailing policy considerations. These issues will be explored in greater detail in the remaining chapters.

CHAPTER 12

DUTY OF CARE

■ ■ ■

A. CARE, RISK-TAKING, AND BUSINESS JUDGMENT

Based on the managerial prerogatives of directors to manage the business and affairs of the corporation, the law defers to their decisions in most situations—right, wrong, bad, unlucky, or otherwise. This deference is found in the business judgment rule, which is the "presumption that in making a business decision the directors of a corporation acted on an informed basis, in good faith and in the honest belief that the action taken was in the best interests of the company." Aronson v. Lewis, 473 A.2d 805, 812 (Del. 1984). The law presumes that directors acted in accordance with their duties. Note the legal wrongs implied in the statement of the business judgment rule: *i.e.*, not acting *informedly*, not acting *in good faith*, and not acting with *the honest belief* that the action was in the corporation's best interest. Based on the business judgment rule, it is clear that directors and officers cannot be held liable for merely making substantively erroneous or bad decisions. Delaware courts have been emphatic on this point.

> Whether a judge or jury considering the matter after the fact, believes a decision substantively wrong, or degrees of wrong extending through "stupid" to "egregious" or "irrational," provides no ground for director liability, so long as the court determines that the process employed was either rational or employed in a good faith effort to advance corporate interests.

In re Caremark Int'l Inc. Derivative Litig., 698 A.2d 959, 967 (Del. Ch. 1996).

> If, however, corporate directors were to be found liable for a corporate loss from a risky project on the ground that the investment was too risky (foolishly risky! stupidly risky! egregiously risky!—you supply the adverb), their liability would be joint and several for the whole loss.

Gagliardi v. TriFoods Int'l, Inc., 683 A.2d 1049, 1052 (Del. Ch. 1996).

> As for the plaintiffs' contention that the directors failed to exercise "substantive due care," we should note that such a concept is foreign to the business judgment rule. Courts do not measure, weigh or quantify directors' judgments. We do not even decide if

> they are reasonable in this context. Due care in the decisionmaking context is *process* due care only.

Brehm v. Eisner, 746 A.2d 244, 264 (Del. 2000).

If one analogizes to tort law, the duty of care suggests that directors should be held to a substantive standard of care, a certain minimum level of substantive care that defines the scope of reasonable conduct. Negligent decisions that produce losses should result in liability, the way that liability is imposed on a negligent doctor or driver. However, corporation law does not embrace this concept of substantive care. In reading the excerpt below, think about this question: What should be the theory of a wrongful conduct with respect to the concept of the duty of care?

THE TORT FOUNDATION OF DUTY OF CARE AND BUSINESS JUDGMENT

Robert J. Rhee, 88 Notre Dame L. Rev. 1139, 1156–58 (2013)

The relationship between corporation law and tort law has been distant. Commentators have argued that tort law and corporation law are different because the goal of torts is loss spreading, whereas corporation law seeks to incentivize risk taking. The tort system, it is argued, shifts loss from specific victims to a larger pool of risk-bearers through insurance and tort liability. In the corporate setting, such robust liability scheme would concentrate risk by shifting loss from diversified shareholders to directors. These points are well taken, but they are incomplete. The argument is based on an incomplete conception of the tort system and it does not present a consensus view of the raison d'être of the tort system.

Another important aspect of tort law is deterrence, which is the prevailing law and economics perspective. The most prominent example of this thought is the Hand Formula, which conceptualizes negligence as a cost-benefit analysis of accident and precautionary costs for the purpose of achieving optimal deterrence and social cost. If corporation law imposes liability on directors to deter bad business decisions, the laws of torts and corporations should converge. However, prominent corporate law jurists have referenced a director's care to that of a driver or doctor, and have rejected the analogy as "misleading" and "not well-suited to judicial review." Scholars have also analogized a director's negligence to common torts, and have dismissed tort law as irrelevant.

At first blush, this consensus view seems right. The duty of care is dressed in the language of torts, and yet directors are not held to a negligence standard for business losses. Courts and scholars correctly argue that directors must not be held liable for negligent, stupid, careless, unlucky, or egregious decisions in spite of any visceral impulse to blame and levy liability for a bad outcome. Of course, such a concept is antithetical to tort law. Since tort law finds liability for negligence and corporation law does not, inter-doctrinal divergence seems correct on the surface. But upon a deeper analysis this argument is flawed.

The tort analogy fails because scholars and jurists have focused on the difference in judicial outcomes, and have wrongly assumed that the application of tort law would require a substantive review of business decisions under the negligence standard. However, the divergence of outcomes is not as meaningful, and the better inquiry focuses on the reasons why outcomes diverge, which is a search for a common analytical framework under which courts formulate duty and its limitation.

The case below presents facts that, when viewed through the hindsight of history, makes clear the board performed poorly during the financial crisis of 2008–2009. In reading this case, consider these questions: (1) Is a failure to correctly monitor risk actionable? (2) Can you think of a theory in which the failure to monitor would be actionable?[1] (3) Was this a case of intentional omission? (4) If the board's failure resulted in such grievous injuries to the corporation, why should directors not be liable?

IN RE CITIGROUP INC. SHAREHOLDER DERIVATIVE LITIGATION

964 A.2d 106 (Del. Ch. 2009)

CHANDLER, CHANCELLOR.

This is a derivative action brought on behalf of Citigroup Inc., seeking to recover its losses arising from exposure to the subprime lending market.

Plaintiffs allege that certain defendants are liable to the Company for corporate waste for allowing the Company to purchase $2.7 billion in subprime loans from Accredited Home Lenders in March 2007 and from Ameriquest Home Mortgage in September 2007; and allowing the Company to invest in structured investment vehicles ("SIVs") that were unable to pay off maturing debt.

[These] claims are dismissed for failure to adequately plead demand futility pursuant to Court of Chancery Rule 23.1.

The complaint names thirteen members of the Citigroup board of directors. Plaintiffs allege that a majority of the defendants were members of the Audit and Risk Management Committee ("ARM Committee").

---

[1] Hint: suppose the board failed to monitor regulatory compliance with respect to financial risks, and thus the board's failure was tantamount to a breach of external banking laws. Can this fact change the analysis?

Plaintiffs allege that since as early as 2006, defendants have caused and allowed Citigroup to engage in subprime lending that ultimately left the Company exposed to massive losses by late 2007. Beginning in 2005, house prices, which many believe were artificially inflated by speculation and easily available credit, began to plateau, and then deflate. Adjustable rate mortgages issued earlier in the decade began to reset, leaving many homeowners with significantly increased monthly payments. Defaults and foreclosures increased, and assets backed by income from mortgages began to decrease in value. By February 2007, subprime mortgage lenders began filing for bankruptcy and subprime mortgages packaged into securities began experiencing increasing levels of delinquency. In mid-2007, rating agencies downgraded bonds backed by subprime mortgages.

Much of Citigroup's exposure to the subprime lending market arose from its involvement with collateralized debt obligations ("CDOs")—repackaged pools of lower rated securities that Citigroup created by acquiring asset-backed securities, including residential mortgage backed securities ("RMBSs"), and then selling rights to the cash flows from the securities in classes, or tranches, with different levels of risk and return. Included with at least some of the CDOs created by Citigroup was a "liquidity put"—an option that allowed the purchasers of the CDOs to sell them back to Citigroup at original value.

According to plaintiffs, Citigroup's alleged $55 billion subprime exposure was in two areas of the Company's Securities & Banking Unit. The first portion totaled $11.7 billion and included securities tied to subprime loans that were being held until they could be added to debt pools for investors. The second portion included $43 billion of super-senior securities, which are portions of CDOs backed in part by RMBS collateral.

By late 2007, it was apparent that Citigroup faced significant losses on its subprime-related assets, including the following:

- *October 1, 2007:* Citigroup announced it would write-down approximately $1.4 billion on funded and unfunded highly leveraged finance commitments.

- *October 15, 2007:* Citigroup issued a press release reporting a net income of $2.38 billion, a 57% decline from the Company's prior year results.

- *November 4, 2007:* Citigroup announced significant declines on the fair value of the approximately $55 billion in the Company's U.S. subprime-related direct exposures, and estimated that further write downs would be between $8 and $11 billion.

- *November 6, 2007:* Citigroup disclosed that it provided $7.6 billion of emergency financing to the seven SIVs the Company operated after they were unable to repay maturing debt. The SIVs drew on the $10 billion of so-called committed liquidity provided by Citigroup. On December 13, 2007 Citigroup bailed out seven of its affiliated SIVs by bringing $49 billion in assets onto its balance sheet and taking responsibility for the SIVs' $49 billion of assets.

- *January 15, 2008:* Citigroup announced it would take an additional $18.1 billion write-down for the fourth quarter 2007 and a quarterly loss of $9.83 billion. Citigroup also announced that the Company lowered its dividend to $0.32 per share, a 40% decline from the Company's previous dividend disbursement.

- By March 2008, Citigroup shares traded below book value and the Company announced that it would lay off an additional 2,000 employees, bringing Citigroup's total layoff since the beginning of the subprime market crisis to more than 6,000.

- July 18, 2008: Citigroup announced it lost $2.5 billion in the second quarter, largely caused by $7.2 billion of write-downs of Citigroup's investments in mortgages and other loans and by weakness in the consumer market.

In November 2007, Citigroup disclosed that it provided $7.6 billion of emergency financing to the seven SIVs the Company operated after they were unable to repay maturing debt. Ultimately, Citigroup was forced to bail out seven of its affiliated SIVs by bringing $49 billion in assets onto its balance sheet, notwithstanding that Citigroup previously represented that it would manage the SIVs on an arms-length basis.

Plaintiffs allege that defendants are liable to the Company for breach of fiduciary duty for (1) failing to adequately oversee and manage Citigroup's exposure to the problems in the subprime mortgage market, even in the face of alleged "red flags" and (2) failing to ensure that the Company's financial reporting and other disclosures were thorough and accurate. The "red flags" alleged in the eighty-six page Complaint are generally statements from public documents that reflect worsening conditions in the financial markets, including the subprime and credit markets, and the effects those worsening conditions had on market participants, including Citigroup's peers.

The business judgment rule "is a presumption that in making a business decision the directors of a corporation acted on an informed basis, in good faith and in the honest belief that the action taken was in the best interests of the company." Aronson v. Lewis, 473 A.2d 805, 812 (Del. 1984). The burden is on plaintiffs to rebut this presumption. Absent an allegation of interestedness or disloyalty to the corporation, the rule prevents a judge or jury from second guessing director decisions if they were the product of a rational process and the directors availed themselves of all material and reasonably available information. The standard of director liability under the rule "is predicated upon concepts of gross negligence."

To the extent the Court allows shareholder plaintiffs to succeed on a theory that a director is liable for a failure to monitor business risk, the Court risks undermining the well settled policy of Delaware law by inviting Courts to perform a hindsight evaluation of the reasonableness or prudence of directors' business decisions. Risk has been defined as the chance that a return on an investment will be different than expected. The essence of the business judgment of managers and directors is deciding how the company will evaluate the trade-off between risk and return. Businesses—and particularly financial institutions—make returns by taking on risk; a company or investor that is willing to take on more risk can earn a higher return. Thus, in almost any business transaction, the parties go into the deal with the knowledge that, even if they have evaluated the situation correctly, the return could be different than they expected.

It is almost impossible for a court, in hindsight, to determine whether directors properly evaluated risk and thus made the "right" decision. In any investment there is a chance that returns will turn out lower than expected, and a smaller chance that they will be far lower than expected. When investments turn out poorly, it is possible that the decision-maker evaluated the deal correctly but got "unlucky" in that a huge loss—the probability of which was very small—actually happened. It is also possible that the decision-maker improperly evaluated the risk posed by an investment and that the company suffered large losses as a result.

Business decision-makers must operate in the real world, with imperfect information, limited resources, and an uncertain future. To impose liability on directors for making a "wrong" business decision would cripple their ability to earn returns for investors by taking business risks. Indeed, this kind of judicial second guessing is what the business judgment rule was designed to prevent, and this Court will not abandon such bedrock principles of Delaware fiduciary duty law. With these considerations and the difficult standard required to show director oversight liability in mind, I turn to an evaluation of the allegations in the Complaint.

The allegations amount essentially to a claim that Citigroup suffered large losses and that there were certain warning signs that could or should have put defendants on notice of the business risks related to Citigroup's investments in subprime assets. Plaintiffs then conclude that because defendants failed to prevent the Company's losses associated with certain business risks, they must have consciously ignored these warning signs or knowingly failed to monitor the Company's risk in accordance with their fiduciary duties. Such conclusory allegations, however, are not sufficient to state a claim for failure of oversight that would give rise to a substantial likelihood of personal liability, which would require particularized factual allegations demonstrating bad faith by the director defendants.

Plaintiffs do not contest that Citigroup had procedures and controls in place that were designed to monitor risk. Plaintiffs admit that Citigroup established the ARM Committee and that one of the purposes of the ARM Committee was to assist the board in fulfilling its oversight responsibility relating to policy standards and guidelines for risk assessment and risk management. The ARM Committee was also charged with (1) discussing with management and independent auditors the annual audited financial statements, (2) reviewing with management an evaluation of Citigroup's internal control structure, and (3) discussing with management Citigroup's major credit, market, liquidity, and operational risk exposures and the steps taken by management to monitor and control such exposures, including Citigroup's risk assessment and risk management policies. The ARM Committee met eleven times in 2006 and twelve times in 2007.

Plaintiffs argue that the director defendants breached their duty of oversight either because the oversight mechanisms were not adequate or because the director defendants did not make a good faith effort to comply with the established oversight procedures. To support this claim, the Complaint alleges numerous facts that plaintiffs argue should have put the director defendants on notice of the impending problems in the subprime mortgage market and Citigroup's exposure thereto. Plaintiffs summarized some of these "red flags" in their answering brief as follows:

- the steady decline of the housing market and the impact the collapsing bubble would have on mortgages and subprime backed securities since as early as 2005;
- December 2005 guidance from the FASB staff—"The FASB staff is aware of loan products whose contractual features may increase the exposure of the originator, holder, investor, guarantor, or servicer to risk of nonpayment or realization.";
- the drastic rise in foreclosure rates starting in 2006;
- several large subprime lenders reporting substantial losses and filing for bankruptcy starting in 2006;
- billions of dollars in losses reported by Citigroup's peers, such as Bear Stearns and Merrill Lynch.

The warning signs alleged by plaintiffs are not evidence that the directors consciously disregarded their duties or otherwise acted in bad faith; at most they evidence that the directors made bad business decisions. The "red flags" amount to little more than portions of public documents that reflected the worsening conditions in the subprime mortgage market and in the economy generally. Plaintiffs fail to plead "particularized facts suggesting that the Board was presented with 'red flags' alerting it to potential misconduct" at the Company. That the director defendants knew of signs of a deterioration in the subprime mortgage market, or even signs suggesting that conditions could decline further, is not sufficient to show that the directors were or should have been aware of any wrongdoing at the Company or were consciously disregarding a duty somehow to prevent Citigroup from suffering losses.

To recognize such claims under a theory of director oversight liability would undermine the long-established protections of the business judgment rule. It is well established that the mere fact that a company takes on business risk and suffers losses—even catastrophic losses—does not evidence misconduct, and without more, is not a basis for personal director liability. That there were signs in the market that reflected worsening conditions and suggested that conditions may deteriorate even further is not an invitation for this Court to disregard the presumptions of the business judgment rule and conclude that the directors are liable because they did not properly evaluate business risk. What plaintiffs are asking the Court to conclude from the presence of these "red flags" is that the directors failed to see the extent of Citigroup's business risk and therefore made a "wrong" business decision by allowing Citigroup to be exposed to the subprime mortgage market.

Citigroup has suffered staggering losses, in part, as a result of the recent problems in the United States economy, particularly those in the subprime mortgage market. It is understandable that investors, and others, want to find someone to hold responsible for these losses, and it is often difficult to distinguish between a desire to blame *someone* and a desire to force those responsible to account for their wrongdoing. Our law, fortunately, provides guidance for precisely these situations in the form of doctrines governing the duties owed by officers and directors of Delaware corporations. This law has been refined over hundreds of years, which no doubt included many crises, and we must not let our desire to blame someone for our losses make us lose sight of the purpose of our law. The discretion granted directors and managers allows them to maximize shareholder value in the long term by taking risks without the debilitating fear that they will be held personally liable if the company experiences losses. This doctrine also means, however, that when the company suffers losses, shareholders may not be able to hold the directors personally liable.

[The plaintiff's] claims in the complaint are dismissed.

B. DUTY TO BE INFORMED

Despite the business judgment rule, the duty of care actually exists. But if a director cannot be held liable for "stupid" or "egregious" or "bad" decisions, what actually is the nature of the duty and the standard of care? Any understanding of duty in the legal context requires an examination of the scope of the duty. What type of conduct would breach the duty?

The case below is perhaps the most famous (or infamous) case in all of corporation law. The facts are long and complicated, and they drive the court's analysis. The complexity of the facts is not unusual for merger and acquisition transactions, which are complex deals. This seminal case defines the scope of the duty of care. In reading this case, consider these questions: (1) What does it mean to say that a director breach her duty of care? (2) If care is not based on substantive rightness or wrongness, what is it? (3) What is the legal standard for determining whether a director breached her duty of care? (4) Applying the court's announced standard to the facts of the case, did the court reach the right decision? (5) What was the basic difference in opinion between the majority and the dissent?

SMITH V. VAN GORKOM

488 A.2d 858 (Del. 1985)

HORSEY, JUSTICE (for the majority):

This appeal from the Court of Chancery involves a class action brought by shareholders of the defendant Trans Union Corporation, originally seeking rescission of a cash-out merger of Trans Union into the defendant New T Company, a wholly-owned subsidiary of the defendant, Marmon Group, Inc. Alternate relief in the form of damages is sought against the defendant members of the Board of Directors of Trans Union, New T, and Jay Pritzker and Robert Pritzker, owners of Marmon.

Following trial, the former Chancellor granted judgment for the defendant directors. The plaintiffs appeal.

We reverse and direct that judgment be entered in favor of the plaintiffs and against the defendant directors for the fair value of the plaintiffs' stockholdings in Trans Union, in accordance with *Weinberger v. UOP, Inc.*, 457 A.2d 701 (Del. 1983). We hold that the Board's decision, reached September 20, 1980, to approve the proposed cash-out merger was not the product of an informed business judgment.

Trans Union was a publicly-traded, diversified holding company, the principal earnings of which were generated by its railcar leasing business. During the period here involved, the Company had a cash flow of hundreds of millions of dollars annually. However, the Company had difficulty in generating sufficient taxable income to offset increasingly large investment tax credits (ITCs). Accelerated depreciation deductions had decreased available taxable income against which to offset accumulating ITCs. The Company took these deductions, despite their effect on usable ITCs, because the rental price in the railcar leasing market had already impounded the purported tax savings.

Trans Union lobbied in Congress to have ITCs refundable in cash to firms which could not fully utilize the credit. Defendant Jerome Van Gorkom, Trans Union's chairman and CEO, testified in Congress for refundability of ITCs and against further accelerated depreciation. Van

Gorkom was convinced that Congress would neither accept the refundability concept nor curtail further accelerated depreciation.

Van Gorkom met with Senior Management. Van Gorkom reported on his lobbying efforts and his desire to find a solution to the tax credit problem more permanent than a continued program of acquisitions. Various alternatives were suggested and discussed, including the sale of Trans Union to a company with a large amount of taxable income.

Donald Romans, CFO, stated that his department had done a "very brief bit of work on the possibility of a leveraged buy-out." The work consisted of a "preliminary study" of the cash which could be generated by the Company if it participated in a leveraged buy-out. This analysis "was very first and rough cut at seeing whether a cash flow would support what might be considered a high price for this type of transaction."

On September 5, at another Senior Management meeting which Van Gorkom attended, Romans again brought up the idea of a leveraged buy-out as a "possible strategic alternative." Romans and Bruce Chelberg, President and Chief Operating Officer, had been working on the matter in preparation for the meeting. According to Romans: They did not "come up" with a price for the Company. They merely "ran the numbers" at $50 a share and at $60 a share with the "rough form" of their cash figures at the time. Their "figures indicated that $50 would be very easy to do but $60 would be very difficult to do under those figures." This work did not purport to establish a fair price for either the Company or 100% of the stock. It was intended to determine the cash flow needed to service the debt that would "probably" be incurred in a leveraged buy-out, based on "rough calculations" without "any benefit of experts to identify what the limits were to that, and so forth." These computations were not considered extensive and no conclusion was reached.

At this meeting, Van Gorkom stated that he would be willing to take $55 per share for his own 75,000 shares. He vetoed the suggestion of a leveraged buy-out by Management, however, as involving a potential conflict of interest for Management. Van Gorkom, a certified public accountant and lawyer, had been an officer of Trans Union for 24 years, its Chief Executive Officer for more than 17 years, and Chairman of its Board for 2 years. It is noteworthy in this connection that he was then approaching 65 years of age and mandatory retirement.

Van Gorkom decided to meet with Jay Pritzker, a corporate takeover specialist and a social acquaintance. Van Gorkom assembled a proposed per share price for sale of the Company and a financing structure by which to accomplish the sale. Van Gorkom did so without consulting either his Board or Senior Management except one: Carl Peterson, Trans Union's Controller. Van Gorkom directed Peterson to calculate the feasibility of a leveraged buy-out at an assumed price per share of $55. Apart from the Company's historic stock market price, and Van Gorkom's long association with Trans Union, the record is devoid of any competent evidence that $55 represented the per share intrinsic value of the Company.

Having thus chosen the $55 figure, based solely on the availability of a leveraged buy-out, Van Gorkom multiplied the price by the number of shares outstanding to reach a total value of the Company of $690 million.

Van Gorkom arranged a meeting with Pritzker at the latter's home on Saturday, September 13. Van Gorkom prefaced his presentation by stating to Pritzker: "Now as far as you are concerned, I can, I think, show how you can pay a substantial premium over the present stock price and pay off most of the loan in the first five years. If you could pay $55 for this Company, here is a way in which I think it can be financed."

Van Gorkom then reviewed with Pritzker his calculations based upon his proposed price of $55 per share. Van Gorkom stated that to be sure that $55 was the best price obtainable, Trans Union should be free to accept any better offer. Pritzker demurred, stating that his organization would serve as a "stalking horse" for an "auction contest" only if Trans Union would permit Pritzker to buy 1,750,000 shares of Trans Union stock at market price which Pritzker could then sell to any higher bidder.

On Monday, September 15, Pritzker advised Van Gorkom that he was interested in the $55 cash-out merger proposal and requested more information on Trans Union. Van Gorkom agreed to meet privately with Pritzker, accompanied by Peterson, Chelberg, and Michael Carpenter, Trans Union's consultant from the Boston Consulting Group. The meetings took place on September 16 and 17. Van Gorkom was "astounded that events were moving with such amazing rapidity."

On Thursday, September 18, Van Gorkom met again with Pritzker. At that time, Van Gorkom knew that Pritzker intended to make a cash-out merger offer at Van Gorkom's proposed $55 per share. Pritzker instructed his attorney, a merger and acquisition specialist, to begin drafting merger documents. There was no further discussion of the $55 price. However, the number of shares of Trans Union's treasury stock to be offered to Pritzker was negotiated down to one million shares; the price was set at $38—75 cents above the per share price at the close of the market on September 19.

Van Gorkom called a special meeting of the Trans Union Board for noon the following day. He also called a meeting of the Company's Senior Management to convene, prior to the meeting of the Board. No one, except Chelberg and Peterson, was told the purpose of the meetings. Van Gorkom did not invite Trans Union's investment banker, Salomon Brothers or its Chicago-based partner, to attend.

Of those present at the Senior Management meeting on September 20, only Chelberg and Peterson had prior knowledge of Pritzker's offer. Van Gorkom disclosed the offer and described its terms, but he furnished no copies of the proposed Merger Agreement. Romans announced that his department had done a second study which showed that, for a leveraged buy-out, the price range for Trans Union stock was between $55 and $65 per share. Van Gorkom neither saw the study nor asked Romans to make it available for the Board meeting.

Senior Management's reaction to the Pritzker proposal was completely negative. No member of Management, except Chelberg and Peterson, supported the proposal. Romans objected to the price as being too low; he was critical of the timing and suggested that consideration should be given to the adverse tax consequences of an all-cash deal for low-basis shareholders; and he took the position that the agreement to sell Pritzker one million newly-issued shares at market price would inhibit other offers, as would the prohibitions against soliciting bids and furnishing inside information to other bidders. Romans argued that the Pritzker proposal was a "lock up" and amounted to "an agreed merger as opposed to an offer." Nevertheless, Van Gorkom proceeded to the Board meeting as scheduled.

Ten directors served on the Trans Union Board, five inside (defendants Bonser, O'Boyle, Browder, Chelberg, and Van Gorkom) and five outside (defendants Wallis, Johnson, Lanterman, Morgan and Reneker). Of the outside directors, four were corporate chief executive officers and one was the former Dean of the University of Chicago Business School. None was an investment banker or trained financial analyst.

Van Gorkom began the Special Meeting of the Board with a twenty-minute oral presentation. Copies of the proposed Merger Agreement were delivered too late for study before or during the meeting. He reviewed the Company's ITC and depreciation problems. He discussed his initial meeting with Pritzker and his motivation in arranging that meeting. Van Gorkom did not disclose to the Board, however, the methodology by which he alone had arrived at the $55 figure, or the fact that he first proposed the $55 price in his negotiations with Pritzker.

Van Gorkom outlined the terms of the Pritzker offer as follows: Pritzker would pay $55 in cash for all outstanding shares of Trans Union stock upon completion of which Trans Union would be merged into New T Company, a subsidiary wholly-owned by Pritzker and formed to implement the merger; for a period of 90 days, Trans Union could receive, but could not actively solicit, competing offers; the offer had to be acted on by the next evening, Sunday, September 21; Trans Union could only furnish to competing bidders published information, and not proprietary information; the offer was subject to Pritzker obtaining the necessary financing by October 10, 1980; if the financing contingency were met or waived by Pritzker, Trans Union was required to sell to Pritzker one million newly-issued shares of Trans Union at $38 per share.

Van Gorkom took the position that putting Trans Union "up for auction" through a 90-day market test would validate a decision by the Board that $55 was a fair price. He told the Board that the "free market will have an opportunity to judge whether $55 is a fair price." Van Gorkom framed the decision not as whether $55 per share was the highest price that could be obtained, but as whether the $55 price was a fair price that the stockholders should be given the opportunity to accept or reject.

Attorney James Brennan advised the members of the Board that they might be sued if they failed to accept the offer and that a fairness opinion was not required as a matter of law.

Romans attended the meeting as CFO. He told the Board that he had not been involved in the negotiations with Pritzker and knew nothing about the merger proposal until the morning of the meeting; that his studies did not indicate either a fair price for the stock or a valuation of the Company; that he did not see his role as directly addressing the fairness issue; and that he and his people "were trying to search for ways to justify a price in connection with such a [leveraged buy-out] transaction, rather than to say what the shares are worth." Romans testified:

> I told the Board that the study ran the numbers at 50 and 60, and then the subsequent study at 55 and 65, and that was not the same thing as saying that I have a valuation of the company at X dollars. But it was a way—a first step towards reaching that conclusion.

Romans told the Board that, in his opinion, $55 was "in the range of a fair price," but "at the beginning of the range."

Chelberg, Trans Union's President, supported Van Gorkom's presentation and representations. He testified that he "participated to make sure that the Board members collectively were clear on the details of the agreement or offer from Pritzker;" that he "participated in the discussion with Brennan, inquiring of him about the necessity for valuation opinions in spite of the way in which this particular offer was couched;" and that he was otherwise actively involved in supporting the positions being taken by Van Gorkom before the Board about "the necessity to act immediately on this offer," and about "the adequacy of the $55 and the question of how that would be tested."

The Board meeting of September 20 lasted about two hours. Based solely upon Van Gorkom's oral presentation, Chelberg's supporting representations, Romans' oral statement, Brennan's legal advice, and their knowledge of the market history of the Company's stock, the directors approved the proposed Merger Agreement.

The Merger Agreement was executed by Van Gorkom during the evening of September 20 at a formal social event that he hosted for the opening of the Chicago Lyric Opera. Neither he nor any other director read the agreement prior to its signing and delivery to Pritzker.

On September 22, the Company issued a press release announcing that Trans Union had entered into a "definitive" Merger Agreement with an affiliate of the Marmon Group, Inc., a Pritzker holding company.

On December 19, this litigation was commenced. On January 26, Trans Union's Board met and voted to proceed with the Pritzker merger.

The stockholders of Trans Union approved the Pritzker merger proposal. Of the outstanding shares, 69.9% were voted in favor of the merger; 7.25% were voted against the merger; and 22.85% were not voted.

[Business Judgment Rule]

We turn to the issue of the application of the business judgment rule to the September 20 meeting of the Board.

The business judgment rule is the offspring of the fundamental principle that the business and affairs are managed by or under its board of directors. *Aronson v. Lewis,* 473 A.2d 805, 811 (Del. 1984). In carrying out their managerial roles, directors are charged with an unyielding fiduciary duty to the corporation and its shareholders. *Loft, Inc. v. Guth,* 5 A.2d 503 (Del. 1939). The business judgment rule exists to protect and promote the full and free exercise of the managerial power granted to Delaware directors. The rule itself "is a presumption that in making a business decision, the directors of a corporation acted on an informed basis, in good faith and in the honest belief that the action taken was in the best interests of the company." *Aronson,* 473 A.2d at 812. Thus, the party attacking a board decision as uninformed must rebut the presumption that its business judgment was an informed one.

Whether a business judgment is an informed one turns on whether the directors have informed themselves "prior to making a business decision, of all material information reasonably available to them."

Under the business judgment rule there is no protection for directors who have made "an unintelligent or unadvised judgment." A director's duty to inform himself in preparation for a decision derives from the fiduciary capacity in which he serves the corporation and its stockholders. Since a director is vested with the responsibility for the management of the affairs of the corporation, he must execute that duty with the recognition that he acts on behalf of others. Such obligation does not tolerate faithlessness or self-dealing. But fulfillment of the fiduciary function requires more than the mere absence of bad faith or fraud. Representation of the financial interests of others imposes on a director an affirmative duty to protect those interests and to proceed with a critical eye in assessing information of the type and under the circumstances present here.

A director's duty to exercise an informed business judgment is in the nature of a duty of care, as distinguished from a duty of loyalty. Here, there were no allegations of fraud, bad faith, or self-dealing. Hence, it is presumed that the directors reached their business judgment in good faith, and considerations of motive are irrelevant to the issue before us.

The standard of care applicable to a director's duty of care has been restated by this Court. In *Aronson,* we stated: "our analysis satisfies us that under the business judgment rule director liability is predicated upon concepts of gross negligence." 473 A.2d at 812.

We again confirm that view. We think the concept of gross negligence is also the proper standard for determining whether a business judgment reached by a board of directors was an informed one.

It is against those standards that the conduct of the directors of Trans Union must be tested regarding their exercise of an informed business judgment in voting to approve the Pritzker merger proposal.

[Analysis]

The issue of whether the directors reached an informed decision to "sell" the Company on September 20, 1980 must be determined only upon the basis of the information then reasonably available to the directors and relevant to their decision to accept the Pritzker merger proposal.

We must conclude that the Board of Directors did not reach an informed business judgment on September 20, 1980 in voting to "sell" the Company for $55 per share pursuant to the Pritzker cash-out merger proposal. Our reasons, in summary, are as follows: The directors (1) did not adequately inform themselves as to Van Gorkom's role in forcing the "sale" of the Company and in establishing the per share purchase price; (2) were uninformed as to the intrinsic value of the Company; and (3) given these circumstances, at a minimum, were grossly negligent in approving the "sale" of the Company upon two hours' consideration, without prior notice, and without the exigency of a crisis or emergency.

The Board based its September 20 decision to approve the cash-out merger primarily on Van Gorkom's representations. None of the directors, other than Van Gorkom and Chelberg, had any prior knowledge that the purpose of the meeting was to propose a cash-out merger of Trans Union. No members of Senior Management were present, other than Chelberg, Romans and Peterson; and the latter two had only learned of the proposed sale an hour earlier. Both general counsel Moore and former general counsel Browder attended the meeting, but were equally uninformed as to the purpose of the meeting and the documents to be acted upon.

Without any documents before them concerning the proposed transaction, the members of the Board were required to rely entirely upon Van Gorkom's 20-minute oral presentation of the proposal. No written summary of the terms of the merger was presented; the directors were given no documentation to support the adequacy of $55 price per share; and the Board had before it nothing more than Van Gorkom's statement of his understanding of the substance of an agreement which he admittedly had never read, nor which any member of the Board had ever seen.

Under 8 *Del.C.* § 141(e), "directors are fully protected in relying in good faith on reports made by officers."[15] The term "report" has been liberally construed to include reports of informal personal investigations by corporate officers. However, there is no evidence that any "report," as defined under § 141(e), concerning the Pritzker proposal, was presented to the Board on September 20. Van Gorkom's oral presentation of his understanding of the terms of the proposed Merger Agreement, which he had not seen, and Romans' brief oral statement of his preliminary study regarding the feasibility of a leveraged buy-out of Trans Union do not qualify as § 141(e) "reports" for these reasons: The former lacked substance because Van Gorkom was basically uninformed as to the essential provisions of the very document about which he was talking. Romans' statement was irrelevant to the issues before the Board since it did not purport to be a valuation study. At a minimum for a report to enjoy the status conferred by § 141(e), it must be pertinent to the subject matter upon which a board is called to act, and otherwise be entitled to good faith, not blind, reliance. Considering all of the surrounding circumstances—hastily calling the meeting without prior notice of its subject matter, the proposed sale of the Company without any prior consideration of the issue or necessity therefor, the urgent time constraints imposed by Pritzker, and the total absence of any documentation whatsoever—the directors were duty bound to make reasonable inquiry of Van Gorkom and Romans, and if they had done so, the inadequacy of that upon which they now claim to have relied would have been apparent.

The defendants rely on the magnitude of the premium or spread between the $55 Pritzker offering price and Trans Union's current market price of $38 per share.

A substantial premium may provide one reason to recommend a merger, but in the absence of other sound valuation information, the fact of a premium alone does not provide an adequate basis upon which to assess the fairness of an offering price. Here, the judgment reached as to the adequacy of the premium was based on a comparison between the historically depressed Trans Union market price and the amount of the Pritzker offer. Using market price as a basis for concluding that the premium adequately reflected the true value was a clearly faulty, indeed fallacious, premise, as the defendants' own evidence demonstrates.

The parties do not dispute that a publicly-traded stock price is solely a measure of the value of a minority position and, thus, market price

15 Section 141(e) provides in pertinent part: "A member of the board of directors shall, in the performance of his duties, be fully protected in relying in good faith upon the books of accounts or reports made to the corporation by any of its officers, or by an independent certified public accountant, or by an appraiser selected with reasonable care by the board of directors, or in relying in good faith upon other records of the corporation."

represents only the value of a single share. On September 20, the Board assessed the adequacy of the premium over market solely by comparing it with Trans Union's current and historical stock price.

The Board had no other information on which to base a determination of the intrinsic value of Trans Union as a going concern. The Board had made no evaluation of the Company designed to value the entire enterprise. The adequacy of a premium is indeterminate unless it is assessed in terms of other competent and sound valuation information that reflects the value of the particular business.

Despite the foregoing facts and circumstances, there was no call by the Board for any valuation study or documentation of the $55 price per share as a measure of the fair value of the Company in a cash-out context. It is undisputed that the major asset of Trans Union was its cash flow. Yet, at no time did the Board call for a valuation study taking into account that highly significant element of the Company's assets.

We do not imply that an outside valuation study is essential to support an informed business judgment; nor do we state that fairness opinions by independent investment bankers are required as a matter of law. Often insiders familiar with the business of a going concern are in a better position than are outsiders to gather relevant information; and under appropriate circumstances, such directors may be fully protected in relying in good faith upon the valuation reports of their management.

Here, the record establishes that the Board did not request its CFO, Romans, to make any valuation study or review of the proposal to determine the adequacy of $55 per share for sale of the Company. The Board rested on Romans' elicited response that the $55 figure was within a "fair price range" within the context of a leveraged buy-out. No director sought any further information from Romans. No director asked him why he put $55 at the bottom of his range. No director asked Romans for any details as to his study, the reason why it had been undertaken or its depth. No director asked to see the study; and no director asked Romans whether Trans Union's finance department could do a fairness study within the remaining 36-hour period available under the Pritzker offer.

The record also establishes that the Board accepted without scrutiny Van Gorkom's representation as to the fairness of the $55 price per share for sale of the Company—a subject that the Board had never previously considered. The Board thereby failed to discover that Van Gorkom had suggested the $55 price to Pritzker and, most crucially, that Van Gorkom had arrived at the $55 figure based on calculations designed solely to determine the feasibility of a leveraged buy-out. No questions were raised either as to the tax implications of a cash-out merger or how the price for the one million share option granted Pritzker was calculated.

The record compels the conclusion that on September 20 the Board lacked valuation information adequate to reach an informed business judgment as to the fairness of $55 per share for sale of the Company.

To summarize: we hold that the directors of Trans Union breached their fiduciary duty to their stockholders by their failure to inform themselves of all information reasonably available to them and relevant to their decision to recommend the Pritzker merger.

We hold that the Trial Court committed reversible error in applying the business judgment rule in favor of the director defendants in this case.

On remand, the Court of Chancery shall conduct an evidentiary hearing to determine the fair value of the shares represented by the plaintiffs' class, based on the intrinsic value of Trans Union on September 20, 1980. Such valuation shall be made in accordance with *Weinberger v. UOP,* 457 A.2d at 712–715. An award of damages may be entered to the extent that the fair value of Trans Union exceeds $55 per share.

MCNEILLY, JUSTICE, dissenting:

I have no quarrel with the majority's analysis of the business judgment rule. It is the application of that rule to these facts which is wrong. An overview of the entire record, rather than the limited view of bits and pieces which the majority has exploded like popcorn, convinces me that the directors made an informed business judgment.

At the time of the September 20 meeting the 10 members of Trans Union's Board of Directors were highly qualified and well informed about the affairs and prospects of Trans Union. These directors were acutely aware of the historical problems facing Trans Union which were caused by the tax laws. They had discussed these problems *ad nauseam*. In fact, within two months of the September 20 meeting the board had reviewed and discussed an outside study of the company done by The Boston Consulting Group and an internal five-year forecast prepared by management. At the September 20 meeting Van Gorkom presented the Pritzker offer, and the board heard from James Brennan, the company's counsel in this matter, who discussed the legal documents. The Board directed that certain changes be made in the merger documents. These changes made it clear that the Board was free to accept a better offer than Pritzker's if one was made. The facts reveal that the Board did not act in a grossly negligent manner in informing themselves of the relevant facts before passing on the merger. To the contrary, this record reveals that the directors acted with the utmost care in informing themselves of the relevant and available facts before passing on the merger.

CHRISTIE, JUSTICE, dissenting:

I respectfully dissent. Considering the standard and scope of our review, I believe that the record taken as a whole supports a conclusion that the actions of the defendants are protected by the business judgment rule. *Aronson v. Lewis,* 473 A.2d 805, 812 (Del. 1984). Under the circumstances I would affirm the judgment of the Court of Chancery.

NOTES

1. The controversial nature of *Van Gorkom* is evinced by the fact that the court issued a split decision with two dissenters. While a split court may not be so unusual for the U.S. Supreme Court, the Delaware Supreme Court embraces a "unanimity norm." Randy J. Holland & David A. Skeel, Jr., *Deciding Cases Without Controversy*, 5 Del. L. Rev. 115, 118–19 (2002) ("The Delaware Supreme Court, which has long been recognized as the definitive authority on corporate law, rarely issues separate opinions. Even on deeply controversial issues, Delaware's justices almost invariably speak with a single voice. . . . Over the fifty-year history of the separate Delaware Supreme Court, its nineteen justices have written separately on the average in only about three percent of the reported cases each year."). *Van Gorkom* was the first case in which the Delaware Supreme Court imposed personal liability on directors for a breach of the duty of care. The defendants ultimately settled the case for $23.5 million, of which the directors' liability insurance provided $10 million and the Pritzker group (the acquirer) paid the balance of $13.5 million. *Roundtable Discussion: Corporate Governance*, 77 Chi.-Kent L. Rev. 235, 237–38 (2001). The case was extremely controversial. It generated a legion of commentary criticizing the decision. *E.g.*, Larry E. Ribstein, *Takeover Defenses and the Corporate Contract*, 78 Geo. L.J. 71, 96 (1989) ("Van Gorkom has been heavily criticized for the scope of the duty of care applied by the court."); Jonathan R. Macey & Geoffrey P. Miller, *Trans Union Reconsidered*, 98 Yale L.J. 127, 139 (1988) (noting that the case exhibited a "mysterious anti-management bias"); Richard A. Booth, *The Emerging Conflict Between Federal Securities Law and State Corporation Law*, 12 J. Corp. L. 73, 94 n.109 (1986) ("While there are many good reasons for requiring directors to investigate the terms of mergers to which they commit, the *Van Gorkom* court's reason is patently absurd."); Daniel R. Fischel, *The Business Judgment Rule and the Trans Union Case*, 40 Bus. Law. 1437, 1454 (1985) ("Van Gorkom [is] surely one of the worst decisions in the history of corporate law.").

2. What happens when a plaintiff shareholder rebuts the presumption of the business judgment rule?

> The [business judgment] rule posits a powerful presumption in favor of actions taken by the directors in that a decision made by a loyal and informed board will not be overturned by the courts unless it cannot be "attributed to any rational business purpose." Thus, a shareholder plaintiff challenging a board decision has the burden at the outset to rebut the rule's presumption. To rebut the rule, a shareholder plaintiff assumes the burden of providing evidence that directors, in reaching their challenged decision, breached any one of the *triads* of their fiduciary duty—good faith, loyalty or due care. If a shareholder plaintiff fails to meet this evidentiary burden, the

business judgment rule attaches to protect corporate officers and directors and the decisions they make, and our courts will not second-guess these business judgments. If the rule is rebutted, the burden shifts to the defendant directors, the proponents of the challenged transaction, to prove to the trier of fact the "entire fairness" of the transaction to the shareholder plaintiff.

Under the entire fairness standard of judicial review, the defendant directors must establish to the *court's* satisfaction that the transaction was the product of both fair dealing *and* fair price. Further, in the review of a transaction involving a sale of a company, the directors have the burden of establishing that the price offered was the highest value reasonably available under the circumstances.

Cede & Co. v. Technicolor, Inc., 634 A.2d 345, 361 (Del. 1993). Upon a rebuttal of the presumption of the business judgment, the burden of proof shifts to the defendants to show that the challenged transaction satisfies the entire fairness standard. *See* Mills Acquisition Co. v. Macmillan, Inc., 559 A.2d 1261 (Del. 1989) ("The challenged transaction must withstand rigorous judicial scrutiny under the exacting standards of entire fairness. *Weinberger v. UOP, Inc.*, 457 A.2d 701, 710 (Del. 1983)."). Unlike the business judgment standard which requires judicial deference to business decisions, the entire fairness standard requires no deference and imposes a rigorous, independent judicial analysis of the entire fairness of the transaction.

The concept of fairness has two basic aspects: fair dealing and fair price. The former embraces questions of when the transaction was timed, how it was initiated, structured, negotiated, disclosed to the directors, and how the approvals of the directors and the stockholders were obtained. The latter aspect of fairness relates to the economic and financial considerations of the proposed merger, including all relevant factors: assets, market value, earnings, future prospects, and any other elements that affect the intrinsic or inherent value of a company's stock. However, the test for fairness is not a bifurcated one as between fair dealing and price. All aspects of the issue must be examined as a whole since the question is one of entire fairness. However, in a non-fraudulent transaction we recognize that price may be the preponderant consideration outweighing other features of the merger. Here, we address the two basic aspects of fairness separately because we find reversible error as to both.

Weinberger v. UOP, Inc., 457 A.2d 701, 711 (Del. 1983).

3. The application of the business judgment rule is frequently outcome determinative. It precludes judicial review of the challenged action, unless the plaintiff shareholder can rebut the presumption.

It is sometimes thought that the decision whether to apply the business judgment rule or the entire fairness test can be outcome-determinative. Because the effect of the proper invocation of the business judgment rule is so powerful and the standard of entire

> fairness so exacting, the determination of the appropriate standard of judicial review frequently is determinative of the outcome of derivative litigation.

Nixon v. Blackwell, 626 A.2d 1366, 1376 (Del. 1993).

C. EXCULPATION

In direct response to *Van Gorkom* and the deluge of criticism, the Delaware legislature, always sensitive to market perceptions in light of its desire to protect the state's incorporation franchise, amended the corporation statute to include section 102(b)(7).

DGCL § 102(b)

The certificate of incorporation may also contain . . .

(7) A provision eliminating or limiting the personal liability of a director to the corporation or its stockholders for monetary damages for breach of fiduciary duty as a director, provided that such provision shall not eliminate or limit the liability of a director:

> (i) For any breach of the director's duty of loyalty to the corporation or its stockholders;
>
> (ii) for acts or omissions not in good faith or which involve intentional misconduct or a knowing violation of law;
>
> (iii) under § 174 of this title;[2] or
>
> (iv) for any transaction from which the director derived an improper personal benefit.

Section 102(b)(7) permits the exculpation of liability for money damages for a breach of the duty of care only.

> When the General Assembly enacted Section 102(b)(7), three years after this Court's landmark decision in *Weinberger v. UOP, Inc.*, 457 A.2d 701 (Del. 1983), it not only recognized but reinforced *Weinberger's* restatement of a venerable and fundamental principle of our common law corporate fiduciary jurisprudence: there is no "safe harbor" for divided loyalties in Delaware. The fact that Section 102(b)(7) does not permit shareholders to exculpate directors for violations of loyalty or good faith reflects that the provision was a thoughtfully crafted legislative response to our

[2] DGCL § 174 is titled "Liability of directors for unlawful payment of dividend or unlawful stock purchase or redemption; exoneration from liability; contribution among directors; subrogation." A board generally has discretion, subject to the business judgment rule, to declare and pay dividends. However, a corporation may not pay dividends or make a distribution to shareholders under certain circumstances set forth in § 160. Section 174 imposes liability for directors who make an unlawful payment of dividends.

holding in *Van Gorkom* and, simultaneously, reflected the General Assembly's own expression of support for our assertion in *Weinberger* that when the standard of review is entire fairness the requirement of fairness is unflinching in its demand.

Emerald Partners v. Berlin, 787 A.2d 85, 96 (Del. 2001).

Section 102(b)(7) does not preclude a shareholder from seeking nonmonetary remedies, such as an injunction or rescission, for a breach of the duty of care. For example, it would not preclude a shareholder in a case like *Van Gorkom* from seeking an injunction against the merger.

The certificates of incorporation of most public companies contain a section 102(b)(7) exculpation provision. The following are examples in the certificates of Facebook and Google (Alphabet Inc.).

Facebook, Inc. Restated Certificate of Incorporation

To the fullest extent permitted by law, nor no director of the corporation shall be personally liable to the corporation or its stockholders for monetary damages for breach of fiduciary duty as a director. Without limiting the effect of the preceding sentence, if the General Corporation Law is hereafter amended to authorize the further elimination or limitation of the liability of a director, then the liability of a director of the corporation shall be eliminated or limited to the fullest extent permitted by the General Corporation Law, as so amended.

Alphabet Inc. Amended and Restated Certificate of Incorporation

To the fullest extent permitted by the General Corporation Law of Delaware as the same exists or as may hereafter be amended, a director of the Corporation shall not be personally liable to the Corporation or its stockholders for monetary damages for breach of fiduciary duty as a director. If the General Corporation Law of Delaware is amended to authorize corporate action further eliminating or limiting the personal liability of directors, then the liability of a director of the Corporation shall be eliminated to the fullest extent permitted by the General Corporation Law of Delaware, as so amended.

The above certificates provide an insight into the link between the risk of liability and the incentives of directors, the core policy consideration of the business judgment rule. Both Facebook and Google have controlling shareholders who, presumably, could dictate the terms of any optional provisions in the certificate of incorporation, such as the choice of including or not an exculpation clause. Yet both companies, like many other public companies, chose to include one, presumably with the tacit consent of controlling shareholders who are advised by sophisticated lawyers. Why?

D. AIDING AND ABETTING BREACH OF DUTIES

In light of *Van Gorkom* and the possibility of section 102(b)(7) exculpation, one must question whether the duty of care has any *practical* effect on incentives. What is the point of saying there is a "duty," when there is effectively no personal liability against a director?

> Liability for a wrong should ultimately matter, a point amply demonstrated by the shocked reaction to the finding of liability in *Smith v. Van Gorkom*. A mountain of papers on aspiration does not hold a candle to a single-page order of judgment. Directors do not need aspirational sermons on the boardroom mount, when we consider that it comes with the price tag of Wall Street investment banks and law firms who must divine what the sermons actually mean, a significant cost attached to every meaningful transaction. . . . If we are left only with an aspirational norm, the whole thing strikes of kabuki theater. This indulgence of judicial ceremony comes at the heavy cost of legal uncertainty and its progeny of derivative suits. And, if the duty of care is simply an aspirational norm, one wonders whether the psychological effect of having a friendly reminder of the aspiration is really worth it, or whether the Sunday boardroom can do without the sermons.

Robert J. Rhee, *The Tort Foundation of Duty of Care and Business Judgment*, 88 Notre Dame L. Rev. 1139, 1154–55 (2013).

One answer to this question of relevance is that the duty of care imposes liability and provides remedies so long as they are not money damages against directors. A plaintiff shareholder can seek injunction or rescission of the subject transaction. But still, what about incentives?

Another answer is that section 102(b)(7) exculpates only directors for personal liability for money damages. It does not exculpate officers or third persons. A non-director person can be held liable for aiding and abetting a breach of fiduciary duty, including the duty of care. *See In re Del Monte Foods Co. Shareholders Litigation,* 25 A.3d 813, 838 (Del. Ch. 2011) ("By their terms, Sections 102(b)(7) and 141(e) do not protect aiders and abetters."); *Gantler v. Stephens,* 965 A.2d 695, 709 n.37 (Del.2009) ("Although legislatively possible, there currently is no statutory provision authorizing comparable exculpation of corporate officers.").

The elements of an action for aiding and abetting the breach of fiduciary duty are: (1) the existence of a fiduciary relationship, (2) the fiduciary's breach of duty, (3) the defendant's knowing participation in that breach, and (4) damages proximately caused by the breach. Malpiede v. Townson, 780 A.2d 1075, 1096 (Del. 2001). When a corporation engages in a significant transaction such as a merger or acquisition, directors and officers do not execute transactions in a vacuum. They always depend on outside advisers, *e.g.*, lawyers, accountants, bankers, and consultants. If directors breached their duty of care, outside advisers and others may be liable if they aided and abetted the breach. For non-directors, the breach of the duty of care may have a painful personal bite.

The case below deals with the liability of an investment bank resulting from the board's breach of the duty of care. In reading this case, consider these questions: (1) In what way did the board breach its duty? (2) In what way did the investment bank aid and abet this breach? (3) In what way was the investment bank's conduct more culpable than the board's? (4) In what way is this case an example of agency cost?

RBC CAPITAL MARKETS, LLC v. JERVIS

129 A.3d 816 (Del. 2015)

VALIHURA, JUSTICE:

Pending before this Court is an appeal and cross-appeal arising out of a final judgment of the Court of Chancery finding that RBC Capital Markets, LLC ("RBC" or "Appellant") aided and abetted breaches of fiduciary duty by former directors of Rural/Metro Corporation ("Rural" or the "Company") in connection with the sale of the Company to an affiliate of Warburg Pincus LLC ("Warburg"), a private equity firm.

The Court of Chancery issued a post-trial decision and held RBC liable to a class of Rural stockholders (the "Class") for aiding and abetting breaches of fiduciary duty by Rural's board of directors.

The Court of Chancery issued a decision setting the amount of RBC's liability at $75,798,550, constituting 83% of the $91,323,554 in total damages that the Class suffered, which represented the difference between the value the Company's stockholders received in the merger and Rural's going concern value.

We affirm the principal legal holdings of the Court of Chancery.

Rural is a Delaware corporation headquartered in Scottsdale, Arizona. The Company is a leading national provider of ambulance and private fire protection services that serves more than 400 communities across 22 states. Rural's shares traded on NASDAQ from July 1993 until the merger closed. Upon closing, each publicly held share of Rural common stock was converted into the right to receive $17.25 in cash.

Before the merger, the board of directors had seven members: Christopher Shackelton, Eugene Davis, Earl Holland, Henry Walker, Robert Wilson, Conrad Conrad, and Michael DiMino (the "Board").

Shackelton, Davis, and Walker comprised the special committee (the "Special Committee" or "Committee"). Shackelton was its Chair.

[Plaintiffs settled with Moelis & Co. for a payment of $5 million and the individual defendants for a contemplated payment of $6.6 million.] Thus, the case proceeded to trial solely against RBC.

The Board hired Michael DiMino as the Company's new President and CEO and gave him a mandate to grow the Company. To carry out his mandate, DiMino developed new growth strategies.

RBC was hired by the Special Committee as Rural's primary financial advisor in connection with the Company's decision to explore strategic alternatives. Anthony Munoz, a Managing Director at RBC, was Rural's lead banker. Marc Daniel, RBC's lead M & A banker, participated in the Rural sale process alongside Munoz. Moelis was brought on as Rural's secondary financial advisor. Richard Harding, a Managing Director, was Rural's contact at Moelis.

The Special Committee was first formed in August 2010, after RBC advanced the idea of Rural acquiring American Medical Response, Inc. ("AMR"), its primary national competitor in the ambulance business. AMR was a subsidiary of Emergency Medical Services Corporation ("EMS"). The Board formed the Special Committee with the authority to oversee the process of formulating Rural's acquisition strategy concerning AMR.

The Rural Auction Process

The decision to initiate a sale process in December 2010 was unreasonable at the outset because the Board did not make the decision to launch a sale process, nor did it authorize the Special Committee to start one. The initiation of the sale process was unreasonable because RBC did not disclose that proceeding in parallel with the EMS process served RBC's interest in gaining a role on the financing trees of bidders for EMS. It found that RBC designed a process that favored its own interest in gaining financing work from bidders for EMS. RBC's sale process design prioritized the EMS participants so they would include RBC in their financing trees. RBC did not disclose the disadvantages of its proposed schedule. The Board failed to oversee the Special Committee, failed to become informed about strategic alternatives and about potential conflicts of interests faced by the advisors, and approved the merger without adequate information, including the value of not engaging in any transaction.

The evidence supports these findings and reflects that RBC viewed Rural as an "angle" to obtain EMS work. RBC scheduled first round bids for late January 2011 because that tracked with the EMS process and Rural's ability "to act as an 'angle.'" RBC hoped to generate up to $60.1 million in fees from the Rural and EMS deals. The maximum financing fees of $55 million were more than ten times the advisory fee.

Rural encountered readily foreseeable problems associated with trying to induce financial buyers to engage in two parallel processes for targets that were direct competitors. The Special Committee had not previously considered this complication.

RBC developed a two-track bidding process, with the first classification of buyers constituted primarily of those participating in the EMS process and the second grouping generally composed of "those that have dropped out of the EMS process and/or [those that] have/should have interest in [Rural] as a standalone deal."

In late December 2010 and early January 2011, participants in the process provided negative feedback about its timing and design. As the auction developed, Moelis's concerns regarding transaction complexity were realized; Harding, the Rural point person for Moelis, commented that a potential bidder for Rural, KKR, suggested it "would be tough" to participate in "simultaneous auctions." KKR told Rural's bankers that it "would be ideal" if the EMS deal and the Company's deal were "staggered." After speaking with Bain Capital Partners, Harding shared with Shackelton and RBC that the private equity firm thought that "lining up two deals for public companies simultaneously is tough but staggered, even fairly closely, could work." Clayton, Dubilier & Rice ("CD & R") also urged delaying the Rural process until the EMS sale was completed.

The Special Committee met on February 6, 2011. RBC and Moelis reviewed the six indications of interest. A joint presentation by RBC and Moelis summarized the initial indications of interest:

American Securities:	\$16.00–\$17.00;
Ares Management:	\$14.50–\$16.50;
CD & R:	\$15.50–\$16.50;
Leonard, Green & Partners:	\$17.00–\$19.00;
Kelso & Company:	\$14.75–\$16.50;
Warburg:	\$17.00.

RBC's presentation to the Special Committee at the February 6 meeting was four pages long, provided no opinion, preliminarily or otherwise, on the quality of the bids, and, as the Court of Chancery observed, failed to include any valuation metrics.

On March 15, 2011, the Board met to consider the Special Committee's progress for the first time since December 8, 2010. Akin to its previous presentations, RBC failed to include valuation metrics and provided no opinion, preliminarily or otherwise, on the quality of the bids during its March 15, 2011 sale process update.

At the March 15 meeting of the Board, RBC and Moelis discussed the final bid deadline of March 21, 2011. RBC had designed the sale process ostensibly to give the winner of the EMS auction the opportunity to make a bid for Rural that included synergies.

RBC's faulty design prevented the type of competitive dynamic among multiple bidders that is necessary for reliable price discovery. Because Warburg had withdrawn from the EMS process, it was able to pursue Rural aggressively, thus giving Warburg an advantage over others who were still involved in evaluating EMS. Warburg knew that its competitors in the process lacked similar resources and that it did not need to incorporate as much of its anticipated gains in its price to outbid the other firms.

The Board adopted a resolution which the trial court characterized as "granting the Special Committee the authority that Shackelton and RBC had assumed for themselves."

RBC's Efforts to Secure Staple Financing and Warburg's Final Bid

On March 18, 2011, RBC sent Warburg executed commitment papers, but Warburg did not respond.

As part of its push to secure Warburg's business, RBC bankers sought internal approval to underwrite 100% of a $590 million financing package for Warburg.

Before the bid deadline, [Sean Carney, a Warburg partner] emailed a Warburg colleague with an update on the Rural process: "I think we are in a good position. [DiMino] likes us a lot, the bankers are pulling for us, and we are the premier firm involved in the process."

Warburg submitted a bid at $17.00 per share, and CD & R submitted an indication of interest at $17.00 per share, subject to further diligence.

On March 23, the Special Committee met to discuss the offers received from Warburg and CD & R.

The Special Committee decided not to engage further with CD & R, and that "the Special Committee directed RBC and Moelis to engage in final negotiations with Warburg over price."

RBC's internal communications before the March 23 meeting of the Special Committee reflect the bank's position that closing on the Warburg offer and obtaining the private equity firm's buy-side financing business were its priorities when advising the Board.

On March 25, Warburg increased its bid to $17.25 per share. Warburg's bid materials did not include staple financing from RBC.

Following Warburg's submission of its bid, RBC did not disclose to its client that it continued to seek a buy-side financing role with the private equity firm.

RBC's Manipulation of the Valuation Process

On Saturday, March 26, 2011, the RBC fairness opinion committee met to discuss Warburg's bid for Rural. The committee members reviewed the fairness presentation and letter, and "recommended certain changes."

On the deal front, RBC worked to lower the analyses in its fairness presentation so Warburg's bid looked more attractive. [The court described several ways in which RBC unreasonably lowered the valuation of Rural in its analysis of valuation given to the board.]

The Board's Acceptance of the Revised Warburg Offer

The Board failed to provide active and direct oversight of RBC. It observed that when the Board approved the merger, the directors were unaware of RBC's last minute efforts to solicit a buy-side financing role from Warburg, had not received any valuation information until three hours before the meeting to approve the deal, and did not know about RBC's manipulation of its valuation metrics.

Unbeknownst to the Rural directors, RBC had been communicating with Warburg in the lead up to the private equity firm's revised bid. [Sean Carney, a Warburg partner] emailed his colleagues the following:

> I have spoken to a number of bankers on our side (for advice) and theirs (for back-channel feedback). There are definitely two other offers as we suspected, both say they need another week of work but the company's bankers think it is more like 2–3 weeks. Sounds like both are higher but again not a knock-out, I haven't been able to get more specific info than that.
>
> The BOD is split. Some are ready to vote yes for us now. Others want to try to get a little more from us, and some a lot more, with silly numbers like $18 being thrown around in the BOD room. The company's bankers think this may just be posturing in front of the bankers, and the bankers have told the BOD that a number like that is not likely to happen ever and certainly not from us.

On March 25, Warburg submitted its best and final offer of $17.25 per share. Warburg determined to proceed without utilizing RBC's commitment papers, despite the offer to fund the sponsor's revolver and the bank's other inducements.

On March 27, 2011, the Board met to consider the potential merger. The Rural directors received written valuation analyses from RBC and Moelis at 9:42 p.m. The valuation materials were the first the Board had received since December 2010. At 11 p.m., without knowledge of RBC's downward modifications to its analysis, back-channel communications with Warburg, and late push to get on the private equity firm's financing tree, the Board and Special Committee held a joint meeting. Shackelton led the meeting before turning it over to RBC, which discussed "the implied transaction multiples" and the premium that Warburg's offer represented over Rural's current and historical trading prices. Daniel "reviewed RBC's valuation methodologies" with the Board. Shackelton later requested that RBC deliver its financial analysis "and an oral fairness opinion to the Board." RBC opined that the transaction was fair from a financial point of view. The Board approved the merger with Warburg after midnight.

Revlon

RBC argues that the court erred by holding that the Board breached its duty of care under the enhanced scrutiny articulated in *Revlon, Inc. v. MacAndrews & Forbes Holdings, Inc.*, 506 A.2d 173 (Del.1986).

Revlon "requires us to examine whether a board's overall course of action was reasonable under the circumstances as a good faith attempt to secure the highest value reasonably attainable." As we recently reiterated, "there is no single blueprint that a board must follow to fulfill its duties, and a court applying *Revlon*'s enhanced scrutiny must decide whether the directors made a *reasonable* decision, not a *perfect* decision."

We agree with the Court of Chancery's principal conclusion that the Board's overall course of conduct fails *Revlon* scrutiny.

The reasonableness of initiating a sale process to run in tandem with the EMS auction, absent conflicts of interest, "would be one of the many debatable choices that fiduciaries and their advisors must make and it would fall within the range of reasonableness." But where undisclosed conflicts of interest exist, such decisions must be viewed more skeptically.

The record indicates that Rural's Board was unaware of the implications of the dual-track structure of the bidding process and that the design was driven by RBC's motivation to obtain financing fees in another transaction with Rural's competitor.

The Board violated its situational duty by failing to take reasonable steps to attain the best value reasonably available to the stockholders. We agree that the individual defendants breached their duties by engaging in conduct that fell outside the range of reasonableness, and that this was a sufficient predicate for [the] aiding and abetting liability against RBC.

RBC Aided and Abetted the Board's Breaches

The elements of aiding and abetting breaches of fiduciary duty [are]: (i) the existence of a fiduciary relationship, (ii) a breach of the fiduciary's duty, (iii) knowing participation in that breach by the defendants, and (iv) damages proximately caused by the breach.

As to the third element, "a third party may be liable for aiding and abetting a breach of a corporate fiduciary's duty to the stockholders if the third party knowingly participates in the breach." The trial court held that "if the third party knows that the board is breaching its duty of care and participates in the breach by misleading the board or creating the informational vacuum, then the third party can be liable for aiding and abetting." We affirm this narrow holding.

The aider and abettor must act with *scienter*. The aider and abettor must act "knowingly, intentionally, or with reckless indifference;" that is, with an "illicit state of mind." "RBC acted with the necessary degree of *scienter*." The evidence supports this finding.

RBC knowingly induced the breach by exploiting its own conflicted interests to the detriment of Rural and by creating an informational vacuum. RBC's knowing participation included its failure to disclose its interest in obtaining a financing role in the EMS transaction and how it planned to use its engagement as Rural's advisor to capture buy-side financing work from bidders for EMS; its knowledge that the Board and Special Committee were uninformed about Rural's value; and its failure to disclose to the Board its interest in providing the winning bidder in the Rural process with buy-side financing and its eleventh-hour attempts to secure that role while simultaneously leading the negotiations on price. RBC's desire for Warburg's business also manifested itself in its financial analysis, provided by RBC the day the Board approved the merger. RBC's illicit manipulation of the Board's deliberative processes for self-interested purposes was enabled by the Board's own lack of oversight, affording RBC "the opportunity to indulge in the misconduct which occurred." The Board was unaware of RBC's modifications to the valuation analysis, back-channel communications with Warburg, and eleventh-hour attempt to capture a portion of the acquirer's buy-side financing business. RBC made no effort to advise the Rural directors about these contextually shaping points. The result was a poorly timed sale at a price that was not the product of appropriate efforts to obtain the best value reasonably available.

The Court of Chancery determined compensatory damages in the amount of $4.17 per share. Relying on this Court's holding in *Weinberger v. UOP, Inc.* 457 A.2d 701 (Del. 1983), the Court of Chancery undertook to discover the "fair value" or "intrinsic value" of the shares held by the Class "using the same methodologies employed in an appraisal [proceeding]."

The Court of Chancery properly exercised its broad discretionary powers in fashioning a remedy and award of damages. The trial court's judgment awarding damages [of $75,798,550] is affirmed.

CHAPTER 13

DUTY OF LOYALTY

■ ■ ■

A. SELF-DEALING AND CONFLICT OF INTEREST TRANSACTIONS

Directors and officers owe the fiduciary duty of loyalty. The reasons and policies are well known.

> Corporate officers and directors are not permitted to use their position of trust and confidence to further their private interests. While technically not trustees, they stand in a fiduciary relation to the corporation and its stockholders. A public policy, existing through the years, and derived from a profound knowledge of human characteristics and motives, has established a rule that demands of a corporate officer or director, peremptorily and inexorably, the most scrupulous observance of his duty, not only affirmatively to protect the interests of the corporation committed to his charge, but also to refrain from doing anything that would work injury to the corporation, or to deprive it of profit or advantage which his skill and ability might properly bring to it, or to enable it to make in the reasonable and lawful exercise of its powers. The rule that requires an undivided and unselfish loyalty to the corporation demands that there shall be no conflict between duty and self-interest. The occasions for the determination of honesty, good faith and loyal conduct are many and varied, and no hard and fast rule can be formulated. The standard of loyalty is measured by no fixed scale.

Guth v. Loft, Inc., 5 A.2d 503, 510 (Del. 1939).[1]

How much harm can disloyal directors and officers inflict on the corporation and its shareholders? As the above quote suggests, the duty of loyalty is "derived from a profound knowledge of human characteristics and motives." How can directors and officers breach their duty of loyalty? The ways are myriad. Consider these simple hypotheticals.

---

[1] This formulation echoes the expected standard for partners in a partnership set forth in *Meinhard v. Salmon*, 164 N.E. 545, 546 (N.Y. 1928): "Joint adventurers, like copartners, owe to one another, while the enterprise continues, the duty of the finest loyalty. Many forms of conduct permissible in a workaday world for those acting at arm's length, are forbidden to those bound by fiduciary ties. A trustee is held to something stricter than the morals of the marketplace. Not honesty alone, but the punctilio of an honor the most sensitive, is then the standard of behavior."

- **Self-dealing:** Alex is a director at Boston Inc., but is also the sole owner of Alexandria Inc. Boston is a real estate company that owns a portfolio of high-end malls. A major asset is Boulder mall, which has a fair market value of $100. Alex causes Boston to sell Boulder to Alexandria for the below market price of $50. The interests of Alex and Boston are misaligned.
- **Conflict of interest:** Alex and Avery are spouses. Alex is a director at Boston Inc. Avery is the CEO of Avery Inc. Alex causes Boston to enter into a transaction with Avery Inc. in which Avery Inc. received a return that was out of line with an arm's length market transaction. The interests of Alex and Boston are misaligned.
- **Business opportunity:** Alex is a director at Boston Inc., but is also a controlling shareholder and chief executive of Alexandria Inc. By virtue of Alex's directorship at Boston and Boston's business connections, Alex learns of a highly profitable business opportunity to do a deal with Dallas Inc., a deal that Boston was actively considering. Alex causes Alexandria to intercede, and Alexandria takes away the business opportunity from Boston and enters into a contract with Dallas. The interests of Alex and Boston are misaligned.

Transactions can involve a director who has a personal interest in the matter. For example, a director has an asset that he wishes to sell to the corporation. He has a personal interest in achieving the highest price, but is also a fiduciary of the corporation, which has an interest in buying the asset at the lowest price. There is a conflict of interest.

Delaware General Corporation Law: § 144 Interested Directors; Quorum.

(a) No contract or transaction between a corporation and 1 or more of its directors or officers, or between a corporation and any other corporation, partnership, association, or other organization in which 1 or more of its directors or officers, are directors or officers, or have a financial interest, shall be void or voidable solely for this reason, or solely because the director or officer is present at or participates in the meeting of the board or committee which authorizes the contract or transaction, or solely because any such director's or officer's votes are counted for such purpose, if:

(1) The material facts as to the director's or officer's relationship or interest and as to the contract or transaction are disclosed or are

known to the board of directors or the committee, and the board or committee in good faith authorizes the contract or transaction by the affirmative votes of a majority of the disinterested directors, even though the disinterested directors be less than a quorum; or

(2) The material facts as to the director's or officer's relationship or interest and as to the contract or transaction are disclosed or are known to the stockholders entitled to vote thereon, and the contract or transaction is specifically approved in good faith by vote of the stockholders; [2] or

(3) The contract or transaction is fair as to the corporation as of the time it is authorized, approved or ratified, by the board of directors, a committee or the stockholders.

(b) Common or interested directors may be counted in determining the presence of a quorum at a meeting of the board of directors or of a committee which authorizes the contract or transaction.

The case below deals with a situation in which a director seeks to do a transaction with the corporation, a prototypical self-dealing scenario. A director is in a position to sit on both sides of the bargaining table. In reading this case, consider these questions: (1) Does a conflict of interest between a director and the corporation void the contemplated transaction? (2) How should the transaction be structured to achieve a benefit for the corporation, but at the same time to protect against the potential for harmful outcome? (3) What is the function of DGCL § 144?

BENIHANA OF TOKYO, INC. V. BENIHANA, INC.

906 A.2d 114 (Del. 2006)

BERGER, JUSTICE:

Rocky Aoki founded Benihana of Tokyo, Inc. (BOT), and its subsidiary, Benihana, which own and operate Benihana restaurants in the United States and other countries. Aoki owned 100% of BOT until 1998, when he pled guilty to insider trading charges. In order to avoid licensing problems created by his status as a convicted felon, Aoki transferred his stock to the Benihana Protective Trust. The trustees of the Trust were Aoki's three children (Kana Aoki Nootenboom, Kyle Aoki and Kevin Aoki) and Darwin

---

[2] Although Section 144(a)(2) does not refer to "disinterested" stockholders in the way that Section 144(a)(1) refers to "disinterested directors," the Delaware Supreme Court interpreted Section 144(a)(2) to require disinterested shareholder vote to receive the benefit of the statute's safe harbor. *See* Marciano v. Nakash, 535 A.2d 400, 405 n.3 (Del. 1987) ("approval by fully-informed disinterested directors under section 144(a)(1), or disinterested stockholders under section 144(a)(2), permits invocation of the business judgment rule and limits judicial review to issues of gift or waste with the burden of proof upon the party attacking the transaction.").

Dornbush (who was then the family's attorney, a Benihana director, and, effectively, the company's general counsel).

Benihana has two classes of common stock. There are approximately 6 million shares of Class A common stock outstanding. Each share has 1/10 vote and the holders of Class A common are entitled to elect 25% of the directors. There are approximately 3 million shares of Common stock outstanding. Each share of Common has one vote and the holders of Common stock are entitled to elect the remaining 75% of Benihana's directors. Before the transaction at issue, BOT owned 50.9% of the Common stock and 2% of the Class A stock. The nine-member board of directors is classified and the directors serve three-year terms.*

Shortly after Aoki married Keiko Aoki, conflicts arose between Aoki and his children. The children were upset to learn that Aoki had changed his will to give Keiko control over BOT. Joel Schwartz, Benihana's president and chief executive officer, also was concerned about this change in control. He discussed the situation with Dornbush, and they briefly considered various options, including the issuance of sufficient Class A stock to trigger a provision in the certificate of incorporation that would allow the Common and Class A to vote together for 75% of the directors.

The Aoki family's turmoil came at a time when Benihana also was facing challenges. Many of its restaurants were old and outmoded. Benihana hired WD Partners to evaluate its facilities and to plan and design appropriate renovations. The resulting Construction and Renovation Plan anticipated that the project would take at least five years and cost $56 million or more. Wachovia offered to provide Benihana a $60 million line of credit for the Construction and Renovation Plan, but the restrictions Wachovia imposed made it unlikely that Benihana would be able to borrow the full amount. Because the Wachovia line of credit did not assure that Benihana would have the capital it needed, the company retained Morgan Joseph & Co. to develop other financing options.

After evaluating Benihana's financial situation and needs, Fred Joseph, of Morgan Joseph, met with Schwartz, Dornbush and John E. Abdo, the board's executive committee. Joseph expressed concern that Benihana would not have sufficient available capital to complete the Construction and Renovation Plan and pursue appropriate acquisitions. Benihana was conservatively leveraged, and Joseph discussed various

* Author's note: A classified board is a staggered board in which only a portion of the board comes up for election each year. *See* DGCL § 141(d) ("The directors of any corporation organized under this chapter may, by the certificate of incorporation or by an initial bylaw, or by a bylaw adopted by a vote of the stockholders, be divided into 1, 2 or 3 classes; the term of office of those of the first class to expire at the first annual meeting held after such classification becomes effective; of the second class 1 year thereafter; of the third class 2 years thereafter; and at each annual election held after such classification becomes effective, directors shall be chosen for a full term, as the case may be, to succeed those whose terms expire.").

financing alternatives, including bank debt, high yield debt, convertible debt or preferred stock, equity and sale/leaseback options.

The full board met with Joseph. He reviewed all the financing alternatives that he had discussed with the executive committee, and recommended that Benihana issue convertible preferred stock. Joseph explained that the preferred stock would provide the funds needed for the Construction and Renovation Plan and also put the company in a better negotiating position if it sought additional financing from Wachovia.

Joseph gave the directors a board book, marked "Confidential," containing an analysis of the proposed stock issuance (the Transaction). The book included, among others, the following anticipated terms: (i) issuance of $20,000,000 of preferred stock, convertible into Common stock; (ii) dividend of 6% +/− 0.5%; (iii) conversion premium of 20% +/− 2.5%; (iv) buyer's approval required for material corporate transactions; and (v) one to two board seats to the buyer.

The board met again to review the terms of the Transaction. The directors discussed Benihana's preferences and Joseph predicted what a buyer likely would expect or require. The board understood that the preferred terms were akin to a "wish list."

Shortly after [this] meeting, Abdo contacted Joseph and told him that BFC Financial Corporation was interested in buying the new convertible stock. Joseph sent BFC a private placement memorandum. Abdo negotiated with Joseph for several weeks. They agreed to the Transaction on the following basic terms: (i) $20 million issuance in two tranches of $10 million each, with the second tranche to be issued one to three years after the first; (ii) BFC obtained one seat on the board, and one additional seat if Benihana failed to pay dividends for two consecutive quarters; (iii) BFC obtained preemptive rights on any new voting securities; (iv) 5% dividend; (v) 15% conversion premium; (vi) BFC had the right to force Benihana to redeem the preferred stock in full after ten years; and (vii) the stock would have immediate "as if converted" voting rights. Joseph testified that he was satisfied with the negotiations, as he had obtained what he wanted with respect to the most important points.

Abdo sent a memorandum to Dornbush, Schwartz and Joseph, listing the agreed terms of the Transaction. He did not send the memorandum to any other members of the Benihana board. Schwartz did tell Becker, Sturges, Sano, and possibly Pine that BFC was the potential buyer. At its next meeting, held on May 6, 2004, the entire board was officially informed of BFC's involvement in the Transaction. Abdo made a presentation on behalf of BFC and then left the meeting. Joseph distributed an updated board book, which explained that Abdo had approached Morgan Joseph on behalf of BFC, and included the negotiated terms. The board was not informed that Abdo had negotiated the deal on behalf of BFC. But the board did know that Abdo was a principal of BFC. After discussion, the board reviewed and approved the Transaction, subject to the receipt of a fairness opinion.

After he learned that Morgan Joseph was providing a fairness opinion, Schwartz publicly announced the stock issuance. Two days later, Aoki's counsel sent a letter asking the board to abandon the Transaction and pursue other, more favorable, financing alternatives. The letter expressed concern about the directors' conflicts, the dilutive effect of the stock issuance, and its "questionable legality." Schwartz gave copies of the letter to the directors at the May 20 board meeting, and Dornbush advised that he did not believe that Aoki's concerns had merit. Joseph and another Morgan Joseph representative then joined the meeting by telephone and opined that the Transaction was fair from a financial point of view. The board then approved the Transaction.

During the following two weeks, Benihana received three alternative financing proposals. Schwartz asked Becker, Pine and Sturges to act as an independent committee and review the first offer. The committee decided that the offer was inferior and not worth pursuing. Morgan Joseph agreed with that assessment. Schwartz referred the next two proposals to Morgan Joseph, with the same result.

Benihana and BFC executed the Stock Purchase Agreement. The board met and approved resolutions ratifying the execution of the Stock Purchase Agreement and authorizing the stock issuance. Schwartz then reported on the three alternative proposals that had been rejected by the ad hoc committee and Morgan Joseph. BOT filed this action against all of Benihana's directors, except Kevin Aoki, alleging breaches of fiduciary duties; and against BFC, alleging that it aided and abetted the fiduciary violations. The Court of Chancery held a trial. The court issued an opinion holding that Benihana was authorized to issue the preferred stock with preemptive rights, and that the board's approval of the Transaction was a valid exercise of business judgement.

A. Section 144(a)(1) Approval

Section 144(a)(1) provides a safe harbor for interested transactions, like this one, if "the material facts as to the director's relationship or interest and as to the contract or transaction are disclosed or are known to the board of directors and the board in good faith authorizes the contract or transaction by the affirmative votes of a majority of the disinterested directors." After approval by disinterested directors, courts review the interested transaction under the business judgment rule.

BOT argues that § 144(a)(1) is inapplicable because, when they approved the Transaction, the disinterested directors did not know that Abdo had negotiated the terms for BFC. Abdo's role as negotiator is material, according to BOT, because Abdo had been given the confidential term sheet prepared by Joseph and knew which of those terms Benihana was prepared to give up during negotiations. We agree that the board needed to know about Abdo's involvement in order to make an informed decision. The record clearly establishes, however, that the board possessed that material information when it approved the Transaction.

Before the May 6 meeting, Schwartz told Becker, Sturges and Sano that BFC was the proposed buyer. At the meeting, Abdo made the presentation on behalf of BFC. Joseph's board book explained that Abdo had made the initial contact that precipitated the negotiations. The board members knew that Abdo is a director and one of two people who control BFC. Thus, although no one ever said, "Abdo negotiated this deal for BFC," the directors understood that he was BFC's representative in the Transaction. We conclude that the disinterested directors possessed all the material information on Abdo's interest in the Transaction, and their approval at the May 6 and May 20 board meetings satisfies § 144(a)(1).

B. Abdo's alleged fiduciary violation

BOT next argues that the Court of Chancery should have reviewed the Transaction under an entire fairness standard because Abdo breached his duty of loyalty when he used Benihana's confidential information to negotiate on behalf of BFC. This argument starts with a flawed premise. The record does not support BOT's contention that Abdo used any confidential information against Benihana. Abdo knew the terms a buyer could expect to obtain in a deal like this. As the trial court found, "the negotiations involved give and take on a number of points" and Benihana "ended up where [it] wanted to be" for the most important terms. Abdo did not set the terms of the deal; he did not deceive the board; and he did not dominate or control the other directors' approval of the Transaction. The record does not support the claim that Abdo breached his duty of loyalty.

C. Dilution of BOT's voting power

BOT argues that the board's primary purpose in approving the Transaction was to dilute BOT's voting control. BOT points out that Schwartz was concerned about BOT's control in 2003 and even discussed with Dornbush the possibility of issuing a huge number of Class A shares. Despite the availability of other financing options, the board decided on a stock issuance, and agreed to give BFC "as if converted" voting rights. According to BOT, the trial court overlooked this powerful evidence of the board's improper purpose.

It is settled law that, "corporate action may not be taken for the sole or primary purpose of entrenchment." Here, however, the trial court found that "the primary purpose of the Transaction was to provide what the directors subjectively believed to be the best financing vehicle available for securing the necessary funds to pursue the agreed upon Construction and Renovation Plan for the Benihana restaurants." That factual determination has ample record support, especially in light of the trial court's credibility determinations. We defer to the Court of Chancery's conclusion that the board's approval of the Transaction was a valid exercise of its business judgment, for a proper corporate purpose. The judgment of the Court of Chancery is affirmed.

The case below discusses the actions of the board and officers in connection with a perceived threat to the corporation's independence, a threat of an unwanted offer to buy the corporation by a potential acquirer. In reading this case, consider these questions: (1) What motivations explain the conduct of the directors and officers? (2) In what way is a corporate manager's loyalty at stake in this situation? (3) How should the rule of law be structured to handle these kinds of situations?

GANTLER V. STEPHENS

965 A.2d 695 (Del. 2009)

JACOBS, JUSTICE.

First Niles is a holding company whose sole business is to own and operate the Home Federal Savings and Loan Association of Niles ("Home Federal" or the "Bank"). The Bank operates a single branch in Niles, Ohio.

The plaintiffs own First Niles shares. Plaintiff Leonard Gantler was a First Niles director from April 2003 until April 2006.

In late 2003, First Niles was operating in a depressed local economy, with little to no growth in the Bank's assets and anticipated low growth for the future. At that time Stephens, who was Chairman, President, CEO and founder of First Niles and the Bank, was beyond retirement age and there was no heir apparent among the Company's officers. The acquisition market for banks like Home Federal was brisk, however, and First Niles was thought to be an excellent acquisition for another financial institution. Accordingly, the First Niles Board sought advice on strategic opportunities available to the Company, and in August 2004, decided that First Niles should put itself up for sale (the "Sales Process").

After authorizing the sale of the Company, the First Niles Board specially retained an investment bank, Keefe, Bruyette & Woods (the "Financial Advisor"), and a law firm, Silver, Freedman & Taft ("Legal Counsel"). At the next Board meeting, Management advocated abandoning the Sales Process in favor of a proposal to "privatize" the Company. Under Management's proposal, First Niles would delist its shares from the NASDAQ SmallCap Market, convert the Bank from a federally chartered to a state chartered bank, and reincorporate in Maryland. The Board did not act on that proposal, and the Sales Process continued.

[Three bidders expressed interest, including First Place Financial Corp. First Place proposed a stock-for-stock transaction valued at $18 to $18.50 per First Niles Share, representing a 3.4% to 6.3% premium.]

The Board considered these bids at its next regularly scheduled meeting. At that meeting the Financial Advisor opined that all three bids were within the range suggested by its financial models, and that accepting the stock-based offers would be superior to retaining First Niles shares. The Board took no action at that time. At that same meeting, Stephens also discussed in further detail Management's proposed privatization.

[After due diligence] First Place increased the exchange ratio of its offer to provide an implied value of $17.37 per First Niles share. At the special Board meeting, Stephens distributed a memorandum from the Financial Advisor describing First Place's revised offer in positive terms. Without any discussion or deliberation, however, the Board voted 4 to 1 to reject that offer, with only Gantler voting to accept it. After the vote, Stephens discussed Management's privatization plan and instructed Legal Counsel to further investigate that plan.

Five weeks later, [the board] a proposed privatization of First Niles ("Privatization Proposal"). That Proposal recommended reclassifying the shares of holders of 300 or fewer shares of common stock into a new issue of Series A Preferred Stock on a one-to-one basis (the "Reclassification"). The Series A would pay higher dividends and have the same liquidation rights as the common stock, but the Preferred holders would lose all voting rights except in the event of a proposed sale of the Company.

First Niles' outside counsel specially retained for the Privatization orally presented the Reclassification proposal to the Board. The Board was not furnished any written materials. After the presentation, the Board voted 3 to 1 to direct Outside Counsel to proceed with the Reclassification program. Gantler cast the only dissenting vote.

Thereafter, the makeup of the Board changed. Csontos replaced Gantler. The Board consisted of Stephens, Kramer, Shaker and Csontos.

The Board voted unanimously to amend the Company's certificate of incorporation to reclassify the shares held by owners of 300 or fewer shares of common stock into shares of Series A Preferred Stock that would have the features and terms described in the Privatization Proposal. The Board disseminated a definitive proxy statement ("Reclassification Proxy" or "Proxy") to the First Niles shareholders.

In the Proxy, the Board represented that the Reclassification would allow First Niles to "save significant legal, accounting and administrative expenses" relating to public disclosure and reporting requirements under [federal securities law]. The Proxy also disclosed the benefits of deregistration as including annual savings of $142,500 by reducing the number of common shareholders, $81,000 by avoiding Sarbanes-Oxley related compliance costs, and $174,000 by avoiding a one-time consulting fee to design a system to improve the internal control structure.

The Proxy also disclosed alternative transactions that the Board had considered, including a cash-out merger, a reverse stock-split, an issue tender offer, expense reduction and a business combination. The Proxy stated that each of the directors and officers of First Niles had "a conflict of interest with respect to [the Reclassification] because he or she is in a position to structure it in such a way that benefits his or her interests differently from the interests of unaffiliated shareholders." The Proxy further disclosed that the Company had received one firm merger offer, and that "after careful deliberations, the board determined in its business judgment the proposal was not in the best interests of the Company or our shareholders and rejected the proposal."

The Company's shareholders approved the Reclassification. Of the 1,384,533 shares outstanding and eligible to vote, 793,092 shares (or 57.3%) were voted in favor and 11,060 shares abstained. Of the unaffiliated shares, however, the proposal passed by a bare 50.28% majority vote.

The Court of Chancery Erroneously Dismissed Count I of the Complaint

Count I of the complaint alleges that the defendants breached their duties of loyalty and care as directors and officers of First Niles by abandoning the Sales Process. Plaintiffs claim that the defendants improperly: (1) sabotaged the due diligence aspect of the Sales Process, (2) rejected the First Place offer, and (3) terminated the Sales Process, all for the purpose of retaining the benefits of continued incumbency.

The Court of Chancery analyzed Count I under the business judgment standard, and concluded that the Count I allegations failed to rebut the presumption of business judgment.

The Court of Chancery erroneously dismissed Count I of the complaint.

The plaintiffs claim that the legal sufficiency of Count I should have been reviewed under the entire fairness standard. That claim is assessed within the framework of the business judgment standard.

The plaintiffs have the burden to plead facts sufficient to rebut that presumption. On a motion to dismiss, the pled facts must support a reasonable inference that in making the challenged decision, the board breached either its duty of loyalty or its duty of care. If the plaintiff fails to satisfy that burden, "a court will not substitute its judgment for that of the board if the decision can be attributed to any rational business purpose."

A board's decision not to pursue a merger opportunity is normally reviewed within the traditional business judgment framework. In that context the board is entitled to a strong presumption in its favor, because implicit in the board's statutory authority to propose a merger, is also the power to decline to do so.

Our analysis of whether the Board's termination of the Sales Process merits the business judgment presumption is two pronged. First, did the Board reach its decision in the good faith pursuit of a legitimate corporate interest? Second, did the Board do so advisedly? For the Board's decision here to be entitled to the business judgment presumption, both questions must be answered affirmatively.

A board's decision to decline a merger is often rooted in distinctively corporate concerns, such as enhancing the corporation's long term share value, or "a plausible concern that the level of debt likely to be borne by [the target company] following any merger would be detrimental to the long term function of that company." A good faith pursuit of legitimate concerns of this kind will satisfy the first prong of the analysis.

The plaintiffs allege that the Director Defendants had a disqualifying self-interest because they were financially motivated to maintain the status quo. A claim of this kind must be viewed with caution, because to argue that directors have an entrenchment motive solely because they could lose their positions following an acquisition is, to an extent, tautological. By its very nature, a board decision to reject a merger proposal could always enable a plaintiff to assert that a majority of the directors had an entrenchment motive. For that reason, the plaintiffs must plead, in addition to a motive to retain corporate control, other facts sufficient to state a cognizable claim that the Director Defendants acted disloyally.

[At the time the Sales Process was terminated, the Board members were William Stephens, James Kramer, William Eddy, Ralph Zuzolo, and the plaintiff Gantler. Only Gantler voted to accept the First Place merger bid. Stephens is the chairman of the board, and CEO of both First Niles and the Bank. Kramer, a director of First Niles and the Bank, is president of William Kramer & Son, a heating and air conditioning company in Niles that provides heating and air conditioning services to the Bank. Zuzolo, who later died, was a partner in a law firm that frequently provided legal services to the Bank and an owner of title company that provided title services to all of the Bank's real estate deals.]

The pled facts are sufficient to establish disloyalty of at least three (*i.e.*, a majority) of the remaining directors, which suffices to rebut the business judgment presumption. A director-specific analysis establishes that a majority of the Board was conflicted.

Stephens: Aside from Stephens losing his long held positions as President, Chairman and CEO of First Niles and the Bank, the plaintiffs have alleged specific conduct from which a duty of loyalty violation can reasonably be inferred. [The court described how Stephens engaged in conduct that sabotaged the sale process.] Thus, the pled facts provide a sufficient basis to conclude that Stephens acted disloyally.

Kramer: Kramer was the President of William Kramer & Son, a heating and air conditioning company in Niles that provided services to the Bank. It is reasonable to infer that Kramer feared that if the Company were sold his firm would lose the Bank as a client. The loss of such a major client would be economically significant, because the complaint alleges that Kramer was a man of comparatively modest means, and that his company had few major assets and was completely leveraged.

Zuzolo: Director Zuzolo was a principal in a small law firm in Niles that frequently provided legal services to First Niles and the Bank. Zuzolo was also the sole owner of a real estate title company that provided title services in nearly all of Home Federal's real estate transactions. Because Zuzolo, like Kramer, had a strong personal interest in having the Sales Process not go forward, the same reasonable inferences that flow from Kramer's personal business interest can be drawn in Zuzolo's case.

The plaintiffs have alleged facts sufficient to establish, for purposes of a motion to dismiss, that a majority of the First Niles Board acted disloyally. Because the claim of disloyalty was subject to entire fairness review, the Court of Chancery erred in dismissing Count I as to the Director Defendants on the basis of the business judgment presumption.

In dismissing Count I as to the Officer Defendants, the Court of Chancery similarly erred. In the past, we have implied that officers of Delaware corporations, like directors, owe fiduciary duties of care and loyalty, and that the fiduciary duties of officers are the same as those of directors.[36] We now explicitly so hold.[37]

The alleged facts that make it reasonable to infer that Stephens violated his duty of loyalty as a director, also establish his violation of that same duty as an officer. It also is reasonably inferable that Lawrence Safarek aided and abetted Stephens' separate loyalty breach. [Safarek is the Treasurer and Vice President of both First Niles and the Bank, and he depended upon Stephen's continued good will to retain his job and the benefits that it generated.] It may be inferred that by assisting Stephens to "sabotage" the [sale] process, Safarek also breached his duty of loyalty.

---

36 That officers and directors of Delaware corporations have identical fiduciary duties has long been an articulated principle of Delaware law. *See, e.g., Guth v. Loft, Inc.*, 5 A.2d 503, 510 (Del.1939) (discussing the duty of loyalty applicable to officers and directors); *Cede & Co. v. Technicolor, Inc.*, 634 A.2d 345, 361 (Del.1993) (same).

37 That does not mean, however, that the consequences of a fiduciary breach by directors or officers, respectively, would necessarily be the same. Under 8 *Del. C.* § 102(b)(7), a corporation may adopt a provision in its certificate of incorporation exculpating its directors from monetary liability for an adjudicated breach of their duty of care. Although legislatively possible, there currently is no statutory provision authorizing comparable exculpation of corporate officers.

The Court of Chancery Erroneously Dismissed Count II of the Complaint

With respect to the Sales Process, the plaintiffs claim that the complaint adequately alleges that the defendants failed to disclose: (i) the circumstances of Cortland's withdrawal and (ii) insufficient deliberations by the Board before deciding to reject the First Place bid. With respect to the Reclassification, plaintiffs claim that the complaint adequately alleges that (iii) the defendants were motivated by a desire to increase their ability to effect stock buy-backs and increase the liquidity of participants in the Employee Stock Ownership Plan.

The Proxy disclosures concerning the Board's deliberations about the First Place bid were materially misleading. We reverse the dismissal of Count II on that basis.

It is well-settled law that "directors [have] a fiduciary duty to disclose fully and fairly all material information within the board's control when it seeks shareholder action." That duty "attaches to proxy statements and any other disclosures in contemplation of stockholder action." The inquiry here is whether the alleged omission or misrepresentation is material. The burden of establishing materiality rests with the plaintiff, who must demonstrate "a substantial likelihood that the disclosure of the omitted fact would have been viewed by the reasonable investor as having significantly altered the 'total mix' of information made available."

In the Proxy, the Board disclosed that "after careful deliberations, the board determined in its business judgment that the [First Place merger] proposal was not in the best interest of the Company or our shareholders and rejected the [merger] proposal." Although boards are "not required to disclose all available information," "once [they] travel down the road of partial disclosure of [prior bids] using vague language, they have an obligation to provide the stockholders with an accurate, full, and fair characterization of those historic events."

By stating that they "carefully deliberated," the Board was representing to the shareholders that it had considered the Sales Process on its objective merits and had determined that the Reclassification would better serve the Company than a merger. The Court of Chancery found, however, that the Board's Proxy disclosure of "careful deliberations" about terminating the Sales Process was immaterial, because it would not alter the total mix of information to "omit that phrase in its entirety." We disagree and conclude that that disclosure was materially misleading.

The Proxy specifically represented that the First Niles officers and directors "had a conflict of interest with respect to the [Reclassification] because he or she is in a position to structure it in a way that benefits his or her interests differently from the interests of unaffiliated shareholders." Given the defendant fiduciaries' admitted conflict of interest, a reasonable shareholder would likely find significant—indeed, reassuring—a representation by a conflicted Board that the Reclassification was superior to a potential merger which, after "careful deliberations," the Board had "carefully considered" and rejected. It cannot be concluded as a matter of law, that disclosing that there was little or no deliberation would not alter the total mix of information provided to the shareholders. On this basis, the dismissal of Count II must be reversed.

The Court of Chancery Erroneously Dismissed Count III of the Complaint

That Count [III] alleges that the defendants breached their duty of loyalty by recommending the Reclassification Proposal to the shareholders for purely self-interested reasons. The court dismissed the claim on the ground that a disinterested majority of the shareholders had "ratified" the Reclassification by voting to approve it.

We conclude that the Court of Chancery legally erred in upholding Count III on shareholder ratification grounds, for two reasons. First, because a shareholder vote was required to amend the certificate of incorporation, that approving vote could not also operate to "ratify" the challenged conduct of the interested directors. Second, the adjudicated cognizable claim that the Reclassification Proxy contained a material misrepresentation, eliminates an essential predicate for applying the doctrine, namely, that the shareholder vote was fully informed.

Under current Delaware case law, the scope and effect of the common law doctrine of shareholder ratification is unclear, making it difficult to apply that doctrine in a coherent manner.

To restore coherence and clarity to this area of our law, we hold that the scope of the shareholder ratification doctrine must be limited to its so-called "classic" form; that is, to circumstances where a fully informed shareholder vote approves director action that does *not* legally require shareholder approval to become legally effective. The only director action or conduct that can be ratified is that which the shareholders are specifically asked to approve. With one exception, the "cleansing" effect of such a ratifying shareholder vote is to subject the challenged director action to business judgment review, as opposed to "extinguishing" the claim altogether (*i.e.,* obviating all judicial review of the challenged action).

The Court of Chancery held that although Count III of the complaint pled facts establishing that the Reclassification Proposal was an interested transaction not entitled to business judgment protection, the shareholders' fully informed vote "ratifying" that Proposal reinstated the business judgment presumption. That ruling was legally erroneous, for several reasons. First, the ratification doctrine does not apply to transactions where shareholder approval is statutorily required. Here, the Reclassification could not become legally effective without a statutorily mandated shareholder vote approving the amendment to First Niles' certificate of incorporation. Second, because we have determined that the complaint states a cognizable claim that the Proxy was materially misleading, that precludes ruling at this procedural juncture, as a matter of law, that the Reclassification was fully informed. Therefore, the approving shareholder vote did not operate as a "ratification" of the challenged conduct in any legally meaningful sense. We conclude that the Court of Chancery erroneously dismissed Count III of the complaint.

NOTES

1. In *Corwin v. KKR Financial Holdings LLC*, 125 A.3d 304 (Del. 2015), the court limited the scope of *Gantler*. It held that the business judgment rule becomes the appropriate standard of review for a post-closing damages action when a merger that is not subject to the entire fairness standard of review has been approved by a fully informed, uncoerced majority of the disinterested stockholders. The plaintiff shareholder broadly interpreted *Gantler* to give no effect to an informed shareholder vote in determining the standard of review. The court disagreed and provided this comment on *Gantler*.

> To erase any doubt on the part of practitioners, we embrace an interpretation of *Gantler* as a narrow decision focused on defining a specific legal term, "ratification," and not on the question of what standard of review applies if a transaction not subject to the entire fairness standard is approved by an informed, voluntary vote of disinterested stockholders. This view is consistent with well-reasoned Delaware precedent.

The case below discusses the doctrine of corporate opportunity. A fiduciary is in a position to acquire sensitive company information. The company may have business opportunities or clients that a director may usurp. In reading this case, consider this question: What is the standard to determine whether an opportunity belongs to the corporation?

BROZ V. CELLULAR INFORMATION SYSTEMS, INC.

673 A.2d 148 (Del. 1996)

VEASEY, CHIEF JUSTICE:

Robert Broz is the President and sole stockholder of RFB Cellular, Inc., a Delaware corporation engaged in the business of providing cellular telephone service in the Midwestern United States. Broz was also a member of the board of directors of Cellular Information Systems, Inc. ("CIS"). CIS is a public Delaware corporation and a competitor of RFBC.

The conduct before the Court involves the purchase by Broz of a cellular telephone service license for the benefit of RFBC. The license in question, known as the Michigan-2 Rural Service Area Cellular License ("Michigan-2"), entitles its holder to provide cellular telephone service to a portion of northern Michigan. CIS brought an action against Broz and RFBC for equitable relief, contending that the purchase of this license by Broz constituted a usurpation of a corporate opportunity properly belonging to CIS, irrespective of whether or not CIS was interested in the Michigan-2 opportunity at the time it was offered to Broz.

The principal basis for the contention of CIS is that PriCellular, Inc., another cellular communications company which was contemporaneously engaged in an acquisition of CIS, was interested in the Michigan-2 opportunity. CIS contends that, in determining whether the Michigan-2 opportunity rightfully belonged to CIS, Broz was required to consider the interests of PriCellular insofar as those interests would come into alignment with those of CIS as a result of PriCellular's acquisition plans.

After trial, the Court of Chancery agreed with the contentions of CIS and entered judgment against Broz and RFBC. The court held that: (1) irrespective of the fact that the Michigan-2 opportunity came to Broz in a manner wholly independent of his status as a director of CIS, the Michigan-2 license was an opportunity that properly belonged to CIS; (2) due to an alignment of the interests of CIS and PriCellular arising out of PriCellular's efforts to acquire CIS, Broz breached his fiduciary duty by failing to consider whether the opportunity was one in which PriCellular would be interested; (3) despite the fact that CIS was aware of the opportunity and expressed no interest in pursuing it, Broz was required formally to present the transaction to the CIS board prior to seizing the opportunity for his own; and (4) absent formal presentation to the board, Broz' acquisition of Michigan-2 constituted an impermissible usurpation of a corporate opportunity. The trial court imposed a constructive trust on the agreement to purchase Michigan-2 and directed that the right to purchase the license be transferred to CIS. Broz and RFBC appeal.

RFBC owns and operates a license area, known as the Michigan-4 Rural Service Area Cellular License. CIS was at all times fully aware of Broz' relationship with RFBC and the obligations incumbent upon him by virtue of that relationship.

Mackinac Cellular Corp. sought to divest itself of Michigan-2, the license area immediately adjacent to Michigan-4. To this end, Mackinac contacted Daniels & Associates and arranged for the brokerage firm to seek potential purchasers for Michigan-2. In compiling a list of prospects, Daniels included RFBC as a likely candidate. David Rhodes, a representative of Daniels, contacted Broz and broached the subject of RFBC's possible acquisition of Michigan-2. Broz later signed a confidentiality agreement at the request of Mackinac, and received the offering materials pertaining to Michigan-2.

Michigan-2 was not, however, offered to CIS. Apparently, Daniels did not consider CIS to be a viable purchaser for Michigan-2 in light of CIS' recent financial difficulties. The record shows that, at the time Michigan-2 was offered to Broz, CIS had recently emerged from lengthy and contentious Chapter 11 proceedings. Pursuant to the Chapter 11 Plan of Reorganization, CIS entered into a loan agreement that substantially impaired the company's ability to undertake new acquisitions or to incur new debt. In fact, CIS would have been unable to purchase Michigan-2 without the approval of its creditors.

Following a meeting of the CIS board, Broz spoke with CIS' Chief Executive Officer, Richard Treibick, concerning his interest in acquiring Michigan-2. Treibick communicated to Broz that CIS was not interested in Michigan-2. Treibick further stated that he had been made aware of the Michigan-2 opportunity prior to the conversation with Broz, and that any offer to acquire Michigan-2 was rejected. After the commencement of the PriCellular tender offer, Broz contacted another CIS director, Peter Schiff, to discuss the possible acquisition of Michigan-2 by RFBC. Schiff, like Treibick, indicated that CIS had neither the wherewithal nor the inclination to purchase Michigan-2. Broz also contacted Stanley Bloch, a director and counsel for CIS, to request that Bloch represent RFBC in its dealings with Mackinac. Bloch agreed to represent RFBC, and, like Schiff and Treibick, expressed his belief that CIS was not at all interested in the transaction. Ultimately, all the CIS directors testified at trial that, had Broz inquired at that time, they each would have expressed the opinion that CIS was not interested in Michigan-2.

Following overtures from PriCellular concerning an acquisition of CIS, six CIS directors entered into agreements with PriCellular to sell their shares in CIS at a price of $2.00 per share. These agreements were contingent upon the consummation of a PriCellular tender offer for all CIS shares at the same price. CIS directors also entered into a "standstill" agreement which prevented the directors from engaging in any transaction outside the regular course of CIS' business or incurring any new liabilities until the close of the PriCellular tender offer. PriCellular commenced a tender offer for all outstanding shares of CIS at $2.00 per share.

At the time the tender offer was launched, however, the source of the $106,000,000 in financing required to consummate the transaction was still in doubt. PriCellular originally planned to structure the transaction around bank loans. When this financing fell through, PriCellular resorted to a junk bond offering. PriCellular's financing difficulties generated a great deal of concern among the CIS insiders whether the tender offer was, in fact, viable. Financing difficulties ultimately caused PriCellular to delay the closing date of the tender offer.

Broz submitted written offers to Mackinac for the purchase of Michigan-2. During this time period, PriCellular also began negotiations with Mackinac to arrange an option for the purchase of Michigan-2. CIS was fully aware that PriCellular and Broz were bidding for Michigan-2 and did not interpose CIS in this bidding war.

PriCellular reached agreement with Mackinac on an option to purchase Michigan-2. The exercise price of the option agreement was set at $6.7 million. The agreement further provided that Mackinac was free to sell Michigan-2 to any party who was willing to exceed the exercise price of the Mackinac-PriCellular option contract by at least $500,000. Broz agreed to pay Mackinac $7.2 million for the Michigan-2 license, thereby meeting the terms of the option agreement. An asset purchase agreement was thereafter executed by Mackinac and RFBC.

Nine days later, PriCellular completed its financing and closed its tender offer for CIS. Prior to that point, PriCellular owned no equity interest in CIS. Subsequent to the consummation of the PriCellular tender offer for CIS, members of the CIS board of directors, including Broz, were discharged and replaced with a slate of PriCellular nominees. This action was commenced by CIS in the Court of Chancery.

The doctrine of corporate opportunity represents but one species of broad fiduciary duties assumed by a corporate director or officer. A corporate fiduciary agrees to place the interests of the corporation before his or her own in appropriate circumstances. In light of the diverse and often competing obligations faced by directors and officers, the corporate opportunity doctrine arose as a means of defining the parameters of fiduciary duty in instances of potential conflict. The classic statement of the doctrine is derived from the venerable case of *Guth v. Loft, Inc.*

> If there is presented to a corporate officer or director a business opportunity which the corporation is financially able to undertake, is in the line of the corporation's business and is of practical advantage to it, is one in which the corporation has an interest or a reasonable expectancy, and, by embracing the opportunity, the self-interest of the officer or director will be brought into conflict with that of the corporation, the law will not permit him to seize the opportunity for himself.

5 A.2d 503, 510–11 (Del. 1939).

The corporate opportunity doctrine, as delineated by *Guth* and its progeny, holds that a corporate officer or director may not take a business opportunity for his own if: (1) the corporation is financially able to exploit the opportunity; (2) the opportunity is within the corporation's line of business; (3) the corporation has an interest or expectancy in the opportunity; and (4) by taking the opportunity for his own, the corporate fiduciary will thereby be placed in a position inimical to his duties to the corporation. The Court in *Guth* also derived a corollary which states that a director or officer *may* take a corporate opportunity if: (1) the opportunity is presented to the director or officer in his individual and not his corporate capacity; (2) the opportunity is not essential to the corporation; (3) the corporation holds no interest or expectancy in the opportunity; and (4) the director or officer has not wrongfully employed the resources of the corporation in pursuing or exploiting the opportunity.

The tests enunciated in *Guth* provide guidelines to be considered by a reviewing court in balancing the equities of an individual case. No one factor is dispositive and all factors must be taken into account insofar as they are applicable. Cases involving a claim of usurpation of a corporate opportunity range over a multitude of factual settings. Hard and fast rules are not easily crafted to deal with such an array of complex situations. The determination of "whether or not a director has appropriated for himself something that in fairness should belong to the corporation is a factual question to be decided by reasonable inference from objective facts." In the instant case, we find that the facts do not support the conclusion that Broz misappropriated a corporate opportunity.

We note at the outset that Broz became aware of the Michigan-2 opportunity in his individual and not his corporate capacity. As the Court of Chancery found, "Broz did not misuse proprietary information that came to him in a corporate capacity nor did he otherwise use any power he might have over the governance of the corporation to advance his own interests." This fact is not the subject of serious dispute. In fact, it is clear from the record that Mackinac did not consider CIS a viable candidate for the acquisition of Michigan-2. Accordingly, Mackinac did not offer the property to CIS. In this factual posture, many of the fundamental concerns undergirding the law of corporate opportunity are not present (*e.g.*, misappropriation of the corporation's proprietary information). The burden imposed upon Broz to show adherence to his fiduciary duties to CIS is thus lessened to some extent. Nevertheless, this fact is not dispositive. The determination of whether a particular fiduciary has usurped a corporate opportunity necessitates a careful examination of the circumstances, giving due credence to the factors enunciated in *Guth* and subsequent cases.

We turn now to an analysis of the factors relied on by the trial court. First, we find that CIS was not financially capable of exploiting the Michigan-2 opportunity. The record shows that CIS was in a precarious financial position at the time Mackinac presented the Michigan-2 opportunity to Broz. Having recently emerged from lengthy and contentious bankruptcy proceedings, CIS was not in a position to commit capital to the acquisition of new assets. Further, the loan agreement entered into by CIS and its creditors severely limited the discretion of CIS as to the acquisition of new assets and substantially restricted the ability of CIS to incur new debt.

PriCellular's own financial situation was not particularly stable. PriCellular was unable to finance the acquisition of CIS through conventional bank loans and was forced to use the more risky mechanism of a junk bond offering to raise the required capital. The fact that PriCellular had available sources of financing is immaterial to the analysis. At the time that Broz was required to decide whether to accept the Michigan-2 opportunity, PriCellular had not yet acquired CIS, and any plans to do so were wholly speculative. Broz was required to consider the facts only as they existed at the time he determined to accept the Mackinac offer and embark on his efforts to bring the transaction to fruition.

Second, while it may be said with some certainty that the Michigan-2 opportunity was within CIS' line of business, it is not equally clear that CIS had a cognizable interest or expectancy in the license. Under the third factor laid down by this Court in *Guth,* for an opportunity to be deemed to belong to the fiduciary's corporation, the corporation must have an interest or expectancy in that opportunity. "For the corporation to have an actual or expectant interest in any specific property, there must be some tie between that property and the nature of the corporate business." Despite the fact that the nature of the Michigan-2 opportunity was historically close to the core operations of CIS, changes were in process. At the time the opportunity was presented, CIS was actively engaged in the process of divesting its cellular license holdings. CIS' articulated business plan did not involve any new acquisitions. Further, as indicated by the testimony of the entire CIS board, the Michigan-2 license would not have been of interest to CIS even absent CIS' financial difficulties and CIS' then current desire to liquidate its cellular license holdings. Thus, CIS had no interest or expectancy in the Michigan-2 opportunity.

Finally, the corporate opportunity doctrine is implicated only in cases where the fiduciary's seizure of an opportunity results in a conflict between the fiduciary's duties to the corporation and the self-interest of the director as actualized by the exploitation of the opportunity. In the instant case, Broz' interest in acquiring and profiting from Michigan-2 created no duties that were inimicable to his obligations to CIS. Broz, at all times relevant to the instant appeal, was the sole party in interest in RFBC, a competitor of CIS. CIS was fully aware of Broz' potentially conflicting duties. Broz, however, comported himself in a manner that was wholly in accord with his obligations to CIS. Broz took care not to usurp any opportunity which CIS was willing and able to pursue. Broz sought only to compete with an outside entity, PriCellular, for acquisition of an opportunity which both sought to possess. Broz was not obligated to refrain from competition with PriCellular. Therefore, the totality of the circumstances indicates that Broz did not usurp an opportunity that properly belonged to CIS.

The director or officer must analyze the situation *ex ante* to determine whether the opportunity is one rightfully belonging to the corporation. If the director or officer believes, based on one of the factors articulated above, that the corporation is not entitled to the opportunity, then he may take it for himself. Of course, presenting the opportunity to the board creates a kind of "safe harbor" for the director, which removes the specter of a *post hoc* judicial determination that the director or officer has improperly usurped a corporate opportunity. Thus, presentation avoids the possibility that an error in the fiduciary's assessment of the situation will create future liability for breach of fiduciary duty. It is not the law of Delaware that presentation to the board is a necessary prerequisite to a finding that a corporate opportunity has not been usurped.

Thus, we hold that Broz was not required to make formal presentation of the Michigan-2 opportunity to the CIS board prior to taking the opportunity for his own. In so holding, we necessarily conclude that the Court of Chancery erred in grafting the additional requirement of formal presentation onto Delaware's corporate opportunity jurisprudence.

The trial court concluded that Broz was required to consider PriCellular's prospective, post-acquisition plans for CIS in determining whether to forego the opportunity or seize it for himself. Had Broz done this, the Court of Chancery determined that he would have concluded that CIS was entitled to the opportunity by virtue of the alignment of its interests with those of PriCellular.

We disagree. Broz was under no duty to consider the interests of PriCellular when he chose to purchase Michigan-2. At the time Broz purchased Michigan-2, PriCellular had not yet acquired CIS. Any plans to do so would still have been wholly speculative. Accordingly, Broz was not required to consider the contingent and uncertain plans of PriCellular in reaching his determination of how to proceed.

We note that certainty and predictability are values to be promoted in our corporation law. Broz, as an active participant in the cellular telephone industry, was entitled to proceed in his own economic interest in the absence of any countervailing duty. The right of a director or officer to engage in business affairs outside of his or her fiduciary capacity would be illusory if these individuals were required to consider every potential, future occurrence in determining whether a particular business strategy would implicate fiduciary duty concerns. In order for a director to engage meaningfully in business unrelated to his or her corporate role, the director must be allowed to make decisions based on the situation as it exists at the time a given opportunity is presented. Absent such a rule, the corporate fiduciary would be constrained to refrain from exploiting any opportunity for fear of liability based on the occurrence of subsequent events. This state of affairs would unduly restrict officers and directors and would be antithetical to certainty in corporation law.

We hold that Broz did not breach his fiduciary duties to CIS.

B. BAD FAITH

Self-dealing, conflict of interest, and usurping business opportunity are classic loyalty problems. They are generally easy to spot: Does a fiduciary stand in posture adverse to the corporation's interest? He stands in an adversarial posture if he directly transacts with the corporation, is advancing the interest of a person transacting with the corporation, or is taking corporate property or benefit. Aside from these transactions, there is another type of disloyal conduct. Recall the business judgment rule: "the presumption that in making a business decision the directors of a corporation acted on [1] an informed basis, [2] *in good faith* and [3] in the honest belief that the action taken was in the best interests of the company." "Informed basis" relates to the duty of care. "Best interests of the company" relates to self-dealing, conflict of interest, and usurping business opportunity. Fiduciaries also have a duty to act "in good faith." What does good faith mean? Consider the following hypotheticals.

- **Violating positive law:** Alex is a director at Berkeley Inc., a medical devices company. The medical devices industry is regulated. Alex causes Berkeley to violate safety regulations for the purpose of skimping on costs and maximizing profits. Due to the company's persistent violation of law, regulators impose severe monetary penalties on the company.
- **Failure of legal compliance:** Alex is a director at Bel Air Inc., a mining company. Mining is a regulated industry. Alex is responsible for the efficacy of an oversight process to ensure legal compliance with the regulatory agency in charge of mine safety. Alex never installs a program of compliance. As a result of the utter failure of legal compliance, a mine accident occurs that kills several miners.
- **Subjective bad faith:** Alex is a director at Baltimore Inc. The company is involved in internal negotiation over strategy and business plan. Alex has a viewpoint that is different from the rest of the board. Alex leaks sensitive, confidential board discussion to the media. Alex knows that the media leaks would hurt the corporation, but they serve Alex's goal of creating discord within the board. As a result of the ensuing havoc, Baltimore's stock price suffers a steep decline.

At one point, there was a question whether "good faith" was a separate category of fiduciary duty. For a while, the Delaware courts referred to a "triad" of duties. *See* Emerald Partners v. Berlin, 787 A.2d 85, 90 (Del. 2001) ("The directors of Delaware corporations have a triad of primary fiduciary duties: due care, loyalty, and good faith."); McMullin v. Beran, 765 A.2d 910, 920 (Del. 2000) ("McMullin had to successfully allege that the Chemical Board had breached any one of its triad of fiduciary duties of care, loyalty, and good faith."); Malone v. Brincat, 722 A.2d 5, 10 (Del. 1998) ("The director's fiduciary duty to both the corporation and its shareholders has been characterized by this Court as a triad: due care, good faith, and loyalty."); Cede & Co. v. Technicolor, Inc., 634 A.2d 345, 361 (Del. 1993) (referring to "the triad of fiduciary duty—good faith, loyalty, and due care"). The moniker "triad" did little to clarify the concept: What does "good faith" mean? How is it different from care or loyalty? What is the implication of bad faith on section 102(b)(7) exculpation?

The Delaware courts subsequently developed the rules on bad faith. A key development was a ruling that "good faith" is not an independent duty in a "triad" of duties, but is subsumed as a part of the duty of loyalty.

> Although good faith may be described colloquially as part of a "triad" of fiduciary duties that includes the duties of care and loyalty, the obligation to act in good faith does not establish an independent fiduciary duty that stands on the same footing as the duties of care and loyalty. The doctrinal consequence is that the fiduciary duty of loyalty is not limited to cases involving a financial or other cognizable fiduciary conflict of interest. It also encompasses cases where the fiduciary fails to act in good faith.

Stone v. Ritter, 911 A.2d 362, 370 (Del. 2006). An important implication of this ruling is that a breach of the duty of loyalty, including the obligation to act in good faith, cannot be protected by an exculpation clause under section 102(b)(7), which excludes "acts or omissions not in good faith or which involve intentional misconduct or a knowing violation of law." If a director acted in bad faith, he breached his duty of loyalty and cannot be exculpated from personal liability for money damages.

1. DEFINING BAD FAITH

The Delaware Supreme Court took a large step toward formulating a doctrine of good faith in *In re Walt Disney Co. Derivative Litigation*, 906 A.2d 27 (Del. 2006). The case arose from a bad decision to hire a senior executive, Michael Ovitz, to serve under the CEO Michael Eisner. Eisner and Ovitz had enjoyed a social and professional relationship that spanned nearly 25 years. Eisner initiated the hiring process. Ovitz began work at Disney on October 1, 1995, but by fall 1996, the board realized that he was "a poor fit with his fellow executives," that the relationship between Ovitz and the company was irreparably damaged, and that he would have to be fired. The board faced a decision to terminate "for fault" or "non-fault." The decision determined the amount of severance payment to Ovitz. Effective December 31, 1996, 15 months after the start of employment, the board fired him on a non-fault termination basis, resulting in a massive severance payment of about $130 million. He earned about $11,800 per hour in every single hour of the day, including sleeping time. The question was whether the Disney board breached its fiduciary duty when it negotiated with Ovitz for his employment agreement and when it designated his firing as "non-fault." Although the general public is oblivious to most corporate law cases, the Disney case touched a social nerve. It became a *cause célèbre* for an era of conspicuous compensation.[3]

The court provided this comment on the distinction between deviating from "best practice" and breaching the duty of care.

> A helpful approach is to compare what actually happened to what would have occurred had the committee followed "best practices" from a process standpoint. In a "best case" scenario, all committee members would have received, before or at the committee's first meeting, a spreadsheet or similar document prepared by a compensation expert. Making different, alternative assumptions, the spreadsheet would disclose the amounts that Ovitz could receive under the [contract] in each circumstance that might foreseeably arise. One variable in that matrix of possibilities would be the cost to Disney of a non-fault termination for each of the five years of the initial term of the [contract]. The contents of the spreadsheet would be explained to the committee members, either by the expert who prepared it or by a fellow committee member similarly knowledgeable about the subject. That spreadsheet, which ultimately would become an exhibit to the minutes of the compensation committee meeting, would form the basis of the committee's deliberations and decision.
>
> Had that scenario been followed, there would be no dispute (and no basis for litigation) over what information was furnished to the committee members or when it was furnished. Regrettably, the committee's informational and decisionmaking process used here was not so tidy. That is one reason why the Chancellor found that although the committee's process did not fall below the level required for a proper exercise of due care, it did fall short of what best practices would have counseled.

The case below provides the legal analysis related to the issue of good faith. In reading this case, consider these questions: (1) What are the ways in which a director or officer can be deemed to have acted in bad faith? (2) What is the relationship between good faith and section 102(b)(7)?

---

[3] *See* Laura M. Holson, *Ruling Upholds Disney's Payment in Firing of Ovitz*, N.Y. Times (Aug. 10, 2005); Bloomberg News, *Ex-Disney Director Says Ovitz Was 'Like a Cancer'*, N.Y. Times (Dec. 10, 2004); Laura M. Holston, *Eisner Regrets Praising Ovitz on 'Larry King'*, N.Y. Times (Nov. 19, 2004); Rita K. Farrell, *Ovitz Fired for Management Style, Ex-Disney Director Testifies*, N.Y. Times (Nov. 13, 2004); Rita K. Farrell, *Ex-Official Says Outside Advice Wasn't Sought on Ovitz Firing*, N.Y. Times (Nov. 9, 2004); Laura M. Holson, *Ovitz Testifies He Was Sabotaged at Disney*, N.Y. Times (Oct. 27, 2004); Bloomberg News, *Disney Defends Chief*, N.Y. Times (Feb. 10, 2004).

IN RE WALT DISNEY CO. DERIVATIVE LITIGATION

906 A.2d 27 (Del. 2006)

JACOBS, JUSTICE.

The Court of Chancery held that the business judgment rule presumptions protected the decisions of the compensation committee and the remaining Disney directors, not only because they had acted with due care but also because they had not acted in bad faith. That latter ruling, the appellants claim, was reversible error because the Chancellor formulated and then applied an incorrect definition of bad faith.

In its Opinion the Court of Chancery defined bad faith as follows:

> Upon long and careful consideration, I am of the opinion that the concept of *intentional dereliction of duty, a conscious disregard for one's responsibilities,* is an appropriate (although not the only) standard for determining whether fiduciaries have acted in good faith. Deliberate indifference and inaction *in the face of a duty to act* is, in my mind, conduct that is clearly disloyal to the corporation. It is the epitome of faithless conduct.

This case is one in which the duty to act in good faith has played a prominent role, yet to date is not a well-developed area of our corporate fiduciary law. Because of the increased recognition of the importance of good faith, some conceptual guidance to the corporate community may be helpful. For that reason we proceed to address the merits of the appellants' second argument.

The precise question is whether the Chancellor's articulated standard for bad faith corporate fiduciary conduct—intentional dereliction of duty, a conscious disregard for one's responsibilities—is legally correct. We note that the Chancellor characterized that definition as "*an* appropriate *(although not the only)* standard for determining whether fiduciaries have acted in good faith." That observation is accurate and helpful, because as a matter of simple logic, at least three different categories of fiduciary behavior are candidates for the "bad faith" pejorative label.

The first category involves so-called "subjective bad faith," that is, fiduciary conduct motivated by an actual intent to do harm. That such conduct constitutes classic, quintessential bad faith is a proposition so well accepted in the liturgy of fiduciary law that it borders on axiomatic. We need not dwell further on this category, because no such conduct is claimed to have occurred, or did occur, in this case.

The second category of conduct, which is at the opposite end of the spectrum, involves lack of due care—that is, fiduciary action taken solely by reason of gross negligence and without any malevolent intent. In this case, appellants assert claims of gross negligence to establish breaches not only of director due care but also of the directors' duty to act in good faith.

Although the Chancellor found, and we agree, that the appellants failed to establish gross negligence, to afford guidance we address the issue of whether gross negligence (including a failure to inform one's self of available material facts), without more, can also constitute bad faith. The answer is clearly no.

In the pragmatic, conduct-regulating legal realm which calls for conceptual line drawing, grossly negligent conduct, without more, cannot constitute a breach of the fiduciary duty to act in good faith. The conduct that is the subject of due care may overlap with the conduct that comes within the rubric of good faith in a psychological sense, but from a legal standpoint those duties must remain quite distinct. Both our legislative history and our common law jurisprudence distinguish sharply between the duties to exercise due care and to act in good faith, and highly significant consequences flow from that distinction.

The General Assembly has addressed the distinction between bad faith and a failure to exercise due care (*i.e.*, gross negligence) in two separate contexts. The first is Section 102(b)(7) of the DGCL, which authorizes a provision in the certificate of incorporation to exculpate their directors from monetary damage liability for a breach of the duty of care. That exculpatory provision affords significant protection to directors. The statute carves out several exceptions, however, including most relevantly, "for acts or omissions not in good faith." Thus, a corporation can exculpate its directors from monetary liability for a breach of the duty of care, but not for conduct that is not in good faith. To adopt a definition of bad faith that would cause a violation of the duty of care automatically to become an act or omission "not in good faith," would eviscerate the protections accorded to directors by the General Assembly's adoption of Section 102(b)(7).

That leaves the third category of fiduciary conduct, which falls in between the first two categories. This third category is what the Chancellor's definition of bad faith—intentional dereliction of duty, a conscious disregard for one's responsibilities—is intended to capture. The question is whether such misconduct is properly treated as a non-exculpable, non-indemnifiable violation of the fiduciary duty to act in good faith. In our view it must be, for at least two reasons.

First, the universe of fiduciary misconduct is not limited to either disloyalty in the classic sense (*i.e.*, preferring the adverse self-interest of the fiduciary or of a related person to the interest of the corporation) or gross negligence. Cases have arisen where corporate directors have no conflicting self-interest in a decision, yet engage in misconduct that is more culpable than simple inattention or failure to be informed of all facts material to the decision. To protect the interests of the corporation and its shareholders, fiduciary conduct of this kind, which does not involve disloyalty (as traditionally defined) but is qualitatively more culpable than gross negligence, should be proscribed. A vehicle is needed to address such violations doctrinally, and that doctrinal vehicle is the duty to act in good faith. The Chancellor implicitly so recognized in his Opinion, where he identified different examples of bad faith as follows:

> The good faith required of a corporate fiduciary includes not simply the duties of care and loyalty, in the narrow sense that I have discussed them above, but all actions required by a true faithfulness and devotion to the interests of the corporation and its shareholders. A failure to act in good faith may be shown, for instance, where the fiduciary intentionally acts with a purpose other than that of advancing the best interests of the corporation, where the fiduciary acts with the intent to violate applicable positive law, or where the fiduciary intentionally fails to act in the face of a known duty to act, demonstrating a conscious disregard for his duties. There may be other examples of bad faith yet to be proven or alleged, but these three are the most salient.

Those articulated examples of bad faith are not new to our jurisprudence. Indeed, they echo pronouncements our courts have made throughout the decades.

Second, the legislature has also recognized this intermediate category of fiduciary misconduct, which ranks between conduct involving subjective bad faith and gross negligence. Section 102(b)(7)(ii) of the DGCL expressly denies money damage exculpation for "acts or omissions not in good faith or which involve intentional misconduct or a knowing violation of law." By its very terms that provision distinguishes between "intentional misconduct" and a "knowing violation of law" (both examples of subjective bad faith) on the one hand, and "acts not in good faith," on the other. Because the statute exculpates directors only for conduct amounting to gross negligence, the statutory denial of exculpation for "acts not in good faith" must encompass the intermediate category of misconduct captured by the Chancellor's definition of bad faith.

We uphold the Court of Chancery's definition as a legally appropriate, although not the exclusive, definition of fiduciary bad faith. We need go no further. To engage in an effort to craft "a definitive and categorical definition of the universe of acts that would constitute bad faith" would be unwise and is unnecessary to dispose of the issues presented on this appeal.

2. FAILURE TO MONITOR COMPLIANCE

In *Walt Disney*, the Delaware Supreme Court characterized one of the three nonexclusive examples of bad faith as: "where the fiduciary intentionally fails to act in the face of a known duty to act, demonstrating a conscious disregard for his duties." What sort of "failure to act" constitutes bad faith and thus a breach of the duty of loyalty?

The case below provides an important framework for thinking about the issue of failing to properly monitor the corporation. In reading this case, consider these questions: (1) What is the procedural posture of this case, and why is the standard of liability relevant to the question of judicial approval of settlement? (2) What function within a corporation must a board monitor, lest a potential for liability based on a breach of fiduciary duty? (3) What is the legal standard for determining whether a board breached its duty by failing to monitor sufficiently?

IN RE CAREMARK INTERNATIONAL INC. DERIVATIVE LITIGATION

698 A.2d 959 (Del. Ch. 1996)

ALLEN, CHANCELLOR.

Pending is a motion pursuant to Chancery Rule 23.1* to approve as fair and reasonable a proposed settlement of a consolidated derivative action on behalf of Caremark International, Inc. The suit involves claims that the members of Caremark's board of directors breached their duty of care to Caremark in connection with violations by Caremark employees of federal and state laws and regulations applicable to health care providers. Caremark was subject to an extensive four year investigation by the U.S. Department of Health and Human Services and the Department of Justice. Caremark was charged in an indictment with multiple felonies. It thereafter entered into a number of agreements with the Department of Justice and others. Those agreements included a plea agreement in which Caremark pleaded guilty to a single felony of mail fraud and agreed to pay civil and criminal fines. Caremark agreed to make reimbursements to various private and public parties. The payments that Caremark has been required to make total approximately $250 million.

This suit was filed, purporting to seek on behalf of the company recovery of these losses from the individual defendants who constitute the board of directors of Caremark. The parties now propose that it be settled.

A motion of this type requires the court to assess the strengths and weaknesses of the claims asserted in light of the discovery record and to evaluate the fairness and adequacy of the consideration offered to the corporation in exchange for the release of all claims arising from the facts alleged. The ultimate issue is whether the proposed settlement appears to be fair to the corporation and its absent shareholders.

Evaluation of the central claim made entails consideration of the legal standard governing a board of directors' obligation to supervise or monitor corporate performance. I conclude that there is a very low probability that

---

* Author's note: Rule 23.1(c) provides that a derivative "action shall not be dismissed or compromised without the approval of the Court."

it would be determined that the directors of Caremark breached any duty to appropriately monitor and supervise the enterprise.

Caremark [provides] patient care and managed care services. As part of its patient care business, which accounted for the majority of Caremark's revenues, Caremark provided alternative site health care services. Caremark's managed care services included prescription drug programs and the operation of multi-specialty group practices.

A substantial part of revenues generated by Caremark's businesses is derived from third party payments, insurers, and Medicare and Medicaid reimbursement programs. The latter source of payments [is] subject to the terms of the Anti-Referral Payments Law ("ARPL") which prohibits health care providers from paying any form of remuneration to induce the referral of Medicare or Medicaid patients. Caremark entered into a variety of agreements with hospitals, physicians, and health care providers for advice and services, as well as distribution agreements with drug manufacturers. Specifically, Caremark did have a practice of entering into contracts for services with physicians at least some of whom prescribed or recommended services or products that Caremark provided to Medicare recipients. Such contracts were not prohibited by the ARPL but they obviously raised a possibility of unlawful "kickbacks."

The U.S. Department of Health and Human Services ("HHS") issued "safe harbor" regulations stating conditions under which financial relationships between health care service providers and patient referral sources, such as physicians, would *not* violate the ARPL. Caremark's predecessor amended many of its standard forms of agreement with health care providers and revised the Guide in an apparent attempt to comply with the new regulations.

The HHS Office of the Inspector General ("OIG") initiated an investigation of Caremark's predecessor. The Department of Justice joined the OIG investigation.

During the relevant period, Caremark had approximately 7,000 employees and ninety branch operations. It had a decentralized management structure. Caremark asserts that it had begun making attempts to centralize its management structure in order to increase supervision over its branch operations.

The first action taken by management, as a result of the initiation of the OIG investigation, was an announcement that Caremark's predecessor would no longer pay management fees to physicians for services to Medicare and Medicaid patients.

Caremark published a fourth revised version of its Guide apparently designed to assure that its agreements either complied with the ARPL and regulations or excluded Medicare and Medicaid patients altogether.

Caremark had an internal audit plan designed to assure compliance with business and ethics policies. Caremark employed Price Waterhouse as its outside auditor. The Ethics Committee of Caremark's Board reviewed an outside auditor report by Price Waterhouse which concluded that there were no material weaknesses in Caremark's control structure.

The Board appears to have been informed about this project and other efforts to assure compliance with the law. The new ethics manual, expressly prohibiting payments in exchange for referrals and requiring employees to report all illegal conduct to a toll free confidential ethics hotline, was approved and allegedly disseminated.

Caremark took several additional steps which appear to have been aimed at increasing management supervision. These steps included new policies requiring local branch managers to secure home office approval for all disbursements under agreements with health care providers and to certify compliance with the ethics program.

A federal grand jury issued a 47 page indictment charging Caremark, two of its officers (not the firm's chief officer), an individual who had been a sales employee of Genentech, Inc., and David Brown, a physician practicing in Minneapolis, with violating the ARPL over a lengthy period.

Five stockholder derivative actions were filed in this court.

In relevant part the terms upon which these claims asserted are proposed to be settled are as follows:

> 1. That Caremark, undertakes that it and its employees, and agents not pay any form of compensation to a third party in exchange for the referral of a patient to a Caremark facility or service or the prescription of drugs marketed or distributed by Caremark for which reimbursement may be sought from Medicare, Medicaid, or a similar state reimbursement program;
>
> 2. That Caremark, undertakes for itself and its employees, and agents not to pay to or split fees with physicians, joint ventures, any business combination in which Caremark maintains a direct financial interest, or other health care providers with whom Caremark has a financial relationship or interest, in exchange for the referral of a patient to a Caremark facility or service or the prescription of drugs marketed or distributed by Caremark for which reimbursement may be sought from Medicare, Medicaid, or a similar reimbursement program;
>
> 3. That the full Board shall discuss all relevant material changes in government health care regulations and their effect on relationships with health care providers on a semi-annual basis;
>
> 4. That Caremark's officers will remove all personnel from health care facilities or hospitals who have been placed in such

facility for the purpose of providing remuneration in exchange for a patient referral for which reimbursement may be sought from Medicare, Medicaid, or a similar state reimbursement program;

5. That every patient will receive written disclosure of any financial relationship between Caremark and the health care professional or provider who made the referral;

6. That the Board will establish a Compliance and Ethics Committee of four directors, two of which will be non-management directors, to meet at least four times a year to effectuate these policies and monitor business segment compliance with the ARPL, and to report to the Board semi-annually concerning compliance by each business segment; and

7. That corporate officers responsible for business segments shall serve as compliance officers who must report semi-annually to the Compliance and Ethics Committee and, with the assistance of outside counsel, review existing contracts and get advanced approval of any new contract forms.

LEGAL PRINCIPLES

The complaint charges the director defendants with breach of their duty of attention or care in connection with the on-going operation of the corporation's business. The claim is that the directors allowed a situation to develop and continue which exposed the corporation to enormous legal liability and that in so doing they violated a duty to be active monitors of corporate performance. The complaint thus does not charge either director self-dealing or the more difficult loyalty-type problems arising from cases of suspect director motivation, such as entrenchment or sale of control contexts. The theory here advanced is possibly the most difficult theory in corporation law upon which a plaintiff might hope to win a judgment.

1. ***Potential liability for directorial decisions:*** Director liability for a breach of the duty to exercise appropriate attention may, in theory, arise in two distinct contexts. First, such liability may be said to follow *from a board decision* that results in a loss because that decision was ill advised or "negligent." The first class of cases will typically be subject to review under the business judgment rule, assuming the decision made was the product of *a process* was either deliberately considered in good faith or was otherwise rational. *See* Aronson v. Lewis, 473 A.2d 805 (Del. 1984). What should be understood but may not widely be understood by courts or commentators who are not often required to face such questions, is that compliance with a director's duty of care can never appropriately be judicially determined by reference to *the content of the board decision* that leads to a corporate loss, apart from consideration of the good faith *or* rationality of the process employed. That is, whether a judge or jury considering the matter after the fact, believes a decision substantively

wrong, or degrees of wrong extending through "stupid" to "egregious" or "irrational", provides no ground for director liability, so long as the court determines that the process employed was either rational or employed in *a good faith* effort to advance corporate interests. To employ a different rule—one that permitted an "objective" evaluation of the decision—would expose directors to substantive second guessing by ill-equipped judges or juries, which would, in the long-run, be injurious to investor interests. Thus, the business judgment rule is process oriented and informed by a deep respect for all *good faith* board decisions.

Indeed, one wonders on what moral basis might shareholders attack a *good faith* business decision of a director as "unreasonable" or "irrational." Where a director *in fact exercises a good faith effort to be informed and to exercise appropriate judgment,* he or she should be deemed to satisfy fully the duty of attention. If the shareholders thought themselves entitled to some other quality of judgment than such a director produces in the good faith exercise of the powers of office, then the shareholders should have elected other directors.

2. ***Liability for failure to monitor:*** The second class of cases in which director liability for inattention is theoretically possible entail circumstances in which a loss eventuates not from a decision but, from unconsidered inaction. Most of the decisions that a corporation, acting through its human agents, makes are, of course, not the subject of director attention. Legally, the board itself will be required only to authorize the most significant corporate acts or transactions: mergers, changes in capital structure, fundamental changes in business, appointment and compensation of the CEO, etc. As the facts of this case graphically demonstrate, ordinary business decisions that are made by officers and employees deeper in the interior of the organization can, however, vitally affect the welfare of the corporation and its ability to achieve its various strategic and financial goals. What is the board's responsibility with respect to the organization and monitoring of the enterprise to assure that the corporation functions within the law to achieve its purposes?

The Delaware Supreme Court in *Graham v. Allis-Chalmers Mfg. Co.,* 188 A.2d 125 (Del. 1963), addressed the question of potential liability of board members for losses experienced by the corporation as a result of the corporation having violated the anti-trust laws of the United States. There was no claim in that case that the directors knew about the behavior of subordinate employees of the corporation that had resulted in the liability. Rather, as in this case, the claim asserted was that the directors *ought to have known* of it and if they had known they would have been under a duty to bring the corporation into compliance with the law and thus save the corporation from the loss. The Delaware Supreme Court concluded that, under the facts as they appeared, there was no basis to find that the directors had breached a duty to be informed of the ongoing operations of the firm. In notably colorful terms, the court stated that "absent cause for suspicion there is no duty upon the directors to install and operate a corporate system of espionage to ferret out wrongdoing which they have no reason to suspect exists." The Court found that there were no grounds for suspicion in that case and, thus, concluded that the directors were blamelessly unaware of the conduct leading to the corporate liability.

How does one generalize this holding today? Can it be said today that, absent some ground giving rise to suspicion of violation of law, that corporate directors have no duty to assure that a corporate information gathering and reporting systems exists which represents a good faith attempt to provide senior management and the Board with information respecting material acts, events or conditions within the corporation, including compliance with applicable statutes and regulations? I certainly do not believe so. The case can be more narrowly interpreted as standing for the proposition that, absent grounds to suspect deception, neither corporate boards nor senior officers can be charged with wrongdoing simply for assuming the integrity of employees and the honesty of their dealings on the company's behalf.

It would be a mistake to conclude that our Supreme Court's statement in *Graham* concerning "espionage" means that corporate boards may satisfy their obligation to be reasonably informed concerning the corporation, without assuring themselves that information and reporting systems exist in the organization that are reasonably designed to provide to senior management and to the board itself timely, accurate information sufficient to allow management and the board, each within its scope, to reach informed judgments concerning both the corporation's compliance with law and its business performance.

Obviously, he level of detail that is appropriate for such an information system is a question of business judgment. Obviously too, no rationally designed information and reporting system will remove the possibility that the corporation will violate laws or regulations, or that senior officers or directors may nevertheless sometimes be misled or fail reasonably to detect acts material to the corporation's compliance with the law. But it is important that the board exercise a good faith judgment that the corporation's information and reporting system is in concept and design adequate to assure the board that appropriate information will come to its attention in a timely manner as a matter of ordinary operations, so that it may satisfy its responsibility.

Thus, I am of the view that a director's obligation includes a duty to attempt in good faith to assure that a corporate information and reporting system, which the board concludes is adequate, exists, and that failure to do so under some circumstances may, in theory at least, render a director liable for losses caused by non-compliance with applicable legal standards.

ANALYSIS OF COMPLAINT AND SETTLEMENT

On balance, I conclude that this settlement is fair and reasonable. In light of the fact that the Caremark Board already has a functioning committee charged with overseeing corporate compliance, the changes in corporate practice that are presented as consideration for the settlement do not impress one as very significant. That consideration appears fully adequate to support dismissal of the claims of director fault asserted, because those claims find no substantial evidentiary support in the record and quite likely were susceptible to a motion to dismiss in all events.

To show that the Caremark directors breached their duty of care by failing adequately to control Caremark's employees, plaintiffs would have to show either (1) that the directors knew or (2) should have known that violations of law were occurring and, in either event, (3) that the directors took no steps in a good faith effort to prevent or remedy that situation, and (4) that such failure proximately resulted in the losses complained of.

1. ***Knowing violation for statute:*** Concerning the possibility that the Caremark directors knew of violations of law, none of the documents submitted for review, nor any of the deposition transcripts appear to provide evidence of it. The Board appears to have been informed by experts that the company's practices while contestable, were lawful. There is no evidence that reliance on such reports was not reasonable.

2. ***Failure to monitor:*** Where a claim of liability for corporate loss is predicated upon ignorance of liability creating activities within the corporation, as in *Graham* or in this case, only a sustained or systematic failure of the board to exercise oversight—such as an utter failure to attempt to assure a reasonable information and reporting system exists—will establish the lack of good faith that is a necessary condition to liability. Such a test of liability—lack of good faith as evidenced by sustained or systematic failure to exercise reasonable oversight—is quite high.

The record supplies no evidence that the defendants were guilty of a sustained failure to exercise their oversight function. The corporation's information systems appear to have represented a good faith attempt to be informed of relevant facts. If the directors did not know the specifics of the activities that lead to the indictments, they cannot be faulted.

The fact that [a huge loss] resulted from a violation of criminal law alone does not create a breach of fiduciary duty by directors. The record does not support the conclusion that the defendants either lacked good faith in the exercise of their monitoring responsibilities or conscientiously permitted a known violation of law by the corporation to occur. The claims asserted against them must be viewed at this stage as extremely weak.

The proposed settlement provides very modest benefits. The settlement mandates duties to be performed by the newly named Compliance and Ethics Committee on an ongoing basis and increases the responsibility for monitoring compliance with the law at the lower levels of management. In adopting the resolutions required under the settlement, Caremark has further clarified its policies concerning the prohibition of providing remuneration for referrals. These appear to be positive consequences of the [proposed] settlement, even if they are not highly significant. Given the weakness of the plaintiffs' claims the proposed settlement appears to be an adequate, reasonable, and beneficial outcome for all of the parties. The proposed settlement will be approved.

The case below concerns an action brought by a plaintiff shareholder under a *Caremark* theory. Like Caremark, the bank here paid large penalties because it failed to adequately comply with the Bank Secrecy Act and anti-money laundering regulations. *Caremark* was brought under a theory of a breach of the duty of care. In this case, the Delaware Supreme Court's affirmed and recharacterized *Caremark*. In reading this case, consider these questions: (1) Is *Caremark* violation still a violation of the duty of care? (2) If a system of legal compliance is necessary, why did *Caremark* set the liability threshold so high ("an utter failure to attempt to assure a reasonable information and reporting system exists")? (3) Aside from—perhaps—an impulse to protect directors from potential personal liability and to curb the private incentive of plaintiff lawyers, is there a more rational explanation for the high threshold?

STONE V. RITTER

911 A.2d 362 (Del. 2006)

HOLLAND, JUSTICE:

This is an appeal from a final judgment of the Court of Chancery dismissing a derivative complaint against fifteen present and former directors of AmSouth Bancorporation. The plaintiffs-appellants, William and Sandra Stone, filed their derivative complaint [against] AmSouth's board of directors (the "Board").

The Court of Chancery characterized the allegations in the derivative complaint as a "classic *Caremark* claim." In *In re Caremark Int'l Inc. Deriv. Litig.*, 698 A.2d 959 (Del. Ch. 1996), the Court of Chancery recognized that: "generally where a claim of directorial liability for corporate loss is predicated upon ignorance of liability creating activities within the corporation only a sustained or systematic failure of the board to exercise oversight—such as an utter failure to attempt to assure a reasonable information and reporting system exists—will establish the lack of good faith that is a necessary condition to liability."

Consistent with *In re Walt Disney Co. Deriv. Litig,* 906 A.2d 27 (Del. 2006), we hold that *Caremark* articulates the necessary conditions for assessing director oversight liability. We conclude that the *Caremark* standard was properly applied to evaluate the derivative complaint in this case. The judgment of the Court of Chancery must be affirmed.

Caremark Standard Approved

As evidenced by the language quoted above, the *Caremark* standard for so-called "oversight" liability draws heavily upon the concept of director failure to act in good faith. That is consistent with the definitions of bad faith recently approved by this Court in its recent *Disney* decision, where we held that a failure to act in good faith requires conduct that is qualitatively different from, and more culpable than, the conduct giving rise to a violation of the fiduciary duty of care (*i.e.*, gross negligence). In *Disney,* we identified the following examples of conduct that would establish a failure to act in good faith:

> A failure to act in good faith may be shown, for instance, where the fiduciary intentionally acts with a purpose other than that of advancing the best interests of the corporation, where the fiduciary acts with the intent to violate applicable positive law, or where the fiduciary intentionally fails to act in the face of a known duty to act, demonstrating a conscious disregard for his duties. There may be other examples of bad faith yet to be proven or alleged, but these three are the most salient.

The third of these examples describes, and is fully consistent with, the lack of good faith conduct that the *Caremark* court held was a "necessary condition" for director oversight liability, *i.e.*, "a sustained or systematic failure of the board to exercise oversight—such as an utter failure to attempt to assure a reasonable information and reporting system exists." Our opinion in *Disney* cited *Caremark* with approval for that proposition.

The phraseology used in *Caremark* and that we employ here—describing the lack of good faith as a "necessary condition to liability"—is deliberate. The purpose of that formulation is to communicate that a failure to act in good faith is not conduct that results, *ipso facto,* in the direct imposition of fiduciary liability. The failure to act in good faith may result in liability because the requirement to act in good faith "is a subsidiary element," *i.e.*, a condition, "of the fundamental duty of loyalty." It follows that because a showing of bad faith conduct, in the sense described in *Disney* and *Caremark,* is essential to establish director oversight liability, the duty violated by that conduct is the duty of loyalty.

This view of a failure to act in good faith results in two additional doctrinal consequences. First, although good faith may be described colloquially as part of a "triad" of fiduciary duties that includes the duties of care and loyalty, the obligation to act in good faith does not establish an independent fiduciary duty that stands on the same footing as the duties of care and loyalty. Only the latter two duties, where violated, may directly result in liability, whereas a failure to act in good faith may do so, but indirectly. The second doctrinal consequence is that the fiduciary duty of loyalty is not limited to cases involving a financial or other cognizable fiduciary conflict of interest. It also encompasses cases where the fiduciary fails to act in good faith. "A director cannot act loyally towards the corporation unless she acts in the good faith belief that her actions are in the corporation's best interest."

We hold that *Caremark* articulates the necessary conditions predicate for director oversight liability: (a) the directors utterly failed to implement any reporting or information system or controls; *or* (b) having implemented such a system or controls, consciously failed to monitor or oversee its operations thus disabling themselves from being informed of risks or problems requiring their attention. In either case, imposition of liability requires a showing that the directors knew that they were not discharging their fiduciary obligations. Where directors fail to act in the face of a known duty to act, thereby demonstrating a conscious disregard for their responsibilities, they breach their duty of loyalty by failing to discharge that fiduciary obligation in good faith.

[The court also held that the board met its duty under *Caremark*: "Although there ultimately may have been failures by employees to report deficiencies to the Board, there is no basis for an oversight claim seeking to hold the directors personally liable for such failures by the employees." The court further reasoned: "In the absence of red flags, good faith in the context of oversight must be measured by the directors' actions to assure a reasonable information and reporting system exists and not by second-guessing after the occurrence of employee conduct that results in an unintended adverse outcome."]

The case below revisits *In re Citigroup Inc. Shareholder Derivative Litig.*, presented in a prior chapter. The factual recitation is not repeated here. In reading this case, consider these questions: (1) What type of activity or function does *Caremark*'s failure to monitor theory address? (2) Why is the failure to monitor business risk, which resulted in catastrophic losses for the company, not a legally sufficient *Caremark* violation?

IN RE CITIGROUP INC. SHAREHOLDER DERIVATIVE LITIGATION

964 A.2d 106 (Del. Ch. 2009)

CHANDLER, CHANCELLOR.

Plaintiffs' argument is based on a theory famously articulated in *In re Caremark Int'l Inc. Derivative Litig.*, 698 A.2d 959 (Del. Ch. 1996).

With regard to director liability standards, the Court distinguished between (1) "*a board decision* that results in a loss because that decision was ill advised or negligent" and (2) "an *unconsidered failure of the board to act* in circumstances in which due attention would, arguably, have prevented the loss." In the former class of cases, director action is analyzed under the business judgment rule, which prevents judicial second guessing of the decision if the directors employed a rational process and considered all material information reasonably available—a standard measured by concepts of gross negligence. As former-Chancellor Allen explained:

> What should be understood, but may not widely be understood by courts or commentators who are not often required to face such questions, is that compliance with a director's duty of care can never appropriately be judicially determined by reference to *the content of the board decision* that leads to a corporate loss, apart from consideration of the good faith *or* rationality of the process employed. That is, whether a judge or jury considering the matter after the fact, believes a decision substantively wrong, or degrees of wrong extending through "stupid" to "egregious" or "irrational", provides no ground for director liability, so long as the court determines that the process employed was either rational or employed in *a good faith* effort to advance corporate interests. To employ a different rule—one that permitted an "objective" evaluation of the decision—would expose directors to substantive second guessing by ill-equipped judges or juries, which would, in the long-run, be injurious to investor interests. Thus, the business judgment rule is process oriented and informed by a deep respect for all *good faith* board decisions.

In the latter class of cases, where directors are alleged to be liable for a failure to monitor liability creating activities, the *Caremark* Court stated that while directors could be liable for a failure to monitor, "only a sustained or systematic failure of the board to exercise oversight—such as an utter failure to attempt to assure a reasonable information and reporting system exists—will establish the lack of good faith that is a necessary condition to liability."

In *Stone v. Ritter*, 911 A.2d 362 (Del. 2006), the Delaware Supreme Court approved the *Caremark* standard for director oversight liability and made clear that liability was based on the concept of good faith, which was embedded in the fiduciary duty of loyalty and did not constitute a freestanding fiduciary duty that could independently give rise to liability.

To establish oversight liability a plaintiff must show that the directors *knew* they were not discharging their fiduciary obligations or that the directors demonstrated a *conscious* disregard for their responsibilities such as by failing to act in the face of a known duty to act. The test is rooted in concepts of bad faith; indeed, a showing of bad faith is a *necessary condition* to director oversight liability.

Plaintiffs' theory of how the director defendants will face personal liability is a bit of a twist on the traditional *Caremark* claim. In a typical *Caremark* case, plaintiffs argue that the defendants are liable for damages that arise from a failure to properly monitor or oversee employee misconduct or violations of law. For example, in *Caremark* the board allegedly failed to monitor employee actions in violation of the federal Anti-Referral Payments Law; in *Stone,* the directors were charged with a failure of oversight that resulted in liability for the company because of employee violations of the federal Bank Secrecy Act.

In contrast, plaintiffs' *Caremark* claims are based on defendants' alleged failure to properly monitor Citigroup's *business risk,* specifically its exposure to the subprime mortgage market. Plaintiffs allege that the director defendants are personally liable under *Caremark* for failing to "make a good faith attempt to follow the procedures put in place or failing to assure that adequate and proper corporate information and reporting systems existed that would enable them to be fully informed regarding Citigroup's risk to the subprime mortgage market." Plaintiffs point to so-called "red flags" that should have put defendants on notice of the problems in the subprime mortgage market and further allege that the board should have been especially conscious of these red flags because a majority of the directors (1) served on the Citigroup board during its previous Enron related conduct and (2) were members of the ARM Committee and considered financial experts.

Although these claims are framed by plaintiffs as *Caremark* claims, plaintiffs' theory amounts to a claim that the director defendants should be personally liable to the Company because they failed to fully recognize the risk posed by subprime securities. When one looks past the lofty allegations of duties of oversight and red flags used to dress up these claims, what is left appears to be plaintiff shareholders attempting to hold the director defendants liable for making business decisions that, in hindsight, turned out poorly. Delaware courts have faced these types of claims many times and have developed doctrines to deal with them—the fiduciary duty of care and the business judgment rule. These doctrines properly focus on the decision-making process rather than on a substantive evaluation of the merits of the decision. This follows from the inadequacy of the Court, due in part to a concept known as hindsight bias, to properly evaluate whether corporate decision-makers made a "right" or "wrong" decision.

The Delaware Supreme Court made clear in *Stone* that directors of Delaware corporations have certain responsibilities to implement and monitor a system of oversight; however, this obligation does not eviscerate the core protections of the business judgment rule—protections designed to allow corporate managers and directors to pursue risky transactions without the specter of being held personally liable if those decisions turn out poorly. The burden required for a plaintiff to rebut the presumption of the business judgment rule by showing gross negligence is a difficult one, and the burden to show bad faith is even higher. As noted in *Caremark,* liability based on the duty of oversight "is possibly the most difficult theory in corporation law upon which a plaintiff might hope to win a judgment."

Plaintiffs argue that the Complaint supports the reasonable conclusion that the director defendants acted in bad faith by failing to see the warning signs of a deterioration in the subprime mortgage market and failing to cause Citigroup to change its investment policy to limit its exposure to the subprime market. Director oversight duties are designed to ensure reasonable reporting and information systems exist that would allow directors to know about and prevent wrongdoing that could cause losses for the Company. There are significant differences between failing to oversee employee fraudulent or criminal conduct and failing to recognize the extent of a Company's business risk. Directors should, indeed must under Delaware law, ensure that reasonable information and reporting systems exist that would put them on notice of fraudulent or criminal conduct within the company. Such oversight programs allow directors to intervene and prevent frauds or other wrongdoing that could expose the company to risk of loss as a result of such conduct. While it may be tempting to say that directors have the same duties to monitor and oversee business risk, imposing *Caremark*-type duties on directors to monitor business risk is fundamentally different. Citigroup was in the business of taking on and managing investment and other business risks. To impose oversight liability on directors for failure to monitor "excessive" risk would involve courts in conducting hindsight evaluations of decisions at the heart of the business judgment of directors. Oversight duties are not designed to subject directors, even expert directors, to *personal liability* for failure to predict the future and to properly evaluate business risk.

Instead of alleging facts that could demonstrate bad faith on the part of the directors, by presenting the Court with the so called "red flags," plaintiffs are inviting the Court to engage in the exact kind of judicial second guessing that is proscribed by the business judgment rule. In any business decision that turns out poorly there will likely be signs that one could point to and argue are evidence that the decision was wrong. Indeed, it is tempting in a case with such staggering losses for one to think that they could have made the "right" decision if they had been in the directors' position. This temptation is one of the reasons for the presumption against an objective review of business decisions by judges, a presumption that is no less applicable when the losses to the Company are large.

[The above] claims in the complaint are dismissed.

The case below provides an example of a pleading that survived a motion to dismiss on a *Caremark* claim. The chancery court ruled: "What Plaintiff really attempts to challenge is not the existence of monitoring and reporting controls, but the effectiveness of monitoring and reporting controls in particular instances," and "This is not a valid theory under *Caremark*." The supreme court reversed the dismissal. In reading this case, consider these questions: (1) What facts contributed to the shareholder satisfying the *Caremark* standard at the pleading stage? (2) Are there aggravating facts here that may distinguish this case from those in *Caremark* or *Stone*? (3) In what two ways can a board breach *Caremark*?

MARCHAND V. BARNHILL

212 A.3d 805 (Del. 2019)

STRINE, CHIEF JUSTICE:

Blue Bell Creameries USA, Inc., one of the country's largest ice cream manufacturers, suffered a *listeria* outbreak in early 2015, causing the company to recall all of its products, shut down production at all of its plants, and lay off over a third of its workforce. Blue Bell's failure to contain *listeria*'s spread in its manufacturing plants caused *listeria* to be present in its products and had sad consequences. Three people died as a result of the *listeria* outbreak. Less consequentially, but nonetheless important for this litigation, stockholders also suffered losses because, after the operational shutdown, Blue Bell suffered a liquidity crisis that forced it to accept a dilutive private equity investment.

Based on these unfortunate events, a stockholder brought a derivative suit against two key executives and against Blue Bell's directors claiming breaches of the defendants' fiduciary duties. The complaint alleges that the executives—Paul Kruse, the President and CEO, and Greg Bridges, the Vice President of Operations—breached their duties of care and loyalty by knowingly disregarding contamination risks and failing to oversee the safety of Blue Bell's food-making operations, and that the directors breached their duty of loyalty under *In re Caremark Int'l Inc. Derivative Litig.*, 698 A.2d 959 (Del. Ch.1996).

Blue Bell Creameries USA, Inc. ("Blue Bell"), a Delaware corporation, produces and distributes ice cream under the Blue Bell banner.

As a food manufacturer, Blue Bell operates in a regulated industry. Under federal law, the Food and Drug Administration ("FDA") may set food quality standards, require food manufacturing facilities to register with the FDA, prohibit regulated manufacturers from placing adulterated food into interstate commerce, and hold companies liable if they place any adulterated foods into interstate commerce in violation of FDA rules.

Not only is Blue Bell subject to federal regulations, but it must also adhere to state regulations. At the time of the *listeria* outbreak, Blue Bell operated in three states, and each had issued rules and regulations regarding the proper handling and production of food to ensure food safety.

The complaint alleges that management turned a blind eye to red and yellow flags that were waved in front of it by regulators and its own tests, and the board—by failing to implement any system to monitor the company's food safety compliance programs—was unaware of any problems until it was too late.

Blue Bell's issues began to emerge in 2009. Paul Kruse, Blue Bell's President and CEO, and his cousin, Paul Bridges, were responsible for the three plants Blue Bell operated in Texas, Oklahoma, and Alabama. The complaint alleges that, despite being responsible for overseeing plant operations, Paul Kruse and Bridges failed to respond to signs of trouble in the run up to the *listeria* outbreak. From 2009 to 2013 several regulators found troubling compliance failures at Blue Bell's facilities:

- In July 2009, the FDA's inspection of the Texas facility revealed "two instances of condensation, one from a pipe carrying liquid caramel [that] was dripping into three gallon cartons waiting to be filled, and one dripping into ice cream sandwich wafers." The FDA reported these observations directly to Paul Kruse, who assured the FDA that "condensation is treated by Blue Bell as a serious concern."

- In March 2010, the Alabama Department of Health inspected the Alabama plant and "found equipment left on the floor and a ceiling in disrepair in the container forming room."

- Two months later, in May 2010, the FDA returned to the Texas plant "and observed ten violations that were cited to Paul Kruse including, again, a condensation drip." While the condensation drip persisted from the FDA's last inspection of the Texas plant, the FDA also observed "ripped and open containers of ingredients, inconsistent hand-washing and glove use and a spider and its web near the ingredients."

- In July 2011, an inspection by "the Alabama Department of Public Health cited drips from a ceiling unit and pipelines, standing water, open tank lids and unprotected measuring cups."

- Nine months later, in March 2012, an inspection of the Oklahoma facility revealed the plant's "failure to manufacture foods under conditions and controls necessary to minimize contamination and failure to handle and maintain equipment, containers and utensils used to hold food in manner that protects against contamination."

- That same month, in March 2012, "the Alabama Department of Public Health required five changes" to the Alabama facility, "including instructions to clean various rooms and items, make repairs after fruit processing to prevent contamination." A year later, "in March 2013, the Alabama Department of Public Health again ordered cleaning and repairs and observed an uncapped fruit tank." The Alabama Department of Public Health made similar observations in a July 2014 inspection.

Regulatory inspections during this time were not the only signal that Blue Bell faced potential health safety risks. In 2013, "the Company had five positive tests" for *listeria*, and in January 2014, "the Company received a presumptive positive *listeria* result reports from the third party laboratory for the [Oklahoma] facility on January 20, 2014 and the samples reported positive for a second time on January 24, 2014."

Although management had received reports about *listeria*'s presence in Blue Bell's plants, the complaint alleges that the board never received any information about *listeria* or more generally about food safety issues.

During the rest of 2014, Blue Bell's problems accelerated, but the board remained uninformed about Blue Bell's problems.

Over 2014, Blue Bell received ten positive tests for *listeria*.

Despite management's knowledge of the growing problem, the complaint alleges that this information never made its way to the board, and the board continued to be uninformed about the problem.

At this stage of the case, we are bound to draw all fair inferences in the plaintiff's favor from the well-pled facts. Based on this chronology of events, the plaintiffs have fairly pled that:

- Blue Bell had no board committee charged with monitoring food safety;
- Blue Bell's full board did not have a process where a portion of the board's meetings each year, either quarterly or biannually, were specifically devoted to food safety compliance; and
- The Blue Bell board did not have a protocol requiring or have any expectation that management would deliver key food safety compliance reports or summaries of these reports to the board on a consistent and mandatory basis. In fact, it is inferable that there was no expectation of reporting to the board of any kind.

The complaint pleads that the Blue Bell board had made no effort at all to implement a board-level system of mandatory reporting of any kind.

Blue Bell's *listeria* problem spread in 2015. Starting in January 2015, one of Blue Bell's product tests had positive coliform levels above legal limits. The same result appeared in February 2015. And by this point, the problem spread to Blue Bell's products and spiraled out of control.

On February 13, 2015, "Blue Bell received notification that the Texas Department of State Health Services also had positive tests for *listeria* in Blue Bell samples."

Four days later, Blue Bell initiated a limited recall. Two days after that, Blue Bell's board met, and Bridges reported that "the FDA is working with Texas health inspectors regarding the Company's recent recall of products. More information is developing and should be known within the next days or weeks." Despite two years of evidence that *listeria* was a growing problem for Blue Bell, this is the first time the board discussed the issue, according to the board minutes. Instead of holding more frequent emergency board meetings to receive constant updates on the troubling fact that life-threatening bacteria was found in its products, Blue Bell's board left the company's response to management.

The problem got worse, with awful effects. "In early March 2015, health authorities reported that they suspected a connection between human *listeria* infections in Kansas and products made by Blue Bell's [Texas] facility." The outbreak in Kansas matched a *listeria* strain found in Blue Bell's products in South Carolina. By March 23, 2015, Blue Bell was forced to recall more products. Two days later, Blue Bell's board met and adopted a resolution "expressing support for Blue Bell's CEO, management, and employees and encouraging them to ensure that everything Blue Bell manufactures and distributes is a wholesome and good testing [sic] product that our consumers deserve and expect."

Blue Bell expanded the recall two weeks later, and less than a month later Blue Bell "instituted a recall of all products." By this point, the Center for Disease Controls and Prevention ("CDC") had begun an investigation and discovered that the source of the *listeria* outbreak in Kansas was caused by Blue Bell's Texas and Oklahoma plants. Ultimately, five adults in Kansas and three adults in Texas were sickened by Blue Bell's products; three of the five Kansas adults died because of complications due to *listeria* infection. The CDC issued a recall to grocers and retailers, alerting them to the contamination and warning them against selling the products.

After Blue Bell's full product recall, the FDA inspected each of the company's three plants. Each was found to have major deficiencies.

The Court of Chancery rejected the plaintiff's claim that Blue Bell's directors breached their duty of loyalty under *Caremark* by failing to "institute a system of controls and reporting" regarding food safety.

At bottom, the Court of Chancery opined that "what Plaintiff really attempts to challenge is not the *existence* of monitoring and reporting controls, but the *effectiveness* of monitoring and reporting controls in particular instances." That, the Court of Chancery held, does not state a *Caremark* claim. As a result, the court held that demand was not excused as to the *Caremark* claims and dismissed the complaint.

The Caremark *Claim*

Although *Caremark* claims are difficult to plead and ultimately to prove out,[99] we nonetheless disagree with the Court of Chancery's decision to dismiss the plaintiff's claim against the Blue Bell board.

Under *Caremark* and *Stone v. Ritter*, a director must make a good faith effort to oversee the company's operations. Failing to make that good faith effort breaches the duty of loyalty and can expose a director to liability. In other words, for a plaintiff to prevail on a *Caremark* claim, the plaintiff must show that a fiduciary acted in bad faith—"the state of mind traditionally used to define the mindset of a disloyal director."

Bad faith is established, under *Caremark*, when "the directors [completely] fail to implement any reporting or information system or controls, or having implemented such a system or controls, consciously fail to monitor or oversee its operations thus disabling themselves from being informed of risks or problems requiring their attention." In short, to satisfy their duty of loyalty, directors must make a good faith effort to implement an oversight system and then monitor it.

As with any other disinterested business judgment, directors have great discretion to design context—and industry-specific approaches tailored to their companies' businesses and resources. But *Caremark* does have a bottom-line requirement that is important: the board must make a good faith effort—*i.e.*, try—to put in place a reasonable board-level system of monitoring and reporting. Thus, our case law gives deference to boards and has dismissed *Caremark* cases even when illegal or harmful company activities escaped detection, when the plaintiffs have been unable to plead that the board failed to make the required good faith effort to put a reasonable compliance and reporting system in place.

The key issue [is] whether the plaintiff has pled facts from which we can infer that Blue Bell's board made no effort to put in place a board-level compliance system. We are not examining the effectiveness of a board-level compliance and reporting system after the fact. Rather, we are focusing on whether the complaint pleads facts supporting a reasonable inference that the board did not undertake good faith efforts to put a board-level system of monitoring and reporting in place.

Under *Caremark*, a director may be held liable if she acts in bad faith in the sense that she made no good faith effort to ensure that the company had in place any "system of controls." Here, the plaintiff did as our law encourages and sought out books and records about the extent of board-

[99] *See Stone v. Ritter*, 911 A.2d 362, 372 (Del. 2006) ("A claim that directors are subject to personal liability for employee failures is possibly the most difficult theory in corporation law upon which a plaintiff might hope to win a judgment."); *Guttman v. Huang*, 823 A.2d 492, 506 (Del. Ch. 2003) ("A *Caremark* claim is a difficult one to prove."); *In re Caremark Int'l Inc. Derivative Litig.*, 698 A.2d 959, 967 (Del. Ch. 1996) ("The theory here advanced is possibly the most difficult theory in corporation law upon which a plaintiff might hope to win a judgment.").

level compliance efforts at Blue Bell regarding the most central issues at the company: whether it is ensuring that the only product it makes—ice cream—is safe to eat. Using these books and records, the complaint fairly alleges that before the *listeria* outbreak engulfed the company:

- No board committee that addressed food safety existed;
- No regular process or protocols that required management to keep the board apprised of food safety compliance practices, risks, or reports existed;
- No schedule for the board to consider on a regular basis, such as quarterly or biannually, any key food safety risks existed;
- During a key period leading up to the deaths of three customers, management received reports that contained what could be considered red, or at least yellow, flags, and the board minutes of the relevant period revealed no evidence that these were disclosed to the board;
- The board was given certain favorable information about food safety by management, but was not given important reports that presented a much different picture; and
- The board meetings are devoid of any suggestion that there was any regular discussion of food safety issues.

And the complaint goes on to allege that after the *listeria* outbreak, the FDA discovered a number of systematic deficiencies in all of Blue Bell's plants—such as plants being constructed "in such a manner as to [not] prevent drip and condensate from contaminating food, food-contact surfaces, and food-packing material"—that might have been rectified had any reasonable reporting system that required management to relay food safety information to the board on an ongoing basis been in place.

In sum, the complaint supports an inference that no system of board-level compliance monitoring and reporting existed at Blue Bell. Although *Caremark* is a tough standard, the plaintiff has met it here. When a plaintiff can plead an inference that a board has undertaken no efforts to make sure it is informed of a compliance issue intrinsically critical to the company's business operation, then that supports an inference that the board has not made the good faith effort that *Caremark* requires.

The directors largely point out that by law Blue Bell had to meet FDA and state regulatory requirements for food safety, and that the company had in place certain manuals for employees regarding safety practices and commissioned audits from time to time. In the same vein, the directors emphasize that the government regularly inspected Blue Bell's facilities, and Blue Bell management got the results.

But the fact that Blue Bell nominally complied with FDA regulations does not imply that the *board* implemented a system to monitor food safety *at the board level.* These types of routine regulatory requirements, although important, are not typically directed at the board. At best, Blue Bell's compliance with these requirements shows only that management was following, in a nominal way, certain standard requirements of state and federal law. It does not suggest that the board implemented a reporting system to monitor food safety or Blue Bell's operational performance. The mundane reality that Blue Bell is in a highly regulated industry and complied with some of the applicable regulations does not foreclose any pleading-stage inference that the directors' lack of attentiveness rose to the level of bad faith indifference required to state a *Caremark* claim.

The Blue Bell directors also stress that management regularly reported to them on "operational issues." This response is telling. In decisions dismissing *Caremark* claims, the plaintiffs usually lose because they must concede the existence of board-level systems of monitoring and oversight such as a relevant committee, a regular protocol requiring board-level reports about the relevant risks, or the board's use of third-party monitors, auditors, or consultants. Here, the Blue Bell directors just argue that because Blue Bell management, in its discretion, discussed general operations with the board, a *Caremark* claim is not stated.

But if that were the case, *Caremark* would be a chimera. At every board meeting, it is likely that management will touch on some operational issue. Although *Caremark* may not require as much as some commentators wish, it does require that a board make a good faith effort to put in place a reasonable system of monitoring and reporting about the corporation's central compliance risks. In Blue Bell's case, food safety was essential and mission critical. The complaint pled facts supporting a fair inference that no board-level system of monitoring or reporting on food safety existed.

If *Caremark* means anything, it is that a corporate board must make a good faith effort to exercise its duty of care. A failure to make that effort constitutes a breach of the duty of loyalty. Where, as here, a plaintiff has followed our admonishment to seek out relevant books and records and then uses those books and records to plead facts supporting a fair inference that no reasonable compliance system and protocols were established as to the obviously most central consumer safety and legal compliance issue facing the company, that the board's lack of efforts resulted in it not receiving official notices of food safety deficiencies for several years, and that, as a failure to take remedial action, the company exposed consumers to *listeria*-infected ice cream, resulting in the death and injury of company customers, the plaintiff has met his onerous pleading burden and is entitled to discovery to prove out his claim.

We therefore reverse the Court of Chancery's decision and remand for proceedings consistent with this opinion.

NOTES

1. In *In re Clovis Oncology, Inc. Derivative Litigation*, 2019 WL 4850188 (Del. Ch. 2019), the trial court relied on *Marchand* to deny the board's motion to dismiss the *Caremark* claim. Clovis Oncology is an upstart pharmaceutical company that is regulated by the Food and Drug Administration. The clinical trial for its drug Roci was named "TIGER-X" and it used an FDA-regulated protocol named "RECIST." The plaintiff averred that the board failed to oversee the clinical trials and to comply with FDA regulations. The court ruled:

> *Caremark*'s second prong is implicated when it is alleged the company implemented an oversight system but the board failed to "monitor it." To state a claim under this prong, Plaintiffs must well-plead that a "red flag" of non-compliance waived before the Board Defendants but they chose to ignore it. In this regard, the court must remain mindful that "red flags are only useful when they are either waived in one's face or displayed so that they are visible to the careful observer." But, as *Marchand* makes clear, the careful observer is one whose gaze is fixed on the company's mission critical regulatory issues. For Clovis, this was Roci's TIGER-X trial and the clinical trial protocols and related FDA regulations governing that study.
>
> Plaintiffs have alleged particularized facts supporting reasonable inferences that: (i) the Board knew the TIGER-X protocol incorporated RECIST; (ii) RECIST requires reporting only confirmed responses; (iii) industry practice and FDA guidance require that the study managers report only confirmed responses; (iv) management was publicly reporting unconfirmed responses to keep up with Tagrisso's response rate; and (v) the Board knew management was incorrectly reporting responses but did nothing to address this fundamental departure from the RECIST protocol. When Clovis' serial non-compliance with RECIST was finally revealed to the regulators, Roci was doomed. And when the drug's failure was revealed to the market, Clovis' stock price tumbled.
>
> ORR [a success-defining metric called "objective response rate"] was the crucible in which Roci's safety and efficacy were to be tested. Roci was Clovis' mission critical product. And the Board knew, upon completion of the TIGER-X trial, the FDA would consider only confirmed responses when determining whether to approve Roci's [new drug application] per the agency's own regulations. As pled, these regulations, and the reporting requirements of the RECIST protocol, were not nuanced. The Board was comprised of experts and the RECIST criteria are well-known in the pharmaceutical industry. Moreover, given the degree to which Clovis relied upon ORR when raising capital, it is reasonable to infer the Board would have understood the concept and would have appreciated the distinction between confirmed and unconfirmed responses. The inference of Board knowledge is further enhanced by the fact the Board knew that

even after FDA approval, physicians (*i.e.*, future prescribers) would evaluate Roci based on its ORR.

Drawing all reasonable inferences in Plaintiffs' favor, I am satisfied they have well-pled that the Board consciously ignored red flags that revealed a mission critical failure to comply with the RECIST protocol and associated FDA regulations. At this stage, Plaintiffs' allegation that this failure of oversight caused monetary and reputational harm to the Company is sufficient to provide a causal nexus between the breach of fiduciary duty and the corporate trauma. Therefore, Defendants' motion to dismiss Plaintiffs' *Caremark* claim under Rules 23.1 and 12(b)(6) must be denied.

2. In *Teamsters Local 443 Health Servs. & Ins. Plan v. Chou*, 2020 WL 5028065 (Del. Ch. 2020), the trial court relied on *Marchand* and *Clovis* to deny the defendant board's motion to dismiss the *Caremark* claim.

It has become among the hoariest of Chancery clichés for an opinion to note that a derivative claim against a company's directors, on the grounds that they have failed to comply with oversight duties under *Caremark*, is among the most difficult of claims in this Court to plead successfully. As with many a cliché, there is truth in the notion. A pleading must allege with particularity facts which imply that the directors utterly failed to provide a corporate reporting system to permit board-level review of compliance with law, or that the directors were provided sufficient notice of corporate non-compliance with law such that their failure to remediate amounts to bad faith. This is a formidable burden.

It is of little wonder that *Caremark* liability is rarely imposed, as it is fortunately rare that directors, otherwise unconflicted, should nonetheless take actions knowingly inimical to the corporate interest, such as ignoring a known duty to act to prevent the corporation from violating positive law.

The Plaintiffs are stockholders in AmerisourceBergen Corp. ("ABC"). ABC acquired Oncology Supply Pharmacy Services ("Pharmacy"). Pharmacy, per the complaint, was run as a criminal organization. Pharmacy was not a state-licensed pharmacy, although it operated in a way that made it appear as such to avoid Food and Drug Administration oversight. Pharmacy's business was to buy single-dose sterile vials of oncology drugs, put those drugs into syringes, and sell the syringes for injection into a cancer patient's body. As acquired by Pharmacy, these single-dose vials had been intentionally overfilled by the manufacturer to account for human error in filling syringes and to permit the medical provider to discharge a small amount before injection to avoid air bubbles, but still have a full dose. Instead of discarding this overfill, which was not intended for patient use, Pharmacy illegally "pooled" the overfill and used it to fill additional syringes. This process was unsterile and led to the contamination of the drugs so pooled.

Having thus created extra product, ABC both pocketed the extra revenue, and undercut the competition by providing kickbacks to buyers to increase market share. The operation used sham prescriptions to make it appear that Pharmacy was a pharmacy, and thus shielded from FDA oversight. When the pooled drugs were so grossly contaminated that particulates were visible to the naked eye, Pharmacy filtered out these "floaters" and sold the drug, nonetheless.

The criminal activities at Pharmacy and other ABC subsidiaries were uncovered, and corporate criminal and civil penalties ensued.

Caremark claims can take two forms. A "prong one" claim arises where "the directors utterly failed to implement any reporting or information system or controls." A "prong two" claim arises where "having implemented such a system or controls, [the directors] consciously failed to monitor or oversee its operations thus disabling themselves from being informed of risks or problems requiring their attention." To state a "prong two" claim, the Plaintiffs must "plead [particularized facts] that the board knew of evidence of corporate misconduct—the proverbial 'red flag'—yet acted in bad faith by consciously disregarding its duty to address that misconduct."

The Plaintiffs allege that the Director Defendants face a substantial likelihood of liability under *both* prongs of *Caremark*.

To state a "prong two" *Caremark* claim requires a pleading of particularized facts that the board knew of red flags but consciously disregarded them in bad faith. That is, to survive the Motion to Dismiss under Rule 23.1, the Complaint must plead particularized facts that the Defendant Directors knew of red flags, but acted in bad faith by consciously disregarding their duty to address the misconduct alerted to by such red flags. "In this context, bad faith means the directors were conscious of the fact that they were not doing their jobs, and that they ignored red flags indicating misconduct in defiance of their duties."

The concept of mission critical compliance risk emanates from our Supreme Court's decision in *Marchand v. Barnhill*. In *Marchand*, the company, Blue Bell Creameries, distributed ice cream containing the deadly bacteria *listeria*. The Supreme Court found that Blue Bell's board had failed to put in place a reasonable system of monitoring and reporting on food safety, which for a "monoline company that makes a single product ice cream" was an "essential and mission critical" compliance risk.

The Plaintiffs have pled that "compliance with FDA regulations is [ABC's] primary regulatory concern and is absolutely critical to its business." Laws governing the health and safety of drugs are thus the "most central safety and legal compliance issue facing the company."

> And "when a company operates in an environment where externally imposed regulations govern its 'mission critical' operations, the board's oversight function must be more rigorously exercised." Thus, when regulations governing drug health and safety are at issue, ABC's Board must actively exercise its oversight duties in order to properly discharge its duties in good faith. The allegations here are a prime example: flouting laws meant to ensure the safety and purity of drugs destined for patients suffering from cancer is directly inimical to the central purpose of ABC's business.

The court denied the motion to dismiss Count I because the plaintiffs have adequately pled that a majority of the board consciously ignored red flags rising to bad faith under *Caremark*. The court determined that the board failed to respond in light of sufficient red flags raised in an attorney's report and a *qui tam* complaint alleging the company's failure to comply with regulations and potential illegal activities.

3. INTENTIONAL VIOLATION OF LAW

Caremark and *Stone* can be seen as upholding one of the most fundamental and mandatory terms in corporation law. A system of legal compliance is required because corporation law makes clear that a corporation can engage in only *lawful* activity. *See* DGCL § 101(b) ("A corporation may be incorporated to conduct or promote any lawful business or purposes"); *id.* § 102(a)(3) ("It shall be sufficient to state, either alone or with other businesses or purposes, that the purpose of the corporation is to engage in any lawful act or activity").

Disney approved the chancery court's formulation of one example of bad faith: "where the fiduciary acts with the intent to violate applicable positive law." The intentional violation of law to pursue profit is an example of bad faith conduct. *E.g.,* Metro Communication Corp. BVI v. Advanced Mobilecomm Technologies Inc., 854 A.2d 121, 164 (Del. Ch. 2004) ("These allegations [of a bribery scheme] are sufficient to state a claim for breach of fiduciary duty of loyalty."). In this context, the motive to maximize profit for the corporation and its shareholders is irrelevant as a matter of law to the question of whether the fiduciary has acted in good faith.

The case below discusses the implication of violating positive law. In reading this case, consider these questions: (1) In terms of a theory of the case, what is the difference between *Caremark* and the case below? (2) What factor distinguishes a director's role in the violation of law as opposed to the corporation's violation of law?

IN RE MASSEY ENERGY CO. DERIVATIVE LITIGATION

2011 WL 2176479 (Del. Ch. 2011)

STRINE, VICE CHANCELLOR.

[Massey Energy pled guilty to criminal charges arising from violations of mine safety regulations and a massive explosion that killed 29 miners. The plaintiff brought a *Caremark* derivative action. As a result of Massey's problems, it entered into a merger agreement with an acquirer, Alpha Natural Resources. The plaintiff sought to enjoin the merger because the Massey board did not negotiate a litigation trust for the derivative claim. The court denied the petition for preliminary injunction. With respect to the *Caremark* claims, the court noted that the claims would survive the merger and pass to Alpha.* As for the substance of the claims at the pleading stage, the court provided the following opinion.]

At a trial when a crucial issue would be the state of mind of each individual defendant charged with a *Caremark* violation, these arguments would require careful consideration. At a pleading stage, however, they are of little moment in light of the particularized facts pled by the plaintiffs. Despite the straw man arguments of certain academics, Delaware law does not charter law breakers. Delaware law allows corporations to pursue diverse means to make a profit, subject to a critical statutory floor, which is the requirement that Delaware corporations only pursue "lawful business" by "lawful acts." As a result, a fiduciary of a Delaware corporation cannot be loyal to a Delaware corporation by knowingly causing it to seek profit by violating the law.

Regrettably, a myriad of particularized facts have been pled that create a pleading-stage inference that the top management of Massey did just that. The objective facts are that Massey had pled guilty to criminal charges, had suffered other serious judgments and settlements as a result of violations of law, had been caught trying to hide violations of law and suppress material evidence, and had miners suffer death and serious injuries at its facilities. Instead of becoming a corporation with a new attitude and commitment to safety that won recognition for that change from its regulators, Massey continued to think it knew better than those charged with enforcing the law, and in fact, often argued with the law itself. Following that continued period of adversarialness, the Upper Big Branch

* Author's note: The court hinted that ultimately the plaintiff would not be able to pursue the derivative suit because the claim would pass to Alpha and the Alpha board rather than the plaintiff under the doctrine of demand futility because the Alpha board has no liability exposure to the Massey board's prior actions. The Alpha board would thus have the prerogative to control the litigation. The court stated: "It seems likely in the end that Alpha will control the Derivative Claims, leaving the current derivative plaintiffs in the position of having to prove demand excusal as Alpha, not Massey, stockholders, and thus receive leave to proceed in a double derivative action on behalf of Alpha. Although that is a possibility, it is not one that an objective mind ought to consider probable, given that the Alpha board has no exposure to liability for the Derivative Claims and the myriad of rational business reasons why Alpha may later decide that prosecuting those Claims does or does not make sense for Alpha as a corporation."

Disaster occurred, Massey miners have lost their lives at other facilities, and the [the federal regulator] has alleged that serious safety violations and an attitude of law-flouting has continued at other Massey facilities.

To be plain, when a company already has been proven to have engaged in illegal conduct, it is a high risk strategy for it to embrace the idea that its regulators are wrongheaded and to view itself as simply a victim of a governmental conspiracy. Relatedly, when a company has a "record" as a recidivist, its directors and officers cannot take comfort in the appearance of compliance motion at the pleading stage, when the plaintiffs are able to plead particularized facts creating an inference that the Board and management were aware of a troubling continuing pattern of non-compliance in fact and of a managerial attitude suggestive of a desire to fight with and hide evidence from the company's regulators. As a kid, most of us are taught that it is not a good excuse to argue with the rules. Telling your parents that all the kids are getting caught shoplifting, cheating, or imbibing illegal substances is not, fortunately, a good excuse. For fiduciaries of Delaware corporations, there is no room to flout the law governing the corporation's affairs. If the fiduciaries of a Delaware corporation do not like the applicable law, they can lobby to get it changed. But until it is changed, they must act in good faith to ensure that the corporation tries to comply with its legal duties.

It may well be that after a trial, the Massey directors and officers will be found to have acted in a manner that does not subject them to liability under the *Caremark* standard. But for purposes of this motion, candor requires acknowledging that the plaintiffs have likely pled Derivative Claims that would survive a motion to dismiss, even under the heightened pleading standard applicable under Rule 23.1.

C. CONTROLLING SHAREHOLDERS

Shareholders with minority stakes do not control the corporation. They are owed fiduciary duties, but do not owe duties to the corporation or other shareholders. But a controlling shareholder can exert control to extract gain at the cost of unfair disadvantage to minority shareholders. How can a controlling shareholder do this? Consider these simple hypotheticals.

- **Distributions:** Catherine is a controlling shareholder who owns 150 shares of Class B common stock of Barstow Inc. The minority shareholders own 1,000 shares of Class A common stock. The Class B stock has supervoting rights, 10 votes per share as opposed to 1 vote per share. By virtue of her 60% control, Catherine causes the board to declare and pay a one-time extraordinary dividend to only the Class B stock of $10,000 per share. The $1.5 million in extraordinary distribution constitutes 75% of the firm's assets.

- **Self-dealing:** Charles is a controlling shareholder with a 40% stake in Burbank Inc., a public company with diffuse remaining shareholders. He is also the sole owner of Albany LLC. He causes Burbank to sell a major asset with a fair value of $100,000 to Albany for $50,000.
- **Cash-out transaction:** Claremont Inc. has a 51% stake in Burlington Inc. The remaining 49% of shares in Burlington is held by public shareholders. Each share held by the minority shareholder has a fair value of $10 per share. Claremont causes Burlington to merge into Chevy Chase Inc., a wholly-owned subsidiary, at $5 per share.

All three transactions constitute a simple form of self-dealing. A controlling shareholder has this power. By virtue of control, a controlling shareholder owes fiduciary duty to minority shareholders.

1. DETERMINATION OF CONTROL AND FIDUCIARY DUTY

Who is a controlling shareholder? Courts view the issue of control pragmatically, elevating substance over form. A controlling shareholder is one who has de jure control over the corporation, a majority of the voting shares. A shareholder with less than a majority of shares is presumptively not a controlling shareholder. Weinstein Enters., Inc. v. Orloff, 870 A.2d 499, 507 (Del. 2005). Such shareholder is a controlling shareholder if it exerts actual control.[4] It is possible that, for example, a 30% shareholder of a public corporation can be seen as a controlling shareholder if the remaining shares are diffusely owned. *See* In re Zhongpin Inc. S'holder Litig., 2014 WL 673547, at *8 (Del. Ch. 2014) (holding that 17.3% stake was a controlling interest); Kahn v. Lynch Comm'n Sys., Inc., 638 A.2d 1110, 1115 (Del. 1994) ("notwithstanding its 43.3 percent minority shareholder interest, Alcatel did exercise actual control over Lynch by dominating its corporate affairs").

Substance over form controls the analysis. A controlling stockholder includes a "control group," which is a group of shareholders who collectively exerts control through joint action even though each shareholder individually is not a controlling shareholder. *See* Sheldon v. Pinto Tech. Ventures, L.P., 220 A.3d 245, 251 (Del. 2019) ("Our law recognizes that multiple stockholders together can constitute a control group exercising

---

[4] *See* In re Crimson Exploration Inc. S'holder Litig., 2014 WL 5449419, at *12 (Del. Ch. 2014) (stating that control depends on whether a shareholder "actually controls the board's decisions about the challenged transaction"); Feeley v. NHAOCG, LLC, 62 A.3d 649, 668 (Del. Ch. 2012) ("Delaware corporate decisions consistently have looked to who wields control in substance and have imposed the risk of fiduciary liability on the actual controllers."); Ivanhoe Partners v. Newmont Mining Corp., 535 A.2d 1334, 1344 (Del. 1987) ("a shareholder owes a fiduciary duty only if it owns a majority interest in or exercises control over the business affairs of the corporation").

majority or effective control, with each member subject to the fiduciary duties of a controller."). The key fact in finding a control group is not just common or parallel interests, but concerted action toward a shared goal. *See* Gilbert v. Perlman, 2020 WL 2062285, at *6 (Del. Ch. 2020) ("By pooling resources in a plan by which they control the corporation, they become fiduciaries."). Shareholders must be "connected in some legally significant way—*e.g.*, by contract, common ownership, agreement, or other arrangement—to work together toward a shared goal." Dubroff v. Wren Hldgs., LLC, 2009 WL 1478697, at *3 (Del. Ch. May 22, 2009).

A controlling shareholder owes fiduciary duties to the corporation and minority shareholder. The duty of loyalty is most commonly implicated. The typical claim alleges that a controlling shareholder misappropriated corporate assets or abused the minority in transactions that the controlling shareholder controls or influences.

The case below discusses the contours of duty. Obviously, a controlling shareholder has control. Obviously too, the exercise of control is not per se a breach of duty in every instance. In reading this case, consider this question: Under what circumstance would a court apply the entire fairness standard of review, as opposed to the business judgment rule, to a controlling shareholder's action?

SINCLAIR OIL CORP. V. LEVIEN

280 A.2d 717 (Del. 1971)

WOLCOTT, CHIEF JUSTICE.

This is an appeal by the defendant, Sinclair Oil Corporation (hereafter Sinclair), from an order of the Court of Chancery in a derivative action requiring Sinclair to account for damages sustained by its subsidiary, Sinclair Venezuelan Oil Company (hereafter Sinven), organized by Sinclair for the purpose of operating in Venezuela, as a result of dividends paid by Sinven, the denial to Sinven of industrial development, and a breach of contract between Sinclair's wholly-owned subsidiary, Sinclair International Oil Company, and Sinven.

Sinclair, operating primarily as a holding company, is in the business of exploring for oil and of producing and marketing crude oil and oil products. At all times relevant to this litigation, it owned about 97% of Sinven's stock. The plaintiff owns about 3,000 of 120,000 publicly held shares of Sinven. Sinven has been engaged in petroleum operations primarily in Venezuela and has operated exclusively in Venezuela.

Sinclair nominates all members of Sinven's board. The Chancellor found as a fact that the directors were not independent of Sinclair. Almost without exception, they were officers, directors, or employees of corporations in the Sinclair complex. By reason of Sinclair's domination, it is clear that Sinclair owed Sinven a fiduciary duty. Sinclair concedes this.

The Chancellor held that because of Sinclair's fiduciary duty and its control over Sinven, its relationship with Sinven must meet the test of intrinsic [entire] fairness. The standard of intrinsic fairness involves both a high degree of fairness and a shift in the burden of proof. Under this standard the burden is on Sinclair to prove, subject to careful judicial scrutiny, that its transactions with Sinven were objectively fair. Guth v. Loft, Inc., 5 A.2d 503 (Del. 1939).

When the situation involves a parent and a subsidiary, with the parent controlling the transaction and fixing the terms, the test of intrinsic fairness, with its resulting shifting of the burden of proof, is applied. The basic situation for the application of the rule is the one in which the parent has received a benefit to the exclusion and at the expense of the subsidiary.

A parent does indeed owe a fiduciary duty to its subsidiary when there are parent-subsidiary dealings. However, this alone will not evoke the intrinsic fairness standard. This standard will be applied only when the fiduciary duty is accompanied by self-dealing—the situation when a parent is on both sides of a transaction with its subsidiary. Self-dealing occurs when the parent, by virtue of its domination of the subsidiary, causes the subsidiary to act in such a way that the parent receives something from the subsidiary to the exclusion of, and detriment to, the minority stockholders.

We turn now to the facts. The plaintiff argues that, from 1960 through 1966, Sinclair caused Sinven to pay out such excessive dividends that the industrial development of Sinven was effectively prevented, and it became in reality a corporation in dissolution.

From 1960 through 1966, Sinven paid out $108,000,000 in dividends ($38,000,000 in excess of Sinven's earnings during the same period). The Chancellor, applying the intrinsic fairness standard, held that Sinclair did not sustain its burden of proving that these dividends were intrinsically fair to the minority stockholders of Sinven.

Since it is admitted that the dividends were paid in strict compliance with 8 Del.C. § 170, the alleged excessiveness of the payments alone would not state a cause of action.

We do not accept the argument that the intrinsic fairness test can never be applied to a dividend declaration by a dominated board, although a dividend declaration by a dominated board will not inevitably demand the application of the intrinsic fairness standard. If such a dividend is in essence self-dealing by the parent, the intrinsic fairness standard is the proper standard. For example, suppose a parent dominates a subsidiary and its board of directors. The subsidiary has outstanding two classes of stock, X and Y. Class X is owned by the parent and Class Y is owned by minority stockholders of the subsidiary. If the subsidiary, at the direction of the parent, declares a dividend on its Class X stock only, this might well be self-dealing by the parent. It would be receiving something from the subsidiary to the exclusion of and detrimental to its minority stockholders. This self-dealing, coupled with the parent's duty, would make intrinsic fairness the proper standard by which to evaluate the dividend payments.

It must be determined whether the dividend payments by Sinven were self-dealing by Sinclair. The dividends resulted in great sums of money being transferred from Sinven to Sinclair. However, a proportionate share of this money was received by the minority shareholders of Sinven. Sinclair received nothing from Sinven to the exclusion of its minority stockholders. As such, these dividends were not self-dealing. We hold that the Chancellor erred in applying the intrinsic fairness test as to these dividend payments. The business judgment standard should have been applied.

We conclude that the facts demonstrate that the dividend payments complied with the business judgment standard and with 8 Del.C. § 170. The motives for causing the declaration of dividends are immaterial unless the plaintiff can show that the dividend payments resulted from improper motives and amounted to waste. The plaintiff contends only that the dividend payments drained Sinven of cash to such an extent that it was prevented from expanding.

Next, Sinclair argues that the Chancellor committed error when he held it liable to Sinven for breach of contract.

Sinclair created Sinclair International Oil Company (International), a wholly owned subsidiary used for the purpose of coordinating all of Sinclair's foreign operations. All crude purchases by Sinclair were made thereafter through International.

Sinclair caused Sinven to contract with International whereby Sinven agreed to sell all of its crude oil and refined products to International at specified prices. The contract provided for minimum and maximum quantities and prices. The plaintiff contends that Sinclair caused this contract to be breached in two respects. Although the contract called for payment on receipt, International's payments lagged as much as 30 days after receipt. Also, the contract required International to purchase at least a fixed minimum amount of crude and refined products from Sinven. International did not comply with this requirement.

Clearly, Sinclair's act of contracting with its dominated subsidiary was self-dealing. Under the contract Sinclair received the products produced by Sinven, and of course the minority shareholders of Sinven were not able to share in the receipt of these products. If the contract was breached, then Sinclair received these products to the detriment of Sinven's minority shareholders. The contract was breached by Sinclair, both as to the time of payments and the amounts purchased.

Under the intrinsic fairness standard, Sinclair must prove that its causing Sinven not to enforce the contract was intrinsically fair to the minority shareholders of Sinven. Sinclair has failed to meet this burden. Late payments were clearly breaches for which Sinven should have sought and received adequate damages. As to the quantities purchased, Sinclair argues that it purchased all the products produced by Sinven. This does not satisfy the standard of intrinsic fairness. Sinclair has failed to prove that Sinven could not possibly have produced or have obtained the contract minimums. As such, Sinclair must account on this claim.

We reverse that part of the Chancellor's order that requires Sinclair to account to Sinven for damages sustained as a result of dividends paid. We affirm the remaining portion of that order and remand.

2. CONTROLLING SHAREHOLDER CASH-OUT TRANSACTIONS

A typical and consequential conflict between a controlling shareholder and minority shareholders involves the former seeking to cash out the latter, thus acquiring the entire corporation. The potential for opportunism is significant. Suppose a controlling shareholder influences the board to set an unfairly low price, or to steer the deal toward its affiliate rather than an independent acquirer. A number of good reasons may exist to acquire the entire company. The corporation may be valuable and owning it whole may be desired. A controlling shareholder owes the minority, even to a 3% holder as was the case in *Sinclair*, fiduciary duties and so eliminating other shareholders may be good. Minority shareholders too may benefit from a cash out at a fair value including a premium. With these benefits in mind, a controlling shareholder must be careful in doing a cash out deal because there is an inherent conflict of interest. How should corporation law balance these competing tensions?

The case below provides the basic framework for dealing with a controlling shareholder cash-out transaction. In reading this case, consider these questions: (1) Why did Signal seek to cash out UOP's minority shareholders, and is this motivation itself illicit? (2) What was the problem with the conduct of the Signal directors? (3) What is the role of information, access to information, and information asymmetry in the dynamics of this transaction? (4) In light of the problems identified by the court, what is the standard of review on remand, who has the burden of proof, and what must the trial court do on remand? (5) In light of the court's opinion, how should the transaction process have been changed to comply with the controlling shareholder's duty to minority shareholders?

WEINBERGER V. UOP INC.

457 A.2d 701 (Del. 1983)

MOORE, JUSTICE:

A former shareholder of UOP, Inc. challenged the elimination of UOP's minority shareholders by a cash-out merger between UOP and its majority owner, The Signal Companies, Inc. The defendants in this action were Signal, UOP, certain officers and directors of those companies, and UOP's investment banker, Lehman Brothers Kuhn Loeb, Inc. The present Chancellor held that the terms of the merger were fair to the plaintiff and the other minority shareholders of UOP.

We conclude that this merger does not meet the test of fairness, at least as we address that concept, and no burden thus shifted to the plaintiff by reason of the minority shareholder vote. Accordingly, we reverse and remand for further proceedings consistent herewith.

Signal is a diversified, technically based company operating through various subsidiaries.

Signal sold one of its wholly-owned subsidiaries for $420,000,000 in cash. While looking to invest this cash surplus, Signal became interested in UOP as a possible acquisition. The negotiations between Signal and UOP occurred. [At the time, UOP's common stock had been trading on the New York Stock Exchange at around $14 per share. Signal ultimately purchased 5.8 million shares at $21 per share, and as a result became a 50.5% controlling shareholder and parent corporation of UOP].

Although UOP's board consisted of 13 directors, Signal nominated and elected only 6. Of these, 5 were either directors or employees of Signal. The sixth, a partner in the banking firm of Lazard Freres & Co., had been one of Signal's representatives in the negotiations and bargaining with UOP concerning the tender offer and purchase price of the UOP shares.

[Signal appointed James Crawford, a long-time employee and senior executive vice president of one of Signal's wholly-owned subsidiaries, as CEO of UOP. He was became a director on UOP's board and was made a director of Signal.]

At the instigation of certain Signal management personnel, including William Walkup, its board chairman, and Forrest Shumway, its president, a feasibility study was made concerning the possible acquisition of the balance of UOP's outstanding shares. This study was performed by two Signal officers, Charles Arledge, vice president (director of planning), and Andrew Chitiea, senior vice president (chief financial officer). Walkup, Shumway, Arledge and Chitiea were all directors of UOP in addition to their membership on the Signal board.

Arledge and Chitiea concluded that it would be a good investment for Signal to acquire the remaining 49.5% of UOP shares at any price up to

$24 each. Their report was discussed between Walkup and Shumway who, along with Arledge, Chitiea and Brewster Arms, internal counsel for Signal, constituted Signal's senior management. They talked about the proper price to be paid if the acquisition was pursued, purportedly keeping in mind that as UOP's majority shareholder, Signal owed a fiduciary responsibility to both its own stockholders as well as to UOP's minority. It was agreed that a meeting of Signal's executive committee would be called to propose that Signal acquire the remaining outstanding stock of UOP through a cash-out merger in the range of $20 to $21 per share.

The executive committee meeting was set for February 28, 1978. As a courtesy, UOP's president, Crawford, was invited to attend, although he was not a member of Signal's executive committee. On his arrival, and prior to the meeting, Crawford was asked to meet privately with Walkup and Shumway. He was then told of Signal's plan to acquire full ownership of UOP and was asked for his reaction to the proposed price range of $20 to $21 per share. Crawford said he thought such a price would be "generous," and that it was certainly one which should be submitted to UOP's minority shareholders for their ultimate consideration.

Crawford voiced no objection to the $20 to $21 price range, nor did he suggest that Signal should consider paying more than $21 per share for the minority interests. Signal's management concluded that the acquisition of UOP's minority shares provided the solution to its business problems.

It was the consensus that a price of $20 to $21 per share would be fair to both Signal and the minority shareholders of UOP. Signal's executive committee authorized its management "to negotiate" with UOP "for a cash acquisition of the minority ownership in UOP, Inc., with the intention of presenting a proposal to [Signal's] board of directors on March 6, 1978."

[Signal then issued a press release of its intent to acquire the remaining 49.5 percent of UOP, and the announcement referred to the fact that the closing price of UOP's common stock on that day was $14.50 per share.] Two days later, on March 2, Signal issued a second press release stating that its management would recommend a price in the range of $20 to $21 per share for UOP's 49.5% minority interest.

Between February 28 and March 6, a total of four business days, Crawford spoke by telephone with all of UOP's non-Signal directors.

During this period Crawford also had several telephone contacts with Signal officials. In only one of them, however, was the price of the shares discussed. In a conversation with Walkup, Crawford advised that as a result of his communications with UOP's non-Signal directors, it was his feeling that the price would have to be the top of the proposed range, or $21 per share, if the approval of UOP's outside directors was to be obtained. But again, he did not seek any price higher than $21.

On March 6, both the Signal and UOP boards were convened to consider the proposed merger. Communications were maintained between the two meetings. Walkup, Signal's board chairman, and also a UOP director, attended UOP's meeting in order to present Signal's position and answer any questions that UOP's non-Signal directors might have. Arledge and Chitiea, along with Signal's other designees on UOP's board, participated by conference telephone. All of UOP's outside directors attended the meeting either in person or by conference telephone.

First, Signal's board unanimously adopted a resolution authorizing Signal to propose to UOP a cash merger of $21 per share as outlined in a certain merger agreement and other supporting documents. This proposal required that the merger be approved by a majority of UOP's outstanding minority shares voting at the stockholders meeting at which the merger would be considered, and that the minority shares voting in favor of the merger, when coupled with Signal's 50.5% interest would have to comprise at least two-thirds of all UOP shares. Otherwise the proposed merger would be deemed disapproved.

UOP's board then considered the proposal. Copies of the agreement were delivered to the directors in attendance, and other copies had been forwarded earlier to the directors participating by telephone. They also had before them UOP financial data for 1974–1977, market price information, and budget projections for 1978.

There was no discussion of [the Arledge-Chitiea feasibility study] at UOP's board meeting. Nothing in that report was ever disclosed to UOP's minority shareholders prior to their approval of the merger.

After consideration of Signal's proposal, Walkup and Crawford left the meeting to permit a free and uninhibited exchange between UOP's non-Signal directors. Upon their return a resolution to accept Signal's offer was then proposed and adopted. While Signal's men on UOP's board participated in various aspects of the meeting, they abstained from voting.

Despite the swift board action of the two companies, the merger was not submitted to UOP's shareholders until their annual meeting on May 26. In the notice of that meeting and proxy statement sent to shareholders in May, UOP's management and board urged that the merger be approved.

The proxy statement indicated that the vote of UOP's board in approving the merger had been unanimous.

As of the record date of UOP's annual meeting, there were 11,488,302 shares of UOP common stock outstanding, 5,688,302 of which were owned by the minority. At the meeting only 56%, or 3,208,652, of the minority shares were voted. Of these, 2,953,812, or 51.9% of the total minority, voted for the merger, and 254,840 voted against it. When Signal's stock was added to the minority shares voting in favor, a total of 76.2% of UOP's outstanding shares approved the merger while only 2.2% opposed it.

By its terms the merger became effective on May 26, 1978, and each share of UOP's stock held by the minority was automatically converted into a right to receive $21 cash.

[Analysis of Fiduciary Duty]

A primary issue mandating reversal is the preparation by two UOP directors, Arledge and Chitiea, of their feasibility study for the exclusive use and benefit of Signal. This document was of obvious significance to both Signal and UOP. Using UOP data, it described the advantages to Signal of ousting the minority at a price range of $21–$24 per share. Arledge, one of the authors, outlined the benefits to Signal:

Purpose Of The Merger

> (1) Provides an outstanding investment opportunity for Signal—(Better than any recent acquisition we have seen.)
>
> (2) Increases Signal's earnings.
>
> (3) Facilitates the flow of resources between Signal and its subsidiaries—(Big factor—works both ways.)
>
> (4) Provides cost savings potential for Signal and UOP.
>
> (5) Improves the percentage of Signal's "operating earnings" as opposed to "holding company earnings."
>
> (6) Simplifies the understanding of Signal.
>
> (7) Facilitates technological exchange among Signal's subsidiaries.
>
> (8) Eliminates potential conflicts of interest.

Having written those words, solely for the use of Signal, neither Arledge nor Chitiea shared this report with their fellow directors of UOP. We are satisfied that no one else did either. This conduct hardly meets the fiduciary standards applicable to such a transaction.

Crawford, UOP's president, could not recall that any documents, other than a draft of the merger agreement, were sent to UOP's directors before the March 6 UOP meeting. Chitiea, an author of the report, testified that it was made available to Signal's directors, but was not circulated to the outside directors of UOP. He testified that he "didn't share" that information with the outside directors of UOP with whom he served.

It appears that a three-page summary of figures was given to all UOP directors. Its first page is identical to one page of the Arledge-Chitiea report, but this dealt with nothing more than a justification of the $21 price. Nothing contained in either the minutes or this three-page summary reflects Signal's study regarding the $24 price.

The Arledge-Chitiea report speaks for itself in supporting the Chancellor's finding that a price of up to $24 was a "good investment" for

Signal. It shows that a return on the investment at $21 would be 15.7% versus 15.5% at $24 per share. This was a difference of only two-tenths of one percent, while it meant over $17,000,000 to the minority. Under such circumstances, paying UOP's minority shareholders $24 would have had relatively little long-term effect on Signal, and the Chancellor's findings concerning the benefit to Signal, even at a price of $24, were correct.

Certainly, this was a matter of material significance to UOP and its shareholders. Since the study was prepared by two UOP directors, using UOP information for the exclusive benefit of Signal, and nothing whatever was done to disclose it to the outside UOP directors or the minority shareholders, a question of breach of fiduciary duty arises. This problem occurs because there were common Signal-UOP directors participating, at least to some extent, in the UOP board's decision-making processes without full disclosure of the conflicts they faced.

[There is a] long-existing principle of Delaware law that these Signal designated directors on UOP's board still owed UOP and its shareholders an uncompromising duty of loyalty. The classic language of *Guth v. Loft, Inc.*, 5 A.2d 503, 510 (Del. 1939), requires no embellishment: "A public policy, existing through the years, and derived from a profound knowledge of human characteristics and motives, has established a rule that demands of a corporate officer or director, peremptorily and inexorably, the most scrupulous observance of his duty."

Given the absence of any attempt to structure this transaction on an arm's length basis, Signal cannot escape the effects of the conflicts it faced, particularly when its designees on UOP's board did not totally abstain from participation in the matter. There is no "safe harbor" for such divided loyalties in Delaware. When directors of a Delaware corporation are on both sides of a transaction, they are required to demonstrate their utmost good faith and the most scrupulous inherent fairness of the bargain. The requirement of fairness is unflinching in its demand that where one stands on both sides of a transaction, he has the burden of establishing its entire fairness, sufficient to pass the test of careful scrutiny by the courts.

There is no dilution of this obligation where one holds dual or multiple directorships, as in a parent-subsidiary context. Thus, individuals who act in a dual capacity as directors of two corporations, one of whom is parent and the other subsidiary, owe the same duty of good management to both corporations, and in the absence of an independent negotiating structure, or the directors' total abstention from any participation in the matter, this duty is to be exercised in light of what is best for both companies. The record demonstrates that Signal has not met this obligation.

[Analysis of Entire Fairness]

The concept of fairness has two basic aspects: fair dealing and fair price. The former embraces questions of when the transaction was timed, how it was initiated, structured, negotiated, disclosed to the directors, and how the approvals of the directors and the stockholders were obtained. The latter aspect of fairness relates to the economic and financial considerations of the proposed merger, including all relevant factors: assets, market value, earnings, future prospects, and any other elements that affect the intrinsic or inherent value of a company's stock. However, the test for fairness is not a bifurcated one as between fair dealing and price. All aspects of the issue must be examined as a whole since the question is one of entire fairness. However, in a non-fraudulent transaction we recognize that price may be the preponderant consideration outweighing other features of the merger. Here, we address the two basic aspects of fairness separately because we find reversible error as to both.

The Arledge-Chitiea report is but one aspect of the element of fair dealing. How did this merger evolve? It is clear that it was entirely initiated by Signal. The serious time constraints under which the principals acted were all set by Signal.

The structure of the transaction, again, was Signal's doing. So far as negotiations were concerned, it is clear that they were modest at best. Crawford, Signal's man at UOP, never really talked price with Signal, except to accede to its management's statements on the subject, and to convey to Signal the UOP outside directors' view that as between the \$20–\$21 range under consideration, it would have to be \$21. The latter is not a surprising outcome, but hardly arm's length negotiations.

Finally, the minority stockholders were denied the critical information that Signal considered a price of \$24 to be a good investment. Since this would have meant over \$17,000,000 more to the minority, we cannot conclude that the shareholder vote was an informed one. Under the circumstances, an approval by a majority of the minority was meaningless.

Given these particulars and Delaware law, the record does not establish that this transaction satisfies any reasonable concept of fair dealing, and the Chancellor's findings in that regard must be reversed.

Turning to the matter of price, plaintiff also challenges its fairness. His evidence was that on the date the merger was approved the stock was worth at least \$26 per share.

The Chancellor perceived that the approach to valuation was the same as that in an appraisal proceeding. Consistent with precedent, he rejected plaintiff's method of proof and accepted defendants' evidence of value as being in accord with practice under prior case law. This means that the so-called "Delaware block" or weighted average method was employed wherein the elements of value, *i.e.*, assets, market price, earnings, etc., were assigned a particular weight and the resulting amounts added to determine the value per share. This procedure has been in use for decades. However, to the extent it excludes other generally accepted techniques used in the financial community and the courts, it is now clearly outmoded. It is time we recognize this in appraisal and other stock valuation proceedings and bring our law current on the subject.

While the Chancellor rejected plaintiff's discounted cash flow method of valuing UOP's stock, as not corresponding with "either logic or the existing law," it is significant that this was essentially the focus, *i.e.*, earnings potential of UOP, of Arledge and Chitiea in their evaluation of the merger. Accordingly, the standard "Delaware block" or weighted average method of valuation, formerly employed in appraisal and other stock valuation cases, shall no longer exclusively control such proceedings. We believe that a more liberal approach must include proof of value by any techniques or methods which are generally considered acceptable in the financial community and otherwise admissible in court, subject only to our interpretation of 8 *Del.C.* § 262(h). This will obviate the very structured and mechanistic procedure that has heretofore governed such matters.

Fair price requires consideration of all relevant factors involving the value of a company.

This is not only in accord with the realities of present day affairs, but it is thoroughly consonant with the purpose and intent of our statutory law. Under 8 *Del.C.* § 262(h), the Court of Chancery:

> shall appraise the shares, determining their *fair* value exclusive of any element of value arising from the accomplishment or expectation of the merger, together with a fair rate of interest, if any, to be paid upon the amount determined to be the *fair* value. In determining such *fair* value, the Court shall take into account *all relevant factors*.

It is significant that section 262 now mandates the determination of "fair" value based upon "all relevant factors." Only the speculative elements of value that may arise from the "accomplishment or expectation" of the merger are excluded.

The judgment of the Court of Chancery, finding both the circumstances of the merger and the price paid the minority shareholders to be fair, is reversed. The matter is remanded for further proceedings.

NOTES

1. The fact that a corporate parent owns entirely or substantially a subsidiary does not mean that the parent can ignore the separateness of corporate entities or that the subsidiary's directors and officers are or should be the agents of the parent corporation in a principal-agent relationship.

> For publicly held corporations, the Delaware General Corporation Law contemplates a separation of control and ownership. The board of directors has the legal responsibility to manage the business of the corporation for the benefit of its stockholders. This

> Court has consistently held that the fact the directors of a corporation are elected by the majority stockholder does not relieve those directors of their fiduciary duties to the corporation and its minority stockholders. The parent, once having elected directors, does not have a right thereafter to interfere. To impose a duty of obedience on directors, moreover, would conflict with the fundamental point that corporate law assigns ultimate managerial power and responsibility to directors. The parent thus lacks the right to assert control through interim instructions, a defining hallmark of a legal relationship of agency. This is not a point of merely formal or definitional significance. The distinction between a right of control and the effective power to control often has practical consequences. In the absence of a right to control the directors it elects, the parent must either disregard their existence, a move disrespectful of the corporate paraphernalia that jeopardizes the corporate veil insulating the parent from subsidiary-level liabilities, or the parent must take steps to exercise its power by coercing the directors or removing them, moves that have drawbacks of their own.

Weinstein Enterprises, Inc. v. Orloff, 870 A.2d 499, 508–09 (Del. 2005).

The case below concerns a situation where a controlling shareholder makes a tender offer to minority shareholders to acquire their shares. In reading this case, consider these questions: (1) From the perspective of a controlling shareholder's duty to minority shareholders, what is the difference between a cash-out merger and a tender offer? (2) In a tender offer, why is there no "right of the shareholders to receive a particular price"? (3) Are there ways in which a controlling shareholder structures a tender offer that violates its duty to the minority?

SOLOMON V. PATHE COMMUNICATIONS CORP.

672 A.2d 35 (Del. 1996)

HARTNETT, JUSTICE.

The suit is a putative shareholder class action that challenges the fairness of a tender offer made by Credit Lyonnais Banque Nederland N.V. ("CLBN") to purchase 5.9 million shares of the publicly traded common stock of Pathe Communications Corp. ("Pathe"). The tender offer was proposed in conjunction with CLBN's planned foreclosure on a security interest it held. Robert Solomon is a shareholder who purportedly represents a class holding ten percent of Pathe's common stock.

Pathe purchased MGM/UA Communications Corporation ("MGM"). The purchase price was funded principally by loans from CLBN totalling approximately $1 billion. As part of this loan transaction, CLBN took a perfected security interest in 89 percent of Pathe's stock and 98 percent of

MGM's stock. Additionally, in exchange for the granting of credit, CLBN acquired the right, under two voting trust agreements, to vote 89.5% of Pathe's shares and substantially all of MGM's shares.

Because of alleged defaults, CLBN foreclosed on the stock of both corporations.

To help ensure that Pathe would not attempt to delay the foreclosure, CLBN offered to make a tender offer for an unspecified number of Pathe's publicly held shares of common stock. In response, Pathe appointed a special committee to review the proposal with the assistance of its own legal and financial advisers.

Pathe and CLBN executed an agreement in which Pathe agreed not to delay the foreclosure. CLBN agreed to make a tender offer of $1.50 per share for up to 5.8 million of Pathe's publicly held shares. CLBN initiated the foreclosure. CLBN made the promised tender offer for the Pathe shares.

One day prior to the announcement of the tender offer, Solomon filed the present action. The complaint asserted that the tender offer was unfair to all shareholders. It asserted that the tender offer price was "coercive" and amounted to a breach of loyalty by CLBN as controlling shareholder of Pathe and MGM. Solomon also asserted in his amended complaint that the Pathe Board was under the control of CLBN; that the Defendants exhibited impropriety by failing to retain independent advisers; and that the Defendants failed "to assure that no conflict of interest existed."

CLBN moved to dismiss the suit. The Court of Chancery granted the motion to dismiss for failure to state a claim under Chancery Rule 12(b)(6).

After a careful review of the amended complaint, we agree with the Chancellor that it fails to state a claim upon which relief can be granted.

The complaint contains two counts. Count I attempts to assert a claim for the breach of the duty of care by the individual Defendants by alleging that they did not negotiate a sufficient tender offer price for the shares.

Count II attempts to assert a breach of the duty of fair dealing by the directors because they did not oppose the tender offer. The asserted unfairness of the tender offer is based on its allegedly inadequate price.

In the case of totally voluntary tender offers, courts do not impose any right of the shareholders to receive a particular price. *Weinberger v. U.O.P., Inc.*, 457 A.2d 701, 703 (Del. 1983). Delaware law recognizes that, as to allegedly voluntary tender offers (in contrast to cash-out mergers), the determinative factor as to voluntariness is whether coercion is present, or whether there is "materially false or misleading disclosures made to shareholders in connection with the offer." A transaction may be considered involuntary, despite being voluntary in appearance and form, if one of these factors is present. There is no well-plead allegation of any coercion or false or misleading disclosures in the present case, however.

In the absence of coercion or disclosure violations, the adequacy of the price in a voluntary tender offer cannot be an issue. *Weinberger,* 457 A.2d at 703. Solomon has plead no facts from which there could be drawn a reasonable inference that there was coercion or lack of complete disclosure.

The case below is another cash-out transaction. In reading this case, consider these questions: (1) What is the role of an independent committee? (2) What is the standard of review, who bore the burden of proof, and why? (3) In light of this opinion, what should the parent corporation Alcatel and the independent committee of Lynch? (4) What is the most important principle that governs an independent committee representing minority shareholders? (5) What is the relationship between the standard of review and the evidentiary burden of proof?

KAHN V. LYNCH COMMUNICATIONS SYSTEM, INC.

638 A.2d 1110 (Del. 1994)

HOLLAND, JUSTICE:

This is an appeal by the plaintiff-appellant, Alan Kahn, from a final judgment of the Court of Chancery which was entered after a trial. The action originally sought to enjoin the acquisition of the defendant-appellee, Lynch Communication Systems, Inc., by the defendant-appellee, Alcatel U.S.A. Corporation, pursuant to a tender offer and cash-out merger. Kahn amended his complaint to seek monetary damages.

A trial was held. Kahn alleged that Alcatel was a controlling shareholder of Lynch and breached its fiduciary duties to Lynch and its shareholders. According to Kahn, Alcatel dictated the terms of the merger and paid an unfair price.

The Court of Chancery concluded that Alcatel was, in fact, a controlling shareholder that owed fiduciary duties to Lynch and its shareholders. It concluded that Alcatel had not breached those fiduciary duties. The Court of Chancery entered judgment in favor of the defendants.

Lynch manufactured telecommunications equipment for sale to telephone operating companies. Alcatel, a holding company, is a subsidiary of Alcatel (S.A.), a French company. Alcatel (S.A.), in turn, is a subsidiary of Compagnie Generale d'Electricite ("CGE"), a French corporation.

As part of [Alcatel's purchase agreement of Lynch stock], Lynch amended its certificate of incorporation to require an 80 percent vote of its shareholders for approval of any business combination. Alcatel obtained proportional representation on the Lynch board of directors and the right to purchase 40 percent of any equity securities offered by Lynch to third parties. The agreement also precluded Alcatel from holding more than 45 percent of Lynch's stock. Alcatel owned 43.3 percent of Lynch's outstanding stock; designated 5 of the 11 members of Lynch's board of directors and 2 of 4 members of the compensation committee.

[Alcatel and Lynch disagreed over several proposals for Lynch to combine with other companies, including an Alcatel affiliate.] Alcatel made [an] offer to acquire the entire equity interest in Lynch, constituting the approximately 57 percent of Lynch shares not owned by Alcatel. The offering price was $14 cash per share.

The Lynch board of directors [authorized an] Independent Committee to negotiate the cash merger offer with Alcatel. At a meeting held that same day, the Independent Committee determined that the $14 per share offer was inadequate. The Independent's Committee's own legal counsel, Skadden, Arps, Slate, Meagher & Flom ("Skadden Arps"), suggested that the Independent Committee should review alternatives to a cash-out merger with Alcatel, including a "white knight" third party acquiror, a repurchase of Alcatel's shares, or the adoption of a shareholder rights plan.

Stuart Beringer, as chairman of the Independent Committee, contacted Michiel McCarty ("McCarty") of Dillon Read, Alcatel's representative in the negotiations, with a counteroffer at a price of $17 per share. McCarty responded on behalf of Alcatel with an offer of $15 per share. When Beringer informed McCarty of the Independent Committee's view that $15 was also insufficient, Alcatel raised its offer to $15.25 per share. The Independent Committee also rejected this offer. Alcatel then made its final offer of $15.50 per share.

At a meeting of the Independent Committee, Beringer advised its other two members that Alcatel was "ready to proceed with an unfriendly tender at a lower price" if the $15.50 per share price was not recommended by the Independent Committee and approved by the Lynch board of directors. Beringer also told the other members of the Independent Committee that the alternatives to a cash-out merger had been investigated but were impracticable. After meeting with its financial and legal advisors, the Independent Committee voted unanimously to recommend that the Lynch board of directors approve Alcatel's $15.50 cash per share price for a merger with Alcatel. The Lynch board met later that day. With Alcatel's nominees abstaining, it approved the merger.

Alcatel Dominated Lynch Controlling Shareholder Status

This Court has held that "a shareholder owes a fiduciary duty only if it owns a majority interest in or *exercises control* over the business affairs of the corporation." This Court has stated:

> A shareholder who owns less than 50% of outstanding stocks does not, without more, become a controlling shareholder of that corporation, with a concomitant fiduciary status. For a dominating relationship to exist in the absence of controlling stock

ownership, a plaintiff must allege domination by a minority shareholder through actual control of corporation conduct.

Alcatel held a 43.3 percent minority share of stock in Lynch. Based upon the testimony and the minutes of the August 1 Lynch board meeting, the Court of Chancery concluded that Alcatel did exercise control over Lynch's business decisions.

The record supports the Court of Chancery's factual finding that Alcatel dominated Lynch.

At the August 1 meeting, Alcatel opposed the renewal of compensation contracts for Lynch's top five managers. According to Dertinger, Christian Fayard, an Alcatel director, told the board members, "you must listen to us. We are 43 percent owner. You have to do what we tell you." The minutes confirm Dertinger's testimony. They recite that Fayard declared, "you are pushing us very much to take control of the company. Our opinion is not taken into consideration."

Although Beringer and Hubert Kertz, two of the independent directors, favored renewal of the contracts, the third independent director, Paul Wineman, admonished the board as follows:

> Wineman pointed out that the vote on the contracts is a "watershed vote" and the motion, due to Alcatel's "strong feelings," might not carry if taken now. Wineman clarified that "you [management] might win the battle and lose the war." With Alcatel's opinion so clear, Wineman questioned "if management wants the contracts renewed under these circumstances." He recommended that management "think twice." Wineman declared: "I want to keep the management. I can't think of a better management." Kertz agreed, again advising consideration of the "critical" period the company is entering.

The minutes reflect that the management directors left the room after this statement. The remaining board members then voted not to renew the contracts.

At the same meeting, Alcatel vetoed Lynch's acquisition of the target company, which, according to the minutes, Beringer considered "an immediate fit" for Lynch. Dertinger agreed with Beringer, stating that the "target company is extremely important as they have the products that Lynch needs now." Nonetheless, Alcatel prevailed. The minutes reflect that Fayard advised the board: "Alcatel, with its 44% equity position, would not approve such an acquisition as it does not wish to be diluted from being the main shareholder in Lynch."

The record supports the Court of Chancery's underlying factual finding that "the non-Alcatel [independent] directors deferred to Alcatel because of its position as a significant stockholder and not because they decided in the exercise of their own business judgment that Alcatel's position was correct." The record also supports the subsequent factual finding that, notwithstanding its 43.3 percent minority shareholder interest, Alcatel did exercise actual control over Lynch by dominating its corporate affairs.

Entire Fairness Requirement Dominating Interested Shareholder

A controlling or dominating shareholder standing on both sides of a transaction, as in a parent-subsidiary context, bears the burden of proving its entire fairness. *Weinberger v. UOP, Inc.*, 457 A.2d 701, 710 (Del. 1983). The demonstration of fairness that is required was set forth by this Court in *Weinberger*: "The concept of fairness has two basic aspects: fair dealing and fair price. The test for fairness is not a bifurcated one as between fair dealing and price. All aspects of the issue must be examined as a whole since the question is one of entire fairness."

Once again, this Court holds that the exclusive standard of judicial review in examining the propriety of an interested cash-out merger transaction by a controlling or dominating shareholder is entire fairness. The initial burden of establishing entire fairness rests upon the party who stands on both sides of the transaction. However, [1] an approval of the transaction by an independent committee of directors or [2] an informed majority of minority shareholders shifts the burden of proof on the issue of fairness from the controlling or dominating shareholder to the challenging shareholder-plaintiff. Nevertheless, even when an interested cash-out merger transaction receives the informed approval of a majority of minority stockholders or an independent committee of disinterested directors, an entire fairness analysis is the only proper standard of judicial review.

In *Weinberger*, this Court noted that "particularly in a parent-subsidiary context, a showing that the action taken was as though each of the contending parties had *in fact* exerted its bargaining power against the other at arm's length is strong evidence that the transaction meets the test of fairness."

The same policy rationale which requires judicial review of interested cash-out mergers exclusively for entire fairness also mandates careful judicial scrutiny of a special committee's real bargaining power before shifting the burden of proof on the issue of entire fairness.

> The mere existence of an independent special committee does not itself shift the burden. At least two factors are required. First, the majority shareholder must not dictate the terms of the merger. Second, the special committee must have real bargaining power that it can exercise with the majority shareholder on an arms length basis.

This Court expressed its agreement with [the above] statement.

Lynch's Independent Committee

The performance of the Independent Committee merits careful judicial scrutiny to determine whether Alcatel's demonstrated pattern of domination was effectively neutralized so that "contending parties had in fact exerted its bargaining power against the other at arm's length."

The Independent Committee's original assignment was to examine the merger with Celwave which had been proposed by Alcatel. The Independent Committee effectively discharged that assignment and, in fact, recommended that the Lynch board reject the merger on Alcatel's terms. Alcatel's response to the Independent Committee's adverse recommendation was not the pursuit of further negotiations regarding its Celwave proposal, but rather its response was an offer to buy Lynch. That offer was consistent with Alcatel's August 1 expressions of an intention to dominate Lynch, since an acquisition would effectively eliminate once and for all Lynch's remaining vestiges of independence.

The Independent Committee's second assignment was to consider Alcatel's proposal to purchase Lynch. The Independent Committee proceeded on that task with full knowledge of Alcatel's demonstrated pattern of domination. The Independent Committee was also obviously aware of Alcatel's refusal to negotiate with it on the Celwave matter.

Burden of Proof Shifted Court of Chancery's Finding

The Court of Chancery gave credence to the testimony of Kertz, one of the members of the Independent Committee, to the effect that he did not believe that $15.50 was a fair price but that he voted in favor of the merger because he felt there was no alternative.

The Court of Chancery also found that Kertz understood Alcatel's position to be that it was ready to proceed with an unfriendly tender offer at a lower price if Lynch did not accept the $15.50 offer, and that Kertz perceived this to be a threat by Alcatel. The Court of Chancery concluded that Kertz ultimately decided that, "although $15.50 was not fair, a tender offer and merger at that price would be better for Lynch's stockholders than an unfriendly tender offer at a significantly lower price." The Court of Chancery determined that "Kertz failed either to satisfy himself that the offered price was fair or oppose the merger."

In addition to Kertz, the other members of the Independent Committee were Beringer, its chairman, and Wineman. Wineman did not testify at trial. Beringer was called by Alcatel to testify at trial. Beringer testified that at the time of the Committee's vote to recommend the $15.50 offer to the Lynch board, he thought "that *under the circumstances,* a price of $15.50 was fair and should be accepted."

The record reflects that Alcatel was "ready to proceed" with a hostile bid. This was a conclusion reached by Beringer, the Independent

Committee's chairman and spokesman, based upon communications to him from Alcatel. Beringer testified that although there was no reference to a particular price for a hostile bid during his discussions with Alcatel, or even specific mention of a "lower" price, "the implication was clear to [him] that it probably would be at a lower price."

According to the Court of Chancery, the Independent Committee rejected three lower offers for Lynch from Alcatel and then accepted the $15.50 offer "after being advised that [it] was fair and after considering the absence of alternatives." The Vice Chancellor expressly acknowledged the impracticability of Lynch's Independent Committee's alternatives to a merger with Alcatel:

> Lynch was not in a position to shop for other acquirors, since Alcatel could block any alternative transaction. Alcatel also made it clear that it was not interested in having its shares repurchased by Lynch. The Independent Committee decided that a stockholder rights plan was not viable because of the increased debt it would entail.

The Power to Say No, The Parties' Contentions, Arm's Length Bargaining

The Court of Chancery properly noted that limitations on the alternatives to Alcatel's offer did not mean that the Independent Committee should have agreed to a price that was unfair:

> The power to say no is a significant power. It is the duty of directors serving on [an independent] committee to approve only a transaction that is in the best interests of the public shareholders, to say no to any transaction that is not fair to those shareholders and is not the best transaction available. It is not sufficient for such directors to achieve the best price that a fiduciary will pay if that price is not a fair price.

Kahn contends the record reflects that the conduct of Alcatel deprived the Independent Committee of an effective "power to say no." Kahn argues that Alcatel not only threatened the Committee with a hostile tender offer in the event its $15.50 offer was not recommended and approved, but also directed the affairs of Lynch for Alcatel's benefit in such a way as to make it impossible for Lynch to continue as a public company under Alcatel's control without injury to itself and its minority shareholders.

In this case the coercion was extant and directed to a specific price offer which was, in effect, presented in the form of a "take it or leave it" ultimatum by a controlling shareholder with the capability of following through on its threat of a hostile takeover.

Alcatel's Entire Fairness Burden Did Not Shift to Kahn

The Court of Chancery's determination that the Independent Committee "appropriately simulated a third-party transaction, where negotiations are conducted at arm's-length and there is no compulsion to reach an agreement," is not supported by the record. Under the circumstances present in the case, the Court of Chancery erred in shifting the burden of proof with regard to entire fairness to the contesting Lynch shareholder-plaintiff, Kahn. The record reflects that the ability of the Committee effectively to negotiate at arm's length was compromised by Alcatel's threats to proceed with a hostile tender offer if the $15.50 price was not approved by the Committee and the Lynch board. The fact that the Independent Committee rejected three initial offers, which were well below the Independent Committee's estimated valuation for Lynch and were not combined with an explicit threat that Alcatel was "ready to proceed" with a hostile bid, cannot alter the conclusion that any semblance of arm's length bargaining ended when the Independent Committee surrendered to the ultimatum that accompanied Alcatel's final offer.

Accordingly, the judgment of the Court of Chancery is reversed. This matter is remanded for further proceedings, including a redetermination of the entire fairness of the cash-out merger to Lynch minority shareholders with the burden of proof remaining on Alcatel.

NOTES

1. On remand, the chancery court, it seems, was less impressed with the supreme court's leaning and the plaintiff's case. The court reevaluated the record under the appropriate burden of proof and concluded that the transaction was entirely fair to Lynch minority shareholders. The court rejected plaintiff's claim that the defendants violated their duty of disclosure in failing to describe specifically the threat of a lower priced tender offer. On the second appeal, the supreme court determined that the trial court applied the proper legal standard and affirmed the factual finding that the transaction was fair to the minority shareholders.

> After reassessing the record under an entire fairness standard, with the burden of proof upon Alcatel, the Court of Chancery determined that the timing and structure of negotiations and the disclosure to shareholders of such event were the product of fair dealing. The trial court concluded that the merger price was fair. Thus the non-bifurcated standard of *Weinberger* was satisfied. Under our standard of review, we defer to the trial court's evidentiary findings if supported by the record and logically determined.
>
> In deciding the ultimate question of entire fairness, the Court of Chancery was required to carefully analyze the factual circumstances in the context of how the board discharged all of its fiduciary duties, apply a disciplined balancing approach to its findings, and articulate the basis for its decision. The record reflects that was done. We find no error in the trial court's application of legal standards.

Kahn v. Lynch Communications System, Inc., 669 A.2d 79, 90 (Del. 1995).

The case below explores whether a controlling shareholder cash out can be reviewed under the business judgment rule rather than the entire fairness standard. In reading this case, consider these questions: How can the transaction process be structured to receive the business judgment rule protection? (2) What is the fundamental rationale?

KAHN V. M & F WORLDWIDE CORP.

88 A.3d 635 (Del. 2014)

HOLLAND, JUSTICE:

This appeal arises from an acquisition by MacAndrews & Forbes Holdings, Inc. ("M & F" or "MacAndrews & Forbes")—a 43% stockholder in M & F Worldwide Corp. ("MFW")—of the remaining common stock of MFW (the "Merger"). From the outset, M & F's proposal to take MFW private was made contingent upon two stockholder-protective procedural conditions. First, M & F required the Merger to be negotiated and approved by a special committee of independent MFW directors (the "Special Committee"). Second, M & F required that the Merger be approved by a majority of stockholders unaffiliated with M & F. The Merger closed, after it was approved by a vote of 65.4% of MFW's minority stockholders.

The Appellants sought post-closing relief against M & F, Ronald Perelman, and MFW's directors (including the members of the Special Committee) for breach of fiduciary duty. The Defendants moved for summary judgment, which the Court of Chancery granted.

The Appellants raise two main arguments on this appeal. First, they contend that the Court of Chancery erred in concluding that no material disputed facts existed regarding the conditions precedent to business judgment review. The Appellants submit that the Special Committee was not disinterested and independent, was not fully empowered, and was not effective. The Appellants also contend, as a legal matter, that the majority-of-the-minority provision did not afford MFW stockholders protection sufficient to displace entire fairness review.

Second, the Appellants submit that the Court of Chancery erred in holding that the business judgment standard applies to controller freeze-out mergers where the controller's proposal is conditioned on both Special Committee approval and a favorable majority-of-the-minority vote. Even if both procedural protections are adopted, the Appellants argue, entire fairness should be retained as the applicable standard of review.

MFW is a holding company. Before the Merger that is the subject of this dispute, MFW was 43.4% owned by MacAndrews & Forbes, which in turn is entirely owned by Ronald O. Perelman.

The MFW board had thirteen members. They were: Ronald Perelman, Barry Schwartz, William Bevins, Bruce Slovin, Charles Dawson, Stephen Taub, John Keane, Theo Folz, Philip Beekman, Martha Byorum, Viet Dinh, Paul Meister, and Carl Webb. Perelman, Schwartz, and Bevins were officers of both MFW and MacAndrews & Forbes. Perelman was the Chairman of MFW and the Chairman and CEO of MacAndrews & Forbes; Schwartz was the President and CEO of MFW and the Vice Chairman and Chief Administrative Officer of MacAndrews & Forbes; and Bevins was a Vice President at MacAndrews & Forbes.

Perelman began to explore the possibility of taking MFW private. MFW's stock price traded in the $20 to $24 per share range. MacAndrews & Forbes engaged Moelis & Co. to advise it. After preparing valuations based on projections that had been supplied to lenders by MFW in April and May 2011, Moelis valued MFW at between $10 and $32 a share.

On June 10, 2011, MFW's shares closed on the New York Stock Exchange at $16.96. The next business day, Schwartz sent a letter proposal ("Proposal") to the MFW board to buy the remaining MFW shares for $24 in cash. The Proposal stated, in relevant part:

> The proposed transaction would be subject to the approval of the Board of Directors of the Company [*i.e.*, MFW] and the negotiation and execution of mutually acceptable definitive transaction documents. It is our expectation that the Board of Directors will appoint a special committee of independent directors to consider our proposal and make a recommendation to the Board of Directors. *We will not move forward with the transaction unless it is approved by such a special committee. In addition, the transaction will be subject to a non-waivable condition requiring the approval of a majority of the shares of the Company not owned by M & F or its affiliates.*

The MFW board met the following day to consider the Proposal. At the meeting, Schwartz presented the offer on behalf of MacAndrews & Forbes. Subsequently, Schwartz and Bevins, as the two directors present who were also directors of MacAndrews & Forbes, recused themselves from the meeting, as did Dawson, the CEO of HCHC, who had previously expressed support for the proposed offer.

The independent directors then invited counsel from Willkie Farr & Gallagher to join the meeting. The independent directors decided to form the Special Committee, and resolved further that:

> The Special Committee is empowered to: (i) make such investigation of the Proposal as the Special Committee deems appropriate; (ii) evaluate the terms of the Proposal; (iii) negotiate with [MacAndrews & Forbes] and its representatives any element of the Proposal; (iv) negotiate the terms of any definitive

> agreement with respect to the Proposal (it being understood that the execution thereof shall be subject to the approval of the Board); (v) report to the Board its recommendations and conclusions with respect to the Proposal, including a determination and *recommendation as to whether the Proposal is fair and in the best interests of the stockholders of the Company other than Holdings* and its affiliates and should be approved by the Board; and (vi) determine to elect not to pursue the Proposal.
>
> The Board shall not approve the Proposal without a prior favorable recommendation of the Special Committee.
>
> The Special Committee [is] empowered to retain and employ legal counsel, a financial advisor, and such other agents as the Special Committee shall deem necessary or desirable in connection with these matters.

The Special Committee consisted of Byorum, Dinh, Meister (the chair), and Webb.

What Should Be The Review Standard?

Where a transaction involving self-dealing by a controlling stockholder is challenged, the applicable standard of judicial review is "entire fairness," with the defendants having the burden of persuasion. In other words, the defendants bear the ultimate burden of proving that the transaction with the controlling stockholder was entirely fair to the minority stockholders. In *Kahn v. Lynch Communication Systems, Inc.*, 638 A.2d 1110 (Del. 1994), however, this Court held that in "entire fairness" cases, the defendants may shift the burden of persuasion to the plaintiff if either (1) they show that the transaction was approved by a well-functioning committee of independent directors; **or** (2) they show that the transaction was approved by an informed vote of a majority of the minority stockholders.

This appeal presents a question of first impression: what should be the standard of review for a merger between a controlling stockholder and its subsidiary, where the merger is conditioned *ab initio* upon the approval of **both** an independent, adequately-empowered Special Committee that fulfills its duty of care, and the uncoerced, informed vote of a majority of the minority stockholders.

Business Judgment Review Standard Adopted

We hold that business judgment is the standard of review that should govern mergers between a controlling stockholder and its corporate subsidiary, where the merger is conditioned *ab initio* upon both [1] the approval of an independent, adequately-empowered Special Committee that fulfills its duty of care; and [2] the uncoerced, informed vote of a majority of the minority stockholders. We so conclude for several reasons.

First, entire fairness is the highest standard of review in corporate law. It is applied in the controller merger context as a substitute for the dual statutory protections of disinterested board and stockholder approval, because both protections are potentially undermined by the influence of the controller. However, as this case establishes, that undermining influence does not exist in every controlled merger setting, regardless of the circumstances. The simultaneous deployment of the procedural protections employed here create a countervailing, offsetting influence of equal—if not greater—force. That is, where the controller irrevocably and publicly disables itself from using its control to dictate the outcome of the negotiations and the shareholder vote, the controlled merger then acquires the shareholder-protective characteristics of third-party, arm's-length mergers, which are reviewed under the business judgment standard.

Second, the dual procedural protection merger structure optimally protects the minority stockholders in controller buyouts. As the Court of Chancery explained:

> When these two protections are established up-front, a potent tool to extract good value for the minority is established. From inception, the controlling stockholder knows that it cannot bypass the special committee's ability to say no. And, the controlling stockholder knows it cannot dangle a majority-of-the-minority vote before the special committee late in the process as a deal-closer rather than having to make a price move.

Third, applying the business judgment standard to the dual protection merger structure:

> is consistent with the central tradition of Delaware law, which defers to the informed decisions of impartial directors, especially when those decisions have been approved by the disinterested stockholders on full information and without coercion. Not only that, the adoption of this rule will be of benefit to minority stockholders because it will provide a strong incentive for controlling stockholders to accord minority investors the transactional structure where stockholders get the benefits of independent, empowered negotiating agents to **bargain for the best price and say no** if the agents believe the deal is not advisable for any proper reason, plus the critical ability to determine for themselves whether to accept any deal that their negotiating agents recommend to them.

Fourth, the underlying purposes of the dual protection merger structure utilized here and the entire fairness standard of review both converge and are fulfilled at the same critical point: **price.** Following *Weinberger v. UOP, Inc.*, 457 A.2d 701, 711 (Del. 1983), this Court has consistently held that, although entire fairness review comprises the dual components of fair dealing and fair price, in a non-fraudulent transaction "price may be the preponderant consideration outweighing other features of the merger." The dual protection merger structure requires two price-related pretrial determinations: first, that a fair price was achieved by an empowered, independent committee that acted with care; and, second, that a fully-informed, uncoerced majority of the minority stockholders voted in favor of the price that was recommended by the independent committee.

The New Standard Summarized

To summarize our holding, in controller buyouts, the business judgment standard of review will be applied *if and only if:*

(i) the controller conditions the procession of the transaction on the approval of both a Special Committee and a majority of the minority stockholders;

(ii) the Special Committee is independent;

(iii) the Special Committee is empowered to freely select its own advisors and to say no definitively;

(iv) the Special Committee meets its duty of care in negotiating a fair price;

(v) the vote of the minority is informed; and

(vi) there is no coercion of the minority.[14]

If a plaintiff that can plead a reasonably conceivable set of facts showing that any or all of those enumerated conditions did not exist, that complaint would state a claim for relief that would entitle the plaintiff to proceed and conduct discovery. If, after discovery, triable issues of fact remain about whether either or both of the dual procedural protections were established, or if established were effective, the case will proceed to a trial in which the court will conduct an entire fairness review.

Unless *both* procedural protections for the minority stockholders are established *prior to trial,* the ultimate judicial scrutiny of controller buyouts will continue to be the entire fairness standard of review.

---

[14] The Complaint would have survived a motion to dismiss under this new standard. First, the complaint alleged that Perelman's offer "valued the company at just four times" MFW's profits per share and "five times 2010 pre-tax cash flow," and that these ratios were "well below" those calculated for recent similar transactions. Second, the complaint alleged that the final Merger price was two dollars per share *lower* than the trading price only about two months earlier. Third, the complaint alleged particularized facts indicating that MFW's share price was depressed at the times of Perelman's offer and the Merger announcement due to short-term factors such as MFW's acquisition of other entities and Standard & Poor's downgrading of the United States' creditworthiness. Fourth, the complaint alleged that commentators viewed both Perelman's initial $24 per share offer and the final $25 per share Merger price as being surprisingly low. These allegations about the sufficiency of the price call into question the adequacy of the Special Committee's negotiations, thereby necessitating discovery on all of the new prerequisites to the application of the business judgment rule.

The Special Committee Was Empowered

[After a thorough review of the independence of the directors on the Special Committee, the court held that they were independent of the controlling shareholder and Ronald Perelman.*]

It is undisputed that the Special Committee was empowered to hire its own legal and financial advisors, and it retained Willkie Farr & Gallagher LLP [and] Evercore Partners. The qualifications and independence of Evercore and Willkie Farr & Gallagher LLP are not contested.

Among the powers given the Special Committee was the authority to "report to the Board its recommendations and conclusions with respect to the [Merger], including a determination and recommendation as to whether the Proposal is fair and in the best interests of the stockholders." The Court of Chancery found that it was "undisputed that the Special Committee was empowered not simply to 'evaluate' the offer, like some special committees with weak mandates, but to negotiate with [M & F] over the terms of its offer to buy out the noncontrolling stockholders. This negotiating power was accompanied by the clear authority to say no definitively to [M & F]" and to "make that decision stick." MacAndrews & Forbes promised that it would not proceed with any going private proposal that did not have the support of the Special Committee. The Court of Chancery concluded, "the MFW committee did not have to fear that if it bargained too hard, MacAndrews & Forbes could bypass the committee and make a tender offer directly to the minority stockholders."

The Special Committee Exercised Due Care

[After review of the transaction process, the court upheld the lower court's determination that the special committee exercised due care.]

Majority of Minority Stockholder Vote

We consider the second procedural protection invoked by M & F—the majority-of-the-minority stockholder vote. Consistent with the second condition imposed by M & F, the Merger was put before MFW's stockholders for a vote. The proxy statement contained the history of the Special Committee's work and recommended that they vote in favor of the transaction at a price of $25 per share.

The proxy statement disclosed, among other things, that the Special Committee had countered M & F's initial $24 per share offer at $30 per share, but only was able to achieve a final offer of $25 per share. The proxy statement disclosed that the MFW business divisions had discussed with Evercore whether the initial projections Evercore received reflected management's latest thinking. It disclosed that the updated projections were lower. The proxy statement also included the five separate price

* Author's note: This part of the analysis is presented in the next chapter.

ranges for the value of MFW's stock that Evercore had generated with its different valuation analyses.

Knowing the proxy statement's disclosures of the background of the Special Committee's work, of Evercore's valuation ranges, and of the analyses supporting Evercore's *fairness opinion,* MFW's stockholders—representing more than 65% of the minority shares—approved the Merger. In the controlling stockholder merger context, it is settled Delaware law that an uncoerced, informed majority-of-the-minority vote, without any other procedural protection, is itself sufficient to shift the burden of persuasion to the plaintiff under the entire fairness standard of review. The Court of Chancery found that "the plaintiffs themselves do not dispute that the majority-of-the-minority vote was fully informed and uncoerced, because they fail to allege any failure of disclosure or any act of coercion."

Both Procedural Protections Established

Based on a highly extensive record, the Court of Chancery concluded that the procedural protections upon which the Merger was conditioned—approval by an independent and empowered Special Committee and by a uncoerced informed majority of MFW's minority stockholders—had *both* been undisputedly established. We agree and conclude the Defendants' motion for summary judgment was properly granted on all of those issues.

We have determined that the business judgment rule standard of review applies to this controlling stockholder buyout. Under that standard, the claims against the Defendants must be dismissed unless no rational person could have believed that the merger was favorable to MFW's minority stockholders. In this case, it cannot be credibly argued (let alone concluded) that no rational person would find the Merger favorable to MFW's minority stockholders.

The judgment of the Court of Chancery is affirmed.

NOTES

1. In this case, the court held that "the merger [must be] conditioned *ab initio* upon both" the approvals of the special committee and the minority shareholders." In *Flood v. Synutra International, Inc.*, 195 A.3d 754 (Del. 2018), the initial proposal of a shareholder with 63.5% control did not contain the *MFW* conditions. The board met and formed a special committee, but did not substantively evaluate the initial proposal. The controlling shareholder then engaged a top law firm. Two weeks after the initial offer, and only one week after the formation of the special committee, the controlling shareholder, now advised by the newly engaged law firm (and presumably under its advice), sent a second letter that conditioned the transaction on the *MFW* conditions. The question was whether the second letter met the "ab initio" condition set forth in *MFW*. The court held that it did: "So long as the controller conditions its offer on the key protections at the germination stage of the Special Committee process, when it is selecting its advisors, establishing its method of

proceeding, beginning its due diligence, and has not commenced substantive economic negotiations with the controller, the purpose of the pre-condition requirement of *MFW* is satisfied." *Id.* at 763. The court held that substantive negotiations had not taken place before the controlling shareholder conditioned the offer on the *MFW* conditions. *Id.* at 764.

The court also rejected *MFW*'s dicta in footnote 14, which stated that "the sufficiency of the price call into question the adequacy of the Special Committee's negotiations, thereby necessitating discovery on all of the new prerequisites to the application of the business judgment rule." This footnote suggests that, despite an adequate process conducted by an independent special committee advised by independent advisors, a plaintiff may avoid the business judgment rule by raising questions about whether the special committee was sufficiently adroit in bargaining with the controlling shareholder to achieve an adequate price. The court rejected this argument and footnote 14 in *MFW*: "a plaintiff can plead a duty of care violation only by showing that the Special Committee acted with gross negligence, not by questioning the sufficiency of the price." *Id.* at 768.

2. A short-form merger is one in which a parent corporation with a substantial stake, generally 90% or more, initiates a merger involving a majority owned subsidiary without a vote of the minority shareholders. DGLC § 253(a). A short-form merger recognizes that, by virtue of overwhelming ownership, the majority shareholder should be permitted to engage in a merger without the approval of minority shareholders. The process for a merger is truncated and minority shareholders have no say. A dissenting shareholder is entitled to an appraisal of its shares under DGCL § 262. Clearly, a short-form merger is a controlling shareholder cash out of minority shareholders. In *Glassman v. Unocal Exploration Corp.*, 777 A.2d 242 (Del. 2001), the court considered whether a minority shareholder has a claim under equity for a breach of duty for inadequate merger consideration. The court reasoned:

> Under settled principles, a parent corporation and its directors undertaking a short-form merger are self-dealing fiduciaries who should be required to establish entire fairness, including fair dealing and fair price. The problem is that § 253 authorizes a summary procedure that is inconsistent with any reasonable notion of fair dealing. In a short-form merger, there is no agreement of merger negotiated by two companies; there is only a unilateral act—a decision by the parent company that its 90% owned subsidiary shall no longer exist as a separate entity. The minority stockholders receive no advance notice of the merger; their directors do not consider or approve it; and there is no vote. Those who object are given the right to obtain fair value for their shares through appraisal.

Id. at 247. Thus, the court held that "absent fraud or illegality, appraisal is the exclusive remedy available to a minority stockholder who objects to a short form merger." *Id.* at 248.

CHAPTER 14

SHAREHOLDER LITIGATION

■ ■ ■

A. INFORMATION RIGHTS

The right to have certain information from the firm is essential to ownership. It enables owners to monitor the firm and management, to exercise rights informedly, and to assess the value of one's stake. Business organization laws grant information rights to owners. However, because the production of information is costly and because some owners may not have the proper motive or may be misguided, information rights are not absolute as to right or total as to content.

Delaware General Corporation Law: § 220 Inspection of Books and Records

(b) Any stockholder, in person or by attorney or other agent, shall, upon written demand under oath stating the purpose thereof, have the right during the usual hours for business to inspect for any proper purpose, and to make copies and extracts from:

(1) The corporation's stock ledger, a list of its stockholders, and its other books and records; and

(2) A subsidiary's books and records, to the extent that:

a. The corporation has actual possession and control of such records of such subsidiary; or

b. The corporation could obtain such records through the exercise of control over such subsidiary, provided that as of the date of the making of the demand:

1. The stockholder inspection of such books and records of the subsidiary would not constitute a breach of an agreement between the corporation or the subsidiary and a person or persons not affiliated with the corporation; and

2. The subsidiary would not have the right under the law applicable to it to deny the corporation access to such books and records upon demand by the corporation.

In every instance where the stockholder is other than a record holder of stock in a stock corporation, or a member of a nonstock corporation, the demand under oath shall state the person's status as a stockholder, be accompanied by documentary evidence of beneficial ownership of the stock, and state that such documentary evidence is a true and correct copy of what it purports to be. A proper purpose shall mean a purpose reasonably related to such person's interest as a stockholder.

The case below discusses the legal standard under which a plaintiff shareholder can obtain information for a "proper purpose" under DGCL § 220. In reading this case, consider these questions: (1) How can a plaintiff show a "credible basis from some evidence" of wrongdoing to warrant an order for the production of information under section 220? (2) What are the competing policy rationales supporting the rule in this case?

SEINFELD V. VERIZON COMMUNICATIONS, INC.

909 A.2d 117 (Del. 2006)

HOLLAND, JUSTICE.

The plaintiff, Frank Seinfeld, brought suit under section 220 to compel the defendant Verizon Communications to produce, for his inspection, its books and records related to the compensation of Verizon's three highest corporate officers. Seinfeld claimed that their executive compensation was excessive and wasteful. On cross-motions for summary judgment, the Court of Chancery applied well-established Delaware law and held that Seinfeld had not met his evidentiary burden to demonstrate a proper purpose to justify the inspection of Verizon's records.

We reaffirm the well-established law of Delaware that stockholders seeking inspection under section 220 must present "some evidence" to suggest a "credible basis" from which a court can infer that mismanagement, waste or wrongdoing may have occurred. The "credible basis" standard achieves an appropriate balance between providing stockholders who can offer some evidence of possible wrongdoing with access to corporate records and safeguarding the right of the corporation to deny requests for inspections that are based only upon suspicion or curiosity. The judgment of the Court of Chancery must be affirmed.

[Seinfeld's] stated purpose for seeking Verizon's books and records was to investigate mismanagement and corporate waste regarding the executive compensations of Ivan Seidenberg, Lawrence Babbio, and Charles Lee. Seinfeld alleges that the three executives were all performing in the same job and were paid amounts, including stock options, above the compensation provided for in their employment contracts. Seinfeld's section 220 claim for inspection is further premised on various computations he performed which indicate that the three executives' compensation totaled $205 million over three years and was, therefore, excessive, given their responsibilities to the corporation.

During his deposition, Seinfeld acknowledged he had no factual support for his claim that mismanagement had taken place. He admitted that the three executives did not perform any duplicative work. Seinfeld conceded he had no factual basis to allege the executives "did not earn" the amounts paid to them under their respective employment agreements.

The issue before us is quite narrow: should a stockholder seeking inspection under section 220 be entitled to relief without being required to show some evidence to suggest a credible basis for wrongdoing? We conclude that the answer must be no.

Section 220 provides stockholders with a "powerful right." By properly asserting that right under section 220, stockholders are able to obtain information that can be used in a variety of contexts. Stockholders may use information about corporate mismanagement, waste or wrongdoing in several ways. For example, they may: institute derivative litigation; "seek an audience with the board [of directors] to discuss proposed reform or, failing in that, they may prepare a stockholder resolution for the next annual meeting, or mount a proxy fight to elect new directors."

More than a decade ago, we noted that "surprisingly, little use has been made of section 220 as an information-gathering tool in the derivative [suit] context." Today, however, stockholders who have concerns about corporate governance are increasingly making a broad array of section 220 demands. The rise in books and records litigation is directly attributable to this Court's encouragement of stockholders, who can show a proper purpose, to use the "tools at hand" to obtain the necessary information before filing a derivative action. Section 220 is now recognized as "an important part of the corporate governance landscape."

In a section 220 action, a stockholder has the burden of proof to demonstrate a proper purpose by a preponderance of the evidence. A stockholder's desire to investigate wrongdoing or mismanagement is a "proper purpose." Such investigations are proper, because where the allegations of mismanagement prove meritorious, investigation furthers the interest of all stockholders and should increase stockholder return.

The evolution of Delaware's jurisprudence in section 220 actions reflects judicial efforts to maintain a proper balance between the rights of shareholders to obtain information based upon credible allegations of corporation mismanagement and the rights of directors to manage the business of the corporation without undue interference from stockholders.

A mere statement of a purpose to investigate possible general mismanagement, without more, will not entitle a shareholder to broad § 220 inspection relief. There must be *some evidence* of possible mismanagement as would warrant further investigation of the matter.

Investigations of meritorious allegations of possible mismanagement, waste or wrongdoing, benefit the corporation, but investigations that are "indiscriminate fishing expeditions" do not. "At some point, the costs of generating more information fall short of the benefits of having more information. At that point, compelling production of information would be wealth-reducing, and so shareholders would not want it produced." This Court has held that an inspection to investigate possible wrongdoing where there is no "credible basis," is a license for "fishing expeditions" and thus adverse to the interests of the corporation.

A stockholder is "not required to prove by a preponderance of the evidence that waste and [mis]management are occurring." Stockholders need only show, by a preponderance of the evidence, a credible basis from which the court can infer there is possible mismanagement that would warrant further investigation—a showing that "may ultimately fall well short of demonstrating that anything wrong occurred." That "threshold may be satisfied by a credible showing, through documents, logic, testimony or otherwise, that there are legitimate issues of wrongdoing."

Although the threshold for a stockholder in a section 220 proceeding is not insubstantial, the "credible basis" standard sets the lowest possible burden of proof. The only way to reduce the burden of proof further would be to eliminate any requirement that a stockholder show *some evidence* of possible wrongdoing. That would be tantamount to permitting inspection based on the "mere suspicion" standard that Seinfeld advances in this appeal. However, such a standard has been repeatedly rejected as a basis to justify the enterprise cost of an inspection.

Requiring stockholders to establish a "credible basis" for the Court of Chancery to infer possible wrongdoing by presenting "some evidence" has not impeded stockholder inspections. There are a myriad of cases where stockholders have successfully presented "some evidence" to establish a "credible basis" to infer possible mismanagement and thus received some narrowly tailored right of inspection.

We remain convinced that the rights of stockholders and the interests of the corporation in a section 220 proceeding are properly balanced by requiring a stockholder to show "some evidence of *possible* mismanagement as would warrant further investigation." The "credible basis" standard maximizes stockholder value by limiting the range of permitted stockholder inspections to those that might have merit.

The judgment of the Court of Chancery is affirmed.

NOTES

1. There seems to be a Catch-22 aspect to the court's standard. A plaintiff must first show a "credible basis of some evidence of possible wrongdoing," but how can a plaintiff make the necessary investigation without first some

information from a section 220 production of information? One answer is that a public company provides an enormous volume of information to shareholders and the capital markets. Much of this disclosure is mandated and governed by federal securities law. Companies must provide standardized disclosures of financial statements (Forms 10-K and 10-Q), annual and special proxy statement to shareholders, and current events (Form 8-K). The markets also produce and report enormous amount of information.

2. What is a "proper purpose"? The following is a nonexclusive list of purposes that Delaware courts have found to be proper.

> A stockholder states a "proper purpose" when he seeks to investigate allegedly improper transactions or mismanagement; to clarify an unexplained discrepancy in the corporation's financial statements regarding assets; to investigate the possibility of an improper transfer of assets out of the corporation; to ascertain the value of his stock; to aid litigation he has instituted and to contact other stockholders regarding litigation and invite their association with him in the case; "to inform fellow shareholders of one's view concerning the wisdom or fairness, from the point of view of the shareholders, of a proposed recapitalization and to encourage fellow shareholders to seek appraisal"; "to discuss corporate finances and management's inadequacies, and then, depending on the responses, determine stockholder sentiment for either a change in management or a sale pursuant to a tender offer"; to inquire into the independence, good faith, and due care of a special committee formed to consider a demand to institute derivative litigation; to communicate with other stockholders regarding a tender offer; to communicate with other shareholders in order to effectuate changes in management policies; to investigate the stockholder's possible entitlement to oversubscription privileges in connection with a rights offering; to determine an individual's suitability to serve as a director; to obtain names and addresses of stockholders for a contemplated proxy solicitation; or to obtain particularized facts needed to adequately allege demand futility after the corporation had admitted engaging in backdating stock options.

City of Westland Police & Fire Retirement Sys. v. Axcelis Techns., Inc., 1 A.3d 281, 289 n.30 (Del. 2010).

B. DIRECT AND DERIVATIVE SUITS

A shareholder may sue to enforce a right that belongs to her in a direct action and a right that belongs to the corporation in a derivative action. The difference between a direct and derivative action is consequential. A direct action is one that belongs to the shareholder. She is entitled to any recovery or remedy, and ordinary litigation procedure applies in advancing the litigation. On the other hand, in a derivative action, any recovery by a plaintiff shareholder goes to the corporation since the corporation is the injured party. To advance a derivative suit, a shareholder must satisfy a number of procedural hurdles—specifically, a demand on the board or a showing of demand futility.

The case below discusses the legal standard to determine whether an action is direct or derivative. In reading this case, consider these questions: (1) What kinds of claims are derivative? (2) What are direct?

TOOLEY V. DONALDSON, LUFKIN & JENRETTE, INC.

845 A.2d 1031 (Del. 2004)

VEASEY, CHIEF JUSTICE:

Patrick Tooley and Kevin Lewis are former minority stockholders of Donaldson, Lufkin & Jenrette, Inc. (DLJ), a Delaware corporation engaged in investment banking. DLJ was acquired by Credit Suisse Group. Before that acquisition, AXA Financial, Inc., which owned 71% of DLJ stock, controlled DLJ. Pursuant to a stockholder agreement between AXA and Credit Suisse, AXA agreed to exchange with Credit Suisse its DLJ stockholdings for a mix of stock and cash. The consideration received by AXA consisted primarily of stock. Cash made up one-third of the purchase price. Credit Suisse intended to acquire the remaining minority interests of publicly-held DLJ stock through a cash tender offer, followed by a merger of DLJ into a Credit Suisse subsidiary.

The tender offer price was set at $90 per share in cash. The tender offer was to expire 20 days after commencement. The merger agreement, however, authorized extensions. DLJ and Credit Suisse could agree to postpone acceptance by Credit Suisse of DLJ stock tendered by the minority stockholders.

By agreement between DLJ and Credit Suisse, [Credit Suisse] postponed the merger.

Plaintiffs challenge the extension that resulted in a 22-day delay. They contend that this delay harmed minority stockholders while improperly benefitting AXA. They claim damages representing the time-value of money lost through the delay.

[The Court of Chancery ruled that "because this delay affected all DLJ shareholders equally, plaintiffs' injury was not a special injury, and this action is, thus, a derivative action." The court dismissed the complaint because the plaintiffs lost standing to file a derivative suit when they tendered their shares and thus did not continuously hold their shares.]

The concept of "special injury" that appears in some Supreme Court and Court of Chancery cases is not helpful to a proper analytical distinction between direct and derivative actions. We now disapprove the use of the concept of "special injury" as a tool in that analysis.

The analysis must be based solely on the questions: [1] Who suffered the alleged harm—the corporation or the suing stockholder individually—and [2] who would receive the benefit of the recovery or other remedy?

In the context of a claim for breach of fiduciary duty, the Chancellor articulated the inquiry as follows: "Looking at the body of the complaint and considering the nature of the wrong alleged and the relief requested, has the plaintiff demonstrated that he or she can prevail without showing an injury to the corporation?" We believe that this approach is helpful in analyzing the first prong of the analysis: what person or entity has suffered the alleged harm? The second prong of the analysis should logically follow.

The derivative suit has been generally described as "one of the most interesting and ingenious of accountability mechanisms for large formal organizations." It enables a stockholder to bring suit on behalf of the corporation for harm done to the corporation. Because a derivative suit is being brought on behalf of the corporation, the recovery, if any, must go to the corporation. A stockholder who is directly injured, however, does retain the right to bring an individual action for injuries affecting his or her legal rights as a stockholder. Such a claim is distinct from an injury caused to the corporation alone. In such individual suits, the recovery or other relief flows directly to the stockholders, not to the corporation.

Determining whether an action is derivative or direct is sometimes difficult and has many legal consequences, some of which may have an expensive impact on the parties to the action. For example, if an action is derivative, the plaintiffs are then required to comply with the requirements of Court of Chancery Rule 23.1, that the stockholder: (a) retain ownership of the shares throughout the litigation; (b) make pre-suit demand on the board; and (c) obtain court approval of any settlement. Further, the recovery, if any, flows only to the corporation. The decision whether a suit is direct or derivative may be outcome-determinative. Therefore, it is necessary that a standard to distinguish such actions be clear, simple and consistently articulated and applied by our courts.

A court should look to the nature of the wrong and to whom the relief should go. The stockholder's claimed direct injury must be independent of any alleged injury to the corporation. The stockholder must demonstrate that the duty breached was owed to the stockholder and that he or she can prevail without showing an injury to the corporation.

In this case it cannot be concluded that the complaint alleges a derivative claim. There is no derivative claim asserting injury to the corporate entity. No relief would go the corporation. There is no basis to hold that the complaint states a derivative claim.

NOTES

1. The quintessential derivative suits are actions alleging mismanagement, typically grounded in a claim for breach of the duty of care and the duty of loyalty including claims for self-dealing, entrenchment, and bad faith. A direct claim arises when the "structural relationship" between the firm and owners is harmed by the actions of managers.

> The DGCL establishes a structural relationship between the corporation and its officers, directors, and shareholders. Although the DGCL empowers corporate directors and officers to act for the corporation, the DGCL also imposes certain restraints on the use of this authority. If a corporate officer acts in a manner that the DGCL prohibits, then the officer has violated this structural relationship by disregarding the specific restraints placed on him or her by the shareholders. It is consequently the rights of the shareholders, not those of the corporation, that are injured by the encroachment. Thus, any shareholder who was harmed by the violation of the structural relationship established between the corporation and the shareholder is harmed directly and has an individual cause of action.

Grayson v. Imagination Station, Inc., 2010 WL 3221951, at *5 (Del. Ch. 2010). Examples of direct claims include a failure to enforce a shareholder's voting agreement, discrimination against particular shareholders, unlawful denial of dividends, denial of preferred shareholder's contract-based rights, interference with shareholder voting rights, challenges to a merger on the ground of price or process, and abdication of a board's duties.

C. PLAINTIFF STANDING IN DERIVATIVE ACTIONS

A shareholder's equitable standing to bring a derivative action on behalf of the corporation exists "to prevent a complete failure of justice on behalf of the corporation." Schoon v. Smith, 953 A.2d 196, 208 (Del. 2008). Shareholder standing may be necessary because in certain situations directors and officers are not inclined to sue themselves or pursue claims based on allegations of their defective action and wrongful conduct.

A plaintiff must have standing to bring a derivative action. She must have been a shareholder at the time of the transaction that is the subject of the complaint or her shares devolved upon her by operation of law. DGCL § 327; Delaware Court of Chancery Rule 23.1(a). She must continuously own the stock throughout the litigation. Lewis v. Anderson, 477 A.2d 1040, 1046 (Del. 1984). This requirement precludes a person from purchasing shares after-the-fact to obtain standing. The standing rule assures that the plaintiff's economic interest is aligned with the interest of the corporation for whom the plaintiff pursues the action.

A plaintiff cannot receive any compensation or share in an award, except that she may be entitled to recoupment of fees and costs as approved by the court and reasonable out-of-pocket expenses paid by the plaintiff's attorneys. Delaware Court of Chancery Rule 23.1(b). A plaintiff cannot share in the award because the corporation is the injured party.

The case below discusses the legal standard to determine whether a shareholder has standing to bring a derivative suit. In reading this case, consider these questions: (1) Who is the real party of interest in a derivative suit? (2) What is the benefit and cost of a private attorney general model of shareholder litigation?

IN RE FUQUA INDUSTRIES, INC. SHAREHOLDER LITIGATION

752 A.2d 126 (Del. Ch. 1999)

CHANDLER, CHANCELLOR.

In the eighth year of this protracted derivative litigation, defendants deposed the two derivative plaintiffs in whose names this litigation is prosecuted, Virginia Abrams and Alan Freberg. Defendants determined that Abrams and Freberg were unfamiliar with many of the facts and allegations involved in this lawsuit. Defendants now point to plaintiffs' alleged unfamiliarity and ask this Court to disqualify Abrams and Freberg because they cannot adequately and fairly protect the interests of Fuqua Industries, Inc. and its shareholders as mandated by Rule 23.1. The question is whether I should disqualify a derivative plaintiff who is unfamiliar with the basic facts of his or her lawsuit and who exercises little, if any, control over the conduct of such suit?

Defendants predicate their entire claim on plaintiffs' alleged ignorance of the lawsuit's facts. I deny defendants' motions.

Mrs. Abrams has held Fuqua shares for over thirty years. The quantity of her holdings has ranged from as much as 12,008 Fuqua shares to the current level of 8000 shares.

During the long pendency of this litigation Mrs. Abrams fell ill. As she concedes, her memory and faculties have suffered as a result. In a 1998 deposition, it was evident that Mrs. Abrams lacked a meaningful grasp of the facts and allegations of the case prosecuted in her name. While at times she appeared able to provide a general understanding of her claim, she was unable to articulate the understanding with any particularity and she was obviously confused about basic facts regarding her lawsuit.

Freberg's deposition testimony evidences that his knowledge of the case is at best elliptical. Defendants argue that before his "cram" session immediately before the deposition, Freberg knew absolutely nothing about this matter and had not even been privy to the third amended complaint. Defendants also point out (with much scorn) Freberg's general ignorance of the six or seven other lawsuits in which he was, or still is, the named representative plaintiff. The subtext of defendants' motion is that Freberg has no knowledge of this case because he has no real economic interest at stake. In defendants' view, Freberg is a puppet for his fee-hungry lawyers.

The allegation that attorneys bring actions through puppet plaintiffs while the real parties in interest are the attorneys themselves in search of fees is an oft-heard complaint from defendants in derivative suits. Sometimes, no doubt, the allegation rings true.

By the same token, however, the mere fact that lawyers pursue their own economic interest in bringing derivative litigation cannot be held as grounds to disqualify a derivative plaintiff. To do so is to impeach a cornerstone of sound corporate governance. Our legal system has privatized in part the enforcement mechanism for policing fiduciaries by allowing private attorneys to bring suits on behalf of nominal shareholder plaintiffs. In so doing, corporations are safeguarded from fiduciary breaches and shareholders thereby benefit. Through the use of cost and fee shifting mechanisms, private attorneys are economically incentivized to perform this service on behalf of shareholders.

A real possibility exists that the economic motives of attorneys may influence the remedy sought or the conduct of the litigation. This influence is inherent in private enforcement mechanisms and does not necessarily vitiate the substantial beneficial impact upon the conduct of fiduciaries.

Nonetheless, in some instances, the attorney in pursuit of his own economic interests may usurp the role of the plaintiff and exploit the judicial system entirely for his own private gain. Indeed, the Court in [other cases] dismissed derivative actions when defendants demonstrated that derivative plaintiffs were not even aware of the complaints filed in their name. Such extreme facts call for the court to exercise its discretion and to curb the agency costs inherent in private regulatory and enforcement mechanisms. These agency costs should not be borne by society, defendant corporations, directors or the courts.

[The court found that both plaintiffs, while lacking detailed knowledge of the case, did not have a disabling conflict with the corporation and had a basic understanding of the case.] I deny defendants' motions to disqualify Abrams and Freberg as representative plaintiffs in this action.

The case below discusses the issue of standing in a double derivative action. In reading this case, consider these questions: (1) What is a double derivative action? (2) What are the policies associated with giving a shareholder standing in a double derivative action?

LAMBRECHT V. O'NEAL

3 A.3d 277 (Del. 2010)

JACOBS, JUSTICE:

This is a proceeding, under Article IV, Section 11(8) of the Delaware Constitution,* on a question of law certified to, and accepted by us, from the U.S. District Court for the Southern District of New York ("Southern District"). The certified question arises out of two factually related actions. In those actions (the "double derivative actions"), claims are asserted double derivatively on behalf of Bank of America Corp. ("BofA") and its wholly owned subsidiary, Merrill Lynch & Co., Inc. Originally, the plaintiffs in those actions filed standard derivative actions on behalf of Merrill Lynch to recover losses Merrill Lynch suffered in transactions that occurred before BofA acquired Merrill Lynch in a stock-for-stock merger. After the merger, the complaints were amended to take the form of double derivative actions in which the plaintiffs seek that same relief. The issue posed by the certified question implicates Delaware's legal requirements for standing to sue double derivatively in these circumstances.

In the merger, Merrill Lynch became a wholly-owned subsidiary of BofA and the plaintiffs' Merrill Lynch shares were converted to shares of BofA. Shortly thereafter, the defendants moved to dismiss the then-pending Southern District derivative actions on the ground that the plaintiffs, who were no longer shareholders of Merrill Lynch by reason of the merger, had lost their standing to assert derivative claims on Merrill Lynch's behalf. The dismissal motions were grounded on the settled Delaware law precept that, to have standing to bring a derivative action, the plaintiff must be a shareholder of the corporation at the time of the acts complained of and must also remain a shareholder of that company throughout the litigation. The Southern District dismissed both actions, but "without prejudice to plaintiffs repleading their actions as so-called 'double derivative' actions, whereby they would seek to force the board of BofA, as 100% owner of the stock in BofA's Merrill Lynch subsidiary, [in turn] to force the Merrill board to bring the action that the plaintiffs had originally sought to have Merrill bring." Thereafter, one of the Southern District plaintiffs repled her claim to be double derivative, and the other filed a new lawsuit that took the form of a double derivative action.

The defendants again moved to dismiss for lack of standing. The defendants asserted that to have standing to sue double derivatively, the plaintiffs must be able to show: (a) that they were (and remain) shareholders of BofA both after the merger and also at the time of the pre-merger Merrill Lynch wrongdoing complained of, and (b) that BofA itself was a shareholder of Merrill Lynch at the time of that pre-merger conduct.

* Author's note: Article IV, § 11(8) of the Delaware Constitution grants the supreme court the jurisdiction to issue advisory opinions in response to certified questions from federal courts.

That new argument prompted the Southern District certifying to this Court the following question:

> Whether plaintiffs in a double derivative action, who were pre-merger shareholders in the acquired company and who are current shareholders, by virtue of a stock-for-stock merger, in the post-merger parent company, must also demonstrate that, at the time of the alleged wrongdoing at the acquired company, (a) they owned stock in the acquiring company, and (b) the acquiring company owned stock in the acquired company.

[We answer the question certified to us in the negative.]

The Southern District derivative actions against certain Merrill Lynch officers and directors rest primarily on alleged fiduciary misconduct that predated the merger. The plaintiffs claim that Merrill Lynch's senior management and directors breached their fiduciary duties by involving Merrill Lynch in underwriting collateralized debt obligations and by disregarding warnings about risks concerning its mortgage-related activities, thereby causing Merrill Lynch to lose billions of dollars. In addition, plaintiffs claim that on the eve of the merger, Merrill Lynch, with the assent of BofA, improperly paid bonuses totaling $3.6 billion to various Merrill Lynch employees.

Plaintiff Lambrecht was not a BofA shareholder at the time of the transactions complained of. She became a BofA shareholder only when her Merrill Lynch shares were converted to BofA shares in the merger. Plaintiff Loveman's Merrill Lynch shares were similarly converted, although it appears that Loveman also owned BofA shares before the merger. The record does not disclose, however, whether her ownership of BofA shares was contemporaneous with the alleged wrongdoing at Merrill Lynch. Therefore, it is assumed, for purposes of this Opinion, that Loveman's ownership was not contemporaneous.

The parties have assumed (as does this Court) that BofA was not a Merrill Lynch shareholder at the time of the conduct complained of in the double derivative actions.

Preliminary: The Legal Landscape

Any discussion of a double derivative action must be with reference to the baseline "standard" derivative action. To illustrate, in a standard derivative action, a shareholder brings a lawsuit asserting a claim belonging to a corporate entity in which the shareholder owns shares ("corporation A"). A double derivative action, in contrast, involves two entities: corporation A (the corporation whose claim is being asserted), and corporation B, which owns or controls corporation A.

By its nature a double derivative suit is one brought by a shareholder of a parent corporation to enforce a claim belonging to a subsidiary that is either wholly owned or majority controlled. Normally, such a claim is one that only the parent corporation, acting through its board of directors, is empowered to enforce. Cases may arise, however, where the parent corporation's board is shown to be incapable of making an impartial business judgment regarding whether to assert the subsidiary's claim. In those cases a shareholder of the parent will be permitted to enforce that claim on the parent corporation's behalf, that is, double derivatively.

Double derivative actions fall into two distinct categories. The first are lawsuits that are brought originally as double-derivative actions on behalf of a parent corporation that has a pre-existing, wholly owned subsidiary at the time of the alleged wrongful conduct at the subsidiary level. In this category, no intervening merger takes place. The second category involves cases, such as this, where the action is brought originally as a standard derivative action on behalf of a corporation that thereafter is acquired by another corporation in an intervening stock-for-stock merger.

In the first category—cases where the wholly-owned subsidiary pre-existed the alleged wrongdoing and where no intervening merger took place—corporation A is already a subsidiary of corporation B at the time of the alleged wrongdoing at corporation A. In those cases, only the parent corporation owns the subsidiary's stock at the time of the alleged wrongdoing, and the plaintiff owns stock only in the parent. Therefore, a Rule 23.1 demand could only be made—and a derivative action could only be brought—at the parent, not the subsidiary, level.[11]

The second category involves actions brought derivatively on behalf of a corporation that was originally a stand-alone entity but where, as a result of being acquired in a later stock-for-stock merger, (1) the acquired corporation became a wholly-owned subsidiary of the acquiring corporation and (2) the shareholders of the (pre-merger) entity became shareholders of the acquiring corporation. What materially differentiates the second category from the first is that in this second category, as a matter of law the merger operates to divest the original shareholder plaintiff of standing to maintain the standard derivative action brought originally on behalf of the acquired corporation. That result, in turn, creates issues relating to whether—and, if so, in what circumstances—the original stockholder plaintiff, as a newly incarnated shareholder of the acquirer-parent corporation can have standing to assert the (now wholly-owned) subsidiary's claim double-derivatively. That brings us to the second subject of this preliminary sketch of the current legal roadmap: standing.

[11] Ct. of Ch. R. 23.1(a) ("In a derivative action brought by one or more shareholders to enforce a right of a corporation the complaint shall allege that the plaintiff was a shareholder at the time of the transaction of which the plaintiff complains. The complaint shall also allege with particularity the efforts, if any, made by the plaintiff to obtain the action the plaintiff desires from the directors and the reasons for the plaintiff's failure to obtain the action or for not making the effort.").

The standing issue is a consequence of the doctrine articulated in *Lewis v. Anderson*, 477 A.2d 1040 (Del. 1984). There, a standard derivative action was brought in the Court of Chancery on behalf of Conoco Inc. (Old Conoco) charging its directors with breaches of fiduciary duty. Thereafter, and while that action was pending, E.I. duPont de Nemours, Inc. (DuPont) acquired Old Conoco in a stock-for-stock merger. As a result, Old Conoco disappeared and the surviving corporation—a wholly owned subsidiary of DuPont—was renamed Conoco, Inc. (New Conoco). After the merger, the defendants moved to dismiss the derivative action, arguing that the plaintiff had lost his standing to maintain it because as a matter of law the derivative claim became the property of New Conoco, which post-merger was the only party with standing to assert the claim. The Court of Chancery dismissed the action, and this Court affirmed. The reasoning which supports that outcome is critical to understanding how the standing issue arises in the double derivative context.

The *Anderson* court held that for a shareholder to have standing to maintain a derivative action, the plaintiff "must not only be a stockholder at the time of the alleged wrong and at the time of commencement of suit but must also maintain shareholder status throughout the litigation." These two imperatives are referred to as the "contemporaneous ownership" and the "continuous ownership" requirements. The contemporaneous ownership requirement is imposed by statute;[18] while the continuous ownership requirement is a creature of common law. *Anderson* holds that where the corporation on whose behalf a derivative action is pending is later acquired in a merger that deprives the derivative plaintiff of his shares, the derivative claim—originally belonging to the acquired corporation—is transferred to and becomes an asset of the acquiring corporation as a matter of statutory law. Because as a consequence the original derivative shareholder plaintiff can no longer satisfy the continuous ownership requirement, the plaintiff loses standing to maintain the derivative action. And, because the claim is now (post merger) the property of the acquiring corporation, that corporation is now the only party with standing to enforce the claim, either by substituting itself as the plaintiff or by authorizing the original plaintiff to continue prosecuting the suit on the acquiring company's behalf.

That rationale generates the question presented here, which may be stated thusly: where a shareholder has lost standing to maintain a standard derivative action by reason of an acquisition of the corporation in a stock-for-stock merger, may that shareholder, in his new capacity as a shareholder of the acquiring corporation, assert the claim double derivatively and, if so, what requirements must the plaintiff satisfy? That

[18] 8 *Del. C.* § 327 provides: "In any derivative suit instituted by a stockholder of a corporation, it shall be averred in the complaint that the plaintiff was a stockholder of the corporation at the time of the transaction of which such stockholder complains or that such stockholder's stock thereafter devolved upon such stockholder by operation of law."

issue did not arise in *Lewis v. Anderson* because the plaintiff there did not sue double derivatively, but the issue did arise in *Rales v. Blasband,* 634 A.2d 927 (Del. 1993), which involved facts similar (although not identical) to those presented here.

[In *Rales*] the plaintiff brought a derivative action on behalf of a Delaware parent corporation that had previously acquired a subsidiary in a stock-for-stock merger. The action sought to remedy alleged pre-merger misconduct of the subsidiary's board. The defendants moved to dismiss on the basis that the plaintiffs had not adequately pled that demand on the parent corporation's board was excused.

In *Rales* we held that the traditional *Aronson v. Lewis,* 473 A.2d 805 (Del. 1984), demand excusal test would not be employed in considering whether a demand on the parent board was required in a double derivative action. Rather, a different test (the "*Rales* test") would apply, which is whether the particularized factual allegations of the complaint create a reasonable doubt that the parent's board of directors could properly have exercised its independent and disinterested business judgment in responding to a demand. This Court further held that in a double derivative action the *Rales* test would apply as of the time the complaint was filed, as distinguished from the time of the alleged wrongdoing.

The foregoing legal background shows that Delaware case law clearly endorses the double derivative action as a post-merger remedy. It also shows that to date this Court has determined some, but not all, of the procedural requirements that must be satisfied for a shareholder to proceed double derivatively.

The Legal Issue Analyzed

The defendants' new argument in the Southern District action generates the issue presented: whether, have standing to assert Merrill Lynch's pre-merger claims double derivatively, the plaintiffs must demonstrate that at the time of the alleged wrongdoing at Merrill Lynch, (1) they owned stock in BofA and (2) BofA owned stock in Merrill Lynch.

The defendants' support for their position [is based on] a conceptual argument. The defendants' conceptual argument is premised on a model of a double derivative action as being two separate derivative lawsuits, one stacked on top of the other. As defendants describe it:

> A double derivative action could be viewed as two lawsuits in one: (1) a derivative action brought by the stockholder of the parent corporation through which the parent-stockholder gains authority over the parent corporation's litigation rights from the parent's board of directors; and (2) a second derivative action on behalf of the parent corporation as stockholder of the subsidiary in which the parent corporation, qua stockholder and acting through the

stockholder-plaintiff, takes control of the subsidiary's litigation rights from the subsidiary's board of directors.

We conclude that the defendants' model is conceptually flawed. Accordingly, the certified question must be answered in the negative.

First, as [the Southern District observed], "such requirements would render double derivative lawsuits virtually impossible to bring except in bizarrely happenstance circumstances." Yet, our precedents not only validate but also encourage the bringing of double derivative actions in cases where standing to maintain a standard derivative action is extinguished as a result of an intervening merger. This Court should not undermine its own precedents by imposing procedural requirements that effectively would defeat that remedy.

Second, the fact that requirement (2) finds no support in Delaware law should come as no surprise, because any such requirement would run afoul of *Lewis v. Anderson* and its progeny. Requirement (2)—that BofA must have owned Merrill Lynch stock at the time of the pre-merger wrongdoing—incorrectly presupposes that to be legally capable of enforcing Merrill Lynch's pre-merger claim, BofA must proceed *derivatively* against the persons who were Merrill Lynch directors at the time of the alleged wrongdoing. That assumption ignores the legal precept, confirmed in *Lewis v. Anderson,* that as a result of the merger, Merrill Lynch's claim becomes the property of BofA as a matter of statutory law. As the sole owner of Merrill Lynch, BofA is not required to proceed derivatively; it may enforce that claim by the direct exercise of its 100 percent control.

To illustrate why this must be the correct result, suppose that the merger is structured as a two party transaction in which Merrill Lynch disappears and the surviving corporation is BofA. Because Merrill Lynch would no longer exist, BofA could not—and would not be required to—sue derivatively on Merrill Lynch's behalf. As sole owner of the (former) Merrill Lynch claim, BofA could sue directly and in its own name. BofA would not be required to own any Merrill Lynch shares before the merger occurred.

No different result should obtain where, as here, the merger is structured as a three party transaction with Merrill Lynch ending up as BofA's wholly owned subsidiary. Because BofA owns 100 percent of the shares of its (post-merger) Merrill Lynch subsidiary, there is no basis in law or logic to treat BofA as if it were a minority shareholder of Merrill Lynch and require it to sue derivatively to enforce Merrill Lynch's pre-merger claim. BofA's sole ownership, alone and without more, empowers and entitles BofA, acting through its own board of directors or authorized officers, to use its direct control to cause its wholly owned subsidiary, Merrill Lynch, to do what is necessary to enforce Merrill Lynch's pre-merger claim. To accomplish that, the only Merrill Lynch shares BofA would have to own would be those it acquired as a result of the merger.

Third, requirement (1) of the defendants' double derivative model—that the original derivative plaintiffs must have owned BofA shares at the time of the alleged wrongdoing at Merrill Lynch—is also fatally flawed. BofA is not required to have been a shareholder of Merrill Lynch at the time of the alleged wrongdoing to enforce Merrill Lynch's pre-merger claim. In a double derivative action the plaintiffs stand in the shoes of BofA; that is, they are enforcing BofA's *post-merger* right, as 100 percent owner, to prosecute Merrill Lynch's *pre-merger* claim. Just as BofA is not required to have owned Merrill Lynch shares at the time of the alleged wrongdoing, neither are the plaintiffs required to have owned BofA shares at that point in time. It suffices that the plaintiffs own shares of BofA at the time they seek to proceed double derivatively on its behalf. For the plaintiffs in this specific case, that requirement is easily satisfied, because they acquired their BofA shares in the merger, and their double derivative claim is based on post-merger conduct by the BofA board, *viz.,* its failure to prosecute Merrill Lynch's pre-merger claim, which BofA now (indirectly) owns.

Fourth, the preceding analysis answers the defendants' policy argument that allowing the plaintiffs' post-merger double derivative action to proceed would disrespect the corporate separateness of BofA and Merrill Lynch. This argument lacks merit, because it rests upon an unstated—and incorrect—premise, namely, that the post-merger double derivative action must be viewed as a *de facto* continuation of the pre-merger original derivative action, only with a different label.

If that premise were correct, then the defendants' position might have merit, because allowing the original derivative action to proceed would undo the plaintiffs' loss-of-standing recognized by *Lewis v. Anderson,* and arguably would constitute, *de facto,* a piercing of BofA's corporate veil. The defendants' argument is flawed, however. A post-merger double derivative action is not a *de facto* continuation of the pre-merger derivative action. It is a new, distinct action in which standing to sue double derivatively rests on a different temporal and factual basis—namely, the failure of the BofA board, post-merger, to enforce the premerger claim of its wholly-owned subsidiary. In this quite different structure, the policies favoring both the preservation of the corporate separateness of the parent and subsidiary and the prevention of abusive derivative suits are fully respected. That is because the double derivative suit cannot go forward except in the unusual case where the parent company board is shown to be incapable of deciding impartially whether or not to enforce the claim that the parent company now (indirectly) owns.

D. DEMAND AND DEMAND FUTILITY IN DERIVATIVE ACTIONS

In a direct action, a shareholder does not need to make a demand on the board of directors because the action belongs to her. She sues and the success of the action depends on the usual procedures for disposition of a civil action, *viz.*, the procedural procession of motion to dismiss, discovery, summary judgment, trial, and post-judgment motions.

A derivative action is procedurally different, and its procedures are much more intricate. It is a suit that belongs to the corporation, but the corporation cannot speak for itself. The cause of action is a litigation asset, and the disposition of any business asset is typically a board function and thus a managerial prerogative. The board should ordinarily decide if and how to proceed with a legal claim that belongs to the corporation. A shareholder must ordinarily make a demand on the board.

There is a countervailing consideration. A demand on the board would be infeasible in some circumstances. Suppose the essence of the complaint is that the board breached its fiduciary duty to the corporation and its shareholders. The board may be disinclined to investigate its prior actions that are the subject of the complaint or to sue its fellow directors.

> Equity came to the relief of the stockholder, who had no standing to bring civil action at law against faithless directors and managers. Equity, however, allowed him to step into the corporation's shoes and to seek in its right the restitution he could not demand in his own. It required him first to demand that the corporation vindicate its own rights but when, as was usual, those who perpetrated the wrongs also were able to obstruct any remedy, equity would hear and adjudge the corporation's cause through its stockholder with the corporation as a defendant, albeit a rather nominal one. This remedy born of stockholder helplessness was long the chief regulator of corporate management and has afforded no small incentive to avoid at least grosser forms of betrayal of stockholders' interests. It is argued, and not without reason, that without it there would be little practical check on such abuses.

Cohen v. Beneficial Indus. Loan Corp., 337 U.S. 541, 548 (1949).

Pragmatically, a shareholder and her attorney will not want to make a demand on the board. A demand is tantamount to relinquishing control of the case. The board's disposition of the matter would be subject to the protection of the business judgment rule. A shareholder and her attorney will want to maintain control of the action by pleading demand futility. Delaware law recognizes a rule of demand futility under which a shareholder may pursue a derivative suit without making a demand on the board. The rule of demand futility is really about an important practical question: Who should control the litigation?

There is yet one more pragmatic policy consideration. A corporation could have potentially millions of shareholders, each of whom may have idiosyncratic beliefs about whether it has been wrongfully injured. Should every shareholder have unconditional standing to sue on behalf of the corporation so that she has easy, unvetted access to the litigation process?

Delaware Rules of the Court of Chancery: Rule 23.1 Derivative Actions by Shareholders

(a) In a derivative action brought by one or more shareholders or members to enforce a right of a corporation or of an unincorporated association, the corporation or association having failed to enforce a right which may properly be asserted by it, the complaint shall allege that the plaintiff was a shareholder or member at the time of the transaction of which the plaintiff complains or that the plaintiff's share or membership thereafter devolved on the plaintiff by operation of law. The complaint shall also allege with particularity the efforts, if any, made by the plaintiff to obtain the action the plaintiff desires from the directors or comparable authority and the reasons for the plaintiff's failure to obtain the action or for not making the effort.

Federal Rules of Civil Procedure: Rule 23.1 Derivative Actions

(b) *Pleading Requirements.* The complaint must be verified and must:

(1) allege that the plaintiff was a shareholder or member at the time of the transaction complained of, or that the plaintiff's share or membership later devolved on it by operation of law;

(2) allege that the action is not a collusive one to confer jurisdiction that the court would otherwise lack; and

(3) state with particularity: (A) any effort by the plaintiff to obtain the desired action from the directors or comparable authority and, if necessary, from the shareholders or members; and (B) the reasons for not obtaining the action or not making the effort.

The cases below discusses the legal standard to determine whether demand would be futile. In reading these cases, consider these questions: (1) What are the competing policies underlying the demand futility doctrine? (2) What does it mean when the court says that demand futility is shown when there is a reasonable doubt that "the challenged transaction was otherwise the product of a valid exercise of business judgment"? (3) How might information rights under DGCL § 220 relate to the demand futility doctrine? (4) What is the relationship between the demand requirement, demand futility, and the business judgment rule?

ARONSON V. LEWIS

473 A.2d 805 (Del. 1984)

MOORE, JUSTICE:

When is a stockholder's demand upon a board of directors, to redress an alleged wrong to the corporation, excused as futile prior to the filing of a derivative suit?

The issues of demand futility rest upon the allegations of the complaint. The plaintiff, Harry Lewis, is a stockholder of Meyers Parking System, Inc. The defendants are Meyers and its ten directors, some of whom are also company officers.

This suit challenges certain transactions between Meyers and one of its directors, Leo Fink, who owns 47% of its outstanding stock. Plaintiff claims that these transactions were approved only because Fink personally selected each director and officer of Meyers.

Fink had an employment agreement with Prudential which provided that upon retirement he was to become a consultant to that company for ten years. This provision became operable when Fink retired in April 1980. Thereafter, Meyers agreed with Prudential to share Fink's consulting services and reimburse Prudential for 25% of the fees paid Fink. Under this arrangement Meyers paid Prudential $48,332 in 1980 and $45,832 in 1981.

The defendants approved an employment agreement between Meyers and Fink for a five year term with provision for automatic renewal each year thereafter, indefinitely. Meyers agreed to pay Fink $150,000 per year, plus a bonus of 5% of its pre-tax profits over $2,400,000. Fink could terminate the contract at any time, but Meyers could do so only upon six months' notice. At termination, Fink was to become a consultant to Meyers and be paid $150,000 per year for the first three years, $125,000 for the next three years, and $100,000 thereafter for life. Death benefits were also included. Fink was 75 years old when his employment agreement with Meyers was approved by the directors.

The complaint charges that these transactions had "no valid business purpose," and were a "waste of corporate assets" because the amounts to be paid are "grossly excessive," that Fink performs "no or little services," and because of his "advanced age" cannot be "expected to perform any such services." It is alleged that the loans to Fink were in reality "additional compensation" without any "consideration" or "benefit" to Meyers.

The complaint alleged that no demand had been made on the Meyers board because:

> 13. Such attempt would be futile for the following reasons:
>
> (a) All of the directors in office are named as defendants herein and they have participated in, expressly approved

and/or acquiesced in, and are personally liable for, the wrongs complained of herein.

(b) Defendant Fink, having selected each director, controls and dominates every member of the Board and every officer of Meyers.

(c) Institution of this action by present directors would require the defendant-directors to sue themselves, thereby placing the conduct of this action in hostile hands and preventing its effective prosecution.

Defendants moved to dismiss for plaintiff's failure to make demand on the Meyers board prior to suit, or to allege with factual particularity why demand is excused. [The chancery court ruled that demand would have been futile under the facts as pled.]

A cardinal precept of the General Corporation Law of the State of Delaware is that directors, rather than shareholders, manage the business and affairs of the corporation. Section 141(a) states in pertinent part: "The *business and affairs* of a corporation organized under this chapter *shall be managed by or under the direction* of a board of directors except as may be otherwise provided in this chapter or in its certificate of incorporation." The existence and exercise of this power carries with it certain fundamental fiduciary obligations to the corporation and its shareholders. Moreover, a stockholder is not powerless to challenge director action which results in harm to the corporation. The machinery of corporate democracy and the derivative suit are potent tools to redress the conduct of a torpid or unfaithful management. The derivative action developed in equity to enable shareholders to sue in the corporation's name where those in control of the company refused to assert a claim belonging to it. The nature of the action is two-fold. First, it is the equivalent of a suit by the shareholders to compel the corporation to sue. Second, it is a suit by the corporation, asserted by the shareholders on its behalf, against those liable to it.

By its very nature the derivative action impinges on the managerial freedom of directors. Hence, the demand requirement of Chancery Rule 23.1 exists at the threshold, first to insure that a stockholder exhausts his intracorporate remedies, and then to provide a safeguard against strike suits. Thus, by promoting this form of alternate dispute resolution, rather than immediate recourse to litigation, the demand requirement is a recognition of the fundamental precept that directors manage the business and affairs of corporations.

In our view the entire question of demand futility is inextricably bound to issues of business judgment and the standards of that doctrine's applicability. The business judgment rule is an acknowledgment of the managerial prerogatives of Delaware directors under Section 141(a). It is a presumption that in making a business decision the directors of a corporation acted on an informed basis, in good faith and in the honest belief that the action taken was in the best interests of the company. Absent an abuse of discretion, that judgment will be respected by the courts. The burden is on the party challenging the decision to establish facts rebutting the presumption.

The business judgment rule is of paramount significance in the context of a derivative action. It comes into play in several ways—in addressing a demand, in the determination of demand futility, in efforts by independent disinterested directors to dismiss the action as inimical to the corporation's best interests, and generally, as a defense to the merits of the suit. However, in each of these circumstances there are certain common principles governing the application and operation of the rule.

First, its protections can only be claimed by disinterested directors whose conduct otherwise meets the tests of business judgment. From the standpoint of interest, this means that directors can neither appear on both sides of a transaction nor expect to derive any personal financial benefit from it in the sense of self-dealing, as opposed to a benefit which devolves upon the corporation or all stockholders generally. Thus, if such director interest is present, and the transaction is not approved by a majority consisting of the disinterested directors, then the business judgment rule has no application whatever in determining demand futility.

Second, to invoke the rule's protection directors have a duty to inform themselves, prior to making a business decision, of all material information reasonably available to them. Having become so informed, they must then act with requisite care in the discharge of their duties. While the Delaware cases use a variety of terms to describe the applicable standard of care, our analysis satisfies us that under the business judgment rule director liability is predicated upon concepts of gross negligence.

However, it should be noted that the business judgment rule operates only in the context of director action. Technically speaking, it has no role where directors have either abdicated their functions, or absent a conscious decision, failed to act. But it also follows that under applicable principles, a conscious decision to refrain from acting may nonetheless be a valid exercise of business judgment and enjoy the protections of the rule.

Our view is that in determining demand futility the Court of Chancery in the proper exercise of its discretion must decide whether, under the particularized facts alleged, a reasonable doubt is created that: (1) the directors are disinterested [or] independent [or]* (2) the challenged

---

* Author's note: This sentence is the key rule on demand futility. The original opinion stated the test in the conjunctive "and." However, the Delaware Supreme Court later clarified (corrected) that the test should be stated in the disjunctive "or." *See* Levine v. Smith, 591 A.2d 194, 205 (Del. 1991) ("The premise of a shareholder claim of futility of demand is that a majority of the board of directors *either* has a financial interest in the challenged transaction *or* lacks independence or otherwise failed to exercise due care. On either showing, it may be inferred that the Board is *incapable* of exercising its power and authority to pursue the derivative claims directly."); Rales v.

transaction was otherwise the product of a valid exercise of business judgment. The Court of Chancery must make two inquiries, one into the independence and disinterestedness of the directors and the other into the substantive nature of the challenged transaction and the board's approval thereof. As to the latter inquiry the court does not assume that the transaction is a wrong to the corporation requiring corrective steps by the board. Rather, the alleged wrong is substantively reviewed against the factual background alleged in the complaint. As to the former inquiry, directorial independence and disinterestedness, the court reviews the factual allegations to decide whether they raise a reasonable doubt, as a threshold matter, that the protections of the business judgment rule are available to the board. Certainly, if this is an "interested" director transaction, such that the business judgment rule is inapplicable to the board majority approving the transaction, then the inquiry ceases. In that event futility of demand has been established by any objective or subjective standard. This includes situations involving self-dealing directors.

The mere threat of personal liability for approving a transaction, standing alone, is insufficient to challenge either the independence or disinterestedness of directors, although in rare cases a transaction may be so egregious on its face that board approval cannot meet the test of business judgment, and a substantial likelihood of director liability therefore exists. The entire review is factual in nature. The Court of Chancery in the exercise of its sound discretion must be satisfied that a plaintiff has alleged facts with particularity which, taken as true, support a reasonable doubt that the challenged transaction was the product of a valid exercise of business judgment. Only in that context is demand excused.

Plaintiff's claim that Fink dominates and controls the Meyers' board is based on: (1) Fink's 47% ownership of Meyers' outstanding stock, and (2) that he "personally selected" each Meyers director. Plaintiff also alleges that mere approval of the employment agreement illustrates Fink's domination and control of the board. In addition, plaintiff argued on appeal that 47% stock ownership, though less than a majority, constituted control given the large number of shares outstanding, 1,245,745.

Such contentions do not support any claim under Delaware law that these directors lack independence. "Stock ownership alone, at least when it amounts to less than a majority, is not sufficient proof of domination or control." Moreover, in the demand context even proof of majority ownership of a company does not strip the directors of the presumptions of independence, and that their acts have been taken in good faith and in the best interests of the corporation. There must be coupled with the allegation

Blasband, 634 A.2d 927, 933 (Del. 1993) ("Our decision in *Aronson* enunciated the test for determining a derivative plaintiff's compliance with this fundamental threshold obligation: "whether, under the particularized facts alleged, a reasonable doubt is created that: (1) the directors are disinterested and independent [or] (2) the challenged transaction was otherwise the product of a valid exercise of business judgment.") (bracketed "[or]" in original).

of control such facts as would demonstrate that through personal or other relationships the directors are beholden to the controlling person. To date the principal decisions dealing with the issue of control or domination arose only after a full trial on the merits. Thus, they are distinguishable in the demand context unless similar particularized facts are alleged to meet the test of Chancery Rule 23.1.

The requirement of director independence inheres in the conception and rationale of the business judgment rule. The presumption of propriety that flows from an exercise of business judgment is based in part on this unyielding precept. Independence means that a director's decision is based on the corporate merits of the subject before the board rather than extraneous considerations or influences. While directors may confer, debate, and resolve their differences through compromise, or by reasonable reliance upon the expertise of their colleagues and other qualified persons, the end result must be that each director has brought his or her own informed business judgment to bear with specificity upon the corporate merits of the issues without regard for or succumbing to influences which convert an otherwise valid business decision into a faithless act.

Thus, it is not enough to charge that a director was nominated by or elected at the behest of those controlling the outcome of a corporate election. That is the usual way a person becomes a corporate director. It is the care, attention and sense of individual responsibility to the performance of one's duties, not the method of election, that generally touches on independence.

We conclude that in the demand-futile context a plaintiff charging domination and control of one or more directors must allege particularized facts manifesting "a direction of corporate conduct in such a way as to comport with the wishes or interests of the corporation (or persons) doing the controlling." The shorthand shibboleth of "dominated and controlled directors" is insufficient. We stress that the plaintiff need only allege specific facts; he need not plead evidence.

Here, plaintiff has not alleged any facts sufficient to support a claim of control. The personal-selection-of-directors allegation stands alone, unsupported. At best it is a conclusion devoid of factual support. The causal link between Fink's control and approval of the employment agreement is alluded to, but nowhere specified. The director's approval, alone, does not establish control, even in the face of Fink's 47% stock ownership. The claim that Fink is unlikely to perform any services under the agreement, because of his age, and his conflicting consultant work with Prudential, adds nothing to the control claim. Therefore, we cannot conclude that the complaint factually particularizes any circumstances of control and domination to overcome the presumption of board independence, and thus render the demand futile.

Turning to the board's approval of the Meyers-Fink employment agreement, plaintiff's argument is simple: all of the Meyers directors are named defendants, because they approved the wasteful agreement; if plaintiff prevails on the merits all the directors will be jointly and severally liable; therefore, the directors' interest in avoiding personal liability automatically and absolutely disqualifies them from passing on a shareholder's demand.

Such allegations are conclusory at best. In Delaware mere directorial approval of a transaction, absent particularized facts supporting a breach of fiduciary duty claim, or otherwise establishing the lack of independence or disinterestedness of a majority of the directors, is insufficient to excuse demand. Here, plaintiff's suit is premised on the notion that the Meyers-Fink employment agreement was a waste of corporate assets. So, the argument goes, by approving such waste the directors now face potential personal liability, thereby rendering futile any demand on them to bring suit. Unfortunately, plaintiff's claim falls in its initial premise. The complaint does not allege particularized facts indicating that the agreement is a waste of corporate assets. Indeed, the complaint as now drafted may not even state a cause of action, given the directors' broad corporate power to fix the compensation of officers.

Plaintiff's final argument is the incantation that demand is excused because the directors otherwise would have to sue themselves, thereby placing the conduct of the litigation in hostile hands and preventing its effective prosecution. This bootstrap argument has been made to and dismissed by other courts. Its acceptance would effectively abrogate Rule 23.1 and weaken the managerial power of directors. Unless facts are alleged with particularity to overcome the presumptions of independence and a proper exercise of business judgment, in which case the directors could not be expected to sue themselves, a bare claim of this sort raises no legally cognizable issue under Delaware corporate law.

We conclude that the plaintiff has failed to allege facts with particularity indicating that the Meyers directors were tainted by interest, lacked independence, or took action contrary to Meyers' best interests in order to create a reasonable doubt as to the applicability of the business judgment rule. Only in the presence of such a reasonable doubt may a demand be deemed futile. We reverse the denial of the motion to dismiss.

NOTES

1. There are occasions when the *Aronson* test may not apply well. The test assumes that the board made the challenged action, and thus the complaint must show a lack of independence, disinterestedness, or proper exercise of business judgment. In *Rales v. Blasband*, 634 A.2d 927 (Del. 1993), the court identified some circumstance where a board may be considering a demand but did not make a decision that is being challenged in the derivative suit. "This

situation would arise in three principal scenarios: (1) where a business decision was made by the board of a company, but a majority of the directors making the decision have been replaced; (2) where the subject of the derivative suit is not a business decision of the board; and (3) where the decision being challenged was made by the board of a different corporation." *Id.* at 934. The court set forth the demand futility standard for these kinds of situations:

> It is appropriate in these situations to examine whether the board that would be addressing the demand can impartially consider its merits without being influenced by improper considerations. Thus, a court must determine whether or not the particularized factual allegations of a derivative stockholder complaint create a reasonable doubt that, as of the time the complaint is filed, the board of directors could have properly exercised its independent and disinterested business judgment in responding to a demand. If the derivative plaintiff satisfies this burden, then demand will be excused as futile.

The *Rales* standard encompasses the same core principle in *Aronson*: Is the board competent to pass proper judgment on the shareholder demand? A board would be incompetent to make such a decision if: (1) the board is not independent or disinterested; (2) it made a decision that would not receive the business judgment rule presumption; or (3) it is not capable of making a proper business judgment on the demand.

2. A court will not excuse demand simply because the plaintiff alleges that directors approved the challenged transaction or participated in the alleged wrongdoing. A plaintiff cannot evade demand futility by simply naming directors as defendants in the complaint. Otherwise, a plaintiff can accomplish a complete end-around Rule 23.1 by simply suing all directors irrespective of evidence supporting a "reasonable doubt" as to disinterestedness, independence, or valid exercise of business judgment." Mere allegations to support demand futility are not enough.

A derivative action presents a special procedural challenge. Unlike a direct action, a derivative action requires a shareholder either to show demand futility or to relinquish control of the action to the board. If demand is made, the board controls the process and ultimately determines the course of action, which may be a decision that pursuing the action is not in the best interest of the corporation. A board may decide, quite plausibly, that rather than pursue an action against an officer or a director and recoup certain losses, the best course of action is to fire the manager and avoid the negative publicity. If demand is made, the board's decision concerning it endowed with the protection of the business judgment rule. A shareholder's challenge would not be easy. From the perspective of a shareholder and her attorney, making a demand is undesirable.

The rule of demand futility enables a shareholder to bypass the board. At the outset of the litigation, a failure to show demand futility would be outcome determinative. If a plaintiff cannot aver with particularity the reasons why demand would be futile, a court will dismiss the derivative suit under Rule 23.1. Only when a plaintiff satisfies the *Aronson/Rales* standard can the shareholder proceed with the derivative action.

Delaware Demand Futility Flowchart

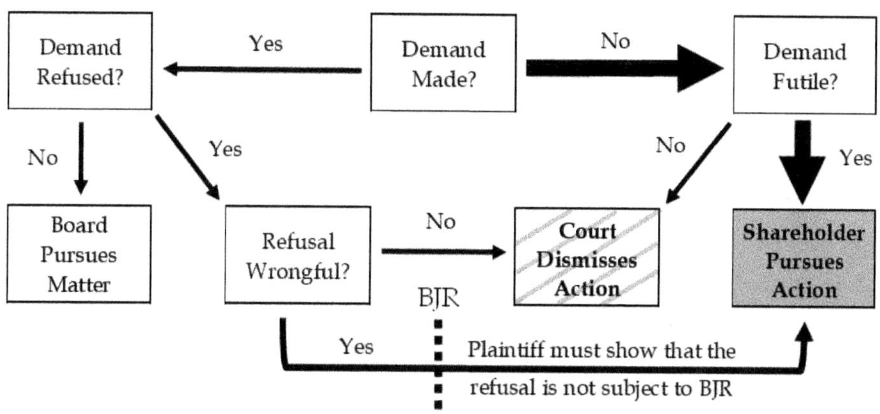

If the shareholder desires to control the suit, the most direct way is to plead demand futility. If a demand would not be futile and a plaintiff fails to make a demand, the court will dismiss the action. If a plaintiff makes a demand, the board controls the matter. It pursues the action. Strictly speaking, the action would no longer be a derivative suit, but instead an action by the corporation initiated by the board. A more likely possibility is that the board rejects the shareholder's demand. A board's refusal, decided informedly and in good faith, becomes a business decision endowed with the presumption of the business judgment rule. If the shareholder is not satisfied with the board's decision, he must challenge it as a wrongful refusal. *See* Zapata Corp. v. Maldonado, 430 A.2d 779, 784 (Del. 1981) ("A board decision to cause a derivative suit to be dismissed as detrimental to the company, after demand has been made and refused, will be respected unless it was wrongful. Absent a wrongful refusal, the stockholder in such a situation simply lacks legal managerial power."). The dissatisfied shareholder must show that any board decision (*e.g.*, a refusal, disposal, settlement, etc.) is not subject to the business judgment rule. A shareholder is better off if he can plead demand futility and thereby control the action.

Aronson and *Rales* establish the bases to plead demand futility: (1) the directors are not independent or disinterested; (2) the challenged action was not the product of a valid business judgment; or (3) the directors are not otherwise capable of making a proper business judgment.

1. NOT VALID EXERCISE OF BUSINESS JUDGMENT

Under *Aronson,* one way to plead demand futility is to plead particularized facts that create a reasonable doubt that the challenged transaction was the product of a valid exercise of business judgment. The business judgment rule is intricately tied to the doctrine of demand futility. The rule has both a substantive and procedural facet.

The case below discusses the nature of the business judgment rule. In reading this case, consider these questions: (1) How can a plaintiff rebut the presumption of the business judgment rule? (2) How does a rebuttal of the business judgment rule relate to the doctrine of demand futility? (3) What is the relationship between the business judgment rule and the entire fairness standard?

CEDE & CO. V. TECHNICOLOR, INC.

634 A.2d 345 (Del. 1993)

Our starting point is the fundamental principle of Delaware law that the business and affairs of a corporation are managed by or under the direction of its board. 8 *Del.C.* § 141(a). In exercising these powers, directors are charged with an unyielding fiduciary duty to protect the interests of the corporation and to act in the best interests of shareholders. Guth v. Loft, Inc., 5 A.2d 503, 510 (Del. 1939); Aronson v. Lewis, 473 A.2d 805, 811 (Del. 1984); Smith v. Van Gorkom, 488 A.2d 858, 872 (Del. 1985).

The business judgment rule is an extension of these basic principles. The rule operates to preclude a court from imposing itself unreasonably on the business and affairs of a corporation. *See* Unocal Corp. v. Mesa Petroleum Co., 493 A.2d 946, 954 (Del. 1985); Sinclair Oil Corp. v. Levien, 280 A.2d 717, 720 (Del. 1971). The rule, though formulated many years ago, was most recently restated by this Court as follows:

> The rule operates as both a procedural guide for litigants and a substantive rule of law. As a rule of evidence, it creates a "presumption that in making a business decision, the directors of a corporation acted on an informed basis [*i.e.*, with due care], in good faith and in the honest belief that the action taken was in the best interest of the company." *Aronson v. Lewis,* 473 A.2d 805, 812 (Del. 1984). The presumption initially attaches to a director-approved transaction within a board's conferred or apparent authority in the absence of any evidence of "fraud, bad faith, or self-dealing in the usual sense of personal profit or betterment."

The rule posits a powerful presumption in favor of actions taken by the directors in that a decision made by a loyal and informed board will not be overturned by the courts unless it cannot be "attributed to any rational business purpose." Sinclair Oil Corp., 280 A.2d at 720. Thus, a shareholder plaintiff challenging a board decision has the burden at the outset to rebut the rule's presumption. Aronson, 473 A.2d at 812; Van Gorkom, 488 A.2d at 872. To rebut the rule, a shareholder plaintiff assumes the burden of providing evidence that directors, in reaching their challenged decision, breached any one of the *triads* of their fiduciary duty—good faith, loyalty or due care. *See* Van Gorkom, 488 A.2d at 872; *Aronson,* 473 A.2d at 812. If a shareholder plaintiff fails to meet this evidentiary burden, the business judgment rule attaches to protect corporate officers and directors and the decisions they make, and our courts will not second-guess these business judgments. *See, e.g.,* Van Gorkom, 488 A.2d at 872; *see also* 8 *Del.C.* § 141(a). If the rule is rebutted, the burden shifts to the defendant directors, the proponents of the challenged transaction, to prove to the trier of fact the "entire fairness" of the transaction to the shareholder plaintiff. Weinberger v. UOP, Inc., 457 A.2d 701, 710 (Del. 1983).

Under the entire fairness standard of judicial review, the defendant directors must establish to the *court's* satisfaction that the transaction was the product of both fair dealing *and* fair price. *Id.* at 710. Further, in the review of a transaction involving a sale of a company, the directors have the burden of establishing that the price offered was the highest value reasonably available under the circumstances.

2. DISINTERESTEDNESS AND INDEPENDENCE OF DIRECTORS

Under *Aronson,* demand futility is satisfied if a shareholder pleads particularized facts that create a reasonable doubt the directors are disinterested or independent. The lack of these qualities would compromise the director's ability to exercise proper business judgment on the demand, in which case demand would be excused as futile. Disinterestedness and independence are separate concepts.

> Although interest and independence are two separate and distinct issues, these two attributes are sometimes confused by parties. Many plaintiffs allege facts which they assert establish that the defendant "lacked the disinterest and/or independence" necessary to consider the challenged transaction objectively. The plaintiff then asks the Court to select whichever type of disabling attribute is consistent with the facts alleged and that will support the plaintiff's claim. But it is not for the Court to divine the claims being made. A plaintiff must make clear to the Court the bases upon which his claims rest.
>
> A disabling "interest," as defined by Delaware common law, exists in two instances. The first is when (1) a director personally receives a benefit (or suffers a detriment), (2) as a result of, or from, the challenged transaction, (3) which is not generally shared

with (or suffered by) the other shareholders of his corporation, and (4) that benefit (or detriment) is of such subjective material significance to that particular director that it is reasonable to question whether that director objectively considered the advisability of the challenged transaction to the corporation and its shareholders. The second instance is when a director stands on both sides of the challenged transaction. *See* 8 *Del.C.* § 144. This latter situation frequently involves the first three elements listed above. As for the fourth element, whenever a director stands on both sides of the challenged transaction he is deemed interested and allegations of materiality have not been required.

"Independence" does not involve a question of whether the challenged director derives a benefit *from the transaction* that is not generally shared with the other shareholders. Rather, it involves an inquiry into whether the director's decision resulted from that director being *controlled* by another. A director can be controlled by another if in fact he is *dominated* by that other party, whether through close personal or familial relationship or through force of will. A director can also be controlled by another if the challenged director is *beholden* to the allegedly controlling entity. A director may be considered beholden to (and thus controlled by) another when the allegedly controlling entity has the unilateral power (whether direct or indirect through control over other decision makers), to decide whether the challenged director continues to receive a benefit, financial or otherwise, upon which the challenged director is so dependent or is of such subjective material importance to him that the threatened loss of that benefit might create a reason to question whether the controlled director is able to consider the corporate merits of the challenged transaction objectively.

Confusion over whether specific facts raise a question of interest or independence arises from the reality that similar factual circumstances may implicate *both* interest and independence, one but not the other, or neither. By way of example, consider the following: Director *A* is both a director and officer of company *X*. Company *X* is to be merged into company *Z*. Director *A*'s vote in favor of recommending shareholder approval of the merger is challenged by a plaintiff shareholder.

Scenario One. Assume that one of the terms of the merger agreement is that director *A* was to be an officer in surviving company *Z, and* that maintaining his position as a corporate officer in the surviving company was material to director *A*. That fact might, when considered in light of *all* of the facts alleged, lead the Court to conclude that director *A* had a disabling interest.

> Scenario Two. Assume that director *C* is both a director and the majority shareholder of company *X*. Director *C* had the power plausibly to threaten director *A*'s position as officer of corporation *X* should director *A* vote against the merger. Assume further that director *A*'s position as a corporate officer is material to director *A*. Those circumstances, when considered in light of *all* of the facts alleged, might lead the Court to question director *A*'s independence from director *C*, because it could reasonably be assumed that director *A* was controlled by director *C*, since director *A* was beholden to director *C* for his position as officer of the corporation. Confusion over whether to label this disability as a disqualifying "interest" or as a "lack of independence" may stem from the fact that, colloquially, director *A* was "interested" in keeping his job as a corporate officer. Scenario Two, however, raises only a question as to director *A*'s independence since there is nothing that suggests that director *A* would receive something *from the transaction* that might implicate a disabling interest.
>
> If a plaintiff's allegations combined all facts described in both Scenario One *and* Scenario Two, it might be reasonable to question *both* director *A*'s interest and independence. Conversely, if all the facts in both scenarios were alleged *except* for the materiality of Director *A*'s position as a corporate officer (perhaps because director *A* is a billionaire and his officer's position pays $20,000 per year and is not even of prestige value to him) then *neither* director *A*'s interest nor his independence would be reasonably questioned. The key issue is not simply whether a particular director receives a benefit from a challenged transaction not shared with the other shareholders, or solely whether another person or entity has the ability to take some benefit away from a particular director, but whether the possibility of gaining some benefit or the fear of losing a benefit is likely to be of such importance to that director that it is reasonable for the Court to question whether valid business judgment or selfish considerations animated that director's vote on the challenged transaction.

Orman v. Cullman, 794 A.2d 5, 25 n.50 (Del. Ch. 2002).

A director is interested "whenever divided loyalties are present, or a director either has received, or is entitled to receive, a personal benefit from the challenged transaction which is not equally shared by the stockholders." Pogostin v. Rice, 480 A.2d 619, 624 (Del. 1984). A plaintiff must show that the director's action resulted in some personal benefit. Such personal benefit can take many forms.

Example 1: Financial interest.—The most common way in which a director may be interested is when a director has a financial interest in the challenged transaction. Suppose director Darwin of Galapagos Inc. secures from the board a sale of assets to Beagle Corp., a company that Darwin owns, on favorable terms to Beagle. Darwin has a financial interest that conflicts with the interest of Galapagos and its shareholders.

Example 2: Personal benefit.—A director can have a personal benefit in the challenged transaction. Suppose director Darwin of Galapagos Inc. secures from the board an investment in Beagle Corp. in which Darwin's spouse is the founding entrepreneur, and the investment is favorable to Beagle.[1] Darwin has a conflict of interest.

Example 3: Entrenchment.—A board can pursue actions that entrenches the positions of directors. Suppose a board approves the issuance of special stock to all directors and officers that has super-voting rights when the company is facing a potential hostile bidder. Or suppose a board attempts to rig a shareholder vote to its advantage for the purpose of entrenching the positions of directors and officers.[2]

The cases below discuss the legal standard to determine whether a director is disinterested or independent. In reading these cases, consider these questions: (1) How should a court deal with the practical fact that directors are colleagues, may know each other well, and may in fact be friends? (2) When is a director's relationship to a defendant so substantial that he is said to be not independent? (3) What does it mean to say that a director is not disinterested?

---

1 *See* Bayer v. Beran, 49 N.Y.S.2d 2, 9 (Sup. Ct. 1944) ("Where a close relative of the chief executive officer, and one of its dominant directors, takes a position closely associated with a new and expensive field of activity, the motives of the directors are likely to be questioned. The board would be placed in a position where selfish, personal interests might be in conflict with the duty it owed to the corporation."); Albright v. Jefferson County National Bank, 53 N.E.2d 753, 756 (N.Y. 1944) ("The rule is inflexible that a trustee may not deal with himself or put himself in a position where his interest might be in conflict with his duty. Included within its scope is every situation in which a trustee chooses to deal with another in such close relation with the trustee that possible advantage to such other person might influence, consciously or unconsciously, the judgment of the trustee who is in duty bound to consider only the interest of his cestui que trust.").

2 *See* Schnell v. Chris-Craft Industries, Inc., 285 A.2d 437, 439 (Del. 1971) ("Management has attempted to utilize the corporate machinery and the Delaware Law for the purpose of perpetuating itself in office; and, to that end, for the purpose of obstructing the legitimate efforts of dissident stockholders in the exercise of their rights to undertake a proxy contest against management. These are inequitable purposes, contrary to established principles of corporate democracy."); Gantler v. Stephens, 965 A.2d 695, 714 (Del. 2009) (holding that shareholder ratification was invalid when directors and officers had a disabling conflict of interest in the reclassification transaction arising from an entrenchment motive).

IN RE EBAY, INC. SHAREHOLDER LITIGATION

2004 WL 253521 (Del. Ch. 2004)

CHANDLER, J.

Shareholders of eBay, Inc. filed these consolidated derivative actions against certain eBay directors and officers for usurping corporate opportunities. Plaintiffs allege that eBay's investment banking advisor, Goldman Sachs Group, engaged in "spinning," a practice that involves allocating shares of lucrative initial public offerings of stock to favored clients. In effect, the plaintiff shareholders allege that Goldman Sachs bribed certain eBay insiders, using the currency of highly profitable investment opportunities-opportunities that should have been offered to, or provided for the benefit of, eBay rather than the favored insiders.

The individual eBay defendants have moved to dismiss these consolidated actions for failure to state a claim and for failure to make a pre-suit demand on eBay's board of directors as required under Chancery Court Rule 23.1. For reasons I briefly discuss below, I deny all of the defendants' motions to dismiss.

The facts, as alleged in the complaint, are straightforward. In 1995, defendants Pierre Omidyar and Jeffrey Skoll founded nominal defendant eBay, a Delaware corporation, as a sole proprietorship. In 1998, eBay retained Goldman Sachs and other investment banks to underwrite an initial public offering of common stock. Goldman Sachs was the lead underwriter. Shares of eBay stock became immensely valuable during 1998 and 1999, rising to $175 per share in early April 1999. Around that time, eBay made a secondary offering, issuing 6.5 million shares of common stock at $170 per share for a total of $1.1 billion. Goldman Sachs again served as lead underwriter. Goldman Sachs was asked in 2001 to serve as eBay's financial advisor in connection with an acquisition by eBay of PayPal, Inc. For these services, eBay has paid Goldman Sachs over $8 million.

During this same time period, Goldman Sachs "rewarded" the individual defendants by allocating to them thousands of IPO shares, managed by Goldman Sachs, at the initial offering price. Because the IPO market during this particular period of time was extremely active, prices of initial stock offerings often doubled or tripled in a single day. Investors who were well connected, either to Goldman Sachs or to similarly situated investment banks serving as IPO underwriters, were able to flip these investments into instant profit by selling the equities in a few days or even in a few hours after they were initially purchased.

The essential allegation of the complaint is that Goldman Sachs provided these IPO share allocations to the individual defendants to show appreciation for eBay's business and to enhance Goldman Sachs' chances of obtaining future eBay business. In addition to co-founding eBay, defendant Omidyar has been eBay's CEO, CFO and President. He is eBay's largest stockholder, owning more than 23% of the company's equity. Goldman Sachs allocated Omidyar shares in at least forty IPOs at the initial offering price. Omidyar resold these securities in the public market for millions of dollars in profit. Defendant Whitman owns 3.3% of eBay stock and has been President, CEO and a director since early 1998. Whitman also has been a director of Goldman Sachs since 2001. Goldman Sachs allocated Whitman shares in over a 100 IPOs at the initial offering price. Whitman sold these equities in the open market and reaped millions of dollars in profit. Defendant Skoll, in addition to co-founding eBay, has served in various positions at the company, including Vice-President of Strategic Planning and Analysis and President. He served as an eBay director from December 1996 to March 1998. Skoll is eBay's second largest stockholder, owning about 13% of the company. Goldman Sachs has allocated Skoll shares in at least 75 IPOs at the initial offering price, which Skoll promptly resold on the open market, allowing him to realize millions of dollars in profit. Finally, defendant Robert C. Kagle has served as an eBay director since June 1997. Goldman Sachs allocated Kagle shares in at least 25 IPOs at the initial offering price. Kagle promptly resold these equities, and recorded millions of dollars in profit.

Demand Futility

Plaintiffs bring these actions on behalf of eBay, seeking an accounting from the individual director defendants of their profits from the IPO transactions as well as compensatory damages from Goldman Sachs for its participation (aiding and abetting) in the eBay insiders' breach of fiduciary duty. Court of Chancery Rule 23.1 requires that a shareholder make a demand that the corporation's board pursue potential litigation before initiating such litigation on the corporation's behalf. When a plaintiff fails to make a demand on the board of directors, the plaintiff must plead with factual particularity why the demand is excused.

eBay's board of directors consists of seven members. Three are the individual defendants—Whitman, Omidyar and Kagle; defendant Skoll is not presently a director. All four of these individual defendants received IPO allocations from Goldman Sachs. The three current directors of eBay who received IPO allocations (Omidyar, Whitman and Kagle) are clearly interested in the transactions at the core of this controversy.

Although the other four directors of eBay (Cook, Lepore, Schultz and Bourguignon) did not participate in the "spinning," plaintiffs allege that they are not independent of the interested directors and, thus, demand is excused as futile. Since three of the seven present eBay directors are interested in the transactions that give rise to this litigation, plaintiffs need only demonstrate a reason to doubt the independence of one of the remaining four directors. Plaintiffs allege that directors Cook, Lepore, Schultz and Bourguignon all have "close business and personal ties with the individual defendants" and are incapable of exercising independent judgment to determine whether eBay should bring a breach of fiduciary duty action against the individual defendants. Plaintiffs allege, for example, that Schultz is a member of Maveron LLC, an investment advisory company in which Whitman has made significant personal investments. More significantly, plaintiffs allege that Cook, Lepore, Schultz and Bourguignon have received huge financial benefits as a result of their positions as eBay directors and, furthermore, that they owe their positions on the board to Omidyar, Whitman, Kagle and Skoll.

eBay pays no cash compensation to its directors, but it does award substantial stock options. For example, in 1998, when Cook joined eBay's board, it awarded him 900,000 options at an exercise price of $1.555. One fourth of these options (225,000) vested immediately, and an additional 2% vests each subsequent month so long as Cook remains a director. In 1998, after Cook had joined the board, eBay adopted a director's stock option plan pursuant to which each non-employee director was to be awarded 30,000 options each year (except for 1999, when no additional options were awarded). As of early 2002, Cook beneficially owned 903,750 currently exercisable options, and an additional 200,000 shares of eBay stock. The complaint notes that the exercise price on 900,000 of the options originally awarded to Cook is $1.555 per share. At the time the complaint was filed in this case, eBay stock was valued at $62.13 per share. At an exercise price of $1.555, Cook's original option grant is thus worth millions of dollars. In addition, the stock options awarded in 2000, 2001 and 2002, which are not yet fully vested, and will never vest unless Cook retains his position as a director, are worth potentially millions of dollars.

The complaint further alleges that director Schultz, Lepore and Bourguignon are similarly situated. That is, the stock options granted to these directors, which are both vested and unvested, are so valuable that they create a financial incentive for these directors to retain their positions as directors and make them beholden to the defendant directors. As a result, plaintiffs contend that it is more than reasonable to assume that an individual who has already received, and who expects to receive still more, options of such significant value could not objectively decide whether to commence legal proceedings against fellow directors who are directly responsible for the outside directors" continuing positions on the board.

I need not address each of the four outside directors, as I agree with plaintiffs that the particularized allegations of the complaint are sufficient to raise a reasonable doubt as to Cook's independence from the eBay insider directors who accepted Goldman Sachs' IPO allocations. Defendants resist this conclusion by pointing out that Whitman, Kagle, Omidyar and Skoll, collectively with management, control 40% of eBay's common stock, which they argue is insufficient to allege control or domination. Defendants also contend that the options represent past compensation and would not effectively disable a director from acting fairly and impartially with respect to a demand. These arguments are unpersuasive in these circumstances.

First, defendants must concede that certain stockholders, executive officers and directors control eBay. For example, eBay's form 10-K for the fiscal year ending December 31, 2000 notes that eBay's executive officers and directors Whitman, Omidyar, Kagle and Skoll (and their affiliates) own about one-half of eBay's outstanding common stock. As a result, these eBay officers and directors effectively have the ability to control eBay and to direct its affairs and business, including the election of directors and the approval of significant corporate transactions. Although the percentage of ownership may have decreased slightly from the time eBay filed the 2000 10-K, the decrease is insufficient to detract from the company's acknowledgement that these four individual defendants control the company and the election of directors.

Second, although many of the options awarded to Cook and the other purported outside directors have in fact vested, a significant number of options have not yet vested and will never vest unless the outside directors remain directors of eBay. Given that the value of the options for Cook (and allegedly for the other outside directors) potentially run into the millions of dollars, one cannot conclude realistically that Cook would be able to objectively and impartially consider a demand to bring litigation against those to whom he is beholden for his current position and future position on eBay's board. With the specific allegations of the complaint in mind, I conclude that plaintiffs have adequately demonstrated that demand on eBay's board should be excused as futile.

[The court ruled that, for the purpose of a motion to dismiss, the plaintiff shareholders have stated a claim that defendant directors usurped a corporate opportunity of eBay. It declined to dismiss the claim against Goldman Sachs for aiding and abetting a breach of fiduciary duty.]

BEAM EX REL. MARTHA STEWART LIVING OMNIMEDIA V. STEWART

845 A.2d 1040 (Del. 2004)

VEASEY, CHIEF JUSTICE.

We review and affirm the judgment of the Court of Chancery in dismissing under Rule 23.1 a claim in a derivative suit because the plaintiff failed to make pre-suit demand on the board and failed to demonstrate demand futility. The single issue before us is that of demand futility.

The Chancellor analyzed in detail the plaintiff's demand futility allegations. We agree with the Chancellor's well-reasoned opinion. But, pursuant to our plenary appellate review, we undertake a further explication of certain points covered by the Chancellor, including the matter of director independence.

The plaintiff, Monica Beam, owns shares of Martha Stewart Living Omnimedia, Inc. (MSO). Beam filed a derivative action in the Court of Chancery against Martha Stewart, the five other members of MSO's board of directors, and former board member John Doerr.

Beam alleged that Stewart breached her fiduciary duties of loyalty and care by illegally selling ImClone stock in December of 2001 and by mishandling the media attention that followed, thereby jeopardizing the financial future of MSO. The Court of Chancery dismissed under Court of Chancery Rule 23.1 because Beam failed to plead particularized facts demonstrating presuit demand futility.

When Beam filed the complaint in the Court of Chancery, the MSO board of directors consisted of six members: Stewart, Sharon Patrick, Arthur Martinez, Darla Moore, Naomi Seligman, and Jeffrey Ubben.

Stewart's potential civil and criminal liability for the acts underlying Beam's claim rendered Stewart an interested party and therefore unable to consider demand.[3] Patrick's position as an officer and inside director, together with the substantial compensation she receives from the company, raised a reasonable doubt as to her ability objectively to consider demand.

We must determine if the following allegations of the complaint, and the reasonable inferences that may flow from them, create a reasonable doubt of the independence of either Martinez, Moore or Seligman:

> 4. Defendant Arthur Martinez is a director, a position that he has held since January 2001. Until December 2000, Martinez served as Chairman of the board of directors of Sears Roebuck and Co., and was its Chief Executive Officer from August 1995 until October 2000. Martinez joined Sears, Roebuck in September 1992 as the Chief Executive Officer of Sears Merchandise Group, Sears's former retail arm. From 1990 to 1992, he was Vice Chairman of Saks Fifth Avenue and was a member of Saks Fifth Avenue's board of directors. Martinez is currently a member of the board of directors of PepsiCo, Inc., Liz Claiborne, Inc. and International Flavors & Fragrances, Inc., and is the Chairman of the Federal Reserve Bank of Chicago. *Martinez is a longstanding personal friend of defendants Stewart and Patrick. While at Sears, Martinez established a relationship with the Company, which marketed a substantial volume of products through Sears. Martinez was recruited for the board by Stewart's longtime personal friend, Charlotte Beers. Defendant Patrick was quoted in an article dated March 22, 2001 appearing in Directors & Board as follows: "Arthur is an old friend to both me and Martha."*

[3] Stewart was, at all relevant times, MSO's chairman and chief executive. She controls over 94% of the shareholder vote. She also personifies MSO's brands and was its primary creative force.

5. Defendant Darla Moore is a director, a position she has held since September 2001. Moore has been a partner of Rainwater, Inc., a private investment firm, since 1994. Before that, Moore was a Managing Director of Chase Bank. Moore is also a trustee of Magellan Health Services, Inc. *Moore is a longstanding friend of defendant Stewart. In November 1995, she attended a wedding reception hosted by Stewart's personal lawyer, Allen Grubman, for his daughter. Also in attendance were Stewart and Stewart's friend, Samuel Waksal. In August 1996, Fortune carried an article highlighting Moore's close personal relationship with Charlotte Beers and defendant Stewart. When Beers, a longtime friend and confidante to Stewart, resigned from the Company's board in September 2001, Moore was nominated to replace her.*

6. Defendant Naomi Seligman is a director, a position that she has held since September 1999. Seligman was a co-founder of Cassius Advisers, an e-commerce consultancy, where she has served as a senior partner since 1999, and is a co-founder of the Research Board, Inc., an information technology research group, where she served as a senior partner from 1975 until 1999. Seligman currently serves as a director of Akamai Technologies, Inc., The Dun & Bradstreet Corporation, John Wiley & Sons and Sun Microsystems, Inc. *According to a story appearing on July 2, 2002 in The Wall Street Journal, Seligman contacted the Chief Executive Officer of John Wiley & Sons (a publishing house) at defendant Stewart's behest last year to express concern over its planned publication of a biography that was critical of Stewart.*

8. Martinez, Moore, Seligman, and Ubben are referred to collectively as the Director Defendants. By reason of Stewart's overwhelming voting control over the Company, each of the Director Defendants serves at her sufferance. Each of the Director Defendants receives valuable perquisites and benefits by reason of their service on the Company's Board.

* * *

<u>DEMAND ALLEGATIONS</u>

73 No demand on the Board of Directors was made prior to institution of this action, as a majority of the Board of Directors is not independent or disinterested with respect to the claims asserted herein.

77. *Defendant Martinez is not disinterested in view of his longstanding personal friendship with both Patrick and Stewart.*

78. *Defendant Moore is not disinterested in view of her longstanding personal relationship with defendant Stewart.*

79. *Defendant Seligman is not disinterested; she has already shown that she will use her position as a director at another corporation to act at the behest of defendant Stewart when she contacted the Chief Executive Officer of John Wiley & Sons in an effort to dissuade the publishing house from publishing a biography that was critical of Stewart.*

80. The Director Defendants are not disinterested as they are jointly and severally liable with Stewart in view of their failure to monitor Stewart's actions. Pursuit of these claims would imperil the substantial benefits that accrue to them by reason of their service on the Board, given Stewart's voting control.

Demand Futility and Director Independence

The Court should draw all *reasonable* inferences in the plaintiff's favor. Such reasonable inferences must logically flow from particularized facts alleged by the plaintiff. "Conclusory allegations are not considered as expressly pleaded facts or factual inferences." Likewise, inferences that are not objectively reasonable cannot be drawn in the plaintiff's favor.

Under the first prong of *Aronson,*[14] a stockholder may not pursue a derivative suit to assert a claim of the corporation unless: (a) she has first demanded that the directors pursue the corporate claim and they have wrongfully refused to do so; or (b) such demand is excused because the directors are deemed incapable of making an impartial decision regarding the pursuit of the litigation.[15] The issue in this case is the quantum of doubt about a director's independence that is "reasonable" in order to excuse a pre-suit demand. The parties argue opposite sides of that issue.

The key principle upon which this area of our jurisprudence is based is that the directors are entitled to a *presumption* that they were faithful to their fiduciary duties.[16] In the context of pre-suit demand, the burden is upon the plaintiff in a derivative action to overcome that presumption. The Court must determine whether a plaintiff has alleged particularized facts creating a reasonable doubt of a director's independence to rebut the presumption at the pleading stage.[18] If the Court determines that the pleaded facts create a reasonable doubt that a majority of the board could have acted independently in responding to the demand, the presumption is rebutted for pleading purposes and demand will be excused as futile.

---

[14] *See Aronson v. Lewis,* 473 A.2d 805, 814 (Del. 1984) (setting forth two steps of a demand futility analysis: whether (1) "the directors are disinterested and independent [or] (2) the challenged transaction was otherwise the product of a valid exercise of business judgment").

[15] *Rales v. Blasband,* 634 A.2d 927, 932 (Del.1993).

[16] *See Aronson,* 473 A.2d at 812 ("It is a presumption that in making a business decision the directors of a corporation acted on an informed basis, in good faith and in the honest belief that the action taken was in the best interests of the company.").

[18] *Rales,* 634 A.2d at 934.

A director will be considered unable to act objectively with respect to a pre-suit demand if he or she is interested in the outcome of the litigation or is otherwise not independent.[20] A director's interest may be shown by demonstrating a potential personal benefit or detriment to the director as a result of the decision.[21] "In such circumstances, a director cannot be expected to exercise his or her independent business judgment without being influenced by the personal consequences resulting from the decision." The primary basis upon which a director's independence must be measured is whether the director's decision is based on the corporate merits of the subject before the board, rather than extraneous considerations or influences. This broad statement of the law requires an analysis of whether the director is disinterested in the underlying transaction and, even if disinterested, whether the director is independent. The independence inquiry requires us to determine whether there is a reasonable doubt that any one of these three directors is capable of objectively making a business decision to assert or not assert a corporate claim against Stewart.

Independence Is a Contextual Inquiry

Independence is a fact-specific determination made in the context of a particular case. The court must make that determination by answering the inquiries: independent from whom and independent for what purpose? The plaintiff has the burden to plead particularized facts that create a reasonable doubt sufficient to rebut the presumption that either Moore, Seligman or Martinez was independent of defendant Stewart.

To show lack of independence, the complaint of a stockholder-plaintiff must create a reasonable doubt that a director is not so "beholden" to an interested director (in this case Stewart) that his or her "discretion would be sterilized." Our jurisprudence explicating the demand requirement

> is designed to create a balanced environment which will: (1) on the one hand, deter costly, baseless suits by creating a screening mechanism to eliminate claims where there is only a suspicion expressed solely in conclusory terms; and (2) on the other hand, permit suit by a stockholder who is able to articulate particularized facts showing that there is a reasonable doubt either that (a) a majority of the board is independent for purposes of responding to the demand, or (b) the underlying transaction is protected by the business judgment rule.

---

20 *See Grimes v. Donald*, 673 A.2d 1207, 1216 (Del.1996) ("The basis for claiming excusal would normally be that: (1) a majority of the board has a material financial or familial interest; (2) a majority of the board is incapable of acting independently for some other reason such as domination or control; or (3) the underlying transaction is not the product of a valid exercise of business judgment.").

21 *Cf. Rales*, 634 A.2d at 936 ("A director is considered interested where he or she will receive a personal financial benefit from a transaction that is not equally shared by the stockholders. Directorial interest also exists where a corporate decision will have a materially detrimental impact on a director, but not on the corporation and the stockholders.").

The "reasonable doubt" standard "is sufficiently flexible and workable to provide the stockholder with the keys to the courthouse in an appropriate case where the claim is not based on mere suspicions or stated solely in conclusory terms."

Personal Friendship

A variety of motivations, including friendship, may influence the demand futility inquiry. But, to render a director unable to consider demand, a relationship must be of a bias-producing nature. Allegations of mere personal friendship or a mere outside business relationship, standing alone, are insufficient to raise a reasonable doubt about a director's independence. We adopt as our own the Chancellor's analysis in this case:

> Some professional or personal friendships, which may border on or even exceed familial loyalty and closeness, may raise a reasonable doubt whether a director can appropriately consider demand. This is particularly true when the allegations raise serious questions of either civil or criminal liability of such a close friend. Not all friendships, or even most of them, rise to this level and the Court cannot make a *reasonable* inference that a particular friendship does so without specific factual allegations to support such a conclusion.

The facts alleged by Beam regarding the relationships between Stewart and these other members of MSO's board of directors largely boil down to a "structural bias" argument, which presupposes that the professional and social relationships that naturally develop among members of a board impede independent decisionmaking. This Court addressed the structural bias argument in *Aronson v. Lewis:*

> Critics will charge that [by requiring the independence of only a majority of the board] we are ignoring the structural bias common to corporate boards throughout America, as well as the other unseen socialization processes cutting against independent discussion and decisionmaking in the boardroom. The difficulty with structural bias in a demand futile case is simply one of establishing it in the complaint for purposes of Rule 23.1. We are satisfied that discretionary review by the Court of Chancery of complaints alleging specific facts pointing to bias on a particular board will be sufficient for determining demand futility.

The plaintiff attempted to plead affinity beyond mere friendship between Stewart and the other directors, but her attempt is not sufficient to demonstrate demand futility. Even if the alleged friendships may have preceded the directors' membership on MSO's board and did not necessarily arise out of that membership, these relationships are of the same nature as those giving rise to the structural bias argument.

Allegations that Stewart and the other directors moved in the same social circles, attended the same weddings, developed business relationships before joining the board, and described each other as "friends," even when coupled with Stewart's 94% voting power, are insufficient, without more, to rebut the presumption of independence. They do not provide a sufficient basis from which reasonably to infer that Martinez, Moore and Seligman may have been beholden to Stewart. Whether they arise before board membership or later as a result of collegial relationships among the board of directors, such affinities—standing alone—will not render pre-suit demand futile.

The Court of Chancery must review the complaint on a case-by-case basis to determine whether it states with particularity facts indicating that a relationship—whether it preceded or followed board membership—is so close that the director's independence may *reasonably* be doubted. This doubt might arise either because of financial ties, familial affinity, a particularly close or intimate personal or business affinity or because of evidence that in the past the relationship caused the director to act non-independently vis à vis an interested director. No such allegations are made here. Mere allegations that they move in the same business and social circles, or a characterization that they are close friends, is not enough to negate independence for demand excusal purposes.

That is not to say that personal friendship is always irrelevant to the independence calculus. But, for pre-suit demand purposes, friendship must be accompanied by substantially more in the nature of serious allegations that would lead to a reasonable doubt as to a director's independence. That a much stronger relationship is necessary to overcome the presumption of independence at the demand futility stage becomes especially compelling when one considers the risks that directors would take by protecting their social acquaintances in the face of allegations that those friends engaged in misconduct. To create a reasonable doubt about an outside director's independence, a plaintiff must plead facts that would support the inference that because of the nature of a relationship or additional circumstances other than the interested director's stock ownership or voting power, the non-interested director would be more willing to risk his or her reputation than risk the relationship with the interested director.

Specific Allegations Concerning Seligman and Moore

1. Seligman

Beam's allegations concerning Seligman's lack of independence raise an additional issue not present in the Moore and Martinez relationships. Those allegations are not necessarily based on a purported friendship between Seligman and Stewart. Rather, they are based on a specific past act by Seligman that, Beam claims, indicates Seligman's lack of independence from Stewart. Beam alleges that Seligman called John Wiley & Sons (Wiley) at Stewart's request in order to prevent an unfavorable publication reference to Stewart. The Chancellor concluded, properly in our view, that this allegation does not provide particularized facts from which one may reasonably infer improper influence.

The bare fact that Seligman contacted Wiley, on whose board Seligman also served, to dissuade Wiley from publishing unfavorable references to Stewart, even if done at Stewart's request, is insufficient to create a reasonable doubt that Seligman is capable of considering presuit demand free of Stewart's influence. Although the court should draw all *reasonable* inferences in Beam's favor, neither improper influence by Stewart over Seligman nor that Seligman was beholden to Stewart is a reasonable inference from these allegations.

The reasonable inference is that Seligman's purported intervention on Stewart's behalf was of benefit to MSO and *its* reputation, which is allegedly tied to *Stewart's* reputation, as the Chancellor noted. A motivation by Seligman to benefit the company every bit as much as Stewart herself is the only reasonable inference supported by the complaint, when all of its allegations are read in context.

2. Moore

The Court of Chancery concluded that the plaintiff's allegations with respect to Moore's social relationship with Stewart presented "quite a close call" and suggested ways that the "balance could have been tipped." Although we agree that there are ways that the balance could be tipped so that mere allegations of social relationships would become allegations casting reasonable doubt on independence, we do not agree that the facts as alleged present a "close call" with respect to Moore's independence. These allegations center on: (a) Moore's attendance at a wedding reception for the daughter of Stewart's lawyer where Stewart and Waksal were also present; (b) a *Fortune* magazine article focusing on the close personal relationships among Moore, Stewart and Beers; and (c) the fact that Moore replaced Beers on the MSO board. In our view, these bare social relationships clearly do not create a reasonable doubt of independence.

3. Stewart's 94% Stock Ownership

Beam attempts to bolster her allegations regarding the relationships between Stewart and Seligman and Moore by emphasizing Stewart's overwhelming voting control of MSO. That attempt also fails to create a reasonable doubt of independence. A stockholder's control of a corporation does not excuse pre-suit demand on the board without particularized allegations of relationships between the directors and the controlling stockholder demonstrating that the directors are beholden to the stockholder. As noted earlier, the relationships alleged by Beam do not lead to the inference that the directors were beholden to Stewart and, thus, unable independently to consider demand. Coupling those relationships with Stewart's overwhelming voting control of MSO does not close that gap.

Because Beam did not plead facts sufficient to support a reasonable inference that at least one MSO director in addition to Stewart and Patrick was incapable of considering demand, Beam was required to make demand on the board. Hence, pre-suit demand was not excused. The Court of Chancery did not err by dismissing Count 1 under Rule 23.1.

KAHN V. M & F WORLDWIDE CORP.

88 A.3d 635 (Del. 2014)

HOLLAND, JUSTICE:

[This case is presented in a prior chapter. The opinion is the same, and so the factual recitation is briefly summarized. MacAndrews & Forbes Holdings, Inc. ("M & F") is a 43% controlling shareholder of M & F Worldwide Corp. ("MFW"). M & F was owned by Ronald Perelman. It sought to acquire the remaining common stock of MFW from minority shareholders. Because M & F was a controlling shareholder, it owed fiduciary duty to the minority shareholders. One way to protect minority shareholder is to appoint a special committee of the board composed of independent directors—directors who are independent from M & F. *Ab initio*, M & F's proposal to acquire all of MFW was made contingent upon two shareholder-protective conditions: the transaction must be negotiated and approved by a special committee of independent MFW directors (the "Special Committee"), and then approved by a majority of the minority shareholders. The purpose of the Special Committee was to protect the interest of the minority shareholders. The critical inquiry was whether in fact the Special Committee was independent.]

The Special Committee Was Independent

The Appellants do not challenge the independence of the Special Committee's Chairman, Meister. They claim, however, that the three other Special Committee members—Webb, Dinh, and Byorum—were beholden to Perelman because of their prior business and/or social dealings with Perelman or Perelman-related entities.

The Appellants first challenge the independence of Webb. They urged that Webb and Perelman shared a "longstanding and lucrative business partnership" between 1983 and 2002 which included acquisitions of thrifts and financial institutions, and which led to a 2002 asset sale to Citibank in which Webb made "a significant amount of money." The Court of Chancery concluded, however, that the fact of Webb having engaged in business dealings with Perelman nine years earlier did not raise a triable fact issue regarding his ability to evaluate the Merger impartially.[21] We agree.

---

21 *Beam ex rel. Martha Stewart Living Omnimedia, Inc. v. Stewart*, 845 A.2d 1040, 1051 (Del. 2004) ("Allegations that [the controller] and the other directors developed business relationships before joining the board are insufficient to rebut the presumption of independence.").

Second, the Appellants argued that there were triable issues of fact regarding Dinh's independence. The Appellants demonstrated that between 2009 and 2011, Dinh's law firm, Bancroft PLLC, advised M & F and Scientific Games (in which M & F owned a 37.6% stake), during which time the Bancroft firm earned $200,000 in fees. The record reflects that Bancroft's limited prior engagements, which were inactive by the time the Merger proposal was announced, were fully disclosed to the Special Committee soon after it was formed. The Court of Chancery found that the Appellants failed to proffer any evidence to show that compensation received by Dinh's law firm was material to Dinh, in the sense that it would have influenced his decisionmaking with respect to the M & F proposal. The only evidence of record, the Court of Chancery concluded, was that these fees were "*de minimis*" and that the Appellants had offered no contrary evidence that would create a genuine issue of material fact.

The Court of Chancery found that the relationship between Dinh, a Georgetown University Law Center professor, and M & F's Barry Schwartz, who sits on the Georgetown Board of Visitors, did not create a triable issue of fact as to Dinh's independence. No evidence suggested that Schwartz could exert influence on Dinh's position at Georgetown based on his recommendation regarding the Merger. Indeed, Dinh had earned tenure as a professor at Georgetown before he ever knew Schwartz.

The Appellants argue that Schwartz's later invitation to Dinh to join the board of Revlon "illustrates the ongoing personal relationship between Schwartz and Dinh." There is no record evidence that Dinh expected to be asked to join Revlon's board at the time he served on the Special Committee. The Court of Chancery noted, Schwartz's invitation for Dinh to join the Revlon board occurred months after the Merger was approved and did not raise a triable fact issue concerning Dinh's independence from Perelman. We uphold the Court of Chancery's findings relating to Dinh.

Third, the Appellants urge that issues of material fact permeate Byorum's independence and, specifically, that Byorum "had a business relationship with Perelman from 1991 to 1996 through her executive position at Citibank." The Court of Chancery concluded, however, the Appellants presented no evidence of the nature of Byorum's interactions with Perelman while she was at Citibank. Nor was there evidence that after 1996 Byorum had an ongoing economic relationship with Perelman that was material to her in any way. Byorum testified that any interactions she had with Perelman while she was at Citibank resulted from her role as a senior executive, because Perelman was a client of the bank at the time. Byorum also testified that she had no business relationship with Perelman between 1996 and 2007, when she joined the MFW Board.

The Appellants contend that Byorum performed advisory work for Scientific Games in 2007 and 2008 as a senior managing director of Stephens Cori Capital Advisors. The Court of Chancery found that the

Appellants had adduced no evidence tending to establish that the $100,000 fee Stephens Cori received for that work was material to either Stephens Cori or to Byorum. Stephens Cori's engagement for Scientific Games, which occurred years before the Special Committee was convened, was fully disclosed to the Special Committee, which concluded that "it was not material, and it would not represent a conflict." We uphold the Court of Chancery's findings relating to Byorum as well.

To show that a director is not independent, a plaintiff must demonstrate that the director is "beholden" to the controlling party. *Rales v. Blasband,* 634 A.2d 927, 936 (Del. 1993) (citing *Aronson v. Lewis,* 473 A.2d 805, 815 (Del. 1984)). Bare allegations that directors are friendly with, travel in the same social circles as, or have past business relationships with the proponent of a transaction or the person they are investigating are not enough to rebut the presumption of independence. *Beam ex rel. Martha Stewart Living Omnimedia v. Stewart,* 845 A.2d 1040, 1051–52 (Del. 2004).

A plaintiff seeking to show that a director was not independent must satisfy a materiality standard. The court must conclude that the director in question had ties to the person whose proposal or actions he or she is evaluating that are sufficiently substantial that he or she could not objectively discharge his or her fiduciary duties.[29] Consistent with that predicate materiality requirement, the existence of some financial ties between the interested party and the director, without more, is not disqualifying. The inquiry must be whether, applying a subjective standard, those ties were *material,* in the sense that the alleged ties could have affected the impartiality of the individual director.[30]

To the extent the Appellants claimed the Special Committee members, Webb, Dinh, and Byorum, were beholden to Perelman based on prior economic relationships with him, the Appellants never developed or proffered evidence showing the materiality of those relationships.

The record supports the Court of Chancery's holding that none of the Appellants' claims relating to Webb, Dinh or Byorum raised a triable issue of material fact concerning their or the Special Committee's independence.

---

[29] *Cinerama, Inc. v. Technicolor, Inc.,* 663 A.2d 1156, 1167 (Del.1995) ("A plaintiff [must] show the materiality of a director's self-interest to the director's independence."); *see Brehm v. Eisner,* 746 A.2d 244, 259 n. 49 (Del.2000) ("'Material' is used to mean relevant and of a magnitude to be important to directors in carrying out their fiduciary duty of care in decisionmaking.").

[30] *See Cinerama, Inc. v. Technicolor, Inc.,* 663 A.2d 1156 (Del. 1995) (adopting a subjective standard for determining an individual director's financial self-interest). *See also, Cede & Co. v. Technicolor, Inc.,* 634 A.2d 345, 363 (Del. 1993) (affirming that "a shareholder show the materiality of a director's self-interest to the given director's independence"); *see also, e.g., Grimes v. Donald,* 673 A.2d 1207, 1216 (Del. 1996) (stating, in the context of demand futility, that a stockholder must show that "a majority of the board has a *material* financial or familial interest").

CHAPTER 15

ISSUES IN MERGERS & ACQUISITIONS

■ ■ ■

A. M&A BASICS

1. REASONS FOR M&A TRANSACTION

"Mergers and acquisitions" (M&A) is the term used to describe deals in which businesses and assets combine or disaggregate. For example, two companies combine to form one company; shareholders of one company sell their shares to a buyer; one company sells substantial assets to another company. These kinds of transactions fall under the rubric of M&A.

There are many reasons for engaging in M&A transactions. A company may want to expand geographic markets, product lines, or customer base. Two companies may combine because they envision revenue synergies. Synergy may arise out of opportunities to sell each company's products to a combined customer base. Below is an example of how a merger can be justified. Firms A and B are exactly identical. Each has profit of 1,000 and shares outstanding of 100 shares. Profit per share is $10, and capital markets value each firm at 15 times profit, which means that each firm has a market value of stock of 15,000.

	A Co.	B Co.	Synergy	New Co.
Revenue	2,000	2,000	200	4,200
Expense	1,000	1,000	100	2,100
Net profit	1,000	1,000	100	2,100
Shares outstanding	100	100		200
Profit/share	$10.00	$10.00		**$10.50**
Profit multiple	15 x	15 x		15 x
Market value of firm	15,000	15,000		**31,500**

Suppose A and B combine. They expect revenue synergy of 200, and after expenses and taxes, the synergy yields a net profit contribution of 100. This results in a profit per share of $10.50. At the same valuation multiple of 15 time, the new merged company would be valued at 31,500, or 1,500 more than the sum of the parts.

Mergers can result in cost synergies. The expense of the new company would be lower than the aggregate expense of the two companies operating as independent companies. Consider again the above hypothetical of the merger of firms A and B. There are no revenue synergies, but the firms expect to save on duplicative expenses.

	A Co.	B Co.	Synergy	New Co.
Revenue	2,000	2,000		4,000
Expense	1,000	1,000	(100)	1,900
Net profit	1,000	1,000	100	2,100
Shares outstanding	100	100		200
Profit/share	$10.00	$10.00		**$10.50**
Profit multiple	15 x	15 x		15 x
Market value of firm	15,000	15,000		**31,500**

M&A deals can create opportunities to cut costs such as excess production capacity or overhead costs. A combined firm may not need two human resources, legal, or finance departments. Cost synergies result from rationing assets, which is often a euphemism for employee layoffs.[1]

A company may wish to buy substantial assets of another company, but not want the whole company. For example, a transportation logistics company may wish to distribute cash to shareholders and terminate business. Its major assets are a terminal in Aeropostale Airport and a dock at Puerto Port. A possible deal may be to sell the whole company for cash. But it may be difficult because there may be few buyers of the unique package of assets. A sale of assets might be better. An airliner may want the terminal but not its dock, and a shipping company may want the dock but not the terminal. In asset sales, the company may realize more value than if it sold itself as a whole to a single buyer.

M&A transactions often originate from strategic considerations involving financial synergies or expansion of capabilities, markets, or products. However, they may be useful in other situations. For example, in *Smith v. Van Gorkom*, Trans Union sought to sell itself to the acquirer for the purpose of monetizing tax credits. 488 A.2d 858, 865 (Del. 1985) ("Van Gorkom met with Senior Management of Trans Union. Van Gorkom reported on his lobbying efforts in Washington and his desire to find a

---

1 M&A transactions have consequences, which explain the fact that there is much human drama behind these transactions, and which sometimes are gleaned in the facts of judicial opinions. In *Smith v. Van Gorkom*, recall that when the CEO Van Gorkom announced the news that he was negotiating with an acquirer to sell Trans Union, the court noted: "Senior Management's reaction to the Pritzker proposal was completely negative. Within 10 days of the public announcement, dissent among Senior Management over the merger had become widespread." 488 A.2d 858, 867, 869 (Del. 1985). In response, senior management proposed a management buyout of Trans Union rather than submit to a takeover. *Id.* at 865 ("[Van Gorkom] vetoed the suggestion of a leveraged buy-out by Management, however, as involving a potential conflict of interest for Management."). Might some of the negativity have been related to the personal interests of management?

solution to the tax credit problem more permanent than a continued program of acquisitions. Various alternatives were suggested and discussed preliminarily, including the sale of Trans Union to a company with a large amount of taxable income."). The reasons for engaging in M&A transactions are many, and such transactions have broad utility. Corporation law permits M&A transaction subject to stated limitations.

The case below describes a merger of an operating company with a shell company, a company that exists in paper only. In reading this case, consider these questions: (1) Why did the company engage in this transaction? (2) Was this a legitimate transaction? (3) How should "legitimacy" of the transaction be conceptualized? (4) In what way did the merger device solve a business problem?

BOVE V. COMMUNITY HOTEL CORP. OF NEWPORT, R.I.

249 A.2d 89 (R.I. 1969)

JOSLIN, JUSTICE.

This civil action was brought in the superior court to enjoin a proposed merger of The Community Hotel Corporation of Newport, Rhode Island, a defendant herein, into Newport Hotel Corp. Both corporations were organized under the general corporation law of this state and are hereinafter referred to respectively as Community Hotel and Newport. No oral testimony was presented and a trial justice sitting without a jury decided the case on the facts appearing in the exhibits and as assented to by the parties in the pretrial order. The case is here on the plaintiffs' appeal from a judgment denying injunctive relief and dismissing the action.

Community Hotel was incorporated for the stated purpose of erecting, maintaining, operating, managing and leasing hotels. Its authorized capital stock consists of 6,000 shares of $100 par value six per cent prior preference cumulative preferred stock, and 6,000 shares of no par common stock of which 2,106 shares are issued and outstanding. The plaintiffs as well as the individual defendants are holders and owners of preferred stock, plaintiffs having acquired their holdings of approximately 900 shares not later than 1930. At the time this suit was commenced, dividends on the 4,335 then-issued and outstanding preferred shares had accrued, but had not been declared, for approximately 24 years, and totaled about $645,000 or $148.75 per share.

Newport was organized at the request of the board of directors of Community Hotel solely for the purpose of effectuating the merger which is the subject matter of this action. Its authorized capital stock consists of 80,000 shares of common stock, par value $1.00, of which only one share has been issued, and that to Community Hotel for a consideration of $10.

The essentials of the merger plan call for Community Hotel to merge into Newport, which will then become the surviving corporation. Although without assets, Newport will, if the merger is effectuated, acquire the sole ownership of all the property and assets now owned by Community Hotel. The plan also calls for the outstanding shares of Community Hotel's capital stock to be converted into shares of the capital stock of Newport upon the following basis: Each outstanding share of the constituent corporation's preferred stock, together with all accrued dividends thereon, will be changed and converted into five shares of the $1.00 par value common stock of the surviving corporation; and each share of the constituent corporation's no par common stock will be changed and converted into one share of the common stock, $1.00 par value, of the surviving corporation.

Consistent with the requirements of G.L.1956, § 7 G.L.1956, § 7–55–33,[1] the merger will become effective only if the plan receives the affirmative votes of the stockholders of each of the corporations representing at least two-thirds of the shares of each class of its capital stock. For the purpose of obtaining the required approval, notice was given to both common and preferred stockholders of Community Hotel that a special meeting would be held for the purpose of considering and voting upon the proposed merger. Before the scheduled meeting date arrived, this action was commenced and the meeting was postponed to a future time and place. So far, it has not yet been held.

The plaintiffs argue that the primary, and indeed, the only purpose of the proposed merger is to eliminate the priorities of the preferred stock with less than the unanimous consent of its holders. Assuming that premise, a preliminary matter for our consideration concerns the merger of a parent corporation into a wholly-owned subsidiary created for the sole purpose of achieving a recapitalization which will eliminate the parent's preferred stock and the dividends accumulated thereon, and whether such a merger qualifies within the contemplation of the statute permitting any two or more corporations to merge into a single corporation.

It is true, of course, that to accomplish the proposed recapitalization by amending Community Hotel's articles of association under relevant provisions of the general corporation law[2] would require the unanimous

[1] Section 7–55–33 in pertinent part provides: "Said agreement shall be submitted to the stockholders of each constituent corporation at a meeting thereof called separately for the purpose of taking the same into consideration. At said meeting said agreement shall be considered and the stockholders of said corporation shall vote by ballot, in person or by proxy, for the adoption or rejection of the said agreement, each share entitling the holder thereof to one (1) vote, and if the votes of the stockholders of each such corporation representing at least two-thirds of the shares of each class of its capital stock shall be for the adoption of said agreement the agreement so adopted and certified shall thence be taken and deemed to be the agreement and act of consolidation or merger of said corporations."

[2] Section 7–2–18, as amended, provides that a corporation may "from time to time when and as desired amend its articles of association" and § 7–2–19, as amended, provides that "unless otherwise provided in the articles of association, every such amendment shall require the affirmative vote of the following proportion of the stockholders, passed at a meeting duly called for

vote of the preferred shareholders, whereas under the merger statute, only a two-third vote of those stockholders will be needed. Concededly, unanimity of the preferred stockholders is unobtainable in this case, and plaintiffs argue, therefore, that to permit the less restrictive provisions of the merger statute to be used to accomplish indirectly what otherwise would be incapable of being accomplished directly by the more stringent amendment procedures of the general corporation law is tantamount to sanctioning a circumvention or perversion of that law.

The question, however, is not whether recapitalization by the merger route is a subterfuge, but whether a merger which is designed for the sole purpose of cancelling the rights of preferred stockholders with the consent of less than all has been authorized by the legislature. The controlling statute is § 7–5–2. Its language is clear, all-embracing and unqualified. It authorizes any two or more business corporations which were or might have been organized under the general corporation law to merge into a single corporation; and it provides that the merger agreement shall prescribe "the terms and conditions of consolidation or merger, the mode of carrying the same into effect as well as the manner of converting the shares of each of the constituent corporations into shares or other securities of the corporation resulting from or surviving such consolidation or merger, with such other details and provisions as are deemed necessary." Nothing in that language even suggests that the legislature intended to make underlying purpose a standard for determining permissibility. Indeed, the contrary is apparent since the very breadth of the language selected presupposes a complete lack of concern with whether the merger is designed to further the mutual interests of two existing and nonaffiliated corporations or whether alternatively it is purposed solely upon effecting a substantial change in an existing corporation's capital structure.

Moreover, that a possible effect of corporate action under the merger statute is not possible, or is even forbidden, under another section of the general corporation law is of no import, it being settled that the several sections of that law may have independent legal significance, and that the validity of corporate action taken pursuant to one section is not necessarily dependent upon its being valid under another.

We hold that nothing within our statute forbids a merger between a parent and a subsidiary corporation even under circumstances where the merger device has been resorted to solely for the purpose of obviating the necessity for the unanimous vote which would otherwise be required in order to cancel the priorities of preferred shareholders.

For the reasons stated, the judgment appealed from is affirmed.

---

the purpose: (b) Where the amendment diminishes the stipulated rate of dividends on any class of stock or the stipulated amount to be paid thereon in case of call or liquidation, the unanimous vote of the stockholders of such class and the vote of a majority in interest of all other stockholders entitled to vote."

2. BASIC TRANSACTION STRUCTURES

Two companies can execute a business combination through several basic deal structures. The most basic structures are: statutory merger, triangular merger, asset sale, and tender offer. Each of these methods have unique characteristics that may be more or less suitable for a particular situation. Two major considerations are: whether shareholders of either company must vote to approve the transaction; whether dissenting shareholders have appraisal rights.[2]

Statutory Merger

Statutory merger provisions provide that two or more companies may merge or consolidate. *See* DGCL § 251(a) (domestic corporations), § 252(a) (domestic and foreign corporations). A "merger" is a transaction in which one of the combining entities survive: A and B merge, and either A or B is the surviving entity. A "consolidation" is a transaction in which they combine to form a new entity: A and B consolidate, and C is the new entity. (With this understanding of technical distinctions in terms, transactions between two companies will be generically referred to as a "merger" or an "acquisition," *i.e.*, M&A.)

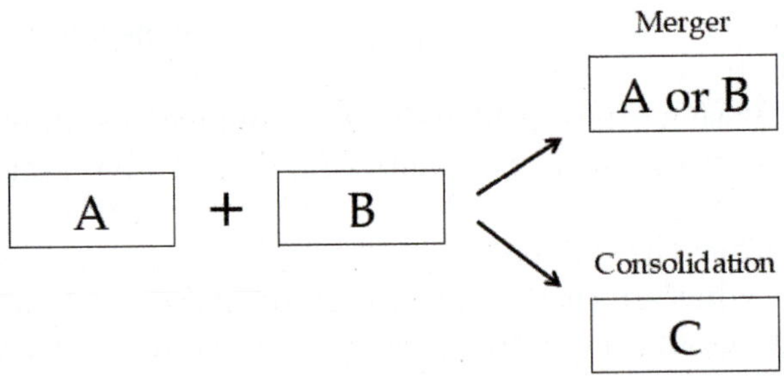

The boards of each company must approve the transaction agreement. *Id.* § 251(b), § 252(b). Upon approval by the boards, shareholders of both companies must vote to approve the agreement. *Id.* § 251(c), § 252(c). The voting threshold is usually the majority of the shares entitled to vote.[3] However, the shareholders of the surviving corporation do not have a right to vote if its shares "do not exceed 20% of the shares of common stock of such constituent corporation outstanding immediately prior to the effective date of the merger." *Id.* § 251(f).[4]

---

2 The exercise of appraisal right is a judicial proceeding in which a dissenting shareholder seeks a judicial appraisal of the "fair value" of shares. *See* DGCL § 262.

3 Some classes of shares may have different voting rights including nonvoting shares and supervoting shares, and the certificate of incorporation may provide for different voting thresholds.

4 *See* MBCA § 11.04(h) (no vote required by surviving corporation's shareholder if issuance of shares satisfies § 6.21(f)), § 6.21(f) (no vote required if issuance will not "comprise more than 20% of the voting power of the shares of the corporation that were outstanding immediately before the transaction"). For example, a corporation has 2,000,000 shares of common stock. Thus, 20% of the voting power represents 400,000 voting shares. The company proposes to issue 200,000 shares of common stock, and 100,000 shares of nonvoting preferred stock that is convertible into 2.5

Section 251(b) states that the acquisition agreement must provide, among other things:

> The terms and conditions of the merger or consolidation. The mode of carrying the same into effect. The manner, if any, of converting the shares of each of the constituent corporations into shares or other securities of the corporation surviving or resulting from the merger or consolidation, or of cancelling some or all of such shares, and, if any shares of any of the constituent corporations are not to remain outstanding, to be converted solely into shares or other securities of the surviving or resulting corporation or to be cancelled, the cash, property, rights or securities of any other corporation or entity which the holders of such shares are to receive in exchange for, or upon conversion of such shares and the surrender of any certificates evidencing them, which cash, property, rights or securities of any other corporation or entity may be in addition to or in lieu of shares or other securities of the surviving or resulting corporation.

When one considers these requirements, we can imagine the work that is necessary to get to the point of board approval, followed by shareholder affirmation. Two companies begin discussion and negotiation over the merger transaction. There are many complex issues to work out.

- What is the strategic or financial rationale?
- What is the transaction structure?
- How will the transaction be financed?
- What will shareholders get in consideration?
- What will be the effect on all constituents?

The legal contract—the acquisition agreement—is also complex. It sets forth the parties, consideration, rights and obligations of parties, representations and warranties, and conditions. Assuming that all hurdles are cleared and conditions are satisfied or waived, the transaction would close and become effective.

Upon closing, "the separate existence of all the constituent corporations shall cease and the constituent corporations shall become a new corporation, or be merged into 1 of such corporations." *Id.* § 259(a). One or both of the old corporations would disappear by operation of law, and there would be a surviving corporation or a new corporation. What happens to all the properties, contracts, rights, obligations, powers, and liabilities, including debts to creditors, of the merging corporations? They survive and pass to the surviving or new corporation. *Id.* There is a

---

shares of common stock. This issuance would require a shareholder vote under section 6.21(f) because it represents 450,000 voting shares, which is greater than 20% of the voting power immediately before the transaction.

seamless transition from merging corporations to the new or surviving corporation by operation of law.

With respect to appraisal rights, "any stockholder who continuously holds such shares through the effective date of the merger or consolidation, who has otherwise complied with [procedural perfection requirements] and who has neither voted in favor of the merger or consolidation nor consented thereto shall be entitled to an appraisal by the Court of Chancery of the fair value of the stockholder's shares." *Id.* § 262(a). "No appraisal rights shall be available for any shares of stock of the constituent corporation surviving a merger if the merger did not require for its approval the vote of the stockholders of the surviving corporation." *Id.* § 262(b)(1). These provisions link appraisal rights to voting. All shareholders in a consolidation and target shareholders in a merger, including those with nonvoting shares,[5] have appraisal rights, but shareholders of the surviving corporation have appraisal rights only if they were required to vote.

The statute has a "market exception" to appraisal rights: "no appraisal rights shall be available for the shares of any class or series of stock [that] were either: (i) listed on a national securities exchange or (ii) held of record by more than 2,000 holders." *Id.* § 262(b)(1). Why this exception?

> The states that have market exceptions (with or without exemptions) do so for many of the policy reasons proposed by the MBCA. They recognize the considerable court and legal expenses as well as the procedural difficulties involved in pursuing appraisal, and they are unconvinced that judicial appraisals inevitably result in accurate or "fair" assessments. Recognizing that the courts need to assess fair value for private company shareholders because no established market price for private company shares exists, they note that, in contrast, public shareholders presumptively have an available market. These states prescribe that when a public market exists (or is deemed to exist), public shareholders must employ market price instead of court-appraisal as the measure of their interests.

Gil Matthews, *The "Market Exception" in Appraisal Statutes*, Harv. L. Sch. Forum on Corp. Gov. (Mar. 30, 2020).

The "market exception" has an exception. Notwithstanding the fact that shares were publicly traded or widely held, shareholders still have appraisal rights if the consideration is not one of the following: "[1] Shares of stock of the corporation surviving or resulting from such merger or consolidation; [2] Shares [that] will be either listed on a national securities

---

[5] "Appraisal rights shall be available for the shares of *any class or series of stock* of a constituent corporation in a merger or consolidation." DGCL § 262(b).

exchange or held of record by more than 2,000 holders; [3] Cash; or [4] Any combination of the shares of stock and cash." DGCL § 262(b)(2).[6]

Triangular Merger

In addition to statutory mergers, other transaction structures can be used. A popular structure is the triangular merger. In a triangular merger, an acquirer creates a subsidiary, which is a shell company formed for the purpose of merging with the target company. In a "forward" triangular merger, the target merges into the subsidiary. In a "reverse" triangular merger, the subsidiary merges into the target.

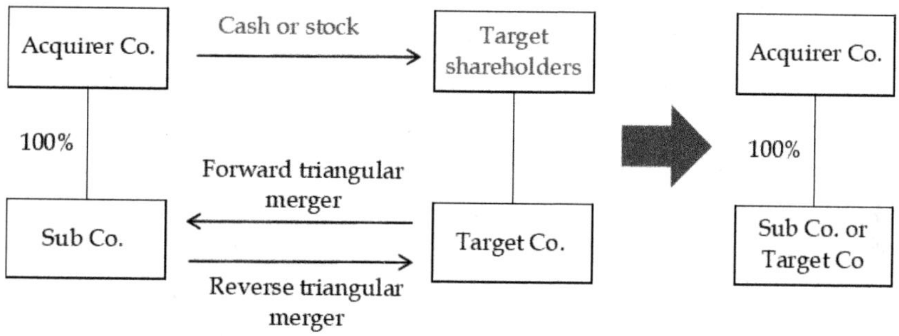

Upon closing, the acquirer would own the target's operating business as a wholly-owned subsidiary.

The triangular merger can serve several purposes. First, as a matter of transaction structuring, the shareholders of Acquirer do not vote on the transaction. Sub and Target are the merging corporations. The sole shareholder of Sub is Acquirer. A fundamental principle of corporation law is that a corporation is separate and distinct from its shareholders. Sub's sole shareholder is Acquirer, and thus the board would vote Acquirer's shares in favor of the merger between Sub and Target. Second, as a matter of business strategy, Acquirer may not want to merge directly with Target for the purpose of separating risks and assets. This rationale is based on the basic logic of corporate separateness and limited liability. The two companies may operate entirely different business lines. They may have a different mix of risk and management skill sets, which may justify keeping the companies separate. A triangular merger produces an outcome in which Target becomes a wholly-owned subsidiary of Acquirer.

---

[6] "Section 262 generally grants appraisal rights for all shareholders who have not voted in favor of a merger or consolidation and have timely perfected such rights. 8 *Del.C.* § 262(a), (d). However the statute also contains a market exception to appraisal rights: appraisal is not available if the shares to be appraised were widely held or traded on a national securities exchange. 8 *Del.C.* § 262(b)(1). Subsection (b) sets out two exclusions to the market exception. The first, contained in § 262(b)(2), provides that appraisal rights are available notwithstanding the fact that the shares are widely held or publicly traded if those shares must be exchanged for anything other than (a) shares of the surviving or resulting corporation; (b) other publicly traded or widely held shares; (c) cash in lieu of fractional shares of the corporations described in (a) and (b); or (d) any combination of (a), (b) and (c)." Klotz v. Warner Communications, Inc., 674 A.2d 878, 879–80 (Del. 1995).

Because Acquirer's shareholders do not vote on the transaction, they are not entitled to appraisal rights. With respect to Target shareholders, they are entitled to vote. Because they vote, they have appraisal rights unless the "market exception" to appraisal rights apply.

Short-Form Merger

In a short-form merger, a parent corporation with a substantial stake, usually at least 90%, initiates a merger with its majority-owned subsidiary without a vote of minority shareholders. DGLC § 253(a) (requiring "at least 90% of the outstanding shares of each class of the stock that, absent this subsection, would be entitled to vote on such merger"). A short-form merger recognizes that, by virtue of overwhelming ownership and control, the majority shareholder should be permitted to engage in a merger without the approval of minority shareholders.

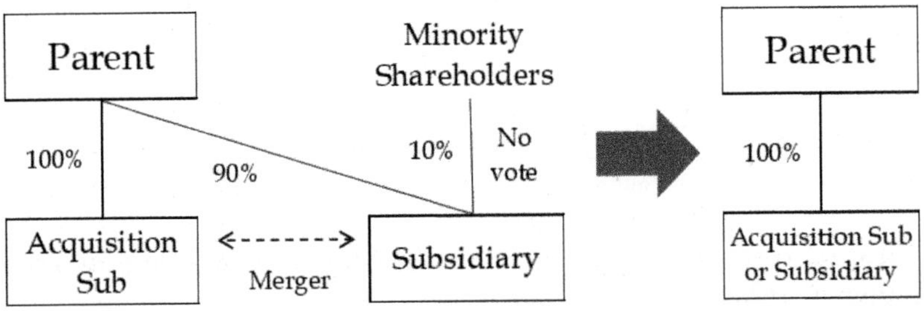

A dissenting shareholder's sole remedy is an appraisal. *Id.* § 262(b)(3) ("appraisal rights shall be available for the shares of the subsidiary"). Absent fraud or illegality, minority shareholders do not have a right to challenge a short-form merger for inequity or unfairness. Glassman v. Unocal Exploration Corp., 777 A.2d 242, 247–48 (Del. 2001).

Asset Sale

Another transaction structure is the sale of all or substantially all assets. This transaction is a sale of assets, and at all times buyer and seller remain separate and independent. They do not combine. When the selling company disposes of all or substantially all assets, it usually distributes the cash and remaining assets to its shareholders and then dissolves. With respect to its liabilities, the general rule is that the buyer does not acquire the seller's liabilities. The seller can presumably satisfy its liabilities with the consideration received and other assets it owns.

Under the doctrine of successor liability, the buyer may sometimes incur liability for the debts and obligations of the seller.

> It is a general rule that where one company sells or otherwise transfers all its assets to another company, the latter is not liable for the debts and liabilities of the transferor, including those arising out of the former's tortious conduct.

> Despite the general rule, in some limited situations where an avoidance of liability would be unjust, a purported sale of assets for cash or other consideration may be found to transfer liabilities of the predecessor corporation. A buyer may be found to have assumed the selling corporation's liabilities, for example, if there has been a de facto merger or consolidation or if the successor corporation is a mere continuation of the predecessor under a different corporate name. If the seller corporation is absorbed into the buyer, and if the seller's stockholders continue to have an ownership interest in the buyer, a merger may be found even though statutory requirements were not followed. Similarly, if a new corporation is formed to acquire the assets of an existing corporation, which then ceases to exist, the successor may be found to be a mere continuation of the predecessor. "There is in effect but one corporation which merely changed its form and ordinarily ceases to exist upon the creation of the new corporation which is its successor."

Fehl v. S.W.C. Corp., 433 F.Supp. 939, 945–46 (D. Del. 1977). The *Fehl* court noted that Delaware would adopt the rule of successor liability. *Id. See* Spring Real Estate, LLC v. Echo/RT Holdings, LLC, 2013 WL 6916277, at *4–*5 (Del. Ch. 2013) (recognizing *Fehl* but not rejecting or endorsing the successor liability rule).

The shareholders of the buyer corporation do not vote. It incurs only the economic effect of buying new assets, but no change in ownership. The shareholders of the seller corporation must vote to approve the sale. DGCL § 271(a) ("Every corporation may sell, lease or exchange all or substantially all of its property and assets when and as authorized by a resolution adopted by the holders of a majority of the outstanding stock of the corporation entitled to vote thereon"). Shareholders do not have appraisal rights because they still retain the shares in the corporation.

Tender Offer

Another transaction structure is a tender offer. Mergers and asset sales involve negotiation between the two companies and their boards. They are friendly transactions, subject to the condition of a successful shareholder vote. In a tender offer, the target board is not involved in a cooperative process with the acquirer's board, and neither company's shareholders vote. The tender offer is a direct transaction between the target's shareholders and the acquirer, who makes an offer to purchase shares. If the acquirer gains sufficient shares, it gains control of the target. The target board can be passive, but takes an adversarial posture when it views the tender offer as an attempted hostile takeover.

After a successful tender offer ("success" defined as voting control), an acquirer will not own all shares because some target shareholders will not tender. What does it do with the minority stub? It can accept the situation and be happy with control. Or it can execute a second-step merger to cash out the minority. There are several ways to do a second-step cash out.

Most corporation statutes, including Delaware's, provide for a short-form merger. An acquirer can merge out the minority as a matter of right if it acquired at least 90% of shares. If it did not meet this threshold but still has voting control, it can vote its shares to do a second-step merger. Clearly, the minority shareholders would lack the votes to stop a merger. However, the acquirer would be a controlling shareholder and would owe fiduciary duties to the minority in a cash-out transaction.

In Delaware, following a tender offer for all shares, a corporation can do a second-step merger without a shareholder vote if it meets certain conditions, including: (1) the corporation's ownership stake "equals at least such percentage of the shares [that] would be required to adopt the agreement of merger" (in most cases a majority of shares); and (2) shareholders receive "the same amount and kind of cash, property, rights or securities to be paid for shares" as the shareholders who tendered their shares. DGCL § 251(h). Section 251(h) facilitates and streamlines the process to acquire a company through a tender offer.

3. VOTING IN DILUTIVE TRANSACTIONS

A shareholder vote is a significant transaction contingency. In a friendly deal in which the boards of both companies want to do the deal, a negative shareholder vote would terminate it. Deals may be structured with the shareholder vote in mind. The acquirer's shareholders are not required to vote in a triangular merger, an asset sale, and a tender offer.

Shareholders who would not have a right to vote under corporation law may still have a right to approve the deal under stock exchange rules if their corporation issues shares. The typical situation is when an acquirer issues its shares as a part of the consideration given to target shareholders. For example, in a triangular merger, the acquirer's shareholders would not vote on the transaction, but suppose the acquirer issues its shares to target shareholders. Under the stock exchange rules, shareholders must vote if:

> (1) the common stock has, or will have upon issuance, voting power equal to or in excess of 20 percent of the voting power outstanding before the issuance of such stock or of securities convertible into or exercisable for common stock; or
>
> (2) the number of shares of common stock to be issued is, or will be upon issuance, equal to or in excess of 20 percent of the number of shares of common stock outstanding before the issuance of the common stock or of securities convertible into or exercisable for common stock.

NYSE Rule 312.03(c), Shareholder Approval. *See also* NASDAQ 5635(a), Shareholder Approval (same).

4. ROLE OF FIDUCIARY DUTIES

An M&A transaction can result in dramatic changes to a shareholder's interest. The company may be eliminated through a transaction. Its capital and economic structure may have changed. The shareholder may own shares in a new company. How are shareholders protected in transactions that can result in such fundamental changes to their interest?

Shareholders are protected in a number of ways. Corporation law or stock exchange rules may require a vote. Dissenting shareholders may have appraisal rights. Voting and appraisal provide some protection when the conditions call for them, but the most fundamental protection is that directors and officers owe fiduciary duty to shareholders. Unlike voting and appraisal, fiduciary duty is a constant. Mergers require the approval of the two boards: "*The board of directors* of each corporation which desires to merge or consolidate *shall adopt a resolution approving an agreement* of merger or consolidation and declaring its advisability." *Id.* § 251(b). This is an action of the board, which is subject to fiduciary duty. When a board approved a merger, did it act in accordance with its fiduciary duty of care? When it approved or rejected an offer, did it act in accordance with the duty of loyalty? Did the board act in its self-interest, either because it had an economic interest or an interest in entrenching their positions? Was the board-approved offer fair to shareholders? Was the board improperly influenced by someone, say a controlling shareholder?

Shareholders are not the only constituents who experience dramatic changes in an M&A transaction. Directors and managers may be out of their jobs. Creditors may experience adverse changes due to a new capital structure. Employees may painfully realize the meaning of "cost synergies." Creditors and employees, generally speaking, have lesser voice in corporate governance. That is not the case with directors and managers. The risk to shareholders of wayward directors and managers is significant in an M&A transaction. Corporation law imposes fiduciary duties on the board. The board must act in accordance with the duty of care. *E.g.,* Smith v. Van Gorkom, 488 A.2d 858 (Del. 1985). It must also be loyal to the corporation and all shareholders. The risk of disloyal conduct is significant. Wrongful conduct can arise in several context. The board may be beholden to a particular shareholder or interest group. Consider the situation of a controlling shareholder to whom directors feel a gravitational allegiance due to hierarchical compunction or self-interest and thus undermine the interest of other shareholders. *E.g.,* Weinberger v. UOP Inc., 457 A.2d 701 (Del. 1983). The board may be motivated by reasons other than the best interest of the corporation and shareholders. Both the board and the management of a target corporation may have personal interest in ensuring that the corporation remains independent, thus entrenching their positions, rather than advancing the interest of all shareholders. *E.g.,* Gantler v. Stephens, 965 A.2d 695 (Del. 2009).

When there are no agency problems, the court applies the business judgment rule. This was the essential holding in *Corwin v. KKR Financial Holdings,* LLC, 125 A.3d 304 (Del. 2015): "where the stockholders have had the voluntary choice to accept or reject a transaction, the business judgment rule standard of review is the presumptively correct one and best facilitates wealth creation through the corporate form." Delaware courts have applied *Corwin* to corporate transactions. *E.g.*, In re USG Corp. Stockholder Litig., 2020 WL 5126671 (Del. Ch. 2020). In *USG*, the court dealt with the issue of whether *Corwin* applies when stockholder approval was based on faulty disclosure. The court held that it did not.

> This matter involves the acquisition (the "Acquisition") of USG Corporation, a building materials company, by a strategic buyer. The Plaintiffs, former USG stockholders, allege that USG's directors breached fiduciary duties in connection with USG's sale to Knauf. They seek monetary damages.
>
> USG's stockholders overwhelmingly approved the sale. The Defendants have moved to dismiss; first, they seek a dismissal under the rubric of *Corwin v. KKR Financial Holdings, LLC.* That case stands for the proposition that where the stockholder-owners of a corporation are given an opportunity to approve a transaction, are fully informed of the facts material to the transaction, and where the transaction is not coercive, there is no agency problem for a court to review, and litigation challenging the transaction is subject to dismissal under the business judgment rule. The Defendants' Motion in reliance on *Corwin* is rather easy to deal with, as the Complaint specifically pleads facts, which I must assume at this pleading stage are true, that make it reasonably conceivable that USG's stockholders were not fully informed at the time they approved the Acquisition. The Plaintiffs allege that USG's Board of Directors had reached a subjective belief that USG had an intrinsic value nearly 15% higher than the deal price, yet the directors failed to disclose this fact to USG's stockholders. Breaches of duty inherent in the Acquisition, therefore, cannot be deemed cleansed under the *Corwin* rationale.
>
> This raises the question of what bearing the determination described above has on the balance of the Defendants' Motion to Dismiss, which alleges that the Plaintiffs have failed to state a claim upon which relief can be granted against the Defendants. Due to an exculpation clause in USG's charter, the Plaintiffs will be required to demonstrate a breach of the duty of loyalty, or its doppelganger bad faith, to recover damages. It became clear that the Plaintiffs make two assumptions that I find unwarranted. The first is that, having pled facts that raise a reasonable inference of disclosure deficiencies sufficient to scuttle the *Corwin* defense,

they have necessarily cleared the bar of pleading bad faith on the part of the Defendant directors for purpose of withstanding a dismissal under Rule 12(b)(6). Doctrinally, the concept of bad faith and the determination of adequate disclosure for *Corwin* purposes are fundamentally separate. They involve different inquiries, the outcomes of which are not necessarily mutually supportive.

A series of hypotheticals may help illustrate the distinction. First, consider an allegation, for example, that directors omitted from a proxy statement the fact that they had received a kickback from the buyer, in return for which they cut short a sales process. Such an allegation, if adequately pled, would easily support a rejection of *Corwin* cleansing *and* a pleading of breach of loyalty. But the focus of the two inquires would be different. For *Corwin* purposes, the focus would be on what the stockholders were told; the 12(b)(6) analysis would focus on the director's allegedly faithless actions. By counterexample, this hypothetical bribe, if fully disclosed to the stockholders in way of a non-coercive vote, and in the (unlikely) scenario that the stockholders nonetheless approved the transaction, theoretically would result in dismissal under *Corwin* despite adequate pleading of a clear breach of loyalty on the part of the directors.

Conversely, posit a situation where the defendant directors have approved and submitted a merger in which the stockholders will receive \$9.50/share. They authorize a proxy statement that discloses, truthfully and completely, that their financial advisor has opined that a range of fair value for the company is \$9.00–\$9.99 per share. Now assume that, via a printer's error, half the proxies issued erroneously give the fairness range as \$6.00–\$6.66 per share. The stockholders approve the sale, half of them in theoretical reliance on the erroneous fairness range. Clearly, the error would be material and would render *Corwin* inapplicable. Such a finding by the court would have no bearing, however, on whether the complaint otherwise adequately pled bad faith or breach of the duty of loyalty against the directors sufficient to withstand a motion under Rule 12(b)(6).

Viewed in that light, and having determined that *Corwin* does not cleanse the transaction here, I must turn to the allegations of the Complaint to see whether a claim has been pled upon which I may grant relief.

B. ENTRENCHMENT AND DEFENSES

The power of a target board to just say "no" is substantial. A merger transaction does not occur unless the "board of directors of each corporation which desires to merge or consolidate adopts a resolution approving an agreement." DGCL § 251(b). The assent of the board is the first and most important hurdle in the merger process. If a target board says "no," in most cases that ends the matter. *See* Gantler v. Stephens, 965 A.2d 695, 706 (Del. 2009) ("A board's decision not to pursue a merger opportunity is normally reviewed within the traditional business judgment framework."). There is no duty to disclose this fact, and shareholders never hear of the offer. In the halls of corporate suites, preliminary advances and summary rejections are common. These matters are confidential conversations, and the public and investors seldom hear about them.[7]

Although a target board can always reject an approach, an acquirer sometimes may not go quietly into the good night. There is a divide between friendly and hostile deals. If the target is appealing enough, an acquirer may "go hostile." The target board and the acquirer battle for control. The fight may occur on several levels. The acquirer may buy shares from target shareholders through a tender offer or a purchase large blocks of shares. It may seek to enlist other shareholders to the cause. A part of this strategy might be to change the composition of the target board through a proxy contest where it present an alternative slate of directors and solicit shareholder proxies.

A target board too may not go quietly into the good night. It has defensive tactics to discourage a hostile takeover, including erecting transaction barriers between an acquirer and target shareholders. If shareholders are susceptible to the temptation of a tender offer, the target company can do in a self-tender and repurchase shares, thus removing from circulation shares more likely to tender and leaving more obstinate shares. Another strategy is to fight the public relations battle for the minds of shareholders, typically in a proxy contest. Aside from these strategies, target boards have two substantial tools.

First, corporation law permits a staggered (or classified) board in which only a certain portion of the board is up for election each year. *See* DGCL § 141(d) (providing that the corporate charter may "be divided into 1, 2 or 3 classes; the term of office of those of the first class to expire at the first annual meeting held after such classification becomes effective; of the second class 1 year thereafter; of the third class 2 years thereafter"). This defense is usually installed ex ante in anticipation of a possible hostile takeover at some point. With a staggered board, an acquirer can replace the majority of the board at the earliest in two election cycles, which would slow down the acquisition process.

---

[7] In light of the power to just say no, some commentators have argued that, in face of a tender offer, incumbent management should be severely restrained and remain passive. *See* Frank H. Easterbrook & Daniel R. Fischel, *The Proper Role of a Target's Management in Responding to a Tender Offer*, 94 Harv. L. Rev. 1161, 1164 (1981). This view, expressed among some, is not the law today. Such a law would raise a significant policy issue that can be summed in these questions: Should every corporation have a "for sale" sign in its corporate headquarters as a matter of law? Or should the decision to place a "for sale" sign be made by the board in charge of the company?

Second, perhaps the most effective weapon against a hostile takeover is a poison pill. A poison pill is a shareholder right, issuable by the board to shareholders other than the hostile acquirer. It gives them the right to purchase additional shares in the company ("flip-in" version) or in the acquiring company ("flip-over" version) at deeply discounted prices upon a triggering event, which is the hostile acquirer's acquisition of a specified percentage stake (*e.g.*, 30% ownership). A poison pill dilutes an acquirer's stake in the target (*e.g.*, from 30% to 15%). It does not theoretically preclude an acquisition; if the acquirer wants the target, it can simply "power through" the pill by just throwing more money into the acquisition. It makes the acquisition more difficult and expensive. Like most commercial purchases, there is a break point in price. Most acquisitions are based on careful economic analysis, and if the total purchase price exceeds a certain point the deal economics would not work. The company would not be desirable. The concept of the poison pill has long been validated. *See* Moran v. Household International, Inc., 500 A.2d 1346 (Del. 1985).

An important facet of the poison pill is that the rights can be redeemed by the board. This means that if the acquirer and the target ultimately agree on the terms of an acquisition, the target board can take down the defense. The poison pill, and all other takeover defenses, can be an important bridge to go from the hostile to the friendly. Takeover defenses, including the poison pill, can be an effective negotiation tool for target boards to use in negotiating a better deal on behalf of target shareholders.

> When a corporation lacks a classified board, it risks bordering on malpractice for it not to have a standard form of poison pill to allow the board, in the event of an offer for the company, to: (i) negotiate on behalf of the stockholders to secure a better price; (ii) encourage market competition by seeing whether other bidders will pay a higher price; (iii) educate the stockholders about the board's view of the merits of the offer in light of the company's standalone prospects; and (iv) channel the debate over whether a bid represents a better value for the stockholders than if the company remains independent into the less coercive context of an election contest for control of the board. Without a pill, a bidder can act quickly under the tender offer rules without the board having the chance to act for stockholders to get the highest price reasonably available."

Leo E. Strine, Jr., *Can We Do Better by Ordinary Investors? A Pragmatic Reaction to the Dueling Ideological Mythologists of Corporate Law*, 114 Colum. L. Rev. 449, 497 (2014).

There is a flip side to defensive tactics. Target boards can use takeover defenses to thwart a takeover when it believes that independence would be better. The utility of takeover defenses assumes that a board acts in the best interest of the corporation and shareholders, and so with a pure heart.

Does this assumption merit deference to the point where the business judgment rule should apply to such board actions? What else can motivate a board to erect defenses? Suppose the target board deploys them to advance an illicit cause, such as its interest in entrenchment of position and perquisites or tilting the scale for a specific person favored by the board but not in the best interest of shareholders. Such a motive, if proven, would rebut the presumption of the business judgment rule. Should the powerful presumption of the business judgment rule—being potentially outcome determinative—automatically apply in situations where a target board seeks to defend the corporation against an unwanted acquisition?

The case below discusses the legal standard applicable for reviewing a board's actions in the face of a hostile takeover. It states that under certain circumstances the court will apply an intermediate or "enhanced" standard of review, something between the deferential business judgment rule and the exacting scrutiny of an entire fairness review. In reading this case, consider these questions: (1) What is the key factor that distinguishes actions taken by a board in response to an unwanted takeover overture from other kinds of board actions? (2) What standard of review should apply when assessing a target board's defensive actions? (3) Under what circumstances should that standard of review apply?

UNOCAL CORP. V. MESA PETROLEUM CO.

493 A.2d 946 (Del. 1985)

MOORE, JUSTICE.

We confront an issue of first impression in Delaware—the validity of a corporation's self-tender which excludes from participation a stockholder making a hostile tender offer for the company's stock.

The Court of Chancery granted a preliminary injunction to Mesa Petroleum Co., enjoining an exchange offer of the defendant, Unocal Corp. for its own stock. The trial court concluded that a selective exchange offer, excluding Mesa, was legally impermissible. We cannot agree with such a blanket rule. We reverse the decision of the Court of Chancery and order the preliminary injunction vacated.

Mesa, the owner of 13% of Unocal's stock, commenced a two-tier "front loaded" cash tender offer for 64 million shares, or approximately 37%, of Unocal's outstanding stock at a price of $54 per share. The "back-end" was designed to eliminate the remaining publicly held shares by an exchange of securities purportedly worth $54 per share. Mesa issued a supplemental proxy statement to Unocal's stockholders disclosing that the securities offered in the second-step merger would be highly subordinated, and that

Unocal's capitalization would differ significantly from its present structure. Unocal has rather aptly termed such securities "junk bonds."

Unocal's board consists of eight independent outside directors and six insiders. It met on April 13, 1985, to consider the Mesa tender offer. Detailed presentations were made by legal counsel regarding the board's obligations under both Delaware corporate law and the federal securities laws. The board received a presentation from Peter Sachs on behalf of Goldman Sachs & Co. and Dillon, Read & Co. discussing the bases for their opinions that the Mesa proposal was wholly inadequate. Sachs opined that the minimum cash value that could be expected from a sale or orderly liquidation for 100% of Unocal's stock was in excess of $60 per share.

Sachs presented various defensive strategies available to the board if it concluded that Mesa's two-step tender offer was inadequate and should be opposed. One of the devices outlined was a self-tender by Unocal for its own stock with a reasonable price range of $70 to $75 per share. The cost of such a proposal would cause the company to incur $6.1–6.5 billion of additional debt, and a presentation was made informing the board of Unocal's ability to handle it.

The board adopted a resolution rejecting as grossly inadequate Mesa's tender offer. Despite the nine and one-half hour length of the meeting, no formal decision was made on the proposed defensive self-tender.

On April 15, the board met again. Unocal's Vice President of Finance and its Assistant General Counsel made a detailed presentation of the proposed terms of the exchange offer. A price range between $70 and $80 per share was considered, and ultimately the directors agreed upon $72. The board's decisions were made in reliance on the advice of its investment bankers, including the terms and conditions upon which the securities were to be issued. Based upon this advice, and the board's own deliberations, the directors unanimously approved the exchange offer. Their resolution provided that if Mesa acquired 64 million shares of Unocal stock through its own offer (the Mesa Purchase Condition), Unocal would buy the remaining 49% outstanding for an exchange of debt securities having an aggregate par value of $72 per share.

Unocal's exchange offer was commenced on April 17, and Mesa promptly challenged it by filing this suit in the Court of Chancery.

The issues we address involve these fundamental questions: Did the Unocal board have the power and duty to oppose a takeover threat it reasonably perceived to be harmful to the corporate enterprise, and if so, is its action here entitled to the protection of the business judgment rule?

We begin with the basic issue of the power of a board of directors of a Delaware corporation to adopt a defensive measure of this type. Neither issues of fairness nor business judgment are pertinent without the basic underpinning of a board's legal power to act.

The board has a large reservoir of authority upon which to draw. Its duties and responsibilities proceed from the inherent powers conferred by 8 *Del.C.* § 141(a), respecting management of the corporation's "business and affairs." The powers here being exercised derive from 8 *Del.C.* § 160(a), conferring broad authority upon a corporation to deal in its own stock. It is now well established that in the acquisition of its shares a corporation may deal selectively with its stockholders, provided the directors have not acted out of a sole or primary purpose to entrench themselves in office.

The board's power to act derives from its fundamental duty and obligation to protect the corporate enterprise, which includes stockholders, from harm reasonably perceived, irrespective of its source. In the broad context of corporate governance, including issues of fundamental corporate change, a board of directors is not a passive instrumentality.

The business judgment rule, including the standards by which director conduct is judged, is applicable in the context of a takeover. The rule is a "presumption that in making a business decision the directors of a corporation acted on an informed basis, in good faith and in the honest belief that the action taken was in the best interests of the company." *Aronson v. Lewis,* 473 A.2d 805, 812 (Del. 1984). A hallmark of the business judgment rule is that a court will not substitute its judgment for that of the board if the latter's decision can be "attributed to any rational business purpose." *Sinclair Oil Corp. v. Levien,* 280 A.2d 717, 720 (Del. 1971).

When a board addresses a pending takeover bid it has an obligation to determine whether the offer is in the best interests of the corporation and its shareholders. In that respect a board's duty is no different from any other responsibility it shoulders, and its decisions should be no less entitled to the respect they otherwise would be accorded in the realm of business judgment. There are, however, certain caveats to a proper exercise of this function. Because of the omnipresent specter that a board may be acting primarily in its own interests, rather than those of the corporation and its shareholders, there is an enhanced duty which calls for judicial examination at the threshold before the protections of the business judgment rule may be conferred.

> We must bear in mind the inherent danger in the purchase of shares with corporate funds to remove a threat to corporate policy when a threat to control is involved. The directors are of necessity confronted with a conflict of interest, and an objective decision is difficult.

In the face of this inherent conflict directors must show that they had reasonable grounds for believing that a danger to corporate policy and effectiveness existed because of another person's stock ownership. They satisfy that burden "by showing good faith and reasonable investigation."

In the board's exercise of corporate power to forestall a takeover bid our analysis begins with the basic principle that corporate directors have a fiduciary duty to act in the best interests of the corporation's stockholders. *Guth v. Loft, Inc.*, 5 A.2d 503, 510 (Del. 1939). Their duty of care extends to protecting the corporation and its owners from perceived harm whether a threat originates from third parties or other shareholders. But such powers are not absolute. A corporation does not have unbridled discretion to defeat any perceived threat by any Draconian means available.

The restriction placed upon a selective stock repurchase is that the directors may not have acted solely or primarily out of a desire to perpetuate themselves in office. To this is added the further caveat that inequitable action may not be taken under the guise of law. *Schnell v. Chris-Craft Industries, Inc.*, 285 A.2d 437, 439 (Del. 1971). The standard of proof established is designed to ensure that a defensive measure to thwart or impede a takeover is motivated by a good faith concern for the corporation and its stockholders, which in all circumstances must be free of any fraud or other misconduct. However, this does not end the inquiry.

A further aspect is the element of balance. If a defensive measure is to come within the ambit of the business judgment rule, it must be reasonable in relation to the threat posed. This entails an analysis by the directors of the nature of the takeover bid and its effect on the corporate enterprise. Examples of such concerns may include: inadequacy of the price offered, nature and timing of the offer, questions of illegality, the impact on "constituencies" other than shareholders (*i.e.*, creditors, customers, employees, and perhaps even the community generally), the risk of nonconsummation, and the quality of securities being offered in the exchange. While not a controlling factor, it also seems to us that a board may reasonably consider the basic stockholder interests at stake, including those of short term speculators, whose actions may have fueled the coercive aspect of the offer at the expense of the long term investor. Here, the threat posed was viewed by the Unocal board as a grossly inadequate two-tier coercive tender offer coupled with the threat of greenmail.

The Unocal directors had concluded that the value of Unocal was substantially above the $54 per share offered in cash at the front end. Furthermore, they determined that the subordinated securities to be exchanged in Mesa's announced squeeze out of the remaining shareholders in the "back-end" merger were "junk bonds" worth far less than $54. It is now well recognized that such offers are a classic coercive measure designed to stampede shareholders into tendering at the first tier, even if the price is inadequate, out of fear of what they will receive at the back end of the transaction. Wholly beyond the coercive aspect of an inadequate two-tier tender offer, the threat was posed by a corporate raider with a national reputation as a "greenmailer."

In adopting the selective exchange offer, the board stated that its objective was either to defeat the inadequate Mesa offer or, should the offer still succeed, provide the 49% of its stockholders, who would otherwise be forced to accept "junk bonds," with $72 worth of senior debt. We find that both purposes are valid.

Such efforts would have been thwarted by Mesa's participation in the exchange offer. If Mesa could tender its shares, Unocal would effectively be subsidizing the former's continuing effort to buy Unocal stock at $54 per share. Mesa could not, by definition, fit within the class of shareholders being protected from its own coercive and inadequate tender offer.

We are satisfied that the selective exchange offer is reasonably related to the threats posed. It is consistent with the principle that "the minority stockholder shall receive the substantial equivalent in value of what he had before." This concept of fairness, while stated in the merger context, is also relevant in the area of tender offer law. The board's decision to offer what it determined to be the fair value of the corporation to the 49% of its shareholders, who would otherwise be forced to accept highly subordinated "junk bonds," is reasonable and consistent with the directors' duty to ensure that the minority stockholders receive equal value for their shares.

While the exchange offer is a form of selective treatment, given the nature of the threat posed here the response is neither unlawful nor unreasonable. If the board of directors is disinterested, has acted in good faith and with due care, its decision in the absence of an abuse of discretion will be upheld as a proper exercise of business judgment.

In conclusion, there was directorial power to oppose the Mesa tender offer, and to undertake a selective stock exchange made in good faith and upon a reasonable investigation pursuant to a clear duty to protect the corporate enterprise. The selective stock repurchase plan chosen by Unocal is reasonable in relation to the threat that the board reasonably believed was posed by Mesa's inadequate and coercive two-tier tender offer. Under those circumstances the board's action is entitled to be measured by the standards of the business judgment rule. Unless it is shown by a preponderance of the evidence that the directors' decisions were primarily based on perpetuating themselves in office, or some other breach of fiduciary duty such as fraud, overreaching, lack of good faith, or being uninformed, a Court will not substitute its judgment for that of the board.

The decision of the Court of Chancery is reversed, and the preliminary injunction is vacated.

C. REVLON AND ITS PROGENY

The board of a target company confronts a fundamental choice when it is approached by an acquirer: Sell? Not sell? Often, an unexpected, uninvited approach is a jarring event. It triggers many questions. The board cannot make this decision willy-nilly or pursue its preference for preference sake. It is always subject to fiduciary duty. But to evaluate the propriety of the board's action, we must know the exact nature of the duty and the legal standard by which we review board action. When a board determines that the company should be sold or not sold, what are the board's duties? If a board desires to keep the company independent, in what way can it do so without violating its duties?

The case below addresses the nature of a board's fiduciary duties when the company is subject to an offer. In reading this case, consider these questions: (1) What is a board's duty when confronting a hostile takeover attempt? (2) In what way does this case doctrinally augment *Unocal Corp. v. Mesa Petroleum Co.*? (3) What is the rule of law announced in this case (what is the "Revlon duty")? (4) What is the standard of review if the Revlon duty is triggered? (5) Why did the court rule that the board did not have a duty to consider the interest of Revlon's creditors?

REVLON, INC. V. MACANDREWS & FORBES HOLDINGS, INC.

506 A.2d 173 (Del. 1986)

MOORE, JUSTICE:

In this battle for corporate control of Revlon, Inc., the Court of Chancery enjoined certain transactions designed to thwart the efforts of Pantry Pride, Inc. to acquire Revlon. The defendants are Revlon, its board of directors, and Forstmann Little & Co. The injunction barred consummation of an option granted Forstmann to purchase certain Revlon assets (the lock-up option), a promise by Revlon to deal exclusively with Forstmann in the face of a takeover (the no-shop provision), and the payment of a $25 million cancellation fee to Forstmann if the transaction was aborted. The Court of Chancery found that the Revlon directors had breached their duty of care by entering into the foregoing transactions and effectively ending an active auction for the company. The trial court ruled that such arrangements are not illegal *per se* under Delaware law, but that their use under the circumstances here was impermissible. We agree. We consider for the first time the validity of such defensive measures in the face of an active bidding contest for corporate control. Additionally, we address for the first time the extent to which a corporation may consider the impact of a takeover threat on constituencies other than shareholders. *See Unocal Corp. v. Mesa Petroleum Co.*, 493 A.2d 946, 955 (Del. 1985).

Ronald Perelman, chairman of the board and chief executive officer of Pantry Pride, met with his counterpart at Revlon, Michel Bergerac, to discuss a friendly acquisition of Revlon. Perelman suggested a price in the range of $40–50 per share, but the meeting ended with Bergerac dismissing those figures as considerably below Revlon's intrinsic value. All subsequent

Pantry Pride overtures were rebuffed, perhaps in part based on Bergerac's strong personal antipathy to Perelman.

The Revlon board met specially to consider the impending threat of a hostile bid by Pantry Pride. At the meeting, Lazard Freres, Revlon's investment banker, advised the directors that $45 per share was a grossly inadequate price for the company. Felix Rohatyn and William Loomis of Lazard Freres explained to the board that Pantry Pride's financial strategy for acquiring Revlon would be through "junk bond" financing followed by a break-up of Revlon and the disposition of its assets. With proper timing, according to the experts, such transactions could produce a return to Pantry Pride of $60 to $70 per share, while a sale of the company as a whole would be in the "mid 50" dollar range. Martin Lipton, special counsel for Revlon, recommended two defensive measures: first, that the company repurchase up to 5 million of its nearly 30 million outstanding shares; and second, that it adopt a Note Purchase Rights Plan. Under this plan, each Revlon shareholder would receive as a dividend one Note Purchase Right (the Rights) for each share of common stock, with the Rights entitling the holder to exchange one common share for a $65 principal Revlon note at 12% interest with a one-year maturity. The Rights would become effective whenever anyone acquired beneficial ownership of 20% or more of Revlon's shares, unless the purchaser acquired all the company's stock for cash at $65 or more per share. The Rights would not be available to the acquiror, and prior to the 20% triggering event the Revlon board could redeem the rights for 10 cents each. Both proposals were unanimously adopted.

Pantry Pride made its first hostile move with a cash tender offer for any and all shares of Revlon at $47.50 per common share and $26.67 per preferred share, subject to (1) Pantry Pride's obtaining financing for the purchase, and (2) the Rights being redeemed, rescinded or voided.

The directors advised the stockholders to reject the offer. Further defensive measures also were planned. Revlon commenced its own offer for up to 10 million shares, exchanging for each share of common stock tendered one Senior Subordinated Note (the Notes) of $47.50 principal at 11.75% interest, due 1995, and one-tenth of a share of $9.00 Cumulative Convertible Exchangeable Preferred Stock valued at $100 per share. Lazard Freres opined that the notes would trade at their face value on a fully distributed basis. Revlon stockholders tendered 87 percent of the outstanding shares (approximately 33 million), and the company accepted the full 10 million shares on a pro rata basis. The new Notes contained covenants which limited Revlon's ability to incur additional debt, sell assets, or pay dividends unless otherwise approved by the "independent" (non-management) members of the board.

Pantry Pride remained determined in its efforts and continued to make cash bids for the company, raising its bid to $53.

The Revlon directors met to consider Pantry Pride's $53 bid and to examine possible alternatives to the offer. Forstmann made certain proposals to the board. As a result, the directors unanimously agreed to a leveraged buyout by Forstmann. The terms of this accord were as follows: each stockholder would get $56 cash per share; management would purchase stock in the new company by the exercise of their Revlon "golden parachutes"; Forstmann would assume Revlon's $475 million debt incurred by the issuance of the Notes; and Revlon would redeem the Rights and waive the Notes covenants for Forstmann or in connection with any other offer superior to Forstmann's. The board did not actually remove the covenants, because Forstmann then lacked a firm commitment on its financing, but accepted the Forstmann capital structure, and indicated that the outside directors would waive the covenants in due course.

When the merger, and thus the waiver of the Notes covenants, was announced, the market value of these securities began to fall. The Notes, which originally traded near par, around 100, dropped to 87.50. The Wall Street Journal reported threats of litigation by these creditors.

Pantry Pride [raised its] offer to $56.25, subject to nullification of the Rights, a waiver of the Notes covenants, and the election of three Pantry Pride directors to the Revlon board.

Forstmann made a new $57.25 per share offer, based on several conditions. The principal demand was a lock-up option to purchase Revlon's Vision Care and National Health Laboratories divisions for $525 million, some $100–$175 million below the value ascribed to them by Lazard Freres, if another acquiror got 40% of Revlon's shares. Revlon also was required to accept a no-shop provision. The Rights and Notes covenants had to be removed as in the October 3 agreement. There would be a $25 million cancellation fee to be placed in escrow, and released to Forstmann if the new agreement terminated or if another acquiror got more than 19.9% of Revlon's stock. Finally, there would be no participation by Revlon management in the merger. In return, Forstmann agreed to support the par value of the Notes, which had faltered in the market, by an exchange of new notes. Forstmann also demanded immediate acceptance of its offer, or it would be withdrawn. The board unanimously approved Forstmann's proposal because: (1) it was for a higher price than the Pantry Pride bid, (2) it protected the noteholders, and (3) Forstmann's financing was firmly in place. The board further agreed to redeem the rights and waive the covenants on the preferred stock in response to any offer above $57 cash per share. The covenants were waived, contingent upon receipt of an investment banking opinion that the Notes would trade near par value once the offer was consummated.

Pantry Pride filed an amended complaint challenging the lock-up, the cancellation fee, and the exercise of the Rights and the Notes covenants. Pantry Pride again raised its bid, with a cash offer of $58 per share conditioned upon nullification of the Rights, waiver of the covenants, and an injunction of the Forstmann lock-up.

The Court of Chancery prohibited the further transfer of assets, and eight days later enjoined the lock-up, no-shop, and cancellation fee provisions of the agreement.

The ultimate responsibility for managing the business and affairs of a corporation falls on its board of directors. 8 *Del.C.* § 141(a). In discharging this function the directors owe fiduciary duties of care and loyalty to the corporation and its shareholders. *Guth v. Loft, Inc.*, 5 A.2d 503, 510 (Del. 1939); *Aronson v. Lewis,* 473 A.2d 805, 811 (Del. 1984). These principles apply with equal force when a board approves a corporate merger pursuant to 8 *Del.C.* § 251(b);[9] *Smith v. Van Gorkom,* 488 A.2d 858, 873 (Del. 1985); and of course they are the bedrock of our law regarding corporate takeover issues. *Unocal Corp. v. Mesa Petroleum Co.,* 493 A.2d 946, 953, 955 (Del. 1985). While the business judgment rule may be applicable to the actions of corporate directors responding to takeover threats, the principles upon which it is founded—care, loyalty and independence—must first be satisfied. *Aronson v. Lewis,* 473 A.2d at 812.

If the business judgment rule applies, there is a "presumption that in making a business decision the directors of a corporation acted on an informed basis, in good faith and in the honest belief that the action taken was in the best interests of the company." *Aronson v. Lewis,* 473 A.2d at 812. However, when a board implements anti-takeover measures there arises "the omnipresent specter that a board may be acting primarily in its own interests, rather than those of the corporation and its shareholders." *Unocal Corp. v. Mesa Petroleum Co.,* 493 A.2d at 954. This potential for conflict places upon the directors the burden of proving that they had reasonable grounds for believing there was a danger to corporate policy and effectiveness, a burden satisfied by a showing of good faith and reasonable investigation. The directors must analyze the nature of the takeover and its effect on the corporation in order to ensure balance—that the responsive action taken is reasonable in relation to the threat posed.

The first relevant defensive measure adopted by the Revlon board was the Rights Plan, which would be considered a "poison pill" in the current language of corporate takeovers—a plan by which shareholders receive the right to be bought out by the corporation at a substantial premium on the occurrence of a stated triggering event. The focus becomes one of reasonableness and purpose.

The Revlon board approved the Rights Plan in the face of an impending hostile takeover bid by Pantry Pride at $45 per share, a price which Revlon reasonably concluded was grossly inadequate. Lazard Freres had so

[9] The statute provides in pertinent part: "(b) The board of directors of each corporation which desires to merge or consolidate shall adopt a resolution approving an agreement of merger or consolidation."

advised the directors, and had also informed them that Pantry Pride was a small, highly leveraged company bent on a "bust-up" takeover by using "junk bond" financing to buy Revlon cheaply, sell the acquired assets to pay the debts incurred, and retain the profit for itself. In adopting the Plan, the board protected the shareholders from a hostile takeover at a price below the company's intrinsic value, while retaining sufficient flexibility to address any proposal deemed to be in the stockholders' best interests.

To that extent the board acted in good faith and upon reasonable investigation. Under the circumstances it cannot be said that the Rights Plan as employed was unreasonable, considering the threat posed.

The second defensive measure adopted by Revlon to thwart a Pantry Pride takeover was the company's own exchange offer for 10 million of its shares. However, when exercising that power in an effort to forestall a hostile takeover, the board's actions are strictly held to the fiduciary standards outlined in *Unocal*. These standards require the directors to determine the best interests of the corporation and its stockholders, and impose an enhanced duty to abjure any action that is motivated by considerations other than a good faith concern for such interests.

The Revlon directors concluded that Pantry Pride's $47.50 offer was grossly inadequate. In that regard the board acted in good faith, and on an informed basis, with reasonable grounds to believe that there existed a harmful threat to the corporate enterprise.

However, when Pantry Pride increased its offer to $50 per share, and then to $53, it became apparent to all that the break-up of the company was inevitable. The Revlon board's authorization permitting management to negotiate a merger or buyout with a third party was a recognition that the company was for sale. The duty of the board had thus changed from the preservation of Revlon as a corporate entity to the maximization of the company's value at a sale for the stockholders' benefit. This significantly altered the board's responsibilities under the *Unocal* standards. It no longer faced threats to corporate policy and effectiveness, or to the stockholders' interests, from a grossly inadequate bid. The whole question of defensive measures became moot. The directors' role changed from defenders of the corporate bastion to auctioneers charged with getting the best price for the stockholders at a sale of the company.

This brings us to the lock-up with Forstmann and its emphasis on shoring up the sagging market value of the Notes in the face of threatened litigation by their holders. Such a focus was inconsistent with the changed concept of the directors' responsibilities at this stage of the developments. The impending waiver of the Notes covenants had caused the value of the Notes to fall, and the board was aware of the noteholders' ire as well as their subsequent threats of suit. The directors thus made support of the Notes an integral part of the company's dealings with Forstmann, even though their primary responsibility at this stage was to the equity owners.

The original threat posed by Pantry Pride—the break-up of the company—had become a reality which even the directors embraced. Selective dealing to fend off a hostile but determined bidder was no longer a proper objective. Instead, obtaining the highest price for the benefit of the stockholders should have been the central theme guiding director action. Thus, the Revlon board could not make the requisite showing of good faith by preferring the noteholders and ignoring its duty of loyalty to the shareholders. The rights of the former already were fixed by contract. The noteholders required no further protection, and when the Revlon board entered into an auction-ending lock-up agreement with Forstmann on the basis of impermissible considerations at the expense of the shareholders, the directors breached their primary duty of loyalty.

The Revlon board argued that it acted in good faith in protecting the noteholders because *Unocal* permits consideration of other corporate constituencies. Although such considerations may be permissible, there are fundamental limitations upon that prerogative. A board may have regard for various constituencies in discharging its responsibilities, provided there are rationally related benefits accruing to the stockholders. However, such concern for non-stockholder interests is inappropriate when an auction among active bidders is in progress, and the object no longer is to protect or maintain the corporate enterprise but to sell it to the highest bidder.

The rights of the noteholders were fixed by agreement, and there is nothing of substance to suggest that any of those terms were violated. The Notes covenants specifically contemplated a waiver to permit sale of the company at a fair price. The Notes were accepted by the holders on that basis, including the risk of an adverse market effect stemming from a waiver. Thus, nothing remained for Revlon to legitimately protect, and no rationally related benefit thereby accrued to the stockholders. Under such circumstances we must conclude that the merger agreement with Forstmann was unreasonable in relation to the threat posed.

A lock-up is not *per se* illegal under Delaware law. Such options can entice other bidders to enter a contest for control of the corporation, creating an auction for the company and maximizing shareholder profit. Current economic conditions in the takeover market are such that a "white knight" like Forstmann might only enter the bidding for the target company if it receives some form of compensation to cover the risks and costs involved. However, while those lock-ups which draw bidders into the battle benefit shareholders, similar measures which end an active auction and foreclose further bidding operate to the shareholders' detriment.

The Forstmann option had a similar destructive effect on the auction process. Forstmann had already been drawn into the contest on a preferred basis, so the result of the lock-up was not to foster bidding, but to destroy it. The board's stated reasons for approving the transactions were: (1) better financing, (2) noteholder protection, and (3) higher price. As the

Court of Chancery found, and we agree, any distinctions between the rival bidders' methods of financing the proposal were nominal at best, and such a consideration has little or no significance in a cash offer for any and all shares. The principal object, contrary to the board's duty of care, appears to have been protection of the noteholders over the shareholders' interests.

While Forstmann's $57.25 offer was objectively higher than Pantry Pride's $56.25 bid, the margin of superiority is less when the Forstmann price is adjusted for the time value of money. In reality, the Revlon board ended the auction in return for very little actual improvement in the final bid. The principal benefit went to the directors, who avoided personal liability to a class of creditors to whom the board owed no further duty under the circumstances. Thus, when a board ends an intense bidding contest on an insubstantial basis, and where a significant by-product of that action is to protect the directors against a perceived threat of personal liability for consequences stemming from the adoption of previous defensive measures, the action cannot withstand the enhanced scrutiny which *Unocal* requires of director conduct.

In conclusion, a hostile and determined bidder sought the company at a price the board was convinced was inadequate. The initial defensive tactics worked to the benefit of the shareholders, and thus the board was able to sustain its *Unocal* burdens in justifying those measures. However, in granting an asset option lock-up to Forstmann, we must conclude that under all the circumstances the directors allowed considerations other than the maximization of shareholder profit to affect their judgment, and followed a course that ended the auction for Revlon, absent court intervention, to the ultimate detriment of its shareholders. No such defensive measure can be sustained when it represents a breach of the directors' fundamental duty of care. In that context the board's action is not entitled to the deference accorded it by the business judgment rule. The measures were properly enjoined.

NOTES

1. When is *Revlon* triggered? Beyond an all cash sale of the company, three scenarios trigger the *Revlon* duty: (1) a corporation initiates a bidding process for the sale or breakup of the company; (2) a target abandons its long-term strategy and acquiesces to a sale to a bidder; and (3) a transaction results in a change of control. Arnold v. Soc'y for Sav. Bancorp, Inc., 650 A.2d 1270, 1289-90 (Del. 1994). Courts do not provide boards with a judicial blueprint to advance shareholder wealth maximization. Since each deal is unique with different factors and dynamics, the rule does not provide an algorithmic or deterministic path. "No court can tell directors exactly how to accomplish that goal, because they will be facing a unique combination of circumstances, many of which will be outside their control." Lyondell Chem. Co. v. Ryan, 970 A.2d 235, 242 (Del. 2009). Courts do not defer to a board under the business judgment, and instead apply a heightened scrutiny for reasonableness under

which "directors are generally free to select the path to value maximization." In re Thrifty S'holder Litig., 14 A.3d 573, 595-96 (Del. Ch. 2010).

The cases below involve two situations where companies confronted hostile acquirers. Both involving Paramount Communications and are seen as doctrinally linked in the field of Delaware takeover law. In the first case, Paramount was the hostile acquirer. Then the tables turned, and in the second case Paramount was the target in a hostile bid. In reading these cases, consider these questions: (1) How did *Revlon* and *Unocal* apply? (2) Can a board just say "no"? (3) What explains the difference in the outcomes of the two Paramount cases?

PARAMOUNT COMMUNICATIONS, INC. V. TIME INC.

571 A.2d 1140 (Del. 1989)

HORSEY, JUSTICE:

Paramount Communications, Inc. and two other groups of plaintiffs ("Shareholder Plaintiffs"), shareholders of Time Incorporated separately filed suits in the Delaware Court of Chancery seeking a preliminary injunction to halt Time's tender offer for 51% of Warner Communication, Inc.'s outstanding shares at $70 cash per share. The Chancellor refused to enjoin Time's consummation of its tender offer, concluding that the plaintiffs were unlikely to prevail on the merits.

The principal ground for reversal, asserted by all plaintiffs, is that Paramount's uninvited all-cash, all-shares, "fully negotiable" (though conditional) tender offer for Time triggered duties under *Unocal Corp. v. Mesa Petroleum Co.,* 493 A.2d 946 (Del. 1985), and that Time's board of directors, in responding to Paramount's offer, breached those duties.

Plaintiffs assert a claim based on *Revlon v. MacAndrews & Forbes Holdings, Inc.,* 506 A.2d 173 (Del. 1986). Those plaintiffs argue that Time's board breached its *Revlon* duties by failing, in the face of the change of control, to maximize shareholder value in the immediate term.

We affirm the Chancellor's ultimate finding and conclusion under *Unocal.* We find that Paramount's tender offer was reasonably perceived by Time's board to pose a threat to Time and that the Time board's "response" to that threat was reasonable and proportionate.

We find that Time's board did not by entering into its initial merger agreement with Warner come under a *Revlon* duty either to auction the company or to maximize short-term shareholder value, notwithstanding the unequal share exchange. Therefore, the Time board's original plan of merger with Warner was subject only to a business judgment rule analysis. *See Smith v. Van Gorkom,* 488 A.2d 858, 873–74 (Del. 1985).

In 1987, Time established a special committee of executives to consider and propose corporate strategies for the 1990s. The consensus of the committee was that Time should move ahead in the area of ownership and creation of video programming. Some of Time's outside directors, especially Luce and Temple, had opposed this move as a threat to the editorial integrity and journalistic focus of Time.[4]

[Time considered various strategic options, and it engaged in discussions with Steve Ross, CEO of Warner Brothers.] Time's board met, with all outside directors present. Management presented the board with a profile of various entertainment companies in addition to Warner, including Disney, 20th Century Fox, Universal, and Paramount.

Of a wide range of companies considered by Time's board as possible merger candidates, the board concluded that Warner was the superior candidate for a consolidation. Warner stood out on a number of counts.

From the outset, Time's board favored an all-cash or cash and securities acquisition of Warner as the basis for consolidation. However, Steve Ross, Warner's CEO, was adamant that a business combination was only practicable on a stock-for-stock basis.

The parties ultimately agreed upon an exchange rate favoring Warner of 0.465. On that basis, Warner stockholders would have owned approximately 62% of the common stock of Time-Warner.

On March 3, 1989, Time's board met and unanimously approved the stock-for-stock merger with Warner. Warner's board likewise approved the merger. The agreement called for Warner to be merged into a wholly-owned Time subsidiary with Warner becoming the surviving corporation. The common stock of Warner would then be converted into common stock of Time at the agreed upon ratio.

The rules of the New York Stock Exchange required that Time's issuance of shares to effectuate the merger be approved by a vote of Time's stockholders. The Delaware General Corporation Law required approval of the merger by a majority of the Warner stockholders. Delaware law did not require any vote by Time stockholders.

By May, the merger appeared to be an accomplished fact.

On June 7, 1989, Paramount [made an] all-cash offer to purchase all outstanding shares of Time for $175 per share. The trading price of Time's stock rose from $126 to $170 per share.

[4] The primary concern of Time's outside directors was the preservation of the "Time Culture." They believed that Time had become recognized in this country as an institution built upon a foundation of journalistic integrity. Time's management made a studious effort to refrain from involvement in Time's editorial policy. Several of Time's outside directors feared that a merger with an entertainment company would divert Time's focus from news journalism and threaten the Time Culture.

Over the following eight days, Time's board met three times to discuss Paramount's $175 offer. The board viewed Paramount's offer as inadequate and concluded that its proposed merger with Warner was the better course of action. Therefore, the board declined to open any negotiations with Paramount and held steady its course toward a merger with Warner.

Time's financial advisors informed the board that, on an auction basis, Time's per share value was materially higher than Warner's $175 per share offer. The board concluded that Paramount's $175 offer was inadequate.

At these meetings, certain Time directors expressed their concern that Time stockholders would not comprehend the long-term benefits of the Warner merger. Large quantities of Time shares were held by institutional investors. The board feared that even though there appeared to be wide support for the Warner transaction, Paramount's cash premium would be a tempting prospect to these investors.

The following day, Time's board met to take up Paramount's offer. The board's prevailing belief was that Paramount's bid posed a threat to Time's control of its own destiny and retention of the "Time Culture." Time's board maintained its position that a combination with Warner offered greater potential for Time. Time's board formally rejected Paramount's offer.

Time's board decided to recast its consolidation with Warner into a cash and securities acquisition of Warner by Time. Time restructured its proposal to acquire Warner as follows: Time would make an immediate all-cash offer for 51% of Warner's outstanding stock at $70 per share. The remaining 49% would be purchased at some later date for a mixture of cash and securities worth $70 per share. To provide the funds required for its outright acquisition of Warner, Time would assume 7–10 billion dollars of debt, thus eliminating one of the principal transaction-related benefits of the original merger agreement.

Paramount raised its all-cash offer to buy Time's outstanding stock to $200 per share. Time's board formally rejected Paramount's $200 per share second offer. The board reiterated its belief that the offer was still inadequate. The Time board maintained that the Warner transaction offered a greater long-term value for the stockholders and, unlike Paramount's offer, did not pose a threat to Time's survival and its "culture."

The Court of Chancery posed the pivotal question: Under what circumstances must a board of directors abandon an in-place plan of corporate development in order to provide its shareholders with the option to elect and realize an immediate control premium? As applied to this case, the question becomes: Did Time's board, having developed a strategic plan of global expansion to be launched through a business combination with Warner, come under a fiduciary duty to jettison its plan and put the corporation's future in the hands of its shareholders?

While we affirm the result reached by the Chancellor, we think it unwise to place undue emphasis upon long-term versus short-term corporate strategy. First, Delaware law imposes on a board of directors the duty to manage the business and affairs of the corporation. This broad mandate includes a conferred authority to set a corporate course of action, including time frame, designed to enhance corporate profitability. Thus, the question of "long-term" versus "short-term" values is largely irrelevant because directors, generally, are obliged to chart a course for a corporation which is in its best interests without regard to a fixed investment horizon. Second, absent a limited set of circumstances as defined under *Revlon,* a board of directors, while always required to act in an informed manner, is not under any *per se* duty to maximize shareholder value in the short term, even in the context of a takeover. In our view, the pivotal question presented by this case is: "Did Time, by entering into the proposed merger with Warner, put itself up for sale?"

We first take up plaintiffs' principal *Revlon* argument, summarized above. We premise our rejection of plaintiffs' *Revlon* claim on the absence of any substantial evidence to conclude that Time's board, in negotiating with Warner, made the dissolution or break-up of the corporate entity inevitable, as was the case in *Revlon.*

Under Delaware law there are, without excluding other possibilities, two circumstances which may implicate *Revlon* duties. The first, and clearer one, is when a corporation initiates an active bidding process seeking to sell itself or to effect a business reorganization involving a clear break-up of the company. However, *Revlon* duties may also be triggered where, in response to a bidder's offer, a target abandons its long-term strategy and seeks an alternative transaction involving the breakup of the company.[13] Thus, in *Revlon,* when the board responded to Pantry Pride's offer by contemplating a "bust-up" sale of assets in a leveraged acquisition, we imposed upon the board a duty to maximize immediate shareholder value and an obligation to auction the company fairly. If, however, the board's reaction to a hostile tender offer is found to constitute only a defensive response and not an abandonment of the corporation's continued existence, *Revlon* duties are not triggered, though *Unocal* duties attach.[14]

---

[13] As we stated in *Revlon,* in both such cases, "the duty of the board [has] changed from the preservation of [the] corporate entity to the maximization of the company's value at a sale for the stockholder's benefit. [The board] no longer faces threats to corporate policy and effectiveness, or to the stockholders' interests, from a grossly inadequate bid." *Revlon v. MacAndrews & Forbes Holdings, Inc.,* 506 A.2d 173, 182 (Del. 1986).

[14] Within the auction process, any action taken by the board must be reasonably related to the threat posed or reasonable in relation to the advantage sought. Thus, a *Unocal* analysis may be appropriate when a corporation is in a *Revlon* situation and *Revlon* duties may be triggered by a defensive action taken in response to a hostile offer. Since *Revlon,* we have stated that differing treatment of various bidders is not actionable when such action reasonably relates to achieving the best price available for the stockholders.

Plaintiffs argue that the use of a lock-up agreement, a no-shop clause, and so-called "dry-up" agreements prevented shareholders from obtaining a control premium in the immediate future and thus violated *Revlon.*

We decline to extend *Revlon*'s application to corporate transactions simply because they might be construed as putting a corporation either "in play" or "up for sale." The adoption of structural safety devices alone does not trigger *Revlon.* Such devices are properly subject to a *Unocal* analysis.

We do not find in Time's recasting of its merger agreement with Warner from a share exchange to a share purchase a basis to conclude that Time had either abandoned its strategic plan or made a sale of Time inevitable. The legal consequence is that *Unocal* alone applies to determine whether the business judgment rule attaches to the revised agreement.

We turn now to plaintiffs' *Unocal* claim. Our decision does not require us to pass on the wisdom of the board's decision to enter into the original Time-Warner agreement. That is not a court's task.

We have purposely detailed the evidence of the Time board's deliberative approach, beginning in 1983–84, to expand itself. Time's decision in 1988 to combine with Warner was made only after what could be fairly characterized as an exhaustive appraisal of Time's future as a corporation. Time's board was convinced that Warner would provide the best "fit" for Time to achieve its strategic objectives. The record attests to the zealousness of Time's executives, fully supported by their directors, in seeing to the preservation of Time's "culture," *i.e.*, its perceived editorial integrity in journalism. We find ample evidence in the record to support the Chancellor's conclusion that the Time board's decision to expand the business of the company through its merger with Warner was entitled to the protection of the business judgment rule.

In *Unocal,* we held that before the business judgment rule is applied to a board's adoption of a defensive measure, the burden will lie with the board to prove (a) reasonable grounds for believing that a danger to corporate policy and effectiveness existed; and (b) that the defensive measure adopted was reasonable in relation to the threat posed. Directors satisfy the first part of the *Unocal* test by demonstrating good faith and reasonable investigation. We have stated that the refusal to entertain an offer may comport with a valid exercise of a board's business judgment.

Paramount and the individual plaintiffs extrapolate a rule of law that an all-cash, all-shares offer with values reasonably in the range of acceptable price cannot pose any objective threat to a corporation or its shareholders. Thus, Paramount would have us hold that only if the value of Paramount's offer were determined to be clearly inferior to the value created by management's plan to merge with Warner could the offer be viewed—objectively—as a threat.

Implicit in the plaintiffs' argument is the view that a hostile tender offer can pose only two types of threats: the threat of coercion that results from a two-tier offer promising unequal treatment for nontendering shareholders; and the threat of inadequate value from an all-shares, all-cash offer at a price below what a target board in good faith deems to be the present value of its shares. Since Paramount's offer was all-cash, the only conceivable "threat," plaintiffs argue, was inadequate value. We disapprove of such a narrow and rigid construction of *Unocal,* for the reasons which follow.

Plaintiffs' position represents a fundamental misconception of our standard of review under *Unocal* principally because it would involve the court in substituting its judgment as to what is a "better" deal for that of a corporation's board of directors.

The usefulness of *Unocal* as an analytical tool is precisely its flexibility in the face of a variety of scenarios. *Unocal* is not intended as an abstract standard; neither is it a structured and mechanistic procedure of appraisal. The open-ended analysis mandated by *Unocal* is not intended to lead to a simple mathematical exercise: that is, of comparing the discounted value of Time-Warner's expected trading price at some future date with Paramount's offer and determining which is the higher. Precepts underlying the business judgment rule militate against a court's engaging in the process of attempting to appraise and evaluate the relative merits of a long-term versus a short-term investment goal for shareholders.

In this case, the Time board reasonably determined that inadequate value was not the only legally cognizable threat that Paramount's all-cash, all-shares offer could present. Time's board concluded that Paramount's eleventh hour offer posed other threats. One concern was that Time shareholders might elect to tender into Paramount's cash offer in ignorance or a mistaken belief of the strategic benefit which a business combination with Warner might produce. We cannot conclude that the Time board's decision that Paramount's offer posed a threat to corporate policy and effectiveness was lacking in good faith or dominated by motives of either entrenchment or self-interest.

We turn to the second part of the *Unocal* analysis. The obvious requisite to determining the reasonableness of a defensive action is a clear identification of the nature of the threat.

Paramount argues that Time's response was unreasonable in precluding Time's shareholders from accepting the tender offer or receiving a control premium in the immediately foreseeable future. The contention stems, we believe, from a fundamental misunderstanding of where the power of corporate governance lies. Delaware law confers the management of the corporate enterprise to the stockholders' duly elected board representatives. 8 *Del.C.* § 141(a). The fiduciary duty to manage a corporate enterprise includes the selection of a time frame for achievement of corporate goals. That duty may not be delegated to the stockholders. Directors are not obliged to abandon a deliberately conceived corporate plan for a short-term shareholder profit unless there is clearly no basis to sustain the corporate strategy. *See, e.g., Revlon,* 506 A.2d 173.

The Chancellor found that Time's responsive action to Paramount's tender offer was not aimed at "cramming down" on its shareholders a management-sponsored alternative, but rather had as its goal the carrying forward of a pre-existing transaction in an altered form. Thus, the response was reasonably related to the threat.

We find plaintiffs failed to establish a reasonable likelihood of ultimate success on the merits. Therefore, we affirm.

PARAMOUNT COMMUNICATIONS, INC. v. QVC NETWORK INC.

637 A.2d 34 (Del. 1994)

VEASEY, CHIEF JUSTICE.

We review an order of the Court of Chancery dated November 24, 1993 (the "November 24 Order"), preliminarily enjoining certain defensive measures designed to facilitate a so-called strategic alliance between Viacom Inc. and Paramount Communications Inc. approved by the board of Paramount and to thwart an unsolicited, more valuable, tender offer by QVC Network Inc. In affirming, we hold that the sale of control in this case, which is at the heart of the proposed strategic alliance, implicates enhanced judicial scrutiny of the conduct of the Paramount Board under *Unocal Corp. v. Mesa Petroleum Co.,* 493 A.2d 946 (Del. 1985), and *Revlon, Inc. v. MacAndrews & Forbes Holdings, Inc.,* 506 A.2d 173 (Del. 1986).

Approximately 118 million shares of Paramount's common stock are outstanding and traded on the New York Stock Exchange. The majority of Paramount's stock is publicly held by numerous unaffiliated investors.

Viacom is controlled by Sumner Redstone, who owns indirectly approximately 85.2 percent of Viacom's voting Class A stock and approximately 69.2 percent of Viacom's nonvoting Class B stock.

Beginning in the late 1980s, Paramount investigated the possibility of acquiring or merging with other companies in the entertainment, media, or communications industry. Paramount made a tender offer for Time Inc. in 1989, but was ultimately unsuccessful. *See Paramount Communications, Inc. v. Time Inc.,* 571 A.2d 1140 (Del. 1990).

Recent efforts to explore such a transaction [between Paramount and Viacom] began at a dinner meeting between Redstone and [Martin Davis, Paramount's Chairman and CEO]. Robert Greenhill [an investment banker] attended and helped facilitate this meeting. [After a series of negotiations that followed, Paramount and Viacom agreed to a deal.]

The Paramount Board met and unanimously approved the Original Merger Agreement whereby Paramount would merge with and into Viacom. The terms of the merger provided that each share of Paramount common stock would be converted into 0.10 shares of Viacom Class A voting stock, 0.90 shares of Viacom Class B nonvoting stock, and $9.10 in cash. The Paramount Board agreed to amend its "poison pill" Rights Agreement to exempt the proposed merger with Viacom. The Original Merger Agreement also contained several provisions designed to make it more difficult for a potential competing bid to succeed. We focus on three of these defensive provisions: a "no-shop" provision (the "No-Shop Provision"), the Termination Fee, and the Stock Option Agreement.

First, under the No-Shop Provision, the Paramount Board agreed that Paramount would not solicit, encourage, discuss, negotiate, or endorse any competing transaction unless: (a) a third party "makes an unsolicited written, bona fide proposal, which is not subject to any material contingencies relating to financing"; and (b) the Paramount Board determines that discussions or negotiations with the third party are necessary for the Paramount Board to comply with its fiduciary duties.

Second, under the Termination Fee provision, Viacom would receive a $100 million termination fee if: (a) Paramount terminated the Original Merger Agreement because of a competing transaction; (b) Paramount's stockholders did not approve the merger; or (c) the Paramount Board recommended a competing transaction.

The third and most significant deterrent device was the Stock Option Agreement, which granted to Viacom an option to purchase 19.9 percent (23,699,000 shares) of Paramount's common stock at $69.14 per share if any of the triggering events for the Termination Fee occurred. The Stock Option Agreement contained two provisions that were both unusual and highly beneficial to Viacom: (a) Viacom was permitted to pay for the shares with a senior subordinated note of questionable marketability instead of cash, thereby avoiding the need to raise the $1.6 billion purchase price (the "Note Feature"); and (b) Viacom could elect to require Paramount to pay Viacom in cash a sum equal to the difference between the purchase price and the market price of Paramount's stock (the "Put Feature").

On September 12, 1993, Paramount and Viacom announced their proposed merger. In a number of public statements, the parties indicated that the pending transaction was a virtual certainty. Redstone described it as a "marriage" that would "never be torn asunder" and stated that only a "nuclear attack" could break the deal.

[Barry Diller, chairman and CEO of QVC] sent a letter to Davis on September 20, proposing a merger in which QVC would acquire Paramount for approximately $80 per share, consisting of 0.893 shares of QVC common stock and $30 in cash.

On October 21, QVC filed this action and publicly announced an $80 cash tender offer for 51 percent of Paramount's outstanding shares. Each remaining share of Paramount common stock would be converted into 1.42857 shares of QVC common stock in a second-step merger. The tender offer was conditioned on, among other things, the invalidation of the Stock Option Agreement, which was worth over $200 million by that point.

On October 24, the Paramount Board approved the Amended Merger Agreement and an amendment to the Stock Option Agreement. The Amended Merger Agreement was essentially the same as the Original Merger Agreement, except a few new provisions. One provision related to an $80 per share cash tender offer by Viacom for 51 percent of Paramount's stock, and another changed the merger consideration so that each share of Paramount would be converted into 0.20408 shares of Viacom Class A voting stock, 1.08317 shares of Viacom Class B nonvoting stock, and 0.20408 shares of a new series of Viacom convertible preferred stock.

Although the Amended Merger Agreement offered more consideration to the Paramount stockholders and somewhat more flexibility to the Paramount Board than did the Original Merger Agreement, the defensive measures designed to make a competing bid more difficult were not removed or modified.

On November 6, Viacom unilaterally raised its tender offer price to $85 per share in cash and offered a comparable increase in the value of the securities being proposed in the second-step merger. The Paramount Board agreed to recommend Viacom's higher bid to Paramount's stockholders.

QVC responded to Viacom's higher bid on November 12 by increasing its tender offer to $90 per share and by increasing the securities for its second-step merger by a similar amount.

The Paramount Board determined that the new QVC offer was not in the best interests of the stockholders. The purported basis for this conclusion was that QVC's bid was excessively conditional. The Paramount Board did not communicate with QVC regarding the status of the conditions because it believed that the No-Shop Provision prevented such communication in the absence of firm financing.

On November 24, the Court of Chancery issued its decision granting a preliminary injunction in favor of QVC and the plaintiff stockholders.

APPLICABLE PRINCIPLES OF ESTABLISHED DELAWARE LAW

The management of the business and affairs of a Delaware corporation is entrusted to its directors. 8 *Del.C.* § 141(a); *Aronson v. Lewis,* 473 A.2d 805, 811–12 (Del. 1984). Under normal circumstances, neither the courts nor the stockholders should interfere with the managerial decisions of the directors. The business judgment rule embodies the deference to which such decisions are entitled. *Aronson,* 473 A.2d at 812.

Nevertheless, there are rare situations which mandate that a court take a more direct and active role in overseeing the decisions made and actions taken by directors. In these situations, a court subjects the directors' conduct to enhanced scrutiny to ensure that it is reasonable.[9] The decisions of this Court have clearly established the circumstances where such enhanced scrutiny will be applied. *E.g., Unocal,* 493 A.2d 946; *Revlon,* 506 A.2d 173. The case at bar implicates two such circumstances: (1) the approval of a transaction resulting in a sale of control, and (2) the adoption of defensive measures in response to a threat to corporate control.

In the case before us, the public stockholders (in the aggregate) currently own a majority of Paramount's voting stock. Control of the corporation is not vested in a single person, entity, or group, but vested in the fluid aggregation of unaffiliated stockholders. In the event the Paramount-Viacom transaction is consummated, the public stockholders will receive cash and a minority equity voting position in the surviving corporation. Following such consummation, there will be a controlling stockholder who will have the voting power. Irrespective of the present Paramount Board's vision of a long-term strategic alliance with Viacom, the proposed sale of control would provide the new controlling stockholder with the power to alter that vision.

The consequences of a sale of control impose special obligations on the directors of a corporation. In particular, they have the obligation of acting reasonably to seek the transaction offering the best value reasonably available to the stockholders. The courts will apply enhanced scrutiny to ensure that the directors have acted reasonably. The obligations of the directors and the enhanced scrutiny of the courts are well-established by the decisions of this Court. The directors' fiduciary duties in a sale of control context are those which generally attach. In short, "the directors must act in accordance with their fundamental duties of care and loyalty."

In the sale of control context, the directors must focus on one primary objective—to secure the transaction offering the best value reasonably available for the stockholders—and they must exercise their fiduciary duties to further that end. *Revlon,* 506 A.2d at 182 ("The duty of the board [is] the maximization of the company's value at a sale for the stockholders' benefit.").

[There are] methods by which a board can fulfill its obligation to seek the best value reasonably available to the stockholders. These methods are designed to determine the existence and viability of possible alternatives. They include conducting an auction, canvassing the market, etc. Delaware law recognizes that there is "no single blueprint" that directors must follow.

---

[9] Where actual self-interest is present and affects a majority of the directors approving a transaction, a court will apply even more exacting scrutiny to determine whether the transaction is entirely fair to the stockholders. *E.g., Weinberger v. UOP, Inc.,* 457 A.2d 701, 710–11 (Del. 1983).

Board action in the circumstances presented here is subject to enhanced scrutiny. Such scrutiny is mandated by: (a) the threatened diminution of the current stockholders' voting power; (b) the fact that an asset belonging to public stockholders (a control premium) is being sold and may never be available again; and (c) the traditional concern of Delaware courts for actions which impair or impede stockholder voting rights.

The key features of an enhanced scrutiny test are: (a) a judicial determination regarding the adequacy of the decisionmaking process employed by the directors, including the information on which the directors based their decision; and (b) a judicial examination of the reasonableness of the directors' action in light of the circumstances then existing. The directors have the burden of proving that they were adequately informed and acted reasonably.

Although an enhanced scrutiny test involves a review of the reasonableness of the substantive merits of a board's actions,[17] a court should not ignore the complexity of the directors' task in a sale of control. There are many business and financial considerations implicated in investigating and selecting the best value reasonably available. The board of directors is the corporate decisionmaking body best equipped to make these judgments. A court applying enhanced judicial scrutiny should be deciding whether the directors made **a reasonable** decision, not **a perfect** decision. Thus, courts will not substitute their business judgment for that of the directors, but will determine if the directors' decision was, on balance, within a range of reasonableness. *See Unocal,* 493 A.2d at 955–56.

It is true that one of the circumstances bearing on these holdings was the fact that "the break-up of the company had become a reality which even the directors embraced." It does not follow, however, that a "break-up" must be present and "inevitable" before directors are subject to enhanced judicial scrutiny and are required to pursue a transaction that is calculated to produce the best value reasonably available to the stockholders.

The Paramount defendants have interpreted our decision in *Time-Warner* as requiring a corporate break-up in order for that obligation to apply. In *Time-Warner,* the Chancellor held that there was no change of control in the original stock-for-stock merger between Time and Warner because Time would be owned by a fluid aggregation of unaffiliated stockholders both before and after the merger:

> Where the shares of both constituent corporations are widely held, corporate control can be expected to remain unaffected by a

[17] In cases where the traditional business judgment rule is applicable and the board acted with due care, in good faith, and in the honest belief that they are acting in the best interests of the stockholders (which is not this case), the Court gives great deference to the substance of the directors' decision and will not invalidate the decision, will not examine its reasonableness, and "will not substitute our views for those of the board if the latter's decision can be attributed to any rational business purpose." *Unocal,* 493 A.2d at 949 (*quoting Sinclair Oil Corp. v. Levien,* Del.Supr., 280 A.2d 717, 720 (Del. 1971)). *See Aronson,* 473 A.2d at 812.

stock for stock merger. Neither corporation could be said to be acquiring the other. **Control of both remained in a large, fluid, changeable and changing market.**

The existence of a control block of stock in the hands of a single shareholder or a group with loyalty to each other does have real consequences to the financial value of "minority" stock. **But here, the merger would not have subjected Time shareholders to the risks and consequences of holders of minority shares. No control passed to anyone in the transaction contemplated.** The shareholders of Time would have "suffered" dilution, of course, but they would suffer the same type of dilution upon the public distribution of new stock.

Paramount Commc'n Inc. v. Time Inc., 1989 WL 79880 (Del. Ch. 1989).

Our decision in *Time-Warner* expressly states that the two general scenarios discussed in the above-quoted paragraph are not the **only** instances where "*Revlon* duties" may be implicated. The instant case is clearly within the first general scenario set forth in *Time-Warner*. The Paramount Board, albeit unintentionally, had "initiated an active bidding process seeking to sell itself" by agreeing to sell control of the corporation to Viacom in circumstances where another potential acquiror (QVC) was equally interested in being a bidder.

When a corporation undertakes a transaction which will cause: (a) a change in corporate control; **or** (b) a break-up of the corporate entity, the directors' obligation is to seek the best value reasonably available to the stockholders. This obligation arises because the effect of the Viacom-Paramount transaction, if consummated, is to shift control of Paramount from the public stockholders to a controlling stockholder, Viacom.

BREACH OF FIDUCIARY DUTIES BY PARAMOUNT BOARD

Having decided to sell control of the corporation, the Paramount directors were required to evaluate critically whether or not all material aspects of the Paramount-Viacom transaction (separately and in the aggregate) were reasonable and in the best interests of the Paramount stockholders in light of current circumstances.

When entering into the Original Merger Agreement, and thereafter, the Paramount Board clearly gave insufficient attention to the potential consequences of the defensive measures demanded by Viacom. The Stock Option Agreement had a number of unusual and potentially "draconian" provisions, including the Note Feature and the Put Feature. Furthermore, the Termination Fee, whether or not unreasonable by itself, clearly made Paramount less attractive to other bidders, when coupled with the Stock Option Agreement. The No-Shop Provision inhibited the Paramount Board's ability to negotiate with other potential bidders, particularly QVC which had already expressed an interest in Paramount.

From the first QVC merger proposal on September 20 through the Paramount Board meeting on November 15, QVC's interest in Paramount provided the **opportunity** for the Paramount Board to seek significantly higher value for the Paramount stockholders than that being offered by Viacom. QVC persistently demonstrated its intention to meet and exceed the Viacom offers, and frequently expressed its willingness to negotiate possible further increases.

The Paramount directors had the opportunity in the October 23–24 time frame, when the Original Merger Agreement was renegotiated, to take appropriate action to modify the improper defensive measures as well as to improve the economic terms of the Paramount-Viacom transaction. Under the circumstances existing at that time, it should have been clear to the Paramount Board that the Stock Option Agreement, coupled with the Termination Fee and the No-Shop Clause, were impeding the realization of the best value reasonably available to the Paramount stockholders. Nevertheless, the Paramount Board made no effort to eliminate or modify these counterproductive devices, and instead continued to cling to its vision of a strategic alliance with Viacom.

By November 12, 1993, the value of the revised QVC offer on its face exceeded that of the Viacom offer by over $1 billion at then current values. This significant disparity of value cannot be justified on the basis of the directors' vision of future strategy, primarily because the change of control would supplant the authority of the current Paramount Board to continue to hold and implement their strategic vision in any meaningful way.

When the directors met on November 15 to consider QVC's increased tender offer, they remained prisoners of their own misconceptions and missed opportunities to eliminate the restrictions they had imposed on themselves. The circumstances existing on November 15 made it clear that the defensive measures, taken as a whole, were problematic. The directors remained paralyzed by their uninformed belief that the QVC offer was "illusory." This final opportunity to negotiate on the stockholders' behalf and to fulfill their obligation to seek the best value reasonably available was thereby squandered.

VIACOM'S CLAIM OF VESTED CONTRACT RIGHTS

The No-Shop Provision could not validly define or limit the fiduciary duties of the Paramount directors. To the extent that a contract, or a provision thereof, purports to require a board to act or not act in such a fashion as to limit the exercise of fiduciary duties, it is invalid and unenforceable. Despite the arguments of Paramount and Viacom to the contrary, the Paramount directors could not contract away their fiduciary obligations. Since the No-Shop Provision was invalid, Viacom never had any vested contract rights in the provision.

The Stock Option Agreement contained several "draconian" aspects, including the Note Feature and the Put Feature. While we have held that lock-up options are not *per se* illegal, no options with similar features have ever been upheld by this Court. Under the circumstances of this case, the Stock Option Agreement clearly is invalid. Accordingly, Viacom never had any vested contract rights in that Agreement.

For the reasons set forth herein, the November 24, 1993, Order of the Court of Chancery has been AFFIRMED.

In *Air Products & Chemicals, Inc. v. Airgas, Inc.*, 16 A.3d 48, 67 (Del. Ch. 2011), the Delaware Court of Chancery analyzed the issue of whether the propriety of the poison pill defense in light of evidence that a majority of fully informed shareholders wanted to cash out through a hostile tender offer. The case tests the doctrines set forth by the Delaware Supreme Court in the *Unocal, Revlon*, and the two *Paramount* cases. The court's analysis shows that the intertemporal choice confronting the target board, the choice between "longterm" and "short-term" profit discussed in *Paramount Communications, Inc. v. Time Inc.*, was complex and contextual, even with the benefit of hindsight, and that the optimal choice ultimately depended on the relative profitability of the short-term choice versus the expectation of the long-term. The law review excerpt below provides the factual context. In reading this case, consider these questions: (1) Who should have the ultimate power to sell the company? (2) What is the limit of that power? (3) Can a board have a "preclusive forever" (*i.e.*, "forever no" to hostile acquirers) frame of strategic thinking?

CORPORATE SHORT-TERMISM AND INTERTEMPORAL CHOICE

Robert J. Rhee, 96 Wash. U. L. Rev. 495 (2018)

On October 15, 2009, Air Products and Chemicals ("Air Products"), a market leader in the industrial gas industry, privately approached Airgas, a midsize firm, about a potential acquisition. Private talks between the companies ensued. Air Products first offered $60 per share and then later upped the offer to $62 per share. On January 4, 2010, the Airgas board rejected this offer because it "grossly undervalued Airgas." The bid was opportunistic, the board believed, because Air Products timed the offer during the stock market crash related to the financial crisis of 2008–2009.

Undeterred, Air Products commenced a hostile takeover on February 4, 2010. The tender offer was a fully-financed, all-shares, all-cash offer at $60 per share, conditioned on the redemption of Airgas's poison pill. The next day, Airgas shares incorporated the information into the price, which closed at $60.96.[112] The offer provided a significant premium to Airgas's trading price. Air Products later raised its offer several times: on July 8 to $63.50 per share and again on September 6 to $65.50 per share. The Airgas board rejected these offers as "grossly inadequate."

After the offer went public, the composition of Airgas's shareholders changed abruptly. Short-term shareholders, who were merger arbitrageurs (hedge funds), rushed in to buy Airgas shares. The following chart shows the changing composition of shareholders over time.

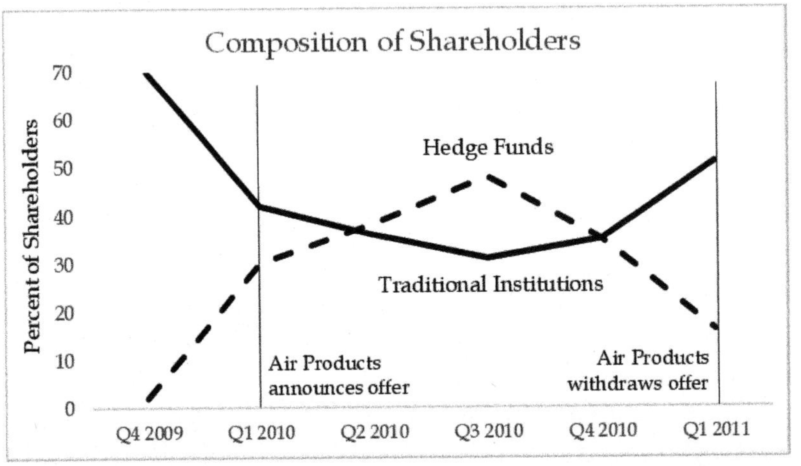

In the fourth quarter of 2009, before the public offer, about 70% of Airgas stock was held by traditional institutional shareholders with very little held by hedge funds. In the first quarter of 2010, when Air Products made its public offer, hedge funds seeking short-term profit on merger arbitrage rushed in to take a significant stake.[117] They bought most of their shares from traditional institutional shareholders who were presumably longer-term investors. These short-term shareholders sought to influence the Airgas management, and they clearly wanted the Airgas board to sell the company.[120] This new shareholder composition and the intent of hedge

112 The offer provided a premium of 38% to Airgas's closing share price on February 4, 27% over the thirty-day trading average, 29% over the fifty-two-week average, and 18% over the fifty-two-week high.

117 Airgas's chief financial officer commented on the sudden change in the shareholder base and its implication for Airgas: "Within 3 months of February, 40% of Airgas shares were transferred into the hands of arbitrage firms. That was a huge change in the complexion of the shareholder base. We continued to talk about long-term value creation and how it would exceed that provided by Air Products but long-term was not really a part of their lexicon because the arbs were in it for the quick deal. They're all about quick money rather than making longer-term return. Their time horizon is very short." CHARLES C.Y WANG, PAUL M. HEALY, PENELOPE ROSSANO & KYLE THOMAS, HARVARD BUS. SCH., AIR PRODUCTS' PURSUIT OF AIRGAS (A), CASE STUDY 9–116–024, at 7 (Nov. 12, 2015).

120 "Air Products' tender offer would almost certainly result in a change of control transaction, as the offer would likely succeed in achieving greater than 50% support from Airgas's stockholders, which largely consist of merger arbitrageurs and hedge funds who would gladly tender into Air Products' offer." *Airgas,* 16 A.3d at 95 n.312.

funds to force a sale presented the key legal issue: whether short-term shareholders posed a threat to corporate policy under the *Unocal* analysis.

Airgas had a staggered board and a shareholder rights plan ("poison pill"). This combination constitutes a formidable takeover defense. To successfully win a proxy battle, an acquirer must wage a two-year battle for control and redemption of the poison pill. The combined defense could potentially give a target board a "preclusive forever" power to rebuff all sales.[125] Air Products fought the takeover battle on two fronts: a proxy contest for the control of the Airgas board, and a lawsuit to force the Airgas board to redeem the poison pill.

Airgas had a nine-member staggered board. For the coming election cycle, Air Products nominated three independent directors for election. On September 15, 2010, it won and installed its three nominees to the Airgas board. Merger arbitrageurs delivered the necessary votes in this proxy battle. But Air Products needed to wait a full year to nominate another slate of three directors and thereby install a majority of the board.

The takeover saga reached a fever pitch on December 9, 2010, when Air Products made its "best and final" offer of $70 per share and set it to expire on February 15, 2011. The Airgas board rejected this bid as "clearly inadequate" and stated that Airgas was worth at least $78 per share. In a surprising turn of events, the three newly elected Air Products nominees agreed as a part of a unanimous Airgas board (they "changed teams" as the court loosely characterized this unexpected turn).

In light of the Airgas board's continued resistance, Air Products could succeed in its tender offer only if the court ordered the board to redeem the poison pill. The key question was: When shareholders are fully informed of all information related to the value of the company and are not subject to structural coercion in the tender offer,[135] "who gets to decide when and if the corporation is for sale?"[136] The court applied the *Unocal* two-prong test to determine the propriety of the poison pill.

AIR PRODUCTS AND CHEMICALS, INC. V. AIRGAS, INC.

16 A.3d 48 (Del. Ch. 2011)

A. *Has the Airgas Board Established That It Reasonably Perceived the Existence of a Legally Cognizable Threat?*

Under the first prong of *Unocal,* defendants bear the burden of showing that the Airgas board, "after a reasonable investigation determined in good faith, that the [Air Products offer] presented a threat

[125] *Airgas,* 16 A.3d at 113–14.

[135] *Airgas,* 16 A.3d at 54, 77, 106.

[136] *Airgas,* 16 A.3d at 54.

that warranted a defensive response." I focus my analysis on the defendants' actions in response to Air Products' current $70 offer.

In examining defendants' actions under this first prong of *Unocal,* "the presence of a majority of outside independent directors coupled with a showing of reliance on advice by legal and financial advisors, constitutes a prima facie showing of good faith and reasonable investigation." Here, it is undeniable that the Airgas board meets this test.

First, it is currently comprised of a majority of outside independent directors—including the three recently-elected insurgent directors who were nominated to the board by Air Products.

Second, the Airgas board relied on not one, not two, but three outside independent financial advisors in reaching its conclusion that Air Products' offer is "clearly inadequate." In short, the Airgas board's process easily passes the smell test.

The first part of *Unocal* review requires the board to show that its good faith and reasonable investigation ultimately gave the board "grounds for concluding that a threat to the corporate enterprise existed."

The only threat that the board discussed—the threat that has been the central issue since the beginning of this case—is the inadequate price of Air Products' offer. Thus, inadequate price, coupled with the fact that a majority of Airgas's stock is held by merger arbitrageurs who might be willing to tender into such an inadequate offer, is the only real "threat" alleged. In fact, Airgas directors have admitted as much.

Airgas's directors concede that the Airgas stockholder base is sophisticated and well-informed, and that they have all the information necessary to decide whether to tender into Air Products' offer.[389]

Inadequate price and the concept of substantive coercion are inextricably related. The Delaware Supreme Court has defined substantive coercion as "the risk that [Airgas's] stockholders might accept [Air Products'] inadequate Offer because of 'ignorance or mistaken belief' regarding the Board's assessment of the long-term value of [Airgas's] stock." If management advises stockholders, in good faith, that it believes Air Products' hostile offer is inadequate because in its view the future earnings potential of the company is greater than the price offered, Airgas's stockholders might nevertheless reject the board's advice and tender.

In essence, Airgas's argument is that "the substantial ownership of Airgas stock by these short-term, deal-driven investors poses a threat to

[389] For example, Clancey testified that the Airgas stockholders have access to "more than adequate" information upon which to base their decision whether or not to tender into Air Products' offer—"all the information that they could ever want is available." This includes the public and well-known opinion of the Airgas board, as well as that of its financial advisors and numerous analysts' reports with numbers that are "very close or almost identical to management's own internal projections for this company going forward."

the company and its shareholders"—the threat that, because it is likely that the arbs would support the $70 offer, "shareholders will be coerced into tendering into an inadequate offer." The threat of "arbs" is a new facet of substantive coercion, different from the substantive coercion claim recognized in *Paramount*.[410] Airgas's claim is that it needs to maintain its defensive measures to prevent control from being surrendered for an unfair or inadequate price. The argument is premised on the fact that a large percentage (almost half) of Airgas's stockholders are merger arbitrageurs—many of whom bought into the stock when Air Products first announced its interest in acquiring Airgas, at a time when the stock was trading much lower than it is today—who would be willing to tender into an inadequate offer because they stand to make a significant return on their investment even if the offer grossly undervalues Airgas in a sale. "They don't care a thing about the fundamental value of Airgas." The risk is that a majority of Airgas's stockholders will tender into Air Products' offer despite its inadequate price tag, leaving the minority "coerced" into taking $70 as well.

The threat that merger arbs will tender into an inadequately priced offer is only a legitimate threat if the offer is indeed inadequate. "The only way to protect stockholders [from a threat of substantive coercion] is for courts to ensure that the threat is real and that the board asserting the threat is not imagining or exaggerating it."

If a majority of stockholders *want* to tender into an inadequately priced offer, is that substantive coercion? Is that a threat that justifies continued maintenance of the poison pill? Put differently, is there evidence in the record that Airgas stockholders are so "focused on the short-term" that they would "take a smaller harvest in the swelter of August over a larger one in Indian Summer"? Air Products argues that there is none whatsoever. They argue that there is "no evidence in the record that [Airgas's short-term] holders [*i.e.*, arbitrageurs and hedge funds] would not reject the $70 offer if it was viewed by them to be inadequate. Defendants have not demonstrated a single fact supporting their argument that a threat to Airgas stockholders exists because the Airgas stock is held by investors with varying time horizons."

Both Airgas's expert and well as *Air Products' own expert* testified that a large number—if not all—of the arbitrageurs who bought into Airgas's stock at prices significantly below the $70 offer price would be happy to tender their shares at that price regardless of the potential long-term value of the company.[425] I find sufficient evidence that a majority of stockholders

---

[410] *Paramount Commc'ns, Inc. v. Time, Inc.*, 571 A.2d 1140 (Del.1990). Similar concerns about short-term investors were noted in *Paramount*, however: "Large quantities of Time shares were held by institutional investors. The board feared that even though there appeared to be wide support for the Warner transaction, Paramount's cash premium would be a tempting prospect to these investors." *Id.* at 1148.

[425] SEH Tr. 567–68 (Harkins) ("Arbitrageurs typically purchase their shares at elevated levels in order to profit by realizing the spread between the price they paid and the deal price. If the offer fails and the stock returns to pre-bid levels or to anticipated post-tender trading levels,

might be willing to tender their shares regardless of whether the price is adequate or not—thereby ceding control of Airgas to Air Products. This is a clear "risk" under the teachings of *Paramount*[427] because it would essentially thrust Airgas into *Revlon* mode.

When a company is not in *Revlon* mode, a board of directors "is not under any *per se* duty to maximize shareholder value in the short term, even in the context of a takeover."[429] The Supreme Court has unequivocally "endorsed [the] conclusion that it is not a breach of faith for directors to determine that the present stock market price of shares is not representative of true value or that there may indeed be several market values for any corporation's stock." I find that the Airgas board acted in good faith and relied on the advice of its financial and legal advisors in coming to the conclusion that Air Products' offer is inadequate. And as the Supreme Court has held, a board that in good faith believes that a hostile offer is inadequate may "properly employ a poison pill as a proportionate defensive response to protect its stockholders from a 'low ball' bid."

B. Is the Continued Maintenance of Airgas's Defensive Measures Proportionate to the "Threat" Posed by Air Products' Offer?

Turning now to the second part of the *Unocal* test, I must determine whether the Airgas board's defensive measures are a proportionate response to the threat posed by Air Products' offer. Defendants bear the burden of showing that their defenses are not preclusive or coercive, and if neither, that they fall within a "range of reasonableness."

Airgas's defensive measures are certainly not coercive in [the sense that] Airgas is specifically *not* trying to cram down a management sponsored alternative, but rather [it] simply wants to maintain the status quo and manage the company for the long term.

Air Products and Shareholder Plaintiffs argue that Airgas's defensive measures are preclusive because they render the possibility of an effective proxy contest realistically unattainable. The real issue posed is whether defensive measures are "preclusive" if they make gaining control of the board realistically unattainable in the short term (but still realistically attainable sometime in the future), or if "preclusive" actually means "preclusive"—*i.e.*, forever unattainable. In practice, these two formulations ("preclusive for now" or "preclusive forever") may be one and the same

the arbitrageurs would suffer huge losses. I think it's widely understood that short-term investors own close to if not a majority of this company. So if you decided to not tender, you would be making that decision knowing and believing that owners of a majority were likely to tender."); SEH Tr. 735–36 (Morrow) ("Q. You don't know any merger arb who, given a choice between tendering for 70 bucks and waiting for a second-step merger three or four months later at the same price, would choose not to tender and wait for that second-step merger instead; right? A. That's correct.").

[427] Airgas's board is not under "a fiduciary duty to jettison its plan and put the corporation's future in the hands of its stockholders." *Paramount Commc'ns, Inc. v. Time, Inc.*, 571 A.2d 1140, 1149–50 (Del.1990).

[429] *Paramount*, 571 A.2d at 1150.

when examining the combination of a staggered board plus a poison pill, because no bidder to my knowledge has ever successfully stuck around for two years and waged two successful proxy contests to gain control of a classified board in order to remove a pill. So does that make the combination of a staggered board and a poison pill preclusive?

This precise question was asked and answered four months ago in *Versata Enterprises, Inc. v. Selectica, Inc.* The Delaware Supreme Court rejected this argument, stating that "*that the combination of a classified board and a Rights Plan do not constitute a preclusive defense.*"

Air Products has already run one successful slate of insurgents. Their three independent nominees were elected to the Airgas board in September. Airgas's next annual meeting will be held sometime around September 2011. Accordingly, if Airgas's defensive measures remain in place, Air Products has two options if it wants to continue to pursue Airgas at this time: (1) It can call a special meeting and remove the entire board with a supermajority vote of the outstanding shares, or (2) It can wait until Airgas's 2011 annual meeting to nominate a slate of directors. I will address the viability of each of these options in turn.

If Air Products is unwilling to wait another eight months to run another slate of nominees, that is a business decision of the Air Products board, but as the Supreme Court has held, waiting until the next annual meeting "delays—but [does] not prevent—[Air Products] from obtaining control of the board."[479] I thus am constrained to conclude that Airgas's defensive measures are not preclusive.

"If a defensive measure is neither coercive nor preclusive, the *Unocal* proportionality test requires the focus of enhanced judicial scrutiny to shift to the range of reasonableness." The reasonableness of a board's response is evaluated in the context of the specific threat identified—the "specific nature of the threat sets the parameters for the range of permissible defensive tactics at any given time."

Here, the record demonstrates that Airgas's board, composed of a majority of outside, independent directors, acting in good faith and with numerous outside advisors concluded that Air Products' offer clearly undervalues Airgas in a sale transaction. The board believes in good faith that the offer price is inadequate by no small margin. Thus, the board is responding to a legitimately articulated threat.

[479] Although the three Air Products Nominees from the September 2010 election all have joined the rest of the Airgas board in its current views on value, if Air Products nominated another slate of directors who were elected, there is no question that it would have "control" of the Airgas board—*i.e.*, it will have nominated and elected the majority of the board members. There is no way to know at this point whether or not those three hypothetical New Air Products Nominees would join the rest of the board in its view, or whether the entire board would then decide to remove its defensive measures. The preclusivity test is whether obtaining control of the board is realistically unattainable, and here I find that it is not. Considering whether some future hypothetical Air-Products-Controlled Airgas board would vote to redeem the pill is not the relevant inquiry.

This conclusion is bolstered by the fact that the three Air Products Nominees on the Airgas board have now wholeheartedly joined in the board's determination—what is more, they believe it is their fiduciary duty to keep Airgas's defenses in place. And Air Products' *own directors* have testified that (1) they have no reason to believe that the Airgas directors have breached their fiduciary duties, (2) even though plenty of information has been made available to the stockholders, they "agree that Airgas management is in the best position to understand the intrinsic value of the company," and (3) if the shoe were on the other foot, they would act in the same way as Airgas's directors have.

What occurred here is not what Air Products expected to happen. Air Products ran its slate on the promise that its nominees would "consider without any bias [Air Products'] Offer," and that they would "be willing to be outspoken in the boardroom about their views on these issues." Air Products *got what it wanted.* Its three nominees got elected to the Airgas board and then questioned the directors about their assumptions. (They got answers.) They looked at the numbers themselves. (They were impressed.) They requested outside legal counsel. (They got it.) They requested a third outside financial advisor. (They got it.) And in the end, they *joined in the board's view* that Air Products' offer was inadequate. John Clancey, one of the Air Products Nominees, grabbed the flag and championed Airgas's defensive measures, telling the rest of the board, "*We have to protect the pill.*"

The Supreme Court has clearly held that "the inadequate value of an all cash for all shares offer is a legally cognizable threat." Moreover, "the fiduciary duty to manage a corporate enterprise includes the selection of a time frame for achievement of corporate goals. *That duty may not be delegated to the stockholders.*"[493] The Court continued, "Directors are not obligated to abandon a deliberately conceived corporate plan for a short-term shareholder profit unless there is clearly no basis to sustain the corporate strategy." Based on all of the foregoing factual findings, I cannot conclude that there is "clearly no basis" for the Airgas board's belief in the sustainability of its long-term plan.

On the contrary, the maintenance of the board's defensive measures must fall within a range of reasonableness. The board is not "cramming down" a management-sponsored alternative—or *any* company-changing alternative. The board is simply maintaining the status quo, running the company for the long-term, and consistently showing improved financial results each passing quarter. The board's actions do not *forever* preclude Air Products, or any bidder, from acquiring Airgas or from getting around Airgas's defensive measures if the price is right. In the meantime, the board is preventing a change of control from occurring at an inadequate price. This course of action has been clearly recognized under Delaware

[493] *Paramount Commc'ns, Inc. v. Time, Inc.*, 571 A.2d 1140, 1154 (Del.1990).

law: "directors, when acting deliberately, in an informed way, and in the good faith pursuit of corporate interests, may follow a course designed to achieve long-term value even at the cost of immediate value maximization."

There is no question that poison pills act as potent anti-takeover drugs with the potential to be abused. Counsel for plaintiffs make compelling policy arguments in favor of redeeming the pill—to do otherwise, they say, would essentially make all companies with staggered boards and poison pills "takeover proof." The argument is an excellent sound bite, but it is ultimately not the holding of this fact-specific case.

In order to have any effectiveness, pills do not—and can not—have a set expiration date. To be clear, though, this case does not endorse "just say never." What it does endorse is Delaware's long-understood respect for reasonably exercised managerial discretion, so long as boards are found to be acting in good faith and in accordance with their fiduciary duties (after rigorous judicial fact-finding and enhanced scrutiny of their defensive actions). The Airgas board serves as a quintessential example.

Directors still owe fiduciary duties to *all stockholders*—this includes short-term as well as long-term holders. At the same time, a board cannot be forced into *Revlon* mode any time a hostile bidder makes a tender offer that is at a premium to market value. The mechanisms in place to get around the poison pill—even a poison pill in combination with a staggered board, which no doubt makes the process prohibitively more difficult—have been in place since 1985, when the Delaware Supreme Court first decided to uphold the pill as a legal defense to an unwanted bid. That is the current state of Delaware law until the Supreme Court changes it.

Air Products' requests for relief are denied, and all claims asserted against defendants are dismissed with prejudice.

NOTES

1. After fending off Air Products, Airgas stayed independent for a few years. Then it ultimately sold to a bigger company in a friendly deal.

> After the chancery court's decision, Air Products ended its bid. But the Airgas saga lived on. Airgas stayed independent for a few more years, but continued to be the apple of acquirers' eyes. It faced another informal approach from Air Products, and it had to contend with an influential activist shareholder who took a stake in Airgas. These events pressured Airgas to seek a friendly deal. On November 17, 2015, it agreed to be acquired by Air Liquide, another industry leader, for $143 per share, and the acquisition closed in 2016.

Robert J. Rhee, *Corporate Short-Termism and Intertemporal Choice*, 96 Wash. U.L. Rev. 495, 525 (2018). Does the fact that Airgas ultimately sold for $143 per share validate the Airgas board's decision and the chancery court's ruling?

APPENDIX A

OPERATING AGREEMENT OF CHRYSLER GROUP LLC

■ ■ ■

FOURTH AMENDED AND RESTATED LIMITED LIABILITY COMPANY AGREEMENT OF CHRYSLER GROUP LLC[1]

Dated as of June 10, 2014

THE MEMBERSHIP INTERESTS REPRESENTED BY THIS FOURTH AMENDED AND RESTATED LIMITED LIABILITY COMPANY AGREEMENT HAVE NOT BEEN REGISTERED UNDER THE UNITED STATES SECURITIES ACT OF 1933, AS AMENDED.

THE MEMBERSHIP INTERESTS REPRESENTED BY THIS FOURTH AMENDED AND RESTATED LIMITED LIABILITY COMPANY AGREEMENT ARE ALSO SUBJECT TO ADDITIONAL RESTRICTIONS ON TRANSFER SET FORTH IN THIS FOURTH AMENDED AND RESTATED LIMITED LIABILITY COMPANY AGREEMENT OR IN THE CERTIFICATE ATTACHED AS EXHIBIT A HERETO.

TABLE OF CONTENTS

ARTICLE I: DEFINITIONS

Section 1.1 Specific Definitions
Section 1.2 Other Definitions

ARTICLE II: ORGANIZATIONAL MATTERS; GENERAL PROVISIONS

Section 2.1 Name
Section 2.2 Formation and Continuation
Section 2.3 Purposes
Section 2.4 Powers
Section 2.5 Principal Business Office
Section 2.6 Registered Agent
Section 2.7 Limited Liability
Section 2.8 Duration
Section 2.9 Filings; Qualification in Other Jurisdictions

ARTICLE III: CAPITALIZATION; MEMBERSHIP INTERESTS

Section 3.1 Membership Interests; Capitalization; Capital Accounts

[1] Chrysler Group LLC Form 8-K (June 13, 2014), *available at* https://www.sec.gov/Archives/edgar/data/1513153/000119312514235676/d743061dex31.htm. The company subsequently amended the operating agreement to rename the company as FCA US LLC. The amendment follows the operating agreement.

Section 3.2 Application of Article 8 of the Uniform Commercial Code
Section 3.3 Certification of Membership Interests

ARTICLE IV: CONTRIBUTION; ALLOCATIONS; DISTRIBUTIONS

Section 4.1 Additional Contributions
Section 4.2 Allocation of Profits and Losses
Section 4.3 Tax Matters
Section 4.4 Distributions

ARTICLE V: BOARD OF MANAGERS; OFFICERS

Section 5.1 Establishment of Board of Directors
Section 5.2 General Powers of the Board of Directors
Section 5.3 Election of Directors
Section 5.4 Meetings
Section 5.5 Notice of Meetings
Section 5.6 Quorum
Section 5.7 Voting
Section 5.8 Action Without a Meeting; Telephonic Meetings
Section 5.9 Compensation of Directors; Expense Reimbursement
Section 5.10 Committees of the Board of Directors
Section 5.11 Delegation of Authority
Section 5.12 Officers
Section 5.13 Standard of Care; Fiduciary Duties; Liability of Directors and Officers

ARTICLE VI: INDEMNIFICATION

Section 6.1 General Indemnity
Section 6.2 Rights Non-Exclusive
Section 6.3 Merger or Consolidation; Other Entities
Section 6.4 No Member Recourse

ARTICLE VII: ADMISSION OF ADDITIONAL MEMBERS

Section 7.1 Admission Requirements
Section 7.2 Acceptance of Prior Acts
Section 7.3 Transfers; Admission of Transferees

ARTICLE VIII: DISSOLUTION

Section 8.1 In General
Section 8.2 Reasonable Time for Winding Up

ARTICLE IX: RIGHTS AND DUTIES OF MEMBERS

Section 9.1 Members
Section 9.2 No Member Fiduciary Duties

ARTICLE X: MEETINGS OF MEMBERS

Section 10.1 Meetings of the Members
Section 10.2 Notice of Meetings
Section 10.3 Adjournments
Section 10.4 Quorum
Section 10.5 Organization
Section 10.6 Waiver of Notice of Meetings of Members
Section 10.7 Determination of Members of Record

ARTICLE XI: INFORMATION RIGHTS; BOOKS AND RECORDS

Section 11.1 Schedule of Members
Section 11.2 Books and Records; Other Documents
Section 11.3 Reports and Audits
Section 11.4 Financial Statements and Other Information
Section 11.5 Independent Auditor

ARTICLE XII: MISCELLANEOUS PROVISIONS

Section 12.1 Separability of Provision
Section 12.2 Notices
Section 12.3 Entire Agreement
Section 12.4 Governing Law
Section 12.5 Amendments
Section 12.6 Sole Benefit of Members
Section 12.7 Independent Contractors; Expenses
Section 12.8 Creditors
Section 12.9 Further Action
Section 12.10 Delivery by Facsimile or Email
Section 12.11 Interpretative Matters

DEFINITIONS ADDENDUM

SCHEDULE OF MEMBERS

ANNEX A—Form of Certificate

ANNEX B—Schedule of Authority

This Fourth Amended and Restated Limited Liability Company Agreement (this "Agreement") of Chrysler Group LLC (the "Company"), dated and effective as of June 10, 2014 (the "Effective Date"), is entered into by and among those persons or entities signing below or identified on the Schedule of Members (as the same may be amended from time to time) as members (the "Members") of the Company.

WHEREAS, the Company was formed as a limited liability company pursuant to the Delaware Limited Liability Company Act, 6 *Del. C.* § 18–101 et seq. (the "LLC Act") by causing the filing of a Certificate of Formation of the Company (the "Certificate of Formation") with the office of the Secretary of State of the State of Delaware on April 28, 2009, and entering into the Limited Liability Company Agreement of the Company, dated as of April 28, 2009 (the "Original Agreement").

WHEREAS, the Company subsequently amended and restated the Original Agreement on May 14, 2009, and entered into additional amended and restated agreements on June 10, 2009 (which was amended by that certain First Amendment, dated August 7, 2009, that certain Second Amendment, dated January 29, 2010 and that certain Third Amendment, dated April 5, 2011, the "2009 Agreement") and through a third amended and restated agreement on February 24, 2012 (as amended by that certain First Amendment, dated July 27, 2012, and that certain Second Amendment, dated January 21, 2014, the "2012 Agreement").

WHEREAS, following acquisition by FNA (as herein defined) of all of the Membership Interests (as herein defined) not previously held by FNA, the Company wishes to amend and restate the 2012 Agreement.

NOW, THEREFORE, the Members, by execution of this Agreement, hereby agree as follows:

ARTICLE I: DEFINITIONS

Section 1.1 Specific Definitions. As used in this Agreement, and unless the context requires a different meaning, the terms defined in Part I of the Definitions Addendum have the meanings specified or referred to therein.

Section 1.2 Other Definitions. Other terms may be defined elsewhere in the text of this Agreement and, unless otherwise indicated, shall have such meaning indicated throughout this Agreement in the various Sections identified in Part II of the Definitions Addendum.

ARTICLE II: ORGANIZATIONAL MATTERS; GENERAL PROVISIONS

Section 2.1 Name. The name of the limited liability company shall be Chrysler Group LLC.

Section 2.2 Formation and Continuation.

(a) The Company was organized and hereby continues as a limited liability company under the LLC Act, upon the terms and subject to the conditions set forth in this Agreement.

(b) The rights, duties and liabilities of the Members shall be as provided in the LLC Act, except as otherwise provided herein. To the extent that the rights, powers, duties, obligations and liabilities of any Members are different by reason of any provision of this Agreement than they would be in the absence of such provision, this Agreement shall, to the extent permitted by the LLC Act, control.

(c) This Agreement completely amends, restates and supersedes in all respects the 2012 Agreement and each of its predecessor agreements.

Section 2.3 Purposes. The Company is formed for the object and purpose of, and the nature of the business to be conducted and promoted by the Company is, engaging in any lawful act or activity for which limited liability companies may be formed under the LLC Act, as such acts or activities may be determined by the Board of Directors (as herein defined) from time to time.

Section 2.4 Powers.

(a) The nature of the business or purposes to be conducted or promoted by the Company is to engage in any lawful act or activity for which limited liability companies may be organized under the LLC Act. The Company may engage in any and all activities necessary, desirable or incidental to the accomplishment of the foregoing. Notwithstanding anything herein to the contrary, nothing set forth herein shall be construed as authorizing the Company to possess any purpose or power, or to do any act or thing, forbidden by Law to a limited liability company organized under the Laws of the State of Delaware.

(b) Subject to the provisions of this Agreement and except as prohibited by Law, (i) the Company may enter into, deliver and perform any and all agreements, consents, deeds, contracts, proxies, covenants, bonds, checks, drafts, bills of exchange, notes, acceptances and endorsements, and all evidences of indebtedness and other documents, instruments or writings of any nature whatsoever, all without any further act, vote or approval of any Member, and (ii) the Company may authorize (including by general delegated authority) any Person to enter into, deliver and perform on behalf of the Company any and all agreements, consents, deeds, contracts, proxies, covenants, bonds, checks, drafts, bills of exchange, notes, acceptances and endorsements, and all evidences of indebtedness and other documents, instruments or writings of any nature whatsoever.

(c) Subject to the other provisions of this Agreement, the Company shall do all things necessary to maintain its existence separate and apart from each Member and any Affiliate of any Member and shall maintain its books and records separate from those of any Affiliate of the Company or any other Person.

Section 2.5 **Principal Business Office**. The principal business office of the Company shall be located at 1000 Chrysler Drive, Auburn Hills, Michigan 48326, or at such other location as the Company as determined by the Board of Directors may designate from time to time in writing to be filed with the records of the Company.

Section 2.6 **Registered Agent**. The Company's initial registered agent in the State of Delaware for service of process is identified in the Certificate of Formation filed with the Secretary of State of the State of Delaware. The Company may, as determined by the Board of Directors, from time to time change the registered agent, and any such change shall be reflected in appropriate filings with the Secretary of State of the State of Delaware.

Section 2.7 **Limited Liability**. Except as otherwise provided by the LLC Act, the debts, obligations and liabilities of the Company, whether arising in contract, tort or otherwise, shall be solely the debts, obligations and liabilities of the Company, and no Member shall be obligated personally for any such debt, obligation or liability of the Company solely by reason of being a member of the Company.

Section 2.8 **Duration**. The period of the Company's duration commenced on April 28, 2009 and shall continue in full force and effect in perpetuity; provided that the Company may be dissolved and wound up in accordance with the provisions of this Agreement and the LLC Act.

Section 2.9 **Filings; Qualification in Other Jurisdictions**. The Company may prepare any documents required to be filed or appropriate for filing under the LLC Act, and the Company shall cause each such document to be filed in accordance with the LLC Act, and, to the extent required by Law, to be filed and recorded, and/or notice thereof to be published, in the appropriate place in any jurisdiction in which the Company may have established, or after the Effective Date may establish, a place of business. The Company may be qualified, formed or registered under assumed or fictitious name statutes or similar Laws in any jurisdiction in which the Company transacts business where the Company is not currently so qualified, formed or registered. Any Officer, acting individually as an authorized person within the meaning of the LLC Act, may execute, deliver and file any such documents (and any amendments and/or restatements thereof) necessary for the Company to accomplish the foregoing. The Company may appoint any other authorized persons to execute, deliver and file any such documents.

ARTICLE III: CAPITALIZATION; MEMBERSHIP INTERESTS

Section 3.1 **Membership Interests; Capitalization; Capital Accounts.**

(a) The Company shall have one authorized class of Membership Interests, consisting of 1,632,654 Membership Interests which may be issued in one or more series. A Membership Interest shall for all purposes be personal property. For purposes of this Agreement, Membership Interests held by the Company or any of its Subsidiaries shall be deemed not to be outstanding. The Company may issue fractional Membership Interests pursuant to the terms of this Agreement, and all fractional Membership Interests shall be rounded to the fourth decimal place.

(b) The Members of the Company consist of the Persons named as Members on the Schedule of Members. The Company shall update the Schedule of Members to reflect any changes in the Members, the Membership Interests and the Total Interest of the Members in accordance with the terms of this Agreement. The Company shall maintain a separate capital account (a "Capital Account") for each Member in accordance with Section 1.704–1(b)(2)(iv) of the Treasury Regulations.

Section 3.2 Application of Article 8 of the Uniform Commercial Code. Each Membership Interest shall constitute a "security" within the meaning of, and governed by, (i) Article 8 of the Uniform Commercial Code (including Section 8–102(a)(15) thereof) as in effect from time to time in the State of Delaware (the "UCC"), and (ii) the corresponding provisions of the Uniform Commercial Code of any other applicable jurisdiction that now or hereafter substantially includes the 1994 revisions to Article 8 thereof as adopted by the American Law Institute and the National Conference of Commissioners on Uniform State Laws and approved by the American Bar Association on February 14, 1995. Notwithstanding any provision of this Agreement to the contrary, to the extent that any provision of this Agreement is inconsistent with any non-waivable provision of Article 8 of the UCC, such provision of Article 8 of the UCC shall be controlling.

Section 3.3 Certification of Membership Interests.

(a) Membership Interests shall be issued in non-certificated form; provided that any Member may request that the Company issue certificates to such Member representing the Membership Interests held by such Member. Upon request by a Member for issuance of Membership Interests in certificated form the Company shall issue one or more non-negotiable certificates in the name of such Member substantially in the form of Annex A hereto (a "Certificate"), which evidences the ownership of the Membership Interests of such Member. Each such Certificate shall be denominated in terms of the number of the Membership Interests evidenced by such Certificate and shall be signed by an Officer on behalf of the Company.

(b) The Company shall issue a new Certificate in place of any Certificate previously issued if the holder of the Membership Interests represented by such Certificate, as reflected on the books and records of the Company:

(i) makes proof by affidavit, in form and substance satisfactory to the Company, that such previously issued Certificate has been lost, stolen or destroyed;

(ii) requests the issuance of a new Certificate before the Company has notice that such previously issued Certificate has been acquired by a purchaser for value in good faith and without notice of an adverse claim;

(iii) if reasonably requested by the Company, delivers to the Company a bond, in form and substance satisfactory to the Company, with such surety or sureties as the Company may direct, to indemnify the Company against any claim that may be made on account of the alleged loss, destruction or theft of the previously issued Certificate; and

(iv) satisfies any other reasonable requirements imposed by the Company.

(c) Upon a Member's transfer in accordance with the provisions of this Agreement of any or all Membership Interests represented by a Certificate, the transferor of such Membership Interests shall deliver such Certificate to the Company for cancellation (executed by such transferor and the transferee on the reverse side thereof), and the Company shall thereupon issue a new Certificate to such transferee for the Membership Interests being transferred and, if applicable, cause to be issued to such transferor a new Certificate for the Membership Interests that were represented by the canceled Certificate and that are not being transferred.

ARTICLE IV: CONTRIBUTION; ALLOCATIONS; DISTRIBUTIONS

Section 4.1 **Additional Contributions**. No Member shall be required to make any additional capital contribution to the Company in respect of the Membership Interests then held by such Member or to provide any financing to the Company; provided that a Member may, at the request or with the consent of the Company, make additional capital contributions or provide financing to the Company.

Section 4.2 **Allocation of Profits and Losses.**

(a) Subject to the other provisions in this Section 4.2 and other than in the case of a liquidation of the Company, for each Fiscal Year or other shorter period in which allocations of profits and losses are to be made among the Members (an "Allocation Period"), the Company's Book Profits and Book Losses shall be allocated for each Allocation Period to the Members in proportion to the Total Interest of each Member.

(b) The Members agree to allocate gross income or, at the discretion of the Tax Matters Member, other items of income to FNA in the amount of any payments described as royalties and provided for under the Master Industrial Agreement (and related agreements) ("PDARs") made to FNA, until the aggregate amount allocated and previously allocated under this Section 4.2(b) equals the aggregate amount of such PDARs paid and previously paid to FNA, and to treat such payments as distributions for the purposes of maintaining Members' Capital Accounts. At the discretion of the Tax Matters Member, such PDARs may be treated, in whole or in part, as guaranteed payments within the meaning of Section 707(c) of the Code and the Treasury Regulations thereunder (instead of as allocations of gross income and corresponding distributions as described in the immediately preceding sentence), and the Tax Matters Member is hereby authorized to make such allocations of the deduction for such guaranteed payment as it may deem appropriate to give effect to the purposes of this Section 4.2(b). For the avoidance of doubt, amounts treated as distributions for the purposes of maintaining Members' Capital Accounts under this Section 4.2 shall not be considered distributions for purposes of determining the amount distributable under Section 4.4.

(c) **Tax-Free Contribution Treatment**. The Company and each of the Members shall continue to be bound by Section 4.2(c) of the 2009 Agreement.

(d) For purposes of determining the Book Profits, Book Losses, or any other items allocable to any Allocation Period, Book Profits, Book Losses, and any such other items shall be determined on a daily, monthly, or other basis, as selected by the Tax Matters Member using any permissible method under Section 706 of the Code and the Treasury Regulations issued thereunder.

(e) **Regulatory Allocations**

(i) The allocations made under this Section 4.2 are intended to comply with Treasury Regulations issued pursuant to Section 704(b) of the Code as in effect on the date hereof and therefore shall be considered to include a "Qualified Income Offset" and "Minimum Gain Chargeback" as defined in the Treasury Regulations.

(ii) In accordance with Section 704(c) of the Code and the Treasury Regulations issued thereunder, income, gain, loss and deduction with respect to any property contributed to the capital of the Company shall, solely for income tax purposes, be allocated among the Members so as to take account of any variation between the adjusted basis of such property to the Company for federal income tax purposes and its Fair Market Value at the time of contribution, and, in the event that the Book Value of any Company asset is adjusted in accordance with the last sentence of the definition of Book Value, allocations of items of income, gain, loss and deduction with respect to such asset shall thereafter take into account any variation between the adjusted tax basis of the asset to the Company and its Book Value in accordance with Section 704(c) of the Code and any Treasury Regulations issued thereunder. Any allocation made pursuant to the immediately preceding sentence shall be made solely for tax purposes and shall not affect, or in any way be taken into account in computing, any Member's Capital Account or shares of Book Profits or Book Losses, and any elections or other decisions relating to such allocations made under the immediately preceding sentence shall be made in the discretion of the Tax Matters Member consistent with the economic arrangement of this Agreement.

(iii) Nonrecourse Deductions, other than Member Nonrecourse Deductions which shall be allocated (as required) in accordance with Section 1.704–2(i)(1) of the Treasury Regulations, shall be allocated among the Members in accordance with their Total Interests.

(iv) Nonrecourse Debts of the Company to the extent that they constitute Excess Nonrecourse Liabilities shall be allocated among the Members in accordance with their respective Total Interests.

(f) Recognizing the complexity of the allocations pursuant to this ARTICLE IV, the Tax Matters Member is authorized to modify these allocations to ensure that they achieve results that are consistent with and to achieve the objectives of the distribution provisions, and it is intended that the provisions of this Section 4.2 shall be interpreted in a manner (consistent with the requirements of "substantial economic effect" of Section 704 and the Treasury Regulations issued thereunder) such that each Member's Capital Account, after allocations of income, gain, deduction, loss or items thereof, shall equal as much as possible, immediately before the liquidation of the Company, the amount of distribution that such Member would be entitled to receive upon liquidation if Section 8.1(d)(ii) provided that all remaining assets of the Company shall be distributed to the Members in accordance with Section 4.4 of this Agreement (but without giving effect to the cross-reference in Section 4.4 to Section 8.1). For the avoidance of doubt, if, as a result of any determination by a relevant Taxing Authority or if such allocation or other change is otherwise required by law, an amount of income, gain, deduction, loss or items thereof is imputed and required to be allocated to or otherwise taken into account by any of the Members that is different from the amount originally allocated to or otherwise taken into account by such Member, the Tax Matters Member is hereby authorized to take such imputed amount into account in allocating other items of income, gain, loss and deduction among the Members so that, to the extent possible, the net amount of such allocations of other items and the imputed items to each Member shall be equal to the net amount that would have been allocated to each such Member if the allocation of the imputed amount had not occurred.

(g) The Members are aware of the income tax consequences of the allocations made by this ARTICLE IV and hereby agree to be bound by the provisions of this ARTICLE IV in reporting their shares of Company income and loss for income tax purposes.

Section 4.3 Tax Matters.

(a) **Tax Treatment.** The Members agree to treat the Company as an entity other than as a corporation for U.S. tax purposes, and to report consistent with this treatment on their respective U.S. federal, state and local tax returns and related correspondences with any Taxing Authority, until they, acting at a meeting or by written consent as contemplated in ARTICLE X or pursuant to an amendment to this Agreement, shall agree otherwise.

(b) **Taxable Year**. The taxable year of the Company shall be the Fiscal Year unless another year end is selected by the Tax Matters Member, or is required under the Code or the Treasury Regulations.

(c) **Tax Returns, Reports and Payments**. At the direction of the Tax Matters Member, the Company shall prepare and file, or cause to be prepared and filed, at the expense of the Company, all Tax Returns of the Company and each Subsidiary thereof. As soon as practicable following the end of each Fiscal Year, the Company shall prepare and deliver, or cause to be prepared and delivered, at the expense of the Company, to each Member, in respect of each class of Membership Interests, a completed report (which may be on IRS Schedule K-1 or an equivalent) indicating such Member's share of all items of income or gain, expense, loss or other deduction and tax credit of the Company for such year, as well as the status of such Member's Capital Account, and its Capital Account balance, as of the end of such year. The Board of Directors shall cause the Company to pay all taxes, levies, assessments, rents and other impositions imposed on the Company.

(d) **Tax Elections**. All elections and decisions for purposes of Federal, state, local and foreign taxes shall be made by the Tax Matters Member in its discretion, provided, however, that the Tax Matters Member shall not take a position inconsistent with the positions of the Members agreed to under Section 4.2(c)(i) of the 2009 Agreement and Section 8.1(d)(ii) of this Agreement without the consent of the Board of Directors.

(e) **Appointment of Tax Matters Member**. The Company shall appoint a Tax Matters Member as the "tax matters partner" of the Company, as such term is defined under the Code, and each of the Company and the Members hereby agrees to appoint FNA (or such other Affiliate of Fiat Parent that is a Member and as Fiat Parent may designate) as such Tax Matters Member so long as FNA (or such other Affiliate) remains a Member of the Company. Each Member shall have a continuing obligation to provide the Tax Matters Member with sufficient information and the Tax Matters Member has a continuing obligation to provide such information to the Internal Revenue Service, such that each Member is eligible to be a "a notice partner" within the meaning of Section 6231(a)(8) of the Code, unless a Member elects not to be a notice partner and so informs the Tax Matters Member in writing. To the extent permitted by law, each Member further agrees that such Member shall not treat any Company item inconsistently on such Member's own income tax return with the treatment of the item on the Company's tax return, and each Member agrees that such Member will not independently take any position inconsistent with the position taken by the Company with respect to tax audits or tax litigation affecting the Company, in each case except to the extent of (a) adjustments required by the final outcome of such tax audits or tax litigation or (b) written advice of independent counsel received by such Member that a challenge by a U.S. Taxing Authority to such position is likely to be successful. The Company shall indemnify the Tax Matters Member for, and hold it harmless against, any claims made against it in its capacity as Tax Matters Member in accordance with ARTICLE VI. All reasonable out-of-pocket expenses and costs incurred by the Tax Matters Member in its capacity as Tax Matters Member shall be paid by the Company as an ordinary expense of the Company's business.

Section 4.4 Distributions.

(a) Subject to Section 8.1, distributions may be made to the Members, at the times and in the aggregate amounts determined by the Board of Directors.

(b) Any distributions shall be made pro rata to the Members in proportion to their Total Interests at the record date established therefor by the Board of Directors (or if no such record date is established then at the time of such distribution), such that no Member receives under this Section 4.4(b) an amount less than such Member's Tax Amount (i.e., for the avoidance of doubt, the resulting distribution shall satisfy two conditions: (i) the distribution must be pro rata in proportion to the Members' Total Interests and (ii) each Member must receive no less than its Tax Amount). For the avoidance of doubt, any amounts distributable to a Member under this Section 4.4(b) shall be reduced by any amounts withheld under Section 4.4(d) (including any amounts required to be withheld under Section 1446 of the Code). If it is determined that the Company does not have and cannot reasonably obtain cash sufficient to distribute the aggregate amount distributable under the first sentence of this Section 4.4(b) with respect to any period, (i) the Company shall make distributions to the Members under this Section 4.4(b), to the extent practicable, pro rata in proportion to the Members' Total Interests (the excess of the aggregate amount distributable under the first sentence of this Section 4.4(b) over the amount actually distributed under this Section 4.4(b), the "Shortfall Amount"), and (ii) the Company shall, as quickly as reasonably possible, make additional distributions to the Members under this Section 4.4(b) pro rata in proportion to their Total Interests as of the time that the Shortfall Amount arose, as and when the Board of Directors determines in its discretion that cash becomes available for distribution, to reduce the Shortfall Amount to zero.

(c) Notwithstanding any provision to the contrary contained in this Agreement, the Company shall not make any distribution to a Member that would violate the LLC Act or other applicable Law.

(d) The Company may withhold from amounts otherwise distributable to a Member under this ARTICLE IV the amount of any tax required to be withheld by the Company under U.S. federal, state or local law, or foreign law, provided that such amounts shall be deemed to have been actually distributed to such Member for purposes of this Agreement, including for purposes of this ARTICLE IV.

(e) The term "distribution" for purposes of this Section 4.4 does not include any payment of PDARs, even though such payments may be treated as distributions for the purposes of maintaining Members' Capital Accounts as otherwise provided in this Agreement. For the avoidance of doubt, PDARs shall be deducted from amounts otherwise available for distribution under this Section 4.4.

ARTICLE V: BOARD OF MANAGERS; OFFICERS

Section 5.1 Establishment of Board of Directors. There is hereby established a committee of Member representatives (the "Board of Directors") comprised of natural Persons (the "Directors") having the authority and duties set forth in this Agreement. The Board of Directors shall number between five and thirteen persons as determined from time to time by the Members acting at a meeting or by written consent as contemplated in ARTICLE X. The Directors shall be elected pursuant to Section 5.3 for terms not to exceed one year; provided that Directors may serve an unlimited number of consecutive terms. Each Director elected shall hold office until a successor is duly elected and qualified or until his or her earlier death, resignation or removal as provided in this ARTICLE V.

Section 5.2 General Powers of the Board of Directors. The property, affairs and business of the Company shall be overseen by the Board of Directors, except as otherwise provided in this Agreement. Each Director shall be a "manager" (as such term is defined in the LLC Act) of the Company but, notwithstanding the foregoing, no Director shall have any rights or powers beyond the rights and powers granted to such Director in this Agreement or properly delegated to such Director by the Board of Directors. Except as such power is delegated pursuant to Section 5.11, no Director acting alone, or with any other Directors, shall have the power to act for or on behalf of, or to bind, the Company. For the avoidance of doubt, any act or thing that may be done under the authority or direction of the Board of Directors may also be done under the authority of a resolution duly adopted by Members holding a majority of the Membership Interests acting at a meeting or by written consent as contemplated in ARTICLE X.

Section 5.3 Election of Directors. The Members shall take all such actions as are necessary to appoint and duly elect Directors to the Board of Directors under the following terms:

(a) FNA may, for so long as it holds a majority of the Membership Interests, nominate for election each of the Directors and the Members agree to vote their Membership Interests in favor of such nominees. The Board of Directors shall from time to time elect from among the Directors the chairman of the Board of Directors (the "Chairman").

(b) The Board of Directors may (but is not required to) include one or more Independent Directors.

(c) Any Director may be removed from the Board of Directors or any committee of the Board of Directors with or without cause at the written request of FNA for so long as FNA holds a majority of the Membership Interests.

(d) Any Director may resign at any time by giving written notice to the Chairman or the Secretary. The resignation of any Director shall take effect upon receipt of notice thereof or at such later time as shall be specified in such notice, and, unless otherwise specified therein, acceptance of such resignation shall not be necessary to make it effective.

(e) If any Director for any reason ceases to serve as a member of the Board of Directors either during such Director's term of office or because such Director's term of office has concluded, the resulting vacancy on the Board of Directors shall be filled pursuant to the procedures set forth in Section 5.3(a).

Section 5.4 **Meetings.**

(a) Meetings of the Board of Directors may be held in Auburn Hills, Michigan or at such other place, within or without the State of Delaware, as shall from time to time be determined by the Chairman, but in no event less than one time during any 12-month period. Special meetings of the Board of Directors may be called by or at the request of (i) the Chairman or (ii) Member(s) holding a majority of the Membership Interests.

(b) Any Director or any member of a committee of the Board of Directors present at a meeting shall be conclusively presumed to have waived notice of such meeting. Such Director shall be conclusively presumed to have assented to any action taken unless his or her dissent or abstention shall be entered in the minutes of the meeting or unless his or her written dissent or abstention to such action shall be filed with the secretary of the meeting before the adjournment thereof. Such right to dissent or abstain shall not apply to any Director who voted in favor of such action.

Section 5.5 Notice of Meetings. Written notice stating the place, day and time of every meeting of the Board of Directors shall be given to each Director in the manner contemplated by Section 12.2 not less than two nor more than 20 calendar days before the date of the meeting, in each case to each Director at his or her notice address maintained in the records of the Company by the Secretary. Such further notice shall be given as may be required by Law, but meetings may be held without notice if all the

Directors entitled to vote at the meeting are present in person or by telephone or represented by proxy or if notice is waived in writing by those not present, either before or after the meeting.

Section 5.6 Quorum. Unless otherwise provided by Law or this Agreement, the presence of Directors constituting a majority of the Directors then in office shall constitute a quorum for the transaction of business. If such quorum is not present within 60 minutes after the time appointed for such meeting, such meeting shall be adjourned and the Chairman shall reschedule the meeting to be held not fewer than one nor more than 10 Business Days thereafter. If such meeting is rescheduled, then those Directors who are present or represented by proxy at the rescheduled meeting shall constitute a valid quorum for all purposes hereunder; provided that written notice of any rescheduled meeting shall have been delivered to all Directors at least twelve hours prior to the time of such rescheduled meeting. Each Director may designate by proxy any other Director to attend and act on behalf of the Director (including voting on all matters brought before the Board of Directors) at a meeting of the Board of Directors, a copy of which proxy shall be delivered to the Chairman at or prior to the meeting. Notwithstanding any provision to the contrary contained herein, interested Directors may be counted in determining the presence of a quorum at a meeting of the Board of Directors or of a committee that authorizes any interested party contract or transaction.

Section 5.7 Voting.

(a) Each Director shall be entitled to cast one vote with respect to each matter brought before the Board of Directors (or any committee of the Board of Directors of which such Director is a member) for approval.

(b) Except as otherwise provided by this Agreement, the LLC Act, other Law or the Certificate of Formation, all matters to be determined by the Board of Directors shall be determined by a majority vote of the Directors present at a meeting at which a quorum is present. No Director shall be disqualified from voting on matters as to which such Director or any Member may have a conflict of interest, whether such matter is a direct conflict of interest in connection with which such Director or Member or any Affiliate of such Person will engage in a transaction with the Company or one or more of its Subsidiaries.

Section 5.8 Action Without a Meeting; Telephonic Meetings.

(a) On any matter requiring an approval or consent of Directors under this Agreement or the LLC Act, the Directors may take such action without a meeting, without prior notice and without a vote if a consent or consents in writing, setting forth the action so taken and presented for approval to all applicable Directors, shall be signed by a majority of such Directors.

(b) Any Director may at such Director's discretion, participate in meetings of the Board of Directors by means of conference telephone or similar communications equipment by means of which all Persons participating in the meeting can hear one another. Participation in a telephonic meeting pursuant to this Section 5.8(b) shall constitute presence at such meeting and shall constitute a waiver of any deficiency of notice.

Section 5.9 Compensation of Directors; Expense Reimbursement. Directors may receive a stated compensation as determined from time to time by the Board of Directors. All Directors shall receive the same compensation for service as a Director with the exception of the Chairman of the Board and Committee chairs who may receive additional compensation as determined by the Board of Directors. Directors who are also Officers (as defined herein) of the Company or employees of any Member or its Affiliates may receive a fee for services in their capacity as Directors and nothing herein contained shall be construed to preclude any Director from serving the Company or any of its Affiliates in any other capacity and receiving compensation therefor.

Section 5.10 Committees of the Board of Directors.

(a) The Board of Directors may designate one or more committees, each of which shall be comprised of one or more Directors and may designate one or more of the Directors as alternate members to replace absent or disqualified Directors at any meeting of that committee subject to any limitation imposed by the Board of Directors.

(b) Any committee of the Board of Directors shall have and may exercise the authority of the Board of Directors, subject to any limitations set forth in the resolutions establishing such committee. Any committee members may be removed, or any authority granted to any committee may be revoked, at any time for any reason by the Board of Directors. Each committee of Directors may fix its own rules of procedure and shall hold its meetings as provided by such rules, except as may otherwise be provided in this Agreement, the charter for such committee or by a resolution of the Board of Directors designating such committee.

(c) There is hereby established the audit committee of the Board of Directors (the "Audit Committee"). The composition of the Audit Committee shall be set forth in the Audit Committee charter adopted from time to time by the Board of Directors, but in any event shall consist of two or more Directors. The Board of Directors shall appoint a chairman of the Audit Committee. The Audit Committee shall have and may exercise such powers, authority and responsibilities as set forth in the Audit Committee charter. The Audit Committee shall report its actions, findings and reports to the Board of Directors on a regular basis.

Section 5.11 Delegation of Authority. The Board of Directors may, from time to time (acting in any applicable case with any required consent under this Agreement), delegate to any Person authority to act on behalf of the Company as it shall deem advisable. Any delegation pursuant to this Section 5.11 may be revoked by the Board of Directors at any time and for any reason or no reason.

Section 5.12 Officers.

(a) The officers of the Company (the "Officers") shall consist of a Chief Executive Officer and such other Officers as the Chief Executive Officer may deem appropriate. Appointment of a Chief Executive Officer will require the prior written approval of Fiat Parent. Other Officers shall be approved and appointed by the Chief Executive Officer (which designation shall be in writing). One Person may hold, and perform the duties of, any two or more of such offices.

(b) Any Officer may be removed, with or without cause, at any time by the Board of Directors (in the case of the Chief Executive Officer) or by the Chief Executive Officer (in the case of other Officers), except that the Chief Executive Officer may be removed only with the prior written approval of Fiat Parent. For the avoidance of doubt, any of the Officers, including the Chief Executive Officer, may be employees of Fiat Parent or any of its Affiliates. Any seconded Officer may receive supplemental employment compensation from Fiat Parent or any of its Affiliates related to such secondment. The Board of Directors or the Chief Executive Officer may from time to time adopt a schedule of authority setting forth the specific powers and authorities delegated to each of the Officers and other authorized representatives (if any) of the Company. The initial schedule of authority is set forth in Annex B and shall be in force until amended, modified or terminated (in total or as applicable to any particular Officers(s) or other authorized representative(s)) by the Board of Directors, solely with respect to any power or authority delegated to the Chief Executive Officer, or the Chief Executive Officer (except as it applies to any power or authority delegated to the Chief Executive Officer).

Section 5.13 **Standard of Care; Fiduciary Duties; Liability of Directors and Officers.**

(a) The Board of Directors shall adopt corporate ethics, anti-bribery, anti-corruption, safety, environmental and other policies at least equivalent to those applicable to Fiat Parent.

(b) Any Director or Officer, in the performance of such Director's or Officer's duties, shall be entitled to rely in good faith on the provisions of this Agreement and on opinions, reports or statements (including financial statements, books of account or any other financial information, opinions, reports or statements as to the value or amount of the assets, liabilities, profits or losses of the Company and its Subsidiaries) of the following other Persons or groups: (i) one or more Officers or employees of such Member or the Company or any of their respective Subsidiaries, (ii) any legal counsel, accountants or other Person employed or engaged by any Member, the Board of Directors or the Company or any of its Subsidiaries or (iii) any other Person who has been selected with reasonable care as to matters which such relying Person reasonably believes to be within such other Person's professional or expert competence. The preceding sentence shall in no way limit any Person's right to rely on information to the extent provided in Section 18–406 of the LLC Act.

(c) On any matter involving a conflict of interest not provided for in this Agreement, each Director and Officer shall be guided by his or her good faith judgment as to the best interests of the Company and shall take such actions, if any, as are determined by such Person to be necessary or appropriate to ameliorate such conflict of interest.

(d) Subject to, and as limited by the provisions of this Agreement, the Directors and the Officers, in the performance of their duties as such, shall owe to the Company and its Members duties of loyalty and due care of the type owed under Law by directors and officers of a business corporation incorporated under the Delaware General Corporation Law; provided that the doctrine of corporate opportunity or any analogous doctrine shall not apply to the Directors and provided, further, that, no Director and no Person that elected such Director shall have any duty to disclose to the Company or the Board of Directors confidential information in such Director's or Person's possession even if it is material and relevant information to the Company and/or the Board of Directors and neither such Director nor such Person shall be liable to the Company or the Members for breach of any duty (including the duty of loyalty and any other fiduciary duties) as a Director or Person that has the right to nominate or elect such Director by reason of such lack of disclosure of such confidential information. The provisions of this Agreement, to the extent that they restrict or eliminate the duties (including the duty of loyalty and other fiduciary duties) and liabilities of a Director or Officer otherwise existing at Law or in equity or by operation of the preceding sentence, are agreed by the Members to replace such duties and liabilities of such Director or Officer. Notwithstanding the foregoing provisions and Section 5.13(f), except as otherwise expressly provided in this Agreement or any other written agreement entered into by the Company or any of its Subsidiaries and any Director, if a Director acquires knowledge of a potential transaction or matter that may be a business opportunity for the Company, such Director shall have no duty to communicate or offer such business opportunity to the Company and shall not be liable to the Company for breach of any duty (including the duty of loyalty and any other fiduciary duties) as a Director by reason of the fact that such Director directs such opportunity to any other Person, or does not communicate information regarding such opportunity to the Company, and any such direction of an opportunity by such Director, and any action with respect to such an opportunity by such Person, shall not be wrongful or improper or constitute a breach of any duty hereunder, at law, in equity or otherwise.

(e) Except as required by the LLC Act, no individual who is a Director or an Officer, or any combination of the foregoing, shall be personally liable under any judgment of a court, or in any other manner, for any debt, obligation or liability of the Company, whether that liability or obligation arises in contract, tort or otherwise by reason of being a Director or an Officer or any combination of the foregoing.

(f) No Director or Officer shall be liable to the Company or the Members (whether for monetary damages or otherwise) for any act or omission (including any breach of duty (fiduciary or otherwise)), including any mistake of fact or error in judgment taken, suffered or made by such Person if such Person acted in good faith and in a manner such Person reasonably believed to be in or not opposed to the best interests of the Company.

ARTICLE VI: INDEMNIFICATION

Section 6.1 General Indemnity.

(a) To the fullest extent permitted by the LLC Act, the Company, to the extent of its assets legally available for that purpose, shall indemnify and hold harmless each Person who was or is made a party or is threatened to be made a party to or is involved in or participates as a witness with respect to any action, suit or proceeding, whether civil, criminal, administrative or investigative (each a "Proceeding"), by reason of the fact that he or she, or a Person of whom he or she is the legal representative, is or was a Director, an officer or employee, or is or was serving at the request of the Company as a manager, director, officer, employee, fiduciary or agent of another Entity (collectively, the "Indemnified Persons") from and against any and all loss, cost, damage, fine, expense (including reasonable fees and expenses of attorneys and other advisors and any court costs incurred by any Indemnified Person) or liability actually and reasonably incurred by such Person in connection with such Proceeding if such Person acted in good faith and in a manner such Person reasonably believed to be in or not opposed to the best interests of the Company and except that no indemnification shall be made in respect of any claim, issue or matter as to which such Person shall have been adjudged to be liable to the Company unless and only to the extent that the Court of Chancery of the State of Delaware or the court in which such action or suit was brought shall determine upon application that, despite the adjudication of liability but in view of all the circumstances of the case, such Person is fairly and reasonably entitled to indemnity for such expenses which the Court of Chancery or such other court shall deem proper. The termination of any Proceeding by judgment, order, settlement, conviction or upon a plea of nolo contendere or its equivalent, shall not, of itself, create a presumption that the Person did not act in good faith or in a manner such Person reasonably believed to be in or not opposed to the best interests of the Company.

(b) The Company shall pay in advance or reimburse reasonable expenses (including advancing reasonable costs of defense) incurred by an Indemnified Person who is or is threatened to be named or made a defendant or a respondent in a Proceeding; provided, however, that as a condition to any such advance or reimbursement, such Indemnified Person shall agree that it shall repay the same to the Company if such Indemnified Person is finally judicially determined by a court of competent jurisdiction not to be entitled to indemnification under this ARTICLE VI.

(c) The Company shall not be required to indemnify a Person in connection with a Proceeding initiated by such Person against the Company or any of its Subsidiaries if the Proceeding was not authorized by the Board of Directors. The ultimate determination of entitlement to indemnification of any Indemnified Person shall be made by the Board of Directors in such manner as the Board of Directors may determine.

(d) Any and all indemnity obligations of the Company with respect to any Indemnified Person shall survive any termination of this Agreement. The indemnification and other rights provided for in this ARTICLE VI shall inure to the benefit of the heirs, executors and administrators of any Person entitled to such indemnification.

Section 6.2 **Rights Non-Exclusive**. The rights to indemnification and the payment of expenses incurred in defending any Proceeding in advance of its final disposition conferred in this ARTICLE VI shall not be exclusive of any other right which any Person may have or hereafter acquire under any Law, provision of this Agreement, any other agreement, any vote of Members or Directors or otherwise.

Section 6.3 **Merger or Consolidation; Other Entities**. For purposes of this ARTICLE VI, references to "the Company" shall include, in addition to the resulting company, any constituent company (including any constituent of a constituent) absorbed in a consolidation or merger which, if its separate existence had continued, would have had power and authority to indemnify its managers, directors, officers, employees, fiduciaries or agents, so that any Person who is or was a manager, director, officer, employee, fiduciary or agent of such constituent company, or is or was serving at the request of such constituent company as a manager, director, officer, employee, fiduciary or agent of another company, partnership, joint venture, trust or other enterprise, shall stand in the same position under this ARTICLE VI with respect to the resulting or surviving company as he or she would have with respect to such constituent company if its separate existence had continued. For purposes of this ARTICLE VI, references to "another Entity" shall include employee benefit plans; references to "fines" shall include any excise taxes assessed on a Person with respect to any employee benefit plan; and references to "serving at the request of the Company" shall include any service as a manager, director, officer, employee or agent of the Company that imposes duties on, or involves services by, such manager, director, officer, employee or agent with respect to an employee benefit plan, its participants or beneficiaries; and a Person who acted in good faith and in a manner such Person reasonably believed to be in or not opposed to the best interests of the participants and beneficiaries of an employee benefit plan shall be deemed to have acted in a manner "not opposed to the best interests of the Company" as referred to in this ARTICLE VI.

Section 6.4 **No Member Recourse**. Anything herein to the contrary notwithstanding, any indemnity by the Company relating to the matters covered in this ARTICLE VI shall be provided out of and to the extent of Company assets only and no Member shall have personal liability on account thereof or shall be required to make additional capital contributions to help satisfy such indemnity of the Company.

ARTICLE VII: ADMISSION OF ADDITIONAL MEMBERS

Section 7.1 **Admission Requirements**. One or more additional Persons may be admitted to the Company as Members only upon furnishing to the Company: (i) a joinder agreement pursuant to which such Person agrees to be bound by all of the terms and conditions of this Agreement and (ii) such other documents or instruments as may be necessary or appropriate to effect such Person's admission as a Member (including entering into an investor representation agreement or such other documents as the

Company may deem appropriate). Such admission shall become effective on the date on which the Company determines that the foregoing conditions have been satisfied and when any such admission is shown on the books and records of the Company. Upon the admission of an Additional Member, the Schedule of Members shall be amended to reflect the name, notice address, Membership Interests and other interests in the Company. Such Member's capital contributions and initial Capital Account shall be reflected in the Company's books and records.

Section 7.2 Acceptance of Prior Acts. Any Person who is admitted pursuant to Section 7.1 hereby accepts, ratifies and agrees to be bound by all actions duly taken pursuant to the terms and provisions of this Agreement by the Company prior to the date it was admitted to the Company and, without limiting the generality of the foregoing, specifically ratifies and approves all agreements and other instruments as may have been executed and delivered on behalf of the Company prior to such date and which are in force and effect on such date.

Section 7.3 Transfers; Admission of Transferees.

(a) No Member may Transfer its Membership Interests unless such Transfer complies with the provisions of this Agreement and any Certificate representing such Membership Interests. Notwithstanding the foregoing, any Member may Transfer its Membership Interests to any other Member.

(b) Upon admission as a Member pursuant to a Transfer conducted in accordance with this Agreement, a Transferee shall succeed to the rights, duties and obligations of the Transferor under this Agreement, the Certificate of Formation and the LLC Act and any references in this Agreement to the Transferor (unless such Transferor remains a Member) shall be deemed to refer to such Transferee for purposes of this Agreement.

(c) Until a Transferee is admitted as a Member pursuant to Section 7.1, the Transferor shall continue to be a Member and to be entitled to exercise any rights or powers of a Member with respect to the Membership Interest transferred.

ARTICLE VIII: DISSOLUTION

Section 8.1 In General. The Company shall dissolve and its affairs shall be wound up upon the first to occur of the following: (i) the written consent of the Members holding a majority of the Membership Interests, (ii) at any time there are no Members of the Company unless the Company is continued in accordance with the LLC Act or (iii) the entry of a decree of judicial dissolution under Section 18–802 of the LLC Act.

(a) The bankruptcy (within the meaning of Sections 18–101(1) and 18–304 of the LLC Act) of any of the Members shall not cause such Member to cease to be a member of the Company and upon the occurrence of such an event, the business of the Company shall continue without dissolution.

(b) In the event of dissolution, the Company shall conduct only such activities as are necessary to wind up its affairs (including the sale of the assets of the Company in an orderly manner), and the assets of the Company shall be applied in the manner, and in the order of priority, set forth in Section 18–804 of the LLC Act.

(c) Upon the cancellation of the Certificate of Formation in accordance with the LLC Act, the Company and this Agreement shall terminate.

(d) In the event of a Liquidation Proceeding:

(i) the liquidators shall pay, satisfy or discharge from the Company funds all of the debts, liabilities and obligations of the Company (including all expenses incurred in such Liquidation Proceeding) or otherwise make adequate provision for payment and discharge thereof (including the establishment of a cash fund for contingent liabilities in such amount and for such term as the liquidators may reasonably determine); and

(ii) after payment or provision for payment of all of the Company's debts, liabilities and obligations has been made in accordance with Section 8.1(d)(i), and after all allocations have been made in accordance with Section 4.2, all remaining assets of the Company shall be distributed to the Members in accordance with their positive Capital Account balances, subject to any applicable waiting periods or consents required under applicable law.

Section 8.2 Reasonable Time for Winding Up. A reasonable time shall be allowed for the orderly winding up of the business and affairs of the Company and the liquidation of its assets pursuant to Section 8.1 to minimize any losses otherwise attendant upon such winding up.

ARTICLE IX: RIGHTS AND DUTIES OF MEMBERS

Section 9.1 Members. The Members of the Company, and their respective numbers of Membership Interests, are listed on the Schedule of Members. No Person may be a Member without the ownership of a Membership Interest. Except as otherwise expressly provided in this Agreement, no Member, in such capacity, shall have any authority to bind, to act for, to sign for or to assume any obligation or responsibility on behalf of any other Member or the Company.

Section 9.2 No Member Fiduciary Duties.

(a) No Member shall, except as expressly required by the LLC Act and other applicable Law, owe any duties (including fiduciary duties) as a Member to (i) the other Members or (ii) the Company, except for duties arising under contracts between such Members and the Company, in each case notwithstanding anything to the contrary existing at Law, in equity or otherwise.

(b) Except as otherwise expressly provided in this Agreement, any Member may engage in or possess any interest in another business or venture of any nature and description, independently or with others, whether or not such business or venture is competitive with the Company or any of its Subsidiaries, and neither the Company nor any other Member shall have any rights in or to any such independent business or venture or the income or profits derived therefrom, and the doctrine of corporate opportunity or any analogous doctrine shall not apply to the Members and the members, shareholders, partners and Affiliates thereof. The pursuit of any such business or venture shall not be deemed wrongful, improper or a breach of any duty hereunder, at Law, in equity or otherwise. Any Member and the members, shareholders, partners and Affiliates thereof shall be able to transact business or enter into agreements with the Company to the fullest extent permissible under the LLC Act, subject to the terms and conditions of this Agreement.

(c) If a Member acquires knowledge of a potential transaction or matter that may be a business opportunity for both such Member and the Company or another Member, such Member shall have no duty to communicate or offer such business opportunity to the Company or any other Member and shall not be liable to the Company or the other Members for breach of any duty (including fiduciary duties) as a Member by reason of the fact that such Member pursues or acquires such business opportunity for itself, directs such opportunity to another Person, or does not communicate information regarding such opportunity to the Company.

(d) The provisions of this Agreement, to the extent that they restrict or eliminate the duties (including fiduciary duties) and liabilities of a Member otherwise existing or implied at law or in equity, are agreed by the Members to replace such duties and liabilities of such Member.

ARTICLE X: MEETINGS OF MEMBERS

Section 10.1 Meetings of the Members. Meetings of the Members may be called at any time by the Board of Directors, the Chairman, the Chief Executive Officer or as provided by this Agreement. Except to the extent otherwise provided in this Agreement, the following provisions shall apply to meetings of Members. For the avoidance of doubt, any matter that may be presented for approval or consent at a meeting of Members whether under this Agreement or the LLC Act or otherwise, the Members may take such action without a meeting, without prior notice, and without a vote if a consent or consents in writing, setting forth the action so taken, shall be signed by Members holding a majority of the Membership Interests.

Section 10.2 Notice of Meetings. The written notice of any meeting of Members shall be given not fewer than two (2) nor more than twenty (20) calendar days before the date of the meeting to each Member entitled to vote at such meeting.

Section 10.3 Adjournments. Any meeting of Members may be adjourned from time to time, to reconvene at the same or some other place, and notice need not be given of any such adjourned meeting if the time and place thereof are announced at the meeting at which the adjournment is taken. At the adjourned meeting the Members may transact any business which might have been transacted at the original meeting.

Section 10.4 Quorum. Except as otherwise provided in this Agreement, at each meeting of Members, the Members holding a majority of outstanding voting Membership Interests, present in person or represented by proxy, shall constitute a quorum.

Section 10.5 Organization. Meetings of Members shall be presided over by the Chairman, or in his absence, by the Chief Executive Officer or another Director designated by the Board of Directors. The Secretary shall act as secretary of the meeting, but in the absence of the Secretary, the chairman of the meeting may appoint an Officer to act as secretary of the meeting.

Section 10.6 Waiver of Notice of Meetings of Members. Whenever notice is required to be given by law or under any provision of this Agreement, a written waiver thereof, signed by the Person entitled to notice, whether before or after the time stated therein, shall be deemed equivalent to notice. Attendance of a Person at a meeting shall constitute a waiver of notice of such meeting. Neither the business to be transacted at, nor the purpose of, any regular or special meeting of the Members need be specified in any written notice or waiver of notice of meeting.

Section 10.7 Determination of Members of Record. In order that the Company may determine the Members entitled to notice of, or to vote at, any meeting or any adjournment thereof or to consent to action in writing without a meeting, the Board of Directors or any Officer of the Company may fix a record date, which record date shall not be more than sixty (60) nor less than five (5) days before the date of such meeting or consent, as applicable. If no record date is set, the record date for determining Members entitled to notice of, or to vote at, a meeting shall be at the close of business on the day next preceding the day on which notice is given, or, if notice is waived, at the close of business on the day next preceding the day on which the meeting is held. If no record date is set, the record date for determining Members entitled to consent to action in writing without a meeting shall be the first date on which a signed written consent setting forth the action taken or proposed to be taken is delivered to the Company. A determination of Members of record entitled to notice of or to vote at a meeting shall apply to any adjournment of the meeting; provided, however, that a new record date for the adjourned meeting may be established.

ARTICLE XI: INFORMATION RIGHTS; BOOKS AND RECORDS

Section 11.1 Schedule of Members. The Company shall maintain and keep at its principal office the Schedule of Members on which it shall set forth the name and notice address of each Member, and the aggregate number of Membership Interests of such Member at any time.

Section 11.2 Books and Records; Other Documents.

(a) The Company shall keep, or cause to be kept, (i) complete and accurate books and records of account of the Company, (ii) minutes of the proceedings of meetings of the Members, the Board of Directors and any committee thereof and (iii) a current list of the Directors and Officers and their notice addresses. Any of the foregoing books, minutes or records may be in written form or in any other form capable of being accurately and completely converted into written form within a reasonable time. The Company shall, and shall cause its Subsidiaries to, (A) make and keep financial records in reasonable detail that accurately and fairly reflect all financial transactions and dispositions of the assets of the Company and its Subsidiaries and (B) maintain a system of internal accounting controls sufficient to provide reasonable assurances that (1) transactions are executed in accordance with authorization by the Person in charge and are recorded so as to provide proper financial statements and maintain accountability for assets and (2) safeguards are established to prevent unauthorized persons from having access to the assets.

(b) At all times the Company shall maintain at its principal office a copy of the Certificate of Formation, including any amendments thereto, copies of this Agreement and all amendments hereto, and all other records required to be maintained pursuant to the LLC Act.

(c) The Company shall maintain books for the purpose of registering the Transfer of Membership Interests.

Section 11.3 Reports and Audits.

(a) Promptly upon request, the Company shall, at its cost and expense, furnish, or cause to be furnished, to each Member such information relating to the financial condition, operations of the Company or any other aspect of the Company or its business in possession of the Company as any such Member may from time to time reasonably request.

(b) Each Member shall have the right, at all reasonable times and upon reasonable notice during normal business hours, and at its own expense, so long as such access does not unreasonably interfere with the normal operation of the Company, to examine and make copies of or extracts from the books of account of the Company or any other Company record for any purpose reasonably related to such Member's interest as a Member of the Company, including to satisfy any public reporting obligations of such Member under applicable law and the rules of any securities exchange, and for federal, state, local or foreign income or franchise tax purposes. Such examination rights may be exercised through any designated agent or employee of such Members, as applicable, or their respective Affiliates. The parties agree that any such examination is not intended to duplicate in its entirety the audit conducted by the Independent Auditor.

Section 11.4 Financial Statements and Other Information.

(a) The Members shall be supplied with annual (audited) and condensed quarterly (unaudited but reviewed) consolidated financial statements of the Company in form and substance reasonably satisfactory to Fiat Parent, together with such other financial statements and supporting information as Fiat Parent may reasonably request to facilitate compliance with its financial reporting, record keeping and internal control requirements.

(b) The Members shall be supplied with all Company information reasonably necessary to enable each Member to prepare its federal, state, local and foreign income Tax Returns. Such information shall be prepared by the Company, and the Company shall use its reasonable best efforts to deliver such information to each Member promptly in light of the timing applicable to the purpose for which such information is to be used by such Member.

(c) If a Member or Affiliate of such Member is required by Law or any accounting principles (including GAAP) applied by such Member to consolidate or otherwise reflect the financial results of the Company into such Member's financial statements, then the Company shall provide to such Member, reasonably promptly upon request (and, so long as such Member has timely made such request, within a sufficient period of time so as to enable such Member to comply with any Law or accounting requirement applicable to it), any information reasonably requested for such purposes.

Section 11.5 Independent Auditor. The Company and its Subsidiaries shall engage a Person to audit its financial statements (the "Independent Auditor") that (a) is an independent public accounting firm within the meaning of the American Institute of Certified Public Accountants' Code of Professional Conduct (American Institute of Certified Public Accountants, Professional Standards, vol. 2, et seq. 101), (b) is a registered public accounting firm (as defined in Section 2(a)(12) of the Sarbanes Oxley Act of 2002 (the "Sarbanes-Oxley Act")), and (c) would not be in violation of the auditor independence requirements of the Sarbanes-Oxley Act by reason of its acting as the auditor of the Company and its Subsidiaries.

ARTICLE XII: MISCELLANEOUS PROVISIONS

Section 12.1 Separability of Provision. Each provision of this Agreement shall be considered separable, and if for any reason any provision or provisions herein are determined to be invalid, unenforceable or illegal under any existing or future Law, such invalidity, unenforceability or illegality shall not impair the operation of or affect those portions of this Agreement that are valid, enforceable and legal.

Section 12.2 Notices. All notices, demands, financial reports, other reports and other communications to be given or delivered under or by reason of the provisions of this Agreement shall be in writing and shall be deemed to have been given or made when (a) delivered personally to the recipient, (b) sent by facsimile to the recipient (with hard copy sent to the recipient by reputable overnight courier service (charges prepaid) that same day) if sent by facsimile before 5:00 p.m. New York time on a Business Day, and otherwise on the next Business Day, or (c) one Business Day after being sent to the recipient by reputable overnight courier service (charges prepaid) to the following addresses:

if to the Company or Board of Directors:

Chrysler Group LLC
1000 Chrysler Drive
Auburn Hills, MI 48326
United States of America

if to FNA:

Fiat North America LLC
c/o Fiat Finance NA Inc.
7 Times Square Tower, Ste. 4306
New York, NY 10036

Attention: General Counsel Attention: General Counsel

Section 12.3 Entire Agreement. This Agreement and the other documents referred to herein, constitute the entire agreement among the parties and contain all of the agreements among the parties with respect to the subject matter hereof as of the date of this Agreement and supersede all prior agreements, undertakings and negotiations (in each case, both oral and written) between the parties concerning the subject matter herein. Failure by any party hereto to enforce any covenant, duty, agreement, term or condition of this Agreement, or to exercise any right hereunder, shall not be construed as thereafter waiving such covenant, duty, term, condition or right; and in no event shall any course of dealing, custom or usage of trade modify, alter or supplement any term of this Agreement.

Section 12.4 Governing Law. This Agreement shall be governed by, and construed and enforced in accordance with, the Laws of the State of Delaware, without giving effect to any choice of law or conflict of law rules or provisions (whether of the State of Delaware or any other jurisdiction) that would cause the application of the Laws of any jurisdiction other than the State of Delaware.

Section 12.5 Amendments. This Agreement may not be amended, modified, waived or supplemented except pursuant to a written instrument signed by the Company and the holders of a majority of the Membership Interests outstanding at such time.

Section 12.6 Sole Benefit of Members. Except as expressly provided in ARTICLE VI, the provisions of this Agreement (including without limitation Section 4.1) are intended solely to benefit the Members and, to the fullest extent permitted by applicable Law, shall not be construed as conferring any benefit upon any creditor of the Company (and no such creditor shall be a third-party beneficiary of this Agreement), and no Member shall have any duty or obligation to any creditor of the Company to make any contributions or payments to the Company; provided, that FNA and Fiat Parent shall be third party beneficiaries with respect to each provision of this Agreement that explicitly designates rights to FNA or Fiat Parent, including but not limited to each provision of this Agreement that relates to the Directors.

Section 12.7 Independent Contractors; Expenses. This Agreement does not constitute any party hereto the partner, agent or legal representative of any other party hereto, except to the extent that the Company is classified as a partnership for United States federal income tax purposes and the Members are treated as "partners" for such tax purposes. Each party hereto is independent and responsible for its own expenses (except as otherwise agreed pursuant to ARTICLE VI), including attorneys' and other professional fees incurred in connection with the transactions contemplated by this Agreement.

Section 12.8 Creditors. None of the provisions of this Agreement shall be for the benefit of or enforceable by any creditors of the Members, the Company or any of its Affiliates (other than Indemnified Persons), and no Person that makes a loan or otherwise extends credit to any Member, the Company or any of its Affiliates may have or acquire (except pursuant to the terms of a separate agreement executed by the Company in favor of such Person) at any time as a result of making the loan any direct or indirect interest in Company profits, losses, Distributions, capital or property other than as a secured creditor.

Section 12.9 Further Action. The parties hereto agree to execute and deliver all documents, provide all information and take or refrain from taking such actions as may be necessary or appropriate to achieve the purposes of this Agreement.

Section 12.10 **Delivery by Facsimile or Email**. This Agreement, the agreements referred to herein, and each other agreement or instrument entered into in connection herewith or therewith or contemplated hereby or thereby, and any amendments hereto or thereto, to the extent signed and delivered by means of a facsimile machine or email with scan or facsimile attachment, shall be treated in all manner and respects as an original agreement or instrument and shall be considered to have the same binding legal effect as if it were the original signed version thereof delivered in person.

Section 12.11 **Interpretative Matters**. In this Agreement, unless otherwise specified or where the context otherwise requires:

(a) the headings of particular provisions of this Agreement are inserted for convenience only and will not be construed as a part of this Agreement or serve as a limitation or expansion on the scope of any term or provision of this Agreement;

(b) words importing any gender shall include other genders;

(c) words importing the singular only shall include the plural and vice versa;

(d) whenever the words "include," "includes" or "including" are used in this Agreement, they will be deemed to be followed by the words "without limitation";

(e) whenever the words "herein" or "hereunder" are used in this Agreement, they will be deemed to refer to this Agreement as a whole and not to any specific Section, unless otherwise indicated;

(f) references to "Articles," "Exhibits," "Sections" or "Schedules" shall be to Articles, Exhibits, Sections or Schedules of or to this Agreement;

(g) references to any Person include the heirs, executors, administrators, legal representatives, successors and permitted assigns of such Person where the context so permits;

(h) the use of the words "or," "either" and "any" shall not be exclusive;

(i) wherever a conflict exists between this Agreement and any other agreement, this Agreement shall control but solely to the extent of such conflict;

(j) the terms "dollars" and "$" shall mean dollars of the United States of America; and

(k) references to any agreement, contract, guideline, exhibit or schedule, unless otherwise stated, are to such agreement, contract, guideline, exhibit or schedule as amended, amended and restated, replaced, substituted, modified or supplemented from time to time in accordance with the terms hereof and thereof; and references to any Law or a particular provision of any Law, unless otherwise stated, are to such Law and any successor Law or to such provision of Law and the corresponding provision in any successor Law, as applicable.

IN WITNESS WHEREOF, the undersigned has executed or caused to be executed on their behalf this Fourth Amended and Restated Limited Liability Company Agreement pursuant to the requirements of Section 5.8 and Section 15.5 of the 2012 Agreement as of the date first written above.

CHRYSLER GROUP LLC

By: /s/ Marjorie Harris Loeb

Name: Marjorie Harris Loeb

Title: Senior Vice President, General Counsel and Secretary

By: FIAT NORTH AMERICA LLC

By: /s/ Giorgio Fossati

Name: Giorgio Fossati

Title: Attorney in Fact

FNA HOLDCO 00, LLC
FNA HOLDCO 01, LLC
FNA HOLDCO 02, LLC
FNA HOLDCO 03, LLC
FNA HOLDCO 04, LLC
FNA HOLDCO 05, LLC
FNA HOLDCO 06, LLC
FNA HOLDCO 07, LLC
FNA HOLDCO 08, LLC
FNA HOLDCO 09, LLC
FNA HOLDCO 10, LLC
FNA HOLDCO 11, LLC
FNA HOLDCO 12, LLC

By: FIAT NORTH AMERICA LLC

(sole member of each)

By: /s/ Giorgio Fossati

Name: Giorgio Fossati

Title: Attorney in Fact

DEFINITIONS ADDENDUM

Part I. Definitions.

"Additional Member" means any Person that has been admitted to the Company as a Member after the Effective Date pursuant to Section 7.1.

"Affiliate" means, with respect to any Person, any other Person that, directly or indirectly, whether through one or more intermediaries, Controls, is Controlled by or is under common Control with such Person.

"Book Profit" and "Book Loss" means, for each Fiscal Year, or other period, an amount equal to the Company's taxable income or loss for such year or period, determined in accordance with Section 703(a) of the Code; provided that for this purpose, all items of income, gain, loss or deduction required to be stated separately pursuant to Section 703(a)(1) of the Code shall be included in taxable income or loss, with the following adjustments:

(i) any income of the Company that is exempt from federal income tax and not otherwise taken in account in computing Book Profit or Book Loss pursuant to this provision shall be added to such taxable income or loss;

(ii) any expenditures of the Company described in Section 705(a)(2)(B) of the Code or treated as Code Section 705(a)(2)(B) expenditures pursuant to Section 1.704–1(b)(2)(iv)(i) of the Treasury Regulations, and not otherwise taken into account in computing Book Profit or Book Loss pursuant to this provision, shall be subtracted from such taxable income or loss;

(iii) gain or loss resulting from any disposition of any asset of the Company with respect to which gain or loss is recognized for federal income tax purposes shall be computed by reference to the Book Value of the asset disposed of as determined under Treasury Regulations Section 1.704–1(b)(2)(iv), notwithstanding that the adjusted tax basis of such asset may differ from such Book Value;

(iv) in lieu of depreciation, amortization and other cost recovery deductions taken into account in computing such taxable income or loss, there shall be taken in account Depreciation for such Fiscal Year, computed as provided in this Agreement; and

(v) in the event the Book Value of any Company asset is adjusted to reflect the Fair Market Value of such asset in accordance with the last sentence of the definition of "Book Value," the amount of such adjustment shall be taken into account as gain or loss from the disposition of such asset for purposes of computing Book Profit or Book Loss.

If the Company's taxable income or loss for such Fiscal Year, as adjusted in the manner provided above, is a positive amount, such amount shall be the Company's Book Profit for such Fiscal Year, and, if a negative amount, such amount shall be the Company's Book Loss for such Fiscal Year. Notwithstanding the other provisions of this definition of Book Profit and Book Loss, any gross items specially allocated pursuant to ARTICLE IV shall not be taken into account in computing Book Profit and Book Loss.

"Book Value" of an asset means, as of any particular date, the value at which the asset is properly reflected on the books and records of the Company as of such date in accordance with Section 1.704–1(b)(2)(iv) of the Treasury Regulations as follows:

(i) The initial Book Value of each asset shall be its cost, unless such asset was contributed to the Company by a Member, in which case the initial Book Value shall be the Fair Market Value for such asset, and, in each case, such Book Value shall thereafter be adjusted for Depreciation with respect to such asset rather than for the cost recovery deductions to which Company is entitled for federal income tax purposes with respect thereto.

(ii) The Book Values of all Company assets shall be adjusted to equal their respective Fair Market Values, as reasonably determined by the Tax Matters Member, as of the following times:

(A) the acquisition of an additional interest in the Company by any new or existing Member in exchange for more than a de minimis additional capital contribution or, as provided in Treasury Regulations Section 1.704–1(b)(2)(iv)(f)(5)(iii), in exchange for services;

(B) the distribution by the Company to a Member of more than a de minimis amount of the Company assets, including money, if, as a result of such distribution, such Member's interest in the Company is reduced;

(C) the liquidation of the Company within the meaning of Treasury Regulations Section 1.704–1(b)(2)(ii)(g); and

(D) at any other time, as permitted by the Treasury Regulations, at the discretion of the Tax Matters Member.

"Business Day" means any calendar day other than a Saturday, a Sunday or any other day on which commercial banks are authorized or required by Law to be closed in Torino, Italy, Detroit, Michigan or New York, New York.

"Certificate of Formation" means the Certificate of Formation of the Company filed with the Secretary of State of the State of Delaware on April 28, 2009, which became effective on such date.

"Code" means the United States Internal Revenue Code of 1986, as amended from time to time.

"Consent" means any consent, approval, authorization, waiver, grant, franchise, concession, agreement, license, exemption or other permit or order of, registration, declaration or filing with, or report or notice to, any Person.

"Control," "Controlled" or "Controlling" means, with respect to any Person, any circumstance in which such Person is directly or indirectly controlled by another Person by virtue of the latter Person having the power to (i) elect, or cause the election of (whether by way of voting capital stock, by contract, trust or otherwise), the majority of the members of the Board of Directors or a similar governing body of the first Person; or (ii) direct (whether by way of voting capital stock, by contract, trust or otherwise) the affairs and policies of such Person.

"Depreciation" means, for each Fiscal Year, an amount equal to the depreciation, amortization or other cost recovery deduction as reported for federal income tax purposes with respect to an asset for such year or other period, except that if the Book Value of an asset differs from its adjusted basis for federal income tax purposes, Depreciation shall be an amount which bears the same ratio to such beginning Book Value as the federal income tax depreciation, amortization or other cost recovery deduction for such Fiscal Year bears to such beginning adjusted tax basis; provided, however, that if the adjusted basis for federal income tax purposes of an asset at the beginning of such Fiscal Year is zero, Depreciation shall be determined with reference to such beginning Book Value using any reasonable method selected by the Tax Matters Member.

"Distribution" means each distribution after the Effective Date made by the Company to a Member, whether in cash, property or securities of the Company, pursuant to, or in respect of, Section 4.4 or ARTICLE VIII.

"Entity" means any general partnership, limited partnership, corporation, association, cooperative, joint stock company, trust, limited liability company, business or statutory trust, joint venture, unincorporated organization or Governmental Entity.

"Excess Nonrecourse Liability" means an "excess nonrecourse liability" within the meaning of Section 1.752–3(a)(3) of the Treasury Regulations.

"Fair Market Value" means, in reference to property or assets owned by the Company, the fair market value of such property or assets as reasonably determined by the Tax Matters Member.

"Fiat Group" means Fiat Parent and FNA and their respective Subsidiaries, but excludes the Company and its Subsidiaries.

"Fiat Parent" means Fiat S.p.A., a *Societa per Azioni* organized under the laws of Italy or its legal successor regardless of jurisdiction of organization.

"Fiscal Year" means the fiscal year of the Company, which shall be the year ending December 31. Each Fiscal Year shall commence on the day immediately following the last day of the immediately preceding Fiscal Year.

"FNA" means Fiat North America LLC, a limited liability company organized under the laws of the State of Delaware, and its Subsidiaries (including unless the context otherwise requires any Person through which FNA holds its ownership interest in the Company, but excluding the Company and its Subsidiaries).

"GAAP" means accounting principles generally accepted in the United States of America as in effect from time to time, consistently applied and maintained throughout the applicable periods both as to classification or items and amounts.

"Governmental Entity" means the United States of America or any other nation, any state, province or other political subdivision, any international or supra-national entity, or any entity exercising executive, legislative, judicial, regulatory or administrative functions of government, including any court, tribunal or arbitral body, and any self-regulatory organization, in each case having jurisdiction over the Company or any of its Subsidiaries or any of the property or other assets of the Company or any of its Subsidiaries.

"Independent Director" means a Director who is independent of the Company as determined by reference to the list of enumerated relationships precluding independence under the listing rules of the New York Stock Exchange.

"IRS" means the United States Internal Revenue Service.

"Law" means any law, statute, ordinance, rule, regulation, code, order, judgment, tax ruling, injunction or decree of any Governmental Entity.

"Liquidation Proceeding" means any liquidation, dissolution or winding up of the Company or any of its Subsidiaries or the commencement of proceedings to adjudicate the Company or any of its Subsidiaries as bankrupt, or consenting to the filing of a bankruptcy proceeding against any of them, or filing a petition or answer or consent seeking reorganization of any of them under any bankruptcy or insolvency law, or consenting to the filing of any such petition, or consenting to the appointment of a receiver or liquidator or trustee or assignee in bankruptcy or insolvency, or making an assignment for the benefit of creditors, or admitting inability to pay debts generally as they become due.

"Master Industrial Agreement" means the Master Industrial Agreement, dated as of June 10, 2009, between Persons within the Fiat Group and the Company.

"Member" means each Person who appears on the Schedule of Members, as amended from time to time, or is hereafter admitted as a member of the Company in accordance with the terms of this Agreement and the LLC Act. The Members shall constitute the "members" (as such term is defined in the LLC Act) of the Company. Except as otherwise set forth herein or in the LLC Act, the Members shall constitute a single class or group of members of the Company for all purposes of the LLC Act and this Agreement.

"Membership Interest" means the limited liability company interests of a Member in the Company, as set forth opposite such Member's name on the Schedule of Members hereto, as amended from time to time, and also the right of such Member to any and all of the benefits to which such Member may be entitled as provided in this Agreement and the LLC Act, together with the obligations of such Member to comply with all the provisions of this Agreement and the LLC Act. The Company may issue whole or fractional Membership Interests pursuant to the terms of this Agreement.

"Member Nonrecourse Deductions" has the meaning given to "partner nonrecourse deductions" set forth in Treasury Regulations Section 1.704–2(i)(2).

"Nonrecourse Debt" means any Company liability to the extent that no Member or related Person bears the economic risk of loss for such liability under Section 1.752–2 of the Treasury Regulations.

"Nonrecourse Deductions" has the meaning set forth in Treasury Regulations Section 1.704–2(b)(1).

"Person" means any individual or Entity.

"Securities Act" means the Securities Act of 1933, and the rules and regulations promulgated thereunder, as amended from time to time.

"Subsidiary" means, with respect to any Person, a second Person in which the first Person has an amount of voting securities, other voting rights or voting partnership interests that are sufficient to elect a majority of the second Person's board of directors or other governing body, or, if there are no such voting interests, if the first Person has more than 50% of the equity interest of the second Person.

"Tax Amount" means, in respect of any Member, the product of (x) the sum of the highest U.S. Federal rate of tax (expressed as a percentage) generally applicable to corporations plus five (5) percent in respect of state and local taxes (reduced by the net federal tax benefit deemed to arise from such state and local taxes at the relevant assumed rates) and (y) the net amount of income allocable to such Member (excluding any allocations of income in respect of PDARs) for the applicable period.

"Tax Matters Member" means any Person that has been designated the Tax Matters Member pursuant to Section 4.3(e).

"Tax Return" means any and all returns, reports and forms (including declarations, amendments, schedules, information returns or attachments thereto) required to be filed with a Governmental Entity with respect to any taxes.

"Taxing Authority" means, with respect to any tax, the Governmental Entity or political subdivision thereof that imposes such tax, and the agency (if any) charged with the collection of such tax for such entity or subdivision, including any governmental or quasi-governmental entity or agency that imposes, or is charged with collecting, social security or similar charges or premiums.

"Total Interest" means, with respect to a particular Member at any time, the percentage obtained from the quotient of (i) the number of Membership Interests held by such Member divided by (ii) the number of Membership Interests in the aggregate held by all Members.

"Transfer" means any sale, transfer, assignment (other than a contingent assignment for the benefit of creditors), exchange, or other disposition of an interest (whether with or without consideration, whether voluntarily or involuntarily or by operation of Law). The terms "Transferee," "Transferor," "Transferred," and other forms of the word "Transfer" shall have the correlative meanings. A Transfer shall also include the entering into of any financial instrument or contract the value of which is determined by reference to the Company (including the amount of the Company's distributions, the value of the Company's assets or the results of the Company's operations).

"Treasury Regulations" means the regulations, including temporary regulations, promulgated by the US Treasury under the Code, as amended from time to time.

Part II. Cross-References. In addition to the terms set forth in Part I of the Definitions Addendum, the following terms are defined in the text of this Agreement in the locations specified below:

Term	Cross-Reference
Agreement	Preamble
Allocation Period	Section 4.2(a)
Audit Committee	Section 5.10(c)
Board of Directors	Section 5.1
Capital Account	Section 3.1(b)
Certificate	Section 3.3(a)
Chairman	Section 5.3(a)
Company	Preamble
Directors	Section 5.1
Effective Date	Preamble
Indemnified Persons	Section 6.1(a)
Independent Auditor	Section 11.5
LLC Act	Recitals

Members	Preamble
Officers	Section 5.12(a)
Original Agreement	Preamble
PDARs	Section 4.2(b)
Proceeding	Section 6.1(a)
Sarbanes-Oxley Act	Section 11.5
Secretary	Annex B
Shortfall Amount	Section 4.4(b)

SCHEDULE OF MEMBERS

Name and Notice Address of Members	Membership Interests		
	Number of Units	Total Interest	
Fiat North America LLC	955,730.00	58.5384	%
c/o Fiat Finance NA Inc. 7 Times Square Tower, Ste. 4306 New York, NY 10036			
FNA Holdcos:			
All c/o Fiat Finance NA Inc. 7 Times Square Tower, Ste. 4306 New York, NY 10036			
FNA Holdco 00, LLC	54,153.92	3.3169	%
FNA Holdco 01, LLC	54,153.92	3.3169	%
FNA Holdco 02, LLC	54,153.92	3.3169	%
FNA Holdco 03, LLC	54,153.92	3.3169	%
FNA Holdco 04, LLC	54,153.92	3.3169	%
FNA Holdco 05, LLC	54,153.92	3.3169	%
FNA Holdco 06, LLC	54,153.92	3.3169	%
FNA Holdco 07, LLC	54,153.92	3.3169	%
FNA Holdco 08, LLC	54,153.92	3.3169	%
FNA Holdco 09, LLC	54,153.92	3.3169	%
FNA Holdco 10, LLC	54,153.92	3.3169	%
FNA Holdco 11, LLC	54,153.92	3.3169	%
FNA Holdco 12, LLC	27,076.96	1.6585	%
Total for FNA Holdcos:	676,924.00	41.4616	%
TOTAL	1,632,654.00	100	%

ANNEX A

CERTIFICATE FOR LIMITED LIABILITY COMPANY INTERESTS IN CHRYSLER GROUP LLC

THE MEMBERSHIP INTEREST IN CHRYSLER GROUP LLC HAS NOT BEEN REGISTERED UNDER THE SECURITIES ACT OF 1933, AS AMENDED. THE HOLDER OF THIS CERTIFICATE, BY ITS ACCEPTANCE HEREOF, REPRESENTS THAT IT IS ACQUIRING THIS SECURITY FOR INVESTMENT AND NOT WITH A VIEW TO ANY SALE OR DISTRIBUTION HEREOF. THE MEMBERSHIP

INTEREST MAY NOT BE SOLD, ASSIGNED, PLEDGED OR OTHERWISE DISPOSED OF AT ANY TIME EXCEPT IN A TRANSACTION REGISTERED UNDER SUCH SECURITIES ACT AND LAWS OR, A TRANSACTION THAT IS EXEMPT FROM AND NOT SUBJECT THERETO.

THE SALE, ASSIGNMENT, HYPOTHECATION, PLEDGE, ENCUMBRANCE OR OTHER DISPOSITION (EACH, A "TRANSFER") AND VOTING OF THE MEMBERSHIP INTERESTS REPRESENTED BY THIS CERTIFICATE IS RESTRICTED BY THE TERMS OF THE LIMITED LIABILITY COMPANY AGREEMENT (AS DEFINED BELOW), A COPY OF WHICH IS ON FILE WITH THE SECRETARY OF THE COMPANY. THE COMPANY WILL NOT REGISTER THE TRANSFER OF SUCH SECURITIES ON THE BOOKS OF THE COMPANY UNLESS AND UNTIL THE TRANSFER HAS BEEN MADE IN COMPLIANCE WITH THE TERMS OF THE LIMITED LIABILITY COMPANY AGREEMENT.

Certificate Number [ ]   [ ] Membership Interests

Chrysler Group LLC, a Delaware limited liability company (the "Company"), hereby certifies that [ ] (together with any assignee of this Certificate, the "Holder") is the registered owner of [ ] Membership Interests in the Company. The rights, powers, preferences, restrictions and limitations of the interests in the Company are set forth in, and this Certificate and the limited liability company interests in the Company represented hereby are issued and shall in all respects be subject to the terms and provisions of, the Fourth Amended and Restated Limited Liability Company Agreement of the Company dated as of June [10], 2014, as the same may be further amended or restated from time to time (the "Limited Liability Company Agreement"). By acceptance of this Certificate, and as a condition to being entitled to any rights and/or benefits with respect to the limited liability company interests evidenced hereby, the Holder is deemed to have agreed to comply with and be bound by all the terms and conditions of the Limited Liability Company Agreement. The Company will furnish a copy of the Limited Liability Company Agreement to the Holder without charge upon written request to the Company at its principal place of business. Transfer of any or all of the limited liability company interests in the Company evidenced by this Certificate is subject to certain restrictions in the Limited Liability Company Agreement and can be effected only after compliance with all of those restrictions and the presentation to the Company of the Certificate, accompanied by an assignment in the form appearing on the reverse side of this Certificate, duly completed and executed by and on behalf of the transferor in such Transfer, and an application for transfer in the form appearing on the reverse side of this Certificate, duly completed and executed by and on behalf of the transferee in such Transfer.

Each Membership Interest in the Company shall constitute a "security" within the meaning of (i) Section 8–102(a)(15) of the Uniform Commercial Code as in effect from time to time in the States of Delaware and New York and (ii) the Uniform Commercial Code of any other applicable jurisdiction that now or hereafter substantially includes the 1994 revisions to Article 8 thereof as adopted by the American Law Institute and the National Conference of Commissioners on Uniform State Laws and approved by the American Bar Association on February 14, 1995 (and each limited liability company interest in the Company shall be treated as such a "security" for all purposes, including, without limitation perfection of the security interest therein under Article 8 of each applicable Uniform Commercial Code).

This Certificate and the limited liability company interests evidenced hereby shall be governed by and construed in accordance with the laws of the State of Delaware without regard to principles of conflicts of laws.

IN WITNESS WHEREOF, the Company has caused this Certificate to be executed as of the date set forth below.

Dated: [ ], 20___

CHRYSLER GROUP LLC, A DELAWARE LIMITED LIABILITY COMPANY

BY: _____________

NAME:

TITLE:

(REVERSE SIDE OF CERTIFICATE)

ASSIGNMENT OF INTEREST

FOR VALUE RECEIVED, the undersigned hereby sells, assigns and transfers unto (print or typewrite name of transferee), (insert Social Security or other taxpayer identification number of transferee), the following Membership Interests in the Company: (identify the percentage interest being transferred) effective as of the date specified in the Application for Transfer of Interests below, and irrevocably constitutes and appoints and its authorized Officers, as attorney-in-fact, to transfer the same on the books and records of the Company, with full power of substitution in the premises.

Dated: [ ], 20___

BY: _____________

NAME:

TITLE:

APPLICATION FOR TRANSFER OF INTERESTS

The undersigned applicant (the "Applicant") hereby (a) applies for a transfer of Membership Interests in the Company described above (the "Transfer") and applies to be admitted to the Company as a substitute member of the Company, (b) agrees to comply with and be bound by all of the terms and provisions of the Limited Liability Company Agreement, (c) represents that the Transfer complies with the terms and conditions of the Limited Liability Company Agreement, (d) represents that the Transfer does not violate any applicable laws and regulations, and (e) agrees to execute and acknowledge such instruments (including, without limitation, a counterpart of the Limited Liability Company Agreement), in form and substance satisfactory to the Company, as the Company reasonably deems necessary or desirable to effect the Applicant's admission to the Company as a substitute member of the Company and to confirm the agreement of the Applicant to be bound by all the terms and provisions of the Limited Liability Company Agreement with respect to the limited liability company interests in the Company described above. Initially capitalized terms used herein and not otherwise defined herein are used as defined in the Limited Liability Company Agreement.

The Applicant directs that the foregoing Transfer and the Applicant's admission to the Company as a Substitute Member shall be effective as of ___, 20___.

Name of Transferee (Print)

____

Dated: ______________________ Signature: ______________________

Address: ____________________

The Company (a) has determined that the Transfer described above is permitted by the Limited Liability Company Agreement, (b) hereby agrees to effect such Transfer and the admission of the Applicant as a substitute member of the Company effective as of the date and time directed above, and (c) agrees to record, as promptly as possible, in the books and records of the Company the admission of the Applicant as a substitute member.

CHRYSLER GROUP LLC,
a Delaware limited liability company

By: ______________
Name:
Title:

ANNEX B

SCHEDULE OF AUTHORITY

Chief Executive Officer. The Chief Executive Officer of the Company (the "Chief Executive Officer") shall perform such duties as may be assigned to him or her from time to time by the Board of Directors. Subject to the direction of the Board of Directors, he or she shall have, and exercise, direct charge of, and general supervision over, the business and affairs of the Company. He or she shall from time to time report to the Board of Directors all matters within his or her knowledge that the interest of the Company may require to be brought to its notice, and shall also have such other powers and perform such other duties as may be specifically assigned to him or her from time to time by the Board of Directors. The Chief Executive Officer shall see that all resolutions and orders of the Board of Directors are carried into effect, and in connection with the foregoing, shall be authorized to delegate to any President and the other Officers such of his or her powers and such of his or her duties as he or she or the Board of Directors may deem to be advisable.

Chief Financial Officer. The Chief Financial Officer of the Company (the "Chief Financial Officer") shall have the custody of the Company's funds and securities and shall keep full and accurate accounts of receipts and disbursements in books belonging to the Company and shall deposit all monies and other valuable effects in the name and to the credit of the Company, in such depositories as may be designated by the Chief Executive Officer. The Chief Financial Officer shall exercise such powers and perform such duties as generally pertain or are necessarily incident to his or her office and shall perform such other duties as may be specifically assigned to him or her from time to time by the Chief Executive Officer.

Secretary. The Secretary of the Company (the "Secretary") or any Assistant Secretary of the Company (the "Assistant Secretary") designated by the Secretary shall attend all meetings of the Members and the Board of Directors, except to the extent the Secretary or such Assistant Secretary is excused, by the Members or the Board of Directors, as the case may be, and record all votes and the minutes of all proceedings in a book to be kept for that purpose and shall perform like duties for any committee when required. He or she shall give, or cause to be given, notice of all meetings of the Members and, when necessary, of the Board of Directors. The Secretary or such designated Assistant Secretary, as the case may be, shall exercise such powers and perform such duties as generally pertain or are necessarily incident to his or her office, and he or she shall perform such other duties as may be assigned to him or her from time to time by the

Chief Executive Officer. To the greatest extent possible, the Secretary or such designated Assistant Secretary, as the case may be, shall vote, or cause to be voted, all of the Equity Securities of any Subsidiary of the Company.

FIRST AMENDMENT TO FOURTH AMENDED AND RESTATED LIMITED LIABILITY COMPANY AGREEMENT OF CHRYSLER GROUP LLC[2]

This First Amendment (this "Amendment") to the Fourth Amended and Restated Limited Liability Company Agreement (the "LLC Agreement") of Chrysler Group LLC (the "Company"), dated and effective as of June 10, 2014, as amended, is made and entered into as of December 15, 2014 by and among the members (the "Members") of the Company.

WHEREAS, the Company is a limited liability company pursuant to the Delaware Limited Liability Company Act, 6 Del. C. § 18–101 et seq., as amended from time to time (the "Act"), and its Members have entered into the LLC Agreement, in accordance with the provisions of the Act, governing the business and affairs of the Company and the conduct of its business;

WHEREAS, pursuant to Section 12.5 of the LLC Agreement, the LLC Agreement may be amended by an affirmative vote of the majority of the holders of a majority of the Membership Interests outstanding; and

WHEREAS, all of the Members of the Company have previously executed a unanimous written consent authorizing any officer of the Company to execute an amendment to the LLC agreement to reflect a change in the name of the Company.

NOW, THEREFORE, the Members, by the execution of this Amendment, agree as follows. Any capitalized terms used herein and not defined shall have the meanings set forth in the LLC Agreement:

ARTICLE I

The LLC Agreement is hereby amended as set forth in the following section:

Section 2.1 **Name.** The name of the limited liability company shall be **FCA US LLC**

IN WITNESS WHEREOF, the undersigned has executed or caused to be executed on their behalf this First Amendment to the Fourth Amended and Restated Limited Liability Company Agreement pursuant to the requirements of Section 12.5 of the Fourth Amended and Restated Limited Liability Company Agreement as of the date first written above.

CHRYSLER GROUP LLC
BY: /S/ MARJORIE H. LOEB
NAME: MARJORIE H. LOEB
TITLE: SENIOR VICE PRESIDENT,
GENERAL COUNSEL & SECRETARY

---

[2] FCA US LLC Form 10-K (March 4, 2015), available at https://www.sec.gov/Archives/edgar/data/1513153/000151315315000010/exhibit33.htm.

APPENDIX B

REVISED UNIFORM LIMITED LIABILITY COMPANY ACT (2006 & 2013 HARMONIZED) (EXCERPTED)

■ ■ ■

ARTICLE 1: GENERAL PROVISIONS

Section 101. Short Title.

Section 102. Definitions.

Section 103. Knowledge; Notice.

Section 104. Governing Law.

The law of this state governs:

(1) the internal affairs of a limited liability company; and

(2) the liability of a member as member and a manager as manager for a debt, obligation, or other liability of a limited liability company.

Section 105. Operating Agreement; Scope, Function, and Limitations.

(a) Except as otherwise provided in subsections (c) and (d), the operating agreement governs:

(1) relations among the members as members and between the members and the limited liability company;

(2) the rights and duties under this [act] of a person in the capacity of manager;

(3) the activities and affairs of the company and the conduct of those activities and affairs; and

(4) the means and conditions for amending the operating agreement.

(b) To the extent the operating agreement does not provide for a matter described in subsection (a), this [act] governs the matter.

(c) An operating agreement may not:

(1) vary the law applicable under Section 104;

(2) vary a limited liability company's capacity under Section 109 to sue and be sued in its own name;

(3) vary any requirement, procedure, or other provision of this [act] pertaining to:

(A) registered agents; or

(B) the [Secretary of State], including provisions pertaining to records authorized or required to be delivered to the [Secretary of State] for filing under this [act];

(4) vary the provisions of Section 204;

(5) alter or eliminate the duty of loyalty or the duty of care, except as otherwise provided in subsection (d);

(6) eliminate the contractual obligation of good faith and fair dealing under Section 409(d), but the operating agreement may prescribe the standards, if not manifestly unreasonable, by which the performance of the obligation is to be measured;

(7) relieve or exonerate a person from liability for conduct involving bad faith, willful or intentional misconduct, or knowing violation of law;

(8) unreasonably restrict the duties and rights under Section 410, but the operating agreement may impose reasonable restrictions on the availability and use of information obtained under that section and may define appropriate remedies, including liquidated damages, for a breach of any reasonable restriction on use;

(9) vary the causes of dissolution specified in Section 701(a)(4);

(10) vary the requirement to wind up the company's activities and affairs as specified in Section 702(a), (b)(1), and (e);

(11) unreasonably restrict the right of a member to maintain an action under [Article] 8;

(12) vary the provisions of Section 805, but the operating agreement may provide that the company may not have a special litigation committee;

(13) vary the right of a member to approve a merger, interest exchange, conversion, or domestication under Section 1023(a)(2), 1033(a)(2), 1043(a)(2), or 1053(a)(2);

(14) vary the required contents of a plan of merger under Section 1022(a), plan of interest exchange under Section 1032(a), plan of conversion under Section 1042(a), or plan of domestication under Section 1052(a); or

(15) except as otherwise provided in Sections 106 and 107(b), restrict the rights under this [act] of a person other than a member or manager.

(d) Subject to subsection (c)(7), without limiting other terms that may be included in an operating agreement, the following rules apply:

(1) The operating agreement may:

(A) specify the method by which a specific act or transaction that would otherwise violate the duty of loyalty may be authorized or ratified by one or more disinterested and independent persons after full disclosure of all material facts; and

(B) alter the prohibition in Section 405(a)(2) so that the prohibition requires only that the company's total assets not be less than the sum of its total liabilities.

(2) To the extent the operating agreement of a member-managed limited liability company expressly relieves a member of a responsibility that the member otherwise would have under this [act] and imposes the responsibility on one or more other members, the agreement also may eliminate or limit any fiduciary duty of the member relieved of the responsibility which would have pertained to the responsibility.

(3) If not manifestly unreasonable, the operating agreement may:

(A) alter or eliminate the aspects of the duty of loyalty stated in Section 409(b) and (i);

(B) identify specific types or categories of activities that do not violate the duty of loyalty;

(C) alter the duty of care, but may not authorize conduct involving bad faith, willful or intentional misconduct, or knowing violation of law; and

(D) alter or eliminate any other fiduciary duty.

(e) The court shall decide as a matter of law whether a term of an operating agreement is manifestly unreasonable under subsection (c)(6) or (d)(3). The court:

(1) shall make its determination as of the time the challenged term became part of the operating agreement and by considering only circumstances existing at that time; and

(2) may invalidate the term only if, in light of the purposes, activities, and affairs of the limited liability company, it is readily apparent that:

(A) the objective of the term is unreasonable; or

(B) the term is an unreasonable means to achieve the term's objective.

Section 106. Operating Agreement; Effect on Limited Liability Company and Person Becoming Member; Preformation Agreement.

(a) A limited liability company is bound by and may enforce the operating agreement, whether or not the company has itself manifested assent to the operating agreement.

(b) A person that becomes a member is deemed to assent to the operating agreement.

(c) Two or more persons intending to become the initial members of a limited liability company may make an agreement providing that upon the formation of the company the agreement will become the operating agreement. One person intending to become the initial member of a limited liability company may assent to terms providing that upon the formation of the company the terms will become the operating agreement.

Section 107. Operating Agreement; Effect on Third Parties and Relationship to Records Effective on Behalf of Limited Liability Company.

(a) An operating agreement may specify that its amendment requires the approval of a person that is not a party to the agreement or the satisfaction of a condition. An amendment is ineffective if its adoption does not include the required approval or satisfy the specified condition.

(b) The obligations of a limited liability company and its members to a person in the person's capacity as a transferee or a person dissociated as a member are governed by the operating agreement. Subject only to a court order issued under Section 503(b)(2) to effectuate a charging order, an amendment to the operating agreement made after a person becomes a transferee or is dissociated as a member:

(1) is effective with regard to any debt, obligation, or other liability of the limited liability company or its members to the person in the person's capacity as a transferee or person dissociated as a member; and

(2) is not effective to the extent the amendment imposes a new debt, obligation, or other liability on the transferee or person dissociated as a member.

(c) If a record delivered by a limited liability company to the [Secretary of State] for filing becomes effective and contains a provision that would be ineffective under Section

105(c) or (d)(3) if contained in the operating agreement, the provision is ineffective in the record.

(d) Subject to subsection (c), if a record delivered by a limited liability company to the [Secretary of State] for filing becomes effective and conflicts with a provision of the operating agreement:

(1) the agreement prevails as to members, persons dissociated as members, transferees, and managers; and

(2) the record prevails as to other persons to the extent they reasonably rely on the record.

Section 108. Nature, Purpose, and Duration of Limited Liability Company.

(a) A limited liability company is an entity distinct from its member or members.

(b) A limited liability company may have any lawful purpose, regardless of whether for profit.

(c) A limited liability company has perpetual duration.

Section 109. Powers.

A limited liability company has the capacity to sue and be sued in its own name and the power to do all things necessary or convenient to carry on its activities and affairs.

Section 110. Application to Existing Relationships.

Section 111. Supplemental Principles of Law.

Unless displaced by particular provisions of this [act], the principles of law and equity supplement this [act].

Section 112. Permitted Names.

Section 113. Reservation of Name.

Section 114. Registration of Name.

Section 115. Registered Agent.

Section 116. Change of Registered Agent or Address for Registered Agent by Limited Liability Company.

Section 117. Resignation of Registered Agent.

Section 118. Change of Name or Address by Registered Agent.

Section 119. Service of Process, Notice, or Demand.

Section 120. Delivery of Record.

Section 121. Reservation of Power to Amend or Repeal.

ARTICLE 2: FORMATION; CERTIFICATE OF ORGANIZATION AND OTHER FILINGS

Section 201. Formation of Limited Liability Company; Certificate of Organization.

Section 202. Amendment or Restatement of Certificate of Organization.

Section 203. Signing of Records to be Delivered for Filing to [Secretary of State].

Section 204. Signing and Filing Pursuant to Judicial Order.

Section 205. Liability for Inaccurate Information in Filed Record.

Section 206. Filing Requirements.

Section 207. Effective Date and Time.

Section 208. Withdrawal of Filed Record Before Effectiveness.

Section 209. Correcting Filed Record.

Section 210. Duty of [Secretary of State] to File; Review of Refusal to File; Delivery of Record by [Secretary of State].

Section 211. Certificate of Good Standing or Registration.

Section 212. [Annual] [Biennial] Report for [Secretary of State].

ARTICLE 3: RELATIONS OF MEMBERS AND MANAGERS TO PERSONS DEALING WITH LIMITED LIABILITY COMPANY

Section 301. No Agency Power of Member as Member.

(a) A member is not an agent of a limited liability company solely by reason of being a member.

(b) A person's status as a member does not prevent or restrict law other than this [act] from imposing liability on a limited liability company because of the person's conduct.

Section 302. Statement of Limited Liability Company Authority.

Section 303. Statement of Denial.

Section 304. Liability of Members and Managers.

(a) A debt, obligation, or other liability of a limited liability company is solely the debt, obligation, or other liability of the company. A member or manager is not personally liable, directly or indirectly, by way of contribution or otherwise, for a debt, obligation, or other liability of the company solely by reason of being or acting as a member or manager. This subsection applies regardless of the dissolution of the company.

(b) The failure of a limited liability company to observe formalities relating to the exercise of its powers or management of its activities and affairs is not a ground for imposing liability on a member or manager for a debt, obligation, or other liability of the company.

ARTICLE 4: RELATIONS OF MEMBERS TO EACH OTHER AND TO LIMITED LIABILITY COMPANY

Section 401. Becoming Member.

(a) If a limited liability company is to have only one member upon formation, the person becomes a member as agreed by that person and the organizer of the company. That person and the organizer may be, but need not be, different persons. If different, the organizer acts on behalf of the initial member.

(b) If a limited liability company is to have more than one member upon formation, those persons become members as agreed by the persons before the formation of the company. The organizer acts on behalf of the persons in forming the company and may be, but need not be, one of the persons.

(c) After formation of a limited liability company, a person becomes a member:

(1) as provided in the operating agreement;

(2) as the result of a transaction effective under [Article] 10;

(3) with the affirmative vote or consent of all the members; or

(4) as provided in Section 701(a)(3).

(d) A person may become a member without:

(1) acquiring a transferable interest; or

(2) making or being obligated to make a contribution to the limited liability company.

Section 402. Form of Contribution.

A contribution may consist of property transferred to, services performed for, or another benefit provided to the limited liability company or an agreement to transfer property to, perform services for, or provide another benefit to the company.

Section 403. Liability for Contributions.

Section 404. Sharing of and Right to Distributions Before Dissolution.

(a) Any distribution made by a limited liability company before its dissolution and winding up must be in equal shares among members and persons dissociated as members, except to the extent necessary to comply with a transfer effective under Section 502 or charging order in effect under Section 503.

(b) A person has a right to a distribution before the dissolution and winding up of a limited liability company only if the company decides to make an interim distribution. A person's dissociation does not entitle the person to a distribution.

(c) A person does not have a right to demand or receive a distribution from a limited liability company in any form other than money. Except as otherwise provided in Section 707(d), a company may distribute an asset in kind only if each part of the asset is fungible with each other part and each person receives a percentage of the asset equal in value to the person's share of distributions.

(d) If a member or transferee becomes entitled to receive a distribution, the member or transferee has the status of, and is entitled to all remedies available to, a creditor of the limited liability company with respect to the distribution. However, the company's obligation to make a distribution is subject to offset for any amount owed to the company by the member or a person dissociated as a member on whose account the distribution is made.

Section 405. Limitations on Distributions.

(a) A limited liability company may not make a distribution, including a distribution under Section 707, if after the distribution:

(1) the company would not be able to pay its debts as they become due in the ordinary course of the company's activities and affairs; or

(2) the company's total assets would be less than the sum of its total liabilities plus the amount that would be needed, if the company were to be dissolved and wound up at the time of the distribution, to satisfy the preferential rights upon dissolution and winding up of members and transferees whose preferential rights are superior to the rights of persons receiving the distribution.

(b) A limited liability company may base a determination that a distribution is not prohibited under subsection (a) on:

(1) financial statements prepared on the basis of accounting practices and principles that are reasonable in the circumstances; or

(2) a fair valuation or other method that is reasonable under the circumstances.

(c) Except as otherwise provided in subsection (e), the effect of a distribution under subsection (a) is measured:

(1) in the case of a distribution as defined in Section 102(4)(A), as of the earlier of:

(A) the date money or other property is transferred or debt is incurred by the limited liability company; or

(B) the date the person entitled to the distribution ceases to own the interest or right being acquired by the company in return for the distribution;

(2) in the case of any other distribution of indebtedness, as of the date the indebtedness is distributed; and

(3) in all other cases, as of the date:

(A) the distribution is authorized, if the payment occurs not later than 120 days after that date; or

(B) the payment is made, if the payment occurs more than 120 days after the distribution is authorized.

(d) A limited liability company's indebtedness to a member or transferee incurred by reason of a distribution made in accordance with this section is at parity with the company's indebtedness to its general, unsecured creditors, except to the extent subordinated by agreement.

(e) A limited liability company's indebtedness, including indebtedness issued as a distribution, is not a liability for purposes of subsection (a) if the terms of the indebtedness provide that payment of principal and interest is made only if and to the extent that payment of a distribution could then be made under this section. If the indebtedness is issued as a distribution, each payment of principal or interest is treated as a distribution, the effect of which is measured on the date the payment is made.

(f) In measuring the effect of a distribution under Section 707, the liabilities of a dissolved limited liability company do not include any claim that has been disposed of under Section 704, 705, or 706.

Section 406. Liability for Improper Distributions.

Section 407. Management of Limited Liability Company.

(a) A limited liability company is a member-managed limited liability company unless the operating agreement:

(1) expressly provides that:

(A) the company is or will be "manager-managed";

(B) the company is or will be "managed by managers"; or

(C) management of the company is or will be "vested in managers"; or

(2) includes words of similar import.

(b) In a member-managed limited liability company, the following rules apply:

(1) Except as expressly provided in this [act], the management and conduct of the company are vested in the members.

(2) Each member has equal rights in the management and conduct of the company's activities and affairs.

(3) A difference arising among members as to a matter in the ordinary course of the activities and affairs of the company may be decided by a majority of the members.

(4) The affirmative vote or consent of all the members is required to:

(A) undertake an act outside the ordinary course of the activities and affairs of the company; or

(B) amend the operating agreement.

(c) In a manager-managed limited liability company, the following rules apply:

(1) Except as expressly provided in this [act], any matter relating to the activities and affairs of the company is decided exclusively by the manager, or, if there is more than one manager, by a majority of the managers.

(2) Each manager has equal rights in the management and conduct of the company's activities and affairs.

(3) The affirmative vote or consent of all members is required to:

(A) undertake an act outside the ordinary course of the company's activities and affairs; or

(B) amend the operating agreement.

(4) A manager may be chosen at any time by the affirmative vote or consent of a majority of the members and remains a manager until a successor has been chosen, unless the manager at an earlier time resigns, is removed, or dies, or, in the case of a manager that is not an individual, terminates. A manager may be removed at any time by the affirmative vote or consent of a majority of the members without notice or cause.

(5) A person need not be a member to be a manager, but the dissociation of a member that is also a manager removes the person as a manager. If a person that is both a manager and a member ceases to be a manager, that cessation does not by itself dissociate the person as a member.

(6) A person's ceasing to be a manager does not discharge any debt, obligation, or other liability to the limited liability company or members which the person incurred while a manager.

(d) An action requiring the vote or consent of members under this [act] may be taken without a meeting, and a member may appoint a proxy or other agent to vote, consent, or otherwise act for the member by signing an appointing record, personally or by the member's agent.

(e) The dissolution of a limited liability company does not affect the applicability of this section. However, a person that wrongfully causes dissolution of the company loses the right to participate in management as a member and a manager.

(f) A limited liability company shall reimburse a member for an advance to the company beyond the amount of capital the member agreed to contribute.

(g) A payment or advance made by a member which gives rise to a limited liability company obligation under subsection (f) or Section 408(a) constitutes a loan to the company which accrues interest from the date of the payment or advance.

(h) A member is not entitled to remuneration for services performed for a member-managed limited liability company, except for reasonable compensation for services rendered in winding up the activities of the company.

Section 408. Reimbursement; Indemnification; Advancement; and Insurance.

Section 409. Standards of Conduct for Members and Managers.

(a) A member of a member-managed limited liability company owes to the company and, subject to Section 801, the other members the duties of loyalty and care stated in subsections (b) and (c).

(b) The fiduciary duty of loyalty of a member in a member-managed limited liability company includes the duties:

(1) to account to the company and hold as trustee for it any property, profit, or benefit derived by the member:

(A) in the conduct or winding up of the company's activities and affairs;

(B) from a use by the member of the company's property; or

(C) from the appropriation of a company opportunity;

(2) to refrain from dealing with the company in the conduct or winding up of the company's activities and affairs as or on behalf of a person having an interest adverse to the company; and

(3) to refrain from competing with the company in the conduct of the company's activities and affairs before the dissolution of the company.

(c) The duty of care of a member of a member-managed limited liability company in the conduct or winding up of the company's activities and affairs is to refrain from engaging in grossly negligent or reckless conduct, willful or intentional misconduct, or knowing violation of law.

(d) A member shall discharge the duties and obligations under this [act] or under the operating agreement and exercise any rights consistently with the contractual obligation of good faith and fair dealing.

(e) A member does not violate a duty or obligation under this [act] or under the operating agreement solely because the member's conduct furthers the member's own interest.

(f) All the members of a member-managed limited liability company or a manager-managed limited liability company may authorize or ratify, after full disclosure of all material facts, a specific act or transaction that otherwise would violate the duty of loyalty.

(g) It is a defense to a claim under subsection (b)(2) and any comparable claim in equity or at common law that the transaction was fair to the limited liability company.

(h) If, as permitted by subsection (f) or (i)(6) or the operating agreement, a member enters into a transaction with the limited liability company which otherwise would be prohibited by subsection (b)(2), the member's rights and obligations arising from the transaction are the same as those of a person that is not a member.

(i) In a manager-managed limited liability company, the following rules apply:

(1) Subsections (a), (b), (c), and (g) apply to the manager or managers and not the members.

(2) The duty stated under subsection (b)(3) continues until winding up is completed.

(3) Subsection (d) applies to managers and members.

(4) Subsection (e) applies only to members.

(5) The power to ratify under subsection (f) applies only to the members.

(6) Subject to subsection (d), a member does not have any duty to the company or to any other member solely by reason of being a member.

Section 410. Rights to Information of Member, Manager, and Person Dissociated as Member.

ARTICLE 5: TRANSFERABLE INTERESTS AND RIGHTS OF TRANSFEREES AND CREDITORS

Section 501. Nature of Transferable Interest.

A transferable interest is personal property.

Section 502. Transfer of Transferable Interest.

(a) Subject to Section 503(f), a transfer, in whole or in part, of a transferable interest:

(1) is permissible;

(2) does not by itself cause a person's dissociation as a member or a dissolution and winding up of the limited liability company's activities and affairs; and

(3) subject to Section 504, does not entitle the transferee to:

(A) participate in the management or conduct of the company's activities and affairs; or

(B) except as otherwise provided in subsection (c), have access to records or other information concerning the company's activities and affairs.

(b) A transferee has the right to receive, in accordance with the transfer, distributions to which the transferor would otherwise be entitled.

(c) In a dissolution and winding up of a limited liability company, a transferee is entitled to an account of the company's transactions only from the date of dissolution.

(d) A transferable interest may be evidenced by a certificate of the interest issued by a limited liability company in a record, and, subject to this section, the interest represented by the certificate may be transferred by a transfer of the certificate.

(e) A limited liability company need not give effect to a transferee's rights under this section until the company knows or has notice of the transfer.

(f) A transfer of a transferable interest in violation of a restriction on transfer contained in the operating agreement is ineffective if the intended transferee has knowledge or notice of the restriction at the time of transfer.

(g) Except as otherwise provided in Section 602(5)(B), if a member transfers a transferable interest, the transferor retains the rights of a member other than the transferable interest transferred and retains all the duties and obligations of a member.

(h) If a member transfers a transferable interest to a person that becomes a member with respect to the transferred interest, the transferee is liable for the member's obligations under Sections 403 and 406 known to the transferee when the transferee becomes a member.

Section 503. Charging Order.

(a) On application by a judgment creditor of a member or transferee, a court may enter a charging order against the transferable interest of the judgment debtor for the unsatisfied amount of the judgment. Except as otherwise provided in subsection (f), a charging order constitutes a lien on a judgment debtor's transferable interest and requires the limited liability company to pay over to the person to which the charging order was issued any distribution that otherwise would be paid to the judgment debtor.

(b) To the extent necessary to effectuate the collection of distributions pursuant to a charging order in effect under subsection (a), the court may:

(1) appoint a receiver of the distributions subject to the charging order, with the power to make all inquiries the judgment debtor might have made; and

(2) make all other orders necessary to give effect to the charging order.

(c) Upon a showing that distributions under a charging order will not pay the judgment debt within a reasonable time, the court may foreclose the lien and order the sale of the transferable interest. Except as otherwise provided in subsection (f), the purchaser at the foreclosure sale obtains only the transferable interest, does not thereby become a member, and is subject to Section 502.

(d) At any time before foreclosure under subsection (c), the member or transferee whose transferable interest is subject to a charging order under subsection (a) may extinguish the charging order by satisfying the judgment and filing a certified copy of the satisfaction with the court that issued the charging order.

(e) At any time before foreclosure under subsection (c), a limited liability company or one or more members whose transferable interests are not subject to the charging order may pay to the judgment creditor the full amount due under the judgment and thereby succeed to the rights of the judgment creditor, including the charging order.

(f) If a court orders foreclosure of a charging order lien against the sole member of a limited liability company:

(1) the court shall confirm the sale;

(2) the purchaser at the sale obtains the member's entire interest, not only the member's transferable interest;

(3) the purchaser thereby becomes a member; and

(4) the person whose interest was subject to the foreclosed charging order is dissociated as a member.

(g) This [act] does not deprive any member or transferee of the benefit of any exemption law applicable to the transferable interest of the member or transferee.

(h) This section provides the exclusive remedy by which a person seeking in the capacity of judgment creditor to enforce a judgment against a member or transferee may satisfy the judgment from the judgment debtor's transferable interest.

Section 504. Power of Legal Representative of Deceased Member.

ARTICLE 6: DISSOCIATION

Section 601. Power to Dissociate as Member; Wrongful Dissociation.

(a) A person has the power to dissociate as a member at any time, rightfully or wrongfully, by withdrawing as a member by express will under Section 602(1).

(b) A person's dissociation as a member is wrongful only if the dissociation:

(1) is in breach of an express provision of the operating agreement; or

(2) occurs before the completion of the winding up of the limited liability company and:

(A) the person withdraws as a member by express will;

(B) the person is expelled as a member by judicial order under Section 602(6);

(C) the person is dissociated under Section 602(8); or

(D) in the case of a person that is not a trust other than a business trust, an estate, or an individual, the person is expelled or otherwise dissociated as a member because it willfully dissolved or terminated.

(c) A person that wrongfully dissociates as a member is liable to the limited liability company and, subject to Section 801, to the other members for damages caused by the dissociation. The liability is in addition to any debt, obligation, or other liability of the member to the company or the other members.

Section 602. Events Causing Dissociation.

A person is dissociated as a member when:

(1) the limited liability company knows or has notice of the person's express will to withdraw as a member, but, if the person has specified a withdrawal date later than the date the company knew or had notice, on that later date;

(2) an event stated in the operating agreement as causing the person's dissociation occurs;

(3) the person's entire interest is transferred in a foreclosure sale under Section 503(f);

(4) the person is expelled as a member pursuant to the operating agreement;

(5) the person is expelled as a member by the affirmative vote or consent of all the other members if:

(A) it is unlawful to carry on the limited liability company's activities and affairs with the person as a member;

(B) there has been a transfer of all the person's transferable interest in the company, other than:

(i) a transfer for security purposes; or

(ii) a charging order in effect under Section 503 which has not been foreclosed;

(C) the person is an entity and:

(i) the company notifies the person that it will be expelled as a member because the person has filed a statement of dissolution or the equivalent, the person has been administratively dissolved, the person's charter or the equivalent has been revoked, or the person's right to conduct business has been suspended by the person's jurisdiction of formation; and

(ii) not later than 90 days after the notification, the statement of dissolution or the equivalent has not been withdrawn, rescinded, or revoked, the person has not been reinstated, or the person's charter or the equivalent or right to conduct business has not been reinstated; or

(D) the person is an unincorporated entity that has been dissolved and whose activities and affairs are being wound up;

(6) on application by the limited liability company or a member in a direct action under Section 801, the person is expelled as a member by judicial order because the person:

(A) has engaged or is engaging in wrongful conduct that has affected adversely and materially, or will affect adversely and materially, the company's activities and affairs;

(B) has committed willfully or persistently, or is committing willfully or persistently, a material breach of the operating agreement or a duty or obligation under Section 409; or

(C) has engaged or is engaging in conduct relating to the company's activities and affairs which makes it not reasonably practicable to carry on the activities and affairs with the person as a member;

(7) in the case of an individual:

(A) the individual dies; or

(B) in a member-managed limited liability company:

(i) a guardian or general conservator for the individual is appointed; or

(ii) a court orders that the individual has otherwise become incapable of performing the individual's duties as a member under this [act] or the operating agreement;

(8) in a member-managed limited liability company, the person:

(A) becomes a debtor in bankruptcy;

(B) signs an assignment for the benefit of creditors; or

(C) seeks, consents to, or acquiesces in the appointment of a trustee, receiver, or liquidator of the person or of all or substantially all the person's property;

(9) in the case of a person that is a testamentary or inter vivos trust or is acting as a member by virtue of being a trustee of such a trust, the trust's entire transferable interest in the limited liability company is distributed;

(10) in the case of a person that is an estate or is acting as a member by virtue of being a personal representative of an estate, the estate's entire transferable interest in the limited liability company is distributed;

(11) in the case of a person that is not an individual, the existence of the person terminates;

(12) the limited liability company participates in a merger under [Article] 10 and:

(A) the company is not the surviving entity; or

(B) otherwise as a result of the merger, the person ceases to be a member;

(13) the limited liability company participates in an interest exchange under [Article] 10 and, as a result of the interest exchange, the person ceases to be a member;

(14) the limited liability company participates in a conversion under [Article] 10;

(15) the limited liability company participates in a domestication under [Article] 10 and, as a result of the domestication, the person ceases to be a member; or

(16) the limited liability company dissolves and completes winding up.

Section 603. Effect of Dissociation.

(a) If a person is dissociated as a member:

(1) the person's right to participate as a member in the management and conduct of the limited liability company's activities and affairs terminates;

(2) the person's duties and obligations under Section 409 as a member end with regard to matters arising and events occurring after the person's dissociation; and

(3) subject to Section 504 and [Article] 10, any transferable interest owned by the person in the person's capacity as a member immediately before dissociation is owned by the person solely as a transferee.

(b) A person's dissociation as a member does not of itself discharge the person from any debt, obligation, or other liability to the limited liability company or the other members which the person incurred while a member.

ARTICLE 7: DISSOLUTION AND WINDING UP

Section 701. Events Causing Dissolution.

(a) A limited liability company is dissolved, and its activities and affairs must be wound up, upon the occurrence of any of the following:

(1) an event or circumstance that the operating agreement states causes dissolution;

(2) the affirmative vote or consent of all the members;

(3) the passage of 90 consecutive days during which the company has no members unless before the end of the period:

(A) consent to admit at least one specified person as a member is given by transferees owning the rights to receive a majority of distributions as transferees at the time the consent is to be effective; and

(B) at least one person becomes a member in accordance with the consent;

(4) on application by a member, the entry by [the appropriate court] of an order dissolving the company on the grounds that:

(A) the conduct of all or substantially all the company's activities and affairs is unlawful;

(B) it is not reasonably practicable to carry on the company's activities and affairs in conformity with the certificate of organization and the operating agreement; or

(C) the managers or those members in control of the company:

(i) have acted, are acting, or will act in a manner that is illegal or fraudulent; or

(ii) have acted or are acting in a manner that is oppressive and was, is, or will be directly harmful to the applicant; or

(5) the signing and filing of a statement of administrative dissolution by the [Secretary of State] under Section 708.

(b) In a proceeding brought under subsection (a)(4)(C), the court may order a remedy other than dissolution.

Section 702. Winding Up.

(a) A dissolved limited liability company shall wind up its activities and affairs and, except as otherwise provided in Section 703, the company continues after dissolution only for the purpose of winding up.

(b) In winding up its activities and affairs, a limited liability company:

(1) shall discharge the company's debts, obligations, and other liabilities, settle and close the company's activities and affairs, and marshal and distribute the assets of the company; and

(2) may:

(A) deliver to the [Secretary of State] for filing a statement of dissolution stating the name of the company and that the company is dissolved;

(B) preserve the company activities, affairs, and property as a going concern for a reasonable time;

(C) prosecute and defend actions and proceedings, whether civil, criminal, or administrative;

(D) transfer the company's property;

(E) settle disputes by mediation or arbitration;

(F) deliver to the [Secretary of State] for filing a statement of termination stating the name of the company and that the company is terminated; and

(G) perform other acts necessary or appropriate to the winding up.

(c) If a dissolved limited liability company has no members, the legal representative of the last person to have been a member may wind up the activities and affairs of the company. If the person does so, the person has the powers of a sole manager under Section 407(c) and is deemed to be a manager for the purposes of Section 304(a).

(d) If the legal representative under subsection (c) declines or fails to wind up the limited liability company's activities and affairs, a person may be appointed to do so by the consent of transferees owning a majority of the rights to receive distributions as transferees at the time the consent is to be effective. A person appointed under this subsection:

(1) has the powers of a sole manager under Section 407(c) and is deemed to be a manager for the purposes of Section 304(a); and

(2) shall deliver promptly to the [Secretary of State] for filing an amendment to the company's certificate of organization stating:

(A) that the company has no members;

(B) the name and street and mailing addresses of the person; and

(C) that the person has been appointed pursuant to this subsection to wind up the company.

(e) [The appropriate court] may order judicial supervision of the winding up of a dissolved limited liability company, including the appointment of a person to wind up the company's activities and affairs:

(1) on the application of a member, if the applicant establishes good cause;

(2) on the application of a transferee, if:

(A) the company does not have any members;

(B) the legal representative of the last person to have been a member declines or fails to wind up the company's activities; and

(C) within a reasonable time following the dissolution a person has not been appointed pursuant to subsection (c); or

(3) in connection with a proceeding under Section 701(a)(4).

Section 703. Rescinding Dissolution.

Section 704. Known Claims Against Dissolved Limited Liability Company.

Section 705. Other Claims Against Dissolved Limited Liability Company.

Section 706. Court Proceedings.

Section 707. Disposition of Assets in Winding Up.

(a) In winding up its activities and affairs, a limited liability company shall apply its assets to discharge the company's obligations to creditors, including members that are creditors.

(b) After a limited liability company complies with subsection (a), any surplus must be distributed in the following order, subject to any charging order in effect under Section 503:

(1) to each person owning a transferable interest that reflects contributions made and not previously returned, an amount equal to the value of the unreturned contributions; and

(2) among persons owning transferable interests in proportion to their respective rights to share in distributions immediately before the dissolution of the company.

(c) If a limited liability company does not have sufficient surplus to comply with subsection (b)(1), any surplus must be distributed among the owners of transferable interests in proportion to the value of the respective unreturned contributions.

(d) All distributions made under subsections (b) and (c) must be paid in money.

Section 708. Administrative Dissolution.

Section 709. Reinstatement.

Section 710. Judicial Review of Denial of Reinstatement.

ARTICLE 8: ACTIONS BY MEMBERS

Section 801. Direct Action by Member.

(a) Subject to subsection (b), a member may maintain a direct action against another member, a manager, or the limited liability company to enforce the member's rights and protect the member's interests, including rights and interests under the operating agreement or this [act] or arising independently of the membership relationship.

(b) A member maintaining a direct action under this section must plead and prove an actual or threatened injury that is not solely the result of an injury suffered or threatened to be suffered by the limited liability company.

Section 802. Derivative Action.

A member may maintain a derivative action to enforce a right of a limited liability company if:

(1) the member first makes a demand on the other members in a member-managed limited liability company, or the managers of a manager-managed limited liability company, requesting that they cause the company to bring an action to enforce the right, and the managers or other members do not bring the action within a reasonable time; or

(2) a demand under paragraph (1) would be futile.

Section 803. Proper Plaintiff.

A derivative action to enforce a right of a limited liability company may be maintained only by a person that is a member at the time the action is commenced and:

(1) was a member when the conduct giving rise to the action occurred; or

(2) whose status as a member devolved on the person by operation of law or pursuant to the terms of the operating agreement from a person that was a member at the time of the conduct.

Section 804. Pleading.

In a derivative action, the complaint must state with particularity:

(1) the date and content of plaintiff's demand and the response to the demand by the managers or other members; or

(2) why demand should be excused as futile.

Section 805. Special Litigation Committee.

Section 806. Proceeds and Expenses.

(a) Except as otherwise provided in subsection (b):

> (1) any proceeds or other benefits of a derivative action, whether by judgment, compromise, or settlement, belong to the limited liability company and not to the plaintiff; and
>
> (2) if the plaintiff receives any proceeds, the plaintiff shall remit them immediately to the company.

(b) If a derivative action is successful in whole or in part, the court may award the plaintiff reasonable expenses, including reasonable attorney's fees and costs, from the recovery of the limited liability company.

(c) A derivative action on behalf of a limited liability company may not be voluntarily dismissed or settled without the court's approval.

ARTICLE 9: FOREIGN LIMITED LIABILITY COMPANIES

Section 901. Governing Law.

(a) The law of the jurisdiction of formation of a foreign limited liability company governs:

> (1) the internal affairs of the company;
>
> (2) the liability of a member as member and a manager as manager for a debt, obligation, or other liability of the company; and
>
> (3) the liability of a series of the company.

(b) A foreign limited liability company is not precluded from registering to do business in this state because of any difference between the law of its jurisdiction of formation and the law of this state.

(c) Registration of a foreign limited liability company to do business in this state does not authorize the foreign company to engage in any activities and affairs or exercise any power that a limited liability company may not engage in or exercise in this state.

Section 902. Registration to Do Business in This State.

(a) A foreign limited liability company may not do business in this state until it registers with the [Secretary of State] under this [article].

(b) A foreign limited liability company doing business in this state may not maintain an action or proceeding in this state unless it is registered to do business in this state.

(c) The failure of a foreign limited liability company to register to do business in this state does not impair the validity of a contract or act of the company or preclude it from defending an action or proceeding in this state.

(d) A limitation on the liability of a member or manager of a foreign limited liability company is not waived solely because the company does business in this state without registering to do business in this state.

(e) Section 901(a) and (b) applies even if a foreign limited liability company fails to register under this [article].

Section 903. Foreign Registration Statement.

Section 904. Amendment of Foreign Registration Statement.

Section 905. Activities Not Constituting Doing Business.

(a) Activities of a foreign limited liability company which do not constitute doing business in this state under this [article] include:

(1) maintaining, defending, mediating, arbitrating, or settling an action or proceeding;

(2) carrying on any activity concerning its internal affairs, including holding meetings of its members or managers;

(3) maintaining accounts in financial institutions;

(4) maintaining offices or agencies for the transfer, exchange, and registration of securities of the company or maintaining trustees or depositories with respect to those securities;

(5) selling through independent contractors;

(6) soliciting or obtaining orders by any means if the orders require acceptance outside this state before they become contracts;

(7) creating or acquiring indebtedness, mortgages, or security interests in property;

(8) securing or collecting debts or enforcing mortgages or security interests in property securing the debts and holding, protecting, or maintaining property;

(9) conducting an isolated transaction that is not in the course of similar transactions;

(10) owning, without more, property; and

(11) doing business in interstate commerce.

(b) A person does not do business in this state solely by being a member or manager of a foreign limited liability company that does business in this state.

(c) This section does not apply in determining the contacts or activities that may subject a foreign limited liability company to service of process, taxation, or regulation under law of this state other than this [act].

Section 906. Noncomplying Name of Foreign Limited Liability Company.

Section 907. Withdrawal Deemed on Conversion to Domestic Filing Entity or Domestic Limited Liability Partnership.

Section 908. Withdrawal on Dissolution or Conversion or Conversion to Nonfiling Entity Other than Limited Liability Partnership.

Section 909. Transfer of Registration.

Section 910. Termination of Registration.

Section 911. Withdrawal of Registration of Registered Foreign Limited Liability Company.

Section 912. Action by [Attorney General].

ARTICLE 10: MERGER, INTEREST EXCHANGE, CONVERSION, AND DOMESTICATION

PART 1: GENERAL PROVISIONS

Section 1001. Definitions.

Section 1002. Relationship of [Article] to Other Laws.

Section 1003. Required Notice or Approval.

Section 1004. Nonexclusivity.

Section 1005. Reference to External Facts.

Section 1006. Appraisal Rights.

Section 1007. Excluded Entities and Transactions.

PART 2: MERGER

Section 1021. Merger Authorized.

Section 1022. Plan of Merger.

Section 1023. Approval of Merger.

Section 1024. Amendment or Abandonment of Plan of Merger.

Section 1025. Statement of Merger; Effective Date of Merger.

Section 1026. Effect of Merger.

PART 3: INTEREST EXCHANGE

Section 1031. Interest Exchange Authorized.

Section 1032. Plan of Interest Exchange.

Section 1033. Approval of Interest Exchange.

Section 1034. Amendment or Abandonment of Plan of Interest Exchange.

Section 1035. Statement of Interest Exchange; Effective Date of Interest Exchange.

Section 1036. Effect of Interest Exchange.

PART 4: CONVERSION

Section 1041. Conversion Authorized.

Section 1042. Plan of Conversion.

Section 1043. Approval of Conversion.

Section 1044. Amendment or Abandonment of Plan of Conversion.

Section 1045. Statement of Conversion; Effective Date of Conversion.

Section 1046. Effect of Conversion.

PART 5: DOMESTICATION

Section 1051. Domestication Authorized.

Section 1052. Plan of Domestication.

Section 1053. Approval of Domestication.

Section 1054. Amendment or Abandonment of Plan of Domestication.

Section 1055. Statement of Domestication; Effective Date of Domestication.

Section 1056. Effect of Domestication.

ARTICLE 11: MISCELLANEOUS PROVISIONS

Section 1101. Uniformity of Application and Construction.

In applying and construing this uniform act, consideration must be given to the need to promote uniformity of the law with respect to its subject matter among states that enact it.

Section 1102. Relation to Electronic Signatures in Global and National Commerce Act.

Section 1103. Savings Clause.

This [act] does not affect an action commenced, proceeding brought, or right accrued before [the effective date of this [act]].

Section 1104. Severability Clause.

If any provision of this [act] or its application to any person or circumstance is held invalid, the invalidity does not affect other provisions or applications of this [act] which can be given effect without the invalid provision or application, and to this end the provisions of this [act] are severable.

Section 1105. Repeals.

Section 1106. Effective Date.

This [act] takes effect . . . .

APPENDIX C

REVISED UNIFORM PARTNERSHIP ACT (1997 & 2013 HARMONIZED) (EXCERPTED)

■ ■ ■

ARTICLE 1: GENERAL PROVISIONS

Section 101. Short Title.

Section 102. Definitions.

Section 103. Knowledge; Notice.

Section 104. Governing Law.

The internal affairs of a partnership and the liability of a partner as a partner for a debt, obligation, or other liability of the partnership are governed by:

(1) in the case of a limited liability partnership, the law of this state; and

(2) in the case of a partnership that is not a limited liability partnership, the law of the jurisdiction in which the partnership has its principal office.

Section 105. Partnership Agreement; Scope, Function, and Limitations.

(a) Except as otherwise provided in subsections (c) and (d), the partnership agreement governs:

(1) relations among the partners as partners and between the partners and the partnership;

(2) the business of the partnership and the conduct of that business; and

(3) the means and conditions for amending the partnership agreement.

(b) To the extent the partnership agreement does not provide for a matter described in subsection (a), this [act] governs the matter.

(c) A partnership agreement may not:

(1) vary the law applicable under Section 104(1);

(2) vary the provisions of Section 110;

(3) vary the provisions of Section 307;

(4) unreasonably restrict the duties and rights under Section 408, but the partnership agreement may impose reasonable restrictions on the availability and use of information obtained under that section and may define appropriate remedies, including liquidated damages, for a breach of any reasonable restriction on use;

(5) alter or eliminate the duty of loyalty or the duty of care, except as otherwise provided in subsection (d);

(6) eliminate the contractual obligation of good faith and fair dealing under Section 409(d), but the partnership agreement may prescribe the standards, if not

manifestly unreasonable, by which the performance of the obligation is to be measured;

(7) unreasonably restrict the right of a person to maintain an action under Section 410(b);

(8) relieve or exonerate a person from liability for conduct involving bad faith, willful or intentional misconduct, or knowing violation of law;

(9) vary the power of a person to dissociate as a partner under Section 602(a), except to require that the notice under Section 601(1) be in a record;

(10) vary the grounds for expulsion specified in Section 601(5);

(11) vary the causes of dissolution specified in Section 801(4) or (5);

(12) vary the requirement to wind up the partnership's business as specified in Section 802(a), (b)(1), and (d);

(13) vary the right of a partner under Section 901(f) to vote on or consent to a cancellation of a statement of qualification;

(14) vary the right of a partner to approve a merger, interest exchange, conversion, or domestication under Section 1123(a)(2), 1133(a)(2), 1143(a)(2), or 1153(a)(2);

(15) vary the required contents of a plan of merger under Section 1122(a), plan of interest exchange under Section 1132(a), plan of conversion under Section 1142(a), or plan of domestication under Section 1152(a);

(16) vary any requirement, procedure, or other provision of this [act] pertaining to:

(A) registered agents; or

(B) the [Secretary of State], including provisions pertaining to records authorized or required to be delivered to the [Secretary of State] for filing under this [act]; or

(17) except as otherwise provided in Sections 106 and 107(b), restrict the rights under this [act] of a person other than a partner.

(d) Subject to subsection (c)(8), without limiting other terms that may be included in a partnership agreement, the following rules apply:

(1) The partnership agreement may:

(A) specify the method by which a specific act or transaction that would otherwise violate the duty of loyalty may be authorized or ratified by one or more disinterested and independent persons after full disclosure of all material facts; and

(B) alter the prohibition in Section 406(a)(2) so that the prohibition requires only that the partnership's total assets not be less than the sum of its total liabilities.

(2) To the extent the partnership agreement expressly relieves a partner of a responsibility that the partner would otherwise have under this [act] and imposes the responsibility on one or more other partners, the agreement also may eliminate or limit any fiduciary duty of the partner relieved of the responsibility which would have pertained to the responsibility.

(3) If not manifestly unreasonable, the partnership agreement may:

(A) alter or eliminate the aspects of the duty of loyalty stated in Section 409(b);

(B) identify specific types or categories of activities that do not violate the duty of loyalty;

(C) alter the duty of care, but may not authorize conduct involving bad faith, willful or intentional misconduct, or knowing violation of law; and

(D) alter or eliminate any other fiduciary duty.

(e) The court shall decide as a matter of law whether a term of a partnership agreement is manifestly unreasonable under subsection (c)(6) or (d)(3). The court:

(1) shall make its determination as of the time the challenged term became part of the partnership agreement and by considering only circumstances existing at that time; and

(2) may invalidate the term only if, in light of the purposes and business of the partnership, it is readily apparent that:

(A) the objective of the term is unreasonable; or

(B) the term is an unreasonable means to achieve the term's objective.

Section 106. Partnership Agreement; Effect on Partnership and Person Becoming Partner; Preformation Agreement.

(a) A partnership is bound by and may enforce the partnership agreement, whether or not the partnership has itself manifested assent to the agreement.

(b) A person that becomes a partner is deemed to assent to the partnership agreement.

(c) Two or more persons intending to become the initial partners of a partnership may make an agreement providing that upon the formation of the partnership the agreement will become the partnership agreement.

Section 107. Partnership Agreement; Effect on Third Parties and Relationship to Records Effective on Behalf of Partnership.

(a) A partnership agreement may specify that its amendment requires the approval of a person that is not a party to the agreement or the satisfaction of a condition. An amendment is ineffective if its adoption does not include the required approval or satisfy the specified condition.

(b) The obligations of a partnership and its partners to a person in the person's capacity as a transferee or person dissociated as a partner are governed by the partnership agreement. Subject only to a court order issued under Section 504(b)(2) to effectuate a charging order, an amendment to the partnership agreement made after a person becomes a transferee or is dissociated as a partner:

(1) is effective with regard to any debt, obligation, or other liability of the partnership or its partners to the person in the person's capacity as a transferee or person dissociated as a partner; and

(2) is not effective to the extent the amendment:

(A) imposes a new debt, obligation, or other liability on the transferee or person dissociated as a partner; or

(B) prejudices the rights under Section 701 of a person that dissociated as a partner before the amendment was made.

(c) If a record delivered by a partnership to the [Secretary of State] for filing becomes effective and contains a provision that would be ineffective under Section 105(c) or (d)(3) if contained in the partnership agreement, the provision is ineffective in the record.

(d) Subject to subsection (c), if a record delivered by a partnership to the [Secretary of State] for filing becomes effective and conflicts with a provision of the partnership agreement:

(1) the agreement prevails as to partners, persons dissociated as partners, and transferees; and

(2) the record prevails as to other persons to the extent they reasonably rely on the record.

Section 108. Signing of Records to be Delivered to be Delivered for Filing to [Secretary of State].

Section 109. Liability for Inaccurate Information in Filed Record.

Section 110. Application to Existing Relationships.

Section 111. Delivery of Record.

Section 112. Signing and Filing Pursuant to Judicial Order.

Section 113. Filing Requirements.

Section 114. Effective Date and Time.

Section 115. Withdrawal of Filed Record Before Effectiveness.

Section 116. Correcting Filed Record.

Section 117. Duty of [Secretary of State] to File; Review of Refusal to File; Delivery of Record by [Secretary of State].

Section 118. Reservation of Power to Amend or Repeal.

The [legislature of this state] has power to amend or repeal all or part of this [act] at any time, and all limited liability partnerships and foreign limited liability partnerships subject to this [act] are governed by the amendment or repeal.

Section 119. Supplemental Principles of Law.

Unless displaced by particular provisions of this [act], the principles of law and equity supplement this [act].

ARTICLE 2: NATURE OF PARTNERSHIP

Section 201. Partnership as Entity.

(a) A partnership is an entity distinct from its partners.

(b) A partnership is the same entity regardless of whether the partnership has a statement of qualification in effect under Section 901.

Section 202. Formation of Partnership.

(a) Except as otherwise provided in subsection (b), the association of two or more persons to carry on as co-owners a business for profit forms a partnership, whether or not the persons intend to form a partnership.

(b) An association formed under a statute other than this [act], a predecessor statute, or a comparable statute of another jurisdiction is not a partnership under this [act].

(c) In determining whether a partnership is formed, the following rules apply:

(1) Joint tenancy, tenancy in common, tenancy by the entireties, joint property, common property, or part ownership does not by itself establish a partnership, even if the co-owners share profits made by the use of the property.

(2) The sharing of gross returns does not by itself establish a partnership, even if the persons sharing them have a joint or common right or interest in property from which the returns are derived.

(3) A person who receives a share of the profits of a business is presumed to be a partner in the business, unless the profits were received in payment:

(A) of a debt by installments or otherwise;

(B) for services as an independent contractor or of wages or other compensation to an employee;

(C) of rent;

(D) of an annuity or other retirement or health benefit to a deceased or retired partner or a beneficiary, representative, or designee of a deceased or retired partner;

(E) of interest or other charge on a loan, even if the amount of payment varies with the profits of the business, including a direct or indirect present or future ownership of the collateral, or rights to income, proceeds, or increase in value derived from the collateral; or

(F) for the sale of the goodwill of a business or other property by installments or otherwise.

Section 203. Partnership Property.

Property acquired by a partnership is property of the partnership and not of the partners individually.

Section 204. When Property is Partnership Property.

ARTICLE 3: RELATIONS OF PARTNERS TO PERSONS DEALING WITH PARTNERSHIP

Section 301. Partner Agent of Partnership.

Subject to the effect of a statement of partnership authority under Section 303, the following rules apply:

(1) Each partner is an agent of the partnership for the purpose of its business. An act of a partner, including the signing of an instrument in the partnership name, for apparently carrying on in the ordinary course the partnership business or business of the kind carried on by the partnership binds the partnership, unless the partner did not have authority to act for the partnership in the particular matter and the person with which the partner was dealing knew or had notice that the partner lacked authority.

(2) An act of a partner which is not apparently for carrying on in the ordinary course the partnership's business or business of the kind carried on by the partnership binds the partnership only if the act was actually authorized by all the other partners.

Section 302. Transfer of Partnership Property.

Section 303. Statement of Partnership Authority.

Section 304. Statement of Denial.

Section 305. Partnership Liable for Partner's Actionable Conduct.

(a) A partnership is liable for loss or injury caused to a person, or for a penalty incurred, as a result of a wrongful act or omission, or other actionable conduct, of a partner acting in the ordinary course of business of the partnership or with the actual or apparent authority of the partnership.

(b) If, in the course of the partnership's business or while acting with actual or apparent authority of the partnership, a partner receives or causes the partnership to receive money or property of a person not a partner, and the money or property is misapplied by a partner, the partnership is liable for the loss.

Section 306. Partner's Liability.

(a) Except as otherwise provided in subsections (b) and (c), all partners are liable jointly and severally for all debts, obligations, and other liabilities of the partnership unless otherwise agreed by the claimant or provided by law.

(b) A person that becomes a partner is not personally liable for a debt, obligation, or other liability of the partnership incurred before the person became a partner.

(c) A debt, obligation, or other liability of a partnership incurred while the partnership is a limited liability partnership is solely the debt, obligation, or other liability of the limited liability partnership. A partner is not personally liable, directly or indirectly, by way of contribution or otherwise, for a debt, obligation, or other liability of the limited liability partnership solely by reason of being or acting as a partner. This subsection applies:

(1) despite anything inconsistent in the partnership agreement that existed immediately before the vote or consent required to become a limited liability partnership under Section 901(b); and

(2) regardless of the dissolution of the limited liability partnership.

(d) The failure of a limited liability partnership to observe formalities relating to the exercise of its powers or management of its business is not a ground for imposing liability on a partner for a debt, obligation, or other liability of the partnership.

(e) The cancellation or administrative revocation of a limited liability partnership's statement of qualification does not affect the limitation in this section on the liability of a partner for a debt, obligation, or other liability of the partnership incurred while the statement was in effect.

Section 307. Actions By and Against Partnership and Partners.

(a) A partnership may sue and be sued in the name of the partnership.

(b) To the extent not inconsistent with Section 306, a partner may be joined in an action against the partnership or named in a separate action.

(c) A judgment against a partnership is not by itself a judgment against a partner. A judgment against a partnership may not be satisfied from a partner's assets unless there is also a judgment against the partner.

(d) A judgment creditor of a partner may not levy execution against the assets of the partner to satisfy a judgment based on a claim against the partnership unless the partner is personally liable for the claim under Section 306 and:

(1) a judgment based on the same claim has been obtained against the partnership and a writ of execution on the judgment has been returned unsatisfied in whole or in part;

(2) the partnership is a debtor in bankruptcy;

(3) the partner has agreed that the creditor need not exhaust partnership assets;

(4) a court grants permission to the judgment creditor to levy execution against the assets of a partner based on a finding that partnership assets subject to execution are clearly insufficient to satisfy the judgment, that exhaustion of partnership assets is excessively burdensome, or that the grant of permission is an appropriate exercise of the court's equitable powers; or

(5) liability is imposed on the partner by law or contract independent of the existence of the partnership.

(e) This section applies to any debt, liability, or other obligation of a partnership which results from a representation by a partner or purported partner under Section 308.

Section 308. Liability of Purported Partner.

ARTICLE 4: RELATIONS OF PARTNERS TO EACH OTHER AND TO PARTNERSHIP

Section 401. Partner's Rights and Duties.

(a) Each partner is entitled to an equal share of the partnership distributions and, except in the case of a limited liability partnership, is chargeable with a share of the partnership losses in proportion to the partner's share of the distributions.

(b) A partnership shall reimburse a partner for any payment made by the partner in the course of the partner's activities on behalf of the partnership, if the partner complied with this section and Section 409 in making the payment.

(c) A partnership shall indemnify and hold harmless a person with respect to any claim or demand against the person and any debt, obligation, or other liability incurred by the person by reason of the person's former or present capacity as a partner, if the claim, demand, debt, obligation, or other liability does not arise from the person's breach of this section or Section 407 or 409.

(d) In the ordinary course of its business, a partnership may advance reasonable expenses, including attorney's fees and costs, incurred by a person in connection with a claim or demand against the person by reason of the person's former or present capacity as a partner, if the person promises to repay the partnership if the person ultimately is determined not to be entitled to be indemnified under subsection (c).

(e) A partnership may purchase and maintain insurance on behalf of a partner against liability asserted against or incurred by the partner in that capacity or arising from that status even if, under Section 105(c)(7), the partnership agreement could not eliminate or limit the person's liability to the partnership for the conduct giving rise to the liability.

(f) A partnership shall reimburse a partner for an advance to the partnership beyond the amount of capital the partner agreed to contribute.

(g) A payment or advance made by a partner which gives rise to a partnership obligation under subsection (b) or (f) constitutes a loan to the partnership which accrues interest from the date of the payment or advance.

(h) Each partner has equal rights in the management and conduct of the partnership's business.

(i) A partner may use or possess partnership property only on behalf of the partnership.

(j) A partner is not entitled to remuneration for services performed for the partnership, except for reasonable compensation for services rendered in winding up the business of the partnership.

(k) A difference arising as to a matter in the ordinary course of business of a partnership may be decided by a majority of the partners. An act outside the ordinary course of business of a partnership and an amendment to the partnership agreement may be undertaken only with the affirmative vote or consent of all the partners.

Section 402. Becoming Partner.

(a) Upon formation of a partnership, a person becomes a partner under Section 202(a).

(b) After formation of a partnership, a person becomes a partner:

(1) as provided in the partnership agreement;

(2) as a result of a transaction effective under [Article] 11; or

(3) with the affirmative vote or consent of all the partners.

(c) A person may become a partner without:

(1) acquiring a transferable interest; or

(2) making or being obligated to make a contribution to the partnership.

Section 403. Form of Contribution.

A contribution may consist of property transferred to, services performed for, or another benefit provided to the partnership or an agreement to transfer property to, perform services for, or provide another benefit to the partnership.

Section 404. Liability for Contribution.

Section 405. Sharing of and Right to Distributions Before Dissolution.

(a) Any distribution made by a partnership before its dissolution and winding up must be in equal shares among partners, except to the extent necessary to comply with a transfer effective under Section 503 or charging order in effect under Section 504.

(b) Subject to Section 701, a person has a right to a distribution before the dissolution and winding up of a partnership only if the partnership decides to make an interim distribution.

(c) A person does not have a right to demand or receive a distribution from a partnership in any form other than money. Except as otherwise provided in Section 806, a partnership may distribute an asset in kind only if each part of the asset is fungible with each other part and each person receives a percentage of the asset equal in value to the person's share of distributions.

(d) If a partner or transferee becomes entitled to receive a distribution, the partner or transferee has the status of, and is entitled to all remedies available to, a creditor of the partnership with respect to the distribution. However, the partnership's obligation to make a distribution is subject to offset for any amount owed to the partnership by the partner or a person dissociated as partner on whose account the distribution is made.

Section 406. Limitations on Distributions by Limited Liability Partnership.

(a) A limited liability partnership may not make a distribution, including a distribution under Section 806, if after the distribution:

(1) the partnership would not be able to pay its debts as they become due in the ordinary course of the partnership's business; or

(2) the partnership's total assets would be less than the sum of its total liabilities plus the amount that would be needed, if the partnership were to be dissolved and wound up at the time of the distribution, to satisfy the preferential rights upon dissolution and winding up of partners and transferees whose preferential rights are superior to the rights of persons receiving the distribution.

(b) A limited liability partnership may base a determination that a distribution is not prohibited under subsection (a) on:

(1) financial statements prepared on the basis of accounting practices and principles that are reasonable in the circumstances; or

(2) a fair valuation or other method that is reasonable under the circumstances.

(c) Except as otherwise provided in subsection (e), the effect of a distribution under subsection (a) is measured:

(1) in the case of a distribution as defined in Section 102(4)(A), as of the earlier of:

(A) the date money or other property is transferred or debt is incurred by the limited liability partnership; or

(B) the date the person entitled to the distribution ceases to own the interest or rights being acquired by the partnership in return for the distribution;

(2) in the case of any other distribution of indebtedness, as of the date the indebtedness is distributed; and

(3) in all other cases, as of the date:

(A) the distribution is authorized, if the payment occurs not later than 120 days after that date; or

(B) the payment is made, if the payment occurs more than 120 days after the distribution is authorized.

(d) A limited liability partnership's indebtedness to a partner or transferee incurred by reason of a distribution made in accordance with this section is at parity with the partnership's indebtedness to its general, unsecured creditors, except to the extent subordinated by agreement.

(e) A limited liability partnership's indebtedness, including indebtedness issued as a distribution, is not a liability for purposes of subsection (a) if the terms of the indebtedness provide that payment of principal and interest is made only if and to the extent that a payment of a distribution could then be made under this section. If the indebtedness is issued as a distribution, each payment of principal or interest is treated as a distribution, the effect of which is measured on the date the payment is made.

(f) In measuring the effect of a distribution under Section 806, the liabilities of a dissolved limited liability partnership do not include any claim that has been disposed of under Section 807, 808, or 809.

Section 407. Liability for Improper Distributions by Limited Liability Partnership.

Section 408. Rights to Information of Partners and Persons Dissociated as Partner.

Section 409. Standards of Conduct for Partners.

(a) A partner owes to the partnership and the other partners the duties of loyalty and care stated in subsections (b) and (c).

(b) The fiduciary duty of loyalty of a partner includes the duties:

(1) to account to the partnership and hold as trustee for it any property, profit, or benefit derived by the partner:

(A) in the conduct or winding up of the partnership's business;

(B) from a use by the partner of the partnership's property; or

(C) from the appropriation of a partnership opportunity;

(2) to refrain from dealing with the partnership in the conduct or winding up of the partnership business as or on behalf of a person having an interest adverse to the partnership; and

(3) to refrain from competing with the partnership in the conduct of the partnership's business before the dissolution of the partnership.

(c) The duty of care of a partner in the conduct or winding up of the partnership business is to refrain from engaging in grossly negligent or reckless conduct, willful or intentional misconduct, or a knowing violation of law.

(d) A partner shall discharge the duties and obligations under this [act] or under the partnership agreement and exercise any rights consistently with the contractual obligation of good faith and fair dealing.

(e) A partner does not violate a duty or obligation under this [act] or under the partnership agreement solely because the partner's conduct furthers the partner's own interest.

(f) All the partners may authorize or ratify, after full disclosure of all material facts, a specific act or transaction by a partner that otherwise would violate the duty of loyalty.

(g) It is a defense to a claim under subsection (b)(2) and any comparable claim in equity or at common law that the transaction was fair to the partnership.

(h) If, as permitted by subsection (f) or the partnership agreement, a partner enters into a transaction with the partnership which otherwise would be prohibited by subsection (b)(2), the partner's rights and obligations arising from the transaction are the same as those of a person that is not a partner.

Section 410. Actions by Partnership and Partners.

(a) A partnership may maintain an action against a partner for a breach of the partnership agreement, or for the violation of a duty to the partnership, causing harm to the partnership.

(b) A partner may maintain an action against the partnership or another partner, with or without an accounting as to partnership business, to enforce the partner's rights and protect the partner's interests, including rights and interests under the partnership agreement or this [act] or arising independently of the partnership relationship.

(c) A right to an accounting on dissolution and winding up does not revive a claim barred by law.

Section 411. Continuation of Partnership Beyond Definite Term or Particular Undertaking.

(a) If a partnership for a definite term or particular undertaking is continued, without an express agreement, after the expiration of the term or completion of the undertaking, the rights and duties of the partners remain the same as they were at the expiration or completion, so far as is consistent with a partnership at will.

(b) If the partners, or those of them who habitually acted in the business during the term or undertaking, continue the business without any settlement or liquidation of the partnership, they are presumed to have agreed that the partnership will continue.

ARTICLE 5: TRANSFERABLE INTERESTS AND RIGHTS OF TRANSFEREES AND CREDITORS

Section 501. Partner Not Co-owner of Partnership Property.

A partner is not a co-owner of partnership property and has no interest in partnership property which can be transferred, either voluntarily or involuntarily.

Section 502. Nature of Transferable Interest.

A transferable interest is personal property.

Section 503. Transfer of Transferable Interest.

(a) A transfer, in whole or in part, of a transferable interest:

(1) is permissible;

(2) does not by itself cause a person's dissociation as a partner or a dissolution and winding up of the partnership business; and

(3) subject to Section 505, does not entitle the transferee to:

(A) participate in the management or conduct of the partnership's business; or

(B) except as otherwise provided in subsection (c), have access to records or other information concerning the partnership's business.

(b) A transferee has the right to:

(1) receive, in accordance with the transfer, distributions to which the transferor would otherwise be entitled; and

(2) seek under Section 801(5) a judicial determination that it is equitable to wind up the partnership business.

(c) In a dissolution and winding up of a partnership, a transferee is entitled to an account of the partnership's transactions only from the date of dissolution.

(d) A partnership need not give effect to a transferee's rights under this section until the partnership knows or has notice of the transfer.

(e) A transfer of a transferable interest in violation of a restriction on transfer contained in the partnership agreement is ineffective if the intended transferee has knowledge or notice of the restriction at the time of transfer.

(f) Except as otherwise provided in Section 601(4)(B), if a partner transfers a transferable interest, the transferor retains the rights of a partner other than the transferable interest transferred and retains all the duties and obligations of a partner.

(g) If a partner transfers a transferable interest to a person that becomes a partner with respect to the transferred interest, the transferee is liable for the partner's obligations under Sections 404 and 407 known to the transferee when the transferee becomes a partner.

Section 504. Charging Order.

(a) On application by a judgment creditor of a partner or transferee, a court may enter a charging order against the transferable interest of the judgment debtor for the unsatisfied amount of the judgment. A charging order constitutes a lien on a judgment debtor's transferable interest and requires the partnership to pay over to the person to which the charging order was issued any distribution that otherwise would be paid to the judgment debtor.

(b) To the extent necessary to effectuate the collection of distributions pursuant to a charging order in effect under subsection (a), the court may:

(1) appoint a receiver of the distributions subject to the charging order, with the power to make all inquiries the judgment debtor might have made; and

(2) make all other orders necessary to give effect to the charging order.

(c) Upon a showing that distributions under a charging order will not pay the judgment debt within a reasonable time, the court may foreclose the lien and order the sale of the transferable interest. The purchaser at the foreclosure sale obtains only the transferable interest, does not thereby become a partner, and is subject to Section 503.

(d) At any time before foreclosure under subsection (c), the partner or transferee whose transferable interest is subject to a charging order under subsection (a) may extinguish the charging order by satisfying the judgment and filing a certified copy of the satisfaction with the court that issued the charging order.

(e) At any time before foreclosure under subsection (c), a partnership or one or more partners whose transferable interests are not subject to the charging order may pay to the judgment creditor the full amount due under the judgment and thereby succeed to the rights of the judgment creditor, including the charging order.

(f) This [act] does not deprive any partner or transferee of the benefit of any exemption law applicable to the transferable interest of the partner or transferee.

(g) This section provides the exclusive remedy by which a person seeking in the capacity of a judgment creditor to enforce a judgment against a partner or transferee may satisfy the judgment from the judgment debtor's transferable interest.

Section 505. Power of Legal Representative of Deceased Partner.

ARTICLE 6: DISSOCIATION

Section 601. Events Causing Dissociation.

A person is dissociated as a partner when:

(1) the partnership knows or has notice of the person's express will to withdraw as a partner, but, if the person has specified a withdrawal date later than the date the partnership knew or had notice, on that later date;

(2) an event stated in the partnership agreement as causing the person's dissociation occurs;

(3) the person is expelled as a partner pursuant to the partnership agreement;

(4) the person is expelled as a partner by the affirmative vote or consent of all the other partners if:

(A) it is unlawful to carry on the partnership business with the person as a partner;

(B) there has been a transfer of all of the person's transferable interest in the partnership, other than:

(i) a transfer for security purposes; or

(ii) a charging order in effect under Section 504 which has not been foreclosed;

(C) the person is an entity and:

(i) the partnership notifies the person that it will be expelled as a partner because the person has filed a statement of dissolution or the equivalent, the person has been administratively dissolved, the person's charter or the equivalent has been revoked, or the person's right to conduct business has been suspended by the person's jurisdiction of formation; and

(ii) not later than 90 days after the notification, the statement of dissolution or the equivalent has not been withdrawn, rescinded, or revoked, or the person's charter or the equivalent or right to conduct business has not been reinstated; or

(D) the person is an unincorporated entity that has been dissolved and whose activities and affairs are being wound up;

(5) on application by the partnership or another partner, the person is expelled as a partner by judicial order because the person:

(A) has engaged or is engaging in wrongful conduct that has affected adversely and materially, or will affect adversely and materially, the partnership's business;

(B) has committed willfully or persistently, or is committing willfully or persistently, a material breach of the partnership agreement or a duty or obligation under Section 409; or

(C) has engaged or is engaging in conduct relating to the partnership's business which makes it not reasonably practicable to carry on the business with the person as a partner;

(6) the person:

(A) becomes a debtor in bankruptcy;

(B) signs an assignment for the benefit of creditors; or

(C) seeks, consents to, or acquiesces in the appointment of a trustee, receiver, or liquidator of the person or of all or substantially all the person's property;

(7) in the case of an individual:

(A) the individual dies;

(B) a guardian or general conservator for the individual is appointed; or

(C) a court orders that the individual has otherwise become incapable of performing the individual's duties as a partner under this [act] or the partnership agreement;

(8) in the case of a person that is a testamentary or inter vivos trust or is acting as a partner by virtue of being a trustee of such a trust, the trust's entire transferable interest in the partnership is distributed;

(9) in the case of a person that is an estate or is acting as a partner by virtue of being a personal representative of an estate, the estate's entire transferable interest in the partnership is distributed;

(10) in the case of a person that is not an individual, the existence of the person terminates;

(11) the partnership participates in a merger under [Article] 11 and:

(A) the partnership is not the surviving entity; or

(B) otherwise as a result of the merger, the person ceases to be a partner;

(12) the partnership participates in an interest exchange under [Article] 11 and, as a result of the interest exchange, the person ceases to be a partner;

(13) the partnership participates in a conversion under [Article] 11;

(14) the partnership participates in a domestication under [Article] 11 and, as a result of the domestication, the person ceases to be a partner; or

(15) the partnership dissolves and completes winding up.

Section 602. Power to Dissociate as Partner; Wrongful Dissociation.

(a) A person has the power to dissociate as a partner at any time, rightfully or wrongfully, by withdrawing as a partner by express will under Section 601(1).

(b) A person's dissociation as a partner is wrongful only if the dissociation:

(1) is in breach of an express provision of the partnership agreement; or

(2) in the case of a partnership for a definite term or particular undertaking, occurs before the expiration of the term or the completion of the undertaking and:

(A) the person withdraws as a partner by express will, unless the withdrawal follows not later than 90 days after another person's dissociation by death or otherwise under Section 601(6) through (10) or wrongful dissociation under this subsection;

(B) the person is expelled as a partner by judicial order under Section 601(5);

(C) the person is dissociated under Section 601(6); or

(D) in the case of a person that is not a trust other than a business trust, an estate, or an individual, the person is expelled or otherwise dissociated because it willfully dissolved or terminated.

(c) A person that wrongfully dissociates as a partner is liable to the partnership and to the other partners for damages caused by the dissociation. The liability is in addition to any debt, obligation, or other liability of the partner to the partnership or the other partners.

Section 603. Effect of Dissociation.

(a) If a person's dissociation results in a dissolution and winding up of the partnership business, [Article] 8 applies; otherwise, [Article] 7 applies.

(b) If a person is dissociated as a partner:

(1) the person's right to participate in the management and conduct of the partnership's business terminates, except as otherwise provided in Section 802(c); and

(2) the person's duties and obligations under Section 409 end with regard to matters arising and events occurring after the person's dissociation, except to the

extent the partner participates in winding up the partnership's business pursuant to Section 802.

(c) A person's dissociation does not of itself discharge the person from any debt, obligation, or other liability to the partnership or the other partners which the person incurred while a partner.

ARTICLE 7: PERSON'S DISSOCIATION AS A PARTNER WHEN BUSINESS NOT WOUND UP

Section 701. Purchase of Interest of Person Dissociated as Partner.

(a) If a person is dissociated as a partner without the dissociation resulting in a dissolution and winding up of the partnership business under Section 801, the partnership shall cause the person's interest in the partnership to be purchased for a buyout price determined pursuant to subsection (b).

(b) The buyout price of the interest of a person dissociated as a partner is the amount that would have been distributable to the person under Section 806(b) if, on the date of dissociation, the assets of the partnership were sold and the partnership were wound up, with the sale price equal to the greater of:

(1) the liquidation value; or

(2) the value based on a sale of the entire business as a going concern without the person.

(c) Interest accrues on the buyout price from the date of dissociation to the date of payment, but damages for wrongful dissociation under Section 602(b), and all other amounts owing, whether or not presently due, from the person dissociated as a partner to the partnership, must be offset against the buyout price.

(d) A partnership shall defend, indemnify, and hold harmless a person dissociated as a partner whose interest is being purchased against all partnership liabilities, whether incurred before or after the dissociation, except liabilities incurred by an act of the person under Section 702.

(e) If no agreement for the purchase of the interest of a person dissociated as a partner is reached not later than 120 days after a written demand for payment, the partnership shall pay, or cause to be paid, in money to the person the amount the partnership estimates to be the buyout price and accrued interest, reduced by any offsets and accrued interest under subsection (c).

(f) If a deferred payment is authorized under subsection (h), the partnership may tender a written offer to pay the amount it estimates to be the buyout price and accrued interest, reduced by any offsets under subsection (c), stating the time of payment, the amount and type of security for payment, and the other terms and conditions of the obligation.

(g) The payment or tender required by subsection (e) or (f) must be accompanied by the following:

(1) a statement of partnership assets and liabilities as of the date of dissociation;

(2) the latest available partnership balance sheet and income statement, if any;

(3) an explanation of how the estimated amount of the payment was calculated; and

(4) written notice that the payment is in full satisfaction of the obligation to purchase unless, not later than 120 days after the written notice, the person

dissociated as a partner commences an action to determine the buyout price, any offsets under subsection (c), or other terms of the obligation to purchase.

(h) A person that wrongfully dissociates as a partner before the expiration of a definite term or the completion of a particular undertaking is not entitled to payment of any part of the buyout price until the expiration of the term or completion of the undertaking, unless the person establishes to the satisfaction of the court that earlier payment will not cause undue hardship to the business of the partnership. A deferred payment must be adequately secured and bear interest.

(i) A person dissociated as a partner may maintain an action against the partnership, pursuant to Section 410(b)(2), to determine the buyout price of that person's interest, any offsets under subsection (c), or other terms of the obligation to purchase. The action must be commenced not later than 120 days after the partnership has tendered payment or an offer to pay or within one year after written demand for payment if no payment or offer to pay is tendered. The court shall determine the buyout price of the person's interest, any offset due under subsection (c), and accrued interest, and enter judgment for any additional payment or refund. If deferred payment is authorized under subsection (h), the court shall also determine the security for payment and other terms of the obligation to purchase. The court may assess reasonable attorney's fees and the fees and expenses of appraisers or other experts for a party to the action, in amounts the court finds equitable, against a party that the court finds acted arbitrarily, vexatiously, or not in good faith. The finding may be based on the partnership's failure to tender payment or an offer to pay or to comply with subsection (g).

Section 702. Power to Bind and Liability of Person Dissociated as Partner.

Section 703. Liability of Person Dissociated as Partner to Other Persons.

Section 704. Statement of Dissociation.

Section 705. Continued Use of Partnership Name.

ARTICLE 8: DISSOLUTION AND WINDING UP

Section 801. Events Causing Dissolution.

A partnership is dissolved, and its business must be wound up, upon the occurrence of any of the following:

(1) in a partnership at will, the partnership knows or has notice of a person's express will to withdraw as a partner, other than a partner that has dissociated under Section 601(2) through (10), but, if the person has specified a withdrawal date later than the date the partnership knew or had notice, on the later date;

(2) in a partnership for a definite term or particular undertaking:

(A) within 90 days after a person's dissociation by death or otherwise under Section 601(6) through (10) or wrongful dissociation under Section 602(b), the affirmative vote or consent of at least half of the remaining partners to wind up the partnership business, for which purpose a person's rightful dissociation pursuant to Section 602(b)(2)(A) constitutes that partner's consent to wind up the partnership business;

(B) the affirmative vote or consent of all the partners to wind up the partnership business; or

(C) the expiration of the term or the completion of the undertaking;

(3) an event or circumstance that the partnership agreement states causes dissolution;

(4) on application by a partner, the entry by [the appropriate court] of an order dissolving the partnership on the grounds that:

(A) the conduct of all or substantially all the partnership's business is unlawful;

(B) the economic purpose of the partnership is likely to be unreasonably frustrated;

(C) another partner has engaged in conduct relating to the partnership business which makes it not reasonably practicable to carry on the business in partnership with that partner; or

(D) it is otherwise not reasonably practicable to carry on the partnership business in conformity with the partnership agreement;

(5) on application by a transferee, the entry by [the appropriate court] of an order dissolving the partnership on the ground that it is equitable to wind up the partnership business:

(A) after the expiration of the term or completion of the undertaking, if the partnership was for a definite term or particular undertaking at the time of the transfer or entry of the charging order that gave rise to the transfer; or

(B) at any time, if the partnership was a partnership at will at the time of the transfer or entry of the charging order that gave rise to the transfer; or

(6) the passage of 90 consecutive days during which the partnership does not have at least two partners.

Section 802. Winding Up.

(a) A dissolved partnership shall wind up its business and, except as otherwise provided in Section 803, the partnership continues after dissolution only for the purpose of winding up.

(b) In winding up its business, the partnership:

(1) shall discharge the partnership's debts, obligations, and other liabilities, settle and close the partnership's business, and marshal and distribute the assets of the partnership; and

(2) may:

(A) deliver to the [Secretary of State] for filing a statement of dissolution stating the name of the partnership and that the partnership is dissolved;

(B) preserve the partnership business and property as a going concern for a reasonable time;

(C) prosecute and defend actions and proceedings, whether civil, criminal, or administrative;

(D) transfer the partnership's property;

(E) settle disputes by mediation or arbitration;

(F) deliver to the [Secretary of State] for filing a statement of termination stating the name of the partnership and that the partnership is terminated; and

(G) perform other acts necessary or appropriate to the winding up.

(c) A person whose dissociation as a partner resulted in dissolution may participate in winding up as if still a partner, unless the dissociation was wrongful.

(d) If a dissolved partnership does not have a partner and no person has the right to participate in winding up under subsection (c), the personal or legal representative of the last person to have been a partner may wind up the partnership's business. If the representative does not exercise that right, a person to wind up the partnership's business may be appointed by the affirmative vote or consent of transferees owning a majority of the rights to receive distributions at the time the consent is to be effective. A person appointed under this subsection has the powers of a partner under Section 804 but is not liable for the debts, obligations, and other liabilities of the partnership solely by reason of having or exercising those powers or otherwise acting to wind up the partnership's business.

(e) On the application of any partner or person entitled under subsection (c) to participate in winding up, the [appropriate court] may order judicial supervision of the winding up of a dissolved partnership, including the appointment of a person to wind up the partnership's business, if:

(1) the partnership does not have a partner and within a reasonable time following the dissolution no person has been appointed under subsection (d); or

(2) the applicant establishes other good cause.

Section 803. Rescinding Dissolution.

Section 804. Power to Bind Partnership After Dissolution.

Section 805. Liability After Dissolution of Partner and Person Dissociated as Partner.

Section 806. Disposition of Assets in Winding Up; When Contributions Required.

(a) In winding up its business, a partnership shall apply its assets, including the contributions required by this section, to discharge the partnership's obligations to creditors, including partners that are creditors.

(b) After a partnership complies with subsection (a), any surplus must be distributed in the following order, subject to any charging order in effect under Section 504:

(1) to each person owning a transferable interest that reflects contributions made and not previously returned, an amount equal to the value of the unreturned contributions; and

(2) among persons owning transferable interests in proportion to their respective rights to share in distributions immediately before the dissolution of the partnership.

(c) If a partnership's assets are insufficient to satisfy all its obligations under subsection (a), with respect to each unsatisfied obligation incurred when the partnership was not a limited liability partnership, the following rules apply:

(1) Each person that was a partner when the obligation was incurred and that has not been released from the obligation under Section 703(c) and (d) shall contribute to the partnership for the purpose of enabling the partnership to satisfy the obligation. The contribution due from each of those persons is in proportion to the right to receive distributions in the capacity of a partner in effect for each of those persons when the obligation was incurred.

(2) If a person does not contribute the full amount required under paragraph (1) with respect to an unsatisfied obligation of the partnership, the other persons required to contribute by paragraph (1) on account of the obligation shall contribute the additional amount necessary to discharge the obligation. The

additional contribution due from each of those other persons is in proportion to the right to receive distributions in the capacity of a partner in effect for each of those other persons when the obligation was incurred.

(3) If a person does not make the additional contribution required by paragraph (2), further additional contributions are determined and due in the same manner as provided in that paragraph.

(d) A person that makes an additional contribution under subsection (c)(2) or (3) may recover from any person whose failure to contribute under subsection (c)(1) or (2) necessitated the additional contribution. A person may not recover under this subsection more than the amount additionally contributed. A person's liability under this subsection may not exceed the amount the person failed to contribute.

(e) If a partnership does not have sufficient surplus to comply with subsection (b)(1), any surplus must be distributed among the owners of transferable interests in proportion to the value of the respective unreturned contributions.

(f) All distributions made under subsections (b) and (c) must be paid in money.

Section 807. Known Claims Against Dissolved Limited Liability Partnership.

Section 808. Other Claims Against Dissolved Limited Liability Partnership.

Section 809. Court Proceedings.

Section 810. Liability of Partner and Person Dissociated as Partner When Claim Against Partnership Barred.

ARTICLE 9: LIMITED LIABILITY PARTNERSHIP

Section 901. Statement of Qualification.

Section 902. Permitted Names.

Section 903. Administrative Revocation of Statement of Qualification.

Section 904. Reinstatement.

Section 905. Judicial Review of Denial of Reinstatement.

Section 906. Reservation of Name.

Section 907. Registration of Name.

Section 908. Registered Agent.

Section 909. Change of Registered Agent or Address for Registered Agent by Limited Liability Partnership.

Section 910. Resignation of Registered Agent.

Section 911. Change of Name or Address by Registered Agent.

Section 912. Service of Process, Notice, or Demand.

Section 913. [Annual] [Biennial] Report for [Secretary of State].

ARTICLE 10: FOREIGN LIMITED LIABILITY PARTNERSHIP

Section 1001. Governing Law.

(a) The law of the jurisdiction of formation of a foreign limited liability partnership governs:

(1) the internal affairs of the partnership; and

(2) the liability of a partner as partner for a debt, obligation, or other liability of the foreign partnership.

(b) A foreign limited liability partnership is not precluded from registering to do business in this state because of any difference between the law of its jurisdiction of formation and the law of this state.

(c) Registration of a foreign limited liability partnership to do business in this state does not authorize the foreign partnership to engage in any business or exercise any power that a limited liability partnership may not engage in or exercise in this state.

Section 1002. Registration to Do Business in This State.

(a) A foreign limited liability partnership may not do business in this state until it registers with the [Secretary of State] under this [article].

(b) A foreign limited liability partnership doing business in this state may not maintain an action or proceeding in this state unless it has registered to do business in this state.

(c) The failure of a foreign limited liability partnership to register to do business in this state does not impair the validity of a contract or act of the foreign partnership or preclude it from defending an action or proceeding in this state.

(d) A limitation on the liability of a partner of a foreign limited liability partnership is not waived solely because the foreign partnership does business in this state without registering to do business in this state.

(e) Section 1001(a) and (b) applies even if a foreign limited liability partnership fails to register under this [article].

Section 1003. Foreign Registration Statement.

Section 1004. Amendment of Foreign Registration Statement.

Section 1005. Activities Not Constituting Doing Business.

(a) Activities of a foreign limited liability partnership which do not constitute doing business in this state under this [article] include:

(1) maintaining, defending, mediating, arbitrating, or settling an action or proceeding;

(2) carrying on any activity concerning its internal affairs, including holding meetings of its partners;

(3) maintaining accounts in financial institutions;

(4) maintaining offices or agencies for the transfer, exchange, and registration of securities of the partnership or maintaining trustees or depositories with respect to those securities;

(5) selling through independent contractors;

(6) soliciting or obtaining orders by any means if the orders require acceptance outside this state before they become contracts;

(7) creating or acquiring indebtedness, mortgages, or security interests in property;

(8) securing or collecting debts or enforcing mortgages or security interests in property securing the debts and holding, protecting, or maintaining property;

(9) conducting an isolated transaction that is not in the course of similar transactions;

(10) owning, without more, property; and

(11) doing business in interstate commerce.

(b) A person does not do business in this state solely by being a partner of a foreign limited liability partnership that does business in this state.

(c) This section does not apply in determining the contacts or activities that may subject a foreign limited liability partnership to service of process, taxation, or regulation under law of this state other than this [act].

Section 1006. Noncomplying Name of Foreign Limited Liability Partnership.

Section 1007. Withdrawal Deemed on Conversion to Domestic Filing Entity or Domestic Limited Liability Partnership.

Section 1008. Withdrawal on Dissolution or Conversion to Nonfiling Entity Other Than Limited Liability Partnership.

Section 1009. Transfer of Registration.

Section 1010. Termination of Registration.

Section 1011. Withdrawal of Registration of Registered Foreign Limited Liability Partnership.

Section 1012. Action by [Attorney General].

ARTICLE 11: MERGER, INTEREST EXCHANGE, CONVERSION, AND DOMESTICATION

PART 1: GENERAL PROVISIONS

Section 1101. Definitions.

Section 1102. Relationship of [Article] to Other Laws.

Section 1103. Required Notice or Approval.

Section 1104. Nonexclusivity.

Section 1105. Reference to External Facts.

Section 1106. Appraisal Rights.

Section 1107. Excluded Entities and Transactions.

PART 2: MERGER

Section 1121. Merger Authorized.

Section 1122. Plan of Merger.

Section 1123. Approval of Merger.

Section 1124. Amendment or Abandonment of Plan of Merger.

Section 1125. Statement of Merger; Effective Date of Merger.

Section 1126. Effect of Merger.

PART 3: INTEREST EXCHANGE

Section 1131. Interest Exchange Authorized.

Section 1132. Plan of Interest Exchange.

Section 1133. Approval of Interest Exchange.

Section 1134. Amendment or Abandonment of Plan of Interest Exchange.

Section 1135. Statement of Interest Exchange; Effective Date of Interest Exchange.

Section 1136. Effect of Interest Exchange.

PART 4: CONVERSION

Section 1141. Conversion Authorized.

Section 1142. Plan of Conversion.

Section 1143. Approval of Conversion.

Section 1144. Amendment or Abandonment of Plan of Conversion.

Section 1145. Statement of Conversion; Effective Date of Conversion.

Section 1146. Effect of Conversion.

PART 5: DOMESTICATION

Section 1151. Domestication Authorized.

Section 1152. Plan of Domestication.

Section 1153. Approval of Domestication.

Section 1154. Amendment or Abandonment of Plan of Domestication.

Section 1155. Statement of Domestication; Effective Date of Domestication.

Section 1156. Effect of Domestication.

ARTICLE 12: MISCELLANEOUS PROVISIONS

Section 1201. Uniformity of Application and Construction.

In applying and construing this uniform act, consideration must be given to the need to promote uniformity of the law with respect to its subject matter among states that enact it.

Section 1202. Relation to Electronic Signatures in Global and National Commerce Act.

Section 1203. Savings Clause.

This [act] does not affect an action commenced, proceeding brought, or right accrued before [the effective date of this [act]].

Section 1204. Severability Clause.

If any provision of this [act] or its application to any person or circumstance is held invalid, the invalidity does not affect other provisions or applications of this [act] which can be given effect without the invalid provision or application, and to this end the provisions of this [act] are severable.]

Section 1205. Repeals.

Section 1206. Effective Date.

This [act] takes effect . . . .

APPENDIX D

UNIFORM LIMITED PARTNERSHIP ACT (2001 & 2013 HARMONIZED) (EXCERPTED)

■ ■ ■

ARTICLE 1: GENERAL PROVISIONS

Section 101. Short Title.

Section 102. Definitions.

Section 103. Knowledge; Notice.

Section 104. Governing Law.

The law of this state governs:

(1) the internal affairs of a limited partnership; and

(2) the liability of a partner as partner for a debt, obligation, or other liability of a limited partnership.

Section 105. Partnership Agreement; Scope, Function, and Limitations.

(a) Except as otherwise provided in subsections (c) and (d), the partnership agreement governs:

(1) relations among the partners as partners and between the partners and the limited partnership;

(2) the activities and affairs of the partnership and the conduct of those activities and affairs; and

(3) the means and conditions for amending the partnership agreement.

(b) To the extent the partnership agreement does not provide for a matter described in subsection (a), this [act] governs the matter.

(c) A partnership agreement may not:

(1) vary the law applicable under Section 104;

(2) vary a limited partnership's capacity under Section 111 to sue and be sued in its own name;

(3) vary any requirement, procedure, or other provision of this [act] pertaining to:

(A) registered agents; or

(B) the [Secretary of State], including provisions pertaining to records authorized or required to be delivered to the [Secretary of State] for filing under this [act];

(4) vary the provisions of Section 204;

(5) vary the right of a general partner under Section 406(b)(2) to vote on or consent to an amendment to the certificate of limited partnership which deletes a statement that the limited partnership is a limited liability limited partnership;

(6) alter or eliminate the duty of loyalty or the duty of care except as otherwise provided in subsection (d);

(7) eliminate the contractual obligation of good faith and fair dealing under Sections 305(a) and 409(d), but the partnership agreement may prescribe the standards, if not manifestly unreasonable, by which the performance of the obligation is to be measured;

(8) relieve or exonerate a person from liability for conduct involving bad faith, willful or intentional misconduct, or knowing violation of law;

(9) vary the information required under Section 108 or unreasonably restrict the duties and rights under Section 304 or 407, but the partnership agreement may impose reasonable restrictions on the availability and use of information obtained under those sections and may define appropriate remedies, including liquidated damages, for a breach of any reasonable restriction on use;

(10) vary the grounds for expulsion specified in Section 603(5)(B);

(11) vary the power of a person to dissociate as a general partner under Section 604(a), except to require that the notice under Section 603(1) be in a record;

(12) vary the causes of dissolution specified in Section 801(a)(6);

(13) vary the requirement to wind up the partnership's activities and affairs as specified in Section 802(a), (b)(1), and (d);

(14) unreasonably restrict the right of a partner to maintain an action under [Article] 9;

(15) vary the provisions of Section 905, but the partnership agreement may provide that the partnership may not have a special litigation committee;

(16) vary the right of a partner to approve a merger, interest exchange, conversion, or domestication under Section 1123(a)(2), 1133(a)(2), 1143(a)(2), or 1153(a)(2);

(17) vary the required contents of a plan of merger under Section 1122(a), plan of interest exchange under Section 1132(a), plan of conversion under Section 1142(a), or plan of domestication under Section 1152(a); or

(18) except as otherwise provided in Sections 106 and 107(b), restrict the rights under this [act] of a person other than a partner.

(d) Subject to subsection (c)(8), without limiting other terms that may be included in a partnership agreement, the following rules apply:

(1) The partnership agreement may:

(A) specify the method by which a specific act or transaction that would otherwise violate the duty of loyalty may be authorized or ratified by one or more disinterested and independent persons after full disclosure of all material facts; and

(B) alter the prohibition in Section 504(a)(2) so that the prohibition requires only that the partnership's total assets not be less than the sum of its total liabilities.

(2) If not manifestly unreasonable, the partnership agreement may:

(A) alter or eliminate the aspects of the duty of loyalty stated in Section 409(b);

(B) identify specific types or categories of activities that do not violate the duty of loyalty;

(C) alter the duty of care, but may not authorize conduct involving bad faith, willful or intentional misconduct, or knowing violation of law; and

(D) alter or eliminate any other fiduciary duty.

(e) The court shall decide as a matter of law whether a term of a partnership agreement is manifestly unreasonable under subsection (c)(7) or (d)(2). The court:

(1) shall make its determination as of the time the challenged term became part of the partnership agreement and by considering only circumstances existing at that time; and

(2) may invalidate the term only if, in light of the purposes, activities, and affairs of the limited partnership, it is readily apparent that:

(A) the objective of the term is unreasonable; or

(B) the term is an unreasonable means to achieve its objective.

Section 106. Partnership Agreement; Effect on Partnership and Person Becoming Partner; Preformation Agreement.

(a) A limited partnership is bound by and may enforce the partnership agreement, whether or not the partnership has itself manifested assent to the agreement.

(b) A person that becomes a partner is deemed to assent to the partnership agreement.

(c) Two or more persons intending to become the initial partners of a limited partnership may make an agreement providing that upon the formation of the partnership the agreement will become the partnership agreement.

Section 107. Partnership Agreement; Effect on Third Parties and Relationship to Records Effective on Behalf of Partnership.

(a) A partnership agreement may specify that its amendment requires the approval of a person that is not a party to the agreement or the satisfaction of a condition. An amendment is ineffective if its adoption does not include the required approval or satisfy the specified condition.

(b) The obligations of a limited partnership and its partners to a person in the person's capacity as a transferee or person dissociated as a partner are governed by the partnership agreement. Subject only to a court order issued under Section 703(b)(2) to effectuate a charging order, an amendment to the partnership agreement made after a person becomes a transferee or is dissociated as a partner:

(1) is effective with regard to any debt, obligation, or other liability of the partnership or its partners to the person in the person's capacity as a transferee or person dissociated as a partner; and

(2) is not effective to the extent the amendment imposes a new debt, obligation, or other liability on the transferee or person dissociated as a partner.

(c) If a record delivered by a limited partnership to the [Secretary of State] for filing becomes effective and contains a provision that would be ineffective under Section

105(c) or (d)(2) if contained in the partnership agreement, the provision is ineffective in the record.

(d) Subject to subsection (c), if a record delivered by a limited partnership to the [Secretary of State] for filing becomes effective and conflicts with a provision of the partnership agreement:

(1) the agreement prevails as to partners, persons dissociated as partners, and transferees; and

(2) the record prevails as to other persons to the extent they reasonably rely on the record.

Section 108. Required Information.

A limited partnership shall maintain at its principal office the following information:

(1) a current list showing the full name and last known street and mailing address of each partner, separately identifying the general partners, in alphabetical order, and the limited partners, in alphabetical order;

(2) a copy of the initial certificate of limited partnership and all amendments to and restatements of the certificate, together with signed copies of any powers of attorney under which any certificate, amendment, or restatement has been signed;

(3) a copy of any filed articles of merger, interest exchange, conversion, or domestication;

(4) a copy of the partnership's federal, state, and local income tax returns and reports, if any, for the three most recent years;

(5) a copy of any partnership agreement made in a record and any amendment made in a record to any partnership agreement;

(6) a copy of any financial statement of the partnership for the three most recent years;

(7) a copy of the three most recent [annual] [biennial] reports delivered by the partnership to the [Secretary of State] pursuant to Section 212;

(8) a copy of any record made by the partnership during the past three years of any consent given by or vote taken of any partner pursuant to this [act] or the partnership agreement; and

(9) unless contained in a partnership agreement made in a record, a record stating:

(A) a description and statement of the agreed value of contributions other than money made and agreed to be made by each partner;

(B) the times at which, or events on the happening of which, any additional contributions agreed to be made by each partner are to be made;

(C) for any person that is both a general partner and a limited partner, a specification of what transferable interest the person owns in each capacity; and

(D) any events upon the happening of which the partnership is to be dissolved and its activities and affairs wound up.

Section 109. Dual Capacity.

A person may be both a general partner and a limited partner. A person that is both a general and limited partner has the rights, powers, duties, and obligations provided by this [act] and the partnership agreement in each of those capacities. When the person acts as a general partner, the person is subject to the obligations, duties, and restrictions under this [act] and the partnership agreement for general partners. When the person acts as a limited partner, the person is subject to the obligations, duties, and restrictions under this [act] and the partnership agreement for limited partners.

Section 110. Nature, Purpose, and Duration of Limited Partnership.

(a) A limited partnership is an entity distinct from its partners. A limited partnership is the same entity regardless of whether its certificate states that the limited partnership is a limited liability limited partnership.

(b) A limited partnership may have any lawful purpose, regardless of whether for profit.

(c) A limited partnership has perpetual duration.

Section 111. Powers.

A limited partnership has the capacity to sue and be sued in the name of the partnership and the power to do all things necessary or convenient to carry on the partnership's activities and affairs.

Section 112. Application to Existing Relationships.

Section 113. Supplemental Principles of Law.

Unless displaced by particular provisions of this [act], the principles of law and equity supplement this [act].

Section 114. Permitted Names.

Section 115. Reservation of Name.

Section 116. Registration of Name.

Section 117. Registered Agent.

Section 118. Change of Registered Agent or Address for Registered Agent by Limited Partnership.

Section 119. Resignation of Registered Agent.

Section 120. Change of Name or Address by Registered Agent.

Section 121. Service of Process, Notice, or Demand.

Section 122. Delivery of Record.

Section 123. Reservation of Power to Amend or Repeal.

ARTICLE 2: FORMATION; CERTIFICATE OF LIMITED PARTNERSHIP AND OTHER FILINGS

Section 201. Formation of Limited Partnership; Certificate of Limited Partnership.

Section 202. Amendment or Restatement of Certificate of Limited Partnership.

Section 203. Signing of Records to be Delivered for Filing to [Secretary of State].

Section 204. Signing and Filing Pursuant to Judicial Order.

Section 205. Liability for Inaccurate Information in Filed Record.

Section 206. Filing Requirements.

Section 207. Effective Date and Time.

Section 208. Withdrawal of Filed Record Before Effectiveness.

Section 209. Correcting Filed Record.

Section 210. Duty of [Secretary of State] to File; Review of Refusal to File; Delivery of Record by [Secretary of State].

Section 211. Certificate of Good Standing or Registration.

Section 212. [Annual] [Biennial] Report for [Secretary of State].

ARTICLE 3: LIMITED PARTNERS

Section 301. Becoming Limited Partner.

(a) Upon formation of a limited partnership, a person becomes a limited partner as agreed among the persons that are to be the initial partners.

(b) After formation, a person becomes a limited partner:

(1) as provided in the partnership agreement;

(2) as the result of a transaction effective under [Article] 11;

(3) with the affirmative vote or consent of all the partners; or

(4) as provided in Section 801(a)(4) or (a)(5).

(c) A person may become a limited partner without:

(1) acquiring a transferable interest; or

(2) making or being obligated to make a contribution to the limited partnership.

Section 302. No Agency Power of Limited Partner as Limited Partner.

(a) A limited partner is not an agent of a limited partnership solely by reason of being a limited partner.

(b) A person's status as a limited partner does not prevent or restrict law other than this [act] from imposing liability on a limited partnership because of the person's conduct.

Section 303. No Liability as Limited Partner for Limited Partnership Obligations.

(a) A debt, obligation, or other liability of a limited partnership is not the debt, obligation, or other liability of a limited partner. A limited partner is not personally liable, directly or indirectly, by way of contribution or otherwise, for a debt, obligation, or other liability of the partnership solely by reason of being or acting as a limited partner, even if the limited partner participates in the management and control of the limited partnership. This subsection applies regardless of the dissolution of the partnership.

(b) The failure of a limited partnership to observe formalities relating to the exercise of its powers or management of its activities and affairs is not a ground for imposing liability on a limited partner for a debt, obligation, or other liability of the partnership.

Section 304. Rights to Information of Limited Partner and Person Dissociated as Limited Partner.

Section 305. Limited Duties of Limited Partners.

(a) A limited partner shall discharge any duties to the partnership and the other partners under the partnership agreement and exercise any rights under this [act] or the partnership agreement consistently with the contractual obligation of good faith and fair dealing.

(b) Except as otherwise provided in subsection (a), a limited partner does not have any duty to the limited partnership or to any other partner solely by reason of acting as a limited partner.

(c) If a limited partner enters into a transaction with a limited partnership, the limited partner's rights and obligations arising from the transaction are the same as those of a person that is not a partner.

Section 306. Person Erroneously Believing Self to Be Limited Partner.

ARTICLE 4: GENERAL PARTNERS

Section 401. Becoming General Partner.

(a) Upon formation of a limited partnership, a person becomes a general partner as agreed among the persons that are to be the initial partners.

(b) After formation of a limited partnership, a person becomes a general partner:

(1) as provided in the partnership agreement;

(2) as the result of a transaction effective under [Article] 11;

(3) with the affirmative vote or consent of all the partners; or

(4) as provided in Section 801(a)(3)(B).

(c) A person may become a general partner without:

(1) acquiring a transferable interest; or

(2) making or being obligated to make a contribution to the partnership.

Section 402. General Partner Agent of Limited Partnership.

(a) Each general partner is an agent of the limited partnership for the purposes of its activities and affairs. An act of a general partner, including the signing of a record in the partnership's name, for apparently carrying on in the ordinary course the partnership's activities and affairs or activities and affairs of the kind carried on by the partnership binds the partnership, unless the general partner did not have authority to act for the partnership in the particular matter and the person with which the general partner was dealing knew or had notice that the general partner lacked authority.

(b) An act of a general partner which is not apparently for carrying on in the ordinary course the limited partnership's activities and affairs or activities and affairs of the kind carried on by the partnership binds the partnership only if the act was actually authorized by all the other partners.

Section 403. Limited Partnership Liable for General Partner's Actionable Conduct.

(a) A limited partnership is liable for loss or injury caused to a person, or for a penalty incurred, as a result of a wrongful act or omission, or other actionable conduct, of a general partner acting in the ordinary course of activities and affairs of the partnership or with the actual or apparent authority of the partnership.

(b) If, in the course of a limited partnership's activities and affairs or while acting with actual or apparent authority of the partnership, a general partner receives or causes the partnership to receive money or property of a person not a partner, and the money or property is misapplied by a general partner, the partnership is liable for the loss.

Section 404. General Partner's Liability.

(a) Except as otherwise provided in subsections (b) and (c), all general partners are liable jointly and severally for all debts, obligations, and other liabilities of the limited partnership unless otherwise agreed by the claimant or provided by law.

(b) A person that becomes a general partner is not personally liable for a debt, obligation, or other liability of the limited partnership incurred before the person became a general partner.

(c) A debt, obligation, or other liability of a limited partnership incurred while the partnership is a limited liability limited partnership is solely the debt, obligation, or other liability of the limited liability limited partnership. A general partner is not personally liable, directly or indirectly, by way of contribution or otherwise, for a debt, obligation, or other liability of the limited liability limited partnership solely by reason of being or acting as a general partner. This subsection applies:

(1) despite anything inconsistent in the partnership agreement that existed immediately before the vote or consent required to become a limited liability limited partnership under Section 406(b)(2); and

(2) regardless of the dissolution of the partnership.

(d) The failure of a limited liability limited partnership to observe formalities relating to the exercise of its powers or management of its activities and affairs is not a ground for imposing liability on a general partner for a debt, obligation, or other liability of the partnership.

(e) An amendment of a certificate of limited partnership which deletes a statement that the limited partnership is a limited liability limited partnership does not affect the limitation in this section on the liability of a general partner for a debt, obligation, or other liability of the limited partnership incurred before the amendment became effective.

Section 405. Actions By and Against Partnership and Partners.

(a) To the extent not inconsistent with Section 404, a general partner may be joined in an action against the limited partnership or named in a separate action.

(b) A judgment against a limited partnership is not by itself a judgment against a general partner. A judgment against a partnership may not be satisfied from a general partner's assets unless there is also a judgment against the general partner.

(c) A judgment creditor of a general partner may not levy execution against the assets of the general partner to satisfy a judgment based on a claim against the limited partnership, unless the partner is personally liable for the claim under Section 404 and:

(1) a judgment based on the same claim has been obtained against the limited partnership and a writ of execution on the judgment has been returned unsatisfied in whole or in part;

(2) the partnership is a debtor in bankruptcy;

(3) the general partner has agreed that the creditor need not exhaust partnership assets;

(4) a court grants permission to the judgment creditor to levy execution against the assets of a general partner based on a finding that partnership assets subject to execution are clearly insufficient to satisfy the judgment, that exhaustion of assets is excessively burdensome, or that the grant of permission is an appropriate exercise of the court's equitable powers; or

(5) liability is imposed on the general partner by law or contract independent of the existence of the partnership.

Section 406. Management Rights of General Partner.

(a) Each general partner has equal rights in the management and conduct of the limited partnership's activities and affairs. Except as otherwise provided in this [act], any matter relating to the activities and affairs of the partnership is decided exclusively by the general partner or, if there is more than one general partner, by a majority of the general partners.

(b) The affirmative vote or consent of all the partners is required to:

(1) amend the partnership agreement;

(2) amend the certificate of limited partnership to add or delete a statement that the limited partnership is a limited liability limited partnership; and

(3) sell, lease, exchange, or otherwise dispose of all, or substantially all, of the limited partnership's property, with or without the good will, other than in the usual and regular course of the limited partnership's activities and affairs.

(c) A limited partnership shall reimburse a general partner for an advance to the partnership beyond the amount of capital the general partner agreed to contribute.

(d) A payment or advance made by a general partner which gives rise to a limited partnership obligation under subsection (c) or Section 408(a) constitutes a loan to the limited partnership which accrues interest from the date of the payment or advance.

(e) A general partner is not entitled to remuneration for services performed for the limited partnership.

Section 407. Rights to Information of General Partner and Person Dissociated as General Partner.

Section 408. Reimbursement; Indemnification; Advancement; and Insurance.

Section 409. Standards of Conduct for General Partners.

(a) A general partner owes to the limited partnership and, subject to Section 901, the other partners the duties of loyalty and care stated in subsections (b) and (c).

(b) The fiduciary duty of loyalty of a general partner includes the duties:

(1) to account to the limited partnership and hold as trustee for it any property, profit, or benefit derived by the general partner:

(A) in the conduct or winding up of the partnership's activities and affairs;

(B) from a use by the general partner of the partnership's property; or

(C) from the appropriation of a partnership opportunity;

(2) to refrain from dealing with the partnership in the conduct or winding up of the partnership's activities and affairs as or on behalf of a person having an interest adverse to the partnership; and

(3) to refrain from competing with the partnership in the conduct or winding up of the partnership's activities and affairs.

(c) The duty of care of a general partner in the conduct or winding up of the limited partnership's activities and affairs is to refrain from engaging in grossly negligent or reckless conduct, willful or intentional misconduct, or knowing violation of law.

(d) A general partner shall discharge the duties and obligations under this [act] or under the partnership agreement and exercise any rights consistently with the contractual obligation of good faith and fair dealing.

(e) A general partner does not violate a duty or obligation under this [act] or under the partnership agreement solely because the general partner's conduct furthers the general partner's own interest.

(f) All the partners of a limited partnership may authorize or ratify, after full disclosure of all material facts, a specific act or transaction by a general partner that otherwise would violate the duty of loyalty.

(g) It is a defense to a claim under subsection (b)(2) and any comparable claim in equity or at common law that the transaction was fair to the limited partnership.

(h) If, as permitted by subsection (f) or the partnership agreement, a general partner enters into a transaction with the limited partnership which otherwise would be prohibited by subsection (b)(2), the general partner's rights and obligations arising from the transaction are the same as those of a person that is not a general partner.

ARTICLE 5: CONTRIBUTIONS AND DISTRIBUTIONS

Section 501. Form of Contribution.

A contribution may consist of property transferred to, services performed for, or another benefit provided to the limited partnership or an agreement to transfer property to, perform services for, or provide another benefit to the partnership.

Section 502. Liability for Contribution.

Section 503. Sharing of and Right to Distributions Before Dissolution.

(a) Any distribution made by a limited partnership before its dissolution and winding up must be shared among the partners on the basis of the value, as stated in the required information when the limited partnership decides to make the distribution, of the contributions the limited partnership has received from each partner, except to the extent necessary to comply with a transfer effective under Section 702 or charging order in effect under Section 703.

(b) A person has a right to a distribution before the dissolution and winding up of a limited partnership only if the partnership decides to make an interim distribution. A person's dissociation does not entitle the person to a distribution.

(c) A person does not have a right to demand or receive a distribution from a limited partnership in any form other than money. Except as otherwise provided in Section 810(f), a partnership may distribute an asset in kind only if each part of the asset is fungible with each other part and each person receives a percentage of the asset equal in value to the person's share of distributions.

(d) If a partner or transferee becomes entitled to receive a distribution, the partner or transferee has the status of, and is entitled to all remedies available to, a creditor of the limited partnership with respect to the distribution. However, the partnership's obligation to make a distribution is subject to offset for any amount owed to the partnership by the partner or a person dissociated as a partner on whose account the distribution is made.

Section 504. Limitations on Distributions.

(a) A limited partnership may not make a distribution, including a distribution under Section 810, if after the distribution:

(1) the partnership would not be able to pay its debts as they become due in the ordinary course of the partnership's activities and affairs; or

(2) the partnership's total assets would be less than the sum of its total liabilities plus the amount that would be needed, if the partnership were to be dissolved and wound up at the time of the distribution, to satisfy the preferential rights upon dissolution and winding up of partners and transferees whose preferential rights are superior to the rights of persons receiving the distribution.

(b) A limited partnership may base a determination that a distribution is not prohibited under subsection (a) on:

(1) financial statements prepared on the basis of accounting practices and principles that are reasonable in the circumstances; or

(2) a fair valuation or other method that is reasonable under the circumstances.

(c) Except as otherwise provided in subsection (e), the effect of a distribution under subsection (a) is measured:

(1) in the case of a distribution as defined in Section 102(4)(A), as of the earlier of:

(A) the date money or other property is transferred or debt is incurred by the limited partnership; or

(B) the date the person entitled to the distribution ceases to own the interest or right being acquired by the partnership in return for the distribution;

(2) in the case of any other distribution of indebtedness, as of the date the indebtedness is distributed; and

(3) in all other cases, as of the date:

(A) the distribution is authorized, if the payment occurs not later than 120 days after that date; or

(B) the payment is made, if the payment occurs more than 120 days after the distribution is authorized.

(d) A limited partnership's indebtedness to a partner or transferee incurred by reason of a distribution made in accordance with this section is at parity with the partnership's indebtedness to its general, unsecured creditors, except to the extent subordinated by agreement.

(e) A limited partnership's indebtedness, including indebtedness issued as a distribution, is not a liability for purposes of subsection (a) if the terms of the indebtedness provide that payment of principal and interest is made only if and to the extent that payment of a distribution could then be made under this section. If the indebtedness is issued as a distribution, each payment of principal or interest is treated as a distribution, the effect of which is measured on the date the payment is made.

(f) In measuring the effect of a distribution under Section 810, the liabilities of a dissolved limited partnership do not include any claim that has been disposed of under Section 806, 807, or 808.

Section 505. Liability for Improper Distributions.

ARTICLE 6: DISSOCIATION

Section 601. Dissociation as Limited Partner.

(a) A person does not have a right to dissociate as a limited partner before the completion of the winding up of the limited partnership.

(b) A person is dissociated as a limited partner when:

(1) the limited partnership knows or has notice of the person's express will to withdraw as a limited partner, but, if the person has specified a withdrawal date later than the date the partnership knew or had notice, on that later date;

(2) an event stated in the partnership agreement as causing the person's dissociation as a limited partner occurs;

(3) the person is expelled as a limited partner pursuant to the partnership agreement;

(4) the person is expelled as a limited partner by the affirmative vote or consent of all the other partners if:

(A) it is unlawful to carry on the limited partnership's activities and affairs with the person as a limited partner;

(B) there has been a transfer of all the person's transferable interest in the partnership, other than:

(i) a transfer for security purposes; or

(ii) a charging order in effect under Section 703 which has not been foreclosed;

(C) the person is an entity and:

(i) the partnership notifies the person that it will be expelled as a limited partner because the person has filed a statement of dissolution or the equivalent, the person has been administratively dissolved, the person's charter or the equivalent has been revoked, or the person's right to conduct business has been suspended by the person's jurisdiction of formation; and

(ii) not later than 90 days after the notification, the statement of dissolution or the equivalent has not been withdrawn, rescinded, or revoked, the person has not been reinstated, or the person's charter or the equivalent or right to conduct business has not been reinstated; or

(D) the person is an unincorporated entity that has been dissolved and whose activities and affairs are being would up;

(5) on application by the limited partnership or a partner in a direct action under Section 901, the person is expelled as a limited partner by judicial order because the person:

(A) has engaged or is engaging in wrongful conduct that has affected adversely and materially, or will affect adversely and materially, the partnership's activities and affairs;

(B) has committed willfully or persistently, or is committing willfully and persistently, a material breach of the partnership agreement or the contractual obligation of good faith and fair dealing under Section 305(a); or

(C) has engaged or is engaging in conduct relating to the partnership's activities and affairs which makes it not reasonably practicable to carry on the activities and affairs with the person as a limited partner;

(6) in the case of an individual, the individual dies;

(7) in the case of a person that is a testamentary or inter vivos trust or is acting as a limited partner by virtue of being a trustee of such a trust, the trust's entire transferable interest in the limited partnership is distributed;

(8) in the case of a person that is an estate or is acting as a limited partner by virtue of being a personal representative of an estate, the estate's entire transferable interest in the limited partnership is distributed;

(9) in the case of a person that is not an individual, the existence of the person terminates;

(10) the limited partnership participates in a merger under [Article] 11 and:

(A) the partnership is not the surviving entity; or

(B) otherwise as a result of the merger, the person ceases to be a limited partner;

(11) the limited partnership participates in an interest exchange under [Article] 11 and, as a result of the interest exchange, the person ceases to be a limited partner;

(12) the limited partnership participates in a conversion under [Article] 11;

(13) the limited partnership participates in a domestication under [Article] 11 and, as a result of the domestication, the person ceases to be a limited partner; or

(14) the limited partnership dissolves and completes winding up.

Section 602. Effect of Dissociation as Limited Partner.

(a) If a person is dissociated as a limited partner:

(1) subject to Section 704, the person does not have further rights as a limited partner;

(2) the person's contractual obligation of good faith and fair dealing as a limited partner under Section 305(a) ends with regard to matters arising and events occurring after the person's dissociation; and

(3) subject to Section 704 and [Article] 11, any transferable interest owned by the person in the person's capacity as a limited partner immediately before dissociation is owned by the person solely as a transferee.

(b) A person's dissociation as a limited partner does not of itself discharge the person from any debt, obligation, or other liability to the limited partnership or the other partners which the person incurred while a limited partner.

Section 603. Dissociation as General Partner.

A person is dissociated as a general partner when:

(1) the limited partnership knows or has notice of the person's express will to withdraw as a general partner, but, if the person has specified a withdrawal date later than the date the partnership knew or had notice, on that later date;

(2) an event stated in the partnership agreement as causing the person's dissociation as a general partner occurs;

(3) the person is expelled as a general partner pursuant to the partnership agreement;

(4) the person is expelled as a general partner by the affirmative vote or consent of all the other partners if:

(A) it is unlawful to carry on the limited partnership's activities and affairs with the person as a general partner;

(B) there has been a transfer of all the person's transferable interest in the partnership, other than:

(i) a transfer for security purposes; or

(ii) a charging order in effect under Section 703 which has not been foreclosed;

(C) the person is an entity and:

(i) the partnership notifies the person that it will be expelled as a general partner because the person has filed a statement of dissolution or the equivalent, the person has been administratively dissolved, the person's charter or the equivalent has been revoked, or the person's right to conduct business has been suspended by the person's jurisdiction of formation; and

(ii) not later than 90 days after the notification, the statement of dissolution or the equivalent has not been withdrawn, rescinded, or revoked, the person has not been reinstated, or the person's charter or the equivalent or right to conduct business has not been reinstated; or

(D) the person is an unincorporated entity that has been dissolved and whose activities and affairs are being would up;

(5) on application by the limited partnership or a partner in a direct action under Section 901, the person is expelled as a general partner by judicial order because the person:

(A) has engaged or is engaging in wrongful conduct that has affected adversely and materially, or will affect adversely and materially, the partnership's activities and affairs;

(B) has committed willfully or persistently, or is committing willfully or persistently, a material breach of the partnership agreement or a duty or obligation under Section 409; or

(C) has engaged or is engaging in conduct relating to the partnership's activities and affairs which makes it not reasonably practicable to carry on the activities and affairs of the limited partnership with the person as a general partner;

(6) in the case of an individual:

(A) the individual dies;

(B) a guardian or general conservator for the individual is appointed; or

(C) a court orders that the individual has otherwise become incapable of performing the individual's duties as a general partner under this [act] or the partnership agreement;

(7) the person:

(A) becomes a debtor in bankruptcy;

(B) executes an assignment for the benefit of creditors; or

(C) seeks, consents to, or acquiesces in the appointment of a trustee, receiver, or liquidator of the person or of all or substantially all the person's property;

(8) in the case of a person that is a testamentary or inter vivos trust or is acting as a general partner by virtue of being a trustee of such a trust, the trust's entire transferable interest in the limited partnership is distributed;

(9) in the case of a person that is an estate or is acting as a general partner by virtue of being a personal representative of an estate, the estate's entire transferable interest in the limited partnership is distributed;

(10) in the case of a person that is not an individual, the existence of the person terminates;

(11) the limited partnership participates in a merger under [Article] 11 and:

(A) the partnership is not the surviving entity; or

(B) otherwise as a result of the merger, the person ceases to be a general partner;

(12) the limited partnership participates in an interest exchange under [Article] 11 and, as a result of the interest exchange, the person ceases to be a general partner;

(13) the limited partnership participates in a conversion under [Article] 11;

(14) the limited partnership participates in a domestication under [Article] 11 and, as a result of the domestication, the person ceases to be a general partner; or

(15) the limited partnership dissolves and completes winding up.

Section 604. Power to Dissociate as General Partner; Wrongful Dissociation.

(a) A person has the power to dissociate as a general partner at any time, rightfully or wrongfully, by withdrawing as a general partner by express will under Section 603(1).

(b) A person's dissociation as a general partner is wrongful only if the dissociation:

(1) is in breach of an express provision of the partnership agreement; or

(2) occurs before the completion of the winding up of the limited partnership, and:

(A) the person withdraws as a general partner by express will;

(B) the person is expelled as a general partner by judicial order under Section 603(5);

(C) the person is dissociated as a general partner under Section 603(7); or

(D) in the case of a person that is not a trust other than a business trust, an estate, or an individual, the person is expelled or otherwise dissociated as a general partner because it willfully dissolved or terminated.

(c) A person that wrongfully dissociates as a general partner is liable to the limited partnership and, subject to Section 901, to the other partners for damages caused by the dissociation. The liability is in addition to any debt, obligation, or other liability of the general partner to the partnership or the other partners.

Section 605. Effect of Dissociation as General Partner.

(a) If a person is dissociated as a general partner:

(1) the person's right to participate as a general partner in the management and conduct of the limited partnership's activities and affairs terminates;

(2) the person's duties and obligations as a general partner under Section 409 end with regard to matters arising and events occurring after the person's dissociation;

(3) the person may sign and deliver to the [Secretary of State] for filing a statement of dissociation pertaining to the person and, at the request of the limited partnership, shall sign an amendment to the certificate of limited partnership which states that the person has dissociated as a general partner; and

(4) subject to Section 704 and [Article] 11, any transferable interest owned by the person in the person's capacity as a general partner immediately before dissociation is owned by the person solely as a transferee.

(b) A person's dissociation as a general partner does not of itself discharge the person from any debt, obligation, or other liability to the limited partnership or the other partners which the person incurred while a general partner.

Section 606. Power to Bind and Liability of Person Dissociated as General Partner.

(a) After a person is dissociated as a general partner and before the limited partnership is merged out of existence, converted, or domesticated under [Article] 11, or dissolved, the partnership is bound by an act of the person only if:

(1) the act would have bound the partnership under Section 402 before the dissociation; and

(2) at the time the other party enters into the transaction:

(A) less than two years has passed since the dissociation; and

(B) the other party does not know or have notice of the dissociation and reasonably believes that the person is a general partner.

(b) If a limited partnership is bound under subsection (a), the person dissociated as a general partner which caused the partnership to be bound is liable:

(1) to the partnership for any damage caused to the partnership arising from the obligation incurred under subsection (a); and

(2) if a general partner or another person dissociated as a general partner is liable for the obligation, to the general partner or other person for any damage caused to the general partner or other person arising from the liability.

Section 607. Liability of Person Dissociated as General Partner to Other Persons.

ARTICLE 7: TRANSFERABLE INTERESTS AND RIGHTS OF TRANSFEREES AND CREDITORS

Section 701. Nature of Transferable Interest.

A transferable interest is personal property.

Section 702. Transfer of Transferable Interest.

(a) A transfer, in whole or in part, of a transferable interest:

(1) is permissible;

(2) does not by itself cause a person's dissociation as a partner or a dissolution and winding up of the limited partnership's activities and affairs; and

(3) subject to Section 704, does not entitle the transferee to:

(A) participate in the management or conduct of the partnership's activities and affairs; or

(B) except as otherwise provided in subsection (c), have access to required information, records, or other information concerning the partnership's activities and affairs.

(b) A transferee has the right to receive, in accordance with the transfer, distributions to which the transferor would otherwise be entitled.

(c) In a dissolution and winding up of a limited partnership, a transferee is entitled to an account of the partnership's transactions only from the date of dissolution.

(d) A transferable interest may be evidenced by a certificate of the interest issued by a limited partnership in a record, and, subject to this section, the interest represented by the certificate may be transferred by a transfer of the certificate.

(e) A limited partnership need not give effect to a transferee's rights under this section until the partnership knows or has notice of the transfer.

(f) A transfer of a transferable interest in violation of a restriction on transfer contained in the partnership agreement is ineffective if the intended transferee has knowledge or notice of the restriction at the time of transfer.

(g) Except as otherwise provided in Sections 601(b)(4)(B) and 603(4)(B), if a general or limited partner transfers a transferable interest, the transferor retains the rights of a general or limited partner other than the transferable interest transferred and retains all the duties and obligations of a general or limited partner.

(h) If a general or limited partner transfers a transferable interest to a person that becomes a general or limited partner with respect to the transferred interest, the transferee is liable for the transferor's obligations under Sections 502 and 505 known to the transferee when the transferee becomes a partner.

Section 703. Charging Order.

(a) On application by a judgment creditor of a partner or transferee, a court may enter a charging order against the transferable interest of the judgment debtor for the unsatisfied amount of the judgment. A charging order constitutes a lien on a judgment debtor's transferable interest and requires the limited partnership to pay over to the person to which the charging order was issued any distribution that otherwise would be paid to the judgment debtor.

(b) To the extent necessary to effectuate the collection of distributions pursuant to a charging order in effect under subsection (a), the court may:

(1) appoint a receiver of the distributions subject to the charging order, with the power to make all inquiries the judgment debtor might have made; and

(2) make all other orders necessary to give effect to the charging order.

(c) Upon a showing that distributions under a charging order will not pay the judgment debt within a reasonable time, the court may foreclose the lien and order the sale of the transferable interest. The purchaser at the foreclosure sale obtains only the transferable interest, does not thereby become a partner, and is subject to Section 702.

(d) At any time before foreclosure under subsection (c), the partner or transferee whose transferable interest is subject to a charging order under subsection (a) may extinguish the charging order by satisfying the judgment and filing a certified copy of the satisfaction with the court that issued the charging order.

(e) At any time before foreclosure under subsection (c), a limited partnership or one or more partners whose transferable interests are not subject to the charging order may pay to the judgment creditor the full amount due under the judgment and thereby succeed to the rights of the judgment creditor, including the charging order.

(f) This [act] does not deprive any partner or transferee of the benefit of any exemption law applicable to the transferable interest of the partner or transferee.

(g) This section provides the exclusive remedy by which a person seeking in the capacity of a judgment creditor to enforce a judgment against a partner or transferee may satisfy the judgment from the judgment debtor's transferable interest.

Section 704. Power of Legal Representative of Deceased Partner.

ARTICLE 8: DISSOLUTION AND WINDING UP

Section 801. Events Causing Dissolution.

(a) A limited partnership is dissolved, and its activities and affairs must be wound up, upon the occurrence of any of the following:

(1) an event or circumstance that the partnership agreement states causes dissolution;

(2) the affirmative vote or consent of all general partners and of limited partners owning a majority of the rights to receive distributions as limited partners at the time the vote or consent is to be effective;

(3) after the dissociation of a person as a general partner:

(A) if the partnership has at least one remaining general partner, the affirmative vote or consent to dissolve the partnership not later than 90 days after the dissociation by partners owning a majority of the rights to receive distributions as partners at the time the vote or consent is to be effective; or

(B) if the partnership does not have a remaining general partner, the passage of 90 days after the dissociation, unless before the end of the period:

(i) consent to continue the activities and affairs of the partnership and admit at least one general partner is given by limited partners owning a majority of the rights to receive distributions as limited partners at the time the consent is to be effective; and

(ii) at least one person is admitted as a general partner in accordance with the consent;

(4) the passage of 90 consecutive days after the dissociation of the partnership's last limited partner, unless before the end of the period the partnership admits at least one limited partner;

(5) the passage of 90 consecutive days during which the partnership has only one partner, unless before the end of the period:

(A) the partnership admits at least one person as a partner;

(B) if the previously sole remaining partner is only a general partner, the partnership admits the person as a limited partner; and

(C) if the previously sole remaining partner is only a limited partner, the partnership admits a person as a general partner;

(6) on application by a partner, the entry by [the appropriate court] of an order dissolving the partnership on the grounds that:

(A) the conduct of all or substantially all the partnership's activities and affairs is unlawful; or

(B) it is not reasonably practicable to carry on the partnership's activities and affairs in conformity with the certificate of limited partnership and partnership agreement; or

(7) the signing and filing of a statement of administrative dissolution by the [Secretary of State] under Section 811.

(b) If an event occurs that imposes a deadline on a limited partnership under subsection (a) and before the partnership has met the requirements of the deadline, another event occurs that imposes a different deadline on the partnership under subsection (a):

(1) the occurrence of the second event does not affect the deadline caused by the first event; and

(2) the partnership's meeting of the requirements of the first deadline does not extend the second deadline.

Section 802. Winding Up.

(a) A dissolved limited partnership shall wind up its activities and affairs and, except as otherwise provided in Section 803, the partnership continues after dissolution only for the purpose of winding up.

(b) In winding up its activities and affairs, the limited partnership:

(1) shall discharge the partnership's debts, obligations, and other liabilities, settle and close the partnership's activities and affairs, and marshal and distribute the assets of the partnership; and

(2) may:

(A) amend its certificate of limited partnership to state that the partnership is dissolved;

(B) preserve the partnership activities, affairs, and property as a going concern for a reasonable time;

(C) prosecute and defend actions and proceedings, whether civil, criminal, or administrative;

(D) transfer the partnership's property;

(E) settle disputes by mediation or arbitration;

(F) deliver to the [Secretary of State] for filing a statement of termination stating the name of the partnership and that the partnership is terminated; and

(G) perform other acts necessary or appropriate to the winding up.

(c) If a dissolved limited partnership does not have a general partner, a person to wind up the dissolved partnership's activities and affairs may be appointed by the affirmative vote or consent of limited partners owning a majority of the rights to receive distributions as limited partners at the time the vote or consent is to be effective. A person appointed under this subsection:

(1) has the powers of a general partner under Section 804 but is not liable for the debts, obligations, and other liabilities of the partnership solely by reason of having or exercising those powers or otherwise acting to wind up the dissolved partnership's activities and affairs; and

(2) shall deliver promptly to the [Secretary of State] for filing an amendment to the partnership's certificate of limited partnership stating:

(A) that the partnership does not have a general partner;

(B) the name and street and mailing addresses of the person; and

(C) that the person has been appointed pursuant to this subsection to wind up the partnership.

(d) On the application of a partner, the [appropriate court] may order judicial supervision of the winding up of a dissolved limited partnership, including the appointment of a person to wind up the partnership's activities and affairs, if:

(1) the partnership does not have a general partner and within a reasonable time following the dissolution no person has been appointed pursuant to subsection (c); or

(2) the applicant establishes other good cause.

Section 803. Rescinding Dissolution.

Section 804. Power to Bind Partnership After Dissolution.

Section 805. Liability After Dissolution of General Partner and Person Dissociated as General Partner.

Section 806. Known Claims Against Dissolved Limited Partnership.

Section 807. Other Claims Against Dissolved Limited Partnership.

Section 808. Court Proceedings.

Section 809. Liability of General Partner and Person Dissociated as General Partner When Claim Against Limited Partnership Barred.

Section 810. Disposition of Assets in Winding Up; When Contributions Required.

(a) In winding up its activities and affairs, a limited partnership shall apply its assets, including the contributions required by this section, to discharge the partnership's obligations to creditors, including partners that are creditors.

(b) After a limited partnership complies with subsection (a), any surplus must be distributed in the following order, subject to any charging order in effect under Section 703:

(1) to each person owning a transferable interest that reflects contributions made and not previously returned, an amount equal to the value of the unreturned contributions; and

(2) among persons owning transferable interests in proportion to their respective rights to share in distributions immediately before the dissolution of the partnership.

(c) If a limited partnership's assets are insufficient to satisfy all of its obligations under subsection (a), with respect to each unsatisfied obligation incurred when the partnership was not a limited liability limited partnership, the following rules apply:

(1) Each person that was a general partner when the obligation was incurred and that has not been released from the obligation under Section 607 shall contribute to the partnership for the purpose of enabling the partnership to satisfy the obligation. The contribution due from each of those persons is in proportion to the right to receive distributions in the capacity of a general partner in effect for each of those persons when the obligation was incurred.

(2) If a person does not contribute the full amount required under paragraph (1) with respect to an unsatisfied obligation of the partnership, the other persons required to contribute by paragraph (1) on account of the obligation shall contribute the additional amount necessary to discharge the obligation. The additional contribution due from each of those other persons is in proportion to the right to receive distributions in the capacity of a general partner in effect for each of those other persons when the obligation was incurred.

(3) If a person does not make the additional contribution required by paragraph (2), further additional contributions are determined and due in the same manner as provided in that paragraph.

(d) A person that makes an additional contribution under subsection (c)(2) or (3) may recover from any person whose failure to contribute under subsection (c)(1) or (2) necessitated the additional contribution. A person may not recover under this subsection more than the amount additionally contributed. A person's liability under this subsection may not exceed the amount the person failed to contribute.

(e) All distributions made under subsections (b) and (c) must be paid in money.

Section 811. Administrative Dissolution.

Section 812. Reinstatement.

Section 813. Judicial Review of Denial of Reinstatement.

ARTICLE 9: ACTIONS BY PARTNERS

Section 901. Direct Action by Partner.

(a) Subject to subsection (b), a partner may maintain a direct action against another partner or the limited partnership, with or without an accounting as to the partnership's activities and affairs, to enforce the partner's rights and otherwise protect the partner's interests, including rights and interests under the partnership agreement or this [act] or arising independently of the partnership relationship.

(b) A partner maintaining a direct action under this section must plead and prove an actual or threatened injury that is not solely the result of an injury suffered or threatened to be suffered by the limited partnership.

(c) A right to an accounting on a dissolution and winding up does not revive a claim barred by law.

Section 902. Derivative Action.

A partner may maintain a derivative action to enforce a right of a limited partnership if:

(1) the partner first makes a demand on the general partners, requesting that they cause the partnership to bring an action to enforce the right, and the general partners do not bring the action within a reasonable time; or

(2) a demand under paragraph (1) would be futile.

Section 903. Proper Plaintiff.

A derivative action to enforce a right of a limited partnership may be maintained only by a person that is a partner at the time the action is commenced and:

(1) was a partner when the conduct giving rise to the action occurred; or

(2) whose status as a partner devolved on the person by operation of law or pursuant to the terms of the partnership agreement from a person that was a partner at the time of the conduct.

Section 904. Pleading.

In a derivative action, the complaint must state with particularity:

(1) the date and content of plaintiff's demand and the response to the demand by the general partner; or

(2) why demand should be excused as futile.

Section 905. Special Litigation Committee.

Section 906. Proceeds and Expenses.

(a) Except as otherwise provided in subsection (b):

(1) any proceeds or other benefits of a derivative action, whether by judgment, compromise, or settlement, belong to the limited partnership and not to the plaintiff; and

(2) if the plaintiff receives any proceeds, the plaintiff shall remit them immediately to the partnership.

(b) If a derivative action is successful in whole or in part, the court may award the plaintiff reasonable expenses, including reasonable attorney's fees and costs, from the recovery of the limited partnership.

(c) A derivative action on behalf of a limited partnership may not be voluntarily dismissed or settled without the court's approval.

ARTICLE 10: FOREIGN LIMITED PARTNERSHIPS

Section 1001. Governing Law.

(a) The law of the jurisdiction of formation of a foreign limited partnership governs:

(1) the internal affairs of the partnership;

(2) the liability of a partner as partner for a debt, obligation, or other liability of the partnership; and

(3) the liability of a series of the partnership.

(b) A foreign limited partnership is not precluded from registering to do business in this state because of any difference between the law of its jurisdiction of formation and the law of this state.

(c) Registration of a foreign limited partnership to do business in this state does not authorize the foreign partnership to engage in any activities and affairs or exercise any power that a limited partnership may not engage in or exercise in this state.

Section 1002. Registration to Do Business in This State.

(a) A foreign limited partnership may not do business in this state until it registers with the [Secretary of State] under this [article].

(b) A foreign limited partnership doing business in this state may not maintain an action or proceeding in this state unless it is registered to do business in this state.

(c) The failure of a foreign limited partnership to register to do business in this state does not impair the validity of a contract or act of the partnership or preclude it from defending an action or proceeding in this state.

(d) A limitation on the liability of a general partner or limited partner of a foreign limited partnership is not waived solely because the partnership does business in this state without registering to do business in this state.

(e) Section 1001(a) and (b) applies even if the foreign limited partnership fails to register under this [article].

Section 1003. Foreign Registration Statement.

Section 1004. Amendment of Foreign Registration Statement.

Section 1005. Activities Not Constituting Doing Business.

(a) Activities of a foreign limited partnership which do not constitute doing business in this state under this [article] include:

(1) maintaining, defending, mediating, arbitrating, or settling an action or proceeding;

(2) carrying on any activity concerning its internal affairs, including holding meetings of its partners;

(3) maintaining accounts in financial institutions;

(4) maintaining offices or agencies for the transfer, exchange, and registration of securities of the partnership or maintaining trustees or depositories with respect to those securities;

(5) selling through independent contractors;

(6) soliciting or obtaining orders by any means if the orders require acceptance outside this state before they become contracts;

(7) creating or acquiring indebtedness, mortgages, or security interests in property;

(8) securing or collecting debts or enforcing mortgages or security interests in property securing the debts and holding, protecting, or maintaining property;

(9) conducting an isolated transaction that is not in the course of similar transactions;

(10) owning, without more, property; and

(11) doing business in interstate commerce.

(b) A person does not do business in this state solely by being a partner of a foreign limited partnership that does business in this state.

(c) This section does not apply in determining the contacts or activities that may subject a foreign limited partnership to service of process, taxation, or regulation under law of this state other than this [act].

Section 1006. Noncomplying Name of Foreign Limited Partnership.

Section 1007. Withdrawal Deemed on Conversion to Domestic Filing Entity or Domestic Limited Liability Partnership.

Section 1008. Withdrawal on Dissolution or Conversion to Nonfiling Entity Other Than Limited Liability Partnership.

Section 1009. Transfer of Registration.

Section 1010. Termination of Registration.

Section 1011. Withdrawal of Registration of Registered Foreign Limited Partnership.

Section 1012. Action by [Attorney General].

ARTICLE 11: MERGER, INTEREST EXCHANGE, CONVERSION, AND DOMESTICATION

PART 1: GENERAL PROVISIONS

Section 1101. Definitions.

Section 1102. Relationship of [Article] to Other Laws.

Section 1103. Required Notice or Approval.

Section 1104. Nonexclusivity.

Section 1105. Reference to External Facts.

Section 1106. Appraisal Rights.

Section 1107. Excluded Entities and Transactions.

PART 2: MERGER

Section 1121. Merger Authorized.

Section 1122. Plan of Merger.

Section 1123. Approval of Merger.

Section 1124. Amendment or Abandonment of Plan of Merger.

Section 1125. Statement of Merger; Effective Date of Merger.

Section 1126. Effect of Merger.

PART 3: INTEREST EXCHANGE

Section 1131. Interest Exchange Authorized.

Section 1132. Plan of Interest Exchange.

Section 1133. Approval of Interest Exchange.

Section 1134. Amendment or Abandonment of Plan of Interest Exchange.

Section 1135. Statement of Interest Exchange; Effective Date of Interest Exchange.

Section 1136. Effect of Interest Exchange.

PART 4: CONVERSION

Section 1141. Conversion Authorized.

Section 1142. Plan of Conversion.

Section 1143. Approval of Conversion.

Section 1144. Amendment or Abandonment of Plan of Conversion.

Section 1145. Statement of Conversion; Effective Date of Conversion.

Section 1146. Effect of Conversion.

PART 5: DOMESTICATION

Section 1151. Domestication Authorized.

Section 1152. Plan of Domestication.

Section 1153. Approval of Domestication.

Section 1154. Amendment or Abandonment of Plan of Domestication.

Section 1155. Statement of Domestication; Effective Date of Domestication.

Section 1156. Effect of Domestication.

ARTICLE 12: MISCELLANEOUS PROVISIONS

Section 1201. Uniformity of Application and Construction.

In applying and construing this uniform act, consideration must be given to the need to promote uniformity of the law with respect to its subject matter among states that enact it.

Section 1202. Relation to Electronic Signatures in Global and National Commerce Act.

Section 1203. Savings Clause.

This [act] does not affect an action commenced, proceeding brought, or right accrued before [the effective date of this [act]].

Section 1204. Severability Clause.

If any provision of this [act] or its application to any person or circumstance is held invalid, the invalidity does not affect other provisions or applications of this [act] which can be given effect without the invalid provision or application, and to this end the provisions of this [act] are severable.]

Section 1205. Repeals.

Section 1206. Effective Date.

This [act] takes effect . . . .

INDEX

References are to Pages

ACTION (LEGAL ACTION)
Arbitration, 459–460
Corporation
    Direct and derivative actions, 781–782
    Shareholder standing, 784–785
Demand in derivative suit
    Demand futility, 794, 802–803
    Demand requirement, 794–795, 802–803
    Disinterestedness, 805–808
    Independence, 805–808
Limited partnership and limited liability company, 423–428
    Demand futility, 427
    Derivative suit, 423–424
    Tooley test, 426, 432
Partnership, 420–422
    Accounting, action for, 420–422
    Exclusivity rule, 421

ADMISSION
Becoming an owner, 198–199
Financial effect, 230–231
New owner, 204–205
    Issues to consider, 244

AGENCY
Agency cost, 658–659
Authority
    Actual, 266–267
    Apparent, 267–268
Estoppel, 270
Inherent agency power, 269
Legal definition, 249–250
Liability of principal
    Contract, 277–278
    Wrongful conduct and torts, 279
Limited liability, relationship to, 288–289
Ratification, 270–271
Separation of ownership and control, 610–611
Theory and reasons for, 247–249

ATTORNEYS
Clients, identification of, 52–53
    Aggregate theory, 54
    Entity rule, 54
    Reasonable expectation, 54–55
Conflict of interest, 55–57
Organizations, 58–59
Pro se representation of entities, 52

BOARD OF DIRECTORS (See "CORPORATION")

BUSINESS ENTITY FORMS
Choice of entity, 32–33
Difference forms, 3–6
    Entity formation over time, 5
Differences between corporations and NBEs, 10–15
Formation over time, 5–6
Nature of firms, 37–39
Sources of law
    Corporations, 20–22
    Delaware General Corporation Law, 20–21
    Model Business Corporation Act, 21
    NBEs, 23–24
    Uniform laws, 23–24
Taxonomy, 17–18
Theory of firms, 37–39
    Coase, 37
    Nexus of contract, 38

BUSINESS JUDGMENT RULE
Limited liability company, 301–302
Nature and limits of, 665–666
Outcome determinative, 684–685
Procedural aspect, 300–301
Statement of rule, 299, 636–637

BUSINESS PLANNING
Basic questions to consider, 1–3
Choice of entity, 32–33, 622
Choice of law, 33–35, 116
Corporation by estoppel, 92
De facto corporation, 92
Formation
    Limited liability entities, 81–86
    Partnership, 63–66
Issues to consider in contracting for fiduciary duties, 460–465
Issues to consider in dissolution, 599–602
Issues to consider in financing, 240–244
Issues to consider in forming NBEs, 119–123
Issues to consider in liability management, 187–188
Issues to consider in structuring management, 337–339
Issues to consider in transfer of interest and dissociation, 546–550

Preformation rights and liabilities, 90–91
Corporation by estoppel, 92
De facto corporation, 92

BUY-SELL AGREEMENT (See "DISSOCIATION")

CAPITAL ACCOUNT
Admission, 230–231
Definition and description, 209–211
Dissociation, 231–232
Profit and loss
Allocation methods, 223–225
Issues to consider, 243–244
Partnership, allocation, 217–218

CHARGING ORDER (See "TRANSFERABLE INTEREST")

CHARTER AGREEMENT
Amendment, 119–120
Arbitration, 459–460
Assent, 120–121
Contract interpretation (see "Contract interpretation principles")
Definition, 101–102
Fiduciary duties, 460–465
Drafting considerations, 460–461
Duty of care, 461–462
Duty of loyalty, 462–465
Function of, 103–105
Implied terms, 102
Oral terms, 102
Organization, example of Chrysler Group LLC, 121–123
Structure, 121–123
Voting to amend, 116
Writing, 101–102, 119

CONTRACT INTERPRETATION PRINCIPLES
General principles, 116–118
Contra proferentem, 118
Expressio unius exclusion alterius, 117
Unambiguous (plain), meaning, 117

CONTRIBUTION
Default rule, 211–212
Issues to consider, 240–243
Liability, 212–213

CONVERSION
General consideration, 587–588

CORPORATE GOVERNANCE (See "CORPORATION")

CORPORATION
Accountability, mechanisms of, 663–664
Basic requirements, 633–636
Business judgment rule, 636–637
Disinterestedness, directors, 805–808
Exculpation for money damages, 84
Functions of, 636
Independence, directors, 805–808
Professional management, 623
Public company boards, 634–635
Separation of ownership and control (see separate heading)
Agency cost, 658–659
Accountability mechanisms, 663–664
Board of directors, 298
Choice of corporate form, 622–626
Close corporation, 16
Closely held corporation, 15–16
Constitutional rights, 611, 616–617
Criticism of *Citizens United*, 616–617
Free speech, 611
Controlling shareholder, 747
Cash out transactions, 752
Determination of control, 748–749
Corporate governance, 656–658
Corporation by estoppel, 92
De facto corporation, 92
Delaware law
Equity, principles of, 627
Generally, 626–627
Differences with NBEs
Fiduciary duty, 12
Generally, 10–15, 617–622
Limited liability, 13
Management structure, 11–12, 617–619
Mandatory fiduciary duties, 621
Mandatory rules, 14, 619–621, 622–623
Separation of ownership and control, 12
Taxation, 11, 622
Transferability of interest, 13
Entire fairness standard, 684
Exculpation for money damages, 84, 685–686
Fiduciary duty, 342–344
Mandatory duties, 621
Formation, 82–84
Market for corporate control, 664
Officers, 646–647
Private corporation, 15
Professional management, 623
Public corporation, 16–17, 606
Reasons for selecting corporate form, 622–626
Shareholder, types, 648–651
Inside shareholders, 651
Institutional shareholders, 648–651
Society, relationship to, 605–607
Fortune 500 companies, 605
Stock, 192–195
Classes and series of, 194–195
Fungibility, 193
Issuance of, 193–194
Preferred stock, 192–193, 195
Tax, 622
Voting
Plurality rule, 653–654
Proxy, 655–656
Quorum, 653

Shareholder, 371–318
Voting rights, 651–653

DISSOCIATION
Buy-sell agreement, 542–546, 548–549
Comparisons, 116
Financial effect, 231–232
General consideration, 548
Limited liability company, 534–535
Limited partnership, 532–534
Partnership, 501–505
Price and valuation, 550

DISSOLUTION
Administrative dissolution, 575
Events of dissolution, 553–555, 602
Exit mechanisms, 548–549
Issue to consider in voluntary dissolution, 599–600
Judicial dissolution, 600–602
Wind up, 577–580

DISTRIBUTION
Improper distribution
Corporation, 225–227
NBEs, 227–229
Limited liability company, 221–222
Limited partnership, 221
Market value of assets and liabilities, 229
Book value, distinguished from, 229
Partnership, 217–218

ENTITY FORMS (See **"BUSINESS ENTITY FORMS"**)

FIDUCIARY DUTY
Aiding and abetting breach of duty, 687–688
Bad faith, corporation (see "Duty of loyalty" below)
Contracting for duties
Contracting in NBEs, 382–383
Delaware's approach, 391–392
Drafting considerations, 460–461
Duty of care, 461–462
Duty of loyalty, 462–465
Corporation, 342–344
Mandatory fiduciary duties, 621
Creditors, 414–415
Differences between corporations and NBEs, 12
Duty of care, 462–465
Duty to be informed and *Van Gorkom*, 672–673
Duty of loyalty, 462–465, 695–697
Bad faith, *Caremark*, 721–722
Bad faith, defined, 716–718
Bad faith, violation of law, 745
Business opportunity, 696
Cash out transactions by controlling shareholder, 752
Conflict of interest, 696
Policy, 695
Self-dealing, 696
Elimination, 116
Exculpation, 685–686
Good faith, contractual obligation in NBEs, 403–405
Good faith (bad faith) in corporation, 404
Limited liability company (members and managers), 365–367
Limited partnership (general and limited partners), 349–353
Mergers, 835–837
Minority oppression, 374–375
Nature of, 341–342
Partnership, 344, 348–349

FOREIGN ENTITIES
Activities not constituting doing business, 94
Filing requirement, 93
Meaning of, 93

GENERAL PARTNERSHIP (See **"PARTNERSHIP"**)

GOOD FAITH
Fiduciary duty in corporation, 404
Obligation of good faith in NBEs, 403–405

INDEMNIFICATION
General, 188, 323–324

INFORMATION RIGHTS
Corporation, 332–333, 777–778
NBEs, 333–335

INSURANCE
General, 323–324

INTERNAL AFFAIRS
Choice of law, 33–35, 116
Federalism, 21
Internal affairs doctrine, corporation, 21–22
Internal affairs doctrine, NBEs, 24–25

LEGAL PERSONHOOD (See **"PERSONHOOD"**)

LIMITED LIABILITY
Agent, relationship to, 288–289
Basic features, 18–19
Control rule in limited partnerships, 143
Corporation, 127
Differences between corporations and NBEs, 13
Direct liability, 125, 155, 188
Forming limited liability entities, 81–86
Limited liability company, 145–46
Series LLC, 147–148
Limited partnership, 140–143
Limited liability limited partnership, 141
Partnership, 137–139
Limited liability partnership, 139
Personal guarantee, 188
Series LLCs, 147–151
Veil piercing (see "Veil piercing")

Vicarious liability, 125–126

LIMITED LIABILITY COMPANY
Basic features, 19–20
Check the box regulation, 7
Different entity forms, 32
Fiduciary duty, 362, 365–367
Formation, 84–85
Growth of, 5–8
  Tax status, 6–7
Liability, 145–146
  Series LLC, 147–148, 150–151
  Veil piercing, 164–165
Management, 305–301
  Manager-managed, 306
  Member-managed, 306
Member
  Becoming, 198, 204–205, 230–231
  Dissociation, 231–232
Profit and loss
  Allocation of profit and loss, 221–222

LIMITED LIABILITY PARTNERSHIP
Formation, 85–86
Liability, 139

LIMITED PARTNERSHIP
Basic features, 18–19
Fiduciary duty, 349–353
  General partner conflict, 351–352
Formation, 85
Liability, 140–143
  Control rule, 143
  General partner, 140–141
  Limited partner, 140–141
  Veil piercing, 164, 180–181
Management, 303–305
Partner
  Becoming, 198, 204–205, 230–231
  Dissociation, 231–232
Profit and loss
  Allocation of profit and loss, 221

MANAGEMENT
Basic forms, 293–295
Business judgment rule, 299–302
Centralized management
  Fiduciary duties, 297
  Professional management, 623
  Reasons for, 295
Corporation, 298–299
  Board of directors, 298
  Natural persons, 299
Differences between corporations and NBEs, 11–12
Limited liability company, 305–310
  Agency, 309–310
  Contractual flexibility of management structure, 305–306, 308
  Two types of LLCs, 305
Limited partnership, 303–305
  General partner as manager, 303, 305
Partnership, 302–303
Removing managers, 338–339
Representative management, in corporation, 617–619
Selecting and removing managers, 338–339
Structuring management, 337–338

MANDATORY RULES
Corporations, compared to, 112, 622–623
Default rules, 11, 14, 113
Differences between corporations and NBEs, 14, 619–621
Elasticity of private ordering, 14, 111–114
Enabling rules, 113
NBEs, compared to, 113–114
Private ordering, 14

MERGER
Asset sale, 832–833
Controlling shareholder cash out transaction, 752
Fiduciary duties, 592, 835–837
  Entrenchment and takeover defenses, 837–840
General consideration, 587–590
NBE, 587–590
Reasons for, 823–825
Revlon doctrine, 844–845
  Short-termism, 865
Short-form merger, 832
Statutory merger, 828–831
Tender offer, 833–834
Triangular merger, forward and reverse, 831–832
Voting, 834

OPERATING AGREEMENT (See "CHARTER AGREEMENT")

PARTNERSHIP
Basic features, 18
Definition of, 63
Fiduciary duty, 344, 348–349
Formation, 63–66
  "Accidental" (unintended) partnership, 64
  Factors in determining existence, 65–66
  Specific intent, 64
Liability, 137–139
Management, 302–303
Partner
  Becoming, 198, 204–205, 230–231
  Definition, 138
  Dissociation, 231–232
  Legal person as partner, 138
Profit and loss
  Allocation of profit and loss, 217–218
  Meaning of profit, 63–64

PARTNERSHIP AGREEMENT (See "CHARTER AGREEMENT")

PERSONHOOD
Constitutional rights, 48–49, 611, 616–617

Instrumental functions, 43–44
Limited liability, relationship to, 42–43
NBEs, 44–45

PRE-FORMATION LIABILITY (See "BUSINESS PLANNING")

PRIVATE ORDERING (See "MANDATORY RULES")

REVERSE VEIL PIERCING (See "VEIL PIERCING")

SECURITIES
Definition of, 232–233
Federal securities law, 232–234
NBE interests as, 233–234

SEPARATION OF OWNERSHIP AND CONTROL
Agency problem, 610–611
Berle-Means, 607
Corporate management, 623–624
Differences between corporations and NBEs, 12
Theory, 12

SERIES LLCS
General, 147–151

SHAREHOLDER (See "CORPORATION")

STOCK
Characteristics, 192–193
Classes and series, 194–195
Issuing stock, 193–194
Standardized units, 624–626
Transferability, 624–626

SUCCESSOR LIABILITY
General, 181–182

TAXATION
Different entity forms, 32
Limited liability companies, growth of, 6–7
Partnership tax under Subchapter K, 11
S corporation, 11

TRANSFERABLE INTEREST
Charging order, 482–483
    Foreclosure on, 500–501
Corporation, transferability of stock, 469, 624–626
Definition, 469
Differences between corporations and NBEs, 13
NBEs, 469–471, 546–547

VEIL PIERCING
Avoiding, 187–188
Corporation, 127
Equitable veil piercing, 137
Limited partnerships, 180–181
NBEs, 164–165
Personal guarantee, 188
Reverse veil piercing, 174–175

VOTING
Corporation, 317–318, 651–654
Horizontal voting (voting among voting group), 319–321
Matters voted upon, 321–322
Mergers, 834
NBEs, 318–319
Purpose, 316–317
Shareholder voting
    Default rule, 651–652
    Full voting power, 652
    Incentives to vote, 656–657
    Plurality rule, 653–654
    Proxy, 655–656
    Rational apathy, 652
Threshold, 320
Vertical voting (approval of manager decisions or choices), 322–323